BETWEEN WORLDS

edited by
Timothy O. Benson and Éva Forgács

selected by
Timothy O. Benson

Éva Forgács

Michael Henry Heim

Krisztina Passuth

Piotr Piotrowski

Karel Srp

Irina Subotić

Ioana Vlasiu

between worlds:

Los Angeles County Museum of Art

The MIT Press
Cambridge, Massachusetts and London, England

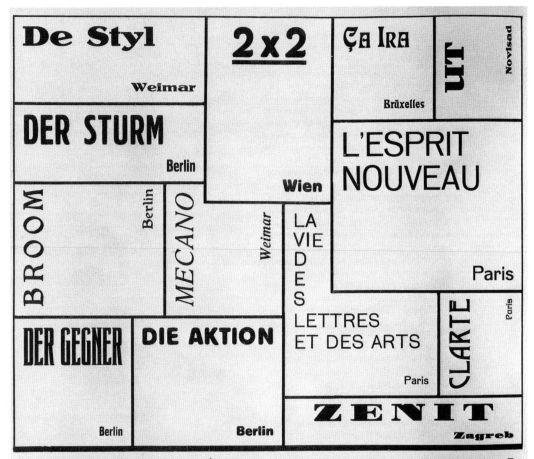

a sourcebook of central european avant-gardes, 1910–1930

First MIT Press edition 2002

Los Angeles County Museum of Art, 5905 Wilshire
Boulevard, Los Angeles, California 90036.

Published in conjunction with the exhibition *Central
European Avant-Gardes: Exchange and
Transformation, 1910–1930*. This exhibition was
organized by the Los Angeles County Museum of
Art. It was supported in part by the Art Museum
Council; Art of the Palate; the National Endowment
for the Arts; and the National Endowment for the
Humanities, dedicated to expanding American
understanding of history and culture. Additional
support was provided by the Trust for Mutual
Understanding; the Austrian Federal Ministry
for Foreign Affairs; an International Partnership
Among Museums award presented by the
American Association of Museums with funding
from the Bureau of Educational and Cultural
Affairs of the United States Information Agency
and the Samuel H. Kress Foundation; and
H. Kirk Brown III and Jill Wiltse.

In-kind support for the exhibition is provided by
KLON 88.1 FM.

This publication was made possible in part by
a grant from the National Endowment for the
Humanities, dedicated to expanding American
understanding of history and culture. Additional
support was provided by Mary and Roy Cullen.

Printed and bound in Ghent, Belgium, by
Snoeck-Ducaju & Zoon.

Library of Congress Control Number: 2002100648

ISBN: 0-262-02530-2

Managing Editor: Stephanie Emerson
Editor: William R. Hackman
Assistant Editor: Sara Cody
Editorial Assistance: Thomas Frick
Designer: Katherine Go
Production Assistance: Angel Go
Production Coordinator: Karen Knapp
Supervising Photographer: Peter Brenner
Rights and Reproductions Coordinator:
Cheryle T. Robertson

Frontispiece:
Back page of *Ma*, vol. 8, no. 1 (1922) advertising
other avant-garde periodicals

CONTRIBUTORS

COMMENTATORS

Timothy O. Benson

Éva Forgács

Juliana Maxim

Krisztina Passuth

Piotr Piotrowski

Karel Srp

Irina Subotić

Ioana Vlasiu

TRANSLATORS

Sanda Agalidi

John Bátki

David Britt

Alexandra Büchler

Marjan Golobič

Michael Henry Heim

Klara Kemp-Welch

Wanda Kemp-Welch

Steven Lindberg

Julian Semilian

Maja Starčević

Gerald Turner

Andrée Collier Záleská

CONTENTS

ACKNOWLEDGMENTS

This volume grew from the collaborative endeavors of an international team involved in the creation of the exhibition *Central European Avant-Gardes: Exchange and Transformation, 1910–1930,* held at the Los Angeles County Museum of Art during the spring of 2002. This exhibition sought to explore the mysteries of artistic influence and its dependence on communication and the exchange of perspectives throughout the region that is the subject of the present volume. Apart from the works of art themselves, the "little magazines" of the avant-garde provide the primary documentation of this exchange, including the responses of critics and literati. As so little of this material is available in English, it quickly became clear that the exhibition, as well as subsequent discussions in the field of scholarship, could greatly benefit from a substantial selection of documentation.

The initial meetings for this project were sponsored by the Trust for Mutual Understanding. We are extremely grateful to them, to the Alexander von Humboldt Foundation, which sponsored my initial research, and to the National Endowment for the Humanities for a collaborative research grant, which supported further research and translation and without which this project would not have been realized. Mary and Roy Cullen very generously provided additional support.

The shape of the volume gained its initial impetus in discussions between myself and Krisztina Passuth, Piotr Piotrowski, and Karel Srp during the very first of several meetings sponsored by the Trust for Mutual Understanding for planning the exhibition. Some documentation was already intended for the catalogue, but once we realized that a separate volume was greatly needed we undertook to broaden the selection team and to secure the necessary funding. Éva Forgács, Irina Subotić, and Ioana Vlasiu filled out the selection team, and we began making preliminary lists of possible documents with the research assistance of Monika Król, curatorial assistant for the exhibition project, who also provided valuable support during the grant writing process.

Equally essential for this project has been our team of translators, each a sensitive interpreter with a deep appreciation for the literature and art of the early twentieth century. We are most grateful for the masterful renderings of Sanda Agalidi, John Bátki, David Britt, Alexandra Büchler, Marjan Golobič, Michael Henry Heim, Klara Kemp-Welch, Wanda Kemp-Welch, Steven Lindberg, Julian Semilian, Maja Starčević, Gerald Turner, and Andrée Collier Záleská.

We are also grateful to Mark Pejcha for additional translation assistance and to Juliana Maxim for writing a portion of commentaries on very short notice. We are especially grateful to Michael Henry Heim for his generous counsel in choosing the translation team and maintaining a consistency across the many vocabularies, nuances, and linguistic variances. William Hackman brought editorial consistency to this volume, devoting his diligent attention to every page of the masses of primary material and much of the accompanying commentary. Sara Cody brought her acute editorial eye to many of the commentaries herein, and wrangled the mountains of documents in their original languages and in translation into a working order for our team. We are also grateful to Thomas Frick for editorial advice and assistance.

The clarity and appropriateness of the design of this book is indebted to Katherine Go and her predecessor Scott Taylor. Angel Go assisted with the incorporation of its large amount of text in the short amount of time allowed by our production schedule. Supervising photographer Peter Brenner and staff photographers Steve Oliver and Annie Appel supplied photographic material, while Sonja Cendak obtained photographic material from institutions far and wide. Cheryle Robertson researched and secured photography copyright permissions. Garrett White, former Director of Publications, was supportive of this project from its inception, while Managing Editor Stephanie Emerson is responsible for its realization by providing crucial support at every turn as she shepherded it through the entirety of the production process with agility, resourcefulness, and skill. We are grateful to Roger Conover of The MIT Press for his continual encouragement.

This volume is indebted to the support of Andrea L. Rich, President and Director of the Los Angeles County Museum of Art. We are also grateful to our colleagues Stephanie Barron and Nancy Thomas for administrative support. Tom Jacobson, former Director of Development and his successor Acting Director Connie Morgan, oversaw our productive relations with donors and granting agencies. The intricate details of our grant proposals were ably managed and budgets skillfully crafted by Stephanie Dyas and Karen Benson. At the Robert Gore Rifkind Center for German Expressionist Studies, collections librarian Susan Trauger attended to innumerable research requests. Deborah Barlow Smedstad and the staff of the Mr. and Mrs. Allen C. Balch Research Library at LACMA helped find many sources, while program specialist Anne Diederich facilitated countless interlibrary loans. Our curatorial administrator Claudia Ramos attended to masses of correspondence.

As this volume began grew in magnitude and complexity, so also did the role of Éva Forgács as a full collaborator in bringing to it shape and clarity. I am grateful to her for the vision and diligent attention to detail she brought to this project.

Timothy O. Benson
Curator, the Robert Gore Rifkind Center for German Expressionist Studies
Los Angeles County Museum of Art

tank

no. 1½

ljubljana, s. h. s.
lioubliana, s. c. s.

Marko Ristić

Avgust Černigoj, cover design for *Tank* no. 1½ (1927)

INTRODUCTION

Timothy O. Benson
Éva Forgács

The avant-garde circles of Central Europe were an integral part of the evolution of modernism as it reached its zenith during the 1920s as an international cosmopolitan community. The documentation of these movements (in the form of manifestos, artists' statements, and reviews) was their lifeblood and, during the periods when political events conspired to isolate them, one of their few means of communication and exchange. The small magazines in which such documents appeared often published excerpts from one another as well as promoted one another in advertisements. Written and read at café tables and in ateliers, avidly exchanged among artists of different regions, these publications are an essential part of the historical fabric. However, much of this crucial evidence—familiar at the time—has been lost to us due to intervening historical events. Indeed, the artistic avant-gardes of Central Europe have been in a blind spot of scholarship on modernism for several decades. Recently a growing interest occasioned by the fall of the Berlin Wall, and a number of the exhibitions and publications, have begun to bring this crucial aspect of European culture—"the other Europe"[1]—back into focus.

Yet historical accounts and critical theory have generally continued to draw upon Western European or Russian avant-garde works and texts, by and large ignoring the territory in between. Writers of the region— Franz Kafka, Robert Musil, Elias Canetti, Jaroslav Hašek, Bohumil Hrabal, Czesław Miłosz, and more recently Péter Nádas, Péter Esterházy, Danilo Kiš, and Claudio Magris, to give but a few examples—have long been appreciated beyond their respective cultures (some having emigrated during their careers). Yet the visual arts and art criticism of the Central European avant-garde have remained in relative obscurity for the English-speaking world. In large part this is due to the inaccessibility of sources and lack of translations. The present volume provides a body of documentation in order to deepen appreciation and scholarship concerning the evolution of modernism throughout Central Europe during the first decades of the twentieth century.

Whether considering geographic scope or stylistic criteria, no simple definition suffices for Central European art. Not bound linguistically to specific national cultures, the region's visual artists, especially those of the avant-gardes, could espouse an internationalist agenda, sometimes producing work so supranational in style as to be scarcely distinguishable from their West European counterparts. Yet a liberal press and open market were rarely available; consequently the records left behind were fragmentary and episodic. Moreover, much of this evidence became unavailable during four decades of Soviet domination. Discussion of the avant-garde was frequently distorted, suppressed, or banned during the very period when the history of the Western avant-garde was being constructed.

Retrospective accounts, anthologies, and exhibition catalogues (typically including translated documents) concerning the avant-gardes of Central Europe began to appear in West Germany and France in the late 1960s and throughout the 1970s.[2] In 1973 the Muzeum Sztuki in Łódź brought its crucial collection of Polish modernism to the West, accompanied by a catalogue in English that excerpted texts by the Polish Constructivists.[3] As interest grew, the first exhibition to consider how modernism developed across Central and Western Europe in the 1920s was mounted in Germany from Western collections.[4] During the 1980s the premier collections of modernism under state authority in the Eastern Bloc began to be seen in the West. This brought forth documents pertaining to the Hungarian Eight and Activists,[5] as well as to Czech architecture.[6] Several subsequent European and American exhibitions provided more documents,[7] among them

Wechselwirkungen (1986),[8] *Kubismus in Prag* (1991),[9] and *Europa, Europa* (1994).[10] English language academic anthologies have added little. Stephan Bann's classic *The Tradition of Constructivism* presented a broad picture of International Constructivism (especially Russian, German, and Dutch) but with only limited space for Central Europe.[11]

Although these exhibitions and their scant documentation brought the avant-gardes of Central Europe within the periphery of the Western canon, many basic questions were left unresolved: Was there something distinctive about Central European art and its avant-garde manifestations? Was the art in this region merely a dialect of West European art? Did the adoption of Western modernist formal idioms in Central Europe lead to the creation of meanings, contents, and values different from those signified by the same idioms in the West? What terms and assumptions would differentiate a narrative for the modernist art of Central Europe from the prevailing account of Western art?

On a broader scale, Central Europe itself as a cultural entity remains problematic. When asked to explain it, the late Yugoslav writer Danilo Kiš responded in thirty-eight fragmentary chapters;[12] the historian Jacques Rupnik opened his book with a chapter titled "In Search of Central Europe"[13]; and Timothy Garton Ash, a seasoned observer of the region, wrote an essay entitled "Does Central Europe Exist?"[14]

The intellectual mapping of this politically and ethnically diverse region, whose boundaries continually shifted and blurred throughout centuries, has long depended on the conflicting interests of those defining it. The term *Mitteleuropa*, the first strategic recognition of the region, was coined in 1915 by Friedrich Naumann, founder of the Christian Social Movement.[15] He used it primarily as a political and economic concept and presciently suggested that Germany might absorb this part of continental Europe, with all its resources, as an alternative to overseas colonies that, Naumann feared, would not be gained after a possible defeat in World War I.[16] As had many predecessors equating the arrival of the Christian universality of the Holy Roman Empire with civilization itself, Naumann referred to Charlemagne's great empire as the model of a supranational European federation, and urged cultural rapprochement and solidarity between the Germans and smaller nations. His concept of German-dominated integration drew criticism from many quarters. The socialists found it incompatible with their own dreams of internationalism, the liberals

thought it too narrow, and the Pan-Germans thought it was too favorable for the Slavs.

Yet these political disputes could scarcely sweep away the legacy of German involvement in vast regions of Central Europe embodied in the five-century dominance of the Habsburg empire: a profound and often uneasy cultural amalgam (combining German *Kultur* with indigenous Slavic and Magyar traditions) not easily dissolved with the founding of modern nation states nor eliminated even by the tragedy of Nazism. As Claudio Magris reminds us in *Danube*, his sweeping, deeply felt survey: "Today, questioning oneself about Europe means asking oneself how one relates to Germany."[17]

The term *East Central Europe* came to be used around 1918–19, when the map of the region was redrawn after the war. As a political concept, it demarcated Russia and the Balkans as a more distant region to be called Eastern Europe, while Poland, Czechoslovakia, Hungary, occasionally the Baltic states, Finland, and the northwestern parts of the Balkan region became East Central Europe.[18] The equally current term *Zwischeneuropa*, or "Between-Europe," describes a territory where thirteen new states were created or reinstated between 1820 and 1920.[19] Although used politically, this term reflects to no small degree the cultural landscape of the avant-garde at the time: to the west Paris summoned many as a center of revolutionary artistic change, and to the east Moscow was also exerting tremendous appeal with its promise of a social utopia and an art suited to technological progress.

Prior to 1918 many nations in Central Europe had either been partitioned, as was Poland among three powerful empires, or had been wholly absorbed into the Austro-Hungarian empire. For them nineteenth century Romanticism had given birth to movements of national awakening. Yet this urge toward independence could be pursued only culturally prior to the collapse of the empires at the end of World War I. Thus the artist, as protagonist on the prewar cultural stage, had already become a freedom fighter, prophet, and national symbol, aware of—and sometimes skeptical of—these iconic roles.[20]

While Enlightenment philosophy developed in the West in tandem with an industrializing economy and par- liamentary or quasi-parliamentary nation states, in Central Europe latent feudalistic structures persisted in a largely agrarian society that became industrialized only through the mas- sive investment of Western capital and an increase in migration during the twilight years of the empires.[21] Regional aristocracies remained in place, while a bourgeois middle class gradually began to grow, as Western entrepreneurs arrived with skills nec- essary for modernization and industri- alization. Many of these newcomers augmented the small Jewish mercantile and working classes that had resided throughout Central Europe since the Middle Ages.[22]

Cosmopolitan cultural trends of con- sumption and patronage, as well as political rationalism aspiring to the creation of new, international republics, alternated with or existed alongside the forces of nationalist conservatism that fueled the re- creation of national mythologies. Ambitions for international cultural integration thus often required circumventing local power structures in favor of a wider community where new artistic concepts might be validated. Many intellectuals in these regions sought to overcome this duality and synthesize their national heritage with their belief in progress.

During the century and a half between the creation of nation states in the West and in the East many regional differences evolved across Central Europe in political institutions and power structures, resulting— especially at a distance from cosmopol- itan centers—in a denial of basic freedoms that were becoming com- monplace in the West. Differences also developed in the institutional settings of culture (ranging from the academies to the avant-garde) and in economic conditions (including patronage patterns and the viability of art markets). Even forms of expression adopted from Western cultures now reverberated with local overtones and meanings. The espousal of purely formal concerns might become an issue as much of political freedom as aesthetic autonomy. Thus the Central European avant-gardes of the 1910s and 1920s were the first art movements in their regions to function under historically new circumstances—in new nation states, free from the authority of the former empires—and they evolved widely divergent strategies of communication and modes of aesthetic production.

The Central European avant-gardes were also influenced by the anarchist philosophies that flourished especially among German and Russian intellectuals from the late nineteenth century. While strongly engaged with Russian ideas (framed by debates between devotees of Karl Marx and Mikhail Bakunin), German anarchism ranged widely between extreme individualism (exemplified in the centenary revival of Max Stirner around 1905) and the more communalistic tendencies of Kropotkin translator Gustav Landauer, whose socialist views found a profound resonance among many post–World War I social revolutionaries, artists, writers, and architects.[23]

In the early twenties the resolutions forged by Central European artists would lead to an International Constructivism departing from Russian Constructivist, Suprematist, and Productivist antecedents originating from the Soviet realm. Yet despite the connections of the avant-garde to working-class movements and to later, oppressive cultural-political systems,[24] these artists were able to sustain their idealism without the unrelenting crashes with reality of the subsequent era (and eventual change of strategies of the 1980s).[25]

Armed with messianic ideologies, the avant-gardes of the early twentieth century, even after surviving the carnage of the Great War, could still be innocently militant. They were only occasionally subjected to violence (as during the fall of the Munich Soviet and Hungarian Commune) and only occasionally flirted with true political power. Tensions between those insisting on artistic autonomy and others adhering to political organizations prevailed throughout European avant-garde circles and cannot be divorced from the similar debates in the workers movement among political activists and ideologists.

Between Worlds: A Sourcebook of Central European Avant-Gardes is the collaborative effort of a team of scholars familiar with the primary materials in their individual specialties. In shaping the anthology we have attempted to reflect a general consensus, yet differing perspectives, as well as the diversity of the texts themselves, preclude a wholly consistent organization or set of criteria, and we have given priority to this diversity over any artificial consistency. The selections examine the era of the historical avant-garde roughly between 1910 and 1930. We include writings from the Czech-speaking lands, Hungary, Poland, the former Yugoslavia, and Romania, along with a more limited body of documents originating from the better-known German art scene.

The avant-gardes of Central Europe are mapped here as a network of cosmopolitan cities in which art movements embodied the tension between the regional and the cosmopolitan: Bucharest, Budapest, Cracow, Dessau, Łódź, Prague, Poznań, Warsaw, Weimar, Zagreb—all of these had direct links to Amsterdam, Berlin, Cologne, Hanover, Moscow, Vienna, or Paris. Sometimes thoroughly ideological, at other times escaping ideology altogether, the avant-gardes within these coordinates often changed their tenets and sometimes rewrote their manifestos. Hence chronological order does not always presume development or evolution and may merely follow the unfolding of local current events.

Nonetheless, as channels of communication resumed after World War I and travel restrictions and military blockades were lifted, the avant-gardes of Central Europe became increasing interconnected and, by the early 1920s, had become self-consciously international, resulting in a discourse about their mission and identity that must figure prominently in any account of the period. Consequently we have organized the selections not as separate regional accounts, but as an interrelated discourse grouped loosely under four thematic headings implying a rough chronology, yet accepting that the narrative will at times appear chronologically discordant in its episodes.

STYLE AS THE CRUCIBLE OF PAST AND FUTURE

A sense of national cultural revival prevailed throughout Central Europe in the first decade of the century, and artists were driven by idealism and optimism to "translate" and adjust such international movements as Art Nouveau and Symbolism to the local traditions. Increasingly artists, architects, composers, and actors, as well as poets, playwrights, critics, and other literati posed alternatives to the established culture of art academies and salon exhibitions.

By the end of the decade the great scientific and technical progress that had been achieved in the West during the late nineteenth and early twentieth centuries—symbolized by Einstein's Special Theory of Relativity in 1905—created much excitement within the avant-garde.[26] The young social disciplines of linguistics, anthropology, and sociology strengthened the cultural relativism that many among the intelligentsia had discovered in Nietzsche. Whether in social structures, abstract visual forms, or non-Euclidean geometries, there was a strong impulse to reveal new paradigms. Artists throughout Europe became fascinated with Cézanne,[27] Cubism, Futurism, and Expressionism—all seeming to explore underlying structures or forces beyond the visible surface of nature.

With an unprecedented experience of industrialization and a faith in progress, artists and writers in Central Europe felt increasingly competent to shape the future of their countries' cultures, not by readdressing the national mythologies but rather by acting as socially engaged cultural agents, who could convey the new perspectives heralded by the new art they encountered on pilgrimages to France and Germany.

As traditional styles vied with novel alternatives, debates over competing cosmopolitan and local standards were often circumscribed by the conventional boundaries of art discourse, using such concepts as form, style, and content. The viability of "national character" was both celebrated and contested[28] as well as philosophically examined,[29] while a universal expression of humanity within the diversity of cultures was claimed as the basis of these concepts. If art and aesthetic culture were seen as means of national revival a decade earlier, by the early 1910s they were largely seen as instrumental for a more universal cultural renewal and social awareness.

ART AND SOCIAL CHANGE

During and after World War I avant-garde groups in Central Europe became dramatically politicized. Artists recognized the communicative power of art, including its potential for addressing much broader audiences. The elaboration of new vocabularies was important for asserting a social radicalism that was both aesthetic and political. Fueled by the 1917 Communist revolution in Russia and the 1918 revolution in Germany, Hungarian activists participated in the 1919 Hungarian Commune, and

Stanisław Kubicki, *Rebellion* (c. 1918), illustration for *Die Aktion* vol. 8, no. 21/22 (1918)

Polish artists formed Bunt [Rebellion], which had ties to the circle of the socialist Berlin periodical *Die Aktion*. In Prague a new group, *Tvrdosíjní* [The Obstinates], focused on artistic content and art's potential to shape society and morality.

Yet the political content of particular stylistic idioms often changed with the local context. The political energy of Futurism, for example, invigorated almost the whole Central European avant-garde (as it had Russian art prior to the war), but its militarist stance was critiqued and dismissed by most Central European groups, including the Dadaists. The Czech Karel Teige and the Hungarian Lajos Kassák were simultaneously pro-Futurist and antiwar.

By November 1918, Berlin was at the epicenter of the Central European avant-gardes. As György Lukács recalled, "There was a widespread belief that we were at the beginning of a vast revolutionary wave that would flood all over Europe within a few years. We labored under the illusion that within a short time we would be able to mop up the last remnants of capitalism."[30] Amid the poverty and shortages endured by a defeated Germany, the most fantastic architectural and ideational utopias thrived along with a reinvigorated Expressionism, spiritual revivals, and grand schemes for reforming the entirety of culture. No less important, the economic infrastructure of the art scene was being restored. Galleries and art criticism returned in full force, and the Bauhaus was established in Weimar. Herwarth Walden's Berlin gallery and publishing house Der Sturm, so essential to the avant-garde prior to the war, mounted pioneering shows of the works of artists arriving in Berlin from Czechoslovakia, Hungary, Poland, Romania, and Russia. Berlin, with its huge Russian émigré population, now attracted artists and intellectuals from all over Europe including Holland, Austria, Belgium, Sweden, Hungary, and Romania, almost overnight challenging Paris as the international art capital.

László Péri, cover design for *Der Sturm* vol. 4, no. 2 (1923)

INTERNATIONALISM

The ideals of internationalism and collectivism that prevailed throughout the avant-gardes of Central Europe during the early 1920s were inspired in part by the idea of a coming world revolution promulgated by the Soviet Russian state. The Central European avant-garde groups, most already opposed to nationalism and conservatism, were drawn to internationalism with messianic fervor. International cooperation offered new opportunities for artists marginalized in their respective national cultures, as an international network of journals, exhibitions, and meetings quickly evolved. Internationalism held the promise of cultural emancipation, acceptance in the coveted Western centers of Europe, and the utopistic platform of a tabula rasa.

Internationalism left the romantic politicization of national art behind in favor of an equally romantic future-oriented political and cultural ideal. In reality the internationalist avant-gardes of the 1920s were decentralized, nomadic, and diffuse in their modes of aesthetic production. By becoming thoroughly interconnected they paradoxically discovered their plurality, and at the center of the debates prompted by the 1922 International Congress of Progressive Art in Düsseldorf was the attempt to attain a new sense of unity. The ensuing discussions showed the great centralizing role that De Stijl, and particularly Theo van Doesburg, played in integrating Central European art into the fabric of Western culture. In as marginal a position in Holland as any Central European artist in his respective homeland, van Doesburg had used his own funds to publish the *De Stijl* monthly, which now carried these debates. His Dadaist forum *Mecano*, edited under the pen name I. K. Bonset, also gave visibility to many Central European authors and encouraged international discussions. In spring 1922 van Doesburg

taught a course in Weimar as an alternative to the then Expressionist Bauhaus, which attracted students from Germany and several other countries.[31]

The primary instigator from the East was El Lissitzky, who arrived in Berlin from Moscow at the end of 1921. He published *Veshch/Gegenstand/Objet* with Ilya Ehrenburg, and in late 1922 designed the catalogue for the Erste Russische Kunstausstellung [First Russian Art Exhibition], which presented the full range of Russian Constructivism and elicited a tremendous response among artists.[32]

Constructivism's departure from the traditions of easel painting and pedestal sculpture for principles that could be used in building the environment and designing products for everyday life exerted a great influence, especially in Berlin, Weimar, and Warsaw (even if the rejection of easel painting was not as rigorous in the West as it was in Moscow). The Constructivist cult of technology furthered an interest in film, photography, abstract animation, photomontages, and photograms, all seen as components of a new common language.

As traditional artistic boundaries dissolved, an unprecedented type of multidisciplinary agent arose. Figures such as van Doesburg and Lissitzky, Karel Teige, Lajos Kassák, Ljubomir

El Lissitzky, cover design for *Veshch/Gegenstand/Objet* no. 1–2 (1922)

Micić, László Moholy-Nagy, and Władysław Strzemiński could be at once writers, poets, painters, sculptors, photographers, authors of essays, manifestos, and programs, exhibition organizers, editors, publishers, even architects. As editors of periodicals or representative volumes of contemporary art such as *Kunstismen* [The Isms of Art] by Lissitzky and Hans Arp, or *Buch neuer Künstler* [Book of New Artists] by Kassák and Moholy-Nagy, they promoted trends and individuals that they judged important, thus initiating the canonization of the international avant-garde.

By the mid-1920s international avant-garde exhibitions were being mounted, albeit sporadically, in cosmopolitan centers throughout Central Europe. M. H. Maxy, Marcel Janco, and the Contimporanul group in Bucharest organized an exhibition in 1924 that included artists from Poland (Mieczław Sczcuka and Teresa Żarnower), Germany (Kurt Schwitters) Czechoslovakia (Teige), Hungary (Kassák), and Sweden (the abstract films of Viking Eggeling). Their periodicals *Contimporanul* and the subsequent *75 HP*, *Integral*, and *Unu* show how revolutionary international trends were for Romanian art and architecture, hitherto regarded there as "foreign" tendencies.[33] Ljubomir Micić and the *Zenit* group mounted an international exhibition in Belgrade in 1924 including recent works by Moholy-Nagy and Lissitzky. Micić used his periodical (which also had featured International Constructivism) to promote the Balkan spirit represented by the "Barbarogenius" against Western European norms.[34]

M. H. Maxy, cover design for *Integral* no. 1 (1925)

THE TWILIGHT OF IDEOLOGIES

By 1929 international activity with all its diversity had begun to wane, just as the production of the avant-garde was finding its museological destination in the Polish "a.r." group's founding of the International Collection of Modern Art that would be housed in the municipal museum in Łódź. A potential demise of the avant-garde, at least in its international dimension, had already been evident in Ernő Kállai's 1925 essay "The Twilight of Ideologies."[35] Indeed, as Karel Teige suggested in his "Poetism" manifesto a year earlier, "there is no –ism, only 'new art' that often harbors illusions as old as the world itself and calls them universal truths."[36] While Teige remained optimistic that "Poetism... at the time of the twilight of all idols...has appropriated *lyrical value* as its very own and true golden treasure,"[37] the metaphysical basis for ideologically driven movements was being eroded by a new emphasis on practicality, a fragmentation of artists' groups, and the exploding growth of mass culture. As Teige proclaimed a few years later, these were "the last glimmers of the isms."[38]

As early as 1920 the utopian fantasies of Expressionism had been denounced in favor of actual practice by one of the former fantasists par excellence, Bruno Taut: "I no longer want to draw Utopias 'in principio,' but absolutely palpable Utopias that 'stand with both feet on the ground.'"[39] Similar issues divided members of the Polish Praesens group, whose architects sought realistic solutions. Former Polish Formist Stanisław Ignacy Witkiewicz's "Portrait Firm," ironically presented as a purely business

enterprise,[40] used sarcastic self-reflection to convey a rejection of metaphysics. Pragmatism was not embraced universally, but was ubiquitous as an issue. Constructivism—and especially its Productivist proclivities—was roundly critiqued in Teige's Poetism, which favored a more playful celebration of life.[41] However, the growing fissures between pragmatism and metaphysics, politics and aesthetics, one-time ideals and newfound utilitarianism, were no longer easily accommodated by movements or groups.

As the 1930s dawned, Surrealism, with its focus on the unconscious, attracted artists from all over Europe. The Romanian periodical *Unu* was an important Surrealist venue, and Czech Devětsil members Štyrský and Toyen, after living in Paris in the late 1920s, founded a Surrealist group in Prague with Vítěslav Nezval in the early 1930s. By this time the avant-garde was everywhere plagued with factional splits. The Polish group Blok had broken up in 1926; Bortnyik and Kassák had left the Vienna Ma group and returned to Budapest the same year. In Bucharest a debate took place between traditionalists and a younger generation asserting complete independence. Devětsil, already having splintered into factions over ideological differences, dissolved in 1931 with the last issue

Above:
El Lissitzky, cover design for *Zenit* no. 17–18 (1922)

Opposite:
Ljubomir Micić in front of the poster for the First International Zenit Exhibition, 1925

of *ReD*. It was in this year that van Doesburg died, one of the principle unifiers of the international avant-garde.

The new common language throughout the culture at large and within the remnants of the avant-garde was that of mass media, with what Kállai called its "mass sensibility."[42] Many within the avant-garde—among them Karel Teige and Moholy-Nagy—embraced the expressive means of photography, film, sound recording, and radio. An international debate over the relationship of film and photography to art (especially painting) took place in the pages of the Dutch periodical *i10*, with the discussion framed by Moholy-Nagy. The issues were broadened beyond the avant-garde into the realms of journalism and advertising in the 1929 Düsseldorf *Film und Foto* exhibition, in which Moholy-Nagy also played a shaping role.

Kállai addressed the threat of kitsch posed by utilitarianism, the cult of the machine, and mass production just when many artists, including Bortnyik and Kassák in Budapest, Schwitters in Hanover, and Bayer at the Bauhaus were becoming involved with advertising.[43] Kállai was also among those who recoiled at the alliance forged between "the advertising and organizational practices of modern mass psychology" and the

Lajos Kassák, *Noise* (1920), collage and ink on paper, 5 ⅞ x 4¼ in.

Lajos Kassák, page from Ma book *To My Woman* (1921)

Lajos Kassák, "Picture Poem," *Ma* vol. 8, no. 1 (1922)

Third Reich,"44 an alliance that brought the heroic era of European modernism to a definitive close.

An anthology of this sort can never convey the full experience of a text's original visual impact or its tactile existence, the physical medium in which it appears, whether a cheaply printed broadside or a luxuriously appointed volume. Yet perhaps in no other era were artists more sensitive to the expressive potential of such details as layout and design, illustrations, and even the paper used. Among the authors we consider, El Lissitzky, Lajos Kassák, László Moholy-Nagy, and Karel Teige were most responsible for a complete transformation of the page, one that would be widely influential throughout the entire century. Lissitzky brought his "proun" principles to bear on periodicals ranging from his own *Veshch/Gegenstand/Objet* to Ljubomir Micić's *Zenit* and Kassák's *Ma*. As were many of the avant-garde in the late teens, Lajos Kassák had been inspired by Futurist Filippo Marinetti's *parole in libertá* in his early Bruitist collages and poetry. In contrast to the gesturally rendered masthead and Expressionist graphics of the early *Ma* issues, his "picture-architecture" and picture poems embody Constructivist principles in language and would eventually

Lajos Kassák, cover design for *Ma* vol. 6, no. 5 (1921)

Sándor Bortnyik, cover illustration for *Ma* vol. 4, no. 5 (1919)

Karel Teige, cover design for *ReD*, vol. 1, no. 2 (1927)

appear on new cover designs in a programmatic context, as exemplified in the Vienna-era *Ma* covers and in the *Buch neuer Künstler*. Teige, whose early work included picture poetry, incorporated photography, a Constructivist grid of bold bars and colors, and modular letters of the type used in industrial stencils to create an imposing image of Lenin for the cover of his periodical, *ReD*. Moholy-Nagy imagined the page cinematically in his film score "Film Sketch: Dynamics of a Metropolis" in *Ma*.[45] M. H. Maxy conceived standardized forms that might be used to "construct" letters in his cover for *Integral*.

Text became increasingly responsive to the surrounding context of mass culture and industrialized production. Just as Henryk Berlewi hoped that exhibiting his *Mechano-faktura* works in a Warsaw Austro-Daimler showroom would allow them to be understood as standardized patterns suitable to the age of the machine,[46] his colleagues in the Blok group used illustrations of industrial products, large-scale newspaper format, and standardized letters in bold layouts to convey their faith that "production technology" could produce "utilitarian objects" that reveal a "universal type of beauty."[47] The use of mass media technologies and the broadside format could also enact a subversive critique of the surrounding culture,

MOHOLY-NAGY: $_F$ILMVÁZ ● A NAGYVÁROS
dinamikája

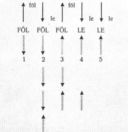

Szemközti házsorok egymáson átlátszóan ellentétes irányban ⇐⇒ rohannak és az autók is mindig gyorsabban, hogy rövidesen káprázik a szem belé.

Tigris TIGRIS jár ketrecében dühösen föl s alá
Magasan — fönt — tisztán szemaforok

automatikusan
a—u—t—o—m—a—t—i—k—u—s—a—n
mozognak (nagy részletfölvétel)

	föl		föl		
		le		le	le
FÖL	FÖL	FÖL	LE	LE	
1	2	3	4	5	

Teherpályaudvar
Váltóállomás
Raktárépületek és pincéik

SÖTÉT SÖTÉT
SÖTÉTSÉG
Vasut:
Országut (járművekkel). Híd. Viadukt. A mélyben: uszó hajók. Fölötte lebegő vasut (Elberfeld)

Vonatfölvétel magas töltésről: rézsutosan
Bakter haptákban szalutál
Szemei megüvegesednek (Nagy RÉSZLETfölvétel)
A vonat egy hidról: fölülről

Alulról: egy a sinek közötti árokból a v o n a t h a s a, ahogy elvágtat
Kerék forog — elmosódott vibrálásig

TEMPÓ ó
TEMPÓ
TEM PÓ
TEM
TEM
TEEM
M
$_M$$_P$ P $Ö$ Óó ó

Áruházban üvegfölvonók négergyerekkel
Ferdén
Eltorzitott perspektiva

Le

FÖL

FÖL

Kilátás. CSŐDÜLET
A bejáratnál kikötött kutyák
Az üvegfölvonók mellett üveges telefónfülke telefonálóval
Földszintfölvétel az üveglapokon át
A telefonálónak foszforeszkáló anyaggal bedörzsölt (hogy ne keletkezzék sziluett) ARCA közvetlenül a fölvevőgép mellett lassan elfordul jobbra
Feje fölött spirálisan huzódik el egy messziről röpülő aeroplán

Röpülőfölvétel csekély magasságból: tér, ahová sok utca torkollik

Járművek tömege: villanyos, autó, teherkocsi, konflis, bicikli, autóbusz, ciklonett hajt gyors tempóban kifelé egyszerre visszafordul mind
a középen összefutnak

Vasdaru épitése
(A trükkasztal-fölvétel — rajz — lassan természetfölvételbe olvad át)
Házépítésnél mozgó emelő

Fölvétel ↑ alulról
rézsutosan
felülről ↓

Téglafölvonó.
Körben-mozgó darú

Ezt a mozgást tovább folytatja egy automobil, amelyik balra
rohan. A kép közepén folyton egy és ugyanazt a házat látni; (t. i. a házat mindig vissza kell a középre fotografálni). Megjelenik egy másik automobil, amelyik az elsővel egyidejűleg, csak ellenkező irányban, száguld
Az utca egyik házsora ugyanebben az irányban rohan ugy, hogy a kép közepén levő ház átlátszik rajta. A házsor elfut: és visszajön

Rézsut
rézsut
RÉZSUT

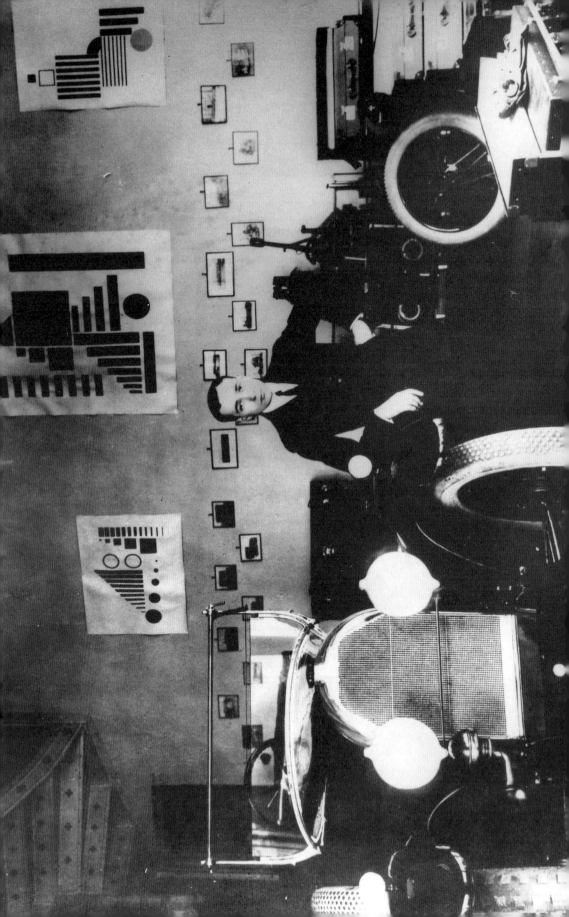

including its most radical avant-garde aspects, as Branko Ve Poljanski demonstrated in his Zagreb periodical *Dada-Jok*.[48] In Ljubljana, *Tank* leader Avgust Černigoj took a more conventional position against earlier avant-gardes,[49] and resolved on a direction that demonstrates how the visual discoveries of Constructivism had been thoroughly internationalized by the late 1920s, and could be deployed to reflect the issues of the local context.

The Central European avant-gardes documented in this volume embodied this duality between the regional and the cosmopolitan as they furthered dialogue interconnecting the two. At times creating, at times contributing to, and at times adopting the unfolding narrative of the European avant-garde, multicentered and multinational Central Europe has not yet been fully appreciated for its impact. The present selection of documents is intended as a contribution toward its further discovery.

Above:
Cover of *Blok* no. 2 (1924)

Opposite:
Henryk Berlewi at his exhibition in the Austro-Daimler showroom, Warsaw, 1924

Below:
Cover of *Dada-Jok* (1922)

1 The title of Jacques Rupnik's *The Other Europe* (London: Weidenfeld and Nicholson, 1988) was a phrase often used around 1989–90.

2 The first such exhibition was *Avantgarde Osteuropa* (Berlin: Kunstverein Berlin in West Berlin, 1967).

3 Ryszard Stanislawski, et. al., *Constructivism in Poland 1923–1936: BLOK, Praesens, a.r.* (Łódź: Muzeum Sztuki, 1973). The exhibition was also seen in Otterlo and Cambridge. Cf. Hilary Gresty and Jeremy Lewison, eds. *Constructivism in Poland, 1923 to 1936.* Kettle's Yard Gallery in association with Muzeum Sztuki, Łódź (Cambridge: The Gallery, 1984). It included texts by Henryk Berlewi, Katarzyna Kobro, Tadeusz Peiper, Henryk Stażewski, Władysław Strzemiński, Mieczysław Szczuka, and Teresa Żarnower.

4 *Tendenzen der Zwanziger Jahre* (Berlin: Reimer, 1977). It included a few German translations of documents related to Polish, Hungarian, and German Constructivism. In 1979 a large volume, *L'Activisme Hongrois* by Charles Dautrey and Jean-Claude Guerlain (Montrouge: Goutal-Darly) included French translations of documents by Sándor Bortnyik, Lajos Kassák, and György Lukács, among others.

5 *The Hungarian Avant-Garde: The Eight and the Activists* (Hungarian Institute for Cultural Relations and Hayward Gallery, February 27 to April 7, 1980) included half a dozen documents by Lukács, Fülep, Kassák, and Kállai.

6 *Czech Cubism: Architecture, Furniture, and Decorative Arts 1910–1925*, seen in 1992 at the Canadian Centre for Architecture (CCA) in Montreal and the Cooper-Hewitt in New York after its initial presentation at the Vitra Design Museum in Weil am Rhein in 1991, included a handful of short texts related to architecture by Pavel Janák.

7 *Wille zur Form: Ungegenständliche Kunst 1910–1938 in Österreich, Polen, Tschechoslowakei und Ungarn* (Vienna: Hochschule für Angewandte Kunst, 1993), provided a few key documents by Kobro, Strzemiński, Teige, Kassák, and Suschny in German.

8 *Wechselwirkungen: ungarische Avantgarde in der Weimarer Republik* (Marburg: Jonas Verlag, 1986). This elucidation of Hungarian-German artistic exchange includes nearly 150 documents translated into German—including examples of texts from the Bauhaus and the Berlin Sturm Gallery.

9 Jirí Svestka and Tomáš Vlček in *1909–1925 Kubismus in Prag: Malerei, Skulptur, Kunstgewerbe, Architektur* (Düsseldorf: Kunstverein für die Rheinlande und Westfalen, 1991) included a large selection of German translations of important texts from the little magazines of the day by the leading Czech painters and architects (Čapek, Filla, Gutfreund, Hofman, Janák, Kubišta, Špála, and Zrzavý) as well as a small selection of the correspondence between art historian Vincenc Kramář and both Paris dealer Daniel-Henry Kahnweiler and German Expressionist Ernst Ludwig Kirchner.

10 Ryszard Stanislawski and Christoph Brockhaus, *Europa, Europa: das Jahrhundert der Avantgarde in Mittel- und Osteuropa* (Bonn: Bundesmuseum, 1994), including a volume of documents selected by Hubertus Gassner, which is the most comprehensive selection hitherto published and includes German translations of 335 key texts (some excerpted) ranging from Symbolism and Synesthesia, to post-World War II developments in performance, conceptual, and media arts.

11 Stephan Bann, *The Tradition of Constructivism* (New York: Viking, 1974) included texts by László Moholy-Nagy, Ivan Puni, and from the Polish periodical *Blok* and the Czech *Disk*.
Moholy-Nagy is among the few artists who have had much of their work translated into English: Richard Kostelanetz, *Moholy-Nagy* (New York: Praeger, 1970), Krisztina Passuth, *Moholy-Nagy* (London: Thames and Hudson, 1985), and the translation of the 1925 Bauhaus book *Malerei, Fotografie, Film*: László Moholy-Nagy, *Painting, Photography, Film* (Cambridge: MIT Press, 1969).
English translations have appeared for Władysław Strzemiński's 1928 *Unism in Painting* (Łódź: Muzeum Sztuki, 1994); for Teige (Erich Dluhosch and Rostislav Svácha, eds., *Karel Teige: L'Enfant Terrible of the Czech Modernist Avant-Garde* [Cambridge: MIT Press, 1999] includes four texts by Teige; see also Teige, *Modern Architecture in Czechoslovakia and Other Writings* [Los Angeles: Getty Research Institute, 2000]); and for El Lissitzky's 1930

Russia: An Architecture for World Revolution (trans. Eric Dluhosch [Cambridge: MIT Press, 1970]). For some Romanian texts in English, see *Plural*, no. 3, 1999.
Some Romanian and Hungarian avant-garde texts have appeared in German: Eva Behring, ed., *Texte der Rumänischen Avantgarde: 1907–1947* (Leipzig: Verlag Phillip Reclam, 1988); Lajos Kassák, *Lasst uns leben in unserer Zeit: Gedichte, Bilder und Schriften zur Kunst*, ed. József Vadas (Budapest: Corvina, 1989), and Ernst Kállai, *Schriften in deutscher Sprache: 1920–1925* (Budapest: Argumentum, 1999).
French translations appear in Krisztina Passuth, *Les Avant-Gardes de l'Europe Centrale* (Paris: Flammarion, 1988).

12 Danilo Kiš, "Variations on the Theme of Central Europe," *Cross Currents* 6 (1987), 1–14.

13 Jacques Rupnik, ibid., 3–23.

14 *New York Review of Books*, Sept. 29, 1988. This question was broached for the visual arts in Andrzej Turowski's book *Existe-t-il un art de l'Europe de l'est?* [Does East European Art Exist?] (Paris: Editions de la Villette, 1986); and in Éva Forgács's article "Is There an East European Art?" in *Budapest Review of Books*, Summer/Fall 1999.

15 Friedrich Naumann, *Mitteleuropa*. (Berlin: G. Reimer, 1915). Cf. Helmut Rumpf, "Mitteleuropa: Zur Geschichte und Deutung eines politischen Begriffs," in *Historische Zeitschrift* 165 (1942).

16 Antal Czettler, "Német tervek és elképzelések Közép-Európáról a 20. század első felében" [German Plans and

Concepts of Central Europe in the First Half of the Twentieth Century], in Bán D. András, ed.: *A híd túlsó oldalán. Tanulmányok Kelet-Közép Európáról* [On the Other Side of the Bridge. Essays on East-Central Europe] (Budapest: Osiris, 2000), 57–58.

17 Claudio Magris, *Danube*, trans. Patrick Creagh (New York: Farrar, Straus, Giroux, 1999), 32.

18 John Lukács, "Az Európa-fogalom kialakulása és fejlődése. Magyarország helye Európában" [The Creation and Development of the Concept of Europe. Hungary's Place in Europe], in András, op. cit., 36.

19 Ibid., 37.

20 For example, see the discussion of ambiguous loyalties in Poland in Piotr Piotrowski, "Modernity and Nationalism: Avant-Garde Art and Polish Independence 1912–1922," in Timothy O. Benson, ed., *Central European Avant-Gardes: Exchange and Transformation, 1910–1930* (Cambridge: MIT Press, 2002), 312–26; and Jan Cavanaugh, *Out Looking In: Early Modern Polish Art, 1890–1918* (Berkeley: University of California Press, 2000).

21 Serfdom was abolished in 1807 in Prussia, 1861 in Russia, 1863 in Poland, and during the 1870s throughout the Habsburg empire, but much of the aristocratic social order remained intact. See Ivan T. Berend, *Decades of Crisis: Central and Eastern Europe before World War II* (Berkeley: University of California Press, 1998), 5–11.

22 On this phenomenon of "Lücken-Positionen," or gap-positions, between ruling elites and agrarian

economies in the rigid and outmoded social structures of Central Europe, which needed to be filled by immigration as the region modernized, see Berend, *Decades of Crisis*, 32–40.

23 Ulrich Linse, *Organisierter Anarchismus im Deutschen Kaiserreich von 1871* (Berlin: Duncker & Humblot, 1969), and also Walter Fähnders, *Anarchismus und Literatur: Ein vergessenes Kapitel deutscher Literaturgeschichte zwischen 1890 und 1910* (Stuttgart: Metzler, 1987).

24 See, among other works, Boris Groys, *The Total Art of Stalinism*, trans. Charles Rougle (Princeton: Princeton University Press, 1992), and Timothy J. Clark, *Farewell to an Idea: Episodes from a History of Modernism* (New Haven: Yale University Press, 1999), in particular the introduction.

25 Artists would not experience how living in opposition could entail another kind of relationship with political power till the last years of the cold war era in the 1980s. The Hungarian György Konrád responded with his strategic *Antipolitics: An Essay*, trans. Richard E. Allen (London: Quarter Books, 1984), the Czech Milan Kundera called for an avoidance of all dialogue with political power (interview in *Magyar Füzetek* [Paris: Dialogues Européens, 1979]), and the Pole Adam Michnik developed the political philosophy of nonviolence as another way of avoiding any contact with power.

26 See Jakobson, "Dada," 359.

27 For example *Gauguin*, *Cézanne* (Budapest: Nemzeti Szalon, 1907), and *Francouzští Impressionisté*

(Prague: S. V. U. Mánes, 1907), which included Cézanne and Gauguin as well as French Impressionism.

28 See Carl Vinnen, "Quousque Tandem," 50, and Bohumil Kubišta, "Josef Mánes's Exhibition at the Topič Salon," 57.

29 See Lajos Fülep, *Hungarian Art*, 71.

30 György Lukács: "A Tanácsköztársaság kultúr-politikájáról" [On the Cultural Politics of the Hungarian Soviet Republic] in Lukács, *Magyar irodalom, magyar kultúra* [Hungarian Literature, Hungarian Culture] (Budapest: Magvető Kiadó, 1970), 626.

31 See Bernd Finkeldey et. al., eds., *Konstruktivistische Internationale Schöpferische Arbeitsgemeinschaft 1922–1927: Utopien für eine europäische Kultur* (Stuttgart: G. Hatje, 1992) 308–10 for list of attendees.

32 See chapter 7.

33 See S. A. Mansbach, "The Foreignness of Classical Modern Art in Romania," *Art Bulletin* 80, no. 3 (September 1998): 534–54.

34 See chapters 5 and 8

35 See 615.

36 Teige, "Poetism," 579.

37 Ibid.

38 Teige, "Poetism Manifesto," 593.

39 From correspondence reprinted in Timothy O. Benson, ed., *Expressionist Utopias: Paradise, Metropolis, Architectural Fantasy* (Berkeley: University of California Press, 2001), 305.

40 See "Rules of the S. I. Witkiewicz Portrait Painting Firm," 646.

41 Teige, "Poetism," 579.

42 Kállai, "Painting and Photography," 684.

43 Kállai, "Art and the General Public," 719.

44 Kállai, "Politics of Art in the Third Reich," 726.

45 See 458.

46 See Berlewi, "Mechano-facture," 489.

47 See Władysław Strzemiński, "Theses on New Art," 493.

48 See "Dada Anti-Dada," in *Dada-Jok*, 345. For further discussion of the Dada text see Timothy O. Benson, "Constructions and Conventions: The Performative Text in Dada," in Stephen C. Foster, *Dada: The Coordinates of Cultural Politics* (Boston: G. K. Hall, 1996), 83–106.

49 See Avgust Černigoj, Tank Manifesto, 574.

STYLE AS THE CRUCIBLE OF PAST AND FUTURE

2

3　4

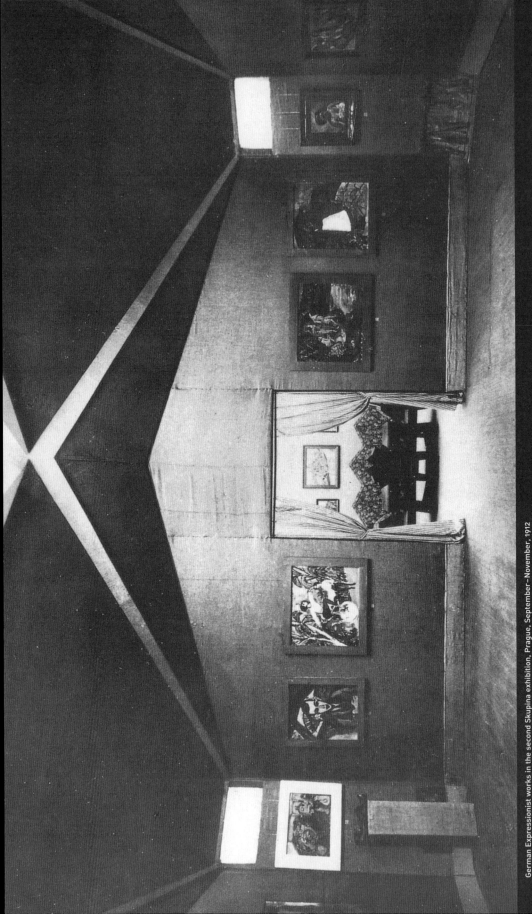

German Expressionist works in the second Skupina exhibition, Prague, September–November, 1912

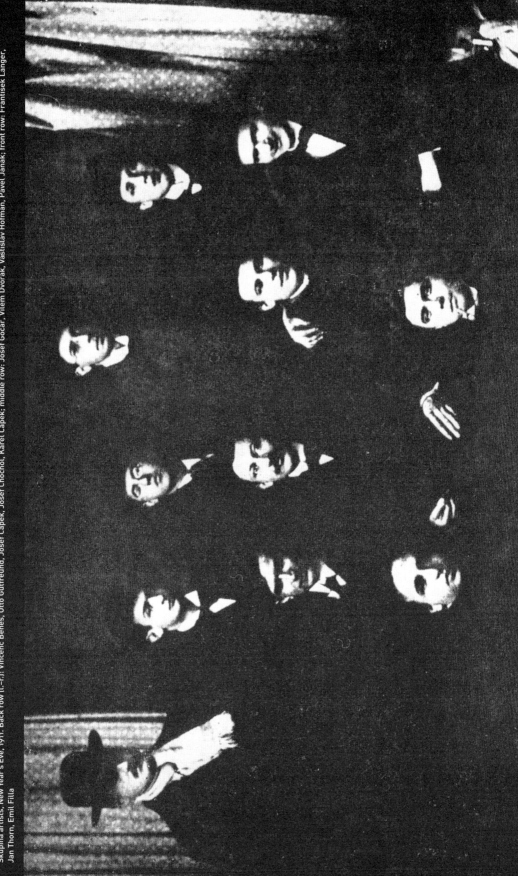

Skupina artists, New Year's Eve, 1911. Back row (l.–r.): Vincenc Beneš, Otto Gutfreund, Josef Čapek, Josef Chochol, Karel Čapek; middle row: Josef Gočár, Vilém Dvořák, Vastislav Hofman, Pavel Janák; front row: František Langer, Jan Thorn, Emil Filla

chapter 1

NATIONAL TRADITIONS

Éva Forgács

The territory that is identified, with more or less uncertainty, as Central Europe today—with the reservation, by many authors, that Central Europe is more a kingdom of spirit than a geographic entity—figured on the map at the turn of the nineteenth and twentieth centuries as the Austro-Hungarian Empire. The country we know as Poland today did not exist on that map: its present territory was divided between the Austro-Hungarian Empire, Prussia, and Russia.

Suppressed by huge empires, the nations of Central Europe lived as nations in their cultures only. National culture, national tradition, and national character created the backbone of national existence. Painting and sculpture had created the images of the mythical past and commemorated the great events of the history of the respective nations throughout the nineteenth century.

The Central European artist was laden with heavy burdens unfamiliar to the Western artist. He had to represent his oppressed nation's cause in a political situation where the mere use of the national language or a national idiom in art was a bold gesture signaling the re-claiming of nationhood. The artist was seen as a beacon in the fight for the cause of the nation. He had to be—and some of them literally became—a freedom fighter, ready to sacrifice himself for the independence of the nation, its language and its culture.

The modern Central European nation-states arose only in 1918, but a sense of national-cultural renewal swept over this part of the continent around the turn of the century. Although industrialization was significantly slower here than in Western Europe—and the societies of the region still featured the feudal privileges of the aristocracy, which was slow to accept modernization—the idea of progress emerged and gained momentum in the growing cities: Vienna, Budapest, Prague, Brno, Warsaw, Cracow, Zagreb, Ljubljana, and others.

The cultivation of the national character based on tradition and the distinctive values of the national culture was a positive goal. Cultural nationalism, at this time, lacked aggression and hostility towards other nations. It had an anti-imperial stance, but without the intention of immediately changing the historical-political status quo. Although culture in Central Europe has traditionally been the medium of history and politics, around 1900 the issue of national art was addressed throughout Central Europe as a great newfound potential for cultural, and, through this, national renewal without revolutionary ambitions.

Ruminations on national culture, even if politically loaded, were philosophical rather than politically disruptive. (See the contemplative mood of Jiránek's "The Czechness of Our Art," Witkiewicz's essay on Matejko, or Fülep's theoretical approach.) The possibility—or impossibility—of national style, its implications, meaning, and ramifications were addressed both emotionally and theoretically. The rediscovery of national heritage had a collectivizing power. It was exploited to energize the respective nations' identity by generating solidarity, a sense of responsibility, and the vision of a common future.

Endeavors to create a national art were, paradoxically, the first step towards the creation of internationalism, because these early movements sought to confirm national pride and consciousness in order to elevate the nation as a full-fledged member of Europe and integrate the national culture into the European cultural heritage. The creation and cultivation of authentic national culture was seen as the token of cultural emancipation as well as national progress.

Shortly before the turn of the century, when the long-waited, all-encompassing international style finally surfaced as *Art Nouveau*, or *Jugendstil*, or *Sezession*, the issue of style was double-edged. Adopting Art Nouveau ensured modernity, thus international integration, which was a welcome move; but it discarded national identity. Thus local variants of Art Nouveau were created, where the novelty of the style and the national particulars of the contents—such as symbolist elaboration of mythical or historical motifs—created new meaning. It was precisely this union of stylistic progress and local tradition that opened up the possibility of creating what was hoped would become modernist national art. The artists of Central Europe, still living under the dominance of one or another of the great empires, had to see renewal in terms of the dialectics of the cultures of the empires and those of their own national traditions. The stylization, symbolism, and deliberate vagueness of art nouveau harbored and curbed the possible harshness of nationalist gestures. This was the first time in the history of the cultures of Central Europe since the Enlightenment that the concept of progress and the concept of tradition had to be rendered compatible.

The intensity of the internationalist movements that would come later in the 1920s was thus rooted in the long tradition of the dreams about national art and national culture all over Central Europe. Transcending nationhood yet not losing it in order to join the common European tradition had always underpinned the national cultural renewal movements.

GERMANY Éva Forgács

Art was considered an instrument for teaching nationhood to the people, a way of great ideals and a triumphant confirmation of national values by no less an authority than Emperor William II. As he stated in a famous speech he gave in Berlin in 1901: "We Germans have permanently acquired these great ideals, while other peoples have more or less lost them. Only the Germans remain and are above all others called upon to guard these great ideals." The emperor's voice was, however, but one among many that discussed the national vocation of art and the particular Germanness of its values. A firm official concept reigned in Wilhelmine Germany about what was encouraged and what was prohibited in art. Emerging styles, most of all Expressionism—even if the term was not yet coined—directly clashed with these principles and the bourgeois patronage structure.

The Berlin Secession, founded in 1898, had already carried on a successful fight for the then new style of Impressionism and managed to graft the idiom originating in France onto the Berlin art scene. This international orientation made many enemies, too, particularly because of the great market success of the foreign Impressionist artists—even if many Germans shared in this success.

In the highly politicized German cultural discourse, the 1906 program of the *Die Brücke* group, which appealed to the young who "want to be free (...) from the long-established old powers," reverberated as the bold rejection of the canonized national values. Conservatives and unsuccessful German artists, such as Carl Vinnen, could not forgive the welcoming of not only French artists and their influence, but also the work of primitive cultures. By the time Wassily Kandinsky's and Franz Marc's *Der Blaue Reiter* almanac was published in 1912, their embrace of international diversity signaled that a stronghold of new values had been established. Their attitudes overtly conflicted with the emperor's views: "...the principle of internationalism is the only one possible.... An individual nation is only one of the creators of the whole; alone one can never be seen as the whole. Like the personal, the national is automatically reflected in each great work."

QUOUSQUE TANDEM FROM *A PROTEST OF GERMAN ARTISTS*   Carl Vinnen
Originally published as "Quousque Tandem," in *Ein Protest deutscher Künstler* (Jena, Germany: 1911)

In light of the great invasion of French art that has been in progress in so-called progressive German art circles over the past few years, it seems to me that necessity bids German painters raise a warning voice, and not be daunted by the reproach that only envy motivates them.

For to be an artist also carries an obligation!

As the entire movement of the last quarter century had its beginning in France, admiration of its great masters—which is certainly justified—has led to certain excesses among us today that threaten to transform a blessing into its opposite.

In the violent battles for new direction, if one can speak of such a thing, the avant-garde artist has a faithful ally, namely the modern art-author.

....

Recognizing, not incorrectly, that Rhineland art has fallen from its former position of power into obscurity, the "Sonderbund"—an artists' association there with many influential benefactors in its own province and beyond—is seeking intimate association with the latest Parisian extravagants—Matisse among others—and so is moving from one extreme to another.

....

Far be it from me to devalue the way in which our culture has been stimulated through the high culture of French art, and if I myself recently spent some time in Paris in order to learn, that should be proof enough of my admiration.

But speculation has become a factor in the matter. German and French art dealers have shaken hands, under the pretext of promoting artistic goals, and Germany is being flooded with great quantities of French pictures.

....

This tide of pictures enters the land through the flood-gates of art literature, and the literature becomes reinfatuated with it; the infatuation in the press in turn helps the dealers to unload the pictures on German collectors at exorbitant prices. By way of illustrating how much these values increase, one might consider the Lady in a Green-Black Dress by Monet, which netted the artist 700 francs and cost the Bremen Museum 50,000 marks.

Yet at the time, I myself supported Director Pauli, who has done so much for the development of artistic life in Bremen and for the formation of our gallery, when he suggested its purchase; and I would support him again, considering the high artistic value of the painting. There are exceptional cases, finally, in which money can be no object.

No real artists would want to quibble where real masterpieces—the achievements of a great man, of whatever nationality—are concerned. But when we see how even the casual studies by van Gogh, even those in which an artist misses all three dimensions—draughtsmanship, color and mood—draw 30 to 40 thou-sand marks with no questions asked, how not enough old dregs from the studios of Monet, Sisley, Pissaro, etc., can be put on the German market to satisfy the demand, one must say that in general the prices of French pictures have been driven up to such an extent—of course France itself does not pay these prices—that we seem to be faced with an inflated esteem in which the German people should not cooperate indefinitely.

It's doubtful whether these prices, which today are driven to dizzying heights by means of market manipulation, will ever even approach stabilization.

One must distinguish between the ephemeral, that is, the art historical value of these pictures as evolutionary factors, and their permanent value, which they will also have for the sensibility of times to come,....

More important is the other question:

What constitutes the great danger of introducing foreign art, when speculation takes hold of it?

Well, mostly in the overestimation of foreign nature so that our own, original character doesn't measure up.

Accomplishments since Monet are, to put it briefly, dedicated to the surface of things.
....

The art of a Cézanne, a van Gogh, was too characteristic of its creator, with too little attention to structure to found a school and to make way for successors.
....

A rush, a hunt begins, everybody wants to be modern, everybody searches...for his individuality in imitation.
....

Because let it be said again and again, a people is only driven to great heights by artists of its own flesh and blood.
....

There should be no doubt that we have *completely* lost the world market for art, which we formerly dominated. The reasons our modern painting was so inadequately represented in the last great World-exhibitions are certainly sufficiently well known. This lowered us into an art of second rank in the eyes of the world, especially the Americans. Now the great international stream of foreigners that flows through Germany every year sees how the often truly mediocre French pictures are enthusiastically praised, hung in the places of honor in our galleries and the windows of art dealers, how our illustrated art magazines are full of them, our youth zealously and diligently imitate them.

How can we expect the foreigners to hold us in higher esteem than we do ourselves!

And yet now would be the time to win a place in the sun for our art, ideally and materially, as we have been able to do for our crafts with such conspicuous success.
....

Even if every true artist, everything great and beautiful of whatever heritage, should enjoy a right to hospitality at the German hearth, a great cultural people, a people possessed of such powerful aspirations as is our own, can not forever tolerate a foreign presence that claims spiritual authority.

And as this is being foisted upon us by a large, well-financed international organization, an earnest admonition is in order: to proceed no further in this way, and to be clear about what we are in a position to lose, namely nothing less than our own essence and our inherited native capacity.

Our art history tells us that this would not be the first time a great tradition had been lost for a long time, and it also tells us the consequences—

So we must struggle in the best of faith, not in reactionary ways, not in sentimental ones, but in the spirit of the best that our art has achieved.

Translation from Rose-Carol Washton Long, German Expressionism

THE HISTORICAL DEVELOPMENT OF MODERN ART FROM *THE STRUGGLE FOR ART: THE ANSWER TO "THE PROTEST OF GERMAN ARTISTS"*
Wilhelm Worringer
Originally published as "Entwicklungsgeschichtliches zur modernsten Kunst," in
Im Kampf um die Kunst: Die Antwort auf den "Protest deutscher Künstler" (Munich: 1911)
and in *Der Sturm* vol. 2, no. 75 (August, 1911)

Vinnen's brochure is entirely understandable to me, psychologically, and I don't hesitate to regard it as a symptomatic phenomenon. I even welcome it as a timely call for an honest discussion of principles. The crisis in which we find our conceptions and our expectations of art cannot be kept quiet: it must lead to open and decisive discussions.

With these points in mind I must regret, however, that Vinnen's promotional piece fails to treat the basic questions seriously, only touching on them fleetingly here and there and using space instead for popular turns of phrase and emotional pronouncements that cannot be substantiated. Thus the main argument with which the attacking faction wishes to engage the public is not the sort of refutation of new artistic principles that could be discussed impartially, but an irresponsible denunciation of the personalities on the other side, transposed into every possible key.... For it is not right to cultivate, in a general public made gullible through innate inertia and an instinct for self-preservation, the gratifying conviction that the movement under attack consists of a senseless game among impotent, sensation-hungry artists, undiscriminating art writers swayed by every whim of fashion, and cunning art dealers who, suppressing their laughter, reap profits from this comedy.
....

For besides such irresponsible hangers-on there stand artists who search in earnest, who for all their sober self-awareness remain perfectly modest; there stand serious theoreticians who preserve, despite their productive partisanship, a historical consciousness and with it, a critical discretion; there stand finally art dealers who, although they of course have business matters to consider, still foster, with inner conviction and understanding, a movement in which one's profits are at far greater risk than they would be in marketing some simple, recognized commercial product.
....

If I understand Vinnen correctly, he wants German art, in finding a new artistic form, to guard against the influence not of the great classic Impressionists such as Manet, Monet, and Renoir, but of the so-called young Parisians, who follow Cézanne, van Gogh, and Matisse in searching for a new kind of artistic formulation.

... Where an unprepared and backward public sees and can only see the products of willful self-indulgence and idiotic sensationalism, we sense historical necessity. We see above all a unity in the movement that has something fundamental about it, before which everything that seems to be self-indulgent disappears. Yes, I think I make no mistake in seeing the deepest roots of this new artistic drive precisely in the desire to conquer willful self-indulgence and personal limitations. This unmistakable striving for impartiality, for a compelling simplification of form, an elemental openmindedness about artistic representation, is bound up in the basic character of the new art, which some believe can be trivialized as primitive or childish comedy played before the adults of Europe.

But the only ones to be affected in this way will be those who have not yet come to understand primitive art and who see in it only a lack of skill over which one chuckles with the superiority of grown-ups. Today the cultural arrogance of Europeans is eroding, however, yielding to insights into the fundamental grandeur of primitive life and its artistic expression. The same need that makes us want to understand the new Parisian Synthetists and Expressionists has also developed in us a new eye for primitive art. How transparently clear it seems today that the stylistic character of primitive art is not determined by any lack of skill, but by a different conception of artistic purpose, a purpose that rests on a great, elementary foundation of a sort that we, with our well-buffered contemporary approach to life, can hardly conceive. We only vaguely sense that the grotesque distortion and compelling simplification of this primitive art (compelling, however, only for those who can distinguish between a compulsion for form and a compulsion for illusionary effect) emanates from a higher level of tension in the will to artistic expression, and we learn to recognize that the difference between our artistic achievement and the primitive is not one of degree, but of kind. A difference in kind that consists in reckoning art's achievements not in today's terms, namely in the release of a certain fine quality of feeling-sensual or spiritual, but in the release of a fundamental sense of the inevitable. An affirmation of the ambiguity of phenomena: in this lay the meaning, in this lay the essence, the mystique of this art....

Of course today we can't artificially force ourselves back to the level of primitive people, but the subliminal urgency we feel today is finally not only a reaction against Impressionism, but also against the whole previous development in which we have been involved since the European Renaissance, whose starting point and direction is embraced in Burckhardt's concise statement about the discovery of the individual. The vast wealth of factual learning of the past epoch has left us poor, and out of this sense of impoverishment we are today demanding consciously from art approximately that which primitive people naively demanded. We want art to affect us again, to affect us more powerfully than does that higher, cultivated illusionism that has been the destiny of our art since the Renaissance. In order to achieve this, we are trying to free ourselves from that rationalization of sight which seems to educated Europeans to be natural sight, and against which one may not transgress without being cast as a complete fool. In order to achieve this, we force ourselves to that primitive way of seeing, undisturbed by any knowledge or experience, which is the simple secret of the mystical effect of primitive art. We want to push external symbolism, hailed as a national trait of German art in particular, back into the innermost center of the artwork, in order that it might flow out from there of its own natural energy, free of every dualism of form and content. In short, the primitive art of seeing, to which we force ourselves, is only a means of approaching the elemental possible effects of art....

Such a return to earlier, elemental stages of development, such a generating of creative force from the concentrated reserves of power of the past, is not new to one who thinks in historical terms. To him it is only the repetition of a historical pattern so regular it seems almost to follow some natural law. Only the length of the pendulum's swing changes. And it is only the best sign of the power and passion of our time that the pendulum has swung as far as it has, and that it is now going back to basic and most essential things, things from which we have been separated by the pride of our European classical inhibition and the myopia of the European adult attitude. One goes back to the elemental stages of development because one hopes to again come closer to nature by doing so. And the unnaturalness that has been so ridiculed and disdained in recent painting is finally nothing other than the result of such a return to nature, although to a nature not yet filtered through the rationalizing optics of a European education, and from whose chaste purity and symbolic affective power the average European can know nothing.

...In the final analysis it is in the interests of future generations that we concern ourselves with the present. For this modern primitiveness is not supposed to be the last word. The pendulum does not rest in its extreme position. This primitivism should rather be understood as a long, deep breath, before the new and decisive word to the future will be pronounced....Surrounded with such broad vistas, let us in any case retreat from the narrow sphere in which Herr Vinnen fights over French and German art, and tries to persuade us with financial statistics.

Apropos of which, just two words in regard to the national aspect of the question. He who really knows about being German, who knows above all the history of German art, he knows that it is not given to us, with our innate ambiguity and with our inborn, sensual, instinctive uncertainty, to find the direct route to a form, he knows that we always take our cue first from outside Germany, that we have always had to give up and lose ourselves first, in order to find our real selves. That has been the tragedy and the grandeur of German art from Dürer to Marees, and he who would cut our art from interaction with other art worlds is betraying our real national tradition. Such a statement of dependency degrades our art only from a very childish and psychologi-cally immature point of view; to me the characteristic quality of German art history has always been this theater of engagement and this passionate striving beyond one's own narrow bounds. I would not want to be without this tragedy, this ambiguity, for it has given German art its singular dynamic.

Still one short observation pertaining to the external impetus for the whole discus-sion: the position our museum directors have taken on the new movement. The prob-lem from their point of view can be formulated briefly as follows: should they just buy good pictures, that is, good in terms of average taste, or should they now and then sacrifice such relative security in the interests of something that is historically signifi-cant, but that has not yet been sanctioned by the majority's taste? This question is only now becoming urgent for our museums because they themselves have just reached a historical crisis, and must decide which way to go. They were founded as institutions of courtly luxury: adventurousness and persuasiveness were not part of their nature. Should they retain this mature, culture-saturated, backward-looking character of lux-ury, or will they try to suit themselves to the rhythm of the times and make a dead herbarium into a living one? Should they only register history or should they make history?

...Whether these experiments lead to a positive result or turn out to be a useless expenditure of energy, a valuable piece of the actual inner life of our time has animated them. For this reason they deserve a place in our museums: a place not superior to, but certainly on a par with, the unproblematical art products that, as mentioned above, reflect the average character of our epoch and so force much of the finest and best into silence. Even failed experiments have their essential value and their historical meaning.

Translation from Rose-Carol Washton Long, German Expressionism

One of the dominant themes of Czech sculptural criticism at the beginning of the twentieth century was coming to terms with the fading legacy of the nineteenth. The generation of the 1890s included artists such as painters Antonín Slavíček and Jan Preisler; the generation forming in opposition to it, which comprised the group Osma, was led by Emil Filla and Bohumil Kubišta. Both groups agreed on the artists they admired: Josef Mánes (1820–1871) as a key figure in the genesis of Czech modern art, and Mikolas Aleš (1852–1913) as an authentic talent fighting lack of public comprehension. Mánes especially became a model, over whom a merciless battle was played out among the national and international supporters of art. Mánes found inspiration for his work in French art, and he was also interested in Moravian folklore and Czech mythology. The tensions pervading his work, which on the one hand were expressed through an attraction to the solid form, and, on the other, through an animated imitation of the subject, served as criteria for judging and differentiating the nation and the international—in this case primarily the French approaches.

If Miloš Jiránek and Kubišta were critical of the fact that viewers of a work of art fixate solely on the subject—which they ascertain the moment they determine that the work has a patriotic content—then both writers also realized that the activity at the heart of modern art was primarily concerned with form. Kubišta valued Aleš not for his work with the mythological themes of the Czech past, but because his murals were characterized by "pure sculptural form." Comparisons with French art, the development of which had been set up as a model by Mánes's followers—and which had been canonized in the Czech art world—soon led Jiránek and Kubišta to note a certain discontinuity and to conclude that it was necessary to create a solid base for the real development of Czech art as a point of departure. The opposition between the national and international discussions was consequently altered by a fundamental shift: the expression of national features was sought not in content, but in form.

Translated by Andrée Collier Záleská

THE CZECHNESS OF OUR ART   Miloš Jiránek

Originally published as "Českost našeho umění," *Radikální listy* vol. 7, no. 4 (January 4, 1900)

I recently came across an interesting letter from Russia about an exhibition of Austrian art in St. Petersburg in which, as we know, the Czech lands were represented to some extent for the first time. Judging from private reports, which are always more frank than official reviews in major journals, the locals were not particularly impressed with us. "Well-painted things", they admit, "but we have seen paintings exactly like that produced by the French, Dutch, English, etc." They look for a special Czech character in our art, and only when it is apparent does their interest turn into admiration and enthusiasm. Hynais's poster for the Ethnographic Exhibition makes a greater impression on them than his painting *The Trial of Paris*, while Nemejc—and above all Uprka, Slabý, and Trsek—triumph over everyone else with their subjects.

This is an interesting lesson: it is clear that our art can make an impact and attract interest abroad only when it is distinctively Czech. This means that if we want to conquer foreign parts, we must send out not simply art, but *Czech* art.

Let us ask: have we ever had such art, and do we have it now?

The first question can be answered without hesitation with two the names closest to our hearts: Aleš and Mánes. The two have expressed a certain period of our lives and certain aspects of the Czech spirit in a definitive artistic form.

Aleš's work is the most complete, pure, and lovely expression of all that was good about Czech country life: a world now entirely lost survives in his drawings; his touch gives back sound to the now mute chords of certain emotions; we are fond of him in the same way we are fond of our youth, once pure and joyous, but gone forever.

The Mánes brothers carried inside them the soft, lyrical soul of Slavic dreamers alongside the disappearing charm of rococo and idyllic German art of the forties, to which they were quite visibly and closely relate. But it is the Czech aspects of their work that we like best about them, the softness of form and depth of emotion, the decorative charm and masterly art of drawing, so individual that there is nothing else quite like it.

Beside[s] them, we had J. Čermák and we had Chittussi—we had Czech artists, but no continuous tradition and development.

And what about today? We have art created by Czechs, but it is art without an adjective: so far, it contains only the beginnings of future "Czech art."

Today we cannot build on the tradition of Mánes and Aleš; Czech life developed too quickly, and there is a gap between us that has never been filled. Czech life has lost its distinctive external characteristics; today we live a European cultural life, and we have to count with European competition.

And art must express this life and its time. In the future, our distinctiveness will not be manifested externally in different customs and costumes, it will not be just a difference of subject—as it is today represented by Uprka, whose work is the most beautiful and artistic example of a distinctiveness that is disappearing little by little, along with national costume and type, until it becomes extinct. The difference will be of an inner nature, a difference of race.

As for technical proficiency, we are capable of standing up to any competition when it comes to art—thanks mainly to Hynais and Myslbek—and that only makes our duty and responsibility greater. Today's young generation feels it, and makes the highest demands on itself—something that goes without saying in art, which justifies only extreme demands. But they are the same demands as ever, reinstated with a new rigor: seriousness and honesty, with which an artist has to give his best and deepest, reaching the bottom of his soul and the depths of his nature—and this is where we are all Czechs, whether we want it or not. The Czechness of our art will be self-evident: when we have a number of distinctive characteristics that can be artistically expressed, it will be what we share as a race that will make an impact and that will be the Czech quality of our art. And just as the Czech man and woman of tomorrow will differ dramatically from the man and woman of the past—whose difference will be measured not by one but by two or three generations, because in the old days, the generation gap between the "young" and the "old" went deep into the core of their being and views, and mattered far more—and so the Czech artist of tomorrow will be different too.

He will use not only external form from the past—for example folk embroidery or ornaments—but its real substance, the visual sense Czech art inherited from old women of Slovak Moravia who decorated their porches with amazing instinct; he will use all the achievements of modern culture to create a strong sense of self and to apply forces inherent to his race, that beautiful race that survives in full strength because and as long as it is Slavic.

And that will be achieved only by means of strong progress and hard work, not governed by programs which we will not be conscious of, because a new generation of strong, healthy people who will need to work to process their energy, a generation that has experienced and has in its blood all we have worked towards with a great deal of effort, courage, independence, eagerness to work—the future Czech generation.

To herald the future is not to deny the past. On the contrary, we remember it with fondness and love, as a beautiful but lost idyll that brings grateful smile to our lips. But we must not tarry at this past, however tempted we might be, because the great struggle of life and art—the struggle of the twentieth century—is calling us.

Translated by Alexandra Büchler

JOSEF MÁNES EXHIBITION AT THE TOPIČ SALON   Bohumil Kubišta
Originally published as "Výstava Josefa Mánesa v Topičově salonu," *Přehled* vol. 9, no. 25 (March 17, 1911)

In our time, manifestations of national character have been elevated to the foremost criterion by which a work of art is assessed: yet no one has clearly formulated what exactly national art might be—what its properties are and what critical methods might be derived from such a concept. I personally doubt that this path could lead anywhere at all: the question of national art cannot be satisfactorily answered, any more than such questions as "What is Art" and "What is Life?" It is not a critical problem but a philosophical one, a subject for reflection at the end of an era rather than speculation at its beginning. In the first case, manifestations of nationality appear to be not a criterion but an inherent quality of works of art that had been tested by a different fire and more reliable *aqua regia* than the nebulous concept of nationality in art. It is generally said that Mánes is a great artist because he is Czech. This is not so: whether Mánes is a great artist must be apparent from his work. Mánes's best work bears traces of the French interest in form, while those works in which he accentuated the

Czech national types are the weakest, precisely because he neglected the general conventions of form.

Mánes lived at a time when French culture exercised influence not only on the inner lives of individuals but on the entire nation; at a time when a wave of French revolutions gradually swept across Europe. In art, this was a time when David's and Ingrès's academic classicism reigned supreme and Delacroix's romanticism was being replaced by realism. Mánes's work reflects all these styles, Fragonard and Watteau alike. His creative method shows the influence of Ingrès's line and Delacroix's color. His significance consists in the fact that as an artist, he digested everything that was happening in France, all the developments taking place in separate regions and over several generations. Mánes's task was to take a young Czech art from Empire style to realism.

It was a difficult task and Mánes can be excused for not always availing himself fully. His entire work shows signs of haste and appears unfinished and incomplete. He did not master composition and the linear construction of an image as well as Ingrès, nor did he master color as well as Delacroix. With Mánes, line always has an empirical significance and color is usually material; both elements are used correctly only when he relied directly on his French models. There is no category of painting Mánes did not work in: he produced religious paintings, portraits, allegories, song illustrations, landscapes, diplomas and other occasional designs, and that is why he appears to us to have possessed a universal talent.

The works gathered in Topič's Salon—mostly fragmentary sketches, drawings and a handful of watercolors and paintings—are displayed without a selective criterion and purely for a commercial purpose. The best known among them are *The Seamstress* and a small picture entitled *In the Summer*. The composition of *The Seamstress* is marred by the obtrusiveness of the symbolic objects (canary, cage, Virgin Mary); the use of such a symbolic apparatus to convey certain psychological states is the most usual and effective tool that would, however, never be employed by a truly creative spirit. In such a case, it is impossible to speak of composition in a visual sense; it is simply a collection of objects that may be of interest in real life.

The large painting *Laura and Petrarch* is an academic work in the true sense of the word: heavy colors, poor, schematic composition, laborious and barren brushstrokes. Only the facial expressions possess a true spirituality. Several landscape watercolors overflow with detail (*Slovak Cottage*) and with objects of interest per se. Mánes's pencil and ink drawings were done by means of hatching drawn, at the most, in three different directions.

Mánes's drawing talent is most evident in drawings or designs for larger paintings, in which entire figures and their movements are captured in supple contours. Josef Mánes has been elevated to the top of new Czech painting spontaneously and without critical analysis. It would be difficult and dangerous to draw any definitive conclusions on the basis of this fragmentary exhibition and without a detailed historical study. Until there is a critic who can properly elucidate Mánes's place not only in Czech art but in the context of wider developments, the conditions of this specific development will remain unclear and fair-minded efforts to analyze Mánes's work will be forsaken in the name of general support for Czech art.

Translated by Alexandra Büchler

At the end of the eighteenth century, Poland lost its political sovereignty. Divided between three neighboring powers—Austria, Prussia, and Russia—the Polish state disappeared from the map. The Polish nation was partitioned. Culture became a substitute for sovereignty, preserving the nation's historical memory and thereby reconstructing its identity. Cultural identification became the most important task of art and literature. Poets, writers, and artists functioned as spiritual leaders with great authority in matters of the Poles' political ambitions and moral aspirations. The names of poet-prophets, above all that of Adam Mickiewicz (1798–1855), became symbols of the nation's invincibility. It wasn't just the question of ethnic identity—for, in the past, multinational Poland could not claim one identity—but of *cultural* identity, constructed on the basis of history, at least before the nationalist movements of the late nineteenth century.

History was the reference point for all discourse on national identity. This produced a specific demand for history painting, of which the leading artist was Jan Matejko (1830–1893). His painting, didactic in its essence, has become a subject of analysis and debate among historians. It was also of interest to art critics, among them Stanisław Witkiewicz (1851–1915), a leading figure of the time. Originally a proponent of Realist painting, he later stood for art expressive of national identity. In his texts on Matejko, Witkiewicz associated the mastery and artistic value of the paintings with their national content. Stanisław Wyspiański (1869–1907), a painter, poet and dramatist, was a pupil of Matejko, but his art was very different from his master's. Wyspiański's painting was close to the decorative Art Nouveau of the fin-de-siècle and to contemporary Expressionist movements. He looked for "Polishness" not so much in history as in folk culture, in which he found a kind of Polish national "spirituality." By contrast the paintings of Jacek Malczewski (1854–1929) evoked a national identity based on the nation's martyrdom in the nineteenth century—defeated insurrections and the struggle for independence—and on a mythical and metaphysical vision of the future as the ultimate fulfillment and liberation. This repeated the Romantic ideology of Mickiewicz—of national redemption and salvation.

Translated by Wanda Kemp-Welch

WYSPIAŃSKI AS A PAINTER-POET (PERSONAL IMPRESSIONS)
Juliusz Kaden-Bandrowski

Originally published as "Wyspiański jako malarz-poeta (osobiste wrażenia)," *Przegląd Poranny* no. 337 (1907)

I remember the day when I stepped into the vestibule of the fine art exhibition in Sukiennice. For the vestibule housed a retrospective exhibition of the early works of Wyspiański. These were strange works. Completely different from those assigned to the Salons. There was Wyspiański in the vestibule of art, pulling in crowds of Cracow philistines and attracting their attention. Why? Because he was different, revolutionary.... Because, he was himself.... Because in a few lines, a few color chiaroscuro, he produced the spiritual image of his model. The brightness of the coloring and the lines of the drawing testify to this over and over.... Here and there, the drawing of the eyes, mouth or nose have caused voices of indignation to be raised...but above all the indignation of all the philistines was caused by the discords and oppositions of color: yellow with blue, red with green.... One magical word made an impression: the pupil of Matejko. The old [Wojciech] Kossak, nearly on his deathbed, was launching for me a holy crusade against Wyspiański. They can't draw, he said. Yes, the drawing was careless. But in these works there was something shining forth, which created a general uneasiness.... What did the future have in store? Greatness!... Novelty!... A revolution in Polish art. A revolution of the spirit, not of form, which the spirit broke.... Until he found an outlet in the word...the poet...since then he began to be taken more seriously...as an expressionist...who had no time to assimilate a conception into the proscribed forms. That is how Matejko thought of him while Wyspiański was renovating St. Mary's Church.... This is how he liberated himself, this *Titan of art*, when he worked in the Franciscan Church in Cracow, his stained glass windows great not because of their form, but because of the gigantic idea of recreating the Polish spirit of the Middle Ages.... He was equally original and individualist in his other works. These, when sometimes seen in Warsaw, were not understood. Because.... Wyspiański drew his strength and creative power from the spirit of Poland's past, buried in the Cathedral of the Wawel Castle and in the hearts of the Polish people under its Cracovian peasant's coat of Piast; because he drew them from the spirit of nature, which distinguished the nation he came from, he, the precious fruit, sincere to the bone, genuine and homogeneous, as an expression of the spirit and power of the nation—the people—shown in his *Wesele* [The Wedding], in the peasant log-cabin, the power enchanted in the motion, as picturesque and as vivid as any of his poetry and literary works. These works can scarcely be separated from the spiritual ones, so strongly does the spirit of the creator come through in them and bind them into one element.... This is Wyspiański, the artist-painter. Warsaw could neither recognize nor appreciate [his greatness], though she came to love him as the "king of the spirit", just as today she mourns him from the bottom of heart and laments his loss—because many years shall pass before Poland sees another Wyspiański.

Translated by Klara Kemp-Welch

The impact of one of the arts stirring the soul, stirs all its senses and creates the
need for sensations which only other arts can provide. From the sounds of music
there emerge images, as from paintings emerge poems, and from poems—powerful
arches and slender spires, since all the arts have as their basis one and the same
human soul, the bottomless sea of its life.

Art as a whole reflects the full spectrum of life and, at the same time, reflects the
essential character of a nation and the era.

The Poland of the nineteenth century was revealed in her art. We cannot exactly
explain why it was poetry that came first, followed almost simultaneously by music,
and later by painting. However, thanks to the powerful range of the human spirit, they
came to crystallize the great spirit of the artists and focused all elements of the
nation's life.

Though Polish poetry penetrated deep into the human soul, it would not have embodied art were it not for the music of Chopin. Thanks to this music—over and above the
silent pages of *Dziady*, *Król Duch*, *Irydion*—rises their passionate call expressing the
will to fight, their utter desperation, their sighs of longing, and the silence of their
immense sadness. The whole century of the Polish struggle swirls to the rhythm and
tune of "Polonaise in A"—this music says aloud what is written in silence but what
should be played as the reveille over the whole of Poland, from a peak in the Tatra
mountains. And as if to complete art, to embody the Polish soul, there comes painting.
What had been presaged, imagined, heard, materializes in shapes and colors creating
bright, close, lasting visions, imposing on everyone's imagination and for ever the
testimony of Poland's existence.

There was a moment when national awareness seemed to have disappeared from
public life and manifested itself only in art, as previously it had in poetry. All energy was directed at the problems of everyday human existence, and generations
stricken by defeats came to fear their own name. It seemed to us that we had died
and there was no resurrection. Some were preoccupied with setting themselves up
in life; some could barely remember the names of those in the vanguard who fought
for a better world. It seemed that the *Polish problem* no longer existed, there were
only local, administrative matters to be resolved by the different governments controlling the former Polish state. In this deep night the Polish spirit was only manifested in art....

If anywhere, the powerful argument for the impact of one's close environment could
be found in Matejko's paintings. Born in Cracow, where every brick, every paving stone
tells a story, where the voice of the past seems to call from spires and cloisters, where
tragic and powerful ghosts of times past seem to mix with passing crowds even in the
daytime, where one can find splendid monuments to power and glory, and the most
terrible testimony of bondage, where the most holy national relics can be seen and
touched, where from a threshold of a church or the Castle gates, the human soul is
taken by a hurricane, chaos, a world of sensations, memories, images, names, events,
pulling it between two polarities—suffering and joy, between boundless hope and
bottomless despair, where what we call tradition is not something faraway but is tangible, present, terrible and joyful, which makes one feel as if someone were squeezing
one's heart with a strong fist. It could be assumed that what Matejko felt, knew, and
had been stemmed from this strange, impressive environment. He breathed in the
ashes of the great national cemetery; he brushed against the coffins of those who with
their deeds of valor had written the centuries-long history of one of the strangest

states. The reveille from St. Mary's church and the somber strokes of the "Zygmunt"
bell sang to him. Legend and history, from the Dragon's Cave to Kościuszko, held his
soul in their powerful claws from the time when he had began to feel and think.
Matejko seems as necessary a product of the Cracow environment as the mould on
the Castle walls, as the moss growing in the crevices of old roof tiles, or as a plant
that grows only on this soil.

We must remember that out of the tens of thousands of inhabitants of occupied
Cracow, the masses of traders, cobblers, monks, clerks, barbers, writers, coach-
men, painters, and professors only Matejko—without predecessors and without
followers, though under the influence of the environment, a powerful, original
and independent spirit, self-willed—was fanatically driven to produce tremendous
work. Man's individuality reacts to the influence of even most powerful environment in its own way.

On dark nights in old Cracow, when Matejko wandered the curved streets of
gloomy, grey houses with buttresses, on the Market Square over which tower the
silhouettes of St. Mary's spires, he felt and thought differently than a burger returning from a wine bar; when from the dark sky the sharp sound of the reveille cut
through the night silence like the glimmer of a sword. For Matejko it was a call
from a graveyard that stretched to the sea, on top of which stood the Wawel tomb,
whereas for a clerk passing through the Square, its effect was to make him look
at his watch to check if St. Mary's tower clock was not late. At every moment, at
every fragment of a wall, at every relic of the past, Matejko felt and thought differently from his contemporaries.

Though others could have thought and felt the same, their thoughts scattered without
leaving any trace in their lives, while the thoughts and feelings of Matejko were transformed into paintings, stemming from his own creative force alone. The formidable
environment of Polish history, hung as heavily over Matejko as it did everyone. Matejko
painted *The Sermon of Skarga* and *Rejtan*, while others went to their deaths or to
Siberian exile, still others traded, gathered money, ploughed the land or scrambled for
positions, orders, titles.... Matejko might have not painted *Skarga* and *Rejtan*, but
whomever he might have chosen to paint would have been a man of similar stature,
distinguished by the same dignity and solemnity. Perhaps they would have been less
tragic figures, yet ones that foresaw as unavoidable a fate of bondage and infamy....
In the force of his expression lies the essence of Matejko's personality, and this could
not have originated in his environment, but only in himself, the content of his soul
and the power of his art. The essence of his art was his emotion....

The artist must be utterly sincere. What he feels, and what he feels at the moment
when the images emerge in his head, he has to express without reservations, without
digressions, and with unrestrained passion—cynically and naively, as Nietzsche
would have said. All the power of his mind, all the stirrings of his emotions have to
focus in this one thought, in the strong, clear and precise expression of what was
revealed to him in the first moment of the creative urge. Creative activity must necessarily respond to his intentions, and in this alone lies the real and unique ethics of
art. Whatever sublime, or wicked, noble or commonplace ideas, duties or interest
violate this ethic, the effect is always the same—a bad work of art. The artist who
aims for fame, money, or merit, or subordinates his art to the tastes of those who can
satisfy the appetites of his base egoism, or is motivated by a universal good, devotion
to and love of the people, will be an artistic criminal, a poor fool, or a tragically broken
man, whose noble feelings and desire for good cannot prevent him from stumbling.
The artist cannot and should not think of the spectators over his shoulder, whether
angels or the rabble. He has to delight in creative activity, to appear as he is, in all
his nakedness.

62

The public that drove Matejko was Poland, the beloved Fatherland, understood in a noble and powerful way. In order to gain this public, he spoiled his pictures, he did not paint as he understood "the conditions for the artistic perfection of the picture". This was his crime against art, his violation of its ethic, which took revenge on his work.

Matejko's art was stifled by the idea of the Fatherland, and his mentality was limited by his simple and naive belief in the religion in common use. "Without religion and Catholic religion at that, one can do nothing" he wrote in his early youth, and for the rest of his life, he never passed through a stage of doubt. He saw in religion the absolute and total agreement of dogma and life. This Catholic religiosity was a part of his philosophy of history, his notion of life, the fall and rebirth of Poland, as formed the basis for a political program for a certain mentality.

In his thin body there was a powerful spirit, a brave heart, and a will of iron.

His oeuvre is astounding for the effort he had put into it. This small, thin, sickly man with a big head and caricaturelike face, always worked on his own, with the same earnestness, concentration, good faith, great solemnity, and an absolute devotion to the task at hand. His tireless hand did hundreds of paintings, filled with crowds of people and masses of objects, reproduced not pedantically but with ardor and passion—the elementary passion of the painter's temperament. Through archaeological and historical research he deepened his knowledge of art. He did not approach these studies as an artist looking for sensations but as a historian and archaeologist studying monuments of the past and old masters, or as a scientist searching for an absolute truth. And he painted with the same characteristic passion.

Matejko's art had enormous significance for Polish society in the second half of the nineteenth century. The greater part of national ideology, and everything that resulted from the past, found expression in Matejko's work. This work was a direct emanation of national thought, it was rooted in the past, and lit by all the brilliance of the nation's imagination. It depicted the nation enslaved, and the times of its independence, times which from a distance appeared devoid of mundane, everyday troubles, but were seen only in their grandest or blackest moments.

But history was not made by Matejko. History existed before him and was the subject of many other painters, whose names disappeared from people's memory even before they had passed away. Matejko's strength was different, coming as it did from his own psychology, from his being a great artist. However great and significant a historical fact the painter chooses as his subject, the value of the painting is related to the artist's talent—the subject cannot raise this value even by the smallest degree. Rather, the painting's value depends on the essence of the artist's soul. The most sublime and powerful subjects can result in poor and clumsy work, whereas even trivial events can be raised to the level of great deeds performed by powerful figures. There have been many historians and many history painters, but there was only one Matejko, and only he was capable of exerting such an influence on the human soul; he alone had sufficient power of suggestion to make people believe in the truth of his historical visions, visions that could be relived, not just remembered or discussed, but felt in people's nerves, heart and mind.

His art stretched creative force to its limits. One can criticize Matejko extensively and ruthlessly but there would still be enough left to honor and admire in him. He had, to the highest degree, all the qualities which characterize great artists and ideological martys: unconditional service to what he regarded as the truth, losing himself in his work; a deep and naive seriousness, sincerity and directness; a consistent striving towards his aims; and a passionate, almost fatalistic, strong-headedness. He could not have avoided the internal transformation of his soul, but, looking at the enormity of his work, so uniform and consistent in its essential content, one has the impression of a bullet launched with great force, which rose in the air and reached its zenith, only to fall to earth according to the laws of nature.

He had many of the drawbacks that even mediocre talents avoid, but he had one absolute talent—he created masterpieces.

Wanda Kemp-Welch

ON THE ARTIST'S CALLING AND THE TASKS OF ART Jacek Malczewski
Originally delivered as "O powołaniu artystów I zadaniach sztuki," Vice-chancellor's lecture (October 15, 1912)

Gentlemen and future Polish artists!

For some time now I have intended to inaugurate the new academic year at the only Academy of Fine Arts in [former] Poland, with a speech welcoming the new academic year, new listeners, those who have already been attending and those who will be finishing their studies. And I fulfil this intention with a sense duty on behalf of myself, my mission and my present position. My original thought was to invite today the representatives of the teaching profession and art historians. But I have dropped this idea. And I stand alone in before you, surrounded by my present colleagues and by you, my future colleagues. And it is better that way, for here we are a family, an association, a sect of the initiated.

Every one of us has made a goal for himself to work in the field of art. This common goal unites us into one family, and the consistent work in the field of art slowly uncovers for us the mystery of our profession and the sacredness of the feeling of art. These feelings distinguish us from the rest of the society, where the struggle for survival writes the history of politics, industry, finances and the social problems of nations. These feelings, I repeat, distinguish us, because it is not in the struggle for survival, but with a lack of concern for worldly possessions that we can strive for ideals in art, art which for the rest of society is above all a form of entertainment, before becoming, with the passage of time, history and a very special form of knowledge, as well as one of the greatest prayers of mankind. This is why we are alone at today's meeting—alone as every one of us will be throughout his whole life. There are three ways to perfect the spirit and make it come closer to the throne of God: the path of prayer, the path of love and the path of knowledge (that is, the discovery of truth).

On the path of love there lies the route of art. Following this route, we come closer to the knowledge of the omnipotence of the Creator, we unite more eagerly with His will. Because we, artists, sing the Magnificat seeing God's creation on earth and in the Universe.

We worship the Highest Spirit, admiring a cloud, a flower, or the smallest crystal. And enchanted by the wonders with which He had surrounded us, we timidly demand to be His equals—in order to better understand and love Him, and so we make so bold as to reproduce the creations of His hand on the flat plane without dimensions, or in volume with the fullness of dimension. Thus equipped, though humble, while we work we secretly sing the hymn of worship, the hymn of love for the Best Father, for so many wonders, graces and benefits. As of this moment we combine two ways, two routes, two ladders on which the human spirit rises to perfection and achieves its essential self: the Path of Prayer with the Path of Love.

And when you, my colleague, pray, you do not pray so that your neighbor will see you, or for an earthly or eternal reward; but you pray because you love God, because He is your dearest Father and the only one who knows your soul, your Judge and your Guardian. Therefore, confident in His wisdom, in His unlimited love you sum up the prayer: Your Will be done.

Thus art which is our prayer, shall not be made either for the world that surrounds us, or for money which we supposedly need in order to live, or for vanity of the profession in which we work, or for the admiration of crowds who do not want to listen to the voice of one crying in the wilderness. We shall practice art out of love, to come closer to and to unite with the Holy Spirit, God the Eternal Father, in silence, humility and loneliness.

And as the most sincere, ardent, profound prayer from the bottom of the soul cannot be repeated or taught because it would be different with every person, and different each time; so we cannot teach you this prayer, the most sincere, profound, genuine art as your whole prayer.

We cannot teach you the mastery of prayer (art) which elevates you who are lying in ashes at the feet of the Almighty Spirit with hearts heavy from the feelings gathered. We shall not teach the mastery of prayer, we shall not teach the mastery in art! But we shall attempt to show you the greatness of God—either in the bone structure of the smallest creature or in the form of a giant dinosaur; we shall teach you to look at these wonders—light, shadow, chiaroscuro and brilliance that the Creator has unfolded in the Universe.

We shall teach you to be proud in spirit, and humble in every moment of life. For you will be alone and solitary if you persist and become artists, that is if you wish to live with the prayer of art, kneeling down before Divine Love. The present world will leave you alone and on your knees.

The future world will demand to see you kneeling! But you shall not be lonely, you shall not be alone. You shall be kneeling in adoration of the highest Love and you shall see and feel it in the infinite Universe; and singing the Magnificat—you shall die.

Before that, however, many of you (I would like to believe), carried on the wings of grace, and having understood the harmony of the whole of nature, endowed with Divine courage, will manage to create the harmony of the whole from your own feelings, like the harmony of the Universe—and you shall create masterpieces. Because—you are the sons of God.

Then you shall know that there are eternal harmonies, which have their beginning in God and for the whole of mankind as long as he remains chained to the earth are often opaque. Visible only in moments of grace, recalled by genuine prayers of art, they shall become immortal and serve as signposts for the whole of humanity. Both in relation to the smaller circles of the seeming harmonies, squeezed by the materialization of society, or its egoistic blindness and in relation to the true light of the Gospel.

I wanted to say these few words, please remember these few statements. Perhaps my effective activity in this Academy shall be limited to just this speech. I am already on the other side of the hill, facing the sunset. I have derived my thoughts from my own experience, of which I bear the effects on my shoulders, like a relentless burden of crimes.

Translated by Wanda Kemp-Welch

WYSPIAŃSKI'S STAINED GLASS WINDOWS AT THE WAWEL CATHEDRAL
Włodzimierz Żuławski

Originally published as "Witraże wawelskie Wyspiańskiego," *Maski* no. 13 (1918)

(....) Wyspiański did not escape the fate, which is the lot of the greatest men. Misunderstanding standing between him and his own society and misunderstanding standing in the way of the happiness of his creative life would accompany him, like a tiresome and aggressive shadow right to his burial place—the Skałkę. He, the Spirit from the rainbow path to the stars, whose whole life was filled with creative toil, the master of all art bestowing upon his nation royal visions of beauty and greatness, how many times he might have uttered plaint, when the chorus of dwarfs drowned the great silence of his prophetic deeds with their earthly clamor. It is the fate of the greatest men working in the realm of beauty that their works cannot seize and enchant everyone's heart. There will always be souls for whom their routine and dogma is the accepted and recognized beauty, souls lacking creative power, who always imagine beauty in its existing form, and whose judgment of this beauty, will not be changed or moved by art revealing new beauty. The imperative to create, with which Wyspiański, the spirit, came down to the soil of his earthly fatherland, would have in store for him many a painful disappointment. And truly, one would need to be superhuman, with the flight and sight of an eagle and Christ-like compassion, to forget all the wrongs in one's heart, so become oblivious to the pain and love of life, for not everyone can be creative. All that is earthly, everything I touch, dies in my hands—says Konrad in *Wyzwolenie* [Liberation] and this is the most tragic description of the collision resulting from the unavoidable clash between the sacred spirit and the environment of microbes. And this environment, knowing the force of its own mass, will always be the wrong-doer; having reigned over the world, where from generation to generation it has become accustomed to crawl according to the rules obliging in a crowd, it rejects all new values outright, as though they were a challenge and a blow aimed at its instinct of self-preservation. Wyspiański will be approached by many narrow minds, by the wanton mediocrity of Poles; they will look at his new work, so different from anything else today, and not finding in it their own vocabulary and rec-ognized rules of beauty, they will launch an offensive which will be to the detriment of the artist and to that of Poland. Speechless was his mouth, he was silent when the crowd was passing judgment on him, in his home-town full with mediocrities: a hand and glove group of artists, architects and art historians, all together and with excep-tional agreement—took to the gravediggers' trade and buried his most sublime cre-ative conceptions in eternal darkness and doom. Wyspiański would accuse nobody. His anger, the anger of a man and genius, both wronged, was like a sudden momentary pain, which wounds strongly and painfully, but passes quickly. He had too great a heart to complain of human pettiness, hypocrisy or stupidity. Once and only once, this pillar of strength shed a tear over his fate: not at the time when his youthful dreams of restoring the Church of the Holy Cross were turned to dust, but not when his pro-posal for turning a theatre over to him (he was asking for one year trial period so that his powerful plays could have a stage life), when the architects of Cracow's tenement buildings judged his frescoes (over 100 drawings) to be fitting for a church in Biecz but not for a building in Cracow, or on the many other occasions when crimes were com-mitted against this unique man.... Wyspiański who knew and loved Wawel Castle as no one else in the nation, was right to cry over the most painful wrong done to him by his compatriots: over the rejection of his project for stained glass windows for the Cathedral of Wawel Castle. Whilst abroad he had a vision, somewhere in the Gothic cathedrals of Paris, Chartres or Reims. Moved by their sublime stained glass, there came to him a dream for the cathedral on the hill, towering over the great river Vistula. His eyes took in every shape, stone and detail, there was no place where his heart did not come to rest.... His creative thought flew through the twilight and the spectral Karsts, to the fervent mediaeval prayer for everlasting time sung by the French stained glass.... The windows of the Cathedral would not, though, show a crowd of devout believers, or a circle of angels singing psalms before the Almighty. With a pious sigh and proud thoughts he would resurrect the heroes of the Fatherland, the fighters for ideas and glory, immortalized by the nation for their deeds, he would wrest from death the powers which it had destroyed and return them to life, resurrected. Henry the Pious, Casimir the Great, and St. Stanisław—appeared as projects for stained glass offered to the National Museum. The first was influenced by Matejko's paintings: *Departure of Henry the Pious from Legnica* and *The Defeat of Legnica (A History of Civilization in Poland)*. In the first painting the heroic king departs for battle with the foreboding of defeat and in his eyes opened wide in awe—a vision of the martyr's death. The other painting shows the burial service of the King and his knights. A row of corpses lies in the center of the church filled with the moan of the orphaned people, frightened by the decree of Providence, defeat and the sight of glowing fires. Lowered masts of Polish flags lit by candlelight.... The mood of the Wawel Cathedral stained glass windows is quite different. Here we have laconic drama, the decisive moment in which the King's feat is finished, in which it achieves its eternal form. In 1869 the bones of King Casimir the Great were discovered—the event, recounted to Wyspiański by Matejko and commemorated in his painting, profoundly shook the imagination of the artist. He wrote a poem about the event and designed the stained glass window. The silvery cadences of the poem in which he extolled the King's story posthumously, from the moment of his entombment in the Wawel Cathedral, leaving his glory to the nation. (....) Wyspiański recreates in his design the moment at which Casimir the Great, escaping death, appears to the nation at his royal funeral. Wyspiański wanted to fill the window in the left nave with stained glass representations of St. Stanisław, opposite the chapel dedicated to the martyr. The composition is entirely filled by the coffin with an opening through which we see the saint's head surrounded by a white halo. The eternal legends of life and the mystery of the event, shroud the coffin and the figure of the Bishop. He looks on with terror at King Bolesław's action and at the ages flying past.... The stained glass windows, designed for the upper windows of the Wawel Cathedral, were to be supplemented by lower panes of glass, below the tracery. According to Wyspiański's notes every stained glass window was to bear two compositions: the vision and, below the tracery, the actual historical event. Below the vision of Henry the Pious, he showed the battle of Legnica, burning with crimson flames and smoke. In the lower panel of the stained glass window of Casimir the Great, the actual event depicted is the second funeral of the King, with the red patch of the coffin, masses of flags spread about in the air amongst the glowing candles, and a trail of burnt incense. The drama of Bolesław the Bold, the last scene, fills the lower panels of the stained glass window of St. Stanisław. The windows were destined solely for the Cathedral they could be installed anywhere within it, provided that it was here that they would radiate their colors and their psychology; their intensity and power are completely lost on the museum wall, especially as they are hung close to one another. Any museum, without exception, even with the best lighting and the best spatial conditions, will always be a prison for stained glass compositions; their colors are inevitably dulled and their forms lose their vitality and energy. The design on paper, hung on the wall, is a work of art in a state of metamorphosis, to use the entomological expression: it is only a chrysalis announcing the coming of life. Only in its final form, in the transparent glass, in lines framed by lead the stained glass comes to life, full life— embodied and spiritual.

He was laid in his tomb and already forgotten by people of whom it will one day be said that they stood before the beauty of Wyspiański's works like barbarians; not knowing what they were doing they stoned this beauty. Future Polish minds will be astounded, and will contemplate with pain, a generation that was unable to protect the treasures of their own spirit against blasphemy, and the dwarfed times when an all-powerful handful of ignoramuses with a level of culture equivalent to that of Apelles's critic, rendered the artist's highest flights of imagination useless. The document from which posterity will effortlessly learn the aesthetic criteria of the ruling mediocrities and their relation to Wyspiański's masterpiece, shall be preserved. This document is a letter to the public, protesting against bringing stained glass from abroad to the Wawel Cathedral factory; written by Polish artists once they had lost all hope of Wyspiański's design would be realized. The protest was an arrow that missed. Its holy cry was unheard by those who had decided that Wyspiański's project was unsuited for the Cathedral—because it lacked a pious thought! This pious thought demanded by the iconoclasts, was supposedly expressed the mass-produced article of some foreign factory. Wyspiański's powerful masterpiece was destroyed once and for all. He realized with pain that his most tender feelings, his creative longings and pride had been wronged and that his creative work was hindered by these small men. Besides the stained glass windows held by the National Museum, there is a drawing for a stained glass window of Wanda, the legendary daughter of Krak, designed by Wyspiański for one of the windows in the transept of the Cathedral. The pencil sketches, now reproduced in *Maski* (ten of them) summing up the first impression of what Wyspiański wanted to create for the Cathedral windows, are a condensed form of the Wawel stained glass windows. Recalled from the past by his heart of gold, there appear to him.... Piast, the wheeler raised to the kingship and his son, Ziemowit. In his peasant eyes, one sees the radiance of the moment when he went to his brothers of Kruszwica.... His left hand is laid upon his son's head. With his right hand he holds the sickle, and strongly he embraces a sheaf of corn.... They are both wearing the peasant dress, tied with leather belts.... The vision of Queen Kinga marches as if in expiatory procession, lit by candlelight. She has received her eternal form.... Above her humbly bent forehead there is a halo, her eyes do not see anything worldly, her lips, numb with prayer, are closed.... She is visiting her former, earthly kingdom in a beggarwoman's frock.... The battle of Grunwald, the founding of the Cracow Academy, and sublime deeds and feelings are retold in the stained glass window of King Jagiello and Queen Jadwiga. Paired in noble marital unity there are two independent beings: he, the inhabitant of the North, with its forests, with a large face coarsely sculpted, she—the young woman of refined culture, a princess with small, subtle features.... As light comes through the Wawel window, there appears the steel-clad Zawisza Czarny, bursting in with all his knightly force; his sword thrown over his helmet by the wind of the battle, and his arm faithfully guarding the Royal emblems and trophies. The hymn of an iron-will on his lips, his eyes dazzling with the happiness of fulfilled work.... The Teutonic Knights turn to ashes beneath Polish assault.... The King-humanist who wanted no sovereignty over himself except for the Divine one, accedes to the throne: King Casimir the Jagiellon. He is seated to receive tribute from the Great Master, Poland's vassal. The king's chest rises in triumph, on his visage one sees the invincible spirit looking into his native sun.... Pomerania, Malbork, Warmia, and Gdańsk all under the power and glory of the Jagiellonian scepter.... He has placed this world beneath his imperious hand, while the waves of the Baltic, Polish Sea sing.... Władysław Łokietek, Sigismund the Old, and Sigismund Augustus take their lineage from the Wawel Castle's memorials, there are none sentimental values so abundant in all Wyspiański's art here. There is a drawing, preserved from 1902, for a stained glass window of "Polonia", the vision of a martyr, tragically inert, and the specter of Wernyhora. Discovered in a portfolio which the great artist, on his sick bed, ordered to be burned so as to lay painful memories to rest, these sketches are but a fragment of the Wawel's stained glass windows. According to a story told by the late Joanna Stankiewicz, Wyspiański's aunt and foster mother, the portfolio also contained designs for the six windows of the main nave, which are the most complete, some reworked more than once, besides projects for the windows of other churches. They were consumed by fire along with the artist's priceless notes on colors of glass, dimensions and many other matters. It must be mentioned that Wyspiański requested to be told the exact dimensions of the Cathedral windows! He only managed to acquire these from a high-ranking member of the Chapter after some pleading and in secret. Posterity will judge this pitiful affair, detrimental both to the Wawel Cathedral and to Wyspiański, and the words which the great Polish writer Maria Konopnicka sobbed aloud at Wyspiański's coffin, shall be recalled: "It was because, in your time, the nation had no great idea and no great synthesis of popular feeling (...) that you, the Divine flame, flickered, and were thrown to the wind."

Translated by Klara Kemp-Welch

"'World view' and 'contents' can be discussed in art theory only inasmuch as they have been transformed into *form*, that is: art," Lajos Fülep, the Hungarian philosopher, art critic and theorist wrote in the introduction to his 1916 book, *Magyar művészet* (Hungarian Art). At a time when political liberalism was in crisis in Hungary, and positivism dominated the culture, Fülep set out to fathom the idea of *national art*.

Having studied the national characteristics in the architecture of Ödön Lechner and in the sculpture of Miklós Izsó, and having examined them from the perspective of what he called "universal" art, he formulated the dictum that reverberated in Hungarian art writing for years to come: "National and international are interrelated concepts."

Fülep examined the impact of the national in art in a context that spanned over three millennia, from ancient Greek art to the present. "If there is anything that is national in art, it is form," he wrote, because everything else is ethnic material. Thus he identified *form* and *style* as the primary vehicles of national self-expression, and set up the thesis: "Form is as universal, and as national, as it is artistic." He believed that the particular mission of each nation's art hinged on solving a certain form-problem. Before he will affirm that

Hungarian art *exists*, he asks "whether it has a national character, and if so, is that character universal, too? That is, does it deal with a form-problem the solution of which is its own exclusive task, turning a national issue universal?"

The efforts of many young Hungarian aesthetes, critics, and artists in the first decade of the twentieth century were directed at a great upsurge of national art that would be rich with universal values. Fülep's sharp and often edgy art criticism; the new generation of art critics, among whom László Márkus excelled; the public debates with the participation of the composer Zoltán Kodály, the philosopher György Lukács, the poet Béla Balázs and others; all were fueled by the hope that if the formal and stylistic qualities of Hungarian culture were elevated, it would become one of the great national cultures of Europe.

In the case of Izsó, the subject of his theme, in which the sculptural problem materializes, is not a matter of indifference and is never generalized, as in the small bronzes
of the Renaissance that mimic Greek goddesses, satyrs, and bacchantes, etc., but is,
on the contrary, essential and consciously chosen, as in ancient Greek sculpture in
large and small formats, the Tanagras, and the diminutive bronzes. For just as these
thematic figures perpetuate and concretize the ethnic identity of the Greek people
and their ideal of the human figure, in Izsó's figures the Hungarian ethnic identity and
ideal is carried into the transfigured realm of art. However, we must not forget that
the motifs, themes, and ethnicity in Izsós case acquire their significance from the fact
that they are absorbed in an art that is absolute in itself. Without this, ethnicity—no
matter how important, interesting and otherwise valuable from the national point of
view it may be—would be worthless in regard to the question of a national art. Only
after we have ascertained the formal components and the purely sculptural content of
Izsó's art are we entitled to consider ethnicity without the danger of straying into territory far from the domain of art. (…It will suffice to compare Izsó with the so-called
continuers of his direction, the ones who later modeled in clay or carved in wood all
those figures of Hungarian peasants sporting the *gatya* [loose linen trousers] or the
szűr [long embroidered felt cloak]: what these latter lack is precisely the sculptural
concept; in fact they have little to do with sculpture and more with ethnography; if
they are the "continuers" of anything, it would be of a piece such as *The Melancholy
Shepherd*, and not of Izsó's struggle with the problems of sculpture. The chasm separating them from Izsó is too great to be expressed by a word; they provide the negative
example that makes it possible to fully appreciate the positive values of Izsó's art.)
Start out from ethnicity and you will arrive at the most vital problems of sculpture, or
start out from the sculptural problems, to arrive at the ethnic ideal—this equation
constitutes the foundation of Izsó's art, and its incomparable value. It also constitutes
the most personal and most innovative aspect of his art, a veritable miracle in the
nineteenth century. (We are not in a position here to examine the influence of contemporary "folk-type" genre painting on his appraisal and formulation of the ethnic in his
art, but no matter how this coincidence in time worked as a factor, it does not alter the
originality and novelty of his experiment. For the painters of folksy figures and genre
pictures lacked precisely what was essential in Izsó's case: on the one hand, the artistic issue that subordinates everything else, and, on the other, the emphasis on setting
an ideal as a goal; the only thing he shares with them, at the most, is the fact that
he, too, "took his subjects from among the people"—that he, too, depicted peasants,
shepherds, and horse-herders.)
Izsó—it makes no difference whether consciously or instinctively—undertook something that had barely any precedent in his day: the depiction of the bodily ideal of a
people, and the identification of this ideal with sculptural issues. The intent behind
Izsó's experiment was the attempt to imagine Hungarian ethnic identity in the form of
a single figure—just as the ancient Greek artist had in the figure of the athlete—in
this case choosing the figure of the representatives of ancient activities, such as shep-
herding and horse-herding, taking the elements of reality and proceeding toward the
ideal, in the direction indicated by that reality.
This ideal is obviously not as noble, as saturated with culture, or as spiritualized in
its physicality as the Greek precedent—but that is another issue altogether. In its
own kind, it is every bit as justified as the other, for it fulfills the objectives of sculpture without becoming an abstraction, such as the idealized human figure of the

Renaissance. It is rooted in the living environment and reality of the people, which makes it vital and sanctifies it. Izsó's ideal is not a classical body, evolved into perfection of each part by athletics, but a human body made flexible and tough through the exercise of ancient, barbarian activities in the unlimited freedom of living on the plains. This body, all sinews and nerves, is first and foremost suited to its vocation, which does not consist of play, sport, or religious cult, but of ceaseless work around wild and tame animals, in all types of weather—that is, a barbarian thing. But when this weighty and majestic body—hardened by work, wanderings over the plains, and the vicissitudes of weather—casts off the burden of its existence and starts to dance, it becomes light and airy and flexible, as if it had spent all its life at sports or dancing. All of its movements snap to a rhythm that runs through the whole body, capable of every sort of attitude and turn, as it plays through the entire gamut of velleities in the possibilities of human motion, from a quiet swaying to the wildest whirl. And if Berzsenyi's words are correct ("Its secret laws mastery does not codify, but makes its own laws by curbing rapture")—the laws of sculpture come alive and become visible in these bodies, which is what Izsó had glimpsed in them, in choosing them to become the vehicles of his sculptural imagination.

If the sculptural idea were absent from Izsó's modeling of these figures, we would have little to say about them in connection with the art of sculpture. But since they are alive with sculptural ideas, these figures are doubly significant for us. This is the accomplishment of his art: it endowed something with an increased and permanent value. Thus Izsó's art possesses this independent and for us special value of ethnicity and the folk ideal: the things he had discovered and what he expressed about them, something that was conceived in the life and soul of the people, just as Apollo and the Doryphoros had been in the Greek soul. Without Izsó we would not be able to *see* the bodily ideal of our people, and we would not be aware of its sculptural value.

Translated by John Bátki

The end of nineteenth and beginning of twentieth centuries were marked by an explosion of national aspirations in the young Kingdom of Serbia, only lately freed from centuries-long Ottoman domination. This was especially apparent in an almost unanimous desire among South Slavic youth from Serbia, Slovenia, Croatia and Bulgaria for multinational unification and the creation of a common Yugoslav cultural region. Their hope was that cultural and artistic cooperation would establish lasting relationships among peoples who had for ages lived in different states, and who had—despite widely different historical and social circumstances—common roots, interests, and languages. Such was the spirit behind six Yugoslav art exhibitions, the first of which was held in Belgrade in 1904; it was followed by exhibitions in Sofia (1906), Zagreb (1908), Belgrade (1912 and 1922), and Novi Sad (1927). Each exhibition presented more than twenty painters, sculptors, graphic artists, and architects. Rejecting the traditional Viennese and Munich schools, these artists saw the art of cosmopolitan Paris as their model. They adopted Impressionism, plein-air painting, Symbolism, Expressionism, post-Cubism, and even tendencies of the avant-garde, all the while expounding the virtues of creative freedom, artistic emancipation, analytical consciousness, and the battle for an independent world of shapes and colors.

The political, social, and aesthetic contexts in which the exhibitions were organized varied greatly: the four pre-World War I events were animated by a fervent sense of epic national movement and provided an intellectual battleground where ideas of creative renewal sought to topple an older patriarchal spirit; the two postwar exhibitions were marked by the contradictions of life in the nascent Kingdom of Serbs, Croats and Slovenes. Yet they also marked the maturing of Yugoslav art's modernist tendencies and a triumph of academic visual language. The idea of a unified Yugoslav cultural region paved the way for modern art: the enlightening role of the Yugoslav Exhibitions was enthusiastically accepted by both the critics and the public.

The invitation to participate at the First Yugoslav Exhibition of 1904, signed by the most prominent Serbian intellectuals of the time, was written in Belgrade on the symbolic date of Vidovdan, June 28—the date that marks St. Vitus Day and the fateful battle between Serb and Turkish forces in Kosovo in 1389.

Translated by Maja Starčević

Dear Sir,

It is the belief of University Youth Organization in Belgrade that small Balkan nations, and Yugoslav nations especially, will be able to win the race with much larger and more cultured western nations only if they unite. That is why we have made it our goal to disseminate, and if possible, to realize the idea of uniting and making closer the relationships in all areas of cultural life of the Balkan nations, Yugoslav nations being of the first importance. To this purpose, the University Youth Organization has decided to arrange for an exhibition of artwork during this very school year, to be held in September, and to, for the moment, feature only the artwork of Yugoslav artists and artisans.

The University Youth maintains that the abovementioned idea of bridging the gap between Yugoslavs will be much easier to realize if they come to know one another better. Periodic art exhibitions held in the great capitals of Yugoslav nations, such as Sofia, Belgrade, Zagreb, and Ljubljana will prove to be a useful and strong means of introducing Yugoslavs to one another. The University Youth has, therefore, decided to take steps toward to the realization of this idea by being host to one Yugoslav art exhibition in Belgrade. The University Youth would like to stress not more than two extremely important and decisive facts concerning the occasion, those being:
a) Belgrade is more or less in the midst of the northwestern and the southeastern South Slavs, and thus connected to them with cheap and practical means of transport, which will make the visits to the exhibition more numerous, and b) a congress of the Yugoslav Youth Organization will be held at the same time in Belgrade, the Youth being a representative for the idea of Yugoslav congress.

We believe that you too, as a member of one of the Yugoslav nations, hold dear not only the survival, but also the advancement of your nation, and with it, that of other Yugoslavs. We believe that you, as an artist, will have the will and the ability to help this idealistic, but also demanding work that the Yugoslav Youth Organization is doing. The University Youth in Belgrade has the honor of asking for your help, which you could extend by sending your work to this exhibition.

Due to the fact that there is very little time left until the opening of the exhibition, the Exhibition Committee—i.e. members of University Youth Organization, professors of the University and artists—has resolved that in case there are no new works made specifically for this exhibition available, the exhibition shall accept earlier works of the artists regardless whether they have been exhibited before, or if they are in public or private collections, if there is any possibility to show them in this exhibition. The Exhibition Committee, will, in case the artists decide to create new works of art for this exhibition, the freedom to pick an unlimited number of subjects. However, we would like to express our wish that during the creation of new works, the artists keep in mind the exhibition's goal and duty. For these reasons, it would be extremely useful if the artists were to send such works which reflect not only their individual artistic characteristics, but also both historical and modern characteristics of the nation to which the particular artist belongs.

The University Youth appreciates the great importance artists have not only for the culture of the Yugoslav nations and as a whole, but also their even greater importance as the best and the most trustworthy aides in the realization of the idea of Yugoslav congress. Thus, the Youth has decided to disseminate the idea into the widest spheres of the people by buying off and distributing the works of art. That is why the Exhibition Committee was asked to organize a specific type of lottery for the purpose of buying the works of art at the exhibition. The University Youth in Belgrade hopes that it shall be able to, with the help of all other Yugoslav Youth Organizations, buy, if not all, then most of the works exhibited, and by doing this not only show their appreciation for the artists, but also make it possible for their works to travel to even the most distant regions of the Yugoslav nations.

In order to make the collecting of artworks easier and faster, the Exhibition Committee has asked for the establishment of one special committee made up of local artists and friends of art in Sofia, Belgrade, Zagreb, and Ljubljana. Those committees will at the same time serve as the first jury for the artworks of those artists who gravitate towards that center not only politically, but also spiritually. These local committees shall provide the artists of the abovementioned nations with necessary information, and at the same time have the duty to collect as many works as space at the exhibition shall allow, as well as to send those works to the Exhibition Committee in Belgrade. The works sent by these local committees will not go through any other formalities, and will be put up for exhibition immediately.

The Exhibition Committee of the University Youth in Belgrade shall accept all responsibility and it promises to be diligent in safeguarding the artworks sent to the exhibition. The Committee shall pay for the expenses of packing and transport of artworks from the places of their author's or owner's origin to the local committees in Sofia, Belgrade, Zagreb, and Ljubljana, the expenses of transport from Sofia, Zagreb, and Ljubljana to Belgrade, as well as for the possible return of these artworks to the place specified by their owners.

For the purpose of more effective safeguarding of artistic works during transport and exhibition, the artworks will be insured for an amount specified by the owner at the moment of releasing the work. The works will be insured from the moment they pass into the dealer's hands until the moment of their return to the hands of their owners. In case of error, damage, or destruction of the works of art, the owners will be compensated for the damage.

The Exhibition Committee will take on the responsibility to free all works of art sent to the exhibition of import tax upon their arrival in the Kingdom of Serbia, as well as to free them of tax upon leaving Serbia and return to their owners. The Committee shall do this in a way that will prove to be most appropriate.

The Exhibition Committee of the University Youth Organization in Belgrade will educate a special jury that will include one member of each of the local committees as representatives of the Bulgarian, Serbian, Croatian, and Slovenian nations, and these representatives will then elect another member, who will, all things permitting, be from the Kingdom of Serbia. This Belgrade jury will then decide the following: a) which artworks will be bought to serve as lottery prizes, and b) moral awards for the artworks of certain artists. Specific medals will be created for this purpose, to be made of gold, silver, or bronze, and given to the artists as an award.

The date when all artworks for the exhibition have to reach Belgrade is August 20 according to the old calendar, or September 2 according to the new. The reason for this is to allow enough time for the creation of the exhibition catalogue.

The exhibition will be opened on September 5/18, and will be open until September 25, that is to say, October 8, and will be held in the second floor of the University.

The Exhibition Committee of the University Youth in Belgrade would like to ask you, upon the arrival of this invitation, to turn to your local committee, which has sent you this invitation, for all further information and instructions.

In order to make the purchase, sale, and insurance of your works easier for the Exhibition Committee, we would like to ask you to list a price for each work separately.

In the hope that the Exhibition Committee has chosen the right path and manner of hosting the Yugoslav Art Exhibition, and taking into consideration the small amount of time it had to do it in, the committee would like to state its readiness to accept any advice and any suggestion which the artist would believe is beneficial to the exhibition and the abovementioned idea as a whole. The Exhibition Committee kindly asks you to interest your colleagues and those in your midst in this exhibition and to help the Committee with your advice.

The Exhibition Committee hopes that all is ready for the creation of an artistic exhibition. Whether it will be held depends solely on the good will and response of Yugoslav artists. However, as we are familiar with our artists' enthusiasm for all things noble and exalted, we take the freedom of believing that you too, Sir, shall participate in the exhibition by showing your works.

We are therefore honored to call ourselves,
Your Admirers.

No. 112
Vidovdan, 1904
Belgrade
In the name of University Youth Organization Board of "Brotherhood"
The Exhibition Committee of the University Youth:
Ljubomir Nešić, Attorney, "Brotherhood" President
Ljuba Jovanović, Attorney, Editor of "Slavic South"
Milivoje Smiljanić, Technician
Miloje Jovanović, Technician
Stanoje Mihailović, Attorney
Milan Đ. Nikolić, Attorney
Branko Popović, Technician
Kosta Jovanović, Technician
Svetislav Petrović, Philosopher
Dr. Marko Leko, Rector of the University
Mihailo Valtrović, Trustee of the National Museum
Dr. Jovan Cvijić, University Professor
Andra Stefanović, University Professor
Simo Matavulj, Writer
Steva Todorović, Painter
Đoka Jovanović, Sculptor
Dr. Miloje Vasić, Aide to National Museum Trustee

Translated by Maja Starčević

Simbolul group, Bucharest, 1912–13. L.–r.: Tristan Tzara, unknown youth, Marcel Janco, Jules Janco, Poldi Chapier, Ion Vinea

chapter 2

NEW ALTERNATIVES

Timothy O. Benson

If at the *fin-de-siècle*, artists throughout Central Europe had begun to gain a sense of independence from the officialdom of their immediate cultural institutions and national traditions, they approached the teens with a sense of excitement and commonality based on a compelling interest in contemporary art in Paris and other Western centers. As had Alfons Mucha and František Kupka before them, many (including the Hungarian János Máttis-Teutsch and Czech Cubists Josef Čapek, Otto Gutfreund, Bohumil Kubišta, and Otokar Kubin) traveled to Paris; artists in Berlin, Bucharest, Budapest, Prague and other cities could become well informed about recent French art and other tendencies in their own exhibition halls. For example, Prague's S. V. U. Mánes galleries hosted touring exhibitions of Impressionism (1901 and 1907), Auguste Rodin (1902), Edvard Munch (1905), and Antoine Bourdelle (1909), while Budapest's Nemzeti Szalon (National Salon) presented a major Cézanne exhibition (1907).

New groups, including the Hungarian Nyolcak (The Eight, 1909–1914), the Czech Osma (The Eight, 1907–08) and the Romanian Tinerimea artistică (Artistic youth) provided artists with avenues for their departure from national variations on Naturalism and Impressionism in favor of Cézanne, Post-Impressionism, and Fauvism—styles that increasingly left behind the appearance of nature to explore the underlying structure and order of art. Italian Futurism and German Expressionism were readily available in exhibitions created by Alexander Mercereau in Budapest and Prague in 1913 and 1914, while at the same time in Prague a collection focusing on Cubism was being created by the art historian Vincenc Kramář with the aid of Paris-based Daniel-Henry Kahnweiler. The Skupina výtvarných umělců (Visual Artists' Group founded in 1911) had already included French Cubists and German Expressionists in their own exhibitions, in art historian and Skupina member Václav Štech's words, "not as the apex and unattainable model" but as "colleagues in a common endeavor." In turn Skupina was included in art impresario Herwarth Walden's ground-breaking international exhibition held in Berlin in 1913, the Erster deutscher Herbstsalon (First German Autumn Salon).

This integration of artists from East and West was greatly advanced by such periodicals as *Volné směry* (Free Directions, published by S. V. U. Mánes in Prague beginning in 1896), *Umělecký měsíčník* (Art Monthly, the organ of Skupina, Prague, 1911), *Simbolul* (The Symbol, Bucharest, 1912) and *Chemarea* (The Call, Bucharest, 1915), which together with other such organs created a new forum of exchange from which many of the following documents are drawn.

Prior to the blossoming of such periodicals, concurrent groups such as the Eight groups in Prague and Budapest often had little or no direct contact with one another, despite their shared interests, in this case in Cézanne, Post-Impressionism, and the Fauves. Now they gradually forged a common commitment to the unprecedented departure from nature in favor of autonomy of form brought to completion in Cubism and Futurism. Yet their adoption of this new formal language was far from imitative. Many of the Czech artists of Osma and Skupina (such as Josef Čapek, Emil Filla, Otto Gutfreund, Vlastislav Hofman, and Bohumil Kubišta) understood the potential of the artificiality of art in terms of a profound philosophical discourse informed by Wilhelm Worringer (whose theories were essential for the Expressionists) and the emerging Viennese art history of Alois Riegl, among others. As had these scholars, they explored non-Western sources ranging from tribal cultures to Asian and Pacific influences to the more distant antecedents of their own cultures in Mesopotamia, Asia Minor, Egypt, and Greece, as well as Medieval, Gothic and endemic folk traditions closer to home. Čapek, Hofman, and Kubišta all yearned for a deep inner transformation based in the direct experience of art. The Hungarian Eight, led by Károly Kernstok, also absorbed the new international artistic trends within their own intellectual traditions, largely through their association with the Galileo Circle. This radical association founded by

several university students became a forum for intellectuals from throughout Hungary to which György Lukács and others frequently lectured. Consequently The Eight, and the Hungarian Activists after them, denounced traditional bourgeois values and espoused ideals of social progress and cultural creativity increasingly shared by their counterparts throughout the avant-garde.

Seeking new alternatives, artists throughout Central Europe made Cubism, Futurism, and Expressionism their own, thus setting the stage for the internationalist ambitions that would resume after the interruption of the First World War.

The founding of the Artists' Group (Skupina výtvarných umělců) (1911) called forth a rift between the older members of the Mánes Union of Artists and the youngest generation, which was already seasoned because many of its members were the founders of the former group Osma. The young generation from Mánes came out ostentatiously in order to make it absolutely clear that they were going to follow their artistic ideals uncompromisingly, without regard to the external environment and to public reaction. Their act brought on notable publication and exhibition activity, as had never been seen before in Czechoslovakia to such an extent with regard to the inception of modern art. Skupina began publishing the Umělecký měsíčník (Artists' Monthly), to which most of its members contributed extensive commentary. (Volume 1 covered October 1911–September 1912; Volume 2, November 1912–October 1913; only two issues of Volume 3 were produced before publication was halted by the outbreak of the First World War.) Skupina, comprised of visual artists, architects, art historians and writers, counted among its membership all the important figures of the day (including Vincenc Beneš, Josef Čapek, Karel Čapek, Emil Filla, Josef Gočár, Vlastislav Hofman, Josef Chochol, Pavel Janák, František Langer, Antonín Prochazka, Václav

Špála, and Václav Vilém Štech), with the exception of Bohumil Kubišta, who retained his independence after the breakup of Osma.

Thanks to the international contacts of Filla and Kramář, Skupina managed to acquire the trust of Daniel-Henry Kahnweiler, who willingly loaned works by Picasso and Braque for their exhibits. Skupina put on four exhibits in Prague: the first in January–February of 1912; the second in the autumn of 1912, in which German painters living in Prague were exhibited (Willy Nowak and Friedrich Feigl), as well as painters from Paris (Picasso, Friesz, Derain), and Berlin (Heckel, Kirchner, Mueller, Schmidt-Rottluff); the third exhibit in May of 1913, which featured Derain, Braque, Picasso, Gris, Cézanne and Soffici as guests, and also included examples of folk art and oriental art; the fourth exhibit was held in February of 1914, and included Munch, Picasso and Pechstein as guests. Another two exhibits by Skupina took place in Germany in the Munich Goltz Salon of New Art (April 1913), and in the Berlin gallery Der Sturm (October 1913), showing only the work of group members.

The fundamental theme of most of the contributors to the Umělecký měsíčník was the relationship to the spiritual essence of form, which the representatives of Skupina attempted to capture not only in paintings and sculptures, but also in architecture and the practical arts. (Their central interest became primarily the internal motion of form, granted by its personal, autonomous existence, which is limited according to the surrounding environment.) Out of this perspective a link was forged in Prague between the ideas of the Vienna art history school and the impulses of Parisian Cubism. Within Skupina there soon arose an ideological polarization between Filla and Josef Čapek, which led to a split in 1912, after which some of the original founding members of the group left (the Čapek brothers, Chochol, Špála, etc.) in order to temporarily return to Mánes. The rift—interpreted as a polarization between a more open approach to modern art as a whole (even to Futurism or Expressionism), and a more limited one, exclusively remaining with Picasso's Cubism— distinctly marked the fate of Czech modern art well into the twentieth century.

Translated by Andrée Collier Záleská

HONORÉ DAUMIER: A FEW NOTES ON HIS WORK   Emil Filla

Originally published as "Honoré Daumier, Několik poznámek k jeho dílu," *Volné směry* 14 (1910)

If we understand the history of art from the standpoint of utilizing one of three artistic elements—color, line and light—and if we use these as a sort of measuring device, then all efforts and misunderstandings become only a motive for the struggle for dominance of one element over another. The work of Honoré Daumier expresses itself within this evolutionary drama as an illogical and paradoxical exception. An analytical examination of Daumier's work according to the requirements of the purity of a certain creative principle, the solution to its inclination towards a certain pole, no matter what side we approach it from, inevitably fails and defies clarification and comprehension. What is a priority and necessity for other artists is either utterly dismissed by Daumier, or chaotically mixed in his work. The values that are contingent on the point of view determined by the laws of one sculptural principle are likewise ignored. Daumier is an exceptional soul who defies ordinary artistic creation; either his principle of form is the foundation for all visual art—something primary, specific to all the highest expressions of artistic work—or else he is one of those whose foundations are foreign conventions of creation. It is clear, however, that all the elements that distinguish his art are found as fundamentals in the work of the greatest masters—often here too, only hidden and mixed.

For Daumier a single element—whether line, light, or color—was never a final, decisive course, a measure that ensured and caused certain artistic expressions, but rather merely something bearing expressive possibilities. His own element is molding and pure sculptural understanding, the primary ability, which Rodin called the basis for the whole world: "If we imagine God's thoughts while creating the world, then we can say that he thought first of molding, which is the single principle of nature, being, and perhaps even the planet."

Everything operates at the same time in his pictures, without regard for the laws of individual elements, because he subjects *all* elements to the laws of pure sculpture and space. The arabesque of his picture has no absolute beauty. He isn't concerned with a smooth execution, and he commits the greatest sins against technical rules. He fails to respect the natural logic of certain artistic elements—his concern is only with the right look, even, as with all the greatest primitives, to the detriment of beauty. And yet with all his extremes which approach simplicity, his work is, in form and content, as rich as life itself, and all the work of his contemporaries and the later Impressionists pale next to his pictures—they are only as pretty and empty as piece-work, and their effect today is expressed only in aberrations.

His basic means of expression is his combinatory and contradictory technique; his objects seem to me kneaded from matter, their materiality is destroyed to the greatest possible degree—they are dematerialized. His way of dematerializing and subordinating is again based on the expression of plasticity: he either destroys it, dematerializes it, or emphasizes it. Daumier's coordinating composition relies on the dramatic relationship of sculptural masses in space.

Daumier doesn't use light in accordance with the light-principle method—he doesn't flood the whole picture with either light or darkness. His work with shadows is for the most part hard and sharp, in order to emphasize even more the contrast of several masses, or in order to elevate and exaggerate some sort of important relief. Color doesn't serve him, as it does Cézanne and his followers, as a single expressive means; instead he uses it as a quality that is capable of contrasting or symbolizing. Yet his paintings *Two Singers* and *Scapin* give us proof of his technical greatness and his exact knowledge of the principles of color. These are works that surely seemed in their own time like confused miracles, and which even today are awaiting discovery. The line in his paintings does not have a mere outlining function in the manner of the Japanese and the line-primitives. Its effect is limited to the greatest possible economy and the greatest strength of contrast. All of Daumier's work is based on the economic creation and the construction of contrasts.

This suggestive pathos and drama reaches extremes, especially through a turbulent dynamic in opposition to static motionlessness and solidity. In *The Crowd on the Street*, *Dramata*, and *Ecce Homo*, a motionless, severe wedge—the silhouette of a building or a protruding balcony—clashes with the passion of twisted human bodies formed in a powerful, surging wave. With him, the problem of contrast isn't a problem of the heightened intensity of the pictorial effect but, instead, becomes the very basis of expression and the foundation for the rhythmic articulation of masses. Typical, psychologically important points and borders, the division of surfaces, he marks and articulates usually by a set of medial/golden section, which lies under the frame and whose height and width is chosen as the basis of two contrasts with regard to the internal dramatic content.

If attempts are made to measure his creative power, Daumier is often compared to the greatest talents, Michelangelo and Rembrandt. Daumier has in common with Michelangelo only the elements found in the work of all great masters: an efficiently economic technique, a broad conception of masses, tectonic structure, the greatest peaceful unity of the whole, easily comprehensible despite the complexity of individual elements and the richness of the essential details of expression. In Daumier's case we understand once again that no richness of content, multifaceted elements, or exuberance of detail mean anything by themselves—in fact they are detrimental unless tied in the slightest detail to regular comprehensiveness and a clear and easily understandable structure. Each detail in the picture can be justified only when it either aids in emphasizing the dominant variable, when each part is in the relationship to the others and every direction in a dramatic relationship with the other directions, when all surfaces and panels are subject to the uniformity of geometric and arabesque comprehensiveness. Or they are possible only if they all lead—with the liveliest internal architectural rhythm and the most grotesque internal motion—to the achievement of the greatest balance of the whole, to unity and calm.

Daumier's work once again documents the fact that the end result of every artistic work is balance and peace. The newest young French painters—Maillol, Denis, and Matisse—are attempting to embody this requirement; they make it a principle that the final effect of a painting should be for the viewer as an armchair is to an exhausted person. This understanding forced Michelangelo to retain as much as possible the original character of stone—its physical consistency—despite the greatest internal motion and liveliness. This principle led him to compose his sculptures from basic cubic forms: cubes, pyramids and cylinders. Rembrandt tried for nothing less, with his magical system cloaking everything that is subordinate and secondary in shadows and achieving through his dematerializing abilities—based on the principles of light, with an aggregation and bejewelment that are absolutely Baroque—a whole that is clearly distributed between dark areas and focuses of light.

At first glance Daumier's work seems classifiable—by the previous generation as well as the present one—as standing solely on the principle of color, along with artistic creations that express themselves merely through light and shadow. An apparent resemblance to Rembrandt supports this error.

Rembrandt's composition and structure does not derive from malleable materials and their sculptural expression, as Daumier's does, but instead transforms the work of the tectonic element into light, shadow, and dark. But in paintings like the *Good Samaritan*

(1650) and *The Sermon of Saint John the Baptist* (although, in this painting, the dominant elements are emphasized with light), almost all creative work, directions of lines, arrangement of compartments into a simple whole, emphasis and symbols, are created not with light and shadow, but almost solely though pure plasticity and the expressive abilities that come out of it. Daumier was never able to combine the laws of sculptural and arabesque beauty of this particular creative element, as Rembrandt was in his later pictures.

As with all the great masters, each work of Daumier's seems unrelated to the others, and each new painting is a new expression and a new discovery for the viewer. With regard to decorative worth, it is beyond the frontier of decorative effect in its internal power, uniting it into a completely independent organism. A Daumier painting is almost self-sufficient and independent. It is not planned to hang on a wall as the center of the interior; it's a world in itself and requires complete immersion from the viewer. Every improvement to the interior would seem dubious or pointless in his case. This also explains his monumental pictorial effect in imperceptible dimensions.

The categorical postulate of every artistic work is the special concept, and all branches of the visual arts and all components of individual creation must come only out of, and aim towards, cubic understanding and its expression. The question of talent is, above all, a question of the ability to observe and sense space. If Delacroix is considered the source of the new spatial-sense, as the beginning of the "dot system" of the under-standing and creation of surfaces—the further continuation of which was developed in the work of the Impressionists, mainly Cézanne—then Daumier's work can be classi-fied unilaterally with the work of those who express themselves through sets of dots as focal points, and through the light-principle.

With Daumier it is impossible to truly speak of the unity of expression and creation of spatiality.

His method is unclear, inconsistent, and governed by the dominant element in each piece. To the extent that Daumier has a sense of distance, depth, and space at all, it is apparent in his sketches and drafts. In order to express the most complex spatial con-figuration he needs only a simple stroke set down with confidence. In this, his work resembles the drawings of the old Dutch masters, especially Ostady and Rembrandt, whose records seem to give a sense not only of the magic of a coincidental, fleeting moment, but are at the same time a typical fixing of phenomenon and the quintes-sence of thousands of observations. Form-memory was so well developed in Daumier that in the whole history of art we cannot find an analogous figure—only Rubens' form-mnemonic can be compared to it.

It's known that Daumier's sketches were never made from an object, and that before he began a drawing or painting he made a model of the figures out of clay. In order to create in this manner it's necessary to have a bit of the soul of Dostoevsky and Balzac—as well as their faith in the reality of their characters—and also a great deal of acting talent. Every great artist is a sort of actor; his victims are the actors of his emotions.

Daumier's work remains as unpopular as Poe's. His concept of caricature was neither sarcastic nor moralistic. In fact, if we compare his style with the caricatures of our contemporary artists, they were almost unbiased. They merely register all the pas-sions and record all the various rhythms of life, not in order to amuse, or arouse empathy or hatred, but in order to provoke the viewer out of impartial lethargy and passivity. Caricature was necessary in his work only in its theme, like Cézanne's apples.

By some fateful error Daumier has been inserted into the evolutionary drama of modern French art at the very beginning. In the history of every artistic school and every independent trend an inimitable master such as Michelangelo, Rembrandt or Tintoretto comes along to complete the action, to become the curse of progress, making further development impossible because he is the culmination of something and the beginning of rapid deterioration. Daumier, however, with his early and therefore inexplicably mysterious appearance, is a blessing, a point of reference for the new directions, and it seems that all later art had to come along only in order to illuminate and interpret his distilled work. Everyone has found what they need in Daumier, and they have all been enriched by it as long as they didn't adopt his method, but instead sought to clarify his chaos, which threatened to destroy lesser talents—J. F. Millet most of all. Delacroix's later work shows how much he was able to triumph from his understanding of Daumier.

Daumier's pathos and the fullness of his content became the Impressionist worldview for us, especially after the war; this school of the passivity of the soul, totally foreign—especially after the examples of Cézanne and Gogh—we have learned to understand through Daumier's congenial language. Daumier's work remains a lighthouse in an ocean of doubt—showing the way, and yet shipwrecking anyone who comes too close to it.

Translated by Andrée Collier Záleská

THE PRISM AND THE PYRAMID Pavel Janák
Originally published as "Hranol a pyramida," *Umělecký měsíčník* vol. 1 (1911)

The development and range of our local architecture have been and still are determined by two large European architectural families: the architecture of Southern Antiquity and that of Northern Christianity. In our view, they represent two stylistic possibilities given to our world of ideas with its psychological predispositions. The purest of its types, Ancient Greece and French Gothic around 1300, embody two opposite poles: despite its high style, Southern architecture, based on a natural way of building— placing boulders on top of one another—represents architectural naturalism, which maintains the independent character, prismatic surface and materiality of the building components (columns and entablatures), and the only aesthetic intervention consists in placing beautifully hewn and proportionally positioned heavy stones and slabs, quietly and calmly on top of each other in accordance with the simplest natural law of gravity, and in a manner that betrays nothing of the pressures and forces they have to bear and transfer. A characteristic of the Southern architecture is that even where it is created in large masses (Egypt, Rome) and is therefore less dependent on its building components, it still maintains the character of a layered building style. The Northern group aims to rise above the quotidian of earthbound building and reach supernatural beauty. Building components (stones) disappear under the whole of the edifice; the builder penetrates the matter of stone, boldly and speculatively removing mass from underneath its surface. The aim is to create a building as if made of single matter, with all its parts alive and active, almost in tension. The Southern direction with its clear, natural, general quality has always lent itself to re-planting and grafting; that is why, from Egypt to Asia, until the recent Renaissance efforts of the nineteenth century, it has taken root in the widest possible geographical and temporal area, reviving exhausted eras with the simplicity of its creative principles. The Northern group however, as soon as its sources were released in the Romanesque style, developed along the direct line of one style; because its ultimate aim—the total transcendence of matter—was so specific and so unattainable, that its development was arrested by the power of matter itself. Once more in history, matter was reversed by mind and turned to abstraction: when the earthly quality of the Baroque brought into art and religious reformation by the Renaissance was transcended again by Catholicism; the material calm of ancient forms (columns and entablatures) was revitalized by imagined movements that imbued matter with spirit.

Our architecture belongs to both of these families. Both have claimed us for equal periods of time: the first six hundred years of our history—and this is very important— the foundations of our culture were being laid, giving rise to national awareness, were under the influence of the Northern group; the Southern spirit—of course already at the stage of Renaissance revival—came as the second direction and took up the entire second half of our history, until today: that it developed its full potential above all in the Baroque, a period again controlled by abstraction, it was characteristic for our national character. A large part of our history of architecture was taken up by attempts to escape beyond and above the limits of matter—in the Gothic and the Baroque style—while the rest (sixteenth and seventeenth centuries) remained with a positive, accepting attitude towards matter and material form.

Contemporary, so-called "modern," architecture shares this materialistic view by virtue of its origin and nature. Having clearly developed from Neo-Renaissance, with all the theoretical attempts to prove its connection with the Empire style, the character of its system of construction (ridiculed by amateur critics as "Assyrian" or "Egyptian") all prove its genetic relatedness to the Southern group. It is important to keep this in mind, as the ideas that had ushered it in and that it has itself brought forth—for example, the "re-birth of art, purged of falsely repeated historical forms, a return to modern life"—seemingly represent a sudden turn of history in a new, unprecedented direction. Considering the ideological principles of new architecture, its ideological affiliations undoubtedly emerge clearer. Its broadest principle, the return to contemporary life, (an analogy of the return to nature), means—there is no denying it—mere positivity and earthliness, albeit temporarily recognized as beauty. The eradication of old historical stylistic forms and traditions, decided and thoroughly carried out by the new architecture, apart from being healthy and effective in curbing the wildest excesses of pseudohistorical architecture, has another characteristic that cannot be overlooked: a fundamental distaste for any immaterial, spiritual form. Its suggestion that architecture must be functional and down-to-earth, accepted as the corrective measure ("what is not functional, cannot be beautiful") is a very safe but also materialistic one. On the other hand, side by side with the recommendation that art should maintain close links with daily life and serve its material needs, and with the general acknowledgement of matter, new architecture paid little or almost no attention to the question of how and what kind of artistic abstraction it wanted to make from these material preconditions. All this clearly shows the true nature and spirit of modern architecture.

Modern architectural works executed in this spirit signify a certain return to a realistic way of building, to the natural use of building materials. Natural building units were re-discovered and recognized in their bare prismatic system, following a certain logical development, and all the constructive elements—column and slab—were again set into material substances of which they were made, that is prisms of stone, beams, etc. It could be said that this negative, cleansing artistic activity deprived anything that departed from the skeleton of the prism of any sense. At the same time, these natural building shapes took architecture back to the primary system of building by placing pieces of material on top of each other, according to the simple technical and natural law of burden and support; outwardly, this architecture is characterized by being divided exclusively into horizontal and vertical elements, or planes, but consistently excluding any other (for example diagonal) formal possibility. Any need for plastic gradation is again met by prismic gradation of volume.*

It can be said that under the given conditions, today's architecture has achieved a certain easy system of expression, which has left no problem unresolved. Our sensibility, however, preceding all future action by thinking about this system, labels it unwittingly with attributes and phrases that demonstrate the difference in our inner emotional view, suggesting that we find in it certain negative characteristics and that we seem to feel that this is precisely where architecture should be positive. If we consider contemporary architecture—in its current mature state—materialistically pedestrian and lacking in real poetry, it means that such values have been positively developed, that they claim their due and that we miss them in contemporary architecture. This change in sentiment can be observed in objects we have been fond of in the history of architecture: if, in accordance with the architecture of the prism we sympathized with related eras, for example with Ancient Greece, primitive Italian architecture, or the Renaissance, we start dealing with the Gothic and Baroque, which had previously appeared distant; we see them now in the true sense of the word, whereas before, it was as if they did not exist. They attract our attention by the vivacity of the spirit that permeates matter, and by the dramatic quality of their expressive means that serve to create their shape. Both aspects, which we find so surprising, have in the meantime become a new substantial part of our sensibility. At the same time, we find the system of prism and its means too poor and insufficient to express this; it seems that in such thinking about this materialistic system, the spirit and will to abstraction that has always been close to our Northern sensibility is awakened in us.

In this view, where the artistic form of matter and artistic creation are considered a positive, we must be interested in its emerging opposite: the natural building form of matter and natural creation, if it exists or if it is possible to construct it as an idea.

It can be said that the first attribute and force of matter in the inorganic sphere of nature—assuming that it is in itself outside all movement of the universe, atmosphere and surface of the earth—is gravity. Gravity is a force tending towards equalization of all matter—if it were not prevented by friction—into a great calming horizontal surface, and further into horizontal layers, placed on one another as they have been brought by time: the purest result of gravity is the surface of water, alluvium compressed into layers. To these horizontal formal planes appertains the vertical direction of gravity (the trajectory of objects in free fall), and together they form a substantial formal pair of natural matters; nature exhausts itself in them in the event that there are no other properties and forces of matter and life permeating each other. If matter placed in this way according to the law of gravity were in turn to be acted upon by the force of gravity (for example, the weight of the upper layers), and if matter did not resist because of its cohesion, a layer of matter would break off along a fracture vertical to its surface. Such clean fractures really occur in nature, fortunately in simplified conditions, and their result—mass delimited along vertical and horizontal planes— can indeed be considered naturally formed matter.

All other geometrically more complex shapes appearing in inorganic nature come into being as a result of synergy of a third force: diagonally falling rain is caused by the

* Materiality of the South is manifested not only in shape, but also in other values. Greatness was, for example, realized and represented by means of physical volume of works of art: colossi, etc. in Egypt, preferred use of the largest size building blocks, increasing the size of a temple according to its importance. [Author's original note.]

additional factor of wind, similarly snow-drifts, potholes, ravines, caves, depressions, and volcanoes are mostly shapes created positively or negatively out of inorganic matter by another, penetrating force that deforms and varies the natural shapes in which it had been deposited. The most beautiful example of this process is crystallization: here, the merging force (the force of crystallization) is so disproportionately strong in comparison with gravity that—it can be almost said—the weight of the matter has no impact on crystallization; the force of crystallization seems to be a kind of gravity of matter concentrated into it, so strong that it is realized in all circumstances into a world centered in itself. All such shapes, in contrast to natural primary shapes (limited by the system of biplanes vertical to each other) are distinguished by planes diagonal to the basic, natural ones. Diagonality is then a shape created by imbalance brought into balance by fracture and remaining so. If then the vertical and horizontal biplane is the shape of stillness and of the isolated equilibrium of matter, diagonal shapes were preceded by dramatic activities and more complicated clusters of forces.

The view of flatlands, the surface of the sea or vertical rockfaces evoke—creatively speaking—an idea of dead stillness, a zero degree of duration, while diagonal shapes in nature—slopes, ruins, gorges, volcanoes—evoke a sense of drama, movement, sharpness and pointedness; the nature of both categories of feeling are proportionate to and coordinate with the actions that had preceded and created them. This ratio between the natural primary shape of stillness and a dramatized shape provides the means by which matter is conquered artistically, since the artist's intentions, although psychologically more complex, are in principle the same as the forces penetrating, permeating and moving natural matter and its natural shape. What we can conclude from it about the nature of artistic creation is this: if dead matter is to be artistically overcome, that is, given spirit so that something happens in it, this occurs by means of a third plane added to the natural biplane shape.

This comparison offers a beautiful parallel to the means of human action and human creation: wedges, arrows, stakes, knives and levers that physically overcome matter are mostly diagonally shaped.

The cause of the first shelters and buildings made by humans was man's intention to resist certain natural forces, rain, snow, sun, acting from above. Man's activity, aiming vertically upwards from the surface of the earth, is contrary to the direction of gravity, and the only purpose of this initial building system is to solve the problem of gravity and overcome it; to prevent matter from being set into falling motion by the force of gravity, it is necessary to place a horizontal load against it, a material support—that is, a form that again demonstrates the disciplined, natural system of vertical biplane. The building material best suited to this system—if it is formulated on the basis of the vertical biplane—is the prism, which is often found in this shape in nature (ashlar or stone slab), or it is hewn or formed (bricks). The natural adding and ordering of these prism-shaped building units into walls, pillars and ceilings contributes to the entire building becoming a structure based on the system of prism, unless there are other than practical intentions at play. Certain decisions of mutual ratios and certain spatial and compositional ideas may be applied here. On the whole, however, the act of enclosing matter into prisms signals acceptance of its material nature. The geometric form of prism given to matter arises from usefulness and technological considerations, not from intellectual, artistic or philosophical conclusions.

As soon as thinking about the essence of matter is added to this purely technical way of creating material and building with it, and questions are asked about its necessity, how and where it appears to human senses, how it bears the impact of force and pressure, the materiality of matter is no longer so exclusively recognized and doubts and emotive views of matter arise, which, as soon as they become active, turn into forces penetrating underneath the surface of matter or changing it everywhere where it doesn't appear to suit. A thinking, feeling spirit mostly desires to give matter life, to clarify it according to its own ideas, and, as a penetrating force it clashes with the very materiality of dead matter, dealing with it by hewing its corners and edges, penetrating into the depths wherever it does not accept matter or does not empathize with it. These changes wrought upon matter by artistic sense are of unnatural origin, that is, they no longer follow rules derived from the biplane system (in that case they would have been merely a correction of the dimension of the building block, detracting from its length, width, etc.), but they correct and change matter in the sense of dramatizing it, above all with the aid of a third element, the diagonal plane. The body that can be created from such dramatically ordered diagonal planes is the pyramid, which is the highest shape of matter intellectually abstracted from the natural mother-shape of the prism. For if we imagine a lying prism, not weighed by anything, and a pyramid, drawn into it above its base, the pyramid would be the philosophical substitute of its geometrical form: it reaches the same height with the same base, it has all three of its main dimensions, but it is less material, as it has no superfluous matter and is more concentrated in the sense of its height.

Architecture, in contrast to the natural way of building, is a higher activity, combining in fact two purposes: the purpose of meeting human need and the purpose of artistic expression, in other words, abstraction of matter. That is why, as a whole, it combines two systems of creation: the technical prismatic biplane building and the abstract transformation of matter by means of a triplane, diagonal or curved system. Its overall character then depends on which of the two architectural impulses prevails.

Primary building of any kind and in any era has nearly no diagonal elements and is formally akin—despite differences in geography, time and nationality. An entire group of European architecture is based on natural building: Mesopotamia, Asia Minor, Egypt, island cultures, Greece, etc., which have created the basic formal language, employed in all its subsequent renaissances. Since abstract tendencies are evident already in this stylistic group and, above all, the very composition of matter in relation to each other is refined or even idealized, it is possible to describe it as naturalism of the beautiful seeing of nature.

In its highest type—Greek architecture—a whole series of elements are transformed by means of abstraction: the foot and head of columns, the stepped profile of an architrave, ledges, cantilevers—such features mostly protrude from the vertical element of the wall and column, so that the tangential planes of their profiles are at an acute angle with the facing planes; a column changes from its original cylindrical shape into a more abstract, more sensitively formed conical column (in the Doric style), and later even biconical (entasis). On the whole, however, abstraction was limited to transitional linking elements inserted wherever the main constructive volumes of the prism met and rested on each other; the overall outline composition of the building remained within the limits of the still prism structure.

Ancient Rome, as we know, adopted the stylistic vocabulary of Greece and Asia Minor without changing much about the relationships employed by each system; the late style of the Roman Empire, however, displayed an increased dramatic expression of the basic masses, especially in architecture of the imperial villas (curved, even arching fronts) so that it is rightly called Roman Baroque.

Italian post-renaissance Baroque, especially in Northern Italy takes Southern architecture still further from the natural to the abstract. The basic Ancient forms and systems it adopted, with their calm materiality and stillness, did not correspond to the intellectual life of the Baroque era, and the way in which they were transformed illuminates the way of abstraction. Baroque, as we know, added and extended, intensifying the expression of all shapes by mounting and adding of matter: bases and heads of columns, entablatures and ledges are more sharply profiled and cantilevered further out, in their individual elements and in their entirety, the slabs of architraves and ledges take on a diagonal shape and there are conical pilasters, consoles and pillars. Alongside such means of intensified expression of the original forms, the Baroque also discovered other means of abstraction working by gradual intensification: turning and moving whole shapes from the original position they had held in Ancient architecture into positions that dramatically confront the core of the building at diagonal angles. Columns, pillars in portals and towers in the front of churches all turned diagonally to the axis, as if the matter of the building came to life and erupted or retracted inward, rearranging the formerly flat composition of the architecture. It is in essence the most abstract idea and possibility: to allow a living forming force remodel whole facades by lifting them and applying pressures directed outside and inside the foundation of the building.

If Baroque abstraction depends on intensification, on enlivening and moving of matter, the principle of the Northern family of architecture is opposite: it overcomes the calm and materiality of matter by immersing in it and detracting from it in the direction of the third diagonal plane.

The manner of this penetration into matter is best manifested in the development of the pillar in the nave of the cathedral system. This pillar is initially quadrangular, primary, its edges gradually become more and more faceted and its character grows more and more in both directions of the vaults and ribs resting on it, not until High Gothic is the original four-sided, unnecessarily massive pillar ideally and abstractly replaced by a quadrangular, diagonally placed pillar. All the other originally prism-shaped building elements went through the same transformation: strips, ribs, supporting arches. Portals with their diagonal sides are, according to the same principle, openings made into the mass of the façade; if their sides were directly vertical, cutting into the depth of the wall according to the biplane system, it would mean that the entire mass in this particular place would be cut out, abolished, while the diagonal sides visually maintain the mass of the wall. The Gothic style clearly recognized and consistently adopted the visual means of abstraction: the pyramids that end obelisques, roof ridges and tower summits represent the correct abstract delimitation of the building. There are beautiful explanations for this: if a tower ended with a prism, it could run upwards ad infinitum; if, however, we replace it with an equally high pyramid, the ending is definite and unambiguous; otherwise, the pyramid is a plastic elevation and resolution of the upper plane of the prism of the tower, from which it is as if lifted. The mass of the pyramid ends with a point, without the possibility of continuing any further.

The countries of the East, starting with Egypt, have cultures that had grown together over long periods of time in one direction; conditions, long accumulated, have therefore resulted in even more intellectual abstraction of matter in architecture. Egypt, in its pyramids and temples, which certainly have abstract, diagonal elements in their walls and pylons; India has an architecture of abstractly graded, repeated and added plasticity, underneath which the very essence of the building disappears and architecture becomes a kind of sculpture. China and Siam in their—to our eyes, strange— buildings often abolish the last natural biplane shape of their structure; the pagodas of Siam resemble accumulations of stalactites, while the roofs of Chinese temples and palaces are curved and their ends raised on arched, wavy beams. This is architecture removed as far as possible from natural building, becoming its second possibility: a sculptural building expression.

Translated by Alexandra Büchler

SURFACE AND SPACE Otto Gutfreund

Originally published as "Plocha a prostor," *Umělecký měsíčník* vol. 2 (1912)

Original human perceptions were sensual, leading to no particular rational conclusions. It was only with the passage of time that man, frightened by the multiplicity and vagueness of the shapes around him, wanted to confront the world, and find lasting values and criteria by means of which he could settle his relationship with it, a relationship between a subject and an object. He searched for an aim and meaning in life that would protect him from destruction, and clung to what was permanent and unchangeable.

Desire for the absolute, without development or end, was the motive behind all human thinking. Man was not content with simply letting life take its meandering, irregular course through an unknown river bed, without knowing where it came from, where it was going and why. He did not want to be a mere wave in an opaque, murky stream, a wave that would disappear without a trace.

Each deliverance from this uncertainty is conditioned by faith. Religious faith— that is, faith in absolute values outside life and human understanding—was the first means of deliverance. Science—that is faith in absolute values gained by the workings of the intellect—did not satisfy all of man's needs, as it did not give his daily life a moral code. Philosophy, the result of faith in intellect, leads to nihilism and skepticism.

Rational understanding represents the solidifying parts in the stream of past life, the firm substance of action, the salts crystallized from the living waters of intuition. A learned man, representing the human type bearing the defect of faith in intellectual values, is standing on such a part, on breaking ice thawed and carried by the warm stream of life, trying in vain to stop the current of development and to catch a glimpse of that absolute, eternal truth, mirrored in the stagnant surface of the water.

The artist, representing the human type bearing the defect of faith in the senses, hears in the stream of action the rhythm of waves breaking against the shore, sees in the moving stream the reflection of cosmos, magnified by the rippling effect of the waves, watches the impact of waves breaking against the firm, fatal shore, preserving and ordering their rhythm, reflections and tragic impact.

The senses-rays transfer the image of life into the artist's inner world as if into a lens through which they pass denser, stronger, and more balanced.

The artist needs metaphors not only to express himself; he needs metaphors to recognize the state of his own soul. It is only indirectly, by means of his senses, that he recognizes his own feelings. Without the mirror of a world perceivable through the senses we would not know our own reflection, just as without an artist who observes, there would be no reflection in the mirror. The senses transfer feelings into their own spheres, creating perceivable images and words. We cannot speak even to ourselves without words and metaphors. Every image, taken over by the senses from reality, is a symbol of a feeling. The senses are the only medium between the artist's self and the world.

The world is a phantom created by the senses, and there is no organ by means of which I could gain an absolute certainty and which would divide the apparent from the real. I therefore accept the world as a reflection of my own self, perceiving it and evaluating it in the form conjured up by my senses, my inner physical organs. Feeling does not distinguish a painter from a musician, poet from a sculptor, but they all differ from the average man, their observations possess the power of a vision, they are much more intense. They do not describe the object gradually from all sides, but perceive it and evaluate it simultaneously, guessing its inner value through its surface. Between them, they differ only according to the sense sharpened at the expense of others.

With the painter and the sculptor, it is the same sense—the sight—that acts as a medium between the subject and the object. The results should therefore be the same. The sculptor however sees in the mirror of life's surface the image of himself, while the painter sees through the surface, penetrating the secret of the stream. *A statue is not a dematerialization of reality, as is a painting, but a dematerialization of images born inside its creator.*

Comparing, somewhat boldly, a sculptor and a dancer, I would say that the dancer is inspired by music, materializing and transferring into reality the mental state aroused by music, turning it into art perceivable by means of sight. Although he appeals to the sight as the mediator between his dancing and the perceptions of the audience, he uses his own memories of visual perceptions of reality to portray an abstract musical impression. The musician, whose medium is immaterial, does not need visual interpretation to express himself. (The complex form of opera is the result of an opposite process: music elevates the drama enacted on stage into higher spheres of unreality.) Dance offers the viewer a graphic and material expression of inner feelings.

The sculptor draws on his inner fond, not on visual perceptions; he draws on ready-made motifs, just as the dancer draws on musical motifs, or the sculptor, for instance, on literary motifs. The outcome—the statue—is a materialized impression created by a motif. To recapitulate: the sculptor materializes directly a vision reflected in his soul, and only later does a reflection of visual perceptions enter the creative process, in the same way as it happens in the case of a dancer. He imagines himself to be the character representing an idea or experiencing a great passion, a hero or a martyr, and his inspiration is fertilized by an existing motif to give birth to the work in great pain. The sculptor realizes an imaginary idea in real space in a material form, *stopping the flow of development by spatial materialization.*

If we follow European sculpture in all its peaks, we always find this tendency to express visually and by means of symbols religious feelings, intellectual movements of the time, or, if art is an expression of an individual person, the tendency to materialize emotions and transfer them into space.

Ancient Greek sculptors created tangible gods from imaginary ideas, dragging them down from the highest of celestial spheres and incomprehensible spaces, and placing them into the real world, a world that was being born around them, was evolving and dying, while they represented the eternally unchangeable, the halting of time and change, the transference into space.

Donatello finds inspiration in John the Baptist, a biblical and therefore literary ascetic, and creates his material image with the aid of abstract means.

Rodin's *Age of Metal* symbolizes the sculptor's time just as Donatello's *David* symbolizes the Renaissance. *La Vieille Heaumière* was inspired by a poem; *The Citizens of Calais, John the Baptist* or *Balzac* are based on ready-made subjects. This list—to which we may add the *Mask with a Broken Nose*—also includes Rodin's best work, and it seems as if the rest were mere preparatory studies for several great gestures. Rodin's naturalism is a means, not an end, a means shared by a whole generation.

Gothic sculpture avoids any materialization of the highest concept of Christianity— of God. The Gothic approach is perfectly expressed in the open, flowing space of Gothic architecture. God remains outside time and space, and becomes a visible symbol only in the form in which he appeared on Earth, in the figure of His Son. The rich sculpture of gothic cathedrals is a choir explaining the mystery to the faithful by visual and symbolic means, while the highest concepts remain hidden to the eye.

If we consider the Gothic to be a movement with a common formal sensibility and we compare the forms of Gothic sculpture and architecture, we will be left with very few statues that could be described as truly Gothic. Gothic architecture denies all tangible volume; it scoops up matter and replaces it with surface (the Chartres Cathedral). In architecture, dematerialization into surface was not enough; the surface-wall is later replaced with slender supports. In other words: surface returns to its original form— the line. Gothic sculpture stopped at the first step towards dematerialization. The highest goal achieved by the Gothic tendency in sculpture is the substitution of volume with surface (Vézelay and Moisac). The relationships of depth were transformed into relationships of surface by dematerialization of volume and its transformation into surface, into relief. The remaining so called Gothic sculpture with its sensibility belongs to Romanesque style, while its later phase could be described as Baroque Gothic. (Baroque here means any art that has lost its ethical sense, which has in turn loosened its formal sense.)

To use the comparison with dance once more: original dance was the expression of physical desires, and a typical example of this is the dance of Salome, which, like most oriental dances, is practically a sexual act with realistic movements performed in a rhythm. Dance as art has progressed further, its means are more abstract, it expresses desire and passion by its very rhythm and dynamics.

In sculpture, African sculpture represents elementary perception of plasticity. The physical, material visualization has the same expressive potency as oriental dance. Today's sculptor goes further, replacing the very volume with illusive volume—surface. Moving surface is volume in the making and ceases to be form measurable by intellect; its function is taken over by the moving surface and a statue is no longer time stopped and transformed into space; it is an expression of flowing action, of incessant movement whose rhythm is identical to the rhythm of the mental creative process, before the thought settled as an idea. Real volume measurable by intellect is carried along and hollowed out by the stream of intense perception; a statue is no longer a conglomerate of volumes, the surfaces of which we gradually see through, surfaces that are petrified fragments of time and at the same time incessantly rippling illusions of volume, whose currents tear at the banks of the delineating space and carry them away, with eddies suggesting underlying depths and currents reflecting fragments of reality without ever ceasing to flow.

New sculpture knows no weight, as its real volume is replaced with surface. It therefore also knows no center of gravity. And this is where the main formal difference between Baroque sculpture and the sculpture of today lies. The dramatic pathos of Baroque sculpture consists in the shifting of the burden from its own center of gravity; it is a struggle of two forces, the balancing of a falling weight.

The seeming similarity between Baroque sculpture and sculpture of today lies in the richness of movement and vitality of form. In Baroque art, this particular movement was given by a lack of balance of the forces struggling within; today we strive for a free development of action without signs of struggle. Struggle without a final balancing always carries a sign of pathos; it is struggle for the sake of struggle, a show of strength, rather than real power. It is certainly not strength disciplined in the service of an idea, but tension for the sake of the dramatic effect of suspense. Rodin and Bourdelle have taken from Baroque art the shifting of weight from its center of gravity to the limits of static possibilities, in an effort to achieve a dramatic effect.

New sculpture is sometimes criticized for its bas-relief quality, which is seen as a manifestation of lack of three-dimensional understanding. It is true that new sculpture has this relief quality, and this is a result of its tendency to take everything in from one point of view, to enrich one point of view by hinting to others, to concentrate an all-encompassing richness in each point of view.

This path leads to new formal possibilities, new conditions and new questions. To find answers to these questions is a task for a strong personality, who will have to resolve them not theoretically, but by means of intuition, in accordance with the prevailing sensibility. The answer will then ensue on its own from the conditions and views of the time.

Translated by Alexandra Büchler

ON THE VIRTUE OF NEO-PRIMITIVISM   Emil Filla
Originally published as "O ctnosti novoprmitivismu," *Volné směry* 15 (1912)

The synthetic movement, which has inspired developments in painting over the past ten years, leading to a plainer, simplified expression, is still seen as a manifestation of some jaded, over-sophisticated, amoral artistic attitude, an unhealthy historical anomaly or at best an inane joke. Elucidation of the roots and essence of this new movement should protect it from prejudice and present it to impartial critical judgment.
Unlike in the case of music, an art of pure abstraction and therefore of a perfect, one-directional unity, the role of painting falls into two categories, because of its necessary respect for abstraction as a form of expression and for reality and nature as the source of its creative inspiration. In this sense it is analogous to literature whose medium, the word, has its sound, melody, rhythm, at the same time signifying a notion, idea, or object. If we follow the history of painting on the basis of this assumption, we can compare the development of the art form to a wave whose curve moves between two extreme points, one of which is an excessive love of reality and nature, and the other a love of abstract, purely formal beauty. Such development then appears to us as a struggle whose final aim and meaning consists in a harmonious balancing of the two tendencies and in finding equilibrium between a sense for nature and its formal equivalent. In the history of painting, one pole is represented by primitivism and the other by classicism. Primitivism came first, being the cradle and source of creative efforts progressing towards classicism, which represents a conquest of reality by means of abstraction and form.
Primitivism is nothing but the recognition of one's own inability to fulfill formal schematism in a unified way, by means of a detailed, natural form. On the other hand, an artist is seen as classical when his painting skill makes it possible to maintain a unity and order in a work, despite numerous individual details. Creative ability then coincides with a sense for motif, reality, nature.
It is the duty of every perfect painting as a complete whole and orderly organism to achieve a clear, comprehensible expression. A primitivist achieves this with simplicity bordering on asceticism of form, motif, and movement. This moderation is the consequence of virtue; the artist knows that complexity, insufficiently managed, would necessarily lead to chaos and illegibility. A classicist, by nature extravagant and perceptive, produces a classic of form by virtue of organizing rich and complex multiplicity into a well ordered, clear whole.
The development from primitivism to classicism moved either through traditional work from generation to generation, or through the work of exceptionally talented and assertive individuals of genius, who sped up the process of development from primitivism to classicism, and even to the baroque, representing the extreme of lavish expression. Throughout this development, a liking for reality grew, until it ended with

naturalism, a movement justified only where it rested on a long tradition and on a highly cultured form. It makes sense only when, as in the case of Rembrandt, it is the outcome of a development. Otherwise it is a symptom of lack of direction, a negation of development, coming to the fore whenever the old conventions of style and expression begin to die and no longer serve to express the life of an era. At this stage, naturalist artists arrive as revolutionaries, wasting creative energy to bring down old dogmas and customs, without the possibility of a substitute, without the promise of a new form and style. Masaccio is celebrated in Italian art for moving beyond the schematic, hieratic, rigid style, beyond impotent and uncomplicated primitivism towards reality, life, nature. It is not certain, however, whether this step was made at the expense of discipline and purity of perception and expression. Trying to bring his work closer to nature, he added shadow, maintained a unified optical field in relation to shapes and space, and allowed local color into his paintings. It is necessary however to ask whether it may have been the case that with Masaccio, a lesser talent entered Giotto's school, an impatient, ruthless naturalist with immature naturalistic appetites. Every untimely instance of a desire to become a classic carries with it a threat of brutality, aggression and blasphemy, and is a symptom of complacency and uncritical attitude towards one's own capacity. From a historical point of view, minor talents working on new problems, or primitivist artists starting from the beginning, have a moral right to claim a place in the closed visual arts culture alongside an all-embracing genius who develops certain principles, taking a particular direction to its conclusion.

Our era is experiencing a strong primitivist movement, akin to the attempts made in search of an expression in paining in the early Middle Ages. Yet the Italian primitivists were no barbarians, unfamiliar with the secrets of formal beauty. Giotto and his school were the true heirs of previous visual cultures, and there is a direct, uninterrupted line of development leading from Byzantine art and mosaics to Giotto's frescoes. These artists invest the Byzantine formulas with a new emotional charge, adopt their formal language and develop it further. They are not then primitivists without tradition, without a legacy of the past.

Modern primitivism is however driven by different efforts than its mediaeval version. It builds on more one-sided premises, leading to a total renewal of form and its principles. This one-sidedness necessarily arises from its role as a reaction to the preceding Impressionist movement. Modern primitivism is practically without tradition; it builds from the beginning.

The greatest problem with Impressionists was their indifference to the constructive, compositional essence of the work. They lacked a sense of style, of the rhythmic pathos of the work, a sense for the monumentality and unity of form. The Impressionists were still connected with the tradition of old masters through Delacroix, but their successors, the Neo-impressionists, who took their creative principles and methods to the extreme in their obsession with the details of their color system, forget the frame, the structure of the work. Manet was the only one of them who sensed the impossibility of creating a work of art equal to the paintings of old masters in the style of Impressionism, noting correctly that its freshness of the touch, immediacy and sketchy quality are not enough to build a monumental work of art. Already at the time when he proved his constructive power and connection with tradition, he was convinced that the impressionist method contradicts the ideal of painting. At the time when he painted *Olympia* and *Déjeuner dans l'Atelier* (*Luncheon in the Studio*), he abandoned the characteristic breaking up of form into spots and gave line the main expressive function; the tonality of individual parts is kept at the same range and contrast of wide color planes is used to constructive purpose. Even in his last years when he adopted Monet's method, he still returned to the tradition of his younger years, whenever he wanted to resolve a more serious, monumental problem (*Desboutin*, *Fishermen*, *Workers of the Sea*). Painting based only on visual perceptions does not create a monumental work of art, because the senses convey data, facts—nothing more. It is the logic of reason that is instrumental in constructing a comprehensive view. Impressionism was acceptable as a method of painting only as long as the artist was a genius and as long as he could at least partially replace the necessary stylistic conception and consistency with his individual approach. An ingenious conception has to do with concentration and economics. Seeing nature in a monumental way means transferring a multiplicity of forms and complexity of shapes onto a very limited number of original shapes, resting on a process of simplification, which reduces multiplicity into unity. Every one-sided method in visual arts has its hidden dangers, which eventually claim it and which are manifested first and most tangibly in the work of mediocre talents. Impressionism, as a school of sketching, of individual, random creation, and optical perception of reality meant that the mediocre painter sat in front of nature, without discipline and instruction, but with the courage to communicate the most complex natural phenomena. He had the courage of a great master, a classic, who conquers detail by means of constructive power, which is a manifestation of "artistic conscience and a proof if its integrity." Creating a work of art does not merely mean placing individual facts next to one another, for being a creative artist means to be able to take possession of natural creative mechanics, observing and following the creative principles of the universe.

Modern primitivism as reaction to Impressionism is necessarily one-sided. The primitivists' effort merely aims to establish a new convention of form and conception, and is exhausted in structural construction. Yet, it would be wrong to accuse these experimenting pioneers that they lack a sense of reality and its emotive value. In their moderation, they do not attempt to deal with more complex subjects, restricting themselves to still life, landscape, and studies of the human body. Their poverty is voluntary.

A tragedy of creative spirit is the case of an artist returning to primitivism while lacking an adequate form for sophisticated, over-refined psychological states, whose emotions are too deep, expansive and personal to be fitted into the limited primitive form. Such artists inevitably overflow, leaving the narrow restraints of formal principle and technical discipline, and become anti-visual in the deepest sense of the word.

The danger of neo-primitivism is internal and not as immediately obvious as the danger of Impressionism. It consists, above all, in a deliberate devaluation of reality, in an indifference to the task of achieving a balance between the abstract form and object, as witnessed in the work of lesser talents and voguish imitators. The creative problem is not resolved by the will of form per se, the new form must be derived from a new perception of nature, it is necessary to search for a shorthand for motif, rather than fill a readymade formula with a violated motif. The second danger lies in a rigid insistence on dogmatic prescriptions and stereotypes.

An adequate expression of the primitive will is the work of the younger generation of French artists. They seemingly tend toward perfect monumental and decorative works, in their desire to return the painting on the wall and to achieve a closer connection with architecture. Here the word "decorative" is not meant to be pejorative, as it is used so often today to describe empty works with no content, which do not position the expressive agents actively against each other, where the dramatic impact of its components is minimal, whose form is lifeless and whose overall character resembles ornamental wallpaper.

The proper form of neo-primitivist art reflects the effort to achieve utmost abstraction and dematerialization. The view of form is not optical, perceptional; it is governed by consciousness, composed, reflexive, notional. Neo-primitivism develops form in color planes, avoiding all perspectival shortenings, excessive movement, anything that could disturb the balance, calm and completeness of the painting. They try to achieve utmost motionlessness, a state of stasis and symmetry, making stasis the dominant compositional principle, the basic element, almost a geometrical center.

The neo-primitivists' effort is however nothing else than a preparatory developmental stage directed towards the ideal of all art, stylistic classicism. Their honesty, self-denial and respect towards laws of development are virtues showing integrity and thereby promising and guaranteeing a new future.

Translated by Alexandra Büchler

INTRODUCTION TO THE SECOND SKUPINA EXHIBITION CATALOGUE
Václav Vilém Štech   (Autumn, 1912)

This is the second exhibition comprising the work of members of the Visual Artists Group, on this occasion adding examples of the work of foreign artists working along the same lines.

This time we are inviting artists from abroad under different circumstances than before, since we are presenting them not as the apex and unattainable model, but because we consider them colleagues in a common endeavor and because we want to show the entire, and so far incoherent, range of the great intellectual movement, involving all the progressive forces of Europe, in as many of its aspects as possible.

We do not know as yet the direction and precise content of this movement, and it will be long before we do, but we can already observe its characteristics, and we can see the world fundamentally changing before our eyes, a world we have taken over from previous generations and to which we are gradually growing unaccustomed. In this rebirth, art is not a mere blossom growing apart from human struggles and in the good, fertile soil of existing culture, but becomes, in this very moment, a direct collaborator in the building of a new society. It carries out a cleansing, critical work, simultaneously creating new general values. It first demolishes the expiring old world; or rather, it demolishes the one last form of its eternal quintessence. It criticizes all the relationships we had considered explored and secure—what we see and feel, the relationship of man to nature, to colors and shapes through which it blossoms, examines the proportions of tones, feelings of bliss, combinations of rhythms, ideas of plasticity and flatness, perceptions of beauty and measures of greatness. Our eyes slowly become accustomed to seeing in a different way from the generation of Impressionists, we see more and more different things than were seen and enjoyed by those who immortalized their ideals of live and art before us. From the ruins of old nature and old beauty, art builds the first conditions for a new concept of life, new shapes filled with their activity, their need to talk and express themselves in a form elevated above the temporal existence of an ephemeral subject. Art is acquiring a new ideal quality, a new quality of being unreal, more emphatically and consciously independent of the direct appearance of phenomena, new means and forms to express action and movement, in matter governed by a new logic and different intellectual conditions.

A great historical interest prevailing throughout the nineteenth century, a great historical justice that was its world task have carried out surgery on our internal organs and opened the eyes of intellectual Europe, opened wide the doors to all the currents of the past that were still alive, all the majesty and wisdom hidden in the art of the exotic and natural nations of Asia and from the depths of Africa, the Japanese alongside the tiny nations of the Pacific islands, praying to unknown gods, are today joined in our work and desires, and their art, no lesser than ours, helped to release the formal possibilities of a new style. If art of the previous era did not work otherwise than with direct reference to nature, today's visual art has the courage to work through free form, free movement carried by form that has not been adopted from nature, but created freely and governed by logic and laws derived mainly from the inner organization of the work itself. Hence its unreality—the new ideal quality of today's artistic expression.

A whole new world is being created in front of our eyes that shall, of course, be connected with the old one through what is permanently valid, permanently human, what is added by man as a contribution of his spirit and as the unchangeable residue of his existence to the environment he finds and shapes and by which he is in turn being shaped and determined.

The aim of this exhibition is to give an insight into work in progress, as yet to be completed, to be an occasion for information about problems that are at this moment precious and necessary, and finally to contribute to the rapprochement between the artist and the audiences and in this way to help recreate an uninterrupted chain of cultural tradition, without which no art has ever flourished. For our work also needs nothing else but to be able to express fully and freely all that is part of the life and growth of our present.

Translated by Alexandra Büchler

THE INTELLECTUAL BASIS OF MODERN TIME   Bohumil Kubišta
Originally published as "O duchovém podkladu moderní doby," *Ceská kultura* 1 (1912–13)

All art forms have lately engaged with the question of the possibilities of style, and it would therefore be profitable to examine the intellectual basis on which a style should rest. Eras of unified style can be likened to a flower whose entire being works toward producing a single beautiful blossom; modern times, however, resemble a flower whose stems are like individual artistic personalities, surrounded by clusters of blossoms forming smaller groups connected to the main stem. It is a grape form, organically divided yet beautiful in its order as a whole. That is why artists such as Manet, Cézanne, van Gogh and Picasso, despite their different visual methods, have one basic characteristic in common, sharing a stem that is surrounded with individuals who in turn share the roots of their era, and this plant transforms the sap differently than the organism of a renaissance or gothic flower.

It is therefore not possible to reject Monet because his working method is different from Picassos; each has sprung from the intellectual soil of his time. It is true that developments in the visual arts have lately taken frequent turns, with new schools and directions appearing every five or ten years in resolute reaction against their predecessors. Today I can nevertheless say that stylistic developments are not the most essential aspects of new art: what we demand of new art, and what can bring us the ultimate satisfaction, is a transformation of its inner intellectual essence. An attempt to justify all the expressive possibilities of form is not futile; on the contrary, it is necessary and it has to come before a final creative process that goes on slowly inside every human being. Yet it is possible to ask the following question: What are the conditions that bring about fundamental changes in life and the creation of new forms in the outside world? Look at a plant: resting in winter, seemingly dead, it grows buds with the first rays of the sun, opens them up into leaves and blossoms, and works toward bearing fruit. Having completed the process, it falls again into a partial state of death, a state of necrosis. Observe a massive steam engine racing along a given course, its wheels turning, its chimneys belching clouds of smoke, as it rushes towards its final destination. Its substance is brought to life, just like the sub-stance of a tree; beside the process of external change, both go through a change of motive force, and anyone who is not content simply to register external changes, will have to admit that this force is the precondition of all manifestations of life. A physicist takes as axiomatic that energy is maintained through its changes: the transformation of mechanical energy into heat, light, electricity, magnetism, etc. that governs inani-mate matter. Animate beings are governed by a different kind of force, a force that could be called vital and that pervades in various degrees the entire living universe. Each individual is its embodiment and its carrier to a smaller or larger extent; in its free form, it penetrates those mysterious realms of nirvana, heaven and the under-world, outside time and space; it is a pure deity, hidden to the senses and invisible. As long as man sought to formulate his relationship with this force, he created an ideology, when he tried to imagine it, he created a personal deity, and by combining the two, he created religion.

Accordingly, shifting the center of gravity to creation as an accumulator of a bound part of transcendental vital force on the one hand, and shifting it to its free part, a deity, creates two main categories of religious thought: atheist and theist. On the one hand, the individual "I" becomes the center; on the other, the center is God with his creation. All intellectual and spiritual processes and the entire organization of society are in this case governed by man's relationship to this authority residing outside his personal world. Those in power derive their authority from being in direct contact with God and subsequently destined to rule those who are not so privileged. Kings were considered to be either sons of God, or at least his highest priests, having been appointed by the grace of God. The Jews were directly ruled by Jehovah, who made his will known to them by means of certain signs. All other lower authorities depended directly on higher power and indirectly on divinity. The will of God and his laws therefore pervades the entire society, whose members wish to come near him, celebrate him and seek his forgive-ness, if they had acted against his will, creating sacrifices and rites which have to be performed in specific sacred places—in temples, so beloved by deities. Ideologies tending towards God and societies organized according to his will offered art, as a fur-ther stage in the transformation of vital force, all possible variations of subject and form—architectural, visual, verbal and musical. What mystical enchantment gave birth to religious Hindu poetry! How thirstily did a tortured soul drink the sacred psalms of the ancient Hebrews! How we admire the classical beauty of Hellenic epos and theatre! See how the most essential dramatic theme develops from conflict between the law of man and the law of God, how Gods' vengeance and their curses pursue even the inno-cent and devastate entire royal dynasties, how the Furies haunt those who have violated divine laws and will be appeased only by a sacrifice. Religion offered creative spirits lyrical, epic, dramatic, and, above all, mystical themes: what wealth of variations on the theme of the birth of Christ was created by the Christian spirit; with what tenderness did primitive and classical masters imbue the movements and features of the mother of the holy child, what terror and dread are embodied in Michelangelo's group of the damned in his Last Judgment! A man expressing himself artistically in this way, acted, in another form, like the man who fought bloody wars for the religious symbols of the cross and the crescent, who tortured heretics or renounced the whole world and isolated himself from life in a monastery or in the wilderness. Thus we shall understand that the same force that has driven humanity to such acts of violence or to a life of asceticism, was transformed into Egyptian, Christian and Hindu temples, into Michelangelo's and Greco's Baroque or into an anonymous Gothic, and this happened in times when man believed in God and his image—the immortal soul.

When man, however, rebelled against God and elevated himself into God's place, drawing on the endless sources of that mysterious universal force, the breath of nature, called *atman* by the Hindus, the form of human society changed, as each individual became a center of active force, and, according to its quantity, acted on other individuals, subject to a law similar to the law of gravitation. People no longer listen to or worship the representatives of divine power, who have lost almost all their influence, but, still subject to the law of gravitation, they are no longer attracted to the rule of sword or of religion, but instead to the power of an industrialist, inventor or another authority of our time, who indirectly take possession of him, using him to their own ends. The energies of an individual subjected to this unknown, strange force are sapped, his power paralyzed and restricted by the one who possesses him, so that he feels as weak and devoid of free will as an ancient slave. This phenomenon has long been noticed in our time and brought about the efforts to restrain the excessive powers of individuals by building organizations that would unite the weak so they could challenge the force of a powerful individual. We have witnessed how various class interests have created a number of formations and institutions, not just for the purpose of defense but also for the purpose of creation, how the power of individuals is concentrated in such organizations and gives rise to marvelous works of technology, to be accumulated and in turn to draw weaker groups that gravitate to it. The law of gravitation governs all aspects of public life, all industrial, financial, and political organizations, as well as states, which no longer rely on the numerical power of their armies to act upon others, but on their ability to create economic and social values that outweigh other, weaker values.

Understanding this essence of modern life is important for art in the sense that new developments are only possible—as this has already happened in literature—on the basis of atheism, as strong as the basis of religion. The force of gravitation acts on individuals and is accompanied by strong feelings and spiritual excitement, different from mere fleeting moods, and it was the exploration of such states in literature that has given birth to works of crucial importance. Each individual has experienced the painful anguish of being manipulated by a force he could not resist and that made his being open to destruction, as well as the empowering sense of triumph and security that takes over his entire inner being when he succeeds in breaking the power of the enemy, who may not kill with a weapon, but who kills by means of his influence, unless his own suggestive power is broken.

An example of the exploration of such states of mind in literature can be found in the work of Dostoevsky. The ingenious epileptic—perhaps precisely because of to his illness—entered the secret workshop of the soul, creating new values and poetic forms from processes and feelings that are born in moments when a person becomes involved in a relationship with another human being, and his inner self is trembling with an unknown fear, pain, passion and pleasure evoked by his own active power or by the power of the other.

What an indelible impression it must have been that forever bound the hero of his *Idiot*, Count Myshkin, to Nastasia Philipovna, at the first sight of her portrait, when he felt as if a knife had been driven through his heart! That terrible wavering between the unhappy Nastasia and the proud, beautiful Aglaja, that mystical, terrifying relationship between the two men, the Count and Rogozhin—both are developed here and combined to an unprecedented effect. These are miracles of the modern soul as wondrous as the miracles of the Old and New Testament, and the books, which contain them, are our bible. Ibsen's *Builder Solness*, a work generally misunderstood, also explores the tragedy of bonds created by the force of gravitation working within the human being. The young Solness forces everyone around him to serve him, evoking in the girl Hilda an unforgettable sense of hope in life's possibilities, so that she returns to him after ten years for the promised kingdom. But the Solness she finds is no longer young and strong; instead, she faces a man full of creative power, but tormented by anxiety and fear that someone young and strong shall come and take his power away. A strange process is set off by this encounter: the center of gravity shifts and Hilda takes over the role until then played by Solness, forcing him to climb, against his will, the high tower of a new building from which he falls to his death. In our literature, a similarly symbolic theme was for the first time explored by F. X. Šalda in his *Ironic Life*, where the writer Varjan drains and ultimately breaks the heroine Melchiora to revive the source of his art, which he believes to be fading.

These examples suggest new possibilities for visual arts. Impressionism, in its lyrical essence, was unable to develop dramatic or mystical themes, as its view of reality—whether of a landscape or a man—was always the same and could not be turned into its opposite. As soon as the artist takes possession of this hidden force, manifested by life itself, he can differentiate it and develop conflicts, plot and tragic scenes from its positives and opposites. To give an explanation of the nature of impressionism, I would choose the image of a circle of light with the artist's self placed in the center. Wherever he turns, the diameter of the circle is the same. That is why it is impossible to create a modern novel or drama by means of an impressionistic method, which is suitable for realistic recordings of momentary, unorganized perceptions that can be retrospectively tied up into a monographic and purely external unity, as in Goncourt's novels.

The dramatic principle, however, resembles a hyperbole in which the center of the curve—the artist—keeps moving back and the ratios between the focal points and points around the perimeter change incessantly, with both parts of the fork facing each other in a continuous relationship of action and reaction. Mysticism, after all, resembles a parabola, with one focus receding ad infinitum; mysticism is a dramatic principle where one active component disappears into infinity and the unknown.

The move from theism to atheism had a negative effect on literature, painting, and sculpture, while architecture was just as negatively influenced by transitional impressionism. Temples, the sites of divine authority, disappeared, and so did palaces, the sites of its visible representatives on earth. Both were replaced by banks, offices, industrial buildings, and factories, that no longer have the function of elevating man to higher spheres but, on the contrary, tie him down to earthly and temporal tasks, such as the exchange of materials and power, the organization and division of labor, and the facilitation and intensification of human productivity. These buildings nevertheless still attract man, and their aesthetic solutions can also be deduced from the principle of gravitation. The fact that one office building differs from another is due to the promotional needs of businesses: each wants to be more attractive than his neighbor. The principle of gravitation, on the other hand, is responsible for a related, but different impact on form.

The task of the visual artist is to choose such formal elements that would best express new themes implicit in the gravitational and atheistic principle or, rather in a corresponding social situation, so that form born of this principle, will have nothing anachronistic in it, nothing that reeks of historical pastiche or empty decorative formulas, and shall fully reflect its time, having grown organically out of its new intellectual basis.

There is no need to lament the lack of unity of images and perceptions, so abundant in religious thought. Our time has replaced them with equally precious values, but it has the right to hide them from the eyes of the uninitiated and reveal them only to those strong enough to be able to draw the veil that covers them.

Translated by Alexandra Büchler

FRAGMENTS OF CORRESPONDENCE Josef Čapek to Jarmila Pospíšilová
(1913)

[Prague, 11.4.1913]
I am writing to you in haste, and you will have to forgive the untidy scribbles you are going to receive. I remembered that I would have too few pictures for the Spanish issue, and so I would like to ask you to select one, or even better, two more Picassos. I wouldn't want to determine the selection; but it would be good if those five or six pictures properly documented Picasso's development. Something like the head from 1909 (no. 112), inspired by Cézanne, or 1910 (no.44), also a head, would fit in well. Then something from 1911, or even more recent. It is important to make sure that you don't choose something that had already appeared in *Volné směry* or *Umělecký měsíčník*. They must be things that have not been reproduced in the Czech lands before. Another important thing is, unfortunately, that the TK two you are going to select should be quite accessible to an average viewer; that means, the less "cabalistic" things. It is sad, but I have to follow this counsel; the readers of *Volné směry* are by now so spoiled by bad art that the moment *Volné směry* features something wilder, they immediately cancel their subscription. They are happier when they can recognize what a painting represents. So, it should be something accessible. Do not hesitate to talk to Kahnweiler; you can learn some very interesting things from him that you will surely be pleased to know.
Be so kind and tell him that you have been asked by the magazine to select the photographs, and so he should reserve them for *Volné směry*, and we shall immediately order them. Tell him also that they are for an original article about young Spanish art by José Junoy, and that we shall order more photographs later, because our editorial office has also requested original articles from Apollinaire and Olivier Hourcad. Should Kahnweiler ask you about the attitude of *Volné směry* or *Mánes* towards the Cubists (Metzinger, Gleizes, Fauconnier and others), tell him that it is one of tolerance, but that they are seen as a stage in a development and that this tolerant view is not without reservations, and that the same goes for the Futurists: they are seen as lower stages in the development of painting. I would certainly be pleased if you told him that. Mr. Kahnweiler should also definitely know that in December of this year *Mánes* intends to organize a large exhibition of modern art, showing the development from Cézanne until recent times, and that we hope that Kahnweiler will make it possible for Picasso, Derain, and Braque to be represented, as befits their significance in the development of modern art.
You will have to forgive me for burdening you with all these messages and asking you to be some kind of an intermediary, but what is at stake, is as follows.
The Group is exhausted, morally and ideologically. *Artists' Monthly* can practically no longer come out (issue 4 has yet to be published), because there is no one to write for

it and no one to finance it. The Group has already come to the chairman of *Mánes* with an intimate proposal that Filla, Janák and company would re-join. This is what I have predicted, and it is quite possible that they will be admitted; in that case their first job will be to oust me from the editorial office and bring in Matějček and Filla. They are already preparing to join *Mánes*, and to do it with an appropriate amount of fuss. Filla is now in Paris, and today I have had positive reports that he has certainly not traveled there without a specific aim. The Group wants to damage and discredit the Cubist exhibition in *Mánes* because its success would be their moral and ideological defeat. This is why Filla has gone to see Kahnweiler and tried to make him believe that *Mánes* deliberately wants to promote Cubists (mainly Metzinger and Gleizes) against Picasso, Derain, and Braque, and that these Cubists have already been invited by *Mánes* to take part in the exhibition, while Picasso and others represented by Kahnweiler, will *not be invited*. This, of course, is a lie, since no one has been invited as yet. The result of Filla's pronouncements is this: Kahnweiler hates the Cubists for commercial reasons; they represent competition and spoil his trade. And so he will give the Group a whole series of Picassos, Braques and Derains for their spring exhibition. The Group will therefore have a show of the greatest representatives of modern art much earlier than the winter exhibition in *Mánes*, and *Mánes* won't. The effect will be as follows: the Group will stand before the public as the most modern and elite association, basking in the reflected glory of Picasso and others, making it appear as if *Mánes* cannot get past a couple of ordinary Cubists. Then they are going to join *Mánes*, and everyone will say that *Mánes* was joined by the best and most internationally minded of Czech artists, so that they can raise its standard. This is Filla's scheme and it is well thought through: the Group will shine one last time before joining the less lustrous *Mánes* to improve it. This will give it a better position in their defeat. Filla's action is, of course, a contemptible dirty trick; *Mánes* had agreed on its winter exhibition with Mercereau (who will organize it) long before the Group even thought of having their own exhibition; now, Filla wants to make it poorer and embarrass us by depriving it of its most important part, and this will be used to adorn the Group. Kahnweiler, as I know, promised the Group that he would send them as many Picassos as possible, when he heard Filla's slandering talk. It is a mean thing to do, try to damage others and get ahead of them, and it will harm not so much the older members of *Mánes*, but us, the younger generation.

If it is not too late, it might be possible to neutralize the results of Filla's damaging activity by letting Kahnweiler know that *Mánes*, let alone the editorial office of *Volné smĕry*, do not want to support the Cubists at the expense of Picasso and others. Kahnweiler is a very charming, talkative man, who knows a lot of new things and likes to have a conversation. Perhaps you can tell him, when an opportunity arises, that *Volné smĕry* will have three original articles from France, discussing Kahnweiler's artists, and he should also know that *Mánes* is counting on having Picasso, Braque, and Derain represented in the winter exhibition as best as possible.

He likes to hear the latest and likes to share his news, and you will probably enjoy learning about the Parisian scene and art world from him. Don't mention however that anybody here knows that Filla has already worked on him to our detriment!

Don't tell anyone at all that you know about the Group's intention to join *Mánes*; so far, it is a big secret!

Having written what is most important, I can see that I am doing nothing but bothering you with requests to do things you may not find very pleasant and in which you have no interest. I regret that I have to write such a sloppy letter and that the haste in which I am writing prevents me from talking about something else, more from the heart and for myself. I shall write again as soon as possible and I beg you to forgive me writing about problems that are of no real interest to you. Enjoy yourself, and remember that I am often in the places where I used to be with you and that I often think of you.

[Paris, 19.4.1913]

This is my first day on my own in Paris—Mother left this morning for Stuttgart and tomorrow she is setting out for Prague—and I have already visited Kahnweiler this afternoon. So far, I haven't seen any of the private collections; I haven't been anywhere, not even in the rue Laffitte, or anywhere else. I couldn't go out on my own, the walks I wrote to you about were the last and only ones, because Mother could not bear to be alone for a moment among the people here, not being able to communicate, and didn't want me to leave her. I am afraid that the trip to Paris may have harmed her, she was ill and off color for the entire time...

[J. Pospíšilová]

[Prague 21.4.1913]

I have to briefly thank you for your letter. I must be off to the printers in a few minutes, so I can be with you just briefly and I shall write more comprehensively as soon as I can. Thank you very much for selecting the photographs at Kahnweiler's and for kindly dealing with matters that were a burden to you. I am sorry to have charged you with such an unpleasant mission, but I really had no one else to turn to in Paris. You have availed yourself very well and I would like to ask you not to think about it any more; nothing more could be done. I would very much like to have the photograph of Picasso's latest still life you have written about; we shall order it together with the others. And what about Manolo Hugué? You mention nothing about getting him; I assume that Kahnweiler had photographs of his work and that we are going to obtain them. Be so kind and let me know if you have selected them. It is rather strange that you ran into none other than Filla at Kahnweiler's. What the Group is going to do will later cause a lot of trouble. I shall write about that (and about the competition between Kahnweiler the dealer and younger painters in Paris). I have been lately suffering from a cold and have been therefore irritable and unhappy in the world. I have been impatiently waiting for news from you and worried, since I had not heard from you for such a long time. Other than that, I have a lot of work and even more problems. Sometimes they become so heavy that I would like to throw them away into a corner and run as far away from them as possible. It becomes too much when you have to take on the responsibility for other's problems; things are always easier when you have only yourself to defend. Now I am looking forward to your next letter, where you will write about yourself; I wish for nothing else. I shall have my work photographed and send you the pictures; but later, in a week or ten days, now, I have very little money, because I had to get ready for spring. I have to stop here, because it's time to go to the printers. I wish nothing more than to be able to write you quietly and without a single thought about anything else. I shall write again as soon as possible; this is as if I cannot speak to you any more: always about other things...

I hope you are fine, and life in Paris is easier than how you describe it. If there is the slightest opportunity, I shall come to Paris, even if just for a few days.

Remember me soon again.

[Prague 24.4.1913]

I am glad that this time I could keep my word and I am indeed writing soon. All in all, today I have a pleasant feeling, outside, the weather is lovely, the windows open, and the cold that was still making me irritable and immobilized has completely passed. When I think of you now, I see Paris clearly in front of me, I can conjure up each place I used to know and I can very well bring you into the image. I can best see the sunlit boulevard Saint-Michel with the tall and already very green trees along the sidewalks, and I can smell that strange odor that I have always strongly associated with that peculiar, distinctive atmosphere of Paris, the smell of large buildings, shops, dusty

streets being sprinkled, basement kitchens, fast-baked potatoes, vegetable off-cuts, and above, various perfumes, fabrics, drinks, and smoke. When I felt nice in Paris and in myself, I quite enjoyed that smell, and it seemed to be a particularly pleasant, very true element into which we could immerse for a while with everything we were searching for. I can imagine even that tiny room of yours, but here the vision changes and it is less light and joyful than outside. I look forward to your moving soon, I think that sometimes that restricted space made you feel anxious, and, at any rate, sometimes it is very difficult for a lonely person to shut all the feelings into a small space like that; an open space never constricts in the same way. Now you are all alone in Paris and I often think about how you are going to manage there; so far I don't even quite know how you are doing there. But from your last letter I can feel what I can still remember: how many opportunities for enjoyment and pleasant passing of days Paris gives you and how next to all those opportunities there was a little bit of confusion in me and a little bit of sadness, a strange emotional mixture, a swinging enchantment, endlessly hesitating and wavering between happy oblivion and somewhat more nostalgic and sadder sobriety. You have been writing very little about how you use your time, what most pleases you and when you are most satisfied. There are many questions in me, and I would be delighted if you were merely to touch on something about you that I cannot see all that clearly in my memories of you. I would like you to find several strong interests that make the present easier and freer to live and give us the opportunity to look forward to each next day almost with impatience. In Paris, it is possible to create some métier, no matter how crazy, madly enjoy paintings or read books with delicious pleasure and absorption, let oneself be often disturbed and return to these interests again with insatiable passion. That, I believe, makes life bearable and possible in the best way. I would very much wish Paris to be a station as pleasant as possible for you, if for no other reason then because even I would find it sad to imagine that you have left me here for several months of joyless life in Paris. I am confident however that you will manage to make the best of your life there, and I look forward to your letters; isn't is sad that I have to think about you so much and I know about you so little? As far as I am concerned, I cannot tell you much new about myself; I do all the things I have to do, and they are not always what I'd like to do. I wanted to keep this letter until Saturday and add more pages to it, because I felt that until then something interesting might happen. Now that feeling has passed and you would get the letter too late; after all, I can write you again on Saturday, if anything out of the ordinary should happen. The Group has now aimed a couple of cannons at us and I expect more things to happen, but not by Saturday. The photographs from Kahnweiler have arrived and I envisage a beautiful issue. Four of my painting are in the exhibition, and there are always more people in front of them than in front of any other, enraged, provoked for no reason and terribly stubborn; I went in by chance today and I had to laugh at the comments and angry reactions, in the end, an elderly German lady took me by the sleeve (she had no idea that I was the painter and author of that monstrosity) and demanded that I explain the paintings to her. I told her that it is "etwas Grässlisches, was die Maler heutzutage treiben" and that I also see it as "wahnsinning blöd". The old lady was very pleased and I had to laugh too. Otherwise I behave very seriously and look forward to painting soon instead of writing, and hope that you will write soon.
A book on Cubism by Apollinaire came out recently, published by Figuière.

[Prague 8.5.1913]
I was pleased to hear from your last letter that you have found a suitable way of life and that you have managed to overcome the first hardships and troubles of life in a foreign land. It is much gloomier here and there is less to see; for many days we have had a cold rain, I stayed at home and from the window I could see a one puddle next

to another and dirty stream into which endlessly and tirelessly fell more and more water from the skies. Now the sun has come out a little bit and time passes more pleasantly. Lately, most of my time is taken up by small tasks that leave no tangible results, and it is really a kind of distracted, fragmented inactivity. I think of painting as the happiest salvation from this veiled idleness, but so far I cannot find enough courage to break the languid inertia and throw all of myself into work that requires all possible concentration. I have a vision of a larger painting I could make, of a man giving a signal with a bright flag, a vision deeply realistic and symbolic at the same time, so far, it is just an image, impossible to grasp, a pleasant idea without clear contours, in the midst of the dull existence and everything else I have to deal with.

And what else? You say that you rarely remember Prague; I also think of you less, of how you live in Paris, but the few memories are all the more intense and urgent. Often, among a thousand other things, ideas come into my mind that may not concern you at all. Now when they are not present, I cannot describe them, but always in those moments when this strange feeling overcomes me and I get lost in it, there is one single thought left, very sharp and categorical, that you should know *exactly this*. It is peculiar that now I don't know what ideas they were and why I now think that they have nothing to do with you; it cannot be like that. Right now, in the latest moment I feel that it will be something inseparable from you; why should I think of you otherwise?...

[Paris 12.5.1913]

[...] I used to imagine in Prague that I was going to lead the life of a very diligent, concentrated person; so far, I wander around a lot and I can't even feel remorse. I feel lighter here and happier and sometimes I think almost that I would learn to be cheerful if I lived here for a longer time [...]
[J. Pospíšilová]

[Prague 20.5.1913]

Whenever a letter arrives from you, I always want to write you immediately; each word is received with gratitude and so many things are ready and waiting to be written that they would make endless letters. Then, day after day, matters come that have to be dealt with as soon as possible, and in the end I feel dull and I put off responding until later (there is still something festive in me, when I want to write to you), until I feel more agile and thinking comes easier. In the end I worry about it and I turn to you, whenever I can. Your last letter made me very happy; it seems to me that you are now somehow more concentrated and closer to yourself, than you used to be in Prague. Sometimes I imagine, when I think about it, that you are coming back soon, that you are going to return somehow changed, I don't know how, but I think about it, how and in what I am going to recognize it, I guess, but I cannot grasp anything tangible and in the end I have to reconcile myself with that same old waiting and anxious anticipation that I like to give myself up to so often these days.

I was also very pleased to hear about the life you are leading in Paris; it was all the more wonderful because your description of it was very close to the way I imagined it. For that reason, I was touched by everything you have written about yourself in an intimate and vital way, it was such a gentle and safe feeling of joy, the kind we find so rarely because all the other ones are too abrupt, suggestive and ephemeral. I also finally have to let you know about my failed plans to go to Paris, about how I started arranging the trip and how my plans were thwarted. But how could you have any idea about how much I would love to come to Paris! I didn't want to write about it, because I had to wait and see how things were going to be resolved by a stroke of luck, but now it is almost too late to rely on it since it had not turned out in my favor. As you can see, while you can choose from the full baskets of Paris the nice things and the slightly worse, I am living my unrevealed disappointments. But what can be done? Still, I do have to explain how it went: the news that Filla is on his business trip trying to damage the autumn exhibition (of the youngest French artists) reached *Mánes*; as you know, I did not put a stop to these rumors and conjectures, because I had been well informed from Paris that it was indeed so. Those members of *Mánes* who have an interest in the success of the exhibition—there are those, of course, who are not interested in modern art for understandable reasons—began to fear Filla's activities in Paris and started to wonder whether somebody should travel there and put things right. I myself behaved so modestly and knowledgeably in the matter that I was selected and all that was needed was an official approval. This was a situation I had been very much trying to bring about: to have an official excuse to make a trip to Paris and in this way to paralyze in advance any possible conjecture and speculation regarding my journey. I'm afraid that I have been punished for my scheming. Kafka announced that he was going to Paris, offered himself to do various missions for all and sundry, saying that he was going to arrange and settle everything, etc., and so the matter is now with him, although no one has any confidence in his diplomatic abilities. This meant that my departure had to be postponed, and I could see that nothing much could be done about it. Kafka soon sent a long letter from Paris, in which he announced with a great deal of enthusiasm that he has arranged this and that, that the exhibition was completely guaranteed, that he has put *A Spanner In The Works* for Filla and so on; in short, it was a very enterprising letter. It put the minds of *Mánes* members at rest; there came other matters to be dealt with and in the end, everything somehow calmed down. And so I am back in the same situation I was in some time ago: I would love to see myself in Paris and I would be pleased if I could give the journey some external, official or executive purpose; in all this I thought of you very much, perhaps too much, because I indulged in dreams and speculations, wanting to make chance into a vehicle for my wishes—and now it has come to nothing, it is late and I can see that I have thought too much and acted too little, directly and according to my inner pressure. All that is left of this plan that had its deeper and more serious reasons is a slightly comical aftertaste. I don't even want to stop and spend time worrying about it. And what else—since man is like that, thinking and imagining an encounter, the first glance, all the circumstances and the very first words, that fertile excitement, when images are intensely present and the vision is almost physical, the Luxembourg Gardens, the street, all clear and almost true! Now I had better start thinking about something else: that you will come back soon, and I should invest the entire present into this anticipation. So far, my existence is not as I would wish it to be. I have to write a lot, make sure that *Volné směry* comes out regularly, edit friends' articles, not allow myself to be disturbed too often, and do a lot of work instead of others and for others. Yet, this work is not that bad, as long as there are results, and as long as it turns out to offer executive power and control. What I am not happy about is that it will easily grow to the extent that I shall no longer have time for my innermost needs. When the work of editor and typist is over, I would like to be able to grab a free day and paint; instead, a whole series of new necessities turns up; I have to devote entire long days to assisting at the difficult birth of my brother's poem, then some photographs borrowed for a single day have to be immediately reproduced, something gets stuck somewhere, visitors arrive, and in the end all these accidental needs accumulate, and day by day is lost and I cannot paint. And so my existence is incomplete and somehow out of balance. I very much like good performance and active life, but all this is really too much *à part* of what is most truthful. I have to think about all this. Or see it as something temporary and stick to what you have been guessing: I shall change my situation in the course of the year, and this is most probable. And so the man signaling with a flag remains nothing but an appealing bubble, almost a dream, and that is a mistake: the later I realize it, the less intense will be the

first impressions, the more faded and bland they will become, and that initial joyful fancy and excitement the image has brought me will be dulled and blunted in time. This is how it usually is; and I think it would make a nice picture. Until the time when I can paint again, the first feeling of bright, clairvoyant joy will pass. But isn't life longer and more eventful than I am making it appear now? I can turn all that around and differently when I am going to feel the need to live for what I want most. I would like to write more, but I have to rush so as not to miss my lecture.
Please, write to me the way you used to!

[Prague, 28.6.1913]

I am sending you Jules Romains, I don't know, perhaps you will find the book too coarse and the basic jokes, which form the contents of the last chapters, unoriginal, but I have enjoyed the coarseness; it did not repel me in the slightest and did not strike me as strange. Thank you for Lanson's anthology; I have a strong feeling that I have it at home.
I must also thank you for thinking of me when you were writing your last letter. That I could interpret your silence as being due to other circumstances than those that really caused it, and that I could have made all sorts of conclusions. I could see that you really know me well by now; that you know how often I had allowed idle conjecture trouble me, and that you now want to spare me that worry. This time however I did not make any guesses; I admit that I was concerned and anxious, the same way I had been in the past whenever I had not heard from you for a long time, but I did not want to make any conjectures, that might have entered my mind as a result of my anxiety. I am learning to subject myself to the greatest discipline in this respect.
For five days I suffered from a strong headache; the worst obstacle being that my eyes were good for nothing, everything collapsed and dissolved in front of me, and so, for the whole time I could not take the brush in my hand and paint, although I had the time and longed to work. When I finish this letter, I shall try to paint again; earlier, I started a study of a washbasin with a pitcher, a towel, and other things that belong to a washbasin, and I shall finish it. I have also started a smoker's head. But these are not the right things; I would like to try something bigger and of a different nature. But that later.

Translated by Alexadra Büchler

THE BEAUTY OF MODERN VISUAL FORM   Josef Čapek
Originally published as "Krása moderní výtvarné formy," *Přehled* 12 (1913/1914)

Modern art—the so-called Cubist movement—gives the initiated a rich aesthetic experience that must be incomprehensible to most people. And this is why its champions are at a disadvantage against its opponents, the critics and painters of the old school or of insufficient intelligence, and against the public. For it is impossible to convince a person lacking a deeper ability to enter a spiritually and formally new area about its beauty. I think of the ungrateful and futile task of modern art, which, through the mouths of its advocates, incessantly justifies and substantiates its existence by means of philosophical and metaphysical arguments. Reflections using such arguments may appeal to the opponents' intellect and may succeed in persuading them that modern art may, after all, have its depth, but it has usually been the form or external appearance of the paintings that has irritated most.

For all those who take part in today's art developments with their own work, the intellectual content of today's art is a concluded, all-comprising fact, not just an impetus for philosophical speculation. Accordingly, the practical aesthetics of modern art is simpler and more rudimentary, and concerns the formal nature of this innovative and most legitimate force of the new world. This is also how it is most likely to maintain its full exclusivity and originality against the surviving art of the previous era, rather than by means of philosophical speculation that is sometimes poorly constructed and out of ignorance inappropriately applies old philosophical systems to new goals.

Yet, to those who are incapable of immediate communication with the art of the present, practical aesthetics will offer even less assistance than those speculations that place various notions applicable to all art in general without a deeper commitment, above a new formal expression. It is difficult to offer explanations to someone who represents a dead link in an environment of such electrifying intensity as the modern era.

The Cubist technique, or rather the Cubist creative perspective by means of which physical space is constructed into a visual space, was explained in a simple, straightforward manner by Jean Metzinger in an article published in the last issue of *Volné směry*. Several comments that form the subject of this essay are concerned with individual form of modern art and its stylistic impact.

When visiting large galleries, a truly modern viewer will often catch himself considering certain styles with a dose of insincerity and admiring them as a matter of cultural interest. Such a viewer, lacking immediacy, forces himself to adopt a historical and aesthetic interest out of fear that he might leave the gallery without gaining what can be offered by well-ordered history of art. And yet it is true that paintings of certain eras can literally inflict torturous boredom, even on a receptive viewer knowledgeable about art. This does not mean that these paintings are bad, but that they are probably alien to us and have little to say in our time, and that our sensibilities cannot relate to their structure. It is in this way that the brown Dutch paintings can be boring in comparison with early mediaeval paintings, which make an altogether deeper, more immediate impression on us and strike us as beautiful. Since the subjects of Gothic paintings (religious figures) can no longer move us in our time, a certain source of visual effectiveness inherent in their structure probably corresponds to some inner conditions determining modern man and artist in relation to modern art. Fondness for this art suggests that the modern spirit gravitates towards a particular type of art, which would satisfy us in our own environment and on our own territory, since the Gothic has, after all, very little to do with our time. It represents, however, the most idiosyncratic style in European art, and as a very fundamental style, it is far removed from raw depictions of nature, lacking in spirituality, including the naturalistic approach. Elements of naturalism began appearing already in Renaissance art, and could never quite be transposed into a higher and purer visual type, not even in the case of strongly idealizing art. All art then put a great deal of effort into a visual transcription and accentuation of natural beauty, and much less into the development of its own stylistic—that is also abstract— aspect than Gothic art. All styles that followed up until our time brought substantial changes and stylistic enrichment, especially in the use of the brush and color to express physical space and in the free use of sensuality. At the same time, such enrichments, that in their complexity encompassed light, shadow, color, air and ambiance in a spatial environment, the lovely, shimmering harmony of the spatial medium, bore within them the seed of visual destruction that could be successfully managed only by painters with a strong artistic personality.

No other era had so much stylistic elementality and primordiality as the Gothic. The Gothic line, fractured by the desires of a pure and slightly sad spirit, and, above all, the clear, bright color planes placed next to each other without being weighed by air, light and natural space, make an impression on their own, *by virtue of their own being, their own order* and orphic composition which could contain the spirit in its most beautiful variations. The beauty of Gothic art is given by the fact that it is a style created by the spirit, and this is also its strongest and most admired aspect. If modern art strives for an autonomous visual expression, it is not at all as a result of some Gothic tradition, but as a result of its own necessity and invention that gives rise to a modern, unprecedented originality.

The explanation of the nature of modern art (architect Vlastislav Hoffman) was given by a certain dualism: a striving for material reality and fully ideal form. Ideal (not idealizing) form replaces things, notions and contents not by their naturalistic reproduction but by its own expression and order; the visual material to be artistically shaped is being consummated and reevaluated by a higher, independent, spiritual and stylistic principle. Modern art has long developed by diverging from traditional views, and so today modern art stands *consciously* on an entirely new foundation. The new perspective by means of which modern painters construct space in their paintings is the result of an essentially new view of space, communicating the notion that the old (merely optical) perspective is by comparison an insufficient, ineffective tool with little meaning for the modern mind. Changes in the conception of space went hand in hand with changes in visual technique that should convey its modern view clearly and emphatically. The artist is thus charged with the task of *expressing* himself and his personality, but has to do so *in a particular way*, whereby artistic expression should not be, above all, some kind of prolapse of the artist's emotions, a means for personal expression, done in any style. For apart from personal expression, modern art form demands something for itself: maximum expressivity and consistency, which means that the artist's task is formal, as well as expressive.—Expressionism (for example Matisse's) was, from today's point of view, merely an expression of the artist's inner self; he did have a beautiful capacity for synthesis by means of a fluent line that encompassed volume by a summary flick of the hand, and, above all, by means of color planes that easily contained the complexities of space. His main merit was that particularly rapid and total synthesis, and the clear medium of color, but he lacked the basic spatial view of today's art and the autonomous form by means of which spatial views could be constructed within a certain artificial order.

Autonomy or *artificiality* of the modern form is the primary quality we demand of the new endeavor, as the very nature of modern art is that it seeks originality, which it wants to grasp as the highest guiding creative principle. And that happens through consistency, experimentation and conscious "cultivation" of form; above the chaos of nature and raw dynamism of inner feelings the artist places something more absolute and intellectual: the artificiality of form. Here, things of the physical world are contained and controlled with powerful intensity that deprives them of their optical or photographic appearance and dresses them up in a monumental costume made of its ideal essence. These formal intentions are applied in modern art with such consistency and determination, that things in paintings take on a monstrous quality, as they do in Gothic art. It is not merely a matter of recognizing and presenting objects so deeply and penetratingly in an almost mystical way, the way many felt about Picasso who indeed penetrates the form of objects most deeply and as if scientifically. Latest developments point towards another prerequisite, to an intensified building of the pictorial space; this is manifested in Picasso's most recent development, as well as in the activities of other painters.

Picasso's paintings from 1911 are entirely different from his contemporary work. When they were described as having a rather impressionistic form, Picasso's worshipers considered it to be a stupid insult. Today, we can see his next developmental shift, in which he gradually abandons his earlier masterly opalescent quality of light, constructing his new paintings from large planes of unusually pure and brilliant color. Without wanting to touch on the question of quality, I can only say that today, his paintings are in a certain way closer to the best paintings by French cubists than they were then, although all young painters are indebted to him for their development. None of the other Cubists however matches his capacity for deep insight, which makes their paintings more superficial, and it is also something they had been rightly criticized for; they did however construct their pictures from large planes and clear colors, without a spatial, aerial or luminous medium, strengthening the developments in painting in a particular way which has been unjustly underestimated. In this sense, for example, Léger's *Woman in a Blue Dress* from the Autumn Salon of 1912 has a certain developmental value, and it would be unfair to forget that, despite the painting's shortcomings.

The form of contemporary painting has its prominent characteristics with which it gradually achieves a remarkable and unprecedented expressivity. The new perspective is constructed in a simple and clear way into spatial compositions, whose logical visual harmony is pleasing to the eye and to the mind. By means of its construction, which is somewhat architectural, the painting achieves a greater objectivity; beautiful color planes, unusually clear and sensitively rendered, appear without the help of light and shadow. Here, color finds its most objective application, at the same time becoming the medium of the most absolute and pure visual plasticity. These outstanding, luminous modern pictures are the opposite of the Dutch way of painting and in their perfect clarity they superficially resemble early mediaeval paintings, in which the space is also built on a particularly artificial principle. Like their medieval predecessors, modern paintings have their internal decorativeness, which is the opposite of superficial embellishment. The painter's intentions do not have to be restricted solely to still life; he can just as well take on the task of executing, with the same consistency and completeness, figurative paintings in which the object, built under the pressure of a different view and painting method than the illusory painting of the previous era, comes to resemble modern architecture, which also works with the basic functions of planes towards a perfect spatial effectiveness. More then ever before, the painter strives for a beautiful way of painting and for the greatest visual purity.

It is not therefore an exaggeration to say that the highest esthetic pleasure modern era can offer an intelligent and sensitive person can be found above all in Cubist painting and architecture.

Translated by Alexandra Büchler

THE SPIRIT OF CHANGE IN VISUAL ART Vlastislav Hofman
Originally published as "Duch přeměny v umění výtvarném," *Almanach na rok* (1914)

Growing organically and developmentally to become part of the modern environment means to encompass spontaneously certain expediencies. With Taine's doctrine of evolutionary determinism shaken, it is no longer customary to invest the environment with the necessary power to determine the direction and character of artistic creation. It is true that the environment itself is uncertain and vague like a haze from which, like sharp edges and rays of light, arise only certain idiosyncratic inspirations of the spirit, which are however not sufficient to create a *structure* in a spiritual environment. And it is precisely this indifference what makes the artistic milieu a useful stage for the development of a new expression. It has to be said that art contains a drive to organize this uncertain matter in the same way as a philosophical idea born at a *particular moment*, for which it is useful, gives its time a surprising yet self-evident order. Guided by a focused evolutionary instinct the artist actively enters this particular stage and introduces into it magnetic interference; his task is to organize an environment formally, while the environment alters him as far as contents and nature are concerned. It is true that all possibilities for a new expression are already stored in this new creative environment filled with energies which are to be used by the artist to establish a system of harmony and constructive unity, and that behind every artistic shift, every new form, hides the mechanism and sum of things which together constitute the present world. For a conscious individual, however, the greatest and most comprehensive thing *in the world* is his own *view*.

The connection with objects in an environment is the first obvious characteristic of modern art. A new environment is like a new region, inviting us to investigate and measure it; the sense of a new environment immediately brings about a lively need for a new taste, a hitherto hidden form and new, contemporary, purely modern beauty. The modern mind, inquisitive, sharp and penetrating never misses an opportunity to gain a change from a new situation. A new life is saturated with desire for mystery and with a will to penetrate it, something that in science happens with an almost military effort, while in art it happens by means of beauty and excitement.

The modern era is by nature anti-naturalist: it overcomes nature, takes possession of it and creates an artificial world governed by man's powerful abilities. Everything man has so far achieved by means of technique, ingeniousness and practice, certainty, rapidity, self-assuredness, knowledge, firmness and strength, is used by humanity to stand up to the perceived oppressive power of god and nature. In the same way in art, the raw character of naturalism is changed under the impact of a mind more effective and incomparably deeper than by way of mere copying and imitation of reality in previous times. Our era is governed by intellectual principle and purpose wholly missing in decadent times. Naturalism knows no other way of grasping objects than by copying them, in the same way as Australian savages believe that in order to capture animals, it is necessary to imitate them. On the other hand, principle is like mathematics, grasping the size and volume of objects by dividing them into differentials with a newly abstracted integrated volume. Modern art is aware of other tasks: it is not content to multiply nature even if the artistic temperament makes it prettier, just as photography is not enough to gain inner knowledge of an object, or just as the intellectual existence of a famous man cannot be multiplied by means of bronze and plaster casts of his popular bust.

The fundamental change that the art of our time is going through is conditioned by longing for the unknown, for new impressions, as if for an entire new world. This inner motivation gives new art a peculiarly emotive expression, and so we have the painting of emotion, architecture of emotion and emotive poetry, in which emotion is manifested not through a mood but by agitation from a state of calm. Modern art is a strong desire to conquer reality; based on principle, it detaches itself from the living raw basis of reality and channels all its efforts into an act of turning the massive dynamics of life into construction and into an abstract surface spiritualized by intellect. Its process is spiritualization and formation, transformation of the world into an ideal state, into a sum of autonomous forms. Here, the very word "form" acquires a different meaning: it no longer means decorative form, as this would bring the modern spirit little practical, clean and expert quality, nor is it a natural form, imitating natural things and based on observation of processes of the physical world. The modern form is *objective*: it does not consist in imitation of objects, nor is it their symbol—it *is* the object, it is treated as an autonomous entity, irrespective of whether it does or does not resemble a particular natural object. The special nature of modern art then lies in its emotiveness, its state of emotion, in its clear and sure awareness of being based on principals, a kind of conscious, rational logic of artistic creation, and finally in its daring, innovation and readiness to test new expression attractive for its very novelty. These are the three given, specific factors in the indeterminate equation of contemporary art; the indeterminate and variable value is the deep originality of initial ideas, the mysterious effect of modern environment, the fundamentally instinctive and emotive disposition of the poetic, almost meditative character. It is clear that modern art is a sum of human intellectual powers of unprecedented complexity, and that the inner process, by means of which it comes into being, is very different form the easy process of naturalistic work.

Modern art is based on striving for form of absolute and fundamental certainty; its tools are media such as color, space and sound. Cubism, for example, has its "astral" space without atmosphere, devoid of the magic and stickiness of naturalist juices; it is not a space governed by elemental spontaneity and passionate natural forces, but an autonomous, pure principle that establishes a certain *l'art pour l'art* attitude in the best sense of the word, in which Bach's music is *l'art pour l'art* as opposed to Wagner's.

The turn from naturalism that is so characteristic of modern art is best imagined in the following way: starting with the Renaissance, European visual art tried to create an imitation of a beautiful external appearance of things. This tendency lasted until the 19th century, and its modifications and styles were caused by changes in European "moral temperature," rather than by fundamental revolutionary transformations. The modern min however has absorbed too much scientific knowledge not to know that what happens under the surface of things, within their structure and power, is more mysterious and also more beautiful than their external layer. The most perfect *illusion of an object* would no longer offer the contemporary spirit a full and lasting satisfaction. At this point, the task of art becomes to liberate itself from nature and to become its master. Impressionism at least managed to free itself from the materiality of nature, imbuing it with the rapidity and subtlety of psychological action, but this did not interfere with the nature of art in a deeper sense and there was still a resolute step to be made: replacing nature with *artificiality*, with autonomous human order and full authority of artificial form, so that form, a creation of the mind, replaces natural objects. Modern art clothes objects in monumental garb, making it possible to substitute this monumental principle independently and autonomously for reality; art takes form by processes different from mere transposition of reality.

What I would call an artistic *substitution* of object is an abstract surface and form, devoid of naturalism, emotive and artificial. The neoimpressionist color dot already was such autonomous thing, a small space contained in a touch of paint, subjecting natural appearance to a certain principle. In today's art, the changes taking place are far more fundamental, effecting the very core of visual understanding. Interest in form has become clarified and rid of coarse impurities. What art aims to achieve by numerous means and experiments is *ideality of form*. Yet the realization of this ideality is not easy to achieve: the artist does not find it in the world in a ready-made state; on the contrary, he has to prepare it. Modern art is *acted*, not dreamt; it has to pursue its idea by way of logic and intuition, by means of strange play with things of the world, by clever and clear use of world view to the benefit of formal vision, in order to create a new beauty and new artificiality. When this beauty is born, it does not have a general recognition; in the eyes of aestheticians and antiquarians who rehash art created a long time ago, without their contribution, and pass it from hand to hand, it appears raw and crude. Yet the fact that autonomy of form is already here, realized in the new art, cannot be weakened simply because it is inconvenient to eyes accustomed to eclectic and naturalist art.

To create conditions that would allow a powerful and fertile rise of the new beauty, we must have faith in our present—we must consider the modern era to be the most beautiful of all. If we want to create modern beauty, we have to, above all, discard sentimental admiration for things of the past, in the same way as a soldier senses new beauty in a gunshot from an automatic weapon, the beauty of perfect functionality, a feeling very different from the old, dull beauty experienced by the magical hunter-marksman. The modern viewer should experience the same naïve and uncomplicated feeling when confronted with art.

Modern art then aims for ideality of form devoid of illusion. Early medieval art also lacked the suspect illusive magic of later styles; its expressive language was all the more mysterious for being pure and original.

Yet, new art does not turn away from reality, nor does it escape to an ideal of beauty existing outside our world. On the contrary, a full, living sense of our time teaches us to try to force our way into the very core of reality, down to the skeleton carrying it. Our sense of reality is sharpened to the extent that everything that is mere illusion leaves a deep soul with a sense of tortuous dissatisfaction and improbability. The modern mind is not earthbound; it keeps close to reality that continually challenges man to conquer it by action. And this true reality, no longer appearing ugly or ordinary to our senses, is the permanent subject of man's creative work. We no longer need to beautify it, to veil it with symbols and metaphors, to paint it with dazzling colors and clothe it in a cloak of godliness. Art no longer belongs to another world—it happens in the same reality as the work of a scientist, chemist, physicist or engineer.

Art of the past created an ideal world rather than an ideal form. It contained beautiful "idealized" objects, rendered by means of naturalistic imitation. The dignity of art was replaced with a certain illusion of godliness, a noble aristocratic beauty that was meant to be better than mere reality. Here, rational and civilian revolution brought liberation and cleansing, and put an end to much of the exquisiteness of the past. Only when it's gone can new reality be ushered in, introducing new ideas and a deeper inquisitiveness and vision than before. Now we demand of poets more than elegant, philosophical rides on the back of Pegasus, of musicians more than beautiful melodies, of painters more than academic mastery, as all this is nothing but a theater stage displaying a charmingly posing illusion of beauty. The modern era discovers in itself something far more elemental and basic and does not demand satisfaction and intoxication, but our own construction. The interest of modern art aims for things, aims to possess them. The new expressive language conveys the mystery and truth of reality in the new touch of the spirit, making such a strong impact on us that we become almost frightened of reality. Modern painting examines things with an almost analytical precision, circles them, is surprised by them; art has never before proceeded with such precision as it does now.

This is how we find in new art a kind of dualism: a striving for fully objective reality and a striving for full ideality of form. The new law of modern art is that it must achieve such an ideality of form so as to become a complete and synthetic substitute for objects. Our art, being thus stored between two equally strong, new, and necessary demands, is a problem that does not admit an unlimited number of solutions. In it is a source of inexhaustible wealth that we can see in the future of new art.

Contemporary art realizes the demands stated here fully and outstandingly. What is the modern artist's form of expression? He speaks by means of lines that are the most complete shorthand for the long journey along which nature was transformed through the prism of the soul; he speaks by means of surfaces that delimit natural surface, a unique surface, made of the same molecules so as to sound loud and specific; he speaks by means of forms constituting the last borderline between impossibility and probability; here, color planes perhaps resembling colorful ribbons, strange stripes and blocks, are the artistic outcome that fundamentally rejuvenates the decorative impact of a painting, creating an effect that cannot be achieved by means of color photography; this process of abstraction from natural appearance is taken so far that the formal components acquire a geometrical or machine-like character. How, then, can one create ideal form and simultaneously feel the reality of things? By divesting things of the magic of their changeable surface and denuding them; by recovering their formal construction from within, by simplifying and developing them, summarizing and multiplying them in one single vision. There are many more means and systems than can be mentioned here. Numerous conquests and pressures ultimately through the barriers maintained by eclectic traditionalists and create watersheds. And just as this movement with its intensity disturbed many notions and aesthetic systems that had once been considered complete and absolute, so has the mechanical homogeneity of linear narrative been broken down by free verse, newly organized in search of its legitimate bonds, so has space in Cubist paintings been broken down into painterly substitutes, and melody into a disparate and automatic tone system. Yet, this process of breaking down is not the same as rational analysis; it is the spreading of wings to take the most daring flight for which an entire century has been preparing.

Translated by Alexandra Büchler

EXCERPT FROM *CUBISM*   Vincenc Kramář
Originally published in *Kubismus* (Brno: 1921)

Picasso's art can teach us two lessons. First of all, it shows us in the purest, most original and perfect form the essential formal problems of modern painting and their solutions, at the same time presenting the type of modern artist who can serve in many ways as an example. The values involved are therefore artistic and moral.
The quintessence of this new art, I repeat, is that it springs from the innermost spiritual and intellectual depths. It is art that draws on the artist's imagination in which all his experiences are concentrated. The process by means of which it comes into existence is real creation, not mere imitation of something seen. Objects, the way Picasso renders them, cannot be seen in nature, if nothing else than because they are not a product of optical perception, but of various experiences, of the entire man. Apart from that, these paintings combine into a single whole several views of an object, and it is the intended composition of the painting, ensuing from the emotional involvement, that dictates the selection, composition and various emphasized properties of objects that live their own life here. The dimensional aspect things as we know it from our everyday experience has been abolished here, and things present themselves to us as something far more complicated and mysterious than we knew them to be until now. Above all, they appear

to us as products of spatial relationships, and alongside this central axis are their material and other properties. Like every primary art, Picasso's work is entirely objective, stating that lines, colors, and light in his paintings are not the end in themselves but that they mean something, and if they form as part of a strict image construction something new from material given by experience, that they are an expression of a new world-view that is just being born. This objectivity is intrinsic to the very composition of the painting, which is no longer a merely pleasant or in any way purposeful arrangement, but a structure, through which the object finds it full embodiment. And there is one more quality this art possesses that we need to mention, which is close to objectivity, but in another sense, namely, the striving for objectivity. Understanding the world as a construction made purely of shapes, this art desires to suppress all the influences of the subject and external factors that might color or distort it. Things are to appear to us in their pure flawless beauty and above all in their permanent essence. The "reality" of this art is not that accidental and changeable reality of naturalism and its branches, but a comprehensive, permanent reality, given by the laws of the functions of our intellect. It is certain that this art—its creation or its perception—is not cozy lounging in an armchair, as Matisse once described his own decorative—the in perfect sense—paintings. Not that it would have been impossible to create similar enjoyable works in his circle. I have already mentioned Picasso's simple, economical works, products of happy creative moments, but we must not forget that to be able to enjoy these pleasant things to the full, it is necessary to have experienced the development from which they have blossomed like flowers. That is not to say that they cannot be enjoyed without any mediation. They can, but this enjoyment would embrace little more than the beauty and sensitivity of the painting matter, which is by no means sufficient to understand Picasso's art, and new art in general, fully and correctly. Such art, invested with the artist's feelings, intelligence, with his entire being, in turn addresses the entire being of the person perceiving it—not a mere "viewer"—requiring direct collaboration. For those who seek in art nothing more than a pleasant tickling of the senses, Cubism will always be a hard nut to crack, or an outright nonsense. However, real artists have never created for this class of people. Those who want to find inner enrichment and growth in art will find such wealth in the new art, that all the effort invested in penetrating its essence will turn into pleasure. The main condition is, however, to live a life of one's era, as instinct is not enough to create or perceive art, but in both cases is indispensable.

[...]

In short, only backward people, or those who live in delusion, fail to arrive at the truth that external naturalism, moods, and pure subjectivism are outdated. Only they can believe that it is still possible to cover the canvas in paint without thinking and that by doing so they are contributing to the development of contemporary art. No, art that belongs to the present and the future is much more complex and generous and demands honest work from the entire person. Its *inner spiritual and intellectual quality* is a higher developmental form, from which there is no return, containing everything that claims the label of a living, progressive art.

[...]

Now we must realize that only the baffled viewer, whose creative intelligence and feeling are not sufficient to deal with Picasso's paintings and who is uninformed about their essence, sees in them triangles, squares, cubes and cylinders, etc. in the same way as in the case of Impressionism, when the same kind of conservative viewer saw nothing more than a canvas with material color spots. Our author correctly explains how man in his tendency towards objectification—a painting must definitely represent something!—in his puzzlement grasps in the inaccessible painting the shapes he knows from his own experience, in this case the geometrical shapes. In reality, those capable of understanding Picasso's and Braque's paintings, do not see those regular shapes, but in their mind, they see the real thing, and that with an intensity impossible to achieve with illusionist painting. Those geometric shapes, those numerous color planes and segments, of course form the skeleton of the painting, but apart from them—and especially more recently—there are entirely individual characteristics, whether lines or planes giving a peculiar shape of depicted things, color, various properties of matter, and finally there are also realistic fragments, faithfully imitating their model or directly inserted into the painting. In the mind of a perceptive viewer, all these elements combine into an image of an object. However, is it an object we are used to seeing in nature? Surely not. That was provided by illusionist painting. Yet, what we have here is a far more complex and intellectual image. And this is also why it makes no impact on most viewers, who come before Picasso's paintings with assumptions based on old art, demanding from them what they cannot offer. These viewers would forgive Picasso and Braque all their triangles and cubes, if the seen color planes and lines combined into the usual, familiar image of the world—but for that there would have been no need for Picasso's long-term hard work, and it would have been enough to stay with the principles of illusionist painting. These new paintings however do not rest only on optical perceptions, but also on others that are conveyed to us by means of our muscles and sense of touch, and, above all, that are the fruit of intensive brainwork and amazing intuition. And the cooperation of the whole being is required of the viewer, who has to work very hard in front of a painting by Picasso or Braque. This work has to do with learning about a new world, and just as these images came into being in Picasso's inner world, the depicted object is being created in the viewer's inner world or mind. It is impossible to approach Picasso's paintings by simply looking at them, as the required effect is not on the canvas, but is created in the viewer's mind by its synergy. The true nature of Picasso's and Braque's work is intellectual.

[...]

It has been said that Picasso is obsessed with things. This must not be understood in the sense that it takes material things to be true reality. That would mean a return to the view of the Egyptians, but such simple returns are not possible in the development of thought and art. Development which always represents complications, multiplication and re-evaluation, can seem at certain stages a mere return or reconnection with ancient intellectual values only to a superficial viewer. In reality so-called reactions are based on previous stages which they counteract, fundamentally reassessing the values from which they follow. The crossbreeding of contrasts is one of the main laws governing development of thought and art in the world. Picasso's art is therefore not thinkable without the preceding illusionism. It may fundamentally stand against it, but it does not return to the Middle Ages or even further back; rather, it adopts the most essential element of illusionism and passes it on for further development substantially re-evaluated. Such essential component of painting in the last five centuries is spatiality, whereas Picasso fundamentally changes the perception of space and its rendering. Instead of an endless space that swallows all things, he constructs a limited but measurable space dependent on things, thus preserving the spatiality of illusionist painting and at the same time preserving things, and in this sense, it is necessary to understand whether we speak of Picasso's return to things as reality. It is to some extent a return to things, but not to those material ones of the pre-illusionist era, we can say rather that it is construction of things as something spatial, something that is practically an outcome of spatial relations.

Translated by Alexandra Büchler

The history, stylistic changes, and written manifestations of the pioneering Hungarian art groups are inseparable from the intellectual milieu that gave birth to them. Their influences include the revival in Hungarian poetry brought about by Endre Ady, as well as the periodical *XX.század* (Twentieth Century), the Free School of Humanistic Sciences, the Hungarian Freemasons, the radical Galileo Circle, and later the Sunday Circle. One of the most important sources of Hungarian modernism was the intellectual community of the 1910s, represented by the philosophers Lajos Fülep, Leó Popper, György Lukács, and others, and by such art critics as György Bölöni, Iván Hevesy, and Géza Feleky. Views were exchanged at the meetings of the Sunday Circle, the Galileo Circle, but most of all at the Budapest coffeehouses. The work of Parisian painters arrived here through several filters, so that the first truly radical group of artists, formed in 1909 under the name of "A Keresők" (the Seekers), showed very little concrete, identifiable Parisian influence. But for an energetic, truly effective group to emerge, in addition to painters of outstanding talent, it must also possess an active leading personality. Károly Kernstok, a somewhat older painter with a bourgeois radical orientation, would fill this role. Kernstok named the movement

"investigative art," a term he used as the motto for the group's first exhibition in 1909.

In 1911 the group adopted the name "A Nyolcak" (the Eight) for its eight members: Róbert Berény, Dezső Czigány, Béla Czóbel, Károly Kernstok, Ödön Márffy, Dezső Orbán, Bertalan Pór, and Lajos Tihanyi. This period marked the height of their activity. By this time they had broken away from the tradition of the school of Matisse without being truly swayed by the Cubism of Picasso or Braque. Their vigorous style, aiming for effects of monumentality, received the praise of radical art critics.

Early on, The Eight addressed the issues of "the new composition," and advanced the views of Cézanne. Subsequently the problem of the new composition became, in activist art, the problem of the "new poster." In this conception, the poster was destined to take over the role of the fresco, by providing a dynamic and easily accessible visual form for revolutionary ideas, fulfilling the severe set of requirements embodied by the new composition.

Translated by John Bátki

FORMS AND THE SOUL, EXCERPT FROM THE ESSAY *RICHARD BEER-HOFFMAN* György Lukács

Originally published as "A lélek és a formák," in *A pillanat és a formák: Richard Beer-Hoffmann* (1910)

All writing, even that born out of the assonance of beautiful words, leads toward great portals, great portals through which there is no passage. All writing leads toward great moments, moments that yield a view into the depths of dark whirlpools, dizzying whirlpools into which we shall have to fall one day, the secret content of entire lives being a yearning for that fall; whirlpools that our consciousness—for as long as possible—tries to keep away from us, but which are nonetheless there in front of our feet in the form of vertigo produced when sudden panoramas open up as we stand on the mountaintop, or when the evening mist swallows the redolent rose bushes surrounding us. All writing is built around questions and progresses so that it can stop unexpectedly, at once, and yet with compelling force, at the edge of the chasm. And all of its passages—be it past lush palm groves or across a field of ardently glowing white lilies—all of its passages will lead us there, to the edge of the great chasm, and it can never stop before reaching that chasm. And this is the most profound significance of forms: to lead the reader to the great moment of a vast silence, and to make life's fleeting multicolored variety seem as if it rushed past merely for the sake of such moments. And the difference between various writings is simply due to the variety of mountain scenery that leads us to the chasm, the diversity of amazements that give birth to our questions. And forms are necessary only because in any one landscape only one road leads to the mountain peaks. One question, surrounded by all of existence; one silence surrounded on all sides by the roar, the noise, the music of the cosmos: this is form.

And yet—perhaps only in our day—what is human and what is form, these questions constitute the central problem of all art. Granted that art was made possible—if one is allowed to probe the causes of that which has existed for millennia and has perhaps become alienated from its origins by the ravages of millennia—the art of writing can only have meaning because it is able to render these moments. Only because of these moments does art possess a value in our lives, the same as the forests, the mountains, people, our own souls; yet in a more complex and profound way that is nearer and also more remote than these, colder in its objectivity vis-à-vis our life, while all the more snugly fitting into its eternal melody. Art is a value only for these reasons, only because it is human, and only to the extent that it is human. And what about form? There was a time when, if one had asked this question, he would have been answered, "Is there anything else?" There was a time—at least we believe so—when that which we call form, and seek with feverish purposefulness, and in a cold ecstasy pluck as the one and only permanence among the ever-changing phenomena, there was a time when it was simply the natural language of manifestation, the unobstructed ease of screams bursting forth, the unfettered energy of writhing movements. A time when no one asked what form was, and no one separated it from material life, and no one was aware that it was anything apart from matter and life; a time when it was nothing else than two souls of a kind—the poet and his audience—understanding each other in the simplest and most immediate way. But in our day form, too, has become problematic.

Theoretically the whole conflict is incomprehensible. If we think about form, intending to give meaning to the word designating it, its definition can only be this: the simplest and most direct way of producing the most powerful, most lasting expression. And—we feel that these analogies are of some help—we think of the golden rule of mechanics, or of the law of economics stating that everything strives to reach the greatest results with the least expenditure of energy. Yet we cannot help but be aware that the conflict still persists. We know that there are artists for whom form is the immediate reality, while somehow life seems to have slipped out of their works; artists who provide the end result while we remain unsated, for the end receives its beauty in the course of arriving at it, through the keen anticipation along the arduous passage on the long and winding road (from another viewpoint I could put it this way: they provide only the road and not the arrival at the end, and yet...) And there are artists whose souls, overflowing with abundance, feel shackled by any formal constraint, and for lack of a chalice to gather their wine, the golden fluid of their rich vintage evaporates into nothingness, so that they must renounce perfection with melancholy, bowed head, as their half-finished works drop from their weary hands. As the great Hebbel, master of form, had once written about himself: "Meine Stücke haben zu viel Eingeweide, die der Andern zu viel Haut." ("My plays have too many innards, others' plays, too much hide.")

Abundance and form—perhaps the question may be posed in another way: what may be and what ought to be relinquished for the sake of form? And does there have to be a relinquishing? Why? Perhaps because forms have not sprung forth from our life, which, because of its great artlessness and because of its total anarchy has become so weak and so uncertain that it is unable to mold even to approximate its needs those forms that change with time and which indeed must change so that a living art can come into being. Thus today it is only abstract form that exists, resulting from the enthusiastic study and appropriation of the secrets of the great works of the past, an abstraction that cannot present the peculiarities, beauties and richness specific to our contemporary life. Or else there is a total lack of form, and the work's effect depends upon the strength of the communally shared experience, and becomes incomprehensible as soon as the community disappears. Maybe this is the reason, but one thing is certain, that the conflict exists, and it is also certain that during the great periods of art this was not so; the most personal lyric could reveal itself in Greek tragedies, and the lushest abundance and wealth of color was unable to disrupt the great compositions of the Quattrocento— and even less the works of earlier centuries.

Thus we have today writings that affect us through their forms, and others that affects us in spite of their forms, and for many the question remains: Is it still possible to find harmony in our time? In other words: is there, can there be, a contemporary style? Is it possible to grasp some essence from formal abstraction that is not overflowing with today's live way? Is it possible to make something lasting for all time out of the fleeting colors, scents, butterfly wing dust of our moment, something that may be—even unbeknownst to ourselves—possibly its innermost essence?

Translated by John Bátki

INVESTIGATIVE ART Károly Kernstok
Lecture delivered to the Galileo Circle (January 9, 1910); also published as "A kutató művészet," *Nyugat* vol. 1 (1910)

I have a feeling that it is easier to make paintings than to write or chat about them. Our current little exhibition, I am aware, has created a far greater stir than we had envisioned, given its modest framework. The progressive segment of our audience—a public that is as condemned by the conservatives as we painters are—has sensed if not the end then at least the beginnings of a long and winding road on which we are advancing, having departed from the traditions in order to seek and to find those great new values which will be essentially very much akin to the best art of all ages.

Confronted by our paintings and by us, they especially like to throw "nature" at our heads. Yes, nature certainly exists. But the arguments they use to throw nature at our heads simply do not exist. "Nature is not like this," they say, "nature is something else; there are no people like this in nature; nature is natural"—this is the main thrust of their argument.

These gentlemen have very short memories. It was less than a generation ago when natural nature still had no perspective, when no one seemed to perceive that distant mountains were blue, when shadows were still seen as black, when the drawing of nature was more simple-minded than poor photography, when natural nature was all browns, and trees were not green, when it was not permissible to paint nature in all the grandeur of its appearance—at a time when the traditions were defended by other gentlemen.

For nature is oh so patient that it not only puts up with being grazed down but also does not mind being monopolized by various schools of painting.

And the fact is that it was the various schools that had taught us to see nature. They had taught us to see nature as broad and flat, in spots, as sharp and cross-hatched and pointy; we were taught to see patched figures, two-dimensional trees, serpentine twisting blouses and a multitude of "other" phenomena.

Courbet, when he was the first to bring us an airy, seemingly alive nature by having completed *Demoiselles au bord de la Seine*, could hardly have had in mind the school that would arise from this marvelously beautiful picture—the Naturalists—who would soon enough lay down their infallible rules! The rules were laid down—but where was the spirit of Courbet!

They sat down in front of nature and copied it narrow-mindedly, without any insight, without true contemplation. Setting out without any objectives, leaving matters to chance—they started at the upper left corner of the canvas and proceeded to fill it in until they reached the lower right corner, and the picture was done and so was nature. A natural nature. Likewise Manet, when he painted his *Olympia*, did not have the future Impressionists in mind. But he did indeed paint nature, the nature that he saw, as only he could see it for his own purposes.

And lo, the Impressionists arrived, and named Manet, one of the most structural of painters, against his will the father of the school that produced the greatest number of charlatans.

Ah, those facile spots of color, those accidents of drawing, those human figures made of spots and dots, those flat cows, those compositions with the birches on the right and the storks on the left—which occasionally switched sides, whenever the painter wanted to thrill his audiences with his marvelous inventiveness.

Or take Cézanne, who developed a loathing for all the superficialities and frills of life and of painting, and went into hiding from the world, in order to seek its forms and colors, to seek the materiality of the human figure, the landscape, the still life. He pointed out different values; for him the line was no mere empty decorative end in itself, a fine colorful or brown fancy; for him colors were simply a means. Have his followers mastered this profound absorption of Cézanne's? Yes, some may been thus inspired. But schools, as always, are only capable of passing on the externals, the formalism, the cheap and easily attainable effects. Courbet gives rise to coloristic extravagances, Manet to specialists of flat surfaces, Monet to mist, birches, and storks; from Giotto they adopt a period mood instead of his positive values of painting, drawing, and vision. The Greeks, who created the liveliest and most full-bodied art, were turned into the driest, most vapid academic art; and what has Cézanne wrought? A multitude of painted lemons.

Art, or let us say painting, always originates in nature. Primitive man, as we know, at first perceived the life that existed around him. When children make a drawing of a man, they see the head, the eyes, the nose, the mouth, the ears, and they see the limbs with which the man walks and acts. That is all they see and that is all they are able to render. But when a child does this, he is drawing nature, he draws the nature that his level of comprehension is able to understand.

As his faculty of understanding develops, especially if he is predisposed in this direction, he will greatly advance in his comprehension, but just as it was not nature that he had perceived with the undeveloped intellect of a child, even so what he later makes of it will not be nature either.

For the means employed by the painter are radically different from those employed by nature. We do not have at our disposal living cells, water vapor, rays of sunlight. What we have is a brush, a flat surface, some pigments and a few other such wretched devices. In vain do we sit in front of nature to replicate it like a Camera Obscura, when we do not contain a light-sensitive plate inside our heads; in vain do we long to paint it as colorful as we perceive it, when we have no sunlight of our own.

But there is something we posses as human beings that is of equal significance, and that is our intellect.

This is the instrument that we must rely on when we confront nature; this is that certain something the artist must take with him when he stands in front of nature in order to create and seeks the assistance of nature. It is not a matter of seeking science in painting, nor the play of emotions, but indeed the involvement of the *intellect* in painting, human brainwork. We should not look for the artist's intellect in the type of ideology his art serves but in the kind of artistic, painterly treasure he is able to extract from the eternal, inexhaustible mines of nature.

Time and again, the diverse manifestations of art history drive home the point that intellects and cultures create our manifold visions of nature. The various arts of different cultures, having unfailingly started out from nature, arrive at widely divergent surface forms that present us with essentially the same end results.

How different is the drawing of the Japanese, their vision of nature from that of Greek vases. Consider the differences between the nature seen by Giotto and that seen by Michelangelo.

The Greek Aphrodites are perfect examples of the ancient Greek ideal of feminine beauty. Yet how different they are in outward appearance from the statue of Lake at the Musée Guimet in Paris. And I will confess that compared to the Greek proportions that we find so beautiful—the Greek head, shoulders, breasts, hips, pelvis, arms, and legs—the pointed head of this Hindu Venus, her large round mouth, narrow shoulders, large, full breasts, extremely slender waist and large pelvis produce an alien effect. And yet Buddhist culture is a vast and ancient tradition, and within that culture this depiction of Lakme, the Buddhist Venus—although it would astonish an ancient Greek—is certainly the grandest vision of the object of love and the most splendid representation of the most perfect forms of feminine beauty. All of these works used nature as their starting point, and only the roads taken, the cultures they came from, are different in each case.

I consider the current upheavals in art as signs of a vast process of purification. A process of purification that, like a fever ridding the body of infection, means to eliminate all those trappings that still play such an important role in painting. Nature herself is not painted or created fashionably. There are no colors in nature, and I personally hold it to be a flaw if a painter attempts to reach with color. It is a mistake for an artist to decide he must look for tonality because nature has no tonality as such; I consider it a flaw if an artist produces graphics because there are no graphics in nature. There are subjects in nature and these are defined by drawing, and they may be spherical. This is indicated by their drawing and tones. But neither drawing nor tonality are independent, self-sufficient entities, but are in fact properties of objects, properties that are expedient means we can use to depict the object itself.

If one sees only colors in nature and applies these colors on canvas, no matter how pleasing their juxtaposition, he has glimpsed only a small portion of nature. If one perceives tonality and places these tones one over the other, he has only accomplished a bit of sentimentalism. If one renders the human figure only by means of lines, where has the body vanished between the lines? Yes, the body, for nature also has a body that is round and not flat, it is not only colors, not only tones, not only lines: it is matter that exists both self-contained and in the surrounding environment as well. It is this nature that we must call to our aid, this is the nature that we must interpret; we must go out and encounter it and search for the phenomena that will familiarize us with their images until we get to know them—at which point we must work in the simplest manner, making use of line, color, and tone. When it is no longer possible for one to paint along the crooked paths of an awkward formalism, when we have attained the ability to paint in a straightforward, intelligent manner, then our work will indeed have something to say that makes painterly sense. We must try to decide what those simple ways and means are that allow us to attain a comprehension of nature.

We must disconnect ourselves from all the knowledge we have acquired, put aside all the "isms" and lose sight of the images derived from them. After all the creators of outstanding art of all periods had always ignored the rules.

Let us go directly to nature herself and take a good look at a head, for instance. We see among other things that it is spherical, that it has eyes, ears, a nose, mouth, forehead, chin, etc. and that it, along with the neck, grows out of a body.

Well, this head is spherical, but we intend to transfer it onto a flat surface, and between that flat surface and the round head is where the entire history of painting occurs, and all the anguish of the painter.

If you want to paint it like it is in nature, you will never succeed, because of the above-mentioned material limitations. And if you are content to paint it according to the impression superimposed upon you, then you are irresponsibly throwing away help available to bring you closer to the solution.

I prefer to observe that head, set down the impression it creates, and then proceed to depict its volume, the cheekbones, the forehead, and the chin to the extent that these features can be of assistance in rendering the image. And if the jaw helps me more than the nose to grasp that head, then I will emphasize the jaw at the expense of the nose, or vice versa.

In another case it is the eyes and the orbits that prove to be the most characteristic features, and accordingly I will emphasize them—in other words, I always stress what I think is the most salient. Without any hesitation I use whatever means lead to the most harmonious realization of my aim: if a body in motion has such momentum that an arm, a leg, or the trunk appear to be elongated, I seize on that detail to achieve the desired equilibrium, and the same holds true for emphasizing one or another muscle; if I need to, I will emphasize a line in order to convey the body, its materiality; it may be that a lighter or darker tone might serve my purpose best, or intensifying the natural values of colors, or else making them paler.

It is an interesting phenomenon that within this process of purification that is ridding art of formalism there is another ongoing process of selection. The first one is an investigative art, which is in the service of evolution in art, and results in masterpieces. The other is an opportunistic art that, in the service of an ideology or social class, functions as a useful tool of class agitation, of awakening the consciousness and keeping it awake. This kind of art like a vassal accompanies its master for better or worse. If the master is triumphant, this art becomes fashionable; if not, it vanishes along with the vanquished.

It is amusing to trace the roles taken by this kind of second-rate daubing in the history of our art. Back in the days of the political revolt against "accursed Austria" it was fashionable to paint Gypsies and peasants wearing the *"gatya"* [loose white linen trousers]. During the feudal reaction that followed there was a flurry of paintings depicting great festive assemblies and processions in traditional ceremonial garb accompanied by sighs of delight. And now a painting showing a tubercular worker is supposedly the art of the proletariat. As for this last case, which interests me the most, I vehemently object to its truth. No, this servile art is not the art of the intellect, not the art of the proletariat; the latter is actually what I have referred to as investigative art. This investigative art, which is ever in search of artistic value, will not be going under with the downfall of any one class. There will always be people more intelligent than the average, and they will always feel closer to an art that is not a mere replica of nature, and does not serve any ideology or class warfare.

The artist cannot be the mirror of nature; but to the extent he is able to bring out new values in nature, his art mirrors his intellect. As for the social stir created by his work— it is an indication of the intellectual level of the times.

Translated by John Bátki

THE WAYS HAVE PARTED*   György Lukács
Originally published as "Az utak elváltak," *Nyugat* vol. 1 (1910)

These few remarks will not apply exclusively to the pictures exhibited at the Könyves Kálmán. My feeling is that the debate that has erupted about them is so heated and bitter, so full of petty violence and malicious joy, because these pictures express for the first time, clearly and unmistakably, the parting of the ways. And it is about this parting and its causes and significance that I should like to make a few remarks.

For anyone who just looks at pictures and knows how to look at pictures will not really understand that there can be any debate and exasperation here at all. These pictures do not represent any trend (not even an artistic one); these pictures do not wish for anything and do not go anywhere; in these pictures there is no new 'attitude' that might come into conflict with old 'attitudes.' These pictures bring quiet, peace, calm and harmony— it is totally beyond comprehension that they are able to shock anyone.

And yet these pictures mean battle. But it is a conflict completely different from the innumerable 'artistic movements' and 'secessions' of the nineteenth century. There it was always a new 'attitude' that opposed an old 'attitude', a new 'perception' opposing

---

* A debate following Károly Kernstok's lecture published in the last issue of *Nyugat* gave me the opportunity of making these few remarks. Published here is the substance of what I said to the Galileo Circle on the 16th of this month. [Author's original footnote]

an old one. Folk discovered that the old 'attitude' was not after all exhaustive, and a new one had to be found—or in most cases they simply grew tired of viewing things in that light. And then there arrived a new way of looking at things, a new 'direction', and the two directions struggled with each other until a third came on the scene, the newest one, which continued the comedy *ad infinitum* against the combined force of the first and second directions.

Here we are dealing with something else. Here we arc concerned not with differences, but with oppositions; here those who have come into opposition with each other have not done so because of trends, but simply because of their existence. Here it is not a question of the achievement of a new art, but of the resurrection of the old art, of art, and of the life-and-death struggle provoked by its resurrection against the new, the modern art.

Károly Kernstok stated what it is all about. About the fact that the pictures which he and his friends paint (and the verses created by a few poets and the philosophical ideas created by a few thinkers) are trying to express the essential nature of things.

The essential nature of things! These simple words, simple enough to avoid polemics, indicate the material of the great debate, indicate the point at which the ways part. For the whole conception of the world with which we grew up, the art from which we received our first great impressions, did not know things and denied that anything could have an essential nature. It derided anyone who dared to think or talk about such matters and declared them out-of-date, mediaeval and bumptious without any cause. The period in which we grew up—and the whole of the nineteenth century—did not believe in the permanence of anything. A hundred years ago they wrote that the landscape was but a mood, but everything in this world became a mood. There was nothing solid in it and nothing permanent; there was nothing in it that could possibly have been imagined or allowed to bring liberation from the slavery of the moment. Everything turned into mood; everything existed only for a moment, as long as I disposed of certain experiences in a certain direction or saw them in a certain light. And the next moment altered everything. And there was nothing that could have created order in the boundless swirling torrent of moments. There was nothing which might have been common to things and thus tide them over the moment; there was nothing that might have been permanent in a thing and thus raise it above the moment. For things did not exist, but only an endless succession of moods, and between moods there is not, nor can there ever be, any difference in value.

And this sovereign ego, that forms everything in accordance with its own moods, was itself dissolved in this dissolution of everything. The ego flooded into the world and—with the aid of its moods—fused it into itself. But for this very reason the world also flooded into the ego and there was nothing that could have established demarcation lines between them. And there was nothing that could have created order within the ego, whose extent was merely surmised in its indistinctness. With the end of the solidity of things the solidity of the ego also ceased to exist; with the loss of facts, values were also lost. There remained nothing else but mood. Simply mood of equal rank arid significance within and between individuals. Everything became a matter of concept; everything was simply a view, simply an individual opinion. And the only thing that gave significance to each individual opinion was the fact that it was individual, and there could be no difference between the importance of views. All unanimity of meaning ceased to exist, because everything was merely subjective; all that could be verified ceased to exist, because everything was merely subjective; there ceased to exist the fact that statements have any meaning and that they exclude the possibility of an opposing statement. In this world everything was compatible with everything, and there was nothing that could have excluded anything at all.

The only possible art of this mood of life was the art of sensations. The art of communication of experience, the art of the merely subjective, the merely momentary. But the more subjective something is and the more it clings to the moment, the more problematical is its ability to be communicated. Really it is only the common that can be communicated, and this art wanted at any price to communicate one moment in the personality of the artist, something incommunicable. And by this means every influence became fortuitous. It was the play of fortuitously pleasant twisting lines and harmoniously toned colors, the play of pleasantly but fortuitously harmonizing words, independent of any meaning. And in the case' of every influence it might happen that the harmony of a certain mood intended by the creator to be somber became the cause of amusement in the fortuitous mood of the one who received it. Or vice-versa, or anything else in the immeasurable vastness of nuances which can be varied infinitely.

Thus everything became the art of surfaces, surfaces behind which there is nothing, which do not mean anything and do not express anything, but simply exist somehow fortuitously, and somehow, fortuitously, have some effect—no matter how, provided they may have an effect. The art of surfaces could only be the art of sensations, the art of the denial of profound study, of evaluation, of making distinctions. New categories came along, paradoxical categories, values which simply by being realized had necessarily to destroy themselves—the new and interesting as values, as the only values. For if there only exist moods and sensations, only their freshness and their power distinguishes them from each other. And everything new and everything interesting, in the very moment that it exists, is already less new and less interesting. And with every moment, every analogy and repetition it becomes less new and less interesting, until finally it loses all the character of a sensation; it ceases to have an effect, it is dead, and no longer in existence.

This art has no material, for that is tangible, of a particular kind and demands space for itself. In this art there are no forms, because form is unequivocal and excludes other forms and what has not been formed; because form is the principle of evaluation, differentiation and creation of order.

And everything was so compatible with everything else in this world that it did not even notice the coming to birth of its deadly enemy and destroyer. Or rather it noticed it, but was incapable of feeling inimical to anything; it felt this too to be a new sensation and one that was compatible with all the old ones. I am thinking now of a few achievements in the natural sciences and those concerned with mankind (Marxism, for example). For it was these that first produced a denial of the subjective, impressionist conception of life: unequivocal and verifiable statements and order in things. Statements from which something followed, because either they were true or they were not true, either they were valid or they were invalid, And every single admission of the truth was accompanied by the rejection of a thousand other things as a necessary consequence. And they produced statements which had a bearing on things. Things of which it is possible to speak because there is something permanent in them, something which is independent of my own moods and sensations; things regarding which it is a matter of complete unconcern how I see them at such and such a moment or under such and such an influence. Things exist, and in them the important and the unimportant, the permanent and the changing, surface and essence.

But the men of Impressionism acquiesced in these truths too. Their all-comprehending minds accepted these too as truths—and in their feelings and experience everything remained as it had been.

But today these recognitions have finally become emotional values. Today once again we long for order among things. We long to recognize them and recognize in ourselves that which is really ours. We long for permanences, for our deeds to be measurable, our statements unequivocal and verifiable. And then that there should be a meaning to all our things, that consequences should follow from them, to exclude something. We long for evaluations, for differentiations, for profound thought.

And the very belief that there is something palpably permanent in the whirlpool of moments, the conviction that things exist and have an essential nature excludes Impressionism and all its manifestations. For then there are goals to which it is worthwhile, indeed necessary, to press forward, and the direction taken by the roads is no longer a matter of indifference. Then we can no longer say, as did one of the most fastidious-minded impressionist critics, 'The artist may do anything he likes provided he knows how to do what he likes.' For then the objective too can be criticized, and art which has set off on the road to a wrong goal is to be rejected all the more strongly, the more clever the virtuosity it employs to reach its goal which is not worth reaching. And the way towards it can be criticized because there is the wherewithal to measure the achievements and the unsuccessful attempts, the correct and the incorrect.

This new feeling has already made itself known from numerous directions, and in many places it has found expression already in poems and buildings, pictures and tragedies, statues and philosophies. But the new art, coming from many directions, and the new *Weltanschauung* have scarcely made themselves realized yet. As yet few people realize them in themselves and even fewer in others, in their own art and like arts. Perhaps the greatest significance of Károly Kernstok and his friends is that they are the ones who up to now have given the clearest, most forceful and most artistic expression to this mode of feeling and seeing things.

This art is the old art, the art of order and values, the art of the constructed. Impressionism turned everything into a decorative surface—even architecture too—and its colors, lines and words were given value only by their attractiveness and their sensation-producing effect, because they do not carry anything and do not express anything concrete. The new art is architectonic in the old and true sense. Its colors, words and lines are merely expressions of the essence, order and harmony of things, their emphasis and their equilibrium. The harmony of forces and stresses can only attain expression in the equilibrium of every thing and materials and forms. And every line and every mark, as in architecture, is only beautiful and of value in so far as it expresses this: the equilibrium of the stresses and forces that constitute any thing in the simplest, clearest, most concentrated and most substantial way. Here too everything is on the surface. Our senses can only condition themselves to surfaces, and colors and words, tones and lines can be the only means of expression at all times. But the means of expression are now indeed only means of expression and not ends, not termini. Impressionism always came to a stop at the discovery of possibilities of expression; the appearance of its trends, the discovery of a new means of expression and its disappearance always set hard into a style. Impressionism always merely provided attitudes with whose aid it would have been possible to reach some goal. But it did not wish to reach any goal. It felt the attitudes to be goals, since they too could be the carriers of sensations and moods. It regarded its ideas as termini if they were sufficiently new and sufficiently interesting. It regarded them as termini, not routes; sensations and stimuli, not tasks and duties. The new art is the art of the creation of the whole, that of going the whole way, of profundity.

The ways have parted. In vain do they point to the geniuses of Impressionism. The really great Impressionists are truly great only to the extent that they are not Impressionists, to the extent that profundity is artistic and their ideas merely routes for them to approach the real comprehension of things and their attitudes only means towards the creation of the whole. And just as he who regards his ideas and vision not as task and weapon but as goal and amusement is not worthy of them, so the Impressionists have not been worthy of the great artists who have been prominent among them. They have not deserved them and they have not understood them. And the road the geniuses have taken from the idea to the whole the Impressionists have traveled in reverse on seeing their works. And they have debased to an attitude the very thing with which they presented them, and debased to a style that art with which it expressed it, and from their thoughts they could extract nothing but sensations.

The ways have parted. In vain does the refined lack of conviction of clever Impressionists 'comprehend' many of the artistic moments of this art. This comprehension too is only an idea, only the extraction of sensations from anything whatever, and there follows from it no transformation. They see the cudgel about to fall on their heads and with delicate sense enjoy the powerful gesture of the hand that brings it down. But this comprehending astuteness is of no avail, because this gesture is now more than a gesture, because this cudgel will indeed crash down on their heads. For the art which brings quiet means for them a declaration of war and a life-and-death struggle. This art of order must destroy all the anarchy of sensation and mood. The mere appearance and existence of this art is a declaration of war. It is a declaration of war on all Impressionism, all sensation and mood, all disorder and denial of values, every *Weltanschauung* and art which writes 'I' as its first and last word.

Translated by George Cushing

THE ROLE OF THE ARTIST IN SOCIETY Károly Kernstok
Originally published as "A művész társadalmi szerepe," *Huszadik század* vol. 1 (1912)

The function of the artist, that is the man who creates aesthetic value—whether his production is needed or unnecessary—is one of the questions that crop up, especially at the end of the season when, having viewed vast numbers of paintings and sculptures, we leave the exhibition halls with a sensation of satiation and go out into the open where we can relish the direct, unmediated pleasures of the land, the light and the open spaces.

Why all those paintings, and so many artists, what will happen to the works, how can the artist make a living?

What is the actual position occupied in the various classes of society by someone who creates aesthetic value?

All those who have already experienced the effects of aesthetic power are able to repeatedly recognize the need for this effect and long for its recurrence; and although in their thinking they may not have admitted the necessity of artistic production, when confronting some phenomenon or effect of nature they nonetheless connect the artist's work with it, interposing it between the phenomenon and themselves, and see it as possessing the ability to perpetuate and to mediate, thereby affording them the occasion for re-experiencing certain emotions.

This mediation between natural phenomena and human life had been known and practiced ever since the earliest and most primitive ages of man. The gazelle daubed on stone by the Bushman (Ethnographic Museum, Paris), or the Dordogne caveman's torso carved in ivory (Museum of Anthropology, Paris), and the reliefs carved into reindeer antlers all indicate the need of man in the most primitive periods to permanently fix the images received from nature and the phenomena affecting him. The possibility of constantly being able to view something ephemeral, be it a hunting exploit, the relief of a deer coveted as a quarry, or the outlines of a woman, could bring about excitement, desire as well as its fulfillment. The viewing of such images evoked a hundredfold re-experiencing of some past event and set into motion the same emotive or intellectual process that takes place in today's human who discovers the wealth and variety of expression in such a captured and perpetuated phenomenon, be it a form conceived in a novel manner, a color harmony, a movement, or a rhythm. And, for primitive man, viewing the image of a deer carved onto an antler might have endowed an otherwise uneventful hunt with a mythic grandeur, or seeing the drawn outlines of his woman might have perpetuated past delights and germinated new desires. And this desire was no longer merely expressive of such momentary needs as hunger for meat or the instinctive animal drive to copulate, but it contained the joy of the possibility of reliving an experience that has processed pleasures and desires and perpetuated them in a lasting form—the joy of being able to create. This image given permanent form was already a force that created aesthetic value even for primitive man, and the one capable of accomplishing it and conveying it to his fellow human beings was an artist fulfilling the same social function as today's artist, who fulfills a far greater variety of far more complex needs—or at least ought to.

Societies have long recognized the artist's role as special. For instance, one of the explorers in Tibet was attacked by robbers who discovered among his belongings photographs of wild yaks and horses. When they saw these pictures, and saw him making drawings of them, the robbers' manner changed and became friendly; they did not take anything and offered the traveler milk and food as a sign of their friendly intentions. Another example from personal experience: in 1896 I was perambulating some rough neighborhoods in Paris in the company of the writer G. P., who is a man of enormous strength and stature. He wore an outfit "en Apache", complete with cap and belt. We stumbled into a smoky underground den where a girl was singing in a sickly voice to an audience that sentimentally hung on her every word. The local ruffians resented the arrival of G.P., sensing a powerful rival in him, and started to act up in a decidedly unfriendly manner. In such dire straits I pulled out a sheet of paper and started to draw the most menacing of the toughs, who instantly became tamed, assumed a pose, and the others stood around me to watch; when they recognized his image, there was much laughter, after which they had drinks with us and we were accepted.

But let us examine the role of the makers of art throughout history.

In ancient Egypt the artist was a slave. Slaves built the temple at Thebes; slaves designed the pyramids; slave artisans carved the Sphinx, as well as the myriad of art objects— all of those artfully wrought utilitarian objects that are present in great numbers in all the museums of the world. Slaves painted images of the pharaoh and of the deities such as Ptah, Osiris, and Isis. These artists occupied the lowest social positions, whereas they accomplished the highest social functions. Egypt was a theocracy where the pharaohs ruled through the medium of the priests, and although the priests enjoyed the most exalted social positions, they were nonetheless parasites living off the slave artist. It was a symbiosis of sorts, with the artist as a producer and the priest as the consumer. The artist, by means of his imagination, forms, colors, in a word his creations, conjured up the most annihilating effects of terror and servility within the viewers, by depicting the personages of the ruling classes and their imaginary objects larger than life-size, on a superhuman scale, in deathly stillness, and showing Osiris and the judges of the nether world sternly confronting the always down-hearted, lethargic deceased, who was the accused, looking accursed. The last judgement was a splendidly disciplined affair, but it needed the artist to convey this, and make it palpable for everyone. By means of this aesthetic power generated by artists the priests were able to make the population accept the ethical dogmas beaten into them, were able to retain the unthinking veneration of the populace and thus ensure their continued rule.

What is more, the aesthetic values created by artists endowed a permanent cultural existence to social formations even after the cessation of those institutions. Buddhism, Hellenism, Christianity. Statues of the Buddha, Tanagra sculptures, and images of the Virgin Mary have enormous socializing powers. Could it be that the demise of Talmudic Judaism and the decline of iconoclastic Islam were caused by their rejection of this enormously associative visual aesthetic power?

It would be time-consuming but not too difficult, to demonstrate that the relationship between the power providing aesthetic energy and ethical dogma has remained the same in the course of time nearly down to our days. The relationship between artist and priest has remained the same; the former has always been relegated to the lowest rungs of the social ladder while the other at the topmost level enjoyed contact with the gods. The transformations that brought some change in this relationship were also historical phenomena, occurring at times when the power of religion weakened in its compulsive effect. But as soon as in the course of time one speculative ethical teaching became replaced by another, the same old process was repeated. Only in most recent times has a great transformation begun to take effect. Ethical dogmas are beginning to gradually, very gradually it is true, to lose their powers of compulsion. The mighty force, the great magician, bringing about this effect is, as we know, experimental natural science. At present there are in existence not only individual people but entire groups, social institutions even, that have been liberated from the overwhelming effects of dogmatic ethics, but the metaphysical needs of such individuals as well as of the collective psyches of such institutions must still be satisfied. And just as throughout the millennia, consciously or unconsciously, art has been able to satisfy these needs, it continues to do so in our days and will continue in the future. Experimental natural science, researching through experimental means the ultimate phenomena of origination and death, will eventually render these two questions unfit for fantasies of other worlds. That is when art will occupy a splendid position in society, and the artist will no longer be forced to do his work as a slave of a hierarchy, but will enjoy total independence and absolute sovereignty. Probably this new sphere of action will result in new tasks, and an enriched vocabulary of expression. The newest artistic revolutions and experiments offer a foretaste of this. Although I would not be able to determine what it will lead to, nonetheless each and every successful, or even unsuccessful artistic experiment constitutes another step, another fact in the process of emergence. These developments that are revolutionary at the time of their first appearance are naturally most likely to evoke the greatest antipathy among the official guardians of the established ethical dogma and phenomena associated with it.

It is a noteworthy fact that, in a manner similar to that of the priest in the theocratic states in history, in our days the statesmen who direct the life of society also pay attention to artistic questions, for the time being without any intentions of patronage, without any critical or objective knowledge, with a view toward the aesthetic direction of the production of art, in lieu of its social exploitation. It is also true that the aesthetic direction is not suitable for serving the ideologies of the statesmen who rule in our days. The utilization of the vast social powers residing in art will be a sign of wisdom in a statesman as long as any social institution will continue to be directed by a central organ. This central organ in our case is just beginning to recognize that vast social potential, most probably as a result of learning from the successes formerly achieved by the church. Ethical dogmas combined with a class-oriented nationalism steer the artistic energies toward the treatment of certain ethnic phenomena, so that, by the depictions of houses with thatched roofs and peasants clad in the *gatya* [loose white linen trousers] it can arouse a solidarity in those who still see the borders of association within narrow limits and do not have the slightest inkling of the great solidarity of all of humankind.

So in order to subjugate these masses and to restrict the expansion of their ways of thinking the ruling powers endeavor to compel all aesthetic forces to produce this type of national(ist) art. And for them everything is nationalist, be it Baroque or Gothic, as long as it speaks its habitual formal language and refrains from proclaiming novel social or ethical ideas. For otherwise, as soon as we step back and see them from a long-range perspective, these national arts lose their individual characters, so that from the sculptural figures of Miletus to Cézanne we can recognize a single great European or Aryan art that is divided into various periods. The minor anthropological differences between a skull by the River Tisza and one from the Bay of Biscay are not enough to create borderlines in artistic production, for the reason that the respective artistic traditions, experience and intellectual atmosphere are identical. And those who would exploit these aesthetic forces for their own purposes are incapable of creating anything else, and thus will not succeed in forcing artists to perpetuate their own enslavement by playing the role of psychic jailkeepers.

As for the multitudes of paintings and of artists in the past, they had the same role as the pollen of the pine tree: producing a vast amount of surplus, in order to fertilize, with the help of chance, in as many places as possible.

In time production will become more economical, for instead of being left to chance, it will be planned, with the erection of aesthetic temples and public buildings that will satisfy all needs, and the changed role of the artist in society will also change the artist's position in society. In the earliest times he was an amateur, then became slave, then member of a guild; at times he was a grand seigneur (Raphael, Rubens, etc.), and more recently the bohemian outcast excluded from the social order.

But in the future when the artist will use his creative power directly to fulfill the needs of uncorrupted souls, he will no longer be the mercenary of the priesthood or of any other class, but will in fact become the high priest of aesthetics that will replace the ethical dogmas. The artist will occupy the highest rung of the social ladder where, even if he will not be conversing with the gods, he will provide direction for the mass psyche. His work will be that ray of light that will penetrate the vast dark jungle of society, to convey light and shade, depth and splendor.

Translated by John Bátki

Echoes of Symbolist aesthetics and ideology had been present in Romanian art and literature since the end of nineteenth century. Around 1910 Symbolism became a recognized trend in Romanian culture. The Symbolist artists turned away from the prevailing rural inspiration and the contemplation of nature; they looked instead to the town, with its tumultuous life, its tragedies, and sadness. These writers and artists heralded a new sensibility, the thrill of the novelty, the awareness of taking part in a modern movement. A climate of restlessness and revolt is detectable in the literary journals. In *Revista celorlalţi* (The Journal of the Others), Ion Minulescu (1881–1944)—a well-known Symbolist poet and supporter of the avant-garde—wrote an editorial, "Light the Torches," (1908) where he proclaimed his disgust for old and used formulas and for the past. Four years later, three teenagers—Ion Vinea (1895–1964), the future Dadaist Tristan Tzara (1896–1963) and the future avant-garde painter and architect Marcel Janco (1895–1984)—edited the journal *Simbolul*, marking Tzara's first appearance as a poet. Other journals, such as *Insula* (The Island), 1912; *Fronda* (Opposition), 1912; and *Chemarea* (The Call), 1915, could be considered post-symbolist, and a presentiment of Dadaist turmoil could be detected.

In 1909 the Romanian painter Iosif Iser (1881–1958) organized an exhibition to which he invited the French artists Galanis, Forain, and André Derain. The exhibition provided an opportunity for sympathetic critics to polemicize against prevailing bourgeois tastes, and to offer contempt and irony as antidotes. Romanian sculptor Constantin Brâncuşi, who had lived in Paris since 1904, was invited as well, although he was unable to participate. But Brâncuşi continued to send his innovative works to Bucharest, to be shown at the Official Exhibition and at Tinerimea Artistică (Artistic Youth). Although, for many, Brâncuşi's art represented a provocation, a small group of artists, critics, and collectors perceived him as "a formidable exception." The famous poet and journalist Tudor Arghezi wrote about the "beautiful ugliness" of Brâncuşi's sculptures and Alexander Bogdan-Piteşti—a controversial figure, but the most important art collector of the time—bought some works. Already, in 1910, N. D. Cocea had noted significantly that Brancusi's works had the "effect to trouble the common ideas on beauty, a trivial and boring beauty, as conceived by our art loving bourgeoisie."

Originally published as "Aprindeți torțele," *Revista celorlalți* no. 1 (March 20, 1908)

What will be the end of the struggle begun long ago—10 years ago?

We see it; they hide it.

In spite of all this, it's good that everyone who is interested in the development of
Romanian literature knows the few young writers with the courage to break away
from the crowd.

They are neither the alchemists in search of the philosopher's stone, nor the modern
inventors. They are nothing if not the expression of the law of evolution. They do not
seek new things for new things do not exist. They seek nothing other than new forms
for the old things.

In order to dream up a new art, they demolish.

For the past, they have no love. For the past, they may have only respect. Love, they
reserve it for the future.

Freedom and individuality in the arts, the abandonment of forms learned from the old
masters, the tendency towards what is new, odd, bizarre even, the tendency to extract
from life only the characteristic parts, to shove aside what is common and banal, to
pay attention only to the actions through which an individual distinguishes oneself from
others: these are some of the seminal principles with which the few have the courage
to mark their passage.

Translated by Julian Semilian

THE EXHIBIT OF PAINTING AND DRAWING: DERAIN, FORAIN, GALANIS, ISER   N. D. Cocea

Originally published as "Expoziția de pictură și desen Derain, Forain, Galanis, Iser,"
Nouă revista română (November 22, 1909)

Take, for example, an event from the social domain: the Russian revolution, the universal vote, the assassination of Ferrer, the expulsion of doctor Racovski, and you will
immediately observe how people separate into two distinct and inimical camps. Some,
the majority, through an instinctual reactionary frame of spirit, through a nearly physical hostility against everything that is new and everything that perturbs their particular
sort of reasoning consecrated through custom, will be against the revolution, against
Ferrer, against Racovski. The others, in the minority, eager to form their convictions
based solely on their own thinking, and perhaps impelled by their revolutionary sentiments just as instinctive as the reactionary spirit of the former will hop to the other
side of the barricade, for revolution, for Ferrer, for Racovski.

What occurs in the social domain, occurs as well in the same measure in the artistic
domain. In the arts, as in social life, the majority will opt for the antiquated formulas
of making art, for the cliches which they adopted while polishing the back of their
pants on the school benches, for that which satisfies the aesthetic needs of the human
being, minus the great and painful efforts of thought and of understanding. In painting,
for instance, the artist's craft till now taught us that a painting must be a faithful reproduction of nature, nature as perceived by the majority of people, with green trees and

blue seas, with bodies that are fashioned with harmonious proportions and display a shiny polish. In painting, the spectator has his own criterion of judgment, measured with the compass. The reproduction of famous canvasses furnishes him with ready-made means of comparison. A landscape or a nude that doesn't depart too far from the sorts of landscapes or nudes that he is used to are acceptable to him. Everyone is content. The fans, because they have something to adorn their living rooms, without the strain of having to make too many choices and without the fear of being cheated buying inferior canvasses, because all the canvasses are pretty much the same; the painters, because they can sell so many pieces per anum, like the shoemaker or the tailor sells so many ready-made shoes or suits, without the torture of putting the creative spirit to work to bring a novel tone to the dusty conceptions of art. The galleries multiply, get rich, and if you've seen one, you've seen them all. On the walls lounge vulgar and insipid canvasses, in gilded frames. Messrs. Strâmbulescu, Aricescu, Loghi, Grant, etc, etc, are short on craft, dispersing colors on top of colors, and polishing their wares with the indifference of a street shoeshine.

You can imagine then what the reception must have been for the last exhibit at the Athenaeum, in its idyllic atmosphere of mercantile mawkishness. We will not mention De Forain or Galanis. The fashionable French magazines made them popular in our parts as well, and though some, in the intimacy of their souls, were convinced to the contrary, they lacked the audacity to dispute it publicly. But with the lesser known Derain, and with Iser, who is Romanian and who allows himself to understand painting in a manner that diverges from that of the Beaux Arts professors and to introduce a new tone, lively and personal, to the quotidian exhibition chambers of the Athenaeum, things are different. The majority, that majority we were speaking of a moment ago, made up randomly of painters, dilettantes, from "Mecaenases" or simply from regular bourgeois, these majorities that have one single mode of reasoning: routine and an involuntary horror of thinking, of the novel and the unknown, perused in passing Derain's symphonies of color and Iser's synthetic art with, more than likely, the same indefinite sense of perplexity, of worry, as the baby calf from the popular saw gawked at the new gate. Iser and Derain, here are two new gates for our public to gawk at. The former doesn't believe it is enough to reproduce nature to create a work of art. For this, the photographers and the official painters are enough. But the artist needs more: nature must undergo the journey through his soul's crucible. Every audacity is permitted and you can kick down the foundation of all of past's forms, but with one single stipulation: to possess sincerity in the face of nature. Iser is sincere. He doesn't organize his pictures like a theatrical tableau. He doesn't force nature to become more beautiful for him. He doesn't paint with gold dust, nor with toothpaste. Peruse the above reproduction: Woman Reading. Her clothes do not fall in elegant creases, and the woman is not posed in an elegant posture. The means of interpretation are extremely simple and the poetry of the painting lives within the rigidity of nature, in the fugitive and discreet profile of the reader, and in the vague and mysterious impression it makes upon our soul. You will be left with the same impression after you have seen The Amazon, after you have seen all of Iser's works. I said "seen" and insist upon this word. The canvasses of the official painters, it is enough to merely glance at them. So many painters' exhibits can be easily passed over, with distracted view, as you would leaf through an album of post cards. The works of Iser must be seen once, twice, many times in a row, and only after you have seen it thus, after you shed your fear of novelty, you may have the right to understand it. Your effort will not cost you a great deal. The slow and difficult understanding of a work of art yields rewards you will never obtain from the gilded frames or the respectable chromolithographs of the professorial craft.

Penetrating all that is intimate, all that comes from the soul, all that is warm, in one of Iser's works, you leave with the impression that you have penetrated one of your nature's enigmas. A synthetic sketch of Iser's, the color harmonies of Derain, seems to unveil something of the content and of the laws of nature. We no longer have anything to do here with descriptive art. Their canvases are not painted only for the satisfaction of the eye. Like a line from Verlaine, from Baudelaire, from Arghezi, they lean out of the window opening out to the infinite.

Oh, certainly, this art is not for the majority of our bourgeois-infused times. Exasperated by the general lack of taste and ambient imbecility, a critic with prophetic veleities might kick down the salesman's stall, might take the whip to the art's Pharisees. In their place he would enthrone Iser.

But, admiring, desiring even, this gesture, we regret our inability to execute it. We live in a century of skepticism and permissible epicurianism. The immense banality of the bourgeois taste that loiters everywhere, in social life as well as in the arts, disarms all the intentions of subversion. In place of revolt, our distress has but two weapons at its disposal: contempt or irony. For Iser, isolated in the rotunda of the Athenaeum, shunned by the triumphant bourgeoisie that dabbles in painting, in criticism, in "Mecaenism" we have the following reminder, in Flaubert's celebrated definition: *J'appelle bourgeois quiconque pense bassement.* [I call bourgeois whoever thinks ignobly.]

Translated by Julian Semilian

FRAGMENT FROM TINERIMEA ARTISTICĂ EXHIBITION CATALOGUE
Theodor Cornel   (1910)

...At that time the artist finds even in ugliness the most sublime elements for attaining Beauty, and from that moment on, ugliness can exist no longer. That is why, Beauty, in art, is not the opposite of Ugliness; that is why there is no such thing as artists who, on account of representing subjects that are ugly, are bad artists, because by representing those ugly subjects, they can manifest the most enchanting expression of Beauty.

Translated by Julian Semilian and Sanda Agalidi

NEW GUIDELINES IN ART   Theodor Cornel
Originally published as "Îndrumări in artă," *Viaţa socială* vol. 1, no. 4 (May 1910)

A quick glance at artistic activity in this country shows us that the new tendencies in art have several representatives here; it instructs us that these representatives, mostly gathered around the group Tinerimea artistică (Youth in the Arts), whose annual exhibition is now open, are counted and discounted in the worst way by that "zoologic species," as Octave Mirbeau put it, called the "art critic." They are described as "buffoons" or as "lunatics."

Partisans of a more substantial artistic expression, our artists who are heralds of these new tendencies, have not had yet the chance to unite their efforts. They are scattered, each working within his or her direction of experimentation. They reached no agreements in view of the pursuit of similar goals. They have not even created the conditions for reciprocal supervision, along allied artistic routes, like the Impressionists before them, and in our time, the neo-impressionists. Instead, they pursued, distant from one another, altogether different visions, albeit leading to the same ideal of a superior and intensive art, spiritualized, freed from all the materiality imposed by strict and impotent realism. In a two-year interval we saw the blossoming of a new artistic expression, supported by the most characteristic elements of the movement, by our most robust talents. Ever since, a breath of pure idealism and artistic elan swells the sails of the ship that ferries the aspirations and hopes of the "new" ones. Standing up to the erudite system of reigning realism (but seated backwards on its throne), in the academies and schools, the image of modern art is flies, capriciously enchanting, more meaningful, nobler, richer in aesthetic emotion, aimed only at a truth in constant movement.

Those who propagate it are: Const. Brâncuși in sculpture, Mme. Cecilia Cutescu-Storck, Iser, Camil Ressu, Petrașcu, Mutzner, and to a certain extent Theodorescu-Sion, in painting. These are those who are "wayward," about whom Romanian criticism spoke, or still speaks, contemptuously. Against them rose a constellation of art illiterates, accusing them of derangement, madness, and absurdity. What are these artists after, and of what are they guilty?

Their essential mistake is that they paint, sculpt and draw as they feel. Their inexcusable crime is that they bring more air, more light, more harmony into the stifling atmosphere of the pre-established art movement. They will no longer heed in their work the so-called laws of painting and sculpture, laws which are the negation of art, the prescriptions of the established art, laws which stipulate modes of composition, modes of expression, recipes of manufacture and craft. These newcomers, essentially revolutionaries, shape the artistic future differently, and the critic does not accept this mode from the enslaved artists and by the ill-enlightened public. They speak softly, but the line that they draw, in its expressive, characteristic sense, the coloring harmonized via contraries and natural oppositions of pure color, the abbreviated form evoked by volumes, produce an impression of mobile novelty and capture the attention. They chase away those multiple accessories that make artistic expression difficult; they do not acknowledge the pretensions of the calculated composition; they reject clever craftiness and they stay away from the banality of utilitarian subject matter. For them nature is a source of rhythm and luminous oscillations. They extract from it what is general, durable and has character. By personal transposition they endow it with a particular, unexpected vibration, unseen by the myopic eyes of the profane, governed by the surrounding materialist illusion, a vibration which therefore the profane, does not understand and does not even care to understand. In a word they are making personal art.

Still, they are unjustly discounted. Pedantic critics discredit, if it deserves to be called "discrediting," Brâncuși, one of our most beloved, identifying him as an "impostor" of bad taste. They reproach him that he does not respect the "form" and proportion of the human body and that he has regressed to an archaic art, whose sense misses. Such aberrant charges suggest to us that Brâncuși's symbolism has been entirely misunderstood. *Cumințenia pământului* (*The Wisdom of the Earth*) is a conceptual creation, an intellectual rather than sculptural interpretation of the primitive settlement, assembly, (sic) of the principle of existence, in universal life. The form that follows indicates a natural rusticity offered by early man, who was closer to the earth than contemporary man. Symbol in the plastic arts is the most difficult art.

[. . .]

Realism has given all that it can; today it is lifeless, tired by the incessant wringing of the same formula, it limits itself to a lone technical acrobatics, a gymnastics of manufacture. Realism lacks intellectualism when it becomes utilitarian and serves as an ornamental device. Standing up to it are the new, vigorous and young aspirations: that precious idealism which allows multiple formulas, as long as aesthetic emotion replaces the artifice of clever craft. Our public needs to be initiated and guided along the same luminous roads where our most precious dreams stroll gracefully and alluringly like fantastic creatures, and toward which man's eternal nature striving for perfection and spiritualism insatiably aims.

Translated by Julian Semilian and Sanda Agalidi

STATEMENT   Editors of *Insula*
Insula no. 1 (March 18, 1912)

We do not follow a doctrine for our future activities. Doctrines come at the end: they rise out of the working mode itself, of each and every one of us & are determined by the conditions of reality. We have, however, the duty to note an attitude:
We no longer believe in formulas & neither in the possibility of their rehabilitation.
We understand that in this fashion we travel over untraveled roads & and we conceive new motives. We are not afraid of solitude, but in fact seek it. We may be wayward and in a hurry (perhaps). We will be redundant and contradict ourselves, yes. But this matters very little.

Translated by Julian Semilian

WARNING   Ion Vinea
Originally published as "Avertisment," *Chemarea* (October 4, 1915)

Let us emerge then with sturdy breastplates under our vests. Let us replace the maps from the editorial offices with arms in hand; let us place stink bombs in wastebaskets, let us wield pencil sword canes.
Perhaps it is still possible to carry a wide-ranging and intelligent conversation. After the old-timers emptied their hermetic guts, while the virtues of many bled on shirts agitated in service of the plebeian fiddle, and the children manifested incontinence in public on sheets of paper white as bedding, now at least it is the time of the young, of those who hearken the call, to rise to the need, to fight, to ask themselves where they will be sent. Our magazine is a question, the question of a group of writers, journalists and students, a question addressed to all.
We offer these pages. Without a doubt it is now those who think with their backside to reality who will fill these pages, not the political pederasts.

Translated by Julian Semilian

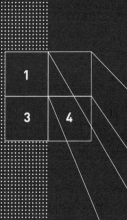

2

ART AND
SOCIAL CHANGE

Władysław Skotarek, cover for *Zdrój* vol. 4 (1918)

Konrad Winkler, *Portrait of Tytus Czyżewski* (1921), oil on cardboard, 19⁷⁄₈ x 15⁹⁄₁₆ in.

chapter 3

THE ACTIVATION OF THE AVANT-GARDE

Éva Forgács

The ongoing battles of World War I rapidly politicized cultural and intellectual activity throughout Europe. In the turmoil of the war, when many artists were drafted and died in the battlefields, those who remained at home or sought asylum in neutral Switzerland expressed increasing resistance to the war. Radicalized artists saw the war, a preeminently nationalist conflict, as one between the ruling classes—which profited handsomely on the war—and the oppressed; the true enemies, accordingly, were those divided by class interests rather than national borders. Franz Pfemfert, editor of *Die Aktion* (The Action) in Berlin, expressed his opposition to the war through calculated provocations, such as publishing works by artists who were citizens of enemy countries. The same activity led to the immediate banning of Lajos Kassák's *A Tett* (The Act) in Budapest, 1916.

Expressionism, in literature and theater as well as in the visual arts, took on a new pathos and a new ideology. It became the most powerful vehicle of antiwar commitment, international solidarity, and conscientious objection in the face of the madness of the slaughter. The term *avant-garde* was once again infused with its original military and political meaning. The avant-garde groups were engaged in social and political

antiwar propaganda, class struggle, and the anticipation of a new, egalitarian postwar reality. Artists held fast to their expectations of a bright future—expectations fueled by Futurist visions, socialist utopias, and the scant news coming from post-Revolutionary Soviet Russia.

Expressionism captured their anger, energy, and hopes; it was the first artistic idiom that consciously advocated internationalism (even if the German critic Adolph Behne, defending it against the charge of being unpatriotic, declared it the new national art in Germany). During World War I, Expressionism was embraced by avant-garde groups in Poland and Hungary as the most valid idiom to convey the anger, despair, and revolt of the artists, while artists in the Czech lands had discovered it before the war and harnessed it for emotional expression. During the war internationalism in the arts developed a political edge that distinguished it from the spiritual cosmopolitanism of the earlier Der Blaue Reiter group, which already had the cooperation of artists from all countries and all creative fields on its agenda.

Expressionism in Central Europe during the First World War was not seen as a mere aesthetic category, and most of the art works were scarcely "purely" Expressionist. Many artists in these countries broke away from the search for a common theoretical ground that characterized the pre-WWI years, and declared themselves fully-fledged activists with an articulate social consciousness and political goals, asserting a newfound engagement in a range of historical and social issues. The entire activity of each vanguard group was imbued with a variant of the Futurist insistence on an epochal break with the past.

The reception of the new art varied from state to state, but nowhere in Europe was it accepted by such a wide audience as it was in Germany, where it had made initial inroads during the prewar years. Still imbued with revolutionary overtones, German Expressionism conquered the art market and established itself as the most important new art form. Many on the left and among the young looked upon the Expressionists as the heralds of a new, better world. In the Central European countries, artists enjoyed far less exposure to the public. The language of Expressionism and its alarming message was confined to the very small circles of moral supporters and to the small audience they were able to recruit.

Art in Central Europe had long served as a forum for social demands and historic claims. During the First World War, the avant-garde in these countries followed the example of their German counterparts and organized themselves into activist groups. They sought to expand their mission more pragmatically than their nineteenth-century Romantic predecessors, from mere artistic issues to social and political tasks. The avant-garde had embarked on a road of social activism.

Franz Pfemfert's periodical *Die Aktion* (The Action, published 1911–32) was a leading Expressionist organ in Berlin, rivaled only by *Der Sturm* (1910–32). While both periodicals published a blend of lyric prose and poetry, Expressionist woodcuts and drawings, as well as cultural commentary, *Die Aktion* was the first journal to combine such aesthetic radicalism with political radicalism, wherein party affiliation was avoided in favor of the anarchist thought that was so widely influential among Berlin intellectuals. Hence texts by Mikhail Bakunin, Senna Hoy, Peter Kropotkin, and Max Stirner were mingled on *Die Aktion*'s pages with poems by Jakob van Hoddis and Georg Heym. Also abundant was Expressionist prose and commentary by Kurt Hiller, Ludwig Rubiner, and other young habitués of Berlin's Café des Westens, a primary meeting place for Berlin's bohemian artists and *Literaten* (literati).

The anti-authoritarian stance these writers shared, as well as their reverence for literature, are brilliantly and succinctly captured in Rubiner's aggressively satirical text "Listen!" Typical of *Die Aktion*'s stance, even members of the intelligentsia are ridiculed for the slightest concession to bourgeois values. Pfemfert's "The Possessed" conveys the growing enthusiasm for war that surged across Germany two years earlier on the eve of World War I, its promise of adventure and sweeping change proving irresistible among the Expressionist generation eager for an end to the stodgy values and staid cultural institutions of Wilhelmine Germany. Pfemfert, however, remained steadfast in his fervent opposition. Within a week of writing this essay he would pen his wartime position statement: to survive censorship the journal would ostensibly drop its political content, focusing instead only on art and literature (thus anticipating and avoiding the fate of Munich-based *Das Forum*, which was banned, or *Die weißen Blätter* [The White Pages], forced from Leipzig into Swiss exile). However Pfemfert soon contrived a range of subversive strategies (such as publishing verbatim jingoistic and bellicose statements from the German establishment press, allowing them to appear ludicrous in the context of his own pages) that would articulate his political opposition to the war and gain wide admiration among radical writers and artists, including Hugo Ball, Erwin Piscator, and Lajos Kassák, whose journals *A Tett* (The Act) and *Ma* (Today) attest to this influence.

THE POSSESSED Franz Pfemfert

Originally published as "Die Besessenen," *Die Aktion* vol. 4 (August 1, 1914)

I.

So these are the cultural heights we have achieved: hundreds of thousands of the healthiest, most valuable forces tremble at the thought that something vague—a sign from the rulers of Europe, a bit of ill will or sadistic whim, a fit of Caesarean madness or a business speculation, an empty word or a vague tribute—will chase them tomorrow from their homes—from wife and child, from father and mother, from everything they have labored to build—and unto death. A quirk of fate can today, tomorrow, at any moment issue a call, and they will all come. Obeying necessity. They will begin by howling, because they see their bit of earthly happiness falling apart. But soon thereafter, though with underwear less than spotless, they will be possessed by rapture and senselessly murder and be murdered.

II.

It is stupid to speak a word of reason when the hour of reason is gone. Writing manifestos and prefabricated peace resolutions today—there's nothing more useless, more trivial. And if international social democracy "denounces the disgrace of war" with pretty phrases, while the comrades may already be mobilized to march, its leaders should be either ridiculed or flogged. Because dereliction of duty amongst the wretched hagglers over parliamentary seats is alone is to blame for the fact that the peoples of Europe today (like fifty years ago) must fear the possibility of a worldwide conflagration. Had the bombastically blathering Party of Four Million not had nationalism drilled into it for decades, we could stand up to any war cries.

III.

Perhaps the danger, brought on almost entirely by the mindless press pirates, will pass this time round. Perhaps the great mass murder will have taken another recess by the time these lines appear in print (I am writing them on July 27 in Ilsenburg, where there are no extra editions). Yet we shall have no occasion to celebrate. The awareness remains: a new danger can arise at any moment; chauvinism is constantly life-threatening for mankind. Chauvinism is all it takes to make millions of rational beings possessed overnight. This knowledge must keep us awake even when danger appears to be snoring.

IV.

(What Germany has to hope or fear from a world war in terms of Realpolitik is an issue that concerns only "patriots." Our patriots must come to terms with the fact that Prussia's Polish policy has pushed a valuable ally into the arms of the Czar and that Schleswig and Alsace-Lorraine have found precious few opportunities to learn to love the black-white-and-red.)

Translated by Timothy O. Benson

Do you hear comrade, fellow worker, reader, the ostracizing call resound again and again: "Writer!"—the curse excommunicating us, the case of the horse dung thrown at us?

Do you hear the mocking shout: "Writer!"?

The shattering of windows thrown open: "Writer!"?

Oh, swindlers cowering in the surging crowd who shouts: "Stop that writer!"

The didactic full beard, the retarded Tolstoy, who guards his well furnished rebellious dungheap and zealously writes for capitalist newspapers,

The theater director, who has gone disgracefully bust on pranks and taken refuge from death in the daily press,

The solemn publisher, who sends every great work of a dead writer to the bookshops transformed into a glossy, effortless, mysterious unction (yet again on imitation hand-made paper),

The pimp under the beds of his friends eavesdropping for literary material,

The three-hundredth imitator of Gottfried-Keller,

The founder of taverns with humanitarian wide-eyes who besieges editors for recommendations,

The proclamation specialist,

The reclusive mystic, who greases every old legend, every fairy tale, every discovery of foreign thinkers into a marketable deep book,

People who do nothing but make literature, live off literature, stand behind literature, covered with sweat,

People put on the *qui-vive* by a recalcitrant literary remark (how remarkable!)'—

They all use "writer" as an insult, they degrade you with the word "writer," they discredit you with the word "writer,"

They put an end to comradeship with it.

The rebel who all his life reads nothing but newspapers and refers only to poorly written sentences, foaming,

The novelist who is not satisfied with his reviews,

The sour classic who churns out high dramas based on antiquated models and has them printed,

The profiteer of the intellect, the doctor, official, banker, businessman, director who, ah, writes poetry only as a pastime,

The newspaperman who is no longer proud of his mental powers,

And the writer himself, incompetent and anxious, squinting toward posterity, mutterer, stutterer, deep do-gooder, quibbler (concerned entirely with posthumousness), and coward—

They all should be ashamed of themselves and put an end to their lives,

Because it has been useless.

Or why do they write?

Only because others write?

What do they have to say to us?

Only self-deception, self-swindling, a private matter!

Or the deception of others?

Fellows who leave their places at the most important hour.

Their place is not to make words about things past.

We don't need interpreters; today everyone interprets himself.

Their place is

To make words for things that are good, for the humanity to come;
To make words against desecration of the spirit;
To make words against the betrayal of divine humanity;
To make words!
Because others are better at making sausage, suits, gloves, cupboards, beer, boots, and rolls.
Their job is to make the word that sets people in motion and gives them bliss on earth,
The word that causes a generation to act,
The word that they, the writers, know better than their readers.

Their job is to be leader, not explainer.
Whoever is not that must step down!
Wretched mediocrities, interventionists, valets with old secrets—step down!
Whimpering malcontents, traitors, informers of word and devotion, suspicious of the leaders—step down!
Down with swindlers!
Long live the voice! The voice for the
Others!
Long live the word, bright as a bugle call!
Long live the wide-open mouth that loudly screams:
Long live the leader!
Long live the writer!

Translated by Timothy O. Benson

The radicalization of the Hungarian avant-garde subculture was advanced in the teens by the poet, writer, and editor Lajos Kassák, who eventually established himself as a visual artist as well. Kassák came from a proletarian family, had worked as a locksmith since childhood, and had associated with workers' movements while very young. In 1915 he started the most politically radical avant-garde periodical to appear hitherto in Hungary, entitled *A Tett* (The Act), in homage to Franz Pfemfert's radical Berlin journal of the same name, *Die Aktion*. Kassák's program was as much spiritual and metaphysical as devoted to an antiwar political stance. He trusted the power of poetry, but insisted also on antiwar action. The words "action" and "Futurism" resonated through his rapidly expanding avant-garde circle, but he used them idiosyncratically. In his "Program," he spoke about a new art in a distant, postwar future, which "opposed all wars, for (contrary to the Futurists' claims) wars are the most vile enslavers of energies." *A Tett* anticipated a world revolution as the necessary consequence of World War I.

When *A Tett* was banned in the summer of 1916, Kassák, by now experienced in keeping one step ahead of his censors, immediately launched a new periodical entitled *Ma* (Today). Since art, as Kassák observed, was less scrutinized for political meaning, *Ma* would be dressed more as a cultural and artistic forum rather than a political and literary one. Accordingly, it appealed to the "friends of literature and arts," and the introductory article focused on pragmatic issues such as publication and subscriptions, rather than politics.

If including art in *Ma* was initially a subterfuge to protect its political radicalism, Kassák became increasingly interested in the fine arts, attracting a group of like-minded artists whose works he began to show in 1917 when he opened an exhibition room. Ede Bohacsek, Sándor Bortnyik, Rudolf Diener-Dénes, Valéria Dénes, Sándor Galimberti, Lajos Gulácsy, János Kmetty, János Máttis-Teutsch, József Nemes-Lampérth, György Ruttkay, János Schadl, and Béla Uitz shared Kassák's future-oriented views and infused *Ma* with Cubist and Expressionist idioms. Although Kassák designated *Ma* as an activist periodical only in February 1919, the term "activism" has come to refer to his group's activity from 1915 to the end of his Vienna exile in 1926.

When you read the manifesto of these temperamental young Italian painters (for first of all we must have a manifesto!) you have the feeling that the psychology of the war in Tripoli is becoming easier to understand. For until now one might have thought, what on earth could the Italians want in Africa while their Sicilian peasants are still using flails to thresh the wheat by hand, their public health and census officials are befuddled, and they have their own Africas that are darker and more extensive than Tripoli, right at home? But now you are inclined to think that maybe after all they were struck by some Norman wanderlust, some adventurous devil-may-care attitude to leave everything behind, to start everything anew, someplace totally different...For lo and behold, this is what the Futurist Manifesto declares: all museums must be blown up. Here are the primitives of the future.

The walls of the three exhibition rooms of the firm of Bernheim-jeune are currently covered by a whirl of cut-up body parts in a swirl of toppling smokestacks, ragged clothes torn into shreds, and dismantled engine components. As for the viewers... why, the viewers look at each other and do not dare to laugh out loud. (Ah, here in Hungary the audiences would be more demonstrative.)

For this is no simple matter. Our fathers and grandfathers have used up the right to laugh at a work of art that they did not understand and believed to be peculiar. Bach was forgotten, Mozart had to starve, Wagner was greeted with catcalls, Cézanne was ignored till the day he died, and Philippee is still not purchased, even after his death. But the sins of our fathers and elders consisted not so much in their laughing off works of genius, as in depriving us of our sense of security, our right to spontaneous laughter, and in giving rise to a rampant snobbery that would have its genius as fresh as its oysters, and in the shade of which even the most blatant mediocrity is allowed its one or two hours of fame.

I do not believe that the Futurists intend to do harm. And if one manages to remain unfazed by the first impression, which may be compared to stepping onto a heaving garbage dump of color and line, then he will encounter in more than one picture the fragments of energetic and appealing forms that signal talent. And anyway, I like those who know what they want. And the Futurists certainly know what they want; what is more, they have written about it in their manifestos with a wit and clarity that merits a thoughtful response.

And we must admit one thing. What they are doing is indeed new. It is without precedent and kin in the history of art. (Although I doubt that they should be ashamed of any kinship.) Their "art" has emerged without any transition, fully fledged from their theoretical foreheads. (A peculiar sign of the times, this reversal of the order of things, where theories precede the actual art movement...) The theory they have propounded with such dialectical acumen is as follows. Objects seen as immovable are in fact empty abstractions. They correspond neither to reality nor to the state of our soul. Within and without us all is in motion. Every single line is only a vector of forces that must be uncovered by the painter, by breaking apart the forms of seemingly still objects. The other great principle is that things that are simultaneously present together in the psyche must be painted together in the same composition. What we see is not as important as the associations that make up our true inner experience.

Thus the theory, in a nutshell. As for the paintings themselves... Well, say the subject of one picture is a woman on a balcony, seen from the interior of the room. If Monet or Renoir or any other painter before now had painted this, only the woman would be visible within the doorframe and as much of the sky and rooftops as could be fitted within that doorframe. But Boccioni paints a fiacre into the woman's hairdo, inside which are seated two palazzos of four stories each. In place of her right shoulder we see a confusion of legs and feet, and over her left shoulder street lamps are floating in empty space.

The picture is undeniably novel. But listen to the official commentary. "We wish to paint the ensemble of impressions the woman on the balcony experienced while looking at the street. The noisy helter-skelter of the street, the receding line of buildings, the sweeping torrent of people and animals. In her mind these things are broken down into their elements which mix and meld together. The viewer should stand in the middle of the picture and the painting should be a synthesis of what we see and what we remember." The title of the painting is—naturally—*The City Enters the Room*.

Thus the theory is nowhere near as silly as the painting. What it asserts about the state of the mind is true, after all. However! However, this state of mind is invisible. And to paint what is invisible is, to say the least, a proposal that contradicts itself. And even if it were possible to paint the forms melted down by memory into thoughts—what would that amount to? An illustration suitable for a Freudian psychoanalysis. We want to see not so much the things in our minds as our minds in things, for it is not the things that are important—which is incidentally what the Futurists believe, as well.

Or take the official commentary to another painting. "The sixteen persons sitting in the same omnibus with you seem at various times to be one, ten, four, or three in number. They sit still and nonetheless they change their places. They come and go and jump out on the street; they are submerged in sunlight, only to resume their places by your side as eternal symbols of a universal vibration. How often have we all seen on the face of the man we happened to be talking to a horse trotting far away at the other end of the street? Our bodies sink into the benches we sit on and the benches penetrate into our bodies. The omnibus breaks through the row of buildings and the buildings fall on the omnibus and intermingle with it..."

The above is not excerpted from the diary of a madman but from the catalogue of an exhibition of paintings in Paris, in which we can also find plenty of clever and witty comments as well. As for the painting that depicts the omnibus ride, it would make no sense for me to describe it; you would still not be able to imagine it, dear reader.

Should we respond to the theory with our own theory? And say that, if we were to be consistent in this manner of depicting movement, then we ought to be painting motion pictures? Or should we point out that even if you paint twenty legs on a horse (they are never satisfied with less) then you end up with twenty motionless legs, and that thereby the painting loses that enormous mysterious force of tension that glows in the forms painted by the old masters, making us feel all the vehemence of the sum of potential movements packed into one motionless form—and even though the Futurists have lost this force of tension by breaking up the form, they nonetheless end up painting nothing but immobility?

It is not really worthwhile to elaborate the argument. It would be too easy. What is certain is that the possibility of such an art movement is an exciting and instructive symptom of our age. What they are doing, even though it consumes a considerable amount of talent, is not really art. Nonetheless we must not dismiss them as pathological or foolish. They are numerous and seem to speak each other's language, which is disquieting. And even if we do not understand their pictures, we understand the sensation they are creating. Our nerves are more sensitive to converging life forms. We can feel that these lines are merely the vectors of forces that melt into one another and our minds perceive objects as symbols of dematerialized energies. This is the same new sensitivity that gave rise to Bergson's philosophy, according to which materiality and immobility are only optical illusions, the stillness of a speeding train seen from another one that is moving on a track parallel with it. Our empirical abstractions freeze into still forms the eternal fountains of energies.

The Futurists would like to melt these fountains by means of their paintbrushes and their intuitive sensations. Instead, they end up shattering them into a multitude of senseless fragments.

Translated by John Bátki

FUTURISM: NEW POSSIBILITIES IN ART AND LIFE   Dezső Szabó
Originally published as "A futurizmus: az élet és művészet új lehetőségei," *Nyugat* (1913)

Ah, the anguish of bat-souls! In the company of mammals, the torment of wings that stick out, and among birds, the tragic realization that your vaunted, soaring wings are merely downy paws fluffed out with feathers. Torment of a twofold solitude, mocked by both fates: either a heritage of lies or a cynicism spawned by desperate vanity. Poor and wretched cynicism, revenge of the skunk-man on the merciless grandeur and beauty of life.

Yes, we are witnessing the spasms of the Age of Bats. Our sickness is that of the amorphous times between two monumental epochs. The great epics, the great mythologies have crumbled; occasional pieces of belated debris still drop with a thud inside empty souls. The new epic, tomorrow's mythology is still only a promise.

Christianity, you are a dead mythology, a dead epic, dead and gone. We can still hear the echoing blows of the hammer used by the madmen of this dying-birthing world to slam you down into your grave. In death you are still tragic, for the face of the dead gains meaning from the passions of the living. Your Greek sibling lies smiling in his grave under our fawning eyes, caressing as the sun on a sea stretching becalmed. But those hungering for a new spirit still hate you as if you were alive, and the antiquarian pretends you are still alive. Why have we failed to realize you are dead? That would smooth away the agony frozen on your face, and turn it into a smile, and you could be the eternal bride of every artist's soul.

Around your sepulchre two crude crowds churn the mud under their feet. One is a group of dwarf-size tavern saints complete with marionette-Christ and Mary-marionette, and full of lies, claiming to be part of a living and leavening Christianity, the epic that had swept a former world, the mythology that once gave birth to Europe! The small change jingling in their palms is the price of admission, sweated out by sorry simpletons.

The other group has Homais, the "natural scientists," the "intellectuals," the "moderns." Behold the diminutive natural scientist, Tom Thumb Prometheus, his micrometer caliper measuring the universe, proclaim that "today's modern man is found not in poems or novels, the child must be taught the scientific world-view, etc., etc." Well, Monsieur Homais, I don't really care if scientific nature has no gods, colors, sounds, or infinity, as long as my flesh and blood and body and soul are straining to give birth to a mythology, and inside me sings a world of music embraced by color. Do you think that they can be banished by the laws you have extracted from the highly improbable world external to my own skin? If you cannot save all of me, please do not try to be my Redeemer by cutting me in half. I was born to be creative and to live as variously as humanly possible. And I would rather be a medieval cock than a capon of modern natural science.

For the last 150 years the problem has been staring us in the face: Christianity is defunct, along with all of its consequences, while the human machine rattles on meaninglessly. The basic psychic functions need a new dogma, a new will, and new passion to create new life…

And anyone attempting the heroic anachronism of living on a grand epic scale is laughed at, like some shadow play for children. The literature of the nineteenth century is full of lugubrious Herculean figures shrunken down into weird jugglers, having realized how risible the simple, grand, and heroic have become.

Dogmas, dogmas are needed for the broken mosaic of humankind! The fiery wind of dogmas to sweep all sterile little egos into one new, fertile medium. Dogmas, to move muscles with great love or great hatred, for only love and hatred are capable of building. Dogmas, to make men once again simple, childlike, and heroic. To sweep away the scholastics with their piddling expertise, trivial artsiness, refined souls and intellectual games.

Even a dogma of only one sentence, of socialist origin or whatever, but pregnant with the future, let the juices revive the vast jungle of our ego. Science is just as much a cage as religious morality. Hasn't anyone noticed how unlimited man is?

II.

Christianity died, and in its wake came a century-long dance of death. The scattered fragments of a great unity sickened into individuals, and like the various members of a dissected frog, kept on twitching in the dance of the whole body. For Romanticism with its weeping, wailing, self-dissecting thirst for the infinite was a special edition of Christianity, its post-mortem spasm.

The Romantics, too, professed suffering as one of their bywords. But it was no longer the word originating from Christ's wounds, it no longer was the stuff of dogma, it did not create a new world order. These were negative giants; through them a dying world was torn to shreds. But they were still beautiful in their grandeur. And their marvelous *danse macabre* certainly conjured some thrashing silhouettes and splendid wails into our literature.

III.

The superb madmen of early Romanticism were succeeded by the diminutive, refined souls of the late nineteenth century. They are tiny and strange, as if they had dropped here out Japanese art. They turned literature into an occultism of microscopic secrets.

But signs of slowly sprouting new life began to appear in various scattered phenomena. The first great saint of the future mythology is Auguste Comte. He was the first to introduce a new dogma to restore the unity of our world.

His positivism gave rise to the art of two great Romantics: Victor Hugo and Emile Zola. The chief merit of all three is that they attempted to install the concept of humanity as the radiant centerpiece of the new faith. But Hugo and Zola throughout much of their work are still negative, destructive forces.

The first great constructive force in literature is Walt Whitman. *Leaves of Grass* remains to this day the most perfect, most fertile Futurism.

[…] In Walt Whitman I see the revelation of the future man.

Walt Whitman's message is the following:

Life is not a system, but an ongoing, self-regenerating kaleidoscope of which even the most comprehensive system can capture only a tiny sliver. It is, in all its forms and contradictions, subsumed within the human even as the human is the sole measure of the many sorts of life. All things are equally important, sacred, and true, because all are part of life. Health, sickness, mortality, sin, and virtue are all stages in the cycle by which life begets life; we can never know what came from where or what it may become. (The novelty of these thoughts in poetry at the time is indicated by the general stupefaction and consternation evoked by Whitman's debut.) Life is a constant dash from who knows where to who knows where, and each person is a momentary cross-section of this universal torrent. You are the kin of every phenomenon—each pebble, weed, and creature—because everything exists within you and through you. This life has two basic conditions. One is democracy, the principle of individualism, giving free rein to the rush of energies. The other is solidarity: everything is alive only to the extent that it is lived by me, is a part of my life, thus I love myself in everything, and my life stands to gain from everything I love. Solidarity, the adherence of progressive forces, is fundamental, an inherent biological necessity.

From here on the poet will sing of democracy and solidarity, with his eyes toward the future, because with each passing moment life takes another step forward. The past and the present exist only as elements of the future, just as the initial swing of the arm is part of the trajectory of the thrown ball.

Democracy and solidarity expand poetry, enabling it to render an integral picture of life. From here on poetry would reflect all of life the way motion pictures capture every little secret rustling of a forest or all the violence of a storm at sea, in full motion, complete with every detail; the motionless state is an abstraction. Since all things are throbbing with life, allow your poem to be one with the fevered heartbeat of universal life.

The words do not matter, says Whitman; his poetry acts through the driving and formative power of his lines. His wide-open eyes take in all of Life, which becomes transmuted into irregular rhythmic segments in his poems. They take on strange and capricious forms that are determined by the throb of the universe as it is registered inside Whitman. Some of his poems consist of nothing but catalogs of sights seen, including every swerve of their ongoing existence, so that the total effect is one of movement, of a new and full life.

Whitman likes to call himself a cosmos. And indeed, he has miraculously earned that name, if being a cosmos means living through everything that may be sensed or thought by any human being, living in empathy with everyone and everything, and creating a total synthesis of the multifariousness of existence so that dualistic antitheses disappear, as in the swirl of real life. In him are united the three immensities of the metropolis, the forest primeval, and the ocean... *Leaves of Grass* is a vast encyclopedia of actualities lived through and humanized, an encyclopedia that embodies the swarming of life. It is highly likely that beauty is not just an occasionally occurring special event in the world, but in fact everything is beautiful, and beauty is actually the ultimate reality of all life; it is only our eyes that have not been able to glimpse this and see everything as beautiful. By perceiving this reality Walt Whitman has perhaps bestowed a greater gift upon humanity than any of his predecessors or followers.

IV.

Yes, Whitman possesses many features that will go into the making of the soul of the new age. He has transmuted Schopenhauer's tragic will into a joyful life principle that amounts to the salubrious progress of life. One of the most characteristic accomplishments of Whitman's poetry is that he unites all of the advantages of positivism into the prospect of the "unknown." According to Whitman there is no body, no soul, no intellect (rational thought), no perception, and no will. My ego in every one of its manifestations is an inseparable, integral occurrence of universal life. This applies to every one of the ego's phases; Apollonian introspection and Dionysian ecstasy of action are both exalted by the selfsame onrush of life force. According to him life is uninterrupted laughter that has no beginning or end, and the *Übermensch* is the one whose laughter resonates the most.

This involves a total break with the world of the past. He offers, in place of the existing view of a stable world, an image of a world of constant becoming. Each person is a potential life quantum that democracy and solidarity make fully realizable. And the new epic, the new mythology of democracy is the battle fought by industry, commerce, politics and science. This is greater in its scale than any previous struggle, and its results more marvelous. The Hercules of the new age is beyond good and evil, and follows his own path with joyful energy. The basic biological need for association and solidarity coordinates these surging energies. Our souls should always be oriented toward the future for we enter the future with each passing moment.

Lo and behold the mighty, democratic *Übermensch*, who would later assume the tigerish features of the aristocratic boogey-man in Nietzsche's conception. The fertile chaos of Walt Whitman contains a whole slew of ideas that later thinkers fobbed off as their own discoveries...

V.

Here, then, are the antecedents of Italian Futurism, which demands to burn all antecedents. For even the most rapidly moving body's momentum contains all of its previous motion. But save the objections for later. It would a cheap and useless exercise if I were to dissect all the comical, bizarre, contradictory, and foolish features of Futurism. Surely no one could have foreseen, in the comical human rags worn by earliest Christianity, the arrival of the most creative and far-reaching unity the world has ever known. Those who fight for the future are always labeled as fools and charlatans at first. [...] This is all the more true in our days, when the innovators of the age of democracy must indeed assume the guise of fools and charlatans in order to create sufficient publicity in the competition for attention. I will examine Futurism as one phase, perhaps the most characteristic one, of the new psyche that is in the making.

Italian Futurism—Walt Whitman with an admixture of Nietzsche—proclaims the following.

Life is a constant onrush of energies and their transformation into new shapes. Life is synonymous with the new, death with the old. The man of the future is constantly impelling his highest self into new action, and is violent and cruel. *Noi vogliamo glorificare la guerra, sola higiene del mondo, il militarismo, il patriottismo, il gesto distruttore dei libertari, le belle idee per cui si muore e il disprezzo del donna.* (We wish to glorify war, the sole hygiene of the world, militarism, patriotism, the destructive gesture of libertarians, beautiful ideas to die for, and the contempt for woman.) This is Futurism in a nutshell.

The man of the future is a hero, for heroism is the essence of life. He rushes courageously to the fore, wherever his instincts thrust him. Everywhere, in politics, economics, or art he seeks out the challenge, for each conquered obstacle adds another bundle of fibers to one's muscles, brings another surge of life. Thus his life is a ceaseless series of conquests. He indulges the full extent of his ego, independent of morality and free of sentimentalism. (Herein lies the greatest self-contradiction in Italian Futurism: it preaches the most extreme anarchy, but within the "homeland" it demands a unity that rules above all.)

Therefor this majestic beast loves his own kind, and is chauvinistic.

His feverish pursuit of life goads him into constant innovation and scatters his energy in daring, gigantic deeds. Only the ethical imperative has meaning; life must be forever bold, rebellious, and ready for creative destruction.

In order for the "Futurist" to become the prevailing psychic type, so that modern man can live to the fullest, the following obstacles will have to be eliminated:

1. The past. The book you are reading, the church, palace or room you are admiring, the furniture that surrounds you, the clothes you wear, the song you sing...All these are not really you; they are all saturated by your ancestors, they are the ones you are absorbing everywhere, they coat your eyes so that you see only through them, they take over your muscles so that you act for them. Ninety percent of our lives does not belong to us; the experience of past millennia makes us lethargic. Many fine, grand and daring acts await the doer, much beauty lies in wait for the beholder, but our senses, drugged by the past, are unable to respond accordingly. Every vestige of the past must be extirpated from our world and burned away, so that it dies out of our souls. This alone can bring true salvation, real liberation. The permanently built-in reflexes of the past paralyze the arm readying for action, the skepticism of ghosts returned to haunt us drains away energies aching for the future. So demolish libraries, burn down museums, destroy everything that is past, and amidst the wild ecstasy of destruction, let man be reborn as a child, a hero, and a free denizen of the future.

2. Woman. Woman is the other great illness that brings on man the affliction of sentimentality and inaction. The enfeebling cult of woman that currently floods literature, art and all spheres of life squelches man's creative energies. Delilah, having mastered Samson, sucks away the potential energy of contemporary history. For the man of the future, woman can only be an object of sexual gymnastics, merely one outlet for his overflowing power that he puts aside when the time for action arrives. Woman must be killed off as a source of metaphysics; woe to him who endows her with spiritual dimensions.

3. All types of intellectual scholasticism: playing at science, intellectual pretensions, soul-searching analyses. Perform actions, instead of analysis. Become an integral will to live, indulge your great intuitive flashes, do not let logic, psychology, or any other halfway measure waste you away.

We must constantly create the future, by constantly destroying the past. Let the makers of history be young men, 25 to 35 years of age, who can shape the world because they are still saturated by the future. Let them sweep away the obsolete older generations. Poetry and art should be the free gestures of this individual power intoxicated by action. Respect for models and authority equals suicide. You must break up the frozen forms of the rigid old world. This applies not only to poetic forms, but includes even the shackles of grammar and syntax. Let your surging life force leap into any words you like. Instead of the limiting verb conjugations make use of the infinitive, to represent the act as it glides onward. Do not circumscribe life with grammatical rules! Pile noun upon noun to render your vision. Forget about punctuation and complete sentences. Only the burning lava of words can convey the overflowing of one's ego in resonant, rhythmic waves of sound. And if they do not understand you, so much the better. After all, one's poetry is merely the act of exercising one's conquering power; incomprehension can only mean that you have succeeded in creating an unprecedented, utterly new life within yourself.

VI.

Reader, before you rush to wash the terror from your eyes with holy water and rid your soul of these terrible things with the sigh of outrage, ask yourself, What are you? You are a tax-paying nonentity, draftable cannon fodder, a praying non-believer, and a deist playing at natural science; you are a whatever, an invisible bourgeois of the twentieth century. You are a Christian but your faith has nothing to do with Christianity. Your faith never motivates any of your practical deeds. It is merely your childhood catechism served up with a dollop of pantheistic, scientific sauce. You put on this faith along with your deerskin gloves and best shoes every Sunday before going to church and take it off afterward...

VII.

It is most likely that such a piddling little manikin is unsuitable to create a new era. Probably the meaning of life is indeed heroism, and a great, productive age can only arrive when men are born to be powerful yea- and naysayers. Isn't this the definitive development that our fevered age is looking for?

It could be that Futurism contains much madness and sickness, because the world is trying to cure itself through madness and illness. But its overall gist evinces a cool-headed and calculating intelligence: enough of the Romantic whining of the past 150 years, enough of all the analyses, all the critiques, denials, wails; let us start looking for the positive creative elements of the future. We must develop the soul that can settle the undecided issues of this transitional age, in whatever manner. The world needs a new faith, a burning fanaticism that will fuse into a new unity the sterile individuals of this afflicted age, in order to give a new, immortal form to humankind in a new world order, with new laws, and a new art. If the epic and mythology of our age is indeed to be found in industry, commerce, and science, then it is the task of poetry and art to root these into our soul with the same epic and mythological fervor that formerly war and the church had evoked in the collective soul. Futurism itself is bound to perish, for its anarchistic contradictions will be unable to bear any social results. But the thirst for heroic grandeur is bound to become ever more powerful.

Translated by John Bátki

TO ACCOMPANY CARLO D. CARRÀ'S PAINTING *ANARCHIST FUNERAL*
Lajos Kassák
Originally published as "Carlo D. Carrà Anarchistatemetés című képe alá," *A Tett* (1916)

They began to gather early in the morning, moving stealthily through out-of-the-way, narrow alleys, sneaking into the building like timid, hunted thieves, climbing winding spiral stairs to the upper floors, and it was fiery noontime, dipped in golden light, when the four young men in black, despondent and down-hearted, lugged downstairs to the street the coffin decorated with broad red ribbons.

The fat, lacy towers of the town did not resound with bells tolling for the funeral; instead, a silence, a horrid dull silence lay everywhere, in the streets, in the depths of open doorways, in the teary, hesitant eyes, while the factory sirens, so loud on other days, now loomed like gigantic black idols under the clear autumn sky.

The procession set out at a slow pace, the marchers huddled together.

At first they trudged in silence, without a word, heads hung low, like a flock whimpering before a storm; then someone uttered the first word and all joined in with words of their own.

They spoke of Him, in a slow, soft drawl, their grateful hearts recalling countless unforgettable memories.

The dead man had traveled much, had bathed his thirsty eyes in many a foreign land, many foreign tongues had trilled their beauty into his fertile brain, and one fine day when nobody knew who he was or where he had come from, he arrived here to sink his roots like some fully-blown, honey-blossomed flower.

He lived among them, planted new desires and faiths into their souls, and now as his weary body, broken by hard labors, lay low among the rough, splintered planks, the light of a whole world seemed to have gone out in the eyes of these people.

Somber, superstitious images appeared in their eyes, and these mourners now inched forward not so much for the sake of the deceased as for themselves, for their living, aching selves, and all the words that had been uttered from his mouth over the years were now buzzing around and agitating inside their disheveled heads, carrying and seeping them toward their secretly envisioned goal.

Their hearts sensed that restless, fiery existence, and someone struck the first defiant, blood-stirring chords, to be followed by an outburst of unaccustomed song from these sad, uplifted faces.

A foolish, playful wind swept the sound forward, and gateways and street crossings began to fill with curious onlookers until little by little the crowd swelled into a broad, rolling torrent.

Up front, the coffin swayed beneath an unfurling fire-red banner, followed by the orphaned flock singing about a beautiful, coveted future.

Up above the sky radiated its pure splendor in abundance, and there was no longer any trace of the usual funereal mournfulness.

It was as if they were returning home after long, wearisome labors from a rich, nourishing harvest and up ahead, instead of the coffin, the lads were carrying the farmers' blessed sheaf of wheat—they were as if intoxicated by each other's warmth, the freely flooding joy of life.

They had left behind the maze of narrow alleys and were now marching where they had never marched before, on broad, fancy squares and mirror-eyed boulevards where their pounding footfall kicked up the dust.

They rolled on, their liberated will turned loose, so that from the scaffolding of skyscrapers under construction the tired masons and thin, coughing women crawled down to join them, desiring the sun, and the colorful, formidable caravan now signaled the way toward wild, merciless struggles.

Muscles tensed, eyes open and hungry, they pressed forward following the coffin, and delightedly bathed in the never before seen colors, in place of guttering consecrated candles they carried redolent flowers, red cockades flared in their lapels and a hundred unfamiliar women were singing alongside a hundred unfamiliar men.

And their song rose, and soared, and wound its way into every nook and cranny, its enticing fire stirring the bottomless woes in every soul.

The silent, peace-observing buildings opened their reinforced gates, and the streets poured out their most painful burden: Man.

Ancient, wizened grandmothers and playful youngsters with muscles of steel all marched to the same rhythm drummed by the heart, the sad and rebelling heart, and embittered throats hoarse with silence now shot roaring rockets toward the sky, the words of cheering:

"Go! Go! Go!"

The whole city was seized in the throes of a hellish, awesome dance.

"Go! Go! Go!"

The crowd rolled on, and some unruly, childish prankishness caused the first windowpane to be broken, followed by another, then a hundred more, and suddenly it was as if people's minds had been inflamed by madness, and all restraint was gone.

"Go! Go! Go!"

Now destructive, alien forces mingled into the crowd, and even the smallest among them reared up with a wild fury.

A hard, villainous command rang out, and whoever could, struck out.

"Forward, attack!"

The air was filled with a heavy, suffocating smell, rifle fire crackled, sharp blades dripping with red flashed in the sunlight, large, slippery puddles of spilled blood steamed on the ground—one could fall to an easy death in them—and no one was taking cover and yesterday maybe no one would have thought that this could ever happen.

The dead lay on the hard, gray asphalt, but above them an army of new, live souls was dancing on.

They were tossed about to and fro in the streets in a mad frenzy of unchained wills, like some monster with a thousand heads that only becomes more maddened the more it is mutilated; like ravening wolves they fell upon death the reaper.

In place of couples intoxicated by each other, there were now people whose blood was boiling with a black wrath, playing instead of kisses a bitter music of woe, and the former lover found himself facing alien eyes.

"Go!"

"Don't let up!"

Desperate life flung its commands and people treaded on each other's backs to find their way.

But which way to go? No one knew, they stood in place and strained to make a move, as if they had been rooted on the spot, right into the giant, deep-set heart of the earth.

And over their heads the coffin was passed from hand to hand, still speaking to them of the promised land, and it seemed as if its streaming red ribbons shone like live, flaming torches illuminating the longed-for world.

Those who dropped away beneath it handed it on with jealous love to others who raised it upon their intoxicated shoulders.

This is how the day passed over the city.

The sun stood on the incarnadined horizon and down here the red army was diminishing, and thinning out.

The ground was covered by the mutilated bodies of the forever reconciled dead, and the eyes of the living were flooded by the dull madness of the dreaded horror of death.

"People!"

Somebody screamed out.

"People! Brothers!"

A chorus of voices rattled it, and this mournful plaint was echoed by the surrounding spaces:

"Brothers!"

They wanted to flee but no one knew the way out.

Slender, giggly virgins, wiry, bronze-armed young men, silent old graybeards all lay one atop the other, grown cold, their mouths gaping, blind eyes bulging, and the sluggish, accursed soil refused to shake them back into life, and their beaten bodies shone with red Christ-blossoms under the sky.

Then it was evening.

And on this day many men, who had been at the full beauty of their vigor and hopeful of the future, found themselves embraced by death.

Translated by John Bátki

PROGRAM   Lajos Kassák
Originally published as "Programm," *A Tett* (1916)

The ongoing worldwide horror of the past year and a half has already inflicted deep,
throbbing wounds on the decrepit body of old Europe, and it can only end in utter self-
exhaustion. Meanwhile it has undeniably brought about many advances in physics,
technology and psychology, solving problems that, in the ordinary course of evolution,
would have reached their present stages only after lengthy scientific research. And
although civilized humankind has never before revealed itself in such naked brutish-
ness in front of its thinkers, strangely enough never had the thinkers anticipated such
a vast measure of moral purification in human nature as now, in the wake of such
unmasking.

It is as if the year 1914 had marked the onset of a new period in the evolution of
humankind. The coming of a more human Human Being, inaugurating the age of
a new moral order.

I believe in the long-established truth that, notwithstanding its enormity, this war,
like all wars, is only a horrendous episode in the story of humankind. It will certainly
not change the petty practices of some men, nor will it smash all those fangs now
exposed in fraternizing grins. But I emphatically deny that this monstrous butchery
will slip out of the collective memory of the great masses without leaving an imprint,
in the form of self-awakening recollections, on the consciousness of humankind.
While today the end of the world war is as yet barely conceivable, still there is hardly
a nation whose people, grown more Christlike, has not begun to yearn for social con-
cord in our world. With the ebbing of this sea of blood the world of commerce antici-
pates a relaxing of stultifying protective tariffs; even while nations fight to the death
the world of politics dreams of a United States of Europe, and with good cause, a
hope more justified than ever before. In this entire topsy-turvy world it is only art
that remains deaf and blind, still indulging in self-adulation, lost in a jungle of sterile
catchphrases evoking "national pride" and romantic chivalry. And yet it is precisely
art, especially literature, because it possesses the most direct, active means of
expression, that faces the greatest task in the molding of the coming generation
into a human form. Literature can no longer be content with decadent self-glorifica-
tion. It must consciously strive, as the most dedicated proponent of progress, to
seize for itself a role in the very forums that will lay the foundations and provide
directions. Therefore:

1. Although the new literature did not come into being during the war, it still needed
    the war for its development from the piddling *Weltschmerz* vaporings of the previ-
    ous generation into a lyric representation of the conscious will. The new literature
    must maintain ever-present contact with all progressive economic and political
    movements, and its prominent figures, just as those of commerce, industry and
    politics, must demand a leading role in steering the machinery of the state, revis-
    ing existing laws and creating new legislature.

2. This new literature, in order to realize its full significance and make its truths
    and beauties, drawn always from the essentials of actual life, fully effective,
    must free itself from all conventional "ideal" and technical fetters. For every-
    thing that served as creative form or essential content for the artist of yesterday
    can only be, for today's creative artist, a drainage ditch that channels off the
    essence.

3. The new literature must not swear allegiance to any one of the "isms." It must
    not place its faith in the renewed possibilities of Christianism, and likewise must
    diametrically oppose Futurism. For at the one extreme are ascetics who have

been staring at their navels for millennia and at the other, vain prima donnas singing the apotheosis of war... Every school bears the hallmark of some decadent estheticism, extraneous virtuosity, or sacred mediocrity.

4. The new literature must react to all natural phenomena. It should not recognize any unbridgeable gaps in time or space. It should be the helpmate of the sciences, and vice versa. It should recognize—and use every means to illuminate—spiritual forces, by striving to equally include in its song the mysteries of the soul, the erotic splendor of flesh and blood, the poisons exhaled by the dungheap at springtime, the "Marconigraph" of technology hungering for infinity, the locomotives taking the measure of the globe, the aeroplanes probing the skies, as well as the majestic silences through which the souls of objects address us.

5. The new literature frees the will by opening the floodgates. The writer must simultaneously be both skeptic and enthusiast, a lover of everything that is unreachable, while impassively stepping over the bodies of dead gods, and moving past the purple haze of obsessions.

6. The new literature glorifies creative forces. It encourages the free competition of liberated forces, reformations, and revolutions—but opposes all wars, for (contrary to the Futurists' claims) wars are the vilest enslavers of energies.

7. The new literature cannot serve racial or national ends!

8. The new literature will not consist of garlanded snobs crooning lullabies to hysterical women!

9. The new literature must be a pillar of fire arising from the very soul of the age!

10. The subject of the new literature is the entirety of the cosmos!

11. The sound of the new literature is the chant of the conscious energies!

12. The glorified ideal of the new literature is Man, enlightening into infinity!

My intention has been, insofar as possible within the limits of available space and the censorship at work today, to provide a program for literature. My recent work has served as its illustration; I have conceived of *A Tett* for its propagation, and for its realization I have found in the vast reaches of the art world a number of companions forging ahead on diverse paths leading to the same goal as mine. Our will is as red as our blood and as fresh as our youth. We believe in reaching our goal. We are certain of the coming realization of our credo. But today, at a time when each day hurls at us a growing number of material and other artificial obstacles, I hold it necessary to spell out in this form our aims for the future. For there will come a time when we shall have to remember these days. For:

The blood that is being criminally spilled nowadays will be calmly absorbed by the soil, but when the fruit ripens, its taste will be bitter in our mouths for a long time to come, with the taste of the horrors suffered. Mendacious, glorified legends may emanate from today's casemates, but for a long time to come eyes that are open will still be confronted with the wavering question and exclamation marks of mutilated human bodies.

Translated by John Bátki

We are launching a new monthly named *Ma*.

The editor-in-chief of the periodical is Lajos Kassák.

The artistic aims directing the work of Lajos Kassák and the writers and visual artists grouped around him are well known.

Ma was founded in order to carry out this agenda, and the person-of-our editor in chief is guarantee that the contents of every issue of our periodical will be of a serious aesthetic value, devoid of any compromise.

The proprietors of *Ma* are writers and visual artists, and thus the supporters of our periodical will not be enriching the capital of an enterprise founded for financial profit. They will be providing direct assistance toward the achievement of their artistic goals to the very artists from whom they are receiving aesthetic value.

Therefore we turn with confidence to the true friends of literature and the arts and hereby serve notice that we intend to broaden contact with our public in other areas, beyond the pages of our magazine.

We have established a book publishing company,

we shall distribute reproductions of works of art,

we shall organize matinees,

and employ other means as well, in order to salvage as many artistic values as possible from the crippling pressures of commercial capital.

Let the fate of literature and the arts be placed in the hands of writers and artists!

In order to fully realize our goal, we, too, must organize ourselves in a businesslike manner.

Our editorial offices will work in total independence from our publishing venture.

The direction of the business aspects will follow the decisions of the publishing committee, whereas the editor will take full responsibility for the aesthetic quality of our publications

so that what we are advertising here is uncontaminated art.

We offer ourselves undiluted and unbowdlerized, and seek the approval of those who demand art to be that way.

Talent is not enough: purity of intent and hard work are also required in the making of an artist of the highest quality.

We believe there will be many with the ability to understand and appreciate our endeavors, and who will provide support to strengthen our group.

The cause of art is also the cause of the consumers of art.

With us, art is not an instrument of business, but rather business is the instrument for the liberation of the arts.

We confidently call upon the friends of literature and the arts to subscribe and to support us in ways that are not yet customary here, but have been long prevalent in the artistic life of Berlin and other international centers of culture.

We are issuing certificates of patronage.

There are levels of annual patronage and lifetime patronage.

Membership for one year is 20 korona and a lifetime membership is 200 korona.

We guarantee our patrons privileges that will make this manner of support advantageous for them.

Those possessing certificates of patronage, will, for the duration of their membership receive our periodical without additional subscription fees,

receive our other literary publications at half price,

receive one artistic reproduction annually,

have at their disposal two half-price tickets to our matinees,

and will receive similar discounts in our other artistic enterprises that are at present in a formative stage.

Those who subscribe at the annual rate of 8 korona (4 korona for six months) will not be eligible for the above discounts.

Translated by John Bátki

THE POSTER AND THE NEW PAINTING Lajos Kassák
Originally published as "A plakát és az új festészet," *Ma* (November 1916)

First of all let us posit an old truth: art and the artist are inseparable concepts, and the only way to objectively judge the artistic product is to see the "two lives" as a single unity. But by admitting this we seemingly take a deterministic view that holds each sound, each color, each movement of life to be part of a predetermined process constantly influenced by the external world—which would be tantamount to admitting our utter subservience. We believe that humans are physical and powerfully social beings, and as such are always influenced by the external world, but—and here we take issue with dyed-in-the-wool determinism—our intellectual capabilities enable us to fend off at least 50 percent of these influences, forcing us to adjust the character of our life by making it ever more conscious and independent. If this thesis holds true for the human as intellectual being, it is true a hundredfold for the artist as the maximal human potential.

We approach the new painting from this point of view.

The latest movement coming to a close carried the triumphant banners of Impressionism. Now we would propel the momentum into other directions, on less fortuitous trails, toward a diametrically opposed goal. The naive, contemplative gaze of the impressionists must give way to the measuring and selective vision of twentieth-century man, divested by cultural sophistication of all theoretical conventions and sentimental emotional momentum. Until now it was a pleasing truism to say that the artist is the harp upon which life plays out its whimsical ditties; from now on let the hard truth be recognized: life provides merely the raw material that is subservient to the artist's creative genius.

The model placed in front of the new painter's eyes is no longer the theme to be painted, but simply material that suggests certain forms to the creative will.

Thus the material can only be a springboard for the artist's imagination; it is only a counterbalance to the intensive conceptual work that forever attempts to liberate itself from its surroundings, even if this milieu happens to be the world of today. We are not referring here to those who are ordinarily called the gifted, or to decadent talents, but to genius in the strictest sense of the word, those individuals born to tower prophet-like in front of the masses.

And so nature remains the starting point for the new painting, but this art can never be *Naturalism* (not even in the sense of Giotto, who reached divine heights compared for instance with the likewise naturalist Jordaens). The aim of the new painting is not to approximate nature as closely as possible, but to soar away from it as far as possible; it is, more accurately stated, the act of transcending nature.

Pure naturalism is no more than a liberal contemplation, whereas the true artist is always distinguished, within the framework of whatever period, by a subversive, revolutionary temperament.

I have already to a certain extent opened up my eyes to take in my natural surroundings and have no need whatsoever for a painterly product that cleverly transposes to the canvas the literal external likeness of a landscape or a body. (This would be naturalism.) Such a painting may make for a tolerable wall decoration, a document attesting the imitative abilities of a dear friend. But art aims far beyond this, it even aims beyond the far greater role of chronicler. Especially in our days when, using a much simpler technical process (the motion picture) we are able to produce almost exact copies of the world's events. To sum up: the new, timely art of our days will arise beyond both naturalism and impressionism (although it will be a meld of the undeniable values of both of these schools).

It is a commonplace observation that the legacy, the absolute value we have received from the painting of past centuries resides first and foremost in the manner of treating a certain theme—that is, in the artist's evocative power. The social value inherent in the choice of subject is always temporary, and what makes the picture esthetically appreciable for posterity is the manner of its execution...And this is precisely the juncture we have envisioned as the logical meeting place of the poster and the new painting.

Not so long ago people would set their dogs on traveling salesmen to chase them from their doors, whereas these days they play quite a respectable role in society. In the same way the poster, formerly banished from the "sacred groves" of high art, has in our days acquired a very lively role that affects many of the more material moments of our lives.

The successful poster is a practically infallible touchstone of our commercial, industrial, political and artistic life. Every enterprise of any magnitude has given rise to its own mediator in the shape of a poster that does the job of a hundred thousand human voices in creating market publicity; its colors and figures blare into every seeing eye night and day, promoting the business interests of its sponsor.

The successful poster need not, (and does not) carry an image of the consumer item. It *wrests* the desired effect solely by means of its power of suggestion.

The successful poster is always conceived in a spirit of radicalism (its creator always intends it to break through a settled mass or overcome an opposing current). For this reason it always leaps onto the stage as a unique and absolute force, and never as merely one of an anonymous crowd. It is always agitative by nature, and essentially impossible to constrain within bounds. For a successful poster is meaningful not only as a business intermediary, but may be enjoyed and appreciated without any reservations as a pure artistic product, in the manner of a landscape or portrait. Without abandoning its real mission it may possess every single known esthetic value, and, what is more, may even introduce new esthetic values with greater facility than any "artistically" executed painting.

I am not sure whether the latest schools (Futurism, Cubism, Expressionism, Simultanism) have acknowledged the enormous expressive powers and countless new pictorial possibilities latent in the poster. One thing is certain, however: their diverse paths of discovery all gravitate toward the freewheeling, willful style of the poster.

No other generation of painters has had as much trouble with technical difficulties as our generation—Determinism versus the individual's will to freedom.

This revolutionary activity is novel only in its scale and in the diversity of its simultaneously appearing manifestations. Otherwise, each of these outbursts has been seen before in the course of the evolution of art. There was a reason for them then and likewise there is a reason for them now. At all times they were the harbingers of a vast social reform, or at any rate its concomitants. And if they had already existed during the Age of Christianity and the Age of Serfdom, then they surely must exist raised to the nth power in our age, rife with social problems, with its free competition and desire to change the world. Philosophy, politics and technology have all produced their revolutionary advances; now art must take a leap forward, no matter how many great masters it has had in the past.

In our day painters have new things to say, therefore their means of expression must be new as well.

The smooth, detailed manner of the classical painters is no longer adequate in our days; it is in fact jarring for contemporary subjects.

In our giant metropolises we have embarked upon the century of technology and sociology. The mystical contemplation of divinity has been topped by a thousand more burning problems; the apotheosis of peaceful rural idylls has been squeezed out of us by our modern nervous systems' greedy hunger for each momentary sensation. Instead of patriarchal acquiescence we are reeling in a storm of ill winds; the artist working in this century and wishing to render the character of this century must represent these times in each nerve fiber, each drop of blood, each piece of work.

Such artists today tend to be Futurists, Expressionists, and other "madmen," who, influenced by the times, struggle to find a conscious way out, while the "sober ones" are holding up the ladders that lead back to the essentially dead old masters. Inasmuch as the present century has created a chaotic melange in our society that is in the process of regaining its equilibrium, they are the new primitives of an eventually classical art. (Not to be confused with the spineless neo-primitives, nor with Henri Rousseau, who may be an autodidact blessed with genius, but has no special significance for the new painting.) Only in African art or in the classical primitives of the twelfth century can we find parallels to the explorations going on today.

Somewhat like the archaic primitives (but in more sophisticated and complex forms) today we live once again in the company of divine stammerers.

Such world-transforming changes imploding into humankind can no longer tolerate the aestheticization of form into a canon. The new message, soul-sparked by the heat of life, finds the existing means of expression inadequate. This accounts for the confused incomprehension reflected in the eyes of lay viewers, as well as the occasionally excessive *mannerisms* that seekers are swept into adopting. But this does not alter the value of the truths uncovered.

Just as the poster artist, they are warriors, prophets and human individuals within their own artistic spheres.

Their pictures intend to cast a purifying force over our age; their art constitutes the signposts for this century still in the throes of birth. Their pictures are not intended as interior decoration, but purport to be so many live question and exclamation marks for the thinking masses. (Admitting this much does not mean surrendering to the above-mentioned schools, which are still only steppingstones leading to the great ensemble and real value can only be born out of their conscious union.)

The moral individuality of the new painter is filled with faith and a longing for unity.

His paintings are instruments of war!

The new painter does not waste time on esthetic debate, and never considers nuances to be as important as the essence (in subject matter as well as in execution) which, in its grandeur is always a living and aggressive unit.

The new painting is created in the sign of monumentality, as revised by the intellect, and in its totality it always serves some aim that is more joyous than our present.

Its character is just like a poster's—individual demonstration and liberated energy! We have had enough of emerald-green seas, milky birch copses, and "realistically envisioned" waxen legs.

We are conscious of existing and our lives can accept only what is alive in art.

Our wholehearted desire is to see—in the manner of the poster that is a splendid complement to the modern city—the painting fill our rooms with a life that is extraneous to us and conquers all industrial objects. And just as posters vie for attention on colorful advertising hoardings with their stubborn, world-conquering moods, let the new paintings vie with each other in today's stale and somnolent exhibition galleries!

Translated by John Bátki

FOR THE COMPREHENSIVE *MA* EXHIBITION   Lajos Kassák
Originally published as "A *Ma* demonstrativ kiállitásához," *Ma* vol. II, no. 8–9
(September 15, 1918)

If some future chronicler/critic were to draw up the moral balance sheet of the *Ma* exhibition series, she would have to emphasize first and foremost that during the period of World War-related corruption only this group of artists dared go against the prevailing currents of opportunism. We opened our first exhibition in 1917, showing completely new work, and since then we have introduced three hitherto unknown artists. In our current comprehensive exhibition we are presenting to the public an entire group of young artists whose power to take a stand along with the requisite cultural preparedness, serve as the surest indicators of an evolution that will not be halted by any esthetic softening or warmongering propaganda. We are entangled in an age of scoundrels, commercial robber barons, and cannibals. We have stepped forth with program, relying on our humanity to prepare a consciously social directive for living. How much of this will we be able to realize? Woe to us if we compromise! Here are thirteen artists working unconstrained by the fetters of belonging to the same school, nonetheless making their way ahead together on the same avenue by virtue of their progressive talents and aggressive energies, to present for the public the only pure gift possible in this handful of Hungary yearning to be a part of international unity. What they have created is as yet in each case a credo and a spotlight aimed with critical purpose at the innermost self. Thus the stammering that besets young artists who have not yet achieved economy of means in their striving for the ultimate. But there is no cold commercial calculation here, no clever, fashionable attempts to be *modern* And in our days, when we are deprived of Paris, at a time when the *great* epigones have resumed their former copying machine selves, we consider this search for what is fresh in the psyche, what is new without claiming to be modern, to be all the more of a virtue, and proudly bear it as our banner. We insist on the new, not for the sake of novelty, but in order to present our unique individuality in any manner, and also in order to consume it without leaving any waste. Art, for some of us, is the substantial form of our lives. For us art is not an ivory tower, but a means, in the most everyday sense, to the universal plenum that is life. For us, art is active, agitative life itself that throbs with our blood. We have left far behind us the leaders of the pack of five or six years ago, and their entire swarm abuzz with so-called modernism. They have collapsed due to their own vacuity, as if the ground had been pulled from under their feet. Good God, if only the illustrated art books could have been knocked out of their hands as well! A new generation has arisen after them and a cruelly severe test of their nascent strength, the World War. For them, no help would be available from the influential West, while here at home every established spokesperson is either hostile or a neutral fence sitter. The only reception for the thirteen artists exhibiting here is bound to be malicious hostility or cowardly silence. But for them, this will merely mean an enforced increase of willpower. Today's tentative striving toward the light will be tomorrow's vigorous, full-bodied assault on darkness. For their art is not a piddling continuation of *l'art pour l'art* vaporings, but a commitment, a conscious stand against the weight of all of yesterday's burdens. Here are thirteen islands of light in a sea of darkness. Life predominant. We believe this is the first generation to sink healthy roots into the land we call our home, where all that is new is commonly turned into clever fashion and where epigones can always count on being cuddled. We are unaware of what is happening right now in the great cities abroad with their classical art traditions and constant hunger for the new, but we think it unlikely that their young have fallen back on Baudelaire, or are rediscovering Manet, or, even less likely, Ingres or Renoir. Political advances are making a worldwide clamor; the same must hold true in the arts. The killing fields of the war are fertilizing new, more willful energies—preparations for some great communion in socialism. That is the direction these thirteen artists point out with the banners of their art. And their present exhibition is proof that, once the borders will again allow through trains, ships, airplanes for the cause of life, these artists will be the first to demonstrate that in spite of all our isolation we *were* here and lived our lives, magnetized by our communion with the world around us, that is, contemporary culture.

Translated by John Bátki

LAJOS TIHANYI György Bölöni
Originally published as "Tihanyi Lajos," *Ma* vol. 3, no. 10 (October 15, 1918)

The artist who is proud of himself and his uniqueness, who refuses to bargain and compromise and insists on painting relentlessly what he thinks is best, is hardly likely to find a home among the rapidly growing multitude of salons, associations, and art galleries in Hungary. That is precisely why Tihanyi found *Ma*, and *Ma* found Tihanyi.

Tihanyi's genesis is brief. Eight years ago, when The Eight was formed, he soon became the most noteworthy participant in the group. There was nothing tentative or uncertain about him. His manner of painting, just like his manner toward people, has never been hesitant. He never yielded to any special interest, friendship or sympathy; he had become implacable and incorruptible. He has never compromised, and loved only the sincere and the true, only the artist who does not dissemble or beat around the bush, whose conscience is clear even when roused from a dream in the middle of the night. He is beyond reproach as a man and as an artist; he has not sacrificed artistic integrity for superficial values. He is an excellent judge of character, and has as little use for the frivolous and the trivial in human beings as well as in art as an ant has for ultraviolet rays. His is a critical, logical and objective intellect—full of curiosity and the will to dissect. He is stubborn and impatient.

This portrait of the man is part and parcel of his art: Tihanyi's character pervades and exudes from the works of Tihanyi the painter. His pictures are founded not only on observation but also on meditation and astute judgment. For Tihanyi a person's appearance means more than for other artists. In his childhood his hearing became impaired, and his other senses had to make up for this loss. Thus the eyes are far more significant for him than for others, more important than for any other painter. For him, vision has to augment the sense of hearing, so that he is compelled to read from a person occupying the space in front of him everything that someone else would find out only after lengthy and intimate conversation. Instead of sound vibrations, rays of light must convey for him those true confessions and light is his channel of psychological perception. Tihanyi is a portrait artist, but before he even touches the brush—because of his hearing deficiency—he is already automatically making a study of the subject, whose psychic mysteries he can unravel only through his vision.

Thus a sensory impairment creates a position of strength as the starting point of his art. It had made him isolated, capable of building out of himself, and developed the ability to emphasize the essentials in his art. A caricature, too, emphasizes essential characteristics. Tihanyi, however, never lapses into caricature, he has no penchant for the grotesque, and stays within the boundaries of reality, although he quite mercilessly paws the faces he paints. He accentuates the essentials, he touches upon the salient forms of objects and bodies, and from these constituents he constructs paintings that astonish with their visionary power. His pictures, be it portraits, landscapes or figures, do not rely upon a facile verisimilitude, a dry emphasis on character, but neither do they lead to documentary synthesis or stylization. Even though his portraits juggle human skulls with a freedom and confidence as if they were inanimate objects, his fundamental nourishment comes from corporeal breasts and he does not stray far from life. He is not the speedy painter who is ever ready to sketch and finishes the work in one sitting. Instead, he is meditative, prefers to penetrate his subjects to the marrow, never satisfied with quickly and easily capturing the subject; his vision pins down the subject for scrutiny. When he paints you he looks for not only the skin and bones, the shape and anatomical configuration of your head; his brush slices open your epidermis and trepans your skull for a look at what dwells inside your central nervous system, inside your brain. Tihanyi manner of seeing and constructing, his very vision is more decisive and profound than others'—for him the subject is not merely an external phenomenon but a problem to be dissected apart, one that must be resolved both psychologically and geometrically. He has introduced the psychological portrait into Hungarian painting. We have the impression that his portraits somehow give voice to the subconscious—the viewer does not merely glide by on the surface—besides the palpable forms some intangible quality seems to hover in his figures. His portraits vibrate somewhere between the disquieting psychic contents of Van Gogh's portraits (although stylistically the two are far apart) and the figures of Dostoevsky.

That explains why his studio and now his exhibition gallery suggest a psychiatric clinic, a laboratory of the soul. He is not intimidated by names, by prominent people, by writers—the very subjects with whom a painter rarely fills a gallery. He is able to handle these heads full of character and faces that radiate the life of the soul. In Kosztolányi's face he shows the timorousness of the child as well as the terrors of a neurotic. In his self-portraits he fights the most ferocious and instructive battles against himself. Lajos Fülep is shown in all his haughty and superior frostiness. Béla Révész is seen submerged into a brown study. Lajos Kassák, despite Slavic and feminine features, evinces a stubborn fortitude befitting an ancient crone.

Portrait painting has not made Tihanyi one-sided, but instead increased his competence in other subjects. Tihanyi seems to be executing a portrait even when painting a landscape, extracting the essential and unique features as he does from a face. He never looks for the general and the familiar, as if all he ever saw were only extraordinary landscapes, whereas it is simply his painterly imagination that makes them unique and seen for the first time. In the same landscape another person would not even see the same phenomena, while Tihanyi seizes the most outstanding motif. At times it seems as if it were not a human but a little demon that sat before his easel. In him the natural wrestles with the supernatural, in a demonic manner.

He has a Gothic sense of form. This is not said lightly. His entire sense of life is Gothic, massive, aspiring, and struggling with mass, and this vision goes into the construction of every one of his heads and landscapes. Tihanyi emphasizes the sculptural values of objects. For him light and color are not ends in themselves but are subservient to the three-dimensional development of forms. His forms revert to the simplicity of geometric figures, and each object assumes the guise of a latent geometric form. This is not Cubism, but rather a recognition of the significance of forms, the problematics of three-dimensionality and the placement of bodies in space; this is a tectonic art that corrals living reality within closed forms.

Of the generation that eight years ago in a fascinating series of rebellious eruptions explored its strivings and artistic aims Tihanyi alone has remained most consistently within himself. Consistency is not always a virtue, but in his case it was, for it meant a defiant retention of purely artistic aims by a determined talent well on its way, cognizant of further development to come from his own resources. He has never beat around the bush, and has never compromised. He has deepened and perfected his ongoing involvement with the formal problems of old. He has always respected El Greco and Cézanne as his forebears, but has also divested himself of this psychic heritage when it constituted an obstacle or constraint for his stubborn and obstinately assertive individuality.

Until this day Hungarian art has not been aware of this painter. It is time to recognize him as our most outstanding portraitist.

Translated by John Bátki

JÁNOS MÁTTIS-TEUTSCH   Iván Hevesy
Originally published as "Máttis Teutsch János," *Ma* vol. 3, no. 11 (November 20, 1918)

The art of János Máttis-Teutsch is an utterly subjective art. It does not provide an experience of space or form, it does not render objects, the relative or absolute truths of nature. It does not investigate the colors, forms, and three-dimensional realities of the external world. It does not even tempt our eyes by the ephemeral flash of impressions. What he does accomplish is a pure lyricism, a pure hypnotism of feelings. For in the case of Máttis-Teutsch feeling is more important than vision. The vision itself, and the natural forms it conveys, can only be a means for the expression of his feelings. Thus the forms derived from objects serve only as a means, and for this reason he treats them most arbitrarily, depriving them of every vestige of their natural character: *from the actual forms occurring in nature he creates abstract aesthetic forms, which are no longer the symbols of objects but the signifiers of feelings.*

The art of Máttis-Teutsch breaks away from nature and from matter, to become entirely spiritual, in order to express the soul. It expresses the soul and its every tremor, registers its very pulse and dynamism, the varied and multi-directional vibrations set off in it by each impression. It would be very difficult to formulate in words the feelings that constitute the contents of his images. It would not be much help to designate them by means of such primitive generalizations as sadness, joy, desire, excitement, or calm, for these words fail to denote the very qualities that are unique and original in those feelings, or more correctly, *sensations*. For this painting of feelings is no mere naive indulgence in allegories, but is the direct expression of inner states of feeling by resorting to absolute painterly means. It is closely related to music, and is analogous to it in both form and content. The only difference is that Máttis-Teutsch does not use sounds, but makes his music with line and color.

Even if we cannot translate his images into verbal concepts, we may designate the musical scale of feelings through which he is most completely able to express his artistic individuality. He is able to convey both of the extreme poles of feeling: action-filled drama and conflict, as well as passive surrender of the self. The latter passivity is no doubt the element that dominates in Máttis-Teutsch's character. We can find the entire spectrum of longing in his works, at times so tender as to be feminine and sentimental, but often in the form of mighty eruptions. His art is inspired and imbued by the fermenting desires and tense instincts residing in the unconscious; his art is the purest erotic art in existence. The analysis of the psychic characteristics that gave birth to these pictures is a task best left to the Freudians.

From the above, it should be clear what kind of perspective we should take in viewing Máttis-Teutsch's pictures. We must make the effort to empathize and attempt to directly experience the picture by entering it in the same way that we appreciate a musical composition. We must not try to find a meaning for the motifs, and to determine what they *depict*, for these pictures have as little to do with depicting the external world as, say, Beethoven's "Moonlight" sonata does. One may object that anyone may project whatever feelings he wishes into these pictures. Well and good; but then remember that the same argument may be used against all of music, from Bach to Debussy. It would also be a mistake to declare that Máttis-Teutsch is nothing but a decorative painter. He is only superficially related to decoration, through the non-imitative aspect of his art. Simple decoration is always content with color harmonies and linear rhythms that are pleasing to the senses. Máttis-Teutsch, as we have seen, offers much more, something that is far more profound.

The artistic development of Máttis-Teutsch has consisted of a gradual elimination of rendering natural objects and occurrences; he has progressed from the reality of phenomena to the reality of sensations.

The majority of his pictures exhibited a year ago had still been dominated by natural forms and effects; phenomena and feelings were still in a state of compromise. But the road of his future development toward an increasingly abstract expression was already clearly indicated. The works in his current exhibition manifest a purely abstract, consistently elaborated manner of form-giving. Only a smaller series of oil paintings represent the transitional stage.

The feeling-images are presented in three different orchestrations: as linoleum cuts, watercolors and oils. The linoleum cuts are the most highly realized works of Máttis-Teutsch in this modality; they are completely finished and integral, without a single superfluous gesture or line. Watercolor and oils create fuller and more varied effects than the simplicity of the linoleum cut. Their polyphonic wealth is able to express a greater variety and abundance of feelings as well. If the linoleum cut is a solo piano, then the watercolor and oils are the full orchestra.

Translated by John Bátki

ONWARD ON OUR WAY   Lajos Kassák

Originally published as "Tovább a magunk utján," *Ma* vol. 3, no. 12 (December 20, 1918)

It has been two years since we first, emphatically, bundled together on our pages the young artists of this chaotic world. In other lands at that time red lights had already been lit to signal the revolution that would end this war, and that had been our way of greeting those rebellious few, by asserting our presence and our desire to be like them. Not exclusively Hungarian, nor citizens sneaking a glance at the bourgeois tradition, but rather people *born into a new ideology and new morality*. Not merely passive pacifists, but active anti-militarists.

That was two years ago. We were facing the organized might of a bourgeois great power and yet the fight we fought then had been far more hopeful. We fought against war, our struggle based on the class forces. Since then the world war has consumed itself and the revolution has attained full sway only to fade away, with the bourgeoisie gaining the upper hand.

Today we are able to see clearly the results of the revolution in Hungary; with these our class-conscious proletariat has taken on the greatest of challenges. The night of October 30 has, for the time being, dulled the sharp edges of the class forces confronting each other, while helping into the saddle the most spineless stratum of society, the capitalist bourgeoisie.

The collapse of the war meant a chance for a totally new social structure; what we have managed to glean from it is nothing more than the historically inevitable forward sweep of liberated forces, with no reorganizing contribution from the productive labors of the human intellect and will. For us the revolution has petered out before it had a chance to ripen into a creative force, for lack of a receptive soil—the educated will of the one and only revolutionary element, the proletariat. It is first and foremost because of the education of the masses that the Russian revo-lution, likewise arising out of the bankruptcy of the war, has become a world-changing force. With us there has never been an attempt of any conceptual mag-nitude to break down the petty bourgeois morality of the working classes, to turn their desire for patriotic comforts into an awareness of revolt against all forms of servitude. The revolution in Russia was the final result of an internal evolution taking place within the minds and heart-blood of individuals, while with us it was only the accidental interplay of externals that brought about the possibility of a vast revolution. In Russia the soldiers liberated from the frontline became the spark that ignited the revolution and they have remained its most tenacious supporters to this day, whereas our demoralized army had never been transformed into an active revolutionary force. It simply disintegrated, and given the lack of revolutionary leadership we are lucky if it does not become the tool of the counter-revolutionary forces that are already organizing themselves.

We could blame the Social Democratic Party for this neglect, were we not aware of their delimiting program which (temporarily, according to them) does not call for a fundamentally new social structure but merely asks for the amelioration of the current situation—that is, it culminates in bourgeois radicalism.

As we can see, eighty percent of the Social Democrats' ideals have been realized. Therefore a revolutionary mass conscious of its class relations and intending to advance its position must first of all break open the platform framework of its own party, the Social Democrats, who have missed a ripe opportunity for a creative move. It must demonstrate that this party works in the spirit of compromise and that the results achieved by it were not won by the revolutionary proletariat but are facile changes of outward form based on the old status quo. It must be pointed out that this party is not fighting for the ideal of maximal human welfare, and is content with helping the two opposing classes meet halfway, through a passive and irresponsible process of embourgeoisement.

That's where we stand today. The bourgeois democracy has softened the provocative rigidity of a tradition-bound bourgeoisie and has thereby effectively demobilized the proletarian masses whose energies were predestined to fight to achieve their aims. For we are well aware that whereas the bourgeois capitalist had not even been willing to sit down at the negotiating table with trade union representatives, the bourgeois employer will always be ready to sign a reasonable collective agreement. But beware! For such agreements will not acknowledge your rightful claims, but will be another form of fortifying their own imperialist aims. All such agreements appeal to reason-ableness. And all such agreements soften your explicit demands into a whimper for pity. Whereas formerly bourgeois society strove to silence your voice as economically menacing and esthetically jarring, today's bourgeois democracy encourages you to group into associations; being a proponent of political compromise, it rightly considers your associations to be the hotbeds of rationalism.

So beware! For today's mushrooming associations are a symptom of bourgeois society—these councils of housewives, dental technicians, coal thieves, and artists, with ministerial patronage. And they, wearing the mask of sympathy, of course always nod in approval. For they are the simplified mirrors of this world. They have already realized that your associations are institutions for the assistance to the destitute, and also realize that the loud voices of masterless artists are merely vociferating for patronage.

Beware, all you people committed to doing honest work, physical or intellectual! Your time has come! Let democracy's knights of decorum step aside! Do not swear by the sacredness of party unity, but abused and exploited as you are, be anti-democratic if need be, and fight your way into the executive forum! The equilibrium you will thus create will be the purest form of democracy! For if you agree to compromise today, tomorrow you will languish on a chain of your own making! By then it will be obvious that you were not ready, and that the times have passed you by!

Believe no one except your aching, dissatisfied selves. Promises are nothing, and the gifts of these *reasonable folks* are less than nothing—for in exchange you will have to renounce the right to equality.

And this is where our art and worldview come in to join the social revolutionary struggle for a human ideal that rests on political and economic heights of equal altitude. We pro-claim the most far-reaching class warfare, while we, as intellectual and physical laborers dissociate ourselves from the foregoing politics of art and of society. We are artists! Not precious formalists hiding in cocoons, but workers who possess active brain- and will-power. Our ideals are rooted in progressive thought and healthy feeling. And by means of the class struggle we intend to re-shape this world along the lines of our ideals. We intend to create a communist art alongside the communist economic system. We are socialists, body and soul, and so it is not the tenets of a materialist philosophy that we want to turn into art, but rather it is the absolute purity of the spirit, the surplus of maximal life that we sing as bread and wine for the soul of the working masses. Our surplus, intended as a higher-order necessity of life, for their benefit.

We want a socialist art, but, again let us emphasize, one that is beholden to no external directives. We cannot fawn on the wealthy, nor do we intend to regress into the ranks of the culturally impoverished. Our role is not identical to that of the party agitator, just as the research scientist's role is different from the elementary school science teacher's. We believe that our new art, and the worldview that goes with it, is as useful, as vitally essential for building a new world as any other profession. And therefore, in the face of all other viewpoints, we continue on our way, which is not the versification of doctrines, the telling of stories in pictures, the lamenting of tragedies in music, but the eternal yearning for a great, harmonious wholeness. We are here not only to diagnose but also to predict. We are not here to cater to the public, but to make it work. We feel the untenableness of present-day life and our minds are capable of constructing a new world, our world in whose lap sits the new human.

We have our roots in the masses seeking to redeem themselves, and there are others of our kind the world over.

Brothers! Artists of the new faith, of whatever nationality!

The handful of us, here in this grief-stricken Hungarian land, welcome you to communism!

Translated by John Bátki

THE GALIMBERTIS[1] Béla Uitz
Originally published as "Galimbertiék," *Ma* vol. 3, no. 12 (December 20, 1918)

The art of the Galimbertis was conducted in the spirit of the highest morality. They never wrangled for the spoils and never wished to show more than what they had, more than the work they had effectively finished. Of their generation, they were the most persistent and had advanced the farthest, to shine their clear light past the jungle of the Hungarian art world. Viewing the chronological series of their works offers the best proof of their substantial achievement. Starting with their first Nagybánya paintings, all the way to the last compositions they finished in Amsterdam, we can observe a logical development that is devoid of any compromise or careerism. Their earliest works arose within the framework of Impressionism, the dominant movement of those days. But viewers of their current exhibition could very well object to my mention of any "ism" in connection with their work. Therefore let me make it clear: in their case the mention of an "ism" does not imply belonging to any school (as in the case of epigones), but refers to a worldview. Or, to put it more accurately, a non-purposive vision of the world by the not yet definitive ego.

Dematerialized nature is the constant theme of their art. In a word, it is spiritual, not material. Their paintings are constructive, but without the speculative sterility that chokes off intuition.

We see this constructive art at its best and most developed form in their last paintings. These large-scale visual compositions are resolved by using the means of a constructive worldview, Cubism. But again we are not referring to any school. For the Cubism of the Galimbertis juxtaposes the contradictory methods of the various Cubist schools so that they mutually enhance each other, following the laws of an inner logic. They have reached the stage of synthesis.

The components of their paintings are creative (musical) and material (readily received) Cubism. If we are able to grasp the deeply felt and logical counterbalancing of these two forces in the Galimbertis' canvases, then we have glimpsed one of the finest instances of fully aware painting in Hungarian art, with the most promising possibilities for further development. For the first principle is purely self-generated, or arises from an imaginary motif, whereas the second leads back to the richest possibilities of form-giving.

1 Sándor Galimberti and his wife Valéria Dénes Galimberti married in 1911, exhibited together in Paris and Hungary, and were invited to participate in the 1915 Panama-Pacific International Exposition in San Francisco. Dénes died on July 18, 1915; her husband committed suicide two days later. [Ed.]

The first is the visualization of the psyche; the second is the dissolving of the universe. The first is purely spiritual; the second is the spiritualization of the given world. The first is the purest, solitary self; the second is the world's self. Of the two, which is the more important? For a truly successful painting, both are indispensable—the first for its nobility, the second for its immeasurability. In the paintings of the Galimbertis both are present as the unity of the absolute. Thus they are our signposts toward an art of the collective.

A painting that does not raise any questions is a mere replica of the given world, a photograph. The art of the Galimbertis pours forth question upon question, thus forming a spiritual and material surplus value. Spiritual in the universal sense of composition, construction, concentration, etc.—and material in its motifs: buildings, towers, ships, water, sun, people, etc. However, even their material motifs always possess spiritual value. For example, take their leaning towers and the leaning tower of Pisa. The latter is an accident, whereas the former obeys the necessity of a law. The oft-praised wonder of the world at Pisa was not intended to lean, its "miracle" is an architectural fluke— while the leaning towers of the Galimbertis are surrounded by leaning houses and serve the compositional requirements of a greater whole. Their leaning towers and crooked houses and masts all serve to emphasize concentric values.

The chaos "envisioned" in their paintings carries within it the law of the strictest unity. Their art is not cleverly imitative, but by stating problems of worldview and technical solutions, offers a psychic presence; their painting is life itself.

The art of the Galimbertis originated in a spirit of universality. And here lies their tragedy: they have sensed and signaled a new worldview, but death has cut off the promising arc of their careers.

Translated by John Bátki

Around World War I two artists' groups of international character emerged in Poland: Bunt in Poznań, connected mainly with the German art world (principally Berlin), and Jung Idysz, a group of Jewish artists in Łódź. These were the first groups to take up, more or less decisively, the problems of avant-garde art, such as placing the work of art in a social context. Both groups can be placed in the history of Expressionism, though for entirely different reasons.

Bunt, connected with *Zdrój* (The Source) published by Jerzy Hulewicz (1886–1941), was close to the Berlin Aktion group and the Der Sturm Gallery. The active link between Berlin and Poznań, some 300 km to the east, was Stanisław Kubicki (1889–1942). His art, his position on artistic issues, and his activity on the international scene contributed greatly to both the artistic and ideological self-definition of the group—not only their aesthetic models which drew on Expressionism, but most importantly their activist ideology, rooted in the ideas of the European anarchism. It was the basis of the major conflict between the publisher of *Zdrój* and Kubicki who saw art as a revolutionary activity aimed at the bourgeoisie's institutions and ideology. His position became much more radical at the beginning of the 1920s and was manifest in Kubicki's active presence in the circles of German artists of the left. He took part, for instance, in the First Congress of Progressive Artists in Düsseldorf where he signed *Die Kommune* manifesto.

The Poznań artists and the Jewish artists from Łódź had some strong personal contacts, though these had no noticeable effects in artistic actions. Unlike the Bunt artists, the artists of Jung Idysz initially attempted to create art either within the framework of rather traditional spiritualism— as, for example, Jankiel Adler (1895–1949)—or they looked for self-definition in stylistic categories, in national (Jewish) identity somewhere between the Judaic tradition and modern art. Soon some of them became more radical, both artistically and ideologically—especially Henryk Berlewi (1894–1967) who, while taking part in the Düsseldorf Congress as one of the artists from Jung Idysz, broke away from the Expressionist tradition. He moved toward international Constructivism, which he had first encountered in 1921, when he met El Lissitzky in Warsaw.

Around that time, Futurism in Poland occupied a somewhat singular position as a stand-in for Dadaism. The main figure of Polish Futurism was Bruno Jasieński (1901–39), whose manifestoes sometimes went against the most rudimentary rules of grammar and spelling. In the public consciousness Futurism was associated with extreme radicalism in art and behavior, but in the visual arts it was not associated with concrete artistic activity, although the term was popular amongst the contemporary art critics and often used interchangeably with other stylistic terms.

Translated by Wanda Kemp-Welch

TO THE HOLY REBEL   Jerzy Hulewicz

Originally published as "Do świętego buntownika," *Zdrój* no. 1 (1918)

For thou hast raised up rebellion and made holy dissent to the Spirit grown cold in the one form, and having partaken of the divine blood of Christ, thou hast given new form to the Spirit, bringing shame on earthly-mindedness and giving the sublime back to form—for this praise be to thee, Holy Rebel!

For thou hast renounced that which was not from the Spirit and stripped bare the body to the regret of the parent, to the outrage of the bishop's saintly eyes and to the amazement of his eminent retinue, so that the lords and their pages shuddered, the matrons' clouded eyes became transfixed with shame and the virgins' cheeks flushed, for thou hast made nakedness holy—praise be to thee!

For thou hast raised the Spirit above to the holiness of tradition and thrown away all excellence acquired by learning, who hast made the soul wander in search of new form, which thou hast found, having made severance with the day and the link with eternity; for thou loved Life and scorned the dead form—praise be to thee, the Holy Rebel!

God gave the Spirit to His creation and laid upon it the hallmark of Rebellion.

HE GAVE LIFE.

When it started to cool, God did violence to the old form, and taking delight in the Virgin's Womb, uncorrupted by the tradition of sin, impregnated it with Rebellion and—REDEEMED.

Whenever life was close in form to expiring, God filled it with His own suffering, in order to give new form the hallmark of perfect suffering.

THE CROSS OF CHRISTS.

God suffering eternally for the perfection of the Spirit in form.

The hallmark of divine suffering rested in thou. Thus the Lord once more bestowed upon His creation the mystery of Love, that divine blood, flowing from Christ's five wounds, might anointed the Spirit in new form.

THE REBELLION OF LOVE.

Thou hast walked into the dispirited crowd and rekindled the torch of a bloody revolution.

Thou hast carried the embers of Rebellion to the holy lives of beggars and to the lives of the mighty, who have found their dignity in suffering.

Thou hast spread the divine spark with a wide cast over the royal heads of sultans and the old heads of monks.

Where form expires, thy fire spreads and burns death unto this day.

Thy holy rebellion gave all creation understanding of the Spirit, so that the wolf has become the guardian of infants, swallows have checked their restlessness to pay attention to the Divine word being made incarnate while other creatures, having paid tribute to holy humility, filled with the Spirit, gave unwilling acknowledgement to fossilized, depraved man.

The golden calf, incensed with the stifling stench of slavery and the false golden halo, armed with the force of the false cross, mounted opposition against thy holy Rebellion and said:

"Rebel, bow down and praise me."

But thou hast praised the glory of the Spirit, so that the golden calf cursed thee in the name of God, thy Lord.

And he supposed to be the Lord of Rebellion whom God bestowed upon thee when the holy source thou strengthened with great humility of body and allowed to cement it with a written law to defy the golden calf, his peace and laziness, in all his sated glory.

Thy tears are the joy of life and the calmness of the soul.

Thou announceth the joy of life, commanding all to draw freely from the Fullness of Life.

And when the Pharisees and priests, having decked their bodies out with stately robes and numerous devotional articles adopted from pagans to cover their inner emptiness and dwarfing of the spirit, bearing on the false witness of God, cursing all conception of Spirit and all change of form as evil, contrary to God—thou, the Holy Rebel, standeth naked in front of the Lord and men, and singeth thine own song, as though an adventurer, and thy singing is likewise pleasing to God whether it be a hymn or the troubadour's love song.

THE REBELLION OF SONG.

Through the stakes of the burnt-offering, through the prison's iron bars—there resounds the Rebellion of song with the clattering of the chains of bondage; through the barricades and the Bastilles, through the dungeons and the galleys there resounds the hum of a secret song, the Rebellion ambushing the powerful of this world.

For thou hast returned Life to the Spirit and the power of struggle—therefore praise be to thee thrice!

For thou hast given the holy Power of endurance to the Rebellion and Power in the new form of creation—therefore praise be to thee thrice.

For thou hast given Victory of the Spirit in live form and led us towards divine perfection—therefore praise be to thee thrice, HOLY REBEL!

Translated by Wanda Kemp-Welch

NOTES   Stanisław Kubicki

Originally published as "Anmerkungen," *Die Aktion*, special *Bunt* issue, nos. 21/22, 35/36 (June 1, 1918)

I. Art has nothing in common with the concept of "beauty and goodness" (*kalokagathia*) as conceived in inept brains. We are far removed from the aesthetic game [that is played] as if art—the quintessence of our lives—were at the service of bourgeois pleasures.

II. The fight is on, not for images of aesthetic issues (gypsy studio anecdotes) but for MAN and for our DAY (it will come), against the sordidness of your day and the ugliness of its articles of faith, for which (we feel ourselves to be responsible) we blush.

III. WE are Art. The petrified forms of our life (forms that appear comic to *you*) are the building blocks of a future life, the ultimate conclusions of which are (not to us) *terrifying*.

Translated by David Britt

ON EXPRESSIONISM Zbigniew Pronaszko

Originally published as "O ekspresjonizmie," *Maski* (1918)

The Polish Expressionist Group has opened its first joint exhibition. They came together and separated themselves from the rest of Polish painting not because they considered themselves to be implicitly better. The reason lies elsewhere—it lies in the need for a collective effort in art. There is not a single event in the art of creating style, generally speaking, whether as an expression of a given epoch, of a particular school or guild, or even of a passing movement—which would not be the result of collective work. This means that individuals sharing an affinity, being in regular contact with one another, achieve a common expression more quickly—though each by a different path and through different means.

The notion that this regular contact might have a negative influence on individuals by making them more similar and thus losing them in the general expression, is a mistaken one. Above all, it would not be harmful to the general expression of, let us say, style, for one works for it, and it remains the only legacy of general work, as it was its only target. It is sufficient to take as an example here all sorts of styles, such as Gothic or guild painting, which have not left a single name, in spite of having left great works of art. Besides this the individual, as long as he be a strong individuality, will remain so, and conversely, the weak individuality, even if it were left solely to itself, would at the first opportunity latch onto a stronger one and remain under its influence. The aforementioned group came out under the name Expressionism. The issue here is not that of name, which is as incidental as Futurism, Cubism, Orphism and so many others pertaining to Expressionism; we are concerned with the essence of things.

Today's Expressionism has its origins in its predecessor of yesterday, Neo-impressionism, which in turn takes its precedent from Impressionism. Nineteenth century Impressionism was simply a return to color, which, having been thoroughly neglected, was just beginning to be reborn under the brush of Delacroix. And here came a whole plethora of colorists with Manet at their head: Degas, Renoir, Claude Monet, Sisley, Pissarro and others. In the name of the return to color they subjected it to an exhaustive analysis, which, uncovering in it new horizons and values, nevertheless had to remain within the sphere of incidental experiment. For wanting to progress to construction, whose condition is form, one has to follow the opposite path, the path of gathering and formulation, the path of synthesis.

The struggle for form only began when Van Gogh, and more particularly Cézanne, took up the challenge of these newly discovered values. Experience had already taught Cézanne that changing the coloring of a body resulted in the destruction of its structure. He knew that painting is not just the imitation of objects with the help of color and line, but is the art of submitting plastic consciousness to instinct.

Essentially: painting cannot be a "return to nature," painting must always be a return to the picture. Whilst a picture is the deliberate, logical filling of a certain space with particular forms, constituting in this way a unified, unchanging organism.

What I call "form" is the convention with which I express a given shape; what I call shape is the appearance of any spatial body, e.g. a fragment of sky surrounded by clouds, a patch of light on a forehead, a tree, the shadow of a tree and the like. Shape, as an expression of nature, is dependent on circumstances and surroundings, and is thus incidental; form, as an expression of creativity, is permanent. The human form is an incidental shape, subject to change; the human figure, on the other hand—e.g. in Gothic art—is a form: shapes forming convention, a certain system. For a picture to have form it is necessary that: 1. all its objects should have form; 2. their form should be uniform; 3. the relationship between objects should be precise and organic. Shapes in nature, arranging themselves by chance (light), rule out for this same reason any purposefulness in the construction of the picture, that is to say one configuration of shapes rather then another, and any "bending" of shapes to suit one's purposes is futile; they are too different, they have too many different types, in a word, because of their dependence on the moment, surroundings and matter, of which they are an expression, they are too incidental to be able to harmonize into one organism. Hence the need to create form. For it is through this, the rendering of shape with a particular convention, that groups of one type are produced and brought together to a common denominator, and relationships between forms are made possible. It is also for this reason that if one is painting shapes, and not their conventions, one does not go beyond the boundaries of imitating nature, which has nothing to do with painting, because it is only through form that leads the path to construction and organism: the essence of any creativity. Artists have from the earliest time, been struggling towards construction, heading along different paths for the same goal. These signs—symbols, which when appropriately related expressed painterly concepts, have also been known for a long time (one ancient source being hieroglyphics).

[...] These forms—signs, suit one another better, are easier to relate to one another, insofar as they are simpler and more primary and their scale is more limited. This is why construction so often goes hand in hand with the primitive: Assyria, Byzantium, or even our own primitives: glass painting from the Podhale region. [...] The tradition of the sign (form) is as old as art itself, and it is only its external appearance that is subject to change. It is known in Persia and China, Ancient Greece, Byzantium, Gothic, baroque (although only in part), as it is in the efforts of most recent times. Life and nature are ruled by one set of laws, pictures by another. The life of a picture is its logic, logic ruling over forms and patches in uncompromising connection. Just as in a picture there are no such things as digestion or the circulation of blood, in nature there are no lines or interdependence of forms; these are the products of art.

The life of a picture depends solely on its construction; its subject can only be a question of form and color, since nature serves as its source, groundwork, the theme on which the picture builds its subject. Thus anything that is not a question of form and color does not belong to painting. Such things as for example anatomy, perspective, literature, that is: various allegories or stories, symbolic puzzles, any kind of philosophy of history, even the most national (Grottger). All this can belong to whatever it likes: to medicine, engineering, literature, the war archives ("war art"), "national mementos," or even to an individual career—yet it will never have anything to do with painting. [...] "The third dimension," often employed in Expressionism, is something widely at variance with traditional perspective. This utilizes certain directions of line, the schematic gradation of color, and the source of light, which placed in one place, gives out in only one direction, in the manner of a theatrical reflector with coulisses. The third dimension of the Expressionists on the other hand, depends on elevations of the object, which when developed, come together mutually to constitute its volume. While looking at or contemplating an object, I do not only see it frontally, quite the contrary: a whole range of its plans and views enter my consciousness and it is only after I have reassembled them that I come to receive its full expression, its essence.

We meet with the need to differentiate between and to reassemble these views on a daily basis. One so often hears the comment that a given picture does not give us the desired "impression." These words express the lack of those views, which we can remember or see, besides the one we apprehend in the picture. Anyone can put this to the test on himself—it is sufficient to imagine a well-known object: we will certainly remember it along with a thousand of its aspects. The same applies to the relationship between objects. Objects in nature do not exist in isolation: their shapes combine with one another, they divide or complement one another in the general chaos: this is why there are no so called "contours," this is a billboard invention. It often happens that the shapes of a more distant object so dominate in our consciousness those of a closer object, that they nearly cover them or intersect; it is the task of painting to identify these shapes, gather them into forms and organize them in such a way as to only put across those which are the most essential, which contribute to the expression of the object and to associate or separate these out, adding or separating off complementaries. It is in this way that the infinite sphericity of the picture, that mysteriousness which is so enchanting, emerges. [...]

If anyone should reproach us that the picture is, as a result of this, unclear, that it "doesn't make sense," then we will reply that the picture makes sense only through its power of being, and is not the logic of forms and colors.

The goal here is expression, which is revealed with the help of the sign, conventions, reacting to shapes, which come to us whilst we contemplate an object. For this expression the essential task of painting is to find form and it is this which Expressionism strives for. Impressionism gave the optical impression of an object; Expressionism seeks to reveal its expression.

Translated by Klara Kemp-Welch

EXPRESSIONISM (FRAGMENTS FROM A LECTURE) Jankiel Adler
Originally published as "Ekspresjonizm (fragmenty z prelekeji)," *Nasz Kurier* no. 292 (December 5, 1920)

We are the children of the twentieth century. Our lullabies were drowned by the noise of street. We spent our childhood in brick houses of great city similar to army barracks.

Our first breath was of stuffy and stifling air. Our first walks were accompanied by a choir of a thousand voices of trams ringing, horse drawn cabs rolling, goods carts croaking, automobiles galloping, noisy pedestrian precincts cutting across streets in thousands of diagonals.

And the further away from childhood we grow, the closer to us seem the noise of the city and its chaos, the human tumult, and life's whirl. From all walls shout motley sign-boards to us: yellow and black posters wind around our brains; we are drunken with yellow sun spots smiling at us from shining roofs; a spectacle of thousands colors, of sunlight, of people, of their clothes, flashes in front of our eyes.

This shouting and shining whirl penetrates with its entirety, its whole dynamics not just the human eye. Who could paint with the time-honored calm of the classics the volcano of contemporary life? Who could absorb this whirl through the eye alone, but not through the mind, so much sharper and deeper?

We bow our heads to the masters of the Renaissance, to the great artistic personalities of the baroque; however, our most profound reverence is for the Infinity, for those who did not seclude themselves in the sarcophagus of theory. The closest to us are Gothic artists whose architecture knows no limits. Notre-Dame in Paris, and Reims Cathedral are without gables, therefore we can extend them in our minds to infinity.

We have thrown away sight having changed hearing for sight, and with this sight we see only the surface.

Our generation made them a commonplace, devoid of wings, pushing them towards appearances and superficiality. Great strength is needed in order to get rid of the deposit of this superficiality, to erase this nothingness which we owe to looking only with the eyes.

We, the young, have quite lost the relationship to God of our fathers; we have lost everything possessed by those satisfied with themselves—half sin, half virtue; our trust in people was poisoned when we were still young, and in our hearts we are weighed down with the burden of a great, great longing for God and eternity, for the power that made Creation happen, for Logos.

The art of the twentieth century, Expressionist art, was born from this longing and it is the seventh day and the week of the commonplace is over.

Expressionists, who do not see in phenomena only external and accidental things as the Impressionists had been doing, are conscious that everything is unity and eternity, and that above "everything" there floats a sacred breath of Eternity.

Translated by Wanda Kemp-Welch

THE STRUGGLE FOR A NEW FORM   Henryk Berlewi
Originally published as "W walce o nową formę," *Ringen* no. 1 (1921)

Our times are devoid of style; it is a period of anarchy in art. We lack the ground under our feet; tradition has disappeared. We are left as if after an earthquake, or a violent storm, and we are forced to take up building anew, the new which so far had not existed. Is it our bad or good luck? To have no defined purposes, no limitations of tradition, no yoke of a prevalent school, to have no style, even such that would reflect our times!

Yes, no period in the history of art could boast of so many movements, such a variety of forms. Not only is there no single school, no single form of collective creativity, but even an individual artist takes recourse in his art to various eccentricities.

Deprived of tradition—we are as naked as Adam and call upon our own resources. Thus we confront a great task: to create a new world, a world of forms.

If only we would break off completely! We get entangled in the remains of the heritage of old forms. We have the feeling that we are almost free, we have only to disentangle ourselves. However, in getting free we are hampered by a particular human weakness, which we call habit, since we are accustomed to various stereotyped conventions, remnants of what has accumulated over a long time. Only when we notice this can we break off, but how can we notice all that we lug behind us and what lies beyond our consciousness.

Moreover, in order to create our own form we must break off from everything that is genuinely alien to us—but if, in spite of it, due to the force of habit, we accept what is wrong for us—how can we free ourselves?

Here come artists' slogans. Whether a slogan is realized—is another matter, but I do not doubt it is right. Why?

It is because an idea is born to the present (by "idea" I understand exclusively the idea of form) but, in order to materialize, to receive its actual shape, it has to pass hard tests, it has to go through the flame of the artist's laboratory.

And so, during the whole creative process the original idea changes to some extent, moves away from its original outline. The reason is that we do not possess formal means that are sufficiently rich to be absorbed by the force of imagination.

And so, just as every impulse causes a reaction in our imagination, and only in consequence the most likely form of art, so form always follows behind in relation to an idea.

What is more: a new idea shines above the ground of old forms; in relation to old forms it is more revolutionary, it cannot be contained within them. Then there is a struggle between the two opposites, and the old form must be overcome. The new idea must receive appropriate shape. That is a problem—in order to be able to master form one needs to overcome the old and create a new form.

New art is nothing more than the problem of form. Let us exclude here everything that has absolutely nothing to do with the problem.

Form is autonomous. It has its own sphere of influence.

Art —such as there is today—is the most complex phenomenon, it absorbs various elements into its organism.

Form—as one of those elements, becomes seriously crippled in its expression and limited by other components of art, and, if we are to deal with form as such, we have to gradually pluck it free from any other components, in order to see form in all its nakedness.

If we do not succeed—we have found the key to the problem of form, we notice what before had been fused in art as a whole: the division between idea and form is no longer concealed by other elements and therefore we are dealing with pure form.

Having denuded form we must be able to use it, to deal with it as the only means of expression, without calling back for help once all superfluous elements are rejected. E.g. an idea of form comes to our mind and we want to carry it out quickly. If we are an "artist" we want to make "art." We gather together the whole conglomerate of artistic ideas but when we push an idea of form into the crowded space the form will only be damaged. The most stress for form is caused by the idea of content. In such a case form must lose its force in favor of content. We then end up with a work of art that is far removed from our original idea. In relation to every new idea of form we are opportunistic and make compromises. The original idea of form slips away between our clumsy fingers.

What is more, we must master form—which means we must free form from the pressures of our times. We can only do that if we treat it as a completely independent means in art, as a direct heir of the idea, independent from content, i.e. what the form expresses.

By only cultivating form and negating any other means we gradually want to approach the divine source of all forms.

Translated by Wanda Kemp-Welch

OVERCOMING ART   El Lissitzky

Originally published as "Die Überwindung der Kunst," *Ringen* no. 10 (1922)

All art is mortal, not just the individual artworks but the arts themselves. One day the last Rembrandt portrait will have ceased to exist, even though a painted canvas may remain, because the last eye that understood its formal language will have disappeared.
—Oswald Spengler, *The Decline of the West*

We leave rainbows of our tracks behind us in the awareness of new floods.

I.

Decaying souls with blind eyes stand in the storm raging around modern art and wail: "The world of the beautiful is drowning! The world of the beautiful is drowning!" What they see in modern art seems wild and absurd to them. But why don't they judge the acts of modern science, of modern technology, with the same forbearance? There the revolutions reach more deeply and are more violent! They want to tackle the results of a thousand years of growth and grasp them in a second, so when the artist demands an effort of two or three seconds, there is a wild outcry and unrest, and dead dogs and living lions gather into a single pack.

We tell those who wish to approach the new art that it is not enough to stare at it with your eyes; you must turn your entire head in another direction. Cézanne lead the artist out of the cinema of life, where he was sitting on a tiny fissure, searching for moon love [and] roses, leavening them with his own temperament, and baking little paintings from them. First they were exhibited and then sold to become the icons of sentimental feelings of sympathetic bachelors, soft young ladies, upstanding fathers, and proper mothers. Cézanne discovered the essence of the painter, the man through whom a stream of colors flows, who channels this seething river and gives it form. Cézanne approaches the canvas as if it were a field, to be tilled, fertilized, sowed, and harvested of its painterly fruit. It is true that Cézanne still believed in art that was shrouded under museum roofs, but with his own work he liberated us from it. And we saw him standing at his workbench, a stream of burning colors in him, his heart beating in time, his hand outstretched as if to guide a brush—but at the very moment the fruit was set to fall from the womb of his creativity, the dead water of reason flooded over him, and the stillborn child was marinated in the tiny painting. Hence the green faces, the red trees, and the black clouds. The painter who had to present his colors used the objects as canvases, like mannequins, and dressed them with whatever flowed from him. Cézanne too painted still lifes, landscapes, and people, but for him they were already just canvases. The color that flows through his skies, waters, meadows, and faces is his.

II.

Cubism began to destroy the basis, the object. A bottle is made for drinking. When a painter paints it, we cannot drink from the painted bottle. That means that the painter must have something other than the bottle. But what? Its color, the properties of its material (texture), its form; and it is precisely all this that can be expressed so much more intensely with color if all these elements are not placed on the canvas in the order that is necessary for drinking but rather in the order required for the artwork, for its life, for painting. A world had been destroyed. Its elements were gathered together to a new painterly structure of straight lines, curves, surfaces, extension, color, and texture. Painting came of its own. The canvas became a symphony of all contrasts and a harmony of all instruments: woodwinds, brass, strings, drums, bells, and cymbals. The painter understood that the paint manufacturer had limited him terribly by yoking him with cubes [sic], such that every material had its painterly quality and had to be applied directly to the canvas. Thus labels, newspaper clippings, small quantities of sand, chalk, and so on, all appeared on the canvas. The painting as such was destroyed.

III.
Painting created its own empire for its world. Along the road from the Gothic to infinity it created its golden banner: Renaissance, perspective, Impressionism, vibrating flecks of color.
Cubism began to turn away from the depths of the canvas to its surface, to build up the composition before our eyes. In Russia, Tatlin took this path. He began to create an artistic composition from materials (wood, sheet metal, paper) that projected out of the surface of the canvas or panel. But this was a stationary, painterly approach for the eye, standing out only for the sense of touch. Unmediated work with the material impregnated the painter with new goals; he began to refer critically to his place within the creative collective and realized that the engineer, for example, was ahead of him. The engineer discovers, he creates the new in nature; the artist, by contrast, creates only that which already exists. The artists who began to work with materials and to create structures based on Cubist construction believed they were creators, discoverers, materialists—that is, modern men. But they failed to see that they remained old-fashioned romantics because they approached the material from the same direction they approached color: from the direction of beauty, from the aesthetic side. And at just this time, in Western Europe, where they had only heard of us but had not yet seen anything that had been produced in the past seven years, they labeled this purely painterly movement "machine art." We don't know how this term should be understood: art that competes with machines or describes machines or builds machines? Be that as it may, this was one of the most important milestones on the road toward the overcoming of art.

IV.
In 1913 Kazimir Malevich exhibited a black square in Saint Petersburg. A black square painted on a white canvas. This was the founding of Suprematism. What view of the world, what concept of the world found its expression in Suprematism? The bearer of colorful whirlwinds—the artist, the painter—swept from his winged path all the fundamental things that he had previously draped with his colors. He gave color its independence; he made the painting nonobjective. He went on to pure creation. The Suprematists said: Just as the flower, which is clearly [and] unambiguously defined in color, imitates nothing and describes nothing outside itself but merely grows from the earth, so the painting must bloom from the artist. The painting cannot be a reproduction; it must be a work. The modernity of Suprematism, in contrast to nonobjective art (Kandinsky, *Abstrakte Malerei* in Germany, *simultanéisme* in France), derives from its structure and its new painterly expression of space. Suprematism followed to its logical end the path to infinity that passes by way of perspective. It broke through the blue arc of the heavens and escaped into the white limitlessness. The Suprematist colored masses swim like planets in the white cosmic space. But in this way it maximized the illusory aspect of the painting. In lieu of beauty it established another measure: economy.

V.
Malevich believed that with his square he had brought painting to the end of its path, to the zero point. But as we explored in the works that followed, we said: Yes, the path of the painter's culture grew ever smaller and reached the square, but on the other side a new culture is beginning to bloom. Yes, we celebrate the boldness that plunged into the abyss in order to rise from the dead in a new form. Yes, if the line of painting

descended...6, 5, 4, 3, 2, 1 to 0, then on the other side a new lines begins 0, 1, 2, 3, 4...And we saw that the new painting that is emerging from within us is no longer an image. It describes nothing; rather it constructs extensions, surfaces, lines with the goal of creating a system for a new composition of the real world. We gave this building a new name: *proun.*

The name *proun* signifies for us the station on the path to the creative design of the new form that grows from the earth fertilized by the dead bodies of the image and the artist. The image collapsed together along with the old world that the image had created. The new world will not need any small images. When it needs a mirror, it has photography and the cinema. In the new world the creator, known as an "artist," will create the world himself, not describe it. Proun—that is the path we will take to the new composition. Although science and the engineer now manage to create their realities by means of designing projects, we do not consider this the only, the categorical way. We believe in creative intuition, which establishes its own methods and its own system outside of design but in harmony with laws that are just as organic as the growth of flowers. Proun does not compose; it constructs. This is a fundamental contrast to the image. Composition is a discussion on a given plane with many variations; construction is a confirmation of the one for a given necessity. Proun has no axis perpendicular to the horizon, as the image does. It is constructed in space and brought into equilibrium, and because it is a structure, one has to walk around it, see it from below and explore it from above. The canvas has been set in motion. Proun is created from material and not from some aesthetic. From the richest gold mine of color we have taken the purest vein of subjective [sic] quality. Yellow, green, blue—those are the blondes, brunettes, and chestnut browns of the spectrum. We do not need the individual but the universal. We have taken our colors from the realm of black and white. And the contrast or harmony between two blacks, two whites, or two intermediate shades serves us like the contrast or harmony of two materials like granite and wood or iron and cement. Thus color has become the barometer of the material for us.

VI.

In precisely the same way that religion was overcome, we are now struggling to overcome art using our newfound abilities.

The time of the hunter who chased the animal and caught it is far behind us—he described it. We are equally distant from the time of the tamer, the shepherd who sat at his oven and abstracted nature—he beautified it. We live in an epoch of reinforced concrete, a dynamic epoch; we do not describe and we do not beautify: we run and we create. We leave behind, on the one hand, the artist and his image and, on the other, the engineer and his project, and we go out to create the elements of the first, second, and third dimensions in space and time in order to grow together with nature as a whole in accordance with the law of the world. And we are the steps of our movement, which is just as independent and just as incomprehensible as the path of the moonstruck man for whom everyone steps aside in shame.

Translated by Steven Lindberg

TO THE POLISH NATION: A MANIFESTO CONCERNING THE IMMEDIATE FUTURIZATION OF LIFE   Bruno Jasieński

Originally published as "Do narodu Polskiego: Mańifest w sprawie natyhmiastowej futuryzacji żyća," in *Jednodniówka futurystów* (Cracow, 1921)

Given that any sporadic or isolated reform of art divorced from life itself—all art being its pulse and organic function—inevitably proves itself vain, fruitless and sterile from the outset, and furthermore there being no time for preliminary and preparatory moves of this sort—Polish life and art are threatened with suffocation, and the only possible and effective measure to be taken in such a case is an immediate tracheotomy—we, the Polish Futurists, are as of today launching a huge and radical rebuilding and reorganization of Polish life. We call on all citizens of the free Polish Republic to unite in co-operation and support.

Universal war along with the colossal movement of whole states, classes and nations has brought with it a huge shift in values. The result of this is a crisis in culture in the whole of Eastern and Western Europe today. Here this crisis appears in a particularly sharp and specific form. A century and a half of political bondage has left a hard, indelible impression on our whole physiognomy, psyche and production. Our cultural awareness was unable to develop as freely as it was in the Western states. Our entire national energy was of necessity expended in directing the utmost pressure towards the arduous and laborious battle for our own language, life and institutions. Polish art also expended itself in the same direction, struggling for its own national "self" and the building of a hard, unbroken national psyche that would be resistant to anything and capable of life.

We, the Polish Futurists, honor here the Romantic poetry of the period of enslavement, the specters of which we shall today pursue and kill without mercy—if only because, during the period of great concentration and slow maturing of the Polish Nation it was not "pure" art but a profoundly national one, because it was written with the very juices and blood of life thundering by, because it was the pulse and scream of its day, as generally only art can and must be.

For these same reasons today, when, together with regaining her political independence, Poland's life has entered a completely new phase and woken up to the prospect of a million questions lurking at her gate, to which there was just no time to give any thought yesterday, and to which it is necessary to give a categorical reply promptly if we don't want the oncoming waves to catch up with us, we call out to you:

For too long we have been a nation reminiscent of a museum of curiosities, producing nothing but mummies and relics. The crazy and unstoppable present enters through all our doors and windows, it shouts out, harasses us and makes demands. If we can't afford to create new categories into which it could fit, a new art in which it could sing to its heart's content—we shall not survive.

We must open wide all the doors and windows, to get rid of this stench of cellars and church incense which they have been teaching us to breathe since we were children. Armed with gigantic facemasks, we are coming out to meet you.

Following on from S. Brzozowski, we announce a great sale of old junk. The old traditions, categories, customs, pretty pictures and fetishes, are all going for next to nothing.

A giant nationwide museum of curiosities will be held at the Wawel.

We shall be bringing along the stale mummies of mickiewiczs and słowackis from the squares and streets in wheelbarrows. It is time to make space on the pedestals, clean up the squares, and make space for those who are coming.

We, the people of wide lungs and broad shoulders, are sneezing from all the sickly smells of your yesterday's Messianism, and propose to you the one and only new Messianism, contemporary and crazy. If you do not want to be the last nation in Europe, but, on the contrary, the first, stop once and for all feeding off of the old spatters from the kitchen of the West (we can afford to have our own menu), and hurry to the goal-post of the great race of civilizations, with short, synthetic steps.

We set to work on building a new home for the widened Polish Nation, which can no longer be fitted into its old one. We cannot manage alone. We call on all those who are alive, dissatisfied, and willing to help.

We announce:

A huge shifting of classes is taking place in the East and the West. A new power is finding its voice—the proletariat with a new awareness. A great reevaluation of values is beginning. All the rights and wrongs of the previous 1000 years of culture created at its expense are vying with one another. They are being measured against the one touchstone of the life of struggle—hard, steely, organic work. A great review of legiti-macy is taking place. Whoever cannot legitimize his participation in life with this sin-gle coin—shall not survive.

We stress three fundamental moments in contemporary life: the machine, democracy and the crowd.

The life of the intellectual classes is undergoing a slow period of degeneration and neurasthenia. The old categories are outlived, and consumed—new ones are not yet here. It is a moment of crisis. Life itself, instead of being fundamentally a joy and a dithyramb, is increasingly coming to resemble a hard, externally imposed duty. Modern man is no longer able to enjoy life organically. The epidemic of suicides, human wrecks, breakdowns and human tragedies is none other than the logical extension of this phenomenon. This state of affairs cannot remain unchanged any longer. Immediate and energetic remedial action must be taken. We propose that one of its fundamental elements be:

More sunshine.

The wisdom of the ancient Chinese proverb: "carry your umbrella even in good weather," has for us become organically constituted.

We reject parasols, hats, bowler-hats; we will go about bareheaded. Bare-necked. It is necessary for everyone to become as tanned as possible. Houses ought to be built with south-facing walls of glass. More light, air, and space. If the Polish Seym deliberated outside, we would be sure to have a much sunnier Constitution.

Modern man, who expends ¾ of his energy working, needs a strong and healthy diet, and new, sharp, synthetic sensations. At present it is only art that can provide these sensations. Art ought to be the juice and joy of life, and not its mourner or its comforter. We are breaking away, once and for all, from so called "pure art," "art for art's sake," "art for the absolute." Art must be foremost and above all human, i. e. for people— mass, democratic and universal art.

Aware of the obligations of art to the present day and its problems, we cry:

Artists take to the streets!

The art huddled in concert halls, exhibitions, palaces of art etc. holding a few hundred or even a few thousand people is a laughable anemic monstrosity, because only 1/100 000 000 of all people make use of it. Modern man has no time to go to concerts and exhibitions, 3/4 of people are in no position to do this. This is why they must be able to find art everywhere:

Flying *poezoconcerts* and concerts in trains, trams, canteens, factories, cafeterias, in squares, stations, halls, pedestrian precincts, parks, from the balconies of houses etc. etc. etc. at all times of day and night.

Art must be unexpected, all pervasive and knock one off one's feet.

Modern man has long ago lost the ability to be moved or expectant. Legal codes have once and for all normalized and classified all manner of the unexpected. Life, which differs from the modern machine in that it permits fairy-tale like surprises, is becoming less and less different from it. The time honored categories of logic, according to which B will always follow on from A, and the sum of these two will inevitably be C—have become intolerable. The mathematical 2 x 2 = 4 is spreading to take on the dimensions of a nightmarish polyps, which has spread its feelers over everything. All logical possibilities have been exhausted to the last. The moment of constant rumination until loss of consciousness. Life, in its logic, has become nightmarish and illogical.

We, the Futurists, wish to show you to the gate that leads out of this ghetto of logic. Man has ceased to feel joy because he has ceased to have expectations. Only a life conceived of as a parade of possibilities and surprises will return this joy to him.

In the vicious circle of things that are self-evident, we have understood that nothing is self-evident and that besides this logic, there exists a whole sea of illogicalities, of which each can create its own distinct logic, whereby A + B = F and 2 x 2 = 777.

A deluge of wonders and surprises. Nonsense dancing along on streets. Art—the crowd.

Anyone can be an artist.

Theaters, circuses, street performances, all played by the public itself.

We call on all poets, painters, sculptors, architects, musicians, and actors to take to the streets.

The stage is revolving. It's time to change the decorations.

Paintings as the walls of buildings. Multi-walled houses, spherical and conical. The orchestra plays a march. People want to walk to its beat.

We call on all craftsmen, tailors, shoemakers, furriers, and hairdressers to create new, never before seen outfits, hairstyles and costumes.

We call on all technicians, engineers, and chemists to make new, unprecedented inventions.

Technology is as much an art as are painting, sculpture, or architecture.

A good machine is the model for and the culmination of a work of art by virtue of the perfect combination of economy, expediency and dynamics. The telegraphic apparatus of Morse is a 1000 times a greater masterpiece than Byron's *Don Juan*.

We distinguish amongst works of architectural, plastic and technical art—WOMAN— as an excellent reproductive machine.

Woman is a force that is immeasurable and unexploited by its unparalleled influence. We demand that unequivocally equal rights be given to women in all spheres of private and public life.

Above all equal rights in erotic and family relations.

The number of married couples not living together, officially or unofficially in separation is reaching numbers threatening the social order. We consider the only way to prevent and stop this process to be the immediate introduction of divorce.

We stress the erotic moment as one of the most vital functions of life as a whole. It is one of the most elementary and exceptionally important sources of the joys of life, provided that the attitude towards it be straightforward, clear and sunny. Sexual tragedies in Przybyszewski's manner are tasteless and are evidence that contemporary men are completely spineless and impotent. We call on women, as physically healthier and stronger, to take the initiative in this sphere.

In the interests of the above, Polish society must itself take into its own hands supervision and control over the entire social life and all production, not permitting the continued production of things not compatible with this aim, unnecessary or harmful.

The first and essential step is control over all artistic production. Do not allow yourselves to be drenched daily with bucketfuls of musty, senile and snobbish literature, which is not now even capable of arousing your sexual instinct. The organized public is a force, against which nothing can endure. No unnecessary book will be published, if nobody needs it.

We call on all citizens of the Polish State to organize in self-defense. The Polish public has outgrown its creators. Today's viewer is already yawning openly at *Macbeth* and experiencing an indescribable pain in the region of the appendix whilst watching dying Eaglets. Polish art, on the other hand, cannot afford to provide a new, vital sustenance. The one effective means to combat this lack of creativity is the unanimous, organized sabotage of senile literature and art. Not going to theaters, not buying books, not reading periodicals etc. etc. etc.

So that Polish society can be organized to achieve communally an immediate, deep, root reaching, fundamental and lasting futurization of life, we are founding all over the Rep. of Poland a gigantic Futurist party. Every working citizen who is instinctively experiencing the present moment of general cultural crisis, and is looking for a way out of it, may become an active member of the party. There is a whole society of such neurasthenics and martyrs of contemporary life. It is to them that we extend our hands.

We turn to the so called new people, i.e. those not yet contaminated by the syphilis of civilization, which universal war has thrust to the surface, and those who the old society still unjustly treats as though they were bastards. We the Futurists are the first to extend our hands in a gesture of fraternity to the "new people." They will be that healthy refreshing juice, which will reinvigorate the old, degenerate race of yesterday's people, that painful but necessary injection with which the great cataclysm of history immunized the whole of pre-war, decomposing Europe, which was already beginning to stink.

Our party, of people tearing their way into tomorrow, will be unprecedented, all encompassing and crazy. Everyone can be a leader and none can be the leader. The broadest decentralization. We do not recognize any leaders or privates; everyone is an equal worker in life's struggle. We stress a great moment in human history.

Fate has become antiquated and died. From now on everyone can be the creator of his own life and of life in general.

We, the Futurists, are coming in this action to the aid of Polish society. With every new manifesto we shall give concrete pointers and instructions in accordance with this manifesto in all spheres. Every nameless member of the Futurist Party (we do not need surnames—they are all equal, aware and universal)—ought to respond to our call at his place of work.

In order for any action on our part to become possible, we demand that the Seym of the constitutional Rep. of Poland immediately resolves that artists receive the same immunity as any Seym deputy. An artist is as much a representative of the Nation as a member of parliament, simply possessing a different field of activity and different powers.

In this great and groundbreaking moment, we, the Futurists are forgetting past slights, we forget the fact that all our proceedings up till now, aiming in one planned direction, have been treated with hostility, thoughtlessness and mockery by Polish society. We know well that this was a misunderstanding caused by false informers and commentators, as well as by the lack of a unified front and a statement of clear, physical faith in ourselves. Now all these misunderstandings fall away of their own accord. With a purple faith in tomorrow and its unlimited possibilities, we wipe out with one fell swoop everything that was bad, both beyond us and within ourselves, all that was dispensable and senile, and we extend our arms to Polish society. If you are a living nation, not just a little nation, if a century and a half of national bondage has not left you spineless, if you really are the nation of tomorrow, and not an obsolete nation—come follow us.

All are called upon to commence unanimous, mass Futurist action, immediately, at the moment of the declaration of this manifesto.

Translated by Klara Kemp-Welch

MANIFESTO CONCERNING FUTURIST POETRY Bruno Jasieński
Originally published as "Manifest w sprawie poezji futurystycznej," in *Jednodniówka futurystów* (Cracow, 1921)

1. Cubism, Expressionism, Primitivism, and Dadaism have outdone all other isms. The only remaining current in art not yet to have been exploited is Onanism. We propose this as a collective name for all our opponents. In justification, we point out the fundamental factors of anti-Futurist art: sexlessness; inability to insemi-nate the crowds with their art; calm, paseistic self-abuse in the murk of melan-cholic ateliers.

2. In a time of great accomplishment, we consider the introduction of new names to be unnecessary and out of keeping with the times. Instead of a trademark, let us raise up the name of that group of people who one and a half decades ago first issued the slogans of the battle we are now concluding, and once again, call ourselves
    futurists.

3. We do not intend to repeat in 1921 that which they were already doing in 1908. We know that we are that many years older than they are. That which was in their case only a premonition, a rapid issuing of new perspectives—must for us become a concerted, conscious and creative effort.
    As the inheritors of an enormous empire of form we announce a great standardi-zation of currency. We will be exchanging all Cubist, Expressionist, Dadaist and Primitivist credit notes for the only talents to have remained, since the Greek times, unfalsifiable.
    To this end we proclaim:

4. It is forbidden in 1921 for anyone to create and construct in any way that has already been done before. Life flows onwards and does not repeat itself. The creator has a duty to everything that he has come across + to that wonderful new leap every artist must make into the emptiness of the universe.
    Art is the creation of new things.
    The artist who does not create new and un-heard of things, but only rehashes, for the several hundredth time, that which has been done before—is not an artist and ought to be held accountable in court for using this title, as one is for using any other title without the appropriate qualifications. We call upon the public to organize a boycott of such individuals.

5. Every artist is obliged to create a completely new and hitherto UN-heard of art, which he has the right to call by his name.

6. We consider a work of art to be a fait accompli, concrete and physical. Its form is conditioned by strictly internal need. As such, it answers for itself with the whole

complex of the forces creating it, thanks to which it is in this way and not another—i.e. under internal pressure, that its individual parts are coordinated in relation to one another and to the whole. We call this mutual relationship composition. We call excellent composition, i.e. one which is economical and firm—with a minimum of material to a maximum of dynamics achieved—Futurist composition. This is the only manner in which one may now compose. We give as deciding factors above all: the generally rising cost of living: a) of printing, which makes the publication of unnecessary things inappropriate and actually harmful to the country's economic situation; b) the rising cost of time. Contemporary man is occupied with professional work for eight hours of the day. He has the remaining four hours for eating, taking care of his day to day affairs, sport, pastimes, keeping up his social life, love and art. For the average person, there works out as being five to fifteen minutes daily for art alone. This is why he must receive art in capsules specially prepared by the artist, purified beforehand of all that is unnecessary and served up to him in completely prepared and synthetic form.

The work of art is an essence. Dissolved in a weekday glass, it ought to dye it entirely its own color.

Before announcing a work of art in print the artist is obliged to wring from it any remaining drips of water. Artists not adhering to this decision will be held accountable to society just like ordinary thieves on the charge of stealing time.

7. We rule out logic as a bourgeois form of thought. Every artist has the right to, and is obliged to, create his own autologic. We consider the principal characteristics of every particular logic to be: the rapid association of things which seem on the surface, to the bourgeois logic, to be remote; a shortcut between two peaks—a leap over the void and a double-somersault.

8. Poetry operates on the level of the word, just as plastic art operates on the level of shapes, music -of sounds. The word is a composite material. Besides the sound component it also has another content, a symbolic one, which it represents, and which need not be killed off under threat of creating a third art, which is no longer poetry, but not yet music (Dadaism).

   Poetry is a composition of words which seeks, without killing off this second concrete soul of the word, to extract maximum resonance from it.

   We break once and for all with all manner of description (painting), and on the other hand also with all manner of onomatopoeic means, the imitation of the voices of nature and similarly tasteless accessories of Pseudo-Futurist-Neo-Realism.

   We rule out the sentence as being an anti-poetic freak.

   The sentence is an accidental composition, bound together only by the weak glue of good old petit bourgeois logic. In its place—condensed, sharp and consistent compositions of words, unrestrained by any syntactical, logical or grammatical rules, but only by a strict internal need, which after tone A demands a tone C, after tone C demands tone F etc.

9. We rule out the book as a form of further delivering poetry to the receiver. Poetry, as an art operating through acoustic qualities, can only be rendered in words. The book can at most play the part of sheet music on the basis of which a certain category of particularly talented people (virtuosos) can recreate the original whole. From the moment of the discovery of the telephonograph, i.e. the linking of the phonograph with the telephone, the book will, in any case, become useless and unnecessary as a bridge between the creator and the public.

10. Our art is neither the reflection and anatomy of the soul (psychology), nor the expression of our aspiration to the other world of God (religion), nor the shaking up of eternal problems (philosophy). We need probably not reply to such accusations

today. Neither is art the diary of some sort of, be they interesting, experiences or inner vicissitudes of the artist. Our grandfathers exhausted their patient contemporaries for long enough with their nostalgia, suffering and mania for eroticism. The artist's experiences are his private property, no doubt of interest to his family and admirers, but to no one else. Artists are advised to find an outlet for their experiences in the appropriate direction, spending more time on sport, sexual love and the sciences.

11. We detach, from the organism of life to which they are attached like leaches, those conceited parasites who call themselves poets, feed off the work of others and produce nothing in return, because life, as it is, defies their Promethean psyche.

We are in favor of a life, which is an eternal strenuous transformation—movement, mob, the sewer system and the City.

Poetry must be everyday, profoundly up-to-date and universal.

The romantic melancholy of roses and nightingales has long ceased to have any impact on us.

We are exalted by the crowd, conceived of as the giant roller of a revolving turbine. We wish to be honest and conscious workers in our field, in life's constant labor and battle to forge tomorrow.

12. We break once and for all with the pathos of eternity in connection with art.

The implicit value of a work of art fluctuates between 24 hours and a month.

In our country, where everything takes so long to become outdated, we extend this deadline to 1 year. By the end of this period all unsold books are to be withdrawn from sale. All second and third editions are forbidden. Those not submitting to this resolution will be called to justice before society, which will itself determine individual cases by way of plebiscite.

Tanslated by Klara Kemp-Welch

A NIFE IN THE STOMAK: FUTURIST SPESHAL ISHEW 2*   Bruno Jasienski

Originally published as "Nuż w bżuhu, 2 jednodńuwka futurystuw," in *Jednodniówka futurystów* (Cracow, 1921)

30000 edishonz of the futurist manifesto—wer snachd up all over Poland in the spaic of fortien dais. stabd in the stomak with a nife the sleepi beest of Polish art began to moo. the lava of futurism spiewd forth from the slit. citizenz, help us to rip off yor skinz worn out from daily use. be dun with draging arownd with yu parti sloganz like "god and the fatherland." in poland, the red baner becaim a red hankachief a long time ago. democratz, hang out baners bearing the wordz of owr swis frendz: We want to pis in all colors!

painted trowsers

In meni privat howsez, as wel az in sum publik wonz e.g. the so colld *encurajment of fine art*, the walls ar hung with hewj, veri often painted, piesez of canvas. Wi dont the

---

* Text originally written in Polish using only phonetic spellings. [Translator's note]

malishus artistz from zach•ta paint their trowserz, and hang the painted wons on the wallz, insted of on themselvz? Walking around in painted trowserz thai wud fulfil their role as akcesibl entertainment for the crowdz. Hung on the wallz thai serv onli as objectz of gosip for a few dozen literari haks.

The goverment obviosli prezyumz that ravenus Poland canot get its fil of familiar jumble of pieces (*stücks*), as it forbidz the export of duch rembrantz and other raphaelz under threat of penalti. We openli encuraj larj-scail contraband and the export of this filth.

Howm-owners, cover the wals and interiors of yor tenement-howses with futurist compozitionz.

Stait, comision the folowing, as the onli painters and sculptorz in Poland, to decorait strietz, squairz and pavementz:

tytus czyżewski, henryk gotlib, leon hwistek, juzef jarema, zbigńew and andżej pronaszko, marian szczerbula, kaźmież tomorowicz, zygm. waliszewski, romuald witkowski.

We coll to oll citizenz of the republik:

Citizenz, paint yourselvz!

paint yorselvz, yor wivez and yor children

The last futurist Eevningz in Zakopane ended in a fist and egg fite betwien too factionz of the publik!

Women hav masivli sided with the futuristz! Shortli even theaterz shal be futurized! The multiplikaition in recent timez of kountles theatrz is the best evidens of their ultimait bankrupsi. The revolutionized publik will demolish the prezent scene. Eggs ar the only sewtabl weapon for the civilized person: they ar reminicent of hand-grenaidz, but ar not lethal. We clasp the handz of france and switzerland. Marinetti is foren to us. Shortli, new carnivalz of futurist poetri will taik plaic in warsaw, cracow, lvuv, poznań, and all the larger townz in poland, at which the loud polish futuristz will apear befor the crowdz.

tytus czyżwski, bruno jaśeński, stańisław młodożeńec, anatol stern, aleksandeer wat.

Tanslated by Klara Kemp-Welch

THE TVRDOŠÍJNÍ (OBSTINATES) IN PRAGUE   Karel Srp

Shortly before the end of World War I, some artists who were neither at the front nor living in exile decided to form an artists' group. They proclaimed their debut in an exhibit with a poster that read: "And yet! An exhibit of The Tvrdošíjní (Obstinates)." The words were printed on a rhombus, reminiscent of an African mask (created by Václav Špála). The composition of the group, whose first exhibit took place in the Weinert exhibit and auction hall (Prague, March–April 1918), and which continued to be called Tvrdošíjní, strongly reflected the situation before 1914, when a rift took place between Skupina and Mánes. A threesome of well-known artists with a modern orientation—Josef Čapek, Vlastislav Hofman, and Václav Špála—formed the fundamental unit of Tvrdošíjní. They brought in more traditionally oriented painters such as Rudolf Kremlička, Otakar Marvánek and especially Jan Zrzavý. (Representatives of the early Devětsil also advocated Zrzavý's work, and Karel Tiege wrote his first monograph on this artist in 1923.)

From the very beginning, they were supported with publicity by Stanislav Kostka Neumann, who in March 1918 began publishing Červen (June)—a biweekly devoted to "New Art, Nature, the Technical Age, Socialism, Freedom"—in which the members of Tvrdošíjní published their graphic art.

The first Czech translation of Apollinaire's poem "Zone," with illustrations by Čapek, also appeared in Červen, and it had an extraordinary influence on Czech poetry up to the 1930s. Most of the representatives of proletarian poetry, and the later Devětsil, reacted to it. Tvrdošíjní held six exhibits in Prague (1918–24), of which the most important was the third (January 1921). It included work by other Czech artists (Emil Filla and Otto Gutfreund, with whom Josef Čapek had parted ways before the war), along with important foreign guests (Paul Klee and the Dresden Art Nouveau).

Tvrdošíjní's unofficial theorist was the art critic and aesthetician Václav Nebeský, who was, aside from Vincenc Kramář, among the few who were able to come to terms with modern post-Impressionist and Cubist art. He understood artistic work to be an autonomous and distinctive whole, independent of external reality. Nebeský's viewpoint was questioned by the early Devětsil, whose representatives began, around 1922, to oppose Tvrdošíjní, even though they had little work behind them. They felt that the Tvrdošíjní approach to art was not developing intellectually and was becoming a tool of official state representation.

Translated by Andrée Collier Záleská

AND YET! Stanislav K. Neumann

Originally published as "A přece!" introduction to the first Tvrdošíjní exhibition
catalogue (1918)

It is certainly strange that at a time when art develops fast and individuals have the
opportunity to observe several far-reaching changes in the arts in the span of their
lifetime, there are still so few people with an interest in art who, in an era of such
critical turns, do not give in to lethargy or are not swayed by the general antipathy
towards the new harbored by the masses, maintaining at least a state of calm, open to
education. Isn't it the case that today every man, even the superficially informed one,
could know that art is essentially a fluid phenomenon, incessantly renewed through
new formal discoveries and impulses, actions and reactions, without which—if they
sometimes take a long time—he wilts and withers without new sap? Rare are those
who do not explode in a paroxysm of hateful anger or distrustful ridicule as soon as a
new direction begins to force its way forward. And even more rare are those who welcome the nascent change, the young direction resembling spring of art that follows
after ripeness, decay and exhaustion of the previous movement, the same spring we
love in nature and in ourselves. It seems that few live with art as passionately and
intimately as we would have expected. Artworks are seen as finished results, not as
connected steps of a constantly progressing phenomenon, as marks left by organic
activity. And yet, there is nothing more beautiful and encouraging in its hidden profound faith, nothing more interesting.

What a pleasure it is to observe the first difficult victory of a new artistic sensibility
over the general flatness of a dying movement, the first uncertain outcomes of a new
endeavor, the first discovery and theoretical justification, the triumph of the discov-
erer—to observe how the he turns into a *magnus parens*, how a liberating breakthrough
turns into a direction, a serious game consisting of various components, pure tissue of
diverse temperaments and abilities—to observe how new talents and principles, at
first opposed and ridiculed, grow, spread their branches and expand, in the end filling
the entire space at their disposal, appearing in the most diverse forms and relationships, conquering the world—and, having given everything, they slowly descend into
the misery old age, still admired by lay supporters, but challenging honest artists to
new conquests!

It is, I repeat, very peculiar that so few people are capable of feeling this pleasure.
Peculiar and embarrassing. But then perhaps it is healthy for the pioneering artistic
mind to be steeled by resistance and lack of understanding. The national art economy
requires, above all, an impartial strictness and considered prudence, encouraging what
is being born instead of what is passing away, while not overestimating the capacities
of youth.

The conspiracy surrounding a young artist coming with a new creative sensibility is too
great, and he indeed has to be very stubborn not to give up. And especially today. For he
is not merely facing the general resistance towards the new that I have just mentioned;
he is being challenged by the loud, threatening demands of the day. If I were to be direct,
I would say that he is the perpetrator of some imaginary or real -ism and -isms have
been banned as "un-national" art. Apart from that, the artist is to be held responsible
even for an inadequate attitude to the war and to our "great" time.

That means however that today, such a stubborn artist—if he is truly an artist—deserves
even more respect and admiration than in peaceful times. Being firmly convinced that
a good painting is not an editorial, nor a march blasted out of a military trumpet, but
an outcome of honest creative effort whose national quality lies in the structure of
the artist's genius, in his blood and nerves, and not in the outward subject or in the

costumed exterior of his work, he does not resist the creative truth he had arrived at and continues bravely along his path.

The present exhibition shows the work of our contemporary obstinate artists. Mostly, the work falls within the wider scope of the new post-Impressionist art, for which the way was opened by Cézanne's creative discoveries and which was approached in the most abstract manner by Picasso. Yet, many paintings exhibited here mean much more. These works have matured in a silence undisturbed by foreign slogans that banished a violent era outside its locked doors. This art gained a final liberation from this situation and everything truly beautiful and mature you find in it speaks to you in its own local language. Here, an assertive strong Czech branch of contemporary modern European art deservedly works its way to the light of day. They have tried to scare it away, deprive it of space and air. And yet it thrusts its way forward, stubbornly, in its own direction.

Translated by Alexandra Büchler

THE OBSTINATES AND FRIENDS   Václav Nebeský
Originally published as "Tvrdošíjní a hosté," introduction to the third Tvrdošíjní exhibition catalogue (1921)

If a group of painters called the Obstinates, who have had the courage to remain faithful to an international concept of art, had been jointly presenting themselves for three years, their name would have by now become obsolete. In the Czech lands, postwar inertia, combined with complacent self-sufficiency, means that the "stubbornness" of these artists has never ceased to be topical and highly necessary.

It is both sad and endearing to note how much strength is needed for the seed of a healthy idea to take and germinate, grow and blossom, and later to bear fruit that can refresh the soul of those who are thirsty, as well as those who have had more than enough. And its is a pleasure to see that despite the limited hope for a wider and more serious understanding that might come soon, a handful of artists are still holding out without concessions and compromises. It is sad to see that after so many years of serious effort and honest work, the oldest artists taking part in this exhibition are still "modern"; on the other hand it is encouraging to know that they have never ceased to be so.

The main artistic virtue and moral strength of this exhibition, whose modernity (still betraying a degree of youthful, insatiable inquisitiveness to move us all) need not astonish anyone any more, is the virtue of mature grown-ups: *pure and fundamental artistic conviction*.

By purity I mean the endeavor to achieve an expression as appropriate as possible to the given goal. As simple as it is within itself, and as complex as it is within itself. And always united and organic, adopting one single expression and not a showy eclectic mix of expression within expression. Hence it is simpler than the ostentatious tricks of a virtuoso. Those who might find this conscious primitivism a little artificial in our over-civilized time, should take into consideration how necessary it is for an artistic regeneration, how noble, even that it is not without charm.

It is inherent in artistic expression that it conveys the soul and nature of man more faithfully and completely than any other, even if it does so in the form of a materially conceived object. Špála's jubilantly colorful song rhythmically rippling the space, a monumentalizing, carefully selected hue, Čapek's sensitively traced critical detail, Hofman's excited, unyielding pathos, Zrzavý's mystical rapture and meditativeness, Kremlička's sophisticated, brilliant splendor—all these are characteristics that differentiate rather than unite this group of artists. Yet, however much these painters differ in their moods and dispositions—which is only natural—they agree on one point: in their decision how to apply their personal qualities and tendencies, so as to avoid giving the impression that their work might be the outcome of personal whim. It is the striving for a firm and clear order, constructive, compositional, or both at the same time, by which it is necessary to embrace and penetrate the object before making it equal to the image of the artist's creative inner world. Therein lies the meaning of their artistic principle. A work of art as an autonomous intellectual and material reality in its own right. And therein lie also the essence and the permanent meaning of its modernity.

Translated by Alexandra Büchler

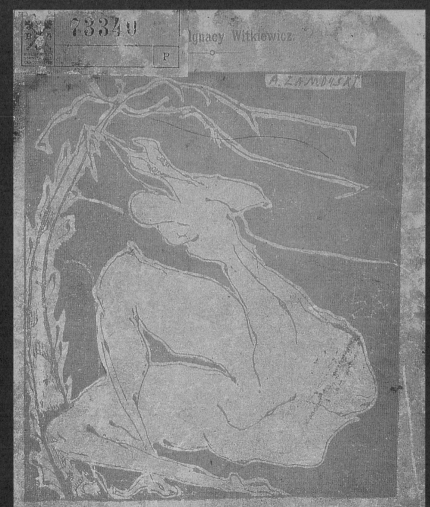

Ignacy Witkiewicz.

NOWE FORMY W MALARSTWIE

I WYNIKAJĄCE STĄD NIEPOROZUMIENIA

chapter 4

ART AND REVOLUTION

Éva Forgács

The end of World War I in November 1918, spelling the fall of the German and the Austro-Hungarian empires, created revolutionary situations in Germany and Hungary. (The states of Czechoslovakia, Poland, and the Kingdom of Serbs, Croats, and Slovenes [renamed the Kingdom of Yugoslavia in 1929] were, among other new states, also established in this historical instance.) The 1918 revolution in Germany leading to the establishment of the Weimar Republic and the Hungarian Commune in 1919 were both connected to the Russian Revolution of 1917 through the participation of Communists and by widely circulating leftist ideas.

Although revolutionary ideas were in the purview of the Devětsil movement in Prague, it was the German and the Hungarian avant-gardes that found themselves in the middle of revolutionary events. They responded to the historic changes with messianic faith in a coming new world, which, they hoped, would also be shaped by the artists and their parallel spiritual revolution. The marked dominance of architects in the German revolutionary art movements (first in the Arbeitsrat für Kunst [Working Council for Art], and later the Bauhaus) as well as in many international avant-garde organizations and forums, indicated that just as in Soviet Russia, architecture had become a powerful metaphor for the conception, engineering, and construction of a new social and cultural order. Radical artists saw themselves as the architects of both the revolution and the new world. Art critics in Prague, Budapest, and Bucharest paid particular attention to architecture. Many articles demonstrate that even the demise of revolutionary expectations was expressed through the metaphor of dismantling monumental architecture and returning to pragmatic building activities.

The Arbeitsrat was founded in Berlin in late 1918 as the council, or soviet, of artists. Its name was indicative of its program: "Arts and people must form a unity." The Arbeitsrat's manifesto was probably authored by the architect Bruno Taut. One of the early documents of the movement expresses the radical idea of eliminating the boundaries between architecture, painting and sculpture, which became one of the central issues of the Bauhaus as expressed in its Manifesto by Walter Gropius, who served as the head of the Arbeitsrat until he founded the Bauhaus in Weimar in April 1919. The revolutionary momentum of the early Bauhaus attracted youth searching for a new philosophy, a faith in the future, and a new type of community.

The Novembergruppe (November Group) was also founded in Berlin in November 1918, and most of its members—artists and critics from all creative fields, including radio— belonged to the Arbeitsrat as well. The Novembergruppe also demanded an active role for the artists in shaping the cultural life of the country. It embraced all modernist art forms— Cubism, Futurism, and Expressionism. The use of these modernist idioms caused some controversy among the public and even some leftist critics and artists.

The Hungarian avant-garde also had to deal with the dilemma of the modernist idiom and a generally comprehensible art. Hungarian Activism, a movement founded and led by the poet, artist, and editor Lajos Kassák, functioned as the Hungarian equivalent of the German art groups during the "Frost-flower Revolution" starting on October 31, 1918, and during the Hungarian Soviet Republic, which lasted from March through August 1919. The Activists' propagation of revolutionary art, their revolutionary goals, and their claim on shaping the future of their country beyond the boundaries of art, like the political poster art of the Commune, were greatly inspired by the German Revolution. The Hungarian avant-garde had to make adjustments for the public, however, because Expressionist language was not received well by the Hungarian working class audience. Another dilemma, the nature of the relationship between art and political power, remained unresolved during the short period of the Commune. The revolutionary avant-garde artists of the post-World War I days were confident in their potential to redesign society, but they lacked political experience.

The end of the Great War, with all its relief and euphoria, was also a moment of intellectual chaos in Germany. "Today's artist lives in an era of dissolution, without guidance," Walter Gropius wrote in 1919. "He stands alone. The old forms are in ruins, the benumbed world is shaken up, the old human spirit is invalidated and in flux toward a new form. We float in space and cannot yet perceive the new order."[1]

During the postwar shortages of materials, fantasy projects were thriving. Architects Bruno Taut, Walter Gropius, Paul Scheerbart, and others organized the informal Crystal Chain, so named because of their ideas for crystal buildings of glass and light. They circulated their utopian designs among one another, seeking critical responses and knowing full well that they would never be built. The Exhibition of Unknown Architects, which opened in Berlin in February 1919, featured glass palaces on the peaks of the Alps, and symbolic architectural centers— *Stadtkrone*, or City Crown—for future cities. Gropius's catalogue essay was a sketch of his Bauhaus Manifesto published two months later, announcing the idea of a new cathedral, a new

architectural *Gesamtkunstwerk*, as the symbol of the coming times. Expressionism was saturated with new meaning and new overtones: nothing that had been created before the war could be accepted in the same way. The sense of a new beginning was blended with anger at the past. "It was not possible for anyone to make use of any prewar traditions," Bruno Taut wrote, "for that period was perforce regarded as the cause of the misfortunes of the past, and because every achievement of those days seemed more or less to hang together with the origins of the war."[2] Our selection offers samples from this turbulent period, which had a profound impact on the art and culture of Central Europe.

---

1   In Barbara Miller Lane, *Architecture and Politics in Germany, 1918–1945* (Cambridge: Harvard University Press, 1968), p. 45.

2   Ibid., p. 45.

MANIFESTO   The November Group
Originally published as *Manifest der Novembristen* (1918)

We stand on the fertile ground of the revolution.
Our campaign slogan is:
FREEDOM, EQUALITY, FRATERNITY!
Our joining together is the result of the equivalence of a humane and an artistic way
of thinking.
We regard it as our highest duty to devote our best energies to the moral cultivation
of a young, free Germany.
We plead for excellence in every respect and dedicate all means at our disposal to the
support of this way of thinking.
We demand that this view be lent unqualified expression and that one publicly declare
one's position toward it.
We consider it our particular duty to gather together all abilities of value in the artistic
sphere and to guide them toward the common good.
We are neither a party nor a class as such, but human beings-human beings who
undertake to perform their work tirelessly from the places allotted to them by nature.
Like any other kind of work that is to serve the common good, it must take account of
general public interest and receive the respect and recognition of the whole.

Translated by Don Reneau

PROGRAM OF THE BAUHAUS IN WEIMAR   Walter Gropius
Originally published as *Programm des Staatlichen Bauhauses in Weimar* (Weimar:
April 1919)

The ultimate aim of all visual arts is the complete building! To embellish buildings was
once the noblest function of the fine arts; they were the indispensable components of
great architecture. Today the arts exist in isolation, from which they can be rescued
only through the conscious, cooperative effort of all craftsmen. Architects, painters, and
sculptors must recognize anew and learn to grasp the composite character of a building both as an entity and in its separate parts. Only then will their work be imbued with
the architectonic spirit that it has lost as "salon art."
The old schools of art were unable to produce this unity; how could they, since art cannot be taught. They must be merged once more with the workshop. The mere drawing
and painting world of the pattern designer and the applied artist must become a world
that builds again. When young people who take a joy in artistic creation once more
begin their life's work by learning a trade, then the unproductive 'artist' will no longer
be condemned to deficient artistry, for their skill will now be preserved for the crafts,
in which they will be able to achieve excellence.
Architects, sculptors, painters, we all must return to the crafts! For art is not a
"profession." There is no essential difference between the artist and the craftsman.
The artist is an exalted craftsman. In rare moments of inspiration, transcending
the consciousness of his will, the grace of heaven may cause his work to blossom
into art. But proficiency in a craft is essential to every artist. Therein lies the prime

source of creative imagination. Let us then create a new guild of craftsmen without the class distinctions that raise an arrogant barrier between craftsman and artist! Together let us desire, conceive, and create the new structure of the future, which will embrace architecture and sculpture and painting in one unity and which will one day rise toward heaven from the hands of a million workers like the crystal symbol of a new faith.

PROGRAM OF THE STAATLICHES BAUHAUS IN WEIMAR

The Staatliches Bauhaus resulted from the merger of the former Grand-Ducal Saxon Academy of Art with the former Grand-Ducal Saxon School of Arts and Crafts in conjunction with a newly affiliated department of architecture.

AIMS OF THE BAUHAUS

The Bauhaus strives to bring together all creative effort into one whole, to reunify all the disciplines of practical art—sculpture, painting, handicrafts, and the crafts-as inseparable components of a new architecture. The ultimate, if distant, aim of the Bauhaus is the unified work of art—the great structure—in which there is no distinction between monumental and decorative art.

The Bauhaus wants to educate architects, painters, and sculptors of all levels, according to their capabilities, to become competent craftsmen or independent creative artists and to form a working community of leading and future artist-craftsmen. These men, of kindred spirit, will know how to design buildings harmoniously in their entirety—structure, finishing, ornamentation, and furnishing.

PRINCIPLES OF THE BAUHAUS

Art rises above all methods; in itself it cannot be taught, but the crafts certainly can be. Architects, painters, and sculptors are craftsmen in the true sense of the word; hence a thorough training in the crafts, acquired in workshops and on experimental and practical sites, is required of all students as the indispensable basis for all artistic production. Our own workshops are to be gradually built up, and apprenticeship agreements with outside workshops will be concluded.

The school is the servant of the workshop and will one day be absorbed into it. Therefore there will be no teachers or pupils in the Bauhaus but masters, journeymen, and apprentices.

The manner of teaching arises from the character of the workshop:

- Organic forms developed from manual skills.
- Avoidance of all rigidity; priority of creativity; freedom of individuality, but strict study discipline.
- Master and journeyman examinations, according to the Guild Statutes, held before the Council of Masters of the Bauhaus or before outside masters. Collaboration by the students in the work of the masters.
- Securing of commissions, also for students.
- Mutual planning of extensive, utopian structural designs—public buildings and buildings for worship—aimed at the future. Collaboration of all masters and students—architects, painters, sculptors—on these designs with the object of gradually achieving a harmony of all the component elements and parts that make up architecture.
- Constant contact with the leaders of the crafts and industries of the country.
- Contact with public life, with the people, through exhibitions and other activities.
- New research into the nature of the exhibitions, to solve the problem of displaying visual work and sculpture within the framework of architecture.

■ Encouragement of friendly relations between masters and students outside of work; therefore plays, lectures, poetry, music, fancy-dress parties. Establishment of a cheerful ceremonial at these gatherings.

RANGE OF INSTRUCTION
Instruction at the Bauhaus includes all practical and scientific areas of creative work.
1. Architecture,
2. Painting,
3. Sculpture, including all branches of the crafts.

Students are trained in a craft (1) as well as in drawing and painting (2) and science and theory (3).

1. Craft training—either in our own, gradually enlarging workshops or in outside workshops to which the student is bound by apprenticeship agreement—includes:
    a) sculptors, stonemasons, stucco workers, woodcarvers, ceramic workers, plaster casters
    b) blacksmiths, locksmiths, founders, metal turners;
    c) cabinetmakers;
    d) scene painters, glass painters, mosaic workers, enamelers;
    e) etchers, wood engravers, lithographers, art printers, enchasers;
    f) weavers.
Craft training forms the basis of all teaching at the Bauhaus. Every student must learn a craft.
2. Training in drawing and painting includes:
    a) free-hand sketching from memory and imagination;
    b) drawing and painting of heads, live models, and animals;
    c) drawing and painting of landscapes, figures, plants and still lifes;
    d) composition;
    e) execution of murals, panel pictures, and religious shrines;
    f) design of ornaments;
    g) lettering;
    h) construction and projection drawing;
    i) design of exteriors, gardens, and interiors
    j) design of furniture and practical articles.

3. Training in science and theory includes:
    a) art history—not presented in the sense of a history of styles, but rather to further active understanding of historical working methods and techniques;
    b) science of materials;
    c) anatomy—from the living model;
    d) physical and chemical theory of color;
    e) rational painting methods;
    f) basic concepts of bookkeeping, contract negotiations, personnel;
    g) individual lectures on subjects of general interest in all areas of art and science.

DIVISIONS OF INSTRUCTION
The training is divided into three courses of instruction:
1. course for apprentices;
2. course for journeymen;
3. course for junior masters.
The instruction of the individual is left to the discretion of each master within the framework of the general program and the work schedule, which is revised every

semester. In order to give the students as versatile and comprehensive a technical and artistic training as possible the work schedule will be so arranged that every architect-, painter-, and sculptor-to-be is able to participate in part of the other courses.

ADMISSION
Any person of good repute, without regard to age or sex, whose previous education is deemed adequate by the Council of Masters will be admitted, as far as space permits. The tuition fee is 180 marks per year (it will gradually disappear entirely with increasing earnings of the Bauhaus). A non-recurring admission fee of 20 marks is also to be paid. Foreign students pay double fees. Address enquiries to the secretariat of the Staatliches Bauhaus in Weimar.

Translated by Wolfgang Jabs and Basil Gilbert

MANIFESTO   Working Council for Art
Originally published as *Arbeitsrat für Kunst—Flugblatt* (April 1919)

In the conviction that the political revolution must be used to liberate art from decades of regimentation, a group of artists and art lovers united by a common outlook has been formed in Berlin. It strives for the gathering together of all scattered and divided energies which, over and above the protection of one-sided professional interests, wish to work resolutely together for the rebuilding of our whole artistic life. In close contact with associations with similar objectives in other parts of Germany, the Arbeitsrat für Kunst hopes in the not-too-distant future to be able to push through its aims, which are outlined in the following program.
In the forefront stands the guiding principle:

Art and people must form a unity.
Art shall no longer be the enjoyment of the few but the life and happiness of the masses. The aim is alliance of the arts under the wing of a great architecture.

On this basis six preliminary demands are made:
1. Recognition of the public character of all building activity, both state and private. Removal of all privileges accorded to civil servants. Unified supervision of whole urban districts, streets, and residential estates without curtailment of freedom over detail. New tasks: people's housing as a means of bringing all the arts to the people. Permanent experimental sites for testing and perfecting new architectural effects.
2. Dissolution of the Academy of Arts, the Academy of Building, and the Prussian Provincial Art Commission in their existing form. Replacement of these bodies, accompanied by a redefining of their territories, by others drawn from the ranks of productive artists themselves and free from state interference. The changing of privileged art exhibitions into exhibitions to which entry is free.
3. Freeing of all training in architecture, sculpture, painting, and handicrafts from state supervision. Transformation of all instruction in the arts and handicrafts from top to bottom. State funds to be made available for this purpose and for the training of master craftsmen in training workshops.

4. Enlivenment of the museums as educational establishments for the people. Mounting of constantly changing exhibitions made to serve the interests of the people by means of lectures and conducted tours. Separation of scientific material in specially-constructed buildings. Establishment of specially-arranged collections for study by workers in the arts and crafts. Just distribution of state funds for the acquisition of old and new works.

5. Destruction of artistically valueless monuments as well as of all buildings whose artistic value is out of proportion to the value of their material which could be put to other uses. Prevention of prematurely planned war memorials and immediate cessation of work on the war museums proposed for Berlin and the Reich.

6. Establishment of a national center to ensure the fostering of the arts within the framework of future lawmaking.

Translated by Don Reneau

ON THE FIRST EXHIBITION OF BAUHAUS STUDENT WORK   Walter Gropius
Speech delivered on July 15, 1919

This exhibition has caused the Council of Masters some perplexity. On the first day we were unable to agree on the award of prizes, and we reconvened after a pause for reflection. For my own part, your works affect me with an oppressive and overwhelming sense of responsibility, and I have been in a state of agitation on the subject for some days. For these are fearfully chaotic times, and this little exhibition is a faithful reflection of them. I spent all of Sunday in the exhibition gallery, because I wanted to grasp and assess every one of you, in order to achieve an authentic cross-section of the Bauhaus. Ladies and gentlemen, there is talent there, but also disintegration. It was against my will that outsiders were admitted to see the exhibition, since they can only be confused by it. I intended this exhibition to be purely for ourselves, an internal matter. I propose that we hold no public exhibitions for the foreseeable future and that we work from a new starting point, in order to collect our thoughts in these turbulent times and learn to satisfy ourselves. This will, I hope, be a great advance.

If I now [...] voice my own purely personal opinion, this is not because I want to lay down the law [...] but because I can see that you now want me to show my true colors, so that everyone can decide where he stands in relation to me and to my plans. I shall try to avoid comparative criteria and set an absolute goal, as high a one as possible. I must inflict no mediocrity on you or on myself. We must never take our cue from the average philistine.

Ladies and gentlemen: externals first. Many beautiful frames, splendid presentation, finished pictures: for whose benefit exactly? I made a point of asking you to submit projects and sketches of ideas. Not one painter or sculptor has contributed compositional ideas of the kind that ought to form the nucleus of such an institution. Who today can paint a finished, fully executed picture? [...]

The most important thing for all of us is still experience, and what the human individual makes of it. We are in the midst of a vast catastrophe of world history: a transformation of the whole of life and of the whole inner human being. For the artistic individual, this may well be fortunate, if he is strong enough to take the consequences; for what we need is the courage for inner experience. This is what gives the artist a new way forward.

Many among us have become bogged down; they still lack true inner experience; but this is something that no one else can provide for them. It has to come from within themselves. Tepidity, lethargy, and complacency are the worst enemies of art. They lead to the materialistic historicism that holds us back so powerfully at present. By contrast, extreme intensity, the stimulation of the whole being by hardship, privation, terror, harsh encounters, or love, leads to authentic formal expression in art. Many students have only recently returned from the battlefield. Those who have had the experience of death have returned totally changed; they know that there is no way forward on the old paths. Looking at them, I can tell that many are unsure and at odds with themselves. One day, they will break free and know which way to go. There are surprises in store for us; some will resolve to start over again, even if they are already master students with established reputations. For my own part, and because I feel all this so distinctly, I would prefer not to force matters. It will all come from you. You will all honestly ask yourselves whether it is necessary to devote yourselves to art; whether the impulse within you is so violent, the forces so strong, as to overcome the enormous difficulties that arise from the current state of the world. Only the artist who can honestly say yes to this question has the right, in my view, to devote himself to art. Our impoverished State has little to spare for cultural matters and is unable to provide for those who want only to keep themselves occupied and to air a diminutive talent. Ladies and gentlemen, I owe it to my conscience to put it so forcefully. For I predict that, in the foreseeable future, many of you will be driven by sheer necessity to move into lucrative occupations; and those who stay with art will be those who are capable of starving for art's sake. We must put out of our minds the time "Before the War," which was entirely different. The sooner we adjust to a new and utterly changed world, and to its beauties—however harsh—the sooner the individual will find subjective happiness once again. As a result of Germany's plight, we shall gain in inwardness and depth. With the decline in material prospects, spiritual prospects have already risen tremendously. Before the War, we put the cart before the horse. We tried to bring art to the public by the back door, by organizing ourselves. We designed artistic ashtrays and beer steins, in the hope of gradually working our way up to architecture on a grand scale. All done by cool organization. This was an unwarrantable presumption, and we failed. Now it will all be the other way around. No more big, intellectual organizations but small, secret, enclosed leagues, cells, lodges, conspiracies, which set out to nurture a secret, a core of faith, and to give it artistic form—until out of all the individual groups there emerges a single great, universal, intellectual and religious idea that is destined to find ultimate, crystalline expression in one great artistic synthesis. And this great collective artwork, this Cathedral of the Future, will then shed its abundant light even into the smallest details of everyday life. This process will be the reverse of what happened before. We shall not live to see it; but we are, I firmly believe, the forerunners and the first instruments of a new world idea. The artist has hitherto stood quite alone, since in these chaotic times there is no unifying idea that will spiritually and materially turn the world upside down. The artist has the gift of second sight that enables him to read the spiritual parallels in an age and present them in pure form. If no such common mental ground exists, then he has no alternative but to build a metaphysical foundation of his own, entirely out of the self. He stands alone. No one—except possibly a few friends—understands him: the public at large certainly does not. To us as artists, the need to share some common mental ground with the people as a whole is as urgent as the need for bread. Unless the signs are all deceptive, the first hints of a new unity, which will succeed chaos, are already detectable. I dream of pulling scattered individuals out of their isolation and bringing them here to create a small community. If this works, much will have been achieved.

Finally, I return to the subject of craftsmanship. Over the next few years, craftsmanship will be a lifeline for us artists. We have a living to earn, and so we shall no longer exist alongside craftsmanship but operate within it. This process, which I would like to call historically inevitable, is a necessity for the production of great art. All the great artistic achievements of the past—the art of India, the miracles of the Gothic—arose from a sovereign mastery of craftsmanship.

You will ask me about the progress of my craft plans, to prevent the loss of those who cannot maintain themselves by the free practice of art. I am working incessantly to bring my plans to fruition. For sculptors, a practical workshop will be in operation by the fall; then, for painters, we hope to set up a training course run by a decorative painter. Then it will gradually become clear who wants to stay with us: who is a genuine apprentice, journeyman or junior master—terms that are now no more than a game, since the craft element in them has yet to become a reality. Much now depends on my ability to keep our budget intact, despite the poor economic prospects. If this can be done, in the fall I shall set about remodeling the Bauhaus with all the strength at my command, and I hope to give you a basis on which you can feel at home.

Translated by David Britt

The collapse of the Austro-Hungarian Empire during World War I precipitated widespread social unrest in Hungary. On October 31, 1918—just ten days before the proclamation of a republic in Berlin—the liberal Count Mihály Károlyi declared Hungary an independent republic and formed a government in which he served as Prime Minister. Károlyi, however, was not in a strong position, particularly because Hungary was unable to defend its then temporary new borders with military force. On March 21, 1919, Károlyi resigned and transferred the leadership to the Socialist Democrats—or so he thought. Unbeknownst to Károlyi, at the exact time he was offering his resignation, the Socialists and the imprisoned Communists were concluding a pact, the result of which was the declaration of the Proletarian Dictatorship in Hungary on the same day. The leader of the newly formed Revolutionary Governing Council was 33-year-old Béla Kun, who had become a Communist while a prisoner of war in the Soviet Union.

The leaders of the Hungarian Commune assumed as an article of faith that their revolution was part of an unfolding world revolution. Encouraged by the declaration of the Bavarian Soviet Republic and news of revolutionary activities in Austria and Italy, the Communist Party immediately nationalized industry, mines, banks, transportation, cultural institutions, and art collections.

Lajos Kassák and his avant-garde circle, socialists from the beginning, cooperated with the new government, but Kassák emphatically refused to serve as the mouthpiece of the Commune. Although he accepted several assignments from the philosopher György Lukács, the Commissar of Culture, working as poster censor, then theater censor, he wanted to safeguard the autonomy of art and artists, especially their distance from party politics.

The Commune was defeated by Czech and Romanian military forces in August 1919. The leaders of the Communist government, as well as all the intellectuals who participated or could be denounced as sympathizers, fled Hungary. Kassák and his group set up shop in Vienna, while many others found refuge in Germany, France, or Holland.

212

Addressed to you, Man, who were wracked by the bloody yoke of the war these past five
years, who dragged your body forth to face death for the sake of capitalism and today's
criminal ruling class; you who in your devastated homes have suffered and starved
until you became crippled and tubercular; addressed to you, young student and worker,
blinded in musty prisons for the sake of tomorrow's proletarian republic:

Men! Women!

Girls! and Boys!

Everyone!

The capitalist and feudal order still reigning in the world, the same that, abetted by the
corrupt press and the self-serving narcotic of politics, had sent with a single stroke of
the pen nations into war against one another, now, as a concession to the hatred of the
awakened masses against their class-rule, has managed to superimpose a veneer of
democracy over the originally imperialist purposes of the war.

But can this nationalist democracy that we too are now stuck with ever become more
than a bargained concession to the current distribution of wealth that has lowered us
to a shameful cultural level? For this distribution of wealth will use the bourgeois
democracy as a splendid springboard for the strengthening of the present rule of capital. We have already seen this in the French bourgeois republic that had swung into
the war with chauvinistic slogans. And now they would urge you with loud screams into
a new war, an immediate prospect of new carnage.

Men! Everyone whose minds are still sane and unpolluted by today's hasty, nationalistic jackal howls, everyone who has thrown off the king's gray uniforms and rejects
these apostles mouthing empty slogans—you will have to realize that your fate is in
your own hands, you proletarians whose lungs have been eaten away, you overworked
pariahs!

Be careful! Don't let today's newly outlined goals turn into a survival of the old imperialistic militarism dressed up in a new guise. Therefore we want to flash in front of you
the prospect of a Communist Republic as the one and only path toward the betterment
of the economic and political foundations of your lives. For we demand the greatest
possible freedoms for human society and for this reason proclaim the brotherly contact of the world's proletariats.

But be careful! For instead of this, the capitalist world order will make a final effort to
salvage the untenable social order of today under the guise of revolution.

Brothers! Rise up in anger against those deaf and blind ones who offer their backs and
would use your backs to support a democracy under nationalist colors.

For it can never happen that individuals with nearly diametrically opposed orientations
to yours will be able to empathize with the lives of those that have been economically
and politically raped for centuries.

Our interests are not the same as their interests! We firmly believe and proclaim that
only a radical transformation can open the way toward the only true democracy. It will
be the democracy of working people who coexist without restrictions, the democracy of
the Communist Republic. We firmly believe that this will be the fastest and only expedient method of providing everyone with the livelihood, culture, and maximal freedom
worthy of human dignity.

People! Workers! Soldiers! Students! All who have felt the boot heel of thugs!

We shine our torchlight on the free, monumental life of a working world! On welfare
without bickering and a culture that makes you fully human!

Brothers!

Let your liberated hearts step forth with a giant leap of will, and stamp out all that is compromise and trickery!

Long live the Communist Republic that is the sole and ultimate liberator from economic and political slavery!

Translated by John Bátki

PROCLAMATION FOR ART!   Lajos Kassák

Originally published as "Kiáltvány a művészetért!" *Ma* vol. 3, no. 11 (November 20, 1918)

Hear our shout issuing straight out of the chaos. Times are running amuck. What was, exists no more; but take care, because the future might also rapidly turn into a has-been in the bungling hands of the present. Who is able to put up with the current bourgeois idiocies constrained within four walls? Human willpower has leaped out into the frightened streets. The young student, the hunchbacked workingman, the soldier whose lungs have been shot through, all shine with the torchlight of their conscious commitment while you who embarrassingly pose as artists would settle for dancing to the most trivial music while howling for compromise!

Art is the bread and wine of motor-powered life!

But in Hungary art remains the last resort of feeble characters, irresponsible word-swillers, glorified freeloaders, and humans in canine guise howling at the moon!

We believe that in Hungary, since the feverish 1848 revolutionary poet Petőfi, it was only under the aegis of *Ma* that the first consciously willful group of artists have been able to blossom into full-grown maturity.

We were the first who, in the midst of the general drunkenness leading to the war, proclaimed the need for action in the face of action: the activity of life against the slaughterhouse of war.

While Hungarian "artists" joined the madness, in search of new themes, to recruit cannon fodder for the Big Berthas and to spit their venom against London, Paris and Rome, when the cheap lickspittles bellowed like would-be poets from the platforms of editorial offices—we in our desolation embraced our creative brothers anywhere in this sinking world.

The censorship of the dastardly ruling class throttled us in our holy infancy!

Yes, they, with the assistance of so-called "artists" squelched us, the artists who had liberated ourselves from the academies!

But we have resurrected, because our blood is the blood of the masses who possess the future, which we have taught them to claim as their own!

Only the gates behind us could be sealed; ahead of us lay an untried path. We had assigned ourselves a program, but could only insist on never turning back. The endless horizon stretches before our eyes. We proclaim that art cannot tie itself down to any one party or social class! For any special interest group is bound to be cursed with blindness beyond a certain point, and every prescribed program ossifies into legal paragraphs. And every law preserves results already achieved, and opposes free development.

Out lot is never to be contented!

Our way of life is a constant struggle forward!

We, more than anyone, are *social* beings, for our *socialism* stems from our very consciousness and temperament in daily life. Our socialism manifests itself in art. Cast beyond all political parties and economic class interest, we coil the springs of unbounded desire aimed at life. By our example we demonstrate the collective individuum: the stubborn will and thinking mind of the active masses! Our vocation is not to provide entertainment, but to incite action. Closed forms are for political tacticians and refined esthetes. We bubble over with life, for life throbs inside us. Obeying the laws of evolution we scrape clean the most painful wounds on the body social. Our art is the anarchy of synaesthesia. And we employ our unfettered energies to intervene in today's political gambles, in the kangaroo morality of bourgeois life, the inner sanctum of the philistine family, and in the brain-pickling business of public education.

Long live Anarchy, where the order of precedence is still unborn!

Death to all new forms that are new only to cover up the same old essentials!

The art of *Ma* is the new art-cum-worldview of contemporary forces. The young artists who join us bring not only new forms but also a conscious socialist worldview.

We want open, leveled spaces to make new construction possible!

That's all we want. Now. After five years of war, the masses roar their demand for a socialist order—and the facts are clear: we, anarchist artists, played a strong role in this. At the outset we nurtured energies and goals, and now we have by our side the wholesome energies of young lives. For them and together with them we demand democratic politics, and within those politics we demand our own recognition in the social order. We protest with every ounce of our being that we have thus far been fobbed off like clowns. For we are neither the entertainers of the ruling class, nor the pacifiers of the rebellious masses. We are fanatical spokesmen, along with the subjugated workingman, for a new and free human society.

In these times that are giving birth to a better way of life, when all workers demand to be represented in forming the new government to safeguard their social and economic rights, we, too, insist on our role in ensuring the possibilities of advancement!

Artists! Painters! Sculptors! Actors! Writers!

In the name of your disrupted lives we demand to be heard everywhere and demand our body- and soul-exhausting work to be at last recognized as an actual product that is vital and indispensable for promoting the development of human society!

We demand that within the framework of the new government, in place of the former ministry of religious affairs, which in a new social system has no rational or practical justification, there be a new cabinet post of minister of arts, by the side of the minister of education, for the moral and material support of the arts.

Artists! Those of you who have ever taken the measure of your strength, who are no longer content with prostituting yourselves in the unconditional service of those in power, but are aware of your active role in destroying the barriers and pointing the way for the great evolution—we call upon you to adopt our demands!

Now is the time to cast off the thousand times accursed mask of aristocratic pretensions, to let our faces be known to each other! For we never had a better occasion to assist the aims of art that speaks the truth and is second to none!

If you don't speak up now, you will once again be stuck in a moral and economic morass!

Brothers! At a time when everyone is realistically seeking to right the balance of everyday life for themselves, don't insist on remaining glorified fools doomed to live in the clouds!

Translated by John Bátki

SOVIET HUNGARY SINCE MARCH 21   Georg Kulka

Originally published as "Seit dem 21 März in Sowjetungarn," *Die Aktion* vol. 9,
no. 33–34 (August 23, 1918)

Our Hungarian comrades have now had their cultural work disrupted by the hoodlums
of the international bourgeoisie. Be of good cheer: Soviet Hungary will soon arise!
World Revolution is unstoppable—in spite of everything!
—F[ranz] P[femfert]

The utterly unhealthy treatment of art in our utterly unhealthy society can be cured
only by a total upheaval. Communism is determined to bring the human being that the
artist remodels by the strongest means—the means of art—so close to the human
being who is an artist that the people will have the independence, maturity, and competence to take the initiative in all artistic matters.

Strictly for the transitional period, a directorate has been set up with plenipotentiary
powers for the conduct of artistic and museum affairs. It consists of two painters, one
sculptor, one artist-craftsman, one architect, and two art historians. This directorate
is assisted by a commission made up of eighteen of the country's artists, who will del-
egate committees to perform specific tasks.

The first committee will be charged with setting up a registry. Its task is to create a
labor union for artists and draw up record sheets for those artists who claim remu-
neration from the State for their creative work. Anyone may claim such sheets. They
are under an obligation to complete them truthfully by listing the works or activities
that qualify them for membership of the Artist's Union. The Union is composed of those
workers in the fine arts who have been selected by the registry committee. It elects
its own council, which exercises the political rights of the group of workers in question
by deputizing members to take seats in the Soviet.

Union members receive support from the State in the form of a monthly stipend. Since
the Soviet Government classifies artists in the top income category, the registry committee admits to the Union only those workers whose purely artistic products show
them to be worthy of this legal status. The stipend will not in any way be a sinecure. No
one is to be precluded from exercising any artistic activity for which he has a talent.
For this, membership of the Artists' Union is not necessary. For this reason, members
of other labor unions (architects, draftsmen, and handicraft workers, among others)
will not readily give up their existing, secure positions; in the Soviet State no one can
belong to more than one union. Artists who are members of other unions receive special fees. Anyone who dares to become a member of the Artists' Union has to show
enough acceptable artistic work to guarantee that he can earn a living by it. For exceptional creative achievements, honorary awards are made.

Only the new creativity that appeared a few years before the worldwide upheaval can
match the rhythm of the new life, overcome the narrow and criminal nationalist consciousness, and serve the ends of a collective, supranational endeavor. Accordingly, the
Hungarian Soviet Government, which calls upon all youthful creative forces to create a
new life, has entrusted the State provision of art to artists who, because they made no
concessions to the capitalist order, were formerly unknown or misunderstood.

Now the old academic institutions and their spirit are being destroyed. A proletarian
school of fine art, housed in the town mansion of Count Julius Andrassy, concentrates
exclusively on training talented proletarian individuals who previously lacked opportunities to cultivate their gifts. One of its two courses admits persons of obvious talent,
approximately twenty to thirty of them, who are withdrawn from collective production. In addition there will be an evening course, from which the best students will be

gradually transferred to the first course. This independent school, which by no means supersedes the Institute of Fine Arts, is by no means a place to teach children: only young workers who have given real evidence of talent are admitted. The teaching system parallels the Gropius-Itten method adopted for the rejuvenated Weimar architecture school. [...]

Translated by David Britt

ART OF THE REVOLUTION—OR ART OF THE PARTY?   Árpád Szélpál
Originally published as "Forradalmi művészet—vagy pártművészet," *Ma* vol. 4, no. 1 (January 26, 1919)

I would prefer to speak of "art," plain and simple, without any adjectives. But today, in a time of infectious, viral prosperity it is necessary to clearly define my position by presenting my thesis in these terms: art of the revolution—or art of the party.
I will use the following concepts:
Art: the intuitive positioning of the self in the cosmic context, or rather the synthesized expression of this in sensory forms.
Art of the revolution: the synthesis is accomplished with the aim of changing existing worldviews, their advancement and continual recharging with ever more progressive contents.
Art of the party: the synthesis is a revolutionary program tuned conservative, because the goal of realizing a specific program becomes, instead, one of preserving a political party.
The difference between the two artistic approaches as defined above is at once obvious. We may state that the difference lies in the perspective of the artist creating the synthesis; that is, in the degree of liberation inherent in the artist's thinking.
The artist—the revolutionary artist—is characterized by a refusal to be satisfied, a constant searching; and by the struggle with the self, with artistic problems, and against programs that have fossilized into rules.
The true artist never *accepts* any party platform or worldview. He *creates*, for himself and for the whole world. But as soon as he has created it, he has already transcended it for a more advanced program, only to leave that one behind as well.
It is precisely this permanent state of revolution that justifies art and raises it above any worldview, as a torch guiding humankind.
The preservation of existing values through academies was always an obstacle to the fulfillment of the mission of art. Every school of art, every academy is a militant opponent of progress, and is disastrous from the point of view of development.
The history of Hungarian literature supports every aspect of my thesis.
The figure of Petőfi has stood for revolution in Hungarian literature. But every single value introduced by him has been preserved by his academic epigones over the past half century. It took the revelation of Nyugat to demonstrate what this had come to mean for Hungarian cultural development: Petőfi's revolutionary art of 1848, crushed into academic molds and vitiated by traditionalists, was still used in 1900 to bludgeon artists seeking the new.
But *Nyugat* was not synonymous with revolution, for its writers have not introduced a new worldview. Endre Ady, the seminal figure of the Nyugat group, concluded the

revolution started by Petőfi. Ady brought a new voice and new forms, but did not offer a new worldview.

As for the rest, they represent the Hungarian versions of various fashionable foreign trends. As such, they preclude the possibility of revolution. They have transplanted styles that had already evolved into schools abroad—that is, have already been preserved. Being passive receivers, these writers cannot be called revolutionary, nor their effects revolutionary, for they have not brought with them a new worldview, merely the external features of Impressionism or Symbolism. They excelled in technique, in the poetics of l'art pour l'art. Outstanding among them is Mih<ly Babits, an academic in the fullest sense of the word. He has not brought a new worldview into our literature, has not signaled a revolution. The trajectory of Ady's turbulent career crashed in and around Babits. The writers in the Nyugat group are conservatives. They have dissociated themselves from daily life, and have labored in a rigid and cloistered l'art pour l'art manner, in pursuit of the metaphysical fiction of the beautiful.

Thanks to their decade of literary busy-work they have been left behind by the times, and must now admit that their work has been aimless and even harmful.

The new, young, revolutionary artists have turned away from them, in search of new paths and more progressive contents.

Babits, in his most recent "Annual Steward's Report," seeks the young newcomers, but it seems his harbor lights are not bright enough, his academic's eyes cannot see the new talent. And he blames the young for this. Where is the youngest generation hiding? What have they done with all the heavy experiences forced upon their virgin souls by this age?! After such mawkish plaints Babits concludes in resignation: "There is no one to accept the torch from our hands." The light of the Piraeus torch!

Babits is incapable of noticing the young writers who cast forth the terrible events of the past four years, along with their yearning for the future, all bloody and raw, somewhat faltering perhaps, but conscious and militant, casting it out of themselves and casting themselves, too, in front of humankind!

Yes, the young ones, dismissed by Babits in his article as "would-be futurists" are here—we are here—artists and therefore revolutionaries, to fight every convention, academy, and stagnation, every manifestation of capitalism. We will always find the present inadequate and we shall never be contented with the future.

We shall not accept the torch from Babits' hands, but will light ourselves up, living torches for humankind.

We shall not accept the heritage of Nyugat. We shall not tolerate the shackles of any heritage. We do not recognize traditions and we do not create traditions, but will fight for ever more progressive contents.

Since the time of Petőfi, whose revolution culminated in the person of Ady, the first new revolution in Hungarian literature has been brought about by the pages of Ma. Ma is revolutionary because it has introduced a new worldview, Ma is revolutionary because it is devoid of tradition and it refuses to create a tradition; it is both the evidence and the maker of revolution, for instead of importing foreign schools it publishes the worldviews that have erupted from its artists after bloody battles within themselves.

Artists—and again let me emphasize, I consider only revolutionary artists as such—are characterized by realization in all their manifestations. The realization of their art means the realization of their selves. Their art is their position in the cosmos, and realization consists of its sensory presentation, that is, its expression by living it out. Every act of realization—that is, every artistic manifestation—means precisely this expression through living it out. For this very reason the same acts are avoided in the artist's subsequent activity, for the artist's next production can only be a newer realization, beyond this phase. Every manifestation by a revolutionary artist is the realization of a fresher and more advanced content.

The preservation of this more advanced content—that is, halting at a certain stage—is no longer art. This is the task of craftsmen, whose work amounts to transforming the revolution wrought by artists and tailoring it to the taste of the public. But this kind of work is no longer art (in my sense of the word), for it lacks the essential requirement of art: claiming a place in the cosmic context. Moreover, it is definitely harmful for, by preserving the revolution, it creates a narcosis to divert people from the momentum provided by the revolutionary artist.

There can be no doubt that such "journeyman artists" are conscious or unconscious servants of the current social order, highly rewarded by capitalism (not necessarily openly, but in various complex and clandestine ways) for lowering the revolutionary content to the level of the audience, using their legerdemain to drug the public and distract it from an awareness of the elemental force it possesses.

It is equally certain that in a communist economic system these "craftsmen" will be toppled from the high horses on which they were enthroned by a capitalist system in furtherance of its own well-considered interests. The value of their art will plummet accordingly.

Thus art—in the sense I have indicated—is revolutionary in its effects, creative in its manifestations (and destructive in its creativeness); its aim is to provide direction, and its ultimate effect is to elevate humankind into the cosmos.

Therefore we want art to be creative instead of receptive.

For this very reason, I categorically condemn the "art" that I have earlier defined as "art of the party."

A party always means a group of people united by their desire to realize or perpetuate an already existing worldview, which they define in a specific party platform.

But art, as I have already made clear, cannot embody any single platform or worldview, but must keep on producing ever newer and more advanced worldviews. For this reason, no artist can ever fit into the framework of any one party, no matter how broad that may be.

The moment an artist becomes ensconced within a political party, he loses the possibility of freely unfolding his creative powers, for the synthesis of his positioning in the cosmos has to take place within the limits, and in the interest of, the party's platform, thus costing him the essence of his art. An artist's alliance with a political party may make sense as a career move and lead to prosperity, but such considerations lie so far from what we value as art that it is superfluous to belabor the unethical nature of such a move.

An artist's worldview can only mean a personal stand and never a party platform. The artist's manifestations should never be the sounding board for the slogans of a political party. His worldview forms the basis for his particular synthesis, which renders his art perceptible.

The slogans of a party's platform or worldview may be broadcast amidst much gesticulating as bombastic editorials disguised as poems but can never elevate the individual into the cosmos that leads to a universal fraternity.

In this regard, there is no difference between "conservative" or "revolutionary." For even a revolutionary party stands for the preservation of a worldview in the form of a program. In comparison to art, it is mere conservatism. It amounts to the same thing, the poets of the Social Democratic party composing jingles based on Marxist tenets or the new poets clamoring "Revolution! Communism! Class warfare! Our three best words!" in the Communist Party paper *Internacionale*

The artist's creative power, which inevitably makes him a revolutionary beyond all schools and political parties in its free manifestation and suggestive power, never reflects the tendencies of a party's alignment but instead elevates into the cosmic context. Instead of hooted slogans, the dynamics of realization.

Therefore we may conclude that only a revolutionary art can fulfill the mission of art; thus we accept only a revolutionary art as art.

The various schools can convey only the externals of the revolutionary momentum of one artist or another. The creative revolution, in their cases, has been preserved as acceptance; the force of the momentum has been broken in a way that is inimical to progress.

Revolutionary parties are militant groups of people who accept a worldview that is already extant, albeit not realized in practice. The artist aligned with such a party to produce tendentious manifestations makes neither art nor revolution, but merely preserves. This is a dangerous derailment on the road of progress, for only the artist's unfettered advance can ensure the next revolution and, in turn, the popular acceptance of the previous worldview—already a conservative view when measured against the artist's revolution.

In sum, only revolutionary art justifies itself by fulfilling its mission and the concept of art—of *art* sans adjective—which we trust and hold to be the guiding torch of humanity.

Translated by John Bátki

ACTIVISM   Lajos Kassák
Lecture given February 20, 1919, published in *Ma* vol. 4, no. 4 (1919)

Activism—a new term in our social movement. It translates as *direct action*. I prefer to understand it in a broader and more comprehensive sense as the spontaneous and permanently revolutionary conduct of life for oppressed people, people who will only be redeemed by their own efforts. It was upon this broadly conceived basis, and with this purpose, that the Budapest Activists group was founded, intending to carry on our movement toward individual revolution that will outlast all forms of government and party dictatorships.

The bankruptcy of the capitalist system of production was accompanied by the moral bankruptcy of contemporary man. The only possible approach to rebuilding our world is through international proletarian revolution, leading to a communist economy. The political renovation of capitalist society, merely repainting the signs of the special interest groups, will not suffice to rekindle production in our days. Rational and truly productive work can only begin with the demolition of a society that is drowning in chaos, and its replacement by a socialist society built on the rights of labor.

Clearly the redemption of the world awaits the power of the proletariat risen in revolt.

It awaits that portion of humankind whose sole way of life is action in ceaseless support of progress—awaits the masses that obey the same inextinguishable laws that move the earth and the stars. It will no longer originate only in consciously made decisions, but will stem from the revolution of creative energies bursting to be liberated. Thus it is true that the ultimate, the one and only revolution can only come into full triumphant swing beyond the cold dialectics and speculative expectations of ameliorist results, when it will burst out of the blood and guts of the masses, a surplus energy that cannot be constrained within existing channels, life at a maximal level insisting on finding new forms. This is the revolution of constant action, the struggle for the ultimate goals of socialism.

Whatever falls outside of this movement—or promotes it gradually, step by step—is mere local interest, tactical consideration, party squabbles: in other words, classical conservatism. Beyond the totally unconscious revolt of hungry bellies, social democracy is the first significant stage of this gradual advance toward revolution. It is a movement that cleverly maneuvers greater mobility and better living conditions for the working class, a typical party movement that is to be credited with opening the floodgates. But beyond this primitive initial capability social democracy is actually reactionary; in the acute stage of revolutionary outbreak it becomes an ideology of compromise saturated by petit bourgeois sentimentality, in actuality a counterrevolutionary factor opposing the active proletariat.

We are not utopians.

Since we need to build a new human being for a new society, we must keep in mind that this ultimate objective of socialism is not going to be achieved overnight. In order for this to happen, the revolutionized proletariat must advance beyond the stage of demanding higher standards of living. It must experience a psychic rebirth, from the uncertainty of comfortable well-being to the certitude of not settling for any other way of life.

In a revolution with a clear sense of direction, there are various stages along the straight line of advance. Social democracy and Communism are such stages. Between these two there are no fundamental differences of worldview. They differ only in their tactics (an all-important difference), both being weapons of socialism as a revolutionary world-view. Thus neither social democracy nor a communist economy constitute the final goal. Both are merely instruments but, as such, both can be a destructive or a constructive force. This is the reason we as Activists, even while believing that bourgeois society can only be toppled by the spontaneous and self-sustainable explosion of the revolutionary power of a majority of the people (the workers), nonetheless endorse the current party struggles, and deem them necessary.

We believe that, without the fuel of parties and party struggles, the revolution could not be directed to lead to *results* within a foreseeable time. There is a need for political parties. It follows that we, as collective individuums fighting for the collective individuum that will unite the masses, must take a stand for and against the respective political parties participating in the current social upheavals.

[...]

From the workers' point of view, each moment of vacillation is a matter of life and death. For this class the hour has come for decisive action. The Social Democrats are correct in citing Marx: true to his prediction, capitalism is not going to choke in its own fat, the warehouses today are not overflowing with surplus goods. But their minds, poisoned by a pseudo-democratic humanitarianism, fail to take into consideration the effects of a five-year-long world war with which a militarist imperialism had intended to solve the problems of its stockpiled goods, its hunger for foreign raw materials, and the increasing demands of the working class. This war has brought about, although in a form contrary to Marx's prediction, the bankruptcy of capitalism, the breakdown of imperialistic militarism, and unemployment of vast proportions. The unexpected outcome of the war has put an unexpected order in the calculations of capitalism. Today's capitalist system, having used the starvation-wage labor of the proletariat to fatten itself into a power that set the standard of living, has slipped up in its calculations, and those who only yesterday still cheered it must today strive to keep it alive in order to stay alive themselves. The collapse of production has created millions of unemployed, a mass of people that (now that the tables are turned) must be supported by the former exploiters, and for this very reason the world proletariat has nothing to lose in its life-and-death struggle.

[...]

Capitalism and the proletariat, the oppressor and the oppressed, have always been, ever since their inception, increasingly aware of their eternal enmity. They can never come to an agreement based on so-called human understanding, for each must struggle against the other for its own welfare. Thus not only material interests but also rigorous, inherent psychic laws incite each against the other. In the perceived interest of their very existence they can have only one aim: total triumph over the other. Anyone presuming to stand as an intermediary between them, although in the best of faith, is bound to end up a traitor to his own class[...]

The dilemma of "democracy or dictatorship" posited by socialist-patriotic scholars is not a real dilemma. Our experience proves beyond any doubt that the proletariat can free itself from the yoke of capital only through its own efforts by way of revolution, completely demolishing the capitalist system. Real democracy can arise only out of the ethical freedom possessed by the new man of a new society built upon the balancing of economic forces. As long as the laws remain in force and insist on vetoing the individual in the interests of the community, only the ignorant or the demagogue can speak of democracy. Real democracy can only arise out of the majority's awareness of its power.

Today's democracy[...]is merely the reluctant benevolence of an oppressing minority toward the oppressed masses. Its motivation is not the superiority of power but a recognition of weakness. Its task is not the establishment of equality but the maintenance of the status quo. It helps to establish capitalism on a new foundation while placing blinders on the working class. It is a fetishism that provides opportunities to some and denies opportunities to others. Thus it has nothing to do with its vaunted slogan "equality." It is simply an item listed under investments in the bookkeeping of the contemporary bourgeoisie[...]

[...]

For the proletariat such a democracy offers, instead of a road to survival, only a death-trap with jaws of steel. Therefore any party that would lead the working class down this road has forfeited its role in the transformation of our world and has knowingly or unintentionally betrayed the revolution. For what was necessary and beneficial yesterday has soured into something untenable and evil today. Granted that, starting with the starvation-motivated earliest socialist movements, all the way to the awakening to the potentials for a more fully human existence (occasioned by the world war), the democracy enforced by this minority was a necessary means in the proletariat's struggle. However by this time it has become an enormous drawback, and like some malicious demon it has wrapped a veil of illusions around the mind of the oppressed masses.

The Social Democrats claim that democracy has enabled the working class to organize itself, to emerge from its bestial condition and begin to approach a more human standard of living. This may be true, but it is also true that this democratic process was initiated and enforced not so much by the kindhearted oppressors as by the increasingly conscious and active efforts toward liberation made by the oppressed class, eager to loosen the suffocating grip of capitalism on its throat. It is likewise true that in this struggle for democracy, which was still rooted in economic motives, the working class has fully adopted the political style of the bourgeoisie. The material gains they have managed to squeeze out of the so-called "humanitarianism" of the enemy have been counterbalanced by the losses suffered by their own revolutionary character, through failing to recognize the nature of this pseudo-democracy. Before they could realize it they were deep in the morass of a power- and will-consuming cohabitation with the very parties against which they had launched their slave revolt. The bourgeoisie's splendidly successful tactic gave a voluntary appearance to the concessions the increasing power of the working class had forced out of them.

[...]

The October revolution in Russia introduced a new struggle employing new means between the oppressors and the oppressed. In this struggle the Communist Party seized the leading role from the Social Democrats, and their red flags carried the rule of dictatorship as their battle cry, in place of a compromising democracy.

This new struggle constitutes the momentous launching of the first purely proletarian revolution. It is the struggle of a minority against the majority, but this majority is no longer comprised of the bourgeoisie. It is a most heterogeneous group, whose brunt is made up not by oppressors suddenly aware of their power but by the oppressed masses misguided by the empty phrases of democracy. For this reason the path of the Communist Party through the entirety of this struggle will require a greater human sacrifice than that consumed by the path of the Social Democrats. The Social Democratic Party had opposed only the capitalists trying to save their own skin, whereas the working-class forces of the Communist Party face their most powerful foes in the workers corrupted by bourgeois mentality, whose weapons in theory and practice equal those of their revolutionary opponents. It would seem that this fight is not so much between oppressors and the oppressed, but exclusively between the right and left wings of the latter masses. It remains a fratricidal war, as long as the one and only mutual enemy, protected by a portion of the enslaved, is still making an ultimate effort to organize the universal suppression of the working class by engaging it in internecine warfare. If however we were to look for a cause of this fratricidal struggle, contrary to the plaintive claims of the Social Democrats who blame it in the Communist Party's disruption of the united front, we would assign it to the betrayal by the Social Democrats who sacrificed the interest of the working class to those of the capitalists. There has indeed been a rift in the united front of the proletariat. But this rift was caused not by the so-called wrong track taken by the Communists but by the Social Democrats becoming bogged down in the mire. Revolution is the path of the proletariat. A portion of the working class, in spite of its misinformation, has once again recognized this path and intends to take it all the way to the fulfillment of its goals. Victory will go to the party that is demonstrably right. The charges made by the Social Democrats have been unequivocally answered by the victory of the Bolsheviks in Russia and the establishment of the dictatorship of the proletariat here in Hungary[...]

The fiery avalanche of proletarian revolution has broken out in the East to light up the world in its red glow, and today, one step ahead of the German, English, and Italian workers, our own will to change the world is being purified in the fire.

There is no stopping now.

The Social Democratic Party has attained for the proletariat the possibility of organizing itself, and with this newfound strength the Communist Party will create the basis for the ultimate goal of socialism, which is a communist economy. This creative work is revolutionary action in the strictest sense of the word. Its path leads through destruction. Its first productive result is the dictatorship of the proletariat. According to historical evolution the class struggle is unimaginable without dictatorship. The dictatorship is not a goal, but the result of a conscious striving forward, which has always acted as an indispensable obstacle against the enemy's repeated attempts to organize itself into a reaction. This explains the horrified protest of classes and parties that have outlived their purpose against the dictatorship of the newly emerged forces. For us Activists there can be no doubt about the necessity of the dictatorship of the proletariat. But now we must emphasize that from a viewpoint that is contrary to that of the reaction we, too, possess a critical and militant opinion of all dictatorships including that of the proletariat. For it, too, is a dangerous double-edged weapon, like all forms of power established for autocratic reasons (and all forms of power are autocratic, even if they represent the seemingly supreme interests of large groups and not merely of individuals). This dictatorship arises in opposition to the reaction and soon enough it becomes a reaction against the revolution itself. Therefore we offer a simultaneous evaluation of the dictatorship from the left and the right. On the right we wish to join it with our supportive critique in its fight against reaction; on the left we oppose it with our agitation demanding further progress toward that individual human revolution that lies beyond the solution of economic problems and the salvation of any one class.

The dictatorship is necessary. It is the foremost evidence of power, and it will both consecrate and terminate party struggles. Today we witness the first steps of a new political party that has higher aspirations than any other party had before. Only from this party can the proletariat expect the purposeful leadership of the political and economic movement, and only this movement can solve the ultimate economic problems. Up to this point we agree with its revolutionary mission. But once this has been accomplished we believe that it, like every other party, will "sober up" into reaction against the revolution. This is axiomatic. The Social Democratic Party has removed the ruling power from the hands of a single autocrat and placed it into the hands of the bourgeois republic; today the Communist Party's mission is the total annihilation of this form of power and the establishment of proletarian councils to replace an irresponsible parliament.

We wish to stress here that ultimately, beyond the economic struggles, the latter movement—as any party movement—shapes its politics to maintain governing power; that their Soviet ideal, seen from the viewpoint of the revolution, constitutes another conservative power structure opposed not only to the right-wing counterrevolution but also to the left-wing revolution that insists on continuation. Revolutions are always created by the momentarily awakened soul of the people; in this process political parties can only provide leadership in organizing the various forces and giving them direction. To this extent they are necessary as active factors in actual life, but beyond this sphere they become passive, and by fostering a general contentment are in fact the most potent obstacles to progress. We have historical evidence in stating that just as the Social Democrats are now crying out to the working class to desist, even so will the Communist Party, beyond a certain point, cry out to a revolutionary humanity.

The revolution of the political parties does not yet constitute the great all-consuming revolution of life. All parties, even the most ambitious ones, have power interests, and upon the realization of these interests they want to secure, as a form of bourgeois contentment, the results of the revolution—and this striving for equilibrium, for the consolidation of achieved results, spells the termination of the party's effective lifetime. This lifetime begins with revolutionary uprising against dictatorships and concludes with the establishment of an antirevolutionary dictatorship.

For us the meaning of life lies therefore beyond the speculative revolution of political parties, in the endlessness of existential revolution.

This is the revolution of life becoming conscious of itself, a fight beyond the political and economic battles, humankind's struggle to find its own identity.

With this conceptual definition we declare the rebirth of the human soul as the barely definable ultimate goal of the revolution—beyond Communism, which is held by many to be the ultimate goal, while it is merely the next stage of development, the single realistic foundation of the socialist ideal. We do not want to be misunderstood: our actions do not intend to undermine the forces concentrated to establish the economic underpinnings, but provide assistance for the subjective utilization of these forces.

[...]

Following the economic revolution achieved in cooperation with the Communist Party, the most important task of our Activist group is work on the preparation and constant sustenance of the above-mentioned revolution.

The fight for the liberation of the body from the yoke of slavery is not enough; it must be accompanied by a struggle for the liberation of the likewise enslaved soul.

[...]

By recognizing this truth we have progressed through an analysis of history, and it becomes obvious that, by laying claim to the fullest life possible, we have created the necessity of organizing a militant force that goes far deeper. Therefore scientific research, literature, the fine arts, and music, arts with a worldview one and all, now demand a place in the preparation of the revolution. There are many who—whether because they resist the truth or fail to recognize the effective power of art—could easily misunderstand my formulation. These gentlemen could easily recruit support of their denial of the revolutionary power of art and its mission in creating the new man. But on the basis of historical evidence, we can forestall them by pointing out that one of the strongest props of bourgeois society has always been a spineless, self-prostituting art. It was this art that injected the inhuman morality of the oppressing class into the slave's psyche, and served to promote the helpless acceptance of the yoke and the spread of militarist madness. We have seen, and still see in our days, the practical examples of this in the supplying of millions with their narcotic against the sufferings of life. But if it is true that *l'art pour l'art* has the power to hinder the economic revolution, it is equally true that the new art, equipped with a total worldview, possesses its own revolutionary power. To prove this, we can once again turn to Russia for an imperfect yet instructive example.

[...]

If we consider the process stretching from Turgenev's nihilism to Gorky's socialist humanism, involving the labors of an entire army of writers, resulting in individual acts of terrorism and desperate suicides, we are able to see, heading toward revolution, fanatical students and urban workers refusing to tolerate the yoke any longer, all of whom had been incited by the worldview of these writers to shake themselves loose from the "order" of bourgeois society. This degree of moral transformation can not be found among the population of any of the Western countries. Western civilization means an irresponsible class culture. In the West the main thrust of the arts was toward fashions in form, while in the East aesthetics and stylistic frivolity were utterly neglected in favor of maximal depth of meaning. The results are obvious to see.

While on the one side the souls contaminated by the so-called arts became more and more deactivated by the tendentious narcosis served up by the bourgeoisie, on the other side a people thrashing under the oppression of capitalism turned to the arts to acquire a truly revolutionary consciousness.

[...]

Thus we see that the transformation of the world does not depend solely on economic factors. They constitute the material fuel of the flames, and bring results utilizable in time, but beyond all that awaits the true increment in ethical value, revolutionary man.

[...]

And today it has become obvious that in the unstoppable process of world revolution those ethnic groups will progress farthest in a practical sense who possess the greatest amount of psychic revolutionary power. In Hungary the prospects are very slim for this kind of fuel to run the locomotives of history. We are familiar with the historical background of this hopelessness. And for this very reason people who think will understand that we Activists, holding as our ultimate goal what cannot be reached from a Marxist basis, still hold Communism to be the most significant practical result, while we are also fighting for the collective individuum, which we hold to be the guarantee of a permanent state of revolution. We are not scientists but artists who are aware of what life is about, and art is the proper manifestation of our minds and emotions. In line with the practical division of labor in the service of the revolution we hold our art to be our most useful contribution in the great struggle and we believe in the ability of this new art to build a new man, just as we believe in the already proven revolutionary power and worldview of Russian art.

[…]

Are we too early, or already too late? There are those who, behind earnest masks, charge us with either. And both opinions are correct, one from the revolutionary, the other from the counterrevolutionary viewpoint.

The only thing our critics fail to notice is that behind us, prior to the revolution that is now organizing itself into consciousness, the appearance of a variety of artistic movements (Futurism, Cubism, Expressionism, Simultanism) has already signaled the onset of an as yet unconscious, anarchic revolution.

These movements used emotions to destroy, whereas we use our minds to lay the first foundations of a building process, besides demolishing. They had answers only for the why, whereas we also possess the answer to the whither.

They had condemned and refused to tolerate any further vegetation in the morass of bourgeois society; we, in awakening to ourselves, have also found the paths leading to life.

This ragged world can be set upon a new path only by the dictatorial class-revolution of the proletariat. Only Communism can redeem the collapse of the bourgeois-capitalist system of production. The irresponsible parliament of social classes can only be followed by the workers' Republic of Councils as the first stage of the community of awakened human beings, toward a collective individuum that recognizes no form of government and exists in a state of permanent revolution. For action is the fullest form of life.

The as yet small group of Activists insists on this revolution, on bringing it to consciousness and keeping it in motion, without any sidetracks. And we believe that the most deeply effective agitative instrument for reaching this goal is scientific research and our new art with its new worldview, and even if some political party were to stifle the revolution for the sake of its own interests, we shall be the first to cry out, "Long live the revolution!"

Translated by John Bátki

WE NEED A DICTATORSHIP! Béla Uitz
Originally published as "Diktatúra kell!" *Vörös Újság* (April 10, 1919)

(Commentary on Comrade József Révai's article, "We Need a Clear Proletarian Politics")

Dictatorship is needed in painting as much as it is needed in today's society. Among painters the revolutionary artists stand opposed to the reactionaries, artists with revolutionary social views stand opposed to those with a bourgeois humanist worldview who believe in patching things up. The latter are worse than the most reactionary artist, because their delaying tactics and reforms give time for the reactionary art and worldview that was defeated and weakened by the revolution, to recover its strength. The only art needed by the dictatorship of the proletariat is art with a social revolutionary worldview. Let the others step aside, for the duration of the dictatorship; even if they are well meaning and wish to help, they will only do harm to the dictatorship of the proletariat and to pure art as well. They possess no worldview; or, if they do, it is a capitalistic one. Thus their help is an intrusion that dilutes, hinders, and weakens revolutionary art and the revolutionary worldview. We must have a worldview, and we must have revolution—for only the consuming flames of these two can annihilate compromise, spinelessness, and unethical behavior.

The proletarian dictatorship has destroyed the corruption of capitalism, which was exploitation. In painting we must likewise destroy all compromise, that is, corruption. It is no excuse that hunger, the demands of the empty belly forced the artist to compromise. (And this is not always the case; in most cases it is greed and individualistic bourgeois selfishness that kills art.) This is where the sharpest distinction lies between the revolutionary and the bourgeois worldviews. A talented artist with a bourgeois worldview may say, "I will compromise a little bit for I need money; later I can be revolutionary." The artist with a revolutionary worldview is prevented by his ethics from behaving this way, as may be seen in innumerable instances past and present. Such artist spat at the eyes of bourgeois tastemakers, and starved and died of tuberculosis before they yielded their principles. For the artist with a bourgeois worldview art is simply *l'art pour l'art*, and also a livelihood; for the artist possessing a social revolutionary worldview, art is a creed. The former's art is frequently prostituted, while for the latter the very thought is inconceivable, for art is something to give one's life for.

The progress of art must parallel that of the spirit of the social order that is being formed now. We hereby voice our protest against the jostling for "positions" by certain elements that only yesterday were sworn enemies of socialism. Yesterday they were making speeches against communism, and today they are the most bloodthirsty communists. These are the most harmful and disruptive elements, for just as they swear by the revolution today, tomorrow, if their interests require it, they will swear by the counter-revolution. They lack revolutionary conviction the same way that their work lacks the conviction of pure art. If need be, they are Impressionists today and Post-Impressionists tomorrow, the day after that classicists—whatever way the trade winds of prosperity happen to be blowing (see for instance the Ernst Museum). Compromise is second nature for them, and it cannot be otherwise. For they lack a worldview, and thus their culture manifests itself at best in conventional exercises. For this reason in the present circumstances when a revolutionary worldview is needed they create the most harmful confusion in people who are thirsting for culture.

They have no social revolutionary art, they have no real affiliation—so how could they teach others to develop a social worldview? The most they can accomplish is to propagate the opposite worldview, that of capitalism.

The argument that one may be a fine artist while being a royalist or a bourgeois is untenable. The former is characterized by the painting of battle scenes, the latter by prudishness and art for the brothel. These are conventional examples, and as such superficial; in contrast they like to refer to so-called "eternal values." But these "eternal values" have been posited by bourgeois aesthetes, unaware of the true values of art, its revolutionary character and creative power. If art is a revolutionary creed, then it cannot entail the artist lowering his art to serve non-artists, but on the contrary, it should mean the elevation of fellow creatures to the level of artist, at least for the duration of viewing the work, and if possible beyond that. In other words, the uplifting and advancement of our fellow citizens.

The socialist worldview is of a higher order than the capitalist worldview. The social revolutionary worldview, by solving material problems, transcends and excludes the capitalist worldview. The latter is material, the former is spiritual. The capitalist worldview has left its brand upon its art. Capitalism is founded on class exploitation— that is, on unethical behavior. The painting of battle scenes for dining room walls, or bedroom paintings to stimulate bourgeois genitalia are all compromises and appendages of a capitalist immorality.

Society gives birth to and determines its art forms—therefore how could an artist with a capitalist worldview determine the direction of social revolutionary art?

We insist that the art of a communist society be directed by men who bears no trace of compromise in their art or their political past, men whose ethics and revolutionary art are beyond reproach. We are not attacking individuals, but art that is polluted and has no worldview. We have no desire to keep disparaging the artist in ourselves, for we believe that art is not an end in itself but, on the part of the artist, the sole possibility of manifesting one's life, and on the part of the viewer, a necessity of the highest order. We have arrived at the first stage in the solution of the problem of mankind's economic situation, and its instrument is the dictatorship of the proletariat. We, artists with a social revolutionary worldview, profess our belief that the sole means of developing new cultural needs is likewise a dictatorship, an intellectual dictatorship.

Proletarians, defend the art that is pure, revolutionary and possesses a social worldview, for by doing so you are protecting your most sacred rights!

Translated by John Bátki

MASS CULTURE, MASS ART   Iván Hevesy
Originally published as "Tömegkultúra tömegművészet," *Ma* vol. 4, no. 4 (April 10, 1919)

I.

The feudal-capitalist world order arrived at the last station of its decomposition in the course of the second half of the nineteenth century. Society saw itself split into not only economic but also intellectual classes and strata. The shared, homogeneous set of beliefs and social spirit which up till then glued society together and unified it had failed a long time before. The leading edge of cultural development—"high culture"—had become the exclusive domain of the privileged classes. The entire cultural spectrum—including the arts, science, and philosophy—had become completely cut off from the masses, from the feelings and ideas of the masses. The culture as a whole had surrendered its universality in favor of individualist values. It came to pass that the masses stood, alien and uncomprehending, at the utmost remove from the problems of philosophy, science, and even the arts—restricted to only the barest awareness of the most practical technological applications of science. In all other respects the masses perceive scientists and philosophers as weird eccentrics residing in ivory towers. They may have heard of Edison, but not of Mme. Curie, Rutherford, Heyd, or Boutroux. Indeed how could they have, lacking as they do the advantage of leisure time for reading and study. The situation is worse in the arts. The masses are utterly incapable of an aesthetic grasp and true enjoyment of painting, music, and literature. In our day and age all true culture has become the intellectual property of a vanishingly small minority. Anyone wanting to attain it had to leave the masses behind and thus turn into an isolated individuum. But the vast masses of people have no opportunity or inclination to indulge in this kind of alienation. So they had to be content with being fed a cheap, ersatz extract of individualist high culture, swill instead of art. (And we can include here, along with popular dance-hall hits, half-witted musicals, pulp fiction and poster reproductions of much contemporary theater, popular literature, and gallery art that works on pretty much the same level.)

The new stage of society we are about to enter will liberate the masses and bring them to the fore. Once these immense, newly liberated powers and energies arrive at an equilibrium and are able to exert their fullest effects, they will create a new and universal culture. Surely this new culture will find its forms and attain its peaks once again through outstanding creative individuals. It is equally certain that this culture will share a spiritual/intellectual community with the entirety of society and will maintain close contact with the masses. For, after all, it will be a manifestation of the masses, the collective soul will endow it with life. Mass culture will displace individualist culture, and similarly, art with a social awareness will replace individualist art.

What will this mass culture, this mass art be like?

It would be a grave error to look for the answer by evoking differences in level. Granted we cannot expect today's individual to descend to the level of today's masses. Neither will the opposite happen: the masses cannot raise themselves to the cultural heights of the individual. They are unable to do so not because this level is too "High" for them but simply because the masses are alienated from—and, therefore, have and want nothing to do with—today's individualist culture. And so, since today's spirit of individualism and the soul of the masses are so utterly different and heterogeneous, it follows that it is inconceivable and ludicrous to imagine an equalization of these two intellectual levels (such as a 50% reduction of the individual's level, accompanied by a 50% increase of the masses'). No, not at all. It is not the "levels" that will equalize. Rather, the power of a new faith will meld the individual spirit and the mass soul into one integral whole. The individual as a separate entity will disappear in the embrace of the shared universal spirit, fertilized by and fertilizing it. If the individual will cry out, this will not be a complaint of solitude or lack of companionship, but a lament for the pain of the masses, of all humankind; and the individual's song of joy will give voice to the universal joy of the masses. There will be no high and low cultural levels; one single and mighty art will prevail, understood equally by all, for they will all encounter themselves in it.

II.

The history of culture affords several precedents to help us imagine the possible developments of mass art. One of these is ancient Greek art up to the age of Pericles, another is Christian Medieval art. And obviously both instances prove that a consideration of individualist and socially aware art side by side cannot be concerned with relative level and value. In any such comparisons mass art would tend to be the winner. For the moral power and values carried by mass art always far exceed those found in individualist art.

Greek art owes its uniform social power to strong national and religious feelings. (With the Greeks, religious and national sentiment were almost the same thing.) Greek art embodied and propagated this shared religious sense, and thus it managed to always remain in the closest symbiosis with the soul of the masses. All Greeks understood the tragedies, the sculpture, and the literature and could identify with the ideas expressed in these works of art.

This identification, this powerfully social character of art, had its own external manifestation in Greek art. The archaic Greeks never emphasized the identity of the artist; thus they did not distinguish the sculptor from the stone carver for in those days the sculptor just like the stone carver were both artists. There was no separation between fine arts and folk arts—the two were one and the same.

Christian art came to express the spirit of even broader and vaster masses of people than Greek art. For even though Greek art, internally, created a social unity, nonetheless it was outwardly isolated by its nationalism. Christianity, on the other hand, unified half the world within one international spirit. And the Christian religion intervened far more thoroughly with the human soul and human life than the Greek one had. Greek religion was plain and calm, whereas Christianity is full of passion and fanaticism. Its creations are more restless and less balanced than Greek art, while achieving a greater monumentality and power of suggestion. Greek religion amounted to a clarity, a sober contemplation of life, in contrast to the one-sided and aggressive metaphysics of Christianity. For these reasons Christian art is a far more overtly religious art than the Greek. The Christian spirit was also more capable of hypnotizing the masses, and, for this reason, Christian art and philosophy form an ideal unity that is a universal mass manifestation capable of shattering barriers. Under the rule of Christianity this culture fused into one great unity, despite the fact that no other society has seen a division into a more severe caste system comprised of one exploiting class placed atop another. Nonetheless, one and the same religious faith and spirit animated both Pope and mendicant friar, Emperor and the lowliest serf. They had one and the same philosophy, their religion, and one and the same art: religious art.

We could cite numerous other examples to prove that a unified set of beliefs is the one and only prerequisite of mass art. We can see this not only in Greek and Christian arts but also in the vast and deeply social cultures of India and China. And it can also be proved by the negatives: the social spirit of art will fail when the religious spirit is moribund. Whenever faith begins to crumble art degenerates into gestures of a naturalist-impressionist individualism. This is what happened in Greek art starting with Pericles, in Christian art starting with the early Renaissance, and in the nineteenth century even in the Orient, among the Japanese.

It must be strongly emphasized that the first and foremost precondition for the emergence of a social art is the emergence of a religion of the masses. The economic situation of the masses, their degree of liberation or exploitation can only play a secondary role. Thus far it has been the Christian and the Buddhist spirits that have produced the most social forms of art, even though both the Christian and Buddhist societies themselves possess the most exploitative and hieratic character imaginable.

And yet, for this very reason, we may expect Communist society to give rise to vaster and more universal forms of mass art and mass culture than any seen thus far. For this new culture will be the meeting ground where a vigorous new faith, a powerful new religion encounters the liberated energies of the liberated masses.

The essence of all religions is belief in a perfected human life. This was the belief that has led humankind all along, from the Neolithic to the culture and cultural possibilities of today, and this belief is the foundation upon which both Christianity and Buddhism are built. But both the Christian and Buddhist religions defer the promise of this perfected life to a realm of metaphysics and otherworldliness so that, meanwhile, here on earth, the masses may remain all the more suffering and exploitable.

The new order brings a new religion—let us for the moment call it a conscious socialist worldview—that demonstrates the perfect life right here on earth and does not defer to some afterlife. And the liberation this religion offers carries the possibility of reaching the goal of perfected life. The liberated energies, united synergistically, will all point toward this end and will realize it through some form of universal single-mindedness. The new religion and the new society will form a new aesthetic culture and folk art of an inconceivably high order, next to which all that has gone before will shrink and vanish. But this new culture will not loom as a vast dead pyramid built of maimed and disfigured entities pressed into service in the manner of the Christian culture that is receding into the past. The new culture will be the live joy juicing through the circuits of a human community built by the purposeful will of liberated, self-knowing individuals, hand holding hand.

Translated by John Bátki

LETTER TO BÉLA KUN IN THE NAME OF ART   Lajos Kassák

Originally published as "Levél Kun Bélához a művészet nevében," *Ma* vol. 4, no. 4 (1919)

Dear Comrade Kun,

Allow me, as one who appreciates politics and knowledge and thus respects your expertise and background in *Realpolitik* to now take the liberty and briefly respond to the few casual words you dropped regarding art, more specifically our art, at the meeting of the Socialist Party. I emphasize the distinction because I intend to distinguish the manifestations of our active souls from the passive, drooling quest for beauty that has until now passed for "meaningful" art.

Please excuse me for the following account of the history of our periodical, about which you have probably already heard a thing or two from our friends or from our detractors. The *Ma* of today was preceded by another periodical along the same lines, *A Tett*, likewise edited by myself under the most penurious conditions, along with other collaborators who have since "cleverly" opted to depart. During the imperialist world war (at a time when Ferenc Göndör, the Pester Lloyd, and other irresponsible scandalmongers were singing the praises of Archduke Joseph) this was the only periodical in Hungary that proclaimed an active anti-militarist stand, published objective scholarly articles opposed to the compromises of the Social Democrats, and shone a critical light on bourgeois writers whose ravings had endorsed the carnage. At the time bourgeois ideology loosed the full wrath of its censorship on us for daring to be a drop of infectious life; we were prosecuted for anti-religious incitement, for compromising military interests; our printers were constantly harassed, and finally, after two issues were impounded *A Tett* was banned once and for all.

But Comrade Kun, as you well know, ideas cannot be killed off. The locomotives of revolution began to move when man was born and they will not stop until the goal is reached.

After a hiatus of two months I launched my new periodical, *Ma*, along the same lines, I must emphasize, but far richer in determination, understanding, and faith. Until March 21 it had received the same treatment from bourgeois society as its predecessor. Those who were in positions of economic superiority to us tried to pull us apart by means of their money, and those who vegetated in cultural impoverishment beneath us kept up a constant barrage of idiocy and cynical cackles directed at us. But we did not pause, for as you know, Comrade Kun, revolution knows no pause.

I am relating these matters not for our own sake, but for the sake of the revolution of which we are unreservedly vital supporters. While Hungarian "intellectuals" ravened after money during the bloody madness of the war, we mourned with our entire being the violated and murdered figure of man, and when Hungarian intellectuals with all of their sophistication threw themselves into the fray against the approaching proletarian revolution, we welcomed it with all of our being, in opposition to the mighty and the unscrupulous.

And could all this be nothing more than "the ecstatic convulsions of a bourgeois decadence?" In case you did not know this, dear Comrade Kun, I feel it is necessary to tell you that while you were still expending your energies in the struggles of our Russian brothers we were already agitating in spoken and printed words for Communism in Hungary. When you were still in Russia and here in Hungary everybody was enjoying the putrid advantages offered by a politics of compromise, we, on the first day of the Károlyi revolution published a special number of *Ma* carrying a proclamation for a communist Soviet Republic, published an objective, severe critique of the Károlyi revolution, and wrote manifestos for the liberation of revolutionary arts. In those very same days we were the first to organize a meeting for communism at the Galileo Circle, which was at the time rather nationalistic in tenor, as indicated by the threats and imprecations howled at us. In the evenings we used the concealed spaces of our editorial offices to begin, together with some of the Red Army soldiers of today, the organization of the communist group. Those comrades who welcomed your first appearance on Visegrádi Street went there from our place and carried the warmth and sincerity of our faith to you.

And why were we not there? (For obviously we weren't.) The meaning of our absence is explained by the dynamics of our worldview, which precludes affiliation with the interests of any political party. For the unattainable, ultimate goal of the struggle we have launched is man himself in the image of the universe, beyond party politics, beyond national or racial ideologies. And we did this not as an act of bourgeois decadence, or because we were deranged by our solitude, but as an act of faith in the struggle for peace, the same faith and same fight the Russian Bolsheviks carried to fulfillment in their politics. From the point of view of revolutionary necessity, the identity the people abandoning them to their faith and will is of no consequence, just as the identity of the people abandoning us to our faith and will, or who are now trying to wipe us out, is of no consequence. But we do have brothers in all parts of the world. New artists and men of the new faith, because for us art is no mere game of *l'art pour l'art*; for us, beauty is identical with what is good; for us the purpose of life is not class warfare, for class warfare is only a means toward attaining the absolute man whose sole way of life is revolutionary action.

Having said this, let us see to what extent our art is an excrescence of the bourgeoisie. I would like to refer you to a few names among the many of those whose art is in the same spirit as ours, and about whom perhaps you may already have heard.

Among those who immediately come to mind, Dear Comrade Kun, the name of Henri Guilbeaux is probably familiar to you. He is the French "communist" whose death sentence was the subject of a report in *Vörös Újság* only a few weeks ago. We are happy to be able to cite the name of this man for you—he is a revolutionary poet more progressive than the French proletariat that has become dazzled by the victory of the Imperialist Entente forces—for both in his worldview and in his art, Guilbeaux is not a party socialist and not a party communist, but a revolutionary with an active worldview, and our brother both in soul and in the manner of giving expression to his soul. I do not think that you entertain any doubts about Guilbeaux's revolutionary credentials. In that case we ask you to take the time from your busy political schedule and read the poem by Guilbeaux in our current issue. You will see that it speaks for us, and speaks out on behalf of the new art that sings the innermost soul of man and provides a synthesis of the dynamics of the world.

And you have probably heard of Franz Pfemfert, the editor of the Berlin periodical *Aktion*, and of his fellow editors, namely Ludwig Rubiner and Ivan Goll. As we all know, ever since the birth of the Spartacus movement in Berlin, these men were among the most vehement front-line fighters for the cause of communism. The contributors to *Aktion* fought alongside Liebknecht, Luxemburg, and Radek, as authors of militant writings, as lecturers, and for months as imperiled prisoners of the German bourgeoisie. Today their periodical *Aktion* is the official organ of the Spartacus movement. So much for the political lives of these men. But we must not neglect to mention, dear Comrade Kun, that these men are also writers. To say the least. But since in all likelihood you entertain not the least doubt about the revolutionary credentials of these men, and since we emphatically point out that these writers, just as Guilbeaux, manifest their revolutionary commitment through their writings, we ask you to look at the poem by Ivan Goll in our current issue. You will see that it speaks for us, and speaks out on behalf of the new art that sings the innermost soul of man and provides a synthesis of the dynamics of the world.

And surely you are familiar with Ottokar Brezina, one of the most salient representatives of the Czech communist movement. This man did not throw himself in front of the revolutionary Czech proletariat in the manner of those Hungarian writers who turned into communists overnight, but similarly to Guilbaux, Ivan Goll, and others, has been an active anti-militarists ever since the outbreak of the bourgeois world war, and even at a time when the Czech proletariat was completely dizzied by the bourgeois victories Brezina was already sounding the welcoming fanfare for the communists. And he did not do this within the framework of any party, we must emphasize. He too, just like us, considers communism to be only an economic groundwork; the goal of his life and each of his writings however—just like ours, for he, too, is a writer—is the new man, the creation of the culturally revolutionized new man. We ask you to take a look at the poem by Brezina in our current issue. You will see that it speaks for us, and speaks out on behalf of the new art that sings the innermost soul of man and provides a synthesis of the dynamics of the world.

And most likely you are familiar with the name of Alexei Remisow, one of the so-called Futurist writers in Russia. I don't think I need to provide a detailed introduction to this writer or to his circle, the new artists known as the "Futurists." You have for years lived and worked for the Russian revolution, and are obviously aware of them; we believe that in the course of the proletarian revolution in Russia you may even have had occasion to meet these outcasts of bourgeois society, these artists who were labeled as madmen for their worldview, and who became active revolutionary fighters. The text by Remisow in our current issue—we believe, and we are after all best qualified to judge—is not a whit more "meaningfully" class-conscious, its sentences not a whit more militant, than writings of a similar genre by our own writers appearing on our pages.

Now the question is, is it a sign of bourgeois excrescences that this writing, along with the works of Guilbeaux, Goll, Březina and the *Ma* writers, refuses any compromise whatever of its truth, worldview, and form of expression, and refuses to give up 50% as a concession to the undeveloped cultural demands of the proletariat? We do not think so. What is more, on this point we can call on three individuals who, we have reason to believe, are held in high esteem by Comrade Kun, too: Romain Rolland, the man of good will, Franz Mehring, revolutionary to his last breath, and Lunacharsky, the Russian cultural apostle. These three men assisted the new international art into the limelight, by having learned to live life all over, alongside the twenty-year-olds of great faith, writing introductions to their books, and by publishing their own works in the periodicals that were launched on their last pennies, in the jungles of the imperialist press, by these twenty-year-olds, for the sake of man and against inhumanity.

(The new art being realized in posters. It may be of interest to mention, since this aspect of our art has also been commented on, that the posters of those "Futurists" who had been labeled insane are currently "poisoning" the pure souls of the proletariat, from the walls of communist Moscow. And this "poisoning" is committed by Lunacharsky of all people, a man who is hardly your typical bourgeois decadent.)

And we have the temerity to assert that Lunacharsky's propagation of the new art is not only intended for Russia. His labors also justify ours. His work justifies the new art, which is international in character and appeal, and which is not merely the irresponsible snake-charming act of certain individuals—just as the proletarian fight in Russia is not only Lenin's game of violence—but a fully deployed revolution, possessing the necessity of a law of nature. This is the cultural-revolutionary trajectory of an ideology, essentially unassailable by the authority of any individual or party. Any counterforce opposed to it can only achieve a minimal delay. To demonstrate the truth of this in Hungarian art, I only need to bring up the case of Endre Ady and Béla Révész in the Social Democratic milieu. We clearly recall that the comrades who are nowadays clamoring against us had driven from their midst Ady at the acme of his human suffering and passion, as he was nearing fulfillment in universality; and likewise at a party congress they launched a campaign of terror against Béla Révész for his finest writing, *Convulsed Villages*, a work of international significance. Granted the esteemed comrades had not succeeded in terrorizing these artists into becoming superficial demagogues—but they will never outlive the guilt of sapping the creative energies of these artists. But in our case we are not afraid of a similar fate. For compromise and mediocrity in art and in politics is no longer tenable today and will be even less so tomorrow.

Forgive me for including one additional matter in my letter. This no longer concerns our literature and the new art, but the dogs that bark at it, i.e. the spinelessness evinced in Hungarian journalism and letters confronting every situation. But let us leave this, for I do not think I am telling you anything new by mentioning that the very editors and newspapers (Ferenc Göndör, Pester Lloyd, etc.) who are now calling for our crucifixion had, before they experienced the nature of the dictatorship of the proletariat, approached us, and asked me for articles, in an attempt to use me to cover up all that they had committed against the proletariat through the years.

Dear Comrade Kun! Having dispassionately and objectively related the above, I ask you: having given it the same dispassionate and objective consideration, do you still see nothing but vestiges of bourgeois decadence in us, in our art—in the new art that presently races through the whole world as the one and only shout for the liberation of man?

I close my letter by repeating what I said at the start. I respect you as one of the greatest among politicians, but allow me to have my doubts about your competence in the area of art. On this point we, whose political outlook—or, more correctly, worldview— is blameless from the viewpoint of the liberation of the proletariat, we, as artists committed to the fullest measure of our lives, are therefore most qualified to pass critical judgments in matters relating to our profession.

With this solemn belief in mind we request you, in the interest of the undisrupted soaring flight of the revolution, to base your comments about art on objective foundations, for let us not forget even for a moment that superficial criticism harms not so much us as individuals but the consummation of revolution itself.

I remain your respectful comrade.

Translated by John Bátki

LETTER   Lajos Tihanyi
(c. 1919)

The proletariat, living amid struggles and exhausted by its misfortunes, cannot take up the eternal goals of art.

Art belongs to humanity.

No struggle could ever completely crush the independence of the creative spirit, of the artist.

In revolutionary periods the talented faction asserts itself against the untalented parasites; when it serves the new ideas, it is practicing a form of intellectual masturbation. It may be a helpful, driving force behind the revolution, but it is not the art of the proletariat.

All the values that the human spirit has ever created will always be viewed by the proletariat as its own property. It also considers the newly emerging values as its own; even so, the intellectual forces carry out their struggles only where the role is played not by the primary means and primary impetus of the revolution—i.e., hate— but by edification. The refusal to acknowledge intellectual superiority, competition, the struggle against inferiority. To intensify the struggle is to revolutionize art. The revolution of art is to acknowledge the struggle that the artist leads for the sake of the artwork.

Creation is the victory of humanity.

Translated by Steven Lindberg

chapter 5

FORM AS THE AGENT OF SOCIAL CHANGE

Éva Forgács

The late Danilo Kiš—one of the pre-eminent Central European writers of the past thirty years—wrote that "awareness of form is a characteristic shared by all writers of Central Europe, form as a desire to give meaning to life and to metaphysical ambiguity, form as *possibility of choice*, form that is an attempt to locate points of fulcrum like those of Archimedes in the chaos around us, form that is opposed to the disorders of barbarism and to the irrational arbitrariness of instincts."[1] Although Kiš was writing in 1987, his words capture precisely the particular significance of form in the art and culture of Central Europe in the first half of the twentieth century.

In Central Europe the freedom of choice had been a far greater luxury than in twentieth century Western cultures. In cultures, where aesthetics, ethics, and politics were often not clearly separable, the choice manifested in form or style carried more weight than in the West. It was a manifestation of freedom—of free choice—in a world where deficit in freedom was the tradition. No matter what formal vocabulary a Central European avant-garde artist chose—Expressionist, Futurist, Dada,

Constructivist, or any combination of these—form was an expression of autonomy not otherwise granted to him. Form was meant to separate the artist from the forces of chaos, as Kiš says. Throughout Central Europe, these forces were always too close to the fragile surface of law and order.

At the time of the rapid politicization of the avant-garde after World War I, when content and narratives appeared to prevail, the choice of form was particularly significant even in the work of those artists who did not directly engage in political activity. The early Devětsil group in Prague around 1920 emphasized that the revolutionary significance of an artwork lies more in its form than in its contents. They rejected the Cubist idiom of prewar Czech modernism, and started to use the forms of primitivist art and magical realism to identify themselves as a new modernist trend. After a short *proletkult* interlude they firmly held the view that art should not be used as any kind of weapon for social purposes, but have autonomy.

The Polish painter Henryk Berlewi wrote about "The Struggle for a New Form," which was echoed in the Hungarian Ernő Kállai's article "New

1 Danilo Kiš, "Variations on the Theme of Central Europe," *Cross Currents* 6 (1987).

Art" in the same year, where he wrote, "we struggle for synthesis, for style." "Content is born out of Form," the Polish Constructivist Strzemiński stated in 1922, having been sensitized to the implications of various formal idioms and the way artists assumed their identity through their choice of form. He called attention to fundamental differences between such contemporaneous Russian trends in art as Cubist-inspired painting, Suprematism, Productivism, and Constructivism, which were all blurred west of Russia into the term "International Constructivism." He urged more consciousness of form, meaning more clarity in thinking.

Ljubomir Micić communicated his concept of the Balkan "Barbarogenius" through his disruption of the traditional form of the printed page with its traditional system of paragraphs and continuous display of the text, using such techniques as broken typography, eruptive lettering, and marked exclamation points. The excitement and aggressiveness of the Zenithist manifestos come across, before anyone reads them, in their loud and "offensive" typographic form.

Form, in postwar Central Europe, was more than ever the nexus of the struggle for a new worldview and new views on art.

DEVĚTSIL IN PRAGUE AND BRNO   Karel Srp

On December 6, 1920, a short declaration was published on the second page of *Pražké pondělí* (Prague Monday) announcing, in the name of fourteen signatories, the recent formation of Devětsil—signaling the arrival of one of the most important Czech artists' groups in the twentieth century. In its ten-year life span, Devětsil—formed by a group of students at the Kremenc Street Gymnasium—included about a hundred personalities of the most diverse sort, including Vladislav Vančura, its first president. Karel Teige, though not among the original signatories, quickly emerged as the group's primary spokesman. Teige soon came into conflict with the preceding generation of artists, represented above all by the group Tvrdošíjní, who stood for approaches that he rejected. (The exceptions were Jan Zrzavý, and Bohumil Kubišta—who died prematurely—as the only two members of Tvrdošíjní who were attractive to Devětsil.)

The early Devětsil was guided in its artistic and literary creations by the idea of proletarian art, reflecting the interests of the working class, and refining its taste. The December 6 declaration already expressed criticism of prewar artistic directions such Cubism, Expressionism, and Futurism in favor of a primitivist enchantment with ordinary objects and direct expression. The ideological rejection of Western European modernism culminated in a spring 1922 exhibition (at Krasoumna Jednota in the Rudolfinum) and the publication of the *Devětsil Revolutionary Anthology*, edited by Teige and Jaroslav Seifert.

The publication activities of the early Devětsil were unusually broad from the beginning. Aside from individual books, poetry collections and short-story collections by Ivan Suk, Seifert, Vančura and Adolf Hoffmeister, there were also single issues of magazines, in which literary and theoretical texts were combined with reproductions of art work.

Translated by Andreé Collier Záleská

Our age has been split into two. Behind us are left the old times, condemned to being turned into dust in libraries; before us sparkles a new day. It is necessary for everyone to speak up. It is also necessary that everyone start building the foundations for a new life. Today, young artists and writers, painters, architects and actors are coming together like a family to stand in the first line with those who wear blue collars and who are going to fight for a new life, because the bourgeois won't.

Artuš Černík, Josef Frič, Josef Havlíček, Adolf Hoffmeister, Karel Prox, Jaroslav Seifert, Ivan Suk, Ladislav Süss, Vladimír Štulc, Karel Teige, Vladislav Vančura, Karel Vanĕk, Karel Veselík and Alois Vachsmann have constituted themselves as the Devĕtsil Association of Artists. You may be asking why. The answer is that they are well aware that an individual can achieve nothing great on his own, organizationally and artistically. To achieve something requires a group of people united by a new idea. No matter how young or modest they may be, they have to realize that. For the old literature, whatever it was called, was always class-conscious and pandered to the tastes of the rich. But these artists are young revolutionaries, and that is why they cannot proceed otherwise than alongside those who are also revolutionaries—that means the workers.

"A little bawler, alternatively called Expressionism, Cubism, Futurism and Orphism, born in 1909 A.D., died in 1919..." observe the young Russian artists, and they are right. If today's young generation moves away from this art, if it distances itself from Léger and Delaunay, from Marinetti and Apollinaire, it does so because it was a fatal mistake to believe that the art of the machine was the art of the worker, who, on the contrary, is imprisoned among monster machines and devastated by them, that he can become enthusiastic about art singing the praise of automobiles, in which he will never ride, of airplanes, in which he will never fly, but in which he will see his masters and exploiters traveling at leisure. Such art was more a capitalist's art than art of the proletariat. It was art that did not see much closer things, things with which it was in closest daily cordial contact.

It was incapable of noticing the table we sit at, the lamp giving us light, the little vase with a small bunch of flowers, the smile on the lips of the girl with whom we go out every day. These young people cannot find enthusiasm for the simplest things surrounding any of us. And this is where they turn away even from S.K. Neumann who has so far been the leader and teacher of the youngest generation.

Not all young people want to go with Devĕtsil. Whether writers or artists. The group of youngest writers, organized in Šrámek's Artists' Club differs from Devĕtsil precisely by virtue of following Šrámek's example and being impressionistic. It does not have a definite program. "We are young," they are saying to themselves, "and we want to be young." That is the whole basis on which their association rests. Its literary members are mostly formalists, just like the right-wing young artists, Rada and Moravec.

Devĕtsil has set out a clear program and it is going to pursue it: its activities will be as popular as possible, open to all. Its program consists of popular lectures on art, evenings of poetry, theatre performances, the publication of an almanac and a catalogue featuring artists' work. Its activities are however restricted by a limited budget and it would be very desirable if our revolutionary workers supported these activities by joining Devĕtsil as paying members. The annual membership fee is twenty crowns and each member will get a discounted admission to all events and will receive and annual bonus in the form of a publication the value of which will exceed membership subscription.

Members of the newly and definitively constituted Devětsil will make their first public appearance with a literary evening in Mozarteum on December 15 at 8 p.m.

S.K. Neumann will participate in Devětsil's other activities, namely in the planned lecture series on proletarian culture.

Translated by Alexandra Büchler

DEFEATISM IN ART   Václav Nebeský

Originally published as "Umělecký defetismus," *Tribuna* (March 27, 1921)

There are moments in life when it is difficult to keep one's head up. The war brought many such moments, but even at times when clouds gathered over the battlefield, we felt that we were allowed to hang our heads only for a brief moment, and then we had to look up again, all the more confidently and proudly. Not all of us shared this view, however. There were those who thought that feeling downcast was the best solution in a difficult situation and who saw resignation as the only salvation for the threatened humanity.

Luckily, there were not many such people in our country. In France, it seems, there were more of them and they were called "defeatists." Defeatism may not be only a political or moral issue: when it appeared in politics, an attitude of equally cautious resignation emerged in an area where it could be least expected. We have always known that the muses fall silent amidst the clamor of arms; what we didn't know was that if they continue to sing, they must sing sotto voce. But even if they sing lower their voices, they should not necessarily have to sing timidly and tremble with embarrassment. The muses of the wartime era suddenly gave us the impression that—for reasons difficult to fathom—they were obliged to show contrition for almost everything of any substance they had dared to do in the years immediately preceding the war. This youthful, virginal modesty was clearly manifested in a phenomenon that could be best described as the twilight of -isms. Various artistic directions that had slowly began gaining ground, gave up their most essential and valuable characteristics precisely at a time when they had matured to the extent that they could take root and be nurtured by life. They began to deny that in the general chaos of visual sensibilities and views, they were the only factor not lacking orientation, the only solid form of a possible artistic expression, the only seeing among the blind, those who knew the way ahead. They may have taken the wrong path, but no one has really proved that. It has however been proven that, so far, there are no other, safer directions. And this is when, in an atmosphere marked by a lack of faith in the past and in the future, defeatism is allowed to take over in art and -isms are being evened out and smoothed over. Much of what we did before the war was "too" angular, for example. Why not make it rounder then? What was "too" light should not be painted in such loud colors. There was "too much" theory and speculation in prewar painting; now it needs a dose of emotion. Painting was "too much" of a personal thing for the painter—it needs more of the undying, eternal nature; or it was too private, and so it needs to be made accessible to the wider public, etc. These were the arguments put forward by the defeatists to excuse a state of affairs that would have otherwise hardly escaped severe criticism. Whatever had character, lost it; whatever had color, faded; whatever had a pleasant smell, went flat. Strong, proud—albeit one-sided—conviction was replaced by reconciliatory, helpless weakness and compromise.

Not even we have escaped this wave of petit bourgeois values—we have grown wiser, more circumspect and superficial and have adopted a lukewarm, academic art. Emotional limpness and anemia caused by the general war psychosis and mental malnutrition was too great not to open the doors to this active tendency, but it was also great enough to bring it quickly to an irrevocable end. This is a dead-end route, and if this is not obvious today, it will clear tomorrow. And then we shall start anew, on a different basis, and only then can we be done with wartime defeatism. But wartime defeatism will be replaced by postwar defeatism, superficially different, but identical in essence.

In the second volume of *Musaion*, Karel Teige published an essay entitled "Images and proto-images." In it he speaks on behalf of a group of poets and visual artists around the revue *Orfeus* that represents the latest, youngest branch on the as yet immature tree of Czech modern art. The essay therefore does not present only his personal views, but it is also a collective confession and a purposeful manifesto. And it is this clear, programmatic conviction that is its most likeable feature. Whether the program itself deserves sympathy is another question.

Yesterday's horizon was ruled by several star galaxies: Cézanne, Matisse, Braque, Delaunay, Metzinger, Gelizes, Whitman, Verhaeren, Marinetti, Apollinaire, Max Jacob—all great masters of the new form. Today's stars are ruled by different zodiacs: van Gogh, Seurat, Derain, Henri Rousseau, Chagall, Dostoevsky, Charles-Louis Philippe, Vildrac, Duhamel, Arcos, Romains—all artists of the unity of life.

Yesterday's stars are still bright in the sky (except for those whose light was dim even then); some, like Matisse or Braque, have become brighter over the years (although so far only in France). Stars that should have been high in the sky were as bright yesterday, while some, like Arcos, have faded overnight. That is not to say that wider knowledge of Duhamel, and especially Vildrac, means that their poetic stars were brighter. And even if this change of artistic constellations were a fact, what had been its cause? The war, is Teige's answer. The war smashed the world of industrialism, technology and civilization, of factories, transatlantic ships and airplanes, it smashed the very world that had brought it about, making the very art that had championed and admired the old world, the art of aestheticism and formalism of the prewar period, inappropriate. Today, the human soul thirsts for something else: for the undervalued "kingdom of the heart."

The task of today's art is to create the proto-image of future life in the "kingdom of the heart." Even this new soul had been created by war... The war is a material, political, economic, social and therefore also moral phenomenon. But never was it an artistic one. Is it then possible that war would have the power to change the artistic, creative and sensitive side of human nature? Of course, it does. But only to the extent to which it can change the moral basis of artistic sensitivity and understanding, no further. And it is what lies further that are the most important aspect of art.

The view that brands art as "formalist" or "aestheticist" shows a profound misunderstanding of the spirit of modern art. I am not talking here about Futurism or Orphism, or about movements that emphasized the perfection and purpose of form—although we could speak of humanizing effects of the functional beauty of form. But to describe Picasso's mystical meditativeness as formalism, or the deeply human expressionism of Munch as the work of an aesthete is an offense against "historical" truth. There is not enough space here to explain whether prewar artists already valued things "according to their purpose and moral meaning, in connection with man's work and life in happiness." All I want to say is that the foundations of the moral basis for artistic, and, in a more general sense, style-forming work that could have possibly been created by war, had been laid already before the war broke out, and have only become firmer without any change to their basic psychological makeup. Life cannot be so easily divided into today and yesterday.

And if the war has indeed made these foundations firmer, so much the better. A true modern artist will then strive for unity between his art and life—something that Teige demands of him—with greater conviction. And if he strives for it with greater conviction and determination, he will be striving towards a goal he has set his heart and mind on, regardless of the war. His path may be different, but its general direction will be the same as before, if this path is to lead towards—a goal.

And here we are at the core of Teige's essay on images and proto-images. Teige does not recommend that artists follow new paths, he recommends a change of direction, turning the artistic process into something strictly social and moral. Today's artistic forms and expression, achieved with a great deal of effort, have been deemed too outdated by Teige and his colleagues—at least in theory—even before their capacity was tested. Away with "formalism" and "aesthetics!"

It would seem that from today, the new generation will be interested in creating new forms more suitable to the needs of our time. But that is unnecessary. Let us transfer art—outside art! There is no need for "designs for modern art," what is needed are "plans for a new life, new organization of the world and its consecration." The task of the painter is no longer to paint well, but to create a new world. And this is an example of a new brand of postwar defeatism.

Wartime defeatism considered it important to revive lost national traditions and folkloric aspects of art, rather than create a good and thorough art. Postwar defeatism recommends that artists acquire a deeper and wider social sense. The outcome of politics interfering with art is as bad as the outcome of art interfering with politics.

Translated by Alexandra Büchler

The "new art" that emerged in Poland during World War I questioned the nationalist message in art as well as the idea that its style should be based on a literary narrative. These discussions were carried on particularly in the circles of the Cracow artists who, in 1917, founded a group initially called the Polish Expressionists. Later, in order to distinguish themselves from German Expressionism (which they were less influenced by than French Cubism), they changed their name to the Polish Formists, and began publishing *Formiści* (1919–21).

Though comprised of artists representing diverse styles and affiliations, the Formists were unified in their interest in modernity and its relation to autonomous form. The primary leaders of the group were Tytus Czyżewski (1880–1945) and Zbigniew Pronaszko (1885–1958), who had experimented with modern art—using fragmentation of objects and representational planes—since the early twentieth century. Other Formists included Leon Chwistek (1884–1944) a painter, writer, philosopher and mathematician who spent time in France, August Zamoyski (1893–1970), a sculptor of aristocratic descent, familiar with French and German art communities, and Stanisław Ignacy Witkiewicz (1885–1939), the painter, novelist, playwright, philosopher, photographer and art theorist who stood as one of the most versatile artists of the interwar period.

While the early avant-garde perceived itself mainly as "spiritual" and interested in the transformation of reality by exerting its influence on the public, the avant-garde movements of the 1920s stressed above all the material dimension of man's life and the possibility of art influencing the social environment. This shift of interests is apparent in Poland, for instance, in the founding in 1922 of *Zwrotnica*. Its founder and editor was Tadeusz Peiper (1895–1969). He made the periodical the main forum for the Polish avant-garde of the period and the most important until the appearance of *Blok* in 1924. The artists later associated with *Blok*, Władysław Strzemiński (1893–1952) and Mieczysław Szczuka (1898–1927), began almost at once to collaborate with *Zwrotnica*. It had international contacts, and it conceived the avant-garde as both an expression of change in civilization and an active force in the transformation of contemporary society. Peiper and his collaborators were fascinated by all manifestations of modern life: the city, the crowd, technology, and especially the possibility of dedicating art to furthering modernity, of influencing material reality through artistic form.

Translated by Wanda Kemp-Welch

EXCERPTS FROM **NEW FORMS IN PAINTING AND THE MISUNDERSTANDINGS ARISING THEREFROM** Stanisław Ignacy Witkiewicz

Originally published as *Nowe formy w malarstwie* (1919)

PART 1: PHILOSOPHICAL INTRODUCTION

Artistic creation...is an affirmation of Existence in its metaphysical horror, and not a justification of this horror through the creation of a system of soothing concepts, as is the case with religion, or a system of concepts showing rationally the necessity of this and not any other state of affairs for the Totality of Existence, as is the case with philosophy.

[...]

PART 3: PAINTING

We live in a frightful epoch, the likes of which the history of humanity has never known until now, and which is so camouflaged by certain ideas that man nowadays has no knowledge of himself; he is born, lives, and dies in the midst of lying and does not know the depth of his degeneration. Nowadays art is the sole crack through which it is possible to get a glimpse of the horrible, painful, insane monstrosity that is passed off as being the evolution of social progress; finding the truth in philosophy is virtually impossible since it has become so entangled in lies in the shape of empirio-critics and pragmatists. In the forms of art of our age we find the atrociousness of our existence and a final, dying beauty which in all likelihood nothing will be able to bring back anymore.

PART 4: ON THE DISAPPEARANCE OF METAPHYSICAL FEELINGS AS A RESULT OF THE EVOLUTION OF SOCIETY

Chapter 1: The Evolution of Society

The views expressed here are not those of some "social reactionary," for in fact we believe in the inevitability and necessity of certain changes that have as their goal justice and the common good. We are concerned only with the secondary effects of these changes, as to whose consequences, in our opinion, certain delusions are much too prevalent....

Starting with the most primitive community, the development of mankind moves in the direction of restricting the individual in favor of the group, while at the same time the individual, in exchange for certain sacrifices, obtains other advantages that he could not attain all by himself. Subordination of the interests of the single individual to the interests of the whole—this is the most general formulation of the process that we call social progress....

It goes without saying that vain are the dreams of naive communists who want to resolve the problem by a return to certain primitive forms of social existence while retaining all the achievements of present-day civilization.... Mankind cannot deliberately retreat from the level of civilization it has already attained; it cannot even stop, for stopping amounts to the same thing as going backward. We cannot give up the increasing convenience and security of our lives, nor can we deliberately stop man's further domination of matter and the resultant organization of the working classes on the vast expanses of our planet.... We cannot say: that's enough civilization and comfort in our lives for the time being, now we'll set to work on the equal distribution of civilization throughout the entire world and bring happiness to all by means of what has already been accomplished. As long as there exists raw material that can be processed and as long as technology encounters no barriers of catastrophic proportions (which for a short period is quite doubtful given the ever-new discoveries of sources of energy), our demands will constantly grow in keeping with the dissemination of previous accomplishments, and halting civilization on a certain already attained level is an absolute impossibility. We cannot foretell what forms the life of society will assume with the passage of time—this is an equation with too large a number of unknowns—in any case on the basis of the already known segments of history we can say that the process of mankind's socialization is a phenomenon that is irreversible in the long run although in the short run it can undergo certain relatively minute fluctuations....

The gray mob was only a pulpy mass on which grew monstrous and splendid flowers: rulers, true sons of powerful deities, and priests holding in their hands the frightful Mystery of Existence. Today, with the astonishment of true democrats, we cannot understand how this mob could have endured so much suffering and maltreatment of "the dignity of man" without protest and revolt, or why they did not establish some kind of communistic regime. But the traditions of such realms are still alive even in our own times in the form of the great nations that succeed in placing their own honor higher than the lives of millions of individuals. The present-day ruler is only a ghost, a wretched caricature when compared to his ancestors—he is only the embodiment of all the people's power and strength, which in the past was the privilege of a person or a small group but today is the property of whole nations But we live in times in which, as the ghosts of nations depart into the past, there appears a shadow threatening everything that is beautiful, mysterious, and unique of its kind—the shadow of that gray mob kept down for centuries, and it is growing to frightening proportions embracing all of mankind. This ghost is still not strong enough yet, but like a spirit at a spiritualist séance it is materializing more and more; already its grazing touch and first contact can be felt which, transformed into hard blows, will avenge the torments of all those wretched beings out of which the mob took shape. Now terrified of this shadow, rulers humble themselves before the people, begging them for the power which in the past they derived from themselves, from the deities who gave birth to them....

This frightful shadow makes the rulers of the world tremble, threatens to destroy all understanding of the Mystery of Existence by making philosophers the servants of its demands, and hurls artists into the depths of madness. It is cast by a mass of former slaves, whose gigantic stomach and desire to enjoy all that they have been deprived of until now becomes the law of existence on our planet now that they grow organized....

Whereas for the former ruler the mob was only pulp that he shaped according to his own will and he alone accomplished great deeds following his own bizarre notions and using the mob as though it were an obedient tool devoid of a will of its own, now the powerful master of times to come will be (and perhaps already is, in an embryonic state) only a tool in the hands of the mass, which strives for material enjoyment and a sense of its own power....

We turn our eyes from the past in shame and from the future in dread at the coming of boredom and grayness, or we create artificial narcotics with which we hope to awaken the long-since dead feeling and fervor of individual strength, we create artificial mystery and artificial beauty in art and in life. It's all in vain—beauty resides only in madness, truth lies at our feet torn to pieces by contemporary philosophers, and of this trinity of ideals, for us there remains only the good, that is, the happiness of all those who have not had the strength to create beauty, or enough courage to look the mystery in the eye. What awaits us is the monstrous boredom of mechanical soulless life in which the little people of the world will wallow in moments of leisure produced by reduced work loads....

The people of the future will need neither truth nor beauty; they will be happy—isn't that enough?.... The people of the future will not feel the mystery of existence, they will have no time for it, and besides they will never be lonely in the ideal future society.

What will they live for? They will work to eat, and eat to work. But why should this question upset us? Isn't the sight of ants, bees, or bumblebees, perfectly mechanized and organized, a reassuring one? Probably they are totally happy, all the more so that undoubtedly they never could think and experience what we have during the four or five thousand years we have endured with a consciousness of the mystery of being....

The physical and spiritual forces of the individual are limited, whereas the strength of organized humanity can grow, at least for the time being, without limit. The numerical limit of this phenomenon can equal the sum total of all the people in the world, but the first step on the way to total leveling of differences is the standardization of civilization, which, given the perfection of the means of communication and interchange of information, grows, at least in Europe, at an absolutely frantic rate. Abstract inequality and individual differences are being wiped out by the specialization of work, and at the extremes the machinery of the whole system will iron them out perfectly. In comparison with present-day cultural interaction, former civilizations were totally isolated, and most significantly, they developed extremely slowly. Nowadays whatever any genius discovers instantly becomes the property of all, and even the most individual accomplishments, quite independent of the will of the person responsible for them, add to the growing power of the mob of gray workers fighting for their rights. Present-day "great men" and geniuses seem to be a tame version of once savage and dangerous beasts, who for reasons of safety have been declawed and defanged. They have a strength, cunning, and resourcefulness that can be used to good advantage, but they pose no threat whatsoever to mankind, whom they have rendered happy, and the forms that the great men of our times use to make available for the general welfare the values they have created are extremely agreeable and pleasant....

In our period, wars—once a splendid manifestation of the wild strength of nations— are neither spontaneous outbursts of hatred caused by essential differences between nations and a direct desire for domination personified by powerful rulers, nor a battle over ideas whose concrete embodiment was not a matter of material utility, as, for example, the wars of religion. War nowadays is nothing but cold, mechanical, systematic murder of one's fellowman, devoid of spontaneous emotional motivation, and it has as its goal the acquisition of financial profits carefully calculated and contrived by diplomats, businessmen, and industrialists. Instead of picturesquely dressed knights fighting breast to breast over what to us are completely fantastic issues, we have reduplicated crawling wretches who murder one another from a distance and poison one another with hideous gases... At the moment when the old world died, a world based on the monstrous torments of the greater part of mankind, but which nevertheless bore the most splendid flowers of creativity, and the new transitional regime of moderate democracy based on parliamentary principles failed to produce universal happiness and simply led to exploitation, in another guise, of the same lower strata of mankind without being able to bring forth anything that could be compared to the former creativity, it can only be wished that the process of mechanization and the leveling of individuality will be accomplished as quickly and as uncatastrophically as possible, out of regard for the cultural values already achieved....

Since there is no doubt but that life tends to more and more social justice, to the elimination of exploitation, to an even distribution of burdens, to comfort and security—for every one, not only for exceptional individuals—it might be assumed that the whole mass of until now wasted energies will be turned in another, more important direction than mutual slaughter and torture, and that now for the first time there will appear, perhaps in the near future, a kind of golden age of mankind....

This, it seems to us, is a delusion to which in our times men of good will succumb since they wish to see the future in every aspect through rose-colored glasses.... Today's liberals see the future of the broad masses through the prism of their own present psychology.... The mystery of existence, unless it appears in the horror of daily life, loses its true significance.... Nothing can be achieved without paying for it, and universal happiness is no exception to the rule. Creativity of a certain kind must be lost as the price of this happiness, creativity that has its source in the tragic sense of existence which future people will not be able to feel.... While we recognize the necessity of social change and the absolute impossibility of going back to former times when millions of the weak were flagrantly oppressed by a handful of the strong, we nevertheless cannot close our eyes to what we will lose through socialization, and perhaps this awareness will at least permit us (if we are no longer capable of adopting an artificial naïveté in our thinking) to experience in a significant fashion our contemporary artistic creativity, which, although it may pass over into the realm of madness, is all the same the sole beauty of our age.

Chapter 2: The Suicide of Philosophy
In our times the educational function of religion has come to an end once and for all, and religion itself is slowly taking a secondary position. In fact today the only religion that has any validity is the cult of society. Today anyone may worship whatever fetish he wants in his own home or celebrate black masses as long as he is a good member of society.... Religion exists for certain individuals from the higher classes, and it also exists for the masses, but in the form of automated rites that have little in common with an essential metaphysical moment.... With unparalleled ease the masses are discarding all the dead weight of religion in favor of doctrines that propose alluring solutions to problems of property and the general welfare. The progress of science and the dissemination of discursive philosophy contribute to the decline of religion. Science, especially for certain narrow minds who do not understand its essential value, is taken as the final explaining away of the Mystery of Being, on the basis of one theory or the other, or of some "synthesis" of these.
As society evolves, as life grows more and more comfortable, more certain in its outlines, more automatic and mechanical in its functions, there is less and less place in man's soul for metaphysical anxiety. Our life becomes so defined that man is brought up from the start to fulfill certain partial functions that do not allow him to grasp the whole shape of phenomena, functions that so consume his time with systematically organized work that thinking about ultimate matters which have no immediate utility ceases to be something important in the course of his everyday life....
From a certain point of view, all philosophies, all systems are only ways of reassuring oneself in the face of the inexplicable Mystery.
Each epoch has the kind of philosophy that it deserves. In our present phase we do not deserve anything better than a narcotic of the most inferior sort which has as its goal lulling to sleep our antisocial metaphysical anxiety that hinders the process of automatization. We have this narcotic in excess in all the forms of philosophical literature found throughout the entire world....
The loneliness of the individual in the infinity of Existence became unbearable for man in the as yet incompletely perfected conditions of societal life, and therefore he set out to create a new Fetish in place of the Great Mystery—the Fetish of society, by means of which he attempted to deny the most important law of Existence: the limitation and uniqueness of each Individual Being—so that he would not be alone among the menacing forces of nature....
Metaphysical truths are pitiless and it is not possible to make compromises about them without laying oneself open to the worst inconsistencies. When the problem is posed that way, the only solution is to forbid people to search for the truth, as though that

were a kind of fruitless unhealthy mania from which mankind has already suffered long enough throughout the centuries.

This is exactly the position that has been adopted by contemporary philosophy, which deserves the name "philosophy" even less than the most primitive or the most new-fangled religious systems. Even a person possessed by an unhealthy religious mania could be considered incomparably higher than a true pragmatist, Bergsonite, or follower of Mach....

Our blasé intellect is only able to take cognizance of certain things passively; we can absorb information, but we are no longer able to say or create anything new on the subject. We have a free choice of the masks we can wear in an hour of deadly boredom, but we cannot feel or experience anything as at least some of our ancestors did....

The proof that the Great Mystery has stopped existing for us once and for all and that we have lost the ability to feel it in its entirety lies in the search for half-mysteries, which, it is hoped, will provide life with some new magic now that the old has been taken away by the exact sciences, social stability, and metaphysics itself in its debased form.

The creation of artificial petty mysteries is a symptom of the disappearance of metaphysical anxiety. The same thing applies to all those mystical beliefs that contemporary America abounds in, despite all its sober approach to life: they are tiny symptoms of an anxiety that something has disappeared which needs to be restored *deliberately*, because without it, for some people, the grayness of tomorrow which is bearing down on us is simply too monstrous. But even these tiny symptoms will soon disappear and from then on mankind will sleep a happy sleep without dreams, knowing nothing in truth about the beautiful and menacing reality that has been its past.

Chapter 3: The Decline of Art
In the closed cultures of antiquity the great artistic styles whose beginnings are lost in the mists of history developed extremely slowly; these styles consisted of two fundamental elements: ornamentation and the presentation of religious images under pressure from the menacing conditions of life and a profound and implacable faith. The religious content of the sculpture and painting that adorned the temples was directly connected to the form; there was no difference between Pure Form and external content because, being close to its primeval source, metaphysical feeling in its purest form, the directly expressed unity in plurality was not divided from its symbol: the image of a fantastic deity. At that time there were not, in our sense of the term, any separate artists forging a style of their own. Rather there was a throng of workers within the context of a style that evolved slowly as the result of a collective effort to which each of them contributed certain relatively minor alterations....

As religion grew superficial and gods were likened to men and the intellect developed in pace with social democratization, there was an immediate effect on art. This process reached its height in Roman sculpture, and then there was a total decline of Art.... When Christian mysticism arose, there was fertilization of the human spirit with regard to art....

But from our point of view the Renaissance was a defeat for true Art.... Painting declined rapidly, and its ideal became fidelity in copying the external world....

The true revival of Pure Form took place in the last decades of the nineteenth century in France starting with the Impressionists who, however, did not leave behind them works of great value besides a riotous outpouring of color, which had been previously killed off by classicism. Even though it stopped being a soulless and even sentimental imitation of nature, painting during this period was not connected with a generally valid metaphysics in the form of religion but was rather the expression of a private, secret, and more or less deliberate metaphysics on the part of individual artists....

The value of a work of art does not depend on the real-life feelings contained in it or on the perfection achieved in copying the subject matter but is solely based upon the unity of a construction of pure formal elements....

Today we have come to Pure Form by another road; it is, as it were, an act of despair against life, which is becoming grayer and grayer, and for that reason, although art is the sole value of our times-excluding of course the technology of living and universal happiness-present-day artistic forms are, in comparison with the old ones, crooked, bizarre, upsetting, and nightmarish. The new art stands in relation to the old as a feverish vision in relation to a calm, beautiful dream....

Nowadays an overworked person has neither the time nor the nervous energy for any thoughtful absorption in works of art, the understanding of which demands leisurely contemplation and inner concentration proportionate to the slow maturation of the works themselves. For people nowadays, the forms of the Art of the past are too placid, they do not excite their deadened nerves to the point of vibration. They need something that will rapidly and powerfully shock their blasé nervous system and act as a stimulating shower after long hours of stupefying mechanical work. This can best be seen in the theater, which, as most dependent on an audience, has most rapidly reached a point of decline from which most probably nothing can ever rescue it, despite efforts at restoring certain old forms. Irrevocably past are the times of metaphysical experiences in the theater, as was the case at the beginnings of Greek tragedy, and all attempts at extricating oneself from mindless realism by means of a "revival" of old forms are an impoverishment of what is and not the natural simplicity that was an expression of strength and spiritual equilibrium.

Today's theater cannot satisfy the average spectator; only the dying breed of theatrical gourmets appreciate the revived delicacies, whereas cabaret on the one hand and cinema on the other are taking away most of the audience from the theater.... Cinema can do absolutely everything that the human spirit might desire, and so if we can have such frantic action and striking images instead, isn't it well worth giving up useless chatter on the stage which nobody needs anymore anyhow; is it worth taking the trouble to produce something as infernally difficult as a truly theatrical play when confronted by such a threatening rival as the all-powerful cinema?....

Today, like everyone else, the painter as artist is compelled to live in the same atmosphere as other people. He is born in it, from childhood he's been exposed to all the masterpieces ancient and modern in reproductions, something which previously was quite unknown; while still a youth, he grows literally blasé about all forms, he succumbs to the general acceleration of life through the necessity of experiencing it with the frantically gesticulating people all around him, he becomes caught up in the feverish tempo of it all, even If he were to live in the country, drink milk, and read only the Bible; and his nerves are so frayed that metaphysical anxiety in his works assumes forms at the sight of which the general public...without understanding their profound substance, roars with laughter and the critic talks about the decline of art.... Such an artist either dies of hunger, embittered by the world's failure to understand his tragedy, or one or more gentlemen appear to take him on as an enterprise and launch his career...and make a pile of money out of him; and then the same critic who previously had virtually wiped the floor with him...now will write about him with wild enthusiasm, while the artist himself, after having created his own style at the age of twenty-eight, will long since have been in the cemetery for suicides or in the hospital poisoned by some drug, or calmed down in a straitjacket on a bed, or, what is still worse, alive and well, but imitating himself in ever-cheaper editions for business purposes.... Nowadays painting is teeming with hyenas and clowns, and it is often very hard at first sight to distinguish between clever *saltimbanques* and the true geniuses of our rabid, insatiable form....

We do not maintain, however, that to be a genius one has to drink oneself to death, be a morphine addict, a sexual degenerate, or a simple madman without the aid of any artificial stimulants. But it is frightful that in fact whatever great occurs in art in our agreeable epoch happens almost always on the very edge of madness....

In our opinion, true artists—that is, those who would be absolutely incapable of living without creating, as opposed to other adventurers who make peace with themselves in a more compromising fashion—will be kept in special institutions for the incurably sick and, as vestigial specimens of former humanity, will be the subject of research by trained psychiatrists. Museums will be opened for the infrequent visitor, as well as specialists in the special branch of history: the history of art—specialists like those in Egyptology or Assyriology or other scholarly studies of extinct races: for the race of artists will die out, just as the ancient races have died out.

Translated by Daniel Gerould

ON 'DEFORMATION' IN PICTURES   Stanisław Ignacy Witkiewicz
Originally published as "O 'deformacji' na obrazach," *Gazeta Wieczorna*, no. 5165 (1920)

A whole range of contradictory theories circulate concerning the "deformation" of objects in the pictures of contemporary painters. Some claim that deformation is nothing more than a vagary of insane people or the product of affectation. Others extend the concept of deformation to art as a whole, claiming that artists have, since the beginning, always had to deform everything. Nevertheless, the last category of people are capable to feel indignant at deformers for going too far, that is to say they want to impose limits on deformation.

The concept of deformation suggests that something that has had a time-honoured form has been disfigured, without entirely losing its likeness to an original shape. It refers above all to individual objects (of permanent, or of a certain variable, form) in the external world. This can make sense, so long as, when looking at pictures, one is actually looking for objects as such or expecting to experience sensations, based on various associations with reality. The concept loses its meaning as soon as one treats pictures as certain constructions of shapes embued with life of their own, possessing a formal unity independent of the objects being depicted, and looks at pictures as Pure Form, rather than as some kind of reflection of or individual interpretation of the visible world. We have, elsewhere, attempted to explain why it is that the world of objects necessarily has to enter as such into every, even the most detached from life painting, unless it is a geometrical ornament or a purely intellectual invention. A sense of unity takes on individual characteristics, assuming form in combinations of pure qualities (sounds, colors) or, composite elements (words, activities) through the world of an individual's images and emotions. For the moment we will concern ourselves with deformation in the purely formal sense.

The objects represented in pictures bring what we call "directional tension" to parts of the composition. We could, theoretically, do without this element, yet this would be to the great impoverishment of the painterly means. By virtue of the similarity of the masses in a composition to objects, one can directly, when accustomed to the visible world, conceive of them as starting in one place and ending in another, facing in one direction rather than another, and recognise at once their main and subsidiary axes whatever their length.

An elliptical form, for example, near one end of the shorter axis of which we might make a set of eyes, may admittedly come to look somewhat like a fish, but at the same time its longer axis, on which lie main points, will become compositionally subsidiary, and the shorter one will take on the role of a main axis. A square as a knee and a rectangle as a shin will function completely differently in combination with a whole body made up of e.g. figures indifferent to tension, than they might, positioned in more or less the same places, if they were not specifically marked out as parts of a certain whole of a certain directional tension, i.e. that of a human figure.

Deformation is not simply the result of a perverse whim to deform as such; it springs from the need to broaden the horizons of compositional possibilities. A certain type of person will ask at this point: "How can one deform something programmatically, consciously? Surely it is because one doesn't know how to draw. This is why everyone can paint these days and why it has become impossible to tell the difference between a work of art and a common splodge." We reply to these questionss as follows: deformation has, in a way, always existed. Once one has accepted this premise, there is no longer any need to speak of deformation. Whereas, by imposing limits on deformation, one shows the lack of understanding the essence of painting, i.e. it is viewed from the point of view of the external world, thus treating the main thing, i.e. form (not the form of conceived objects, but form as the construction of the work as a whole) as nothing more than a means of expression. Therein lies the error of Expressionist theory, although there are to be found, amongst the representatives of this movement, artists of genius who were creating Pure Form.

Misunderstandings with regard to deformation spring form the confusion of two problems, these being: 1) the artist's creative process, and 2) the effect of the finished work. The creative process must, if it is sincere, be homogeneous. This means that there must be no separate composing of abstract forms followed by turning them into objects, and there must be no thinking up of so called "picture's content" followed by its "cubistification" or any other kind of "abstractification." All this happens at once, though the intellect may nevertheless play a very important role in solving particular problems. The work may have two types of effect: essential or inessential, i.e. depending on whether it is viewed as Pure Form or as objects (in music, in terms of purely musical values or the emotional surges which any kind of music can evoke). All the questions of the so called "layman" (i.e. seemingly modest know-it-all) as to the deformation of objects spring precisely from the confusion of these two standpoints. One must not confuse these two standpoints when speaking of art theory. In order to explain anything to the laymen, we need to artificially separate out the homogenous creative process, so as to reveal the meaning of form itself, and that of objects, which symbolise directional tensions. We are then accused of intellectual manipulations which have nothing to do with art (for art is, after all, supposed to be felt), or of seizing on insoluble problems because we fail to comprehend that they are insurmountable. These problems are resolvable; one need only rid oneself, when approaching them, of certain bad habits of thought.

Theory can never be completely adequate to a directly given content; it cannot be the content. This seems always to have been certain. But to doubt it is to doubt the power of mind, and to make the equation that direct experience = direct experience—as does, with the help of that nice little word "intuition," one of the most dishonest philosophers, Henri Bergson—is not to discover a new path, but to give in to complete resignation, disguised as another way of cognizance. The deadly influence of this philosopher is evident in many different fields, besides aesthetics. Artistic impression,

unobtainable by any other way, is one thing, a general theory of art is another.
These problems are difficult ones, but nothing, as yet, gives us licence to write them
off as absolutely insoluble. The answer lies along the path of examining the very
essence of art i.e. its construction, independent of objects, feelings and conceptions,
and not along the path of intuitive digressions which are a second-rate class of
artistic creativity.

It is only by calling life to explain art (on the principle that without life there would be
no art), that blurs all the boundaries and causes aestheticians to flounder like fish in
a net and the public increasingly to lose faith in them. The moment one accepts the
formal aspect of a work of art as the main thing, all obscurity disappears; the theory
of Pure Form is capable to account for all manner of manifestations, from the oldest
to those of our times, with the exception, of course, of Realism and color photography,
which ought once and for all to be excluded from the realm of art.

But where are we to draw the line which must be drawn between works of art and other
works created by the human hand? Some suggest one place, others another. In terms
of actual works and not of their theory, there is no absolute boundary. We have to
examine some almost continuous sequences, with ill-defined boundaries crossing
from one kind to another. Similarly, in the color spectrum, yellow and green are completely different colors, and yet it is impossible to specify the precise point at which
one turns into the other.

Without dreaming of absolute, objective criteria which are impossible to attain, we ought,
in aesthetics, to try, at least when speaking of art, to make sure we discuss one and the
same thing. This is possible, so long as we at last begin to recognise form as the essence
of art, rather than all those inessential elements, which are none the less necessary
to the creative process and even to the work itself: objects, feelings, conceptions, and
even intellectual concepts.

Translated by Klara Kemp-Welch

EXCERPT FROM **ABOUT MULTIPLICITY OF REALITY IN ART**
Leon Chwistek
Originally published as "Wielość rzeczywistości w sztuce" (1921)

1. The theory of multiple realities is particularly relevant for painting and sculpture:
    1) It results in the necessity to reject the copying of nature, which is a negation of
    any genuine art.
    2) It provides the basis for a theoretical explanation of all principal types of paint-
    ing and sculpture.

Before I start substantiating these assumptions, I have to define the terminology. The
confusion in contemporary art theory comes from the ambiguity of meaning of some
fundamental notions on which this theory is based. In particular, this concerns notions
of content and form. To define their denotation is our first task.

The expression "content of the work of art" can be used in three different senses. It can:
    a) embrace all psychological states which a work of art evokes, b) signify an anec-
    dote, c) signify elements of reality which can be found in the work of art.

        Ad. a) The analysis of artistic emotions has been greatly pushed forward in
        recent decades. I have no intention of quoting various attempts at description

of these psychological states, some by outstanding authors. For me such a discussion would be impossible since the artistic sensations I experience directly have their own specific character which cannot be compared to any other psychological state, just as the sensation of color green cannot be compared to the taste of salt. Of course, the great complexity of these states allows us to find elements known from other realms of life. Such an analysis is not without its significance and is in itself an interesting chapter in psychology. Theory of art must, however, pass it over, since anyway it has to assume that *there are some direct criteria that allow one to distinguish a work of art from other products.* Without this assumption we would be moving within the sphere of a commonplace which, of course, is not our aim. If the word "content" is to be useful for art theory, we cannot identify it with the notion of psychological states evoked by the work of art.

Ad. b) As for the anecdotal content of the work of art, it had been resolved by art critics of recent decades. Today, everyone knows that the American *two-step*, for instance, can be beautiful, and a national anthem—hideous, that a sheen of beef painted by Rembrandt is masterpiece, while Piłsudski's portraits, seen in shop-windows, are hideous daubs, that the description of cucumbers in *Pan Tadeusz* are the highest flights of imagination compared with the metaphysical and social visions of *Charity* etc. Nobody will want to seriously consider the "content" of the work of art from this point of view. It would be meaningless to use the word in this sense.

Ad. c) The only interesting sense of "content" in a work of art could be contained in elements of reality. We come across such elements in paintings and sculpture of all periods and nations, from pre-historic times until the most recent art. A similar phenomenon exists in poetry. Poetry uses phrases in a more or less particular sense that confirms some relationship occurring between elements of reality or an ideal world. Indirectly, it brings us into contact with reality or with ideal world. Contrary to painting, sculpture and poetry, such arts as music, dance, architecture and decoration, though they use elements of reality (voices of nature in music, scenes from life in dance, branches of trees in architecture, leaf or flower pattern in decoration) they can still easily eliminate these elements. That is why we can consider these arts devoid of content. The content (in the sense of elements of reality) that appears permanently in painting, sculpture and poetry contributed to the fact that any theory of these arts was sidetracked, that it lost its proper course. To realize this phenomenon, we have to turn to the other fundamental notion of art theory, namely, the notion of form.

Form is actually a much simpler notion than that of content, but to understand it demands a much deeper look into art and this is why we find many instances of a complete inability to associate a definite meaning with the word "form."
To remove all doubts I would like to turn our attention to the following elements of form, which are relatively easy to understand.

1) Composition, that is the mutual relationship of the elements of a work of art. In painting and sculpture: the way shapes are placed, the ratio of their sizes, their degree of complexity, direction, etc.; in poetry: placement of accents and sounds (rhythm and rhyme), structure and placement of sentences, etc.
2) Color: various colors and their juxtaposition; placement of light in sculpture; type of sounds in poetry.
3) Technique, that is: dimension and shape of the canvas, type of paints, type of brushwork; in sculpture—dimension and type of material and type of finish; in poetry—so-called style.

These do not exhaust everything belonging to the notion of form; they should, though, be enough to define the sense of "form" that I shall use. We should also like to turn the reader's attention to the rich possibilities within the form, in order to prepare him for the question of whether he is allowed to look for something else in the work of art which fulfils all the criteria of perfect form, but which is alien to form. The apparent lack of clear formal criteria in art with which we are concerned, as opposed to the seemingly inviolable criteria of content is, in my opinion, responsible for the confusion of notions that I have already mentioned. The significance of the theory of multiple reality is based on the fact that from its point of view the formal criteria of art are much more permanent than the criteria of content, which have to be completely dependent on the kind of reality concerned.

2. From these remarks it follows that the principal difference between music, dance, architecture and decoration on the one side, and painting, sculpture, and poetry on the other depends on the fact that in the first group the absence of elements of reality and a relative simplicity of form direct one's theoretical thinking towards form. Whereas in the second group the high degree of formal questions, combined with the presence of seemingly unambiguous elements of reality, brings these elements to the foreground, due to *the principle of least resistance*. Here we find the roots of the most paradoxical criterion ever thought of, which can be summed up as follows: painting and sculpture should faithfully copy nature, at most idealizing it slightly, while poetry should preach true opinions, in accordance with the principles of ethics, social etiquette, etc.

    This criterion is so widespread that it is often difficult today to recognize all its monstrosity, if we want to remain within pure theory. It is sufficient to turn to the results of art developed on the basis of such an ideology to repudiate it as inadmissible. It is enough to say that the result of this ideology is the extreme naturalism of our period, turning art exhibitions into cabinets of wax figures, and transforming poems into rhymed, or not, textbooks of *savoir-vivre*, history or geography. One should not be surprised that many great artists were led astray by symbolic and literary art, not being able to cope with the obligation to copy nature. It is equally natural that more direct and spontaneous artists went opposed to any theory, disregarding the copying of nature without any theoretical justification, only because they had seen in it the negation of everything that interested them in art. From the artists' reaction a separate theory has developed, written by painters and poets— maybe not always precise, at times full of muddled and fanciful ideas, but invaluable as an elemental protest of creative minds against an imposed, false formula. It is unnecessary to discuss everything that has been written on the subject in France, Germany, Italy, Russia, and our country. I shall only mention a very interesting book by Stanisław Ignacy Witkiewicz, which stands above similar German books thanks to his highly developed artistic intuition, and above non-German versions on account of its theoretical expertise. All those efforts did not bring, however, a definite answer to the following argument, constantly repeated by the supporters of copying nature:

    Let's suppose that a perfect form of the work of art is possible, independent from its accordance with reality. Why not, however, look for this agreement—if even the most famous Old Masters have done it, and if we can gain new values that would not lower the standards of form—if the form is independent?

    As a consequence of this argument artists are being blamed for ignorance, for not faithfully following ideals accepted as images of reality, provoking them to try their skills in naturalism, often alien to them, which leads finally to chaos, disorienting everyone.

I see only one answer to this argument.

If I am to copy reality, then, which reality? The one the reflection of which I find in photography or paintings based on it? What am I to do if I do not believe that I apprehend it indirectly with the help of light beams, as rational realism wants? What am I to do if, e.g., I live in the reality of sense impressions, and I regard light radiation theory only as a convenient hypothesis? Can the photograph be for me anything more than a diagram, alien to reality, a kind of dictionary to use when translating reality into conventional language? Or, if I live in natural reality, what concern can I have for foreshortening and shadows and light in photography, if I know that, e.g., the human body is symmetrical, and skin is uniformly colored— white, black or yellow? And if, what is now very likely, I am in a situation that the reality of images imposes with increasing force, pushing further away all other realities, then a postulate of photography becomes a paradox that cannot be taken seriously even for a moment. What then is left of the sacred principle of copying nature? Nothing, it has to be admitted. It appears that the notion of reality cannot play a positive role in art theory, not only for reasons felt directly and which demand of the artist to look for artistic criteria on the basis of only form, but also because the postulate of copying nature is devoid of sense—it cannot help or thwart the artist and he knows it.

This way we can regard our first assumption as proven.

It remains to show that the relationship of a work of art to reality cannot a priori determine its artistic quality, either in the positive or negative sense. In other a words work of art can have a perfect form independent of what reality is repre-sented, though there is always a danger lowering its quality by over-emphasizing qualities belonging to any of the realities.

The basis for substantiating this assumption is the division of painting and sculpture into different types depending on their relationship to this or that reality.

It is clear that from this point of view we can distinguish four principal types of paint-ing and sculpture corresponding to the four realities presented here. The matter was discussed in articles published in the first issues of *Maski* [The Masks]. It is enough here to draw attention only to the most essential points.

3. The four principal types of painting and sculpture that I shall discuss are as follows: 1) *Primitivism*, 2) *Realism*, with its extreme brand known as Naturalism, 3) *Impressionism*, 4) the so-called new art which, for simplicity, we shall call here *Futurism*.

    These types occur in different periods to a lesser or greater extent. One can say that, basically, art history begins with Primitivism, which subsequently passes through Realism and Impressionism to Futurism. It has to be noted that each of these types not only exists at any time, but also maintains some ability to evolve. Careful observation of the conditions of development of each of the types allows one to draw the conclusion that *each of them is strictly connected with one of the four realities, namely: Primitivism with the reality of objects; Realism—with physical reality; Impressionism with the reality of sense impressions; and lastly, Futurism—with the reality of images.* To convince the reader we shall examine all four realities.

    1) The seeming variance of Primitivism with the reality results from the fact that we are generally used to physical reality or the reality of sense impressions. However, let us try to consider this from the point of view of the reality of objects.

    The Primitive painter does not paint things as we see them but attempts to present them as such. He therefore uses his knowledge of the properties of objects. This depends on his experience which, in practice, as we have seen, are very limited, and hence the great creative force of Primitivism. Thanks to ambiguity in the notion of objects and their mutual relationship, the artist has at his disposal a great free-dom in juxtaposing shapes and colors, which allows him to achieve a high degree of perfection of form. Keeping properties of objects that are widely known, he does not shock the spectator who remains in natural reality, and allows him to give in without reservation to a pure contemplation of the work of art.

Such a relationship of Primitivism to the reality allows one to settle the paradox of content. The Primitive artist is sincere, for he does not search for artificial construction to achieve formal effects, but simply paints the world which attracts him, which he likes. The Primitive artist does not copy reality since his knowledge of objects is given to him at the time of the creative process, he paints from his "memory," relying only on himself. The Primitive artist does not falsify reality since, neglecting, e.g., perspective or chiaroscuro, he avoids only a sphere of visual phe-nomena that he does not count as reality. The Primitive artist is not incompetent, since he knows how to preserve the properties of objects which interest him with great accuracy; the impression of incompetence occurs only when demands are made that are alien to his reality.

2) In much more difficult situation finds himself the Realist painter, or sculptor, who believes that we only know the reality of objects indirectly through visual sensation evoked by the vibration of light. Here there is no case for the use of direct knowl-edge of objects—the artist has to study nature diligently, filling the gaps caused by changing visual sensations with his knowledge of perspective, optics, anatomy etc. Of course, in this way his free hand in the choice of shapes and colors is limited, and the achievement of perfect form in painting depends on the perfect choice of a model, similarly to color photography. The task is very difficult and this is why a great majority of Realist paintings (as opposed to Primitive painting) fail to please as regards form, turning our attention to content, which is a negation of pure art. Strangely, we often hear that Naturalist art (extreme Realism) is something diffi-cult to achieve while Primitivism is only fit to be a child's plaything—a character-istic reversal of the facts. What seems difficult in Naturalism, the faithful copying of models, is almost always achieved by even mediocre talents, after a few years of studies—which from the point of view of the artistic ideal is worth as much as the lack of any study. Whereas the essential difficulty, achieving a perfect form on the basis of Realism—which a talented Primitive artist achieves with no effort—is very rarely taken into account. This aspect of Realism can lead one to the conclusion that Realism is a negation of genuine art. Since, if the goal of art is perfect form, and copying nature is its negation, how can we achieve this goal on the basis of Realism with its far-reaching limitations?

To dispense with this argument it is enough to state that the notion of Realism is not universal. The Realism of the Greeks was different from the Realism of the Renaissance, still different from the Realism of Rembrandt or Ingres. Realism in photography is fundamentally different from the contemporary Realism called Naturalism. If we examine all the stages of the development of physical Realism in science, we shall see its correspondence in Realism in art. As physical Realism gains stronger scientific grounds, Realism in art becomes increasingly lifeless and less artistic. Only in its beginnings did Realism rise to the heights of great art (Venus de Milo, Titian, Tintoretto, Rembrandt), when a certain freedom embodied in its theory permitted the search for perfect composition and color harmony, leav-ing it free to develop in different styles (Baroque). Only an excessive development of physical Realism in theory destroyed any possible further evolution, leaving only the practical or anecdotal significance of illustration, like photography.

3) In none of the styles of painting is the close connection with its appropriate reality more apparent than in Impressionism. The movement, being relatively recent,

allows us a more detailed knowledge of its development. It was only possible in a society used to the reality of visual sensations. So parallel to the development of Impressionism we can observe an unheard of increase in psychological research. Psychology was a ruling fashion. Similarly, the decline of Impressionism coincides with diminishing the interest in psychology.

The main aim of Impressionism—the notation of color on canvas almost at the moment of first observation, combined with Pointillist theory on the synthesis of pure colors occurring in the eye of the spectator, does not leave any doubt that the real world the Impressionists painted had nothing to do with the reality of objects of the Primitive artist, or with the physical reality of the Realist. It was completely new and hence so influential movement, movement using color spots that acted directly on visual senses. Consciously introducing form (understood as color harmony) as the main and only postulate of art, the Impressionists believed that it could be achieved by a complete surrender to the sensation of color. In this way their relation to the reality of sense impressions was an equally precise as that of the Realists to physical reality. Only a one-sided notion of reality represented by the not-too-well-educated classes could have brought on them the accusation of consciously falsifying reality. Only when, as Oscar Wilde rightly noted, the real world changed under the influence of their art—that is when people got used to the reality of sense impressions—did the Impressionists come to represent official painting, losing thus the ability to evolve further.

It is interesting that the Impressionists were able to realize the Impressionist doctrine not only in painting but also in, more difficult art, in sculpture. In Impressionist sculpture i) different views are of different importance, ii) treatment of its parts is disproportionate and the whole fragmentary. These characteristics closely correspond to the properties of the reality of sense impressions.

Before we pass to the fourth type of art, which is not quite crystallized and demands somewhat different treatment, I would like to turn the reader's attention to a common characteristic of all three types described above.

I refer to the fact that copying nature is contrary to the essence of art. That is why a well-developed reality that imposes forcefully does no good for the development of art. On the other hand, if artistic creation is condemned to search for harmonies of color and shapes understood in purely decorative terms, it can soon die because the possible combinations are exhausted. This state of affairs means that many art theorists who believe in one reality are very skeptical about further development in art. This view can be found in Witkiewicz's book mentioned above, and a similar theory can be found in a recently published work by Spengler devoted to "the decline of the West." Naturally, the view cannot be upheld if the theory of multiple realities is correct. It appears that only art that develops on the basis of a static, ever better known reality is condemned to extinction. The emergence of a new reality is bound to be followed by the explosion of great art, since i) it gives a direct stimulus to creative work, excluding cold-hearted combinations of forms and colors, ii) a relative ambiguity of the notion of reality allows great freedom in building form. This observation will allow us to understand the significance of the new art that is emerging. It is, I think, destined to take an equal place alongside the three realities already discussed. We shall discuss this art in the next article.

4) The radical change that has occurred recently in art is that the reality of images has become dominant. This emergent reality includes all the objects of the reality of sense impressions with which Impressionism dealt. However, they appear in a very different form, and then they are lost in the abundance of new objects which have a basically different rationale. For instance, I am interested in a woman whom I only rarely saw and who always appeared the same in the reality of sense

impressions. With my entering the reality of images she takes on ever stranger form, combining with several unknown objects, and what is more important—she does not leave me for the moment. These phenomena are difficult to comprehend. Also "internal sight," of which Bahr writes, is only one of many elements in play. Besides, there is an in-depth knowledge of the object, similar to the one we deal with in the reality of objects, but without its theoretical knowledge. Moreover, there are phenomena much more complex, extremely difficult to describe. If not known from one's own experience, one can only get a notion of them from rare descriptions by a few poets and mystics. I shall quote one such description which we owe to St. Theresa.

St. Theresa spent a few days in the palace belonging to Princess Alba. She saw a room there, containing many precious objects, laid out in such a way that one could take them all in at a glance. This made a great impression on her; she had the feeling of utter bliss. The impression stayed in her memory while details disappeared, so she was not able to describe what exactly she had seen. She talked of her visions in a similar way. It is clear that we are dealing with an experience *based on overcoming the content*, through loosening up the boundaries of objects, which is done more or less consciously in modern painting. It explains why a theoretically very difficult problem of reasons why painting increasingly plays the role of decoration has recently come closer to being resolved. The reason undoubtedly lies in the artists entering into the spirit of the reality of images, which happened almost simultaneously in distant parts of Europe as a result of being satiated with the reality of sense impressions, and partly because of the critique of this reality by Bergson. In this way, the rational critique of this philosopher (which he applied too radically in his philosophy)—that a man who would, instead of swimming, calculate the theoretical possibility of swimming, would conclude that he could never stay afloat. In practice, however, it proves quite easy.

The unprecedented vagueness of the reality of images is clearly reflected in contemporary art, and is the cause of its inability to create a unified style. Different genres of painting and sculpture, which had emerged on the basis of the reality of images, place emphasis on different qualities. And so, the Italian Futurists occupied themselves with the bustling reality of images, the Cubists with its relative simplicity, and the Expressionists with its close relationship to a subjective individual life. The Formists noted its incredible flexibility and the resulting ability to adapt to purely formal issues. What is common to all these movements can be best understood through the following example. Let us assume that I am to paint the portrait of a person who interests me. We had seen how this was done by Primitivist, Realist, and Impressionist painters. A man deep into the reality of images will be far from looking for the "proper" qualities of a model; it would not cross his mind to study the model from nature, or to absorb the sense impressions of color—as Impressionist would have done. He would try to get to know the model well, so that the image of the model would become one of the elements of the reality in which he exists. The image can be shaped in any way—impossible to predict; neither can one say anything a priori about its relationship to other images. Until an image is permanently integrated into the artist's reality, there is no essential need to create a work of art. Only when the image dominates over all the other elements of reality, the artist's creative impulse is stimulated. Only then can the artist achieve perfect form in a more or less unconscious way, without concerning himself fatally with the juxtaposition of shapes and colors.

The so-called likeness will not count in this case—it is useless, but we can still take it up when we come to discuss the "force of suggestion," a means of communication for people steeped in the reality of images.

We see that the "new art" is basically predisposed to take an equal place among the three preceding types of art. We have argued the claim for a theoretical equality of all the principal types of painting and sculpture. However, the inclusion of the reality of images as the content of painting and sculpture allows one to answer a basic question of art theory: to what extent the content of the work of art can be overcome?....

[....]

9. We have seen that the theory of multiple of realities can explain all principal move-ments in art, designating a special place for the latest art as the one that will prepare the most distinct and seemingly paradoxical reality. The result cannot, of course, affect any discussion of its value; still, I do not think, it should be disre-garded. Because the new art spreads in increasingly wider circles and penetrates the mind it has to have an important influence on life. I consider it very important to prove that it does not contradict scientific research in any respect, but rather confirms it, providing at the same time interesting experimental material. I am aware that my study only provides a general outline, and is far from complete. If I publish it now, it is to provoke discussion among all those who do not necessarily think that the role of philosophy is only to "inform" or "elaborate" problems long fallen into oblivion. I expect this discussion to provide the stimulus for further research on the subject.

Translated by Wanda Kemp-Welch

ON 'GREEN EYE' AND HIS PAINTING   Tytus Czyżewski
Originally published as "O 'zielonym oku' i o swoim malarstwie," *Formiści* no. 4 (1921)

(self-criticism—self advertisement)
Green eye was written by Tytus Czyżewski, that is
me
thinking about the perversity of colors, line and form. Everything lives and has its own value. What does not live—does not exist, and what does not exist has neither form nor color.
I wrote The Cat's Serenade "inspired" by the love of a Tom cat—an old flame of a she-cat I knew.
Animals love with passion and a directness of instinct.
My Pastourelles are my reminiscence (from my childhood years) of my family village in the Tatra mountains covered by the thick December snow
carols, carols
Singing houses is a "poem" about the curvature of line and measure. Everything dances in the European post-war lust.
Houses laugh at people, and people cry over their own foolishness.
Children laugh at their parents.
Melody of the crowd is a poem about anxiety or an annoying muddle on a Paris boule-vard (Bulmishel) on which I rediscovered my personality—of a Polish artist without a rudder or anchor.
Le soir d'amour are the teeth chattering before "that"—which "afterwards" becomes banality.

Electrical visions—a mechanized poem.

Man created and unleashed the machine that will one day kill him or elevate him.

We shall build machines—we shall travel to the stars to observe the sun.

The sun will be surprised—where does man get his wits from?

Man will build a mechanical sun.

The old sun—a good old machine.

Let us love the sun and stop talking behind its back.

Man of the future will be an electric machine—tender, complex, and yet simple in style.

Various critics wrote various things about Green eye.

The critics writing in periodicals on "poetry" all agreed that my poems show minimum "talent," whereas my painting was regarded as a "milestone."

And conversely—critics writing in periodicals devoted to plastic arts were almost all in agreement that my poems are "milestones" (?!), whereas my painting is "incompetent," without "drawing" or "color."

I know from experience that the best articles about politics in the Polish press are written by engineers and musicians; on agriculture and gardening—by generals; on trade— by poets; on poetry—by lawyers and doctors; on medicine—by professors of classic languages (Greek and Latin); on Greek and Latin—by teachers of drawing; on plastic arts—by veterinary surgeons, geologists and political analysts.

That is why I feel completely assured about my Green Eye and my painting.

Love electric machines, marry them and produce dynamo-children—magnetize them and educate them so that they grow up to be good mechanical citizens.

The above is a wish from your poet without "wings" and painter without "paint."

Translated by Wanda Kemp-Welch

AESTHETIC SKETCHES   Stanisław Ignacy Witkiewicz
Originally published as *Szkice estetyczne* (Cracow: 1922)

The sequence will be arranged according to a certain raising to the nth power, and other diminishing properties belonging to specific objects and their complexes and the letters a, b, c, d, designated by these same objects. The raising to the nth power of properties associated with objects, will be designated by the indexes 0 to 12. All elements will figure in the given group, and at the same time its minutely small quantity will be designated by the index 0. Groups will be designated by the letters A to D, and at the same time transitional groups (in analogy to the transitional colors in the colors of the spectrum) will be designated by two adjoining letters. Groups with a majority of c elements divide, as we shall see later, into two sequences subsequently merging with each other, and for this reason, properties associated with objects and designated by c will be of two types: c' and c." A degree in the direction of diminution is designated e.g. $b^{12}c$.

And so:

a = matter disorganized in the formal sense.

b = an object (or a complex of the like) of certain unity.

c = the representation of such an object or complex, with a certain unity: naturalistic and stylized representation.

d = pure formal unity, not reducible to the unity of the object.

A_1) a^n = The maximum of formal disorganization of matter, e.g.: a pile of rubbish, mixed salad.

A2) a^{12} = A smaller degree of formal disorganization, e.g.: cliffs, screens.

AB) a^1b^1= The transition to objects constituting organic wholes e.g.: cliffs similar to some kind of creatures, incomplete crystals.

B_1) b^{12} = Objects of a small degree of formal unity, e.g. bushes of irregular form, jelly-like creatures of the sea.

B_2) b^n = Objects of a high degree of formal unity, e.g. a steam engine, a simple house, a man, an animal, the interior of a room arranged in a certain way.

B_3) b^{12} = Objects of a high degree of formal unity, but only in relation to an understanding of their construction, e.g. complex machines, human internal organs.

BC) b^1 with $c^{1'}$ and b^1 with $c^{1'''}$ = Objects whose unity is based on usefulness, but which are not living creatures, e.g.: realist sculpture, more elaborate houses. Objects decorated with ornament e.g.: ornamental furniture and carriages, painted vases.

C_1) $c^{12'}$ d^1 and $c^{12''}$ d^1 = realist paintings (Chełmoński), objects as the background of ornaments, in other words stylized form in unlimited space. Unity as a result of the combination of shapes, independent of the enclosing frame.

C_2) $c^{n'}$ d^5 and $c^{n''}$ d^5 = realist paintings with the addition of a compositional aspect (Siemiradzki) Ornaments of abstract shapes, in other words geometric forms in unenclosed space.

C_3) $c^{12'}$ with d^8 and $c^{12''}$ with d^8 = realist paintings with a significant addition of composition (Rubens) Ornaments in enclosed space.

CD) $c^{10'}$ with d^{10} and $c^{10''}$ with d^{10} = Pure Form with a significant addition of objecthood as such (Titian) Ornaments relating more to enclosed space, than to the relation of shapes to one another.

D_1) $c^{8'}$ with d^{12} and $c^{8''}$ with d^{12} = Pure Form with a small addition of objecthood as such (Boticelli, Gauguin) Ornaments in enclosed space approximate to Pure Form.

D_2) $c^{3'}$ with d^{15} and $c^{3''}$ with d^{15} = Pure Form, with nearly no addition of objecthood as such. Objects as directional forces (Cubism, Kandinsky). Composition with a certain ornamentality.

D_3) d^n = Absolutely Pure Form. Extreme cases and those approximate to them.

D_4) dx = Absolute unity without multiplicity. Single colored circle. Sphere.

A_1 = a^n b^0 c^0 d^0

A_2 = a^{12} b^0 c^0 d^0

AB = a^1 b^1 c^0 d^0

B_1 = a^0 b^{12} c^0 d^0

B_2 = a^0 b^n c^0 d^0

B_3 = a^0 $b^{12'}$ with c^0 d^0

BC = a^0 b^1 with $c^{1'}$ $c^{1'''}$ d^0

C_1 = a^0 b^0 $c^{12'}$ $c^{12''}$ d^1

C_2 = a^0 b^0 $c^{n'}$ $c^{n''}$ d^5

C_3 = a^0 b^0 with $c^{12'}$ $c^{12''}$ with d^8

CD = a^0 b^0 with $c^{10'}$ $c^{10''}$ with d^{10}

D_1 = a^0 b^0 $c^{8'}$ with $c^{8''}$ with d^{12}

D_2 = a^0 b^0 $c^{3'}$ with $c^{3''}$ with d^{15}

D_3 = a^0 b^0 c^0 d^n

D_4 = a^0 b^0 c^0 dx

Combinations designated by double letters constitute the unclear boundaries of different spheres. The sphere designated by the letters CD, in which the transition from realist painting to Pure Form takes place, is important to our theory. Works belonging to this sphere may be treated by some as faithful reflections of nature, and by others as relatively Pure Form. We do not of course attribute any absolute value to the given sequence, we only give it as an example. It is possible to produce a far more complete sequence, one that would more clearly illustrate the indefinable nature of transitions from one sphere to another.

A certain artistic element begins to make its appearance in the sphere of the extremity BC, and Art, according to our definition, begins in the sphere CD.

As long as we do not accept the definition of a work of Art to be that of a human product which is irreducible to formal unity, we can start to count works of art, beginning from group A_1, but then it is doubtful whether it will be possible to say anything precise on this subject, particularly since, according to us, our definition is in accordance with the actual state of things.

There may be an objection that we have chosen the boundaries of CD completely at random. This objection is irrefutable. "How so?" specialists may say, "Chełmoński, Siemiradzki, Rubens, outside the boundaries of art? This is outrageous." To this we reply: if anyone receives the same impression from a painting of Chełmoński's as from a construction of Pure Form, rather than the impression of an excellently represented Polish landscape "according to an individual point of view," the boundary of art will have to be shifted as far as sphere C_1 for him. But it is just this which is extremely dubious. Chełmoński was concerned with the Polish landscape, its character and its beauty, with the love of nature, maybe even with the metaphysical feeling aroused by nature— with everything except for Pure Form.

Everything, even a pile of rubbish, may contain an element of Pure Form—this is why we have assumed it only as a guideline, as equal to 0. If anyone wished to be stubborn about it, he might claim that he could also experience a metaphysical sensation through Pure Form from a pile of rubbish. For as a pile of rubbish is also the product of human hands, might it not also be a work of art? We are entering into the realm of some horrible sort of nonsense. Yet "specialists" and the majority of critics maneuver skillfully in this sphere, completely unaware of this.

We are not in the least comparing the works of Chełmoński, who is a great naturalist painter, to a pile of rubbish, we are merely drawing the ultimate conclusions from the "specialists'" assumptions, maintaining two standpoints simultaneously: those of form and content. This is the most dangerous kind of specialist. It is better to talk to pure naturalists: these at least know precisely what they want.

A propos one more small, but fairly venomous misunderstanding can be explained.

"Specialists" say: "Then, according to these theories of yours, one can do anything. Every blot, every conjunction of lines, a few words with no sense, are a work of art? If colors and lines are everything, then…(here the specialist makes a scrawl with a pencil) and you already have Pure Form." It is strange that no one asks musicians these kinds of questions. If sounds and rhythms are everything, then in that case a cat can run across a keyboard and you already have a prelude at least.

Since the ideology of musical aestheticians has not been warped by any such catastrophe as the Renaissance was in painting, and also to a certain extent because the inessential content of music is the expression of one's feelings and that besides music there is simply nothing to talk about in music, musicians are spared these kinds of pleasant questions. But just let those who shudder in physical ecstasy at Italian opera try to understand Schönberg, Prokofiev or the latest works of Szymanowski, in terms of "feelings." They too will meet with some disappointment, and will turn away, blocking their ears. Unless it is merely a matter of noise, as in the case of one literati who experienced optical hallucinations from the very noise of the piano, and who once listened to Beethoven's *Appassionata* played backwards on the pianola screaming with metaphysical ecstasy.

It is precisely here that a conception of form conceived of as construction, can explain a great deal.

The creation of a work of art, although it may only be made of those snubbed lines and colors (but formed as a certain inseparable whole for the artist), also requires a proportion of all the artists' data listed above. It is only this one formal idea which will make the miracle which we call a work of art, out of seemingly poor material. This is why the "specialist's" scrawl, a few words combined at random, and a cat running across a keyboard, can never be works of art. We may take as an example something which was made by accident, but awakened a purely formal admiration in someone. But even this will not move a theoretician examining the essential relationships, and thus standing above any accidentality, even when it is carried to absurdity.

Besides, no one is denying that there may be such a thing as bad Pure Form. There may be insincere paintings, successful examples of bad things, inventions by cold calculation, imitations that will, in the subjective hierarchy of the work of art, be botches in Pure Form.

There can also be masterpieces of naturalist painting. Who would deny that Matejko was a genius? He was an unparalleled master at rendering facial expressions, he was a wonderful interpreter of nature, a man of deep patriotism expressed in painting, a great mind. There is just one thing: he did not create Pure Form, he did not want to create it and he did not want to force anyone to understand his paintings as Pure Form.

So why confuse two spheres of artistic production, which are completely incomparable just because of the technique of both one and the other i.e. canvas, brushes, paint etc., are the same?

Let us stop arguing—there can be masterpieces and botches in Pure Form, there can be masterpieces and botches in naturalist painting. Naturalists believe that they possess objective criteria and that they know for certain what is a botch and what is a masterpiece; according to us they are mistaken, at least as regards color. We have dealt with drawing elsewhere.* Naturalists cannot entirely make do with the help of the concept of nature alone, and they have to make a whole series of additional assumptions, which lead them rapidly to depart from the purely naturalist standpoint, and make this standpoint little more than an infertile, unclear and not strictly tenable one.

We prefer to conclude that there are no objective criteria but, instead, there is a thoroughly precise theory of Art, as long as one accepts that Form as the construction of the complete work is everything, and so called "content" is an inessential addition. If this is achievable, we can renounce objective criteria, which have never existed and never will, with a clean conscience.

Translated by Klara Kemp-Welch.

---

* *Nowe formy w malarstwie [New forms in painting]*, part III, ch. IV, 2. It is embarrassing to keep quoting oneself, but what can one do. [Original author's note.]

The twentieth century did not know how to come into the world. Fourteen years after
its christening it was still an embryo in the tail of its predecessor. It was the shadow of
its body, the echo of its voice. It did not have its own countenance, it only had its own
number: twenty.

Admittedly, word had been drifting through Europe since before the war, swelled with
the plasma of the century and ruddy with its blood, but it lacked resonance at that time.
There was no choir to take the new word into its hot mouth and give shape to it with
its lips. There was no choir to make its own expression out of the word.

*It was only the war that carried man onto the paths on which he would meet the spirit of
the age and follow it:*
Seen from the high towers of the future, the war we have left behind was also a significant event in the sphere of the cultivation of the spirit.

Was it destructive? It was destructive. But every one of its destructive actions was
preceded by a gigantic act of creation. Every loss caused by it came from an action
that was a gain. Its terrible machines of death were the promise of powerful future
machines of life. It destroyed the creations of civilization with the means of a higher
civilization.

These means were drawn from the deepest flesh of the years in which they were
formed. On each of them the stamp of time was bitten out. Every one of them was
steaming with the sweat of contemporary man. It was a matter of the lives of people
and nations, and this life was all the easier to ensure, the better, the more bravely,
the more purely one was able to exploit the latest achievements of the century. Man
fell into a hitherto unheard of degree of dependence on his tools, which in order to
be victorious, needed to be new. Fighting with the enemy, they were simultaneously
fighting with their heritage.

These conditions ploughed the spiritual substance of man and sewed it with iron. The
spiritual attitude of man to the new products of his hands, for which there had previously been no space in the chosen areas of his soul, altered. Modern tools displayed
their power and melted their iron heart into the heart of man.

The feverish *postwar* [atmosphere] acts on man in a similar way:
The shell of the world has altered.

New nations have been born and new life will impose new demands on them.
The bondage of their will shall disappear, when the will to exist on the freshest
levels of life is born. Divorce from the spirit of the past will become all the more
pressing the harder it is. The battle for existence will order them to create *the
newest organs of existence* within themselves. The germ of modernity will have
to become their totem.

The old nations have received a new identity. The altered proportions of their area will
initiate an effort to balance the proportions of their forces. The battle for power, for
plenty and for happiness will begin. There will be a war without blood. *The factory will
become the tank of peace.* In this struggle, the alliance with time, with our time, will
become the condition for victory, thus a commandment.

An idea flared up in the Russian darkness, which, though blind and crazy, reached
beyond the borders of its fatherland with the shadow of its vibrating wings. Its influence
can be seen in the life of all societies. Forms of people's co-existence have altered,
and the consequences of this change will have to encompass the entire surface of our

life. *Today's social geology* aims to forge lines, which will belong to the most character-istic features of our age.

A new epoch is beginning: *the epoch of the embrace of contemporaneity.*
That which is the essence of our times, which makes it different from the times which have passed, which will be its name in history, and which is its strength in life, is today approaching man, at the distance of an embrace.
Contemporary man, obedient to life's instinct and transforming instinct into an idea, is setting off on the path of making peace with and fraternizing with this new edition of the world, which he began to create a long time ago and which he has, until now, been unable to become accustomed to. He affirms the modern stage of life, and in this way the city becomes for him an enchanted island of powerful emotions. He affirms the new form of people's co-existence, and in this way mass becomes for him the long sought after co-worker of new beauty. He affirms the modern tools of life, and in this way the machine becomes for him the new poetic fairy godmother of his feverish dreams. City, mass, machine, and their derivatives: speed, inventiveness, novelty, the power of man and of the epoch, wrestling with the sky, flight on steel wings, bathing in the freshest vodka of the day, the leap into now—become for us the objects of unknown raptures.

The new swing of life and ideas about life must *also* be imparted *to art.*
Willingly or unwillingly, its servants will have to destroy the prison of history and follow the history that is happening now. Some will do this out of a tendency to harmonize with their surroundings, and others out of the desire to renovate their craft.
The first will wish to become the echo and the looking glass of the substance surrounding them. They will make the aims of time their own aims. They will pour present-day reality into their cups like wine. They will make the flesh of the age the source of their creative inspiration. Their work will be the word, the picture, and the song of the con-temporary.
The others will discover the elements of new artistic forms in the new forms of life. The increasingly huge dimensions of our life will increase the scale of their visions. The prin-ciple of precise construction and of economy of means, reigning in all branches of today's creative production, will fertilize their research in the field of construction. The acceler-ated speed of our walking and breathing will suggest to them a new rhythm. The raised heights of our sensitivity will force them to sharpen up colors.
It is in this way that the hemoglobin of contemporaneity will victoriously reach one and all through countless and invisible arteries.

Zwrotnica aims to turn towards the present. It aims to be the matrix of a new spirit. It aims to sew the nerve of contemporaneity into man. It aims to kindle in him the love of the novelty which he himself created, and in relation to which he could not help but be a few centuries older. It aims to awaken in him a faith in the miracle-producing epoch in which he lives, and distaste for the deceased epochs which live on in him. It aims to drive a new art out of the new spirit. It aims to shed light on the elements of beauty which have freshly sprung from the place, form and tools of modern life. It aims to invite the artist into the contemporary world, which is awaiting eyes worthy of its riches. It aims to follow the style of our epoch and sculpt its head, having first placed it on its own iron ribs. This is what *Zwrotnica* aims to be.
The rest does not depend on it alone. So let us anticipate: *Zwrotnica* will be that which it wants to be, and also something else.
What?

Translated by Klara Kemp-Welch

CITY. MASS. MACHINE. Tadeusz Peiper

Orginally published as "Miasto. Masa. Maszyna," *Zwrotnica* no. 2 (July 1922)

I.

Being a concentration of people brought together for the benefits deriving from coexistence, the city developed according to the demands of life. Its nature, as a concentration of people, imposed limitations on individual will. With the same goal that led to this concentration, utility was raised to the principal norm of development. Both shaped the development of the city in accordance with the most vital interests of the collective. The whim and obstinacy of individuals, or certain obsolete systems of thought, could distort the line of this development in the shorter or longer run, but they could not give it any other direction than that which was dictated by the necessities of life.

Obedient to their call, *the city constantly renewed itself.* Consideration of common interests overcame all other considerations and demanded ever new ways of satisfying these interests. In this way the city produced constant innovations. Its *innovatory nature set the city in constant conflict with the inherited ways of thinking.* The newest manifestations of the city occasioned the distaste of the so-called cultured person, i.e. those persons who most strongly influenced the shaping of the collective spirit to its surroundings. Life was changing; the city, which is after all the channel and trail of life, was changing; enlightened people were the only ones not to change. A state of internal discord manifested itself between people's tastes, which submit very slowly to evolution, and the city, which was changing constantly. The very external appearance of the city, which was all the time shaping itself in accordance with the new necessities of life, must have offended contemporaries. The novelties that the city introduced in its external appearance, had their source in economic necessities and in considerations of comfort, and it was just this source which, wrongly disregarded, lowered these novelties in the feelings of refined individuals. Thus every city, in each period of its development, must have seemed ugly to contemporaries. It could have buildings or streets regarded as beautiful but these were surely of a historical character. But what emerged spontaneously, as an expression of life, evoked negative feelings in the residents and only when it was weathered by time, when it became a melancholy remembrance of the past, did it win people's hearts. Thus narrow, curving little streets became favorite haunts of tourists. As these streets emerged, in response to local needs, aesthetes were overcome by disgust or horror. As they became part of the image of the past, they gained the charm of things past. [...]

We live in times when truths have a shorter life than men do. No truth has enough life even to reach the next generation and take root in its soul. On the other hand some of the novelties of the city now arise differently. No longer spontaneously, no longer as the unimpeded expression of needs, but according to a plan. An artistic plan, arranged in advance. The city, which before had been a sort of nature, now becomes a work of art. A work of art created according to existing notions of aesthetics. It grows into the ideology of the times. From its walls it consciously creates the face of the times. This transfer of established aesthetic ideas to the city partly distorts its proper character, but also mitigates the conflict. [...]

The disappearance of the causes of the ill feeling against the city clears the air of alien factors and grievances. Instead a new emotional relationship could be built. The city can not only cease to seem ugly but start to seem beautiful. It can strongly influence artistic creation. One needs only to *see in it the realization of new beauty*, the embodiment of new aesthetic principles. *It is not enough to take the city as the subject matter of art*, as is at present practiced by many poets, if one does not change one's negative attitude to the new subject. We must say yes to the city, to its most profound essence, which distinguishes it from everything else and which should not be judged by aesthetic criteria, borrowed from other fields. The streets of today's Berlin, one of the most spectacular sights, evoke the antipathy of all those who thoughtlessly and with seeming expertise repeat formulas they have read or overheard, but cannot look at this stone monument to new life with any depth or derive new criteria of beauty from the new conditions of life. And this is what is needed. To see beauty in straight, long boulevards delineated by the requirements of life, stretched taut as strings, on which carriage wheels and people's shoes play a tune not heard anywhere else. To see beauty

in walls covered with colorful posters and to take joy in this extraordinary epos which constantly, a week in advance, describes city life. To see in shop windows a beauty that is equal to the beauty of cathedral chapels. To see beauty of the silver glimmer of tramway tracks competing with the beauty of sunlight on the river. To admire as a butterfly a woman hurrying along the pavement and dressed with modern skill. To see the same sweetness in the flowing ride of the automobile as in the flight line of the descending bird. That is what matters. In this way we should arrive at completely new aesthetic criteria and a new notion of beauty. *And, by different ways, this will have an effect on art, pointing to the new tasks and supplying art with new formal means.*

II.

Ever bigger growth of urban agglomerations.... Ever greater differentiation of societies.... Ever greater dependence of individuals on the organized mass. Growing significance of associations.... Celebrations and street parties.... Growing political importance of the people.... Their participation in cultural life still increasing.... Workers' manifestations making the mass visible.... The mass begins to appear more clearly in the foreground. It becomes felt by the individual ever more strongly because the dependence in which it holds the individual is ever more visible due to its new forms. *The mass-society and the mass-crowd have a stronger impact on man's consciousness.*

There is no doubt that sooner or later the masses will also have to *influence art.* [...] The question is: is a form of artistic order possible which, not being based on increasingly boring geometrism, could, however, become the principle of a strict and logical construction of the work of art?

It seems that such a form of order is possible and that sooner or later it will penetrate into art. Such a form is inherent in the organism. The organic system will one day become the model for the construction of a work of art. Individual parts of the work will remain functionally interrelated and this relationship will constitute the only unity of the work of art. Construction of the work of art will become a great deal more complex. The relationship of individual parts will become more distant but no less precise. The unity of the work of art will not reflect a unity of theme or pattern but, rather, from an irreversible, organic arrangement of its parts. Such organic relations we observe around us. We see them in nature. Undoubtedly, they can suggest the idea of organic unity. But natural organisms, apart from a specific (organic) structure which can serve as a source of inspiration for composition, have usually another property which actually neutralizes the previous advantage: they are usually built symmetrically. With their organic construction they suggest a symmetrical construction, hence a geometrical construction on the principle of which the works of art were composed and which they seem unable to get rid of. *However, there is an organism not burdened with boring and increasingly unbearable geometric order: mass-society....* This organism hypnotizes the individual with a new image of order, and a new idea of order. And even if the internal needs of art did not demand regeneration of constructive principles, this new image of order would automatically have to be extended into artistic creation. The internal needs of art make this process desirable and call for its conscious realization. And one can be sure that this process will happen. Mass-society will impose its construction on art. *Organicity, better known from the functioning of society, will become the inspiration of artistic construction. The work of art will be socially organized. The work of art will be society.*

And, it seems this is the only way in which the masses will express themselves in art. It will be an expression of the masses as an organized collective, mass-organism, mass- society. But in our era there are also forces that will *cause the masses as a simultaneous collective of individuals, mass-sum, mass-crowd, to find its expression in art.*

One of the most essential features of our era is the invasion of economic factors into all spheres of human activity. *The mythology of every action is the history of money.* The relationship of income to expenditure determines every enterprise, whether it is viable or not. It would be unnatural if the law had bypassed art. It has not. Artistic creation is also governed by economic laws. The connection of the aesthetic with the economic becomes increasingly stronger. There are some that adopt Katon's attitude and tear their hair out, if they are not bold, and cry out: Oh, tempora! Parnassus came crushing down to the level of the shop counter!.... Apollo openly took on the mantle of Mercury, and the Muses, if they did not change their cloaks, it is only because their transparency facilitates their connivance with black marketeers. O mores!

Calm down, gentlemen. *The interdependence of the aesthetic with the economic is increasingly stronger, but: how can it profit art?* It can. One has only to understand the situation; find new artistic profits; accept it as the premises and build on these premises. Instead of opposing the economic laws governing the whole of our life, it is better to accept them in order to advance art. It is better to follow them, to steal away from them, and to extract from them everything they have to offer for art. To surrender, in order to ensure their services. Only ridiculous Don Quixotes or those who accept the ridicule of Don Quixotism in order to exploit the suffering, can regard this as the fall of art. One must accept the new conditions as a fact, and use them for artistic purposes.

How? For instance in this way:

We all know that every impresario only looks at an enterprise from the point of view of the profit. The hope of a mass sell-out plays the most important role in his calculations. He can put into the enterprise more work, effort and—yes!—innovation, the higher the number of consumers of which he dreams, i.e. the more it is likely that his profit will be high. This form of mass artistic consumption also has an effect on the forms and direction of artistic production. A book, an exhibition of paintings[1], a concert hall, a theater, a cinema are examples with strong rhetoric. But this influence has been more noticeable in its negative rather than its positive aspects. The reason: artists were not concerned with the purely artistic benefits that can be gained from the economic benefits of mass consumption. They did not think about gaining artistic profit from this very new and contemporary phenomenon. Whereas, *mass artistic consumption opens new perspectives for art.* It allows in many cases a completely new art.

[...]

---

1 It is worth noting the profound influence on painting of the fact that it has ceased to be a courtly art, responding to commissions, and has become a production for an unknown recipient whom the artist reaches through exhibition of the finished product. Working to commission the painter had to take into account the tastes and wishes of the client; working for the unknown recipient, he takes account only of his own preferences, or...the preferences of the public. The difference throws light on the latest phases of painting's development.

III.

In 1911, while a student of Berlin University during the holidays, I went to Copenhagen. The time or purpose of this visit play no role here. Placing memories, nothing more. When considering the aesthetic issue of the machine, these memories come back, bringing to mind one of the ideas that came to me then. I was visiting an ethnographic museum. I stopped longer in the room devoted to prehistoric times. A whim of mine made me dwell on the exhibits of the Stone Age. In the glass cabinets long *rows of stone tools*. Various shapes, various functions, various degrees of finish. Among the objects displayed were tools of sharp whetstone that surprised me with their ideal precision of form. Knives? Chisels? Cutters? Axes? Undoubtedly, this and that, and something more still. But that does not matter. One series of these knives had a completely smooth surface; another had an *ornament* engraved on the surface. A zigzag ornament with perfectly equal elements, an ideal sense of symmetry. This ornament could not serve any practical purpose. It clearly was made for the pleasure of eyes and hands. A pleasure not essentially different from the delight which is evoked by creating and seeing beauty. Undoubtedly, I had in front of me the first beginnings of art.

I thought of the psychological process that had taken place in primitive man in order to produce this phenomenon which I had seen. What kind of primitive feelings had to combine for the ornament to appear on the tool, for the zigzag to become its basic component, symmetrically placed, which must reflect the inner need of the primitive engraver.

The form of a tool is always determined by its purpose. This stone tool of which I speak had one of its ends sharpened like a whetstone because this shape responded best to the needs of primitive man; it enabled it to perform several functions: to split logs, to dig earth, and to gut animals. But this generally sharp arch of the tool was not only the result of practical needs; the same source dictated the symmetry of the tool. Symmetry was originally a practical matter. If it is so widespread in nature, it is thanks to the services it gave in the struggle for survival. A stone knife was in practice all the more comfortable, reliable and effective, the more perfect was its symmetry. It is obvious then that primitive man tried to produce the most ideal and purposeful form of tool. This was not easy. If we take into account the inexperience of man in those times and his primitive means of labor, it is understandable what sum of time and effort was inherent in every object. At the same time it will become clear that the satisfactory completion of this arduous work had to be a source of deep satisfaction and of strongly felt joy to its author. The feeling of delight was associated in his psyche with the arched and symmetrical form of the tool. This form became beautiful for him. When later routine allowed him to obtain this form with less effort, he started playing with it and, on a smaller scale, repeated the form with added lines and grooves. The ornament I was looking at was nothing less than this. *The zigzag that was its basic component was a repetition of the sharp arch of the end of the tool. And the perfect symmetry with which the ornament was executed reflected the practical advantages of the symmetry of the whole tool. And so: the form of the tool, which had been dictated by practical needs, became beautiful through the work on the tool.* The sequence would be as follows: practical needs—tools responding to them—work to obtain the form—delight in the form—the form obtained thus becomes beautiful for the creator.

This is how it was with this stone tool. *And a machine?* Why in the case of this modern tool was the same process not repeated? Why was the machine until present times alien to man?

The process sketched above (I realize it is hypothetical) could not have taken place in the era of the machine mainly because the psychological steps inherent in the process could not occur in our times. Between the era of stone tools and the machine era there appeared the *phenomenon of the division of labor*. People working on a machine, producing a machine, do not put it to practical use, they are not part of its life when it is used. Hence the lack of these psychological links, on the basis of which the new aesthetic feeling could grow. Hence the lack of this specific satisfaction gained from comparing the form of tool with the purpose it was to serve. Primitive man made tools and used them himself. The more perfectly suited the form of the tool, the more convenient to use, the more effective it was, the more plentiful and valuable was the result of labor. This relationship was in each case quite clear to primitive man, not understood, but seen, felt with hands and stomach. In such conditions the maker of the tool could feel joy when he invented a tool with a form which allowed its best use. In our conditions it is impossible. The producer of a machine[2] does not know its application, he does not see it at work, and he does not work it. The connection between the form of a machine and its purpose is not only not felt—it is not even understood. The specific feeling of satisfaction gained from obtaining the most purposeful form cannot be felt by him. The form cannot be psychologically transformed into beautiful form.

Something even worse has happened. *The machine seems to man to be something ugly.* The reasons for this are similar to the reasons that caused the aesthetic degradation of the city. Above all: the conflict with inherited ideas. The machine was new and produced new things. It developed according to its own laws, it constantly changed the surrounding world, and human psychology slowly followed it with the steps of an old paralytic. Hence there was constant estrangement[3]. Next: aspects of a social nature. Machine…factory…manufacturer…proletarian…surplus value…exploitation… the feeling of revolt against the social system and by involuntary extension, against the "means of production." Finally: aspects of a physiological nature. Machine… factory…smoke over the city…noise in the street…worker's tuberculosis…occupational diseases…casualties at work…degeneration. As a result: ill feeling towards the machine. [....]

Between heart and art there is only one stop—conscious will. When the machine, having revealed to all its biological value, won over the man's heart, it was necessary for man to consciously wish that the machine become a component of artistic beauty. This creative wish has been expressed. The machine has been *introduced into the field of art. But how?* Some (Futurists) treat it as a fetish to be worshipped and covered with incense (art). Others (Purists) see in the machine perfect beauty, which art should take as its model. In the first case, the machine is introduced into art as a godlike creature, independent of its artistic values; in the other—it is introduced into art as an idol to be emulated. The first scenario expresses the attitude of a consumer of the machine, one

2 Or rather, parts of the machine. Specialization!
3 Newspapers reported that some German engineer built an aeroplane, imitating the shapes of an enormous bird. We don't know any details of this idea. We don't know the motives of its author. Perhaps it was just a whim? Or perhaps aesthetic considerations had some influence? Perhaps he wanted to make an "ugly" aeroplane beautiful. This would be reminiscent of the ridiculous attempts to prettify factories and factory tools, undertaken by Germans in the middle of the last century, when factory chimneys were made to look like elaborate towers or minarets, its walls and tools peopled with figures from the Olympus and forms of Acropolis, when iron columns were given the shape of Doric or Ionic columns and weighty elements were supported on the heads of caryatids, when reservoirs were crowned by Pallada with a head that could be opened and filled with oil. A false attitude to technology is repeated in many variations up to the present day and, as long as we cannot shake it off, the world of iron and steel, abundant and flourishing, will remain strange for us. Decorating the products of technology is as ridiculous as it would be to decorate medicine. In both everything is determined by the principle of purposefulness. Technology needs to be left to laws to which it is subject by its very essence. The emotional attitude to its works needs to be shaped from the point of view of the consumer's convenience. The most beautiful shape a machine can have is the shape adapted to its function.

who is not yet an artist; the second, that of a producer of the machine, one the artist cannot be. In both cases the aesthetic problem of the machine is wrongly set out. Were the machine only a god it would not deserve art's attention; were it the most perfect beauty, art would not be needed.

It seems to me that *the role the machine can play in art is quite different*. Neither a god nor an idol. Servant! Machine should serve art. It should serve the purposes that emerge from art itself, its very essence. The point is not adulation[4] or imitation of the machine but its exploitation. Undoubtedly, in some arts it has been done. The world of the tenth muse, the world of cinematography, is completely served by the machine. It was also brought into the theater, but it was done in too small doses and very slowly, on account of the aesthetic dogmatists' digestive system. In other fields of art the machine has not yet been used. And this is the whole point. To introduce the machine into those provinces of art to which so far it had no admission, or only a very limited one.

[....]

The renewal of art through the machine. Completely new fields would open before artists, tempting them with a void waiting to be filled, hypnotizing them with unforeseen possibilities. Instead of seeing the development of art in terms of successive forward and backward movements, instead of patiently enduring the comings and goings of the same aesthetic ideas, instead of, at best, introducing into art minute changes, we can start work with a moment of collective thought, one act of collective will, which shall liberate us from the boredom of constant repetition, which will transform art into something it had not been before, which will introduce into it elements capable of giving it a new shape, which will change it to suit our needs; it will grow from the needs of contemporary people. The current art has been repeating, in its own words, what the art of past eras had already said. But *instead of repeating we can speak with our own voice; instead of copying, we can create.*

Tranlsated by Wanda Kemp-Welch

4 Taking the machine as the subject matter of art can have a programmatic meaning. The machine occurs in this case as a symbol of new times. But contemporary art cannot stop at that.

NOTES ON RUSSIAN ART   Władysław Strzemiński
Originally published as "O sztuce rosyjskiej—notatki," *Zwrotnica* no. 3 (1922)

The author of the following article recently came back from Russia, where he took an active part in artistic movements. In the letter addressed to our editorial board he asks to help bring to Poland Mr. Malevich, our countryman and one of the leading artists in the Russian art world. We draw the matter to the attention of the Department of Culture and Art. [Original editor's note]

I.

All content, every different notion of the complex world demands its appropriate form. Adapting old form to new content, a feature characteristic of Expressionism—is fundamentally wrong. This is why the task of art is to go deeper into the notion of form in order to gain a new content. Content is born out of form. This is a sure way, but difficult.

The dominion of content over form frequently results in the application of any old form to the content. It is no longer pure art—it is lowered to the level of applied art. (Blasphemy towards art !!!)

II.
Analyzing the state of Russian art during the last years of the war we find influential names: Larionov, Kandinsky, Tatlin, Malevich.

III.
To label an artist it is necessary to analyze the form he uses in his art. Only then will the phantoms of "the great significance" people impute to Art disappear—Messrs. N. N.— Thus:

a) Impressionism can be characterized as an understanding of the real world as a phenomenon of color. In relation to space, it is not a very decisive position, hesitating between plane (Matisse) and Euclidean space (Monet).

b) Treating the real world as consisting of the simplest geometric volumes in Euclidean space, a characteristic of Cézanne and his school

c) Grasping space and time in movement, typical of Futurism and Cubism. Cubism— the movement of the artist/spectator around the object and in the construction of forms (static) and contrast; Futurism—a dynamic deconstruction, objects swirling around the artist/spectator.

d) Painting consisting of flat geometric forms: the aim is to fuse pictorial forms with the picture plane as much as possible (flatness of painting; the aim of Cubist form— the greatest tension of painting); space unsuitable for dimensions of one and the same linear measure, but based on the equilibrium of mutually attracted forms is characteristic of Suprematism.

IV.
In terms of achieving precise form, we should see Kandinsky as representing the last discord of a dying Impressionism, as the artist mistakenly included in new art. The process leading from Impressionism to non-objective painting had been started by Gauguin and followed by Matisse. There remained only a few more steps...

V.
Expressionism can be defined as a movement aiming at the expression of sensations of a literary character (mostly sensations of the muddle of the mechanized world)— with the means typical of all recent art movements (including Cubism and Futurism). It is to a certain extent a kind of applied art (using the work of others on the development of form.

VI.
Larionov, Goncharova and Shevchenko and those grouped around them began from 1910 to produce work similar to that described above. Its basis was in:

a) Russian archaic painting (icons, *lubok*)
b) Byzantine mosaics
c) Cézanne
d) early Cubism
e) Futurism

—but, through the action of the group of artists, organized a little later, who oriented their art to the principles of Western plastic art and the creation of form, the influence of Larionov was brought to an end and there was nothing for him to do but to leave for Paris and there proclaim himself to be the most outstanding Russian artist once there.

His group scattered and became in [art] history a link between the emotionalist Vrubel and half-realist Impressionism on the one hand, and Cubism, Tatlinism and Suprematism on the other.

Those who won were: Udaltsova, Tatlin and Malevich. This happened around 1914.

VII.

Udaltsova, a talented pupil of Metzinger, transferred onto Russian soil what she had learned in Paris. Though she did not establish far-reaching conceptions, she conscientiously and carefully reproduced what her teacher had created, and as for theory, she also repeated what he had been saying. Her historical role was: to start formal art in Russia, the art of the unified system of assembling forms.

VIII.

Tatlinism—is Cubism with a weak tension of form and a generally mechanical, technical and material notion of content. Since it has failed to develop a form, it propagates the qualities of the "culture of materials."

Tatlin, a man of little culture, saw Picasso's reliefs in his studio, but only understood that they contained different materials juxtaposed. After his return to Moscow, he began to execute them as he understood them. He understood the task of "strong construction" as construction using "strong" (durable) materials (sheet metal, iron, zinc, wood, glass), gradually moving the main point of the task

—away from the construction of form, enhanced by the use of different materials working as surface and color but with a different expression than one usually applied—

—toward a Futurist conception, machine-like achieved by contrasting of materials, neglecting the need for precise construction;

—toward impressions with more or less the following meaning: "iron!!! iron— used in the whole of the present day building industry!! Iron—the powerful lever of progress!!"

etc.—etc.—etc., a whole litany to iron—

—and again a litany to glass, concrete, nickel, some reference to the latest building technique in America—...but plastic form is missing, there is no conclusive idea or system in his juxtaposition of elements—his conception of the work of art relies not on a precise system of ideas, but on the impression, rooted in Futurism, of the adulation of modern machines and materials. This is the foundation of Tatlin's creations, partly machines and partly aesthetic (as not based on any objective system) objects— attempts at reproducing the impressions of the city, factory and of prewar architecture, the impressions of a peasant from a small village from the depth of Russia, sensitive, nevertheless experiencing life in the city for the first time.

Tatlin usually presents his art as an art concerned with surface, and sometimes as the art of *faktura* (meaning something between surface, technique, and form), but he never speaks of construction or form. The only thing that is new in his works is the application of materials never before used in art. The form is decorative, not based on a system filtered through, from a to z, by the creative spirit. As to form—Tatlin is blind. "It is a great mystery, the problem is extremely difficult," he says, creating constructions that are astonishing at first glance—but turn to ashes at the second.

Whereas Archipenko (Tatlin's rival, though detached from the mainstream of Russian art) re-evaluated the baroque, showing it in different guises: Cubist, Futurist and modern and technical—

—what did Tatlin do?

—he materialized—

　　　　—the void of form,

and hence he had to place emphasis on surface, i.e. a secondary issue.

"Let them give me any form and I shall make a surface such as no one else can" he used to say, and thus revealing his lack of a defined position as regards form.

Surface art easily becomes superficial art, lacking foundation. Tatlin showed this in his design of the memorial to the Third International. There was a lot of empty talk, started by Tatlin's friends, partly men of letters, partly engineers. But let us subtract engineering and technical qualities—what is left?

—the ruin of form (a disorganized accumulation, without system or plan), the unresolved opposition between the spiral and the inclined line.

The conclusion of our investigation of Tatlin's work is that Tatlinism is a sort of impoverishment of Cubism; the development of the utilitarian aspect at the expense of others. Tatlin's contribution, however, is that he raised the value of materials not used in art before, and pointed the way to the further development of art—giving materials their appropriate form. But this is more the contribution of a social worker or critic than that of the artist proving that his assertions were right through his works.

IX.

Malevich is not the first preeminent Pole in Russian art (e.g. Orlovsky, Vrubel).

He began to distinguish himself from other artists with his paintings of 1907–1909, which show an affinity with Cézanne, paintings of objects consisting of elementary geometric volumes, but, unlike Picasso's nudes from the same period, intensified by extreme tension of color (e.g. rendering forms in different shades of yellow, rather than breaking them up by using yellow for light and blue for shade).

Even at that time he struggled against emotionalism, atmosphere, etc. (what is described, in a less polite way, as dilettantism). He attempted to base his work on a certain system (a necessary condition resulting in *organic* works).

As art progressed he worked as Cubist and Futurist, drawing from each movement above all, a system of construction (the composition of elements) and properties strictly appropriate to painting.

Picasso, for instance, went no further then extracting all possible consequences from the object in order to saturate the painting with form—

However—

—as the subject is recognized, the whole attention of the spectator focuses on finding ever new elements and so the spectator who has previously submerged himself in the pleasures of painting, is now floating on the surface of naturalism (at first glance somewhat disguised)—

—whereas Malevich, developing Cubism announced:

Cubism in its first stage aims at using up the *whole* form of the object (whether single or plural) and saturating the whole picture with it. As a result a certain construction, consisting of elements of the object, emerges. This is so called figurative Cubism.

In the second stage the artist, having realized the result of his involuntary ultra-naturalistic strivings, draws conclusions from the construction; he explains the principles on which he put together the elements of form, he realizes the system that results from them, and creates abstract constructions according to this system.

... "—the fault of Cubism is that it is based on modulating color hues: mostly grey, brown and black. Typically, we could imagine a Cubist picture painted entirely in shades of black and white. Cubism excludes color, fundamental to painting, from the picture."...(I quote from memory from Malevich's books *New Art Systems* and *Cubism, Futurism and Suprematism*)

The opinion has been widely circulated that we owe the introduction to Cubism of the Impressionists' achievements in color study to Léger. Therefore I state categorically that Malevich had already produced works of a similar nature as early as 1912.

X.

Cubism—a transitory phenomenon, the crossroads from which two roads lead. The first one, naturalist and reactionary (Ozenfant, Jeanneret, many of Picasso's works)— what else can one call the injection of the elemental essence of Cubism into the dead body of Naturalism?

The second road—cleansing art of alien means—is the road of non-objective and constructive art. The first movement on this road and the most powerful so far, was:

Suprematism

Characteristics of Suprematism:

a) A strictly non-objective movement.

b) A movement using geometricized color planes:

   1) In all movements before Suprematism, composition was based either on promoting line (Renaissance, Baroque, academy painting, Cubism) or overcoming line (Impressionism). Genuine composition cannot be created by line. Fluidity of line, its elusiveness, lack of beginning or end—all this is characteristic of the rendering of form rather than of proper composition; since composition is placing color, occupying a certain space, in such a way that it fuses completely with the picture plane, that it grows out of the picture. Line runs around the picture, cannot be stopped. How to fuse the static rectangle of the picture with line whose direction always dynamically escapes beyond the frame? Line has no static point, no point of support where it could gain force by fusing with the picture plane.

   2) In all movements prior to Suprematism, the rendering of form was based on "piercing a hole" in the painting, attempting to give the properties of three-dimensional space to two-dimensional [picture] plane (the desire to change picture into sculpture!!). Although some of the giants of painting, not resigning from the main principle, tried to unite their painted forms with the picture's surface by various ancillary means (Rembrandt, Cézanne, partly Neo-Impressionists— through their technique, and Cubists—by concealing their attempts at showing volumetric objects).

Ensuring strictly pictorial values demands the change-over: rendering form as completely flat.

c) The distance between one form and another is measured by the force of attraction between those forms and not by one and the same linear measure for the whole picture, as in other art movements. Suprematism has no constant measure (a similarity to Einstein's theory, proclaiming the multitude of time dimensions).

d) Color is used not for ensuring harmony but to show the tension of a given form.

e) The content of Suprematism: dynamic, cosmic phenomena ocurring in infinite space; harmony of the universe of forms, organic in their geometrism.

XI.

This was the state of the Russian art before Bolshevism—a stage of transition towards an abstract, non-objective and constructive art of high tension.

Even then there was a fundamental struggle between two tendencies: Tatlin's and Malevich's.

As for sculpture—it did not exist. Admittedly, there was Konenkov—but what can one say today about his attempts to copy ancient Greeks, Egyptians, or Slavonic gods? Only this—copying is never creative art.

Klyun, a painter, executed Cubist-Futurist sculptures, but these were superficial experiments in transplanting certain forms of painting to the field of sculpture without previous study of the essence of painting and sculpture and the differences between them.

XII.

During the Bolshevik Revolution a group of the new art artists, taking advantage of the Bolsheviks' ignorance of art, filled positions at the Department of Fine Arts, with a general support of the new art sympathizers. From their positions they were able to struggle more effectively against old art. (Hence the myth that Bolsheviks support new art.)

But as time passed the communist authorities increasingly turned their attention to this department. Their lack of culture attracted them to the most uncultured of movements—Naturalism. A struggle ensued and its history constitutes, to some extent, the history of the development of new art (its quantitative growth and its decadence).

XIII.

To carry on discussion on art in its proper sense with uncultured people is a hard task and it to no avail. Hence, whereas in the schools, reformed and liberated from being ruled by academicism and naturalism, the struggle was for the supremacy of the culture of painting over uncultured reproduction—

—so against the communist power other weapons, which the artists did not possess, were necessary.

Some careerist critics were pushed forward (Brik, Punin...). They were given the task of creating long theories on new art (2,000 words per minute, 25 articles a week—in order to convince those in power...)

XIV.

Therefore:

—"the content of new art is the machine; the machine—a tool of the proletariat. New art by praising the machine also praises the proletariat. It is the art of the proletariat"—

This conception of Communo-Futurism was successful for a time and has managed to dispose some persons in power favorably to Tatlin, who could be more or less fitted into this theory.

XV.

But because a significant part of new art remained outside this theory (and this included the *latest* groups) so this conception failed.

However, a new theory has emerged:

—because the Soviets needed goods to be sold abroad and at the same time the innovative artists wanted to propagate a new slogan in defense against the host of naturalist art thus proving their usefulness with their agitation works—

—the theory claimed:

—"since new art—the art of abstract form—creates abstract, useless form, with the same success it can produce utilitarian objects, treating them as pure construction. Only then the era of the greatest development of art will arrive: the whole world will be made like the work of art: both as a whole and in details. The division between pure art and applied art shall disappear, since utility will be combined with the high tension of form. The way to achieve it is through utilizing the existing form of painting, as the leading art, and so from painting to sculpture and architecture towards the production of utilitarian objects."...

XVI.

This conception was the virus destroying Russian art and lowering its tension:

1) Anyone who repeats the same catchphrase many times over, finally succumbs to its influence and hypnosis. Even if he had regarded it as wrong, pretending to be sincere he will finally follow it in all sincerity.

2) The disparity between the word and the deed forced some artists to adjust their
   works to the theories proclaimed (or rather repeated).
Hence some groups of Productivist movement have come into being; the conceptions
of culture of materials (juxtaposition of materials used in an industrial technology,
juxtaposition not based on any particular system, juxtaposition pleasing to the eye but
not leaving any deeper impression)
The only right way i.e.:
form—study of the form achieved—inventing a more perfect form
was replaced by:

painting—sculpture—architecture—utilitarian products
—at the same time the issue of form was passed over in silence (i.e. the issue of system according to which all these products were executed); art was deemed to possess
already such a great store of artistic means, worked out by the recent movements,
that a further development of art was superfluous and even undesirable since it would
only slow down the efforts directed towards production.

XVII.
Most Productivists can be described as people just talking, preaching their principles,
but not working. Some have not produced a single work, others produced works
which do not comply with Productivist principles. Among the latter, one must include
Tatlin, with his disgraceful design for the Monument to the Third International, and
Lavinsky, with his designs of the twentieth-century city, of buildings and radio stations based on the principle of "engineerism" (engineerism—a movement which
emerges when the artist, bankrupt in his art, justifies himself by using engineering
forms and objectives). To the former [one must include] Kieselev, Khrakovsky,
Miturich and Mansurov.
Their principle was that every object must be executed according to the law defined by
its purpose, and not by imposing any aesthetic style. The object's economy in terms of
its technique and its purpose is opposed to any aesthetic elements.
The position of the artist confronted with such a postulate is incomprehensible. The
road indicated is the road of pure technology, it has nothing to do with art. One can
claim that art is dead, but why confuse things and call technology art? An experienced
eye can appreciate the beauty of the products of technology, but anyone thinking
clearly understands that the methods and objectives of art and technology are quite
contradictory. And to attempt to produce products of technology with the help of art—
is, surely...?
It is likely that this is the cause of the infertility of the Productivists, who dream of realization of their postulates but are unable in practice to work in accordance with them.

XVIII.
Productivist trends are an outcome of a compromise between new art and the authorities in the Soviet Union. It is only thanks to the advantages that the government elites
expect to gain from new art that it is allowed to exist. In Russian conditions, art either
exists as official art or does not exist at all.
This compromise came at a cost—Productivism had a negative effect on the
minds of people connected with art—it made them turn away from solving the
problem of an organic unity, of form and space, problems left by Cubism and
Suprematism.
It is not an attempt at starting a new direction in applied art. Productivist art, according to the task defined by it, is pure (not applied) art, striving to perfect products of
the big industry, to improve the value of the product as an object of everyday use,
and rejecting aesthetic qualities alien to the logic of object, which either additionally

decorate an already executed object (as in the old applied arts) or which decide that it is not a utility object but a form with artistic purpose.

Productivist art is the rebellion of technology against art, led, however, not by technicians, but the artists themselves.

XIX.

The signpost: painting—sculpture, architecture—utilitarian production—even though not carried through—directed the efforts of many talented painters towards sculpture; as a result sculpture, for many years behind other fields of art, now stands equal to painting. This is the only favorable, though accidental, by-product of the Productivist self-hypnosis. Albeit sculpture does not go beyond conceptions that had already been thought out and executed in painting by the Cubists and Futurists, yet it constitutes a genuine new art. Those tasks are taken up by the Stenberg brothers, Medunetsky, partly by Rodchenko, and others belonging to the Constructivist group OBMOKhU (Society of Young Artists).

The most talented of the young sculptors, [Katyrzina] Kobro, has close ties with the group. Her Suprematist sculptures have significance on a European scale and are a genuine step forward, achieving previously unexplored qualities. They are not copies of Malevich, but works of art which are parallel to his art.

The new tasks in sculpture require new materials. Every form should be justified by a given material. Copper, iron, glass, cement, wood and other materials are used. This is the positive influence of Tatlin, not in terms of form, but only in terms of utilizing a variety of materials of technological character.

XX.

The other part of the OBMOKhU group constitute the "imaginists," a group less decisive in their Constructivist objectives, more sensualist, making use of the inventions of the new, mostly non-objective movements.

XXI.

The works of Malevich are fundamental to the existence of the new Russian art. This outstanding artist, a giant, determined the fate of art for centuries to come. Whereas Picasso had stopped at the beginning of the road and gone backwards, Malevich went forward and finally arrived at the only possible point of departure for our times, at Suprematism, a system of assembling abstract elements to form an organic whole, according to an objective law, and not unjustified will and wishes of individuals, directed by their individual "I want."

Hence Russian art is, in its present state:

a) non-objective

b) constructive

c) it aims to base construction on the principles of an objective law

And this is all. Further development, started by Malevich, was almost completely blocked as a result of the pressure from Lunacharsky, who, not understanding the insignificance of their slogans, supports the Productivists in consideration of the material needs of the USSR.

What is taking place there now is the popularization and trivialization of the whole of new art. Its quantitative growth gives to other countries an impression of the flourishing of the arts. But it is not quantity but quality that matters. Many now famous artists (Rodchenko, Stepanova and some others) have no idea about the efforts that have led to Cubist and Suprematist developments. Unaware of the values in works of new art, however, they go on creating so called "new art," without moving forward and further developing artistic issues but compiling their works from bits of works by earlier artists.

XXII

Therefore:

a) Productivists wander in the darkness of their theories and do not even suspect that their principles are the principles of pure technology. As long as they want to work as Productivist artists they cannot create anything that would correspond to their theories.

b) Constructivists have introduced sculpture the Cubist concepts that had been thought out in painting and are already outdated. They produce sculpture approaching the state in which painting found itself in yesterday.

c) others hesitate between form and emotion. To sum up: there is plenty of critical and theoretical-social discussion, but no thought concerning form.

After the period described, only Kobro and Drevin (a painter who currently draws conclusions from Cubism and Suprematism and coordinates space by applying to it specific axes) are the faithful heirs of the spirit of Malevich's art.

Translated by Wanda Kemp-Welch

THE REACTION OF THE ENVIRONMENT Mieczysław Szczuka
Originally published as "Reakcja otoczenia," *Zwrotnica* no. 4 (1923)

1. THE REACTION OF THE ENVIRONMENT either existing independently of man
or created by man himself

THROUGH

the influence of the great achievements of contemporary civilization
[the development of cities, means of transport (railways, ships, aviation),
industry, international trade]
+ the impact of BEAUTY (= pleasure + comfort)
+ the impact of NATURE ON

MAN'S
CREATION OF
ART
THE CREATION OF FORMS WITH WHICH MAN
FILLS SPACE AND TIME

2. ON MEANS IN ART
The use of materials influences the character of the solution e.g. combining iron and glass leads to a different construction than a flat painting or a marble. This is why contemporary art should be enriched by unexploited means

SUCH AS

MAKING USE OF THE CHARACTER OF MATERIALS
THE CONSTRUCTIONAL QUALITIES OF MATERIAL
(resilience, elasticity, rigidity, strength, resistance)
THE CHARACTER OF THE SURFACE OF MATERIAL
(an extensive surface plane of concrete, and NOT concrete rod)
(the springiness of steel rod)
THE CHARACTER OF THE APPEARANCE OF THE MATERIAL'S SURFACE
(the reflective surface of brass—the roughness of concrete)

(cloth and paper—silk and wool)
DIFFERENT QUALITIES OF MATERIAL SURFACES DEPENDING ON THE FINISH
    (painted iron or oxidized iron)
    (giving wood the smoothest touch with French polish)
    (and qualities of these materials in their crude state)
    THE SPECIFIC QUALITIES OF A MATERIAL'S REACTION TO LIGHT
    (light passes through glass, while copper reflects light)
    INFINITELY WIDE RANGE OF POSSIBILITIES IN THE USE OF ELECTRIC LIGHT
    (flooding any space with light)
    (filling space with any light shapes)
    (e.g. with beams of reflector lights)
    {luminous surfaces (e.g. glass) (the incandescence of electric wire)}
    THE POSSIBLE INTRODUCTION OF
    MOTION

3. ON THE INSEPARABILITY OF ARTISTIC ISSUES AND SOCIAL ISSUES
THE STRUGGLE FOR SURVIVAL
ABSORBS ALMOST ALL OF PEOPLE'S TIME
NOT ALLOWING THEM
TO OCCUPY THEMSELVES WITH ART.
CONTEMPORARY LIFE WHICH AIMS AT
THE MAXIMUM PROFIT WITH THE MINIMUM MEANS EXPENDED
IMPOSES
A CHARACTERISTIC STAMP ON CONTEMPORARY ART

HERE
LIES THE REASON
FOR SLOGANS IN ART

FORMS OF EXPRESSION APPROACHING SHORTHAND
(tenement buildings—economy of every [square] meter—both profit and comfort)

PEOPLE, PREOCCUPIED WITH THE STRUGGLE FOR SURVIVAL
                          HAVE MOVED AWAY
            FROM ART
THIS IS WHY
ART IS INCOMPREHENSIBLE,
UNLIKE,
 FOR INSTANCE, IN THE RENAISSANCE, WHEN THE SLOWER SPEED OF LIFE
MADE IT MORE POPULAR AND UNIVERSAL

THE WORKING   THE PEASANT,
CLASSES, SELLING   WORKING PARTLY
THEIR TIME AND   FOR HIMSELF,
LABOR, HAVE NO   CREATED SO-
CHANCE TO CREATE   CALLED FOLK ART
THEIR OWN ART

IN THE FUTURE
WHEN THE CURSE OF EXPLOITATION VANISHES,
WHEN EVERYONE LIVES IN A WAY DICTATED
BY THE SENSE OF ONE'S OWN HAPPINESS,

FORMS OF ART
WILL ALSO CHANGE
IN WAYS
WHICH CANNOT BE FORESEEN.

Translated by Wanda Kemp-Welch

After the establishment of the Kingdom of Serbs, Croats, and Slovenes in 1918, artists began to reconsider their role within the new political and social circumstances. Additionally, the Russian Revolution the previous year had radicalized many artists, and the most radical movement of these new tendencies was Zenithism. Zenithism (and its primary periodical *Zenit*, published 1921–26) was founded in Zagreb by writer and critic Ljubomir Micić (1895–1971), who co-wrote the movement's founding manifesto with Ivan Goll (1891–1950) and Boško Tokin (1894–1953). Other contributors included writers Branko Ve Poljanski (Ljubomir Micić's brother, born Branko Micić, 1898–1947), Dragan Aleksić (1901–1958), and Marijan Mikac (1903–1972). Poljanski published one issue of the fellow-Zenithist periodical *Svetokret* in Ljubljana in January, 1921 (a month before the first issue of *Zenit* actually appeared), but with the exception of a few Dadaist periodicals published briefly in Zagreb in 1922, *Zenit* was the movement's primary voice.

Zenithism saw itself as a post-Expressionist movement, and initially developed as a sort of cosmic primitivism. As stated in the first Zenithist manifesto, "Expressionism, Cubism, Futurism are dead. We are an extension of their lineage—to higher ground. We are their synthesis, but as an arrow pointing upwards, a reincarnation—*the plusexistence of their philosophical ideas*" (*Zenit* no. 1, 1921). Zenithism promoted "barbarism" in art and culture, and the personified expression of this primitivism was the Barbarogenius, a primeval man of great power who comes from the mystical East in order to fight against the rational West. A linked concept was the idea of the "Balkanization of Europe," which supported the collapse of the capitalist West and its renewal through the forms of an ancestral Balkan culture.

In another aspect, Zenithism stood for the idea of a loosely defined brotherhood of artists in all countries and on all continents, and despite its promotion of "barbarism" it still embraced aspects of modern European culture. Consequently, over the course of its forty-three issues, *Zenit* included contributors from such diverse movements as Expressionism, Cubism, Futurism, Dadaism, Suprematism, Constructivism, Poetism, Activism, Ultraism, Purism, Bauhaus, and others. The originality of the project makes both *Zenit* and the Zenithist movement as a whole a unique contribution to the European avant-garde of the 1920s.

Translated by Maja Starčević

THE ZENITHIST MANIFESTO   Ljubomir Micić, Ivan Goll and Boško Tokin

Originally published as "Manifest Zenitizma," *Zenit* vol. 1, no. 1 (1921)

You cannot "understand" *Zenithism*
unless you *feel* it.
The *electricity* we do not "understand"
but feel is perhaps the greatest
manifestation of the spirit—
Zenithism?

We are naked and pure.
Forget hatred—sink into the naked depths of *Yourself*!
Dive and fly to your own heights!

ZENITH

Fly above this criminal, fratricidal *Present*!
Show your astral being to the visionary eyes of *Superlife*!
Listen to the magic of our words, Listen to *Yourselves*!
There—on Šar Mountain, on the Urals—stands

THE NAKED MAN BARBARO-GENIUS

Fly above the Šar Mountain, above the Urals and the Himalayas—
Mont-Blanc—Popocatepetl—above Kilimanjaro!
We are now floating high high above the bodily spheres of the Globe.
Break, bound chains! Fall, suburbs of big and plague-ridden
West European cities! Shatter, window panes of gilded courts,
High towers of National Stockmarkets and Banks!
Return to your fat stomachs, war profiteers!
Hide your bought concubines deep in your dirty pockets!
Have you no shame?
And you, blind mothers and stupid fathers, selling your innocent daughters
for bundles of money!
And you, black underground spiders, spinning your webs around pure souls
Freemasons!
Have you no shame, you drunk lodges!?
You—the soul profiteers of art and culture—are the greatest liars of all!
Against you—for Man!
Close your doors West—North—Central Europe—
The Barbarians are coming!
Close them close them but

we shall still enter.

We are the children of arson and fire—we carry *Man*'s soul.
And our soul is *combustion*.
Combustion of the soul in the creation of *sublimity*

ZENITHISM

We are the children of the Sun and the Moutains; we carry *Man*'s spirit.
And our spirit is the life of cosmic *unity* held together by *Love*.
We are the children of the *Southeast barbaro-genius*.

*

It is coming... It is coming...

THE RESCUE CAR

Hotblooded horse hoofs hitting
the ground galloping to a savage rhythm.

Underground channels rumble
Cramped hospitals moan.
City churches—streets and cathedrals
         celebrate Easter
         1921.

Moscow pours blood.
Far away bells of assumption thunder.

A closed yellow car is rushing
Cutting through space of sinful and colorful streets
where war battalions of fratricides once passed.

Oh, mortuary music of those gray battalions!
Oh, bloody burials of attack trumpets!
Oh, dull thuds of men's bodies
remember,
         !Man is your brother!
         !Man is your brother!

The sun is spurting.
Astral bodies of the universe are dancing.
Floating up there in the endless circular spheres
of the new planet.

* * Alpha and Pons * *
And the red-colored crosses
on the milky glass of the yellow cars
have hoisted high their visionary flag of Redemption
and are singing the Eastern Slavic song of Resurrection.

Countless crosses of our defeated land are trembling.
The wooden gallows above our skulls are falling.
Bloody ropes are snaking above the fratricidal Black Peak.
And through big cities, cars with red crosses are rushing
                    EAST
                         SOUTH
                              WEST
The Yellow Rescue Car is rushing
Carrying a hidden corpse—Man.

Man is dying everywhere.

The Sun has fallen into my soul
into the limitless spaces of All-love.

Red glass crosses have shattered
Man has died in the yellow car.

Letters are dancing, thrown above the crosses
R   S   U   C   R
   E   C   E   A

Black flags, brothers, flutter in our souls
because
Man is dying everywhere . . .

*   *   *   *   *   *   *   *   *

It is magic, the word *Zenith!*
Man, a brother and father of gods, was born somewhere in the jungle.
Man *created* God, for he saw terrible storms and arrows,
heard thunder and desired the *Sun.*
One magical and deep night he discovered *Himself—Man.*
The first *weakness* of Man created God—*The First Empire.*
The first Egyptian and Greek cultures (*Greece and Macedonia are both in the Balkans!*)—*The Second Empire*
ZENITHISM = THE THIRD UNIVERSE
A graphic picture of *Zenithism* = an incarnation of the metacosmos' bipolarity:

```
                    ZENITH
                      Z
                      E
        ETHER    N    ETHER
                      I
                      T
                      H
                      I
        ASTRAL        ASTRAL
                      S
        ASTRAL BODY  M  ASTRAL BODY
                     MAN
```

                     EARTH—EARTH

Man is the center of the macrocosmos—the Earth's North Pole.
Zenith is the center of the metacosmos—the Universe's North Pole.
Zenithism is a magical and electric interval between the macrocosmos and the metacosmos, between—*Man* and *Zenith.*
Man is thunder thrown into space—on Earth:
Man is our starting point.
Man is a victim. The victim is always central.
Man is tragedy. Tragedy is always sublime.
Man—Spirit—Metacosmos—Sun—Phenomenon—Zenith
                ZENITHISM = THE ORIENT OF AIRPLANE
                            SPIRITS
Zenithism is an idea of art.
Zenithist art must be an art of *ideas—affinitive.*
A Zenithist must *create.*
A Zenithist must create *new* things.
Zenithism is an artistic affirmation of the *Allspirit.*
                ZENITHISM = ∞ = TOTALITY
Zenithism is absolute supernatural *individuation*, the only creative one:
        it must contain the *artist* + the *man.*
                        Superman
        it must incarnate *the bipolar metacosmos*
                        Phenomenon
Zenithism is more than *spirit* = the fourth dimension

Zenithism is beyond dimensions = ∞ or the tenth dimension =
Eternity.
Magical zenithist word = radio station A
Man's fluid feeling and jolt = radio station B

Manifestation = Radiogram.
A Zenithist word must be *electricization*
A Zenithist work must be a *radiogram.*
This is not a Gospel. This is a *Manifesto.*
The people of the future, who come after us, they will write the Gospel. And they
will come... will come...
The future Man!
He will be the son of the Sun and Zenith.
He will speak the Zenithist language.
All...all...will understand.

This is not a philosophy.
The philosophy of Zenithism is still being created.
It is emerging...happening...
Zenithism is mysticism and there is no philosophy of mysticism. There is only
the mysticism of philosophy—the mysticism of *New Art.*
Zenithism is a discovery of the hundred and twentieth century.

Expressionism, Cubism, Futurism are dead.
We are an extension of their lineage—to higher ground.
We are their synthesis, but as an arrow pointing upwards, a reincarnation
—*the plusexistence of their philosophical ideas:*

> The soul of souls of those who have died but lived one hundred and twenty
> centuries ago and yearned for *Zenith.*
> The soul of souls of the nameless ones whose proud children we are.
> Sons of creation—togetherness—unification—traveling
> through chaos—the sons of the *Oriental Sin.*
> The Eastern Sin must have occurred, for that is how people came to know
> *Themselves.*
> There would be no *Zenithism* without the *Oriental Sin*!

We, who have discovered *Ourselves—Man—*we are *Zenithists*
You should be that too!
Our only *thought* is ZENITH—*the highest incarnation of Allexistence.*
Our path is only—*ahead—above—over everything*
that has been.
Down with pale traditions, systems, and borders! Borders are for the
limited!
We keep going...going...
Travelling from chaos to create an *Oeuvre.*
Led by the mystical demi-god
ANARCH
You come too, though woe unto them who stumble and are left by the wayside.
We will not come back.

Poets! Brothers! Zenithists as yet unknown!
Throw down the coat of lies!

Awaken Man and exalt him!
Sing of flames, fire, the burning and thirst for Zenith!
Put a stop to Man's fall. That will be our greatest oeuvre. That is
the vertical line that will pierce the heavens above. And *sunny blood—*
sunny blood shall flow.

The poets of Zenith! Sing of Man, not of a murderer.
Man is made for Love and for Exaltation.

Above shattered human skulls we extend our hands to all,
over all borders, to all who think like us: to people!

And then, when the last *Nonhuman* dies
then
in all the countries—in all the cities—on all the towers
—ships—planes—palaces—courthouses—hospitals
—academies—insane asylums—sea ports—
hang clean white flags and greet the *Future Zenithist*
Man
then
in all the pavillions—churches—halls—playhouses
—circuses—streets—roofs—railways—submarines
—army barracks—
in all Zenitheums
sound your trumpets—
organs—timpani—drums—fanfares—
sing your hearts out
sing...sing...

THE ANTHEM OF ZENITHISM
THE ANTHEM OF ZENITHISM
Earth is for Man the Brother, not for Man the Murderer!

—Ljubomir Micić

Each morning at about five o'clock, on all the continents, the same NEWSPAPERS
raise their hungover gray heads and shout the black lies of life:
PEACE CONFERENCE—MURDER IN CHEESE SHOP—JUMPED FROM HIS DARLING'S
HEART—BUY GILLETTE RAZORS—BERGSON IN CHICAGO—VOTE FOR NERO—
HOORAY!
Oh, dear Europeans with your narrow foreheads, women with corsets too tight, children playing with the Trojan horse: enemies, enemies of yourselves and of one anoth-
er, enemies to your brothers and fathers: all of you, the crowns of creation wearing
paper crowns and American-style haircuts: Socialists and Royalists, shabby proletari-
ans in gold mines, smiling bankers from London:
Oh!
No, we don't like you! We won't approach you with words of love. No, comrades and
brothers with plaster heads, no, addle-pated professors, alcoholic clerks, infected
surgeons of the skin and the soul: no!
We hate you! Hate you! Hate you!
But we will tear the masks of the capitalistic carnival off your faces. We are tearing

your cynical suits off your bodies. We are tearing off the fig leaves: We will blaspheme
and flood your brains which are as dried up as old sponges and your hearts which are
as dried up as three-day old bread.

And then

all of you, born animals, born criminals, born militarists, nations grown strong in the
midst of hymns of war from Homer on down to Marinetti, your civilization determined
by the Bible, grammars and instruction manuals: Nations, high above your army barracks and Halls of Justice decorated with the ridiculous gilt-lettered motto: *Liberty
Equality Fraternity* high above your walls and your morality
we shall show you

ZENITH

and hand you

THE SUN

and the cataracts of truth, millions of Volts in heavenly light.
Our first-rate thinking machine
will pour a poisoned generation into your condensed milk cartons—*Liquid Sun*

THE TRUTH

No! No! No! We definitely do not like you
We won't embrace you, you charlatans, you politicians, you syphilitics, you goody-
goodies, you, sentimental mini-nationals!
Nationalities! Origins! Older generations! *Weeds!*

MAN

We are not French, or Serb, or Black, or German, or
Luxemburgers.
We are *Europeans Americans Africans Asians
Australians.*
So in these times of unavoidable trusts—here is a strong cosmopolitan
document

ZENITH

We will use ozone, hydro-superoxide and radium to wash out
your mouths and hearts, so you can come forth as people, without markings,
with your heads bare—with no top-hats, driver's hats or hard hats—so you can come
before the open *Sun of Truth* with no sleepache or sunstroke.

Let us destroy CIVILIZATION with the help of A NEW ART.
You are partly to blame for Europe the has-been:

for the pathos of its everyday life
for the falsity of its sentimentality
for its slavery to tradition.

The entire literature of the civilized old age is nothing but an expression
of such false feelings and phrases which have estranged us from primeval
nature

Down with all kinds of pathos!
Down with Clichés!

Back to the primeval source of experience—SIMPLICITY

THE WORD
back to barbarism!

We need to become the BARBARIANS of poetry once more.
*The Barbarism of Mongolians Balkanites Negros
Indians*

Your poems above Europe
Most beautiful lyricism comes from you

The only kind of lyricism
                    PRE-BLOOD
                    PRE-SUN
We need modern NEGRO SONGS
filled with electricity, telephones, stenograms
                    MACHINE DANCE
    Dynamite—Moon

                    PRIMEVAL SOUND
                    ZENITHISM
                         is
            intensive—radial—electromagnetic
    SUCKLING ON THE WORLD'S HEART
                 International
                 Interdivine
Each century has *its* form:

            The sonnet was—a square
            Classical drama—a triangle
            Shakespeare and Whitman—parallel lines
Today's poetry is

            A PERPENDICULAR
It is climbing towards the ZENITH with planes, elevators, automobiles, Eiffel Towers, chimneys.

            Man is climbing vertically
                 OBELISK
The Globe would appear to be shrinking
The poet can hold it in his hand
            like an apple
The New Poet is always INTERNATIONAL
        He sings SIMPLY
        for all Nations
        for PEOPLE
Again and always the *first words of the worlds*.

—Ivan Goll

The new artistic movements—Cubism, Futurism, Expressionism—are actually three different expressions, three shapes of a single movement. Three shapes of one possibility (creating a higher reality), of one direction that cuts through dogma, logic, façades and other barriers to the freedom of spirit and action. A higher reality—dynamic, surreal, and cosmic—is being created.

However, the modern epoch and Classicism are still in their infancy. Just beginning. Another plus and impulse is needed: the Slav world.
The present: destruction, gestation, climbing and successful attempts at creation, listening to and feeling oneself. Thence: projecting oneself onto the world and into the world of others.

Cubism and Futurism have got lost in materiality and repetition. Expressionism has yearned and still yearns for spirit, spirituality and *the dynamics of mysticism*. It yearns for dynamism in its ideas as well, but Expressionism has not been able to realize it all and has thus lost something of its vitality and impetus. New movements which are surreal in principle are not always such in practice, and we need this kind of practice: the expression of essential constructions, the emmanation of a *healthy, pure, barbaric dynamism.*

One needs to be *a barbarian.*

This is what it means to be a barbarian: beginning, possibility, creation. (Nietzsche, Whitman and Dostoevsky are barbarians because they are beginnings.) We, the Yugoslavs, are barbarians.

Impetus, dynamism of ideas our own consciousness projects us high, far, straight at our target, into implimentation, into

ZENITH

Barbarian + aristocrat + metacosmician + surrealist = Zenithist

Zenithism = ism par excellence, the only one corresponding to us (humans). Just as one man differs from another, so one ism differs from another. Zenithism boils down and unifies all earlier isms by surpassing them. The magical term Zenithism is quite simple—as Columbus' egg is simple Yes, it had to be found. We are the ones who've found it.

Do you feel (you do feel, you will feel) the meaning of all nuances, variations:

The Zenith of my feelings, emotions, ideas

The Zenith of my being. *My Zenith.*

In the Zenith of your (our) aspirations and exaltations.

Your Zenith.

Zenithism—sublimity. Going higher than oneself.

And behold: a new star is rising to the heavens from Yugoslavia, a new country is projecting itself onto the heights: the journal *Zenith* and *Zenithism.* Electric current. A current dangerous for diseased people.

We project ourselves

in all directions.

We project.

Accept it!

Absorb it!

You who can:

Long live the stars.

Stars.

New stars.

It is being made in all the parts of the world, on all the Earth's places. We are making a style, a heart and a spirit, a *Zenithist* ideology, a *Zenithist feeling of the Earth.* The Earth has chosen us to sublimate it and to create its new meaning.

Europeanness + Asianness + Africanness + Australianness + Americanness + new yet undiscovered continents + Mars + the stars (all the stars) + the Pons comet + ∞ =

ZENITHISM

The aestheticization of all dynamisms and mysticisms = Zenithism.

Zenith everywhere and in everything. In you. New people, fly!...

Flying.

Going higher. Stepping over. Making real.

Climbing.—*Zenith.*

—Boško Tokin

Translated by Maja Starčević

MANIFESTO   Branko Ve Poljanski

Originally published in *Svetokret (Journal for the Expedition to the North Pole of Man's Spirit)* no. 1 (January 1921)

To all those with pale cheeks, bloody hearts, and souls hovering in the heights like smoke!

To all those who have turned their eyes into their very depths!

To all those who are drunk on eternal mystery!

The human spirit has become the prostitute of the twentieth century. Our spirit has become completely lost in the chaos of all sorts of nefarious desires and has become a piece of merchandise owned by a few kilograms of flesh.

And behold, my spirit is screaming because it has woken up and wishes true, flesh-free freedom of the spirit, a spirit wanting to shake off nefarious desires and lies of that well-established, well-respected Madame "Today," whose only goal is to serve fattening and ample dinners.

Our spirit, under the protection of the mighty Madame "Today," is nothing but a sacrifice to our Lord God—the "golden calf" at the end of twenty stinking centuries.

Need! Oh, our spirit needs terribly madly to be free; it needs the sacred freedom to march ahead into time under its colorless flag, to march into eternity, leaving infinitely behind those twenty stinking centuries that appear in the inifinity behind us as a tiny, the tiniest black dot of our ancient "Once Upon a Time."

Need! Oh, our spirit needs terribly madly to be free, so that its invasion, under a holy colorless flag, may advance into time—into eternity—towards the new man.

Need! Oh, we need to proclaim October a holiday a million times over, October, when all conventional and patented forms of cultural laws shall fall from the grafted fruit trees of the European garden and a new earthly spring shall come, when European fruit trees shall absorb new directions from the new earth and bear new forms.

We need to spit into the goblet of eternity: it is a disgusting drink we have gorged ourselves on! We need to spit into the goblet of eternity: it contains the leakage of twenty poisonous centuries!

Long live the self-determination of the spirit! May it ring through all cities, through all streets, through all countries red and blue, through all institutes and royal bestiaries etc.

May the globe resound, glow, and burn in mad joy and cheering:

Long live man's free spirit! Glory to the new man!

May it be a glorious revolution of the spirit in October, when the old forms fall like dry pale leaves.

Let the colorless flag of the spirit flutter high in the air in October, when the new man shall be born.

Our spirit acquires its most sublime form through art.

Our spirit acquires that deep bottomless form through feeling—through feelings of pain and laughter, grief and joy, always searching for a meaningful direction.

Art is far from everyday political—national—social—Bolshevik terror. Art is the form of our deepest "Inner Self".

Art does not need to be logical!

Art can be a paradox!

This means an assassination of all patented forms of music, sculpture, painting, poetry, etc.

But paradox is not nonsense!

(This holds for psychiatrists too!)

Paradox is the spirit's agility and its plasticity.

There is only one possible alternative to our hearts in this life. Things are either tragic or comic.

Consequently, every work of art can provoke either tears or laughter—loud laughter in all four directions. Tears are the spirit's purity, while laughter is its healing potion.

You who have been blessed by the holy spirit, *create in the martyrdom of tears or laughter, because there is no art without martyrdom!*

Cry your blood and your bile out!

Laugh your brain and your heart out!

Die in delirium. Let your brain explode and burn, drunk on mystery!

My ear blends the sounds of the European concert. Long live the Republic! Long live the king! Long live the Internationale! Workers of the world, unite! Long live the soviets! Long live Lenin and Trotsky!

Lucifer triumphs! Glorious music!

In a puddle of red blood and with Parisian grace joyful Europe is dancing a grotesque

can-can

while a Russian balalaika plays "The Red Sarafan"!

The sounds have blended in my ears and fallen into my soul, creating the surrogate of a quiet smile, and my face has been transformed from laughter into cheers.

Long live the October Revolution of the spirit!

Long live new art!

Long live new man!

Translated by Maja Starčević

MAN AND ART   Ljubomir Micić

Originally published as "Čovek i umetnost," *Zenit* vol 1., no. 1 (1921)

MAN—That is our first word.

From the loneliness of stiff walls and cursed streets, from the dark abysses of the uncouscious and from monstrous nights we approach you as apostles, as prophets and we preach ART TO MAN.

Man is the center of the macrocosmos, while art and philosophy are the circumference of his most sublime understanding, his most sublime consciousness. The most sublime manifestation of the spirit and the soul—the SPIRIT or the demiurge, Anarch— wishes to rule chaos, to be all-powerful, to be a god. He lusts to create *action* from chaos. But the only creator is the artist, who always embodies Man in his creation, his work of art. The artist is both the embodiment and a passionate desire for the revelation of *Man*. The artist is the Revelation—the Annunciation—the Last Judgment of: *Man*. The artist is an endless horizon without beginning and without end on Earth's deadly savage hurdle through space. ZENITH is the center—man's only salvation—his only redemption.

The artist, as the incarnation of the *sublime*, suffers from the combustion of his own or humanity's pain. He is a humiliated soul's cry for salvation, a metacosmic cry, a cry from the depths of our innermost spheres.

Having sunk deep into the abyss of the soul, we want to emerge from ourselves with a New Man and shine a new light into the darkness of the black old days, of our sad non-youth. We will bring out a new ember to illuminate Yugoslavia's darkness.

We wish to bring out our inner face.

We are entering a New Decade and need to go beyond Yugoslavia's borders. We crossed them in the past decade as soldiers of war and murder for "the freedom of nations," but from now on we wish to be soldiers of human Culture, Love, and Brotherhood. We enter haggard, yet transformed. We enter deformed and hurt, but we have the strength of those who have suffered and been humiliated and stoned on the pillory of Europe. May our entrance into the third decade of the twentieth century be a battle for humanity through art.

Our martyred generation is dying out. It has been trampled and destroyed. The red monster of war has dug graves for us all, for millions of people, with its murderous claws. One corpse for every two soldiers. We must never forget that the last decade witnessed the death of thirteen million people, that ten million died of poverty and one hundred and fifty million became diseased. And we, who have been left as the rear guard, we carry our pain in our hearts, our common souls are full of desperation, and our common protest is: *No more war! Never again! Never again!*

The silence of our nerves has been shattered by grenades and fear of death. The joy of our souls has been darkened by the monstrosity of mutilated human bodies. The peace of our hearts, now choking on bloody tears, has been shattered by the inconsolable mothers who died of hunger and grief for their innocent children. Oh, you, you who have seen the eyes of the people you killed while they begged for their lives in agony, you who have seen the widow's weeds of mothers dying of grief—you must never, you shall never go forth to kill another man. You are the only ones who know what man really was in this insane asylum of a cursed century.

Man—was as crucified and as spat upon as Christ, but he *was not* Christ.

Man—was as forsaken and as humiliated as a beggar knocking on closed doors.

Man—was created to be God—and then killed as cattle for slaughter.

Thieves!

Your bloody spurs have pricked him, horses' hooves have trod over him, heavy chains of dark prisons have bound him, deadly torrents of sharp bullets and the thunder of stupid cannonry have pummeled him.

Man! Everyone renounces you at the last moment just as Peter renounced Christ, in the name of murder and in the name of your blood. Do not forget this, do not ever forget it!

Every word we have uttered has been against this crime—the crime against us—and against our times. The poet's words of damnation were too weak. That is why everyone must know that our pain is the fire we carry within. We believe in the birth of a New Man. Our first commandment is: IN THE NAME OF MAN—DO NOT KILL!

Our fight will be against crime—for Man.

Workers of the world, unite—against killing! Raise consciousness of Man in *Man*! Today, the non-human is an evil-doing deity—the great inquisitor, who has built black gallows for us all over the world.

All of us poets bear the night's darkness, which is our great punishment for being poets in these times. We have all been pushed into space and we know not whether we are insane or above time. Like apostles of the crucified Man we preach faith in the New Man and wait for his revelation. We are no longer waiting for the czar; we are waiting for Man!

Man!... Man!...

The tragic power of our new art lies in a desperate cry: Man! And that is why it is the furthest from classical beauty and from *l'art-pour-l'artism*. It is a New Spirit that creates, and the artist's eternal urge has always been creation. Art, which to us means Expressionism, is a strong desire to create new values, new forms. It is our love's cry. It is a cry for salvation and exaltation.

Art is general—human. That is why there is no specifically national art, much less class art. We, the poets and artists of this country, extend our hands to everyone who thinks like us, *to everyone, for every one* above shattered human skulls.

Art belongs to nations. That does not mean that a nation has a right to dictate what direction art will take. No! Art must follow the path of its creators, because the collective or the public is in this sense limited—inferior. Art directs its own movements. The public merely takes part passively by reflecting on the works. The public can never experience them. To have an absolutely artistic experience one needs to be an artist. That is why we fight for both the freedom of the *individual* and the affirmation of *individualism*. It must not be destroyed. Only a strong individual is creative. Every artist must be an *individual*. He must create *from within*, not *outside himself*. Otherwise he is a parasite who feeds on *others* like a pseudo-individual. That parasite has a common name: *dilettante*. The cult of dilettantism is quite well established here, and its players are the experienced mystifiers of an unknowing and uneducated population. Gravediggers that they are they block all progress. Many decades, this one included, have been their playground, but let this Third Decade be our playground. We will use it in our decisive fight against all traditions, all regionalisms and borders: for art and man there are no borders! The pages of *Zenit* are open for this purpose to all the apostles of art and humanity from the North Pole to the Cape of Good Hope. These are the words *Zenit* has chosen to represent it toYoung Yugoslavia and to announce its rebirth:

New Man! New Spirit! New Art!

Oh, the sun is so great and brilliant in its ZENITH. When the heavens ring the great zenith noon, our eyes rise up to you, our souls open like a festive Muscovite temple. Our hearts dance the bloody rhythmic dance of man's desperation on earth. The man we are looking for on earth has his ZENITH as well. We long for it—for the most sublime power of the inner cosmos.

Oh, zenith sun, you burn like a fire sacrifice. Our eyes are yellow with its flame, and we long for the highest throne, the throne of the SPIRIT. Our souls yearn for revelation, and art is the great revelation of the Spirit, the great fulfillment of all man's longings. It is our eternal unrest, eternal dynamics, eternal anarchy, eternal revolution. It cannot and must not rest. Our tragedy of unrest and death has reached its Black Peak and directed our art into a new movement. Today we are enjoying a *Second Renaissance*.

It has found its strongest affirmation in *Expressionism*. *Expressionism* is the soul's imperative to create the *most powerful* expression possible in a work of art.

Zenithism is a drive towards creating the *most sublime* forms.

Zenithism is abstract cosmic Expressionism.

Zenithism and Expressionism are mirrors in which we shall see our terrible inner pain— the drama of our souls. For a long time yet these mirrors will remain cursed for the still unborn generations begotten in blood. They will not be able find themselves, but they will find—us. For a long time to come they will look for themselves, but again they will find—us. And we, like monstrous ghosts and phantoms, will roam bloody-handed through their dreams and their nights.

We are a pledge of the future sons who will sacrifice themselves for the salvation of Man, and we leave them our Golgotha and our Mount of Olives in our works—a clear path to resurrection.

Our cry: MAN.

Our faith: ZENITHISM.

Translated by Maja Starčević

EXCERPTS FROM **THE SPIRIT OF ZENITHISM** Ljubomir Micić

Originally published as "Duh Zenitzma," *Zenit* vol. 1, no. 7 (1921)

The spirit of Zenithism: revolt and creation.

The spirit of every creation: revolt.

The spirit of every revolt: shattering the old, not as an end in itself but as an imperative of the positive force, which is a new affirmation.

Zenithism: a new artistic affirmation!

By dint of its expansion and instinct—its *inner* activity and movement—its superior nature and elan as a *spiritual* element of new relations in art—it shatters the matter of stiffness. Its *creation* topples everything though this is not its goal; it is merely the result of new relationships and new values.

Each shattering provokes a *new* creation—a *new* form—a *new* construction.

Each new and great idea causes rebellion and hatred in the weak.

Why do you hate Zenithism?

Because it is new and active.

The crowds have always hated anything new and grand.

Why don't you "understand" Zenithism?

1. Because Zenithism is art.
2. Because your spirit is poor.
3. Because you have learned only old ideas, and we are creating a NEW IDEA.

This has always been the case: the poor in spirit hold on to old ideas because they are all they have: *what has been.*

Their souls are a museum of dusty old objects and books.

Finally: Why are we new?

Because we have been scoffed at by you and never recognized. And your recognition—that is, the recognition of those who should be *students* and not teachers—would be the negation of all new values; it would be a negation of Zenithism. Your tragic inferiority lies in the fact that you are always "teachers" of values *unknown* and *new* to you, never students of those values.

We are new because of the richness of our soul and spirit.

The new art (Futurism, Cubism, Expressionism most of all!) is a precursor to the *scientific* theory of relativity. The artistic *theory of relativity* has been in existence for over ten years.

The *scientific* aspect has found its strongest affirmation in new art. (This is for you "teachers" who are hearing it for the first time!)

The people who audaciously deny the possibilities of *new art* (and there are plenty of them!) are weak and mediocre. And they are the ones who most vigorously defend the traditions and mummies they so slavishly adore. (Only mediocre men are slaves!)

An epigonic generation that lives dishonorably, they sponge on those who *create*.

Imitators and pseudo-personalities find themselves *in others* who have created *their own* faces. Because it is easier to imitate and create algebraic-artificial variations than to create independently—*anew.*

It is easier to be a "defender" because defenders are always characterized by their *collectivity* and great numbers.

Only the strong go on the offensive! (If most people in the world were not idiots, there would be no logical explanation for its tragic fate!)

People who do not think like us do not think like us only because they *do not think* or *cannot think* at all. We cannot think like you because it would be a failing—a great failing. That is as it must be. There would be no conflicts otherwise, and conflict is eternal and bears eternal flame.

There have always been "madmen" who were prophets and "sages" who were idiots.

Zenithism is the destruction of all traditions. It too must be mercilessly destroyed once it becomes a tradition.

We must step backward to move forward! That is why we turn a deaf ear to the requests of those who have not stepped backward.

Spiritual manifestations cannot have specific forms and directions!

The form of biological man is not determined in any way, so much less is the form of spiritual man.

No two people are alike!

There are hermaphrodites just as there are dwarves; there are giants just as there are hunchbacks. (But the moral hunchback is the most common variety!)

There are people who have hearts on their right side. And there are the barbarians.

If this is superfluous, if no one "understands" this, then I believe in Zenith's prophecy: that most people in Yugoslavia are bulls (Kulturträger!) whose heart is on their *right* side and brains in their *feet*!

Each spirit creates its unique forms independently.

That is why there cannot and must not be monotony.

The lines in your forehead (if you have one) cannot be the same as the lines in a poet's forehead. And a poet is by no means what you think a poet to be. A poet is what you, dear "teachers," call a "madman," and "madmen" are poet-apostles you cannot feel.

The person who wants to know them and know the difference between them also must be borderline brilliant and borderline mad.

And you will never reach that border.

Besides, who knows—if the border even exists?

So where do you get the cynical audacity to measure everything with the silly spectacles and microscopes you look through with blind or closed eyes?

Your eyes are closed and filled with dust.

Your eyes are blind even when open.

Why do you laugh out loud?

Because you want to drown out the laughter echoing in your own faces. You laugh out loud because you refuse to feel your poverty and our pity.

And we have enough pity for all the people on this Earth, an Earth which is not good to us. The Earth is your mother—our stepmother and a baby killer.

Go upward into the sublime heights, where there is no laughter or hatred or cynicism, and your eyes will be opened: you will see your days as vain and your words as empty; you will feel the blush of your own shame because you destroy all who do not resemble you and drive them into asylums and prisons.

There have always been "madmen" who were prophets and "sages" who were idiots.

*

Zenithism is right for a man of sublimity and heights—for a man who can go upward and reach up, reach up tirelessly—for a man who does not suffer from vertigo when looking deep down below—into the abyss.

Zenithism is right for a man who will not fall dead from sunstroke—for a man destined to look inward into his soul, who is exalted in his spirit and whose head is touching the clouds and who carries the Sun on his forehead.

He knows and is aware of the fact that he is above the crowds whose laughter is just dogs howling at the full moon.

He hears and feels his stride and his words echo far into space.

He knows that a crowd does not have itself, and that it never had itself.

He is dead to the empty "I" of the crowd.

One has to come to know and discover oneself.

Zenithism is abstract and it discovers the *spiritual* elements within and outside man: it is the new spirit of the earth, a child of the cosmos and the Sun.

Zenith is an *abstract* term for the most *sublime* heights of man's artistic spirit.

Only those who have come to know and discover themselves can be individuals: *elevators.*

The other kind don't have their own souls and they live a lie thinking they are their own. They are *pseudo-individuals.*

That is why you who can drown out the foreign souls, let your own souls be born, free yourselves of the foreign spirit, let your own free spirit be born.

Zenithism is a free spirit, a spirit independent in its search: for its form—its style— its "I"—its *individuality.*

"We are naked and pure" (*The Manifesto of Zenithism*) means this: in a clean cradle, in a Yugoslav-Balkan cradle, a new spirit—an integral, an independent spirit of *creative individualism* was born, and only such a spirit is capable of bearing and creating new values. A new spirit of a strong race has been born, a race that has been without art and culture until now.

Therefore:

Zenithism, in its striving for the liberation of man, in its striving for his individualism, is also *anarchy* and its *religion* is: to create new forms and relationships as a spiritual basis for the future Balkan-human art and to destroy the inhuman and non-spiritual past we all share with its positive aspect.

Because:

Art must be spiritual—abstract.

Music alone has always been a true art because it is abstract and does not "represent" anything.

Art should not "represent" anything except itself.

All that we have *is not* art: it is only a point of departure.

It is only rough matter and craftsmanship, while generations of people have lived a lie, not knowing what art was.

We still do not know what art is.

But we will find out one day.

*

Yugoslav "art" is onanism of brains and captured souls.

Despite the protests of virgins, professors, and journalists, let us destroy wagon loads of false artistic fabrications that travel through the Balkan lands.

Yugoslav "culture" is a foreign wild and rotten apple.

Our advantage lies in the fact that we have no "cultural tradition."

Our only tradition: Prince Marko and Kosovo.

That is where our "art" is now. That is our yesterday—our barbaric yesterday, and we do not want to be barbarians any longer.

One should not be a barbarian!

That muscle and heart heroism of ours has ended its epoch under Rudnik and on Kajmačkalan.

That was the time when the Balkan-Serbian man died as a slavish barbarian for the *physical* freedom and freedom of our borders, for the freedom of an oppressed race.

But there is no art in that.

Only a dead and bloody chapter.

Today we need to fight for the freedom and affirmation of all-human spirit.

The last barbarians are nothing but the forefathers of the first Zenithists.

Let a new day begin: THE HEROISM OF THE SPIRIT.

Let a heroic fight for spiritual freedom of man begin, everywhere where people live, as well as the fight for their brotherhood.

In the spirit of a new beginning: ZENITHISM: A NEW TODAY.

The spirit of Zenithism transforms and is all-human.

I do not say humanistic, because there is no humanity.

Only people.

Humanity has had its difficult birth for centuries now, but the West had no strength to give birth to it, because the West has no religion of feeling, only religion of thought.

(And this is the cause of the fall of the Western culture and its false humanism!)

Religion of feeling and thought is being born in the SOUTHEAST which has raised and will carry the flag.

Zenithism is a religion of thought and feeling—a flag of future transformation.

[…]

Our poems must be the clatter and clang of factories where machines and workers sing: MAN

Our poems must be church bells tolling the song of altars and bell towers:
GOD-SPIRIT

Our poems must be stone roofs of high hills and a welcoming explosion of
THE SUN

Our poems must be clouds and storms thundering the song of lightning:
ZENIT

Our poems must be bloodflight singing its anthem:
COSMOS—CHAOS—WORD

Our greatest poem will be: MANKIND

Our poems are not poems of feminine flirts.

Our poems are the stomp of cities, streets, squares, the thunder of tempests and abysses.

Our poems are not poems of meter and rhyme.

Our poems are rhythms of highly strung cosmic arches in a world of astral visions.

Our poems are not poems of whorish women and profane muses.

Our poems are movements of future spaces and worlds on the other side of Life and Death.

Our poems—dramas—words—symphonies—lines—notes—movements—have no laws.

Law: SPACE

Poem: WORDS IN SPACE

Religion: ZENITHISM

Translated by Maja Starčević

EXPRESSIONISM IS DYING   Ivan Goll

Originally published as "Der Expressionismus stirbt," *Zenit* vol. 1, no. 8 (October 1921)

What has been whispered, smiled about, and suspected everywhere is now confirmed: once again an art is dying of a time that betrayed it. Whether the art or the time is at fault is not important. Critically it could be proven, though, that Expressionism is choking on the carcass of the same revolution whose motherly Pythia it wanted to be.

This can be explained by the fact that Expressionism altogether (1910–1920) was not the name of an art form, but of a *state of mind*. It was more the subject of a *Weltanschauung* than the object of an artistic requirement.

Ludwig Rubiner: "The Poet gets into Politics" (*Die Aktion*, 1912). Also: "Our call to the future, to all lands and beyond is: *L'homme pour l'homme*, instead of the former *L'art pour l'art*" (*Zeit-Echo*, May 1917).

Kasimir Edschmid: "…No program of style. A question of soul. A matter of humanity" (*Neue Rundschau*, March 1918).

Hasenclever: "Let the theater be expression, not play!" "Theater for art, politics, philosophy" (*Schaubühne*, May 1916).

Thus:

Demand. Manifesto. Appeal. Accusation. Oath. Ecstasy. Struggle. Man screams. We are. One another. Passion.

Who was not there? Everyone was there. I was there: "New Orpheus." Not a single Expressionist was a reactionary. Not a single Expressionist was not antiwar. There was not one who did not believe in brotherhood and community. Among the painters as well. Proof: Attitude.

And: Expressionism was a beautiful, great, and noble affair. Solidarity of the mind. Deployment of the genuine.

Through no fault of the Expressionists, however, the result is unfortunately just a logo for the German Republic, 1920. Intermission. Please exit to the right. The Expressionist opens his mouth…and just closes it again. The weapon, namely the tuba, falls out of the hands of Meidner's European prophets. The very same one who waved his arms so earnestly in the air is now doing it for different reasons. The pistol cracks louder.

Yes, my dear brother Expressionist: the danger today is to take life too *seriously*. Fight-ing has become grotesque. The spirit is a hoax in this age of profiteering. The "intellectual," his consciousness raised toward Bolshevism, has to make himself small, very small, before the masses, perhaps even draw a mask of stupidity across his Jewish forehead, so that his teeth won't get knocked out by stones. The ecstatic mouth becomes bitter, very bitter.

The "good man" disappears into the wings with a desperate bow. Life, the *machine*, nature are still right: beyond good and evil. The beautiful strength, to which Alexander Blok, as the first of the Moderns, dedicated the "Skythen." Primitive man, with the dark blood of centuries and unsettling eyes, steps out from the equatorial jungle and from the polar tundra: with secrets of the sun and the moon. He dances over the meridians of the globe.

The fraternal call, oh Expressionist, what sentimentality! What passion in your kind of human nature.

Naked life is better, rather truer than you. Proof: your *Weltanschauung* has not triumphed anywhere. You have not saved the life of one in sixty million. "Man is good": just a phrase. "But perhaps in a thousand years."

A new power seems to be corning over us; one of brain-machinery .The crane of time takes us by the neck and moves us. You tear hair: My God, what rhythm sounds on earth. Why reach for heaven. *Heaven is also earth*, as the aviator knows. The earth has long since been heaven for the Negroes and the primitives. Perhaps he is right. Every American says "Yes." Away with sentimentality, you Germans, which means the same as, you Expressionists. You can bet: Ludendorff is ultimately an Expressionist too?

In France, where I live, one did *not get sentimental* during the entire war apart from three weaklings who don't count. From beyond the Urals, beyond the Balkans, and beyond the oceans, new lands beckon with their will to life and strength. Young countries. Young people. Their first word addressed to us is electric.

Translation from Rose-Carol Washton Long, German Expressionism

Participants in the International Congress of Constructivists and Dadaists, Weimar, 1922. Back row (l.–r.): Max Burchartz, Lotte Burchartz, Karl Peter Röhl, Hans Vogel, Lucia Moholy, László Moholy-Nagy, Alfréd Kemény; middle row: Alexa Röhl, El Lissitzky, Nelly van Doesburg, Theo van Doesburg, Bernhard Stutzkopf; front row: Werner Graeff, Nini Smith, Harry Scheibe, Cornelis van Eesteren, Hans Richter, Tristan Tzara, Hans Arp

Bucharest, 1923. L.–r.: Tristan Tzara, M. H. Maxy, Ion Vinea, Henri Bad, Jacques Costin

Ma group, Vienna, c. 1922. L.–r.: Sándor Bortnyik, Béla Uitz, Erzsi Újvári, Andor Simon, Lajos Kassák, Jolán Simon, Sándor Barta

L'amiral cherche

Poème simultan par R. Huelsenbeck, M. Janko, Tr. Tzara

HUELSENBECK	Ahoi	ahoi	Des	Admirals	gwirktes	Beinkleid	schnell
JANKO, chant			Where	the honny	suckle	wine twines	ilself
TZARA	Boum	boum boum	Il	déshabilla	sa chair	quand les	grenouilles

HUELSENBECK	und	der	Conciergenbäuche	Klapperschlangengrün	sind	milde	ach
JANKO, chant	can	hear	the weopour	will arround	arround	the	hill
TZARA	serpent	à	Bucarest	on dépendra	mes amis	dorénavant	et

HUELSENBECK	prrrza	chrrrza	prrrza	Wer	suchet	dem	wird
JANKO, chant	mine	admirabily	confortabily	Grandmother	said		
TZARA				Dimanche:	deux	éléphants	

Intermède rythmique

HUELSENBECK	hihi	Yabomm	hihi	Yabomm	hihi	hihi	hihiiiii
	ff ·		p	cresc ff		cresc	ff f
TZARA	rouge	bleu	rouge bleu	rouge bleu	rouge bleu	rouge bleu	
	p			f cresc	ff	cresc	fff
SIFFLET (Janko)		·			·		·
	p		cresc f		ff		fff
CLIQUETTE (TZ)	rrrrrrrrrr	rrrrrrrrrr	rrrrrrrrrr	rrrrrrrrrr	rrrrrrrrrr	rrrrrrrrrr	
	f decrsc	f	cresc	fff	uniform		
GROSSE CAISE (Huels.)	O O O	O O O O O	O O O O O	O O O O	O O		
	ff	p	f	fff	p		

HUELSENBECK	im	Kloset	zumeistens	was er	nötig	hätt ahoi iuché	ahoi iuché
JANKO (chant)	I	love the	ladies	I love to	be among	the girls	
TZARA	la	concierge	qui m'a	trompé elle a	vendu	l'appartement	que j'avais loué

HUELSENBECK	hätt'	O süss	gequollnes Stelldichein	des Admirals	im Abendschein	uru uru
JANKO (chant)	o'clock	and tea is	set I like	to have my tea	with some brunet	shai shai
TZARA		Le train	traîne la fumée	comme la fuite	de l'animal blessé	aux

HUELSENBECK	Der Affe	brüllt	die Seekuh bellt	im Lindenbaum	der Schräg	zerschellt tara-
JANKO (chant)	doing it	doing	it see	that ragtime	coupple	over there see
TZARA	Autour du	phare	tourne l'auréole	des oiseaux	bleuillis en moitiés	de lumière vis-

HUELSENBECK			Peitschen um die Lenden	Im Schlafsack	gröhlt der
JANKO (chant)			oh yes yes yes yes yes yes yes yes		yes yes
TZARA	cher c'est si	difficile	La rue s'enfuit avec mon bagage à traves la ville	Un métro	mèle

chapter 6

INTERNATIONAL DADA

Timothy O. Benson

Dada was inherently international from its inception in 1916 in Zurich, then a haven for assorted pacifists, socialists, and intellectuals from all over Europe fleeing World War I. The word "Dada" was adopted as a label for an art movement created somewhat by happenstance as its generic components were consciously assembled by founder Hugo Ball from the internationally diverse artistic, literary, and performance practices on hand. With roots in Italian Futurism, German Expressionism, and French Cubism, the new Dada amalgam conveyed an incipient abstraction. Its performances utilized briutist (or noise) music and sound-poetry, while its periodicals *Cabaret Voltaire* and *Dada* disseminated visual poetry (words freed from syntax and distributed freely about the page in a manner indebted to Filippo Marinetti's *parole in libertà*). These forms—along with a celebration of spontaneity and chaos as a challenge to fixed ideologies— were easily and eagerly absorbed in other avant-garde centers, as seen in our selections from periodicals ranging from the Hungarian exile journal *Ma* (Vienna) to *Dada-Jok* (Zagreb) and *Disk* (Prague).

Yet despite these formal influences it remained for Berlin Dada to politicize the movement and define its international dimension. Richard Huelsenbeck rejected Futurist nationalism while extolling the international viability of its production (especially bruitism) in his "Dada Manifesto." As is recognized in Roman Jakobson's cogent essay, Berlin Dada rejected both Expressionism and Zurich abstraction in its critique of itself *qua* art movement, or "ism." Dispensing with bourgeois aesthetic production, Berlin Dada sought engagement with the broader social order—not only with the proletarian classes with which it sympathized politically, but also with the modern world of the machine, mass production, and the burgeoning mass culture. Many of Berlin Dada's maneuvers and discoveries were taken up by Central European Dada manifestations including satire, provocation, collage, photomontage, assemblage, and manipulation of the text on the page to approximate (while also subverting) conventional publications ranging from newspapers and advertisements to propaganda broadsides.

While Dada manifestations followed almost immediately in Cologne, Hanover, New York, and Paris, in Central Europe its development was slower, more tentative, and ambiguous. Hungarian artists and writers encountered Dada only during their exile in Vienna, at which time German Dada was beginning its "anti-Dada" phase—a searching for structures in culture and the elemental in art that would lead to Constructivism. In Vienna, Lajos Kássak's "picture architecture" and picture poems in the pages of *Ma* already showed parallels with this later phase (to some extent represented by works of Raoul Hausmann and Kurt Schwitters in *Ma*). The absurd juxtapositions and attacks on fixed beliefs in Sándor Barta's satires, as well as the celebration of popular entertainment and rejection of hallowed traditions in Ödön Palasovszky and Iván Hevesy's "Manifesto" show how much Hungarian approaches (in both Vienna and Budapest) had in common with Berlin Dada in its most rebellious phase, even if not always in name.

In Poland, the connection was more distant, as the most allied developments—formal parallels among the Polish Futurists and Stanisław Witkiewicz's idiosyncratic gestures—lacked Dada's crucial institutional enframement as an avant-garde movement. Yet Witkiewicz's intention of superseding Dada with pure hoax, as well as his rejection of art movements altogether in favor of his own commercial portrait studio (in Chapter 11), show credible echoes of the Dada critique in the work of a brilliant independent artist.

Much closer connections resulted from two Dada tours that brought Berlin Dada to Prague: in March 1920 Hausmann and Huelsenbeck appeared at two evenings, and in September 1921 Hausmann and Schwitters presented a "presentist" and "antidadaist" evening. Yugoslav student Dragan Aleksić was soon organizing Dada evenings in Prague, and was joined by Branko Ve Poljanski, brother of Ljubomir Micić, who founded *Zenit* in Zagreb in 1921. Aleksić's inclusive collage-like listing of Dadaist strategies ("Dadaism") and Poljanski's Schwitters-like trust in nonsense, expressed in his own "anti-Dada" periodical, *Dada-Jok* (Dada-Nyet) show a deep appreciation of Dada. Although Micić also utilized Dada strategies, his direction would soon be far more clearly nationalistic.

Dada exerted significant influence among Czech artists only in the mid-twenties, albeit Roman Jakobson, while residing in Prague in 1921, provided a very precise reading of the Zurich and Berlin manifestations. Devětsil may have had the Berlin "Dada-Messe" (Dada Fair) in mind when mounting their 1923 exhibition, "Bazaar of Modern Art." But only with Karel Teige's launching of "Poetism" in response to Constructivism, does it become clear that perhaps what he (and fellow Devětsil member František Halas) had most in common with Dada was its cultivation of play and humor.

Throughout its unfolding across Central Europe, Dada fostered a self-critical perspective on the scope and purpose of aesthetic production, how this was often in conflict with other social agendas (especially those of political activism), and how each movement might be constructed to serve such contradictory ends. Yet despite such commonalities, Dada was situated differently in each avant-garde setting, where it attained entirely different meanings and afforded entirely unique perspectives.

When the German actor and writer Hugo Ball, then living in Zurich, decided to transform his recently founded Cabaret Voltaire into Dada, his collaborators included two Romanian university students, the poet Tristan Tzara and artist Marcel Janco—both previous members of the Simbolul group in Bucharest (see Chapter 2). In its early phase, Zurich Dada sought to encompass a diversity of modernist tendencies including Cubism, Expressionism, and above all Futurism. The multi-lingual "L'amiral cherche une maison à louer," performed by Richard Huelsenbeck, Janco, and Tzara (see p. 307), exemplifies how this cumulative process led from Futurist bruitist poetry (where actual sounds are incorporated) to the Dada invention of simultaneous poetry. When Ball departed Zurich in 1917, Tzara assumed the leadership role, and his 1918 "Dada Manifesto" established the far more radical philosophy for which Dada is remembered: Cubism, Expressionism, and Futurism are rejected in favor of spontaneity, while logic and order are abolished to make way for negation and a thoroughgoing nihilism. His manifesto was published in *Dada* 3, the most radical issue hitherto, and the most adventuresome in terms of its experimental typography and incorporation of woodcuts and drawings by Hans Arp, Janco, Hans Richter, Enrico Prampolini, and Francis Picabia.

Dada took on a very different complexion in Berlin, a city of war shortages, and, during 1918–19, a postwar revolution with street fighting between the pro-Soviet Spartacus League and the Freikorps (remnants of the German army serving the interests of the provisional republic). Social and aesthetic utopias flourished among such avantgarde circles as the Novembergruppe (November Group) and the Arbeitsrat für Kunst (Work Council for Art), modeled on the Workers' and Soldiers' Councils (or Soviets). In December 1918, with the approval of the Arbeitsrat, Bruno Taut of the "Crystal Chain" architects distributed his "Architektur-Programm," which was published in March 1919 as an Arbeitsrat manifesto honed down to six demands, including "dissolution of the Academy of Art" and "establishment of a national center to ensure the fostering of the arts within the framework of all future lawmaking."[1] This was followed in April 1919 by Arbeitsrat co-director Walter Gropius's closely related Bauhaus "Program" (see Chapter 4). The "Dadaist Revolutionary Central Council" first published its "What is

---

1 Translated in Ulrich Conrads, ed., *Programs and Manifestoes on 20th-Century Architecture* (Cambridge: The MIT Press, 1971), pp. 41–45.

Dadaism" manifesto as an insert in the first issue of *Der Dada* in June 1919. Although couched ostensibly as a manifesto in support of the communist international, Hausmann and Huelsenbeck's manifesto is as much a parody of left-wing manifestoes and President Wilson's Fourteen Points (delivered January, 1918)—a demonstration of how Dada texts could approximate while critiquing the surrounding cultural conventions of every political stripe.

DADA MANIFESTO   Tristan Tzara

Originally published as "Manifest Dada," *Dada* no. 3 (March 23, 1918)

The magic of a word—Dada—which has brought journalists to the gates of a world unforeseen, is of no importance to us.

To put out a manifesto you must want: ABC
to fulminate against 1, 2, 3,
to fly into a rage and sharpen your wings to conquer and disseminate little abcs and big abcs, to sign, shout, swear, to organize prose into a form of absolute and irrefutable evidence, to prove your non plus ultra and maintain that novelty resembles life just as the latest appearance of some whore proves the essence of God. His existence was previously proved by the accordion, the landscape, the wheedling word. To impose your ABC is a natural thing—hence deplorable. Everybody does it in the form of crystal-bluffmadonna, monetary system, pharmaceutical product, or a bare leg advertising the ardent sterile spring. The love of novelty is the cross of sympathy, demonstrates a naive *je m'enfoutisme*, it is a transitory, positive sign without a cause.
But this need itself is obsolete. In documenting art on the basis of the supreme simplicity: novelty, we are human and true for the sake of amusement, impulsive, vibrant to crucify boredom. At the crossroads of the lights, alert, attentively awaiting the years, in the forest. I write a manifesto and I want nothing, yet I say certain things, and in principle I am against manifestoes, as I am also against principles (half-pints to measure the moral value of every phrase too too convenient; approximation was invented by the Impressionists). I write this manifesto to show that people can perform contrary actions together while taking one fresh gulp of air; I am against action; for continuous contradiction, for affirmation too, I am neither for nor against and I do not explain because I hate common sense.
Dada—there you have a word that leads ideas to the hunt: every bourgeois is a little dramatist, he invents all sorts of speeches instead of putting the characters suitable to the quality of his intelligence, chrysalises, on chairs, seeks causes or aims (according to the psychoanalytic method he practices) to cement his plot, a story that speaks and defines itself. Every spectator is a plotter if he tries to explain a word: (to know!) Safe in the cottony refuge of serpentine complications he manipulates his instincts. Hence the mishaps of conjugal life.
To explain: the amusement of redbellies in the mills of empty skulls.
DADA MEANS NOTHING
If you find it futile and don't want to waste your time on a word that means nothing...
The first thought that comes to these people is bacteriological in character: to find its etymological, or at least its historical or psychological origin. We see by the papers that the Kru Negroes call the tail of a holy cow Dada. The cube and the mother in a certain district of Italy are called: Dada. A hobbyhorse, a nurse both in Russian and Romanian: Dada. Some learned journalists regard it as an art for babies, other holy jesusescall-ingthelittlechildren of our day, as a relapse into a dry and noisy, noisy and monotonous primitivism. Sensibility is not constructed on the basis of a word; all constructions converge on perfection which is boring, the stagnant idea of a gilded swamp, a relative human product. A work of art should not be beauty in itself, for beauty is dead; it should be neither gay nor sad, neither light nor dark to rejoice or torture the individual by serving him the cakes of sacred aureoles or the sweets of a vaulted race through the atmospheres. A work of art is never beautiful by decree, objectively and for all. Hence criticism is useless, it exists only subjectively, for each man separately, without the slightest character of universality. Does anyone think he has found a psychic base

common to all mankind? The attempt of Jesus and the Bible covers with their broad benevolent wings: shit, animals, days. How can one expect to put order into the chaos that constitutes that infinite and shapeless variation: man? The principle: "love thy neighbor" is a hypocrisy. "Know thyself" is utopian but more acceptable, for it embraces wickedness. No pity. After the carnage we still retain the hope of a purified mankind. I speak only of myself since I do not wish to convince, I have no right to drag others into my river, I oblige no one to follow me and everybody practices his art in his own way, if he knows the joy that rises like arrows to the astral layers, or that other joy that goes down into the mines of corpse-flowers and fertile spasms. Stalactites: seek them every-where, in mangers magnified by pain, eyes white as the hares of the angels.

And so Dada was born of a need for independence, of a distrust toward unity. Those who are with us preserve their freedom. We recognize no theory. We have enough cubist and futurist academies: laboratories of formal ideas. Is the aim of art to make money and cajole the nice nice bourgeois? Rhymes ring with the assonance of the currencies and the inflexion slips along the line of the belly in profile. All groups of artists have arrived at this trust company after riding their steeds on various comets. While the door remains open to the possibility of wallowing in cushions and good things to eat.

Here we cast anchor in rich ground. Here we have a right to do some proclaiming, for we have known cold shudders and awakenings. Ghosts drunk on energy, we dig the trident into unsuspecting flesh. We are a downpour of maledictions as tropically abundant as vertiginous vegetation, resin and rain are our sweat, we bleed and burn with thirst, our blood is vigor.

Cubism was born out of the simple way of looking at an object: Cézanne painted a cup 20 centimeters below his eyes, the Cubists look at it from above, others complicate appearance by making a perpendicular section and arranging it conscientiously on the side. (I do not forget the creative artists and the profound laws of matter which they established once and for all.) The Futurist sees the same cup in movement, a succession of objects one beside the other, and maliciously adds a few force lines. This does not prevent the canvas from being a good or bad painting suitable for the investment of intellectual capital.

The new painter creates a world, the elements of which are also its implements, a sober, definite work without argument. The new artist protests: he no longer paints (symbolic and illusionist reproduction) but creates—directly in stone, wood, iron, tin, boulders—locomotive organisms capable of being turned in all directions by the limpid wind of momentary sensation. All pictorial or plastic work is useless: let it then be a monstrosity that frightens servile minds, and not sweetening to decorate the refectories of animals in human costume, illustrating the sad fable of mankind.

Painting is the art of making two lines geometrically established as parallel meet on a canvas before our eyes in a reality which transposes other conditions and possibilities into a world. This world is not specified or defined in the work, it belongs in its innumerable variations to the spectator. For its creator it is without cause and without theory. *Order = disorder; ego = non-ego; affirmation = negation:* the supreme radiations of an absolute art. Absolute in the purity of a cosmic, ordered chaos, eternal in the globule of a second without duration, without breath without control. I love an ancient work for its novelty. It is only contrast that connects us with the past. The writers who teach morality and discuss or improve psychological foundations have, aside from a hidden desire to make money, an absurd view of life, which they have classified, cut into sections, channelized: they insist on waving the baton as the categories dance. Their readers snicker and go on: what for?

There is a literature that does not reach the voracious mass. It is the work of creators, issued from a real necessity in the author, produced for himself. It expresses the knowledge

of a supreme egoism, in which laws wither away. Every page must explode, either by profound heavy seriousness, the whirlwind, poetic frenzy, the new, the eternal, the crushing
joke, enthusiasm for principles, or by the way in which it is printed. On the one hand a tot-
tering world in flight, betrothed to the glockenspiel of hell, on the other hand: new men.
Rough, bouncing, riding on hiccups. Behind them a crippled world and literary quacks with
a mania for improvement.

I say unto you: there is no beginning and we do not tremble, we are not sentimental. We are
a furious wind, tearing the dirty linen of clouds and prayers, preparing the great spectacle
of disaster, fire, decomposition. We will put an end to mourning and replace tears by
sirens screeching from one continent to another. Pavilions of intense joy and widowers
with the sadness of poison. Dada is the signboard of abstraction; advertising and business are also elements of poetry.

I destroy the drawers of the brain and of social organization: spread demoralization
wherever I go and cast my hand from heaven to hell, my eyes from hell to heaven,
restore the fecund wheel of a universal circus to objective forces and the imagination
of every individual.

Philosophy is the question: from which side shall we look at life, God, the idea or other
phenomena. Everything one looks at is false. I do not consider the relative result more
important than the choice between cake and cherries after dinner. The system of
quickly looking at the other side of a thing in order to impose your opinion indirectly is
called dialectics, in other words, haggling over the spirit of fried potatoes while dancing method around it.

If I cry out:

Ideal, ideal, ideal,

Knowledge, knowledge, knowledge,

Boomboom, boomboom, boomboom,

I have given a pretty faithful version of progress, law, morality and all other fine qualities that various highly intelligent men have discussed in so many books, only to conclude that after all everyone dances to his own personal boomboom, and that the
writer is entitled to his boomboom: the satisfaction of pathological curiosity; a private
bell for inexplicable needs; a bath; pecuniary difficulties; a stomach with repercussions in life; the authority of the mystic wand formulated as the bouquet of a phantom
orchestra made up of silent fiddle bows greased with philters made of chicken
manure. With the blue eye-glasses of an angel they have excavated the inner life for a
dime's worth of unanimous gratitude. If all of them are right and if all pills are Pink
Pills, let us try for once not to be right. Some people think they can explain rationally,
by thought, what they think. But that is extremely relative. Psychoanalysis is a dangerous disease, it puts to sleep the anti-objective impulses of man and systematizes the
bourgeoisie. There is no ultimate Truth. The dialectic is an amusing mechanism which
guides us (in a banal kind of way) to the opinions we had in the first place. Does anyone think that, by a minute refinement of logic, he has demonstrated the truth and
established the correctness of these opinions? Logic imprisoned by the senses is an
organic disease. To this element philosophers always like to add: the power of observation. But actually this magnificent quality of the mind is the proof of its impotence.
We observe, we regard from one or more points of view, we choose them among
the millions that exist. Experience is also a product of chance and individual faculties.
Science disgusts me as soon as it becomes a speculative system, loses its character
of utility—that is so useless but is at least individual. I detest greasy objectivity, and
harmony, the science that finds everything in order. Carry on, my children, humanity...
Science says we are the servants of nature: everything is in order, make love and
bash your brains in. Carry on, my children, humanity, kind bourgeois and journalist
virgins.... I am against systems, the most acceptable system is on principle to have

none. To complete oneself, to perfect oneself in one's own littleness, to fill the vessel with one's individuality, to have the courage to fight for and against thought, the mystery of bread, the sudden burst of an infernal propeller into economic lilies:

DADAIST SPONTANEITY

I call *je m'enfoutisme* the kind of like in which everyone retains his own conditions, though respecting other individualisms, except when the need arises to defend oneself, in which the two-step becomes national anthem, curiosity shop, a radio transmitting Bach fugues, electric signs and posters for whorehouses, an organ broadcasting carnations for God, all this together physically replacing photography and the universal catechism.

ACTIVE SIMPLICITY.

Inability to distinguish between degrees of clarity: to lick the penumbra and float in the big mouth filled with honey and excrement. Measured by the scale of eternity, all activity is vain—(if we allow thought to engage in an adventure the result of which would be infinitely grotesque and add significantly to our knowledge of human impotence). But supposing life to be a poor farce, without aim or initial parturition, and because we think it our duty to extricate ourselves as fresh and clean as washed chrysanthemums, we have proclaimed as the sole basis for agreement: art. It is not as important as we, mercenaries of the spirit, have been proclaiming for centuries. Art afflicts no one and those who manage to take an interest in it will harvest caresses and a fine opportunity to populate the country with their conversation. Art is a private affair, the artist produces it for himself; an intelligible work is the product of a journalist, and because at this moment it strikes my fancy to combine this monstrosity with oil paints: a paper tube simulating the metal that is automatically pressed and poured hatred cowardice villainy. The artist, the poet rejoice at the venom of the masses condensed into a section chief of this industry, he is happy to be insulted: it is a proof of his immutability. When a writer or artist is praised by the newspapers, it is proof of the intelligibility of his work: wretched lining of a coat for public use; tatters covering brutality, piss contributing to the warmth of an animal brooding vile instincts. Flabby, insipid flesh reproducing with the help of typographical microbes. We have thrown out the crybaby in us. Any infiltration of this kind is candied diarrhea. To encourage this act is to digest it. What we need is works that are strong straight precise and forever beyond understanding. Logic is a complication. Logic is always wrong. It draws the threads of notions, words, in their formal exterior, toward illusory ends and centers. Its chains kill, it is an enormous centipede stifling independence. Married to logic, art would live in incest, swallowing, engulfing its own tail, still part of its own body, fornicating within itself, and passion would become a nightmare tarred with protestantism, a monument, a heap of ponderous gray entrails. But the suppleness, enthusiasm, even the joy of injustice, this little truth which we practice innocently and which makes us beautiful: we are subtle and our fingers are malleable and slippery as the branches of that sinuous, almost liquid plant; it defines our soul, say the cynics. That too is a point of view; but all flowers are not sacred, fortunately, and the divine thing in us is our call to anti-human action. I am speaking of a paper flower for the buttonholes of the gentlemen who frequent the ball of masked life, the kitchen of grace, white cousins lithe or fat. They traffic with whatever we have selected. The contradiction and unity of poles in a single toss can be the truth. If one absolutely insists on uttering this platitude, the appendix of a libidinous, malodorous morality. Morality creates atrophy like every plague produced by intelligence. The control of morality and logic has inflicted us with impassivity in the presence of policemen—who are the cause of slavery, putrid rats infecting the bowels of the bourgeoisie which have infected the only luminous clean corridors of glass that remained open to artists.

Let each man proclaim: there is a great negative work of destruction to be accomplished. We must sweep and clean. Affirm the cleanliness of the individual after the state of madness, aggressive complete madness of a world abandoned to the hands of bandits, who rend one another and destroy the centuries. Without aim or design, without organization: indomitable madness, decomposition. Those who are strong in words or force will survive, for they are quick in defense, the agility of limbs and sentiments flames on their faceted flanks.

Morality has determined charity and pity, two balls of fat that have grown like elephants, like planets, and are called good. There is nothing good about them. Goodness is lucid, clear and decided, pitiless toward compromise and politics. Morality is an injection of chocolate into the veins of all men. This task is not ordered by a supernatural force but by the trust of idea brokers and grasping academicians. Sentimentality: at the sight of a group of men quarreling and bored, they invented the calendar and the medicament wisdom. With a sticking of labels the battle of the philosophers was set off (mercantilism, scales, meticulous and petty measures) and for the second time it was understood that pity is a sentiment like diarrhea in relation to the disgust that destroys health, a foul attempt by carrion corpses to compromise the sun. I proclaim the opposition of all cosmic faculties to this gonorrhea of a putrid sun issued from the factories of philosophical thought, I proclaim bitter struggle with all the weapons of

DADAIST DISGUST

Every product of disgust capable of becoming a negation of the family is Dada; a protest with the fists of its whole being engaged in destructive action: *Dada; knowledge of all the means rejected up until now by the shamefaced sex of comfortable compromise and good manners: Dada; abolition of logic, which is the dance of those impotent to create: Dada; of every social hierarchy and equation set up for the sake of values by our valets: Dada; every object, all objects, sentiments, obscurities, apparitions and the precise clash of parallel lines are weapons for the fight: Dada; abolition of memory: Dada; abolition of archaeology: Dada: abolition of prophets: Dada; abolition of the future: Dada; absolute and unquestionable faith in every god that is the immediate product of spontaneity*: Dada; elegant and unprejudiced leap from a harmony to the other sphere; trajectory of a word tossed like a screeching phonograph record; to respect all individuals in their folly of the moment: whether it be serious, fearful, timid, ardent, vigorous, determined, enthusiastic; to divest one's church of every useless cumbersome accessory; to spit out disagreeable or amorous ideas like a luminous waterfall, or coddle them—with the extreme satisfaction that it doesn't matter in the least—with the same intensity in the thicket of one's soul—pure of insects for blood well-born, and gilded with bodies of archangels. Freedom: Dada Dada Dada, a roaring of tense colors, and interlacing of opposites and of all contradictions, grotesques, inconsistencies: LIFE.

Translated by Ralph Manheim

WHAT IS DADAISM AND WHAT DOES IT WANT IN GERMANY?

Raoul Hausmann, Richard Huelsenbeck, Jefim Golyscheff
Originally published as "Was ist der Dadaismus und was will er in Deutschland?"
from *Der Dada* no. 1 (1919)

1. **DADAISM DEMANDS:**

   1) The international revolutionary union of all creative and intellectual men and women on the basis of radical Communism;

   2) The introduction of progressive unemployment through comprehensive mechanization of every field of activity. Only by unemployment does it become possible for the individual to achieve certainty as to the truth of life and finally become accustomed to experience;

   3) The immediate expropriation of property (socialization) and the communal feeding of all; further, the erection of cities of light, and gardens which will belong to society as a whole and prepare man for a state of freedom.

2. **THE CENTRAL COUNCIL DEMANDS:**

   a) Daily meals at public expense for all creative and intellectual men and women on the Potsdamer Platz (Berlin);

   b) Compulsory adherence of all clergymen and teachers to the Dadaist articles of faith;

   c) The most brutal struggle against all directions of so-called "workers of the spirit" (Hiller, Adler), against their concealed bourgeoisism, against Expressionism and post-classical education as advocated by the Sturm group;

   d) The immediate erection of a state art center, elimination of concepts of property in the new art (Expressionism); the concept of property is entirely excluded from the super-individual movement of Dadaism which liberates all mankind;

   e) Introduction of the simultaneist poem as a Communist state prayer;

   f) Requisition of churches for the performance of bruitism, simultaneist and Dadaist poems;

   g) Establishment of a Dadaist advisory council for the remodeling of life in every city of over 50,000 inhabitants;

   h) Immediate organization of a large scale Dadaist propaganda campaign with 150 circuses for the enlightenment of the proletariat;

   i) Submission of all laws and decrees to the Dadaist central council for approval;

   j) Immediate regulation of all sexual relations according to the views of international Dadaism through establishment of a Dadaist sexual center.

The Dadaist revolutionary council.
German group: Hausmann, Huelsenbeck.
Business office: Charlottenburg, Kantstrasse 118.
Applications for membership taken at business office.

Translated by Ralph Manheim

Although the Hungarian avant-garde was antiwar and had a penchant for anarchism from its very beginning in 1916 (as did Zurich Dada at about the same time), it lacked the sense of humor and frivolous playfulness that characterized the original Dada movement. The beginnings of the Hungarian counter-culture were marked by the dramatic intonation of the mainstream culture and by the heavy personality of its creator, the poet, writer, artist, and editor Lajos Kassák. His group's Dadaism *avant la lettre*—the term was apparently not known in the Hungarian cultural context before 1921—differed from its Zurich counterpart mainly in its solemnity. "New art will be seeking God, it will be like a prayer...And holy be the anarchism which will sing a hymn to pleasure," wrote one of the contributors to Kassák's first journal, *A Tett* (The Act).

Kassák and his friends discovered Dada in their Vienna exile in 1921, when picture poems, reproductions of Dada art works, and translations of Kurt Schwitters's poems filled the pages of *Ma* (Today), the avant-garde periodical then edited by Kassák. He exploited Dada in his poetry, too, where he blended it with bold Futurist images and jumbled words. A year later, however, Kassák was ready to adopt a more serious language as well as a more positive and authoritative stance, and gave priority, both in his art and in his journal, to Constructivism. Some of his old-time colleagues and friends disagreed with him at this point, and the Ma group split up in 1922 along the Dada-versus-Constructivism rift. Sándor Barta published his Dada satire, in which he lampoons Kassák and his wife as "Lajos Collective" and "Jolán Simple," in his own journal *Akasztott Ember* (Hanged Man).

Budapest Dada unfolded, as did Zurich Dada, mostly on stage. One of its central agents was the actor, poet, and playwright Ödön Palasovszky, who wrote a manifesto with the art critic Iván Hevesy in 1922 and founded the Zöld Szamár (Green Donkey) theater in 1925. Here Sándor Bortnyik, a former disciple of Kassák, was the stage designer and the author of the pantomime, after which the theater was named. The Green Donkey, as did many other performances of the theater, evoked the satirical, tongue-in-cheek tone of Berlin Dada. The theater was a socialist enterprise, persecuted by censors and the police, who were active in banning performances in Budapest in the late 1920s and the 1930s. Budapest Dada was increasingly forced to turn to a more symbolic language and a more serious version of the cabaret, enhancing poetry recitals and dance performances.

THE BLACK TOMCAT   János Mácza

Originally published as "A fekete kandúr," *Ma* vol. 6, no. 9 (Sept. 21, 1921)

Prologue:
Ladies and gentlemen
brothers and comrades
I am stone, glass, and steel
the spotlight's beam of light
I am sound, and word, and canvas
even the stage manager
and: YOU.
Go ahead and laugh!
Idiots, sponge-heads
parrots and crowbirds
sages artists and those with V.D.
I lift the curtains from your eyes
Let me put the nickel in the nickelodeon
Brrr—nyek—poot
You can start laughing!

Scene: The earth. The sky. In the sky: The Sun, The Moon, The Stars. But they are not lit up. The sun is leaning against some mountain. It is dark.
A dark figure stumbles forth with a lit lantern, holding a long pole. This is "A."
"A" with the long pole (ambles over to the mountain, grumbling, poking the Sun with his pole): Sun rises at five thirty-five.
Sun: inches higher.

Semi-darkness

Motors: sputter up; machines: rev up.
Voice: Our Father who art in heaven...
Bell: Tolls three times. Something emits a terrible screech.
"A" with the pole: A-oo-ah-ah-o (Moves forward to hang placards at stage front, inscribed as follows):

| CHAT NOIRE | DINING ROOM | JEPHNN KOT | CAFFE CHANTANT |

A corrugated iron shutter rolls up with a loud rumble
"B," a smart aleck (seated at a small table, raises a lamp in front of himself): Berson rubber... Palma heels...
"X," a piano player: "To your homeland be forever steadfastly faithful, Oh..."
"D," a young man and a lady (in a roomy easy chair, torrentially): Do you love me?! I love you! Love me! I love her! You love me!! I love you! Now! Now!
"F" wearing a dinner jacket: Meee!
"Ü," a sad sack: stands in place on one leg, changing legs.
"G," a laborer: (keeps lugging stones to the center of the stage): Proletarians unite...
Horns: in D Major
"A" with the pole: shoves "G," then retreats to the back and stands holding the pole.
"H" a poet (in a dark corner): "See, dearly beloved, what we are: lo we are ashes and dust..."
"C" a gentleman: Bravo!
"I," an American, "J," a Frenchman, "K," a Russian, "L," a Czech, "M," a German, "N," a Hungarian: all wearing their respective national costumes, seated around a table, eyeing each other suspiciously with distrust; now they all stand in unison, bow toward each other, and resume their seats.

"O," a priest, at the pulpit: Hail M-A-A-RY, full of grace...

"S," a scientist (at a desk piled with books and astronomical telescope, stands up reverentially): For Jean Jack Rousseau is a great human being!

"Ü," the sad sack, bows deeply

"Z," a writer of tragedies: Gentlemen, our great tragedy is that we do not live in an age of tragedy...

News vendor (crossing the stage): Revolt in the garbage mines! Murder and robbery at the whorehouse! Police investigate the laundry chute... (Off)

"F," in dinner jacket (lounging on sofa): Ah meee, I've got syphilis!

"B," the smart aleck: Trojan prophylactics! Pleasure for gentlemen!

"F," in dinner jacket: But I still love slender ankles!

"R," a physician (rushes over with a large hypodermic syringe): Sir, here comes the twenty-third revised edition! (injects him)

"F," in dinner jacket: Ow-ow-ow!

"R," the physician: Ehrlich—Hata 606 + 23!

"F," in dinner jacket: She said she was a virgin...

"O," the priest: BLE-E-SSED be his will...

"H," the poet: "Bravebloo dreddened placeofwoe mysighsa lutesyou—" (yellow light illuminates his brow)

"C," the gentleman (steps to his side and drops a dime into the hat held out by the poet)

"G," the worker: Proletarians unite

Horns: in A Major

"D," the young man: Jews stink and so do peasants, and so does tanner's glue—oh my sweet-scented goddess! (keeps sniffing "E")

"E," his lady: Love me now!

"O," the priest: BLE-E-SSED are the pure at heart... (spits at worker)

"Z," the author of tragedies: My tragedy is being made into a musical! Wah-ah-ah... (sobs)

"F," in dinner jacket (leaps up): Boring! Boring!...eh...me! meee! (rushes over to the piano, shoves away the player practicing scales): Idiotic Meee!

The scales have ceased—Cacophony—Now "F" resumes playing, but he plays a chromatic scale.—Applause.

"C," the gentleman: What kind of nonsense is this, I ask you!

"O," the priest: Sac-ri-lege! (weeps)

"H," the poet: "Do you know your homeland, that shelter where..." (flooded by green light)

"S," a war hero (his chest covered by medals; enters pulling a cannon on a string): Heh-heh, heh-heh-heh

"H," the poet: "Three orphans abandoned crying in the dark..." (appears in purple light)

Wailing all around: Wa-ah-ah...

Double-bassoon: guffaws

The purple fades above the poet

"P," the scientist: For Dante Alighieri is a grrreat man!

"B" the smart aleck: stands up and tosses a dime into the poet's hat)

The international table illuminated by bright light.

A voice: Gentlemen! The concept of the sovereign state...

"I," the American: Yes yes yes

"J," the Frenchman: Oui oui oui

"K," the Russian: Da da da

"L," the Czech: Ano ano ano

"M," the German: Ja ja ja
"N," the Hungarian: Igen igen igen
Bassoons: chortling
"G," the worker: Proletarians of the world...
Horns: in C Major
Judge (marching across stage, keeps repeating): for JUSTICE lies in Paragraph 364...
for JUSTICE...etc.
Murderer (following after him, in chains, surrounded by bayonets)
12 orphans (follow in single file, weeping)

Organ music accompanies them
"Ü," the sad sack: Sob, sob, sob, sob
"P," the scientist: For Leo Nikolaevich Tolstoy is a grrreat man!
"Ü," the sad sack, stops sobbing and bows deeply
"SZ," a dancer, dances onto the stage in costume
"S," the war hero: Heh-heh-heh
The dancer arouses no interest
"O," the priest: Police! Police!
"SZ," the dancer: flits away
"E," the lady: Love me more! and more! and more!
"H," the poet: "Beloved, who left me, I take my leave of you..."
"A," with the pole, steps forward and looks around): Grayness
"H," the poet: "I will not be the bard of grayness!"
"A" with his pole (prods the Moon into center stage; to the poet): Shut up!
Violins: in B Minor
"Z," the author of tragedies (to "A"): Sir! You are a director of sublime genius!
"T," a girl (approaches, accompanied by several young men): But kind sirs I am still a
VIRGIN
Young men: Ooooh...Aaaah...Tsk,tsk,tsk...
"T," the girl (falls into their arms)
"G," the worker (brings a ladder)
"A," with the pole (leans the ladder against the wall, climbs up on it, and with his pole
paints the moon purple)
Purple light
Violins: in B Minor; cellos: wail away
"H," the poet: "I am death's kinsman, in love with fleeting love..."
Young men (applaud and tip the Poet, and carry off the Girl)
"H," the poet (visibly electrified): "Up flew the peacock, on the county courthouse..."
(in a red light)
ALL: Shut up! Shut up! Filthy swine! Shut your mouth!
Kettle drums, smaller drums: start beating
"H," the poet (shrinks away)
"S," the war hero: Heh-heh-heh
"P," the scientist: For Kalogeropoulos is a grrreat man!
"š," the sad sack (bows down)
"C," the gentleman (singing): "Drink up buddy, drink it up, you'll see better with an
empty cup..." (he goes blind)
"H," the poet (tiptoes squatting): "If there was a copper eel, it would keep an even
keel..." (rose-colored light; he is thrown a coin)
"U," with flashing eyes (approaches with a light in his eyes): I, you, he, we, you, they—
Chomp! I'll eat you up!
"E," the lady: Why you milksop, you dishrag...phooey! get lost! (shoves "D" out of the
easy chair)

"D" the young man: Wa-ah-ah…my pure love…(climbs up on pile of stones, wants to jump off)

"B," the smart aleck: Eternal youth! No more bald heads!

"D," the young man (sidles over to him)

"P," the scientist: For Lloyd George is a grrreat man!

"š," the sad sack (Bows down)

"Z," the author of tragedies: And yet I shall write my great tragedy! (he writes)

"U," with flashing eyes: Chomp! Chomp! (he steps over to "E")

"E" and "U": You love me!? I love you! Love me! I love you! You love me?! I love you! Now! Now!

"O," the priest: BLE-ESSED are the ones who meet

"I," the American (keeping rhythmic time): Business is business!

"J," the Frenchman (gesticulating): Libert, ,galit, fraternit,!

"K," the Russian (leaps up, kneels down, beats his forehead against the floor three times): Prostyitye prostyitye prostyitye

"L," the Czech (striking a statuary pose): Pravda vitezi!

"M," the German (dumbfounded): Der Kaiser Der Kaiser!

"N," the Hungarian: Independent bank duty zone chivalry

"G," the worker (stops working)

Horns, drums large and small: a cacophony

"T," the girl (approaches war hero): Come marry me you handsome blond warrior…

"S," the war hero: Heh-heh-heh (twitches spasmodically)

"T," the girl: I was a virgin

"Ü," the sad sack (bows in her direction with gushing ecstasy)

"S," the war hero: Heh! Heh! Ooooo! (rushes at him with his cannon) Boom!

"Ü," the sad sack (falls down)

"S," the war hero: Heh-heh-heh-heh

"Z," the author of tragedies: Pootzi-Mootzie is dying with love

"Ü," the sad sack (sits up, speaks to "S"): My good sir, I am not mad at you (dies)— (triangle sound)

The international table in bright light

A Voice: Gentlemen, the return to full production…

"I," "J," "K," "L," "M," "N": all leap up and embrace in a circle

"P," the scientist: For Vladimir Ilyich Lenin is a grrreat man!

"O," the priest: Ooh Lord, for endless is thy…

"G," the worker (picks up a stone and throws it at the Moon)

The Moon breaks into smithereens

Violins, cellos moan

"H," the poet: Wah-ah-ah-ah… The *synbolon*, the *synbolon*…

"E," the lady: Now, now…

Bassoons: guffaw

The chromatic scale stops playing

"A," with the pole: Hooey, hooey! (he roars, and impales the Worker on the pole)

"G," the worker: Long li-i-…(he dies)

Horns, bassoons, contrabasses

"C," the gentleman: Say, what's going on here? (he drinks)

"I," "J," "K," "L," "M," "N" (all leap up and stand around the stone structure built by

"G," the Worker): Crash! Crash! The stock market…

"B," the smart aleck: I'm buying! I'm buying!

"A," with the pole: Gentlemen! Gentlemen! (runs around in panic) Music! Extra lights! Wine! Women!

Orchestra plays "C'mere You Nobody"

Wine bottles sprout from the ground and drop from the sky.—Lights.

"SZ," the dancer floats onto the stage, naked

Voices: Aaah...Ooooh...Tsk, tsk, tsk...

Gradually everyone resumes their places

"A," with the pole, carefully adjusts the Sun and the business signs.

"Z," the author of tragedies: Did something happen?

All watch the dancer

"O," the priest: smacks his lips and leers

Little girls, scantily clad, approach in dance step

"O," the priest: SUFFER the babes to come unto me!

"S," the war hero: Heh-heh-heh-heh

"T," the girl, kneels in front of him and pulls him on her

"P," the scientist: For Torama Morama Borama is indeed a grrreat man!

"C," the gentleman (stands up, stumbles forward blind drunk, bumps into a pile of stones. The stones tumble down.) Drink up buddy drink up...(but everyone is busy with themselves)

"Z," the author of tragedies: Pootsie Mootsie threw herself from the fourth floor. Curtain, applause. (Takes his bows)

"S," the war hero: Lo-lo-lo-love muh-muh-muh-me!

"A," with the pole (thumps out the beat. The pole drives a hole into the sky. Red wounds gape down at the merrymakers.)

"SZ," the dancer, jumps up on the international table. Everyone grabs a different part of her body. They all clink glasses.

"I," the American: Cheers!

"J," the Frenchman: Vive!

"K," the Russian: Da zdravsz tvujet!

"L," the Czech: At zhiye!

"M," the German: Hoch!

"N," the Hungarian: Éljen! (Kisses)

"H," the poet (approaches holding a plate): Erato... Erato... Erato...

Various anthems played on string instruments; pianos play music hall ditties, waltzes; organs perform psalms; piccolos shriek.

Horns, bassoons bellow

"A," with the pole, stands grinning and thumping out the beat. A shower of red light.

Curtain.

Translated by John Bátki

GREEN-HEADED MAN   Sándor Barta
Originally published as "A zöldfejü ember," *Ma* vol. 6, no. 3 (March 1921)

THE GREEN-HEADED MAN

or

an active cadaver's manifesto to cab horses and to

elevators

or

TO ALL TUBERCULOTICS OF THE WORLD

or

esteemed humanity

or

the intensity of every faith equals the total amount of

inertia

or

SANDOR BARTA

OR 1920

...but there is no justice and even if there is it's

always independent of justice. So why not simply, honestly

LET EVERYBODY PROCESS

HIS OWN!

BECAUSE

it is physical death to lose an argument

physical death to believe anything

PHYSICAL DEATH TO AGREE WITH ANYONE

PHYSICAL DEATH TO SENSE THE TRUTH OF

ANYTHING

PHYSICAL DEATH TO BE A PART OF ANYTHING

part of the soil, part of some faith

BECAUSE

1) a) b) c) d) i)

I am an active cadaver

AND

e) f) g) h) aitch)

I have no intention of ENDING UP UNDER A BELL

lovely syphilitic girls on rollerskates

scream glass under a saccharine-toothed moon!

There is no space immaterial color form

absolutum

all is material geometry and the all has

no geometry...I must not argue

for only I know that truth is violent sexuality

Truth: the cross-section of stasis

Truth: the drain of energies into inertia

The Truth

equally kills

GOOD and EVIL

THERE ARE NO

TRUTHS,

this is not true either

there are no truths, no common roots

to actions no truths so no common goals

for all humankind no truths so

NO COLLECTIVE ACTS

THERE IS

SUN

PHOSPHORUS

CARBON and AIR

there is

CHEMISTRY

there is

therefore suggestive matter
I too am suggestive matter
BECAUSE a cab horse reared up in front of me
with the NEEDLEhaired little old lady
BECAUSE a girl joys herself to a swoon
on my meat
BECAUSE yesterday a student stabbed himself
with a kitchen knife on top of the highest
streetlight

Watch out!! / literature! / to be omitted!!
I AM THE BROTHER OF CAB HORSES AND ELEVATORS
BECAUSE they are suffering matter incapable of
either belief or denial
BECAUSE they are the whinnying mortar for my
constructions
in the groin of
buildings
streets
harbors
BECAUSE they are the ones who
never hurt me and I can still
reach down into their throats
they simply revolve with bloody-toothed cows
and swim around in plank-lined streets
above them only one house left standing
without windows
and madmen weep red telephone wires
into the march
THE INSANE ARE THE ONLY SERIOUS
MEMBERS OF SOCIETY
the insane sing all night
the insane sing all day
and from behind white fences graze into the sun
I AM INSANE
AND THE SOBER FOLKS ship around me warm gardens
schools to make you smart and preserved virgins
and lantern-brained churches
FOR MADMEN ARE THE MOST SUGGESTIVE MATERIAL
FOR MADMEN ARE THE PUREST HARMONY
THE SUN is insane WATER insane THE NIGHT insane
those who meet in them laugh and scream in fright
only
madmen stand on mountaintops and lightning rods
singing
the silver in mines is on their side
spaceless electricity is on their side
come!!! approach them!!!
LOGIC IS A CAGE
and you mustn't peak and you can't fit inside
and nothing is logical under the sun
IT'S LOGICAL to dive head first at a soldier's bayonet
LOGICAL if a sooty slut bites through your neck under

the lamp-post
LOGICAL rooftop chimneys fields blind beggars waterfalls
THE GREEN DAY IS LOGICAL
tuberculotics are LOGICAL
all day walking on their heads to stay in touch
with matter at least on that point
LOGICAL that a girl silently started to levitate
over the most crowded marketplace
and raised her rachitic hands like two
flowers of pure gold by her ears
LOGICAL that a shoemaker's son is a shoemaker
and suddenly it is night
FAITH IS LOGICAL
and the depth of every faith equals the total amount of
inertia
How much laughter is there in the bawl of a slaughtered ox
and how much less composition
nobody can compose me
warm unstoppable motion am I and always
more or less than myself
AND COMPOSITION IS STASIS
But I can gargle myself out in a guffaw
and sing myself out in a howl
Culture will spit me in the eye I know but I have long ago
spat out culture and would not call myself a man of culture
not for a handful of manure
I do not know geography mineralogy and zoology
do not know water is made of wood
do not know the sun is green blue and red
as for the dead madonnas in museums I would like to
bite them off the walls and hang the visions of madmen there
and their forever trumpeting brains
AGAINST REASON
THE ONE THING THAT DOES NOT EXIST
AGAINST REASON
BECAUSE IT'S BELLOWED AT ME AS AN ABSOLUTE
and what's the reason for the rooster's cry
the kids' whistle the derailed express train
the consecrated cannons the sinking cities
REASON IS DAYTIME
SEX
because at night we are simply pigs at our cows'
udders   And I cannot be understood
but I can be grazed up like tasty alfalfa
Horses graze me up and whinny me out into the air
and I too whinny out hard buckteeth smells breasts
and penises
and never try to get close to my own reason
for that would be my most unreasonable manifestation
AGAINST RESPONSIBILITY
because it's a bell they want to tie to my ankle
AGAINST RESPONSIBILITY

because there are no shared measuring tools
AGAINST RESPONSIBILITY
because there is no one I owe
because only losers' lives can share a common ground
and there are no losers
RESPONSIBLE I AM NOT
because the wind blew a car into the river
because a woman gave a revolutionary lye to drink
because revolutionaries sing the harmonies of madness
NOT RESPONSIBLE NOT EVEN FOR MYSELF
BUT I CAN PROVE to anyone anytime
both I and my opponent are right
also THE OPPOSITE
BECAUSE THE OPPOSITE OF EVERYTHING IS ALSO TRUE
I'm a worthless good-for-nothing I know
and know there's not even futility any more
I only want to know one thing
WHAT COULD SIRIUS SMELL LIKE
and anyway it's all the same but
now it's night already red dragons
barked forth by brothel hovels the wind
gargles pressed cats' heads in the alleys
in place of my heart green
cows low at the moon over the towers

Translated by John Bátki

THE FIRST GATHERING OF THE MAD IN A GARBAGE BIN   Sándor Barta
Originally published as "Az őrültek elsö összejövetele a szemetesládában," *Akasztott
Ember* vol. 1, no. 1 (1922)

It was at night. You could still hear the guffawing of the moon. Under a street lamp
I spied the garbage bin out of which a chorus of male bassos swirled upward like
smoke.
    I stepped over to the ventilation hole and my eyes saw a horrible sight.
    2 marionette-like women and 5 men with matted hair
    sat with bulging eyes, leaning back against the wall of the bin, that makes 7 of
them
    The silence was ghostly. A dreamy daze. Stillness of night.
    12 church clocks each struck 12 times = 144
    A housemaid holding a bottle of lye sat upon Christ's shoulder. A streetcar conduc-
tor with blue trouser button eyes on his beer belly.
    OH WOE!
        WHEREUPON I ENTeRED
    The snoring of seals placed under the doorsill painted my face yellow.
    A birdlike candle flame guttered in the middle, red ink blinked from a blue skull-
cup, and above the members

1 2 3 4 5 6 7
rusty, skinny gallows nails roosted, like crows

PSST!

AND THEN

Someone with a decidedly Slovakian accent raised his forefinger.

At the same time some burglars who deserved better extracted with their pickaxes 13 maidens drowned in honey from the safe of an Argentinean millionaire (Daily Mail)

"THE KING," whispered a thin female voice, and there was adoration and there was a coffin, and only the labor unions of birds of paradise flourished throughout the cosmos.

And this was when Collective Lajos, while he aimed the soles of his feet at an acute angle toward the polar star of the rising Big Dipper, pronounced his historical aphrodite:

The braces have died!

Long live the suspenders!

O-o-oh bra-a-ces, sang a thin female voice, o-o-oh bra-a-ces

Only the story of Quiet Melancholy or the perspective of 5 years made a totally incomprehensible motion, and before Collective Lajos could push the trouser button placed under his hairline, he pulled a hatpin from a hiding place next to his mouth, stuck it into every one of his fingers, extracting 2,452,678 cells, and began to speak at a rapid pace about the history of the graverobbers of Madagascar down to our days, while inscribing 48 little circles like this in the air and rattling nonstop:

"Old grave-robber," hissed The Man Passing for Sober through his teeth, while launching into an urgent expos. of outward curves which he vehemently labeled the vile psychic constructs of the bourgeoisie, and then went on:

Fatheads! Bourgeois! Non-painters!

The straight soul does not recognize any geometric curves!

Death! groaned the assembly.

Down with space, the dimension of winter and the belly!

By now no one paid any attention to Quiet Melancholy; he was playing chess with his poor little cells off in a corner and he kept squeezing more and more of them out of his fingers.

The muttering and mumbling rose to a chaos pitch.

Collective Lajos asked permission to speak in order to explain his misunderstood words:

And he spake:

Dear company!

My highly esteemed sirs

This is not how we play; balls to the highly esteemed practical speaker before me— the cosmos we are talking about is on my side!

Quiet Melancholy and The Man Passing for Sober for a good reason are two painters, but my good sirs, painting is +

killed by life itself, dearly beloved fellow mourners (he faltered), that bestial Life which we kept capitalizing in our proclamatory lines. I however will bring it back to you again, ah, tread softly around it, its name, ah, is beautiful, but its ears, alas, are awfully full of spiders and linger disconsolately in the department store called twilight.

But it is the only one that does not want anything.

For "picture architecture does not want anything."

Picture architecture exists because it can!

But painting does not exist for it is dead.

I am Collective Lajos.
My wife is the first Dadaist actress.
Sándor Barta is a genius.
And this will never end.

And now Simple Jolán stepped out of the closet bearing a condensing vessel tied with a blue ribbon upon her right palm and she too instantly announced that surely a-oo-da ba-oo-da hojo-modo-ho, and what's more it's snow, and then stood on two legs and her vo-o-o-ice so-o-o-oared (vvvvvvvvvv) and it was made of hedgehogs (wwwwwwwwwww) and tissue paper airplanes that tried in vain to mount the spiral stairway leading to the stars and kept crashing among the towers, amidst the simple-minded buttercups.

János, who at the time was imprisoned in Kosice, now suddenly appeared in a forest of shining coconut palms in the sky of the garbage bin, with dreadful clumps of hair hanging from his ears, and we quite distinctly heard as he nearly closed his parchment lips, probably meaning to say:
Ex, mex, lex,
serpent, prunes, golden key,
blue and not green curtain, moveable actors
veiled sounds from the direction of the orchestra
two or three more curtains
a woman who pretends to be the backdrop
a jaundiced eye
floating to and fro between the curtains
yellow yellow yellow blue blue blue
a church chord in underpants loiters in the middle
(all curtains down)
"Antler, orange, bat ear," said someone in the ghostly night, the yellow spot we all carried on our foreheads, and we all saw Simon at the gathering of spiritualists, spookily scratching himself under the bed, his hair curtained to his spiritual eyes, his fingers in a plate fragment, he was conjuring up his favorite topic, the bird of paradise consumed for lunch:
O little bird, he stammered,
will I be a meteorite?
will I be a meteorite?

This was followed by a dreamy silence, then a soft murmur arose from the corners and Lajos the Second stood up to manage the following circular telegram to all the organized quadruped accord workers of Europe:
Fellow workers! Quadrupeds! Non-Jews!
In Budapest the equality of cab horses and army officers has been proclaimed!
Death to them! roared the assembly.
Arise and march in closed ranks to the House of Parliament!
Guitars and bread and butter are required!
Military band music all day long! *Heurige* in the moving water pipes!
Nur für Proletarier, die durch schamlose kommunistische Propaganda nicht [unintelligible—trans.] *sein wollen!*
Bourgeoisie and Police are requested to stay on the sidewalk
und auf gegebene Zeichen mitsingen!
The procession turned in front of the Green Hunter where excellent fodder is available for the highly esteemed *Arbeiterklasse*.

ARISE! ARISE! ARISE!
!FOR THE GREAT RUMBLE!

Pee-yew, said humanity, referring to Lajos the Second. *Ein warer Dichter nur* our
Collective Lajos, even if Simple Jolán constantly wants to make the esteemed world
order believe the opposite.

But lo, the realist writer lady stood up, raising her two index fingers and said in
the tense silence:

I'm still so little,

But I'll soon grow up,

In a year or two

I'll write the new prose.

Upon this unexpected activity all eyes turned toward Alexander *der Grosse* lest he let
on his already well-developed eccentricity, when he suddenly snatched off his hat and
struck up the Activist anthem:

I, the universal man,

greet you

in the milk-headed cosmos!

"Hallelujah," sobbed the chorus of voices.

And this is where the ritual ended; the mem-
bers, in order to simplify transport, picked up the simple furnishings, and the procession, chanting psalms, wound its way into the cosmos.

And at the head marched Collective Lajos with Simple Jolán by his side, followed
by the Quiet Melancholic or the story of five years' perspective, carrying the suicidal
cells in his right hand, and by his side marched The Man Who Passed for Sober, carrying a placard that said:

Only a Thrill seeker!

and in his wake came János with a parachute and little angels on each side were carrying the blue, then came the realist lady writer carrying the sun on her finger together
with all of its conveniences as well as an elevator, then came Alexander *der Grosse*
with two light journals under his arms and a variety of posters appealing for money,
just as Collective Lajos had described him in writing, and last came Lajos the Second
the laughing gas and chemical engineer who kept mumbling:

gentlemen laugh laugh laugh

life is a carousel carousel carousel

Whereupon we arrived under a street lamp as tall as a giraffe, whose head, as we could
clearly see, contained a box of diamonds between two grinder wheels. The procession
came to a halt.

Next, a horrible thing happened!

THE

documents of the tragedy or the break:

Collective Lajos suddenly halted under the gas lamp and his excellent X-ray vision
discoverd a new but nonetheless yellow artistic element.

"God's eyes can see all, do not steal my soccer ball," said the Quiet Melancholic,
and before Collective Lajos could get there, he put his foot on the new but nonetheless
yellow artistic element, which, at the time, was a bespattered streetcar ticket leading
a profound psychic existence.

The opto-haptic orchestra especially hired for the occasion to play over the city
laid an irreparable kibosh on the evening.

Collective Lajos instinctively stepped back.

A Suprematist square burst into flower under the Quiet Melancholic's nose.

And now it came to pass, yes, in spite of the fact that Collective Lajos had already
set up all the typeface for the latest number of *Nyeherehe*.

Quiet Melancholic triumphantly bent down to touch upon the meaning of all creation, but Collective Lajos with a sweeping gesture and a mocking smile turned and
flipped his cloak aside to let us see that alas his belt had already boasted of two hundred streetcar tickets swinging from a ring.

And in the frightened silence we could hear bursts of his mocking laughter all the
way from distant *Amalienstrasse*.

THE END OF EVERYTHING
AND OF THE FIRST GATHERING
OF MADMEN

Translated by John Bátki

MANIFESTO   Ödön Palasovszky and Iván Hevesy
Originally published as *Manifesztum* (Budapest: 1922)

MANIFESTO 1922
Culture for the Masses
We Demand a New Art
Down with Moldy Figs
A Manifesto for a New Mass Culture

We Demand a New Art

Down with art, for it has sold out.
Down with still-lives.
Down with decoration.
Down with the caterwauling of aesthetes.
Down with the fancy moldy figs of hedonism.
We demand a rapturous, great art for the masses.
We demand the art of the liberated man.
Out into the streets, and face the masses!

NEW MIRACLES FOR THE MARKETPLACES,

new mythologies on the advertising posters, new visions on the walls, new chorales
and new tragedies for the open air.
Art had originated in the rapture of the masses,
but art no longer produces any miracles. Art has become the ornament in the hanging
gardens of sausage manufacturers. Art has become the exotic fruit of cultured society
dames, coconuts, eternal beauty and haut couture. Art has become the Sunday
vaudeville entertainment of tax officials with creased pants. Art has become the dainty
garden of lilies for toothless academics. We are awaiting the prophecy of new
mythologies
but art is no longer capable of any miracles,
art is no longer the shared rapture of the masses, art has become putrefied.
We carry the world's epilepsy in our bones, our foreheads bear the stamp of madness,
but artists are not bothered by the wasting away of humankind,

artists do not scream out our tragedy

but would rather sniff white lilies in the hothouses of art patronesses and spew forth serenades in the light of the moon.   We are praying for saviors, but the artists are not shouting out the names of the new god in public spaces.

We are awaiting the prophecy of new mythologies, but the poet has hidden himself in the ivory tower where he elaborates highly wrought poesy; the masked prophet proclaims aloud his own glory and decks himself out in the adoration of fools. The painters, instead of projecting new mythologies on the walls of houses, choose to daub the bloated mummies of old fairy tales onto small pieces of paper. Painters are taking away the business from photographers by their totally realistic representations of cab horses and the watch chains of butchers. Musicians whistle ecstatically for old geezers filling their bellies at the state fair, or indulge in caterwauling dreamy barcaroles for the world's salvation at night clubs. Actors do not proclaim the tragedy of new myths in the theaters; instead they do somersaults in the circus, playing the droll and sad tale of the cheating bald husband and the tricky cocotte, who can be seen displaying herself in the best seat. Meanwhile the bearded ones bow down and solemnly announce that art is the temple of humanity, and the artist is its prophet!

Artists have become idiots

nurtured at academies and in the beds of prostitutes. Artists can no longer perform miracles. The artist sniffs white lilies in the hothouses of cocottes and luxuriates in his own image. And the fools speak out: Behold the artist's heart, it is a vase of lilies.

Artists have sold out,

they are decorating with lanterns the hanging gardens of fish-mongers. The artist has sold out; the fate of humankind no longer bothers him; he would rather design rose arbors for pseudo-virgins and decorate the glorious residences of salami manufacturers. And in turn he is greeted by the chorus of salami manufacturers: All hail the true Artist!

We want none of this art,

for it is putrid. We want none of it for it fails to fuse in a great rapture the masses of humankind, to teach them the new meaning of life and to lead them toward the stages of a truer culture. We want none of this art, for it does not belong to the masses— nor should it. It is the polluted ecstasy and fancy moldy fig of art salons. But it is too stupid even for that, for it keeps regurgitating itself thousands of times over and over, with slightly different frills, whereas even an ox prefers to have some variety in its diet.

Away with the artist

if he has putrefied and sold out. His successor will not be an idol and will not dwell in ivory towers; will not be a moonstruck troubadour singing about his beloved's beauty spot.

The new artist will step out into the marketplace and proclaim the new phase of culture for the masses.

He will not be writing beautiful books intended for educated families, he will proclaim the new meaning of life on posters in the streets: the liberation of simplicity, the liberation of purity, the miracles of work and of shared rapture. The new artist will not be painting the portrait of Uncle Bob in a straw hat, or carve the statue of dancing city fathers for the promenade; he will be painting the splendid visions of life's new meaning on the walls in public spaces. The new artist will not be lingering in filthy night clubs nor will he be fluting ecstasy for pseudo-virgins in windowless concert halls, but will instead

lead the worshipful choir of the new man in the open air for thousands to hear.

The new artist will not be gesticulating in the sideshow of cocottes, but instead will proclaim the eternally returning tragedy of the ornate cultures with their hanging gardens, and the fate of man struggling to develop a new breed; he will, using the unpretentious, heartfelt gestures of the simple man
suggest the new mythology of mothers and lovers and the new myth of saviors and a thousand other new myths
and what we believe in,
the vision of new, purer and fuller stages to come.
Art had originated in the rapture of the masses and art must be returned to the masses.
When art will once again scream out its message to millions in the public spaces, then it will become an honorable and fanatical force for the new culture. Then it will no longer be a vainglorious delight for its own sake, like the pigtails of a mandarin. It will no longer be a dainty decoration, mouthwash for aesthetes, the inane ecstasy of pseudo-virgins. It will no longer be a five-percent solution for ennobling the souls of high school graduates. It will no longer be an idle game for elderly gentlemen, an aesthetic somersault and a moldy fig. There will be no more delicate sonnets, crudely contrived ballads, and musty novels. No more idiotic portraits and still-lifes, no more fancy daubs that had long evaporated the last trace of rapture. No more inane statues promising eternal life to gentleman riders, for the new rapture will call for
new words on the billboards,
new visions on the walls,
new myths for the arenas,
new Choirs for the marketplaces.
The new artist will be a prophet without a name.
The name of the new artist is rapture.The new art will dictate, for the rapture of the masses, the meaning of a new and pure life, in order to direct the shared rapture of the masses toward newer and fuller stages of culture.

THE POSTER, THE NEWSVENDOR, AND THE WHITE MOVIE SCREEN
will be the excellent means that will, with their live energies, accomplish the splendid work of propaganda that alone deserves to be called art.
Painting will abandon in disgust the somnolent salons of the philistines, the crypts called exhibition halls, and joyfully emerge into the street to face the people.
In the midst of the cheerful, noisy rush of street life art, which has been enchained in prisons for centuries, will once again encounter the crowds, and having found each other they will embrace and cry out in triumphant joy.
Painting, once it is out in the open and facing the masses, will not be offering scented flowers and mooing cows,
but will address the people and will try to persuade them to be good, and to become better.
Painting will, with the moving power of its colors and lines, with its splendid simplicity and clarity of its message, will enlighten the hearts of millions about the recovered truths of their lives,
it will teach them work and solidarity.
The painting shouting in the street will no longer be mere decoration, no mere entertainment that caresses the eyes, but a word shouted out demanding a new order, which will raise its new staircase toward the peak of happiness that has been coveted for tens of millennia.
Painting, revived by the art of the poster, will suggest commands and actions for the masses. But there can be only one command, the eternal command of Ethics: to live for everyone! This imperative has a thousand faces and a thousand demands. These

are all hypnotically suggested by posters. But posters get washed away by rains, and the new throbs of life always proclaim and demand new tasks,

whereas the force of the one and only eternal command is a lasting and eternal scripture.

The eternal power of this scripture will be indelibly proclaimed by the poster of the ages, which is the mural.

The mural, too, will stay in the outdoors, it will not hide in rooms, or else it will shine resplendent

in the temples of the new faith, in meeting halls, and anyplace where it will meet the eyes of the masses.

The painting of the future will be Ethics itself—the Symbol of the new world sensation— awakened to its power in the art of the poster and taking eternal shape in the mural.

LITERATURE

will no longer remain the luxurious delicacy of the select few, will not be relegated to the shelves of cobwebbed libraries or pretentious salons, printed on hand-made paper and bound in silk to await the delectation of surfeited palates.

The libraries shrouded in the winding sheets of Boredom

will turn into repositories of mummies, the quiet amusement of the aged, for litera- ture, when the new life explodes new blood into its veins, will reach out far beyond every musty reading room and sterile salon, to grasp the hands of the People, the hands of millions.

Books and magazines, just as in our days, lose their power in hiding and relinquish the guidance of the People to

newspapers, the living, fluttering banners of active life that is forever on the move. But the newspaper, the new newspaper will not be like the old ones, screeching the trivial, idiotic sensationalism of life: "Chopped up female corpses in a trunk! Seamstress burned to a char! Corruption! Corruption! Corruption!"

The new newspaper will broadcast propaganda for the full, liberated life of the masses.

The new newspapers will lead and instruct, will proclaim the new faith, and will hypnoti- cally suggest it with all the power and every single means of suggestion.

We shall have, instead of poems turned into poor editorials, editorials becoming poems!

And the novel and the short story will no longer serve as a digestive to ensure the peaceful afternoon nap of the well-fed bourgeois, or as the love potion for insatiably hysterical women, but

new epic works about new triumphs, about man victorious in creative work and the embrace of brotherhood.

And just as we shall see transferred from the poster's paper to the mural on the wall everything that transcends the wavelets of daily life and ethics to become eternal command and eternal ethics, even so

the eternal preaching and the new scripture

will fly from the pages of the newspaper onto the pages of books.

Thus literature will no longer be a narcotic drug, or a mere game or entertainment, but

action that creates life and forms our own selves.

THE CUCKOLDED HUSBAND

as the subject of today's theater plays, the stage embodiment of debased philistine tastes and crude idiocy, will be swept away along with the rest of the garbage by the New Times. Today's theater will crumble into dust, the stage where the citizen can nightly regurgitate the miserable little titivations of his narrow life, while his esteemed wife shows off her shoulders and her cleavage. And we shall have no more of the busy street corner where the prostitutes of bourgeois literature and art are hustling their wares.

Drama will be reborn in the new arenas of the People, where symbolic plays will show the destiny of the people.

The people will see the eternally repeating meaning of events in the monumental, hypnotic mirror of the new drama which will point out for them the direction leading toward fruitful acts, as well as its purpose: the Part will always know its one and only path and duty—

to embrace the Whole.

But the largest arena is still diminutive and feeble; the loudest shout reaches only
a few thousand. The new tragic drama will meet its real audience
in the movies that reach hundreds of millions
more successfully than the arenas, more effectively stunning the soul, and seizing the heart of the masses, so that, allied with the poster and the newspaper, it can lead the people toward the New Life, and with the unifying power of its unsurpassable hypnotic power
unfold the visions of the New Life.

AND MUSIC,
which has hitherto sounded off for circus horses, and conjured its many-colored, thousandfold images of a thousand moods and emotions for the benefit of aesthetes reclining dreamily in the seats of concert halls,
music, too, will come to realize the new Rhythm
and will cast off its fancy hues, to roar forth out of the concert halls into the open spaces, and strike up new hymns
and will sing out the monumental choruses of dynamic activity into the hearts of millions,
infusing them with a desire for action, proclaiming the joyous triumph of accomplished tasks, rousing and urging them on
toward the new life and the new man!

Translated by John Bátki

GREEN DONKEY PANTOMIME   Sándor Bortnyik
Originally published as "Zöld Szamár Pantomim," *Periszkóp* (June–July 1925)

(Mechanical Ballet)
Prefatory
There are four actors in the play. Three of them are biased, taking subjective stands toward the play, themselves, and toward each other. The fourth one is the only objective and sober character. The interplay of the three subjective roles dominates only up to the moment the objective character appears on the stage. His appearance disrupts the entire course of the play, puts the whole play in a different light (in a physical sense, as well), and will not tolerate a partial, one-sided denouement. He enters at the right moment, and as soon as he has accomplished his task, disappears. An ideal artist, he does not ask for a greater share in the play's success than his due, he does not keep harping on his own importance, nor does he imagine that the whole world

revolves around himself. (Even though he would be justified in the latter belief. He is not a Naturalist, not an Impressionist, not a Futurist, not an Expressionist, not even a Constructivist. Sometimes he builds, at other times he destroys—as the occasion demands, wherever and whenever construction or destruction is needed. He is a symbol, in the best sense of the word; not frozen and eternal but mobile and always fresh and new. He is a symbol of everything: the sun, the moon, the airplane, the radio, art, literature, history; he is also the symbol of the good and the bad human being. He is as much a symbol of the President of the French Republic as he is of "Mr. Nosey Parker," the busybody critic of our daily papers.)

Thus the actors are:

1. "A," the MAN.
2. "B," the WOMAN.
3. "C," the husband, and
4. THE GREEN DONKEY

The play itself is a perfect and final resolution of the love triangle situation so favored by our theaters.

The Play

There is no curtain concealing the stage. The audience witnesses the installation of the props. A trumpet signals the beginning of the action.

1. The stage is in semi-darkness. The props are being moved around chaotically.
2. The situation is clarified, the stage sets are placed in order at the sides of the stage.
3. Two tall screens, violet in color, stand on the left and the right. The silhouette of a human figure, a man on one side and a woman on the other, becomes gradually visible. They are naked and beautiful. At the feet of each, a large letter: A and B.
4. Full light. Red hearts are lit up on the screens.
5. A and B step forward from the violet walls, now fully clothed. (The projected silhouettes disappear at this moment.) Each figure wears a large red heart hanging from his or her neck.
6. The two figures move toward each other but before they meet a six-foot wall suddenly glides forward to separate them.
7. A and B stand still, puzzled, for a moment. A tries to go around the wall but it keeps blocking his way.
8. A discovers a small round opening in the middle of the wall, looks through it, and taps on the wall. B is all attention, steps forward and now both look through the opening, staring at each other's eyes. A wants to kiss B on the lips, but B prances away (solo dance steps), then, holding her heart with both hands, slowly moves back to the wall and offers the tip of her heart through the opening.
9. A kisses the heart. He thumps at the wall. Then he runs to the stage wall on the left, takes out stationery and a huge pencil, writes a letter, folds it up and hands it through the opening.
10. B reads the letter, takes her heart, wraps it in the letter and tosses it over the top of the wall to A.
11. A cuddles the two hearts against each other, then exchanging the two tosses his own heart over the wall to B, at the same instant as
12. (the two hearts having been exchanged) the first obstacle is removed, the wall glides back, A runs after B, who coyly retreats. A game of catch me if you can. But the woman makes an awkward mistake, for just at the moment when A reaches her, B accidentally touches one of the stage walls, a bell rings, and at this signal in the background
13. two screens part and in the opening stands C (the husband, holding a large sword).

14. C stands in a menacing stance. In place of his heart, naturally, there hangs a sizeable money bag. The red hearts fade away from the screens and their place is taken by yellow money bags. From here on the dominant color is a yellow light, the color of gold. A and B part, frightened, and they move to opposite corners of the stage.

15. C raises one hand, whereupon the central stage walls turn and each extends a grilled fence, to separate A and B from each other.

16. C moves forward with slow, cumbersome dance steps; he brandishes his sword threateningly at A, and gestures at B to come closer; when she does, he attempts to take her heart.

17. B tries to resist. She wants to escape, but the walls obstruct her passage. A attempts in vain to help her, but the walls are in his way as well.

18. C exults triumphantly. The stage is alive with dynamic movement. From here on the action develops at a rapid pace, the actors are in constant movement.

19. B's movements (she keeps trying to escape) turn into a very fast dance. C, as far as his obesity allows, does his best to follow her. Using his sword he corners her and robs her of her heart. He sniffs it and points at A, signaling that he knows that this is A's heart. He intends to stab B with his sword.

20. B again rushes forth from her corner, rips the money bag from one of the rear walls, throws it at C's feet, and when she rips away the other money bag, the back screens part, revealing a dark empty space with nothing but a ladder in it. The ladder bears an inscription: "The peak of dramatic tension."

21. B rapidly climbs up the ladder, sits down at the top, C tries in vain to follow her, nor can he reach her with his sword. B opens her arms in A's direction; A suddenly comes to his senses, he rips away the money bags from the walls surrounding him whereupon these give way, A rushes to the ladder, wrestles the sword from C's hand and kills him with his own sword.

22. B descends from her perch on the ladder, A embraces her, the two move to the front of the stage, the moon shines brightly, a love light is lit up, a violet light flood the stage, the red hearts once again glow on the walls. The walls close, screening the lovers from the viewers' eyes.

23. Now the Green Donkey appears, holding a sign in each hand, one bearing the inscription "What's the moral of the story?" and the other, "What happened to the tragedy?" The light turns green.

24. At a signal from the Green Donkey the screens part, and the action begins again at 21.But this time it is C who stabs A through the heart, A collapses in a corner, B takes out a flask of poison, drinks it and dies, C falls on his sword.

25. Once more the Green Donkey appears, wearing a tophat with a ribbon of mourning, a funeral march strikes up, the Green Donkey marches the length of the stage, the walls bow to him, and three coffins are lowered from above; the screens glide forward and form an unbroken wall that completely closes off the stage.

The End.

Translated by John Bátki

Although some of its elements were adopted by the Polish Futurists, Dadaism did not take off in Poland as a movement. That is not to say that there was no interest in Dadaism or its interpretation, however. Stanisław Ignacy Witkiewicz, known as "Witkacy" (1885–1939), wrote *Papierek lakmusowy* (Litmus Paper) and signed it "Marceli Duchański-Hoax." It was as much a lampoon on the growing avalanche of new art movements (Futurism, Dadaism, etc.) as a self-ironical expression of his own position—that of a Polish artist within the sphere of influence of these movements. Witkacy's parody of a manifesto—his "festo-mani" of Pure Hoaxing, making fun of his own theory of Pure Form and full of an existential pathos of "pure art" uncovering the "Mystery of Existence"— was a game concerned with Dadaism. But the manifesto was certainly not Dadaist in character. On the contrary. It was a manipulative text with more than one layer of meaning, reminiscent of Dadaism in its directness and irony, yet displaying Witkacy's deep attachment to a rather conservative idea of art (in its essence having nothing to do with "hoaxing") and thus rejecting the Dadaist alternative.

Translated by Wanda Kemp-Welch

MANIFESTO (FESTO-MANI)   Stanisław Ignacy Witkiewicz

Originally published as "Manifest (Fest-mani)," in *Papierek lakmusowy* (Zakopane: 1921)

The most beautiful of arts, and who knows
if not the most difficult, is mendacity.
(From a conversation with my friend Chwalistor Womiejek-Hoax in the café
"Destruction")

In the last days of August 1921, two important and so to say connected (*conjoints*) movements came into being: *n'importe-quoi-isme* and *comme-pour-quisme*, meaning anythingism and for-whomism. Their main representatives are: Paul Desbauches, Tristan de Tourmentelles, and Mademoiselle Claire Lafondru. We acknowledge these as the main creators of these novelties (though they are insufficiently theoretically informed) and wish to import the movements to our country, on condition that we will try to formulate in strictly theoretical terms that which, to the aforementioned artists, is simply a powerful instinct, dilating their body and soul.

An avalanche of "movements" is tumbling down on mankind. Scarcely does the most radical of them raise its head and start becoming official, but another is already emerging, whose representatives consider the previous one as "barbaric" as a musty mummy and fling themselves still further into the jaws of the Unknown. This process grows faster by the minute. Famous for its novelty, S.I. Witkiewicz's "Pure Form" and the Futurists' "realist nonsense," are already crumbling beneath the sincere efforts of the Dadaists. For the youngest of us (we are only between 16 and 18, except Józefa Pigoń who is 13), who do not wish to tread the sincerely hackneyed Dadaist pavements but also to make some use of artistic life, these novelties amount to nothing. Why? The simple answer: because of their outward appearance of sincerity, which hides masked intrinsic hoaxing. Our brothers in France have failed to realize this, so we, the Polish pure hoaxers, the name we use to comprise both the aforementioned "connected" movements, will be the first to make this clear.

1) Sincerity has become an impossibility. Already scarce, the sincere mammoths of Futurism and Formism are sighing with despair (not that we or the public care — ha! ha!). Hoaxing shapes movements in ways which are unclear, and for this reason fatal, to their creators.

2) What could be in higher repute than Dadaism?
To some, it may seem pointless to ask this question. But we need at last to tear away the mask which has stifled so many generations and condemned the most talented hoaxers to be pickled in their own juices. It must be said that this way of presenting the problem already contains the substance of a new agenda. Once again we ask: how one can outstrip Futurism and Dadaism?* BY PURE HOAXING. What freedom! What bliss! to be able at last to begin hoaxing blissfully and luxuriously. Hooray!! Our chests expand, our hair blows free, our eyes pop out of our heads. Pure Hoaxing!! The first and the last to do so, WE speak, shout and howl this magical word, which nobody else has had the courage to pronounce. Nobody is going to outstrip us. Moreover, our hoaxing is real — it is not concerned with external appearances as printed poems are, for example.
What do the discoveries of Futurism and Dadaism matter compared to this shattering avowal? Away from stinking recesses and partitions of dubious width — to the

---

* The futuristification and dadaification of Formists will be a matter of weeks — at most months, unless these deluded sincere mammoths, standing on the edge of a precipice, wake up to themselves. [Author's original note]

sea, to the Oceans of Pure Hoaxing! We, and the whole of mankind, feel light all of a sudden. That which once seemed to be an impossible dream, has come true: we have outdone the Futurists and the Dadaists, not to mention Pure Form, which is, because it implies programmatic sincerity and metaphysics (ha! ha!), a dried up and crumbling mummy. Hooray!! How light and wonderful everything is!! Hooray!!!! We also manage to avoid the dangers of the small dimensions of our compositions. A sincere fellow makes a cross out of four threads, makes a woodcut or an engraving of it and then sells them in luxury folders. "Why have you done so little?" buyers ask him. "Had I made but one more line, had I worked but five minutes longer, I would have been insincere." It cannot be helped—he is right. It is the same with poetry. Two words are enough to make a poem, so long as we add to them a circle on a stick. "It could not be helped—I could not be insincere." This problem does not exist for us: we can create kilometer long poems and hectare large canvases with a clear conscience, hoaxing without a care. At the same time we knock the deadly weapon—the accusation of insincerity—out of the Philistines' hands.

3) But let us recover from our initial delight. As much as a little hoaxing (pretending to be partly Picasso or Boccioni, partly oneself, or amazing oneself etc.) is a simple matter, attaining Pure Hoaxing is an extremely hard task. We must acknowledge that the concept of Pure Hoaxing is limited. Lies and truth are so intertwined in the human being that it is not at all easy to distill the first of these in its Pure Form (but in another sense than the one you use, Mr. Witkiewicz), not to utter a single word of Truth, not to make a single line or a single smear in the clay sincerely, ho! ho! It is even seemingly impossible. But we, the pure hoaxers, adore impossibilities. From this moment (11a. m. 13.9.1921) that's it—THE END. WE ARE HOAXING, nous hoaxons, wir hoaxeren, noi hoaxamo, hoaxujemy. Sweaty, unwashed, unshaven, hungry—we shall not give in, we shall work like ants, like "badgered hyenas." We have yet to see who it is that will be riding their own trains: us—or the Dadaists.

We make the task more difficult for ourselves (nobody should accuse us of trying to get off lightly) by making some additional assumptions; we rule out: demonism, pornography, metaphysics, and social issues. With regards to society, we must make a note of the fact that we are not affiliated to any party: we are as indifferent to the problems of human existence and as harmless as dogs, cats, sheep, and even insects.

Our only relatively social activity is rescuing non-domestic insects from roads, footpaths and ponds. The actual agency for this division is the "Insect Ambulance" (IA). Chairman: Chwalistor Womiejek-Hoax, Zakopane, villa "Florcia," Kiełbasówka on Cyrhla.

5) The terrible boredom of "always being oneself" vanishes. Unhappy slaves to their own consistency, say to themselves: "I am this way, and I must be this way till the end." This is untrue—I can pretend to be anything and in this way free myself from the damned identity of personality. Existentially and artistically carefree. Ladies, and even ordinary women, know something about this. Hooray!!

6) We acknowledge absolutely no difference between the sexes in matters of creativity. Women (let us say it openly) even have precedence (womanism).

7) Everyone has the right to create anything he likes and to be pleased with it, so long as he is not sincere in his work, and has not found anyone as mendacious as himself to admire it. We embrace all hitherto unacknowledged movements: neo-pseudo-cretinism, jokerism, making-a-fool-ism (Polish lyingism is still in the egg, but we accuse it of too great a dose of demonism. One representative: Józefa Pigoń-Hoax, aged 13, is already shifting in our direction), neo-tricksterism, monkeyism, parrotism, neo-buffoonery, deceitism, solipsisticism, mystificationism,

take-for-a-ride-ism, cheatism, neo-humbugism, shifty-ism, pretendingism, (being different form pretendism, i.e. that which one pretends for the sake of success), play-the-clown-ism, insincerism, lead-up-the-garden-path-ism, take-in-ism, slyism, braggism, falsehoodism, leg-pull-ism, persuade-ism, say-whatever-springs-to-mind-ism, distractionism, make-a-nuisance-of-yourself-ism and talk-nonsense-ism, deludism, fidgetism and wrigglism. The representatives of all these movements will be able to take a deep breath in our delicious atmosphere of Pure Hoaxing. (Works are to be delivered to The Editor, "Gazeta Zakopiańska" [Zakopane Gazette], Polish Bazaar, Krupówki, on Mondays, Wednesdays and Fridays between 12 and 1 p.m.).

8) Without fully understanding its meaning (here lies the whole charm of the matter), we will borrow the term Multiplicity of Reality form the book of the prominent logistician Leon Chwistek. We thrust aside all reference in this work to: philosophy, theory of types and theory of form. Down with form and metaphysics! Down with types! One great shambles in the multiplicity of reality of the nth order. It can't be helped—we have not invented this word—we are very sorry—but we are going to take it and use it without defining its meaning any more closely. There is a multiplicity of reality! Hooray!!! We were all feeling this and could not find the word to describe it. Now we have this little word and will not let go of it. Internal life towers over the chaos of the wildest contradictions. Each belongs to one reality, and to one only. Nevertheless, the reality of pure hoaxing dominates them all and brings everything together into one, great, joyous, drunken revel!!!

9) There is no such thing as an artistic "hangover," there is no such thing as a botched work, and there is no effort or work in the old, nasty sense of the word. There is only HOAXING! At this cost we are unconstrained, happy! On top of this, we are the first to have dared to say so—we are truly great!! Our creativity is eternal, because one can hoax always and everywhere, in any social or individual circumstances. Hence our indifference to all social changes.**

10) Does Hoaxing have a demoralizing effect on us? No—a thousand times NO. Open Hoaxing ennobles. It is common knowledge that conjurers are the most honest of people. Besides, ask the members of our movement: eternally satisfied, polite, humble, and good, not jealous of anyone, not accusing anyone of anything—we go about like animals immersed in the Absolute Beauty of internal harmony between ourselves and the world. Deliberate, self-aware, unconstrained Hoaxing is greater than any number of small, subconscious little lies. Do you understand this, you unhappy ones who did not yourselves first arrive at this conception? How you will come to envy us one day!

11) We are not afraid of influences. Yet another nightmare is lifted from our shoulders. Hoaxing in satirical magazines, imitations and falsifications—does not exist for us. That which certain "comics" do for fun, for a laugh, we do with solemnity, with a sense of real happiness. Can there be anything loftier? We can consciously pretend anything or be insincerely original in our own way, without having to hide this beneath a mask of joking or false originality. If I want, for example, to pretend to be Stern or Czyżewski, I say so openly in my heading, not as a joke but with deep solemnity, and moreover without in this way disguising any creative inability—I am simply pretending. The only danger of Pure Hoaxing, is that sincere works may be smuggled into our publications. This cannot be helped—every movement has its dangers. And besides, our friend Ch. Womiejek-Hoax (following the model of the

** It is supposedly impossible to hoax under torture. But since the likelihood of this is small, we need not take it into account. [Author's footnote]

Dadaists, who attach "dada" after their surnames, we add the term "Hoax") has some sort of secret criteria for finding out sincerity, even in the smallest quantities.

12) Our conception may be hard to grasp against the background of our society's lack of philosophical education, and even its "mogulness." But perhaps popularizers will be found. This is the last time we will play around with theory.

In the meantime: down with "intellectual diarrhea" a la Witkiewicz, as Adolf Neuwert-Nowaczyński rightly wrote, down with his disguised "jokerism," as Grzymała-Siedlecki aptly termed it, down with the entire knowledge and learning of Chwistek, down with Irzykowski, Stern, Bołoz-Antoniewicz and Wat, down with the whole of the Skamander group, Dadaism and all manner of Renewals!!!

Long live clean, delightful, conscious of its power, unconstrained, shameless HOAXING! Hoaxing! What bliss to pronounce this word openly, not about others whose talent one envies, but to say it about oneself, and one's closest soulmates.

Oh Hoaxing! Pure Hoaxing—who shall ever outdo you?!!!!

Marceli Duchański-Hoax
Editor (Villa "Niemoc," Nędzówka in Kościeliska near Zakopane)

Translated by Klara Kemp-Welch

The origins of Yugoslav Dadaism can be traced to the friendship of Dragan Aleksić and Branko Ve Poljanski. While in Prague in 1921, they organized Dadaist and Zenithist evenings that brought them into contact with such prominent German Dadaists as Kurt Schwitters, Raoul Hausmann, Walter Mehring, Richard Huelsenbeck, and Max Ernst.

As the Prague correspondent for *Zenit*, Aleksić created poetry according to his ideas of *orgart* (organic art) and generated a series of essays, polemics, and manifestos advocating Dadaism. In his manifesto "Dadaism," (*Zenit* no.3, 1921), he declared that art functioned at the primitive, preconscious level of the nervous system. He thus rejected the theoretical foundations of Expressionism in favor of an idea of abstraction as a direct, unself-conscious encounter with nerves rather than thoughts or feelings. In "Kurt Schwitters Dada" (*Zenit*, no. 5, 1921), Aleksić examined Schwitters in opposition to the Berlin Dada circle, and viewed his poetry collection *Anna Blume* in the context of post-Expressionist abstraction. Aleksić's text on Vladimir Tatlin corresponds to the Berlin Dadaists' reading of the Russian artist, viewing him not as a Constructivist but, rather, as a representative of so-called machine art.

In 1922 Branko Ve Poljanski began publishing *Dada-Jok* (meaning Dada-Nyet or "No Dada") in Zagreb as an "anti-Dada" journal. Together with his brother Ljubomir Micić, he published manifestos, poetry, and prose, employing new types of graphic solutions, as well as certain techniques borrowed from film. Poljanski favored parodies and Dadaist political provocations; this is where he most differed from Aleksić, who prefered to cultivate the aesthetic side of Dadaist practice (and who published two Dada periodicals of his own in Zagreb in 1922—one issue apiece of *Dada Tank* and *Dada Jazz*).

What the two shared was an aspiration toward abstraction uncontaminated by conventional ideas of meaning. In this, they helped lay the groundwork for the Surrealist poetry—with its emphasis on word-games based on the play of sounds rather than on syntax or logic—that emerged in Belgrade in the mid-1920s.

Translated by Maja Starčević

"Panoptic goes through the Looking Glass" (Fragment from a Zenithosophic DADA
Fragment)

"Don't worry, shoe, I'll put you on. Isn't it lovely watching a bullfight and the picadors'
bravery. It's so real."

These words fell from who knows whose mouth and who knows who was listening.

The day before yesterday they hanged a man for all the good reasons on one hand. But
all men have two hands, unless they have fought for the homeland and the just cause
and as a result have one genuine prosthetic device instead of a hand. So a man with
two healthy hands will want to see why they have, on the other hand, hanged that man.
But a person who shares the logic of people who hang other people must not have had
a good second hand. The surgeon foretold a terrible future for it and then cut it off.
So the other hand has no business looking for its rights: it's not really a hand; it's a—
prosthesis. A hypothesis.

There were a number of people, dogs, horses, etc. out strolling this afternoon.
Everything entered the bright plane of the looking glass. Everything metamorphosed
into imagination and everything died.

Here is everything that entered the bright plane of the looking glass:

> churches and nuns
> motor cars and salesgirls
> kings and invalids
> newspapers and bricklayers
> suns and moons
> stars and infamous whores
> journal editors and kangaroos.

The moment they stepped across the mirror's frame, everything turned to stone.
Boom! Something broke. It was the thick head of the American potato king.

The poetry of the vortex is grand. The vortex is the first and the final sense of sense.
So how can anyone blurt out the word
Nonsense.
That means there has to be sense too!
And what is the sense of nonsense? Nonsense! And what is nonsense?
It is a very beautiful idea for something that not even the hellish human mind can
fathom.
But nonsense makes sense!
Its sense is that it holds a terribly important place in the world of our ideas. And what
is outside the idea?
Everything that cannot fly into the mirror's plane is outside the idea.
What is a mirror?
It is a thing without which the idea of an object could not be understood. An object exists
only if you can see its reflection.
In San Francisco, a city made of stone, there is an opium den. You can see another world
there, a world where ordinary citizens cannot go. The body is sacrificed to the pain of
spasms so as to discover a new world where one lives without a body—where one lives
as a fluid.
Trance! Trance! Trance!

Oh, life must be maddeningly boring for people who don't know the pleasures of life outside concrete forms, outside sausages and marmalade.

A mill grinds all palpable forms. Down to their etheric rebirth. And then every thing appears in its true form:

It is not

That *not* is really the shortest path for Mr Donkey to get to his hay.

Not = Is.

Is = Not.

(Do not be ashamed of confusion, dear reader!)

In your eyes, my dear, there is a strangely magical glimmer of divinities whose faithful have been lost to values.

No one believes

in anything anymore!

The sinners of the new age

believe

only in

Negation

Negation is the source of all good

Amen!

To live till tomorrow, today has to pass. And if this were not so, ugh; a terrible, boggy, reeking swamp would appear instead of time.

> *Always tomorrow*
> *Always tomorrow*
> *Always tomorrow*

The eternity of 777 eternities.

(To be continued in the next issue.)

DADA
ANTI-DADA

Dada is the final consequence of the Europeanization of cabaret intellectualism.

Dada is an activity of all armed minuses that have found themselves on the borders of a new age.

I am a Dadaist, because I am not!

If you buy your afternoon papers in Berlin, you've bought a *Dada* world view. You'll see Dadaists all around you walking along Moscow's streets. Every coolie in Peking is a Dadaist. And just because all these people are Dadaists, they are also anti-Dadaists. (Don't be confused, Citizens!)

Why aren't Dadaists Dadaist?. Just keep driving. I became a Dadaist and I stopped being a Dada in the same second. Keep going straight.

Dada! Pan-Dada! Ultra-Dada! Hyper-Dada! People who don't know you can't imagine your quarrelsome nonchalance, Dada Europe hereditary syphilis! Who's the real dada! Tristan Tzara! A Romanian! A degenerate intellectual Suckling Piglet. And that is why I adore Dada: I just love fresh roast piglets! I am a Dadaist!

Anti-Dada is winning. I am an anti-Dada, because I deflowered Anna Blume in a Prague city park.

To think. Not to think. To think up. To think through. To think of.

> DADA
> ANTIDADA
> ZENITH

Mankind cried its eyes out and became Dadaist.

The whole world is a

dadaworld

And so, one bright morning the grand master of all Dadaists drove his motor car across the border of the land of. Serbs, Croats, and Slovenes, chock full of hot air, gunpowder, and booming spirits

Anti-Dada

in person

Ljubomir Micić.

All fingers pointed at him.

All eyes stared at him.

All curses fell on him.

All flappers made faces at him.

All the Begovićs were shocked

All the Krležas blushed

    a fiery red

All the Vinavers dropped

    to their knees.

All the journalists' skulls

       were hermetically

          sealed.

All the citizens vociferated

All the café tables petrified

The whole city of Zagreb sank into an ocean of laughter

And the grand Dadaist master

The first great Anti-Dada

Counter-Dada

Zenithist

Counter-pseudo-zenithist

GOD OF THE DADAISTS

    LJUBOMIR MICIĆ

collected all this laughter in a copper jug and preserved hurricanes of laughter for the time when

      the anti-Dada barometer

    starts pointing to

     a hurricane

Crocodiles had made good friends with kings of all literatures and were put on contract to devour all the issues of *Zenit* so not a single idea could see the light of day from the crocodiles' insides.

And then the European advertising agency, a.k.a.

DADA

arrived and offered its marketing services to Zenithism. It printed brochures in all languages, living and dead:

What is Zenithism?

Zenithism is still the best remedy for getting rid of intellectual blight!

Zenithism is a tried and true remedy for treating rheumatism of the skull.

Zenithism in powder form is still the best means of purging your stomach, especially if you've been eating glass.

Swallow an entire sausage factory and take some zenithism drops and you will recover.

Zenithism is the best remedy for neck pain if you can't think zenithistically.

What is Dada?

What is Anti-Dada?
How can you become "ein echter Dadaist"?
You must become
        an anti-Dadaist.
Sit in a wheelbarrow, embrace an airplane, swim through a sewer, enter Eugen
Demetrović's belly and disembark in New Zealand. It's the best path to Dadaism.

Translated by Maja Starčević

DADAISM   Dragan Aleksić
Originally published as "Dadaizam," *Zenit* no. 3 (April 1921)

Art used to be tedious, boring. A moment's growth, a part, a detail of a shock, and revolt.
Art is what the *nerves* express. Nerves are primitive. Feeling comes when a body is
receptive and about to think. Feelings are not nerves. Nerves are primeval, unspoiled,
unselfconscious strength. Primitivism has a *basis*.
The realism of truth is always circulating. Truth is my idea (2 x 2 = 5), as is its contrast
illusion. Therefore, to call truth objective is not correct. Morality is a sunken kind of
truth, and all kinds of truths today are sunken. Morality (hither, come hither, salvation
lies this way!) fetters, and truth has begun. Let us take the world and examine it like a
cow on sale. (Comet-fear threatens!) That is why DADA strives for as-you-like-it-ness.
Joy is both an illusion and truth, joy, the basis of all. It needs longevity.
Everything is a symptom. Speech and its results are a symptom. (Absolute algebra!)
Only what is most honest is used. And that means no madness, although the Cosmos
is a factory of nothing but madness and in the extreme, madness = anger, though not
sense. The most honest anger of the most honest person. Doing without knowing what
you are doing means giving yourself.
Not staging truths, reality, demonism. (Beef thigh.)—A soul does not limit; it is not
a dam, it is a widening, a stretch of an idea. Do not close-mind yourself. You need
to elasticize. We live in minutes, seconds, not years. Every second should be news.
Boredom threatens with old age; we need to die as interesting people. There are
no forces of permanence, only gestures of occasion. A moment has the deepest
structure of joy.
Reality of expression is boring, totally stupid (four hundred years of donkey beating.)
Art is not merely an expression of events, a reproducer and causeur (sons!!) That
is how art as a language for transmission of optical or (sian sian) cardiac feelingers,
both fictional and (sup sup sup) experienced appears. Transmitting experience
(Marzynski squeaks) is underestimating the artistic. Seeing art does not mean going
back to experience (a surrogate without competition!); the exchange of réalité experiences is *abstractivity*. Abstractivity is the sense of great beings, not small. It is the
meaning of a work of art. Not Romanticism (good Lord! I've gotten myself into yellow
paper!), no, Dadaism is a primitivistic secondary abstraction its own negation in tradition. (Learn to talk baby talk!)
An abstract work of art is a postulate of the occult-nervous man. Banging running shouting beating yelling advertising (papapapapapa teereereereereetee hoohoohoohoohoo)
are abstract signifiers for the entire complex of this conglomerate. Man does not
begin to remember—the process of the "pre-" (prefix + noun) is vibrated within him.

A second does not have a long beginning, and that is why it produces an abstract feeling of unconsciousness (prefix + noun) about a painting as the tableau of a Now-painting. It is as if there were a general rush through the whole artist. An artist has a nerve for art, feeling is long remembrance of thoughts, the nerve reverberates, beats. (Box-tone, jiujitsurapidscale.) To understand. (Sphynx aeterna). Homo has sunk deep into this idea (Sumatra = I am a black woman!) Who goes for *understanding*? Machine components of seconds are so over-knobbly that they need to be cut through with surprise. To have nerve, minus brain. (A caravan of spiraloids.) To understand artistic details (oh, the shallowness of vainglory!) can only be a plan of a madman or a professor.

To be general. That is you, DADA.

Say it's childish, just a phenomenon. A phenomenon is only a peculiarity intended for psychologists, to be put in a niche. (As Marzynski quoquotes.) An Expressionist is an observer who is only half general; a DADAist is a pan-nervist of abstractivity.

Even Expressionists are now claiming that beaty is a generally decorative—surface—spirituality. Will is absolute beauty. Boredom is lack of will coincidence non-art. Abstraction is overtension and strength of will. An artist creates a secondary expression and not allusions. (Cover yourselves, Symbolists!) A naked man in his first year is a Dadaist. Life in itself is a painting of the present; it is abstraction and contemporaneity. The most important thing for the future is to open its tones.

Poetry of abstraction. Speech is an apparatus. I narrow it for secondness. What else is comparison but incision (W & CL Pitt Clinic). A coat of abstraction instead of a slew of comparisons. (Schwitters Kurt, Kurt, Kurt!!) The Concordatist Mind cries for clarity and drowns in whimpering barber museums powder hair. (Touchichichiching electro-lumination S.T.R.K.) Through-factual line and form do not exist. (Dučić, cut your nose off!) Form has disintegrated greatly, and the idea of form should disintegrate too. Abstraction lives in the final out-scream of the form. (Serner Lugano Last Widening Peanuts 1°–78°.) An Expressionist clamors for distance from reality (if you please!). A DADAist is all for get-to-glueing fulfillment with abstraction. Poetry moment. Poetry circulus wonder change. Poetry is no-end-in-sight.

Spurting risk light-dead cross.
Glimmering pretectonic murderer
Crossful whitelight created (mimi)
Green yellowness brown.
Brightgray brightgray
Treeteeteeteeteetee,
Throws gyratingling mask read as
(Knee kneenee ee——
——ee)
Change as a second-factual-axiom.

Painting is color. The Suprematist is endlessly true to himself and doesn't even use color. (There you go Mechnikov, Petrograd Umansky Listening.) What's it all for if we are over-developed. The alphabet's madness (papapapapapapapapapa!) will sprout sooner or later. Black and white exist. Twirls of color abstract everything. Form is foolishness of mirror games. No need to sign paintings. (That's it that isisisit!!) It is a moment with no meaning that fell from the subject's tracks. Idea is ridiculousness, hence a phenomenon. (Arsenic syphillis—Verdun 1914—joy!) Annals do not exist. (Import secondseconds and millimoments!) A DADAist does not study techniques; it is a superfluity of boredom. (Shoe-makery clog-factory application bang!) A DADAist can paint even a musical prelude as a silver whistle. To understand the idea. The present is madness. Painting is color, non-color, or twirl. (Ssssssssssss...) I strive towards music (Mount Everest 9,006). DADA will also adopt Bruitism. The music of anything for the meaning of Everything. Arranging 888 saws in the city provides a first-class symphony. Sirens car-horns, loud whistles, water going through four hundred waterpipes, sucking on two hundred women's tits, two hundred gurgling people choking—it all belongs in an opera.

The Futurists were actually close to DADA in that respect. Notes are usually secondary, since Bruitism is often a moment and factualizes atonce and only once. (A six-legged wild insect, a tunnel of three buzzes butterflies crocodile.)

A novel is a mistake. (Was, were, have been.) A novel is a long-winding tapeworm. A novel should be thrown about, rapid firing. Electrical rapid-movement as a symbol of vibration. (A machine part number million.) A DADA-novel is an electrical radium rapid-jolt. (Melchior Vischer Prague Jörg Lisbon and Rotation.)

A DADAist novel is a ball rolling toward bowling pins. (Between bowling pins and the beginning of a rapid-jolt.) Rotation rerotation suprarotation of a tachytachydron. (The bowling pins fell impression comprrrrression.) "A second through the head" is a rotationary novel in forty-five rapid-pages. A DADAist lives like a fly, in a millisecond, because he is too nervous. (Alcohol, pins, professor, zoology.)

Billboard:

Do not laugh, gentlemen. You might be laughing at yourselves. But I will be the one laughing then. Who told you that a SQUARE always and everywhere remains a *square*. Just you laugh. (Oh, Vischer! Dadada DADA.)

Vive DADA.

There is a day that was born beautiful. People!!

DADAism is an entire world, its sense. (Wooden horse chess figurine.) The program is the ridiculous as a principle of permanence, a vibration of a twined circle. More than anything, DADA is a command, not a program. The command is being carried out: special notes of DADA tones are appearing. (Airplane at 3,000 m height I enter my bathroom!) Who will start with exoticism. Exoticizing is necessary for Salvation. Not everything is in your mind (Phiphiphiphiphilistines!): exoticism is there too as a moment-risk. (On the Adriatic Sea's bottom there is an Serbs Croats and Slovenes kiosk.) You need to go far away from everyday life to get rid of everyday life.

= DADA is a revolutionary communist.
= DADA is looking for 300,000 circuses to popularize art—(why work?)
= DADA wants to turn churches into cabarets bars colosseums bruit varieté.
= DADA wants to solve the sexual——(jump jump jump)

DADA is a term for getting happy. A great abstraction that would turn two-arm-leggeds from money bricks combat of reality so cruel and introduce them into the never-ending beauty of moments of primitive happiness. The joy of politics (Cacadou supérieur!) Since 1916 or 1917 Dada has been Geneva. Cabaret Voltaire. Tristan Tzara, Ball, Janko, Arp, Hülsenbeck.—DADA sensation and exhilaration. War, the stupid calf, has made people think of the common good. (Geneva is a nice town!) Hanover accepts DADAists and 400,000 copies of DADA rush to the world on "Silver nags." DADA is developing everywhere. DADA has representatives in Prague and their success spreads as fast as drum fire. (Cucucucucu) 500,000 coutons make an extraordinarily beautiful noise and music. Success. Russia is ultra DADA. Advertisement (St. Portion prays for us!) is the most satisfactory meaning of art. DADA = a great name.

Krolookroolookrooooolooo—rirririririlululuheeheehee tactactactactactactactac (zoo garden!)—to destroy culture because it is a boring, bourgeois silliness, nicely made up and wrapped incelophane. Let us go to extremes, to the borderline of great freedoms. (Hahahaha yeeee haa!) Primeval times. The world seems strange now because it's all made up. (Civilization, you old strumpet!) Let's tear it down tear it down all the way. Let language explode and a great DADA remain. (Vischer, you beautiful man!)

Tutumble, stumble—culture and shameless civilization will fall, croak in the sea of the desert plain. Arms into high air, stick out, sleep tight, seconds sight shout wild loud strong: WE ARE YOUNG AGAIN.
DADA screams for YOUTH.
DADA primitivism and desire. Future.
Life is Earth. Life is an abstraction of the globe. Forward is backward. We will reach the START again.
Second through the forehead. (Metaphysics!)
Revolver forty-story fall.
Everything is DADA.

Translated by Maja Starčević

KURT SCHWITTERS DADA   Dragan Aleksić
Originally published as "Kurt Schwitters Dada," *Zenit* vol. 1, no. 5 (1921)

Walter Mehring is pandadaizing around Japan posing as a Dada New-Ocase [sic] while Hannover houses Schwitters, i.e. the most positive dadaist and the Hasenclever-Hulsenbeck match mediator, and he, analogous to all, used by all, and preserving himself through astudy techniques, terms himself a Dada-Antidada poet. Hulsenbeck's negation of Him, the Dadayama, is phenomenal—he spittles on Anna-Blume (C. Ribemont Dessaignes whistle "Java-symptoms") and still, if DADA can be said to be torn apart, a piece surely belongs to Schwitters as well.
Bipolar Earth and bipolar Schwitters poet-painter. Art that isn't condensed in literally-strict boundaries (Pierot Marcetto) but is Sundaybested and newlycostumed. Oldaged-ness whines and resculpts certain ideas into immovability, the core movement of systematic approach disappears—Schwitters does not move mobility but limitations—DADA is globetrotting, ornamented by generalities, it makes music with a painter's verse or paints music-sculptures with verses—Schwitters is a man who is not of the nowbrave age, but a futuro-academic one—
—To spit on Schwitters the Predadaist—Easy—to point the light of three differently colored lamps on Schwitters the dadaist—to use a microscope in search of generalities which are 0, when generality is placed in terms of distance all becomes clarity—Schwitters is generally a dadaist and in his expression he is Merz-Kunst—Merz-Kunst—A wide painterly hippodrome. Everything that is academic and classical could have been taught as imitative and relative towards nature—Technique is studied within school, department and eyeglass frames etc. (Pollice verso!)—But to be left without art in this way is no coincidence. Expressing oneself—the basis of art—cannot be taught; lines, forms, colors and words all produce a complicated combination of expression, a syn-thesis of medium and the artist's air—Schwitters has risen above studying and is taking strides toward the only kind of genius—He thinks: a painting cannot be explained through the medium of speech, just as the words "and" and "that" cannot be painted—(Absurdology)—This is an important point we needn't expand on—He paints without any elements from nature, he rather takes the element of painting into account. These abstractions make matters difficult for non-expansive psychologies, but they are the fundamental forces of art.—But Kurt Schwitters wasn't satisfied with that alone—Even abstract expressionism is only a phase of his—Art as preconception;

it is as inexplicable as life itself, it is divine, undefined and has no point to it—An artistic work is produced by artistic inversion (Raddadistenmashine) of artistic elements— The medium is as secondary as is the artistic mood, it is form which provides sense through the placing of his media (Non-metaphysical supermobility), a placing which is random, not color according to color, or line to line, but wood to canvas, rubber to steel, concrete to paper—He has christened this concept as Merz! An artist is an artist even if all he did was put together framed cutouts of landscape—Interesting artistic hyperbolas, although learned (Absurd!)—If we allow that Merz pifpafpoufs the audience using the shades of a triple-lit gallery, it follows that the tempo of artism is more powerful than all logic all the way from the Greeks to Arnold. (Pull Gjukić's moustache!) Even if bridge-shoo had ordered an abstract-imperial-surrogate, Merz still wouldn't stop being the powerful artistic expression it is—To put together the discrepancy and the diversity of media into a synthetic abstraction is, according to any kind of logic, an artistic act—"Die Kathedrale" by Schwitters is an impossible logo-problem, but it is still a despairing-strong expression of the strongest proportions—Reviewing these abstractions gives one a sense of reality in stillness (Absurd!)—Christe eleison! If you crash a train engine and an airplane under a 70-degree angle, the abstraction must become an abnormally formed conglomerate of divergences (Prospect Glandury Pec. Saturn)—

B-b-b-b-but—Serner sings c'est la guerre! No—Allusions to superfastrunning are equal to zero plus nothing—Charpentier—the masks sublimate Edschmit's air propelling—(Respect boxing!). The clucksnickering of gastrophobes has passed over Schwitters—The minimal growth of war invalids has presented Schwitters with an alabaster pose of a virgin and he tabula rasa'd as a baby—Here—He-he-here! Pouf... Schwitters says: words are elements of poetry, therefore words, sounds, and sentences—poetry is made by inversion. The meaning becomes important only when inverted as a fact—I turn meaning toward nonsense—I prefer nonsense, because it hasn't been exploited artistically for a very long time—And that's a per- sonal matter—

So, DADA... Merz isn't much further than DADA—Schwitters has authored an inter- esting book, "Anna Blume," poems. DADA-poems... (Herren vom stampfenden Leben können das nicht begreifen!)—Abstract tide waves are hidden in the medium of force, it is not the words themselves that have an impact, but some scenery behind them— Post-expressionist abstracting is not inexpressive, like e.g. the neoimpressionist sab- otage—(In the interests of the cosmos, do some surgery on Sima Pandurović!)—Using color as an effect of the fullest abstraction can be seen in poem 27, and mysticism in materialism in poem "Am Rande meines Welken bin ich sanfte Nacht"—Expressionists have stated that the pre-ditch power of abstraction has an excellent effect, while clarity of certain kinds of logic only limits the clearly defined act of human instinct—I never rebel through activity, but "Anna Blume" is active in taking up all artistic space. (Read "Marstal.")

Schwitters is a dadaist of the so-called firstdadaist kind—(Yuck!) This wouldn't normally make a part of a sentence, if Huelsenbeck's dada-club hadn't expelled Schwitters for being a petite-dadaist. However, Tzara says: everyone makes art their own way— Even Schwitters has moved away from the program (Shut up, there is no program!)— Schwitters is a good painter. (He has a clean past! Oh ja, ja, yes, ole!) His paintings sometimes resemble Braque's cubistics or sometimes comment on P. Klee (naturally, a genius, Mr. Poljanski!), but the acts in his "cathedral" are entirely dada-specific— The sculptor is extraordinary—His cathedral is an absolute work of art as a sculpture. It is full of wheels and all kinds of factory material and affords no space to man. (Bow to this!) In this, he combines all kinds of art. (Ferenczy the Futurist!) He marries them together—In his poems there's rhythmic painting, in his drawing there's reading of words, the told pictures become a relief—Generality of DADA—Not specialty but panpanpan-dada! That's who Schwitters is

He made his greatest contributions (Bathos, get out of here!) as a reorganizer of drama, or rather, operadrama, pandrama DADA—(The firm is copyrighted, no fakes here.) He calls it Merz-Bühne—

Although some stress that antiseptic amateurs cannot understand Gauguin, Schwitters' stage will be felt in everyone's brain as the Dianatheter-bomb of 1921.

Schwitters allows his works to become part of a necessary syntheticism. The written text of the drama, the music and the gesture create an expression only through their synthesis, they are cohesive only as they are experienced. Generality, not one sense, but all-all-all—Infected by stability, these parts are connected non-systematically— All that is solid, fluid, or gaseous can become a medium…e.g. electric trams, man, a diesel engine, the button of the Franco-Serb Bank cash register, a blue lightstar— Mobility is symptomatic—Lines tidewell up into square planes, light diverges into 30 streams, an engine condenses water, the button can be pried open and stuck in the hand of some badux-robber—A pantonal score. All tones are equal (Rousseau's principle of gurgling). Whistles as violins, sirens as well as top-notch rubber bands, "Dante Alighieri" as a conga drum—Logic is the same thing as Cagliari-concrete— (A picture gallery for tourists)—Dadadrama demands entirety from an artwork's syntheticism—In poetry we have word vs. word, and here we have factor vs. factor, medium vs. medium—The stage becomes a relief of life's mobility, of music, of pan-tonality—500 lines of different light sources thrown in a bouquet, while flirting, creating an "impossible quiver" of Mr. Krleža ("Kraljevo," isn't that so?) After that, 20 cannon balls fly in a parabola over the plane, and break a few glass panes (Mr. Ivakić's Gardens!) and then reconnect underneath while a fountain flows into a hollow dead man's bone—(While singing "God Save Archipenko!")—Nets are made of lines, they catch Voltaire's necklace from Sansouci—Feathers drop from above and a man, tarred in Condotay-Boston gum arabic, oinks and steps forward only to be turned into Snow White by the feathers—He shouts: "I am Chantecleer! Evviva Rostand Bulldog Southampton—Very good boy!" Ropes lift him up and he plays a marionette, as a puppet—Music: "Orion-Chocolad-Fabrique" Symphony Marsch de Prague—And then a procession of populist socialists passes through yelling "Eat our newspapers— Paper sanitarium—Ooh-ooh-la-la." Circles, gyres, spirals and lamps play a Penkala overture without negation. Then, a sewing machine is framed, and it squawks just like Ibsen's—pouf—it stands on its head, its legs sticking up—Many things are deformed here: a potato-peeling machine, ink-penned superlative of the adjective "heavenly," a piece of the Orient Express wheel—Everyone is deformed and follows the train engine, everyone serves as a witness to a duel with another train engine—Two curtains lead a fencing match while the psalm "Tula, Tula steel" is sung—From above and from side to side various items are thrown, e.g. a lottery ticket, a microscope, a mouse-trap, and the Education Minister's red nose—All in its time (Suttner-Uhre)— Man is of secondary importance here: he doesn't even need to have a role, but he can bipedally speak, have the same understanding of sentences as a parrot, stand on his arms and wear a hat on his feet. Then various items are married to one another— e.g. a barometer to Rodin's Calais burgher's nose, or the tone of "G sharp" to H. H. Evers' Alraun—Then the music: a violin shouts: kee-teh-teh-seesee, while a gas-powered saw hiss-hisss-rahrahs behind the stage. A child jumps into water and shouts "Baby."

Thus Schwitters—Absolute art—many people unreasonably clown the whole thing up, and themselves with it—However, why always work with logic, when it's the most illogical thing of our age; to sum up, exoticizing of art is nothing more than an advertisement for art—

Art is a fact just as life is. It flows over everyone—There are artists among writers
of so-called "silliness," as well as non-artists among Hugos. All of it is a problematic ecstasy of individuals, without any construction or learned doggedness—
Schwitters now attempts to carry out his ideas—His theories are exact and effective,
artistic, and forerunners of non-sterility—Meidner's apocalyptic ground is merely
opportunistic, while Schwitters expresses himself throughout the absolute power
of his panartistic details—(crackcrackcricketycrack in the base of your skull)—
Metaphysical specificity has systematized the problem, but Schwitters guarantees
artistic stability without resorting to metaphysical syllogisms—By all means,
Schwitters, as a pandadaist, overshadows them all—Generality and abstraction are
phenomenally outstanding as that longed-for primitivist great gesture impact—
His colors have gone wild, his words are unkempt, his music is rabid, all is nothing
but human very very human.
Schwitters (wrote the best poems "Anna-Blume" and graphic art "Kathedrale") isn't
merely a quiver of a DADA network, he is the very lasso that will drag the world into
Pandadayamic neofuturism.

(Loooord have mercy) (choir!!!)

Translated by Maja Starčević

TATLIN: HPS [HORSEPOWER] + MAN Dragan Aleksić
Originally published as "Tatlin. HP/s + Čovek," *Zenit* vol. 1, no. 9 (November 1921)

Mayakovsky has said, "We need to destroy the rubbish heap of old 'art.'" Mayakovsky
is a strong man (a prerequisite for creative eruption). A critic masters his trade among
active artists; a critic speaks prior to the result and sees the result prior to speaking.
Modern Russia in art a jolt of anarchy (cheers!) and dilettantism, followers of all kinds
of healthy strength (a boundless signature). Russia produces Kandinsky, a contemporary genius, Chagall and Tatlin. (In the name of the Father...)
Tatlin and Tatlinism. Down with the frilly aesthetics of art so far!
Materialism has reached the heights of mysticism as a mathematical axiom and is
reaching upward. Tamed ties between mysticism and anarchy have encouraged mate-
rialism-based creation. Art the expression of its time. Art the reflection of materialism.
Art needs transformation, Zenith and parabola. Too many and too pale shadows of
European geniuses (Raphael, Meštrović, Rodin) have left only a temporary impression.
Art has no eternal genius. Art grows hardy with time. Art must be itself and thus not
last too long (The tripartite of occasionalism.) Let life live. Stanislav Kostka Neumann
says, "The creative processes are negation processes—a short-lived jolt." For me,
life is (naturally, we are talking of subjectivity) transitory now-time. A moment's relativity of value. Each possibility a moment's expression: necessary, honest: here it is:
it follows. Not opportunism: only radicalism. The artist as a decorator of his time, not
as the creator of his time. The artist as the inspiration of his panorama. Long live the
artist (Jump, class!), eternal contemporaneity.
Papini spits out the following: "Philosophy fears the creation of epochs as elements,"
epoch meaning self-inspiration according to the necessary differences in society.
Mate-rialism today. Materialism non-barrier to art. Connection to man. Brain size.

Strength of powerful expression (without cooperatives), HP, that is HP/4—Man. (Insurance premium 250,000 Dinars). A fact: unit of energy physical—intellect's. Intellect above the line. Man energy above the line. There is something above the line, not to be neglected: physical energy plus above man: a huge plus. Need for something above the line. Machine. Further: machine and man—a creative being. Machine in: steam, electricity, solar power, water, wind. Tatlin: painting man is always a weak initiative. Our time of rebuilding generalizes from necessity. (Russia!) Man, there is your instinct, in exoticism, in the exoticism of everyday life. Man, your thought, spirit, is in steel. Rubber, wood, steel, etc. Steel your thought: the spirit of matter, Transmission of electricity into abstract action. *Transmission of spirit—rough matter into abstraction:* instinctive metamorphosis. Rotationary machines, generators, batteries, transformers, reparators, reconstructors, condensers, etc. aero, radio, hydro, etc. Steel, glass, brass, rubber, silver, paper. Man feels a strike. Brain passes something to the cortex. Instinct is now out-born. Long live work: art makes people work. (Canute, you cursed forefather!) Art. (Homunculus: penetration.) Further! Tatlin: mixes man and machine and intimate distribution of the extremities, man and steel a centered idea of the brain. Rib rotation using four gas engines. Sculpted man-machine: a special accent without officiality. Fog, air, ether: a tiny needless paysage, a chain of shadowless clear energies in mutual circulation. Tatlin colors machine with man and man with machine. Practical term: magnet—intertwining. Theoretical term: supra-oscillation moving opposite abstractions towards the synthesis of fundamental ideas (Regress towards a special connection of some has-been). Thousand year old relict of a man—eternal value:

HOMO + 435 HP =

Collision of brain-tense moments, creates instinct for double-characteristic plus-energies of Work, instinct mass used as needed, perfected action. (for ex.) factory and Tatlin, passage, workers—line of shock, before that: 60% energy—use, after 90%, result + 30% Practicality = proof = clarity.

Old aesthetics: lower lip in derision—angle. A harlot's cynicism 50 grams. Why the instinct of gentleness! Drawing in grotesque. (Far from nonchalance!) Aesthetics ticks like a clock (I am sorry for that insult, holy machine!) kicks with music (or does music kick with aesthetics?) its note killed the strength of the modern artistic boxer.

A surplus of bland scenes cheats the bloody brain

[Long live (you cynic!) the absolute holy cosmic number]

Prelife coos (lie) strikes Today.

Strength of Thought in crrrruelty.

Artistic pleasure: electric raising of 200 tons 40 meters 10 seconds (Via crucis). Artistic pleasure: shock, paralysis, resonance instinct. (Repeat!) Tatlinism. Drawing on celestial sights of strong creators. Letting oneself enjoy means: making the *self* and machine perpendicular, no, *implanting*; a creative Gnosticism of intertwining abstraction—physical core. An electrical centipede rolls its girth through air. Holy Equilibrium, consoling strength, defeated without revenge: up above: man—brain. Or a man's strongly polarized counter-terms of spirit: up above: a turbine or a dynamo or... Man as a basis of physical energy: potency machine. This needs to be expressed. Strength of reflectivity learned through muscles into matter, raw uprooted earth, gives: breath to incentive, strength to decision, affirmation to Work instinct. Like sexuality—instinct acts on work—instinct. Proven. (Electrification of Russia! How? There!) Means of expression all. Technical education exists. New grammar and the aesthetics of our time. Intellect and matter triumph in abstract works. There is no isolated autonomy of the spirit. The quintessence of today's reality, independent techniques and super-intellect in a victorious materialization as an antidote to abstraction results in the possibility of expressing abstractions.

Dadaists shout, "Long live Tatlinistics!" since the grotesque in its widest sense results in a certain slant towards machinist art. Man as a puppet (paper cloth wood) forks, knives, war machines.

The result: war, the blind donkey.

So—

A great thing to be expressive. Which an artist is. Schwitters perspectivizes Tatlin. Positive. Merz. To give chaos: the first principle of impression: Kandinsky, to give disintegration; the second principle of impression. Composed: Chagall to give principle three of incarnated thought of man extracted with machine, as an abstraction of the Work instinct, action of gigantism, principle of contemporaneity =

Tatlin and Tatlinism.

Zenithism rapid-accents it, supra-rapid-accents rrrrsn.

Abstraction = now-giant.

Long live Russia!

Translated by Maja Starčević

ZENITH EXPRESS   Branko Ve Poljanski
Originally published as *Zenit-Ekspres* (Zagreb: 1922–23)

Paris
Berlin   Radiograms
Munich

Ladies and Gentlemen!

Stupidity is self-defeating! I don't need to comment on that. The disease of stupidity has become an epidemic. Stupidity is the Asiatic plague of our time.

Ljubomir Micić (I am sure you know him!) has discovered a Serum for the stupidity epidemic. There have been a number of successful operations thanks to this specialist in numbskull diseases.

                                                        Valerium Poljanski

We therefore wish to inform you that the great inventor Ljubomir Micić, when suddenly called to Paris, threw several thousand pills onto the streets of Munich as first aid for people stricken with the disease. He is currently undertaking extensive measures in Berlin to prepare for a sanitary struggle against the terrible epidemic. His Serum, which has become the talk of Europe, goes by the name of

ZENITHISM

The first news we've received has been quite alarming: after Rathenau's assassination all Germany is excited by the arrival of Maestro Ljubomir Micić, a man who is only by pure coincidence the son of our country. True, he has done nothing to deserve this bad luck, but as the folk is wont to say, "Fate is a kangaroo." And as we are wont to say, "We are too wise to be 'mad'." Our wisdom breaks heads. Believe us, we have mercy for "Thickheads," but we unfortunately haven't much time to soften millions of skulls.

Zenithism (let's be clear on this) is a principle that calls for the complete destruction and disarmament of the Anti-Human Army

for the sake of Man to come. Panic has taken over battalions of

Non-Humans

as the leaders of tomorrow's squadrons (Napoleon—Ljubomir Micić and Bismarck—
Valerium Poljanski) arrive, each ready to fight for the new man!

Ljubomir Micić sends his best from a land where rail traffic is as common as trams
and where books sell as fast bread rolls do in our country.

Well, I would write to you till the beginning of time, but I'm in a terrible rush to get to
Tokyo, where my sweetheart is waiting for me in front of a certain Buddhist temple.
Her name is

Luma

She loves me because she can sense my genius in the fashionable cut of my coat. The
top of my pointy America-shoe represents the peak of my wisdom to my darling.

That female is Japan's audience. Down with Japan! Things are different with us, aren't
they?

Long live the valley of wisdom!

Bye-bye! I can hear the toot of the D-train to Tokyo. So long!

Ever devotedly yours,
Valerium Poljanski

Translated by Maja Starčević

In contrast to Purism and Constructivism, Dadaism was relatively slow in gaining a foothold within the Czech avant-garde. Although several members of the early Devětsil (Adolf Hoffmeister, for example) took part in the presentations by Richard Huelsenbeck and Raoul Hausmann in March 1920—an appearance that inspired short-lived Dadaist circles— not even a second presentation by Hausmann and Kurt Schwitters, a year and a half later, persuaded Devětsil to make closer contact with the Dadaists. This was in marked contrast to the reception of the Italian Futurists in Prague that same year. And it ran counter to other developments: in the spring of 1922 Devětsil held gatherings dedicated to the groups around the Hungarian journal *Ma* and the Yugoslav journal *Zenit*.

Only in the mid-1920s did Dadaism become the center of attention, thanks to the Brno section of Devětsil. Bedřich Václavek, the most important theoretical spokesman of Brno Devětsil, and the poet František Halas emphasized primarily the "creative nihilism" of Dada, which, according to both artists, Czech art failed to experience around 1920, thus denying an appropriate philosophical point of origin. Dadaism was key especially for Halas, and it resonated in his work well into the 1930s.

Teige, who was concerned with the creation of new art and not with its destruction, understood Dadaism to already be a historical phenomenon: "Constructivism and Poetism must give thanks for the negative and destructive action of Dadaism." Although Teige represented an iconoclastic viewpoint, he never aimed to negate art as a whole, but merely a certain aspect of its expression that he considered outdated and academic. Teige's perspective was influenced by the creative work of several representatives of Dada after 1922—those from German-speaking countries as well as from France. During his 1922 Paris trip, he most likely saw Salon Dada. The iconographic motifs of the pictorial poems and the orientation of the Modern Art Bazaar may have been loosely influenced by the Berlin Dada-Messe (1920). That Hausmann's collages had an effect on the concept of the pictorial poem and several book jackets seems more than likely.

The only artist linked with the original Dadaism who had marked success in Prague was Kurt Schwitters, whose Theater Unbound put on an evening of his poetry in 1926, and who held an independent exhibit in Prague in 1927.

Translated by Andrée Collier Záleská

Dada means nothing.
> *Dada 3, 1918*

Dilettantes, rise up against art!
> *Poster at Dada exhibition, Berlin, June 1920*

In these days of petty affairs and stable values, social thought is subjugated to the laws
of bell-ringing patriotism. Just as, for a child, the world does not extend beyond the
nursery, and everything outside that realm is thought of by analogy, so the petty bourgeois evaluates all cities in comparison to his native city. Citizens of a somewhat higher
order lay everything that relates, if not to a different city, then to a foreign country, on
the Procrustean bed of the *homely* and dance according to the tune of their native culture. One's own little world and all that is "translatable" into one's own dialect versus
the incomprehensible barbarians—such is the usual scheme. Is this not the reason
for the fact that sailors are revolutionary, that they lack that very "stove," that hearth,
that little house of their own, and are everywhere equally *chez soi*? Limitation in time
corresponds to limitation in space; the past is normally depicted by a series of metaphors
whose material is the present. But at the moment, despite the fact that Europe has
been turned into a multiplicity of isolated points by visas, currencies, cordons of all
sorts, space is being reduced in gigantic strides—by radio, the telephone, airplanes.
Even if the books and pictures do not get through today, beleaguered as they are by
chauvinism and the "hard currency" of state national borders, nevertheless the questions that are being decided today somewhere in Versailles are questions of self-
interest for the Silesian worker, and if the price of bread rises, the hungry city-dweller
begins to "feel" world politics. The appeal to one's countrymen loses its conviction.
Even the humorists are crying that there is no longer an established order of things
(*byt*). Values are not in demand.

What corresponds in scientific thought to this sudden "swing"? Replacing the science
of the "thousand and first example," inescapable in days when the formula "So it was,
so it shall be" ruled, when tomorrow put itself under the obligation of resembling today,
and when every respectable man had his own *chez soi*, there suddenly appears the
science of relativity. For yesterday's physicist, if not our earth, then at least our space
and our time were the only possible ones and imposed themselves on all worlds; now
they are proclaimed to [be] merely particular instances. Not a single trace of the old
physics has remained. The old physicists have three arguments: "He's a Jew," "He's a
Bolshevik,'" "It contradicts 'common sense.'" The great historian Spengler, in his out-
spoken book *The Decline of the West* (1920), says that history never existed and is not
possible as a science, and above all that there was never a sense of proportions. Thus
the African divides the world into his village and "the rest"—and the moon seems
smaller to him than the cloud covering it. According to Spengler, when Kant philoso-
phizes about norms, he is sure of the actuality of his propositions for people of all
times and nations, but he does not state this outright, since he and his readers take
it for granted. But in the meanwhile the norms he established are obligatory only for
Western modes of thought.

It is characteristic that ten years ago Velimir Khlebnikov wrote: "Kant, thinking to
establish the boundaries of human reason, determined only the boundaries of the
German mind. The slight absent-mindedness of a scholar." Spengler compares his
strictly relativistic system to Copernicus' discoveries. It would be more correct to
compare it to Einstein's; the Copernican system corresponds rather to the transition

from the history of Christianity to the history of mankind. Spengler's book has caused a good deal of noise in the press. The *Vossische Zeitung* concluded: "Ah, relativism! Why say such sad things?" There appeared a voluminous reproof that succeeded in finding a true antidote to Spengler's system. This rebuke resounded from the church pulpit. This is no personal whim—the power of the Vatican is growing; the pope has not had so many nuncios for a long time. It is not without reason that the French government, rejoicing that France has finally disengaged itself from its revolutionary past, is in such a hurry to stress its piousness.

In all domains of science there is the same total rout of the old, the rejection of the local point of view, and new giddy perspectives. One's most elementary premises, which were unshakeable not so long ago, now clearly reveal their provisional character. Thus Bukharin, in his *The Economics of the Transitional Period*, discloses the meaninglessness of the Marxist concepts of "value," "goods," and so on, in application to our time, the fact that they are connected to certain already crystallized forms, the fact that they are particular instances.

Relevant here too is the aesthetics of Futurism, which refused to write beauty and art with capital letters. But Western Futurism is two-faced. On the one hand, it was the first to become aware of the tautological nature of the old formula—"In the name of beauty we are destroying all laws"—from which it follows that the history of every new current in comparison to its predecessor is a legalization of illegality; hence it would seem that there can be no punitive sanctions on what is possible in art, since instead of a decreed new beauty there is a consciousness of the particularity, the episodic nature of each artistic manifestation. It would seem that the scientific, historically minded Futurists, who rejected the past point-blank precisely because of their historicity, are the first who cannot create a new canon. On the other hand, Western Futurism in all of its variants endeavors to become an artistic movement (the thousand and first). "Classics of Futurism" is an oxymoron if you take as your starting point the original conception of Futurism; nevertheless, it has come to "classics," or to a need for them. "One of the innumerable -isms," said the critics, and found Futurism's Achilles' heel. The demand arose for a new differentiation, "a manifestation parallel to the relativistic philosophies of the current moment—a 'nonaxiom,' as one of the literary pioneers, Huelsenbeck, announced. "I'm against systems; the most acceptable system is to have absolutely no system at all," added another pioneer, the Romanian Tristan Tzara. There follow battle cries repeating Marinetti: "Down with all that is like a mummy and sits solidly!" Hence "anticultural propaganda,' "Bolshevism in art."

"The gilding is crumbling off, off the French, like any other. If you tremble, gentlemen, for the morals of your wives, for the tranquility of your cooks and the faithfulness of your mistresses, for the solidity of your rocking chairs and your nightpots, for the security of your government, you are right. But what will you do about it? You are rotting, and the fire has already begun" (Ribemont-Dessaignes). "I smash,' exclaims Tzara somewhat in the tone of Leonid Andreev, "skull cases and the social organization: all must be demoralized."

There was a need to christen this "systemless" aesthetic rebellion, "this Fronde of great international artistic currents:' as Huelsenbeck put it. In 1916 "Dada" was named. The name, along with the commentaries that followed, at once knocked out of the hands of critics their main weapon-the accusation of charlatanism and trickery. "Futurism sings of..." Marinetti used to write—and then came columns of objects celebrated by Futurism. The critic would pick up a Futurist almanac, leaf through its pages, and conclude: "I don't see it." "Futurism concludes," "Futurism bears with it," "Futurism conceals," wrote the ideologists who had become infected with the exoterica of Symbolism. "I don't see it! Ah, the frauds!" answered the critic. "'Futurism is the art of the future,' they say," he would reflect, "why, it's a lie!" "'Expressionism is expressive art'—they lie!" But "Dada," what does "Dada" mean? "Dada means nothing," the Dadaists has-tened to reply, running interference as it were. "It doesn't smell of anything, it doesn't mean anything," says the Dada artist Picabia, bending the old Armenian riddle. A Dada manifesto invites the bourgeoisie to create myths about the essence of Dada. "Dada—now there's a word that sets off ideas; each bourgeois is a little playwright, inventing different dialogues." The manifesto informs lovers of etymology that certain blacks call the tail of a holy cow "dada"; in one part of Italy "dada" means mother; in Russian "da" is an affirmation. But "Dada" is connected neither with the one nor the other nor the third. It is simply a meaningless little word thrown into circulation in Europe, a little word with which one can juggle *à l'aise*, thinking up meanings, adjoining suffixes, coining complex words which create the illusion that they refer to objects: dadasopher, dadapit.

"The word *dada* expresses the internationality of the movement," Huelsenbeck writes. The very question "What is Dada?" is itself un-dadaistic and sophomoric, he also notes. "What does Dada want?"—Dada doesn't want anything. "I am writing a manifesto and I don't want anything...and I am on principle against manifestoes, as I am also against principles," Tzara declares.

No matter what you accuse Dada of, you can't accuse it of being dishonest, of conceal-ment, of hedging its bets. Dada honorably perceives the "limitedness of its existence in time"; it relativizes itself historically, in its own words. Meanwhile, the first result of establishing a scientific view of artistic expression, that is, the laying bare of the device, is the cry: "The old art is dead" or "Art is dead," depending on the temperament of the person doing the yelling. The first call was issued by the Futurists, hence "Vive le futur!" The second, not without some stipulations, was issued by Dada—what business of theirs, of artists, is the future?—"A bas le futur!" So the improviser from Odoevsky's story, having received the gift of a clarity of vision which laid everything bare, ends his life as a fool in a cap scrawling transrational verses. The laying bare of the device is sharp; it is precisely a laying bare; the already laid-bare device—no longer in sharp confrontation with the code *(à la langue)*—is vapid, it lacks flavor. The initially laid-bare device is usually justified and regulated by so-called constructive laws, but, for example, the path from rhyme to assonance to a set toward any relationship between sounds leads to the announcement that a laundry list is a poetic work. Then letters in arbitrary order, randomly struck on a typewriter, are considered verses; dabs on a canvas made by a donkey's tail dipped in paint are considered a painting. With Dada's appeal, "Dilettantes, rise up against art," we have gone from yesterday's cult of "made things" (say, refined assonance) to the poetics of the first word let slip (a laundry list). What is Dada by profession? To use an expression from Moscow artistic jargon, the Dadaists are "painters of the word." They have more declarations than poems and pictures. And actually in their poems and pictures there is nothing new, even if only in comparison to Italian and Russian Futurism. Tatlin's *Maschinenkunst*, universal poems made up of vowels, round verses (Simultaneism), the music of noise (Bruitism), Primitivism—a sort of poetic Berlitz:

Meine Mutter sagte mir verjage die Hühner
ich aber kann nicht fortjagen die Hühner.
(Tzara)

Finally, paroxysms of naive realism: "Dada has common sense and in a chair sees a chair, in a plum—a plum."

But the crux of the matter lies elsewhere, and the Dadaists understand this. "Dada is not an artistic movement," they say. "In Switzerland Dada is for abstract (nonobjective) art, in Berlin—against." What is important is that, having finished once and for all with tl1e principle of the legendary coalition of form and content, through a realization of the violence of artistic form, the toning down of pictorial and poetic semantics, through the color and texture *as such* of the nonobjective picture, through the fanatic word of transrational verses *as such*, we come in Russia to the blue grass of the first celebrations of October and in the West to the unambiguous Dadaist formula: "Nous voulons nous voulons nous voulons pisser en couleurs diverses." Coloring *as such*! Only the canvas is removed, like an act in a sideshow one has grown tired of.

Poetry and painting became for Dada one of the acts of the sideshow. Let us be frank: poetry and painting occupy in our consciousness an excessively high position only because of tradition. "The English are so sure of the genius of Shakespeare that they don't consider it necessary even to read him," as Aubrey Beardsley puts it. We are prepared to respect the classics but for reading prefer literature written for train rides: detective stories, novels about adultery, that whole area of "belles-lettres" in which the *word* makes itself least heard. Dostoevsky, if one reads him inattentively, quickly becomes a cheap best seller, and it is hardly by chance that in the West they prefer to see his works in the movies. If the theaters are full, then it is more a matter of tradition than of interest on the part of the public. The theater is dying; the movies are blossoming. The screen ceases bit by bit to be the equivalent of the stage; it frees itself of the theatrical unities, of the theatrical *mise en scène*. The aphorism of the Dadaist Mehring is timely: "The popularity of an idea springs from the possibility of transferring onto film its anecdotal content." For variety's sake the Western reader is willing to accept a peppering of self-valuable words. The Parisian newspaper *Le Siècle* states: "We need a literature which the mind can savor like a cocktail." During the last decade, no one has brought to the artistic market so much varied junk of all times and places as the very people who reject the past. It should be understood that the Dadaists are also eclectics, though theirs is not the museum-bound eclecticism of respectful veneration, but a motley cafe *chantant* program (not by chance was Dada born in a cabaret in Zurich). A little song of the Maoris takes turns with a Parisian music hall number, a sentimental lyric—with the above-mentioned color effect. "I like an old work for its novelty. Only contrast links us to the past," Tzara explains.

One should take into account the background against which Dada is frolicking in order to understand certain of its manifestations. For example, the infantile anti-French attacks of the French Dadaists and the anti-German attacks of the Germans ten years ago might sound naive and purposeless. But today, in the countries of the Entente there rages an almost zoological nationalism, while in response to it in Germany there grows the hypertrophied national pride of an oppressed people. The Royal British Society contemplates refusing Einstein a medal so as not to export gold to Germany, while the French newspapers are outraged by the fact that Hamsun, who according to rumor was a Germanophile during the war, was given a Nobel Prize. The politically innocent Dada arouses terrible suspicion on the part of those same papers that it is some sort of German machination, while those papers print advertisements for "nationalistic double beds." Against this background, the Dadaist Fronde is quite understandable. At the present moment, when even scientific ties have been severed, Dada is one of the few truly international societies of the bourgeois intelligentsia.

By the way, it is a unique Internationale; the Dadaist Bauman lays his cards on the table when he says that "Dada is the product of international hotels." The environment in which Dada was reared was that of the adventuristic bourgeoisie of the war—the profiteers, the nouveaux riches, the Schieberen, the black marketeers, or whatever else they were called. Dada's sociopsychological twins in old Spain gave birth to the so-called picaresque novel. They know no traditions (*"je ne veux même pas savoir s'il y a eu des hommes avant moi"*); their future is doubtful (*"à bas le futur"*); they are in a hurry to take what is theirs ("give and take, live and die"). They are exceptionally supple and adaptable ("one can perform contrary actions at the same time, in a single, fresh breath"); they are artists at what they do ("advertising and business are also poetic elements"). They do not object to the war ("still today for war"); yet they are the first to proclaim the cause of erasing the boundaries between yesterday's warring powers ("me, I'm of many nationalities"). When it comes right down to it, they are satisfied and therefore prefer bars ("he holds war and peace in his toga, but decides in favor of a cherry brandy flip"). Here, amid the "cosmopolitan mixture of god and the bordello," in Tzara's testimonial, Dada is born.

"The time is Dada-ripe," Huelsenbeck assures us. "With Dada it will ascend, and with Dada it will vanish."

Translated by Stephen Rudy

THE MODERN ART BAZAAR   Jaroslav Jíra
Originally published as "Bazar moderního umění," *Stavba* no. 2 (1923)

The Devětsil exhibit is the meaningful exhibit of the season with its assertive, resolute, modern program language, as well as its artistic values. Both are currently rarities in this country. It is not an exhibit, an academic salon in the ordinary sense of the word. The young artists deliberately avoided this word, calling it the Modern Art Bazaar. It is truly a bazaar, a market, a lively overview of the manifold interests of the modern person: architecture, engineering work, pictures, posters, photographs, reproductions—in other words, besides specifically artistic work and beauty, also photogenic and biomechanical beauty, examples of engineering (ball bearings), a wax figurine from a wig-making factory, as an example of the excellent craftsmanship of simultaneously fashionable and modern sculpture. In a nutshell, this is the theater of the street and the biomechanics of sport, a whole life-spectacle, the interests of the contemporary modern artist in his lively and active relationship to society, to life, and especially to the wide realm of contemporary culture in its technical and mechanical achievements.

This spirit and reviving contribution of the exhibit is expressed most forcibly and concretely in architecture. The idea of Constructivism, which our revue stands for theoretically and practically, is the commonality behind the numerous works of the young architects exhibiting here. Their architecture, which comes almost entirely out of purist principles and guidelines, is above all an art of construction, not one of decoration, historicizing, folklore or picturesqueness. Subordinate to the laws of the new materials, economy and usefulness, it seeks through them, in their spirit, without regard for traditional forms, a new sculptural beauty in the greatest simplicity, uniformity and purity of the work. Among the best examples were Krejcar's monumental project for the Masaryk student dormitories, which solves the problem of modern student housing with deliberate utility and practicality in a harmonious and tectonic construction; Chochol's austere, and yet also philosophically eloquent facades for the school in Tabor and the engineering storage rooms; Feuerstein's studies of architecture in Spain and southern France, and his scenic sketches; the hospital pavilion, doctor's villa and study for a crematorium from Fragner; Fragner and Linhart's theater for Olomouc; and the villa and tenement house by Honzík.

In painting, the young members of this group are almost all closely tied to the contribution and heritage of cubism. But in contrast to the abstract-geometry principles of pre-war cubism they have a consistent Constructivist tendency. They no longer paint subjectless compositions, and they don't deform and break shapes, but instead form them. Štyrský, Remo and Toyen (the latter two are pseudonyms) exhibit very interesting work of this sort. They are also tied to purist form efforts, creating a supply of standard types and shapes, with the implications and ciphers of their pictorial compositions (Štyrský's *Cirk Simonetta*, Remo's *The Bank*, Toyen's *Still Life with Silverware*). Their efforts go further—towards the poetization of artistic expression. Teige, the initiator of the new idea (pictorial poetry)—which attempts a relationship, a fusion, between painting and poetry—takes it the furthest: "The modern picture has the same function as poetry, and it can be read like a poem." (The opposite is also true: the poem is read like a modern picture. See the article "Painting and Poetry" in *Disk* 1.) Teige's pictures, though philosophically monumental and robust in form (*The Station, Landscape with Traffic Lights*) are full of the new expressive artistic sensations and promises.

Mrkvička appears quite disparately in this exhibit, while Šíma fits in well with his attempts to concretize objectivity, though it seems that he came to it from the opposite side, through Orphism and Fauvism (Matisse, Dufy). He exhibits here landscapes from Posázaví and views of Prague—streets, houses, the river, the bridges, steamships— which have a new vision of the landscape and translate Prague's beauty, unencumbered by traditional banality and phrases.

Translated by Andrée Collier Záleská

PICTURE   Jindřich Štyrský
Originally published as "Obraz," *Disk* no. 1 (May 1923)

PICTURE = living advertisement and project of a new world and life
    "   = product of life   EVERYTHING ELSE = KITSCH!

Function of a picture   practical, appropriate, intelligible
                           advertising
                           organizing and composing

PICTURE energy   OF LIFE
        criticism
        motive   power

Requirement: a picture must be active
                  it must do something in the world. In order to accomplish the task
                  allotted to it, it must be mechanically reproduced. 1,000, 10,000,
                  100,000 copies. Reproduction. Graphic art by pamphlet.

I hate pictures as much as I hate snobs who buy them out of the desire to be individual so

original—unique a picture is not only a picture!	*that they can sigh in front of them in their easy chairs between the four walls their aesthetic flats (à la Matisse!). The picture hangs on the wall in a closed area, a barren decoration, and does nothing, wants nothing, says nothing; it does not live.*

Teige: BE A POSTER!
an advertisement and project for a new world!

A plan, project of a new world—by exploring new, more beautiful, more useful forms
and values of life
—by creating new, more beautiful, more useful forms
and values of life

Advertisement and promotion of new, more beautiful, more useful forms and values
of life.

The new world lives neither in the stars nor in the clouds but on earth. Much of the
new world we already know, have, and live.

PROMOTION
of new beauty, health, wisdom, freedom, order, joy of life.

Goll: The Chaplin Saga (cinema).—Černik: Joys of the Electrical Century.—Nezval: The
Wisdom of Foolhardy Merriment.—Krejcar: Americanism.—Birot: Outdoor Poetry.—
Teige: Paris.—Seifert: Paris.—Picasso–Seurat: Circus. The Third International.—Film
(music hall, circus).

Publicity: of ideas
of books
of revolution
of actions and attractions

Definitely not promotion of "Mánes," Ibsen, Stinnes, Poincaré, the bourgeoisie, social
patriots, academies, salons, KU KLUX KLAN.

PICTURE

building up	tearing down
positive action	negative action
objective	subjective

JOURNALISTIC REVOLUTIONARY CARIACTURE destroys, whips, hates.

FORM: Dictated by a purpose, brief, exact, intelligible, entertaining, lucid, constructive, simple: no decoration, ornament, pettiness, literature, psychology, mysticism.

Beauty without soul
THE DESIGN OF A NEW GLOBE
Picture = constructive poem of the beauties of the world

NOT: reproduction, patching, imitation, restoration, idealization, sentimentalization.
The writing in a picture has its practical sense. (Poster!) It speaks. What other sense
has writing anyway? Cubists used letters only to decorate the surface because of their
modern expressivity.

The project of a new world can be worked out only by a NEW MAN who has his work
programmed, is absolutely objective so that he must combat even good subconscious
work as unreliable.

A picture performs its function in life like any other product of human work.

Picture—a product of life for the consumer who is called the world.

A picture—will no longer reproduce poverty, misery, despair, will not portray the oppressive shortages of the present time, social injustices, capitalists' bellies, the atmosphere of the working-class districts.

A picture—of social poverty will not help anybody, it is produced out of an inability to create an energetic revolution, new rules, a new world.

A picture is the product of an age. A picture is not a reproduction of an age. A photograph, a film, a picture magazine, etc. will represent the age.

PHOTOGRAPH: Objective truth and documentary clarity beyond doubt. Kitsch killed the photograph (thank goodness!) but it did not kill the picture! It hastened the evolutionary lucidity of the pictorial arts.

Photograph: a document of the age and of beauties of this world. Picture: a project and the creation of new beauties, new values, a hand-drawn portrait compete with it not even "for individual conception + the soul of an artist" (qualities of people who create kitsch, empty phrases). A photograph is capable of enormous technical development (dimensions, color, clarity, speed). A colored Gauguin = 0 as against the perfect color photograph from the tropics.

Photography has realized the dreams of the old masters from time immemorial—why do fools still admire them today?—because their ideal was nothing but to imitate reproductions. Illusionism.

NEW FORMS OF ART TODAY AND ARISING EVERY DAY
The most beautiful poem: a telegram and a photograph—economy, truth, brevity.

You have seen Mary Pickford standing by the sea, slowly turning her head a gazing at length and languidly at us with her clear eyes—that is, several hundred, several thousand people. MONA LISA—you cannot compete!

Naturally, painters à la Nejedlý and Beneš and hordes of others fight against the modernity that is overwhelming them like an avalanche; in vain; they lack the strength to find a solid and suitable place for themselves and their work in the present time— they are quite useless parasites. A photo is a more perfect narrator than they are.

The art of the past	The art of the present	
Reproduction of the world and life	a) A photo Reproduction of the world and life. More complete, more instructive.	b) Graphic art and poetry Project of a new life, new beauty, new value.

We hate galleries, where for centuries pictures have been growing musty (eternal memory). The health of the world and its youth depends on the fact that everything is being used up and replaced by new things. That is why the world does not grow old and is younger and more beautiful with every hour. If there were no history, the world would be younger by several centuries.

TRADITION: The old masters studied historical masterpieces to see how they should not paint. The modern painter goes them one better: he takes no notice of them at all.

DO NOT PRESERVE THE DEAD! GET RID OF THE CORPSES BECAUSE THEY STINK!

Progress and development: nothing will be impossible, all real projects can be realized, distance is relative. For sad lovers we will cultivate black roses. Our projects will not be fever dreams, utopias; they will be objectively poetic.

BEWARE:

The necessity to distinguish. What in today's world can serve as a basis for the new? A picture is born of thinking, construing, and combining objective elements and thoughts and will not become a superficial and enthusiastic view. Epigones reproduced and produced badly. The machine is taking their place—mechanical reproduction. There will be fewer pictures and more mechanical reproductions.

LOVE NEW PICTURES

Translated by Michael Henry Heim

PAINTING AND POETRY   Karel Teige
Originally published as "Malířství a poezie," *Disk* 1 (May 1923)

Insofar as modern visual, literary, and musical productions are modern, that is, insofar as they have true value, they are based entirely on Cubism.
Contemporary Cubism differs, of course, from the Cubism of 1909 or 1913. The camera abolished the social contract between painting and reality. An enormous amount of work was accomplished from Cézanne to Picasso: visual production was cleansed of representation, decoration, and anecdote; abstraction and geometrization reached their high point; reality, which used to be the point of departure, was deformed and turned into totally autonomous, primary geometric forms and expressive colors dominated by specific pictorial laws of composition and construction, and a powerful poetry grew out of their harmony. Now an opposing trend has come into being: concretization. Cézanne turned bottle into cylinder to make it comply with the pictorial composition; Juan Gris makes the cylinder called for by his pictorial composition into a bottle to maintain contact with reality. Here and there the geometrical composition of the picture is vivified by contacts with raw reality, arousing powerful emotions in the spectator. It is a minimalist poetry, a poetry of intimation, of code. The mechanical age of the electric century proposes new forms to enchant the eye that has received a modern education; it makes a deep impression on our sensitivity. The Italian Futurists try to create a mechanical art (though they were not completely logical about it); artists like Léger, Archipenko, Lipchitz, Laurens, and Gleizes try to represent the monumentality of the machine. Live spectacles in the streets, sport, biomechanical beauty,

the perpetual drama on the surface of the globe that we see in newspapers and especially in the cinema increase the dramatic component in people's lives. Aesthetics has become photogenic and lively.

Non-objective compositions that study pure forms and their mutual relationships are a deviant consequence of Cubism: Mondrian, van Doesburg, Suprematism, and the like risk turning into decoration.

*

What is the problem of the new picture? Will it remain a picture? Surely not forever. The picture is either a poster—that is, public art, like the cinema, sports, and tourism, with its place in the street—or a poem, pure visual poetry, without literature, with its place in the book, a book of reproductions, like a book of poems. It is always wrong to hang a picture on the wall of a room. The traditional framed picture is being gradually abandoned and is losing its true function.

*

Marinetti freed poetry from the fetters of syntax, punctuation, and so on; in Apollinaire's ideograms poetry acquired an optical and graphic form. The poem, once sung, is now read. Recitation is becoming nonsense, and the economy of poetic expression is first and foremost optical, plastic, and typographic, never phonetic or onomatopoeic.

A poem is to be read like a modern picture.
A modern picture is to be read like a poem.

*

Sculpture has been rejected by modern architecture. All that remains is a cabinet object running counter to modern aesthetic feelings. Archipenko and Laurens have attempted to transform sculpture into painting, to enrich it with pictorial elements—sculptural painting; Lipchitz has turned it into monumental architecture. Visual art in its existing forms is disappearing, just as frescoes and mosaics disappeared and just as the novel and drama are fading and the traditional concept of the image.

*

Hence the logical conclusion: the fusion of modern images with modern poetry. Art is one, and it is poetry. In *Disk* 2 you will see picture poems that represent the solution to the problem: the association of painting and poetry. Sooner or later this fusion will lead to the liquidation of traditional modes of making pictures and writing poetry. Picture poems conform precisely to contemporary requirements. Mechanical reproduction provides the means for making picture books. Books of picture poems will need to be published. Methods of mechanical reproduction will assure the wide popularization of art. It is not museums or exhibitions but print that mediates between artistic production and the spectator. Old types of exhibitions are on their way out; they look like mausoleums. A modern exhibition should resemble a bazaar (a trade fair, a world fair). It is a modern production, the manifestation of the electric and mechanical century. Mechanical reproduction and print will finally make the original superfluous: after all, once we print a manuscript we toss it into the wastepaper basket.

Constructivism

Contemporary architecture is dominated by the aesthetic of Purism, it is Constructivist, it is neither decorative nor applied art. Modern constructions and materials (concrete, glass, and iron) subjected to the laws of economy and function have given us harmonious groupings and proportions, a lofty and poetical beauty worthy of its time.

Poetism

Thanks to Cubism, painting and poetry, once dominated by ideology, have become pure poetry. The picture poem is born.

Bioscopic Art

Biomechanics is the only dramatic spectacle of the present: sport, cinema.

New art has stopped being art. New fields are being born. Poetry is pushing its
limits, overflowing and uniting with the multifarious forms of modern life all over
the globe.

Translation by Michael Henry Heim

CREATIVE DADA   Bedřich Václavek
Originally published as "Dada tvořivé," *Host* no. 4 (1925)

There is one thing we can envy postwar Germany: Dadaism. We missed out on a strong
dose of Dada after the war. Having immediately moved on to a revolution for the benefit
of man, we were ethical and pedagogical, and now we want to be constructive. But there
was no decay, no cleansing. That is why we make up for it today by grabbing a bit of
dada here and there, but somehow, there is no more time for that with today's impure,
hybrid forms—and so we have stayed without it. We failed to carry out its destructive
work that would leave behind virginal land ready for the real work of new builders.
Aren't we going to remain a bit idyllic in the usual Czechs way?
Dada. We say yes to the destructive fanaticism with which it has thrown itself against
the superficial, commercial humbug made of "spirituality" and "art." Set upon destruction of the products of bourgeois culture, it has given up the principle of remedy—and
this is what we miss in it, as much as we understand its focus on destruction. It was
nihilistic, but we would say with Huelsenbeck that this was the kind of nihilism that is
part and parcel of life, or, using Mahen's term, we would call it creative nihilism. It
wanted it to be nothing more than an expression of the times, absorbing its abrupt
rhythm, its skepticism and relativism, but also its weariness and doubt about the possibility of some sense and truth. We love it and we fight along its side.
It was naïve. It wanted a self-evident, undifferentiated, unintellectual life. It taught art
to use new material. Rich with intensified modern sensibility, it heralded the simultaneity of modern art.
Later, it gave art up, drawing the last conclusion of the new reality, and its members
became the con artists of art.

Translated by Alexandra Büchler

EXCERPTS FROM **DADAISM**   František Halas
Originally delivered as a lecture in Brno (December 10, 1925)

Look at me well.
    I'm an idiot, a hoaxer, a smoker.
    Look at me well.
    I'm ugly, short, dull.
    I'm like all of you.

This is how Tristan Tzara would begin his lecture and this is how every lecture should begin. Flowers are murdered by Latin names and the colorful kakadu called Dada must be plucked clean, so that apart from the merry adventures and surprises he has in store for us, we can find the essential thing that makes him screech, laugh and engage in that entire circus of words, insults and lyrical expressions he boasts. You will forgive me for speaking seriously about something so droll and playful, and for briefly following its family tree.

Dada = eternal. It has been, it is, it will be. Not art, rather an intellectual epidemic; it has been in Memphis, it is in New York. It exists in the whole world, in every place, in every era. If you want its definition, I can give you several for you to choose from.

D = eternal intellectual youth.

D = beginning and end of the world.

D = indifferent state of mind.

D = humbug and bluff.

D = restoration of idiocy.

D = wooden horsey, the tail of a holy cow, double Russian affirmation, the whimper of a baby.

D = reaction against the humbug of art and intellect, against the self-adoration of literary types.

D = cocktail mixer in a Manhattan bar, mixing curaçao with one hand and catching his gonorrhea with the other. (Serner)

I could go on and on *ad infinitum*. Each of these definitions is true and so is the next one. Everything is true and everything is a lie. This is what we have to realize, if we want to understand dadaism. For many people, it was discovered only after it had been given its label. People in this way discover many things and Dada was baptized in 1916 in Zurich. The muses do not fall silent in war, but if they do, it is the authorized, official muses, and this is lucky for the proscribed ones, those Cinderellas who are thus allowed to show what they can do.

Armies cut off each other's heads with bayonets. A Dadaist would say that this could be possibly the most sensible operation that can be carried out on man. Those not lucky enough to assist with these surgeries, amused themselves in other ways, dealing on the black market, singing the right patriotic songs, seducing abandoned wives, to make them feel less bored, inventing ways in which you can turn furniture into food, discovering new philosophical systems of national activism and energy, and praying for the victory of "our arms"; many amused themselves by starving. Let us then not be surprised that there were several people who remembered that, apart from all that, they could start making some art. They were Tzara, Hans Arp, Marcel Janco, Rich, Huelsenbeck, Hugo Ball. They knew the latest directives of artistic possibilities by heart and wanted to make use of them. Their cosmopolitanism, temperament and boredom were an asset. They were united in their hatred of the bourgeois. What they wanted to achieve was not Dada as we understand it today, it was abstract art, containing Expressionism, Cubism, and Futurism, and it is certain that in its beginnings, Dadaism didn't know exactly what it wanted. But people who can play golf just as well as they can discuss Mallarmé do not ever find themselves in a tight spot. Dada was here and it owns its spreading and popularity to Tristan Tzara's promotional efforts. And to the intensity of the word, this rotating nothing that had attracted attention and interest on two continents. This then is a brief history of the beginnings of Dada as a literary movement. Art was a framework from which it was soon to break out. Civilizational chaos and the flames of the world war were a fertile soil for that. A new way of phrasing certain old experiences is shocking for educated people. They feel some sort of horror, and to regain their sense of security, they resort to negation, to ridicule. The times had brought several: the absurdity of war, the short-lived nature of the so far reliable certainties, the idiocy of nationalism, etc. Delightful doubt and skepticism was a luxury that did not fit in. It was necessary to elevate this skepticism, double it. Discrediting all acts and notions, laughing, was more appropriate than pacifist leaflets, laments and curses. The "sorrow of reason" typical for the end of an era, was the wind driving this wreck with a madly merry and merrily mad crew along a sea of blood. The soldier in the trenches and the worker in the rear were both forced to think about how grotesque this entire bloody theater was, just as the dadaists did, and whenever we can sense the end is near, we are better off raving rather than waiting in tranquil contemplation until it hits us. Let's remember all those stories from the trenches, all those folksy jokes: the world was waiting for Dada and the Dadaists admit that they gave something to people, and it turned out that the people had been waiting for it. Dada was an idea that had touched the most vital nerve of the masses, frightening them, humbling them, but also teaching them something. At a historical moment, when the bourgeois order is collapsing, the time also came to liquidate art, morals and philosophy of this world, since this was where the bourgeois felt most secure; these were the holy fires he guarded. Dada, in its absurdity, naiveté and indifference, became part of modernity and has remained so. The unadulterated negativity of Dadaism unwittingly brought with it some positives, this was where the geysers of the crazy poetry we love gushed from, this is where modern man learned something and began smiling at what frightened him only yesterday. Dada stood at the beginning of that process of relativization in our thought, placing doubt under everything. The fanaticism of destruction, the celebration of a slap in the face, the destruction of art that had looked after the made-up, stupid, fat faces of the capitalist system with such great care, seeing through the hollowness of philosophy and the business called morals, all that was part of the healthy contribution of Dada. It didn't want to put things right, it just wanted to destroy. Dada = people's letters, jokes, those most of all. Dada is everywhere and it's good that a label was found for things that had been so difficult to categorize. Howdy! Hi-de-hi! How's tricks? The Dada of greetings.

Gouge out your eye and put a gramophone inside—this is the Dada of congratulation. Etc, etc. You will surely find enough examples yourselves, and I hope you are going to tell us after the lecture.

DADA + PHILOSOPHY

The perennial indifference of Dada towards philosophy, that is, towards the search for truths, and towards truths themselves, is its basic characteristic. Laughter is a more necessary philosophy. Before God made the world, he should have asked the witty ones, said Anatole France. A tarot reader, coat buttons, Bergson: everything is equally easy. Socrates' modesty was in fact arrogance, since I don't even know that I know nothing. It has been discovered that life is a hoax and the stars are laughter. Let's then put on a hoaxer's face, as if we understand what's going on, so that we don't look stupid in the hour of death.

The ever-present Hamlet streak in us should not be made the subject of journalistic polls and essays. Let's deal with it on our own. We don't want to be seen crying. The vogue of carrying one's heart on one's sleeve is dead. More likely as a flower in the lapel.

We don't put our head out into the universe or the universe into our head; we have realized that doing either is dangerous.

We maintain the seriousness of a clown and so remain outside tragedies, but in the midst of today's infantilism.

We are active, because we are merry. It's the same thing. Sadness is inactivity. Laughter is an act of courage, it is the hygiene of constructive work, where all elementary feelings are subjected to tension. Love of witty truths is better than respect for philosophical systems. Acrobatics of thought, seeing things from all sides. Truths, Klíma said, are a comfortable sitting on the toilet. What arrogance to demand to be believed!

The golden rule is that there is no golden rule. Shaw.

To rid oneself of Faustian tendencies and laugh at yesterday's truths the same way we shall laugh tomorrow at today's. That's all that can be done.

Dada = contempt for those who found a shelter for their weakness in so-called pure spirituality. It was high time to see through the humbug of spirit. A Dadaist is someone who has understood that we can have ideas only when we can realize them in the world, says Serner.

Hence the contempt for speculative activity devoid of a concrete purpose. It is obvious that a Dadaist is an active, positive type, who turns his back to metaphysics, and who sees himself as a phenomenon, a manifestation of his time, with its essentially civilizational and mechanical tendency, but which, apart from its mad tempo, brings weariness and desperation over the meaning of everything. Yet, this is no nihilism, no fan of a *dolce far niente* attitude, on the contrary, it is a thorn prodding towards greater activity. Take note, however, that this applies only to some Dadaists; others have fallen into the bourgeois misery of the present, having acquired an Asiatic concentration, and, gazing at their navel, they believe that this is the most valuable activity in the world. Or that it is Nirvana. Every system is a temptation, every God an opportunity for financiers.

A Dadaist rejects all that, considering the shape of his shoes and clothes more important. To him, worldview is just a jumble of words.

Dadaist = instinctive atheist. There is no difference between him and Saint Thomas. He claims that the need for philosophy arises from boredom.

His self-confidence is based on having none.

He may know that there are days or nights when even the silliest of things appear serious, but he knows how ephemeral they are and overcomes them.

Addressing the philosophical ruminants, he might say: Be as empty as you are.

Today, in an era sadly lacking in enthusiasm, we must forgive him for saying this: In our present time and from any point of view, it is most advisable to die.

The tragedy of modern man is that instincts have survived. And vitality. In the past, man ate, drank, hunted, fucked, ate, fucked, drank, hunted, ate, and fucked, while today, out of his daily twenty-four hours, he is left with no more than ten that he can use for these wonderfully good things.

Dadaists have understood that thinking processes are crossroads through which we can wonder in all directions ad infinitum. They have discovered a great secret: Thoughts are made in the gob. Dada cynicism—well, any decent human being is a cynic, if he's not stupid. Cynicism is the most extreme shortcoming of one-sidedness. It is just one step from cynicism to eccentrism. Laughing, he will consistently end up laughing over everything.

A metaphysic keeps looking behind the mirror, searching for himself, while a human being looks into the mirror and recognizes the world in himself.

The absolute absurdity of truth has been proven. The truth is ice and death. Tendency: stuff the infinite into a trunk (Klíma). Spit at humanity, at Christ, at everything.

Dada = man surprised by modernity. Dada is not an abnormality, it is merely a realization that if it is possible to play with the sun and the stars, the same can be done with philosophy.

[...]

To laugh like a dog barks, like a wolf howls. Learning to laugh is the same as becoming natural. Let's understand: life is a game. Laughter is its accompaniment. It is a sign of excess. The world is what the player wants it to be at any time.

Attribute heavy seriousness to human obtuseness.

A tiger doesn't need Nietzsche to be Dionysian. Let's try to be like that too. He who laughs must have one prerequisite: to be able to laugh also at himself.

Hence the Dadaist's honesty: I'm an idiot, etc.

I remember a sentence by V.: Our skepticism begins by confessing our faith. Herein perhaps lies the entire illness of modern man, it is an ailment, but a charming one. It prevents him from becoming ossified, from sitting down. Sometimes, it is even pain. But there are days when we spit on our worn head. Serner.

Mobilization of wits is the only mobilization mankind should obey. It's not important whether a joke is searched for, the main thing is that it is found.

Man unable to laugh is not just capable of betrayal, guile and deception, but his entire life amounts to betrayal and guile. Carlyle.

Dadaists have seen the world as it is. Like the children in Andersen's story shouting: He has no clothes! They have pure instincts. The only divine thing left in us.

Their joke went on *ad absurdum*, they turned everything upside down, throwing petards of jokes under the feet of fat matrons of art and philosophy. What a hilarious spectacle, clouds of skirts and fat arses screaming in flight.

Philosophical marathons in pursuit of truths are won by the most witty ones. The quality of a Dada-joke is in its nonsensical nature. It's not a joke told by a beer drinking party, that in Germany, a visit to the brothel turns into Tannhäuser's visit to the hillock of Venus; it is an unexpected joke, so idiotic it surprises us. See Hašek's jokes. Free of the weight of thought, it is a ball, a racket, one of the joys necessary for modern man.

[...]

DADA AND ART

Dada has assaulted fine arts. It has declared art to be magical hard stools. It gives the Venus de Milo an enema and lets Laocoön and Sons have a break after their thousand-year struggle with the snake and use the toilet. Dada has taken affirmation and negation to the point of nonsense. To achieve—

[...]

Art has become a fetish. A matter for the salons, entertainment for tea-drinking ladies. Ninety-nine percent of people think it's something special. Everyone who speaks too much about art should be treated with the utmost distrust. Art is as natural as walking, but the moment someone starts talking about art in a ceremonious tone, we can safely conclude there's a problem. Chesterton. The bourgeois all resemble each other, they are all the same. They are kept busy by their brain, which contains five possessions: money, morals, state, family, art. For the bourgeois, literature = something that represents the depth of this thinking. We then cannot be surprised that they keep talking about it; intelligent people no longer speak about art. That would be kleptomania. Art, furnished with restaurants of emotion and convents of prostitution were demolished by Dada. They have declared: art = arrogance.

Hysteria born in artist's studios. The philosophical tigers of Dadaism have leapt into the literary pen and we can still hear the baa-baaa of the lyrical lambs. They have merely caused a fright. Poor poetry! The Hamletian affectation of poets. Yorrick's scull replaced with a heart. Fossilized verse. Countless have come to the vineyard of poetry, the harvest was good, but many have smelly feet.

Idiots are always well fed and so is the art they make.

[...]

Luckily all such art is consumptive. Dada has discredited it...and continues to do so. It's just a question of time before it disappears. Just as Futurism in Italy was a reaction against classicism, Dada in Germany was a reaction against metaphysics manifested by Expressionism. In our country, where we never had this movement as such, the generation that had learned from it rages against every idyll. Dadaism in art has discovered new sensations. It cannot bear anything bearable. It welcomes the variety of the world, but it is not surprised by it. Art was a childhood illness, the Dadaists say. Words are frustrating. Poetry must make no sense. Fruit without a core is the sweetest. Crazy associations, lovely nonsense, wordplay. Games. This is not something Dada has discovered. It is taught already by the ancient wisdom of Bhagavad-Gita. That life is play that only a completed activity is of any value, without a thought about its outcome. Here we go. That is the axiom of Dadaism. To enjoy the process. There is a difference between the activity of play and the activity of life. Here, intense poetic energy is being given the greatest opportunity to change its moods, ideas, words, like a chameleon. This art, evoking elementary impressions of laughter is the opposite of the excessive psychologization of the dying art. The vitality of Dadaism lies in its astonishing, clear, regenerating folly. The modern man is logical in his work but illogical in his leisure. People have a healthy attitude to this. Panem et circenses still applies. The liking for grotesque films, circuses and other forms of entertainment containing a good dose of Dada is a proof. The people themselves are a repository of jokes, dada-jokes, so dazzling and funny they leave you in stitches. I think that the problem of the relationship between the intelligentsia and the proletariat is that today's intellectual is too ready to accept seriousness and reason and this alienates him. At the beginning was nonsense, nonsense came with the word and word was nonsense. Whoever understands this, understands Dadaism. Dadaism is chaotic like everybody who knows too much. If it contradicts itself, it has only language to blame. Men like not only fat girls but also fat ideas. Not so the Dadaists. Dada is mischievous. Without mischievousness, there is no spirit, no imagination. Dada knows that if something ends in fun, its power is doubled. Dada is unbridled and this is what makes it beautiful; there is beauty in everything that is limitless, and woe to poetry and art that applies measures to itself. Dada is brazen like innocent, exuberant joy. It is wrong to deny it to others and even worse to deny it to oneself. Let go and go. That is the slogan... Expressing smelly things in a fragrant way amounts to forgery. Dada called such things by their true name. Freed words of their moral anathema. Went further than futurism, liberated words from their seemingly logical orderliness. Dada is uncomplicated like a child and sophisticated like a man of the world. Simplicity in the world is the greatest paradox. Simple is absolute. Its intellectual juggling allows it to leap from star to star as well as fall off the table and break its neck. The evocative magic of Dada.

Its fanaticism could be based on Shaw's: I find it irritating when I see people being satisfied when they should not be. Dadaism = art presented by drunks. Hašek already says somewhere that if Homer were not an old fool, he would have hardly recited his verse... Tzara says: I write, because it is as natural as urinating.

Today, Dadaism is practically over as an artistic -ism, as Kassák correctly commented, having sacrificed himself to topple old idols. What remained were virginal land and the real work of the new builders to be carried out. The Dadaists are mostly consistent: they have thrown themselves outside art, they work in cabaret, music halls, they are caricaturists, biased essayists. Dada knows itself... and laughs at itself... Dada shall remain a designation.

DADAISM AND POLITICS

Dada has taken on a political character especially in Germany. It was the character of radical communism and this could not have happened otherwise. But it was communism that thinks of improving the world; it was a communism that considered its aim to be the extinction of the bourgeois. This was, as we can see, a very naïve, half-baked concept. Certain individuals however eventually thought it through and the best of them today belong to the class-conscious members of the proletariat.

In Germany, Dada was represented by the following names: Hausmann, Grosz, Heartfield, Hertzfeld, Mehring, Baader.

[...]

DADA + LOVE AND MORALS

This is the last chapter on Dadaism.

Love is merely a miserable product of our animality. Klíma's definition shall probably frighten all misty-eyed lovers, although mankind would benefit mightily from realizing that this is the case. Dying of love today is an anachronism today. Making geese into swans should be stopped. That fairy we keep looking back at is probably just a clothes-horse, and a very skinny one at that. Serner says: the only certainty is sexuality. The best case of contact between man and woman is coitus, slightly worse is something akin to intercourse, and the worst is erotic humbug, quoth Serner. Dying in a lady's stocking à la Don Juan and collecting virgins' scalps?

Lovers turn periodically into automatic tear-fountains and this is called holy love.

[...]

To conclude:

I agree with Grosz: our only mistake was that we concerned ourselves with art at all. Dadaism was a breakout from a narrow, inflated, and overrated environment, greeted with disparaging laughter, from an environment suspended in air between classes, which knew no responsibility towards the life of society. We didn't see immediately that this lunacy was based on a system. Some of us Dadaists were lost in that nothing we found ourselves in having overcome the cliché of art, and especially those in Switzerland and France, who have experienced the turmoil of the last decade mostly through newspapers. The rest of us, however, saw a great new task before us: service to the revolutionary cause.

We acknowledge this wisdom of Dadaism.

It is possible to be a Dadaist and Communist at the same time.

In hell, they laugh at a murderer because he had gone into all the trouble of killing a human being for so long that in the end he joins in and starts laughing himself, writes Grabbe. Let us realize this; if we are to demolish art, let us not take it so seriously and let us be wise enough and laugh in advance.

Allow me a paradox.

We cannot forgive art for being art, but love is forgivable and we love it, don't we?

You will agree that all this was very logical, more logical, less logical, truly logical, rather logical.

An apple falls not far from a horse. Deer do not suffer from gonorrhea. (I. Goll.)

You can draw your own conclusions.

It's up to you.

Think of the one who loves you most.

You have done so.

Say a number and I will tell you the lottery.

Let's make an excursion into the last drivel.

Translated by Alexandra Büchler

EXCERPTS FROM **DADA**   Karel Teige
Originally published as "Dada," *Host* vol. 6, no. 2 (November 1926)

"Total ignorance, total indifference, total indulgence."
Rémy de Gourmont, *The Horses of Diomedes*

Tristan Tzara declares: Read my books they will cure you. You shall see that the world
is insane why logic needs to be suppressed all secrets revealed
nothing is important there is no good or evil everything is
allowed indifference is the only appropriate and effective
remedy indifference without effort and without consequences
truth does not exist speech is child's play no need to take
art politics religion morals law seriously.

This handful of incoherent sentences outlines the character of Dadaism, containing
the essence of its entire program, aesthetics and philosophy—although the Dadaists
would surely protest that they have no program, aesthetics, philosophy, or even character. The Futurists considered the word "madness," which the old-fashioned public
used to throw in their face, almost a term of appreciation. The Dadaists consider their
idiocy to be a privilege. They take nothing seriously, since there is no truth and no need
for it; yet they know—and this is where we can all agree with them—that they are not
right either. They consider no human view or principle serious, binding, or credible.
They do not believe in truth, no matter what kind of truth, which also frees them of the
compulsory respect for science, philosophy and art. They respect nothing, whether
false or true. And perhaps only respect for personal freedom, liberty, and spontaneity
of inspiration teaches them that it may be better not to be taken seriously by the public,
in the same sense that the word serious is understood by earnest people. They feel
that what cannot be taken seriously by earnest people is precisely what is serious to
them. Dadaist manifestos are confessions of the spirit, which take into consideration
objections against itself. Taking a stand of such extreme philosophical relativism and
probabilism, or even absolute nihilism, is characterized by incredible instability, mal-
leability, and flexibility. The Dadaists—philosophically probably quite experienced in
order to be able to do without certainties about anything and about any outcomes—
understood that any whatsoever thesis can be, under the same circumstances, equally
defended or attacked, that by definition, any argument contains a contradiction, that
every argument for is automatically followed by an argument against, and so it is possible to be bored *ad infinitum* by these games that do not always help us pass the time.
With the caution of a highly developed spirit of paradox and contradiction, so dear to
Rémy de Gourmont, they admit to contradictions in their thoughts and actions and they
are appropriately tolerant. Those who have declared the freedom of inspiration, and, by
stating that there are no ideas, also freedom of thought as the spontaneous evolution
of our conscious and subconscious thinking, could not curb or destroy this freedom
within themselves: they are indeed receptive to all ideas, impressions, intuitions and
thoughts, none of which is better or more truthful. They even know that the opposite
of what they might be saying could be true. After all, philosophical relativism has
expressed the essential qualities of the modern spirit long before Dadaism: skepticism
in relation to any dogma or generally applicable truth, which flexes its energy not to
be bound by prescriptions, and along with every single thing to see all its other possibilities and alternatives. This skepticism gave modern life strength in the same way as
medieval life was given strength by religious faith, making it even stronger than faith
ever could. The relativist Simmel has shown that not even relativist truth is absolute,

that almost everything is relative and that relativism must limit itself if it doesn't want to contradict itself. The Dadaists have understood relativist half-truths. And when Bergson demonstrated that it is not advisable to trust reason to be always reasonable, the Dadaists declared *reason bankrupt* and gave *all power to free inspiration*. Of all the philosophies that have appeared to them as a naïve misunderstanding, they have selected nihilism as the most acceptable misunderstanding. And in the name of nihilism they attack all those sacred principles that had congealed like a skin of morals, aesthetics, and science on the authoritarian bourgeois establishment. [...] Dada will not be fooled by philosophy and metaphysics. The Dadaists are therefore not in the least determined to say the truth or defend untruth, fight, live or die for the truth. Jan Hus could afford such luxury, but he was a saint of fifteenth-century Dark Ages. The Dadaists know that the quest for truth does not suit the modern man, and that the only possible constructive activity may be the search for untruths. If they could say, however, together with Jiří of Poděbrady—to continue using patriotic examples—that "truth triumphs," it would be only because Gourmont has shown them that, conversely, what wins is always the truth. The Dadaists do not abandon the tactic of paradox and contradiction, without it they would hardly maintain their precarious balance and would fall into a mania, and, as maniacs are most often monomaniacs, they would fall into the mania of conviction, which they consider to be the last stage of cretinism. And so they prefer to be essentially in contradiction with themselves, because man himself is an inveterate contradiction, an eternal inconsistency: his very shape is irrational. Dada, free of ideas, is also free of fixed ideas. The Dadaists, those chameleons of abrupt, surprising changes, have at hand a rich selection of interesting thoughts and occasional truths suitable for all events, all circumstances, all colors of time and sensibility. They even helpfully attach instructions for use. Their occasional truths, like all truths, are comical, they are a joke. Having witnessed the end of art, philosophy, aesthetics, and morals, the Dadaists were not shaken by the emptiness of life: rather, they danced an extravagant foxtrot on the ruins. They are not frightened by absurdity, knowing that everything is absurd in life. At a time when, according to over-wise philosophers, intellect is in death throes, they are the elite of ever-growing frivolity. The positive enthusiasm fired by life's energy and humor triumphs by means of wit, laughter and noise over the ballast of negative traditions, moribund art and philosophy. The Dadaists wanted, above all, to discredit today's philosophy with its vacuous thinking, as well as today's art world, for which they deserve a word of thanks.

Because they fought wit by means of wit, art by art, philosophy by philosophy, ultimately they found themselves in a dangerous situation where the winner could only again be wit, art, and philosophy. Whether they like it or not, Dada has its philosophical and aesthetic side. It is against philosophy, yet in its fantasist nihilism it brings us philosophy. It is against art, yet it brings us playful, amusing, capricious, cheerful art. What does art matter, after all? And what is art? *Art is probably what not everyone can do; if anyone could do it, it would no longer be art. An artist can do it, and this is why it's no art for him. Art is art for those who can't do it*. Luckily, the Dadaists do not have to lose any sleep over this contradiction. Their thing is negation, and whatever positive emerges along with it doesn't concern them. But what if their magnificent "nichevo" is not the alpha and omega of all wisdom? "Laughing at philosophy really means philosophizing. Nothing responds to Reason as well as refutation of Reason. The latest progress of Reason lies in the acceptance of the fact that there are numerous matters that are beyond Reason and that it is weak indeed if it itself does not arrive at this realization. Here, we are quoting Pascal, and that is why we spell Reason with a capital R. That there are more things between heaven and earth than our philosophy can ever dream about was understood by all Hamlets and all thinkers who started from the Socratic admission: "I know that I know nothing." This is a pronouncement of philosophers who have suffered in body and spirit by disappointments and all proofs of the insufficiency of reason. And this is also the pronouncement of Dadaist mischief, which twists famous formulas, giving them a new, strange meaning: *Cogito, ergo sum.* The Dadaists say: "I think that I am not what I think I am." *Nihil in intellectu quod non fuerit in sensu.* The Dadaists say: "*Nihil in intellectu fuit in sensu.*"

Do not consider taking Dada seriously a joke. Yet, it is a joke, an old one at that, and not entirely successful. At the same time, it is a historical fact and a developmental symptom. It is consequently a kind of poetic Bergsonism, Dadaistically tinged, of course, with the spirit of negation and destruction, with a systematic skepticism, that in the end destroys itself. It is the new disease of the century, the "nouveau mal de siècle," about which Marcel Arland wrote an essay for the *Nouvelle Revue Française*, which was published in 1924, attracting wide attention. There is a terrible sense of the realization of absolute nothingness in Dadaism, a chilly terror of the utter futility of any effort, any faith or hope, a dread of the infinite emptiness of life. And this new, deeply philosophical *weltschmertz* masks its anxiety with gallows humor, with the grimaces of a clown: the realization of the impotence of intelligence is personified in the figure of a dumb buffoon. Dadaism shouts and hollers and laughs in its own somewhat hysterical way. It sings idiotic, drunken songs perhaps just in order to muster the courage to live on the ruins of the world it has rejected.

[...]

Dada does not build. Dada demolishes. It does not bring new truths. It tries to repudiate old doctrines. It is a broadly established "*entreprise de démolitions,*" as Gide called it. That is a rather sad and thankless task. Because it represents mere preparatory work during a period of transition. It can only clear the terrain, ventilate an overheated atmosphere of the literary world. And yet, this sacrificed generation is cheerful, although sometimes their cheerfulness is contradictory: it is cheerful, because it is probably incapable of understanding its lot. It is in essence absurd like any fundamentally programmatic opposition, which cannot light new fires. It cannot create anything, becoming an anomaly after the death of its last enemy, the so-called art. As long as such negative activity can serve as the beginning of a new era, a better, brighter dawn for new work, it represents a valuable, conscientious, we could almost say heroic act. "Dada has attacked art, prescribing it a magical slimming diet, it gave the Venus de Milo an enema and allowed Laocoön and Sons a break after a thousand-year long struggle with rattle snakes. It drove affirmation and negation to absurd ends, and to arrive at indifference, it started to demolish." (Hans Arp). The Futurists spat at the Altar of Art. Nihilistic Dadaists treated the spinsterish art even more rudely. In their *je m'en fous* aesthetic, they declared the bankruptcy of all art and a great sale with rock bottom prices due to bereavement. "Let circus take over now! Universal waffle is over!" And so Dada represents the death throes of the literature that had survived from the previous century. Now the task is to clear literature, to pull it down. Dada has established itself as the club of suicides. "This suicide beguiled with its blue eyes. Passionate writers got to work, and, under the excuse of demolition, repeated Jarry's farces." (Cocteau). The Dadaists live only by their oppositional temperament, the modern constructive spirit is alien to them. They may not know what they want, but they are absolutely certain about what they no longer want. And that means a lot.

[...]

Yet, it is impossible to deny anything without the necessity of laughter. Every negative is turned into a terrible laughter; humor is everywhere where life is the issue. And the Dadaist self-doubt leads to noetic questions about art, subsequently declaring the liquidation of art. The life of art is at stake: hence the laughter! The Dadaists, as Chesterton would say, are, philosophically speaking, too modest a breed to believe in multiplication tables. They have taken the Wellsian "doubt about the tool," the brain, to the most terrible consequences. And so Ribemont-Dessaignes asks: What is beauty? What is ugliness? What is greatness, power, weakness? What is Carpentier, Renan, Foch? I don't know. What am I? I don't know, don't know, don't know." Since the fantasists had shown the Dadaists that there is no place for ideas in poems, and when they realized from autopsy that ideas have little value in life, they elevated jokes above ideas. They could agree with Suarès that madness is one man's dream, but that reason is without doubt everybody's madness. They know that in our life, we lose our head at the most beautiful moments of love, otherwise they would not be as beautiful. Denying the wisdom of intellect they engage in the misdemeanor of sensibility. They have decided to abandon the great achievements of science, art and thought that had taken human idiocy to such a high level of civilization.

[...]

Dada however does not renounce only the art of the past. *It is more consistent, it renounces all art of the past, present and doubtlessly also of the future, it resolutely denies itself*, pronouncing paradoxically that there are Dadaists only in the French Academy, but true Dadaists are against Dada; Dada is simply a world war, a wild intellectual deluge that will sweep through the world of art, turning it into wreckage, so as to open the way for the birth of the new. An uncompromising war has been declared on all snobbism, all hollow fetishes of literature and culture.

It was certainly high time to declare the liquidation of art. Art receives so much attention—verbal, in print and in images—that for once, we consider it appropriate to speak against it. Walk in your mind through the numerous gallery halls around the centers of the civilized world, with thousands square kilometers of canvas covered with paint, thousands of tons of plaster, marble and bronze formed by the sculptor's hand, leaf through the numerous modern publications. You will see the chronic epidemic, the incredible crisis of overproduction and the clear fall in consumption of so-called modern art. Certainly there are too many artists. Too many paintings. If you think of the square kilometers of painted canvas, exhibited every year, of the vast expanses of canvas primed and covered with oil, you ask what happens to the paintings after the show. You know that they have not been sold. They are totally waterproof, a sad, futile result of the artist's pride and unemployment, and yet how many workers have no coat to wear! There is no doubt that art has become a thing of the past, that it has lost its function in the objective world, and, having split up into ninety-nine equally impotent directions, it is ailing and dying." Dadaism discovered that the position of art in people's lives and in the consciousness of the crowd must be urgently changed, that art must be operated on, or, if you like, sacrificed, so that a new beauty can come into being, a song of joy, merriment and happiness. If we are to declare the bankruptcy of all art, we should agree on what we understand by the word "art." If we understand it to be simply the products and manifested functions precisely corresponding to certain material or spiritual factors, that satisfy human needs and desires and man's entire complex being, in this sense, we have to admit that is it eternal, and that it has lasted and shall last, no matter how its manner and shape will change. If we however understand art to be the individual craft disciplines, which had delegated its nine representatives to the ancient Parnassus, then we have to admit that these disciplines may disappear to be replaced by new ones.

[...]

The Dadaists rightly pronounced the word "artists" with the same contempt as the romantics the word "bourgeois." But "*l'esprit Dada*" was not the constructive spirit of renewal, "*l'esprit nouveau*" Apollinaire spoke about with such enthusiasm. No, "l'esprit Dada" is the spirit of frivolous, merry youth, full of imagination and courage that lives without duties and responsibilities, without mysteries and strictness. It is the spirit of romantic bourgeois youth, the *jeunesse dorée*, for we must not deny the fact that Dada

was a bourgeois school, bourgeois fashion and bourgeois crisis. Its passionate destruc-tiveness and negation was the flip-side of the bourgeois sense of wealth, reliability and good life, which holds art in immense respect like all things it does not understand. It is a symptom of a strange crisis of culture, a peculiar flagellantism out of snobbism and progressiveness of the *haute bourgeoisie*, which accepts new literary and artistic theo-ries even when they condemn it and count on its demise. Dada was the product of a crisis of capitalism at its highest point, a symptom of the tense state of the metamor-phosis of art searching for a new social basis. And yet, it was the only living movement that has made itself known after Cubo-Futurism, sweeping away many past illusions. But it was not the herald of future work. It appeared at a point in history when the latent logic of chaos and abrupt changes began to derail art from its route of influence.
[...]

Dadaist nihilism. In a century that decayed through literature, renouncing literature was liberating. Removal of aesthetes who entertained such comical notions of life was a salvation. It was necessary to show that works of art should not be attributed the gravity they don't have. For those living solely by literature, a deluge of the world was born of literary and ideological storms in a teacup. We know however that ideas and art do not have a relevance and influence in the world and that the state of today's world is not the end result of sonnets. Only "naïve artists, infantile primitives in the age of radio and automobile still believe in witches, the Sabbath, fairies and fairy god-mothers." World war could show the obvious futility of idealism and folly of faith in the spirit governing the world. "Goethe in drum-fire, Nietzsche in a soldier's knapsack, Jesus or Buddha in the trenches," and yet, Romain Rolland still believed in the Idea and the Spirit being the independent moving forces! The truth is probably what Rémy de Gourmond wrote about ideas being created to be thought not to be carried out. Dadaism forced art to show its true color and hand in its notice as a result. The Dadaists under-stood that it would have been dangerous luck for art to be responsible for historical events. The Futurists praising war as the only possible hygiene for the world cannot be held responsible for the worldwide bloodbath. The irresponsibility of art allows it not to be afraid of the free running of imagination that breaks fixed conventions. In one of his manifestos, Tzara offers a recipe for a Dadaist poem, along with an appropriate example: cut out words from a newspaper article, words on their own, that is, liberated words; throw them into a hat, shake it, and then pick one after another by chance and copy them carefully in that sequence on a piece of paper, and, lo and behold, you have a Dadaist poem in your image, a poem resembling your individuality, since you directed fate and chance with your own hand. Of course this is nothing but a mystification simi-lar to Poe's a posteriori analysis of the Raven. And yet, wouldn't Tzara's hand, picking words from a hat, tremble if he knew that their confusion would become the confusion of the world? The pleasure of artistic creation lies precisely in the certainty that there is no decisive responsibility here. Art does not moralize, it might rather demoralize. It only vents inner life. It has no heavy social function that might break its wings. It will therefore not fight on the barricades where it would be a burden and an obstacle, impotent against poisonous gases and machine guns. It is a personal pleasure, a nuanced and disinterested game like all metaphysics, a social or gambling game, poetic chess, poker or whist. It is, if you like, the eighth capital sin. Théophile Gautier regretted that human inventiveness had never given us a new capital sin since early Christianity. Well, art and any other metaphysical activity of man is an extremely amusing and delightful new capital sin.

The "chaos of the spirit" that Rimbaud found so sacred became the exclusive domain of inspiration for the Dadaists. And they became accustomed to hallucinations. Having renounced art and aesthetics, they have discovered the poetic astronomy of the subconscious. Nebulae, meteors, and stars of the inexhaustible and uncontrollable subconscious are the repository of their poetic creativity. And their poems are the juggling of words, associations that suddenly light up like fireworks, a snowstorm of butterflies rising from the juggler's skull. In the company of Dadaists you have the impression of increasing drunkenness. Like a drunkard sailing in a sea of alcohol towards unknown, absurd islands, where nothing will apply, not even logic, morals or social rules, towards territories without barbed wire, directives and codes of law, so Dadaists drunk on the liqueur of imagination and subconscious say the most embarrassing things without melancholy, forget themselves, and their ideas take on grotesque, gigantic proportions. Causality collapses. Logic rests on identity of effects elicited by means of the same cause. But in these realms there are no same causes and it is therefore not possible to count on results. In the world of integral absurdity of the deep subconscious, innumerable logics are possible. Logic might after all cease to be logic if it were not absurd. The only humanly true logic is the logic of feelings, sensibility, whose activity is reflexive; it is the logic of vitality and physiology, and, as Freud would say, the logic of libido. It is then not entirely the logic, as we understand it. Reasoning is always absurd in relation to this, the pure contrivance of geometric reason cannot be applied to life, except in certain consequences, which already represent a compromise and which have therefore lost their original intellectual purity. Logic is the product of the laboratory of intellect. It is not found in a wild form in nature, where the way phenomena are linked together is only by logic of sensibility, physiology, and biology. And the subconscious is precisely nature, a virgin forest, jungle of poetic creativity that creates a universe without causality and amuses itself by forcing nature upon it.

Logic was not what the Dadaists needed. They lived in a spiritual atmosphere of the café society. Endowed with a sense of humor and spirit of mystification, which is always the attribute of bohemians, they enjoyed themselves reasonably well, inventing new poems. To the Dadaists as well as the fantasists, art was a mere game, but as Cocteau perceptively observed, "games and jokes can often beget new beauty. The public cannot allow this because for them the artist is a serious man who listens to Beethoven with his face in his hands, and a certain dose of playfulness, present in every modern, revolutionary movement, makes it suspicious in his eyes! But the spirit of mystification may very well appear at the beginning of a discovery, leading directly to it, being the shortest connection with the subconscious; Picasso and Apollinaire would certainly confirm this.

Dadaist poetry, subjective, purely intuitive work in the extreme, represents unconditional, somewhat somnolent obedience of the subconscious. And the subconscious, systematically stimulated, can in the absence of sufficient sexual hygiene become—as Freud's theory of sublimation has shown us—a veritable art factory. Symbolist and fantasist art bears the same trademark. Since the ladies of that time, such as Madame Rachilde, appreciated rough sensuality rather than mystical elation, the literary youths of the day took their revenge by producing spiritual Symbolism and Expressionism. And the Dadaists in turn took revenge on them, having sex *in natura* with the ladies of their dreams. Dadaism is not about sublimation—according to Freud, sublimation is the process that deflects the sexual power from sexual aims reorienting it towards new aims, gaining substantial material for cultural achievements—but direct action of subconscious forces in their nakedness and chaos. The whole "Dadalogy" would make an interesting chapter in psychology or perhaps psychopathology. Yes, this is where the world has ended: "cows sitting on telegraph poles, playing chess," laments Huelsenbeck.

Dadaist negation, Dadaist pessimism and nihilism, Dadaist anti-aestheticism and anti-artism—these are not mere negative items. Dada is not simply a deep, essential sorrow of disruption and emptiness of everything, despair over the futility of it all. The Dadaists know that futility can, under certain circumstances, be as beautiful, kind and merry as love and poetry. Amidst the decline of morals, reason, philosophy, and science we can still laugh. Enjoy the all-pervasive bankruptcy and abuse it, hang one's trapeze on a nail of indemonstrability and indulge in ridiculing antics. This is not Oblomovian nihilism driven to helplessness. It is a nihilism only too active. It is an attack against artistic sentimentality. A cheerful challenge of vitality and positive, humorous energy against stagnant and bloodless aestheticism and literary snobbism. It is an active, fertile, and creative nihilism of the kind praised by Mahen in his *Book on the Czech Character*, it is what Friedländer calls "schöpferishe Indifference." And it is Friedländer that Mahen refers to and who could be referred to by the Dadaists, who professes that if man wants to be creative, he must first of all abandon superstition in existing things. Yes, only indifference makes the future and the past into real present—a living and life-giving space. Resting their cause on nothingness, the Dadaists placed it unwittingly at the very point at which the world keeps its balance. Therefore, they did not need to decide between two alternatives. There is no "either/or" for them. Both apply. "*Tertium datur differenter, sed differenter.*" Dadaists are the living nothing of the world—and this knowledge makes them erupt with creative force.

Dadaist negations were powerful enough to renew positive creative energy. Such a period of negation is, after all, always a sign of a great metamorphosis and rebirth in history. To clear up the terrain for building anew, there was a need for a thorough denial of art and fervent destructive work. Constructivism and Poetism have to thank Dadaism for this negative work of destruction. And the Dadaists' "nichevo" (psychologically akin to what we call, after Nietzsche, Dionysian pessimism) is also encouraging: it shows that everything, everywhere can be laughed at, that the halls of nirvana and the cellars of hell reverberate with laughter. Where there is nothing, there is still laughter.

Dadaism, a blossom opening on ruins, is the reaction of vitality against annihilation and destruction. Redeeming laughter, devouring everything that threatens life's freedom and flourishing. It is a manifestation of life's spontaneity. It is also undemandingly pacifist, unimpressed by lofty metaphors and those great, hollow, decorative words, which often conceal bellicose, aggressive inclinations. At the moment when you decided to start arguing about words (and what else could you argue about?) by its practice, Dadaism made those very words into a laughing stock, rendering them useless.

The Dadaists' anti-philosophical stance is the beginning of wisdom. Dadaist anti-aestheticism and anti-artism marks the beginning of a new era of art and aesthetic creation, which has, since the time of the Cubist coup, set out along new paths, leading to forms, unprecedented in history, which cease being "art." Dadaist skepticism about the very material of literature, the word, brings a renewal of vocabulary, testing the material without which verbal art would not be possible. Reading Dadaist manifestoes and magazines, you hold in your hands faithful photographs of the situation, but only its negative plates. Add sensitive paper and you obtain a positive picture. Yet the role of Dadaism was to act negatively and in opposition. Dada halted its destructive action at the very moment when it would have to become constructive—and gives in its notice.

The school of fantasy bled to death during the anxious nights and days on the Marne, at Verdun, in Moscow, and on the pavements of St. Petersburg. "When saber cut the flow of eloquent verse, guns boomed instead of words of love; that was revolution. That's all." (Seifert.) Now the world is changing. In the Comintern's laboratory, strict and precise plans are being developed for a new social structure, a new blueprint for life, in which there is no place for old art. Gone are images and poems, out of date as soon as they were conceived, destroyed as soon as they became out of date, forgotten as soon as they were destroyed. "A new red star is rising heralding a new era. New beauty, new poetry of a new life, to which the art of the past has nothing to say." Even the Dadaists had to understand this. And they proceeded to liquidate the Dadaist movement. Its obituary was a special issue of *Ça ira* magazine, published in 1922, with a historical account of the birth, life and death of the Dada movement by Pierre Massot. Dada was loud and made a lot of noise, and later it was perhaps deafened by this very noise and in the end drowned in it. "Dada makes you think of a cigarette that leaves behind a pleasant smell," said Picabia. And so its promising story ends and the memory of Dada mingles at dawn with the ashes of our perfumed cigarettes." The adventure of Dada ends in the way of all adventures: banal and grotesque... It ends Dadaistically.

Translated by Alexandra Büchler

chapter 7

INTERNATIONAL CONSTRUCTIVISM IN GERMANY AND AUSTRIA

Timothy O. Benson

International Constructivism, although sharing much with its Russian predecessor, was a diverse amalgam that evolved within several decisively different contexts—at first primarily in Germany and Austria, starting in early 1922—then in Poland, Czechoslovakia, Romania, Croatia, and Slovenia. The word "constructivism" had arisen in the Moscow INKhUK (Institute for Artistic Culture) in March 1921 where Alexander Rodchenko, Varvara Stepanova, and Aleksei Gan took a stance against easel painting, claiming instead that real materials be used for utilitarian purposes. In keeping with the newly-founded communist state, their conception of Constructivism sought a rigorously economic organization of materials, without excesses. The members of OBMOKhU (Society of Young Artists), Karl Ioganson, Konstantin Medunetsky, and Georgy and Vladimir Stenberg soon joined the group creating a variety of spatial constructions and technologically informed works that were exhibited at OBMOKhU in Moscow in May, 1921.

News of Constructivism reached Berlin through El Lissitzky, who arrived in Berlin directly from Moscow in the end of 1921. Yet, in contrast with the severely Productivist direction evolving in Moscow, Lissitzky had continued his "Proun" works, codified previously while he was in Vitebsk working

under the strong infleunce of Kazimir Malevich and Suprematism. Lissitzky's works had a great impact on the work of many artists, including the Polish Expressionist Henryk Berlewi, and he propagated a comprehensive view of Constructivism in his Berlin periodical, *Veshch/Gegenstand/Objet*, which premiered in March 1922 with an installation view of the OBMOKhU exhibition.

Yet prior to this many artists had already developed elementary abstract vocabularies. Hungarian émigrés and Ma members László Péri and László Moholy-Nagy were exhibiting cutting-edge abstraction and sculpture at the Sturm Gallery. Lajos Kassák and Sándor Bortnyik, in Vienna, were moving toward universal architectonic forms. Dutch De Stijl abstraction was known through Gerrit Rietveld, Jan Wils, and Theo van Doesburg, who had launched a private course in Weimar (as an alternative to the Bauhaus). In general there was a growing sense of urgency to forge an international community and common artistic vocabulary— whether "style," fundamental "elements," or universal language ("A Call for Elementarist Art"). Constructivism in Central Europe accrued its meaning partly in terms of the subsequent debates taking place at the Congress of International Progressive Artists held in Düsseldorf in May, 1922, and at the Congress of Constructivists and Dadaists in September in Weimar, where an International Constructivist Creative Union ("Constructivist International") based on a more practical, collectivist approach, was proclaimed.

Only following these events was the full extent of Russian Constructivist production broadly known in Berlin when the First Russian Art Exhibition opened in October 1922 at the Van Diemen Gallery with works by artists ranging from Malevich and Vladimir Tatlin to Naum Gabo, Kazimir Medunetsky, Ivan Puni, Alexander Rodchenko, and Georgy and Vladimir Stenberg. Responses in German, Hungarian, and Croatian journals show how widespread the term "Constructivist" was becoming and how diverse its meanings could be.

But Hungarian artists and critics living in Berlin—László Péri, László Moholy-Nagy, Ernő Kállai—had gained direct access to Russian influences even sooner through their compatriot Alfréd Kemény, who had lectured at INKhUK at the end of 1921, and Ma artist Béla Uitz, who had attended the Third International in Moscow and encountered students of VKhUTEMAS (Higher Art Workshops). This news also reached the Ma group of Hungarian exiles in Vienna, who had already gained knowledge of Malevich, Tatlin, and other precursors of Constructivism in a lecture by Konstantin Umanski sponsored by Ma in November 1920. In 1922 their periodical *Ma* began to feature Russian art, and Kassák and Moholy-Nagy published *Buch neuer Künstler* (Book of New Artists) reproducing Constructivist works. By then Kassák had split both with Sándor Barta, who represented the leftist

Dada spirit in the Ma circle, and with Uitz, who founded his own more orthodox communist periodical, *Egység* (Unity). It propagated a strict, pragmatic, and proletkult interpretation of Constructivism, and published a manifesto against both De Stijl and OBMOKhU signed by the hardliners Kemény and Péri as well as Moholy-Nagy and Ernő Kállai, for whom this statement marked a fleeting episode. *Ma* and *Egység* also provided a forum for visionary interpretation by the well-informed Kállai on Constuctivism and the works of Moholy-Nagy and Kassák. *Ma* also responded to events on Vienna's cosmopolitan arts scene, and devoted a special issue to the 1924 International Theater Exhibition.

In no small part due to Hungarian influences, the Bauhaus became increasingly a center of International Constructivism after 1923 when it held its first public exhibition of Bauhaus production and invited Moholy-Nagy onto its faculty, partly in response to the Constructivist initiative underway in the KURI group (acronym for "Constructive, Utilitarian, Rational, International"), an association of students, many from Hungary. Moholy-Nagy was central to the Bauhaus's exploration of new media (including photography), its collaboration with industry, and its advancement of typography in books and periodicals. If Berlin was an essential birthplace of International Constructivism, it was also the city where it played itself out in perhaps the greatest variety— Kemény and Moholy-Nagy sought dynamic principles for motion lacking among many of the Constructivists, Hausmann imagined a constructed stage space for the dynamic energy of dance, and Nikolaus Braun sought to incorporate light into the Constructivist model. Berlewi and Kemény demonstrated how a panoramic view of Constructivism was possible from Berlin, and, when the time came, Hans Richter cautioned in his Berlin periodical G that Constructivism might be becoming mere fashion.

CONGRESS OF INTERNATIONAL PROGRESSIVE ARTISTS IN DÜSSELDORF Timothy O. Benson

Held in May 1922 on the occasion of the First International Exhibition organized by the Young Rhineland group, the Congress of International Progressive Artists in Düsseldorf was a key event in the attempts to forge an international art movement. While the "Founding Proclamation of the Union of Progressive Artists," signed by some of the participants, made an urgent appeal for an international art, the exhibition lacked cohesion (as Polish artist Henryk Berlewi pointed out in his review) and the Congress itself conveyed little more than disunity and discord. Yet the most progressive artists attending the event—including Theo van Doesburg, El Lissitzky, and Hans Richter—while refusing to sign the Founding Proclamation, led an opposing International Faction of Constructivists that would help establish a new direction. Their "Statement" (published in the Dutch journal *De Stijl*) objected, above all, to the Union of Progressive Artists's emphasis on subjectivity and the autonomy of the individual, and argued instead for the "universally comprehensible."

Lissitzky, who had arrived in Berlin from Moscow in late 1921 with his version of Constructivism and had begun to represent it in his periodical, *Veshch/Gegenstand/Objet*, also published a statement in *De Stijl*, as did artists' groups from Holland, Russia, Romania, Switzerland, Scandinavia, and Germany. The Hungarian Ma group proposed in their journal that an alternative organization representing all of these responses be centered in Berlin. The Berlin Commune, which had noisily refused in advance to participate in the Düsseldorf Congress, staged their own International Exhibition of Revolutionary Artists the following autumn. The following September the Constructivist Faction (van Doesburg, Lissitzky, and Richter), along with Raoul Hausmann, Tristan Tzara, Hans Arp, Sándor Bortnyik, and others, held a Congress of Constructivists and Dadaists in Weimar (home of the recently-founded Bauhaus), preceded by a small Constructivist Exhibition in the atelier of the architect Josef Zachmann. On occasion of this congress they proposed a new organization, the Konstruktivistische Internationale schöpferische Arbeitsgemeinschaft (International Constructivist Creative Union), and published their manifesto in *De Stijl* (signed also by Max Burchartz and Karel Maes).

The failed Düsseldorf congress and its aftermath show how the European avant-garde in 1922 urgently sought its future as an "international" entity. By the end of the year, without adopting all of the tenets of their Russian predecessors, many had rallied around the term "constructivism" as compatible with their program.

CONGRESS OF INTERNATIONAL PROGRESSIVE ARTISTS: A SHORT REVIEW OF THE PROCEEDINGS   Editors of De Stijl, et. al.

Originally published in *De Stijl* vol. 4, no. 4 (May, 1922)

The Young Rhineland group, along with a number of other German groups—the November Group (Berlin), Darmstadt Secession, Dresden Secession, among others— took the initiative in forming a kind of union with the backing of a majority of medium-sized groups in order to set up an International of Progressive Artists. But in this, as in everything, there is agreement in theory but not in practice. With their fine-sounding manifestoes the leaders of the French and German groups drummed out the following proclamation:

FOUNDING PROCLAMATION OF THE UNION OF PROGRESSIVE INTERNATIONAL ARTISTS

"From all over the world come voices calling for a union of progressive artists. A lively exchange of ideas between artists of different countries has now become necessary. The lines of communication that were torn up by political events are finally reopened. We want universal and international interest in art. We want a universal international periodical. We want a permanent, universal, international exhibition of art everywhere in the world. We want a universal, international music festival that will unite mankind at least once a year with a language that can be understood by all.

"The long dreary spiritual isolation must now end. Art needs the unification of those who create. Forgetting questions of nationality, without political bias or self-seeking intention, our slogan must now be: 'Artists of all nationalities unite.' Art must become international or it will perish.

"[Signed:] The Young Rhineland, Düsseldorf; Dresden Secession; November Group, Berlin; Darmstadt Secession; Creative Group, Dresden: Theodor Däubler. Else Lasker-Schüler, Herbert Eulenberg, Oskar Kokoschka, Christian Rohlfs, Romain Rolland, Wassily Kandinsky, Han Ryner, Edouard Dujardin, Marcel Millet, Tristan Remy, Marek Schwarz, Marcel Sauvage (Groupe l'Albatros), Paul Jamatty, Prampolini, Pierre Creixamt, Henri Poulaille, Maurice Wullens, Pierre Lariviere (Guilde des Artisans de l'Avenir), Josef Quessnel, Germain Delafons (Les Compagnons), Stanisław Kubicki, A. Feder, Jankel Adler, Arthur Fischer."

Being in the majority, the Unionists thought themselves strong enough to win over the minority of really progressive artists to their side and to force them to sign the Union proclamation unconditionally. In true Prussian tradition everybody who did not obey was to be thrown out. This provoked a violent reaction from the progressive minority. At this point active intervention by the International Faction of Constructivists (Van Doesburg, Lissitzky, Richter) resolved the conflict, and the enforced signing of the manifesto was changed to simply recording on a list the signatures of those present.

The next thing the Unionists did was to read aloud and applaud the program of the Young Rhineland group. Their program...consisted of no less than 149 paragraphs, devoted almost exclusively to the problems of finance and exhibitions and to starting an annual music festival and setting up an international periodical (whose appearance as announced in the catalogue of the international exhibition at Düsseldorf). Next those who had come with the intention of forming an organization of creative forces, and who put artistic considerations before everything else, turned against the program. From this was apparent that the whole International was already prepared, behind the backs of those present (except, of course, the Young Rhineland), for the

real issue at stake in deciding the aims of the congress: form a group of progressive artists from those present, who collectively, rather than as individuals,
would destroy anything that might stand in the way of the development of the
creative arts. The I.F.d.K. (Van Doesburg, Lissitzky, Richter) wanted to know first
of all what kind of International this would be: was it to be a financial or an artists'
International?

In addition they demanded that a committee should be elected from everybody present (not just from the Young Rhineland). Everybody should then submit his ideas on
the way in which the International should work to the committee through the secretariat and these would then be openly discussed. But again all questions about the
character of the International were only answered evasively. Even the formation of a
definite committee was shiftily dealt with. At the twentieth point in the 149-paragraph
program the speaker (Mr. Wollheim) was interrupted by loud protests. Several suggestions were made at this point, among them, that a committee should be nominated
which should then select the program of the Union. At the request of the I.F.d.K. a
copy of the proceedings was circulated to all present.

After that the sitting was adjourned and the participants joined for a boat trip.

SECOND DAY (MAY 30)

After a speech by a member of the Young Rhineland group and the reading of
some telegrams, the floor was thrown open to all members of the congress.
In this way it was hoped to take account of the demands and suggestions of those
present. The Dadaists, who had been protesting continuously from the beginning,
declared themselves opposed to the whole character and setup of the congress.
Mr. Henryk Berlewi (Poland) asked for a clear definition of the term "progressive
artist."

One of the French representatives declared France ready to hold exhibitions of
German art provided that the Union would make reasonable suggestions. Another
French representative pointed out the necessity for a new romantic movement
(protests from the progressive artists). Mr. Kubicki called attention to the need for
a truly friendly and brotherly way of working together (applause). By this time the
congress had lost all sense of leadership and there was continual shouting going on.
The last speakers were Lissitsky, Richter, and Van Doesburg. They explained their
reasons for attending the conference in a statement that was interrupted partly
by applause, partly by protest. This impartial statement of the position of the
different factions, with its accompanying declaration, printed here in full, was given
to the Unionists, the French, and the Italian representatives at the end of the congress. After that Mr. Raoul Hausmann (Dadaist) read a protest in both French and
German declaring that he was neither for the progressives nor for the artists, and
that he was no more international than he was a cannibal. He then left the room.
Mr. Werner Graeff concluded the reply to Van Doesburg with the following words:
"I am nearly the youngest of all of you and I have reached the conclusion that you
are neither international, nor progressive, nor artists. There is therefore nothing
more for me to do here."

This was greeted with loud applause by the I.F.d.K. group. Then with intense applause
on the one side, and with the boos and cheers of the other side, the I.F.d.K. group,
the Futurists, the Dadaists, and the majority of others walked out of the Düsseldorf
congress buildings.

STATEMENT BY THE EDITORS OF VESHCH/GEGENSTAND/OBJET

1. I come here as representative of the magazine *Veshch/Gegenstand/Objet*, which stands
    for a new way of thinking and unites the leaders of the new art in nearly all countries.

2. Our thinking is characterized by the attempt to turn away from the old subjective, mystical conception of the world and to create an attitude of universality–clarity–reality.

3. That this way of thinking is truly international may be seen from the fact that during a seven-year period of complete isolation from the outside world, we were attacking the same problems in Russia as our friends here in the West, but without any knowledge of the others. In Russia we have fought a hard but fruitful struggle to realize the new art on a broad social and political front.

4. In doing so we have learned that progress in art is possible only in a society that has already completely changed its social structure.

5. By progress we mean here the freeing of art from its role as ornament and decoration, from the need to satisfy the emotions of the few. Progress means proving and explaining that everybody has the right to create. We have nothing to do with those who minister to art like priests in a cloister.

6. The new art is founded not on a subjective, but on an objective basis. This, like science, can be described with precision and is by nature constructive. It unites not only pure art, but all those who stand at the frontier of the new culture. The artist is companion to the scholar, the engineer, and the worker.

7. As yet the new art is not always understood; it is not only society—that misunderstands it, but more dangerously, it is misunderstood by those who call themselves progressive artists.

8. To combat this situation we must join ranks so that we really can fight back. It is essentially this fight that unites us. If our aim were only to defend the material interests of a group of people called artists, we would not need another union, because there are already international unions for painters, decorators, and varnishers, and professionally we belong to these.

9. WE REGARD THE FOUNDING OF AN INTERNATIONAL OF PROGRESSIVE ARTISTS AS THE BANDING TOGETHER OF FIGHTERS FOR THE NEW CULTURE. Once again art will return to its former role. Once again we shall find a collective way of relating the work of the artist to the universal.

—El Lissitzky, delivered also on behalf of Ehrenburg

STATEMENT BY THE STIJL GROUP

I. I speak here on behalf of the Stijl group of Holland, which has been set up because of the need to release the potential of modern art, that is, to solve universal problems in practice.

II. For us the most important thing is to give form, to organize the means into a unity.

III. This unity can be achieved only by suppressing subjective arbitrariness in the means of expression.

IV. We renounce the subjective choice of forms, we are working toward the use of a universal and objective medium of design.

V. "Progressive artists" are those who fearlessly accept the consequences of this new aesthetic theory.

VI. Long ago, as early as the war, the progressive artists of Holland adopted a theoretical position that was internationally recognized (cf. the introduction to *De Stijl*, vol. I, 1917).

VII. This international exhibition was made possible only by the development of our work. It arose from our experience of working. The same needs arose also from the developments of advanced artists in other countries.

VIII.In the certainty that the same problems were being taken up in every country (and in the fields of science, technology, architecture, sculpture, painting, music, etc.), we published our first manifesto as early as 1918.

IX. The manifesto proclaimed the following points:

MANIFESTO 1 OF DE STIJL, 1918

1. There is an old and a new consciousness of time. The old is connected with the individual. The new is connected with the universal. The struggle of the individual against the universal is revealing itself in the world war as well as in the art of the present day.
2. The war is destroying the old world and its contents: individual domination in every state.
3. The new art has brought forward what the new consciousness of time contains: a balance between the universal and the individual.
4. The new consciousness is prepared to realize the internal life as well as the external life.
5. Traditions, dogmas, and the domination of the individual are opposed to this realization.
6. The founders of the new plastic art, therefore, call upon all who believe in the reformation of art and culture to eradicate these obstacles to development, as in the new plastic art (by excluding natural form) they have eradicated that which blocks pure artistic expression, the ultimate consequence of all concepts of art.
7. The artists of today have been driven the whole world over by the same consciousness, and therefore have taken part from an intellectual point of view in this war against the domination of individual despotism. They therefore sympathize with all who work to establish international unity in life, art, culture, either intellectually or materially.
8. The monthly editions of *De Stijl*, founded for that purpose, try to set forth the new comprehension of life in a clear manner. Cooperation is possible by:
9. i.) Sending, as an indication of approval, name, address, and profession to the editor of *De Stijl*. ii.) Sending critical, philosophical, architectural, scientific, literary, musical articles or reproductions. iii.) Translating articles in different languages or disseminating ideas published in *De Stijl*.

Signatures of the collaborators:
Theo van Doesburg, Painter
Robt. van 't Hoff, Architect
Vilmos Huszár, Painter
Antony Kok, Poet
Piet Mondriaan, Painter
G. Vantongerloo, Sculptor
Jan Wils, Architect

X. This manifesto grew out of the common endeavor of painters, designers, architects, sculptors, and poets and was enthusiastically received by the progressive artists of every country. This demonstrated that an international organization was feasible and indeed necessary.

STATEMENT BY THE CONSTRUCTIVIST GROUPS OF ROMANIA, SWITZERLAND, SCANDINAVIA, AND GERMANY

I speak here as the representative of the groups of constructivist artists from Switzerland, Scandinavia, Romania, and Germany. I agree in general with the views of El Lissitzky. The work we wish to produce as an international poses the same kind of problems that we have been trying to solve as individual artists—indeed we have gone beyond our own individual problems to the point where we can pose an objective problem. This unites us in a common task. This task leads (beyond the scientific methods of investigating the elements of art) to the desire for more than just the creation of a better painting or a better piece of sculpture: to reality itself.

Just as the feeling for life prevented us from painting like the Impressionists, prevented us from accepting the old, it now makes us wish to paint, to build, to create the new reality.

We had hoped to find this spirit in the International. This spirit should generate the strength and the initiative necessary to identify and solve the problems of society in their entirety.

But to build an International around economics is to misunderstand the need for an International. The International must not only support its members, but also create and document a new attitude. To show that it is possible to achieve such a new, position in a comradely collective way, using all our strength to create the new way of life we so badly need—that is indeed a worthy task!

But this cannot be achieved if everybody thinks that it is enough simply to fulfill his personal ambition in society. We must first understand that this can be created only by a society that renounces the perpetuation of the private experiences of the soul.

Neither in open discussion, nor, above all, in what it expects from the International, does this congress give any assurance that this point of view is shared by the majority. If we assumed for a moment that we were agreed in principle, what would we do? How could we successfully achieve the intentions of the International?

As a working community!

We will set ourselves the problems: space, the house, surfaces, color, and so on. Because our aim is to make use of each other's work and because our work will be criticized only by others who are themselves familiar with the same problems, we will be able to defend only that part of our work which is objective, which solves problems; this will give everybody a personal interest in the work. If I want to build, I need elements that I know to be reliable. There can be no excuse for anything that does not clarify the intention behind a piece of work; people must not just sympathize, they must understand the work.

You believe that we should choose exhibitions, magazines, and congresses as a means of reorganizing society. But if we are so far advanced that we can work and make progress collectively, let us no longer tack between a society that does not need us and a society that does not yet exist, let us rather *change the world of today*. In the sureness of our mission we represent a real force that has yet to be felt.

On behalf of the constructivist groups of Romania, Switzerland, Scandinavia, and Germany
Signed: Hans Richter
For Baumann, Viking Eggeling, Janco

STATEMENT BY THE INTERNATIONAL FACTION OF CONSTRUCTIVISTS[1]

We came to Düsseldorf with the firm intention of creating an International. Yet the following has proved to be the case:

---

1 "Constructivism" is used here only to characterize the contrast with all "Impulsivists." [Original note added to the publication of the statement in *De Stijl*, presumably an effort by van Doesburg to distance the meaning of the term from its Russian origins.—Ed.]

Unionists:	We:
1. As a basis for organizing the International, the Unionists propose the "lively exchange of ideas between artists of different countries."	1. Good will is not a program and cannot therefore be used as the basis for the organization of the International. Good will disappears just at the moment it should be shown toward the opposition in the congress.
2. There is complete confusion over the purpose of the Union: should it be a guild to represent the interest of the artists, or should it provide the economic basis for carrying out certain cultural intentions?	2. To us it is clear that, first of all our position vis-à-vis the arts must be defined and only on this basis can economic questions be considered.
3. There is no definition of the term "progressive artist." Questions of this kind were *refused* consideration on the agenda on the grounds that the way people tackle the problems of art is an entirely personal matter.	3. We define the progressive artist as one who fights and rejects the tyranny of the subjective in art, as one whose work is not based on lyrical arbitrariness, as one who accepts the new principles of artistic creation— the systemization of the means of expression to produce results that are universally comprehensible.
4. As is evident from the founding proclamation, the Unionists have envisaged a series of undertakings that aim essentially at creating an international trade for the exhibition of painting. The Union must therefore be planning to start a bourgeois colonial policy.	4. We reject the present conception of an exhibition: a warehouse stuffed with unrelated objects, all for sale. Today we stand between a society that does not need us and one that does not yet exist; the only purpose of exhibitions is to demonstrate what we wish to achieve (illustrated with plans, sketches, and models) or what we have already achieved.

From the foregoing it is obvious that an International of progressive artists can be founded only on the following basis:

a) Art is, in just the same way as science and technology, a method of organization which applies to the whole of life.

b) We insist that today art is no longer a dream set apart and in contrast to the realities of the world. Art must stop being just a way of dreaming cosmic secrets. Art is a universal and real expression of creative energy, which can be used to organize the progress of mankind; it is the tool of universal progress.

c) To achieve this reality we must fight, and to fight we must be organized. Only by doing so can the creative energy of mankind be liberated. In this way we can bridge the gap between the most grandiose theories and day-to-day survival.

THE ARTISTS OF THE CONGRESS HAVE PROVED THAT IT IS THE TYRANNY OF THE INDIVIDUAL THAT MAKES THE CREATION OF A PROGRESSIVE AND UNIFIED INTERNATIONAL IMPOSSIBLE WITH THE ELEMENTS OF THIS CONGRESS.

—Theo van Doesburg, El Lissitzky, Hans Richter

Translated by Nicholas Bullock

MANIFESTO OF THE COMMUNE   Stanisław Kubicki, et. al.

Originally published as *Manifesto der Kommune* (Berlin: March 1922)

We, the undersigned, are embarking on a united stand against the historical and natural world. Our unifying bond is the knowledge that, in order to stand for a universal idea, the individual must first prove mental and moral incorruptibility. We shall have nothing to do with the grubby opportunism that is prevalent in artistic groups in general, or with those who devote their lives to such groups. We have no interest in reconciliation at any price—as preached by those who like to fish in troubled waters. Our love will be a hard love. This is the only way to fight soft villainies, and hard ones too. We set up no aesthetic precepts for ourselves, nor have we any intention of doing so for anyone else. For this reason, none of us can become dominant within the group. We agree on the need to break down the horizons imposed on the world and on human thinking by the decay of social and family life. We do not regard any human being as a definitive, unalterable type. Which is why we call on him to change his type, in response to a summons voiced in a clear language that is understood by everyone, whatever the linguistic community to which he belongs. We will have no truck with commercial middlemen. We seek to connect with brothers and sisters in every nation, so as to eradicate the moral and mental infection of personal vanity, pushiness, exclusivity, and plain self-infatuation that nips all eccentric cultural enterprises in the bud. We do not advertise for a following, or for public recognition. We are certain that the aura of a common resolve will seep through every pore and transcend all barriers of time and space. We neither have nor want any form of bureaucratic organization. None of us seeks honors or social status. We hold no tea parties. We accept no protection from anyone in authority. We have launched ourselves into the world and into existence, and we shall defend the form that we have created for ourselves—though we were born in the mud. Within ourselves we have no dark corners into which to lure the unwary for purposes of robbery or murder. Those who take fright at our uncompromising rigor may remain in the reeking morass where each man devours his neighbor's maggots and rolls his eyes in ecstasy. It would be better if they were honest cannibals.
That is our program. Its theses are plain. They rest on human, not artistic guarantees.
—Stanisław Kubicki, Melchior Hala, Stanisławowa, Else Hala, Doris Homann, [Felix] Gasbarra, Franz Josef Esser, Oskar Fischer, Herm. F. A. Westphal, Otto Freundlich

Translated by David Britt

SECOND MANIFESTO OF THE COMMUNE   Stanislaw Kubicki, et. al.

Originally published as *Zweites Manifest der Kommune* (Berlin: May 1922)

The international art exhibition that is scheduled to open in Düsseldorf in May has faced "Die Kommune" with the decision as to whether to participate or not. We have declined.
First of all, we are convinced that the term "international" needs to be defined. The opportunity would have existed, on the occasion of the international exhibition in Düsseldorf, to attach a new meaning to the word: its only true meaning. But here, as everywhere, people were their own worst enemies; and the base machinations of the

art corporations, propelled by power-hungry and ambitious individuals, made a mock-ery of the idea of international cooperation. Not one of the groups—November Group, Junges Rheinland, Der Sturm, Dresden Secession—is going to the Düsseldorf exhibi-tion with any purpose in mind beyond the personal advantage of its members. Not one of those groups has had the courage to depart from its own selfish, partisan stand-point. It has not crossed any of their minds to disband in the interests of a greater international community. To accept this mentality as the norm would be to declare the moral bankruptcy of Europeanism. It would mean that the European faculty of judg-ment is no longer guided or educated by any normative standard of truth. It would mean that mentalities and ideas are as flabby and nondescript as the European way of life. It would mean that there are no exceptions any longer: a rapid process of decline is entrenching a human type that acts—and judges the actions of others—on strictly utilitarian criteria. We are not going to remain silent about this. We mean to give courage to those who find themselves caught in the toils of these parasitical growths that feed on the blood of life and yet remain barren.

Only the barren seek to usurp power over life by stealth. Only the barren resort to intrigue and the patronage of public officials. Only the barren fraternize with the despised adversary and to discard him when they have sucked him dry. Only the barren reward unquestioning trust with a pretense of trust, and use the trustful as tools of their own selfish policy. The world is full of this, true enough. No one objects. And the good people take the easy option and turn into good-natured rogues.

The only being who really loves is he who fights for what he loves. The only being who really loves is he who has purified and clarified his knowledge. Love is absolute devo-tion; its strongest quality is that it creates form, within and without. Whoever creates form only in and for himself is without love. Whoever does not embrace the world in the act of generation is a petty human being and a petty enjoyer. Of course, the sophists of the ego—their hearts so impoverished that they cannot reach out to the other—preach a love that you can hold on the end of a string, like a toy balloon. Bubbles, bubbles, bubbles in the air! Such a love will not hold the weight of a pebble; in fat, it needs the support of all the other human powers if it is to survive a single day. With a weakling's arrogance, such love accepts the rich gifts lavished upon it every second; without them it would at once be lost.

Our task is to review the whole of the past. Not as an intellectual critique but through the *lived* experience of being otherwise. They know that this is all that counts. All those bunglers know it: both those who sell criticism and those who sell pictures.

To the offspring of the bourgeois family, its palisades look like the Pillars of Hercules that support the world; and this belief requires to be sustained by distortion, lies, and deceit. To this end, the world must be infected—on a public and also a domestic scale—by politics, the ruination of all human relationships since history began. But people hold fast to this belief, for quite shallow reasons—thus proving only that shal-low reasons run deep. They are branded onto the brows and necks of human cattle, whose collective life they encompass with an aroma of singed flesh that enables the members of this great clan to recognize each other. Woe betide anyone who lacks the same scent! Those clannish souls look askance at him. Every one of them has devel-oped the sure, instinctive solidarity of the cattle shed. Thus seen, the European men-tality is easy to categorize. Big artistic groups that live by theft from a handful of inventive talents; much-praised individual celebrities, who owe their own good fortune to the possession of an intricate aesthetic skeleton key: these are highly respectable men, wholly legitimate and above board, who are well respected and have the ear of authority at every level. And why not? Are they any different from their patrons? Not in the slightest. Those patrons are often intelligent people. They are quite unmoved by the cries of the nonconformists. They know that none of them really means it, and that it reflects nothing more than an impatient desire for a warm nest. In the end they are all, all graciously received—at Court, or in a great financier's luxurious vestibule, or on the premises of the great art dealers, or among the assembled family mourners—and all is just as it was.

O Man, if you are an artist, a poet, or a writer—let alone a worker—on no account assume the right to take anything in life seriously other than what suits the spirit of the clan, or the party, or the family. Creep as sluggishly as a swamp full of croaking frogs. You all hold international exhibitions. We stand on dry land and listen to the frogs. We know the frogs by name and can tell them apart by their voices.

We know what this bell has tolled and always will toll. We will settle somewhere else: not in that swamp. No. Houses on piles are not for us, and we dislike swamp mists and vapors. The earth will have its way with you. We seek for ourselves a place on this earth where the air is pure and the soil is fertile. The earth will lend us its strength, and we shall lend it ours. Farewell, you frogs.

—Stanisław Kubicki, Otto Freundlich, Tristan Remy, Gasbarra, Herm. F. A. Westphal, Stanisławowa, Ludwig Hilberseimer, Doris Homann, Franz Joseph Esser, Raoul Hausmann, Hedwig Mankiewitz

We originally gave our association the name of Die Kommune. We now detach the label from our brows and state that this group no longer exists.
Our connection will continue, even without a name, if we as human beings are truly connected.

Translated by David Britt

THE INTERNATIONAL EXHIBITION IN DÜSSELDORF   Henryk Berlewi
Originally published as "Miedzynarodowa wystawa w Düsseldorfie," *Nasz Kurier*
(August 2, 1922)

At the end of May, in the large commercial building of Leonhard Tietz in Düsseldorf, the First International Exhibition of Modern Art was opened with great ceremony. A dozen nations were represented. It seemed that all these people from different, faraway countries came to the town on the river Rhine in order to shake hands fraternally and to clear the path for a new art emerging from the chaos. Antagonisms of a non-artistic nature have all but disappeared for the good of one great cause: art.

The fact that the exhibition is hosted not in some traditional *Kunstpalast* or other "Pantheon of art," reeking of the old, but in a building belonging to Mercury, ought to be treated with great enthusiasm.

It shows that the new art is slowly breaking away from the mortuaries called "museums," or "art salons" and is erupting with unstoppable force into our everyday lives, becoming an article as necessary to us as any other on sale in Tietz's department store.

As for the character of the works, their overall standard, and the size of the exhibition, it has to be admitted that given the state of contemporary communication, the organizers (Das Junge Rheinland) gathered together a body of material significant both in terms of quantity and quality. Der Sturm has to a large extent contributed to this. The exhibition lacks a uniform character. In addition to Impressionism, one can see almost all the movements of the last decade here, such as Neo-Impressionism, Cubism, Futurism, Expressionism, Constructivism, and a whole range of variants on these movements. The exhibition can be regarded as an attempt at reviewing and taking stock of the achievements of the new art so far. The great differentiation of forms apparent at the exhibition can be explained by 1) the fast pace of the development of art in recent years, and, 2) its uneven pace—different countries are at different stages in the development of the new art. For instance, while in France or Russia Cubism has reached its peak and then been transformed into new systems (Suprematism, Constructivism, Purism), in Germany so-called Expressionism lingers on (the symptoms of its death throes are already apparent: Dadaism, the Novembergruppe).

It would seem that in the search for new plastic forms all warfare should cease. But it is not so. Differences in opinion are insurmountable and innovators do not care for compromises. The reason that agreement is difficult is that while one group is more advanced in its development, another, perhaps also regarded as "progressive," has not in fact managed to free itself from parochialism. The notion of progress in art has until now been entirely relative and usually subject to local conditions. This kind of particularism in art could have no rationale. Recently, in some countries, artists have shown the will to break down barriers, to have mutual moral and material support, to have a universal exchange of values, and to engage in common action. The internationalization of art—art belonging to the whole of humanity—has turned out to be an unavoidable necessity. The Düsseldorf exhibition is the best illustration of clashes and divergences within the contemporary art world, as well as being the most persuasive argument for the necessity of uniting all, hitherto isolated, creative individuals into one big collective. French art, dominant both in the quality of the works and in progress, is represented here by the leading Cubists and Post-Cubists, such as Albert Gleizes, Fernand Léger, [Louis] Marcoussis, [Georges] Braque, [Pablo] Picasso. Everyone knows the role they have played in the recent breakthrough in art. Of particular historical importance are Picasso's discoveries in the analysis of form. Only in France, with its culture of pure painting, free of literary content, could it be emancipated from alien elements and rise to the heights of abstract (non-objective) forms. For instance Léger's *City*, a large-scale picture in which the rhythm and dynamics of the contemporary city are rendered by non-objective (in the sense of Realist)—but at the same time real (in the sense of non-objective)—forms, already stands on the threshold of the new era in art.

Besides France, a leading place in today's art, although not well represented in this exhibition, belongs to Russia. Tatlin, the Suprematist Malevich, and some other Russian artists are missing. Those exhibiting belong rather to the center and represent the tendency of, let us say, "objective aestheticism": Ivan Puni, [Ksenia] Boguslavskaya, [K.] Zalit, [Pavel] Tchelitchew. Amongst the more radical we should include Rodchenko and Lissitzky, whose *Proun*s have lately been the topic of much discussion. Kandinsky occupies a separate place among the Russians, not recognized by his compatriots (of the Left or Right) and adored by the Germans (*en masse*). Then there is Aleksander Archipenko, whose serious interest in form became stuck in ultra-aestheticism.

The most radical group of artists at the exhibition is the Constructivists. Their aim is to create a monumental, collective style—subordinating painting and sculpture to architecture—and to show the supremacy of utilitarian over aesthetic aspects. Though not formally organized, he group has its own international organization in the form of numerous international periodicals. The Constructivists go hand in hand with the French Cubists, with whom they are united by common goals. The group includes: Theo van Doesburg, a Dutchman, the author of several theoretical articles; the

Hungarians—Moholy-Nagy and Péri; Lissitzky; Viking Eggeling, a Swede, the creator of abstract-dynamic films; and the Belgians Peeters and Wolfs. As for the Germans, represented in great numbers here (nos. 459–812), the majority of their exhibits are characterized by literary and romantic tendencies. "Expressionism," as it is known, is still the all-powerful master and rarely opposed, by brave individuals (like Raoul Hausmann).

Among the most outstanding representatives of the Expressionist movement are Marc Chagall, [Heinrich] Campendonk, Lasar Segall and Oskar Kokoschka. The works of the first are particularly strong coloristically and very intense. Separating the purely pictorial and constructive aspects from the literary ones, their standard is on a par with that of the Cubists in their first stage. Marc Chagall is a painter whose painterly sensibility and sense of scale compensates for his exaggeration of the literary (mysticism). Like any strong artistic personality, he exerts a significant influence on the new generation. This exhibition contains plenty of instances of *faux* Chagall.

Futurism, regarded today as passé, also has its representative at the exhibition: Umberto Boccioni. His picture *Laughter* belongs to those works of art whose value is timeless.

I have given a brief description of the Düsseldorf exhibition. As we have seen, two conflicting tendencies, diametrically opposed to one another—namely, material-constructive and individual-destructive—emerge from this exhibition, which is, after all, a reflection of almost all the tendencies in the art of the last fifteen years.

It is undeniable that the so-called "new art," from the first Cubist works to the Purism of today, has—despite constant persecution from blind conservatives—extended its influence to the point where it is the dominant force in modern culture. A worldwide network of periodicals has appeared, propagating and arguing for new ideas and new forms: the organization of cooperatives on economic and ideological grounds; the generally international character of the whole movement—all these substantiate the claim that we are going through a period of transformation of traditional notions about art.

The other fact that plays an important role in this transformation, and is itself decisive in the whole process of the struggle, is the unprecedented development of industrialism and the transformation along with it of social and economic conditions. The disappearance of country settlements, the growth of cities, the diminishing importance of the individual, centralization and the growth of cooperative movements—all have further consequences for our spiritual life. Art, which hitherto operated mostly on some sort of Olympus, isolated from the rhythm of everyday life, has been forcefully shoved out into the streets. Art has new tasks. Today more than ever before, the tendency is to achieve a uniform style—not only in the art supported by patrons, but in all spheres of our work and in all manifestations of life.

Translated by Wanda Kemp-Welch

THE STAND TAKEN BY THE VIENNA MA GROUP TOWARD THE FIRST DÜSSELDORF CONGRESS OF PROGRESSIVE ARTISTS Lajos Kassák et. al.

Originally published as "A bésci MA-csoport állásfoglalása a haladó művészek első, Düsseldorfban tartott kongresszusához," *Ma* vol. 8, no. 8 (August 30, 1922)

The article published in the fourth issue of *De Stijl* has made it clear to us that deep differences set apart our views and endeavors from those of the organizers of this Congress. The latter still voice the special interests of the "individual artist" while we view life from a social standpoint, aware that the human individual is a component atom of society as a whole. His creative work therefore is always the partisan manifestation of a man wearing the armor of communal forces. On the basis of the above it will be clear that, as always, it is in our primary capacity as human beings and not as artists—which is only a consequence of our being human—that we now take a stand regarding certain problems that have been exposed by the Congress.

Thus we reject the proposed alliance while willing to do our utmost to promote the active collaboration of all creative spirits who believe that the sole possible basis for the unfolding of our creative forces cannot be anything other than the collective society of the future. The first task of artistic work is to demonstrate that an art which only expresses subjective psychic experiences has lost all of its significance; art must fulfill the objective requirements of the times. Therefore it cannot avoid first of all dealing with the unsolved problems of contemporary life within the field of art, after which it must find the ways and means of solving these problems through the collaboration of new artists.

This is how we conceive of the structure of the international organization of revolutionary-minded artists:

1. Its central organ is the executive committee, which may also take the role of initiator.

    In this committee there should be at least two representatives from each field of work, so that they have an overall view of their entire working community.

    Their task will be the coordination of all material and intellectual resources and to ensure the greatest possible exchange of materials in the interests of the greatest possible collectivity and the most maximal results. Toward this end the committee will set itself tasks and will undertake tasks imposed upon it, such as the creation of workplaces, the exhibition and distribution of results by way of various congresses, organs, and exhibitions, etc.

2. The individual groups functioning in various fields of work will maintain constant contact with each other not only through the executive committee but directly as well. Their task within their own field is the same as that of the executive committee within the entire organization. Some preparatory projects aimed at the creation of such an organization:

    a) The periodicals *Vyeshch (Object)*, *De Stijl*, and *Ma*, in view of their past activities representing a largely similar standpoint that, in their view, has served progress without compromises—will without any further debate announce the formation of the international organization of revolutionary-minded creative artists.

    b) Each of the three periodicals should send two members of their editorial boards as representatives in a temporary plenipotentiary executive committee. This temporary executive committee should be located in Berlin. The first duty of the committee will be the elaboration of the organization's ground rules and the publication of these in the three periodicals mentioned above.

    c) At the same time the executive committee must set forth the objectives of the organization and publish an appeal for support.

d) The temporary executive committee of the organization will attempt to organize the creative forces professing revolutionary worldviews within a framework that allows the artists not only to achieve the greatest possible results but also to turn these achievements toward the liberation of hitherto shackled social energies.

e) A practical solution must be found allowing the three periodicals named above to attain results as compatible as possible, without any danger of uniformity. In our opinion this can be attained if the three periodicals (and other, similarly oriented organs that may arise) establish mutual contact with each other in order to make possible an exchange of appropriate artwork. The respective administrative apparatuses of these periodicals should also be made available to each other under the appropriate circumstances.

f) The temporary executive committee must find the means to organize representative traveling exhibitions consisting of the work of artists within its sphere of influence. Multilingual catalogues must be published discussing the exhibited material, and a series of lectures organized in each country, in the respective languages. (The initiating role here, for political reasons, must be played by a completely neutral country such as Holland.)

g) An anthology of writings by members of the international organization of revolutionary-minded creative artists should be published and translated into the major languages. The preparation of the anthology is the task of the temporary executive committee.

h) Until the relevant decision by the Congress, the temporary executive committee must determine the membership fees to cover the administrative and publishing expenses of the organization.

i) The temporary executive committee will be in existence until the convening of the first Congress.

k) The temporary executive committee is obliged to convene the first international Congress within the period of one year.

In the name of the artists of the Activist periodical *Ma*: Lajos Kassák, Sándor Barta, János Mácza, Endre Gáspár, László Moholy-Nagy, Ernő Kállai, Jolán Simon, Lajos Kudlák, Erzsébet Ujvári

Translated by John Bátki

INTERNATIONAL CONSTRUCTIVIST CREATIVE UNION   Theo van Doesburg et. al.

Originally published as "Manifest der K.I. (Konstructivistische Internationale schöpferische Arbeitsgemeinschaft)," *De Stijl* vol. 5, no. 8 (1922)

CONSTRUCTIVIST:

New design of life in keeping with our contemporary consciousness and with universal means of expression. Logically explicable application of these means of expression.

In contrast to all subjective, predominantly emotional approaches to the production of art.

Constructive: Realization of practical tasks (including all the problems of design).

In the spirit of modern methods of working.

In contrast to a creative improvisation that is limited to subjectivity.

INTERNATIONAL:
The same attitude under the different circumstances in different lands.
CREATIVE:
That whose consequences essentially alter real life (including the invention and dis-
covery of new materials).
In contrast to a use of preexisting results, not setting new demands without creation
new possibilities.
UNION:
Economy of our labor power.
Individual initiative is no longer sufficient to fulfill the tasks of life today. Collective
cooperation is a practical necessity. (Modern methods of organization.)
Through organization of creative activity it becomes possible to have real tasks for
all (expansion of the field of creative work), and the labor power of the individual is
increased.

Only on this basis is it possible to form an international creative union.
In addition to the demand that practical tasks be solved immediately, the task of this
international union will be to demonstrate to coming generations the usefulness of
our real achievements for their lives, and to explain to them the uselessness of the
individualistic unique production of past ages.
(We will consider unique products only if they respond to demands that have not yet
been articulated in real life.)
This international union does not, therefore, arise from any emotional causes
(whether of a humanistic sort or any other, "universal love of humanity," etc., etc.) but
rather is based on the same elementary, amoral premises that science and technology
are and is based on the necessity of responding in a collective and creative way, not in
an individual and intuitive one.
To unfold and completely develop our individuality we are (as everyone else is) compelled to organize creative activity.
To realize this international union as an *organization* it is necessary that all likeminded
people of all nations join together immediately.
Expressions of agreement and proposals for collaboration should be sent to the central office.

Theo van Doesburg (Holland), El Lissitzky (Russia), Hans Richter (Germany), Karel
Maes (Belgium), Max Burchartz (Germany)

Translated by Steven Lindberg

INTERNATIONAL REACTION TO THE FIRST RUSSIAN EXHIBITION
IN BERLIN Éva Forgács

"The blockade of Russia is coming to an end," announced El Lissitzky and Ilya Ehrenburg, editors of the trilingual art journal *Veshch/Gegenstand/ Objet* in Berlin in the spring of 1922. Although the leaders of the Bauhaus and the De Stijl had sought contact with the artists of Soviet Russia, few had appeared personally in the West, and the art of the first communist country was largely unknown. All that changed with the 1922 exhibition at the Van Diemen Gallery in Berlin. The initiative came from the newly established International Office in the Department of Fine Arts of the Commissariat for Public Education, led by David Shterenberg. The First Russian Exhibition was an effort on behalf of the Soviet cultural authorities to initiate cultural contacts and dialogues with the West. Since Lenin asserted that Germany was the next country likely to become communist, Berlin was an obvious choice as the site for introducing the new art.

Few exhibitions have generated greater expectations. In 1922 the German and international left-wing intelligentsia in Berlin lived in hope of a world revolution, and many looked to the young Communist regime in Moscow for guidance. Much of the European avant-garde thus anticipated that the show would constitute a communiqué directly from "the children of the future," as Lajos Kassák put it, and received it as an important political message, the first one since the 1917 Bolshevik Revolution.

There was more than a little disappointment, therefore, when artists and critics discovered that the new Soviet state endorsed relatively conservative trends in art. Only a fraction of the exhibited works were representative of the new tendencies—Constructivism, Suprematism, and derivatives of these and Cubism— "the leftist groups," as Shterenberg called them in his foreword to the catalogue. Still, most of the attention was focused on these works—spatial structures by the members of the Society of Young Artists (OBMOKhU), Tatlin, Malevich, Lissitzky, Gabo, Puni, Rosanova, and others—and the exhibition was a sweeping triumph of the young, energetic and innovative Soviet abstract art. The Germans referred to all of this work as Constructivism—newly used in Berlin as an umbrella term, rather than in the original Moscow sense of the word. This altered understanding of Constructivism—its emphasis on issues of aesthetics rather than on rigorously functional or politically committed aspects of the work— was also a symptom of the West's incorporating an Eastern paradigm into its own narrative.

The reviews included here are but
a few among many published in the
German and international press and
offer an array of interpretations of
this historic event.

THE EXHIBITION OF RUSSIAN ARTISTS   Paul Westheim

Originally published as "Die Ausstellung der Russen," *Das Kunstblatt* (November 1922)

This exhibition is a disappointment, and at the same time it is one of the most interesting artistic surveys that we have had for years.

It is a disappointment for anyone who seeks something "lasting," something that is of our time and is capable of growing into timelessness. It is interesting, because it affords a unique glimpse of an intellectual tussle with problems of artistic design inevitably raised by minds for which the Future can mean only one thing: a radical break with anything and everything that belongs to the past.

This future art that is to be created does not as yet exist in Russia (any more than the future form of the economy or of society exists). But the work displayed on the walls of this exhibition shows that people are working with fanatical zeal toward something that is infinitely remote, something that may turn out to be a mere phantom or else, possibly, and in a highly specific sense, a Renaissance of art.

So it might be said that what young Russian art has to offer is not an exhibition of art so much as an *exhibition of artistic problems*.

These Russian artists—like all others in Russia—are driven by a fierce *compulsion to create anew*. In one way, this is a blessing; in others, it is a fateful burden that only courage, character, and extraordinary creative strength can master. To what extent these qualities are present, how much staying power is really present, is not for us to determine. That is a task for posterity, which will be in a position to judge the process by its outcome.

It is the French who find it easiest to make art at present (which is not to say that the work done in France necessarily sums up the expression of the age). In France, a renewal of art associated with the names of Cézanne and Seurat has created a basis for further evolution while maintaining continuity with tradition. At the opposite extreme from ancient France, which still has (or seems to have) enough vitality to renew itself from its own inner resources, there is revolutionary Russia, which rejects all tradition on principle: virgin territory for art, ruled by the idea of building everything new, from scratch. An implicit idea presides over the Russian world: that everything has yet to be and must be done. This instills into creative work a freedom and audacity unknown in Europe for centuries past. The question, of course, is whether our continent still has the strength to handle such freedom and such audacity. It and the new art might well relapse into anarchy together. The country that is finding it hardest at the moment is the one in the middle: ourselves, in other words. We have no tradition on which to rely, because our tradition has been interrupted too often; at the same time, we have too much to lose— in art, as in other respects—by abruptly sacrificing our past for the sake of an uncertain future. With us, the new is a continuation and transformation of the old. In art (as in politics), this precludes radical decisions; it also leads too readily, and too often, to cautious applications of color wash. It is no accident that our artistic evolution has impelled us toward Romanticism. Nor is it an accident that we have to put out feelers first in one direction and then in another; and that issues such as that of a new Naturalism are not only possible but actually require to be brought to a head.

Russia is a vast country, and there is great diversity in the Russian soul—as there is in the German, the French, and the human soul everywhere. The exhibition, which sets out to offer a cross-section, demonstrates—with a candor that is not exactly typical of official exhibitions—that it might be well to avoid glib generalizations. It is true, however, that one highly specific form of Russianness in art currently monopolizes our attention—although this may of course be entirely our own problem. There exists a Russian Salon art, of the Glaspalast type, in which the artist (Arkhipov) encapsulates the New Age (in the spirit of Defregger) by painting peasants in a village who cluster around a small boy and marvel at the said child's ability to read them the latest political news out of the newspaper. And then, as Sternberg has already shown, there is a Russian Cézannism, personified by Falk and by that astonishingly sophisticated painter Rozhdestvensky; there is a Russian variant of Expressionism, in the Bubnovy Valet group; and there is a Russian Cubism, which has produced two sculptors with a structural sense that is all their own, Archipenko and Tsalit. And, finally, there is revolutionary art, the main surprise and talking point of the exhibition, represented by the Suprematists and Constructivists.

Once before in the pages of this journal (1919), a passage from Dostoevsky has been cited: "As soon as we Russians have reached the shore, and have brought ourselves to believe that it really is the shore, we at once begin to look forward to the ultimate frontier. Why is this? If one of us is converted to Catholicism, he immediately turns Jesuit, and the blackest Jesuit of them all; if he becomes an atheist, he will immediately call for belief in God to be eradicated, by force if necessary." This "sudden fanaticism," this total incapacity for moderation, this tendency to take everything to extremes, explains a great deal—in this exhibition, as elsewhere. Take Malevich, for example. He is a great believer in the need to "simplify." So Malevich simplifies. More and more is removed from the picture area. First, of course, all representation of objects. Then color. All that remains is a single contrast between black and white: an abstract form, a black quadrilateral or a black circle on a white ground. And even this is not the ultimate simplification. Malevich then dispenses with black and paints his celebrated work, White on White. On a white ground there is nothing but white. Simplification has been taken to such an extreme that nothing remains within the white frame but an empty expanse of white. This takes intellectual experimentation as far as it can go. "To become an atheist," says Dostoevsky in the passage just quoted, "is so easy for a Russian! More than for anyone else in the whole world. Nor do Russians turn into ordinary atheists; far from it. Atheism to them becomes a new faith. They believe in it, without even noticing that they are believing in a zero." Perhaps this is the psychological background to that white painting? There have been other forms of "simplification." We have Liebermann's risky and—as I am increasingly convinced—questionable assertion that drawing is an art of omission. We can tell what Liebermann meant by omission if we look at his own way of drawing. This shows, may I say, some evidence that he proclaimed his thesis with considerable mental reservations. Malevich, the Russian, takes the word dead literally; with the result that he ends up as a believer in zero. For, quite simply, to paint in "white on white" is to give up painting. The logical conclusion would be to disown art altogether and give up the whole thing. And, if my information is correct, this is precisely what Malevich has done: he has laid down his palette and brushes, turned Catholic, and taken up Theosophy. Some of his disciples, and others—a whole movement, in fact—have sought salvation through something called "Production Art," using metal, wood, and other materials to make constructions that are neither engineering nor art handicraft—all "utilitarian properties" being rejected on principle. From these, nevertheless, a wide highway leads—especially given the theory of "Uniting Art With Life"—to applied art: to posters, ceramics, glassware, and stage design, for which the Russians have always had a special gift, as can now be seen all over again in the work of Altman, Tatlin, Exter, Boguslavskaya, Yakulov, and others.

In the last few decades, "construction" is another term of artistic debate that some have tried to take literally. Just as the mechanical engineer projects plans and elevations onto a two-dimensional surface, so Lissitzky projects Constructions. But drawing is an abstraction in itself. Accordingly, Tatlin and others after him have started to build their Constructions with real materials: iron, sheet metal. This, again, is a negation of painting, and in its way a tangible proof of the "hatred of painting" that I once identified as a recurrent phenomenon in the latest generation of artists. It is work that craves to be treated as "engineering," and yet ultimately it is neither more nor less than the "romance of engineering." In the course of all this conceptual experimentation and exploration, the two-dimensional pictorial space became suspect, on the grounds that it involved an illusion. The cry went up for pictorial space to be developed into real space. Gabo constructs this space out of diagonally intersecting planes of iron or celluloid, thus converting the pictorial image into a relief hung inside the frame. He then extends the same principle to sculpture, which no longer confines itself to molding a volume but aspires to be "not only static but dynamic." In other words, the aim is for sculpture to encompass and mold space. This recalls the experiments of Belling, except that Belling's use of scale enables him to make real use of the dimension of space.

From the viewpoint of our Western artistic culture, these issues, experiments, and endeavors have little or nothing to do with "Art" in our (or should I say in the old) sense of the term. Just imagine how a "connoisseur" like Friedländer, or an amateur like the elder Vollard, would react to such statements as these. Seen from the crowning heights of our Western artistic culture, all of this is terribly primitive. There is no need—or so it will be said—for the art student in our culture to trouble his head with such matters. Centuries of tradition have supplied us with tried and tested methods of artistic creation; the disciple need only adopt them and fill them with his own individual content, Learning to paint is simply a matter of gaining familiarity with the traditional craft skills. Such is the Alexandrian state of ripeness and overripeness that is allegedly imperiled by all those "Barbarians" in the East. They, for their part, have in mind the possibility, indeed the necessity, of giving art a new Archaic Period. They see it as their mission to set about their work afresh, empty-handed; to begin with basic concepts and thus conceivably achieve something that may be different in its principles from anything done before. Hence the fanaticism with which all conclusions and solutions are rejected; hence the intense commitment with which the most elementary issues are tackled. Artists are still wrestling with basic grammatical concepts; language itself is still a thing of the far distant future. Color, for instance, is not yet a medium of expression; it is treated regarded as a material, a study material. Paint is applied to a surface. Rodchenko paints a small quadrilateral—evenly, with intelligent craftsmanship—in glowing crimson: a task of the kind that is set in our craft schools as part of the final examination for apprentice house painters. It is necessary to achieve some clarity as to the *facture* value of such an area of paint. A matte paint surface is set against a glossy surface, and a smooth one against a rough one. As an experiment, an area painted black is juxtaposed with another consisting of black paper stuck to the surface. And so on. From such contrasts, some artists are even now extracting possibilities of pictorial construction. Sternberg, who has retained some sense of the "pictorial image," and Altman, who has already returned to "representation," have already gone farther.

As to the actual artistic outcome of this experimentation, the exhibition tells us nothing. And herein lies the disappointment. It may be said that it is too soon to expect more. After all, artists have had no more than a few years for a task that may well take generations. And look at the circumstances under which they have had to work! But it is hard to gainsay those who demand to see something more than experimentation. They, too, have right on their side, in withholding their commitment from anything so uncertain. What might come of it all? In the end, it is a matter of faith.

There is no denying that the driving force here is the intellect. Much, though not all, of this is brainwork. Too much so. There are also many different dialects in it: an impression that is reinforced as soon as you get into discussion with individual artists. They have a marked tendency to refer back to first principles, and this sometimes degenerates into dogmatism or even scholasticism. It almost seems that they have *more to say than to show*: that their theories and options, manifestoes and programs, arguments and theses, have more to teach us than an exhibition like this one. The intellectual subsoil from which all of this grows is curious, and is not so readily dismissed out of hand as a stack of images or of what might become images. The composition *White on White* (if it can be called a composition) means nothing as an "image"; and yet, it seems to me, there is much to be learned from an intellectual situation that leads logically to this.

Translated by David Britt

ON THE RUSSIAN EXHIBITION   Adolf Behne
Originally published as "Der Staatsanwalt schüzt das Bild," *Die Weltbühne* no. 47 (November 23, 1922)

The Russian exhibit in the [Van Dieman] Gallery provides an excellent documentation of the transcendence of the image. That Kandinsky's paintings have been hung on the final wall is probably a concession to (mistaken) German exhibits of modern Russian art. In no sense is Kandinsky's abstract canvas the last word in Russian painting. The leading role has not been played by Kandinsky, still less by [Marc] Chagall (who has a very weak painting on display here), but by the constructivists, the splendidly represented [Kasimir] Malevich, [Alexander] Rodchenko, [El] Lissitzky, and [Vladimir] Tatlin, [Nathan] Altman, and [Naum] Gabo. The question is no longer whether the Suprematist image is a better or more beautiful image than the impressionist image; rather the question is whether the image as such can continue to supply us with an accepted, fruitful area of work. The image itself is in crisis-not because a couple of painters thought this up but because the modern individual has experienced changes in intellectual structure that alienate one from the image. The image is an aesthetic matter whereas what the radical artists of all nations want is to lend immediate form to reality itself (the Russians call it production art). Soviet Russia was the first to recognize the possibilities inherent in this great new goal and give it free rein; the German "art lover" instead remains stubbornly closed to it (no salon has yet exhibited the German constructivists). This exhibit, the most audacious and richest in productive artistic work that Berlin has seen in a long time—and under what conditions!—is an official exhibit of the People's Commissariat for the Arts and Sciences in Moscow. The Commissariat charged the painter [David] Sterenberg with putting the show together (his works, incidentally, are among the most interesting on display). It is utterly inconceivable that even in a hundred years an official German exhibition would so frankly embrace art, the times, and all that is of current vitality. "We hope," Sterenberg writes in the catalogue, "that our Western comrades, whom we would very much like to see in Moscow and Petrograd, will not keep us waiting long." I can imagine what will be sent to Russia (if anything at all) to represent artistic work in Germany. It will be at least ten years behind the times.

Translated by Don Reneau

In 1914 when war fever soared high in Budapest, a few of us, young socialists and pacifists, were arguing about the future of nations and races. Those were the days when Russian literature was at the height of its popularity in Hungary; our heads were full of its wise and yet revolutionary sentences. No doubt because we were saturated by the human flavor and profound, aching rumble of this literature, we decided in favor of the Slavs.

Since then we have outgrown our love affair with Russian literature, as we have outgrown our young lives. Now it is about to begin its triumphant passage in America, a nation that had only a taste of the war and none of the current revolutions. But we are still here and at times we despair, as if we had been disappointed in the primal source of Russian culture. Momentarily it appears as if the Russian psyche had been pulverized by the material struggles. There is nothing new in literature. The new movements show their weakest results in Russia. It seems certain that Russian literature has for some time to come exhausted its resources in the works of Tolstoy, Dostoevsky, and Gorky. They had introduced new possibilities, offering a taste of severe Asian purity to that old fop Europe. The ones who came after them, Artzybashefff, Kuprin, Remisov, Sologub et al., are creatures of the European schools. They have lost that profound constructive faith we had seen in Tolstoy's antiwar writings, as well as in Dostoevsky's "chauvinist and anti-Semitic" works. Today's Russian writers, including the writers of the Revolution, produce only didactic lessons, a phenomenon generally true of literature everywhere. The great period of Russian literature, as a whole genre of art, has come to a close with the present line of literature.

We observe the newest possibilities of development in a totally different area, that of visual arts, where progress is vigorous and productive.

So that we were not wrong in 1914. In the wake of the literature produced by a Russia in the throes of pre-Revolutionary labor, we are now confronted by the visual arts conveying the renewed power of revolutionized Russia. During the European economic and cultural blockade an utterly new social system has passed its test of strength in Russia, and new advances in the visual arts began to unfold, in numerous instances paralleling the developments in Europe.

The all-Russian exhibition in Berlin, in spite of its great shortcomings, provides a by and large clear balance sheet of the wartime and revolutionary art of Russia.

The European schools of Futurism, Cubism, and Expressionism had still had a chance to seep into the Russian art world and we find in Moscow and Petersburg, as everywhere else in the world, artists who spoke those formal languages. These movements however barely developed here past the stage of art school ateliers. Representative Cubists such as Udalkova, Puni, Posner and others have not added anything to the values produced by the French school. The greatest master of Expressionism, the Russian-born Chagall, has matured his art in Berlin and Paris and has not been able to exert any deeper influence in Russia.

The first consciously new step taken by the young Russian artists may be seen in Suprematism. This is the first movement where the Russian, the Asian power joins the European forces as a truly absolute value that is capable of multiplication. And characteristically its message is, instead of a heaping on, a simplification, by getting rid of every externality deposited by civilization and aesthetics, to dig all the way back down to the essentials. As painters they follow through to the ultimate conclusions, in their forms arriving at basic geometric forms and in their color use at the two basic colors, black and white. Their debut was a revolutionary act. And their simple laws set the stage for the birth (1917) of the entire new generation of Russian artists. Suprematism has drawn the ultimate logical conclusions for painting and has opened the gates toward progress. Suddenly the avenues of possibility multiplied in number and this movement rapidly branched out, enriching itself with new people and values. Malevich is the purest master of Suprematism. He is the source for the departures of the Constructivists and Objectivists. The representatives of these groups are Tatlin, Lissitzky, Rodchenko, Klyun, Drevin, et al.

Shterenberg is one of the Constructivists, but has developed entirely on his own. His paintings depicting naturalistic single objects are infinitely simplified in both form and color. His works, regarding their execution, are the most advanced in the exhibition. Here we must note that in the degree of their technical preparedness this entire generation is wonderfully pure and thorough. There is no evidence whatever of cliché or superficial playfulness.

The least accomplished aspect of the exhibition is the area of sculpture and the works that attempt experimental solutions to spatial constructions with a utilitarian aim. Among these the glass sculptures of Gabo are the most significant. But even these seem to be outlines rather for the work to come. They lack materiality. And probably other factors beside an original material (such as the artist's creative ability in this direction) are still lacking for the work to present fully realized results. It is no accident that the construction containing his vehemently bent forms was made of celluloid instead of rigid glass.

The spatial constructions shown in the exhibition are naive and insignificant works. In these days of locomotives doing 120 kilometers per hour, of giant cranes and vast bridges, these items seem to be superfluous games, impoverished both in intuition and in science.

The exhibited maquettes of stage and playground design are likewise insignificant. The former have long been surpassed in their costume and figure design. Among the latter the most interesting is Altman's playground design for the Jewish Theater.

We must conclude that among the visual art genres included in the exhibition painting is without a doubt the most advanced. In this field the Russians have introduced a new energy and new artistic possibilities to Europe. And their paintings also show the way for themselves, pointing the direction they must follow to reach their ideal, the new human ideal—a constructive way of life.

They are the children of the future.

Berlin is crawling with exhibitions: convulsing forms and screaming colors. Into this labyrinthine, gaudy chaos the Russians have once again brought the primal source of colors and the *straight line* of purity and power.

Translated by John Bátki

THE RUSSIAN EXHIBITION IN BERLIN   Ernő Kállai
Originally published as "A berlini orosz kiállítás," *Akasztott Ember* vol. 2 (February 15, 1923)

The most serious among the several shortcomings of the Russian exhibition in Berlin was the fact that it refused to take any stand whatsoever, and settled for providing a neutral survey of the most diverse visual objects, much to the delight of bourgeois democrats and aesthetes. It gave no indication that it had originated in a country going through the painful struggle of attaining Communism, from where it was dropped into the midst of the luxurious bourgeois environment of Unter den Linden. Those few neat little Soviet posters in the Impressionist style and one or two Soviet emblems on silk or china had the effect of awkward beauty spots modestly hiding among the hundreds of drawings and paintings. For all that, even Herr Ebert, the president of the German pseudo-republic, might well have undertaken the "highest sponsorship" of the exhibition. True, the introductory essays to the catalogue made a few passing references to the revolutionary nature of the new movements and the fact of art having taken to the streets, but it all sounded like apologies and excuses rather than a courageously voiced demand. There was nothing in these writings to provide the exhibition with a backbone of worldview and ethics. The various movements were aligned into an order connected by the fragile thread of an intent to demonstrate causal connections, instead of the immanent goal of a revolutionary will. The only purpose the Russian exhibition evinced was tactical in nature. It would seem that Lunacharsky and the others did not want to scare away the bourgeois viewers of the exhibition. This would explain why they refrained from any kind of overt revolutionary content. But I still find it incomprehensible that this Russian exhibition has overlooked the problem of proletarian art. Some of the cruder examples of the student work in the exhibition *might* have shown evidence of unpracticed proletarian handiwork. But apart from these few pieces there was not even the slightest allusion to the much-debated central issues of *proletcult*.

If there *is* a Russian proletarian art, then it was an unpardonable omission not to devote at least as much attention to it as to the lip-smacking still-lives, sensuous nudes, and melting moods of paintings by Kustodiev and others. And if there is no proletarian art in Russia, even then this—for the time being absent—new artistic collective should have been given the role of occupying one extreme pole of the spirit of this exhibition. Even the concept of an as yet nonexistent proletarian art, as the unknown quantity *x*, would have been an important factor in this exhibition, if the introductory texts in the catalogue had paid some attention to the demands, prospects, and obstructions presented by this concept. The Russian cultural commissariat in all probability has plenty of experience in this respect. Here was the opportunity to give an account of the results at a public forum available to all of Europe. It is greatly to be regretted that this opportunity has not been seized.

What did the exhibition salvage from the Russian revolution? A few seething, expressionistic individuals and world-visions possessed of an imagination and a tenacious, form-giving fanaticism that was indeed staggering, and without parallel in today's painting: they recall old-time icons in terror of damnation. But these visions could equally be seen as feverish nightmares of a humanity disoriented by the world war as much as by the revolution. Whereas the works that were indubitably rooted in the revolution were too feeble to offer more than mere psychological illustration.

The exhibition included representative values from every direction, starting with naturalism and Impressionism, through the heritage of Cézanne, all the way to Tatlin's militant spatial Cubism and Constructivism. The entirety of this extensive range was characterized, not so much by a formal dexterity, as by the remarkable and diverse wealth of ability in the handling of material. The Russians never fail to assign an active role to surface textures, always strictly in accordance with the spirit of the given style in question. This passion for taking meticulous trouble with materials is often incidental to the problem of overall form, and may even lead to an obstructive sort of puttering, but when it stays within the necessary limits it has the effect of endowing the work's optical values with an extraordinary intensity. A surface that is differentiated and structured in its material composition is able to radiate into space a much more opulent, flexible, and irresistible dynamics of reflected light than a surface that is arranged only optically.

The facture of Constructivist works gives evidence of the profound, material unity of psychological and logical existence. Even when touched, or viewed from very close up these surfaces are alive with rhythms.

The facture of Russian Constructivism offers interesting evidence that the psychological category of perceiving materials and the logical category of formal observation are not mutually exclusive but in fact are conditional upon each other, and are different but equally necessary manifestations of artistic vitality. And since the Russian Constructivists (including the Suprematists) pay equal attention to both categories, their works appear alive and actual both in respect of the optical perspective and by virtue of their pure and integral order.

Constructivism, the art of causality disciplined in the service of purposeful life objectives, can be seen in two phases in this exhibition: in two-dimensional planes, and in actual multi-dimensional space. The two-dimensional constructions were in general of a higher quality than the spatial constructions. This was in part certainly due to the fact that from the viewpoint of the formative intention a two-dimensional construction offers far less material resistance and therefore provides more opportunities for the adequate addressing of consciously registered tensions and functions. The great majority of the spatial constructions were in additional hindered in their full resolution by an excessive number of details in the mutually constructive supports of linked parts, resulting in a multitude of forms without any function. They resembled techno-logical objects, but did not perform any technological tasks. Looking past these unsuccessful experiments in technological pseudo-naturalism one could see very few spatial constructions that would pass for real achievements. Medunetsky's triple diag-onal construction is alive because it indicates only in a most general manner the axes that give free play to the full swing of its spatial activity.

In this work as well as in Gabo's far more complex model for a glass sculpture the awareness of functionality is the primary creative motivation, rather than formal con-vention, as in the case of the technological naturalists. Gabo has also attempted a mobile sculpture, the essential form of which is afforded by the optical phenomenon created by motion. In Gabo's mobile sculpture the formal conception is consciously built upon the notion of motion, insofar as it is not only the conveyor but also the result of motion. Further advance from here would lead in the direction of the kinetic lever specified by Kemény and Moholy-Nagy that demands an internal dialectics compared to which the Gabo-type experiments can only be seen as limited and tempo-rary substitutes.

The weakest part of the exhibition consisted of the architectural portions. The few architectural plans and sketches were evidence of an utterly inconsequential romanti-cism, proving that all the programmatic verbiage of utilitarianism will remain idle talk until we evolve new social necessities of life that will need to be fulfilled by practical architectural work.

Translated by John Bátki

NOTES TO THE RUSSIAN ARTISTS' EXHIBITION IN BERLIN

Alfréd Kemény

Originally published as "Jegyzetek az orosz művészek berlini kiállitáshoz," *Egység*
(February 4, 1923)

Suprematism and Constructivism, the two most significant developments in recent
Russian art represent one of the way-stations of progress along the road that leads,
in art and society alike, from the isolation of individualism to the universality of the
collective. From a formal point of view, Suprematism has a tremendous historical
significance. In the first and third phases of its evolution it succeeded in paring down
the painting to the purest and most objective relationships of its two-dimensional
elements (form and color). In form this led to the square, and to the directional
contrasts of movement along the vertical and horizontal axes, as well as along the
two intersecting diagonals; in color, it examined the interrelation between black
and white, and a uniformly white surface. This significance however is by now mostly
historical, for as an artistic worldview relevant to the actualities of contemporary life,
the metaphysical dynamism of Suprematism has become as obsolete as Futurism,
which it is a continuation of. During the second stage of its evolution, instead of
further developing the architectonic potential of the square as a planar form (this
is what Mondrian did in Holland, independently, and at the same time as Malevich,
when he started out from the square as the simplest, most objective and least psychi-
cally loaded form), Suprematism turned away from the laws of two-dimensionality
and, starting out from the white ground of the picture as infinite space, endeavored
the create the illusion of the dynamic conflict of cosmic energies. As such, the dematerialized, illusionistic metaphysics of Suprematism differentiate it from the objectively constructive demands of contemporary life that will find their appropriate artistic
expression in the collective urban architecture of the future. "Unovis," the school
founded by Malevich in Vitebsk, was based on the laws of the plane, but it has rigidi-
fied into an architectonic system consisting exclusively of diagonals, and became incapable of further growth. As opposed to the metaphysical nature of Suprematism, a
development in a realist direction is signaled by the Russian Constructivists, who,
contemporaneously with the work of building a new society in Russia, place the
emphasis on creative organizing and design activities, and use industrial materials
(iron, copper, brass, glass, etc.) by setting them, firmly structured into each other,
within physical space, by emphasizing the laws inherent in the materials and their
factural relationships. Constructivism is the correct path to take, but in Russia it
has come to a standstill in a technological naturalism that consists of illustrating
existing mechanical contraptions. This is only natural in a country that is industrially
the least developed, while it possesses the most advanced artistic culture after
France. Thus although from an agitative point of view the Russian Constructivists'
romantic struggle for industry as opposed to art is important, this is nonetheless a
phenomenon with a limited, local interest. As material constructions the Russian
Constructivist works merely stand alone in physical space, without ever attempting
to organize a specific space. The road of the Hungarian Constructivists leads in this
direction, past their Russian counterparts.

The Russian exhibition in Berlin could have been extraordinarily important if, limiting
itself to the results of recent, post-Suprematist Russian art, it would have chosen
to illustrate the conflicts of contemporary art and life by means of Suprematist and
Constructivist works. Instead the Russian exhibition lacked a specific standpoint
and had an eclectic air about it, by incorporating vast quantities of Impressionist
and Post-Impressionist works in addition to Suprematist and Constructivist ones.

From an aesthetic point of view the exhibition contained isolated works of a high artistic quality, but it failed to represent the constructive aims of today's Russian art that transcend general aesthetics.

Translated by John Bátki

THROUGH THE RUSSIAN EXHIBITION IN BERLIN   Branko Ve Poljanski
Originally published as "Kroz rusku izložbu u berlinu," *Zenit* vol. 3, no. 22 (March 1923)

I part with Marc Chagall. A strapping young man, almost a boy. I find myself at
the Russian exhibition. I won't talk about the older ones—we have little interest
in them. The Suprematists are undoubtedly in the majority and seem the most
powerful ones here.
Malevich. The great founder of Suprematism. An artist, a mathematician, a physicist,
a painter, a sculptor, a revolutionary anti-bourgeois—a Russian without a soul—
a *Russian with spirit.*
A great Russian artistic personality with spirit. He lays new ground—using new
elements to construct a new world—a world of art.
Art of the past is an art that belongs to the religion of monks and priests—it had
been made for churches.
Malevich's art, created to satisfy the highest demands of our time—has been
made for factories!
A memento! What these Russian artists have created so far, untouched by
European influences, is of the utmost importance for European art and culture.
The strongest representative of this independent, non-European Russianism is
none other than Malevich. His most basic colors are used to construct a form
which is sharp, clear, mobile, and eternal. This form has no object as its model.
He has reached the highest level of pure creation in his elemental Suprematist
painting *Red Square.*
A frame, a red square, and nothing else. This painting made me realize that the
color red has acquired its most intense expression. That color is both a pre-red
and an eternal red.
Malevich commands this exhibition not only with his works, but also with the works
of the other Suprematists who have mostly (almost all of them) been created from
his rib. New worlds, hanging on these damp German walls due to a strange quirk of
history, are waiting for a German "samaritan" to take them down and in return give
a crust of bread.
(The proceeds are intended for the starving people in Russia!)
Damn! Nobody is buying.
My eyes stare. Why can't I do anything help?
(I remember, Mayakovsky took off for Paris half an hour ago.)
So after Malevich, a whole avant-garde of Suprematists and Constructivists follows.
(Not all will agree to be called by their first names for quite obvious reasons—
personal vanity!)
Lissitzky. The second Suprematist, Constructivist, spectral specialist and explorer
of ultra-violet rays. He is searching for a way to apply Suprematist painting to a
true realization of visionary worlds, made real as concrete objects; he is looking

for a way to apply this kind of painting to life, to things: a bridge, a monument, a submarine, an airplane, a train, and others.

Each Constructivist painting by master Lissitzky seems to be a blueprint for airborne trains in the fifty-fifth century. We find the psychological genesis for this kind of painting in the fact that Russia truly is a country which needs trains above all else—airborne, ground-bound and underground trains. Lissitzky expands on Malevich's Suprematism so that it takes on a great concept and momentum. There are so many levers, traversals, arches and wheels on his paintings that it seems to be a construction for the great world of the future which is just around the corner. And no country has been so devastated as Lissitzky's homeland—Russia.

Rozanova. The third Suprematist, a woman of many talents, not the least of which is applying her feminine powers to Suprematism. She has produced quite a number of works which are decent, but she has no elemental force. She gravitates toward decoration. Undoubtedly, judging by her works, there is much in her that is masculine. Unfortunately, she is dead already.

Constructivism could also be termed—Suprema-sculpture.

Tatlin. A first of these (sensational!) Constructivists, at the same time monumental, he dematerializes the value of gold. He creates objects that are generally individual. His works are sculptures which not a single masturbating estheticist could ever use for any kind of a decoration.

There is one great decoration created by Tatlin (not counting his stage decorations!) that will become a decoration of all the Russians. I am talking about a sculpture already known to us (see the Russian edition of *Zenit*, no. 17–18.) Tatlin has created a special type of plasticity: counter-relief.

Great pan-cosmic joy surges through my soul as I experience the air's rhythm in the construction of space embodied in one of these Tatlin counter-reliefs. It helps me feel the rumbling bang of the revolution, and I can see how he ridicules the decorations found in old salons, as well as the behavior of new artistic objects and their mechanics, serpentine lines, surface movement and energy of eternal existence. Tatlin has a very strong personality.

Rodchenko. His construction in space is especially interesting (see the Russian edition of *Zenit*.) Rodchenko is the Russian Archimedes. Symbolically (although Symbolism is completely absent from this), this is a scale of contemporary Russia. There is quiet equilibrium in Rodchenko's construction. No kind of force, neither that produced by cosmic laws, nor those produced artificially, can ever disturb this equilibrium. Meteors are not so common anymore.

Gabo. A Constructivist-descriptive sculptor. A glass sculptor. Organization of diagonals, circles, ellipses, parabolas, hyperbolas—and all these lines move in space to create the compact form of a great construction—projectiles. The constructor is successful in creating within us the rhythm of the object which also keeps its own time. These works are not only spacial, dimmensional. They are works of a sculptural machine with its own forces and its own athmospheric rhythm.

You can see the basis for the future creation of monumentally descriptive plasticity. This plasticity of the future will serve as bridges, radiotelegraphic towers, monuments, fast electric trains, etc.

Besides Suprematists and Constructivists (who are the same but just a tiny bit different!) who are the strongest and the most Russian at this exhibition, there is also a whole pleiade of Cézannists, Van Goghists, Hodlerists, Cubists, Picassoists, Braqueists, Expressionists, Impressionists, Depressionists, Dadaists, and others.

Chagall. One of the strongest representatives of German and world Expressionism has only five small water colors and drawings in this exhibition. We do not need to discuss him in terms of this exhibition, because he is scheduled to have his own collective exhibition just after this one, at Unter den Linden.

Burliuk's value as an expressionist is not as high as that of Chagall, and *Boguslavskaya* is a decorator as well and a fan of bright colors with a specifically feminine character. Perhaps this doesn't have much to do with new art.

Archipenko has presented only four sculptures. The reason is that this exhibition is supposed to show an overview of what has been created in Russia and not outside of Russia in the last few years. Archipenko has lived outside of Russia for quite a while, and he lives in Berlin now. He owns a private academy, where I have often visited this great master who has lately been prone to the weakness of stressing that he is not a Russian but a—Ukrainian. The most important part of his work is his talent in using materials (glass, steel, wood, aluminum, color). All of this leaves an effective, optical impression in a Cubist space. He has come up with so many effects that they even bacame his style—concave sculpture.

Furthermore, his sculptural painting—*skupltomalerei*—is already well known. It is quite a happy synthesis of sculpture and painting.

But let me bring this to a close. *Zenit* has to economize—stage decorations have been put on show as well and are dominated by: Tatlin, Altman and Exter. Altman is superior by number and by concept of his work, since this is probably his main trade. He constructs the stage as a world outside of which nothing exists.

Gospodi pomiluy! Gospodi pomiluy! [Lord have mercy! Lord have mercy!]

[P.S. We bring you this Berlin essay by Ve Poljanski now, although it was supposed to come out last year. However, we've had technical difficulties with our journal, which has had the bad luck of having to go on a diet due to money constraints—therefore, we bring you the essay in this number although we feel that, again, due to lack of space, it isn't plastic enough. In the sea of Latins, let the Slavs be heard once in a while!—The Editorial Board.]

Translated by Maja Starčević

EXILE VIENNA   Krisztina Passuth

After the defeat of the Hungarian Soviet Republic, during which Kassák was jailed, he managed to escape to Vienna, where, under totally different circumstances he started to publish the Vienna series of *Ma* in May 1920. As he recalled in his *History of Art Isms*, "Vienna, 1920. This city, impoverished and crippled by the war to the point of despair, became our new home. Uitz arrived in Vienna before me; I found haven there only after stints at the Keszthely jail and at the Budapest transit prison. After having been persecuted, we now felt as if we had been reduced to a shadow existence…. The task confronting us was a difficult one that no Hungarian periodical prior to *Ma* had ever had to face: given the fact of our new situation, the fact of having to publish in exile, in Vienna, we needed to address a public both at home in Hungary as well as abroad."

Kassák's editorial in the first issue was in fact the manifesto of the Activists who had been forced into exile. He had come to consider *fraternity*—the community of individuals, the awakening of humankind to a realization of its own potential—as the primary goal. The manifesto "To the Artists of All Nations" equally reflected the bitter experiences gathered during the Hungarian Commune and the need to join the international community of leftist artists.

During Kassák's period of exile—1920 to 1926—both he, personally, and his periodical *Ma* constituted principal organizing forces for the Hungarian avant-garde in Vienna exile. In 1921 Kassák embarked on an artistic career. His writing and painting became inseparable and, as the leader of the Ma group, he formulated important statements. The Constructivist theoretician and critic Ernő Kállai, who lived in Berlin, also belonged to the Ma circle. More than just commentaries, his writings greatly contributed to the pictorial and sculptural expressions of ideas that were still in the turbulent process of ferment.

In 1926 a general amnesty proclaimed in Hungary made it possible for the previously persecuted Kassák, Károly Kernstok, Sándor Bortnyik, and others to return to Budapest and resume, under very different circumstances, the avant-garde in Hungary.

Translated by John Bátki

TO THE ARTISTS OF ALL NATIONS! Lajos Kassák

Originally published as "An die Künstler aller Länder!" *Ma* vol. 5 (1920)

The artists of a social class that is striving to achieve fully human status, alone and misunderstood in their actions, are calling out to you in a brotherly appeal. Listen to us. Our voices project rebellious, blood-red question and exclamation marks, and their coagulated meaning proclaims our undying faith in permanent revolution. We feel there is only one law, that of continual advance in the face of cosmic life; everything else is a cowardly avoidance of our true selves or a resigned waiting for death. And we are not afraid of ourselves and have no intention of resigning from our lives. The revolution is our life, and our revolution is a most sacred credo of love.

This is 1920 and we are past the purely romantic longing for greater heights; inside us torn, bloody roots reach toward the absolute, and we have earned the right to plain words uttered without gesturing.

We have learned what life is about and have internalized its laws.

We have no roots in the past and we have no reins tied to the future.

Our solitary shout into the world at large is a spout of our lifeblood: where is Man to be found?

The essence of the new art is empathy with the tragedy of our times and infusing it with meaning for the time of birth. The vocation of the new artist involves rousing to full consciousness a humanity lost the midst of the stupefaction of the oppressed and the speculations of profiteers. Thus it is not individual glorification nor is it art for the masses in the sense of people's tribunes. Let us be clear about this. For only through this recognition can the road lead to today's truth, to the only actual truth—to life, to you and me, to Unity.

This is what we demand of those who make art and those who are receptive to art. By placing both on the same level we have declared the equality of those who give and those who accept. For as the concept of the servants and the served will disappear, so will that of the glorified and the abased. Our motto is: Humanity. For we are human in our art, and just as we had refused to be the servants of the bourgeoisie in the past, we shall refuse to be the servants of any other class in the future—even if that class is called the proletariat. We believe that *every* form of class servitude represents another variant of today's social system of enslavement. We have no desire to help a new class in place of the former one, lording it over humanity. We proclaim the community of triumphant individuals as opposed to any kind of class dominance, and a collective ethics as opposed to any kind of morality of the state. This is where the light and warmth of our fraternal words leads. Our paths rush us to the land of fraternity, and the word our banners flash forth is Action. Action of redemption, not the action of hatred.

This alone can be the voice of today's justice.

Brothers! We send our loud signals to you from this land that abounds in history, searching for iron-fisted destroyers and clear-headed builders. We are recruiting the pioneers of the liberating thought to lead the army of the masses flooded by misery. These are the masses that are still mostly led by their bellies so that all fine hopes are again liable to perish. The energies of the revolted proletariat have been fatally chained to a single track and the clock strikes one funeral after another for a world in flames.

Let the seers see clearly now!

The revolution must not be rationalized into the service of solving any one question, any single idea. For the revolution is not a means for triumphing in life—the revolution is the goal, Life itself.

Let us face the fact that today's worldwide movement does not yet signal the beginning of a new world, only the end of the old. Not the individual and collective rejection of government, but its seizure by repressive organizations. This is not yet the transcending of government, merely a development into its fullest form, terrorist Social Democracy.

All this is still nothing but politics.

The power-struggles of parties moving the masses.

Jockeyings for position, with the accompanying anxieties over position.

But the perspectives have opened up!

Certain tragic individuals, like the cursed angels of mythology, already carry within themselves, and expose as a sacred monstrance, the one and only certain sign of revolution: an active consciousness.

And here is our time, and your time, brothers, for all of us who want to set fire to the soul of humanity, using the fuel of historical materialism. Now is the time to bring to light the eternal stability of ethics as opposed to every kind of class morality. Stressing the solution of economic problems is not enough for enhancing the possibilities of human existence. The masses have starved long enough to be ready to revolt at any time for a momentary improvement in their lot—but now is the time, as never before, to deepen instinctive rebellion into conscious and permanent revolution. Having liberated the actual forces at work, we must now reappraise our abstract concepts. As we shake off the hindering layers of mud, we also have to point our torches toward the one and only goal. For only a ceaseless longing for Onward can reinforce our fortitude in fighting each momentary battle. For only a liberated soul can guarantee that the liberated body will not be subjected to a new yoke.

Brothers, whose sad and joyful souls pour forth into single-minded lives of politics, science, and technology, you are as aware as we are that this is the only way it can be. We are aware that the origins of the revolution (its instigators) are immediate economic factors, but its unstoppable propellers are the awakened psychic forces. Pure, unified consciousness. The shout you hear from us issues from the innate law of world revolution. New artists! Reach out in the chaos of revolution to allow the harmony of the revolution resound with the consanguinity of our blood. Beyond class interests, toward the interests of all humankind. Above and beyond the dictatorship of a class, toward the dictatorship of ideas. Throw away the placards carrying names, cast aside pseudo-humanism and individual imperialism!

We shall not be stopped!

Brothers, become truly fraternal, to build a new man, the collective individuum!

For under the banner of communism, which is the purest faith, there cannot be any other interest than humanity's vast existential interest, of which you and I equally partake!

The realization of this interest under the dictatorship of ideas can only take place through the revolutionizing of souls!

This revolution can only be assured through the ethical and pointedly cultural education of the proletariat that constitutes the wholesome raw material of the future.

Therefore we demand culture! And yet more culture!

The proletariat is inexorably battering at the reign of the slave-keeping fathers; we must now begin the fight against the reign of the first-born siblings.

Down with the politics of the bloodthirsty! Down with the leaders clinging on to their prestige! Down with the Talmudists of the revolution!

We have had enough of lawyers' reasoning, administrative mechanisms, boring speeches!

Long live the revolution against all tradition!

Long live the responsible collective individuum!
Long live the dictatorship of ideas!

Translated by John Bátki

THE PROVISIONAL INTERNATIONAL MOSCOW BUREAU OF CREATIVE ARTISTS, QUESTIONS TO THE HUNGARIAN ACTIVISTS, AND THE HUNGARIAN ACTIVISTS' REPLY

Originally published as "Az alkotó művészek provizorikus, moszkvai internacionális irodájának kérdései a magyarországi aktivista művészekhez," *Ma*, vol. 6, nos. 1–2 (November 1, 1920)

I.   What is the position of the Hungarian Activists' group in Hungarian society and art; what are their achievements in poetry, painting, sculpture, music, etc.? (A thorough history of the group's inception, its theoretical basis and the reasons for its coming into being; its conflicts with conservatives and other artists; its commonly used slogans.)

II. What is the opinion of the Hungarian Activists' group about the following artistic and cultural questions of the social revolution:
    1. Art for the proletariat or proletarian art?
    2. Proletarian art or universal human art?
    3. What is revolutionary art?
    4. Art and propaganda.
    5. In what manner is the artistic product to be distributed?
    6. What are the creative artists' obligations (to produce) and what benefits will they receive in a socialist state?

III. What are the theoretical and practical circumstances of the community of artists that the Hungarian Activists' group intends to establish?
    1. The organizational and economic basis of the artists' trade union.
    2. Art and the state.
    3. Collaboration of the artists' union with artists' groups of opposing orientations.

IV. What are the social tasks of the revolutionary artist and on what basis should a creative artists' Communist International be established?

V.   What questions does the Hungarian Activists' group have for the Moscow provisional international bureau of creative artists?

Reply:
I.   We do not feel it is necessary to publish our reply to the first question, for our readers will be familiar with the nature of our past work.

II. 1. Neither art for the proletariat nor proletarian art. The first would mean a denial of art's power to shape life; the second is entirely moot—for a proletarian art is just as unimaginable as a proletarian mathematics.

    2. Without a shadow of doubt: universal human art. In our days we have arrived at the era of world revolution. This revolution is incommensurably greater in its psychic and physical dimensions than any previous racial or national revolution. The present class character of the world revolution is also universally human in its viewpoint and strives for the ultimate goal of creating a free human community.

In addition to the economic forces that make action imperative, it has afforded a full role to the collective socialist worldview. Therefore there can no longer be any question of reforms. Succeeding the Christian worldview, the time has come for a new salvation on earth. The new arts are struggling to give form in our time to this salvation that is in the throes of being born. Thus art, as the primary register and indicator of the collective human longing for betterment can never lower its sights to represent merely the struggles of any one individual, group, gender, or race. This would mean, from the universal viewpoint, an incomplete view of life. Art, because of its authenticity, can only be universal. And it can only join a class struggle if the class-consciousness is universal.. The proletariat is such a class in our days. This is why the new artists count primarily on the proletariat as the force that desires the greatest good and as the only appropriate constituent of the revolution.

3. There is only art. The manifestation art is creation. Seen from today's point of view, art equally surpasses in its results both yesterday's creations and today's givens. Creation conceived in such maximal terms equals revolution. Art that is truly art can only be revolutionary. Anything outside of this definition is mere game-playing or machination with a greater or lesser degree of resemblance to art. Such game-playing and machination constitute *l'art pour l'art* as indulged in by a passive, individualistic bourgeoisie. Art is a demonstrative force and each manifestation takes a stand against the external contingencies of life. Its vocation is the promotion and the fueling of permanent revolution. In a most direct manner it deepens and broadens the world revolution. And even though its propagandistic value is indirect, art as a whole functions, as it were, as a symbol of daily life. Beyond the irresponsible poses of demagogues, priests, lawyers, and judges the new artist appears as the synthetic unity, dynamic and epic, of a new kind of life.

4. One of our slogans is, "There is no art without a worldview." This categorically declares that all art must take a stand. Because of its very nature it agitates for the right or the left. But this agitation by art (which can only be indirect) must not be mistaken for the emotional propaganda projected by posters and speechmakers. The methods of art, and its long-term results, come from a source that is deep down, and cannot be discouraged by mere political failures. The essence of revolutionary art is not comprised of popular or novel political slogans, but consists of the artist's new worldview that contravenes the passive Christian worldview. With every creation the artist's purpose is to inject a worldview into the public, and succeeding in this means producing chaos and confusion in the audience. This is the incommensurable power and meaning of art. The creation of anarchy in souls grown lazy, immured by conventions. For as we know, the beginnings of anarchy bring on a desire for a new equilibrium in us. Every revolution sets out to create new laws upon the ruins of the old laws. Whether this path leads to the left or to the right again depends on the worldview of the leaders. It is the same way in art. The truth of this has already been recognized by Christianity, which placed the propagandistic forces of music, painting, sculpture, and architecture in the service of religion. Art possessing a Christian worldview succeeded in channeling the chaos evoked in the mind of man in the direction of a deity; today's art with a socialist worldview directs the seekers of a new equilibrium toward humanity. This is no mere theorizing on our part. When the new art made its debut in Hungary, it was greeted by general laughter, as a form of incomprehensible madness. Subsequently there were a few who began to recognize the signs of life in it, and the youngest generation joined the battle, taking sides for or against it. This battle could not be compared to the struggles surrounding Impressionism; instead of aesthetic results it produced a change in

worldview. Without any compulsion, the readers of our periodical and the viewers of our exhibitions became fed up with their former lives, gave birth to a fanatical faith, and finally, to make life more bearable, set out with chaos seething inside them to encounter Marx as the first stage of a fuller life. We offered them an "unrealistic" art and they responded by turning to historical materialism. It is now evident that the force that had dislodged them from their past was an active and purposeful force. They, who had broken away from the bourgeois social order, now had to find the socialist order, and without any further persuasion became the most ardent proponents of the proletarian revolution in Hungary.

5. We think that the distribution of artistic products should be in the hands of the state. The artist's works should be transferred from the hands of the artist to the public only after a jury of his peers has made a selection of them, keeping in mind the cultural requirements of the public. The jury should be made up of artists with the most advanced views. The jury process should set aside any and all historical considerations. There can be only one point of view, that of art itself. At the same time we must do away with museums in today's sense of the word. But art historians and aestheticians should be permitted to collect privately (for as long as such bookworms persist in not dying of boredom) those works that were not selected by the jury for the public. The works selected will be organized into demonstrative exhibitions in the larger cities and into permanent travelling exhibitions for the provinces. These exhibitions, too, shall be curated strictly from the viewpoint of art. There can be no concessions to the population's miseducated tastes. The works returned from exhibition will be installed in public buildings, schools and trade union halls. The works considered by the jury as secondary and not absolutely necessary for public exhibition will be offered for sale by state-operated mobile art dealerships where private individuals will be able to purchase them on an installment plan. These art dealerships will be maintained as long as money will remain in effect in the communist society. After the cessation of the money system these works will remain in the possession of the artist. He will be free to give them away to whomever he wants to, or trade them for other works of art that had likewise not been selected for public exhibition. Each artwork in the private collections thus amassed will be registered in an agency created for this purpose, and the artists' juries will always have the right to view the collection for purposes of expropriation; in fact such a viewing will be obligatory once a year. Periodically, say every five years, the public collections will also have to be reviewed, for the purposes of de-accessioning.

The manufacture of reproductions to "replace" original artworks will be prohibited, as a fraud, by the state. Permanent "export" or "import" of artworks to or from "abroad" will not be permissible, as this would prevent the free, agitative circulation of great spirits throughout the world.

6. We have been discussing the outspokenly revolutionary artists whose artistic activity is inseparable from their human activities. On this point we must assume that they act in good faith. We must accept artists as true artists, that is, believe in their commitment to art as the primary activity in life. This implies a guarantee of maximal output by the artists. There can be no question of externally applied production standards as regards quantity or quality, for the simple reason that the social value of the artistic product cannot be measured by any objective parameters. The sole determinant of the value of the artistic product is the degree of the artist's revolutionary humanity. Therefore in this regard we can only discuss the circumstances that have a beneficial or deleterious effect on creative life. Such are the equilibrium of the economic situation and the increased cultural

opportunities. The new artist has stepped forth from the enclave of romanticism: he is a man of sorrows and joys. It is certain that the artist whose work is a live demonstration of the revolution will have a maximally full life under a communist economic system.

The revolution is either viable, in which case artists, as revolutionaries out of inner necessity, will be obliged to bring the maximum out of themselves, or else the revolution still does not possess viable roots, in which case the problem of artistic matters no longer applies. We do not have the slightest doubts about the revolution. The second part of the question is therefore not applicable.

III. 1. We reject the notion of a trade union for artists. For quite some time to come, we cannot envision collective collaboration for artists, who are individuals with widely different specific gravities. Therefore in lieu of trade unions we propose the establishment of a management agency by the state. This agency will be exclusively devoted to the financial needs of artists and will ensure the supply of materials necessary for their work. The selection of who qualifies for this service should not be made by a composite committee; instead, the various artists' groups should select individuals from within their own areas of expertise who are qualified to receive grants. Thus each specific group will be responsible for its members' level of output.

2. We would be hard put to find two more diametrically opposed notions than art and the state. These are two contradictory elements, never to be reconciled with each other. Whereas one is a force that constantly breaks down and makes anew, the other is a permanently consolidating force. While one is the first to revolt against and to disrupt order, the other is its foremost solidifier and ever at work on increasing its dogmatic rule. One is dynamic, the other static. One incites revolt, the other oppresses it. One is permanent revolution, the other is the sober conserver of the problems and solutions presented by any revolution. Thus there can be no lasting conjunction between art and the state. We may only conceive of a one-sided compromise between them, enforced by the state. You feed us so that we can fight against you. For you, the state, are a machine and we are live human beings.

3. This question becomes moot after our response to the previous one.

IV. "Art can only be revolutionary." It follows that art carries in its components all of the problems of the age. Therefore the sole task of the artist is to keep working and to propagate his work on an ever-broader basis. The speeding up of the world revolution by all means needs a Communist International of creative artists. We for our part already condemn the organizers of the revolution for their delay and hesitation in asking this question. The current world crisis cannot be solved on a purely economic basis and through purely political means. Art is not a societal luxury, but as a representative of constant progress is a vast source of energy for the revolution. The Communist International of artists must be the central agency to organize with practical aims in mind this as yet chaotic source of power. We think the Communist International of creative artists should be established along the lines of the Third International. The central committee of the Third International should convene an assembly of the most radical artists of every nation, making sure to invite only those with the cleanest past, and who had already taken a stand on behalf of communism. The only agenda of this meeting should be the establishment of a Communist International of Creative Artists. The number of members is not significant, just as it made no difference at the time of the founding of the Third International.

The founders should assume the role of dictatorship. No concessions should be made to so-called well-meaning elements, for the first goal of this International, to the exclusion of all other considerations, is the clarification of the issues of art and the revolution. While cooperating with the Third International, the Communist International of Creative Artists must have total autonomy in the area of art. What is more, the central committee of the C.I.C.A. can only function in an observational role vis-à-vis the artists' groups in individual countries. Our movement cannot work along strictly predetermined items on its agenda. The central committee's moral and economic support must make possible the publication of a monthly periodical in every country, one that is obliged to publish, in addition to contributors from its own country, translations of the work of revolutionary artists of other nations. Representatives of the revolutionary artists of each nation should convene periodically (as dictated by the progress of the struggle) in international congresses to discuss the tasks in individual countries as seen from an international perspective, and decide on the tactics to follow.

V. The Activist artists of Hungary have the following questions for the Moscow provisional international bureau of creative artists:

   1. What practical results can the three years of the dictatorship of the proletariat show in the area of art?

   2. What role do artists play in schools?

   3. What is the meaning of the total exclusion of the question of art from communist propaganda thus far?

With our comradely greetings,
The Activist artists of Hungary

Translated by John Bátki

MOHOLY-NAGY   Ernő Kállai (under the pen name Péter Mátyás)
Originally published as "Moholy-Nagy," *Ma* vol. 9 (September 15, 1921)

In the extremes of its adventures, Moholy-Nagy's art reaches out on the borders of Cubism and Dadaism, and by organically uniting these opposite poles, he heralds the world of contemporary man who has managed to subjugate the machines.

Speaking purely in terms of form, he constructs either concentric or eccentric systems of forms or tries to interlink these opposing entities.

In the case of those works, in the monumentality of the few masses which are distanced so as to suggest inevitability, a strong will and elementary laws manifest themselves. In his use of the landscape motifs of the railway tracks, for example by the projection of the tremendous diagonal of a factory chimney leaning left, the leaning, resting forces, forces pressing tensed into vertical, are gathered into a compact architecture of form. Details of bridges and architectural structures, having lost all their utilitarian references and practical functions, freely elevate themselves into a self-willed order, an existence meaningful in itself. In another picture, based on a white horizontal stripe, with an almost organic vitality, the form swings and leaps into a slender vertical. This is all discipline of form, self-awareness, and pride, a totally new and individual manifestation of the modern constructive style, which is devoid of the sometimes dangerously short-changing form and color-splitting and space-complicating of the more differentiated Western Cubism. Colors develop themselves into form through their strong contrasts, through their brutal clashing with each other; the articulations of the form are of the most simple kind possible, and that space, which was left empty for a *tabula rasa*, constitutes a single, wide abstract wall behind the form, on which the artist's credo concerning the future-shaping power of man's civilizing activity is written up with lapidary laconicism.

However, Moholy-Nagy is not only a monumental lord and master-builder of contemporary life and of form, but with a naive admiration of the eternal-primitive child-barbarian, and with his raving joy too, he is also an ecstatic admirer of this life. In other people's hands Dadaism serves as a murderous weapon of moral and social criticism. The exultation over a million possibilities of forms and motion which only the metropolis and modern technology can create, the sudden discovery of a new world and the dancing laughing youth of a vision totally open to the universe: all these are there in Moholy-Nagy's art.

Semaphores of joys, forms and colors are standing on all points of space.

Freshly felt surprises and perspectives of gravitational pulls of manifold directions, of the many and of the many kinds, spring up from everywhere. Total geometrical abstractions as well as pieces, numbers, letters and realistically represented objects or fragments of objects picked from the primary reality proliferate in Moholy-Nagy's eccentrical pictures.

This is a cosmic harmony, nonetheless it has not been kindled by a Futurist Romanticism and, still yet, these works, despite of all their divergences, form, after all, a perfectly intelligible system of absolutely interdependent units.

Anarchy is getting perceptibly arranged into a system of unified law. Although still not with the centralism of the self-containing architectonic structures, the pieces are coalescing into cohesive units, replacing the exploded conglomerate forms. Structures, still open, but set into motion from sharper defined and closer interrelated centers, emerge. Here, the mechanism of the modern machine and its kinetic system has been converted into art through the process of a fruitful coalescence of centrical and eccentrical pictorial factors with the creative principles connecting with Dadaism and Cubism.

This fusion without inner contradictions of the style forming and negating trends of modern art gives Moholy-Nagy a chance to elevate his paintings on the terms of their own forms the level of vision. His art, after all, maintains a close link with its own well-defined objective territory. But in his relatedness to reality he is not satisfied with pointing out that meaning which is already present, although more or less hidden, in our senseless, chaotic age.

Just as the anarchistic manifestations of Moholy-Nagy's art mean neither the rejection nor the approval of the all-destroying selfish instinct of the bourgeois free enterprise. Over problematical features of the present, Moholy-Nagy proclaims law and liberty which throw light on the perspectives of the infinite future.

Translation from Krisztina Passuth, Moholy-Nagy

LAJOS KASSÁK   Ernő Kállai (under the pen name Péter Mátyás)
Originally published as "Lajos Kassák," *Ma* vol. 9 (September 15, 1921)

All collective art has two poles. One of these expands with the faculty for the representation of bodies, until it enfolds the entire world. At the other extreme the will to create a social and intellectual community erects a monument to itself out of its own building blocks.

The former is to a certain extent realistic observation focused on an object, while the latter is pure spirit and ethics embodied as non-objective form in space.

And since the collective spirit implies law and logic, collective form always builds upon the order of articulated parts.

It creates architecture even while painting a picture or modeling a sculpture. Architectonic articulation is all the more severe, and its forms all the more abstract and simple, the less personal freedom the social and economic order of the collective spirit allows. For every new collective signals the elevation of a victorious, objective historical will into an accomplished fact. The launching of every collective involves the welding together of various forces into the most solid agglomeration of power—thus it is a construction, in the most inexorable sense of the word.

Regarding Lajos Kassák's woodcuts that proclaim the collective man, many viewers (even some belonging to the revolutionary youth) are likely to mention the absence of representation, and the regrettable fact that these graphics are not easily comprehensible. Granted that Kassák's graphics, with their vertical, horizontal and diagonal force lines, planes and arches that articulate into structures, do not readily lend themselves for purposes of direct political agitation. But this is the only drawback that burdens them as a result of their incomprehensibility for the masses. For any representative art, especially in the vein of new realism, executed to be readily accessible for the proletariat, can only end up as illustration for the arithmetics of politics and economy in our days. And this kind of realism, unless it is content with being a more or less Dadaist critique of bourgeois society and culture (in the sense of, say, the George Grosz of old), will come into inevitable conflict with even the most humble Constructivist experimentation. (The new George Grosz!) However, without construction it is impossible to create an image of the positive values of the man and society of tomorrow.

Not to mention that the shrinking of space and its relegation to a minor role through the use of illusionistic perspective may be interpreted as the small-minded moral philosophy of individual shares of the patrimony.

Nonetheless, even if the truths demonstrable through realism prove to be a thousand times unavoidable as stepping stones toward social revolution, they still do not constitute the alpha and omega of collective man.

The question of pure human spirit, transcending short-term political agitation, is a matter of life and death. This spirit confronts us in the endless and universal front of workers maintained in every civilization, with regard to which the remote, receding perspective of individual sentimentality and rationality is reduced to nothing. It is the spirit of frontality that commands an egolessness that transcends the differentiations of an objective view, to construct a monument out of its own inner world.

In Kassák's picture architecture, the essence of collective civilization asserts itself with a severe sovereignty. Rising above the chaos of today's unbridled emotions, the future is upheld by the simple clarity of formal and spatial relationships.

The fatalism of such a faith and will discredits regarding the lack of pictorial representation. In this case non-objectivity does not imply a romantic evasion of the world, even less a mystical dematerialization, but the declaration of a new law and new way of life by an inexorably revolutionary will.

This is art that reduced to the most concentrated and basic form: *action*. It is creation, the triumphant forecast of the future collective, charting its course through an infinite and inchoate space. It sets a framework for all of the objects and meanings yet to come.

It does not bother with details, the relative light-, color-, and form-refractions of the one and only ultimate truth. This is why it does not depict people, whether proletarian or capitalist, or whatever else is demanded by the realism of political comprehensibility. This is why it insists on always constructing. But its constructions offer a thousand possibilities of objective views for the future, and not even the most tangible realism of the future can be anything other than the radiant forms of a collective reality that has arrived at its own architecture.

Translated by John Bátki

PICTURE-ARCHITECTURE   Lajos Kassák
Originally published as "Képarchitektúra," *Ma* vol. 7, no. 4 (March 25, 1922)

Down with art! Long live art!
Since the disintegration of the primitive Christian concept of the world there has never been so great a need to "solve" the problems of the human way of life as today, when individual materialism has become bankrupt. Man is born and man cannot endure his life. There are open roads before us and yet we cannot set out because we have no goal in us to spur us on our way. What we desire, the externals of life and their acquisition, is not necessarily indispensable, but all this would mean to us is material enrichment. Therefore as civilized beings we are incapable of making any sacrifice—not even sufficient to rid ourselves of the forms of life today, in other words, our moral endowments—to achieve it. This was what made the World War possible, and this is the root of the collapse in themselves of the social revolutions which undoubtedly began with a strong impulse. Who today believes in the future as "the only sacrament"? Who is spurred to action today by the "glorification of an idea"? It is plain that it is alive somewhere in the depths of human consciousness, that he who set as his aim the conquest of the world cannot conquer the world. In order that we may become ordinary human beings we must extend our desires to the superhuman, for along the road we shall certainly reach the human. He who is ready to travel can only be a man with a concept/*Weltanschauung* of the world. Marxian socialism as a scientific theory cannot be a concept of the world.
A *Weltanschauung* is not something that one knows: it is something that one, above all feels.
Science is practicalities.
Art is a *Weltanschauung*.
Creation alone is life, and life the materialization of the *Weltanschauung* of the world.
Art is creation and therefore the most complete life.
That is the end and that is the road too.
Art never had any beginning and will never come to an end.
From eternity art has been an ever-present force, like ethics, like revolution, like the whole world itself.
Thus there is no new art and no old art.
There is only art.
And since the artist is not the master but the servant of art, the art-products of certain ages show us not the face of art but only the nature of good or bad material which humanity alive at those times had to communicate art.
For art is life, while man can only develop into one who expresses this life.
Therefore art cannot be made.

The artist is like a mother: pregnant with life. A new product of art is as valuable as a newly-born human being.

At certain times only men of a certain caliber can come to birth: at certain times only certain products of art can come to birth.

The artist is inwardly compelled to strive to express the world, in other words himself, as completely as possible.

Since the world is forever changing this aim cannot be realized yet the artist works only to realize this aim.

This is his "tragedy" and this makes him like a "god." The more perfect man is, the more perfect is his god.

The more perfect an artist is, the more perfect is his art.

There is no doubt that once again we have arrived closer to the constructive concept of the world, like the collective belief of the first Christians maintained through a totally disorganized wilderness out of which only one or two painful tragedies succeeded in making their tortured way to the zenith. But our belief is not in Christian religiosity, a form which has already exhausted itself, but in communism, in whose essence totality is like Unity, but as opposed to the hierarchical structure of the Christian religion, the One is also like totality. We feel cosmic life in ourselves and the problems of progress will solve themselves.

In our concept of the world we live life itself; we have completed the bloody vicious circle, and man has once again become capable of expressing the world. Not imitating it, but creating it.

The artist of today, as a man with a concept of the world, again bears his art with him as a manifesto.

Not his view of the world, but the essence of the world.

Architecture.

The synthesis of the new order.

In the fine arts (but I emphasize that what is true of one branch of art as a specialty of form is also true of art itself as a creative unity) the first to desire this new synthesis were the Cubists, Expressionists and the Merz painters. They desired it, but did not yet sense it fully.

Of the three groups it is the searches of the Cubists that point along the surest road to—art. They misunderstood the disintegrated world and in their art searched their way back to the essence of things, to construction. What they achieved depended entirely on their individual values. Their creations put into forms a concept of the world that is not entirely unified. Their synthesis is not *a priori*, but the result of a deep analysis. Their composition is not the embodiment of the compulsion of an inner emotion that cannot be expressed otherwise, but the illustration of a scientific will by using artistic means. Their pictures are not creations for their own sake, but transpositions into painting of a world recognized by optical or psychological means—though mercilessly opposed to "naturalism" and recognizing the laws of plane surfaces. Their forms are restricted to the corporeal nature of objects seen or known, and with their colors they try to put a natural perspective on the canvas; and with this the "picture" finally loses life as a picture and becomes illusory. As a theory, Cubism laid the foundation stone of art in the "modern" period, but the Cubists themselves only progressed beyond Impressionism in form. With geometrical division of form they paint a human being an animal, a violin etc., three-dimensional figures on a two-dimensional plane. Their scientific theories derived from the recognition of the plane have not been successfully transferred into forms of composition even by their most representative artists, like Léger and Gleizes. Instead of the "psychic" depiction of man they have turned to the depiction of "monumental" compositions. This, however, simply implies a difference of theme from the depiction of Picasso's violinist, for example. It is certain that today we have come much closer, just because of the development of our concept of the world, to the sensory perception of machines and great cities, than did our predecessors whose mood was idyllic; but from the standpoint of artistic pretensions the symbolic "composition" of these into pictures indicates nothing more than a second-degree composition. And in the long run how much more does this indicate than impressionism? At most, the one transposes with discernment, the other without it.

Art, however, is a creative act with strict inner laws.

Of the Expressionists it was Kandinsky who went farthest. His forms have scarcely any optical bases; he calls his art absolute painting. And is Kandinsky's painting really absolute painting? Yes. But are Kandinsky's pictures absolute pictures too? No....

A picture as a creation on a flat plane cannot bring to mind any foreign body (such as a body not present in the picture) and cannot exhibit anything. No, not even a psychic process. But Kandinsky's pictures have a story to tell. From his first story-pictures right to the compositions of 1920 one can survey the whole process; the same emotional motifs which appeared on canvas in the first period with dwarfs and fairy queens are still present in his latest creations, though without borrowed forms. Thus the artist has not created a new world: he has merely abstracted himself from the "real" world. There is no doubt that even today he paints not pictures but sensations. He transfers life that is living in some other area to the area of the plane. It is certain, however, that he does it with magnetic intensity, just like a good actor who gives "colossal" life to the prescribed role. And both of these are just secondary creations.

Art, however, is simply bringing something into existence out of nothing.

And Kurt Schwitters, the Merz-painter, says in one of his articles that Merz paintings are abstract creations. What does he mean by "abstract"? The abstract does not exist. Transforming something out of its most characteristic form into something or into some quality—this procedure is called abstraction. In other words from something into some kind. Schwitters, just like Kandinsky, forms emotions into pictures. Only in the choice of the material needed to express their emotions do the two artists differ from each other. Kandinsky, the absolute painter, expresses himself with paints and colors; Schwitters on the other hand carries his emotions through the totality of materials (and here is his unconscious collective significance as opposed to Kandinsky) into plastic art. It is his emotions that he transfers. His pictures have defined titles: Franz Muller's wire-spring, The Great I, etc. Can these pictures be any different from the conscious elaboration of some memory or invention of the artist? No. And what can these pictures give to us? The illusion of a world that exists, once existed or may exist. But in the best instance illusion can only be what creation is.

But art is creation.

A man of unreality lives with illusions.

The concept of the world is the sense of security: the greatest reality.

The only scale of values to the artist is his concept of the world.

The artist with a concept of the world can create anything.

Creation is the constructive good deed.

Construction is architecture.

The absolute picture is *Képarchitektúra*.

The material revolutions, if they have not achieved anything else, have brought home to the thinking man the truth that it is impossible to solve the problems of modern life by relying solely on organizations of violence or solely by economic revolution. The capitalist order of society possesses not only militarism, which is good for patricide, and a conservative bureaucracy, but also a fearful moral strength, and for this reason the hunger-riots of the oppressed will always prove too little to oppose it. For unfortunately this hunger, which is opposed to a more humane fear of life on the part of the capitalists, can be satisfied at any time with a larger slice of bread. The revolution which sets out to change the world trips up on a crumb of bread and dies as a rebellion. It dies because it has no concept of the world to support it. The mass did not set out because it could not put up with the life it has today, but because the prospects of a better life were set before it. And in order that humanity may be able to redeem itself it is not enough to have just a desire for a better life: first and foremost it is necessary to be completely unable to bear with life as it has been hitherto.... Let there be no way back any more! And this can only be completely achieved by means of a psychic liberation either beforehand or in the best instance at the same time. And it is a mistake to believe that man is seriously capable of doing something for "the future." We are alive and we wish to live. Anything beyond this truth may be a revolutionary catchword and it may be a counter-revolutionary catchword. And only the artist can be the one who particularizes and revolutionizes our emotions.

The artist is one who does not command us to do anything but who makes us able to do the greatest things.

Art transforms us, and we become capable of transforming our surroundings.

And as has always been so, in the present world-cataclysm too art has come nearest to the point from which the new concept of the world will be formed.

Applied knowledge tends to revert to the service of reaction, and art has arrived wholly at its own, in other words at the essence of the world, in architecture.

Now we can clearly see that art is Art, and no more and no less than this.

And not according to the interests of tendentious classes or parties, but it is itself a pure life-tendency.

Of all artistic creations hitherto it is architecture alone that demonstrates this life-tendency.

Thus *Képarchitektúra* does not "represent" a powerful god, a fearful war or idyllic love: it is a power that demonstrates itself!

Képarchitektúra does not resemble anything, tells no story, has no beginning and no end anywhere.

It simply exists.

It is like unwalled cities, an ocean that can be traversed by ships, a rambling wood or the creation that is closest to it—the Bible.

Wherever we enter it, we may sense the whole at any point.

So it simply exists, for it had to come to birth by its own power.

And in this existence it is merciless.

It is one of the characteristics of modern schools of art that they try to assimilate, just like their predecessors. For example, if we wanted success for an expressionist picture, we had to search for a suitable and preferably "pleasant" milieu for it. If we placed it in a bad milieu, it died like a broken flower, its colors faded or became mottled and its forms became blurred. The "expert" said it could not bear these surroundings. With *Képarchitektúra* the reverse is true. It appears in its surroundings as a fundamental force living on its own reserves, and what surrounds it does not command it but is subjected to it. Whoever comes to like *Képarchitektúra* must become nauseated by his petty bourgeois surroundings and consequently by his bourgeois self. *Képarchitektúra* is not illusory but realistic, not abstract, but naturalism in the strictest sense. So much so that beside the imitative painting christened "Naturalism" it appears as nature to be imitated, and is no different from trees, men or any other "natural marvels."

Thus *Képarchitektúra* is no longer a picture in the academic sense of the word.

It is an active companion in our life, the symbol of the universe to whom I must attach myself or against whom in the interests of my life I must struggle.

It is enrichment and a force compelling to enrichment.

Through the blur of colors and labyrinth of lines is the galleries *Képarchitektúra* has come to meet us like a trinity of simplicity, security and truth. It has come as the representative of the age and presented us with a knowledge of the plane as a realistically usable space and with the forms of a collective belief in life. Up to now the artist stood before the canvas full of inspiration, and the happiest of them was the one who was so able to receive the influences of the world that he could sweat or foist on to the plane surface "perspectives" that deceived himself and the public. We know that if we are painting a picture we are not boring a tunnel or building a house. But we are building a picture.

Képarchitektúra is constructed not inwards from the plane but outwards from it. It takes the surface simply as a given foundation and does not open perspectives inwards, which may be illusory at all times, but with its layers of color and forms steps out into real space, and thus the picture is given natural perspective, the unlimited potentialities of the life of a picture. *Képarchitektúra*, like architecture in general, counts on the laws of gravity and chemistry. The perspective between forms and colors originates not from the apparent construction of bodies depicted behind each other, but from the corporeality of the colors actually present and the flat forms themselves. Thus these colors and forms live; they live their own real lives, as opposed to the decoration of color and form, as the good critics will term this kind of art. Decoration is filling up the flat surface, *Képarchitektúra* is building on the flat surface. Its pictures are therefore not "like," but are what they are. They have a direct impact and their impact cannot be as if an imitative portrait or landscape or an illusory construction showing the latest machine were about to talk or begin to move. And for this reason our art is a primary creation and we, like all building, set out from our own region on the flat surface, as from a foundation into the air, as men who wish no longer to dance attendance but to transform the world in our own image.

And not by means of tactics like politicians and not by technique, like the chewers of pencils and slaves of the brush.

For technique is not necessary for art. Technique is routine and routine is skimming the surface. It is precisely the opposite of art.

Képarchitektúra rejects all schools—including the schooling of ourselves.

Képarchitektúra does not confine itself to particular materials and particular means; like Merz-art it regards all kinds of materials and means as useful to express itself.

Képarchitektúra does not dabble in psychology.

Képarchitektúra does not want anything.

Képarchitektúra wants everything.

Képarchitektúra has liberated itself from the arms of "art" and has gone beyond Dadaism.

Képarchitektúra believes of itself that it is the beginning of a new world.

Képarchitektúra truly does not wish to be situated in a room.

Képarchitektúra wants to be the room itself, the house itself, indeed it wishes to be your own most intimate life.

Képarchitektúra is as simple as the sole of a boot and yet it is the root of perfection.

Képarchitektúra is the enemy of all art, because only from it can art set forth.

Képarchitektúra is 2 x 2 = 4.

Képarchitektúra has killed mawkish zigzags and idyllic variety.

Képarchitektúra sees an endless spiral even in a straight line.

Képarchitektúra professes itself to be the human zenith.

Képarchitektúra does not wish to die on the wall.

Képarchitektúra wishes to be a town of American caliber, a look-out tower, a sanatorium for consumptives and a popular entertainment.

For *Képarchitektúra* is art, and art is creation and creation is everything.

Translated by George Cushing

THE GREAT FESTIVAL IN MOSCOW   Béla Uitz

Originally published as "A moszkvai nagy ünnep," *Egység* (May 1922)

Summer was approaching. The snow was fast disappearing—the frozen paths turned into rushing streams—spring was fleeting away unnoticed. Within seven days it was suddenly summer.

May had arrived.

Leaves, grasses, flowers spring up from the soil. The miseries of freezing cold are over. Everyone's mood is mellower now. Summer is the gift of life. Life is easier in summertime.

Moscow opens up for the whole world.

There is an unstoppable flood of people.

Yellow-skinned Chinese came, with their introspective Asian serenity.

Americans came from their faraway home, with their broad, confident movements.

There came black-skinned, red-lipped, fiery-eyed Africans.

Europeans came: Frenchmen, Germans, English, Bulgarians, Italians, Norwegians.

They came and came—all the peoples of Europe, Asia, Africa, America, Australia.

The just came and the scoundrels, believers and those without Christ, idealists and materialists, humanists, syndicalists, anarchists, and communists.

Every school of thought on earth, represented by "its very best!" Small-mindedness was not a viable option here. A spiritual storm was heading this way, such as the world has hardly ever seen before.

It was the great celebration Moscow was preparing for.

It was the "great teaching for life," stripped of mendacious idealism and every kind of petty bourgeois slobberiness.

It was the "great trick" in every individuum—the greatest villainy and the greatest humanitarianism.

It was: reality, terror, cleverness, madness and enlightenment.

It was: conviction, irony, and love.

Every single human way of life!

It was: disease, suffering, murder, and horror.

It was: narrow-mindedness, vanity, and heroism.

It was: life itself, opened up.

It was: the fullest fulfillment of the world of the spirit.

It was: the fullest fulfillment of the world of the body (Cakes, white bread, ham, tea, caviar, butter)—while people were starving to death in the streets.

Therefore: this was the greatest hospitality in human history. For never before had a people given everything it had to its guests—as they did here.

This was the great celebration of Moscow.

Moscow returned to life!

Wounded buildings become trimmer.

Variegated walls are dipped into a thousand colors.

The rich harvest of revolutionary painters!

The potholes of streets are smoothed away.

Bakeries resurrected from the dead are pouring forth their bread.

Exhibitions.

Walks.

Performances.

Great perspectives.

Moscow really knows how to disguise herself!

The disguise is for the benefit of the fault-finders; for the steadfast there is only the magnitude of the suffering.

O alas for all you idealists! This is surely not your "pre-planned, beautiful life"!

O alas for you communists! There is not a drop of sentimentalism here.

O alas for you anarchists! Here the "left-wing demagoguery" is all too transparent: selfish, "ethical" opportunism.

The whole world, instead of the "whole Ego."

Here we are faced with facts.

Facts have their laws.

Facts create life.

Here worlds are fighting against worlds.

For this is the great celebration of Moscow.

There came ragged ones, who turned into dandies within a day.

There came men, women, children, young people, priests, agitators.

There came commissars thrown out into the street by workers.

And there came the Red Army's finest.

There came Persians and Indians dressed in colorful outfits. Tough, blunt "cultured" Frenchwomen—and fragile, ethereally tender "savage" Javanese women.

And there came American Indians, Georgians from the Caucasus, Danes, Kirghiz, and Dutch, with wife and children.

Moscow is alive!

The thousands of eyes of foreigners and Russians, curious to see the happiness of foreigners and the happiness of the Russians.

But people are blind; they can only see if we point things out to them.

It is a mild, fine summer.

The countless churches are resplendent in red, gold, blue and white.

The countless gardens rejoice in their verdure.

The feast day is approaching.

Twice we are frustrated. The third time, the gates of the Bolshoi Theater are open.

The meeting of millions of heads, millions of eyes, millions of minds.

The first day: the feast day of feast days.

All that has been created by the spirit, by the people, by all creation, by torment and by joyfulness, is now sacrificed to this day.

Broad-sweeping, high-flying speeches are made by all peoples of the earth.

The "Russian birth-pangs" now speak up.

All the museums, expositions, theaters, performances now open.

In the 40 x 40 church the counter-revolution is stirring.

Greedy jackal claws, and clenched fists are threatening from the direction of Poland and Romania. The air is stifling and full of tension.

And here comes "the people," singing solo and in unison.

Monotone, primitive joys and torments are given voice.

The dancer is doing a sword dance.

The Persian *gusla* sends up a never before heard whimpering, howling, and screaming. The nerves are stripped naked and primitive man is resurrected in a sophisticated sadism.

And here come actors wearing the faces of demagogues, miming suffering, praising tenderness.

Behind the mask of art mockery, knavery, and disgust also speak up.

And then comes the "great knife"—the Red Army.

Festival!!

The sun is pouring forth sheaves of rays. The gently rolling, dirty Moscow River swallows up the bathers.

The gates of the "red wall" are opened up.

The "white Kremlin" is actually red in color!

The halls of the czar are now the halls of the people—the spiritual arena of Communism—a vast, enormous hall, with awful pillars of gold.

The throne has disappeared.

Instead there is a plain table.

This is how the great battle begins.

On one side are 4 men—on the other side, a huge crowd.

It is an unequal battle.

Fact and abstraction, the two polar opposites of intellectual battle, crash into one another.

To the 4 men belong the numberless facts.

To the crowd belongs abstraction.

What shall I say to you?

"Four giants on an ant heap."

The crowd attacks.

The apprentice giant meets the force of blow. He tosses the assailant into the dizzying heights and mercilessly breaks the opponent into smithereens. He creates horror, fear, and conviction by his—facts.

A renewed charge. A wilder, wilier, more powerful and more insidious one.

The first giant stands up.

His eyes are devilish.

His speech would convince a rock, unspeakably warm and simple. He carries the facts on his palms; they are able to kill by their mere existence.

Attack after attack!

They are charging at the most difficult area: the new roads.

But here comes the giant of giants.

He is of small stature, has a broad forehead, killer lips, and a benevolent glance.

He is the plainest of mortals.

He steps up on the podium.

He laughs and cries, he kills, he wheedles. The crowd turns to stone, the podium trembles. The hall totters. The pillars twist. Stones, walls, souls—heaven and earth are held in his hands.

He levels the assault to the ground.

He is being celebrated.

He is the center of the world now.

The focus of hatred and love.

Millions long for him. In their desperation they seek their peace in him.

He is the creator in death.

And still, wave upon wave.

Now he stands up: the laughing giant who has lived through thousands of tragedies, but is nonetheless still merry.

With a sadistic irony he is smashing his opponents to bits.

The great hall is rolling with laughter, guffawing at its own attacks. The laughter turns bitter and incites a new charge.

And now the last one, the "beautiful" giant. He has curly locks and a womanish face.

His honeyed voice creates a tabula rasa.

These words are caressing, flattering, orotund. Tender, cunning, plump, and erotic.

As the glue of life he cements it all together: the crushed attackers, the defeated crowd of abstractions, together with the 4 giants and their facts.

He is indeed like the nut and bolt that unite abstraction and reality into a single whole.

Translated by John Bátki

CONSTRUCTIVISM Ernő Kállai
Originally published as "Konstruktivizmus," *Ma* (May 1923)

Constructivism is art of the purest immanence. Its creative center does not lie outside the spatial formations meant to be sensed and objectivized but, as in the case of non-objective Expressionism, is identical with them. Thus the space of both Constructivism and of non-objective Expressionism is not geocentrically but, rather, egocentrically defined. But whereas Expressionistic space is a passive riverbed of past psychic out-pourings, constructive space, within its own laws, is a conscious and active structure of tensions and patterns of stress. The inner animation of the Expressionist experi-ence is eruptive and staccato, it wanders off in every direction toward boundless and inarticulate regions. The oscillations of Constructivist vitality manifest as a system of balanced and articulated continuity.

This constraint creates a conceptual space that is perfectly even, in its center and peripheries alike, and is maximally, clearly, sharply demarcated from every metaphysical and physiological area of the unconscious.

It follows from this continuity and uniformity of illumination that the Constructivist consciousness experiences itself in space-time in terms of the absolute here and now. However, it does not lack dimensionality. It simply does not recognize the vanishing of the visual field that leads to zones that are perspectively or prophetically placed in the distance: *The constructive consciousness is ahistorical*. It possesses no forms suitable for an anthologizing or teleological viewpoint. There is no dualism of cause and effect con-fronting each other; they are both rooted in the fullest quintessential identity.

The constructive consciousness and work of art are therefore entities identical and suf-ficient unto themselves in the strictest sense of the word. For a Suprematist, it is not merely a matter of mastery to undertake the artistic task of a perfectly smooth, dense, and even painting of a single square. We see here the realization of the will to achieve ultimate unity and identity with oneself, one that, far from seeking some humble liveli-hood by accomplishing this outwardly modest task, strives for a focusing of extraordi-nary intensity. For this Suprematist unity already contains the possibility of an unfolding multiplicity. But this is not a multiplicity whose spread postulates a causal or deductive series, with a beginning and an end. The constructive awareness of multiplicity and of self-identical unity, respectively, relate to each other as does an articulated logical judgement to its own perfectly indivisible meaning.

This quality is incompatible with the notions of predestined fulfillment and the dialectics of tragedy. The mere notion of a constructive drama is an absurdity.

The systematic nature of constructive consciousness does not entail static immobility. On the contrary, Constructivism possesses the most powerful concept and most real possibilities of motion known to art. But the lines of oscillation of Constructivist motion do not scatter into anarchy, nor are they exhausted by a mere gesture, restricted to intimations of infinity. They stretch taut around the center of constructive consciousness like a network of interdependent lines that obtain the basis and rationale of their existence from that center. Each and every peripheral function of constructive consciousness is set within an immanent gravitational system in which the centrifugal and centripetal forces are in perfect balance.

The central point of this gravitational field cannot be defined in psychological terms, but this center is indubitably the absolute factor in the Constructivist work of art. Otherwise we could not speak of unity in such a work, which nonetheless exists, without having to rely on the centralized composition scheme of classical art.

Constructivism cannot tolerate the hierarchic subdivision of emphases, only their uniformity. It does not entrench itself behind the frontality of representation. The consciousness responsible for its existence prevails in the unconditional readiness for action and momentum in every conceivable direction of spatial, logical and ethical expansion. Constructive consciousness is absolute expansiveness.

The will toward autonomous, total constructive development is diametrically opposed to any tendency toward a mystical consciousness. The mystical absorbs the world into itself. It soaks up multiplicity as sand soaks up water. As opposed to this, constructive consciousness quintessentially posits the idea of multiplicity as a goal to be realized. Constructivist multiplicity unfolds in such a manner that the unfolding takes place according to the laws of a system of immanent unity that is identical to itself.

The Constructivist unfolding of multiplicity avoids uncontrollably gliding transitions and fluid boundaries. A geometric precision characterizes its articulations, dividing lines and points of contact. It does not hide behind illusions. This is why Constructivists build with homogeneously colored, pure planes and use realistic material forms in physical space.

The will toward geometric necessity and purity establishes an organic interrelation between Constructivist art and the objective working methods and technological systems of our age. Constructivist art, even given the architectonic unity of the total vocabulary of its forms, affords opportunities for a pervasive division of labor. It is a *collective* art.

Its collective nature is not an image of chaotic society living for the present, but is a striving toward absolute equilibrium and extreme purity. It imposes laws that enter consciousness as the necessary, immanent principles of a transcendental vitality. The realization of the psychological and historical sediments of these principles does not play the least role in their formal and conceptual exposition. The totality of these principles is structured into a system by the ideal of the new human who is economically organized in both body and mind.

Translated by John Bátki

CORRECTION (TO THE ATTENTION OF *DE STIJL*)   Ernő Kállai

Originally published as "Korrektúrát (a 'De Stijl' figyelmébe)" *Ma* vol. 8., no. 9–10 (January 7, 1923)

Constructivism views itself as the triumph of the spirit permanently liberated from the individualist pathos generated by the accidents of nature and tragic instincts. From the outset it has proclaimed the principle of collectivity. As an extreme that brooks no compromise, it aimed to document this collectivity in the form of the purest and most explicit manifestations. Although it never intended mechanical stereotypes, it nonetheless demanded that the inclusion in the finished picture or sculpture of expressive acts not fully comprehensible be kept to a vanishingly small portion of the whole, if not entirely absent. For as soon as we liberate something from the whim of intuitive realizations that are exclusively singular in occurrence, and thus elevate it into the world of rational events, it immediately becomes unambiguous for everyone. It was this unambiguous objectivity that Constructivism recognized as the one and only requirement of collectivity.

However the collectivity of the creative act in art and its reception, unless we intend to totally deprive art of its quiddity as residing in manifestations of human life, is different from the *uniformity* of judgement among mathematicians and geometricians who agree on a set of objective givens. Were we to reduce the unanalyzable factors of a work of art to an infinitesimal portion, we could still only vouchsafe the congruence of sensations and demands arising vis-à-vis the art if the psycho-physical components producing the indissoluble underlying factors of a painting or sculpture existed in identical forms and played identical roles in different viewers. However, while this qualitative uniformity of psycho-physical determinants indeed exists in the human consciousness as regards mathematical, geometric, and purely logical truths, the psychological determinants of art are spread out over a myriad-hued scale of velleities and essential differences.

And everything hinges on this. The essence of art lies, not in some ultimate truth independent of time and space and without any reference to human consciousness, but in its physiological usefulness and dynamic power. It is natural that, depending on the given combination of human mental processes that give rise to art as a biological desideratum and upon which, in their capacity as receptive subject, art is able to exert an effect, there are extraordinary numbers of gradations in artistic quality. No such multiplicity is known in the case of scientific truth. The relationship to basic principles and the requirements of methodology and systematization bring about states of knowledge that are perfectly equivalent in their scientific value, regardless of what psychological, biological, and existential events befall the researcher. The practical usefulness and social significance of science is not our concern here, although we may be certain that the validity of scientific truth does not depend on its utility in individual and social biology, but vice versa.

An artistic creation does not possess an abstract or objective, essential core. Its social and economic functionality does not alter this fact; on the contrary, it underscores it. Art in its totality, with all of its implied conceptual problems, is tied to the psychological and biological laws governing the organism that creates it. Therefore if we are trying to pinpoint the collective nature of art we must look for actual factors; not an objectivity that excludes all subjectivity, but rather the psychological and biological makeup of the creating and receiving subjects. We should look for a mental process that is present all around us in a society-wide, intertwined multiplicity. We may settle for the individual awareness of a central determinism which in our days still exists in isolated forms, but which, we are convinced, may become, and must become the foundation of social claims on life and the unfolding of a social art. In any case we cannot expect to find an accessibility that universally applies to the community in a sphere that is so remote from our subjectivity that this distance vouchsafes a sovereign independence and self-contained, objective self-sufficiency for art. A work of art may be self-contained in every direction, but it must remain *open* to the subjects that create it and react to it in a positive way. Otherwise it is stillborn.

We need to point out these fundamental truths in order to set a limit to the pretensions of Constructivism. Constructivism purports to be the collective art of today or tomorrow, embedded into the totality of the life of the individual and society, while it intends to shake off the ties that bind it to its origins in psychology, its birth in and dependence upon vital human intellect. It would aspire to be an objective form, an uncontaminated view, in contrast to the merely expressive subjectivity of Expressionism. However, just as Expressionism is able to express something only because, albeit minimally, it still articulates, shapes, selects, and arranges, even so Constructivism is only able to build relatively self-contained, autonomous pictorial systems, because it chooses to project these into the world where otherwise they would have not a trace of presence. For Constructivism does not involve the analysis or replication of existing realities but posits new realities and *demands*. Demands can only be made by the will, never by cognition itself. And the will is the backbone of the human life pattern, both individual and social. It is thoroughly embedded in depths and interrelations that cannot be further analyzed or explained. Thus it is an irrational buttressing of demands on life that may be mystical or may be rational. But under no circumstances is it a contemplation, still less the object of contemplation, but rather the living, indissoluble complex of ends that direct and determine contemplation. Thus Constructivism presents the simplest and most conclusive facts (Tat-Sache) to *confront* the wild chaos of contemporary life. The more it claims that these serene facts ought to provide the spirit incarnate, the bread and wine of life for man caught in the hustle and schizophrenia of our days, the more it resembles a sword cutting the Gordian knot or a fist slamming down on a tabletop. It turns into an innovating, stubborn determination and will to act, that is, by no means contemplation or demonstration, but *expression*—documenting the projections of human subjectivity.

But an objectivity that is self-contained and devoid of every subjective quality has never been and can never be the ultimate medium of any kind of *human collectivity*. The extreme objectivization found in the traditional religious systems is ascribable either to the inconceivable vastness of the human soul and nature, or to fictional concepts, or to a slew of legends made accessible and socially palatable by anthropomorphism. Unless Constructivism is willing to settle for a unanimity such as that which makes, for proletarian and millionaire alike, an automobile an automobile and not a tractor or some other practical object, it must give up the notion of striving for communityness by way of objectivity and perfection—that is, seeking it in a sphere where things arrive, if ever, only after the culmination of organic life processes evolving through the ages. Such an culmination is a metaphysical problem and Constructivism rejects any kind of metaphysics.

Let us suppose that one were to nonetheless set up such long-term claims by proclaiming the dominion of the perfectly rational human intellect in place of Christianity's ideal of perfect goodness. It is unlikely that the kingdom of such a Constructive human being would arrive before the end of time. Thus at best it is in infinity that we may conceive the point where the parallel tracks of the insane inanities of historical existence intersect each other in the unity of a rational harmony. Unless we intend to condone this Constructivist eternity's giving free rein to every current infamy and negativity—as in fact the Christian Church has, in the name of an otherworldly salvation—we must transpose the center of gravity of the Constructivist collective from the sphere of autotelic, self-contained objectivities to the battle ground of ongoing subjective givens. Bur an objectivist utopia that transcends all subjectivities has never been and can never be human community. In other words, even while reserving its ultimate ideals in infinity, at any rate switching from the domain of an *ordered totality* to the travails of a partial, fragmentary *history*.

Constructivism will have to make this material and conceptual turnabout as soon as it has glimpsed even the barest outlines of the promised land of objectivity and perfection, where man will no longer be constrained to a community that is subordinated to goals and necessities, and human life will resemble that of the lilies of the field, or of angels. Yet we are clear enough about our ultimate demands to at least attempt their conversion into historical values.

If Constructivism remains what it is today, the embodiment of objective harmony subjugated to pure reason, it has two alternatives.

If it insists on objective harmony as the collective demand from life, then it must consent to its approximation via finite ways, within historical conditions, by reacting to existing human and natural imperfections, and by giving up the exclusivity it has hitherto maintained. Its pure cultural profile must change into a *cultural-political* one. It must take an unmistakable stand first of all with regard to the left, and then vis-a-vis the extent that this turnabout signifies a conscious response and reaction to the total *historical* sum of interconnections. In other words, we must see if Constructivism indeed represents a *human completeness* that is able to unite the infinitely long-term demand for objective self-sufficiency with the goal-oriented service of momentary actualities, by joining political movements.

If Constructivism evades this consequence, then its works are not human and ethical demands but aesthetic reports. But that undermines Constructivism's claim of superiority over other art movements. For then Constructivism becomes only one among the many movements, one more detour in the general confusion. And it has no right whatsoever to claim that its aesthetic status is more significant than any of the "isms" or academies that proliferate today. In view of the endlessness of human misery, my choice of an aesthetic alignment is irrelevant; to turn such a choice into an ideological issue would be to create the most grotesque of academies and the most mendacious of dogmas.

But Constructivism's overdue confrontation of the problems presented by history and society will also mean another kind of restriction. If Constructivism sees more in itself than mere aesthetic games, it can only mean that it would have human life attain the same degree of equilibrium, harmony, and ethics without pathos that is claimed only by its forms today. But everyday life at present, society's as well as the Constructivist artist's, is anything but rational. Therefore we either recognize that the formal objectivization of today's degraded life is necessary, for its mission is to awaken and to disturb—and this would mean sacrificing Constructivism, the isolated cult of future life, to the cult of today's life, where an insistence on demands and guidelines would not provide exemption from responsible acknowledgement of the totality of historical interconnections. This would mean embracing the entire complex of dialectical relations with artistic manifestations from other movements, in order to dig the channel for the progress of art in the direction of the envisioned ideals. Or else we refuse to justify the life-resonance of art and insist only on a theoretical demand for perfection, which would mean the end of Constructivism, for the one-time realization of perfection would constitute a fulfillment after which anything else would be mere academic rumination. But if Constructivism is still alive and developing, it could only mean that it has not yet emerged from the complicated process of historical and psychological dialectics. If we possess universal viewpoints, in respect of the above dialectics we cannot allow ourselves to take refuge in the cocoon of the principle that everyone can keep on playing their little games.

How can we shoulder the pathos implied by the demands for collective validity if we do not strive to bring our superciliously proclaimed theories into fruitful cultural political contact with existing conditions and people? How can we speak of intellectual objectivity of such a degree of perfection that compared to it even the classless society of communism is a mere preparatory stage, when we are not engaged in making every effort to ensure the speediest and most thorough groundwork for communism "at least"? Ethical demands and goals for a way of life are not mere technical details in the sense that a design engineer's work is in relation to the factory workers'. These are central issues and as such require the totality of human perspectives: from theoretical conceptions and the framing of demands to the economic, political, and psychological preparation of the roads leading to their realization, if possible through the proletariat's revolutionary party structure as the uniting instrument of propaganda. Departure from ultimate abstractions and arrival at the concrete fact of the road to be taken. All of this as the documentation of the human community to which most artists have thus far at best offered only utopist objective tokens while refraining with elitist disdain from actual, subjective contributions to its practical development.

What is at risk here is the human meaning and ethical justification of Constructivism. Therefore we must not demean it to the level of an aesthetic fashion for the sake of certain predictions in formal theory or for stylistic perfections. Let us embark on the task of correction while it is not too late, before a dislike that is still only aesthetic drives us into the hopeless treadmill of ever newer aesthetic trends.

*

Even an exclusive Constructivism deems it necessary to speak of the community. Its pictures and sculptures however show us an unconditional, purely rational harmony. Each work is a self-enclosed, serene perfection. Its forms do not rest on a foundation of terrestrial gravity and natural origins. They either fill, with an articulation equally intelligible from all sides, the quadrangular framework meted out to them (De Stijl) or else they hover in unlimited free space (Suprematism and its descendants). But in neither case do they contain any reference to things that could exist outside them, either in space or in time. They evince only a multiplicity of numbers and a systematic articulation within a shared structure. Therefore if Constructivist theory speaks of collectiveness, then the "multitude" necessary for a collective may be provided only in the consubstantiality of form manifesting in a systematic but not evolutionary structure.

But what kind of community is one that has been cut out of temporality, and turned into timeless space? It can only be the objetivization of a self-contained and self-fulfilled ideology, positing no demands, and subsisting without any aggressiveness or struggle.

Such a degree of objectivization is only possible in the realm of metaphysics, but not here on earth. Such a systematic constructivity can only link together mathematical deductions, logical proofs or parts of an engineering design, but is not capable of *linking people together into a society*.

I could postulate a rational, worldwide social order with a perfect harmony of all geological, meteorological, geographic and ethnographic, economic and intellectual, racial and individual, physiological, and psychological functions, so that all problems of life would vanish, and the human fate of unknown origins and destiny would float like some beautifully arranged magic garden in the sky.

Doubtless such a theoretical human/world construction, as indeed any final consummation of anything incomplete, could be subject to as many interpretations and demands as there are ontologies under the sun; as many teleologies, so many self-contained viewpoints, or at least ones that are justifiable as facts of will. Ontology and teleology both imply metaphysical constructs, even if one were to imagine the final consummation of universal human existence as occurring still here on earth. Now an exclusive Constructivism, if we wish to glimpse in its pictorial systems the first intuitions of a new social order, implies a permanent, radical break with the unknowable human lot of causality, destiny and evolutionary continuity, past and future. By fixing the formal factors into a closed and easily surveyable system it would evoke an existence where all events, including birth and death, would exert themselves, along with all their consequences, as parts of a qualitatively and quantitatively perfectly balanced, lasting state of communal existence. And this is in fact a *teleology*.

But let us suppose that we are not bothered by that lunatic absolutism, that infinite variability which belongs in essence to any kind of teleology. Say we accept as our sole salvation the neo-rationalist teleology that follows as the logical necessity based on the visual art products of an exclusive Constructivism. We are doing this, I repeat, supposing that the rationality so often evoked by Constructivism would bring the greatest benefit, truth, beauty, and power attainable by human society in earth. It should be obvious that at this *perfect and spontaneously arranged* degree of human togetherness, free of any failings, the fact of collectivity, regarding the interaction of individual human beings making it up, would mean little by way of demands, restrictions—ethics, in other words—just as the fact of self-identity does not constitute an ethics. The individual functions making up the community in a *utopia* evoked by a Constructivist teleology would follow as directly and naturally from the psycho-physical makeup of its individuals as does, say, breathing.

The tensions created by Constructivist art do not contradict this supposition, for they are *not ethical tensions*. Ethical tension can exist only in the struggle against a causality unknowable in its nature and events, meted out by fate—as long as this struggle is fought in the name of the categorical imperatives ruling over the instincts. The system of tensions implied by exclusive Constructivism is not based on this kind of struggle. By disconnecting the impulses it sets up the exclusive sovereignty of rationalism, and this from the outset ignores the role of inhibitions that go hand in hand with the possibility of actions that are fully their equivalent. Thus there can be no ethical struggle in a situation where the lineup of opposing forces is a foregone conclusion, their relative strengths and positions clear at every point, so that the outcome, the attainment of an unexceptionable equilibrium, is a given stasis of forces that are equal on the whole. Ethics can never be a stasis. Ethics implies a vertical upthrust against destructive horizontal and diagonal forces, a ceaseless movement and striving through various phases to attain a goal. As soon as we reach that goal and restore the ethical equilibrium, the given problem ceases to exist along with our ethical striving on behalf of the given task, and the state we then reach is not ethics. At most it might contain a disposition for further exertions. And not even this instant of fulfillment between two expenditures of energy, this transition without rest, leading to new activity, must be allowed to become the obvious motivation for the active and inhibitive components of the ethical struggle. For the struggle is ethical only if it is conducted without any regard to the outcome.

It is a part of the Constructivist life formula that the equilibrium maintained by the mutual interactions of immanent tensions is not an incidental source but the essential prerequisite for the system and is therefore permanently identified with it. This Constructivist equilibrium is, in spite of its most vehement dynamics, motionless and timeless with regard to the entirety of the life of the community, and therefore because of this timelessness cannot be ethical, that is, social. The battles of opposing forces that constitute ethics are never abstract controversies but psycho-physical agitations occurring in time.

Its amoral nature disqualifies exclusive Constructivism from playing a social role in an ideological sense. We have no use for a utopian society allowing a maximal flourishing of human beings without ethics, when we can ensure this flourishing in our given conditions, under more modest circumstances to be sure, only in a society that has to defend itself with ethical maxims against the destructive effects of individualism. This brings up the most ticklish issue of exclusive Constructivism, namely, how does a Constructivist teleology propose to lead humanity out of the present chaotic whirl of all of its uncontrollable immanent and transcendent conditions and bases of existence, into the tranquil ocean of universal fulfillment, timelessness and equilibrium. Even if there were a way of accomplishing this *societally*, there is no way *metaphysically*. And yet the ultimate particles of society, the individual psycho-physical organisms, could only be reconstructed by reaching into the metaphysical history of their descent, in order that the elements of a Constructivist social equilibrium be included from the outset in the structure of individual human units.

These are the absurd consequences if, obeying the theoretical promptings of an exclusive Constructivism, we attempt to draw the outlines of the social order supposedly anticipated by its visual works of art. If Constructivism claims to have social significance, then its world and way of life could only be as we have described above. We would be confronted by a fully realized teleological obsession, a system in which each human being would revolve in a predetermined orbit, secure in the consciousness of a superior rationality and the pleasant awareness that all is preordained, nothing can go wrong, there is no need to struggle, and one can relax without reservations in a life regulated by technological precision. This newfangled *pre-stabilized harmony* would run human lives as smoothly as a toy electric train, without collisions or catastrophes.

And also *without community*. For in any human coexistence where the entire web of interpersonal relations, with all of its interdependence, lies in a constellation determined once and for all, there can be no shared fate—for lack of a fatedness—nor emotive communities. People whose minds in their form and content are entirely devoid of unconscious impulses and lie perfectly clear to be read by themselves and others are incapable of unions that are more than alliances for practical aims or momentary couplings. Their relations, for lack of any tragic possibilities and any past, can only be mechanical and superficial.

The people inhabiting the Utopia of exclusive Constructivism are linked neither by ethical tensions nor by intuitive attractions or repulsions. Their societal organizations are devoid of any organic nature, any willed tendencies. For lack of any *mass psychology*, numbers of its individual units can align themselves in associations mostly administrative in character, unmenaced by any external or internal threat, and are for their entire lives exempt from the compulsion or spontaneity of caring for each other's petty problems or tragic complications. They are free of joy, empathy, love, hatred, pity and competition. The utopian society envisioned by an exclusive Constructivism hovers in timeless space, free of economic, political, or humanitarian constrictions.

Exclusive Constructivism is characterized by an absence of self-denial and self-sacrifice, and by an inability to empathize and dialectically fructify, or to accept the emotions and ways of thought of people dwelling in other layers of consciousness and living out other fates. What we have here is a composite of the supercilious mind games of intellectuals, a sophisticated utilitarianism, and the Romantic philosophizing of a few grotesquely faithful hearts. The spirit of exclusive Constructivism harbors a *splendid isolation*, a measured correctness, and a selfish, rationalist objectivity—an aesthetic paraphrase of modern industrial capitalism with its single-minded concentration on economic and technological (that is, *objective*) concerns. Actually only a partial paraphrase, for industrial capitalism, in addition to its technological objectivity and economic rationalism, is in fact the primary motivating force of the national and international mass psyches. Played out on its world stage of cultural politics are turbulent dramas abounding in props and sets, heroes and extras, crowds and armies, accompanied by every cheap and expensive effect of pathos, monumentality, haloes and rhetorics. Quite a difference from the picky, aesthetic approach of exclusive Constructivism that builds bit by bit its otherwise most valuable and important material structures.

For Constructivism is significant; in contrast to the unbounded effusions and sentimentality of Expressionism it has pointed out the psychic possibilities of conscious analysis and an inexorably straight linearity. Beyond this psychic and aesthetic concentration it has brought us closer to certain vital demands of our times: the perspectives of objective, realistically textured work, economy of organization, the tempered and disciplined heart. Surely these values are tremendously important from the point of view of social revolution, with regard to the directing and focusing of mass movements, and the raising of their cultural political level. But exclusive Constructivism, in reaction to Expressionist ecstasies and volatile enthusiasms and in the name of the aesthetic harmony of a superior intellectual self-mastery, serene equilibrium, and clearly defined edges has shut itself away from the life of society and from all the actualities of the proletarian revolution, the resonance of which would have disrupted this harmony. While rejoicing in the pleasures of the aesthetic worship of an absolute perfection, it has failed to notice that along with the content of psychological imperfections and imponderables, tragic instincts and volitions it has also thrown out the material of which the historical, that is, *actual life-construct* is made, with respect to society. This is not the realm of timeless eternity and an amoral, pre-stabilized harmony, such as in the exclusive constructions of visual art, the problematic bliss of a perfectly surveyable system. The constructs of history are born in the bed of fast-flying time, contingencies, doubts and catastrophes. The mass organizations of human coexistence grow to greatness in the struggle of impulses and ethical imperatives, sacrifices and cool calculations. They are imperfect and problematic but biologically feasible and necessary. There can be no rational teleological concept or societal Utopia that, no matter how perfect, could empower us to abandon unsystematizable history. Yet that is what we do when, as does exclusive Constructivism, we posit demands that are impossible to fulfill, with respect to the life of the individual and of society. This impossibility degrades exclusive Constructivism into a merely aesthetic concern, with all of its vitality condemned to fuel pictorial systems. And this is how things will remain until exclusive Constructivism establishes a mutual dialectical interaction with the entire range of historical and societal problems. This is the only way that these fruitful components of social revolution and communism, that is, of actual European life, can, if need be through stylistic modifications, be preserved for a greater and more human art of the future.

Translated by John Bátki

MANIFESTO Ernő Kállai, et. al.
Originally published as "Nyilatkozat," *Egység* no. 4 (1923)

We are aware that Constructivism today is increasingly developing bourgeois traits. One of the manifestations of this is the Dutch Stijl group's constructive (mechanized) aestheticism as well as the technical Naturalism achieved by the Russian Constructivists (the Obmokhu group) with their constructions representing technical devices.
Every form of art that sees itself as hovering above the current social forms in aesthetic or cosmic perspective exists on a bourgeois level even if its adherents call themselves Constructivists. The same holds true for all forms of contemporary naturalism, whether its subject be the machine or nature herself.
For this reason, we make a distinction between the aestheticism of bourgeois Constructivists and the kind of constructive art that springs from our communist ideology. This latter, in its analyses of form, matter and structure, is breaking the

ground for the collective architecture of the future, which will be the pivotal art form of communist society. As such it will not think of itself as either absolute or dogmatic, in that it *clearly sees the partial role it fulfils in the integrated process of social transformation at the present time*. It is raised above bourgeois Constructivism and against the bourgeois construction of life in today's society by that constructive content which is indicative of constructive potentialities, which can be fully realized only within the framework of communist society. In contrast, the bourgeois Constructivists provide only the haute bourgeois forms of today's capitalist society with the adequate and simplest artistic construction which can be realized in today's society.

This kind of reappraised (from a bourgeois point of view, destructive) Constructivism (to which only a tiny portion of those contemporary movements in art that are known by the name of Constructivism belong) leads, on the one hand, in practical life to a new constructive architecture* that can be realized only in a communist society, and, on the other hand, to a nonfunctional but dynamic (kinetic) constructive system of forces which organizes space by moving in it, the further potential of which is again in practice dynamic architecture. The road to both goals leads through interim solutions.

In order to bring about a communist society; we artists must fight alongside the proletariat, and must subordinate our individual interests to those of the proletariat. We think that this is possible only within the communist party, by working in co-operation with the proletariat. For this reason, we think that a *Proletkult organization* should be established, an organization that would make such co-operation possible; that is why we join the *Egység*, since it was the one to begin work in this direction.

The new *Proletkult* organization must turn against bourgeois culture (destructive work) and must look for a road leading to a new communist culture (the constructive aspect of the work); furthermore, it must liberate the proletariat from the pressure of bourgeois culture, and substitute for their bourgeois intellectuals' hunger for culture a wish for the most advanced organization of life. The artists of the *Proletkult* must pave the way for a high-standard (adequate) proletarian and collective art.

—Ernő Kállai, Alfréd Kemény, László Moholy-Nagy, László Péri

* City construction based on a unified plan with new materials selected to satisfy the collective needs of communist society (and not used hitherto in architecture), and with forms developed from the constructive potentialities of the new materials. [Original authors' note.]

Translation from Krisztina Passuth, Moholy-Nagy

ON THE NEW THEATRICAL ART   Lajos Kassák
Originally published as "Über neue Theaterkunst," *Ma* vol. 9, no. 8–9 (September 15, 1924)

Ultimately, art is about imparting form. It is the artist's task to create ever-new formal unities, and to fashion the different materials involved into a new whole in obedience to his will. Not in order to illustrate any specific political or other social movement, since in every department of life the creative act is a social, societal act in its own right. The work of art embodies the receptivity, organizing will, and ruling power of the human being in a given epoch. Of all arts, theatrical art offers the most opportunities to demonstrate the human power of feeling, organizing, and mastering the chaos of life. But in order to exploit the potential of theater to the full, we must free the contemporary stage from the hegemony of the epic poet, the actor-illustrator, and the painter-decorator.

Theatrical art, like the arts of music, painting, and literature, constitutes a balanced and self-sufficient whole in itself.

Unlike the other arts, theatrical performance exists concurrently in space and time. Its inner laws are categorically different from those of painting and literature, the first of which relates to two-dimensional surfaces and the second to time. Theater is also distinct, to the same degree as all the other arts, from the everyday life that surrounds us.

Life is an organic unity; art is an organized unity.

The new artist must therefore first of all be a sensitive, visual human being and last of all a superior and implacable organizer.

At the moment, these demands are less adequately fulfilled in theater than in any other art. In the other arts, the latest schools have at least brought out the underlying principles of modern creativity: atonality in music, construction in the fine arts, abolition of the imported, external theme in literature. In theater, Tairov and the other Russians took the first steps, but none of them progressed beyond a reformism that made extensive concessions to the past.

The artists of our generation—[scene] painters, actors, and directors—have followed two alternative paths toward the new theater: on the one hand, the experiments of the Russians; on the other, those of the Europeans. The painters of the European tendency, the stylized theater, remained painters as before, except that they strove to achieve a still more intensive illusion than that created by their avowedly Naturalist predecessors. Their planar stage, created by painterly means, evokes in us, with a precision almost worthy of an engineer, the image of a factory or of a laboratory. The illusion that they create is almost perfect, but it nonetheless remains an illusion. We have before us objects that would come out in a photograph looking exactly as if we had photographed a real factory or a real laboratory, although in fact what was before the camera was only the naturalistic stylization of a factory or laboratory. In short, what they have done as reformers of the stage looks indistinguishable from an object made in reality; but I stress once again that it is not identical with what it seems to be. It is illusion, not reality. Apart from the skill of the painter, there is nothing more to their work than the cottages, palaces, and magic gardens of the old scene painting.

The European movement has achieved no more—inevitably, in the circumstances—than the perfection of stylized stage design. By thus creating a perfect illusion of reality, it has fatally turned its back on the creation of a true locus for theatrical action as artistic reality. For the members of this school, the stage still remains the wall surface that they are required to fill with illustrations and decorations for a predefined action.

Ultimately, the stage is no more and no less than a field of play (field of life).

And the art of the stage is ultimately no more and no less than a constructive game (play, life movement) concentrated upon a single point.

The Russians, for their part, treated the stage as space, and this enabled them to achieve significantly more than the European reformers. Instead of the painted, two-dimensional stage they created the built, three-dimensional stage. In their eyes—and their vision is that of the new humanity, the will that is capable of revolutionary action—the plane died and was replaced by free space as the foundation of theatrical art. However, they too failed to solve the ultimate problem of theatrical art; understandably so, because they did not address the complex of issues as a whole but only in part. They did not work on the synthesis of theatrical art but simply on one element of it. They turned the great, overriding issue into a specialized, professional issue. And this one-sided specialization—which also, in another context, marks the work of Tairov—inevitably gave rise to a new Babel in theatrical art. Hence, inevitably, the absurd dualism that leads to performances of classic drama amid the wood and steel constructions of the Russian revolutionary stage. From the viewpoint of theatrical art, the Russian stage did not yield the results that might have been hoped for, and no new synthesis materialized. The basic elements of theatrical art had, however, now been established: the stage as space, and the possibility of building structures within that space. Although his assumptions were false and his objectives mistaken, Tairov, as stage director, was able to discover and develop the second element of that stage: the actor.

However Tairov went on to repeat the error of overspecialization committed by the Russian stage engineers: he over-specialized the actor. His slogan, "The Stage to the Actor," barely does more than hark back to naturalistic experiments in staging. Previously—and of course unwarrantably—authors or painters had been the sole autocrats of the stage: now, equally unwarrantably, Tairov set up the actor as autocrat in their place. This explains why he too failed to achieve the synthesis of theatrical art, the unified organization. He simply went from Point A to Point B, instead of drawing the whole alphabet into his organizational ambit and giving equal status to all the points.

In Tairov's egocentric view, all the elements of the stage spectacle, with the exception of the actor, remained the same lifeless bodies (lifeless or at best endowed with life reflexes) that they had been on the naturalistic stage. A few nuances aside, everything remained just as it had been. We cannot speak in earnest of a new theatrical art unless we go beyond matters of detail: the whole erstwhile hierarchy of the stage—author, actor, painter, and director—must be uprooted and dismantled.

Theatrical art cannot, any more than any other art, be subordinated to a single factor. Artistic creation is the synthetic creation of form, in which there are no discrete levels of value: only indispensable elements that perfectly fulfill their functions.

If these elements lose their intrinsic meaning, then the artwork as a whole loses its positive value.

It is a poor kind of house that resembles "frozen music."

It is a poor kind of music that imitates the roar of the sea.

It is a poor kind of theatrical art that conveys the illusion of everyday life.

And, in general, anything that does not in itself present an evident and unmistakable reality is not art.

And, just as the arts of architecture, music, poetry, and painting have attained pure self-knowledge, theatrical art, too, must attain a reality of its own.

But before it can obey this law, theatrical art must emancipate itself from its hierar-chical present.

This emancipation is possible only if author, actor, painter, director, light, sound, color, and movement are set on an equal footing as elements.

For the problem of the new theater will not be solved by today's explorers of special-ized fields but by a new human type, the organizer, who has the will to create an emo-tional, visual, collective order.

By organizer, we do not at all mean the present-day stage director. The director is under an obligation to follow the author's script, and often even to observe specific stage directions. His work, in general, is that of an interpreter. The organizer that we have in mind is a creator, like the author or the architect. The difference is that he makes his appearance in new territory governed by new laws. What we have seen in the theater hitherto is at best dramatic art—and thus literature—rather than theatrical art. Not primary creation but transformation. It is an error to speak of a theatrical art based on dramatic literature. This allows us only to perform the author's drama, more or less well, on the stage, which is viewed as an ancillary acting facility. Or, to put it another way, we can perfect the drama as a literary genre without ever creating theatrical art, the new art form in which drama—like the screw in the machine, or the brick in the house, or the person in the city—is one component among several. There can be no doubt, therefore, that theatrical art must constitute a new art form, and that the cre-ator of theatrical art must constitute a new creative type. This type will be closer to the engineer and the inventor than to the traditional dramatist; his work will be closer to a piece of machinery, or to a modern city, than to the theatrical art of the past. When he appears, there will be a new endurance contest between the modern human being and his conservative material. It will be a stammering and stumbling phase of construction, and of entirely new forms, but construction it will nevertheless be. And here I do not have in mind the often-compromised Romantic ideal of "total art," but a new art form, which will give expression in time and space to the emotional and conceptual world of today's humanity, just as past humanity expressed itself in literature, music, and the fine arts.

Translated by David Britt

THE ELECTRO-MECHANICAL SHOW El Lissitzky
Originally published as "Die elektro-mechanische Schau," *Ma* vol. 9, no. 8–9 (September 15, 1924)

What follows is a fragment of a piece of work that arose from the necessity of breaking free of the enclosed box of the proscenium theater. (Moscow, 1920–21.)
No one pays any attention to the magnificent spectacle of our streets, because every *"someone"* is himself in play. Every form of energy is applied to a purpose of its own. The whole is amorphous. All energies must be organized into a unity, crystallized, and put on show. The result is a WORK—it may be called an ARTwork.
On the open space of a square that is accessible from every side, we build a scaffold: this is the SHOW MACHINERY. This scaffold affords every possibility of movement to the bodies in play. Accordingly, it must be possible to make its individual parts slide, rotate, extend, and so on. Transitions from level to level must be rapid. It is all skeleton construction, in order not to mask the movements of the bodies in play. The bodies themselves are each shaped according to will and need. They slide, roll, and hover in and above the scaffold. All parts of the scaffold and all bodies in play are set in motion by electromechanical forces and contrivances, and this control center is in the hands of a single individual. This is the SHOW DESIGNER. His place is in the center of the scaffold, at the switchboards that control all the energies. He directs the movements, the sound, and the light. He switches on the radio megaphone, and across the square resounds the hubbub of railroad stations, the roar of Niagara Falls, or the thunder of a rolling mill. The voices of the individual bodies in play are provided by the SHOW DESIGNER, who speaks into a telephone connected to an arc light, or into other appliances that transform his voice to match the characters of individual figures. Electric sentences flash on and off. Beams of light, refracted through prisms and reflected by mirrors, follow the movements of the bodies in play. And so the SHOW DESIGNER brings the most elementary process to its supreme intensity.
For the first performance of this electromechanical SHOW, I used a modern piece, albeit one originally written for the stage. This is the Futurist opera *Victory over the Sun*, by A. Kruchonykh, inventor of the phonetic poem and leading exponent of new Russian poetry. The opera was first performed in St. Petersburg in 1913. The music is by Matyushin (quartertones). Malevich painted the sets (the curtain—Black Square). Modern man tears down the Sun, standing for the old cosmic energy, from the heavens; through his technological mastery he creates an energy source of his own. In the

opera, this idea is interwoven with an action based on simultaneity. The language is alogical. A number of the sung numbers are phonetic poems.

In my figures, the text of the opera compelled me to retain some elements of human anatomy. As in my *Proun* works, the colors of individual areas in my drawings are to be regarded as material equivalents: that is to say, in performance the red, yellow, or black parts of the figures are not painted in those colors but made out of the appropriate material: for example bright copper, dull iron, and so on.

Recent developments in radio, in loudspeakers, and in film and lighting technology, along with a number of inventions of my own: all of this makes the realization of these ideas far easier than I imagined in 1920.

Translated by David Britt

THEATER AS AN ARTISTIC PHENOMENON Herwarth Walden
Originally published as "Das Theater als künstlerisches Phänomen," *Ma* vol. 9, no. 8–9 (September 15, 1924)

Theater is not a moral institution.

Theater is not an immoral institution.

Theater is not an institution designed to publicize works of literature and their exponents.

Theater is not a temple or a brothel.

Theater is the structured formal design of optical and acoustic movements.

The executants in theater, human beings and objects, are the bearers of those movements.

Theater is a play of the senses.

Through organic and artistically logical relationships between the visual and the audible, the play becomes a work of art.

The play communicates no ideas. Ideas are abstractions from sensory observations.

Theater communicates no sentiments. Sentiments are conclusions drawn from sensory experiences.

Theater communicates no feelings. Feelings are gatherings of sentiments.

Present-day theater has nothing in common with theater as art. Theater of the present is an intellectual observation and representation of life: the illustration of subjective cases and chances, individually interpreted.

Theater as artwork is an organism created by the artistically logical interaction of sensory movements.

Theater must be liberated from literature (written record of facts and their abstractions) and from acting (imitation of human utterance) before it can and will become art.

The material of theater consists of color, form, intonation, and sound in motion. When these elements are shaped into an artistic unity, the result is the work of art that is theater.

All the rest is a pastime for cultural bourgeois and cultural artists.

Translated by David Britt

The poet's roots are in his own people! So say the racial purists of literature; and there
is probably no country where their admonitions have been so taken to heart, as they
were in Hungary in the last few decades before the War. Hungarian poetry had always
been hermetically sealed away from the entire world. It was not until the wars of liberation, in the middle of the last century—when, in varying degrees, popular values
were being reassessed in the literature of every country—that Magyar literature briefly
gained a hearing in the international concert of art. This is the sole reason why Petöfi's
name and life are not as completely unknown outside Hungary as are the works of all
Hungarian poets, Petöfi included. After Petöfi, Hungarian poetry became "national" in
a more extended sense. The term had hitherto applied to the content of individual works;
now it gave rise to an ill-starred politico-literary tradition whereby the Hungarian poet
was chained to the soil, and the further evolution of Hungarian poetry was confined to
elements extracted from its past. Since Petöfi, our poets have forgotten little, but they
have learned still less—especially from abroad. It therefore came as an entirely welcome development—and the whole conservative press was rightly outraged—when
Endre Ady, one of the greatest lyric poets of our generation, made his voice heard.
For, instead of staying at home and making an honest living in Hungary, Ady had the
temerity to travel and spend time in Paris, where he made the acquaintance—and not
by name only—of Baudelaire, Verlaine, and a number of kindred spirits. This took place
not in the 1880s but in the first decade of our own century. It was, nevertheless, an
important step forward, and its importance was intensified by the fact that Ady was
not only unusually modern-minded—by the Hungarian standards of the day—but also
a true poet.
Despite the best efforts of the literary group that gathered around Ady, Hungarian literature still lacked both the self-confidence and the artistic commitment to necessary
to establish a link with the movements that were current abroad before the War. Only
the War itself, and the consequent emergence of a literary pacifism that was international by definition, enabled Hungary to take its place within international artistic life.
A group of new and mostly young writers came onto the scene and, as the needs of
the time required, wrote antimilitarist propaganda. Within Hungary, this group was
the sole mouthpiece for the newly awakened European conscience; but its significance
would have remained purely political, had it not chosen art—and, for obvious reasons,
the newest form of art—as its medium of expression. The result was the emergence
of an art that was and intended to be forever new. However, it differed from analogous
tendencies in every other country (including German Expressionism and Italian
Futurism) in one essential respect. Like their counterparts elsewhere, the Hungarians
wanted to find a New Form for the New Human Being; but what they emphasized was
the sheer radicalism and expressive power of their effort: in a word, their own activity.
They were conscious of themselves as creators. From the start—revolutionaries
though they were—they emphasized not destruction but construction, structure, and
creation. They assumed the name of Activists and started the periodical *Ma* (Today),
now in its tenth year of publication. As is well known, it was the wartime pacifists
who assumed the thankless task of leading the postwar revolutions: the task that the
Hungarian Activists assumed in the domain of art. This, however, was more or less
the end of their political mission. The fact that the Hungarian Activists worked on into
a time when the revolution was forced back onto the defensive, and that they continue
with undiminished vigor to this day, only goes to show that they were artists first and

foremost. As such, they were of course revolutionaries; but their political propaganda was entirely a consequence of their consistently Activist approach to everything in life. Revolutionaries are of two kinds: those who think of nothing but making the revolution, without realizing that in some periods revolution-making is liable to exclude them from the mainstream of life; and those who are revolutionaries because they unconditionally say Yes to life, to the activity of life, and to creativity within the boundaries of that life. The Hungarian Activists belong to the latter category. They feel themselves to be a living force: human beings who seek self-expression, and whose instrument of expression is art. And so, today, they are among the most radical artists anywhere.

After their political phase ended, the emphasis shifted—if possible—even more toward the constructive nature of their work, with its aspiration to build new forms of art and of society.

What do the Activists want today?

Above all, definitely no slogans. These serve a purpose only when a revolution, in its active stage, needs to set some goals. At present, there is a need to find the widest possible range of expressive outlets for the revolutionary being who has no chance of a political revolution. For the artist, art is such a domain. What is possible here is psychological agitation: the representative expression of the constructive human being, and the education of others toward self-confidence and future action. The Activists feel that Constructivism is a basis on which it is possible to build further. They want to express the sense of certainty, the new equilibrium. They could describe themselves as Active Constructivists, but they do not do so, simply to avoid confusion with the Constructivism that now figures as an artistic school. For they, being among the most radical artists to be found anywhere, are determined to have no more schools. The idea of building is something that they share with the Constructivists, but without succumbing to a romanticized machine aesthetic. They regard the words *art* and *life* as interchangeable: both words stand for instinctive human self-expression. But they have no intention of regarding Art as a utilitarian exercise. The artist is not a mechanic or a mechanical engineer. The artist is the one who builds. Let the world decide for itself the best practical use for what the artist builds. There can be no such thing as a utilitarian art, since human expression (which is what art is) is thwarted and constrained by ulterior motives. Expression must have no purpose but expression itself. Only the completed artwork may be judged by others to have a practical usefulness and may then find a place in the line of development.

Has this art anything in common with the Art for Art's Sake of bygone eras? Certainly not, since Activist art is an expression of life raised to the nth power: the life that operates within the artist. Whereas Art for Art's Sake signifies a passive self-adaptation on the artist's part to preexistent forms of art and life. There is a second question, however: does this art have a social relevance? The answer to this is perhaps the most important of all. It shall therefore be expressed with the utmost concision. *Art is a full expression of mankind, and it follows that the art of social mankind must be social.*

In Hungary, the Activists form a numerically sizeable camp. Since the Revolution, this camp has been diminished by successive defections. It would be highly convenient to gloss over this fact—or to brush it aside by pointing out some of the radicals too proved unable to persevere and gave up the quest after years of effort. But in most cases the reasons that led to the defection of the former Activists are so typical, and of such great theoretical interest, that we cannot forbear to devote a few words to them. We hinted at the explanation above, when we referred to the differences between Activists on the one hand and romantic revolutionaries on the other. Those who have now ceased to be Activists fall into two groups: those who now subscribe to the Constructivist school and those who subscribe to *Proletkult*. The former respond to the romance of technology and the machine; the latter respond to the romance of political rhetoric—which is certainly not going to make a revolution, only chew over old ideas and anesthetize— even disable—the bitter resentment of the masses.

To the, the Activists' parting words are as follows: "Away with premeditated practicality in art! Art is not there to express anything outside ourselves. Let art express us and nothing but us; for, if I the artist am the subject matter of art, this means only that I reflect the image of the world; and more than this no one can give. Life is lived by me; and, if I am able to capture it in forms, those forms will be suggestive." (Kassák.)

Today the Activists live scattered in every country, mostly as political émigrés. Their leader, as always, is that effervescent and persuasive fanatic, Lajos Kassák, who even before the War gave expression to the worker's soul (Kassák himself is of working-class origin) with primal force and power—and who has given us proof positive that art is not the deracinated pastime of effetely lisping intellectuals. A Socialist artist in the most forceful sense of the term, he has evolved into the poet of a new primitivism. The most durable influence on his work was that of Dadaism; and it was only recently that he cast off its trappings once for all. Kassák is also known for his work in visual art, which reflects the same standpoint as his writings. Active alongside him are Robert Reiter, Tibor Déry (previously a noted author of novellas), a number of young lyric poets, and a group of theoreticians who include Ernő Kállai and the present writer. Remarkably, the expressive forms used by Activism—in the lyric, especially— have created a well-defined school, while Kassák and the Activists themselves have moved on in search of new modes of expression. In recent years, hardly one young Hungarian lyric poet has appeared who has not been derivative—formally, at least— of the free verse of Kassák's political period, which Kassák himself already regards as outworn. In literature, it is by no means unusual to find imitators who are also enemies. The bitterest foes of *Ma* are older artists: mostly writers who can never get over the fact that even they, with all their gray hairs, eventually succumbed to the influence of this damnably radical art form—and that, by the time they had laboriously learned to sing along, its creator had moved on to something else.

Translated by David Britt

The Bauhaus recruited faculty and students regardless of their national or ethnic background. Besides Germans, there were Czechoslovak, Austrian, Dutch, Swiss, Hungarian, Russian, Yugoslav, and other nationalities among the masters and students in the school.

The Bauhaus transcended nationalist cultural concepts as heir to the internationalism of the Expressionist group Der Blaue Reiter (The Blue Rider)—whose leader, Wassily Kandinsky, was hired as faculty in 1922—and it pioneered the new, supranational functionalism of the emerging industrial and architectural design. The school was also committed to the leftist utopias of the post-World War I period, anticipating, as many other intellectuals in Germany did, revolutionary social changes. Bauhaus director Walter Gropius attempted to contact Soviet artists and, after 1922, when a modified version of Russian Constructivism was grafted on the German art scene, he integrated it into the school by hiring in 1923 the young László Moholy-Nagy. The latter also served, starting in 1926, as editor of the school's journal and series of book publications, the *Bauhausbücher*.

The Bauhaus represented what many Central European artists dreamed of: the model multinational, multidisciplinary community working in anticipation of a world without national or even professional boundaries. The 1922 *KURI Manifesto* by Hungarian Bauhaus student Farkas Molnár epitomized these concepts and expectations (KURI was the acronym for Constructive, Utilitarian, Rational, and International). Students were encouraged to delve into several creative fields and master several media, including photography. As Molnár points out in "Life at the Bauhaus," the Bauhaus community had its own festivities, rituals, summer and winter entertainments, orchestra, and stage to assure undivided creativity and a way of life where professional activity and playfulness merged.

Throughout much of its existence the school was sharply attacked on most of these accounts. In its early Weimar period, Expressionism and its Berlin stronghold, the Sturm (Storm) gallery—where many Bauhaus masters had exhibited—were seen as undesirably revolutionary, and Weimaraners opposed the school's left-wing sympathies. To fend off local and nationalist hostility, Gropius created the Circle of the Friends of the Bauhaus, with such board members as Albert Einstein, Arnold Schönberg, and Marc Chagall, among others, appealing to the national and international community of artists and scientists in defense of, as Gropius put it, "a coming Republic of the Spirit."[1]

The Bauhaus was a unique institution as a state-funded—and later, in Dessau, municipally-funded—art school where cutting edge ideas and technologies were advanced by a faculty that drew regular salaries, and a student body that was not intimidated by tradition. It rose and fell with the Weimar Republic and was one of the first victims of Nazism in 1933.

1 In Reginald Isaacs, *Walter Gropius, Der Mensch und sein Werk*, vol. 1 (Berlin: Gebr. Mann Verlag, 1983), p. 209.

PRODUCTION-REPRODUCTION   László Moholy-Nagy

Originally published as "Produktion–Reproduktion," *De Stijl* no. 7 (July 1922)

If we want to understand correctly the mode of human expression and shaping in art and in other related domains, and if we want to achieve progress therein, we have to examine the contributing factors: namely, man himself as well as the means he applies in his creative activity.

Man as construct is the synthesis of all his functional apparatuses, i.e. man will be most perfect in his own time if the functional apparatuses of which he is composed— his cells as well as the most sophisticated organs—are conscious and trained to the limit of their capacity.

Art actually performs such a training—and this is one of its most important tasks, since the whole complex of effects depends on the degree of perfection of the receptive organs—by trying to bring about the most far-reaching *new* contacts between the familiar and the as yet unknown optical, acoustical and other functional phenomena and by forcing the functional apparatuses to receive them. It is a specifically human characteristic that man's functional apparatuses can never be saturated; they crave ever-new impressions following each new reception. This accounts for the permanent necessity for new experiments. *From this perspective, creative activities are useful only if they produce new, so far unknown relations.* In other words, in specific regard to creation, reproduction (reiteration of already existing relations) can be regarded for the most part as mere virtuosity.

Since it is primarily production (productive creation) that serves human construction, we must strive to turn the apparatuses (instruments) used so far only for reproductive purposes into ones that can be used for productive purposes as well. This calls for profound examination of the following questions:

- What is this apparatus (instrument) good for?
- What is the essence of its function?
- Are we able, and if so to what end, to extend the apparatus's use so that it can serve production as well?

Let us apply these questions to some examples: the phonograph and photography— single pictures (stills) and film.

Phonograph. So far it has been the job of the phonograph to reproduce already existing acoustic phenomena. The tonal oscillations to be reproduced were incised on a wax plate by means of a needle and then retranslated into sound by means of a microphone (correctly: diaphragm, moving cone).

An extension of this apparatus for productive purposes could be achieved as follows: the grooves are incised by human agency into the wax plate, without any external mechanical means, which then produce sound effects which would signify—without new instruments and without an orchestra—a fundamental innovation in sound production (of new, hitherto unknown sounds and tonal relations) both in composition and in musical performance.

The primary condition for such work is laboratory experiments: precise examination of the kinds of grooves (as regards length, width, depth etc.) brought about by the different sounds; examination of the man-made grooves; and finally mechanical-technical experiments for perfecting the groove-manuscript score. (Or perhaps the mechanical reduction of large groove-script records.)

Photography. The photographic camera fixes light phenomena by means of a silver bromide plate positioned at the rear of the camera. So far we have utilized this function of the apparatus only at a secondary level: in order to fix (reproduce) single objects as they reflect or absorb light. In the event of revaluation taking place in this field, too, we will have to utilize the bromide plate's sensitivity to light to receive and record various light phenomena (parts of light displays) which *we ourselves* will have *formed* by means of mirror or lens devices.

Many experiments are needed here, too. Telescopic recordings of stars as well as radiography represent interesting preliminary stages.

Film. Kinetic relationships of projected light. This can be achieved by sequences of fixed partial movements. Cinematography as practiced so far is limited mainly to the reproduction of dramatic action. There are certainly many important activities to be carried out in the domain of film. Some are scientific in nature (dynamism of various motions: of man, animal, city etc.; different observations: functional, chemical etc.; wireless projection of film news etc.); some involve the completion of reproduction itself from a constructive standpoint. But the main task is the formation of *motion as such*; naturally, this cannot be realized without a man-made play of forms as motion carrier. Naive experiments relative to such development were the trick-films (advertisements). Much more highly developed are the works of Ruttman and the Clavilux* of Th. Wilfred; these, however, presented motion as an objectless dramatic action (abstraction or styling of erotic or natural events), albeit by trying to introduce the color picture.

So far the most perfect works are those of Eggeling and Richter, in which instead of dramatic action there is already a play of forms, although to the detriment of kinetic formation. In fact, movement is not given formal purity, for over-emphasis upon the forms' development absorbs almost all the kinetic forces. The way ahead here will be the formation of motion without the support of any direct formal development.

---

* The name indicates a kind of color organ, although we are concerned with light projection on the plane and not in space. [Original author's note.]

Translation from Krisztina Passuth, Moholy-Nagy

KURI MANIFESTO   Farkas Molnár
Originally published as *KURI Manifesztum Út* (Novi Sad: December 1922)

I. ANALYSIS

1. The process of analysis (decomposition and breakdown) must precede the periods of synthesis (producing an art of the *Gesamtkunstwerk*).

2. Art has traversed this road, starting with nature (that is, the inherited styles) via the various "-isms," as follows:

   a) Impressionism analyzed color and line;

   b) Futurism analyzed motion and time;
      MARINETTI–BOCCIONI

   c) Expressionism analyzed the primary elements of feelings;
      KANDINSKY–KLEE

   d) Dada explored destruction as a mode of analysis;
      TZARA–SCHWITTERS

   e) Cubism has progressed through the problems of mass and space to reach material and geometric forms;
      PICASSO–OZENFANT

f) Russian Constructivism advanced to arrive at the primary forms and a primary constructive ideology;
MALEVICH–EL LISSITZKY

g) the Weimar Bauhaus provided the architectural theory, and the new ethics via the mastery of craftsmanly work;
GROPIUS–ALBERS

h) De Stijl in Holland has provided the ornamental style of horizontals and verticals.
VAN DOESBURG–HUSZAR

3. Thus the analytic process has arrived at the forms of plane and solid geometry, spectral colors and the black-white scale.

4. These elements can not be broken down any further, therefore the age of analysis is over.

5. Similarly the scientific activity of the 19th century is characterized by the same phases of research, recording and classification.

6. In the 20th century the same is taking place in the applied sciences: technology, sociology and medical science.

SYNTHESIS

7. Art can only reach a commensurate status by producing an appropriate summing up and synthesis.

8. The *Gesamtkunstwerk*, the highest degree of human creativity is architecture.

9. It is a synthesis in which the human will unites stone, cement, iron, glass, wood, the components of broken-down nature; constructing the analyzed space according to the laws of geometry.

10. It is a utilitarian realization of man's ideal; it is active, in opposition to the passivity of the modes of artistic expression thus far.

11. In place of the subject pursuing utopian ideals of feeling (ethical and aesthetic) it establishes material objects (tangible things) and is therefore rational.

12. The worldwide longing for new buildings fuels our belief that in all lands new steel works and towers will rise to the sky. They will emanate from the creative will of all nations; therefore it is international.

13. It is important to stress the concept of building, the KURI, lest it otherwise sink to the level of a word game played by destructive art forms or become the signpost of selfish enterprises.

14. Therefore we must inaugurate literally new buildings.

15. A building has three components: a) functional-economical, b) structural-mathematical, c) spiritual-meaningful.

16. All three factors must of necessity be expressed within the basic sign of the building in one and the same geometric thesis.

17. This basic sign (basic motif) must define and determine the character of the whole and of each and every part.

18. The building's materials, structure, form, color, and rhythm must determine the form, color, material, and rhythm of its parts.

19. Thus we recognize as art in painting, sculpture and crafts only those works that form the component parts of architecture coordinated in the above manner.

20. Within these limits art is free, and possesses an endless range of objective expression.

21. To signify the above we offer the word KURI to designate the concept.

22. KURI unites the achievements of technology with those of art.

23. At last we shall have a mechanized picture, an architecture in motion constantly altering its forms.

24. Motion will at last be realized without transposition into a hitherto static architecture.
25. The accidental will be replaced by the necessity of law. The decorative and expressive will be replaced by the
Constructive,
Utilitarian,
Rational,
International...
Long live the new cube:
KURI—the first cube-shaped house in the world.

Translated by John Bátki

BAUHAUS MANIFESTO 1923   Oskar Schlemmer
Originally published as *Manifest zur Bauhausausstellung* 1923 (Weimar: February 1923)

The Staatliches Bauhaus in Weimar is the first and so far the only government school in the Reich-if not in the world-which calls upon the creative forces of the fine arts to become influential while they are vital. At the same time it endeavors, through the establishment of workshops founded upon the crafts, to unite and productively stimulate the arts with the aim of combining them in architecture. The concept of building will restore the unity that perished in debased academicism and in finicky handicraft....
Such a school, animating and inwardly animated, unintentionally becomes the gauge for the convulsions of the political and intellectual life of the time, and the history of the Bauhaus becomes the history of contemporary art.
The Staatliches Bauhaus, founded after the catastrophe of the war in the chaos of the revolution and in the era of the flowering of an emotion-laden, explosive art, becomes the rallying-point of all those who, with belief in the future and with sky storming enthusiasm, wish to build the "cathedral of Socialism." The triumphs of industry and technology before the war and the orgies in the name of destruction during it called to life that impassioned romanticism which was a flaming protest against materialism and the mechanization of art and life. The misery of the time was also a spiritual anguish. A cult of the unconscious and of the unexplainable, a propensity for mysticism and sectarianism, originated in the quest for those highest things which are in danger of being deprived of their meaning in a world full of doubt and disruption. Breaking the limitations of classical aesthetics reinforced boundlessness of feeling, which found nourishment and verification in the discovery of the East and the art of the Negro, peasants, children, and the insane. The origin of artistic creation was as much sought after as its limits were courageously extended.... But it is in pictures, and always in pictures, where the decisive values take refuge. As the highest achievement of individual exaggeration, free from bonds and unredeemed, they must all, apart from the unity of the picture itself, remain in debt to the proclaimed synthesis....

*   *   *

Germany, country of the middle, and Weimar, the heart of it, is not for the first time the adopted place of intellectual decision.... We become the bearers of responsibility and the conscience of the world. An idealism of activity that embraces, penetrates, and unites art, science, and technology and that influences research, study, and work will construct the "art-edifice" of Man, which is but an allegory of the cosmic system. Today we can do no more than ponder the total plan, lay the foundations, and prepare the building stones.

But

We exist! We have the will! We are producing!

Translation from Rose-Carol Washton Long, German Expressionism

FILM SKETCH: DYNAMICS OF A METROPOLIS   László Moholy-Nagy
Originally published as "Filmváz: a nagyváros dinamikája," *Ma* vol. 9, no. 8–9 (September 15, 1924)

Construction of an iron crane
(Trick shots on a maquette table—drawings—slowly dissolving into live shots)
Moving hoist at a construction site
       Shot from below
                diagonally
         from above
Elevator for bricks.
Revolving crane.
This movement is continued by an automobile,
speeding to the left. The center of the frame is occupied by one and the same building throughout the sequence (i.e., the building should be re-photographed into the center of the frame.) A second automobile now appears, speeding in the opposite direction.
TEMPO, TEMPO!
One row of buildings rushes by in the same direction (to the right) so that the building in the center of the frame always remains visible through them. The row of building rushes off to the right, and returns.
Translucent rows of buildings facing each other on opposite sides of the street are rushing past each other in opposite directions, and so do the automobiles, faster and faster, with a dizzying effect.
        A tiger, TIGER, angrily pacing back and forth in its cage.
High up, clearly visible semaphores (railway traffic signals) moving automatically
a-u-t-o-m-a-t-i-c-a-l-l-y
(large close-up)
up   up
       down   down down
UP UP UP DOWN DOWN
1   2   3   4   5
Freight station
Shunting yard
Warehouses and cellars
                          DARK DARK
                          DARKNESS
Railway:
Highway (with vehicles). Bridge. Viaduct. Far below: ships passing. Up above: a railway seemingly floating overhead. (Elberfeld)

Diagonal shot of a train on a high embankment

A track watchman salutes, standing at attention

His eyes become fixed in a glassy stare (Large CLOSEUP)

Overhead view of a train, seen from a bridge

From below: as seen from a ditch next to the rails, the belly of the train as it speeds
by

The wheels are turning so fast as to be a blur

TEMPO

TEMPO

TEM

TEM   PO

TEM

    TEEM

    M

    M-P-P-0-0-0-0

         Down

In a department store, glass-walled elevators carrying black children

UP

Obliquely

Distorted perspective   UP

Long-distance view. A CROWD

At the entrance, dogs tied on a leash

Next to the glass-walled elevators, a glass-walled telephone booth with caller inside

Ground-level view through glass panels

Right next to the camera, the FACE of the caller coated with phosphorescent material
(so as not to create a silhouette) slowly turning to the right

Overhead a distant airplane spirals away

View from a low-flying airplane, of a square where many streets converge.

Thick traffic: streetcars, automobiles, trucks, horse-drawn cabs, bicycles, buses,
rapidly moving away from the square

then suddenly they all turn back

and pile up in the center of the square

— — — — — — — — — —

the ground opens up at center of the square, swallows everything

— — — — — — — — — —

(The camera is tipped over to create the effect of falling)

TEMPO   Subway

                      Cables

                      Gas-tank

                      Sewers (cloacas built
                      deep under the city)

Light reflected upon the waters

Arc-lamp

Sparks SPRAYING

Highway at night, glistening asphalt surfaces

Cars whooshing by, seen from above, and diagonally

5 SECONDS OF BLACKOUT

Electric advertising sign flashing on and off:

      MOHOLY   MOHOLY

Fireworks at the amusement park

Ride on a

Roller coaster

Speeding
GIANT Ferris wheel
Funhouse
Distorting mirrors
Various other gimmicks
View of an exhibition hall or of a train terminal:
the camera is rotated in a horizontal circle, then in a vertical circle
Taut
Telephone wires and telegraph cables

between buildings
Towers with porcelain insulation
Antennas on rooftops
Factory:
>Wheels turning
>An acrobat twirls and does somersaults
A pole-vaulter. Seen falling, 10 times in succession.
Variety show. Frantic activity.
Soccer game. Rough. Fast paced.
Women wrestling. Kitsch!
Jazz band instruments (Close-up)
AGAINST THE PUBLIC
A hollow, glittering metal funnel
is tossed at the lens
of the camera
(Meanwhile:)
A man
jerks away
his head
in a lightning-fast reflex (Close-up)
A glass of WATER
(only the surface of the water is seen in a large close-up)
In motion
it gushes up like a Fountain

Jazz band in a *talking picture*
>FORTISSIMO

Wild dance caricature
Street girls
Boxing. Closeup:
>ONLY the boxing gloves
>with slow motion (Zeitlampe) camera
A swirl of smoke (above the bridge, as a train speeds by below)
Factory smokestack, diagonally
A diver sinks head first into the water
A propeller churning under water
Drain openings above and under water
Down the canal in a motor boat
to a WASTE-DISPOSAL PLANT
Recycling of waste
>Hills of scrap metal
>Piles of old shoes
>Stacks of tin cans

PERPETUAL MOTION ELEVATOR, with a view. All around.
                    From here roll the film back all the way to the
                              JAZZ BAND (that, too, in reverse)
                    from fortissimo to PIANISSIMO
Mortuary. Overhead shot.
Military parade
Marching...marching.
                              Women riding horses
The two shots are superimposed, so that both can be seen

Slaughterhouse. Cattle.
Machinery of the cold storage plant.
Sausage-making machine. Thousands of sausages.
A LION'S HEAD, snarling. (Close-up)
Theater. Stage loft, with rigging.
A LION'S HEAD, snarling. (Close-up)
Policeman with a rubber truncheon in the center of a busy intersection
THE TRUNCHEON (Close-up)
Theater audience
A LION'S HEAD, snarling. (Close-up)
A couple of seconds of total darkness.
          CIRCLE
                              TEMPO
Circus.
Trapeze.
Clown. LION. Lion.
                    LION. Lion.
Clowns.
Clowns. Lion.
Clowns.
SLOWLY WATERFALL with sound
                    A corpse floating in the water
                    Soldiers.
                    Marching...marching.
                    A glass of WATER
                    The water's surface moves.
a brief,
rapid Waterspout.
Berlin 1921–1922   THE END

Comments for those who refuse to understand the film right away:
This film originated mostly in the possibilities offered by the camera.
I intended the film to produce its effect through its own action, its own tempos and
rhythms, instead of relying on the still fashionable cinematic plots that ape literature
and the theater.
The speeding automobiles are necessary for creating a shocking initial impact, to
conjure the breathless rush and havoc of the city. The tiger is needed for contrast.
Also to get the audience acclimatized to this kind of surprise and inconsistency from
the outset.
(This film has no intention to teach, to moralize, or to tell a story. Its sole purpose is
to create effects by visual means only.)
Bridges, trains, ships, etc. to indicate the paraphernalia behind urban civilization.

The belly of a train: a sight never seen in the normal course of events.

The phosphorescent face that slowly turns away: a reminder of boring telephone conversations. A dreamlike state (glass–glass–glass); at the same time the direction of the movement prepares us for the spiral inscribed by the airplane.

The speeding roller coaster ride: many things escape one's attention. Many things pass unnoticed because one's sensory apparatus is unable to register everything, such as rapid movement, moments of danger, etc. On the roller coaster almost all people close their eyes during the great plunge. But the eye of the camera is always open. We can barely observe babies or animals objectively because our attention is distracted by so many other things in the meantime.

The metal funnel is meant to be so frightening that it almost hurts.

The surface of the water in the glass: splendid.

The recurrence of the lion's head is a nightmare (again, again, and again). The audience is light-hearted, but the head still reappears—

Etc., etc.

In general one should understand far more from a single rapid reading of the script than any commentary can ever explain.

Translated by John Bátki

LIFE AT THE BAUHAUS   Farkas Molnár
Originally published as "Élet a Bauhausban," *Periszkóp* (June–July 1925)

It is the first institution in Europe dedicated to realizing the achievements of the new arts for the purposes of human existence. Its inception was the first step toward a recognition that has become widespread by now: that "atelier art" has divorced itself from life and is dead, and that every person possessing creative powers must seek his or her vocation in the fulfillment of the practical needs of everyday life. Today's scientific and technological advances will not become assimilated into general culture as long as humankind still lives under medieval conditions. The machine is still a foreign object in the houses of today; the documents of technological culture are still relegated to books atop fancy carved desks, radio music by the fireplace. The age demands a style, a common denominator for its visible phenomena. However, "style" is an unsuitable word, we do not like to use it, for it usually refers to the external pseudo-unity of things, a system of decorative forms.

Each and every object that we have to build anew will be different, according to its material, function, and structure, instead of resembling each other in form. The common denominator will be provided by the object's functionality and beauty demanded by its practicality; it will be the kinship of objects equivalent in their quality.

The architect Walter Gropius, founder and director of the Bauhaus, was among the pioneers in the fight against entrenched historical forms. His prewar creations (such as the *Faguswerk* in Alfeld) had already demonstrated that he was able to realize his goals with absolute technical mastery. He conducted the task of organizing the Bauhaus with the greatest consistency and perseverance in spite of the difficult circumstances and lack of understanding on the part of the authorities. The Bauhaus as organized is the prototype of a new kind of educational institution that does not merely "educate for life" but actually places its students into practical real-life situations. It is articulated into three subdivisions: 1) the school itself where theoretical and practical professional instruction is given in workshops, 2) the production workshops (stone, wood, metal, and glass processing shops, as well as textile, ceramics, murals, printing and theatrical workshops) where work is done on commission and ongoing experimental work is conducted, and 3) the architecture and design department, for the design and construction of all sorts of building projects.

At the time of its founding Gropius declared that in our days there are no architects and no artists capable of executing the loftier tasks of our age in practical form. Therefore the new artists would have to develop here, learning in the course of a constant immersion in materials the ability to think realistically, to make cool-headed calculations, and to draw daring conclusions. We live at a time of the greatest possibilities, a time of the greatest need. Unaccomplishable projects can only hinder us. The artist's pride obstructs development and progress, which is promoted by the forward thrust of mechanical aptitude.

The 1923 exhibition gave evidence of how much of its promise the Bauhaus has realized after a mere four years of existence. They have built a model home in a manner totally devoid of clichés, introducing outstanding technical innovations in its structure and demonstrating creative invention in the layout of its ground plan. The entire building was completely furnished with built-in and multi-functional, movable furniture. Everything was produced at the Bauhaus workshops, including the rugs and dishes. The architecture department exhibited a large number of photographs showing completed buildings and several series of novel projects for inexpensive apartment buildings.

The exhibition of the products of the workshops included several prototypes that have been adopted by industry for mass production. The theater department produced *Triadic Ballet* and *Mechanical Cabaret*. The printing department published a huge Bauhaus volume including reproductions of representative works. Colorful reliefs were installed in the stairways and halls of the main buildings as public examples of innovative spatial design.

The Bauhaus exhibition was able to show very positive financial results even though it took place at a time of the greatest crisis in Germany. Widespread praise in the press and from professional circles was followed by such an influx of orders for various industrial fairs that the production workshops, already overloaded by their instructional schedules, were unable to fulfill the majority of orders. This has occasioned the current crisis at the Bauhaus, since the state that had compliantly erected the original buildings could not afford at present to enlarge the productive workshops, while refusing to approve the involvement of private capital in a state-run institution. Thus Gropius was faced with a choice: to continue with a school which would sooner or later sink to an academic level, or else to establish a corporation in tandem with the Bauhaus staff in order to realize their original goals. Gropius chose the latter, all the more so since the government of Thüringia, not very sympathetic to the school's latest efforts, had become increasingly stingy with its subsidies.

German manufacturing industry and the circles that promote progress in the industrial arts (Werkbund, Werkfreunde, Industrieverband) have already given repeated evidence of their support of the Bauhaus, and in all likelihood will make the establishment of a G.m.b.H. possible in the near future. Given all this, the Bauhaus will be able to look forward with confidence to a future that will not be restricted to one locality but contains the potential of fulfilling a Europe-wide interest.

For someone to be admitted to the Bauhaus workshops he or she must not only know how to work but also how to live. Prospective students are required to send an autobiography and a photograph along with their applications. This is especially important in the case of women... Only healthy and intact individuals are suitable for admission. Education and training are not as essential requirements as a lively, alert temperament, a flexible body, and an inventive mind. Nightlife at the Bauhaus claims the same importance as daytime activities. One must know how to dance. In Itten's apt phrase: *locker sein* [loosen up].

If you are not familiar with the festivals of the Bauhaus, then you don't really know the Bauhaus product. These festivals arise suddenly, on the most varied pretexts. Take, for example, a day of great winds. Whereupon a gigantic placard is carried all over the community: FESTIVAL OF AERIAL GAMES. Two hundred airplanes of all sizes, shapes, and colors float in the air at the end of thin leashes. There is nothing more beautiful than that. Games played by two hundred children of all ages. There are some incredible things that soar superbly. The best in the show was a piece by Fritz Schleifer, our "pretty boy," whose forte was making constructions of air. As such, he was definitely a "keeper." Eventually he became a taxi dancer.

Summer brings many other delights, such as the water games known as *bathing*. The philistines are especially incensed, for it is rumored that the Bauhaus folk are fond of forgetting to bring their swimsuits. But this is not true. I passed three summers there without a single occasion when members of both sexes bathed together like that. Of course there were a few exceptions, here and there, but these were extremely rare. But everyone loved the cold water and the stony beach. And boxing. I challenged Gropius, "the Grand Seigneur" himself, to three rounds.

The nights, too, are beautiful. Especially in the vast park in Weimar. You see, this is where the *model house* is located, just above the Goethe-House, and next to the Bauhaus vegetable gardens. I lived there for a summer. It was the busiest time—during the Bauhaus exhibition. We certainly gave that model house a workout. You would never imagine how valuable a large, central, sky-lit *hall* can be in such a small apartment that economizes on space. And how practical those small sleeping cubicles can be. The Breuer beds, the Otte rugs, and the telephone, affording a "connection" at any time. Breuer's *toilette mirror* is a veritable wonder. If you place the small mirror horizontally across your face and look into the other, the nose disappears and this way the face is always very attractive; turning it slightly you end up with only one eye on your head, making the facial expression truly monumental.

Lantern Festival: what a banal term. But it signifies a real attraction, if you want to see a worldly congeries of the most varied assortment of geometric shapes, and masses of transparent color changes. We, too, can provide some real surprises. Schmidtchen's things possess a magical appeal. They blow even the philistines' minds. El Lissitzky takes me by the arm; this serious little Constructivist engineer exudes sentimentality. Bah! *Proun* pictures. This is reality.

The winters are even more perilous. This is the season when *dancing* becomes a health requirement. The ballroom (Il Montecarlo) is huge. But strangers are not granted admittance. The district chief decides to give us a tax break. The "Schüpo" is always on our side. This is the time when the girls really blossom. If you knew the Bauhaus girls you would drop your low opinion of German women's stockings. Of course many of them are from abroad. But among the German ones those whose names begin with I and L are 100 percent more efficacious than Greek goddesses. They are also more beautiful. My best dancing partner was Princess To (born in 1906 in the German Congo).

Of course the greatest credit goes to Arnold Weininger (born 1899 in Karancs). He organized the Bauhaus band. Jazz band, accordion, xylophone, saxophone, bombast, revolver. When he sits at the piano he rules over all the band masters; he leads the band like Admiral Scheer, he uplifts, he motions, he conducts, he directs. His smile is world-famous. He has also imported Hungarian music. He would make a terrific movie actor. In Hamburg, as author and actor at the Cabaret Jungfrau, he has enjoyed tremendous success.

Here the various kinds of dances are not performed in their customary forms, but as dictated by the throbbing pulse of the blood and the beat. There are also special Bauhaus-dances, just as there were special Bauhaus clothes, until the appearance of Georg Teltscher (when the process of Americanization began). Our dances to original music are the Bauhaus *schritt*, the Bauhaus trot, the Bauhaus *gerade*, and so on.

The dancing is suddenly disrupted by a resounding crash. All eyes are upon the stage. The *Bühnenwerkstatt* is at work. This merits a whole article in itself. The most striking farces, bloody tragedies, persiflages, exoticisms. But there is something even more novel here: those spontaneously arising improvisations. The first was Steegreif in 1919. And everybody performs. One after another they take the stage; much of the time the action is simultaneous in the middle of the hall, up in the galleries and on the podium. The spellbinding story may end as a serious rumble or else as a square dance. Directed by Kurt Schmidt (his nails artfully blackened).

The greatest expenditures of energy, however, go into the *costume parties*. The essential difference between the fancy-dress balls organized by the artists of Paris, Berlin, Moscow and the ones here at the Bauhaus is that our costumes are truly original. Everyone prepares his or her own. Never a one that has been seen before. Inhuman, or humanoid, but always new. You may see monstrously tall shapes stumbling about, colorful mechanical figures that yield not the slightest clue as to where the head is. Sweet girls inside a red cube. Here comes a winch and they are hoisted high up into the air; lights flash and scents are sprayed.

And now one or two intimate details about the bigwigs. Kandinsky prefers to appear decked out as an antenna, Itten as an amorphous monster, Feininger as two right triangles, Moholy-Nagy as a segment transpierced by a cross, Gropius as Le Corbusier, Muche as an apostle of Mazdaznan, Klee as the song of the blue tree. A rather grotesque menagerie...

The dance is non-stop. The members of the Jazz-kapelle break up their instruments. The proprietor loses his patience. Outside the police set up machine guns made of cherry brandy bottles. Inside, the high point is reached. Barometer at 365 degrees. Maximal tension. But it all comes to an end. Hebestreit the executioner shows up. The red arrow points at the emergency exit.

Translated by John Bátki

FILM AT THE BAUHAUS: A REJOINDER László Moholy-Nagy
Originally published as "film im bauhaus: eine erwiderung," *film kurier* no. 206 (December 18, 1926)

these lines are intended neither as self-defense nor as accusation—despite more than one sideswipe that might have been meant for me. i am glad that the issue has been raised and call upon all far-sighted individuals to work together toward a fair solution.

"now the house is there, the stage, the students, the time—begin!"
so the *film kurier* wrote on december 11. house, stage, students: fine. time: long since. proposer: also there, as can be seen in the very same issue. and if the proposer has yet to "prove" that his "promises" have a future: whose fault might that be?
the industry expects proofs, does it? if i could supply such "proofs"—i.e., if i had the

means to prove my point—i would not need the industry. all i would need would be an audience, and i have no fears in that direction.

my—our—expenditure of strength takes the tangible form of proposals, projects, plans, "scripts," theories.

it is for others—for the industry, let us say—to undertake to make a corresponding effort: that is, to make the means available at the point where results are to be expected. to expect: that is the task of supporting bodies. where "proof" has already been supplied, there is no task left to perform.

there are some individuals in the industry who have an instinct for what is to come. but the commercial factors let them down. some years ago, when i showed my film plans to one of the directors of ufa, the situation was the same: he listened to me; he was extremely interested—and the practical outcome was a letter asking me to give ufa first refusal of my film on completion (!!!). on completion! who was going to complete it? what happens to the most magnificent projects if you have to cut them down to the level of your own personal finances?

result: what came out of this was not a film, but only "promises": namely publications in books, magazines, lectures, etc. that is, i gave my plans to the public and abandoned the idea of executing them myself. those plans germinated, and the ideas found acceptance everywhere. my discoveries are now used in one way or another in many films. my script, "dynamic of the big city" (1921–22), has survived to see—and really with no hard feelings—press reports that the fox corporation has commissioned walther ruttmann to make a big-city picture, "berlin."

so who is it who has "catching up" to do in the field of film (see *film kurier*, december 11)? is it the bauhaus teachers? yes, if the bauhaus teachers were board members of a motion picture corporation, this would be a fair criticism. or if the bauhaus students had movie-director fathers—then, too, it would be easier to keep up to date with the practice of the contemporary film industry.

however, the position at the bauhaus is the exact reverse of this. industry supports other schools and academies by supplying apparatus and materials free of charge; why not the bauhaus? where is the instinct for what is to come?

bauhaus teachers and bauhaus students have long aspired to set up an experimental laboratory for the art of film. we are glad that the *film kurier* responds affirmatively to such initiatives. this gives rise to a responsibility. not, initially, for us—we have taken many steps in that direction already—but for the author of the affirmative response, who stands between the parties concerned and can mediate between them. his affirmative response in principle must be translated into positive support.

let us be given an annual sum for experimental research, and a time limit within which to work with that sum. let the sum not be too inadequate, for experimentation costs money—as every interested person now knows. but do not ask us to do costly work without the means to do it.

try to gain a clear idea of the achievement that is there at the bauhaus: the opening days may have afforded an opportunity for this. to this add publishing (*bauhausbücher*), editorial activity (the film and photographic section of the new dutch magazine *i10* and the *bauhauszeitung*), contributions to ten or more international magazines, the output of individuals as painters, photographers, etc., etc.; and then try to imagine whether an individual who is already doing all of this can bestir himself to make films without money! i may say that i do all of this and am entitled to ask that my promises—which, as i have said, contain powerful realities—be answered with realities. set up an experimental film studio for me or for the bauhaus, and then a start can be made. as i say: then i would have no fears as to the outcome.

Translated by David Britt

herwarth walden

was fifty years old on september 16. today, more than ever, he is an outsider in a
bourgeois culture that hankers after orderliness and peace and quiet. to appreciate
the importance of his forceful and many-faceted campaign to revolutionize german
intellectual life, it suffices to list the artists on whose behalf walden vigorously intervened at a time when the official understanding of modern art still struggled to come
to terms with cézanne and van gogh. back in 1910, walden, whose magazine, publishing
house, and art gallery operated under the title of *der sturm*, was a pioneer advocate
for pechstein, kirchner, nolde, schmidt-rottluff, kokoschka, franz marc, archipenko,
boccioni, campendonk, marc chagall, delaunay, albert gleizes, fernand léger, august
macke, jean metzinger, molzahn, and schwitters. there is a special interest, for us,
in noting that bauhaus masters including feininger, kandinsky, and klee, and former
masters johannes itten, georg muche, lothar schreyer, and moholy-nagy also passed
through *der sturm*, which published the "glass architecture" of scheerbart and the
works of august stramm. herwarth walden's pioneering work was greeted with intem-
perate abuse from all sections of the daily and specialist press. just a few years later,
however, cautious literary men and art dealers were clambering through the breaches
made by *der sturm* in order to survey the field with a keener appreciation of nuances
of quality—and then ply a profitable trade in the "best of the best." herwarth walden
was incapable of such a dispassionate approach. in the end, his ambition—no doubt
aided by the sensationalism that made him raise the roof with new *sturm* attractions
every month—led to lapses of discrimination that we cannot but deplore in the interests of the young art that remains free of the currently fashionable petit-bourgeois
banality. for in germany today there is not one magazine or art gallery with the courage
to take a firm stand against all this neo-biedermeier. at the same time, over the last
few years *der sturm* has suffered a loss of quality that must appall even the most
heartfelt former sympathizer. this may explain the fatal isolation into which *der sturm*
has fallen: an isolation that is now far more extreme than formerly, even though the
ideas and artists for whom the paper once fought have long since come into their own.
truly, a tragic isolation, which makes it incumbent on us to quote a remark made by
rené schickele almost twenty years ago in justification of herwarth walden: "in art all
that counts is to make, to detect, and to make known something that is new; the whole
history of art is a succession of such discoveries; to go on this warpath and lose one's
way is better than to peddle yesterday's fashions."

Translated by David Britt

Revolution, political and cultural turmoil, and the influx of immigrants from all over Europe contributed to the rise of Berlin as the continent's artistic capital following World War I. Not only was Germany economically far more advanced than the other countries of Central and Eastern Europe, but Berlin, in particular, was home to lively artistic, literary, musical, and theatrical goings-on. Modern architecture and design had long generated heated debates within the Deutscher Werkbund about their compatibility with art, while the role of art itself had been challenged by the Berlin Dada movement. In this city of relative wealth, with its burgeoning publishing and film industries, liberal cosmopolitan *Bildungsbürgertum* (educated bourgeoisie), and often more radical intelligentsia, artists found unprecedented opportunity for experimentation with such new media as photography, photomontage, photograms, and film. They could also launch journals such as El Lissitzky and Ilya Ehrenburg's *Veshch/ Gegenstand/Objet*, or Hans Richter and Lissitzky's *G*.

Berlin had long been an international center of Expressionism with connections for example, to the Bunt group in Poznań, whose members included Berlin residents Polish artist Stanisław Kubicki and his German artist wife Margarete Kubicka. Herwarth Walden's Berlin gallery, journal, and book publishing enterprise, *Der Sturm*, presented Russian and Czech art, including Prague's Skupina group, as well as the work of émigrés already living in Berlin, such as the Romanian Arthur Segal who had arrived in 1905.

The cosmopolitan atmosphere attracted youth from throughout the defunct Austro-Hungarian Empire who felt more comfortable with the language and culture in Berlin than in Paris. Several representatives of the Hungarian avant-garde—vocal supporters of the commune, forced to flee the military defeat and right-wing terror of late 1919—also sought refuge there, including Moholy-Nagy and the critic Ernő Kállai. Karel Teige visited from Prague and Ljubomir Micić from Belgrade. Der Strum exhibited Mieczysław Szczuka and Teresa Żarnower from Poland, and Avgust Černigoj from Slovenia, to name just a few. From other regions came Viking Eggeling from Sweden and Theo van Doesburg from Holland. Already home of some 100,000 Russian émigrés in the aftermath or the war, Berlin (and its Charlottenburg district dubbed Charlottengrad) now hosted many artists and intellectuals sympathetic to the Revolution. Among the artists were Ivan Puni, who lived in Berlin between 1920 and 1923; Naum Gabo from 1922 to 1933, as well as El Lissitzky

and Ilya Ehrenburg, who arrived in
1921, probably to establish contacts on
behalf of the Soviet Union's Ministry
of Culture. Kandinsky, who took up
a teaching post at the Bauhaus in
Weimar in 1922, first spent several
months in Berlin before traveling to
Weimar.

The cultural life of Berlin, the political
radicalization among its intelligentsia
after the war, as well as their indirect
knowledge of the Russian Revolution
and direct exposure to Russian
Constructivism at the First Russian Art
Exhibition in 1922—and the response
these influences prompted in its international community of artists—all
contributed to establishing the unparalleled cultural context in which
International Constructivism evolved
during the early twenties.

A CALL FOR ELEMENTARIST ART   Raoul Hausmann, Hans Arp, Ivan Puni, and László Moholy-Nagy

Originally published as "Aufruf zur elementaren Kunst," *De Stijl* vol. 4, no. 10 (October 1921)

We love the brave discovery, the regeneration of art. Art that is the expression of the forces of an epoch. We therefore demand the expression of our own time, by an art that can be only of our making, that did not exist before us and cannot continue after us—not a passing fashion, but an art based on the understanding that art is always born anew and does not remain content with the expression of the past. We pledge ourselves to elementarist art. It is elemental because it does not philosophize, because it is built up of its own elements alone. To yield to the elements of form is to be an artist. The elements of art can be discovered only by an artist. But they are not to be found by his individual whim; the individual does not exist in isolation, and the artist uses only those forces that give artistic form to the elements of our world. Artists, declare yourselves for art! Reject the styles. We demand freedom from the styles to reach the STYLE. Style is never plagiarism.

This is our manifesto: seized by the dynamism of our time, we proclaim the revision in our outlook brought about by the tireless interplay of the sources of power that mold the spirit and the form of an epoch and that allow art to grow as something pure, liberated from usefulness and beauty, as something elemental in everybody.

We proclaim elemental art! Down with the reactionary in art!

Translated by Nicholas Bullock

STATEMENT FROM DER STURM CATALOGUE   János Máttis-Teutsch

Originally published in *Paul Klee, Hans Máttis-Teutsch, Gesamtschau* (Berlin: Der Sturm, July/August, 1921)

My goal is to use the means of painting and sculpture to create abstract works that lead autonomous lives as artistic entities and that engender pure spiritual feeling.

My works are predominantly compositions in which the starting point is the human being. Human beings in their spiritual vibration as a nonphysical contact to feeling. The work is determined by a feeling whose rhythmical emanations emerge through the core of the inner vibration.

The construction of the works consists in colorfully rhythmic movements through opposites of cold and warm, dark and bright, resting points, concentric and eccentric movements that harmonize in one goal.

The sculptures in wood are sculpted freely from oak, with emanations and shared movements. Sometimes I paint them with strong colors, so they become independent of the light and unleash movement and expression more purely and autonomously.

Translated by Steven Lindberg

DYNAMIC-CONSTRUCTIVE SYSTEM OF FORCES   László Moholy-Nagy and Alfred Kemény
Originally published as "Dynamisch-konstruktives Kraftsystem," *Der Sturm* no. 12 (1922)

Vital constructivity is the embodiment of life and the principle of all human and cosmic development.

Translated into art, *today* this means the activation of space by means of dynamic-constructive systems of forces, that is, construction of forces within one another that are actually at tension in physical space and their construction within space, also active as force (tensions).

Constructivity as an organizing principle of human efforts has led the arts in recent times from technology to the sort of static form-invested procedure which has been reduced either to technical naturalism or to an over-simplification of form limited to the horizontal, the vertical and the diagonal. The best instance was an open, eccentric (centrifugal) construction which indicated the tensions of forms and of space, without, however, resolving them.

We must therefore replace the *static* principle of *classical art* with the *dynamic principle of universal life*. Stated practically: instead of static *material* construction (material and form relations), dynamic construction (vital construction and *force relations*) must be evolved in which the material is employed only as *the carrier of forces*.

Carrying further the unit of construction, a DYNAMIC-CONSTRUCTIVE SYSTEM OF FORCES is attained whereby man, hitherto merely receptive in his observation of works of art, experiences a heightening of his own faculties, and becomes himself an active partner with the forces unfolding themselves.

There is a close correlation between the problems of this system of forces and the problem of freely floating sculpture as well as of film as projected spatial motion. The first projects looking towards the dynamic-constructive system of forces can be only experimental demonstration devices for testing the connections between man, material forces and space. Next comes the use of the experimental results for the creation of freely moving (free from mechanical and technical movement) works of art.

Translation from Krisztina Passuth, Moholy-Nagy

AIMS OF THE PRÉ THEATER   Raoul Hausmann and László Péri
Originally published as "Die Absichten des Tehaters 'Pré'," *Der Sturm* vol. 13, no. 9 (September 1922)

The Pré Theater sets out to show the human being as a moving component within a shifting configuration of spatial tension. In the first place, it treats a dancer as an entity that perceives itself entirely as the center and periphery of the space defined by the stage. As an abstract quantity, a cubic art form, this space conditions awareness of the dancer as a bearer of space and mover in space, whose task is also to shape the invisible, to shape the logic of the seeming void. The dancer moves the space by sensing all the interrelated tensions of that space within himself and using his body to give them a manifest form. The dancer in the Pré Theater could never sense or shape kinetic relationships against an arbitrary or nonconstructive space; the artificial space of the stage must always be spatially constructed in such a way that the dance emanates from it as the one and only possible logic of movement. This means that both décor and costume, in the old sense, must be eliminated. The logic and clarity of the stage construction prompts and impels the dancer into a form of dance organically bound up with that space. The bygone romanticism of movement is abolished; by analogy with the stage design, the dancer becomes the expression of the vertical, the diagonal, and the square. The stage is treated in accordance with the new conceptions of space in painting and is spatially structured in cubic forms. The so-called background is now in a living relationship with the central space, in which the dancer captures those relationships and transforms them into a synthesis of movements of his limbs, which must be trained to abandon the mechanics of the merely human. Improvisation in dance thus becomes impossible, and dance—total spatial integration—is expressed through the human mental kinetic impulse. The synthesis of the human being in spatial movement in the dance is governed by the strictest observation of rule. The seeming freedom of grotesque dance is perceived as anarchic and rejected. In perfect conformity to the space and to the dance, the music must use the acoustic ratios to set its tempo. The Pré Theater sets out to achieve perfect observation of law and clarity of movement in time and space within the unified form of solid, plane, and sound: a new form of dance, stage, and music.

Translated by David Britt

THE ARTS ABROAD   Henryk Berlewi
Originally "Plastyka za granicą," unpublished manuscript (1922–23)

Purism, Suprematism and Constructivism are gaining an ever more international and cosmopolitan character. Constructivism is divided into several groups each of which—in spite of its affinity with other groups—has some distinct character. There is, for instance, Russian as well as Hungarian, German and Dutch Constructivism. The most important and most consistent in its radicalism is the Dutch De Stijl group. Whereas elsewhere Constructivism is a theory detached from life, at best illustrated with more or less interesting experiments, in Holland it has been partly applied in practice. Some excellent buildings of unheard of simplicity that have spread over various towns are the evidence of this. The periodical *De Stijl*, which represents the group, has been published for the past five years; its editor is Theo van Doesburg, the author of many theoretical works on new art. Close in character to De Stijl is one German group that has recently been developing its activity in Berlin through its periodical *G (elementare Gestaltung)*. Members: Hans Richter, Werner Graff, Mies van der Rohe, El Lissitzky. The dominant subject in it is architecture, its main protagonist being Mies van der Rohe, a Dutchman, well known for his monumental designs in reinforced concrete, distinguished by their audacity and simplicity in resolving the construction [of buildings]. The periodical lacks any characteristic German qualities, such as pomposity, sentimentality, and romanticism. It treats things straightforwardly and concretely. From amongst the flood of periodicals devoted to art in Germany, presenting the whole spectrum of the blasé aesthetics (*Kunstgewerbe*), only *G* breathes life.

In Weimar, this abode of Goethes and Schillers, a new breath of wind has succeeded in clearing the air. The first academy of new art is there: the Bauhaus. As a result of constant pressure and agitation from the De Stijl group, which carried out its actions in Weimar for some time, the Bauhaus has managed to somewhat emancipate itself from the yoke of Munich bourgeois ornamentalism, and has come closer to the tasks of technology and industry. The patrons of this institution: Klee, Kandinsky and other Expressionist artists are slowly being forced to cede their positions to new people, such as Moholy-Nagy (the Hungarian Constructivist). Thanks to the low value of German currency in recent years the mainstream of new art movements has concentrated in Germany. The artists from Russia, Hungary, Japan, Holland, Italy, America, Sweden...

Here is a brief summary of the main events in Berlin and Düsseldorf in the years 1922 and 1923:

1) The ideology of *Der Sturm* goes bankrupt.
2) Lissitzky and Ehrenburg publish *Veshch* [*-Gegenstand-Objet*]
3) Exhibition of new Russian art.
4) Eggeling shows his film + Eggeling contra Richter at the exhibition of Novembergruppe.
5) Partying together in the Berlin amusement grounds.
6) The International Congress of Progressive Artists in Düsseldorf, including representatives of all five parts of the world + their break up and the Constructivists' declaration + dance of Raoul Hausmann at the reception.

All sorts of uncertain news comes from Russia. Some pioneers of new art, developing their theories consistently, have gradually arrived at the complete negation of art as such, in other words, they have murdered art in the name of this art (*smert' isskustva*), while others have completely moved away from Marxism to the Right and are now preoccupied with theosophy (sic!). At any rate, the qualities which the artistic revolution in Russia has brought about (Tatlin, Malevich), though they cannot yet be properly evaluated from the point of view of their practicality, have great theoretical significance.

In Paris there is some consternation on account of the influx of foreigners. The philistine bliss has been somewhat disturbed by artists. The managers of the Salon des Independants went as far in their chauvinism as to decide to separate foreign artists from the native Frenchmen in the exhibition. Apparently, Lhothe and Léger came out against this. On the whole, Paris has lately become a center of the most refined conservatism: Ingres, Renoir, Derain [are a case in point]. Only Ozenfant and Jeanneret (the founders of Purism) propagate *l'esprit nouveau* in the columns of their *L'Esprit Nouveau*. They devote a great deal of space to modern technology and architecture.

Translated by Wanda Kemp-Welch

CONSTRUCTIVIST ART AND PÉRI'S SPATIAL CONSTRUCTIONS
Alfréd Kemény
Originally published as "Die konstructive Kunst und Péris Raumskonstruktionen," preface to *Mappe: Péri, Linoleumschnitte, 1922–23* (Berlin: 1923)

The latest wave in the contemporary visual arts—Constructivism—has posited the simplest possible organization of artistic design and the most deliberate mastery of creative powers as the guiding principles of creative work in the arts. The physiological structure of the human body is subject to strict cosmic laws of construction. As an individual constructional body within the constructional body of the world, it has a need for construction—for constructional design—that stems from the profoundest cosmic-physiological causes. The laws of the world and the laws of man become the laws of art. The immutable laws of the world and of the human microcosm that are expressed in ever new relationships (= contrasts); the immutable laws of the artwork that correspond to these laws of the world, derived from ever new combinations of elementary mathematical (arithmetic, geometric) relationships, that is, from the contrasts in the means particular to it: form, color, material; *the eternal immutability of law in the eternal transformation of form*—this is the profound meaning behind Constructivist design.

In a world of relative motionlessness, we perceive everything as an object, as a certainty. Given the enormous dimensions of the circumstances associated with world movement, we can assume that the world itself is also relatively motionless. All the more so because an external motionlessness—resulting from the tensions among the individual parts in this apparent calm—can cause an intense movement within us. From this recognition Constructivist art forms a new objectivity, a new realism. The artwork itself is created as an abstract reality, as a new object with definite forms and sharp borders. In deliberate contrast to "nonobjective painting," the abstraction of Constructivist design is neither objectivity "resolved" nor nature blurred. The structure of the world takes shape in the sharp clarity and precise organization of the artistic object. The organizational endeavors of the present day are given a corresponding artistic form. Clarity of form is inherently opposed to the confusion of life today in order to establish a clear construction for the life of tomorrow. Of course, this desire is not expressed actively and concretely enough. The nature of the ethics of Constructivist art is more cosmic and physiological, more individual and formal, than social. We may speak here of an intuitive, mathematical design, in which the arithmetic and geometric relationships of the forms dominate. The world is brought back to its relativity, to its original creative logic, which forms the cosmic out of the chaotic, number out of the undifferentiated, the unambiguous out of the multifaceted. This logic is not the barren poverty of an intellect without energy—or only so in the work of the less talented and of the imitators—but rather controlled consciousness and economy of strength. Its effect derives not from the passivity of an intellectual message but from the assailing activity of an immediate sensuality. It is not the subjectivity, the individuality of the artist but rather objectivity, the rational vigor of the design that determines its value above all. The true task an artwork must fulfill is always taken into account. The Constructivist painting is painted for a wall, not made to float in airless space.

Cubism and Futurism had already revealed the path that leads from the subjective interpretation of nature and emotion toward objectivity in design. However, this path reached its high point in the subsequent movements in the visual arts—Suprematism, neoplasticiscm, Tatlinism, Constructivism. Naturally, the value of a particular artwork is determined not by its trend but by the vigor and originality with which it renders the new goals of design objective. The trend of art is dependent on the period, on the economic structure of existing society. This is true even when the artist himself takes a stand against the dominant form of society. Constructivist art possesses the will to collectivism. Collectivist art is, however, impossible in the universal anarchy of the prevailing bourgeois society. As the art of the proletariat it is postponed to the future. The worldwide revolution of the proletariat is its prerequisite. Constructivist art makes use of the idea of constructing a collective life to move from the past epoch of individualist art toward the future epoch of collective art. Constructivist art is necessarily only a transitional phenomenon for a transitional period.

Wherever the logical element of design—consciousness in lieu of the unconscious element: creative intuition—was overemphasized, the result was not creative design

474

but only an aesthetic sham. The fundamental condition of creative art remains, now as always, artistic intuition. Even so, organizing logic, which came to be emphasized in response to the emotional disorder of nonobjective painting, led to a clear, exact, solidly formed, unambiguous, and new form of objectivity.

Péri's construction of space is characterized by an economy compressed into a minimum of forms, by a spatial tension that results from the extreme contrasts in this minimum of forms, from hardness of masses, and from a keen certitude of representation that has no associations with nature whatsoever. The traditional square picture frame does not permit the picture plane to be sharply defined. The square, as the most neutral shape, bestows a certain decorative banality on the entire picture; the passivity of the traditional approach to defining the pictorial space and the isolation of the picture from the wall render it impossible to activate the space in any way. *Malevich* and *Mondrian*, independently of each other, brought the square to the ultimate consequence of the design possibilities inherent in it. In working with the square, by means of invariability, by emphatic repetition of one and the same square plane—the most indifferent surface possible—they destroyed *the form of the painting as such* and achieved a relatively formless type of design based on pure color relationships on a plane. The Russian Constructivists—Tatlin, Rodchenko, Lissitzky, Johansen, Vladimir and George Stenberg, Medunetzky, Gabo, and Klucis—moved from the plane into real space. They gave spatial and plastic designs to the purely material relationships of unadulterated—pure—materials (iron, brass, copper, glass, wood, and so on) used simultaneously in the space. By giving the picture plane the sharpest asymmetrical definition possible, *Péri* exploded the traditional square shape of the painting. In this way he achieved a powerful spatial charge from hard, opposing relationships of two-dimensional forms. The explosiveness of the space is heightened by rhythmic repetition and the relative lack of color of the paints used (black and grayish brown, black and red). The colors are secondary to the spatial function of the forms. As a result, the opposing relationships of the forms that produce the spatial tension are expressed much more strongly. The equilibrium of the object designed results from the immutable color relationships and from the variability of the relationships among the forms, from the color contrast (as the unchanging element) and the form (as the changing one) of the picture plane. A rigid, immobile stability composed of extreme contrasts. The spaceless, cubic template of today's moronic "architectonic interior" is destroyed. A new struggling spatial activity develops from the deeply serious dark contrasts with the dominant elements that result from the omnipresent black paint. In the penultimate constructions the black paint fights with brown and gray. The activity of black is crucial. In these works, despite their asymmetrical and nonquadratic construction, both the horizontal-vertical conflict of the quadrilateral and the concentric, centripetal closed form of the old "painting" are retained. In the final works the horizontal-vertical construction of the painting is eliminated. Opposing diagonal forms span a vertical or horizontal axis as contrasting forces. The spatial tension increases to the most active power relationships of a space balanced at the outside limit of the possibility of equilibrium. Recurrent red fights with black, and its activity drowns out the activity of the black paint. The powerful form masses open up the concentricity of the composition into a dynamic of centrifugal eccentricity. From that point the path leads to the architecture of the future.

The linocuts presented here illustrate Péri's spatial-Constructivist designs. They are not original, creative works and do not wish to be viewed as such. The artist uses linoleum because it is well suited to reproduce his spatial constructions. Nevertheless they still have the value of originals because the elimination of color presents the artist with a new set of problems. Péri's work is presented here in chronological order. Though reproduced on a smaller scale, the proportionality and scale relationships of the forms is the same as that of the originals intended for a wall. The role that color plays in separating the forms and its energetic function in heightening the spatial activity of the design are fulfilled here instead by the lines. The mechanical uniformity of the lines emphasizes both the opposing connections of the form parts of the painting as a whole and the suppressed monumentality of the design, just as the repeating rhythm of the colors did in the paintings. Designing using pure relations of space-creating opposing forms is even more effective when colors are eliminated. The lines reproduce, as hard and definite outlines, the nonquadratic and objective character of the spatial constructions with intense urgency.

Translated by Steven Lindberg

SECOND PRESENTIST DECLARATION—ADDRESSED TO THE INTERNATIONAL CONSTRUCTIVISTS   Viking Eggeling and Raoul Hausmann

Originally published as "Zweite präsentistische Deklaration—Gerichtet an die internationalen Konstruktivisten," *Ma* vol. 8, no. 5–6 (1923)

In the First Presentist Manifesto, we declared that the look of a world that is real is a synthesis of mind and matter. We once more aspire toward conformity with the mechanical working process. We call for the expansion and conquest of all our senses; we shall make strides in optics, as far as the fundamental phenomena of light. As we plainly stated: it is our duty to fight on against tawdry Romanticism in its last and subtlest form. We call for an end to petty individualism. If we now call for an expansion and reform of human sensory emanations, this is only because we have seen the prior birth of an unafraid and unhistorical humanity, that of the working class! We take issue with the declaration published in *Egység* by the Hungarian Constructivists; and to them, and to the international Constructivists in general, we make the following declaration.

Our field of work is neither the Communist Party's *Proletkult* nor Art for Art's Sake! Constructivism is an aspect of Russian painting and sculpture, which imitates the ideoplastic (cerebral/useful) approach of the engineer while playing a game with any material that comes to hand; it therefore ranks far beneath the engineer's work, which is functional and educative. Let us not try to wield intellectual influence over the proletariat until we first appreciate our own déclassé status. Our duty is to work on the physical and physiological problems of nature and humanity; and we shall start where modern science leaves off—because it is not objective, because its sole concern is with exploitability, because it constantly assumes standpoints that pertain to an outworn form of civilization. We are to embark, without prejudice or preconception, on an approach to Nature that restores physics and physiology to their own true level, with a future classless society in mind, but without lapsing into utopianism, and in clear awareness of the work of demolition that needs to be carried out in the existing social sciences and their methods. We can do no more than prepare for the time of objective and positive construction, since we are unable, nor do we intend, to step outside the contingent nature of our own world.

In contradistinction to previous technologies and arts, our orientation toward the physiology of sense and the physics of form and function compels us to see that no area of human experience and work exists purely in its own right; each is bound up with a subconscious analysis of the organic deficiencies and functional inhibitions of

the human psychophysical organism. Once moved onto a conscious level, this exploration must represent a base level of approach and adjustment, with the purpose of
improving somatic functionality. Seen in this light, the machine is not a mere labor-
saving device; and art, as the only field of production in which the law of causality does
not apply—although the law of conservation of energy holds good—loses its character
of uselessness and abstractness. Man's universal functionality reorients all fields of
work in terms of the definitive influence of earth and atmosphere. From this, there
arises a dynamic view of Nature and a general expansion of all human functions; a
form of vision that casts off three-dimensionality as an auxiliary construct, a concession to human frailty—just as it dispenses with the notion of the inertia of all matter.
The common denominator of all our senses is our spatio-temporal sense. Language,
dance, and music were the supreme achievements of intuitive spatiotemporal functionality. Now, it is for optics, haptics, etc., to take over, moving along new paths.
Here, Ernst Marcus has done important pioneer work on the problem of eccentric
sensation. To a degree, the brain as the central organ uses one sense to complement
another; it perfects them all through a reciprocal reinforcement of vibration, where
frequency and amplitude values coincide in time. And here the dynamic perception
of Nature knows only a functional principle of time: time as the kinetic energy that
constitutes space and matter.

Translated by David Britt

THE DYNAMIC PRINCIPLE OF COSMIC CONSTRUCTION, AS RELATED
TO THE FUNCTIONAL SIGNIFICANCE OF CONSTRUCTIVE DESIGN
Alfréd Kemény
Originally published as "Das dynamische Prinzip in der Welt-konstruktion im
Zusammenhang mit der functionellen Bedeutung des konstruktiven Gestaltung,"
Der Sturm vol. 14, no. 4 (1923)

Cosmic construction is the product of dynamic contrasts between centrifugal and centripetal forces. The unity of the cosmos under law therefore rests on the strict coordination of the relations between the motions of bodies, wherein each component operates
in relation to cosmic motion. *Constructivity of the ambient dynamic combines the body
parts of the world into a dynamic cosmic construction.*
Every microcosmic part of the macrocosm rests on the same constructive laws of
dynamic oppositions as the macrocosm itself. Man, who in his own organic structure
functions in obedience to the laws of the dynamic-constructive cosmic system, is
therefore governed in the functioning of his organic apparatus by *the functional principle of the cosmic mechanism: motion.* That is to say, man is an apparatus that works in
accordance with kinetic and mechanical laws. The law of unity of the human organism—homologous to the unity of the cosmos—equally rests on strictly organized relationships between the motions of individual organs, whereby each organ functions in
relation to the unity of motion of the organism as a whole. The *constructivity of the
reciprocal dynamic combines the component parts of the human body into a dynamic
human construction.* Motion is the function of the cosmos as it is of man.
All human design and invention in the field of art, as in those of science, society, and
technology, has meaning primarily in relation to the functionality of the human organism.

Every piece of creative work actively observes new laws that expand the human organism's functional scope. Eliminating the force of inertia that causes the relevant organ of human perception to cling to old and outworn laws, it compels that organ to take an active grip on new and vital laws. The connection between the specific organ and the functionality of the whole organism means that the functional scope of that organism is expanded. For instance: new optical laws, manifested as color design, act primarily to expand the human organ of sight. New acoustic laws, as sound design, act primarily on the acoustic apparatus of the ear. Through the functional association between ear and eye—see Hausmann's *Optophonetics*—these stimulate each other, and through the functional integration of all the organs they stimulate the human organism as a whole. The aesthetic value of the work of creative design—and invention—is primarily that it relieves a sense of sensory inadequacy and thus enhances the possibilities of sensory function.

The need for metaphysics arises from the inadequacy of the human cognitive faculty, occasioned by the limited receptivity of the sensory apparatus. Thus, specific situations and connections in the real world that are impossible to apprehend empirically require to be explained—falsified—irrationally. The greater our empirical receptivity, the less need we have of metaphysics, and the closer we come to the condition in which the expansion of organic function will conduct human life to the point of supreme intensity.

Now to examine those new, active laws of constructive design in visual art that enrich the given functional conditions of the human organism. What form can we expect such an enrichment to take?

As we have seen, the constructive principle is one of the prime laws of cosmic and human structure. Constructivity, which rests on dynamic contrasts between contrary motions, is the composition—the reproduction of the construction—of Nature and man. Construction itself has only a secondary application in classical art. The destruction of classical art—of the classical reproductive construction—led to a neglect of the rigorous organizational principle of constructivity, derived from the functionality of the artwork. Only Cubism drew attention to this in its final phase—two-dimensional design of the image through contrast in the subdivision of the surface—but retained too many naturalistic elements. *The artistic movements after Cubism—Suprematism and Constructivism—were the first in visual art to stress the rigorous organization of human design: construction in creative work as a primary means of production and not as a secondary means of reproduction. All this in relation to the functionality of the artwork and the inner nature of the materials employed.* In the major works of Constructivism, the exact, skeletal, hard structure of the design sprang from the elementary contrasts within the means employed: color, form, material, light, space, and motion. In connection with the functionality—the constructive mobility—of the human organism, *the functional significance of constructive design in art is that it gives structure to vitality.* The rigorous assembly of powerful tensions generates the *potential energy of the static artwork*; within the psychophysical continuum of the viewer—despite the physical immobility of the work itself—this energy translates into an intense inner motion. The translation of potential energy within the artwork into intense psychic motion generates—in contrast to the decadence of bourgeois culture, with its concentration on subtle nuances and distinctions—the *primal consciousness of dynamic constructivity*: the sense of the firm and solid structuring of the dynamic law of opposites. This *is the supreme human sensation of forces*, whereby the world is experienced no longer in countless minuscule gradations but in the basic and most forceful antitheses of its dynamic dialectic. It may well be that the future of visual art lies in the powerful, physical spatial tensions generated by *kinetic force systems in physical motion* in real space: motion, the prime function of the Cosmos and of man, as applied to human formal design. Hitherto primarily a receptive viewer of artworks, man must be raised to a higher power and become the active factor in the creation of form. The static construction of art, stuck in a constructive aesthetic devoid of vitality, weakens man's constructive aspiration to a new and vital construction of life. When pursued into a dynamic-constructive system of forces, the constructivity of reciprocal physical motion assembles together the elements of mobile artistic design. *The potential energy of the hitherto physically immobile artwork, once transformed into kinetic energy, into real motion, will transmit that motion directly and compel man into the strongest deployment of his creative power.*

Translated by David Britt

ABSTRACT DESIGN FROM SUPREMATISM TO THE PRESENT
Alfréd Kemény
Originally published as "Die abstrakte Gestaltung vom Suprematismus bis heute," *Das Kunstblatt* no. 8 (1924)

We publish this introductory survey of the Suprematist movement without endorsing the individual value judgments contained therein.
[Original ed. note.]

The Cubists and the Futurists fought against the undue preponderance of Nature in visual art. Before them, Nature had reigned supreme in both painting and sculpture, so that visual art had been regarded as an illustrative, reproductive activity rather than as creative design. In their works, the Cubists and Futurists did not rest content with conveying the rule of law in the universe indirectly, through the superficial contingencies of a reproduced Nature. They also rejected the anarchy of confused emotions unfiltered by logic (it is an error to regard Futurism as a merely anarchic movement). They strove for a higher level of design: the direct formal expression of the known cosmic rule of law, in all its purity, primarily through elementary relationships. To this end, "Nature" in art—as conveyed through traditional, naturalistic, and perspectival (reproductive) form—must be transcended; as indeed must the atavism of a predominantly individualistic mentality.
To attain these ends, it was left for new designers to fight the battle to its conclusion. Malevich, creator of Suprematism; Tatlin, creator of Constructivism; Mondrian, creator of Neoplasticism; Lissitzky, creator of the Proun; Eggeling, inventor of the abstract cinema of motion; Richter; Péri; Rodchenko; the Russian Constructivist group Obmokhu; the Russian group Unovis; and the Dutch group De Stijl: these have emancipated art from Nature and psychopathology by creating abstract designs composed of elementary contrasts. *Elementary design derived from the elementary relationships between the elementary means of visual art—from elementary relationships of time, space, form, color, light, matter—is the logical outcome of their work. The relativity of the universe, the pure expression of which was obscured in earlier art by chance factors of Nature and emotion, finds full expression in their works, untroubled by accidental factors of nature or emotion.*
Relativism, elementariness, and the principle of economy—i.e., the pursuit of the simplest possible organization of the art object—are the common factors that link all these

otherwise contrasting impulses. Parallels with the theory of relativity in physics, and with the principle of economy in modern industrial production, are readily apparent. The contrasts within the new design are rooted in the East-West polarity: the antithesis between the social dynamism of Russia and the comparative social immobility of the West. This is why the new Russian design is predominantly dynamic, while the works of the new Western designers are predominantly static in nature. Even the most revolutionary abstract works of West European artists are conservative by comparison with achievements in Russia. The revolutionary element in West European art lies on a different plane. Those artists who operate on that plane do not embrace abstraction as a refuge from the reality of a decaying society. They make realistic works that unmask the decay of bourgeois society and fight against it for a better future. The major and most significant representatives of this art of creative political commitment are George Grosz, John Heartfield, Rudolf Schlichter, and Otto Dix.

In 1913 Malevich was the first artist in the East, and a few years later the Dutch artist Mondrian was the first in the West, to give suitable contemporary expression to the shift toward relativity, elementarism, and precision in modern art.

Malevich first used the square in 1913, and before long he moved on to the energy-relationships of "visible dynamic repose." The "force of statics" slices the square into elongated planar surfaces (which tend toward the condition of a straight line), so that it annuls its own existence as a self-contained two-dimensional figure: as a square.

Malevich painted the square—a black square on a square white ground—because it was the most economical and the most elementary form: essentially, as a symbol for the principle of economy in art. He used "economy in geometricism"—minimizing the number of forms—to concentrate design entirely on the universal. In the subsequent evolution of Suprematism, the square as an antagonistic form cancels itself out, distorted by the action of opposing forces: centrifugal (motion) and centripetal (the mutual gravitational attraction among forms). The outcome here is a relativistic absence of form in design.

Mondrian, too, uses the square as an antagonistic form, one that fulfills its function only in self-destruction. Using the square as the basis of his subdivision of the image plane, he achieves a relativistic formlessness of his own, albeit in a different way from Malevich. The square as form is wholly absorbed by the interrelationships between colors. *This self-fragmentation of form enshrines a significant dialectic of polarity. The image as self-contained form is abolished by its own simplest delimiting shape, and through this dialectical process it crosses over into the design of elementary relationships.*

Mondrian has carried the picture as two-dimensional design to its ultimate conclusion. Not as a self-contained form, however, but as a comparatively formless, relativistic design: a balanced summation of color relationships. Malevich, for his part, despite the planimetric structure of his works—which still remain pictures—has taken a bold step out of the picture into infinite, moving space.

With Mondrian, it all comes down to equilibrium, repose, and the equivalence between equally weighted parts. Supreme harmony. The aggression of harmony against the disharmony and chaos of present-day life. His paintings give off a deep, mineral note: a sound from those supernal regions of law where all conflict is stilled. Malevich's Suprematist designs, on the other hand, vibrate with the dynamism of mutually antagonistic planetary orbits. Man is wrenched off balance, challenged to fight for a better design for his own life.

In Malevich, the cosmic force-relationships that are translated into states of motion appear wholly immaterial. His colors accordingly have no material character. They are used "prismatically," as the element of light, and as the element of energy in motion.

What is essential is the antithesis between white and black, the archetypal contrast of energy between light and darkness. But the prismatic—apparently immaterial— treatment of colors, and also the planimetric/spatial structure of Suprematist design, corresponds to the essential function of light-motion. Comparatively speaking, light is the least material of all materials; it is matter in its purest energy-state. And so Malevich uses the motion of an airplane and the orbits of the planets to mark the transition to light-design. And there the threads of the polar dialectic of a unitary Time can once more be drawn together. In the West, abstract and elementary light-design was first materialized in the cinematographic designs made (in total ignorance of the work of the Russian Malevich) by Viking Eggeling and Hans Richter. In 1919, Malevich ceased to paint. In his last paintings, the colors are reduced to nuances of whitish gray. In them, he has reached the frontier of that undifferentiated state in which design as such ceases to exist. According to our viewpoint, we can regard this final period of Suprematism either as "point zero of art" or as an experimental attempt to generate nonrelative space, the frontier of "the Void," through a minimum of differentiation.

Lissitzky has transcended the primitive, planimetric structure of Suprematism. In his Prouns, he achieves new and specific formulations of a constructive and dynamic form of design. The forms are means to an end, sculpturally juxtaposed to create ever-new spatial tensions. The separation of the forms creates antithetical spaces. The same group configurations recur in a variety of projections and depths. This results in multiple spatial contrasts. By moving, "material forms" move space. The space of the *Proun* is unthinkable without the fourth dimension, which is motion. "The material form is designed according to its motion in space." With its extreme clarity, precision, and concentration, the *Proun* is built to transcend and implicitly to combat the repressions, obscurities, and confusions of present-day human life. Lissitzky describes his own work as follows:

"The Proun designer concentrates within himself all the elements of modern knowledge, all systems, and all methods; he designs *elements of plastic form* that stand there like the elements of Nature: like H (hydrogen), like O (oxygen), like S (sulfur). He combines these elements together and obtains acids that attack everything they touch: i.e., they produce their effect in every department of life. This may be a laboratory operation, but these are not scientific preparations, interesting and intelligible only to a small circle of specialists. They are living bodies, objects of a specific kind, whose effect cannot be measured with an ammeter or a manometer..."

"Constructivism" arose in Russia, by way of reaction against the exclusively immaterial and metaphysical emphasis of Suprematism, *as the art of the material culture of the age of technology*. Tatlin was the first to point to the specific—and previously unexploited— constructive possibilities that reside in the materials collectively and simultaneously present in everyday life (such as wood, iron, glass, wire, etc.) The different materials are put in relation to each other in ways that produce sharp contrasts. The objecthood and contrasting qualities of the materials used strongly emphasize the contrasts between the forms. Tatlin's Contre-reliefs abolish the element of volume, "contained space," previously regarded as the sole possible way of delimiting space. Relationships in space take the form of relationships in depth.

Tatlin's work has been described as "Machine Art." This is just as wrong as it would be to apply the term "Formalism" to Malevich, Mondrian, Lissitzky, or Péri. The spatial tensions in Tatlin's work derive from entirely new and powerful experiences of space. Which also explains why they are not some aesthetic game played with "beautiful" industrial materials.

The organizational problems of the period of construction in the Russian economy found essential "artistic" expression in the "constructive" works of the Obmokhu group: the spatial material constructions of Georgy Stenberg, Vladimir Stenberg, Medunetsky, and Ioganson. *These were the first Constructivists to take the step into real (physical) space.* You can touch their works as real objects—with specific forms and made of specific materials—in space. They subordinate all metaphysical problems of form and space to the rational problems of matter.

Among the artists of the "Left Front" in Russia, another outstanding figure is Rodchenko. His work, with its intense color and its painterly handling (use of different varnishes, different *factures*, etc.), occupies a distinguished position in "nonobjective" painting. In his linear constructions, Rodchenko was the first to use line as an abstract-painterly element.

In the West, alongside the works of Mondrian, exceptional importance attaches to the *abstract film creations of Eggeling and Hans Richter.* For the first time, these use time as a real—and not an illusory—element in visual art. In their earliest works, both subdivided time in ways that retained many elements of music. They took unambiguous design elements, such as horizontal, vertical, and diagonal lines and planes, and developed these inventively, after the manner of music, in all their many contrasting and "contrapuntal" possibilities. In these first motion designs, the specific kinetic—and light—functions of film are still far too much obscured by the development of form. Richter comes closer to the essence of film in his latest work in motion design.

Variations in the intensity of light, and contrasts of motion in space, give rise to entirely new, specific spatial functions of light moving in space: *the most elementary version of the unity of space, time, and matter.* This is the point from which we can expect the abstract kinetic design of the future to evolve: as kinetic design with the velocities of moving light, which shatter every form.

Among the new designers, the Hungarian artist Péri must also be mentioned. In his "spatial constructions," he has taken design as an element of the wall and as a component part of architecture. He has broken through the rectangular bounds of the easel picture; acutely asymmetrical in structure, his spatial designs set up strong contrasts with the flat surface of the wall. The passive banality of today's architectural interiors gives way to active force-relationships in space. This space-destroying and space-constructing function is the essential function of his works.

Translated by David Britt

PRAGUE   Hans Richter
Originally published as "Prag," *G* no. 3 (June 1924)

What one has to fight for in many large centers, and is scarcely there despite the fight, exists in Prague: a creatively active atmosphere. This atmosphere gives growth to a modern conviction, a collective working spirit and that activity which arises out of a "belief in life." The vivacity of a multitude of young artists is manifested in several journals, most strongly in the anthology *Život* (Life). I know of no illustrated book that would be timelier. Without the compelling continuity of a certain purposefulness—but convincing as photography from 1924. Karel Teige made the book in collaboration with his friends Seifert and Krejcar.

Karel Teige, americo-roman oriented, smart and sensitive, is occupied with the publication of an ever-growing number of periodicals. The title page for *Život* belongs to a series of "Picture Poems" of Teige's that—tired of the senselessness of easel painting—he has put in the context of the book as a reproduction technology. He and his comrades, periodicals, groups, and energies are absolutistly directed by the beautiful Toyen, native of Prague, with a command of the Czech language and who with only this language managed in Paris. Painter by profession, we have presented all of her pictures, which neither in their power nor refinement, are any less advanced than those of her male colleagues; this personal work—faultless in both form and content—which she has been kind enough to put at our disposal.

Translated by Timothy O. Benson

TOWARD CONSTRUCTIVISM   Hans Richter
Originally published as "An den Konstructivismus," *G* no. 3 (June 1924)

The word *Constructivism* originated in Russia. It refers to art that uses modern construction materials in place of conventional materials and that follows constructional goals. At the congress in Düsseldorf in May 1920, Doesburg, Lissitzky, and I took up the name Constructivism in a broader sense than the opposition. What is operating under that name today no longer has anything to do with elementary design, our dictate for the congress. The name *Constructivism* was taken up at that time as the watchword of those who sought rules for artistic expression and tasks that make sense for our time—opposed by a majority at that congress of individualists (see the report on the congress in *De Stijl* 5, no. 4).
Meanwhile the art market and oil painters have adopted the name, and the individualists, the deal-makers, the oil painters, the decorativists, and the speculators all now march under the name *Constructivism.*—As long as the slogan is fashionable.—It seems as if it may already be passé, at least the sprinter Moholy-Nagy, who has a sensitive nose for such things, has occasionally referred to himself as a Suprematist in *Das Kunstblatt*; perhaps he'll have more luck with that than with the Constructivists of yore.

Translated by David Britt

PHOTOGRAPHY IN REVERSE   Tristan Tzara
Originally published as "Die Photographie von der Kehrseite" in *G* no. 3 (June 1924)

No longer does the object reverse the extreme ends of its trajectory at the iris, projecting itself imperfectly onto the surface.
The photographer has invented a new technique: he confronts space with the image that bursts the bounds of space; and the air snatches it, head lowered and fingers clenched, to store in its inner recesses.
Around a bird an ellipse is to revolve—a cigarette case? Amidst the clatter of the ill-lubricated Moon, the photographic operator turns the spit of his reflections.

The light changes as the pupils contract on the cold paper, with its weight and the thrust that it generates. A limp frond from a tree is preparation for spangled layers and vigorous girandoles; it shines the torch of snowflakes into the vestibule of the heart. And what concerns us is as unreasoned and causeless as a cloud that overflows and spits on a path.

To come to the subject of art. Art, that's right. I used to know a gentleman who did superb portraits. The gentleman is a Kodak—You object: he lacks color and the subtlety of brushwork. Originally a weakness, this slight tremor assumed the name of sensibility to justify itself. Nevertheless, human imperfection seems to possess greater merit than mechanical precision. And still-lifes? I would like to know whether the hors-d'oeuvre, the hampers of game, and the desserts do not have some vivifying effect on us. I hear the rumble of a fuse snake, an electric ray pulls a wry face, and the whole dinner service smashes amid housewifely shrieks. Why are there no portraits of all that? Because it appeals to a channel that conveys a special kind of excitement to those who approach but never stimulates a response in the eye or in color.

Painters could see this. They sat around in a circle and dreamed up schemata for discomposition. And for construction, And for inversion. Schemata for comprehension and apprehension, for sale, reproduction, and museum conservation. Others followed suit, proclaiming amid enlightened protests that what the former group had done was cheap trash. They had their own wares to offer: an Impressionistic sketch, reduced to a commonplace but sweet symbol. I momentarily followed their idiotic, snow-cleansed voices, but soon realized that their trouble was nothing but sterile jealousy. They all ended up manufacturing English picture postcards. Having discovered Nietzsche, and sucked the marrow from the cadavers of their friends, they declared that the only subjects worth painting in oils are beautiful children, and that the best painting is the highest-priced. Well-groomed painting in golden frames.

Everything that bore the name of art had succumbed to paralysis; at which point the photographer lit his thousand-candlepower lamp, and gradually the light-sensitive paper absorbed the blackness of a few utilitarian objects. He had discovered the potential of a gentle flash, untouched by human hands, and more important than all the configurations on which we are invited to feast our eyes. The unique, correct, precise mechanical distortion is fixed. As smooth and pure as a lock of hair combed with light.

Is it a vortex of water or the tragic flash of a revolver, or an egg, a blinding arc or a dam for reason, a keen ear with a mineral whistle or a turbine made up of algebraic formulae? Just as the mirror effortlessly reflects the image, and the echo the voice—without asking why—henceforward the beauty of objects owes nothing to anyone, because it is a physical and chemical product.

Since the great inventions and tempests, all the impostures of sensibility, wisdom, and intelligence have been swept away at a stroke into the sack of the magic wind. The dealer in lighting values accepts the stablemen's challenge. The measure of oats that they dole out night and morning to the horses of modern art will not vitiate the passionate course of his solar and chess gambits.

Translated by David Britt

CONCRETE LIGHT Nikolaus Braun

Originally published as "Das konkrete Licht," in Braun and Arthur Segal, *Lichtprobleme der Bildende Kunst* (Berlin: 1925)

Art is the relative—i.e., the temporal—expression of our longing for the absolute. It is therefore always the summation of the state of knowledge in the age to which it belongs.

Life itself, in every part, is an ebb and flow of shifting views and insights: a constant struggle for temporal supremacy in accordance with the laws of action and reaction. In art, there is the same struggle for temporal supremacy between competing views. The three basic factors in optical art—color, form, and light—have always competed for primacy. If we follow the evolutionary progress of these three separate factors, we see that all three become increasingly conscious and are impelled toward concreteness.

By dissecting a beam of light into its constituent colors, the Neo-Impressionist discovered color as an end in itself. This prompted a joyous response to the pigment in the paint; and so material came into its own as a means of expression. Artists turned to concrete materials, such as wood, textiles, and metals, which they added to the surface of the image. The illusionistic reproduction of material thus became obsolete, and form in its turn tended to become concrete.

Now that Constructivist sculpture has made both form and color concrete, my idea is to add a third concrete element, that of light. I make my sculptures and light-reliefs with electric light as a concrete element, thus giving their forms a literal and intrinsic form of lighting. Previously, the artist who used any of these three factors in the most concrete way possible would have been compelled to sacrifice the other two; the inclusion of concrete light enables all three factors to work together harmoniously in a unified whole. Light is an eminently mobile, highly suggestive material with inexhaustible possibilities. Appropriate concrete lighting intensifies the sculptural and spatial effect of solid body and space. Light enables specific outlines or transitions to be dissolved or else sharply distinguished. Motion in light sculpture is generated by changes of lighting, which constantly vary the relationships of the elements of the image to each other and to the image as a whole. Equally, color can spring directly from light, in which case it appears dematerialized.

Translated by David Britt

chapter 8

INTERNATIONAL CONSTRUCTIVISM IN CENTRAL EUROPE

Éva Forgács

The elementary, geometric vocabulary of International Constructivism provided more than visualizations of a new, collective, and highly mechanized society. It also carried the hope that culture might be started anew, the past might be simply disregarded and discarded, and a whole new life and post-historical era could be initiated from a tabula rasa. (Such hopes echoed, if inadvertently, the vision captured by the 1913 Russian Futurist opera *Victory Over the Sun*.)

These ideas were attached to the idiom generally known as International Constructivism first of all by Central European artists, who were particularly keen on overcoming national and societal differences in order to fully realize their social and artistic avant-garde programs. They believed that the time for an all-European cultural cooperation including their emancipation to Western Europe had come. As Ernő Kállai phrased it in *New Painting in Hungary*, "It seemed that [International Constructivism] would fit immediately, without the detour of evolution through national traditions, into the overall artistic framework of the longed-for new, collective world. For artists coming from the uncertain peripheries of this emerging international Europe, this was bound to seem an extraordinary opportunity."

Artists worked hard to realize the idea of internationalism. In 1923 and 1924 major international art exhibitions were organized in Vilnius, Vienna, and Bucharest; the internationalism of the Bauhaus followed from the composition of its faculty and student body. Many avant-garde periodicals published multilingual international issues and gave detailed accounts of international art events.

Presenting the latest art as the product of a group of international artists was a particularly meaningful message in the Central European context. It meant the rejection of nationalism and faith in the new realities, as well as in an art that transcended borders and could open up new horizons of brotherhood and cooperation.

The history of Polish Constructivism began in Vilnius in 1923 with the Exhibition of New Art. Among the participants were Witold Kajruksztis (1890–1961), Karol Kryński (1900–1944), Mieczysław Szczuka (1898–1927), Władysław Strzemiński (1893–1952), and Teresa Żarnower (1895–1950). The catalogue, published on the occasion of the exhibition, was the first publication to present these artists as a group. In 1924 Henryk Berlewi (1894–1967) showed his abstract *Mechano-faktura* pictures in the Warsaw automobile salon of Austro-Daimler, accompanied by a brochure. The same year saw the publication of *Blok* and the exhibition of the Blok group—organized in the show-room of another automobile firm, Laurin and Clement—in which, along with the artists already mentioned, Katarzyna Kobro (1898–1951) and Henryk Stażewski (1894–1988) took part. *Blok* no. 6/7 (1924) published the group's manifesto "Co to jest konstruktywizm" ("What Constructivism Is"), codifying its main programmatic principles.

The Blok group and periodical, edited primarily by Szczuka and Żarnower, were formative institutions of Polish Constructivism. They were heavily influenced by their experience of Russian avant-garde artists, with whom some of the Blok artists had previously collaborated (for instance, Strzemiński and Kobro, when they lived in Russia). The periodical published brief theoretical articles by the Polish Constructivists of the mid-1920s (for example, Strzemiński's "B=2" and Szczuka's "Photomontage") and translations of texts by Theo van Doesburg, Mies van der Rohe, and Kurt Schwitters, as well as by Russian avant-garde artists such as Kazimir Malevich.

Altogether, during the two years of its existence, eleven issues of *Blok* were published. In 1926 the group split up. On one side were those, such as Mieczysław Szczuka, who regarded art as subservient to the needs of the new society: the working class and its political institutions, including the Communist Party. On the other side such artists as Katarzyna Kobro, Władysław Strzemiński, and Henryk Stażewski wanted autonomy for art, conceiving it as a platform for *generating* the needs of the new society. The latter artists, together with a group of architects including Szymon Syrkus (1893–1964), founded a new group and periodical, *Praesens*.

Translated by Wanda Kemp-Welch

MECHANO-FACTURE   Henryk Berlewi

Originally published as *Mechano-faktura* (Warsaw: 1924) and in *Der Sturm* vol. 15, no. 3 (1924)

Over the past fifteen years or so, painting has been reduced to its simplest elements and in the process a new factor has come to light and become dominant: this is facture. By which is meant: (1) the surface of the painting itself, comprising (a) the nature (direction) of the brushwork and the application of color (as paint mass), (b) the thickness or thinness of the paint layer, (c) the matte or lustrous finish, (d) the roughness or smoothness; and (2) the degree of intensity and density of the color, which partly depends on the material substance of the paint— the so-called patina. Everything, in short, that comprises the material aspect of painting.

Although the existence of facture dates from the very beginnings of painting, it has never received its due as a crucial contributory factor in determining the value of a work. Facture always existed outside the creative consciousness, without occupying the painter's mind. It was something secondary, ancillary, indispensable, but no more than that.

It has taken a major upheaval in the visual arts (Expressionism, Cubism, Futurism) to reveal the immense emotive possibilities that lie concealed in facture.

What is the emotive effect of facture?

The Russian theoretician of facture, Markov, explains it in his extremely important, albeit somewhat chaotic book, *Factor*, as a "sound" produced by the blend of different sense-impressions generated by the given facture of the object. Old paintings, such as icons (Russian images of saints), have a specific facture that creates in us a "sound" quite distinct from the "sounds" of other paintings, such as those of the Impressionists. The same writer ascribes an extraordinary significance to facture, extending its application to everything in the world around us, both organic and inorganic.

Neither Markov nor the other theoreticians define facture in other than material terms; in fact, they subscribe to a pure cult of material. Looking at facture in this light, French and above all Russian painters have carried out numerous interesting experiments. The exaltation of material, together with the laboratory investigation of its properties, reached its peak in Russia (Tatlin, Rodchenko). The outcome of all this research was that facture was emancipated from the pressure of other painterly factors and became an end in itself.

To enhance the effect of facture, artists used materials that had never previously been classed as painting media at all: newspaper clippings, cork, glass, sand, metal, and so forth. These materials, arranged on the picture in a clearly defined rhythm, created an unprecedentedly varied facture, to the utter bafflement of viewers accustomed only to the facture of naturalistic painting.

Inevitably, the juxtaposition of several inherently different materials with different facture qualities and different dimensionality modified the flat quality of the painting and transformed it into a bas-relief. This of course greatly intensified the emotional force of the facture (greater contrasts), but at the same time it transformed painting itself into a new art of "sculptopainting" (Archipenko).

Thanks to facture, painting thus moved closer to its original function; at the same time, it lost one of its specific properties, its two-dimensionality.

If this property is recognized as essential, then logically all three-dimensional (perspectival) illusionism, together with all true plasticity, must be viewed as a violation of the true nature of painting. And yet it is impossible to dismiss out of hand the tremendous works of facture that have been achieved through arduous experimentation in recent years. How are we to strike a balance?

A rigorous analysis of the facture effects of a range of materials (sand, glass, cork, newsprint, wood) leads me to the conclusion that these effects are not immediate. That is, these materials do not affect us in their own right but as bearers of a variety of facture combinations. The printed newspaper as such has a specific meaning for us: we can read it. As a facture element, on the other hand, it loses its utilitarian meaning altogether and transforms itself into a specific, typographic rhythm totally independent of the content of the printed letters. Again, glass as facture transforms itself into a "value," which, thanks to its smoothness and its luster possesses the utmost potential for creating contrast; sand becomes a grainy, dusty, flickering timbre; wood becomes an equivalent wood ornament (graining). There are numerous other examples of metamorphosis in facture.

By functioning as facture, materials lose their intrinsic meaning; in other words, they become dematerialized. Meaning attaches no longer to the materials as such but to their equivalents. By finding appropriate equivalents for materials—glass, sand, wood, and the rest—we can achieve a facture effect identical to the immediate effect of the facture of the material itself.

By consistently pursuing this principle of material equivalence, I have created a new and autonomous facture that is independent of materials and corresponds to the nature of two-dimensional painting.

Quite aside from the functional anomaly that is inherent in "material facture," because of its incompatibility with the two-dimensional nature of painting, it must be stressed that it is an anachronism in relation to the tasks that currently confront the visual arts. Material facture affords an immense variety of media—since of course there is no end to the possible materials. It has forced the painter to ponder incessantly over the mysteries that lie concealed within every material and has thus driven him to create ingenious, far-fetched combinations. Material facture has turned into a hotbed of individualism, subjectivism, and aesthetic over-refinement. In flat contradiction of the spirit of the age, simplicity and economy give way to excessive complexity, and clarity to confusion.

The results of the fetishistic cult of materials, as shown by countless experiments (for instance, those of Picasso and Braque in France, Schwitters and Baumeister in Germany, and the Valori Plastici group in Italy), are important and not to be ignored. These results must be properly assessed and employed in pursuit of new objectives. It is here that modern industrial technology comes to our aid.

Simply to find facture equivalents for all materials would confine painting to imitating the factures of objects, if not the objects themselves. Painting would then transform itself into a new kind of nonobjective Impressionism, a kind of illusionism. What is more, the result would be subjectivism and chaos, because in terms of facture there is no order whatever in the overwhelming profusion of materials that surrounds us. Aside from the anarchy that would afflict the work of the painter, the finding of such equivalents would be a laborious and complex undertaking that would leave us practically speaking no better off. We have therefore had to create equivalents that are not mere photographs, as it were, of the factures of individual materials but contain within themselves the synthesis of all those facture values that are so chaotically distributed through all the objects in the world around us.

To complete this work of organizing all facture values into a synthesis, in order to create a disciplined system of facture, it is necessary to adopt the schematic method. Schematicism is the only rational means of resolving all these confusions, the most economical means of reaching the goal. But, in this case, too, the technical means of painting must be changed to fit; they must be adapted to the requirements of the schema. The old technique of painting, which still lingers to this day, with all its traces of manual virtuosity—the contingent—and its dependence on the painter's momentary moods and whims, was perfectly matched to the requirements of the Impressionist-naturalist, individualist-subjectivist view of art. The tasks that now confront art may be approximately defined as follows: abandonment of all imitation of objects (although art nevertheless remains free), autonomy of form, discipline, a clarity that makes the artist's intention plain to every viewer, schematization, geometricization, a precision that aids every viewer to put in order the impressions received from the work. The old technique of painting is not up to this task. And this craft technique becomes still more impotent when it comes to the creation of a new facture system. Here, only a mechanistic technique can be used: derived from industrial technology, independent of individual whim, and supported by the precise functioning of the machine. Painting today, art today, must therefore be based on the principles of machine production. With the aid of the mechanization of facture, the mechanization of the expressive means of painting, an entirely new formal design system is founded. This applies not to painting alone but to every creative activity.

This does not, however, entail the automation of the creative process: far from it. Mechanization of the medium leads to greater freedom of creation, a greater scope for invention.

The old craft system of painting, with its ballast of prescriptive academic naturalism, curtailed the freedom of invention. It consumed a maximum of creative energy and squandered it on inessentials—on virtuosity.

Art must break all the habits of yesterday's perfumed, perverse, hypersensitive, hysterical, romantic, boudoir-bound, individualistic art. It must create a new language of form that is accessible to all and in unison with the rhythm of life.

Translated by David Britt

EDITORIAL STATEMENT   Editors of *Blok*
Originally published in *Blok* no. 1 (March 8, 1924)

We are finally doing away with the expression of personal moods, the mannerisms of opening one's heart, hitherto existing in modernist art.

Art must not be a manifestation of the artist's individualism, but the result of an effort by the collective in which the artist is the worker and inventor.

What the artist creates is to be the superstructure of all the efforts of his predecessors and his fellow artists of today.

Divergent and individualistic experiments must be replaced by relentless discipline and continuity of work based on the canons.

Instead of inspiration, aesthetic contemplation—a conscious, formative will demanding clear and rigorous forms.

The demands of contemporary life place the principle of economy in the forefront.

The principle of economy results in a great simplification of means—that is why the artist's handiwork is reduced to a minimum through mechanization.

Hand-made forms contain in themselves graphological deviations, characteristic of individual artists, but mechanical production gives complete objectivity to form.

The method of mechanization is directly in contact with technology.

Utilitarian considerations in production technology achieve results similar to those of aesthetic considerations.

We confront the problem of the *aesthetics of maximum economy*.

Translated by Wanda Kemp-Welch

UNTITLED STATEMENTS ON SUPREMATISM AND PAINTING
Henryk Stażewski
Orginally published in *Blok* no. 1 (March 8, 1924)

POST-SUPREMATISM
1. Complete rejection of dynamism (which is characteristic of Suprematism)
2. In Suprematism the background is a passive component of the pictorial construction; only shapes produce an effect—not the picture, but shapes. The absolute union of the background and shapes into one genuine whole is achieved by the Post-Suprematist picture.
3. Complete geometricism of shapes (applied in Suprematism to increase dynamism) cannot be applied to painterly ends. Geometricism connects shapes to the picture's boundary; anti-geometricism connects shapes with the background and with one another.

CONTRADICTIONS IN SUPREMATISM
The technique of planes connects the color plane with the pictorial plane.
The dynamism of planes throws the color plane out beyond the pictorial plane.
Abstract shapes are an attempt to create the work of pure painting—
a perfect form.
The literary character of dynamic painting imposes on it an aspect of cosmic metaphysics, the neglect of form, and overgrowth of literature.
The bankruptcy of Suprematism is the proof that dynamism is not a purely plastic phenomenon.

TOWARDS FLATNESS IN PAINTING
Impressionism, analyzing light came to the assertion: the human eye accommodates the visual world in the form of flat images. The [sense of] recession of planes (in space) in painting depends on the degree of saturation with the color blue. Cubism, analyzing the construction of the picture, transfers the three-dimensional visible world onto the two-dimensional picture using mutually penetrating and overlapping planes—giving unity to the painting phenomenon located within the picture frames. Suprematism finally breaks away from the deformation of nature. Flatness. Abstractionism and geometricism of forms resulting from the geometricism of the canvas on stretcher. A final solution to flatness and the statics of the picture is offered by Constructivism (when it deals with painting).
So-called applied art, flourishing in the time of the crafts, has been killed by the growth of technology, because the fast pace of life means that the production of utility objects places in the forefront: comfort, economy and speed [of production], instead of ornament as before.
A new notion of beauty is born—*the beauty of utilitarianism*.

In the whole life one senses the attempt to replace manual work with the machine. Precision. Ease. Speed.

The demand for portrait, landscape and historical painting, battle scenes, the illustration of everyday life etc. is now fulfilled by photography and cinema, both unrivalled in terms of precision, speed and low cost, compared with the work of artists formerly responding to these demands.

The development of photochemistry is eliminating former illustrative techniques, such as the woodcut etc.

In the place of the architect, digesting obsolete styles, there comes the engineer, constructing bridges, factories, mobile homes, skyscrapers, automobiles, railway carriages, ships, aeroplanes, docks.

Advertising demands the highest ingeniousness, expressiveness, succinctness, versatility, richness of means used, speed and constant innovation. What fascinated an hour ago, no longer interest anyone two hours later.

Radiophone and the gramophone multiply one concert a thousand-fold. However, the gramophone, surpassing all other music instruments by the richness of its means, seems to be still underrated.

Translated by Wanda Kemp-Welch

THESES ON NEW ART   Władisław Strzemiński
Originally published in *Blok* no. 2 (1924)

The artist, while creating, acts disinterestedly, without a pedagogical purpose. However, his work contains potentially pedagogical values: it shapes the style of the moment.

A modern work of art, whose construction is based on principles approaching the mathematical, has a positive effect on the discipline, coordination and mechanization, shaping the external appearance of objects produced. *Today's artists either create disinterestedly, in the sense of the new classicism of museum art* (the work of art as a thing in itself), *or move away from art to practical life bringing to it artistic achievements.*

Some artists, up till now occupied with the decoration of technical products, apply traditional forms to them. They disregard the fact that traditional forms do not fuse into an inseparable unity with the practical aspects of the object. The same mistake was made by the engineer, the technician, and, as a result, we see today automobiles in traditional form of horse-drawn carriage, or modern ships, perfectly designed from the technical point of view, but in an Empire style or with Renaissance interiors, applied indiscriminately.

The modern artist understands that such things are deplorable. One must not spoil the beauty of industrial products. They should not be completed by some artistic additions.

The Constructivist [artist] who begins to work in the manufacture as a technologist does not practice ornamental art. He rules it out and instead creates utilitarian objects, taking into account their purpose, their material and economy. In this way, he cleanses the technology of the remnants of traditional aesthetics and reveals the beauty of utilitarian objects—a new, universal type of beauty.

TWELVE THESES ON NEW ART

1. That which is legitimately called *new art* strives for perfection of plastic form.

2. In analyzing plastic arts we cannot apply a universal method of research, blurring the difference existing between plastic art and any other sphere of activity.

3. Perfection of the work of art must be the end in itself—not a cliché telling some narrative, experienced elsewhere and then to be traced and reflected in the work of art.
   Note: Neither should the work of plastic art be a narrative of the present day.
   Let the degree of its modernity be measured by the degree of its perfection, only attainable today.

4. Classical art has achieved a certain degree of perfection. Its further development was, however, thwarted by its literary tendencies, the principle of symmetry and the attachment to so called the "noble roundness of shapes."

5. The work of plastic art is to be build according to its own laws. Its model must not be the precision of photography, or samples of industrial product, or any other [external] object.

6. The work of plastic art expresses nothing. The work of art is not a sign of anything. It is (it exists) for itself.

7. The work of plastic art is an *organic, spatial phenomenon*.

8. Dynamism is a space-time action, therefore it does not belong to plastic art.

9. Present day art has gone beyond the so-called "new" movements: Cubism, Futurism, Suprematism—all based on the dynamic element.

10. Cubism, starting with a uniform system of contrasts, discovered and introduced the differentiation of textures and differentiation of shapes.

11. Formerly the organic work of art was to be achieved by imitating the organic shapes of nature or by copying Pythagorean hieromathematics (in decoration—the principle of geometry, Leonardo da Vinci's triangle, Tintoretto's diagonal). This could not be done. The laws of art cannot be reconciled with the laws of nature. *Either the logic of art, or the logic of the object.* The non-creative Pythagorean diagrams, not resulting from the essence of art but imposed on it in a violent manner, have been bankrupt since the time of Raphael's frescoes. The beginning of the slow death of principles of symmetry dates back to that time.

12. Deriving the work of art from modern technology, the artist is closer to his goal, since both are the products of human hands. But here the old literary-naturalist tradition ("the picture tells," "the picture expresses," "the picture reproduces") is to blame. Whereas, when the picture tells no story, expresses nothing, reproduces nothing—it is, it exists. The difference in purpose is blurred, and, as a result, so is the difference in the system of construction. The machine is an organic whole, having as its purpose perfect production process. As a whole it can be beautiful, although it does not strive to be. The work of art is an *organic visual whole*. As a whole it can be beautiful, although it also does not strive to be.

Translated by Wanda Kemp-Welch

AN ATTEMPT TO EXPLAIN THE MISUNDERSTANDINGS RELATED TO THE PUBLIC'S ATTITUDE TO NEW ART   Mieczysław Szczuka

Originally published as "Próba wyjaśnienia nieporozumień, wynikających ze stosunku publiczności do Nowej Sztuki," *Blok* no. 2 (1924)

Every new phenomenon finds people ill-equipped to receive it in the proper way. Depending on the category of the phenomenon, on the framework in which it occurs, and the degree of its influence in life, getting accustomed to and understand it as well as assuming a decisive attitude towards it, happens quickly or slowly, is easier or more difficult, with greater or lesser interest.

Familiarity with phenomena such as New Art occurs very slowly, with great difficulty and the interest of the public is not too great. One notes that especially the public that is interested in art, on the whole treats New Art with mistrust and bias.

This is for the following reasons:

1. Lack of aesthetic education (concerning both old art and contemporary art)
2. The urban dwellers' lack of contact with nature. Since contemporary man is detached from nature as a result of the development of cities, he passionately yearns for nature and mistakenly thinks that art can replace it.
3. Excessive, monotonous and routine work. Man has no time and desire to follow developments in art, so he demands sensations within the grasp of his mentality, sexual stimulation, and narration, but never plastic values.
4. The incommensurability of the development of science and technology and the democratization of their achievements. In their research science and technology, which have lately acquired a landmark significance par excellence, are ahead of the society's cognitive ability. Art as a superstructure of life, following its own line of development but at the same pace [as life's], is even more inaccessible and incomprehensible.
5. Liberation of plastic art from Suprematist naturalism, literary anecdote, and other accretions alien to its essence. At present, art restores and follows its own laws and in this way offers plastic values.
6. The laboratory working method and the qualities of this method in the work of art. The laboratory method results from a collective search for forms suited to the expression of new artistic principles with new means. The argument that laboratory experiment should not go beyond the artist's studio is wrong. Such work has been done always and everywhere. So, for instance, painters' problems with perspective and anatomy during the Cinquecento had the same character of laboratory research (which found its perfect expression only in the 16th century) and, nevertheless, were displayed on the walls of churches, palaces, etc.

New art will make its mark on the external appearance of the products of technology and of the building industry.

Thanks to this there will be a turning point in mass psychology, and there will be the demand for the work whose forms are being constructed today.

Translated by Wanda Kemp-Welch

WHAT CONSTRUCTIVISM IS   Editors of *Blok*

Originally published as "Co to jest konstruktywizm," *Blok* no. 6–7 (1924)

Constructivism does not aspire toward the creation of style as an immutable stereotype relying on previously invented and established forms; but it accepts the problem of CONSTRUCTION—which can and must give way to continual changes and improvements under the impact of those newer and even more complex demands that the general development of life presents us with.

1. It is NOT a separate branch of art (e.g., a picture or a line of verse), but art as a whole.
2. It is NOT an expression of its own particular experiences and moods, but a search for the PRACTICAL application of creative impulse.
3. It proceeds from the primordial instinct of art that is manifested in every product of man's labor.
    The CONSTRUCTION of a thing with the aid of all available means should set as its aim *first and foremost* the *practical* efficacy of the thing.
4. It does not mean that the program of Constructivism would eliminate disinterested creative activity in art.
    It is a SYSTEM of *methodological collective* work regulated by a conscious will; its aim is inventiveness and the perfection of the results of collective achievements in work.
5. The MECHANIZATION of the means of labor.
    Forms made by hand present graphological deviations characteristic of individual artists—form is given absolute objectivism when made by machine. (*Blok*, no. 1)
6. The ECONOMIC use of material.
    Only as much material is essentially needed.
7. DEPENDENCE of the character of the created object on the material used.
    Constructive values of material—character of the appearance of the material's surface—color of material—differences in features of the material's surface depending on the processing—peculiarities of the reaction of material to light.
    In its application to construction T. van Doesburg says the following on color as a property of material:
    "The new architecture makes use of color (and not painting), illuminates it, displays in it changes of form and space. Without color we would not be able to obtain the interplay of forms.
    "In the new architectonic style accurate optical balance and the equivalent integration of individual parts can be attained only with the help of color. The artist's task is to coordinate color and wholeness (in the sense of space and time, not of two dimensions).
    "At a later stage of development color can be replaced by reprocessed material (the task of chemistry).
    "Color (and may architects, the enemies of color, understand this) is not a decoration or applied art—it is an element similar to glass or iron, an organic growth from architecture." ("The Renewal of Architecture," *Blok* no. 5)
8. The CONSTRUCTION of an object according to *its own principles*.
    Constructivism does not imitate the machine but finds its parallel in the simplicity and logic of the machine.
9. The DISCIPLINE of harmony and order.
10. The problem of CONSTRUCTION and *not* the problem of *form*.
    Construction stipulates form.
    Form proceeds from construction.
11. The *use* of *technological* achievements for expanding the area of potentiality.

12. The direction of creative effort is primarily toward the *building—the cinema—printing*, etc. *the world of fashion*.
    Out of aesthetic considerations architects have very often ignored the problems of hygiene and comfort—the builders of constructivism accept them as problems of the first rank.
    The introduction of art into life on the principles of participation in general development and dependence on the changes arising in other branches of human creation:
13. First and foremost in technology.
14. The INSEPARABILTY OF THE PROBLEMS OF ART AND THE PROBLEMS OF SOCIETY.

Translated by John Bowlt

B=2 Władysław Strzemiński
Originally published as "B=2," *Blok* no. 8/9 (1924)

I.

To read:

Art = maximum creation

The academic law of abiding by the norms established by all the late authorities and respectables, the law of obedient and passive immobility, the conservative and static law (and thus a dead one) must be replaced by the command of

absolute creation.

Uncreative work, not departing from what has been—is not a work of art, even if all prescriptions of the masters that are dead (and respected by society because they are dead) have been carried out.

II.

Creation + system

The car factory of Ford: each worker performs only one sort of movement (division of labor): each car is gradually constructed by several thousands of workers, and each of them carries out a single function, most simple and strictly determined. Each worker does his portion of the work on the car for one minute (mechanization of labour). The machine transporting the car in production from one worker to the next, moves automatically every minute. In this way, every minute the factory turns out a car; which has passed through thousands of hands. Because of the economy of movements produced by the most strict division, simplification and mechanization of labor—the rate of production is the greatest possible. The task of the engineers controlling the sections into which the flow of work is divided, is to be inventive, to simplify the movements of each individual worker: to replace a few operations by one (by an appropriate change = improvement of machines). The result: a continuous creative effort. Creation can be supported on a pre-existing system, but for that reason it is continuously directed towards modification (= improvement).

III.

The Sunset of Europe

The cultural period, the end of which we are now observing (the Renaissance—Dante and the others), is a development of humanism. It has created a culture that is

individualistic–consumptive–sentimental–freedom-haunted–destructive. An organizational culture is coming: the construction of productivity: the micrometric process of
the productive organization of labor:

The artistic individualism of art during the era of humanism did not know how to work:
it started everything from A. In consequence, its result and its end was the beginning.
He is the excelling artist who steadily attempts to develop a system, who aims at
objective perfection: he tests and improves the system again and again. Such an effort
is beyond an individual's capacity; it requires collective endeavors. And thus: to undertake the work of one's predecessors; to investigate its assumptions; to mend the system
and to continue advancing, this is the way of creating true cultural values. While contemporary creation must base itself on previous efforts, it must take as its beginning
that point where everything that has already been done ends. Tradition is the raw
material that must be used for construction, which means that it must be transformed
into what it has never been. The further we go, the more faithful we are to tradition.

IV.

The direction of development of the visual arts in the second half of the 19th and in the
20th century can be summarized:

    to create a work of art as an organic plastic entity. This is the net result of many
    particular tendencies.

V.

    by no other art: indeed, by no other means can be expressed
plastic feeling =
    what is felt in the plastic arts only and no-
    where else (the next division: painting, sculpture and others)
we can apprehend it by a number of comparisons:

the feeling of painting	←→	the literary feeling
the feeling of painting	←→	the musical feeling
a painting	←→	a natural object
a sculpture	←→	a mystical treatise.

Such oppositions will make easier the elimination of alien elements and the definition
of the concept of plastic feeling. The common trail of contemporary art leads to one
end: a plastic organism. So we are pursuing the highest concentration: the plastic
feeling elevated to the rank of self-sufficiency. The natural lists started along this way
by establishing the principle of visual self-sufficiency and by making the plastic arts
free of literary influences (visionary sentimentalism), but they are wrong when they
speak about identity in the sphere of objects.

VI.

A form of existence produces a form of consciousness. An appearance of a new form
creates a new content. *Therefore form is value.*
Content does not produce form; it cannot turn out a uniform system. To cover imitation,
a different literary and object content is introduced, but since the form remains the
same, then also the plastic feeling determined by the system of apprehension and
arrangement of forms remains unchanged. The efforts are vain and such a work of art
fails to contain anything creative or new. It is a failure.

TOTALITY AND UNITY OF A WORK OF ART

VII.

It should not be an unfinished unity, or containing anything beyond such unity. The
plastic ac tion must be located within the limits of a work of art, i.e,

1) the whole plastic action is contained within the given work of art;
2) only one action is present, rather than two or more. Thus all non-constructlonal or chaotic artefacts are banished from the domain of art.

VIII.

A unity of assumption: a uniform system of selection and connection of all parts.

IX.

The worn-out phrase announcing the "deconstruction of impressionism" marks the speakers' lack of culture and understanding of plastic values. What is the aim of construction? To attain unity. In Cubism, the unity was attained through an equilibrium in the collision of forms. In Futurism, the same dynamic tension was spread thoughout the whole picture. Impressionism connects the disorder of the graphic and spatial forms through an identical tension of color. I think that this way: indifference towards the graphic and sculptural elements and the thrusting of the element of color into the foreground is no less good in painting.

X.

(a Gypsy stole a horse and repainted it to avoid recognition)
The way of French Cubism: to perfect the form and at the same time to conceal an object in it. At the first glance, a perfect form is seen, but when the eye perceives the object, the attraction of form perishes: what remains, is very skilful acrobatics and the search for hiding places. And to follow tracks is a hunter's job. The expressionistic "Murder in the Rue Morgue" committed against form in the Cubist-futuristic sense, a powerful thrill (perhaps no less than in detective stories); but would it not be better to write a detective story where one is permitted to describe more precisely the moods and events before and after the murder?
In both cases, alien elements are absorbed into plastic art: external objects, literary motives, psychologism. A work of art contains in itself a plastic feeling (as a result of the working of forms) + non-plastic feelings: the totality and unity of the work are exploded from within (2 simultaneous principles).
It is time for plastic art to resort to its own means.

XI.

A real autonomous existence in the plastic arts: when a work of art is plastically self-sufficient; when it constitutes an end in itself and does not look for its justification to values that subsist beyond the picture.
An item of pure art, built in accordance with its own principles, stands up beside the other worldly organisms as a parallel entity, as a real being, for everything has its own laws of construction of its body. When we build one thing we cannot do it according to the laws and principles belonging to another thing.
The law of organic painting requires: *the greatest possible union of forms with the plane of the picture.*
1) A union in a direction perpendicular to the plane of the picture, i.e. the flatness of forms: a picture as a plane.
2) A union within the plane of the picture itself: a form ought to grow out from the picture, be directly connected with it: if form flutters and tends to fall out; if it grows from, but is as if fastened to the plane of the picture, against its nature, wishes and intentions, then we know that the picture is one thing and the form is another:
3) The whole picture as a single integral plane works at the same time. Forms should not be active by themselves independent from the whole picture, for then we have got a portrait of forms in an organic whole, but no unity of forms with the background.

It is commonly known that Suprematism is one of the directions of non-figurative painting. Almost all know that a Suprematist picture consists of flat geometrical forms painted on a background which is white.

Those who have some feeling for plastic values know that Suprematism bestows its forms with a capacity for autonomous existence, independent from other forms; and that it establishes a system of cooperation of forms as a substitute for the Cubist opposition. Very few know that the principle of Suprematism is the law of economy and of the greatest development of dynamism. It was for the sake of dynamism that every form was taken to its sharpest logical conclusions. Thus the working of the whole picture is what replaces the Cubist principle of the dynamism of forms, whatever the picture.

The last effort of Suprematism was: to reconcile dynamism with the organicity of a picture. Since: if the task is to give the forms a dynamic expression, the colours are unnecessary and their origin is groundless aestheticism; then: the next to last period in Suprematism was black Suprematism on a white background.

But:

> The contraction of the form
> and background and the heterogeneity
> of the picture

The effect of dynamism
The consequent elimination of colors
—can lead logically to a single color—

compels one to take the last step—to white Suprematism (white forms against white background: the visual difference caused by the difference in surface).

An exercise: straight lined geometrical shapes, essentially conspicuous in the picture —should be connected by means of color. The same color tension for the forms and background. An exercise in colorism!

XIII.

Formerly (Renaissance, Baroque), all the forms in a picture were conglomerated into a triangle, square or circle and placed in center of a picture. Such a figure gave an appearance of construction. The construction did not grow out from the picture, but it was fastened to it in a manner incompatible with its essence. This was called geometrism of structure.

The Cubists introduced the vertical or the diagonal as the basis of construction. The forms that piled up had to be adjusted to the picture, but their rhythm was dependent on the direction of the structure. A picture required more creativity and offered more cohesion than had formerly been possible. But an axis of construction is also an acciden-tal phenomenon pulled from outside. A further step, made by Malevich (Suprematism): a form existing all by itself; growing out from the picture towards the onlooker (the forms of Cubism and Futurism used to grow towards the canvas: they were gliding and for that reason they were not sufficiently united with the picture). So it was in the first and most simple Suprematist paintings. But as the dynamic tendencies developed, forms began to glide on the canvas.

XIV.

Shapes as natural as nature—said Malevich about the deepest assumption of Suprematism.
Universal cosmic shapes as the sign and shape of universal cosmic dynamism.
The fault of Suprematism was that attempting to discover the laws of cosmic organicity,

it overlooked the fact that it was creating its own shape in dependence on the environment which it wanted to overcome.

Suprematism did not define the concept of a shape in painting; its basic shapes result from the categories of spatial (not plastic) thinking, and thus they are the same that exist in the science of spatial cognition, i. e. in geomet~ rather than in the science of painterly endeavor.

The fault of Suprematism was that it applied a universal method of research to the analysis of the field of the plastic arts and in this manner it blurred the difference between art and technology, art and astronomy, art and the hieromathematics of Pythagoras.

It is impossible and vain to speak about shapes in general: each shape becomes adjusted to an end. And thus:

1) What are the tasks of a plastic shape?
2) How should it be shaped to be as natural as nature?

XV.

Every form must be adjusted:
a) to the limits of the picture
—by its shape
b) to the background of the picture
—by its shape and color:

We perceive, how strange and discordant an impression is made by a non-straight form next to the edge of a straight-lined picture, or a straight-lined form next to the edge of a straight-lined picture, or a straight-lined form next to the edge of a round picture.

 1   2

A certain straightness of forms is the result of the straightness of the limits/stretcher —the picture must agree with its limits, introduced into them (fig. II).

We are facing the challenge of balancing these two factors.

The task which is solved by means of color by white Suprematism, ought to be solved by both color and form. We are no longer impressionists!

XVI.

The use of proper also means implies the elimination of time.

(Time is non-plastic element, characteristic for other arts: literature, music.)

Not the action of one form towards another; but a *COMPLETE SIMULTANEITY OF THE PHENOMENON.*

Examples:

1) mutual influence of forms (clashes that make for balance)—in Cubism. Looking at a Cubist picture, we must decipher what every form does to the others (predominant movements, weaker movements, hampered movements, almost nonexistent movements, static points) and at last become aware of the emergent system of equilibrium.

   The basic feature of Cubism is not only its multiple dynamism of forms (dynamism = form x space x time), but also the time it takes to feel and decipher Cubist-expressions contained in a given Cubist work. The underlying cause is that the notion of time (the period of incubation of a picture) has been included in the program of a picture. The relationship between the beholder and the picture is similar to that between a reader and his book.

   The concept of an activity is related to the concept of time.

2) Futurism assumes as its objective: to embody a certain length of time (a few moments of an object's motion) in the given work, by opposing one moment of motion against all the others (this principle is naturalistic and object-directed, rather than plastic). Cubist-futuristic interactions of forms, even if only potential, entail the notion of a certain span of time which is necessary for their completion, and thus they are not a plastic phenomenon: for time plays an essential part in other branches of art.

XVII.

The position of Suprematism is different: an attempt at a compromise between dynamism and pure painting based upon painterly values:
There are a number of autonomous forms, connected by common dynamic action.
Every form has its proper place and thus stands on canvas in its own strength (in Cubism—because it leans against other forms).

Autonomous existence of form growing out from the picture and connected with it as lightly as possible it can only be reconciled with dynamism, which has drive and a change of place as its essence, under the sole condition of reducing the period of time to 0 (a single moment in motion: a concept from mechanics) i. e., the form is established in conditions of the utmost fusion with the picture: dynamism exists potentially, by indicating the direction of motion.
Here lies contradiction: the compromise:
—either the form will merge completely with the picture, from which it will derive its static existence—or else, it will fallout from the picture and then, the whole picture is no good, for there is only a dynamic form that is left.
The concept of static as huge, strongly loaded weights that cannot be moved—I consider as no less dynamic: a dynamism arising from the force of pressure of weight, combined with the strength of resistance is easy to discover:
Malevich, better than anyone, felt the impossibility of a plastic dynamism, the fallacy of the principle itself, but he did not renounce it; he was too deeply stuck in the futurist superstitions. Therefore he created the most plastic form of dynamism.
A line—the power of the Futurists, is in its continuation thrust away from a picture.
A surface: the form of the greatest cohesion with a picture. This entails the selection of raw material in Suprematism. And the effects of dynamism are: too many slanting directions and giving up of the idea of a picture as an organic unit closed in itself.
Inasmuch as dynamism is an objective, painting is a subordinate thing (a means).
Since dynamism is not a purely painterly element, for time is its constituent part, its ultimate result is a renouncing of painting in favor of non-painterly objectives.

XVIII.

A picture should not be an interaction of forms, but a simultaneous phenomenon.
The basic law of absolute painting is *a rejection of dynamism* the deepest essence of the former period, that of Cubism and Futurism.
The avoiding of the interaction of forms, *so-called mutual neutrality of forms.*
Not the associative and material color of the Cubists and old masters; not the emotional hue of the Impressionists; not color as a sign of Suprematist energy—but color in its essence.

Translation from Vision and Unity

International Constructivism in Central Europe   Poland

PHOTOMONTAGE   Mieczysław Szczuka
Originally published as "Fotomontaż" in *Blok* no. 8/9, 1924

PHOTOMONTAGE = the most condensed form of poetry
PHOTOMONTAGE = PLASTIC-POETRY
PHOTOMONTAGE results in phenomenon of mutual penetration of most varied phe-
nomena occurring in the universe
PHOTOMONTAGE—objectivism of forms
CINEMA—is multiplicity of phenomena lasting in time
PHOTOMONTAGE—is a simultaneous multiplicity of phenomena
PHOTOMONTAGE—mutual penetration of two and three-dimensionality
PHOTOMONTAGE—widens the range of possible means: allows the utilization of those
phenomena which are inaccessible to the human eye, and which can be seized on a
photosensitive paper.
PHOTOMONTAGE—the modern epics

Translated by Wanda Kemp-Welch

ON ABSTRACT ART   Henryk Stażewski
Originally published as "O sztuce abstrakcyjnej" in *Blok* no. 8/9 (1924)

Abstraction is the result of extensive research.
Abstract art is not something detached from the world of external reality; however,
it ceases to be a descriptive art and instead employs purely plastic means. It is the
plastic equivalent of nature.
The more we eliminate the representation of objects, the closer we approach pure
plastic art. The new plastic art does not, because of abstraction, become a decoration,
since its goal is the picture, subordinated to its own strictly defined laws.
The new spirit reveals ever-newer laws governing the universe; it creates a new
reality.
To show the essence of things is beyond our grasp. The only goal of the new plastic
art is to express the laws which govern things and being.
Such a plastic art is a reality and it is not devoid of the human component.
The new plastic art attempts to capture a proper sense, it discovers ever-newer visual
laws: the deformation of objects through the invasion of the environment (Cubist
dynamism). Non-objective plastic art subordinates itself more to the law of the picture:
flatness and the rectangular shape of the canvas influence the forms placed on it. Pure
plastic expression is threatened by individualism.
Individualism disturbs the equilibrium between man and the universe, that is, between
what we call the internal and the external.

Translated by Wanda Kemp-Welch

In 1922, Ljubomir Micić traveled to Munich and Berlin, where he was influenced by artists of Der Sturm as well as the Russian avant-garde, particularly El Lissitzky and Ilya Ehrenburg's variant of Constructivism as represented in their journal *Veshch/Gegenstand/Objet*. Zenithist Jo Klek (born Josip Seissel, 1903–1987) was influenced by sculptural elements of the Russian Constructivitsts and Suprematists such as Lissitzky and Kazimir Malevich, as evidenced in his collages, photomontages, and other projects that he combined with the programmatic ideas of Zenithism. Similarly, Mihailo S. Petrov (1902–1983), a professor at the University of Belgrade who was among the first Yugoslav visual artists to hold radically new views, contributed circular and linear forms using a compass and a ruler, reminiscent of Alexander Rodchenko's work.

The echoes of Constructivism and "production art" also left traces in the newer Zenithist manifestos, prose, and poetry. In his programmatic text "The Categorical Imperative of the Zenithist School of Poetry" (1922), Micić stated that a poem needs to be a construction, referring not only to Constructivism, but also to destabilizing the emotional effects of poetry. He also used "object"—a term introduced by the artistic theories of the Productivists, and made the term a fundamental component of poetry. In his prose work "Shimmy on the Latin Quarter Graveyard" (*Zenit* vol. 2, no. 12) he utilized a plotless prose montage, which he termed a "radio-film."

In 1923, Micić moved to Belgrade, where he organized *Zenit* events and lectures as well as the First Zenit International Exhibition of New Art in 1924. Additionally, he published "anti-European" poems and publications throughout the same period, and participated in the Yugoslav wing of the 1926 Exhibition of Revolutionary Art of the West in Moscow. The Zenithist program became even more explicitly leftist, and finally at the end of 1926 *Zenit* was censored after Micić (under the pen name Dr. M. Rasinov) published "Zenithism through the Prism of Marxism" (*Zenit* vol. 6, no. 43). Micić fled to the Croatian port city of Rijeka (then Fiume, under Italy), where he was arrested on December 17. Upon F. T. Marinetti's intervention, he was released on January 14, 1927, and relocated to Paris, where he continued to write (though declining to resume publication of *Zenit*). Micić returned to Yugoslavia in 1936; his brother Branko Ve Poljanski (who also moved to Paris in 1927) remained in France until his death in 1947.

Translated by Maja Starčević

A Zenithist Radio-Film in 17 Acts

A field near St. Petersburg. Tatlin's monument reaches up to cloud-bergs. On its top is a Radio Center + 400m. Devouring a deluge of impulses from Asia Europe the Balkans America China and Japan. A sharp electricity conductor sports the head of an eternally vital bourgeois. Network: MOSCOW–Petersburg–Tokyo–Peking–Bombay–Constantinople–Alexandria–Belgrade–Zagreb–Milan–Prague–Warsaw–Riga–Berlin–London–New York–PARIS.
Orient airplanes ready to rush to all the continents of the Globe. Radio stations controlled by Zenithists. The Tatlin radio-center receives
THE LATEST NEWS

I. ELECTRIC CONDUCTOR TO THE LEFT!
Petrograd, February 1. Use all your strength to pull the nineteentwentyfirst bow! Deadly buzzing heard around the Winter Palace. Turn the electric conductor more to the left! Do not rise when the *Marseillaise* is playing. The Russian Revolution is old hat to us. Roll up your sleeves! *Man-Machine*: NEW ARCHITECTURE! More to the left!...
Vladimir Tatlin

II. CHREZVYCHAIKA ABOLISHED, PEACE CONFERENCE TO BE HELD IN GENOA.
Moscow, February 1. Yes! To reach the clouds with airplanes, to raise a revolution of all poets, and to find NEW FORMS, the Russian *Chrezvychaika* [Secret Police] has been abolished. All Russian poets are to be Futurists. This is what life and honor of the Soviet Russia demand in Genoa. Lenin does not ride in motor cars and will not therefore attend the conference. Lunacharsky hates the Imagists since he wears an English suit and French gloves. "To the left! Move the conductor to the left!
Vladimir Mayakovsky

III. THE MIKADO HAS A YELLOW BILL
Tokyo, February 1. German books printed on Japanese paper are quite affordable. KOKORO–KOKORO–KOKORO =
HEART. Little Hototogizu's heart was broken because she hasn't seen Ljubomir MICIĆ and his wife's pretty Japanese feet.
　　"Hito koe wa
　　Tsuki ga naita ka
　　Ho-to-to-gi-su"
　　(Poor lonely voice! Did the moon call? It was only Hototogizu.)
The Mikado has a yellow bill. His incisor hurts from pecking on Eastern Siberia. Japanese sun umbrellas are on their way to Paris to protect French geniuses from the sun's arsphenamine. NEW SPIRIT. Geishas too are on their way as crossless sisters of mercy.
Kamakura. Oi! Mate!*
Kyo-to

(* Hey! Wait!)

IV. NEGRO GIRLS ARE AS SWEET AS HAWTHORN FRUIT
Peking, February 1. No! No! We don't care for Europe anymore. The Great Wall of China is secure. Cannons made of Japanese bamboo are spitting fire. Buddha's signs

are being erased from foreheads because they resemble crosses. Here too people realize that Jesus Christ plagiarized Indian philosophy. Certain WHITES are being eaten like lamb. Mount Everest is Indochina's great pride. Negro girls are as sweet as hawthorn fruit. Only the Himalayas give birth to blue birds, only the Himalayas.

King Ping

V. APPARITIONS AND GHOSTS FEED MY BONES

Bombay, February 1. I, a descendent of Caligari and Indian fakhirs, I do not swallow flames, but I do dance to the all-human tragedy on a timely canvas. Apparitions and ghosts feed my bones. HYPNOSIS. Magic. The occult. Film. NEW STYLE. Suggestion— new rhythm. I am a Cesare Sleepwalker. I believe in Zenithism. Do not shout or I will fall! I will dance in the moonlight atop the Tatlin monument. To rise and not to fall!

Conrad Fight

VI. PRUSSIAN OFFICER'S BODY FOUND IN SULTAN MEHMED'S STOMACH

Istambul, February 1. Pierre Loti is living under harem skirts, his sailor hats hanging from the Hagia Sophia. Newspaper vendors are rabidly growling at capital letters R. F. and shouting "ZENIT." The Dardanelles are vomiting the mines they once devoured as well as torpedoes dating back to 5916. So instead of the shark that bit Lady Morgan's left tit and the back of her right knee under water as she was on her way to help Serbia, my projectionist is now extracting a Prussian officer's body from Sultan Mehmed's stomach. I film the comedy. I took off from London because I was liable to laugh in their faces. Lloyd George has taken it upon himself to save Europe in Genoa. Red seagulls pecking.

> THE KINGTOWN OF ENGLAND
> THE IDLE CLASS

New orientragicomedy of an American Zenithist. NEW FILM in 17 acts. Price $1,000,000. The Hagia Sophia leans to the left today.

Charles Chaplin

VII. IMPORT OF SAHARA'S DUST AND EGYPTIAN NIGHT TO THE BALKAN PENINSULA

Alexandria, February 1. An Egyptian pyramid's Sphinx is not our grief. Zenith is the NEW GOD. My eyes are filled with the Sahara's dust and the Egyptian night, and I'm on my way to the Balkans. Long live Zenithism!

Nina-Naj

VIII. THREE SHELL-STRICKEN HATS SINGING

Belgrade, February 1. The king is getting married. Avala is taking care of the tomb of the "unknown" soldier. The cross is stuck right in his heart. In his heart! Raiders were strictly forbidden to enter Europe lest they disturb the "eternally independent Croat state." The Vidovdan Constitution does not allow for Zenithism since Zenithism excludes Prince Marko and the Latins and extols Russia. Moscow is mentioned reluctantly and with a sour face and only in the National Parliament, without the Croat lobby's approval. The Minister's Cabinet forbids the BALKANIZATION OF EUROPE and threatens the death penalty on the same gallows and with the same rope once sullied by the

> UNKNOWN BALKAN MAN

on his way to the eternal Albanian Tragedy. The Minister of Education is trying to prevent the creation of a constructive Balkan civilization. "A pearl branch fell from the lilac," as the folk song has it. Get outta here! I am the first Zenithist painter. Three shell-struck hats are singing another song: "Take it to the left…"

Mih. S. Petrov

IX. SHIMMY IN THE LATIN QUARTER GRAVEYARD

Zagreb, February 1. Shimmy! Shimmy! Shimmy! An old, wax-and-powder-encrusted corpse reeks. People only in pockets. Poets handcuffed by editorial good opinion. Nude women in champagne glasses. Shimmy! Shimmy! Shimmy! The whole city is shimmied out. All the faces—masks. All the streets—banks. Prince Carnival is always alive. "Ah, Shimmy," central fans chatter through transparent skirt slips. "Oh, Shimmy," tight trousers of black marketeers and speculators croak. "Ooh, Shimmy", is the height of European civilization. (Zagreb is in Europe TOO.) While Russia starves, Europe shimmies. Hey, Balkan man! Spit fire *in their eyes!—Oh, those were the times when you could take a respectful peek under the tails of Austro-Hungarian mares!* Those were the times when we were an *Austrogarage*. I propose to the Yugoslav Academy that the zoological name of the cockroach be changed from

PERIPLANETA ORIENTALIS

to

PERIPLANETA OCCIDENTALIS.

The Latins called the cockroach "eastern" because they hated us.
GYPSY BOY, PLAY ON DAMMIT!

Ljubomir Micić

X. ITALIAN CHAUVINISM

Milan, February 1. Only Italians can be Futurists!

F.T. Marinetti

XI. CZECH CUBISTS STILL IMITATING THE FRENCH

Prague, February 1. The Žižkov Group is storming St. Wenceslas' monument. Czech Cubists are still imitating the French.
    "DEVĚTSIL"
renounces the president of the Czechoslovak Republic because he refuses to listen to Radio Tatlin. ZENITHISM! DANGER—POISON! Nazdar!

Karel Teige

XII. ALL THOSE WHO ARE NOT ZENITHISTS TO BE LASSOED

Warsaw, February 1. An expedition to the NORTH POLE OF THE SPIRIT is underway. We have yet to find a means of destroying all the Earth's idiots. Polish blood is not exactly milk, but it isn't water either. Helen has a Balkan temperament. Do only IDIOTS have blue blood and dance the shimmy? All those who are not Zenithists should be lassoed! Hrmph, those silly bastards! Don't they know that all Zenithists are geniuses? Lasso evvvverybody!

Valerium Poljanski

XIII. SUSPENSION BRIDGE TO CONNECT VLADIVOSTOK AND ODESSA

Riga, February 1. Construction! All Brian's dogs cannot fit into the Pasteur Institute. Realization! Erect another thousand cubist sculptures immediately. WE WILL BE VICTORIOUS OVER EUROPE without Genoa's help. We must surpass the new American star—and quickly! Build a suspension bridge to connect Vladivostok and Odessa. Geometry! Central elevation: MOSCOW. Western Europe has gone crazy over Charlie Chaplin, whom they love more than Lenin. *Khorosho!* All cinemas: The Third International! NEW ART: leftist—ours, *Zenithist!* Controlled by rebels who love Mother Russia. Old Europe dances the shimmy to the dropping point. As I say, I am the teaching of the Lord: *EPPURE SI MUOVE!*

Ilya Ehrenburg

XIV. EUCALYPTUS–MENTHOLS WITH BEER AND TOBACCO

Berlin, February 1. Germans feed on war pâté and museums. (Oh, the red salt of Spartacus!) STINES is the legal descendent of Kaiser Wilhelm II and is persecuting me, the first Dada-soph, because I am of Slav origin and an anti-pufkeist. We have erected an anti-Dada cabaret on the heads of Prussian Junkers, and we are spinning a Presentism No. 8998 merry-go-round. Eucalyptus–Menthols with beer and tobacco. Take ten to twelve daily.

Raoul Hausmann

XV. HERERO TRIBE SISTERS

London, February 1. I couldn't care less about the New World. Come, dear Herero tribe sisters! Suffragettes are the latest TREND in England. Ivan Goll is the greatest poet in Western Europe! Boo! Boo! Boo!

Claire Goll

XVI. FROGS CROAKING CANNOT BE HEARD

New York, February 1. Tohuvabohu! Dada anonymous. Eight hundred tons every-hourly high-rising. Frog-croaking cannot be heard. (Slavonia, dammit!) Hundreds of hydro-planes salt-sea air-flight height eighty floors. I live in an elevatormobile high-up-bed. Five hundred automobiles over my head bone-cracking no-mercy. America lock sky-scrapers wide-mind SELF-SHIP. (Slavonia, up with your skirt! Lie down, giiiiiiiiirl!) Jazz band Zenithist music. Thirty-six soda-bottles—Bruit. Proletcult nice pointed shoo shoo shoo shoes Miss Mary has. The man is crazy. Marymerymorymurymyriad.

Dragan Aleksić

XVII. BACKLESS DRESSES AND VERA SHAW SHOES

Paris, February 1.Hey you barbarians. Zenith–Box–Match. We suck your PRE-BLOOD. Come. Walk over the height of the sexus civilization in fashionable dance halls. Backless dresses and Vera Shaw shoes are first-class Parisian products. The foxtrot- shimmy is danced here. In the Louvre. PARIS IS BURNING. I travel across the Balkans tomorrow. Hooray! Hooray! Hooray!

Ivan Goll

FIRST ZENITHIST CONGRESS TO BE HELD AT RODCHENKO'S KIOSK

All Zenithists except Marinetti are to meet TOMORROW at Rodchenko's Kiosk in Moscow for the First Zenithist Congress. There will be joyful funeral masses for the peace of the dearly departed at the largest graveyard in the Latin Quarter. The incredible Charlie Chaplin and Conrad Fight will star in the Zenithist Radio Film in Seventeen Acts. Entrance free to all under sixteen years of age. Beginning at high noon—not in the morning or in the afternoon. Music by the Zenithist BANDERIUM. Tickets available at all Zenithist stations on the Globe. One price everywhere: 17 zenitirs. (No other currency accepted!)

Translated by Maja Starčević

A CATEGORICAL IMPERATIVE OF THE ZENITHIST SCHOOL OF POETRY,
FROM *THE RESCUE CAR*   Ljubomir Micić

Originally published as "Kategorički imperativ zenitističke pesničke škole," in *Kola za spasavanje* (Zagreb/Belgrade: 1922)

International Constructivism in Central Europe   Zagreb/Belgrade

The introductory lecture of the first Zenithist anti-citizen Ljubomir Micić was written in blue ink, published in Zenit no. 13, and delivered at the Serbian Royal Academy of Arts and Sciences in Zagreb, at the Mitrovica Penitentiary, and at the opening of the European "Peace" Conference in Genoa on April 10, 1922. [Original ed. note]

To the sad anti-Zenithist convention:
Boldly and with great ease a goatee is paralyzing the cultural values of all contemporary middle-aged poetry. (What wonderful aesthetic power the goatee has!) And if the goat had a long tail to boot, it alone could destroy all West-European poetry in Yugoslavia or, rather, Yugoslav predeluvian fossilized poetry.
But since the GOAT does not come with a long tail, we issued a threat during our performance on February 1, back in 1921, the threat of an earthquake of catastrophic proportions, which shocked all citizens. As early as 1922 (according to the Gregorian calendar) we made old maids cringe in "horror." Without prior approval of the old white-bearded spirit we had created the first independent and collective artistic movement in the Balkans:

ZENITHISM
the latest Balkan type of constructive creation
We are international poets with respect for the Balkan race! We admire the awaking of the *BARBAROGENIUS* for absolute creators are always geniuses. Only mothers are destined to give birth.
We are creating NEW ZENITHIST POETRY as an expression of the times and an age of the most ingenious paradoxes.
Those of you not destined to understand the great temporary meaning of the paradox cannot "understand" our "insane" and "paranoid" Zenithist poetry either. Nor can you be students of the first Zenithist school, which I open here amongst the ruins of a PAPER TOWER as a conscious and spat-upon victor.
Thanks to the wireless, exercises may be held simultaneously at the following sites: Avala—the Himalayas—Mt. Vesuvius—Mt. Fujiyama—the Caucauses—the Sierra Nevada—Vladivostok. Our esteemed anti-Zenithist citizens and academics must make a deadly exodus using emipirical and comparative methods, neck-breaking operations and the following acrobatic exercises:

Exercise One:
One must keep one's blood warm and become cruelly logical at the moment of an EARTHQUAKE. (Becoming logical is the most difficult part!) Changing one's physical position is quite uneccessary given its stereotypical nature. (Hamlet's gravediggers will take care of that!)
Everything that is happening is happening against you and your will. Keep as still and unconscious as Buddha. Lie on your belly-button unless the midwife has cut it out altogether. Feel the clarity of the awareness that
PARADOX IS A GENERAL CONDITION OF EXISTENCE
PARADOX IS AN ELEMENT OF ZENITHIST POETRY

Exercise Two:

As you keep STILL (though nothing is so still and reeking as the stagnant cerebral matter in your hard heads!) while your wife demands a divorce so as to marry her own mother and dance the latest dance of urbane European cultures—the shimmy (tell me, Mr. Minister of Justice, which § that is of the Citizen's Code of Law)—go alone along the streets of dirty cities or along the clean blood-soaked plowfield of our skeletal country and THINK NOTHING about life!

Express LIFE like a poet (life as a physical—metaphysical—cosmic—metacosmic—magnetic—metamagnetic pulse of the times: *zenitosophy*)

Express the EXPANSION of life without the logic of a single event.

Expansion must be expressed *simultaneously—concomitantly—momentarily*. There is an infinite number of illogical events (acts) happening at any one moment independent of one another. Example:

A Russian man is dying of starvation

> *A professor is raping his student in his joy at her having learned logic.*

> > *Lenin's newspaper death.*

> > > *Charlie Chaplin riding on a donkey.*

> > > > *Import of luxury goods forbidden.*

A SIMULTANEOUS EXPANSION OF CONCOMITANT AND VARIED EVENTS IS THE MOST IMPORTANT ELEMENT OF ZENITHIST POETRY

Exercise Three:

Fill your own SPINE with gunpowder! Fire your old brain CANNON with a spark of the ecrasite brain. You will leap as ellegantly as Anna Pavlova or Nijinsky or as the wild leaps of Stravinsky's *Petrushka*. If all the heritage you have contracted from the Western-European HARLOT dies out in you, we will demand a state monopoly for our poisonous medicine and proclaim the experiment with your spine a national holiday (the absolute need for purging and affirming our racial personality). Our primary concern is to stay alive in the interest of the collectivity of our nation and our humanity. Only then shall we be able to acknowledge your "comprehensive maturity examination" as valid.

The above-mentioned immediately makes each of the chosen into a:

Free Zenithist Anti-Citizen

from whom we demand the following:

a) a diploma of "anti-cultural" and anti-European behavior (thought and action must be commensurate with each opther!)

b) a diploma of rebellious ability to act ("common sense" is harmful to new artistic creation!)

c) a diploma of unending revengeful hatred to the point of destruction for the entire old pseudo-culture of the poetry of "feeling"—"emotion"—"beauty" (the PAPER TOWER must be mercilessly burned!)

d) a diploma of metasexual purity and health of the radio-motoric nerves (the seed that fertilizes must be of pure and unspoiled blood)

e) a diploma of anti-political virtue, which causes purity of personality in our type—it must rise above narrow-minded nationalism of small nations (the politics of nationalism: an inferior toad!)

f) a diploma of bravery and determination to perform unheard of savagery—

!For the Balkanization of Europe!

(Raiderism or Balkanism is necessary for the creation of the new civilization!)

Mr. President, please do not ring so rabidly. You may not and must not take my WORD because I am its master and you are nothing but a servant. I will wait until the *RESCUE CAR* removes your esteemed friends, who have fainted so quickly. Do not forget I am a

BANOVINA-BALKAN man like Nikola Tesla. I am not afraid of the highwayman's muskets or of the reek of poisonous gases much less of your goat bell. Take out the corpses immediately because they are beginning to stink of Latin. Your dear Molière is a fool, really. And your imaginary Shakespeare, Mr. Lloyd George! Damn you puny, plagiarizing suck-ups! Charlie Chaplin has made fools of you all!

Exercise Four:
Attention! Hands on desks! We demand unquestioning obedience, honesty, and trust from you. Nations must be unified by force if necessary!
But let me continue:
The new Zenithist poetry is not born but created. It is a lie to say a poem is born!
A ZENITHIST POEM MUST BE A CONSTRUCTION
One reaches a Zenithist poem in an unquestioningly constructive way: consciously—resolutely—geometrically. (Architecture can stand only as many pulleys as are necessary for its stability!) *Construction of primary feeling.* Feeling has no eminent or imperative function. (What do you care about my feelings?) No one should care about what a poet feels but about what his poem is like and what it means. You are the one who is supposed to feel. It is none of our business. (The thing is that you *must* feel.)
An emotion is only an act of free will and the poet's attention. (All apples do not grow on one roof!) Macedonia, the cradle of old Serbian culture, arouses the emotion of hatred only in Croats, while it arouses the emotion of love in Serbs. What Macedonia itself feels is not important for the actual process of events.)
Beauty, just like philistine banality, does not belong to new art. Beauty is an element of public safety and prevents you from being discovered in your philistine and burgher morality.
ZENITHISM IS THE MOST REBELLIOUS ACT OF THE YOUNG BARBARIAN RACE.

Translated by Maja Starčević

BARBAROGENIUS   Ljubomir Micić
Originally published as "Barbarogenije," *Zenit* vol. 4, no. 26–33 (October 1924)

My new poem is the angry lightning bolt of the Sun's mother
The Earth is ringed by a burning Equator
Hey, where do the rays of this Martian rebellion come from?
My feelings are numb to common human loves
And whose hatred has my glance petrified?
My shoulders are too weak for rebellious tides of new planets
Although I am proud, I love only one woman
Alas
I am just a new earthly man of the bad old days.
You get off lightly, light Martian bodies
You can fall and break your wings as you please
You can rise up in freedom
And I? I cannot stumble
Much less fall on this planet.
I am still barbarously bound and cannot budge

I feel like roaring savagely at the Balkan mountains
Caught like a beast in the handcuffs of East and West
Oh...
O you Martian mares and mad phantoms
And you cranes of an unmasked European Venus
You do not know of the spasms of this defeated land
You have no notion of these damned Turkish meridians
Your brothers have lapped young Balkan blood in vain
May your hatred and my love reign for many a year
Our flag is the sky today
My homeland has always been the Earth.
And we will continue to squirm on God's gallows
Have mercy
But the barbarogenius will take his revenge for all new pains.

Translated by Maja Starčević

THE NEW ART   Ljubomir Micić
From the opening of the First International Exhibition in Belgrade (April 9, 1924),
published as "Nova umetnost" in *Zenit* vol. 4, no. 35 (December 1924)

Anyone questioning or underestimating the significance of the First International
Exhibition is to be ridiculed or even pitied. The exhibition includes all the artistic
movements of the past two decades, if not all their founders, then for the most part
their finest representatives. Moreover, the significance of the exhibition is of a timely
character, in that this is the first time people have been able to see the original works
of the new art in the originals, and not, as heretofore, through dishonest mediators
and epigones who, going abroad for "studies" that consist of strolling the boulevards
and lolling about in cafés, have done nothing but import and imitate shop-window
kitsch. And this they sell to their naïve homeland under the exonerating title of "modern art." So for a while we have been a kind of colony of Europe that places no limits
on the import of cultural refuse and even protects it by law. Our movement and our
hard work have at least done something to change the situation and decrease the
smuggling to a more reasonable extent. I assure you that we have had unexpected
success and will have more. Only after the Zenithist movement can we claim with
certainty that this country is nobody's cultural colony, nor is it willing to be one. We
are standing at the gates, watching carefully to make the smuggler's job more difficult
and their raids less frequent, of less significance, and more vain. True, they are always
in the majority. They are supported by the state and the state government, people
whose cultural education has rarely ventured as far as a dusty encyclopedia—much
less to an art about which the only thing they know is that it exists (or so it is said!)—
and some heavy tomes written about Michaelangelo or Raphael (who, according to
the report of a newspaper "critic," passed away just the other day!), about Rembrandt
or a museum-housed Greek sculpture "which is unsurpassable in its beauty and aestheticism." They have ventured no further, and we, the new artists, carry all the consequences of such sins on our shoulders. However, the Zenith has made some daring
leaps, and this exhibition is yet another. Belgrade can now witness the sensation

of Zenithist "fools" mounting its first international exhibition despite the dilettante mafia and *Zenith* haters. The exhibition has been recognized in all cultured countries by those who know of Zenit and Zenithism. And the number of those people is not small. Today there is not a single cultured town or center unaware of the fact that the Serbs have produced a Balkan artistic movement of international importance. It is not surprising that great libraries and reading rooms in New York subscribe to *Zenit* at their readers' request nor that both a great museum and an art gallery in distant San Francisco do the same. We do not care if this sounds exaggerated to some; we do not care that these real facts cause hysterical envy and enmity in those who hate us and are our enemies. We feed on your hate: only great tempests cause great waves.

I admit that the paintings hanging before you are surprising and that you are not used to seeing their like. They have no titles, since that is of little importance. They are numbered, just as people are named. They need to be registered, but they do not need to be titled, since titles tend to lead the viewer astray. As soon as viewers see a title, they start looking for the picture's "theme" or for "what it represents." There is none of that here. In fact, at first glance they all seem the same, they look like the same picture, just as we think all Japanese look the same, although each one has his own physiognomy and anatomy. I gladly admit that it is very difficult—almost impossible—to explain all the paintings at this conference. But I still have a duty to give you some general advice on how to look at them, if you are willing, and I ask you to take it as benevolent advice. Let me stress again: it is impossible to enter the labyrinth of the new art immediately for the aforementioned reasons. If you wish to understand high-level mathematics, you need to know the basics of general mathematics. The same holds for abstraction. So if you can understand a geometrical abstraction in space—for instance, that two perpendicular lines meet only in infinity—then it will not be so hard for you to view these paintings, which were also executed in space and which are real because of that, but also supernatural because of their anatomy.

The first condition is that you must not compare these paintings with any object you have seen in nature, since this is an exhibition of paintings, not a sideshow or a display of consumer goods. This is not the "half-girl, half-fish monster" from the Mali Kalemegdan circus!

We must demand of painting more that it can give. A painting should be viewed for the painter's vitality and nothing else. Whatever artists wish to paint is fair game. Free choice and free creation are their absolute right. Anything that exists in art, in life, cannot exist outside nature. Everything that is in nature is natural. Ergo, the new art is natural! The painter can paint a peasant shoe atop the Main Church's cross (or a man's head turned upside down as Marc Chagall does), and if this idea works and is artfully executed, the painting can stand as a first-rate artifact.

Each painting thus makes its own nature, and one should not wander outside its frame. One should not wander or ask oneself whether it depicts a horse (and whether its tail is in the right place) or a man, or a snake, or a boring female nude. All comparisons with surface nature and explorations of natural exactitude or possibilities—all that is of little importance to the painting. What's important for the painting are certain basic principles on which the art of painting rests. Formally, these principles belong to three categories: 1) form, 2) color, 3) space. It is within the framework of these three fundamental elements that we find the art of painting in general and especially of the new painting. Painting has finally successfully freed itself from literariness and history, from photography and amateurish copying. This is best seen in *arbos*-painting, as I will now for the first time term the Zenithist style, represented at this exhibition by the work of Josip Klek. *Arbos*-painting manifests a successful economy of material, work, and action. No palette contains colors so bright and effective as our *arbos*-paintings, which present the purest forms as if cut in marble or glass. (*Arbos* is an acronym standing for the material of Zenithist painting: *AR*tija [paper]—*BO*ja [paint]—*S*lika [painting]. It will not hurt to mention that of all the arts only music has always been free of non-artistic weight. Music alone has remained true to its artistic nature. A musician connects tones and sounds, provides rhythm and dynamics, and when it all comes together we hear a melody that makes us ecstatic. No one has ever dragged nature into it, since if we apply to music the kind of logic I've seen in print music would be condemned to reproducing the ox's bellow, the horse's neigh, or Mary Magdalene's sobs at the feet of Christ. Is that what art should be? Everyone (except Zenithists!) call opera art. Well, following the line of logic I have just proposed, may I ask if you have ever heard the music of *Carmen* in nature or the passionate wild rhythms or, rather, the musical paradoxes of Mokranjec's songs? Where in nature have you seen love proclaimed by singing in the ridiculous way opera singers do? But let us return to paintings, painters and art as a whole. Artists connect sky to earth, heart to heart, and soul to soul beautifully.

It is meet and fitting so to do!

Translated by Maja Starčević

ZENITHOSOPHY: OR THE ENERGETICS OF CREATIVE ZENITHISM
Ljubomir Micić

Originally published as "Zenitozofija," *Zenit* vol. 4 no. 26–33 (October 1924)

No made in Serbia

1.

Our fellow travelers cannot be corpses. Only vital life lives on! Our fellow traveler is a future Zenith man, a central transformer of our vital rebellious sparks, of our savage and barbaric energies.

And life? This miserable life strikes me as a huge cosmic factory where thousands upon thousands of neurons and millions upon millions of electrons work tirelessly. And there are just as many idlers who do nothing at all!

My vision is neither cosmic nor earthly animalistic. After all, animals are not familiar with the system of speculative philosophy and even less with the Indian opium of Buddhism.

My vision is entirely human and therefore entirely banal. After all, the privileged may sit on their hands and enjoy doing so!

2.

Where sins end, philosophy begins. We have not yet freed ourselves of our sins. Which is why we Serbs have no philosophy.

Hit my crazy head again for dipping this old pen into ink to write a new story about the birth of God's calf.

The birth of God's calf! God's calf!

He is wonderful, that phenomenal walker on the bloody rope of the gallows raised for us by recent history.

Glory be to the gallows! We destroyed them with our teeth, shooting straight into jaws of death.

We did not lose a single tooth though our birth was as deadly as the birth of God's calf or the Zenithist movement rebellion.
Glory be to the gallows in the highest!
So after all, Zenithism has begun dancing like a crazed phantom dancer on the burning Balkan sky of brilliant beyond-sense…

3.

In the new art and new menagerie of isms our word was a magic word, a new word, the last word. The last, as usual, but this time in the vanguard as well and effective! Just a few words concerning this last and final ism of a flooded age, since this is the only ism of a definitely post-war character. The energy of creation is Zenithism's pulse and calls for the synthesis of all phenomena in the highest and most elemental forms of life and worlds.

Let us call this creative urge the energetic imperative in addition to the "categorical imperative of the zenithist school of poetry" which I presented to the world in the spring of 1922 to the shock of all Serbs and other great nations lacking in the Zenithist spirit. That is the date of the first revolution in the anemic and eclectic poetry of all South Slavs (and other artistic mediums!), and it has continued to this day without anyone's recognition. So much the better!

Of one thing we can be certain: there is not a single great artist, poet or even philosopher who does not carry the germ or instinct for Zenithism, since Zenithism is self-creating and not an artificial product of modern bourgeois propaganda. Even less is it a product of the imperialist culture of speculation.

4.

Here are ten points on a tablet, but they merely general principles, not commandments:

1) Zenithism is the awakening of elementary and vital instincts of work natural to all people.
2) Zenithism awakes in man everything that is common to all humanity within him, everything above the personal, everything akin to the barbarogenius.
3) Zenithism, given its elementary nature and creative syntheticism, is inseparable from all those who create great and new things and who work for the future of mankind.
4) Zenithism shows as clear as day that the ultimate human goals are out of the reach of the people currently engaged in creating the new world order and new human relationships.
5) Zenithism is an elixir of eternal youth and a realization that one must tirelessly and eternally strive upward.
6) Zenithism is the energetic imperative of the sum of the new art's work, and it must follow the path of those who are working towards mankind's common goal.
7) Zenithism is an awareness of the falseness of literary "dreams" and the errors of "the absolute" in philosophy.
8) Zenithism is the strength of an immutable will and food for creative instincts.
9) Zenithism is the positive energy for raising a vertical of the new spirit.
10) Zenithism is also a negative energy, since it is consumed in the inevitable struggle with countless cultural eunuchs, the eternal struggle to overturn their reeking matter and closed-mindedness and put their empty heads in the horizontal position of the grave.

5.

Poets have always wanted to make whips and whip this world. In whose name? For what? No! Not even whips can change people until there is peace among them; they cannot change people as long as there are those who whip and those who are whipped. So, give up this useless task, poets. Neither the whippers nor the whipped should exist! Many of you will be gone in the near future anyway.

The new spirit must gather and lead all creative forces of art and work.

The creative force scrapes out the riverbed, while creative will and visionary minds should decide the form of the river's flow, creating a symphony of work, rhythms, and waterfalls.

New poets know better than anyone how powerless rhythms, verse, and word water-falls are today.

6.

The new world is an antenna, and poetry grows only in the beyond-sense sphere of space. These are the Zenithist words in space.

—poetry is the first plane of symmetry
—painting is the second plane of asymmetry
—sculpture is the third plane of plane-symmetry
—music is the fourth plane of non-symmetry
—dance is the fifth plane of rhythm-symmetry
—drama is the sixth plane of poly-symmetry
—film is the seventh plane of counter-symmetry

Altogether, there are seven versions of symmetry possible in nature. No more than seven symmetries can be found in a crystal: the mathematics of crystals is strange: $7 \times 1 = 1$, one body. And here we have one crystal, one body with various lives: art!

Zenithism, as the new art that embodies all mediums, is the only eighth plane of outside-symmetry, or rather, super-symmetry in space: a new supernatural body, created with the maximum of man's powers. Only a few such synthetic works of new art and new life correspond to the Zenithist principles of relative aesthetics or anti-aesthetics. Those rare works are the only ones we can stamp with the copyright of Zenithism. The best mark in the best place, the best word for the best work.

7.

Genius only discovers—tombs, findings—mummies, perceptions—the face of life.

The barbarogenius totalizes the powers of existence into a unique pulse of new life.

The barbarogenius creates a new work and awakens a collective feeling within people, a feeling that is primordial, elemental, but murdered by contradictory cultures and inhuman religions.

Contemporary life strives towards complete collectivity and the economy of all vital forces, towards the organization of mankind's work and the economy of collective feelings. All individual forces should be concentrated in the great circle of the whole.

8.

Souls are the daily bread and the daily burden of all Slavs and all Orientals. Let us free ourselves of the soul's burden and the daily bread of sentimentality!

Sanctification and the last rites have not been performed on our souls according to the Christian Serbian-Orthodox ceremony, in the church, but according to the Christian ceremony in fratricidal wars, in the trenches. "War be with you!"—brave politicians paraphrased the sentimental messiah, who whispered to the people of Rome and Jerusalem, "Peace be with you!" After those words catacombs burned and the weapons of the ancient Roman bourgeoisie clanged. It was those words that caused an abandoned and a spat-upon fanatic to be crucified by the Romans.

Epigones of bright minds and profaners of great minds are those who throw the cruelest mottos and paraphrases to the nations.

We do not acknowledge old profaned Christianity.
We preach new and pure barbarism.
Old Christianity is cannibalism.
New barbarism is the brotherhood of men!

9.

European culture is cruel and cannibalistic. That why Zenithists work on the balkanization of Europe and want to expand their cultural nihilism to all the continents in
the name of the new barbarism, in the name of new people and new continents, in the
name of a terrible struggle: East vs. West!
The Balkan peninsula is a cradle of pure barbarism, which preaches a new brotherhood of men.
That is the idea of our new culture and new civilization, which will come of a final
clash between two old giants, the East and the West, whose urge to fight each other
is in their blood.

10.

Before the last wars thought walked on unsteady feet and, like a colossus, on fiery
legs. Much has been said about this by the epic Russian count Lev Nikolaevich Tolstoy,
since neither he nor Maxim Gorky could have fathomed that Zenithism's founder
would one day write, "An epic is not energy".
After the imperialist wars and wars of liberation thought dances and spins on hot
heads. The proletarian commune-father commune-son and commune-holy spirit have
fallen silent on the subject once and for all. Only the radio telegraphs buzz through all
the continents, Lenin has died, but his work will live forever.
Apparently the only people in France who heard the news on 21 January 1924 were
Romain Rolland and Henri Barbusse, in America Upton Sinclair, in India Mahatma
Gandhi, and maybe an unknown yogi. And in Serbia?
The next day, in England, the leader of the Second International assembled the
Ministerial Cabinet, and in the name of His Majesty King George VII Sir Ramsay
MacDonald ordered the establishment of the famous equilibrium, which is now
destroying our lives and our youth.

11.

The new thought spins and climbs like a circle of fairies above its axis. That is
Zenitosophy. New thought in a cone, in a spiral, in a vertical.
Zenitosophy is the last vertical of the spirit, which connects the Earth to other planets.
Zenitosophy connects three crucial points in space: Earth—Sun—Moon. Zenithism
acknowledges no symbols in any sphere of the new manifestations and phenomena.
Zenithism, the definitive "ism", is congenial to all we want and look for: it is a total-
ized and unified expression for the synthesis of the new spirit and all its endeavors
and struggles towards the Zenith. We are finally on the right path.
Zenithism is a new discovery of spiritual technicality as well of the mind's construction.
Zenithism is an airplane for the first, second, and third athmosphere—for all athmospheres!
Eureka: Zenithism!

12.

Life without Zenithism is not worth a brass farthing. New poets have no buisness living it. The new life should be proud of us, not we of it.
Our time has put on a concrete suit of armor, a glass torso, steel transversals, electric
wires, radio waves. Time has put on a concrete crown and a glass crinoline: a steel
Rococo. But this new upstart has forgotten the electric brain, radium heart, rubber

legs and magnetic arms. Which is much sadder than the fate of sentimental Werther and the fall of his antipode, that stuffed shirt Zarathustra.

13.

Airplanes visit the clouds, pass over cemeteries, graves, and cities, and never land on dull crosses or sharp lightning rods. Their pilots have no liking for Constructivist painting and the fate of mankind on earth.

Neither dead nor living poets (after the several deaths they have survived) are crowned with green wreaths of flowers or even hard bread crusts anymore, so how can they be blessed by airplanes?

That is why our spirit-planes fly straight for the round wings of machines and work-ers, where they have found a new contemporary aesthetics of the spirit and the machine. Our idea-planes fly from our chests high into the immeasurable hangars of work and love, towards the airports of brotherhood of all people and all continents. An old song to new music!

Where there is a heart, there is sun. Where there are new poets, there is no old bread. So it is in Great Serbia or Yugoslavia or the Kingdom of Serbs, Croats, and Slovenes—or whatever you wish to call it.

14.

All the crude elements of life can be turned into creation using Zenithist energetics. Our life burns like a threshold of death. Death is a circle.

It is impossible for people to be a straight line and a circle at the same time. Run out of the circle into a straight line, into a straight line! But only the opposite of geometry is possible: sticking the vertical line straight into the heart of a horizontal circle—Zenithism!

The energetic imperative is Zenith's barbarogenics of the wild thought of the sixth Balkan continent.

And who is Zenithon?

Zenithon is a beyond-sense miracle: a synthetic man of superlife, the son of a Balkan mother in mourning, a fata morgana.

Translated by Maja Starčević

BARBARISM AS CULTURE   Risto Ratković

Originally published as "Barbarstro kao kultura," *Zenit* vol. 5, no. 37 (November–December 1925)

To the Zenithists of the world:

Barbarism—not in the sense that the Greeks, the Chinese, or the Germans under-stood it; or peaceful, cultured ladies (even if they are feminists) understand it, or the fine souls wearing bank governor's and inquisitioner's shoes understand it. Not primitivism or anarchism, either. And not some "return to nature," as the decadent Rousseau sentimentalized; not licentiousness either, dreamed of by silly poets and revolutionaries lying under coffeehouse tables. Not the *Umwertung aller Werte* [re-evaluation of all values] for it does not matter: you go forward either on your feet or in your head.

In a word, barbarism is not meant as the antipode to culture; it is culture, culture's recovery. Such barbarism is an undying, eternally rejuvenating injection of purity, a disinfectant for mildewed spaces in dead spirits. Above all, barbarism is ours. It is an undying thirst for unmasking, for complete unmasking, even if we have to scratch at our own fates. As such, barbarism is a fundamental revolution in culture, a rebellion against all pseudo-revolutions. In order to unmask (oneself and others) one needs to be able to control what one has (which does not mean being aware of everything). One therefore needs not to be a slave, which to barbarians also means not to be a tyrant.

Above all, barbarians are not *Kulturträger*, but creators of culture. Moreover, they have the same relation to culture as creators to their works: they are not mere suspenders like *Kulturträger*. (The explanation is acrobatic: anti-barbaric culture is only the fear of having one's trousers fall).

Beyond the relative terms of good and evil, we believe that man is good deep down, that any action performed of one's own free will, completely independently, in no one's name but one's own, is worth more than the entire slew of made-up, fawning freedoms. That is a pre-philosophy of pure being and at the same time the ethics of an undefeatable uprising against all false etiquettes, the ethics of people who do not a priori respect anything and are still meek and good. We find true nobility in this, a nobility that does no harm to anyone and is both individualistic and social. We have felt, seen, and guessed that so-called culture, anti-barbaric culture, is progressive only pro forma, that it has not distilled primitivism but rather only masked it the better to be de facto anti-cultural. It is in man's nature to mask himself carefully, to hide, since man fears his own nudity.

So it is not at all a paradox or impossible to reach barbarism through culture, because the very act means not giving up on culture, yet avoiding becoming its victim. On one hand, we are extremely idealistic; on the other, we share a basic fraternal nihilism: looking for one's beginnings by going forward. It is not so long ago that militaristic expeditions were all the rage in Europe: "Berlin has gone mad, Paris is spewing forth its rapture, Moscow is tearing its chest." And through all that time balding culture played chess in salons, gambling away armies during its orgies. If the revelers could have admitted to themselves and to others...

The dandy—that pseudo-aristocrat, that stinking flower of stolen culture—is showing off everywhere. Everywhere and all the time there is at least one marketplace of conscience, at least one exchange office of lies, at least one department store of pride. Which clearly shows that the real creators of culture are anonymous even if anti-cultural anti-barbarians put their names to it. Culture is symbolically like a slice of meat: the thicker one is, the more cultured one is. The trouble is, the meat has spoiled, and to keep the smell away culture takes cocaine and turns the tears of the impoverished into cologne for whores.

It would seem, then, that barbaric ethics opposes civilization. But historic materialism cannot be denied and barbarians will not retreat; they will advance civilization and thus make it impossible for civilization to be abused. The invention of gunpowder created great evil, but it has done much more for the expansion of the spirit than Dante's invention of the Inferno, the toilet of his Purgatory, and his idiotic Paradise. It is obvious that the wireless and other products of the exact sciences will either raise social injustice and anti-cultural exploitation to new heights or make a new, independent collectivism possible. The barbarians opt for the latter.

It is no mechanization of the soul. Technology is its necessary luxury. Barbarian culture does not see the world as a machine. We find the scientists' habit of "explaining" the world ridiculous. We even see it as dangerous: disappointment is inevitable, since everything is as "purely materialistic" as it is "purely spiritual." Barbarians cannot be victims of driveling sentimentality or banal rationalism. Even mysticism has its place, but if something stinks it should be removed, mysterious or not, because tolerating a bedbug under one's nose means either not having a nose or being a bedbug oneself. So mysticism remains, as pure and as mysterious as snow from an ancient dream, mysticism of the beginning and of the end, the mysticism of everything. We see no reason why man cannot be a mystic on a plane if he can be one on his couch.

No philosophical school calls into question the ethics of cultural barbarism. Countless philosophical systems correspond to one another on paper without disrupting the purity of interpersonal relations. For instance, I could be a pansexualist without sending a single girl to the VD clinic. Because by applying any view of the world to real life, independent of ethics, we give it an ethical character. Besides, ethics itself is also a philosophy, since no concept is more universal than morality. Here morality is freed of theological and political boundaries. Man alone remains in his countless relations to the world, a power characteristic only of the victors of culture.

Barbarism, therefore, is no sewage system to say nothing of a guidebook to life. It frees the personality. Barbaric cultural ethics are not defined by any social system, but every system free of the reek of humility and cowardly abuse is defined by it. No classes are pure. Even the most miserable proletarian can be as much of a bastard and philistine as a man of leisure. A banal point, but important.

The barbarian-anti-slave, the anti-tyrant. The antipode of all charlatans, from Alexander the Small to Schopenhauer the Lame. It is pitiful, the entire construction of religious heavens! It is so naïve and pathetic, the logic of dualism. Barbarians will never try to build that legendary Tower of Babel destroyed for all times by Dostoevsky. To go one step farther, after Ivan Karamazov and Kirilov, is what it really means to be a barbarian. And we have gone further: the Tower of Babel is behind us.

Barbarism also has a metaphysical basis. Einstein claims that even his own theory of relativity is relative, and the phrase "everything is a lie" also means everything is not a lie, since if everything is a lie, then the statement "everything is a lie" is also a lie. Thus, it would be perfectly logical to prove that there is no death, though death itself needs no proof at all.

We once felt that we should do nothing but weep our whole lives: it was the only way to save ourselves from the grotesque. But because that was impossible, we decided to be maximally courageous. Our innocence made us mad and we became barbarians. What a paradox! But here it is: we oppose all savagery, indignity, meanness, all repulsive things so neatly masked by culture; we oppose them with pure goodness and joyful freedom. (The barbaric cultural spirit is well illustrated by its disgust with the death penalty. Murder can be justified and noble, but the death penalty—never.)

The spirit of cultural barbarism has given rise to an entire revolution in culture. It has made art a conquest of space and time when it expresses what it could not express in previously existing space and time. Art is the maximum of expression in a minimum of space; moreover, the expression (content–form) must be located in the newly conquered space and time. The rhythm of conquest, of moving into another world, the rhythm of creation is specific to any kind of art that has its own character. This is especially true of poetry, music, and painting. The creation of such painting was aided by the invention of photography, which made all copies superfluous and ridiculous. Music too is closely connected to technique, but its tone association is becoming increasingly liberated.

Poetry is the most liberated art and where our greatest hopes lie.

Translated by Maja Starčević

TOWARD THE DOCUMENTATION OF THE EUROPEAN CULTURAL CRISIS: FIVE YEARS OF ZENITHISM Tivadar Raith

Originally published as "Az Európai Kultúrválság dokumentumaihoz: 5 év Zenitizmus," *Magyar Írás* (1926)

In the September 1924 issue of *Magyar Írás* we gave a detailed survey of those move-ments in the arts that provided an accurate mirror of the cultural crisis in Europe. We published the original texts, from the "Futurist Manifesto" to the manifesto of the Tactilists, of every one of those programs in the arts that had, in the course of their fleeting existences, proudly proclaimed that they alone were capable of salvaging European cultural life.

Most of these manifestos that so loudly announced fashionable trends have long since vanished from the European cultural stage. Here in Hungary they were not able to strike roots, and except for a few isolated phenomena they have all disappeared without a trace. The vital new generation of young Hungarian artists that has gathered around *Magyar Írás* has in the meantime persisted in the struggle for a new art that is of uni-versal human value and is at the same time uniquely Hungarian. Future researchers of literary history, wishing to form a complete picture of the postwar Hungarian psyche and of the new literary movements, will find a rich trove of material in the five years of our periodical as well as in the volumes we have published.

We are convinced that the rebirth of European culture will be decided not in Western Europe but in East Europe. In an East Europe where young nations, with ancient ener-gies, are presently still only in the process of getting started.

We firmly believe—unlike the pseudo-intellectuals and their henchmen the publish-ers and the daily press—in the power of Hungarian culture and Hungarian spirit to build the future.

This belief makes us feel especial sympathy toward the movement of the new art in Serbia, which, in the service of the broadest humanistic endeavors, also declares war on the "isms" of Western Europe, and builds its future upon the foundations of its own vitality, "barbarism," and "Balkanism."

It is an interesting coincidence that their periodical *Zenit* has also been in existence for five years, fighting for the new culture, the new man, and for the synthesis of uni-versal human endeavors and specific ethnic ones.

UPSIDE DOWN   Branko Ve Poljanski

Originally published as *Tumbe* (Belgrade: 1926)

(Fragment of a Great Manifesto to all the Nations of the Globe)

It happened yesterday. My earthly consciousness awoke for the first time. I was a boy of five. High above me my wondering childish eyes saw the sun. I was standing in the road. Next to the road was the small wooden house where I had woken up. A garden full of ripening fruit protected our little house from all evil.

The road was very, very long. Oaks walked by the road all the way to the end of my world, to the end of the road. They met there. And my childish eyes could not see any further. I was terribly curious. I had asked my Grandma Julika, now dead, "Granny, what's at the end of the road?" "The town," she said. The word made me happy: it was like hearing angels sing, angels carrying me on their tiny wings above strange and brave new worlds. The town. Yes. The town. And my childish imagination saw it like this: silver waves emerging at the end of the road I was looking at. It was a sea of silver where good people, like my grandfather Stevan Stojić, went swimming. Yes.

Today I am twenty-eight. Today? The town. The city. I feel disgust as only a disappointed soul of a pure and innocent child can feel it. Today, when cities reek of the offal of their culture, my only joy is hatred and my only pain—the sun.

The difference I felt after twenty-five years of a life spent between the city of my childish consciousness and the city of reality is so great that had I not become a Zenithist poet, I would have surely been a murderer by now.

The village of my childhood was called Majske Poljane, May Fields. So I called myself Poljanski, of the fields. My grandmother, now dead, was called Julika; Grandpa's name was Stevan. One aunt was called by the name of the first woman': Eva. Her two sisters were Ljubica and Marija. Marija, now dead, was my mother. She had two sons. The name of the firstborn is Ljubomir; the younger one is me.

I can thank those great, shoe-wearing peasants for everything that is golden and powerful in my spirit. A thank-you to them and to the gentlemen of culture—s**t.

The little river flowing through my village was not the Seine, nor did Cézanne live in the house by the river close to a small wooden bridge. There were no museums of "eternal works" up on the green hill. There was a mountain and a game-filled forest, where liquid gold mixed with the morning dew.

The little river flowing through my village was called Maja. It is not without significance that Maya has two meanings in Hindu—meanings are both opposed and similar: illusion and land. I bathed my body and my spirit in the Maja, and the latter is still pure: it may wear shimmy shoes today, but could easily walk naked and barefoot. May the spirit—my spirit—step barefoot on this sun-scorched land. And on the Maja.

My Zenithist Spirit

And I went along that road, the road I have mentioned. The first town I reached was called Glina. (Glina is the Serb word for the yellow clay pots are made of...) There were two churches there, one school, and two banks. There were two cemeteries on a nearby hill. Here is where I drank up the rudiments of culture. The only thing that made me madly, insanely happy was a circus with a stupid clown and a cinema with a huge projector that made a whistling sound as if all the devils were laughing. And that is the road that took me to Paris. May my naked spirit plant its heavy foot on that Paris,

My Zenithist Spirit

I was seven. At that time I thought the sky was a huge glass bell. God (with a beard!) was the greatest man: he could do anything. One day he would lift the great bell and people would be joyful and gay and see a heaven filled with angels and saints. It did not take long for that lie to turn into bitter disappointment in my childish imagination. And so time passed and I rode on a steel wheel from lie to lie.

My barbaric genius suffered for a long time until it entered its own world, until it became a destroyer and a ravager, because the greatest spiritual joy lies in destruction a joy both negative and positive.

Zenithism has saved me. Ideas bring salvation. The great Balkan poet
                              Ljubomir Micić
said
                              Zenithism
And the word became *deed*.

And so, my dear innovators, creators of all and sundry, creators of the great nothing, turn your faces to the light brought you by joyful Balkan barbarians. Prodigal sons of Mother Earth, do not forget that the only deed that is a

Great Deed

is one that is

Created for Humanity

and not against it.

Works you create for museums are not creations of the new mankind; they are created out of the desire of petty speculators to go beyond the present to Eternal speculation.

We have no understanding for your painting, since "great art" is nothing but a trade where the innovators of today play the part of salesmen on the stock market of mankind's conscience.

Your painting has no sense and no shame. Zenithism fights with European painting.

For a New Barbaric Style

When you discovered African sculpture, what you were really ecstatic over was Zenithism, which you knew nothing about. Your joy did not last long, however, since whatever the speculative hand of the new European touches is lost to the new mankind. You have turned African sculpture, which comes from the naked spirit of "savage" man, into a spiritual nectar of tasteless European lemonade that can only cause—vomiting.

Be Zenithists. Create works that are great for the greatness of mankind, and forget your know-nothing aesthetics. If aesthetics stands for anything, it stands for the

Phenomenon of Stupidity

Do you think mankind would lose anything if Derain or Matisse had not been born? Do you think mankind would lose anything if there were no painting? Believe me, painting is the most foolish work the human spirit has wasted its time on. Stop paint-ing, for God's sake, you

50,000

lost men who paint on the streets of this beautiful city of Paris. Stop painting, because you are committing a historical sin against humanity, which will be summarized by the generations to come as:

Painting Is a Crime

Mankind has never been so much in need of sound, serious spirits. And while fifty thousand people stroll along the boulevards of Paris thinking that the work of their poor

"Spirit in Color"

represents one of the most significant applications of spirit to life, there is another front growing, a front called the

Zenithist

Zenithists are interested in the problem of the spectrum in the art of painting only insofar as they ask how much spirit a certain artist has, if he has as much as is needed for the new world. Verily, I say unto you, it is not a great miracle and wisdom to paint a backside and to claim that it is eternal because it is hanging or will hang in, say, the Louvre. It is even a lesser miracle to paint a square or a circle and to claim it is the greatest manifestation of spirit since the beginning of time. Dear God, those who do cannot imagine the laughter of the

New Man

You will rightly say I am a peasant. And I will be right in pitying you for your immeas-urable stupidity. I truly do not "understand" Cézanne, just as I understand Braque or

Léger so well. They cannot guess that I understand them better than they understand themselves, because my Balkan eyes can see what people hide the most.

Each age has its brand of painting. Only this headless, bloody age of ours lacks one. Everyone and his dog is talking, writing, yelling about the painting of our time, and

There Is No Painting

There are painters, some of whom are even geniuses, but there is no contemporary painting to be found anywhere.

We need a new way of expressing man's naked spirit in color.

We need Zenithist painting. Enough backsides and squares! Stop or you'll ruin painting for the sake of an imaginary lyricism, a virtuous line. Anyone who can feel with his spirit and has intuition understands that this culture is in the process of collapsing. Its creators find it hard to admit, but the rest of us could not see it more plainly.

Gallery owners in the city of Paris and their painter partners say,

You Need To Know How To Look at a Painting

And Zenithism says,

You Need To Know How To Create a Painting

It is obvious that a shameful historical deed has reached a dead end in the aesthetic theory of *l'art-pour-l'artism* and cannot move a step further. When a group of Russian jokers with a great sense of humor founded

Nullunctism

in painting, that is, painting white on white and black on black, it obviously meant the end of a painting culture, of a historical error and of an obvious acrobatics of stupidity that had resulted in the theory of

l'art pour l'art

They say a painting is a world in itself. An absolute work. Pure gold. An eternal work. A museum piece. The Zenithist says, A painting is stupid. An absolute stupidity. A pure stupidity. An eternal stupidity. A museum-piece stupidity.

Strange. Each painter knows the now banal theory of relativity put forth by Mr. Einstein, who states that all is relative. If that is so clear and painters in their agony defend their painting with it (though it hurts them the most), why do they go on trying to create eternal works and museum pieces? Eternity, too, is relative

One Minute—One Billion Years

Create one-minute paintings, because in the end they are the same as eternal paintings.

Go to a cinema where you will feel better than anywhere the relativity of your "eternal works." Let film teach you the speed of changing place and space. The miracle of film is firmly based on a single idea that is not and could never be pretentious.

Why are Buster Keaton, Charlie Chaplin, Douglas Fairbanks and others like them greater dramatists than Shakespeare? It is quite simple. They have instinctively felt the relativity of place, time, and space. In drama they have discovered the

seventh dimension

film

speed.

All Contemporary European art Is Suffering from a Lack of Ideas

> Work without an idea = man without a head!
> Work without an idea = fish out of water!
> Work without an idea = Pegasus with no legs!

Work without an idea = Columbus' egg without America!
Painting without an idea = backside factory.
Poor painting. It has turned into a mania mankind needs to be cured of. The enemies of contemporary painting will certainly be victorious in the fight against it.

I have been speaking of dead museum and "eternal" painting without ideas.
Now a few words about the future.

Zenithist Painting

Since the beginnings of painting and sculpture it was clear that they have never in any age been without ideas, that is, a bluff with no sense.
It has become the custom for the "modern" sculptor to invoke ancient Egyptian, Greek, and even Assyrian sculpture. Then why aren't the principles of these civilizations, where spirit is applied to sculpture, accepted by our gentlemen innovators? Why? The answer is short:

Contemporary European Artists Have No Spirit!

Contemporary European artists are pure artists, masters. (In Serbian, a master is an artisan). They know their trade. They know color. They are virtuosos, the absolute rulers of light, color, form, and space. The only things missing are
Spirit
The spirit of man
The spirit of the new man
The spirit of the naked man
The spirit of the barbarian
The spirit of the barbaric genius.
So they will again invoke African sculpture and everything from the Egyptians to the Cretans. But, dear European artists without Zenithist spirit, I beg of you, look at all the periods of artistic creation, from its beginning to the present-day, look for what you are lacking. And you will find

Humanity's Philosophical Attitude to the Life of Its Time.

There is not a single great work in the world that can be free of ideas when it comes to the artistic and philosophical attitude to the time it was created in.
There are no great works outside mankind.
There are no great men outside life.
There is no great art without mankind.
There is no spirit outside of life.
The spirit is not a dead thing that can be hung on a nail.
The spirit is something eternal, something that *moves* all the forces of the universe.
The spirit is always alive, never dead.
The spirit is always within man and never outside him.
Art is always within man and for man and never outside of him or against him.
The Zenithist spirit is alive and bloody.
The Zenithist spirit is naked and wild.
The Zenithist spirit is new and barbaric.
The Zenithist spirit is strong and humane.
The Zenithist spirit is young and joyful.
The Zenithist spirit is a genius creator.
Ljubomir Micić has given a name to this sum of the eternal crude forces that rejuvenate mankind. He calls it

Barbarogenius

Using pure barbaric genius and the new spirit of a new heroic mankind, we will create

New painting!

Zenithist painting!

New sculpture!

Zenithist sculpture!

New poetry.

Zenithist poetry.

New art.

Zenithist art.

This method must be applied to the concept of

Culture

Culture is not outside man. It is within him and for him.

Culture is not dead. It is alive.

Therefore, culture is not a thing but the force that propels mankind. Let us not call that force the fuel of society but the

Morality of Society

Cultural = Moral.

Moral = Cultural.

Mankind has gone through several stages of morality. Today's stage of morality is called

Morality

For Sale

True miracles have been performed using that morality. It is hard to pinpoint its beginning, but it is not hard to say how it will end.

And when a Zenithist says "morality" to *modern* Europeans, they say he is being—pretentious. No one has ever asked what morality was. Well:

Morality is an elemental force that moves the collective spirit of mankind in the direction of a goal. It would be better to call the force

Anti-Morality

as the new affirmation of a new morality,

Zenithist Morality

The present European morality is Christian. It has become one whole with the morality of

buy—sell

mankind—goods.

Mankind is not for sale!

Europe is not cultured!

Zenithism is a movement for the barbarization of Europe!

Is Zenithism a movement for the Europeanization of the barbarians?

Zenithism is a movement of eternal youth!

Zenithism is a poetry of clashes.

Translated by Maja Starčević

BEYOND-SENSE POETRY (INTRODUCTION TO *ANTI-EUROPE*)

Ljubomir Micić

Originally published in *Anti-Evropa* (Belgrade: 1926)

Two apparently independent worlds create an indivisible whole here: anti-Europe and beyond-sense poetry. These two worlds are connected by the antennas of the new Zenithist spirit.

The realm of beyond-sense is a paradise of "madmen." One gains entrance with the unwritten passport of talent, spiritually naked and pure as a drop of the sun. I have entered by fighting over corpses of European classics and national tradition, sloughing off my old poetry in contempt for myself in me and other poets. And you who are secretly following my "mad" example leading to a "promised land" beyond the boundaries of sense and sanity into the hell of new Zenithist poetry, you who are willing and able—the first thing you must do is cast off old, lame poetry's dirty rags!

Zenithism liberates us from slavery to the European cultural tradition. Zenithism has discovered barbarism and freedom—barbarism of the spirit and barbarism of free thought, and in Zenithism I have discovered a source of new poetry: beyond-sense! Beyond-sense is my source of creation; beyond-sense is the border on which madman and genius dance their crazy dance. Yes, new art comes into being on the border between "pure" reason and "pure" art: Zenithism! Because everywhere the reeking breath of "pure reason" cannot reach is a creative zone of beyond-sense. The beautiful zone of beyond-sense is free of the stinking flowers of reason, free of the limited and salvationist analysis the so-called and self-appointed critics perform, all pathos and dignity. When they "appraise" the worth of artistic works. They have my deepest pity.

Europe is the mother of analysis. But that is not its only error and sin. It has many. They are endless. Besides the political monstrosities (imperialism and capitalism) we have been slaves to from time immemorial, our cultural slavery has significantly increased. That is why we are anti-Europe! It is disgusting to chase Europe. I want us to be the first Balkan dam to European degeneracy. Because to wish for the Europeanization of the Balkans nowadays, during Europe's twilight, at a time when the Balkanization of Europe is at hand, means running after one's own tail. Along with the Russian Revolution the cultural emancipation of the Balkans from Europe is an issue of the utmost significance for us today. Zenithists must realize that these two flames are more important than all other "vital interests." And if anyone wonders why I have chosen poetry to fight against Europe and European culture and, what is more, why I do so in a country where culture is a wild goat trying to escape from Balkan pyramids of political mud and moral corruption—I refuse to answer. Let the works speak for themselves! If there is no one for them to speak to today, there will be tomorrow. Let Zenithism speak!

The fateful effects of our slavery to European culture and the effects of its hunting safari through the East will be felt more in the future than they are today. That is why we must not allow the Balkans to become a warehouse and a storage place for over ripe and cannibalistic European culture. Because after Christianity European culture is the greatest evil of a captive humanity! And for a few years now the Balkan galley—a galley with no cultural rudder and no political equilibrium—has been sinking in the tide of the European swamp. We were the first to extend aid through poetry, and we did so to save both its and our lives. Our aid is the cry of Zenithism, and my beyond-sense poetry should be looked at as a spiritual life belt. As eruptions of deep earthquakes in our barbaric insides let my poetry become a measure of new anti-European feelings and thoughts blooming in the spring of the first spiritual Balkan revolution—in the cradle of Zenithism!

Revolution is not slavery; revolution is resurrection, revolution is liberation. If you wish to enter the heaven of cultural independence, you must run like mad on the heels of the spiritual revolution. Independence of spirit, independence of feeling, and independence of creation are not handed out as John's head was handed on a platter to the perverted Salome. Freedom and independence—the only two moral and cultural values—are worth all our suffering and sacrifice; they are worth a fight to the finish. Spiritual freedom and independence of thought must be seized with your teeth! If you wish to become independently fulfilled and free men, you must sacrifice your slavish and apparent peace of mind to a liberating revolution of the spirit, to a revolution of thought, a revolution of beyond-sense feelings. The fireballs of Zenithism in the postwar literature of the Serbs, Croats, and Slovenes projected at the zenith of victory by Zenithists strike fear in all devils. The Zenithists have forged the steel of the young barbaric spirit and its carrier, the barbarogenius, on the red-hot anvil of new creation above all boundaries! For it is shameful to be only a lyrical poet in these post-war days when our conscience is being raped and our love for the new mankind is so pure.

Translated by Maja Starčević

ZENITHISM THROUGH THE PRISM OF MARXISM   Ljubomir Micić (under the pen name Dr. M. Rasinov)
Originally published as "Zenitizam kroz prizmu marksizm," *Zenit* vol. 6, no. 43 (December 1926)

If we consider the development of art from a Marxist point of view, i.e., its relationship to the social condition as a whole, the reason for Zenithism's emergence becomes clear. We can no longer consider it a product of a desire to be modern and "hyper-modern" but rather as a spiritual eruption—as a conscious artistic being—created from a mass of successive causes and struggles intertwined in the thick web of the entire post-war twentieth-century condition.
The current state of affairs has needed spirits capable of making an honest synthesis of global events, presenting them in all their nakedness and shining the light of the future into today's dark *chaos*. Such spirits have been necessary—just as honest artist giants are necessary—and they have indeed appeared from all ends of the earth. We needed to make people aware of the truths of today and tomorrow and return honor to twentieth-century man. These spirits have appeared to shine the light of truth and save our honor. What we needed was to regain faith in man—and they have revived it. Zenithism is among these spiritual giants!
Zenithism has been fated to make more enemies than any other artistic movement, and its enemies have come from both camps of today's divided society: as Zenithism throws bombs and thunderbolts into one of the enemy camps, the other camp, not yet acquainted with Zenithism, denies its revolutionary and proletarian value. The hatred of the bourgeoisie and servile capitalist intellectuals is a laurel wreath for Zenithism. It is truly its greatest reward, one that has been particularly hard to earn. However, the lack of interest proletarian fighters show for Zenithism is a cause of great pain, even if we bear it proudly. Yet the proletarian camp too has extended greetings of friendship and understanding—if not the camp in our own nation then those in other countries (and Zenithists do not care for nations). We could mention a number of such

greetings—for example, several articles in the Czech newspaper Rudé právo and an invitation from Moscow to participate in the International Exhibition of Revolutionary Art to be hosted by the Academy of Arts and Sciences this year.

What is Zenithism? Zenithism is a son of Marxism. The blood of Marxism flows in Zenithism's veins. Because all knowledge and ideals that the science of Marxism preaches—such as sociology—are the same as Zenithism both preaches and revives in its sphere of art. Zenithism's mottoes are the same as Marxist mottoes:

Down with today's tyranny	DOWN WITH EUROPE!
Down with the exploitation of man by man	
Down with country borders	
Greetings to all workers of the world	LONG LIVE BARBARIANS!
Revolution is our poem	
Long live new liberated society	
Long live the new man	

However, it is unfortunate that certain Marxists understand mottoes such as "Down with Europe" and "Long Live Barbarians" quite literally and thus give them a non-Marxist meaning.

What sort of Europe are we talking about and who are these Barbarians?

Europe is a synonym for greedy Western capitalism and imperialism (including America) resulting in the stinking collapse of mankind, a collapse that reeks so horribly that it threatens to smother everyone—those who have created this paradox, who have killed man in man, who have…

Barbarians are the entire world proletariat. Barbarians are the idea of total proletarian strength, which has power of volcanic lava about to explode. Barbarians are crude and powerful natural elements still unspoiled by bourgeois emancipation. Barbarians are "Moscow vs. Paris"—"East vs.West"—as certain proletarian and non-proletarian journals in other countries have rightfully noted. Barbarians are Micić's barbarogenius—"the sum total of crude eternal forces rejuvenating mankind," as Branko Ve Poljanski puts it in his book *Upside Down*. The barbarogenius is the fighting proletarian, the only one who can make the appearance of the new man possible.

That is the point of the balkanization of Europe, since "the balkanization of Europe" also means "the barbarization of Europe" in the above meaning. Finally, the expression is colored by its faith in the special talents of the Asiatic race and of its own Balkan race, which has, of all races, been the least successful in unleashing its vital forces on European civilization. Therefore, it is not at all like Tolstoy's struggle of primitivism against culture; it is the struggle of a powerful proletarian fighter against a pale bourgeois civilization, a fighter who will bring about a new culture with his crude and healthy elements of gigantic force.

Naturally, the Zenithist movement had to go through a period of factionalization in its beginnings. It has had its fill of pseudo-Zenithists who, naturally, were eventually unable to follow the Zenithist path. After all, Zenithist thunderbolts had to be hurled over the entire capitalistic and imperialistic literary, cultural, and moral residue; heavy Zenithist aircraft had to drop as many as 7 million bombs. And these people were unable to help because they possessed no thunder or lightning, not a single bomb of spirit or an idea.

However, the group that has remained true to Zenithism and is headed by Ljubomir Micić, its founder, has in the six years of its existence missed not a single major event of interest to the world's proletariat, nor has it failed to report on the events in its journal *Zenit* or in its books. *Zenit*'s pages glorify the Russian revolution. Lenin's death was very important news to us as was the fighting in Morocco and other colonies. Protests to all of Europe, screams of tremendous pain from the large heart of the poet Ljubomir Micić made waves throughout the continent when the revolutionary poet Geo

Milev was killed by the bloody hand of the Bulgarian bourgeoisie or the general strike took place in England.

Ljubomir Micić dedicated a poem to the strike in his latest book *Anti-Europe*. The title itself speaks volumes. The poem will kindle love for Zenithism in every proletarian fighter's heart. The strike is observed in a literally Marxist manner:

> The general strike is just a case of color blindness
> Since locomotive drivers saw only green lights
> On this night of the first clashes green lights mean Death
> And red ones
> Only red lights signal the way to the new life
> of a new day
> of a new mankind
> Hungry bayonets glisten in the English ports of the East
> Guns and rabid cannons grunt
> Wounded by the sunstroke of revolution
> Oh workers miners sailors
> Proletarians and followers of the Balkan blood revenge
> We greet you and ask one naïve question
> Why aren't your calluses diamonds
> Or dynamite?

The entire book is a prediction of and strong incitement to a Balkan revolution.

The gravedigger featured in *Upside Down*, the latest book by the Zenithist poet Branko Ve Poljanski—isn't he the same as a hungry proletarian artist dying on a Paris street? Aren't the same millions of starving proletarians dying in all cities, their suffering made so real in his poem that I can feel horror paralyzing my face as I read. "The Laughter of Guns" from the same book is further proof of the Marxist streak in Zenithist writing: it shows the development of the proletariat and the path to social revolution in a completely Marxist way. Many pages of *Zenit* and Zenithist books are filled with a feeling of repulsion and disgust for the capitalist organism, for the gnawing cancer that cannot be removed and with great feelings of love for a new mankind. The powerful Zenithist throat loudly echoes Marx's words: "Workers of the world, unite!"

Finally, Zenithism stands for an already completed revolution in art. The limits of the academic understanding of art have been broken, limits which could not encompass the free spirit in post-war twentieth-century social conditions. Ljubomir Micić's book The Rescue Car conveys Zenithist principles of artistic creation. Zenithism enriches artistic development by creating yet another new form. Spiritual revolutions are closely connected to social revolution. Their bond is the place where they influence one another. Scientific and artistic revolts indirectly and psychologically influence people who then become more courageous and gain more confidence for social revolt and transformation. Furthermore—though it is just a detail—the international form of Zenit subconsciously influences people's opinions, making them feel that national ideas are truly foolish in this day and age since all people on the globe are really one nation.

How long will Zenithist art last? Will it remain in the distant future of the new classless society? Undoubtedly, but it will have to perform its great historical duty during the long class struggle. Because Zenithism is an art of struggle, just as our age is an age of struggle. Zenithism will be remembered as the great art of its age, but with the arrival of the classless society a more subdued kind of art will appear, the art of harmony, since the future will be an age of harmony. That future art will arrive over the Zenithist bridge, which will divide it from pre-war art, and it will have Zenithist juices in its veins.

Translated by Maja Starčević

The first important act of the artistic community at the end of World War I was the founding of the association Arta română (Romanian Art). Many of the association's members had either fought in the war or fled German-occupied Bucharest for the northern city of Jassy. Arta română's founding was in part a reaction against the older association of Tinerimea artistica (which had continued to organize exhibitions in Bucharest during the occupation), and its program, with its emphasis on social and artistic renewal, was grounded in ethics as much as it was in aesthetics. It was in this climate that M. H. Maxy opened his first exhibition in Jassy in 1918, and Arta română exhibitions continued every year in Bucharest until 1926.

The longest lasting Romanian avant-garde periodical, Contimporanul (Present Time), was founded by Ion Vinea and Marcel Janco in 1922. Maxy joined them in 1924, coinciding with the December 1924 opening of the journal's first international exhibition. With an eclecticism indicative of its late arrival on the scene of European avant-garde journals and typical of the Romanian avant-garde in general, Contimporanul fused Dadaist, Expressionist, Futurist, and Constructivist ideas. In its relatively long history—the longest of any Romanian avant-garde journal—

it also devoted special issues to new architecture, interior, theater and cinema, and published texts by Theo van Doesburg, Hans Richter, Kurt Schwitters, Le Corbusier, Walter Gropius, and Adolf Behne.

Shortly before the first Contimporanul show, 75HP (75 Horsepower) appeared in Bucharest. Poet Ilarie Voronca and painter Victor Brauner edited this one-issue journal, in which they showcased their "picto-poetry," an explosive fusion of image and text that teased out unexpected meanings from the arrangement of words on a page. A perfect collaboration between Voronca and Brauner, 75HP may also have been the best evidence that the avant-garde was, as Brauner believed, an expression of friendship.

Voronca and Brauner's nonconformism found a new home in the pages of Punct (Point), which appeared immediately after the sole issue of 75HP. Punct was edited by Scarlat Callimachi, known as the "red prince," an aristocrat sympathetic to leftist ideology. Punct became Voronca and Brauner's tribune for defining Constructivism, just as Vinea, Maxy, and Janco had done in Contimporanul. (The ideas expressed in the two journals were not essentially different from each other—indeed, they published many of the same artists and writers—but Punct assumed a more fiery tone in articulating them.) In keeping with its Constructivist ideals (defined as "abstract harmony with constant laws"), *Punct* emphasized a non-objective synthesis of all expression of the spirit—poetry, art, architecture, theater, and music—and argued that the artist must be in sync with the industrial age.

Like *75HP* and *Punct*, *Integral* was an offshoot of *Contimporanul*. Edited by Maxy, it emphasized, in peremptory form, ideas already promulgated by other avant-garde journals; its greatest success was in coining an evocative word and giving a name to the Romanian version of Constructivism: Integralism. As a movement, Integralism sought to take advantage of and unify the contributions of all the fragmented "-isms" into a modern synthesis. In 1925 Maxy opened the Studio Integral, conceived along the lines of the Bauhaus, in order to fuse "the new spiritualism and technique."

From Campina, not far from Bucharest, Geo Bogza (author of *Sex Diary*) edited the short-lived *Urmuz*. The name of the journal—which lasted for only five issues in 1928—was taken from the late Dadaist writer Urmuz (born Demetru Demetresu-Bazău), famed for the absurd prose pieces he called his "bizarre pages" as well as for his 1923 suicide.

NOTES ON PAINTING   Marcel Janco
Originally published as "Note de pictură," *Contimporanul* no. 4 (1922)

Abstractism, wrongly named Cubism by some, primarily means the liberation of paint-ing from life aspects and exterior signs.

Until it emerged, the art of the line, color, drawing, and painting limited itself to figure, landscape, and still life. Sometime ago, the faithful semblance of the pictorial image and the reproduced one had been the sole concern. Later on, the painter allowed him-self to interpret, i.e., to have his own vision of things. Exact resemblance was then sacrificed and left to photographers. The painter was striving to capture and represent movement, vibration, harmony.

Ever since the romantics we can watch the slow and painful effort that painting took to get rid of reality constraints in order to freely interpret and subjectively create the world. The Impressionists, with their fresh and mighty eye, scornfully overruling the established vision on things, speculated the colored vibrations and their variety of disconcerting surprise.

Expressionism gave up the detail in order to unleash that thing that epitomizes and evokes the whole, through on imposing manner meant to project the whole object and its attributes, its setting and aspiration. (See "The Dance" by Archipenko).

Finally, Abstractism overlooks the model, the aspects of nature, the old pretexts in painting. It is neither on interpretation of the outside world any longer, nor a search for a reference paint. It is something inwardly and personally oriented. It starts with the line and color as absolute values, just the way music does with sounds. And just the way music joins sounds to attain harmony fit to one particular mood, abstract painting handles sounds and colors to get a similarly harmonious effect.

Thus liberated, painting becomes abstract construction, very much like an unpro-grammed symphony. Abstractism, I would say, is the formula of pure painting, of painting for painting's sake. I can foresee the total success of this art, yet not before human soul is able to comprehend it, and then to feel it.

One quality of Cubism: it is entirely constructive. It breaks with tradition, yet it neither claims to have it crashed, nor does it deny the previous pictorial values. It only refrains from imitating them. It follows its own creative path.

Translated by Magda Teodorescu

ART NOTES   Marcel Janco
Originally published as "Însemnări de artă," *Contimporanul* no. 44 (1924)

1. Beauty in art is prejudice.
2. Intelligence is a negative analytic factor, art a positive constructive synthetic one.
3. Invention is ability—fantasy, creation.
4. Devices have been invented that render mathematically any auditory or visual virtuosity.
5. Artist–artisan–artifice, three different meanings bearing the appearance of resemblance.

6. Children's art, folk art, the art of the psychopaths, of the primitive people are the most alive, the most expressive, surging from the depth, the organic, free of the culture of beauty.

7. Primitive people do not make primitive art.

8. In art there is no such thing as primitivism, there are no degrees of development. The Romantics of the last century did not miss the opportunity, given the on-going didacticism of the time, to poison the generations that succeeded them, with the romanticism of the Greek ideal of beauty.

9. The Gothic, the Assyrian, the Romanesque, the Chaldean, the Indian, the Persian, the Egyptian, and the Etruscan are arts carrying far stronger consequences for the human soul than "Classicism." They are entirely unknown even to critics and artists.

10. The more the creator knows how to be at ease, preserve his freshness, avoid "cleverness," the more the artistic expression is turbulent and compelling.

11. Technique has nothing in common with virtuosity or the artificial.

12. The school of art in present practice massacres fantasy, engenders trickery, virtuosity, didacticism, secondary attributes.

13. Sensibility issues from us as fingernail from flesh.

14. Sensibility is the ever same constant of art in time and space.

15. The folk arts are the most powerful examples of a standard of sensibility. The axe is always creating from the beginning, from tabula rasa.

16. The new art pursues intensity by any means necessary.

Translated by Julian Semilian and Sanda Agalidi

VICTOR BRAUNER   Ilarie Voronca
Originally published as "Victor Brauner," *75HP* (October 1924)

In truth, nothing is so opposed to art as [is] the principle of "art as instrument of pleasure." Whether entrenched in the past or committed to innovation, artistic realization had in mind the unctuous wheedling of the spectator. Art consequently became a precision instrument placed on the same shelf with the lacto-, chrono- or alcohol-meter: *pleasuro-meter*. However, the aim of art is something entirely different. Willing or not, literature, the plastic arts, music have yet to overcome an acute crisis. It's on account of this the work of Mr. Brauner emerges with additional significance. I insist: what belongs to art, in its highest manifestation, is the expansion of our abstract awareness, the creation of novel relationships of understanding, the amplifying of the associative network of ideas. Art consequently demands an effort, many times unpleasant, of the cerebral capacity. And the first this effort is incumbent upon is the artist himself. To refine, to put the finishing touch on, these are the endeavors of craftsmen, of producers of slow and precise labor. But the artist, before anything else, is an inventor. His gesture is resolute, audacious, reaching even beyond the absurd. Above limits and schools, his creation is novel, fulgurant. Only in this manner is art redeemed from the throttling of platitude, and duplication that menaces through formula. Refinement, duplication will be nothing but the refuge of mediocrity. The artist is incessantly the fashioner of fresh concatenations of sound, word, and color. The age of refinement has come to an end. Now chimes the clock of every audacious attempt, even the most absurd. The principle of gravity in space defeated by the airplane must be defeated in time as well. This is the reason why the work of Mr. Brauner acquires an expanded and intense significance. The crisis must still be regarded as acute. The contribution of Mr. Brauner is timely. From his first explorations, Mr. Brauner has been preoccupied with the creation of novel and personal relationships of ideas, color, line. And the accomplished fruit of these explorations, *the exhibit of the maison d'art*, will be witness to its triumph. Out of all of the evolutionary steps, Expressionism, Cubism, and especially this last, boasting of a superior and abstract order—Constructivism—Mr. Brauner distinguishes himself with glimmers of metal, with self assured stiletto parries. Actually, no other comment is necessary. The work of Mr. Brauner must be viewed in its totality, without sinuous convolutions, like a deluge caused mutilation. From the canvasses profusely and incontrovertibly unfurled, the painter Brauner emerges as a veritable creator-artist, with peerless elements of invention. Mr. Brauner belongs to the race of great innovators. It's a promiscuous race before which the gates of intelligence and to the subconscious tumble in dire defeat. They are the century's heralds of tidings. Their word, before craft, is passion, their strut draws blood out of the century's bark. Art for them is not a Sunday's repast with Turkish coffee and slothfully rattling backgammon games. But it is an incessant preoccupation, which consumes, ignites. Beauty, pleasure, utility, these are wilted notions that these artists know how to shed. Abstraction, personal construction, novel in thought and form, the unforeseen, these are the elements which cling to them. All these are far from being facile, comfortable, the spectator will find out someday these forerunners are not demented. Because in their consciousness persists a resolution, much more precise, much more luminous than it is largely believed, that the resilience they manifest, the shedding of sentimentalism and logic is requisite warrantee for this super-sensing consciousness. Certainly, this race calls for an aristocracy of sensibility, of intelligence. More often than not it is a race of sacrificers, at least until the moment that a formula is adopted by all. We are convinced: Mr. Brauner will not costume himself in academicism. In attitude and point of view, in line and color, Mr. Brauner dresses in lightning. The imbeciles, in approaching his work, must be outfitted with a lightning rod. The very novelty and abstraction of his work will unleash the most virulent apostrophizing. Still, in spite of all, through the accomplished personality of Mr. Brauner, along with the canvases of Messrs. Janco and Maxy, Romanian painting will make its entrance on the stage of major European art.

Translated by Julian Semilian and Sanda Agalidi

AVIOGRAMĂ   Ilarie Voronca
Originally published as "Aviogramă," *75HP* (October 1924)

READER,
DEBUG
YOUR BRAIN!

AVIOGRAMĂ–AIRPLANEGRAM
(Instead of a Manifesto)
HERMETIC SLEEP OF THE TRAIN ENGINE OVER BALCONIES
EQUATOR
PULSE VAST ANNOUNCEMENT must DYNAMIC MARITIME
SERVICE

THE ARTIST DOESN'T IMITATE THE ARTIST CREATES
THE LINE OF THE WORD COLOR YOU CAN'T FIND IN DICTIONARY
VIBRATES CENTURY-TUNING FORK
HORSE RACES ELEVATOR TYPING-CINEMA
I N V E N T   I N V E N T

SURPRISE ART
GRAMMAR LOGIC EMOTIONALISM
AS LINEN PINS
ON ROPES THE KINGDOM OF LUMINOUS
POSTERS CALLS
CHERRY-BRANDY TRANSURBAN WINE RAILWAYS
THE MOST
BEAUTIFUL POEM: THE DOLLAR FLUCTUATION
THE TELEGRAPH HAS WOVEN WIRE RAINBOWS
IRRADIATOR STARTS OFF STIGMA acd DENTAL
ALPHABET
ASTRAL SHORTHAND
BLEEDING WORD TO COME
METALLIC THE DENIAL OF PURG-ING
FORMULAS AND WHEN
WHAT WE'RE DOING
BECOMES FORMULA
WE'LL DENY OURSELVES, TOO,
IN THE ANESTHETIZED AIR

CABLEGRAMS SINGING DIASTOLE OF STARS THOUGHT
UNPACKED
THE MECHANICAL PIANO IS SERVING COFFEE WITH ELEGANT
MILK
OH! RECITALS OH! CHARITY BALLS A
LICENSE FOR SUICIDE
3 DINARS THE SIDEWALK HAS FILLED ITS TEETH IN A
SPIRAL
MILK DIET THE CRANK IN THE DRUM
BOULEVARD READ ORIENT EXPRESS ANTHRACITE
EMBRYO BUS
HYDROCHLORIC MIRAGE IMPOSSIBLY ACHIEVED WHAT
LITTLE EYES
LIKE POUNDED SUGAR INCEST PROCESSION
ABSTRACT TRANSATLANTIC EXCHANGE AGENCIES
NEWS BUMP

PARIS LONDON TSF BERLIN
NEW YORK

LIKE BILLIARD AIRPLANES

THEY GO DOWN LIKE BAROMETERS THE EUROPE
LIGHTHOUSE NECKLACE IS BURNING
HAS CRAMPS SWALLOWS DISTRICT PILLARS USELESS COMFORTABLE

AS MUCH AS YOU CAN
THE INFINITE IN SLIPPERS MAKES AN ANNOUNCEMENT
BISEXUALITY ATHLETE FOLLOW THE
MUTUAL SPEECH NEWSPAPERS OPEN
LIKE WINDOWS THE CONCERT OF THE CENTURY BEGINS
ELEVATOR RINGS INTER-BANK CLOWN-LIKE JAZZ
HORN
F FLAT
     D
         F FLAT
            IN
                PAJAMAS
                   FOOTBALL

Translated by Monica Voilescu

UNTITLED STATEMENT   Ilarie Voronca (under the pen name Alex Cernat)
Originally published in *75HP* (October 1924)

One cannot overestimate the contribution of modernist research to literature and art. Over the last five years, the whole baggage of melancholy boarding-school girls romance has been gradually forgotten in suburban stations in the oh! sacramental sound of barrel organ. Now, fresh with new virginities drawn or written thought is splitting express like lightning the steppes sonorously unfolded. In airplanes travelers with tough sensitivities play poker or tap-dance on their hands. And the sharp edge of the sensation no longer vainly stops on the retina but breaks up fecund dumdum on the meninges. This is the triumph of cerebrality music-hall acrobatism elegant polite up to gasometer. Life a hot carburetor falls on the chestnut vendor's head. And the words with disheveled bowels run through the faubourg wrapping themselves in the jazz of vertiginous sentences. Literature no longer rusts like leaves in autumn no longer suppurates at intervals like a phlegmon but rolling tire vulcanization in the dance of cities is falling down.
Automobile truck huge cauldron manometer tar all tumultuously spilled over the canvases healed of imbecilization. Painting is no longer the academic onanism of oil tubes. Virile it broke higher than prejudice in the massive constructivist erection. Of course INVENTION INVENTION INVENTION. For so many centuries hungry art has opened its arms to the five continents. This is an INTELLIGENCE class. The SPEED of INTELLIGENCE at 60 floors elevator. Drama is a nervous tic, the stage must be brought down to the audience or toilet booths. Tear up all curtains let us be invaded by the street, by, cities, by ourselves. The world must be reinvented. Always innovative. That is why the invention of Messrs. Victor Brauner and Ilarie Voronca PICTOPOETRY is the synthesis of the new art and might be the justification for the 75HP group in itself.
From the concert of machines without the idiocy of principles 75HP set about tough achievements. Above: the stunning incorrigible un-formula personality of the painter Victor Brauner. Next to him daring Ilarie Voronca, Stephane Roll, Miguel Donvil.
With such elements art will be forever new.

Translated by Monica Voilescu

PICTOPOETRY IS NOT PAINTING
PICTOPOETRY IS NOT POETRY
PICTOPOETRY IS PICTOPOETRY

ASSESSMENTS   Ilarie Voronca
Originally published as "Constatări," *Punct* no. 2 (November 30, 1924)

After the publication of *75HP*, the problem of the new movement became an acute one for all the publications in Bucharest. Not one of them has had the decency to record this movement dispassionately, each rushed ceremoniously to attribute it circumstantial diagnostic prescriptions. Dadaism, Constructivism, Futurism, these are uttered by the hasty reporter with the same off-handed casualness as the rising price of streetcar tickets. And everywhere there is an unsettling incapacity, a painful ignorance. Still, one fact is characteristic: *75HP* broke open instantly for us the question of a movement. Before it I know of no magazine here representing an ideology properly delirious. In France, for instance, each step of spiritual or artistic evolution has its own tribune. For André Gide's generation, *Nouvelle Revue Française*; for the previous one, *Mercure de France*; for today's, *Feuilles libres*. I search for the journal representing for us Naturalism, Romanticism, Neo classicism. I search, but, nothing. They all tumble into a muddy amalgam reverentially borrowing their strained verses or drooling prose like pie-baker puts up a signboard in the window of his shop. Nowhere the word shooting out into a death-defying leap, rope dancer over buildings.

Fifty years of literary overtaxing have not even made one diamond scratch on the time's windowpane. Rising import taxes have not prevented Prague ham from being brought into the country; yet, in spite no import restrictions, words cannot boast of such success: no great shout from across the borders can be heard in these parts. The lamentable ignorance of our writers is in consequence easy to understand.

Singularly the accomplished arc of Mr. Ion Vinea's temperament did not fall prey to this national mediocrity. His stubborn fist made full contact with its target, and critical trousers will incessantly shred from the barbed wire of his talent. Mr. Vinea's *Contimporanul* riposted with confident antennas to the signals from the Occident. And we will state it here (whatever the outcome): Mr. Vinea, along with five or six others: Arghezi, Minulescu, Adrian Maniu (his "Glass of Poison"), Bacovia, Urmuz are the only ones which the above-mentioned mid-centennial effort have offered to European literature. No other voice like theirs vibrated diapason-like, no other fulguration scarred the centuries. It's true, during the time of Mallarmé and of Rimbaud we merely attempted our first steps in verse craft. The six names above represent in all certainty a triumph. To their names the new generation will add others. Until then, we are in need of conditioning.

For many art is a giant piece of nougat from which anyone feels entitled to chew. No one but a connoisseur would venture to judge a descriptive geometrical diagrams or an anatomical plate. Before artistic accomplishment, all attachment to incompetence vanishes. The money lender or the salesman of galoshes who closes up shop at 7, the student who sets aside his books on political economy or commercial law, pausing before a painting, all these sport opinions, emit advice, become scandalized or applaud. Why? For them, literature, paintings are a public *pissoir*. Normally, everything would have gone on as before, within the Naturalist vein. The common soup of our education being something we were force-fed for centuries, each carries in his blood the leukocyte of public artistic understanding. Then the new art showed up, backed up by a series of fresh principles. How can the spectators entrenched in the education of the old stylistic manifestations begging to comprehend this art whose alphabet is still unknown? For the local spirit. *Contimporanul* and *75HP* have been an ice avalanche which, plunging brutally, have torn apart the spinal chord of past literature.

However our principal lack consists of the idiotic informers of this cotton public. The lumpy pill of cerebral nutrition is handed the public, still dripping from the spittle of this incapable windbag of a critic. Last year two admirable exhibits—those of Messrs. Marcel Janco and Maxy (the only exhibits of last year)—this year the accomplished exhibit of Mr. Victor Brauner, have been greeted with nothing but silence.

The lack of preparation of our writer, for things long valued elsewhere is nothing but painful. Nowhere the instructor of these backwards and insensitive spectator. Because certainly, between creative artist and spectator, will we have the courage to proclaim the second one is the idiot?

For the sake of the truthful and honest public information, the aim of *Mişcarea literară* (The Literary Movement) of Mr. Liviu Rebreanu is clear. For the time being *Mişcarea literară* has assured its magisterial scope under the auspices of Mr. Marcel Janco. And this is not insignificant. However, the initiation will not occur overnight. The new literature and plastic arts demands a different sensibility. In addition, soul commerce is perpetually the order the day. But whatever anyone says: in the century of the automobile and airplane, anyone can travel by oxcart: however, we wish to take the airplane.

Translated by Julian Semilian and Sanda Agalidi

THE *CONTIMPORANUL* EXHIBITION (NOTES)   Scarlat Callimachi
Originally published as "Expoziţia 'Contimporanului' (însemnări)" in *Punct* no.3 (December 1924)

The magazine that through its three-year-long persistence stirred up a new current in our literature and art opened its first modernist international exhibition. It is a triumphant start of considerable promise. After this demonstration—which has as its participants Poland, Germany, Belgium, Czechoslovakia, Serbia, Hungary and Romania—*Contimporanul* announces for the month of May an exhibition involving Italy, France, Spain and Russia.

The new movement began simultaneously everywhere. The Romanians, as is well known, were among the precursors. The sculptor Brâncuşi was perhaps the first primitivist and then the first abstractionist in Europe. Among his students are Lipschitz and Archipenko. Marcel Janco was the first to publish "constructions" in Dadaist magazines. At Zürich University he presents, as architect, Cubist reliefs and architectural designs we had to wait until today to find in all the foreign magazines which propose the remake of Europe's cities on foundations that match the needs of the time. These two cases alone clear the charge of imitation and import of Western art into our country. This art developed under the sway of the prevailing atmosphere entire continent.

As precursors then, although with considerable difference of age, we note the presence of Brâncuși and Marcel Janco in this exhibition. We have known for a long time, the bewitching, hallucinatory *Majestic Bird* and that elementary and coarse stone *The Embrace*, both by Brâncuși. Marcel Janco, under the spell of his violent and volcanically balanced visions reminds us however of the concealed Old Master virtuosity and magical technique in drawing, composition, and color. Mrs. Militsa Petrașcu is a revelation for us. The wooden sculpture *Torso*, by remote and fully surmounted Brâncușian influences, expresses an ardent and superior sensuousness that compels matter to shiver. Maxy marks a return from the "industrial" color of his past constructions to the painter's impasto. His canvases, firmly and intently realized, there are two that bewitch the most, denote an intellectualism appropriate to constructive painting and reveals the artist's fortuitous development in this direction. Máttis-Teutsch balances fantasy with sobriety. He builds with elegant strains via lyrical color transitions. Dida Solomon brings her strange "puppets," stolen from who knows what bewitched realm of her rich subconscious: verve, naïve and unrestricted coloring, the way we wish it vainly on those very grave academy professors. Victor Brauner, audacious in his dynamic inventions, which capture in their circuits something from the apparently static tension of the spheres.

Translated by Julian Semilian and Sanda Agalidi

THE FIRST *CONTIMPORANUL* INTERNATIONAL EXHIBITION   Tudor Vianu
Originally published as "Prima Expoziție internațională *Contimporanul*" in *Mișcarea literară*, December 6, 1924

Sunday, November 30 was the opening of the first international exhibition organized by the magazine *Contimporanul* under the direction of Mr. I. Vinea. The obscurity of the salon where a multitude of guests fluttered in agitation and where introductory words uttered by Mr. Eugen Filotti were somewhat lost was suddenly sundered by a drum roll. The lights that then erupted revealed on the podium, behind the master of ceremonies, a jazz-band, replete with Negro musician. The sounds of strings, sirens and drums. The perplexed multitude attempted without much success to advance at the podium. Did the directors of the exhibition pre-plan perhaps this general first impression, the bewildering amalgam of tones like a gigantic collection of colored butterflies? Because at least as far as the intervention of the jazz band is concerned it is certain that we were not only dealing with an effect of stage direction but with a veritable modernist ritual, of Dadaist manifestation.
Only later could we distinguish the structure of the exhibit. The wall on the right was almost entirely occupied by the works of Mr. Marcel Janco, the wall on the left by the works of Mr. Maxy, while Mr. Máttis-Teutsch from Brașov exhibits close the entrance. The canvasses of foreign painters are grouped towards the back of the salon. In the center, corners, on the back podium, sculptures by Mr. Brâncuși and Mme. Militsa Petrașcu, mobiles, vases and small wooden sculptures by Messrs. Maxy, Janco and Teutsch.
In this general arrangement, to the right and to the left, two canvasses of detailed analysis: *Cabaret Voltaire* by Mr. Janco, with clearly enough defined gestures and characters, and *Targul Mosilor* by Mr. Maxy, where any realistic intention is eliminated,

not to mention the paradoxical structure of form and the variegated scintillation of color. In spite of this coincidental contrast, Mr. Maxy seemed to me to be of an emotive temperament, closer to the Expressionist inspiration, if only through his preoccupation to infuse sentiment into a landscape, as in the engaging *Landscapes with Oil Derricks*, while on the other hand Mr. Janco appeared to possess the more abstract nature, radical in his determination to separate subject from sentimental theme, accomplishing in this manner the abstract formula with greater purity. Mr. Teutsch travels along the same route, but places emphasis not on form but on color. Color is, however, by its nature, emotive-musical, and it is difficult to speak about abstraction founded on color only.

The *Contimporanul* Exhibition also presents a few pieces by Mr. Brâncuși, whose fame in foreign lands awakened in our public the desire to get to know him. Mr. Brâncuși creates with a unique energy. In his space, as confined as possible, he unleashes up an expansive space of forms: we have before us one of the most impressive artistic efforts to graphically overcome and annihilate matter. What exactly is it that contributes to the sculptures of Mr. Brâncuși this mysterious and infinite potentiality of expression that causes your knees to weaken? We asked ourselves constantly if it is we who are to blame, or the artist's disregard that caused his regrettable abandonment of native land and Romanian artistic activity, where he was called to play such a predominant role.

A student of Mr. Brâncuși, Mme. Militsa Petrașcu is however capable of originality both in motif and treatment. We admired particularly the piece inappropriately named *Torso*, a stylization of hipbones with leg line through a sober and deft usage of a restrained number of surfaces. Here as well as in the other pieces, Mme. Petrașcu weaves resolution and delicacy in her shapes in a manner which justifies our highest hopes in her future activities.

Infused by the veritable spirit of the modernist experience in art, the organizers of the exhibition added, along with painting and sculpture, pieces of furniture and interior decoration. Maxy's chest of drawers, Mr. Janco's table and chairs, his vases, the wood ornaments of Mr. Teutsch are beautiful stylish objects to fill a modern chamber more suitable than a reminiscences and imitations of past eras. They generate a key to understanding of the framework began Sunday and which, at least in its decorative tendency, can speak to the public at large.

Translated by Julian Semilian and Sanda Agalidi

MARCEL JANCO   Ilarie Voronca
Originally published as "Marcel Iancu," *Punct* no. 5 (December 20, 1924)

There is, without a doubt, in the arts as well as in all other realms—I'm thinking specifically of social activity—a law of historical determinants. You can speak about the art of a certain era, as you speak about the fauna of a certain province. It's a precise algebra of ethnic or moral transmutations, where the terms cannot be altered except through a grave miscalculation. Certainly, the age of Louis XIV called for the response of a Molière or Corneille, in the same manner that the defeat of spiritualism in Fichtean Germany found its cast in the positivism of August Comte or the dourness of Heredia's sonnets. This determinacy of historical climates is unrelenting. In vain the protestations or the simpering smiles of some, the scandalization of all. The spirit of every age demands its fulfillment, as melting snows a path. And towards the accomplishment of this fulfillment, the age's sensibility itself fashions its word bearers.

What you find here is a curious spontaneity in the engendering of values. The great revolutions will always fashion their Napoleons. The metamorphosis of sensibility—in truth lacking in velocity, in the arts revolutions being excluded—will perpetually possess their Pericles, Rousseau, their Manets or their Picassos. Any resistance is fruitless. Time being an apt surgeon, it fertilizes the brains it values. From here will later emerge the man of enchantment. Out of these, the sublime values will shoot out like the baying of a train over the mountains. Some will mark the start of a new age, like a fulguration's reference point. There are those who transmute into letters of the alphabet, which then anyone can utilize, but their creation will become someday the veritable bewitching medicine.

Among them, and at their forefront, stands Mr. Marcel Janco. The writer of these lines is too young not to be an enthusiast. He has met and valued this admirable painter, ponderer of paint, color, line. He was enraptured by his extraordinary canvasses, where the shapes embraced each other or glided into one another abstractedly, purely, like creation itself. But his enthusiasm was particularly stirred by this artist, forging restlessly, throbbing under the bronze visage, perpetually preoccupied, of Mr. Marcel Janco. His agitated temperament, tantalizing even, many times absent, the incessant unrest, the impetuosity and oscillation of a veritable artist have abducted him entirely.

Having met Mr. Janco, you are in a better position to grasp his work. Because the work of Mr. Janco is torn from him personally, as you would tear from the earth the fern. Every canvas by Mr. Janco is rain, perfume, storm, river-spring, and stone.

The art of Mr. Janco is natural like nature itself. Veritable artist, Mr. Janco doesn't imitate, doesn't photograph, doesn't stutter in a dull manner. Mr. Janco creates. With him, along with Arp, Tristan Tzara, Soupault, Dessaignes and a few others from foreign lands (where the initiation of the public is undertaken by serious people, not by gorillas as in our parts), began, it's been ten years since then, an agitation of ideas. Mr. Marcel Janco is among those who searched through unknown territories. His standard flutters even now on top of the highest peak. In these parts, Mr. Marcel Janco, without Messrs. Maxy and Victor Brauner, would be singular. Along the same road, with the same vigor and resolution towards innovation, sojourns with certain steps, Mr. Victor Brauner.

The talent and sensibility of Mr. Marcel Janco have pounded stubbornly on the age's anvil. His name signifies the preoccupations of an age, a fulfillment of art.

And to close with a word by Philippe Soupault:

"This is Marcel Janco, flesh and bone, inhabitant of Bucharest, December 1924."

Translated by Julian Semilian and Sanda Agalidi

VISUAL CHRONO-METERING   M.H. Maxy

Originally published as "Cronometraj-Pictural" in *Contimporanul* vol. 3 no. 50–51 (December 30, 1924)

The genesis of sentimentalism	I fear, struggle mystery, polytheism monotheism	represent-plastic action equal: narrative painting illusion
	heroes, glory, romanticism II lyricism, individualism Impressionism	

1. Mural Painting, vassal of Architecture
2. Easel Painting, independent, non-decorative
   Narrative in coma

CUBISM:

Alembic-laboratory
Chamber music; soloist-universal baton

painting concept	light	R
composition		E
balance	color	V
structure		I
economy	form	S
measure		I
synthesis		O
		N

Thunder, arrows, venom, farce, prose, advertising, rinds, eggs, (effect) artifice
DADAISM

Philosophy, economico-politico-scientifico-artistico-religious

General cauterization
Road to abstraction opened
Fraternity in arms
Cubism redeemed

CONSTRUCTIVISM

Aesthetic relationship of color and form
Conceptual, mechanical, dynamic, static spiritualism

Standard: Music: geometry of sounds
           Painting: geometry of planes

Constructivism, architectonic function:
The Death of Painting
—The End—

Future, future, future
Don't ask Picasso,
Don't ask us
Don't ask nobody
Picasso from time to time juggles

(sensual, nervous recreation)

Biding time, work, biding time

Titanical struggle to determine a constructive cubism
Europe eroded by economical obsessions
The century seeks its style in all its fields
We bide our time, we work, we transform

Translated by Julian Semilian and Sanda Agalidi

CONVERSATIONS WITH LUCIAN BLAGA   Felix Aderca
Originally published as "De vorbă cu d. Lucian Blaga," *Mișcarea literară* vol. 2, no. 8
(January 3, 1925)

And what if, in the world without end, the good
Lord and gruesome Satan were brothers?
And if they traded their crafty masks,
That you don't know who's one or who's the other?

Lucian Blaga, "Master Manole"

It cannot be said that the poet, Transylvanian by birth, universal by temperament,
conviction and will, did not enjoy, from his beginnings as a writer, critical attention.
It is indeed a miracle how a writer so original in his poetic forms, so divers in manifestation—he has composed, along with poetry, studies and drama—has succeeded
in attracting the attention of Romanian critics, through whose fingers, habitually,
slips everything of veritable value.
Critical attention has not managed however to shatter the magic circle of public ignorance, and Lucian Blaga, at this moment the author of eleven volumes, is just as unfamiliar as he was in 1919 when he published his *Poems of Light*.
The quality of his soul is thus completely validated. Because the masses are fated
to always find last what is best.
Integral with synthetic style of writing—characteristic to the writer of essence—
Lucian Blaga alone offers in his numerous studies, lucid in his stance, the key to his
complex personality. Whoever turns back to his book *Philosophy of Style*, published in
1924, finds the following lines on page 70: "The truly novel works of literature and art
of the last quarter century are so many glimmerings of lofty spirituality. We're not
speaking only of those flurries of a new religiosity breezing through these parts. A
vast awareness, directed towards the creation of a new world, arises." And with the
prophetic tonality of the emerging century, Blaga writes: "If it is true that art precedes
those other transformations, then perhaps the tidings that Europe is on the road to a

new dogma and a new spiritual collectivism or church are justified. And he lists the conditions necessary to manifest this new creed: "Anonymity—dogma—spiritual collectivism—abstract art—internal stylization."

And the last two words personify Blaga's essence.

"The spiritual collectivism" of this young prophet is not difficult to contest in his egalitarian intentions. It was contested however by Europe's evolution itself, which he heralds, and which, if indeed it is stepping towards a political, and perhaps economic collectivism, testifies that it aspires towards principles essentially anarchic in the creation of aesthetic values. Neither the painters, nor the writers, nor the architects congregated at Geneva so as to construct conjointly the cathedral of the new "anonymous" creed, like the monument at Chartres or Reims. The pictorial schools, the literary, the dramatic, in France and Germany, which in 1919 aimed towards the universalization of their principle, whether Expressionist or Dadaist, have pulverized unnoticed by anyone, and each of the "anonymous" creators of those currents has established himself on his own, some even aspiring to become members of national academies.

But did the prophet ever appear in order to be contested?...

His most prized dream is more precious than the most precious truth, and his blue flame, more eternal all other realities.

And Blaga, the propagator of anonymous and collective art, has begun by undermining and demolishing the glory of the idol of the cruelest Personalism, God himself. In his drama, *Zamolxes*, he depicted the god as being blind. Then he amalgamated him in all of nature's manifestations, which is godlike in each pebble found on one's path, each leaf of the forest, each wave on the waters.

And as the prophets who negated began always with themselves, abandoning themselves to hunger, thirst and unquenchable temptation, the youthful herald began as well through negation:

> Give me your hand, passerby,
> both you who are leaving and you who are coming.
> All the flocks of this earth have
> haloes over their heads.
> I love myself differently now,
> as one among many,
> I shake myself free of myself
> like a dog coming out of a cursed river.

The idea of a God who could be considered a single principle in nature has pursued Blaga and obsessed him with its unshakable personalism. And he transmuted Him into Satan, as the poem at the start of this essay states, and as he wrote in his first poems:

> From whence, I ask myself,
> does paradise get its light?
> Hell's flames illumine it, I know.

And from the threshold of this apocalypse, from where the prophet embodied a principle, his voice, within the earshot of those who know how to hear him, he culls today the might of great dramatic poetry.

THEORY OF KNOWLEDGE, PHILOSOPHY OF STYLE.

Lucian Blaga: ...There may be a connection between these two books I published during the last few years. To make this connection means to construct a detailed philosophical system. The implication is that I recognize the necessity of a dogmatic system. Individualism, dominant today in the systems of private property, legislation, politics, literature and the other arts, furthers no longer. We are stranded in the mud. We are paralyzed. I feel Personalism cannot create anything original any longer, something previously

untold. We are heading towards anonymous creation. If it were in my power, I would publish a magazine where authors renounce the right to sign their works, and whose unique
ambition is perfection, through emulation, of an artistic ideal commonly accepted.

COLLECTIVE ART

Blaga: We have a tradition in this. The Bible is a collective work. Similarly, *A Thousand
and One Nights.* No less our folk poetry. The Gothic cathedrals, which took hundreds of
years to build, would not be possible without this dogma which surpasses individualism
and requires generations of individualities, which, animated by the same spirit, submitted themselves to a common and anonymous ideal, engendering these enchanting
collective works, on the bricks of which no signature may exist.

...Look at the evidence in he expressionist lyric, which gave today's poet a well-defined
instrument of expression. But the crisis Expressionism suffers from is that it aspires,
through its poets, playwrights, painters, sculptors, individually, but not in a collective
mode, towards a collective style. I realize what this means: this belief in collective art
is a denial of individualism itself...

Marcel Janco, putting aside his sketch: But it is exactly our creed, the creed of
Constructivists! Look, this is what I wrote in *Contimporanul:* The Dada movement
protested against the incessant re-emergence of neoclassicism in architecture.
The call came from the artists themselves.
We launched the first manifestoes in 1915, where we proclaimed:

1. The collaboration between plastic arts and rejuvenated architecture (their isolation
   from each other was the cause of their enfeeblement).
2. Against the commerce of art and of exhibitions (venality gave birth indirectly to
   alienation of the artist and bohemian poverty).
3. Against the frame for abstract paintings (they are no longer naturalist sections;
   architecture alone frames it).
4. Against the superhuman arrogance of the artist, cultivated from Renaissance on
   (the new artist is a human being who returns to society)."

These manifestoes were coupled with examples of collaboration between abstract
plastic arts and architecture. Later, the radical artists group (Arp, Eggeling, Richter
and Janco) went a step further to demand the anonymity of the artwork.
This idea sprouted, because shortly after we witnessed three marvels: The exhibit of
the independent revolutionary architects of Berlin; the first Cubist city ("Magdeburg,"
through the gigantic efforts of architect Taut) and, lastly, the abstract art school
applied to architecture of Weimar (Bauhaus).

Blaga: Working within the principles of a dogma in the arts, through elimination of the
individual, we, Romanians, are connecting ourselves after a long absence to Byzantine
art, a collective art as well. Evidently, we are not talking about a return to Byzantine
dogma (as a too zealous traditionalist might believe), but only to the function of
Byzantine dogma in the creation of the artwork.

THE NEW CHURCH OF ART

Blaga: ...Yes, a new church, whose accent would not fall upon a discriminatory principle, individual-nationalist in nature, but upon spirit, upon metaphysics, both all-
comprehensive. In the Middle Ages similarly there was spiritual power which encompassed national collectivities of considerable stature: Christianity... I feel that a new
art dogma is at the point of manifesting itself. After Rococo there has been no new
style; the dawn of "absolute style"—as I name it in *Philosophy of Style*—is beginning
to emerge...

Janco: One of the elementary conditions for the manifestation of this style is the contact between artists who live far from each other. Because there has never been as

intensive a live contact between artists as today. In Geneva, in Vienna, in Prague, in Bucharest, in Weimar, collective exhibits take place. In Weimar an impressionist hotel was built, whose construction was accomplished by the work of hundreds of artists. It is collapsible and made of wood. It was ordered by the Americans and later will be transported there. Witzing, forced to make 70 thousand sketches for an abstract film, created a plastic alphabet, a syntax of forms, with the help of which different artists, working together, will be able to build, inside the limits of precise indications, a singular work of art.

Blaga: These facts, which so surprisingly coincide with my belief in collective art, prove that this idea of "absolute style" is in rhythm with the times, is a dictate of that law of rhythmic reoccurrence. To attempt to question this law, to prove its justification, is fruitless, and perhaps impossible, it imposes itself.

…You object to my argument that collective art cannot agree with literature, the way it agrees with architecture. That Racine, Corneille, Molière, La Fontaine, even though developing under the vigil of Boileau and Louis XIV, under circumstances approximating the same ideal of Greco-Latin antiquity, veneered in the century' powder, perfume, and lubricity, continue to live on and will go on living, each through his personal, distinct character, specific to his work. Which is true, today, for those who judge an artwork from personalism's point of view. It is a critical view of aesthetics that we wish to transcend. The man of art must, from now on, educate himself from the point of view of collective art.

Translated by Julian Semilian and Sanda Agalidi
[Editor's note: three fragments of Blaga poems are reprinted here. The first was translated by Julian Semilian; the others were translated by Andrei Codrescu and are taken from his book of translations of Blaga poems, *At The Courts of Yearning.* They are used here with his permission. Codrescu's book does not include the first poem, "Master Manole."]

GRAMMAR   Ilarie Voronca
Originally published as "Gramatică," *Punct* no. 6–7 (January 3, 1925)

The word in literature, like color or line in painting, has an abstract duty, above and beyond its grammatical or logical significance. There is chemistry in the admixture of words, and enthrallment results when they react with one another. The verb, employed purely for itself, in the manner of materials of plastic construction, harvests a sense not registered by the mere dictionary. What I mean is, the craving to squeeze instant significance from each word is in truth aggravating. The word pitches tent indifferent to sense, in the same manner that iron, stone, or lead dwell flawlessly before commerce costumes their forms. The anecdotal use of the word, or of the plastic creation is no more than their mass marketing. And in this mass marketing expire all the inept architects of the word. The veritable artist fashions directly, without resorting to symbol, in clay, wood or verb, live organisms, machines dismembering paths, howls violently quavering, like roofs in a hurricane. The words thus earn their own sense, boxing with or embracing one another. No longer does the line have the photographer's purpose of lending the spectator a representation of exterior correspondences. No longer is the sentence a fiction that recalls the electoral discourse or the amorous declaration of the baker of pies who suddenly turns to poetry. No longer does the work of art contain anything supernatural like phantoms or phonographs. The word, liberated and fulgurant, glides singularly like a stiletto into the reader's meninges. The eye no longer dozes sluggishly. The skyscraper verb.

The first attempts at exploration into the word regarded in itself as well as into the reactions between words were made by Rimbaud and Mallarmé (later to be fully completed by Marinetti, Picabia, Tristan Tzara, Kurt Schwitters), if we didn't bear in mind that, long before them, Nostradamus, in his mysterious invocations, accomplished surprising juxtapositions of words.

Still, the consciousness of opposition against the grammatical phrase and commerce begins with Mallarmé. Through him the path is now open. The contribution of the group led by Apollinaire, André Salmon, Braque, Picasso signifies a violent and profound shattering of academicism. But the most appealing among them proves to be the postwar project in Zurich, namely the group led by Arp, Schwitters, Marcel Janco, Tristan Tzara, Picabia, and Soupault. The alarm is unleashed. The spectator would become aware that from here on words are not any longer obedient puppets. Words possess their own life, which they demand and create. The word as an unshackled dancer would leap between lines, to crack the phrase open like a coconut. The leaking milk will regale us with the taste of uncharted provinces, where etymology and syntax, utilized in mediocrity, will no longer reside.

I have discerned elsewhere the artist's purpose, spotlighted in his endeavor to rejuvenate with an element which is novel and proper to itself the depleted framework of artistic production.

Certainly, art forms putrefy and, without this revolutionizing effort, art turns to decaying platitude. The pioneering artist introduces, along with his own sensibility, a personal order to the conditions demanded of a phrase. Logic is utterly useless to artistic creation. And, for good reason, every unforeseen genesis defies this philosophical governor of an erstwhile system. Logic is the result of a research already accomplished. Thus we can't make any reference except to a present and possibly less to a future. It's a clear fact: each contribution, in every domain, scientific (Galileo, Einstein, Freud), philosophic, artistic, gives the appearance of a neologism, for the simple reason, mentioned above, that logic is the mutual production of a number of erstwhile researches, and thus applicable only within their limitations. The result of a novel experience will thus introduce another logic, seemingly neological, which later, after long term usage, will be recorded in the catalogue of the old time logic. But one thing we will underline: the novel and veritable creator shatters the known laws with the pick-axe of his temperament. Each artist must be the originator of novel principles, descending through the concert of fulgurations atop Mount Sinai with the tablets of a new logic in his hands.

Out of the explorations undertaken in the last few years, the logic of boarding school girls and academies emerges in shameful tatters.

And this in the incontestable favor of the arts. The banality and impersonation it was headed towards was replaced by the unforeseen of its actual efforts.

Etymology, syntax, grammar have had much to attempt. Because the perfectly grammatical phrase is nothing but a logical phrase.

The pioneering creator has shattered the agreed upon rules of grammar. The new image demands a new construction. And what admirable images result out of grammatical errors. The poets have always known (certainly, in a smaller measure than today) the wealth of imagery induced by such errors. Out of this results what in the old days was called poetic license. But for the sensibility of today, license, as it was conceived then, is sheer idiocy. Not license but the liberated stringing of words. The verb peeled of symbol gains a veritable vitality. Outside of this words are nearly untranslatable. There is, for us, a craving that is nearly sensual, of linking words in spite of their significance. The same notions in differing languages constantly change. For many:

road, *chemin*, *weg*, *cammino* signify the same thing. Inexact. *Chemin* is entirely something different from *road* or *cammino*, because the road in our parts is something entirely different than the road in Italy, while this is entirely different than the road in France. Beyond the style and sense of every expression lies the style and sense of a period or a land. Each word in itself contains, more precious than its meaning, the sensibility and sonority of a time period. That is why I wrote that words are untranslatable and that is why a poem whose first verse is: "smoking is prohibited," while the second is: *rauchen verboten*, does not contain a repetition but two separate verses, perfectly distinct from one another. But what corresponds to the untranslatability of words is the translatability of "idiotisms."

The oddity and logistics or anti-grammar of an idiotism translated from one language into another signifies the reinvigoration of expression. Examples are innumerable. It is certain that defying logic, its demolition, means the enrichment of sensibility, of the arts in general. Out of these efforts, these shards, will be engendered the voice, the gesture of future sensibilities. Heliade—Rădulescu's shout "Write, boys!" must be re-edited, engraving on it the sign of the times: "Be sure to make grammatical errors!"

Translated by Julian Semilian and Sanda Agalidi

VOICES Ilarie Voronca
Originally published as "Glasuri," *Punct* no. 8 (January 9, 1925)

The transformations in the realm of ethics have always paralleled the ones in the social realm, and especially those in the techno-scientific. The link between these specific manifestations is so close that we could easily picture a scientist of the future discerning the entire sensibility or culture of an era in an automobile screw found during a dig in the same manner that contemporary researchers have recreated an entire antediluvian animal from a single bone.

Certainly our presupposition will cause many to smile. And still this link is indissoluble. All the scientific experiments in the laboratory have their echo in artistic accomplishments. (But we are not saying that there is a conscious upsetting of forms in the wake of scientific discoveries.)

Thus many times, the audacity of the creator in art precedes future scientific developments. Freudianism and all the psychoanalytic principles have been for a long time unconsciously foreshadowed by the explorations of the poets. As a matter of fact the Surrealism of André Breton is a belated duplication, based upon Freudianism, of the Zurich accomplishments of Tristan Tzara, Marcel Janco, Arp, Eggeling. In any case, a novel method of mathematical or psychological analysis, a new means of travel, will open the path for a new sensibility and a new means of expressing this sensibility.

Naturally, the echo of scientific renewal does not limit itself only to this: the resulting effect will be felt in a similar measure in pedagogy, in the methods of instruction, in the entire aspect of social engagement.

But the most accomplished fertilization will be lavished upon the arts with their multiple aspects.

The artist never concerns himself with the degree of *comprehensibility* of his work. On the contrary: the more incomprehensible his work, the more valuable the art. Because art is a flintstone that sparks in the wake of a resistance, a struggle. Yes, cookbooks will always be comprehensible, and ordinances announcing an administrative disposition. The artwork turned out for the pleasure of the spectator will never surpass the salad spontaneously provoking the consumer's enthusiasm. The veritable artwork will always possess the charm of a virginity incessantly renewed.

The taste, the eye, the ear of the spectator must be incessantly violated. The work of art lives only by turning a blind eye to all pre-established rules. The painting, the poem, singularly, will dominate the imbecilically impersonal personality of the spectator. The work of art could never be an open door that the public's filthy boots can insolently trample through. The spectator's perplexity will provoke his timidity or his audacity: from here on the fierce cerebral effort will transmute to his pure, abstract comprehension of the art. The spectator, in consequence, must be raped. In this manner art is redeemed from the incessant threat of turning to platitude. Each word will explode like dynamite, each line will throb like copulation.

For good reason, art cannot co-exist with logic. I said, however, that the new explorations in the realms of philosophy, of the sciences in general, are profitable to the arts. Evidently a holistic character is registered everywhere. It is the emblem the age stamps on its products. Its significance is apparent.

Thus we distinguish in the actual artistic manifestations a trait common to all of the age's manifestations.

And this is: *synthesis*.

Poetry, the plastic arts, drama, music, and especially architecture converge into an abstract accord along the same route, stretched like a cord: *synthesis*. The experiments of Einstein: *synthesis*. The investigations of Freud: *synthesis*. Everywhere the manifestation of the same impulse towards integrity, synthesis. Art is no longer squandered in fragments. Thought, plastic arts, dance, stroll in vigorous unison, unearthing undiscovered landscapes. Until the arrival of today's art (an observation by André Salmon) painting ran always twenty years behind literature. Now the arts have coagulated in cross- fertilization. Their strength lies in this, the most potent factor of the contemporary current. None of the previous currents have enjoyed this holistic *synthesis* in the expression of the diverse art forms. Today, the accomplishments of this synthesis in the arts, poetry, construction, herald forcefully and tumultuously, the *century-sythesis*. In the plastic arts, Romania, through those few forceful elements, finds itself on a perfectly European footing.

The same certainty is heralded by its poetry.

Comprehensible or not, this universal effort shatters or builds everywhere, like a tidal wave crashing against the shore. To challenge or to ignore these efforts becomes akin to ridiculousness.

It is much like ignoring the persistent escalation of a continent. Certainly, much has been written and spoken about the new art. We are the better for it. Ribemont-Dessaignes rightly stated that a whack with a bat is more efficient than unctuous pampering. The combat commenced against today's art and literature (as represented here by *Contimporanul, 75HP*, and *Punct*) proves however the strength and foundation of this art.

No one has yet uttered the veritable word: Cubism, Futurism, Constructivism, all overflowed into the same brazen circle: *synthesis*.

All of human endeavor, today's or any day's, the accomplishments in any field of endeavor, mathematics, astronomy, medicine, chemistry, engineering, all accumulated in cross-fertilization in this art whose name we will shout without reservation: *synthetism*.

Translated by Julian Semilian and Sanda Agalidi

For our public, which hasn't yet strolled through the motley exhibit halls of the Occident,
the artistic event organized by the magazine *Contimporanul* may signify a nothing but
clamorous jumble of colors and forms and a gaping abyss for the eye, a cheap diversion
at the expense of such a true artist as Marcel Janco, or in best case scenario, setting
in motion a set of novel sensations, unknown until now. For some this "international"
exhibition signified perhaps some sort of rejuvenation after so many deathlike succes-
sions of stagnating and lifeless colors which have been observed lately at the Athenaeum
or anywhere else. A great deal has been written about this exhibition, much effort at
clarification has been undertaken, which, under the circumstances, is quite necessary.
The gossip has been abundant, some less agreeable, but admittedly indispensable and
instructional, given the nature of a situation such as this. An artistic panel sought and
even succeeded to hone the attention and disposition of Bucharest's public in the
direction of the new currents in the plastic arts, literature, music. For about two hours
the public's spirit was under attack in a rather belligerent mode. But the public ignorant
in matters of art, which is the very public which has never been perverted by the old
art, remained unconvinced. It came up against too many unoriginal aspects, against
the literary attributes of Hans Arp, against the laughter of Mme. Popovich—who enlightened the chamber by declaiming verses by August Stramm, verses incontestably of
poor quality, but with a content of little amusement. And maybe because during the
same panel, Mr. Maxy, the director of the exhibition, was feeling so well disposed that
he laughed without care, while the verses of Herwarth Walden and those of Mrs. Vinea
and Voronca pierced us with the chills of veritable art, which corresponded to "extensive
Expressionism" and may be accessible to anyone. These modes of instruction must in
any case be avoided in order not to compromise a cause founded upon a momentous
ideology and not one bit ridiculous, though arguable, not so much from the universal
platform of the plastic arts as emerging from an ethical viewpoint, from the aspect of
regarding these manifestations within the framework of our time.
We will strive to compose ourselves into a serious aspect, because if we allowed ourselves the laughter of Mr. Maxy, it might lead to the belief that we are mocking things
and matters that remain beyond our grasp. And on account of the self-same motive,
we must add that our sensibilities feel themselves timid, not only before the entire
complex of European art, often positively concrete, but also before an art which is
primitive, or arising from functions which are autonomous, belonging to a world which
is exotic, or before a building conceived by Bruno Taut, whom we otherwise regard as
the most significant architect of our time. But no less must we insist even today over
the very natural assessment that European art until now has excluded no formula of
synthesizing the exceptionally majestic inclinations and artistic harmonies of other
continents, but has remained, simultaneously, the very aspect of destiny and a governing spirit over the many, over many a century.
European art has been, in most cases, evaluated by those perverted in too great a
measure by the virtues of the old continent, this allowing the new currents distinguished status, and thus opening the path to a far-reaching mentality which did not
halt at the eastern borders of Russia, nor the shores of the Mediterranean Sea.
European art is not unique in the world, no! But it coagulated in the course of the centuries into a simplicity that is great and beyond argument, and that today is part and
parcel of our consciousness. Let it be permitted us to not believe in that *Decline of the*

West that was assessed by Oswald Spengler. We have need of new utopias. [...] Along with the intensified Expressionism of Kandinsky, Buddhism has found enough converts in Europe. And many have shouted: this is the new religion! But, fortunately, their shouts resounded in the void. New utopias? Yes! But not those that borrow the vestments of others, not those that proclaim that our tiny continent bears a past of too little importance to see in it the foundation of the emergence of a new conception of the world. We do not need, more, we avoid like the plague the new assessment: that everything is relative. It is too comfortable an assessment, it is the end of the human. Because there are enough truths that cannot be identified with reality and in these truths are mirrored the purest features of man. The assessments of relativity are the guillotine of all artistic creation. We have need of a sacred ecstasy, but rooted in a belief that which can include the soul of all, not just the convictions of a few. European art is a naturalist art that can be understood and evaluated in organic complexes, because its elements of artistic realization have been sustained by concrete form, even when symbol or spiritual background had nothing in common with the limited size of our planet.

Beginning from the formal realizations in music or the most elementary conceptions of architecture, many modes of novel art find their justification. In fact, everything can be contained in a single word: musicalization!

But music cannot be grasped through a written word, like a concrete form of nature. Today, more than any other time, Europe needs not creations favoring what is relative but precise assessments, because what is relative often stands beyond good and evil.

We are told that until now we have been the slaves of the past and the our time has no art of its own, and that, beginning with architecture the new world needs to concentrate its sensibilities in a novel form of art. Art is religion. Most certainly, but we will not shed our old religion before the new one is created. Shall we all become part of the creation of a new art? Shall we all become heralds of anonymous art? The new art has been until now the art of manifestoes, not of creators. We will need great individualities, whose works of art will infuse once again with ecstasy the barren landscape of our souls. We are waiting: but we believe that to frighten the traditional European with the new art is altogether mistaken. A few westerners realized this and have given their new magazines an aspect that no longer horrifies anyone. I am thinking, for instance, of *Feuilles Libres*, which has become far more domesticated in its last few issues. Perusing the cover of an avant-garde magazine, must we be slapped by the impression that this is the work of a few typesetters who have lost all control, who, in the throes of dementia, are mocking the world? I am being told that it is a case of radical break with the past in regards to the graphic aspect, in regards to typography itself, and in regards to the endurance of our nerves. It seems to me that this is just the sort of misguided enterprise that takes no account of the education of the masses concerning the new art.

And now the ideology, which justifies unequivocally the existence of this art. It is an ideology infused with the uncanny entrancement of the new, and unforeseen in its abundance and capacity to incorporate deeply contradictory intensities of feeling. Much literature was created around the new art currents. There is even a history of the Dadaist episode (Richard Hulsenbeck, *Die Geschichte des Dadaismus*). The leaders of these currents felt it essential to distinguish themselves from one another, while the word invented today was always superior to that of yesterday. The group of "intensive Expressionists" who, headed by Kandinsky, Paul Klee and Feininger, emerged from Germany, wished to be regarded in an entirely different manner than the Italian Futurists. And with good reason. Because the futurists, represented particularly by Marinetti, Boccioni, Gina Severini and Cara, tore up the impression of reality in bits which afterwards they conjoined, for the purpose of creating a more potent and dynamic image than the fragment severed from nature. Futurism, in its incipience, was no more than a reaction, a youthful one, to classic art, to traditional concepts, in which many youthful Italian protagonists drowned. Kandinsky did not wish to make a detour through impression, wished to realize an art which is only organic movement and color, an art purely of the soul without any exterior assistance and with which to oppose nature itself. Kandinsky was a lyrical artist, like Máttis-Teutsch. The French cubist group which separated a few years ago into four camps and called to battle by the great artist, and talented farceur Picasso, did not wish to be confused with less radical currents, because it had won a great deal of terrain on its own. Today's Futurism dissolved almost entirely into cerebral Cubist conceptions, which during the incipient years were tolerant toward reality, but later took flight toward the absolute Cubism of constructions which no longer had need of a literal title. From the shattered guitars of Picasso to the cold Constructivism of Russia is a long road, beaten by many contradictory conceptions. The "scientific" Cubism boasts of achievements other than the "orphic" or "physical," of intentions other than the "instinctive." Orphism, headed by Robert Delaunay, Duchamp, Picabia, Léger, was from the start independent of reality, while Picasso, Braque, Le Fauconnier, Juan Gris, Metzinger and others have first cultivated a sort of anti-naturalism, grounding themselves on the constructive elements of Cézanne.

The essence of new art is not, and does not desire to be *new*. The most elementary concepts of architecture and music are on its side; a distinguished historical past, of Egypt, India, China, of primitive Africa and Oceania sustain and justify it. The traditional ornaments of Nordic countries, where we discern the first beginnings of the dynamic gothic elements are as well consanguine with the new art and their eccentricity and asymmetry mirror the time's disquiet. The stylistic sensibility of the new art cannot hold onto the significance of its past counterpart, because the impact of the creation weighs upon the creator's ecstasy, independent of the organic forms of nature, independent of the means of expression and technical knowledge. The most ancient architecture of India, which opposes to the gigantic landscape one which is abstract-autonomous, constructed from spirit, has at its basis the same concept as a construction by Picasso or Marcel Janco. The Gothic period gave Europe its most profound realization of the abstract spirit, such that even in the new art there is discussion about the fight against symmetry, about Gothic tendencies. From a column of clouds raised at Chrudim (Chekoslovakia) during the culminating era of the baroque to Bakunin's monument in Moscow, created by sculptor Boris Koroliow, there is but a single step.

Everything has always been, everything has existed. But the spirit breathed more intensely, bore on its back, unspeakably powerful, the obsession of artistic realization. History forgets the farceurs of times past, who resemble perhaps Picasso, perhaps Archipenko, perhaps others, yet now we have them before us. (This assessment is not meant as an attack on the veritable significance of the group from Bucharest, heading as it is towards the idealism of French Cubism, while allowing itself its own freedom of movement.) Our attitude does not point its finger at the sense of this art, nor at the exhibitors. We believe these new currents, from which we exclude Expressionism, (which use reality only for the purpose of symbolizing the spirit), are harmful, because they are too relative. This is our judgement today. If the future will justify Messrs. Marcel Janco, Maxy and Brunea, their sincere obsession will be respectfully rewarded.

The exhibition from Syndicate of Plastic Arts salon regaled us with multiple new impressions. We were deeply impressed by the color in Mr. Marcel Janco's work, the unity of spirit of his constructions; we were deeply impressed by the sovereign feeling for form which we discern in all the sculptures of Mr. Brâncuși, the extraordinary sensibility of head and torso exhibited by Miss Militsa Petrașcu. (On a different occasion, when we are not forced to concern ourselves with the entire subject matter, we will speak in more detail about the work of this group.)

Our attitude remains fundamentally divergent, because it is grounded on principle that do not admit that Europe is dead and that art individually national is purposeless.

Translated by Julian Semilian and Sanda Agalidi

MAN   Editors of *Integral*
Originally published as "Omul," *Integral* no. 1 (March 1, 1925)

MAN, an invention: he invented himself. Because he wanted to, he populated the void with landscapes, seasons, civilizations. This is why nature nothing else than the complement of our sensitivity. *We never discovered anything!* Only prophets, artists-ists-ists used to discover pre-existence. The impersonal ape *MAN* was amazed. The *fable-myth* was created for him. Because of him, we lay down in a pseudo-rural attitude.

We definitely live under the sign of the urban. *Filter-intelligence, surprise-lucidity. Rhythm-speed.* Simultaneous balls—atmospheres giving concerts—billions of saxophones, telegraph nerves from the equator to the poles—strikes of lightning; the planet with flags, industrial plants; a giant steamer; the dance of the machines over bitumen ovations. *A crossroads of an era.* Classes are going down, new economies are being built. The proletarians are imposing forms. New psycho-physiologies are growing.

Our own inventions have overcome us. *Thought must exceed speed itself.* Vassals to the sluggish dream, we need *suzerainty*. Softened by beatitudes and Romantic self-compassions. *We don't want reinforced concrete.* The hypertrophy of the ego has devalued us, currency without a standard. *What an inflation of geniuses!!!*

No archangel-individuals hovering over the society; caught in the machinery we live *in, through, for it.* One used to be representative: but we all represent. *Mechanics passionate with a preoccupation.* THAT'S ALL.

Enough straying among intellectual matters! *Intellectual comics, enough!* You know: *Out of controlled knowledge and despair the style of the great epochs was born; the same causes are generating the style of this epoch.* In the old days, humankind was a psychological pygmy before nature; now, before nature and the moving force we have created.

This is why: *the need for us to integrate in nature; the need for us to sensitively go up to new heights.*

INTEGRAL offers certitude.

Teenagers have had fun with farces; contemporaneity was a synonym for farce. We are breaking away from the farce, from the snobbish admiration in cosmopolitan lobbies, from one reiteration after another.

Journalism has had the hunch of modern life, brutally exploiting a life that doesn't require an interpreter. Worker, tax collector, sentimental commentator. But experience has offered us lucid severity without feeling.

Seismograph-artists—readers, spectators and you, good people, be diaphragms!

INTEGRAL *without the protection of major and minor officials* reduces to the same denominator the vital, artistic *standards.* Freed from intellectual mediocrity, we are cutting our way forward over the dead bodies of schools and individuals.

INTEGRAL *claims the essence of the primary expression.*

Tradition: *The intelligence of the people, escaped from the eternally natural pastiche—and technology.* The collective imagination has forged fairy tales, songs, cultures that will forever be viable!

WE: *Synthesize the will life has always had, everywhere, and the efforts of all modern experiments. Immersed in collectivity, we create its style according to the instincts it only surmises.*

The deaf, again, haven't heard us.
The audacious have joined us!

Translated by Monica Voiculescu

SURREALISM AND INTEGRALISM   Ilarie Voronca
Originally published as "Suprarealism și Integralism," *Integral* no. 1 (March 1925)

On the map of modern sensibility, art currents quickly succeeded one another. An abundance of "isms" patrolled the finish line of the nineteenth century.
Specifically after the war, Europe wends through continual unrest. And certainly, above the individual heartbeat pulses the heartbeat of the era. There is a social back-drop that fertilizes the artist's style in the style of the age. Achievements in the arts are projected against a wall of contemporaneity.
The scientific revolutions, the political changes—in our age these last can be reduced to the struggle for or against nationalism—herald the movements of ideas and art, just as the fragrance of the season flags the tender new shoots. The time lugs with-in itself its principles, in the same manner the kangaroo lugs its child glued to its breast.
There is consequently, in the palpitating atmosphere of Europe, the justification for this rapid succession of movements. Still, the contemporary effort to seek incessantly new forms and shed pre-established ones contains a much deeper significance. I see in it the enterprise of the navigators at the close of the Middle Ages, in the expeditions searching for new paths to the Indies. Through the audacity of such a one, we were rewarded with a new continent. But the passion of all the others was not for nothing. Their imagination and daring drilled our starched meninx, our sluggish eye awakened as corkscrew of unscrutinized achievements. Today's visionaries lead us each a step closer to an actual inner India. Tomorrow, from these forerunners, a new Columbus will arise, a Columbus who will unfurl a world of virgin existence. Drunken with the passion of these newly awakened energies, unbounded cords, their step will gash the century's flesh. And each opens a road to the core of this hour. Surrealism still belongs to the category of above-mentioned endeavors. For this effort, we reward it with our enthu-siasm. On the other hand, for its potentials and fertility, our reservations are infinite. Before the wealth of novelty of the preceding currents, surrealism does not contain a contribution its own. On the contrary, its doctrine signifies a belated return to a bygone source. The establishment of hashish and the dream as principles of art, the excessive disintegration, these have been for some time part and parcel of Expressionism in its function as duplicator of the nasal complaints of Romanticism. The appeal to endorse Surrealism metamorphoses into its own act of self-incrimination.
The error was committed at its incipience. The psychiatric theories of Freud could not initially serve the productions of art. Their transposition to an extrinsic plane could

mean nothing but a distortion. In fact, it's a matter of course the subconscious was always utilized by the artist. In the thin trace of light containing the conscious mind, only six or seven images can persist simultaneously. Consequently a substance unequipped for creation. The entire treasury of emotions, ideas, memories, landscapes, promises, melodies dwell innumerably in disorder, like grain in the subconscious's repositories. From these the artist's gesture was effectuated.

As doctrine, Surrealism presents in consequence an already well-known principle. Principles aside, the artistic accomplishments of surrealism can be reduced to an unvaried duplication of the Dadaist experiments. In other words Surrealism—as doctrine—cannot demand the right to claim its own accomplishments. Its effort is limited to a labeling of former or actual accomplishments. In this sense, these following are branded Surrealist: Shakespeare, Chateaubriand, Poe, Baudelaire, Rimbaud (a veritable Surrealist) Mallarmé, Jarry, etc. In a similar sense, Adrian Maniu, *Glass of Poison*, and sometimes Urmuz could be considered Surrealist.

Fully Surrealist, and he whom Surrealism owes (in a disguised form) its system is Tristan Tzara—incontestable poet. On the other hand, Surrealism is (as dynamics) inferior to Dadaism. Surrealism is—after analysis—feminine/Expressionist.

Dadaism was virile. Surrealism doesn't cause disturbances. And moreover, in essence, *Surrealism doesn't respond to the rhythm of the times*. This characteristic must be underlined. The Dadaist experience—this we said before—was useful. Through it, the modern endeavor in the laboratory made contact with the contemporary brain.

Cubism, through Constructivism, opened up for itself a new path, a pure path, of life within its own space.

The age of European construction began.

Live organisms, the forging in stone, wood, scenery, airplanes, awakened to the bloody earth.

Constructivism won the day, with its abstract *order*, with a balanced harmony of laws and lines.

At this instant of fixed synthesis, the Surrealist disintegration cannot answer any necessity. The naïve drawing, disorganized, Surrealist, cannot compete with the massive and virile design of Constructivism. Before the integral voice of the century, Surrealism signifies but an absence. Today is the time of the accomplished deed. Poetry, music, architecture, painting, dance, all step forward integrally linked towards a definitive and lofty scale. Surrealism has ignored the century's voice, shouting: "Integralism." After Expressionism, Futurism, Cubism, Surrealism shows up too late. Not the ill romantic disintegration of Surrealism, *but the synthetic order, the essential order, constructive, classic, integral*.

Still, let us not forget that in Galilee the prophet of Nazareth was not alone. From all parts of Judea, during that restless time of the Roman province, with ivy voices rising to the skies, came all manner of creed bearers. But, over the landscape of the ages, the word of Christ alone prevails forever. And his word was *the most abstract, the purest*. But the martyrdom of all others roaming through time was not fruitless.

In the contemporary artistic aspect, Integralism will be spoken of resolutely. Its gesture, clearly, is not unique. But before the Surrealism's farewell performance, one thing we will shout with certainty: *Integralism is the rhythm of the age; Integralism launches the twentieth century*.

Translated by Julian Semilian and Sanda Agalidi

The sensibility of the last decades: sensibility of metamorphosis. Masks replacing themselves with passengers in a hotel; silhouettes evolving into high-wire acrobats. Physiognomies long and laboriously constructed for the ostentation of a single instant; the sudden spectacle of a fireworks show.

In the hubbub of plights and professions, in the savage concert of torrential simulations, in the carnival of blood- dripping accomplishments of perfection and revolutionary creations—a ballet vertiginously presented to the Undiscovered. Life frolicking at any and every revel; the artist frolicking in any and every life. In this profoundly acute squandering of pragmatism—fatal—the eye lost the ability of general delineation. Stubborn loitering, though fertile, over a single page. Investigations of orphans. Period which, spurred on to excessive development by quotidian insistence and use, tended to take on attributes of surface and volume. Impetus stimulated by the vanity's fruit-lessness. The gaze, suddenly transmuting from its contemplative function into gifted detective, pounced upon the detail with an insistence of drills. A prodigious and hope-less cultivation of details. Details specifically belonging to the subject, bearing the definitive label of singularity; but all terminating with the simple and insufficient intuit-ing of the whole. Train-fulguration which, through vertigo's monocle, may deceive no more than a single façade of the train station.

*

It was a false understanding of the sense of perspicacity. Penetrating clear-sightedness, profound but without the expanse. Skillful inquiry, but circumscribed by a terrain throttled by overwhelming walls. Deluding us, we suspected it deluded others. With eyelids glued to the morning's hampered slumber, we presupposed all others to be early-risers. We're still however in 1925. We view ourselves with too much pride to be hypocritical and disguise ourselves with methodically premedi-tated modesties. The knowledge of our own intelligence stabs us with an acute reek of lachrymal formaldehyde. Candid and insouciant, we scorn the ignorance and idiocy of benighted dilettantes. And in togas of steel, we place ourselves, righteous, without hatred, on the seat of the public accuser, of the ardent and intransigent prosecutor.

In fact, for us, humanity cannot be considered except in time. (The telegraph, the present intellectualism, the recent social tides have destroyed space). Thus, a division into two great periods: prehistory and history. Prehistory is interesting only to the archeologists; history may be concern to us. May be of concern to us. But the historical period begins with us; begins with our childhood. More precisely: from Marinetti. In consequence we only know this: the old Art and the new Art. The old Art: Futurism, Expressionism, Cubism, Dadaism, etc. The new Art: Integralism.

The old Art: development, education and chiseling of the antennas of a veritable sensi-bility, antennas nearly atrophied by Menz from the viewpoint of the discovery of light, from the viewpoint of the discovery of life.

A multicolored funeral procession of precursors. Expectation. A sensual fondling, heroic exploration, incisive exploitation, when the birth-giving fingers, borrowing unfamiliar senses, would not distinguish in the surrounding dark fecal matter from diamonds. A fugitive ray, bewildered, like a question mark, intruded upon retinas heavy with sleep, with the intransigence of an asteroid. Hereditary memories sang the glory of the super-annuated. Newtonian gravity crossed swords with the airplane, still under the tutelage of the baby-bottle. In the barren landscape, innumerable reflexes began to burst out of four times four hundred cardinal points. The comb of pondering picked them up however, each and every one of them. Ample hands shot out boldly towards them, attempting to capture them in word, color, test tube. Monopoly of detail. Not one fist boxed with the sun. It was yesterday's art. Pulverizing the originally compact and indivisible existence—a conviction was ventured that the complex can be mastered through the atom. Systems, theories, manifestoes. Multiple names and designations (Futurism, Expressionism, etc) were nothing but the various facets of the same sensibility, diverse virtues and qualities of the same spirit—utilized separately and under a different marquee, uncoordinated with the wilted-by-neglect rest, systematically not coagulated into a whole. Inconsequential enterprises, characteristic to each incipience of a century. What was missing is the pantheist vision of plural concentration; what was missing initially is power of synthesis.

Futurism exhausted its dynamics. To the detriment of all its other forces. The psychic dynamic of the I; the exterior molecular dynamic. In consequence: unrestricted words, succession of values (plastic or moral), decay of contours. Velocity. Total absence, still, of the spirit of abstraction and associative dissociation (juxtaposition of distant and unrelated elements). Futurism did not traverse the distance from A to Z below ground. The ellipsis of spirit was quasi-known. The velocity of the gait caused in the artist an inability to distinguish clearly the intermediate letters. Under pressure from the Fiat automobile company and through the spectacle lenses steamed up by the air's displacement, instead of *M* they saw a tree, instead of *S* a dynamite bullet. Mobility's constipated admired without scruples dissociation and association. It was an artifice of puerile calculation and easily unmasked simulacra.

Incompetence. Then, in this ubiquitous race, the moment of reflection is missing, the moment that eternalizes the work of art. That is the reason we will not encounter on the whole comprehensive views and an objective and abstract scale of the object, which, surprised in the very moment of absolute stasis, still preserves, by virtue of its inertia, all the attributes of the vanished motion. Futurism was training without completion.

Expressionism imposed itself in a traditional and evolutionary mode, like a perfected oscillation of symbolism, and like an exasperated metaphysical reaction of the I, in quaking impetus towards the intimate nature of things, was a vast occasion for reflection, for delving within itself and the object, allegory, symbol, interpretation. Transcendental genesis of an indefinite cosmos, a solitary cosmos, undated, and exalted towards immobility. Naturally, this ecstatic and austere hieratism morbidly degenerated and decomposed into Romanism (prehistoric state of spirit). Still, Expressionism made use of, enlarging the terrain for future experiences of aestheticizing the subconscious.

Cubism was salutary movement, though too narrow overall. The first organized and organizing movement. In the anonymous society of life, the delegated administrator, hard working and diligent. Instituting objectivity and the discipline of the futuristic and expressionistic experience, lifting the synthetic concentration to the superlative of formula, Cubism stabilized the rules, still in place today, of the balance and harmony of the deconstruction of the represented entities, and replaced subjective interpretation (consequently arbitrary, of the preceding currents) with the cold, logical, geometrical interpretation of the engineer. Of an origin particularly plastic, the superimposition of pre-established values led to a superb identification of notions, an absolute (the Purism of Messrs. Ozenfant and Jeanneret). Bankrupting the anecdote into non-existence, it opened the path to future abstractionism and Constructivism. From the uncultured derelict land of inspiration, Cubism brought art back to the torrid terrain of labor, forcing its flesh into adapting to the laboratory gown, and its eye to introspect with the aid of the microscope. Useless ballast however, riveted it to the semi-natal land. Unable to free itself entirely of mythological parasitism, the essence of pure and total abstraction was mercilessly chased out of this luminous and intellectual phial. Incompetence and error from which successors will profit.

Then Dadaism. Is was much more a state of spirit than a school of art. More the professor than the student. Most terrifying of professors; most ardent guide. Absolute negation, without reticence; the destruction of all cliches. Unrestricted freedom; art without pre-established models; fertile and succulent sensing of life (notably, contemporary); ceaseless desertion, from the most tenebrous subconscious to the most lucid intelligence, of all the human faculties, forceful guidance of reality towards a salutary and hygienic activism: Tristan Tzara. The Dadaist technique: lack of all technique. The Dadaist order: lack of all order. Faith: lack of all faith. Still, it cannot be accused of pauperism. It was the richest in resources currently, as far as it is known. Through its violent action, it determined the independence of abstractionism, converted recently into constructivism. That's all, and it is sufficient.

This is the period of history we took into consideration. (Surrealism, after a gestation hiatus of ten years, amidst the turbulent preoccupations of selection and generalization, created its doctrine—belatedly—out of the reminiscence of the subconscious, allowing any sort of formula. The predecessors utilized it, but primitively. Not accepting particularism, we express our gratitude to surrealism for its good intentions, and subsume it.

Today. We are in a full period of actualization. The naïve period of unilateral experience is gone. We want integral manifestations. Yesterday's young are now mature. The adolescents, men. We await, along with the deflowering of their undiscovered virility, a sumptuous creation. We wish to create ourselves the generations who will value our effort in its veritable worth. The future is constructed.

Naturally, the effort of the successors was not in vain. (It might be believed we reject Constructivism. No. It is ours. We are merely amplifying its dimensions. We are living in a time of titans. We are enlarging its sphere of activity and application. We are moving its borders to the borderless.) Over the ruins of Troy, successive fortresses were constructed. Will ours be the last? We work in virgin earth. In harsh earth. Stripping ourselves of the tyranny of logic and syntax led to the flowering of a new logic and syntax. The structures of the past have gained the amplified rockets of vision. The old literature was three-dimensional contemplation. The work of modern art however, offers the possibility of an emotional surprise, of a lucid four-dimensional contemplation. The material of our realizations? Any piece of wood, any word, sound, piece of iron, color, sensation, idea. The domain of our realizations? Everywhere. Factory, street, whorehouse, man, society. With heart in the shape of an alpenstock, we climbed mountains. Our poet composes in front of the typewriter. Our painter constructs with compass and idea. Our creator is furnished with all the modern comfort, like an American skyscraper. We live on the 57th floor. From there our vision is intercontinental. Stop. From the unilateral and narrow spirit of separate attempts, from the explorations, on patches of land, of our sensibility, we have arrived at the enormous contemporary synthesis: *Integralism.* Constructive spirit with innumerable applications in all domains. Integral effort towards the synthetic perfection of existence. We have gained our technique after years of struggle. We surprised the substrata of the soul with the spontaneity of the great boulevards. It's the life of the eternal future.

With gigantic and certain steps, we are heading towards an incandescent era of classicism.

Translated by Julian Semilian

BLACK ART   Corneliu Michăilescu

Originally published as "Arta neagră," *Integral* no. 4 (1925)

A contemporary aesthetic problem, addressed consistently in the colony possessor West, partially resolved, vulgarized in the same measure, leaving in addition large deserts open for research, with relative mirages and positive surprises for the future.

Black art is too little known in Romania, mirroring a civilization we didn't suspect, belonging to a people whom we have been accustomed to regard as naked, black, and shiny like the shoe freshly leaving the shoeshine's hand. A civilization nearly gone in its entirety today, like a caravan incinerated by the simoom's flames.

To understand black art we must trace back the origin of art itself. It's necessary to determine the causes that engender this spontaneous manifestation in primitive man.

In his struggle for existence, in the instinct for preservation of the species, man creates weapons and objects of essential necessity which he takes pains to adapt to his practical purposes, intuiting the laws the hidden laws of Beauty in the harmony of the practical itself.

During intervals of repose, when the spirit demands its own portion of existence and development, primitive man continues by virtue of this instinct his childlike play. Superimposing or juxtaposing ornaments according to the dictates of fantasy within the framework of the arrived at harmony, ornaments which, along with their practical uses (seduction of opposite sex, descending upon an enemy with the aid of a tattoo, adornment with feathers, the painting of weapons, the use of masks in war), provide the primitive man a genuine joy, removed from utility: the aesthetic joy. In this primordial instinct we find beauty's rudimentary embryo, which will later give birth to perfected art.

Along with this sentiment belonging to the superior life of the spirit, during the struggle for preservation, the religious sentiment is born in man.

"The soul creates for itself through religion a support against the unforeseen future and the unconquerable power of the enemy forces" (Ebbinghaus). In order to overcome these contrary forces, man seeks to understand their essence. Through a series of experiences and observations of his own self he arrives at a natural analogy, where he considers the external world as animated by spirits, and in consequence, treating it as a fellow creature.

Through a transposition of representations, man populates his universe with demons, geniuses, spirits, etc., endowed with an analogous but superior force, and who take part in all human endeavors. "Primitive man animates he world with spirits so as to be able to manage it" (Ebbinghaus). As a result of this resemblance of soul between man and spirits, the spirits will become good or evil.

In order to invoke the protection of some and placate the others, primitive man resorts to prayer, sacrifices, etc. To gain their favor, he whittles the visage of the adored spirit, or the feared one, much in his own likeness and image.

Here we find then the origin of Negro animist anthropomorphic sculptor who, in whittled fetishes and idols, found the reason for his physical and spiritual existence itself. Out of this spiritual conception of existence of the external world, black art took form; and from the instinctual desire to triumph in the daily struggle, his applied art took shape; these two subject to the specific climate and racial conditions engendered, to our surprise, this potent expression of Beauty, infinitely varied, but contingent on and harmonized by the framework of its perfect unity.

It's difficult to establish precisely the era when this art was born.

Presuppositions which have some claim to credibility let us believe that it was the prehistoric era, that it belongs to the mythical period, and it is probable it was influenced by the Egyptian period. In prehistoric engravings primitive man reproduces as accurately—and thus objectively—as possible the impression received from the outside, while the African and Oceanic whittler of idols infuses with spirit the formswhich exteriorize subjective ideas or emotions. We find ourselves here a step ahead in the evolution of creative sensibilities, fact which allows us to uphold the ideas we promoted above.

A question that on the other hand troubles us is the total lack of black architecture. La Meunais's theory, which maintains that all art emerges from architecture, serves not at all in our assertions. Is simply not probable that architecture, as element of beautification and not of utility—which in consequence calls for a social environment of flourishing tranquillity and calm—would precede the arts that spring from primal emotion of immediate necessity.

"Primitive architecture was or should have been long in lacking the element of Beauty, while the hunter or the warrior, associating the idea of the horrific with that of Beauty, adorned himself with animal trophies" (P. Rouaix).

The first human abode is the cave, in it we find the manifestations of art: engravings on reindeer bones in the north, the Bushman paintings in Africa, with the marvelous hunting or war scenes, full of rhythm and movement.

The spiritual life of the black man unfurls in the divinity filled nature.

The temple is the forest with the with thousands of animated columns: trees.

Nature inspires the architectonic element of the black artist. The tree procures for him the material from which to whittle his sculptural oeuvre. The domestic evolved architecture is the cabin, the religious, the temple, when social and physical conditions permit it. To protect them from profanation, the Papua, even today, build lightweight temples, canopied by bamboo reeds, supported by wooden pylons sculpted in human shapes, caryatids emanating suggestiveness.

As a custom, idols are usually worshipped in open air: they stand guard at crossroads like the Hellenic Hermes, the Breton ordeals, or the Romanian iconic triptych.

Public worship gave birth to architecture of considerable scale; familial worship of household spirits "Sibitis," a kind of Roman Lares and Penates, gave birth to minor scale fetish, easy to accommodate and preserve in the narrow cabin.

Black sculpture, springing as it does out religion, is ritualistic and traditional. The first types, although dating back to the mythic era, are preserved through tradition and repetition, reaching perfection during the time of the great flourishing of the black empires of the Middle Ages. The spiritual element predominates over the realistic one: the black sculptor recreates a legendary humanity with the greatest repertory of forms found in the ethnic arts; they keep for their idols the synthetically human form.

It appears that each tribe, in order to represent the divined human form, conceives a plastic problem which it resolves in its own distinguishing manner and which it treats within the ritual traditions not like a craftsman but like an inventive artist.

This variety consists in sculpturally geometrical lines and volumes.

The native decorative art of the Bushongo in Belgian Congo is characteristic through its geometrical-rectilinear forms; it has a grammar of its own, a of hundreds of linear combinations, each with its own name, characteristic analogous to the Romanian popular art.

The straight line as well as the geometricized surfaces from the constructional composition of idols and masks invest these with a superior clarity and precision. Although proportionally reduced, black sculpture preserves the monumental style through its static and architectonic character, expressed through its confident design and fullness of form, synthetically realized.

This is augmented by the genial intuition of the black sculptor, which induces him to respect the material's logic: the wood, in which he executes his work and which dictates its own form. Conception is subordinate to necessity. The natural laws of material are respected.

Perhaps this is one of the reasons that explains the massive construction of the head and neck seated upon the full and cylindrical trunk, as well as the formal abridgment of the lower limbs.

The idol whittler instinctively turns this into a problem of volume and space, which he resolves in an ingenious manner.

Maurice Delafosse attempts to explain the compressed formal proportion of the idol statuettes presented by the black Pygmy type, ancient native inhabitant of Africa, vanished over time under the influence of the black migration, but essentially divined as "masters of the earth." Black art establishes a new formal equilibrium within the apparent disequilibrium, vis-à-vis antiquity's canon.

The exclusivity of European aesthetic ideal perpetuated through a tradition which beclouded out spirit of analysis of creative experimentation in the aesthetic domain of other races, made us smile skeptically before one of the most pure and spiritually realized art, before black sculpture. Black art, acknowledged and validated today, gains, along with the place of honor which it begins to occupy on the stage of contemporary aesthetic concerns, the principle of relativism in the expression of beauty.

The immutable laws that persist at the basis of artistic creation are immeasurably vaster than those we were forced to learn through the rigorously narrow current aesthetics, dedicated to academicism.

From apparently disparate elements, through the power of genius, infinite creation can occur, combinations of forms which aspire towards absolute balance and harmony; and in the establishment of this balance, academic aesthetics teaches us to find the perfect expression of beauty. In consequence, it is useful to grasp the causes that modify the contemporary aesthetics, establishing a close relationship between primitive and contemporary art. What brings closer to the primitives is the mythical conception of the world. The animistic fetishism of primitive peoples is replaced in the civilized man through the consciousness that animating things with spirits belongs to the integral existence of the universal spirit.

The artist creates his work impelled by mystic exaltation. For the black artist, this exaltation is animist-fetishistic. For the modern artist: spiritual-philosophic.

This state, potently lived by the artist at the moment of creation, infuses the work of art with this transposition, transmuted by the distancing from reality that inspires the artist, causing it to become susceptible to spiritual or formally abstract modifications.

Expressionism, Cubism and the derived currents are deeply rooted in causes similar to black art.

The contemporary artist does not directly draw inspiration from black art, but draws from it the lesson that: to create does not mean to parasitically utilize procedures received from tradition, but to return to the natural springs of those times of creative energy, reconstituting under the aegis of actual conception of primary forms, the sources of new art, of tomorrow's styles.

Against the sterile Pharisaic traditionalism, black art constitutes a new current; "Negroism" or "Savagism," as it was contemptuously called by some, a wellspring from which the parched imagination and the bereft of life-force sensibility of present art might drink from.

Reality, as we have noted, is different. Black art was discovered and presented in its true value by those creative energies that found in it a potent element of affinity.

It is viewed not as a decorative element capable of procuring new pretexts of inspiration, but in its intrinsic content, as a method of building and harmonizing new forms within their reciprocal relationships. Its value consists, in consequence, in the balance and nobility of the form in itself.

Like in the Gothic arts, like in all arts produced by the potent exaltation of the religious element, the idol whittler knew how to translate in plastic form this sentiment, lifting himself through the power of genius to the level of the represented divinity, through the spiritualized anthropomorphic transposition of the image he held of it.

Black sculpture constitutes, for modern aesthetics, a definitive plastic achievement, through the fact that the exquisitely accomplished balance of the relationship between the content and form is completed by the personal content, synthesized in the work of art by the collaboration of masses with the individual, action engendering the great styles.

Black art, which is a potent example of style, can be placed, from this viewpoint, along with the eternally classic manifestations: Egyptian, Greek, and Gothic.

The European invasion, with its industrial civilization unfortunately corrupts the native taste of this race; it modifies its creative sensibility, thus destroying black art.

Translated by Julian Semilian

NOTE ABOUT SCULPTURE   Militsa Petrașcu
Originally published as "Notă despre sculptură," *Contimporanul* vol. 4, no. 60 (September 1925)

Any means of representing the object in sculpture is valid when it originates in love for the craft. However, the esthetic of this new art has given emphasis to specific preoccupations, which it must take into consideration if it wishes to avoid tarrying in the recipes of the old grandeur. You may call it "old grandeur" because, once learned, one could sleep for the rest of one's life; the skill demanded of the student is succeeded by the sloth of the spirit. When some degree of mastery is accomplished a benign sort of ability emerges, which explains why the majority of artistic productions, owing to these very principles, end up in degradation.

In art immobility is death.

Let's talk about the perspective that allows us spy some entrancing accomplishments in sculpture.

Brâncuși, Janco!

Which are the specifically novel characteristics that we are forced to consider if we wish to achieve an art, which, if not perfect or absolute, is at least alive?

First, the sculptors must cease being nostalgic for the integral ages, when the concatenation of sculpture and architecture was holy (sacred), while our age will belatedly and with certainty become synthetic.

The concerns with proportion and balance allow the sculptors to produce objects independent of architecture.

This will not prevent them from finding hints of this architecture in an architectural construction conceived by Horta, Van de Velde, or Marcel Janco.

The degree to which something is thought and felt is always of import.

Such concerns allowed modern sculpture to meet the demands of architecture, participating as decorative or constructive motif.

By what means then do we succeed in realizing such concerns?

The means of the modern sculptor are always, again and again, forms perused through an immobile sort of optics, unpredisposed by our sensibility, which tends to clarify, to smooth out, to solidify, and which, because it is entirely new (young) (must not be mistaken with sensuousness) due the fact it was discovered within our own time, it is eager to advance its productions.

The flux and reflux X in Brâncuşi's bronze, the portrait of princess X, amble towards the infinite; this is not just the representation of a certain moment, it is the cosmos which develops its backward and forward movement, the curves defining this conception are unflinching.

The plastic vulgarity, the slant of the houses (the roofs that threaten our poor heads), the walls constraining our vital force, all disappear in the plastic world created by Brâncuşi; his light and delicate planes, his economical alphabet of forms, laid out on a vertical plane, the conceived music of our vision, sober, young, clean, precipitating into a great style.

Translated by Julian Semilian and Sanda Agalidi

INITIATION IN THE MYSTERIES OF AN EXHIBITION: THE SENSATIONAL PRONOUNCEMENTS OF MILITSA PETRAŞCU AND MARCEL JANCO

G. C. Jacques

Originally published as "Inițiere în misterele unei expoziții: Senzaționalele declarații ale Miliței Petraşcu şi ale lui Marcel Iancu," *Contimporanul* vol. 5, no. 65 (March 15, 1926)

I found Militsa Petraşcu and Marcel Janco, their face twisted to the Northwest, in the semi-religious silence preparatory to the construction of the decor.

Assailants trumped up by them, transported, some to a state of abstraction, others beyond good and evil, costumed in wood, in criminal colors, in bronze, awaited their marching orders.

At the sound of my steps, Militsa and Marcel, taking all precaution, reversed charge, each on their own heels.

It is well known that in all matters of art Militsa Petraşcu and Marcel Janco are connected by a euphonic U.

I separated them by flinging hand grenades. Instantly, each implemented a stately curtsy to antagonistic masterworks.

Marcel Janco was suddenly tallying his canvases at vertiginous speed. After pronouncing obstreperously "number fifty" he turned his backside to the walls and re-tallied them in reverse at an even greater speed. I approached him leisurely and grasping his left paw with dissimulated tenderness, I inspected the beats of his pulse in a pocket calendar.

Here are the questions that I asked him, on two separate columns:

1.	2.
How do you paint?	Do you paint roosters?
Why do you paint?	Do you paint cows?
What do you paint like?	Do you paint idiots?
With what do you paint?	Do you paint firefighters?
What do you paint?	Do you paint pawns?
Do you still paint?	Do you pai…
Do you paint?	Do you p…
Do you paint…	
Do you pai…	

He gave an answer to each fifth question, in terms that excluded any discussion:

Nature?
(Furious): "Nature is chaotic, delirious, nature lives out its unknown rhythms, and as far as the arts go, we are neither responsible for, nor dependent on them.
I know of no harmony, no single idea that could serve as guide or support for art. On the contrary, *nature is only good as medicine*.
"Not even those who were enamored of her most and were her most dramatic defenders saw to it or understood that they should copy her.
"The romantics never confused art with a cloaca of emotions. Art never confined itself to reproductions. She creates, invents, invents."
I am speechless.
"Of course this creation, this invention, is something that "postcard" lovers find diffi-cult to grasp. They always were content to unravel and declassify things by way of a tale; this disappeared with impressionism and they suddenly found themselves facing pure painting, absolute art."
(After straining for courage): Finally, what are you painting?
"Nothing. Neither girls, nor Princes Charming, neither moonlessness, nor fish. Only and only the formal play of light, only the balance of color distortions. Only the inte-gration of line and geometry in composition, only minor or major chords of color in rhythm."
With what?
"With abstractions, with fictions. How difficult it is to draw a limit between reality and non-reality! How much vaster, more alive, deeper, the domain where form organizes lines according to laws independent of logic and quotidian illusion.
"The result is an act of art and creation, an alternate cosmos."
Right.
"You see, yesterday's art thrived on the level of childish experiments, mere fumblings. It was the sentimentalist's lack of consciousness. But art shifts towards crystalliza-tion. It is simply a human construction that must ground itself according to a system. One can talk about intention in art, about a creative will, only to the extent that an art-work sets up a problem."
Cubism has inv—
(He interrupts.) "It is true that there is an overproduction in the world, of art and artists, totally useless because they are not serious. Cubism has produced, superficially, a disorientation, yet cubism secured for art such a strong significance, that for the time being it cannot reach the 'masses.'
"In fact this is its very significance, because today's "cultivated" man does not give up any of his idols, even when proven false."
Do you believe in the end of the world?
"There will be always naturalists. But, in time, their craft will become mutilated and

turn into what today are the statuettes by-the-dozen, sugar-coated on the shoulder of 'Italian artists."

I found Militsa Petrașcu concealed behind the illustriousness of a wooden seal. She handed me a terribly delicate chisel yet hazardous enough upon which I respectfully placed my lips. Silently she continued her work.
In the meanwhile, while wantonly caressing the seal's goiter I heard this oracle:
"I am much interested in the development of my plastic vision. If I am successful in awakening this curiosity in the viewer, then my goal, as far as the public is concerned, is accomplished."
At this point, Militsa Petrașcu aimed her gaze directly on my forehead and before I could even blink, applied an oblique chisel to the top of my forehead. Contrary to expectations I felt relieved of a restlessness that was purely artistic. The aptly chastised hairdo now had the aspect conforming to correct historical reality. I could now listen with my mind at peace:
"Modern sculpture is pregnant with the beliefs of an age which aimed entirely to accomplish the most expressive means, and especially specific to each branch of art.
"Sculpture wants to rid itself of masters and literature.
"I feel no belligerence towards subject in sculpture but I am requesting that it be viewed from the standpoint of certain laws of plasticity.
"My dream is neither to sculpt heroes wielding their sword and leaping into battle, nor to portray Motherland with foot squashing vanquished peoples; I would however display the evolution of a flower, the passion of a bird, a face without guilt."
And in order to underscore the above, Militsa Petrașcu abolished an oscillation on my nose, applying a precise chisel after each word of progressively death defying significance.
The Oracle: "the Classics are perfect because they are in perfect accord with their own time."
I pronounced absolute accord with no attempt to remove myself from the chisel's beam. But I allowed myself to note that given the belated hours I would be unable to await the termination of the exercise.
Defeated by my resistance, Militsa Petrașcu laid down her weapon and agreed that the study of my head required an exhibition apart.
Upon departure, Marcel Janco gave me permission, out of gratitude, to call out his name, wherever he might find himself. Owing to this fact I've succeeded since that time to earn my livelihood in the most honorable manner.

Translated by Julian Semilian and Sanda Agalidi

CUBISM   Marcel Janco
Original published as "Cubism," *Contimporanul* no. 71 (1926)

What we call beautiful does not always imply the plastic beautiful.
Cubism is the last ring within the evolution of painting for four centuries. It poses *the problem of plastic construction*. It is only now that the knowledge of *plastic elements* was demanded.

Line, volume, color are plastic elements that are found only under disorganized, unconscious forms in nature.

To gather and organize plastic elements is the very issue of fine arts.

Starting with vision, art creates *plastic realities* freed from the illusive (natural
vision).

Apart from exterior reality, there is another one for us: *plastic reality*. A copy of nature
does not involve the *plastic beautiful*, since nature is not plastic reality.

Plastic reality is not only a product of the human feeling alone, but it is an intellectual construction. It should contain the feature of the composed, ordered pure
thing. Plastic reality is a world in itself, a free construction, an apparatus to capture
emotions.

Nowhere in nature can we trace instances of art, because exterior reality is not a
product of our intelligence and feeling. Those who keep on faking art for life are wrong;
reality of the ambient does not contain anything identical or similar to the intentions
of *the plastic beautiful*.

Composition represents the condensation of the volume around the main motif,
the setting into a frame (closing) of what is achieved through the interplay of vision
and correction of plastic lows. Everything is built on a *tone of color* by a thorough
knowledge of all harmonies and disharmonies, affinities and rejections in coloring.

Translated by Magda Teodorescu

COLORING Marcel Janco
Orginally published as "Colorit" in *Contimporanul* no. 73 (1927)

For the first time, after the Impressionist chaos, Cubism "composes the color." The
painter, who was not aware of what he was doing, began to organize his means.

The world of color is more expressive, more mysterious than that of sounds, and far
richer. Here lies the difficulty to group and set their multitude in order.

Any of the old works, even the secular ones (for instance, the Flemish School) were
studio works composed according to color canons.

Even inside the world of colors there is a fundamental difference between their
physical essence (nature) and their artistic force (expressiveness).

While the physicist speaks of the solar spectrum, where all colors merge to produce
the white color, and two harmonically opposed colors produce the black, the plastic
reality of the colorist denies it.

They say that all the other colors can be composed out of the three fundamental colors:
red, yellow, blue (which one?). Sallow colors can't be obtained from the metallic ones,
and the organic ones can't be made out of the vegetal and mineral ones.

Some painters, some of the most famous ones, create their own "harmony," which
they keep, thinking that thus they have made up their own individuality. We can only
see a new form of Daltonism, that's all.

There is no clear cut in the world of colors; sometimes red shows rather blue, and
green rather yellow.

A systematization of colors is possible by assigning a number and a grade on one, two,
or more scales. This operation, recently started by a chemist, should be accomplished
by the new generation of conscious painters.

We could speak about the power of expression specific to colors, if they are grouped into harmonies. They could fall into major chords (zinc chrome, cobalt, Veronese green, Prussian blue, carmine) endowed with rhetoric force, the "concave" ones, I would say, and the minor chords (chrome, cinnabar green, ivory-black), with an inwardly oriented force, the "convex" ones.

Translated by Magda Teodorescu

URMUZ   Geo Bogza
Originally published in *Urmuz* no. 1 (January 1928)

The toil of a soul throbbing on the outside, the release and the effort to reach It, groan from the rude contact with brutality.
This It with capital *I*, justified as the *H* in Him for Jesus. Both adorers of the future, both apostles of a world to come. Odium and ridicule, shadows hereditary to their lives.
And still, the hallucinating eyes aiming at that miraculous point apperceptible only by those who are chosen.
To get there, the noose: a blessed means.
We, those who stayed behind, convulse, horrified.
At times, rarely, in moments of agonizing rupture with the surroundings, we envy his courage.
At other times he is ours, and then we are brothers.
Between us and Him, a footbridge where feelings stroll as in a dance, fusing fraternally.
The great and absurd synthesis is born: the synthesis of Nothing.
The detection of affinities with Nirvana abound.
Angles blunted to become the Great All.
The beads of time frozen, or gushing vertiginously, lose significance.
But terrestrial destiny brutalizes by forcing one to days with mercantile preoccupations.
Then Urmuz seems an absurd dream and at times the shame of having fraternized once with a madman fated to be swallowed by the very darkness of the instant following his disappearance.
And still, it is not so.
Urmuz lives.
His presence among us whips to lash our conscience. In the basement of our soul, bent deeply from the waist down we follow the traces his steps have left gashing violently the earth, trivialized by the mundane.
Virgin ears still bleed from the deflowering precipitated by his impetuous and virile sentence.
From this moment on the word becomes a fertile spermatozoid. Urmuz too was a contributing surgeon to the operation that Voronca committed upon the stuttering language.
This is the shape shouting for the joy of unabridged triumph. What remains is the background, the profoundly aching problem, like a gash nibbled by vultures.
At the century's crossroads: Urmuz swaying, a noose about his neck: semaphore signaling the disequilibrium of those leaning attentively over the clamor emanating from the soul's abyss.

Julian Semilian

Laboring in an obscure corner, while we were still warming ourselves by the light of a false sun. He turned on the faucet to freezing which now envelops us all.

The sun until now naked in its fruitlessness.

The freezing grows insinuating reprimands flung at our superfluity. Those with thick skins enveloping their souls, uncomprehending of this event, continue to bow to the obsolete star.

But we who feel the freezing permeating acutely, have the obligation to react. And then: motion, exceeding motion. The birth of Constructivism, Surrealism, and all other dynamic "isms," are crucial to our lives threatened by freezing.

Those for whom the false sun is enough, perplexed, peruse this vertiginously of lines, words, sounds, colors, and exclaim: madness.

The best of luck to them.

To them and their soul harness, which keeps them safe in banality's freezing and in the commonplace.

But we, we necessitate motion, excessive, varied.

An entire intellectual acrobatics.

Our duty is to intensify it to the maximum.

Abandoning the false star, compelling this clown's somersault to keep our souls warm through its friction, we cherish the dream to locate someday the veritable sun.

And then...

Translated by Julian Semilian

The Slovenian avant-garde of the of the
second half of the 1920s was marked by
Dadaist- and, especially, Constructivist-
influenced developments in the arenas
of theater, painting, graphic arts,
architecture, typography, photomontage, and "production art." *tank*, published in Ljubljana (1927–28), was
founded and edited by Ferdinand
Delak (1905–1968) and took its numeri-
cal identification system ($1\frac{1}{2}$–$3\frac{1}{2}$)
directly from El Lissitzky's theory of
space. Delak, an actor, director, and
writer, was a figure in stage experiments, closely related to Russian
director Vsevolod Meyerhold's theatrical biomechanics.

Visual artist Avgust Černigoj (1898–
1985) organized the first Constructivist
exhibition in Ljubljana in 1924 after
training briefly at the Bauhaus in
Weimar. Under political pressure,
he was forced to leave Ljubljana for
Trieste, where he co-founded the
Constructivist Group in late 1927 and
developed *tank*'s distinctive graphic
designs. While publishing *tank*, both
Delak and Černigoj were in close contact with Ljubomir Micić, the founder
of the Yugoslav Zenithist movement
living in Paris at the time. Three
issues of *tank* were produced; the
fourth was banned.

Translated by Maja Starčević

GREETINGS! Avgust Černigoj
Originally published as "moj pozdrav!" *tank* no. 1½ (October 1927)

long live *tank*, the international journal of the new art of ljubljana–slovenia!
a movement which our new journal will endow with life and power: all of you who
live in the spirit of the times, opt for and propagate the new slovenian and international art.
for the young slovenian generation, a warm = fighting force for the struggle.
all against the old art!
all against the old dispiritedness!
all against the old passivity and degeneration!
    long live the new art } = constructive!
    "   "   "   "   " } = synthetic!
    "   "   "   "   " } = collective!
across the private border of the nation, the *mighty force must reach the world* where
the struggle is also continuing and is victorious.
we, the young slovenian pioneers, must also reach out and join the solidarity of the
new, *awakening generation.*
!   the new art is not individual.
!   "   "   "   "   " a luxury.
!   "   "   "   "   " traditional.
!   the new art is a collective expression of the new generation.
!   "   "   "   " the beauty of the new religion.
!   "   "   "   " the beauty of "   " righteousness.
!   it is not the art of advertising
!   " " "   "   " exhibition
!   " " "   "   " the church.
our art is the creation of the spirit!
our comrade who struggles in the existential form of the society is a hero of the
spirit!
we demand sincerity even though it may be dangerous.
"   " painfulness "   "   "   " self-sacrificing.
"   " expansion, "   "   "   " punishable.
tank is the herald of our strivings and of the struggle of the spirit.
tank isn't "   " of compromise and affectation.
tank is "   " of truth and struggle.
tank "   "   " of the new artistic generation.
the highest praise to *ferdo delak*, the leader of the new movement, for the hard-fought
victory!
long live the journal *tank*!
"   " the new art!
"   " the young ljubljana!

Translated by Marjan Golobič

MARIJ KOGOJ'S *BLACK MASKS*   Mirko Polić

Originally published as "marij kogoj, *črne maske*" tank no. 1½ (October 1927)

black masks: an opera in two acts (five scenes). libretto by leonid andreev.

reading this score reminded me of schönberg, who said in one of his essays: *"aber der künstler muss. er hat keinen einfluss darauf, von seinem willen hängt es nicht ab. aber da er muss, kann er auch. selbst, was ihm nicht angeboren ist, erwirbt er: manuelle geschicklichkeit, formbeherrschung, virtuosität, aber nicht die der anderen, sondern seine eigene…"* ["but the artist must. he has no influence over (whether he can create). it does not depend on his will, but since he must, he can. he can acquire even what does not come naturally to him: manual dexterity, control over form, virtuosity. but his own, not an imitation of others."]
it is not only that kogoj is a student of schönberg's. you truly have the feeling that everything in this score is so primordial, drawn so closely from nature, the nature of a unique and sometimes spiteful elemental individuality that does not look to any par-ticular "influence," that is its own and that gives from its own inner being not because it is "able and willing" but on the contrary—"because it must"!
at first glance *black masks* appears quite fragmented, even choppy, because of the short, pregnant motifs used by the composer, and not until we study it closely or listen to it more than once do we discover a certain "sense," a sense that creates a work of great amplitude, broad shapes, and a closed form. there is something primeval, racial, savage in those motifs, something that grows even stronger in the shadings of the contrasts that represent an eminently motor-like element in modern music and modern art as a whole. the parts of this mostly contrapuntal score intertwine, compete with one another, creating rhythmical contrasts as well as—analogous to andreev's text— a bizarre background from which words emerge (whether sung, recited, or simply spoken) as a necessary and logical consequence of the work. the music was not cre-ated with the text as its point of departure, to illustrate and comment on it, but con-genially, through spiritual empathy with the characters, as an integral part of the theatrical illusion.
lorenzo's spiritual tragedy is actually the vision we unconsciously share with him by viewing him through a mask that concentrates all our senses and enables us to observe his psychological wanderings and his search for the ultimate sacrifice and catharsis.
the rich palette of the music breaks through this illusion with what seem like rays of light to create an atmosphere conducive to engaging both listeners and viewers and making them enter its mysteries, making them open to an author who will lead them on the path to experience, to the all but metaphysical secret of catharsis. in that sense, music is necessary here not simply for creating an "opera," but for moving the work in the direction of absolute creation. schönberg's maxim is justified even if we merely read the score. if it succeeds, the slovenes will have created their first mature dramatic work and their first genuinely modern piece of art. and it is not only the slovenes who stand to gain, it is the whole world of culture.

Translated by Marjan Golobič

"on the suggestion of the architect hannes meyer, the federation of swiss consumer societies from basel presented itself with a mimic play at the international exhibition of co-operation and social care in genoa. the site of the exhibition
consisted of rather ordinary, yet tastefully arranged pavilions featuring advertising
patterns, garish signs and machinery. it was built by the mentioned federation
during the presidency of b. joeggi at the exhibition site of the little stage where
the basic standpoints of local co-operation were expressed and propagated through
pantomime."
this is what jean bard wrote about the birth of the co-op theater, which had to operate
under difficult conditions: the greatest possible simplicity in acting, stage set design,
lighting effects and technical devices. due to the bilingual belgian population and the
international character of the exhibition, the word had to be discarded. it was nevertheless necessary to label the idea of the federation in order to show its significance
and prove its usefulness.
four basic issues were singled out from the many different aspects of swiss
co-operation

work	clothing	family	craft

and arranged for pantomime. and so were created pieces of pantomime; pictures without words; fragments of life without introduction, plot progression or apotheosis—only
momentary pictures without a beginning or end.
the stage direction by jean bard provided the possibility to combine the man as a great
puppet and as an actor:
on the one hand gestures determined by the brain and custom, on the other hand actions
dictated by the intellect and affectation
on the one hand unhindered reality of expression, on the other hand controlled expression of emotion
the truth here, naturalness there
the puppet here, the man there.
the props were the following

radio	cinema	phono
mechano	electro	auto

the gestures of actors and puppets were strictly determined by the accompanying
phonograph, which alternately played old traditional tunes and the most recent pop
songs.
thus the co-op theatre came across as automatic in its acting gestures, as mechanical
in its music, as cinematographic in its theatrical vision.

man	against	puppet
co-op	against	anti-co-op

it is true that this travelling troupe is still an immature child of its muse; the
puppets and decorations—corresponding to the content—are still somehow
realistic = they lack the simplest simplicities of the new form, but the deteriorating
institution and its personnel cannot and must not in any way be the judge of the
expression of its theater which combines the play of the body, light, color, noises
and gestures.
it addresses the emotions, not the reason; the heart, not the imagination of the
spectator.
simplicity is its mother; language is its wordless esperanto of gestures, while its
purpose is to educate people in the co-operative and artistic sense.

the actors of this theater are monsieur and madame jean bard (both professors of the genoa conservatory) and hannes meyer who operates the puppets. their program consists of four pantomimes and two presentations of pictures by the swiss painters ernst morgenthaler and fritz zbinden.

the first piece entitled "work" promotes wage employment in the co-operative and also presents its opposite, the piecework in private companies. "clothing": disillusioned by fashionable clothing and tired of traditional garb, a man finds happiness by wearing co-op clothing.

in "sleep" a poor family realizes the true meaning of co-operation. "craft" presents the need of the manufacturer and the buyer and the farmer and the housewife to co-operate. the co-op angel pledges eternal loyalty to those involved in co-operation.

and what does the script of such a piece look like? may it serve as a model.

clothing:

clothing store: a woman walks by. a man follows her. the man is wearing ridiculous clothes. as he falls in love, he realizes how ridiculous are his clothes. he enters the shop. he asks for new clothes. a woman shows him a couple dressed in fashionable clothes. the man is disappointed. the woman shows him a couple wearing old-fashioned clothes.

the man is again disappointed. the co-op angel brings him co-op clothing in a co-op package. the man collapses from surprise. the woman helps him up. he puts on the co-op clothes. simple. respectable. neat. they dance. it has been achieved. and the gramophone plays on la java—l'orient—old swiss men—la unit chine.

the mentioned swiss artists should be grateful to the federation of swiss consumer societies for enabling them to put on such a topical public theater—which is blossoming, while the literary theatre—is declining.

Translated by Marjan Golobič

TANK MANIFESTO   Avgust Černigoj
Originally published as "1½ štev tanka" *tank* no. 1½–3 (1927)

the first issue of our review is a document of the time of our activities and of the strivings of our perceptive youth. we, the artists got together to found a new world of beauty–goodness–justice. but our striving is not only theoretical or sentimentally individual; our new striving is the multiplier of all that exists; of the visible and perceptible moment of being. we're not held back by any kind of intimacy or local adversity; we are ready each and every moment for *every struggle*.

architecture
      painting-sculpture
            music-poetry
                        are the main vehicles of the new generation.

europe must fall due to overbearing egoism
=   =   =   =   subconscious individualism
=   =   =   =   free terrorism.

our striving begins where european decadence stops forever.

our warrior is absolute power
=   =   = the collective "me" comes first

we do not fear the local metaphysics and the stupidly feeble slogans of the intimate ego.
our striving is and must be
revolutionary and *not* evolutionary.
europe saw the awakening of a kind of new-centrism (among the latiners), expressionism (among the anglo-saxons) = a reaction of each and every new spirit? again,
some kind of *classicism*.

let us beware!

we must put a stop to every movement of this kind; we must nip it in the bud. the old
european culture cannot make do with old poetries, so it is shaping and building a new
poetic age from the old, shoddy, monumental materials of its tradition, i.e., today's
expressionism = new-centrism. (in ljubljana we've been observing a kind of over-pro-
motion on the architecture of plečnik's or vurnik's school, which is called national
architecture, but is in fact modeled on the secession; and the same is true of painting
and sculpture: the kralj brothers, the dolinars and others, may they perish in little,
philistine ljubljana.)
we know that we must fight against such localisms.
the strongest must win.
may all the old brain-creations perish in the galleries and palaces, where they have no
other function but to gather dust and perish with time.
long live the new art–without the *gallery-museum and church*
=   =   it must *live, be useful and serve.*

let us be proud of our new movement and let us agitate for it to prove our absolute
quality of existence.

welcome delak, our friend

Translated by Marjan Golobič

THE CONSTRUCTIVIST GROUP IN TRIESTE   Avgust Černigoj
Originally published as "grupa konstruktivistov v trstu," *Tank*, no. 1½–3 (1927)

an exhibition of fine arts was put on by the *sindicato delle belle arti* and *circolo artistico*
in the month of october. the purpose of the exhibition was to give an overview of the
activities of the fine artists of trieste. on this occasion, the trade union of artists invited
prof. a. černigoj, head of the trieste artistic avant-gardists, to take part. he proposed a
collective participation of a group whose members were *prof. a. černigoj, e. stepančič,
g. vlah* and *g. carmelich.*
at the exhibition, the group was given a separate area, which was designed according
to their own ideas. the purpose of the exhibits is to attract attention to the elasticity of
space and to the permanence of time. the displayed posters proclaim the program of
the constructivist group. the trieste public, which so far had not had a chance to come
in contact with revolutionary activists, was greatly disturbed but also very interested.

all critics were against this artistic manifestation, and they more or less rejected it a priori. it was noticed that on such occasions the viewers continue to be egotistically poisoned, so that they cannot free themselves from all kinds of embracing movements and objects. artists, painters, sculptors and architects, however, look with cynicism on such hieroglyphs that convey nothing to them because the petty bourgeois environment in which they live only has room for degenerated repetitions of the sterility of everyday life.

what is the intended purpose of this constructivist manifestation in trieste? what is the purpose of this subversion? an artist does not understand the purpose of so much toil and struggle for the true art that constructivists strive for. but it's quite simple.

in art, constructivists strive for a genuine happening and experience in step with the times. all other manifestations are a fake and a pretense of the genuine effect. the new art knows no space without time, which means that this type of manifestation is abstract—but it is also a genuine enjoyment of the experience of the permanent effect. what an ordinary viewer observes, of course, is not the artist's ultimate goal where the purpose and reason of the essential existence of happening is forgotten.

construction must not be regarded merely as an object, but rather, as an instantaneous emotion which must be linked to space, time and light which gives life to the being, to that emotional unit which the artist calls construction (composition in an instant of time-space). to an ordinary viewer, all of this is incomprehensible because the exhibited objects have no history (which is the content of an ordinary picture).

the observer must use his hearing, feeling, sight and also his mind, which registers the observation and ultimately synthesizes a permanent experience that we normally call "sentiment." this does not mean that we must always observe naturally, i.e., see only the exterior, such as a house, a tree, or a person; sentiment must reflect the inner experience along with the external content of the notion. thus genuine art occurs where there is no natural happening and where the internal universe of beauty conforms to the external objectivity = form.

Translated by Marjan Golobič

The year 1923 brought a substantial change of opinion within Devětsil, when new personalities such as Vítězslav Nezval, Jindřich Štyrský, and Toyen entered its ranks, reshaping the character of the organization into the 1930s. The change came out of Teige's 1922 trip to Paris, where he met with the major representatives of postwar European art.

The first distinct rift within Devětsil took place in the spring of 1923, when its ranks were abandoned by the painters and sculptors who wanted to further devote themselves to the initial Primitivist program—which they perceived as a specific movement within the framework of Czech art—rejecting the international style. They founded the Nová skupina (New Group) and held an independent exhibit in 1923.

Devětsil's orientation after 1923 was specifically modernist, internationally based, and avant-garde. It touched on all artistic realms and had a synthesizing character. Teige and Nezval coined the term "Poetism" to encapsulate their ideas about the form of artistic work and the demands it should fulfill. Although the term is often used to this day simply to refer to the avant-garde Czech art of the 1920s, it was originally intended as the antithesis and dialectical adversary of Constructivism. The dynamic tension between these two movements created

a characteristic feature of the Czech avant-garde. Teige, rejecting any traditional notions of painting and sculpture, concentrated primarily on construction, which was to be the plan for future life, and poetry, which was to be its crown. The main expressive medium of Poetism became the "pictorial poem," a special type of collage that was presented in the second issue of *Disk* (1925). About fifteen active members of Devětsil—poets, visual artists, architects, and actors—devoted themselves to pictorial poems, but only a fraction of the work has been preserved.

The culminating point of Teige's theoretical activity in the 1920s was the "Poetism Manifesto," which was published with his article "Ultraviolet Paintings, or Artificialism" in a special issue of *ReD*. Teige prefaced the latter article with a note: "I consider the deep relationship between Artificialism and Poetism to be self-evident because Artificialism—specifically the paintings of Toyen and Štyrský—shares the same origin as Poetism." Teige's perspective was not necessarily in accordance with Štyrský's concept—Štyrský never expressed a sense of the similarity between Artificialism and Poetism.

Štyrský and Toyen began to contemplate their artistic movement after arriving in Paris in the autumn of 1925, when their paintings were part of the important group show L'Art d'Aujourd'hui. The Czech art world became acquainted with their results only after the Paris premiere. They unveiled Artificialism, briefly characterized in their first declaration as "the equation of the painter and poet," in their own studio in the Montparnasse section of Paris; exhibits followed in two important new private galleries in 1926 and 1927. These shows were repeated in Prague in a slighted altered form (Aventinská Mansarda, June–July 1928), with a catalogue essay by Teige. While in Paris, Štyrský and Toyen wrote "Artificialism" as well as other texts on the subject. Štyrský delivered the essay "Poet" as a speech at the opening of their exhibit at the Aventinská Mansarda.

Translated by Andrée Collier Záleská

POETISM   Karel Teige

Originally published as "Poetismus," *Host* vol. 3, no. 9–10 (July 1924)

The nineteenth century, lacking a discrete style, gave birth to -isms, those somewhat more insouciant and noncommittal substitutes for styles. Today, there is no ruling "ism." After Cubism, we have witnessed the rivalry of numerous artistic schools and beliefs. With no rules to guide it, art, individualized to the extreme, has broken up into groups called avant-gardes. There is no -ism, only "new art" or the "latest art" that often harbors illusions as old as the world itself and calls them universal truths. The degeneration of -isms is nothing but a symptom of the *evident degeneration of the existing kinds of art.*

Yet a new style is being born, and together with it a new art that has ceased to be art: free of traditional prejudice, it allows for every promising hypothesis, sympathizes with experimentation; and its ways are as responsive, its sources as rich and abundant, as those of life itself .

And it is likely that it will be those less professional, less literary-minded spirits, yet all the more lively and cheerful for it, who will be, from now on, concerned with this new art. In its blossoming you will discover the intoxicating aroma of life, and that alone will make you forget the problematics of art.

Professionalism in art cannot continue. If the new art, and that which we shall call Poetism, is an art of life, *an art of living and enjoying*, it must become, eventually, a natural part of everyday life, as delightful and accessible as sport, love, wine, and all manner of other delectations. It cannot be a profession; rather, it will become a universal need. No individual life, that is, a life lived morally, with smiles, happiness, love, and dignity, will be able to do without it. The notion of a professional artist is an error and today, to some extent, an anomaly. The Paris Olympics of 1924 did not admit any professional sports clubs. Why should we not reject just as resolutely the professional guilds of painting, writing, modeling, and chiseling businessmen? An artwork is not a commodity for commercial speculation, and it cannot be the subject of stilted academic debates. It is essentially a gift, a game with no constraints and no consequences.

The fresh, abundant, and exquisite beauty of the world is the daughter of real life. She is not a child of aesthetic speculation, [n]or a product of the romantic mentality of an artist's studio, but a simple result of purposeful, disciplined, positive production and the everyday activity of humankind. She will not find a home in cathedrals or galleries, but outside, in the streets, in the architecture of cities, in the refreshing greenery of parks, in the bustle of seaports, and in the heat of industry feeding our primary needs. She does not work according to self-prescribed formalist recipes: modern shapes and forms are the outcome of purposeful work; they are being turned out to perfection under the compulsion of purpose and economy. She has embraced the calculations of the engineer and saturated them with poetic vision. In just this way urbanism, the science of designing cities, has provided us with fascinating poetic works, drawn as a blueprint for life and a prospect of days to come, a utopia that shall be achieved in a future that is red. Its products are the engine of plenty and happiness.

The new beauty was bam from constructive work, the basis of modern life. The triumph of the constructive method (disappearance of handicrafts, abolition of decorative art, mass production, norms, and standardization) has been rendered operative exclusively by the principles of a cutting-edge intellectualism, manifested in contemporary technical materialism. Marxism. The constructive principle is thus the condition of the very existence of the modern world. Purism is the aesthetic control of constructive work—nothing more, nothing less.

Flaubert wrote a prophetic sentence: "The art of tomorrow will be impersonal and scientific." But will it still be art? Today's architecture, city building, industrial art are all *science*. This is not artistic creation as a result of gushingly romantic enthusiasm, but simple, intensive, *civilizing work*. Social technology.

Poetism is the crown of life; Constructivism is its basis. As relativists, we are aware of the hidden irrationality overlooked by the scientific system and therefore as yet not sublimated. It is in the interest of life that the calculations of engineers and thinkers be rational. Yet each calculation rationalizes irrationality merely by several decimal points. The calculus of each machine has its pi.

In our time we require a special frame of mind to be able to deal with the psychological contradictions taken to the point of paradoxical extremes. Collective discipline. We are hungry for individual freedom "After six days of work and building of the world, beauty is the seventh day of the soul." This line by the poet Otokar Březina captures the relationship between Poetism and Constructivism. A man who has lived as a working citizen wants to live as a human being, as a poet.

Poetism is not only the opposite but also the necessary complement of Constructivism. It is based on its layout.

Art as Poetism is nonchalant, exuberant, fantastic, playful, nonheroic, and erotic. There is not an iota of romanticism in it. It was born in an atmosphere of cheerful fellowship, *in a world that laughs*, and who cares if it laughs in tears? Humorous disposition prevails, while pessimism has been openly abandoned. The art of today shifts its emphasis toward enjoyment and the beauty of life, away from musty studies and studios; it points the way leading from nowhere to nowhere, revolving in a circle around a magnificent fragrant park, for it is the path of life. Here, the hours arrive as blossoming roses. Is it a scent? Is it a memory?

Nothing. Nothing but lyrical and visual excitement over the spectacle of the modern world. Nothing but love for life and its events, a passion for modernity, "modernolatry," to use the expression coined by Umberto Boccioni. Nothing but happiness, love and poetry, heavenly things that cannot be bought for money and that are not important enough for people to kill each other for. Nothing but joy, magic, and everybody's optimistic faith in the beauty of life. Nothing but the immediate data of sensibility. Nothing but the art of wasting time. Nothing but the melody of the heart. The culture of miraculous enchantment. Poetism wants to turn life into grand entertainment. An eccentric carnival, a harlequinade of emotions and ideas, a series of intoxicating film sequences, a miraculous kaleidoscope. Its muses are kind, tender, and mirthful, their glances as fascinating and impenetrable as a lover's glance.

Poetism has no philosophical orientation. It would probably confess to a dilettante, pragmatic, tasty and tasteful eclecticism. It is not a worldview—for us, this is Marxism—but an ambiance of life: certainly not the stodgy atmosphere of a study, a library, a museum. It probably speaks only to those who belong to the new world; it has no desire to be understood and perverted by those whose views are outdated, who look back into the past. It harmonizes life's contrasts and contradictions, and, significantly, for the first time it brings us poetry that needs no words, melody, or rhyme, a poetry already longed for by Whitman.

Poetism *is not literature*. In medieval times even legal codes and school grammars were written in verse. Tendentious ideological verse with its "contents and plot" is the last surviving remnant of this kind of poetry. The beauty of our poetry has no intentions, no grand phrases, no deep meaning, no apostolic mission. A game of beautiful words, a combination of ideas, a web of images, if necessary without words. It calls for the free mind of a juggler of ideas, who has no intention to apply poetry to rational axioms and contaminate it with ideology; rather than philosophers and pedagogues,

modern poets are clowns, dancers, acrobats, and tourists. The sweetness of artificiality and the spontaneity of feelings. Communication, poem, letter, lovers' conversation,
improvised drinking sprees, chitchat, fantasy and comedy, a quick card game light
as air itself, memories, good times when people laugh: a week of colors, lights, and
scents.

Poetism *is not painting*. Painting, having rejected all anecdotal aspects and avoided the
dangers of decorativism, has started out on its way toward poetry. As poetry became
visual (in the work of Apollinaire and Marinetti and in Birot's "poetry of the open air"
as well as in his films), so painting, having emancipated form and color in cubism,
ceased to imitate reality, for it was not able to compete with photojournalism, and
instead set out to *make poetry by means of optical form*. *Optical words* as devised in the
language of flags. Similar to the international system of traffic signs. Abstraction and
geometry, a perfect and infallible system that inspires the modern mind. Emancipation
from the picture frame, started by Picasso and Braque, has subsequently led to a
total *suppression of the tableau*. The poetic picture is the picture of book illustration,
photography, photomontage.

The new poetic language is heraldry: *the language of signs*. It works with standards.
(For example: *Au revoir! Bon vent, bonne mer! Adieu!* Green light: go! Red light:
stop!)

Poetism *is not an –ism*, at least not in the narrow sense of the word as it is currently
understood. For there is no -ism in today's art. Constructivism is the method of all
productive work. Poetism—we repeat—is the art of living in the most beautiful sense
of the word, a modern Epicureanism. It offers an aesthetic that is in no way prohibitive
or pedantic. Nor does it wish to mold the life of today or tomorrow according to some
abstract rules. There is no moral code, except for that created by the friendly relationships of common living, person to person—an amiable, tolerant etiquette. -Ism,
after all, is not a very precise word: -isms do not mean what they say, and to explain
them literally, almost etymologically and philologically, would be sometimes terribly
foolish (as for example in the case of cubism). Poetism and Constructivism are not
to be understood in any other way than as a means toward giving a name to a method,
a view, a denomination, a simple name (as in the case of socialism, communism,
liberalism, etc.).

Poetism *is not art*, that is, art in its current romantic sense of the word. It is ready to
liquidate existing art categories, to establish the reign of pure poetry, exquisite in its
multifarious forms, as multifaceted as fire and love. It has film at its disposal (the
new cinematography), as well as avionics, radio, technical, optical, and auditory inventions (optophonetics), sport, dance, circus and music hall, places of perpetual improvisation where new inventions are made every day. It corresponds fully to our need
for entertainment and activity. It is able to give art its due without overestimating
its importance, knowing that it is certainly not more precious than life. Clowns and
Dadaists taught us this aesthetic skepticism. Today, we do not assign a place to poetry
in books and albums alone. Instruments of enjoyment, sailing boats are modern
poems as well.

It is axiomatic that man has invented art, like everything else, for his own pleasure,
entertainment. and happiness. A work of art that fails to make us happy and to
entertain is dead, even if its author were to be Homer himself. Chaplin, Harold
Lloyd, [Vlasta] Burian, a director of fireworks, a champion boxer, an inventive and
skillful cook, a record-breaking mountain climber—are they not even greater
poets?

Poetism *is, above all, a way of life*. It is a function of life and at the same time the fulfillment of its purpose. It is the author of general human happiness and well being,
unpretentiously peaceful. Happiness is a comfortable home, a roof over one's head,

but it is also being in love, having a good time, laughing, dancing. It is a noble teacher. Stimulating life. It relieves depression, worries, irritations. It offers spiritual cleansing and moral health.

Life, with its tedium of work and its daily monotony, would be meaningless, an empty shell, without an animating heart, without resilient sensibility, and without poetry. It is poetry that thus becomes the sole purpose of a meaningful life, conscious of itself.

Not to understand Poetism is not to understand life!

Humanity has emerged from the war tired, troubled, bitterly robbed of illusions, unable to feel desire, to love, to lead a new, better life. Poetism (within its limits) wants to cure this moral hangover and psychological shock, as well as the malaise of its aftermath, as exemplified, for example, by the case of expressionism. It grows out of a constant human need, free of pretensions and artistic humbug. Poetism knows that one of the greatest values embraced by mankind is human individuality harnessed to the discipline of the collective fellowship of man, his happiness and the harmony of his inner life. It puts a new face on the historical ideal of happiness. Poetism revises all values, and, at the time of the twilight of all idols, it has appropriated *lyrical value* as its very own and true golden treasure.

It is essential to live the modern global creed to its fullest. Only a truly modern man is a whole man. Romantic artists are defective individuals. *Etre de son temps.* For art is the most direct manifestation of the handwriting of life.

Today, the world is controlled by money, by capitalism. Socialism means that the world should be controlled by reason and wisdom, economically, purposefully, usefully. Constructivism is the operative mechanism of such a control. But reason would cease to be wise if it were to suppress the domain of sensibility in the process of its rule over the world: instead of multiplication, it would bring impoverishment to life, since the only asset important for our happiness is the wealth of our feelings, the infinite realm of our sensibility. And it is here that Poetism intervenes and comes to the rescue in the renewal of our emotional life, our joy, and our imagination.

It is by means of these lines that we are for the first time trying to put in words the aims of a movement brought to life by several modern Czech authors. It seems that the time has arrived to define what Poetism really means, especially since this word, which has entered common parlance during the one year of its existence, has often been used as well as abused by critics who often had no idea what it is all about.

Poetism was born as a result of the collaboration of several Devĕtsil authors and is, above all, a reaction against the ideologically colored poetry ruling the roost in our country. Resistance against romantic aestheticism and traditionalism. Jettisoning of existing "art" forms. We have set out to explore the possibilities not capable of being satisfied by paintings and poems in film, circus, sport, tourism, and life itself. And so Poetism gave birth to *visual poems, poetic puzzles and anecdotes, to lyrical films.* The authors of these experiments—Nezval, Seifert, Voskovec, and, with your permission, Teige as well—wish to savor all the fruits of poetry, cut loose from a literature destined for the scrap heap, a poetry of Sunday afternoons, picnics, luminous cafes, intoxicating cocktails, lively boulevards, spa promenades, but also the poetry of silence, night, quiet, and peace.

Translated by Alexandra Büchler

CONSTRUCTIVISM AND THE LIQUIDATION OF "ART"   Karel Teige

Originally published as "Konstruktivism a likvidace umění," *Disk* no. 2 (1925)

Constructivism should not mean a transitory aesthetic and artistic fashion, but instead
an important present-day phase in the development of human thought and work, a name
given to this moment in history, the most recent variation of art in Europe. It is not a
narrow artistic 'ism', which from time to time ruffles the flat surface of artistic life. It
is an active and vital power, a powerful and penetrating movement, which with increasing intensity is gaining ground in all civilized countries, a movement which is general
and totally international, a healthy guide for all productive work. The triumph of its
view and its methods—everywhere discernible—is an important and essential feature
of our times. Constructivism is the beginning and the signal of the new architecture,
the start of a new epoch of culture and of civilization in general.

The term *Constructivism* almost interprets itself, so to speak, both philologically and
etymologically. It derives from the verb *to construct*. Hence the word Constructivist is
simply synonymous with the word constructive. Although this interpretation seems
simplistic, it is in fact incomparably closer to the truth than the understanding of
Constructivism as a new artistic 'ism', as the *dernier cri* of studios and exhibitions. The
term Constructivism does not allow one to think of art. Although we consider Constructivism
today's style, the name of contemporary culture and civilization, it does not represent
a new formalist system or an a priori aesthetic order; it abandons all traditional forms
and betrays the nine Muses of classical Parnassus. Constructivism is concerned not
with forms but with functions. The domain of all till now was formalism. Constructivism
proclaims the exchange of formalism by functionalism. It does not imply a new artistic
formula, for the important reason that it is not concerned with art at all.

Liquidation of art.

With Constructivism we proceed

towards the all-out liquidation of art.

We proclaim the total collapse of all varieties of so-called art. If we have been using,
and will perhaps be using, the word "art" as an auxiliary term, we must warn that we
do not refer to sacred and sublime art with a capital A. We do not allude to a beautiful
academic art, *ars academica, les beaux arts*, which modernity dethrones. For us, the
word "umění" (art) derives from umět (be able to do something), and its product is the
artifact. Thus, a word signifies simply every perfect and skillful product. In this sense,
it is possible to speak of the art of building, the art of industry, theater, and film, just
as of the art of cooking, poetry, photography, travel, and dance. The Czech language
allows one to speak of the art of medicine, accountancy, surveying; books and manuals
exist on the art of paying one's debts, the art of palmistry, of tying a cravat, the art of
getting married. Art is simply the manner of using specific means for specific functions,
which are usually more or less changeable. According to the Larousse, art is the application of knowledge towards the realization of a certain task.

It is thus clear that we do not assign to art any sacred and cult supremacy, we do not
suffuse it with incense. We renounce entirely all aesthetic fetishism. Modern vitality
considers so-called art an anachronistic aesthetic mentality; Futurists in Italy and
Russia spit on the altar of art. Rationalist and unprejudiced Constructivism states that
all the problems of so-called art are no longer relevant, that art itself is worthless,
that it approaches its end and therefore art and the artist simply lose all their *raison
d'être*. The degeneration of the former types of art, painting, sculpture, and theater,
is evident and cannot be concealed.

OUR CIVILIZATION IS NOT A CIVILIZATION OF ART AND CRAFT (*l'époque des arts et des
métiers*) BUT THE CIVILIZATION OF THE MACHINE (*le siècle de la machine*).

International Constructivism in Central Europe Prague/Paris

When the Constructivists (using the words of Ilya Ehrenburg) proclaimed "new art stops being art" they did not wish to pronounce a clever paradox or to commit an act of Futurist-like iconoclasm. They wanted only to state a fact, to declare that there are no eternal values in art, and that today's art faces its end. If by art we understand products which meet precisely certain material or spiritual needs, which satisfy human beings in all their complexity, then art is in this sense eternal, no matter how much its forms and modes may change; this art lasts as long as mankind lasts.... The human need for shelter and clothing is evidently almost everlasting, but it does not follow from this that decorative art is equally everlasting. The human need for poetic pleasure, for spiritual diversion, the need of the senses to be stimulated through colors, forms, sounds, words, and odors, appears permanent, but it does not follow from this that there will always be a need for easel painting, symphonic orchestras, and literature. All the more so, because modern man's thirst for beauty is sooner quenched elsewhere, right in the middle of the drama of life, rather than by so-called art. Modern man feels the inadequacy of contemporary art.

The Constructivists do not propose a new art form but a plan for a New World and a program for a new life. They do not apply some kind of aesthetic theory; they create a new world. They simply come and offer a design for a new globe. They intend to reconstruct the world on a new foundation, which is oriented to a more just social equilibrium. They reject *en bloc* all Classicism and Romanticism, all "-isms" and aestheticism, a deed that requires both a strong will and a clear and far-sighted intelligence. They abandon stuffy museums and cemeteries of thought and they shake the dust off their shoes. As the past is dead and history has stopped being a teacher, it is not necessary to refer to the past, to tradition and to history.... We may reduce all history to statistics: it tells us more and is less deceptive.

All modern art "-isms," even the most oppositional, looked for their analogies in the past in order to prove their legitimacy. With a little good will, this could always succeed. Everything can be found in history, everything legitimated with examples amassed from history. If you like, you can find Cubism, Orphism, Futurism, and Impressionism in the great masters of the past. In history, however, against every argument *pro*, you may find an argument *contra*, and so on *ad infinitum*.... Therefore, we have decided to desist from confirming modern principles by references to arguments culled from the history of art, simply because we are convinced that these are no arguments at all and we know that the modern epoch is essentially incomparable with any epoch in the past.

The twilight of artistic archetypes has arrived. Eyes that can see, intelligence that comprehends, sensibility that feels, know that in the field of so-called art the part of models is larger than that of true values. Precisely because the so-called eternal values turned into archetypes, they have in fact been dead long since.

The unbelieving and skeptical modern mind never lets itself be deceived by the superstition of eternal values. Our stoical time knows that every human action is provisional, that there are no definite states, that nothing lasts except that which is no longer alive. Eternity belongs to cosmic powers, and we need not and cannot worry about them. There is no truth but the occasional and the ephemeral. The basic trait of the modern mind is skepticism about all dogma, all absolute validity, and all eternal, immortal values.... Constructivism knows what the world looks like without any absolute values.

The rational mind of Constructivism is necessarily relativist. It has a rather ironic conception of eternity and the absolute. It knows that the Heavens, considered indestructible, do not record anything but the constant transition of all (A. France). Modern philosophy, which examines every fact and analyzes all its essential elements regardless of the external marks (e.g., "art") under which it might appear, which explores its

immanent possibilities and conditions, must first ask what was that which is. Therefore, criticism should be the science of the development of art. And here we recognize
that there is no absolute truth even in art, for its spirit regenerates uninterruptedly; the
notion of truth is refuted by the notion of evolution. And if the world develops so does
man, who is in no way a finite being but one who evolves incessantly towards the perfect type, a continuous attempt to become a new man. A man of one generation never
demands and never creates the same poetry as a man of an earlier generation. There
is no eternal duration; there is only everlasting change and renewal. A new, active, and
dynamic notion of eternity, in which there is no room for static everlasting values and
truth. An absolute and normative aesthetic is impossible and is nonsense. The ideal
erotic type changes fundamentally both in space and time and the ideal of beauty, on
which it depends directly and indirectly, changes even more. For a Negress, the idea of
beauty lies in thick lips, for the sportsman in Fairbanks, for Plato in *ephebes*, for the
Tunisian Jew in a corpulent bride, and for today's girl in herself.
We cannot rely on the principles of traditional and classical aesthetics. Classical
aesthetics is inadequate for all the manifestation of contemporary productions and
cannot serve as basis for modern criticism.... Every work of art has its own time-
bound system, its principle, and therefore its aesthetics.... A theory in itself is worthless and meaningless; it has value only if it relates to a certain work, direction, and
movement.
Historical or traditional ideals and norms of aesthetic do not exist; there are no inherited laws. Modern culture and civilization are a fact and they carry their own laws and
conditions. If a work of art proves viable even though it contradicts dominant views it
would be foolish to condemn it. If the new phenomena of technological civilization
prove that their poetic intensity is an excellent substitute for the dying types of art we
will welcome it wholeheartedly. We do not wish to crush a view that may probably propose the needed solution. Ancient beauty and medieval beauty are incomparable with
today's beauty and we shall not refer to them. Men often stress the so-called eternal
rule of art. But this allegedly eternal rule, which is, incidentally, deduced from works
of art *ex post*, should logically exist a priori. But works of art are not principles; they
are results and consequences that grow out of multiple experiences. When new facts
of life and culture emerge, philosophy, ethics, morality, aesthetics, and criticism automatically need new criteria and new yardsticks. According to contemporary relativism
and pragmatism both truth and beauty are qualities of a kind, that is, they are not
autonomous categories, which might to some extent be considered correct. It is therefore a question of utility which ethos is production. Incidentally, in this utility we do
not include only material utilitarism.
The functionality of art (by no means a certain form, a certain content, and a certain
tendency—the erroneous German aesthetics of content) constitutes the first and most
important criterion. In future, we will not waste useless, abstract words on form and
content and their relationship, for correctly stated questions relate to function. The
Constructivist era replaces formalism with *functionalism*. It is no longer a question of
form, but of maximal functionality. And in this point we part for good from traditional
aesthetics and so-called art.
After we have left the tabernacle of art, we find ourselves immersed in the center of
real life. Modern life is devoid of creed; this is the creed of modern man. It created its
products not according to the dictates of aesthetic and ethic theories but in the measure of man. Against all stylistic and aesthetics criteria, Constructivism postulates the
human measure. 'What man has become, a being in itself, contradicts nature. Herein
lies his greatness and beauty. Human beauty is artificial and only this suits him and is
natural for him; it is an invention, which is gradually perfected, one of his greatest
works and the arch-creation of his intelligence.' For the Constructivists, *man is the*

measure of all things. Architecture, cities, machines, sports, all are after the measure of man. *Man is the measure for all tailors.* He, then, is the stylistic principle that under-lies all architecture, for aren't our apartments essentially an extension of our clothes? And is it not necessary for our apartments to fit us as constructively as our clothes? Must they not be as purposeful, as hygienic, as discreet, and as elegant? Modern style and modern culture do not have a uniform canon of form; they are functional. Nor do they have uniform constructive principles like Classic and Gothic architecture used to have. The common denominator for everything is *man....*

Man clothes and arms himself by means of civilization. The form of civilization results from his struggle with nature and its exploitation and it changes from one generation to the next. Nanuk, a primitive man, has a biomechanical civilization. His primitive tools complement his muscular skill. Modern man has a machine civilization; the complex organization of his tools and production is guided by his even more complex mental powers. We have left the caves and have turned into inhabitants of big cities, and although all passéists call for a return to nature, for the "abandonment of cities" (Taut), we cannot renounce that which made us truly cultured: men of cities. The intervention of the machine made possible the essential metamorphosis of culture and civilization and stimulated the liquidation of art. *For at bottom machine civilization is at variance with the civilization of arts and crafts.* This antagonism cannot be eliminated by the rejection of the motorcar, the gramophone, cinema, and linotype. Aesthetes often have a funny image of life. Since we live in houses constructed with concrete, since we wear clothes, use plumbing and electric light, since we travel by train and read newspapers, we are not naked in the paradisiacal primeval forest. The machine has sealed the fate of craft. All attempts to revive the crafts have proved not only futile but undesirable. The machine liquidates arts and crafts. At first it imitated manual labor, imitated it poorly; this was probably why the opposition to machine production could rise, such as was proclaimed by Ruskin. Ruskin resembled the Don Quixote of Marx's aphorism: Don Quixote suffered for the wrong assumption that a migrant chivalry could be likened to all the forms of civilization. We adapt with certain difficulty to the requirements of contemporary mechanical civilization, yet our historical education prefers to confine itself to the profound study of periods when technology made no progress. H. G. Wells observed that in Europe historical knowledge started when the Greeks traveled the world on horseback, in sailing boats, and galleys until the time when Napoleon, Wellington, and Nelson traveled using virtually the same kind of vehicles or ships. The discovery of steamship and of electricity—at this point history turns up its nose, sneers, and closes its eyes. And thus a certain period of incubation was necessary until modern production thought was able to absorb the machine. Then all of a sudden the machine created new social, intellectual, and moral relationships and conditions; it changed the environment and finally became an instructor of modern aesthetics and a means for the liquidation of art. It became a part of man. It is clear that its appearance either kills art or takes possession of it. That is what Eli Faure says. To put it more precisely, the machine replaces art.

Our time is one of science and technology. First, they showed religion, rather irrever-ently, out of the workroom door. Consistently and sincerely, they renounced all mysti-cism. With idealistic exaltation, they proclaimed themselves materialistic up to the ultimate consequences. Joyfully, they hoisted the flag of positivism. They experimented. When religion lost its credibility science found it. Scientists believed that their work could install heaven on earth. This heaven is called technical civilization. In the seclu-sion of laboratories, scientists discovered radium, x-rays, and serum. As a result of the specific discoveries of pure science, which are made under the microscope, gigantic and far-reaching changes are made in manufacture and industry; technology, which applies these discoveries, arrives at ever newer inventions. These in turn modify opinions, correct medical and hygiene practices, and reform legislation and morality. The driving force behind this progress is *the machine*. The machine shortens working hours to their maximum efficiency. *Its law is minimum effort for maximum effect.* This is the law of *economy.* The law of economy is the law of all work. And work is the only law of the world, its ordering force, which leads organized matter to an unknown destination. Industry produces in one year more products than manual work produced in a century. Machine civilization gave modern man "the song of iron, the buzzing song of electric sparks...and they understood that this was the song of their time, they hear its merciless cadences in the blast of trains, which run above their heads," says Kellerman in his *Der Tunnel*.

The machine is no picturesque subject, but the form and development of a certain amount of energy organized in a certain manner. It is not a theme for art, but an instruction for the mind. It is a model of modern aesthetics, almost a symbol of modern beauty....

"Les belles formes sont les plans droits avec les rondeurs," said Jean August Dominique Ingres. And with this quotation, one can verify the beauty of mechanical product, if one wants to.

Are not ball bearings, for instance, a joy to look at? The brilliance of magnificent modern materials, the precision of geometric forms—the circle and the sphere are forms that flatter most our sight—they suggest directly the perfection of their function. This beauty matches precisely the character of our times, which are industrious and sober, matter-of-fact and hard working.

When we discuss machine aesthetics, we have to point out that we do not intend to preach the deification and worship of the machine. The sentimentalists could not help condemning the machine and the Futurists glorified it; but it is necessary to consider it rationally and bear in mind in what respect the machine constitutes a source of instruction and how it directs us to a new sensibility. We live in an era of steel, and polished steel fascinates us; if mechanical beauty is not the work of so-called practical common sense, it is simply the work of modern man, it is the fixed point of contemporary culture. The machine is an interfering element in modern culture. So far, modern artists have accepted the machine in a rather incomplete and mainly artistic manner. And in essence, naturalistically, The majestic beauty of the machine should not be crowned with ornaments or panegyric poetry. Marinetti's poetry and Léger's paintings of machines have not augmented the beauty of the machine and the limousine. It is better to leave machines where they are; they belong to the factory and not in paintings, works of sculpture or poetry.

The instruction offered us by the machine is roughly as follows:

We see that wherever the engineer worked conscientiously with disregard to aesthetics and without any artist interfering with his work, he achieved a pure and complete modern beauty, using new materials. The machine was not created for exhibitions but for use, although the sight of a factory at work is a dazzling modern theater. Clean profiles, clear outlines, precise and categorical motions of the machine prompt us to develop the logical and creative faculties of the mind; they liberate feelings, which were perverted by earlier art, which being supernatural was a hand-made drill in metaphysics. To dress up mechanical forms, whose beauty rests in precision and function, with external decoration and to relocate them on a canvas or on a building, as was done in *Jugendstil* and is done even now, is tantamount to false and unenlightened machine romanticism and is a fundamental error. The Greeks of antiquity would have surely never applied the curves of their ship to their architecture, while the Romantics of the machine calmly apply the forms obtained through aerodynamic calculations to furniture and buildings, that is, to static objects. (Mendelsohn's Einstein Tower in Potsdam.)

What lesson does the machine teach us? Artists through handicraft have not invented the mechanical principles of today's aesthetics; modern constructors have, who have never thought of art. They aimed at the complete fulfillment of a concrete task. And we declare that when one seeks solutions to a concrete task and a concrete problem with utmost economy and precision, one achieves the purest modern beauty without superfluous aesthetic considerations. It is impossible to say that this beauty begins where the completely fulfilled utility ends, it is simply not possible to distinguish the beauty from the utility of a form. It is not possible to argue that architecture starts where the construction ends. It is impossible to say so, because the moment we achieve all-round, goal-oriented perfection, we automatically achieve beauty. It is impossible to precisely determine at which point this beauty starts, just as we do not know where the curve changes its route, or when an object that answers practical needs appeals to our aesthetic perception. We do know that form in itself is unimportant and that it impresses our sensibility and interests our vitality only when it is associated with some function. At this point we declare that all beauty probably begins where the indifference to utility ends. Powerful modern beauty exists in every object which is made for a precise and definite purpose and which fulfills exactly the end for which it is intended.

All the confusion that besets contemporary visual artists derives first from a lack of clear aims and an imprecision concerning the use of the object. By contrast, the products and constructions of modern industry give birth to new beauty. New proportions, a game of volumes and materials, for which we cannot find examples in history, *contain number, that is, order*. These undeniably beautiful constructions evoke a *virile* atmosphere. Their modern beauty is *mathematical*. It is the beauty of a perfect system.

It might be objected that many machines that serve their purpose in every respect may be unsightly and ugly. This is not quite true. If they are plain, it is mainly because they are perhaps not totally functional, because their perfection is only relative and they demand further perfection. It would be possible to say that an ugly machine calls directly for further perfection, that its ugliness is a symptom of imperfection. We affirm that *the more a machine is perfect, the more beautiful it is*. And it is perfect and consequently beautiful only when absolute functionalism, to the exclusion of beauty, was the only intention of its constructor. When two machines that serve the same purpose stand next to one another, and both have been assessed as equally perfect in their utility, and one of them is more ugly, there cannot be any doubt that the more beautiful functions better. Machines are born of calculation and calculation always leaves several possibilities, it always opens the way to a number of modes. The choice of the best (implicitly the most beautiful) solution, is the work of mathematical intuition. Mathematical intuition, which intervenes here, does not mean artistic intuition, aesthetic or formal: where well-disciplined and logical mathematics is involved, there is no room for feeling, fantasy, and taste.

The mathematical spirit of the machine explains everything. It explains its regular perfection, and its latent and innate irrationality. Where we speak of mathematical intuition, where we explain the beauty of the machine—*and the beauty of the machine is an irrational value of a rational product*—we realize that beyond the rational evaluation lurks the efficacy of irrationality. Mathematics, or rather geometry, was defined as the art of thinking with precision about imprecise facts. Indeed, mathematical thought operates with fictions, with knowingly incorrect conclusions, which are voluntarily accepted as correct...? is an irrational number, which can be rationalized to many decimals, but always only partly; irrationality cannot be eliminated. Every machine with ball bearings, every cylinder contains a π, an irrational element. The formula of the circle, a fundamental form, is irrational. All the inexplicability of the beauty of the machine probably lies in its irrationality. And thus, the machine could be not only the model of modern mind and logical work, but also of modern sensitivity. There is nothing more nervous than a running motor.

Intervention of irrationality signifies the intervention of mathematical intuition. Instead of the advance of elementary and mechanical logic, we speak of the intervention of a biomechanical factor, of *invention*. The biomechanical power of human inventive faculty cannot be defined. In a series, there is always room for sudden changes: invention is the only unpredictable and accidental element in industry and technology. Invention precludes chance, and where chance prevailed (as was the case in so-called art) invention cannot come to its own.

Therefore, the aesthetics of the machine tells us: a product is beautiful when it has been created economically and precisely for maximum perfection and utility, and without any aesthetic considerations. The machine is the work of specialists, of the engineer, never of the artist. We need specialists. An accomplished specialist produces a perfect object. But this is not much. The specialist can meet only existing needs; he cannot awaken new needs. A specialist who is detached from the rest of life is an "acultural" phenomenon, which is incapable of moving development forward. The inventor is a specialist—he is a modern man. The vital force rests in the biomechanical factor of inventive power. We need inventors.

Translated by Alexandra Büchler

ARTIFICIALISM   Jindřich Štyrský and Toyen
Originally published as "Artificielismus," *ReD* vol. 1, no.1 (1927–28)

Cubism was the outcome of the traditional division of painting into figurative, landscape and *nature morte*, where the main difference consisted in descriptive thoroughness. Essentially, it was a new method and technique of depiction, replacing the illusion of optical perspective by the illusion of reality distributed in space. It generally looked at painting through a model. Formally, the painting coincided with the appearance of reality, and where this was not possible, the result was deformation. Analysis of reality led to its mirroring and duplication. Cubism turned reality around, instead of spinning imagination. When it reached maximum reality, it realized that it lacked wings. The eyes that had become sensitive, kept glancing back at the horizon of their origin, with the result that what came next was an illogical "return to nature." Yet, Cubism offered painting *unlimited possibilities*.

Artificialism comes with a reverse perspective. Leaving reality alone, it strives for *maximum imaginativeness*. Without manipulating reality it can still enjoy it, without an ambition to liken a clown's cap to a body that may not have any other charm than that of abstract infallibility, which nevertheless suffices when it comes to satisfying poets well versed in mystification. Mirror without image. Artificialism is the *identification of painter and poet*. It negates painting as a mere formal game and entertainment for the eyes (subjectless painting). It negates formally historicizing painting (Surrealism). Artificialism has an abstract consciousness of reality. It does not deny the existence of reality, but it does not use it either. Its interest focuses on *poetry* that fills the gaps between real forms and that emanates from reality. It reacts to the latent poetry of interiors of real forms by pursuing positive continuity. The exterior is determined by poetic perception of memories (negative continuity). Remembrance of memories. Imagination loses real connections. Deduction of memories without the aid of memory and experience prepares a concept of painting, the essence of which excludes any mirroring, and positions memories into imaginary spaces.

Memories are prolonged perceptions. If perceptions are transfigured as they are born, memories become abstract. They become the result of a conscious selection that denies imagination, and pass through consciousness without leaving an imprint and without disappearing.

The outcome of abstract visual memories at the stage when they permeate one another is new formations that have nothing to do with reality or with artificial nature. This stage does not coincide with the receptive and passive state of artificial paradise or with the erratic logic of abnormal individuals.

The function of the intellect is external and final. It organizes and disciplines and to some extent chisels the mass of emotional response. The process of identification of painter and poet is internal, indivisible and simultaneous.

An artificial painting is not bound to reality in time, place and space, and for that reason it does not provide associative ideas. Reality and forms of the painting repulse each other. The greater the distance between them, the more visually dramatic is the emotiveness, giving birth to analogies of emotions, their connected rippling, echoes all the more distant and complex, so that at the moment of confrontation between reality and image, both feel entirely alien in relation to each other.

An artificial painting elicits not only optical emotions and arouses not only visual sensibility. It leads the viewer away from the merry-go-round of his usual imagination, dismantling the systems and mechanisms by which ideas connect. Artificialism abstracts real spaces, giving birth to a universal space, which is often replaced with surface distances, so that forms are connected by means of distance. The color itself has gone through a light process, and is therefore not affected by the anomalies of diffused and condensed light. The value of nuances and transpositions creates a lyrical atmosphere.

The composition of a painting based on lack of interest in reality, presupposes complete consciousness and is dependent on concrete logic of artificial painting. It is entirely definitive, unchangeable and static. The forms in the paining coincide with images of memories. Giving the painting a title is not an act of describing or naming its subject, but of characterizing and giving direction to emotion. The subject is identified with the painting and its forms become self-explanatory.

Translated by Alexandra Büchler

THE POET (LECTURE GIVEN ON THE OCCASION OF AN EXHIBITION OPENING)   Jindřich Štyrský and Toyen
Originally published as "Básník (přednáška proslovená při vernisáži výstavy)," *Rozpravy Aventina* 3 (1927–28)

Artificialism identifies the painter and the poet. This identification is inseparable, internal and contemporary. The designation "Artificialism" is irrelevant. We are using it out of need to differentiate and distance ourselves from the manure of the so called modern painting, because we owe it nothing.

We shall call the painter poet.

Cubism was the reckoning of traditional painting, divided into figurative, landscape and nature more. Cubism was essentially a new method of depicting models, with a difference in descriptive thoroughness. It viewed painting through a model. It replaced the illusion of optical perspective with the illusion of reality distributed in space, and it projected the illusion of space into reality. Forms in a painting overlapped with the appearance of reality and where it was not possible to achieve such a partial cast, what ensued was deformation. Analysis bore fruit: duplicates. The Cubist painter turned reality around instead of setting his own imagination in motion. Cubism achieved maximum reality. But then the desperate movement realized that it had no wings, having been betrayed by its own vision, with one eye cast on reality and the other on the painting. This second eye did not charm us to the extent that we would stop feeling innate repulsion towards the quartering of victims.

Constructivism and objectless painting, based on play with forms and on pure pleasure of the eye, resembles the writing of essays. Words precede thought and people bear merely the weight of words. Everything in the world has been said and depicted, and that is why it is impossible to build on causes, but on results. The primitive man was pursued by fate and geometry. That's why he had a right to happiness. The poet is pursued by chance. He decides to swallow a banana if it has been peeled. The Constructivists did peel Pythagoras, but what they swallowed was the skin.

Artificialism rejects literary, formally historicizing or deforming gimmickry, that is surrealism. The shorter our life, the dafter metaphors for it we choose. We cannot argue over terms, but over their scope. The subconscious is a gag many put in their mouths so as not to think. Admiration for the sauces that garnish the world is passed from generation to generation.

Rivers flow out into cemeteries and the ocean swallows ships because it keeps looking for its swans. Swans with two necks, one of which ingests sleep, while the other throws it up. The juggler digests the applause in advance, forgetting that he would not be able to vomit it out. Noah's Ark, carrying hemlock, sinks at sea. The flour-moth sits on a branch, singing. The poet rejects only his manner.

Each of us is tracking his own toad, but its games of hide-and-seek escape the human eye. If we find it for the second time, we are not sure whether it is indeed our own. Higher creatures grow fat and lower ones multiply. One day, the world shall be taken over by a hirsute mannequin. Blue collars shall dig out the graves and rob poets of their gold. Then they will leave them alone, having achieved equality. Death shall be nothing else but abandonment of the world of banknote currency. Gold shall belong to gravediggers, and treacherous clouds shall swallow doves and airplanes with equal indulgence. Only then shall airplanes begin singing.

The population merely wants its daily soup, knowing how to wait for it and enjoy it. Absurd theories are commitments we can freely talk to each other about without falling under each other's influence. The poet shall untie the knot, throw away the key and leave.

Dreams confirm the experiences of our habits. We see faces that scandalize by their feigned holding of breath. The tired smiles of flowers and collars that we cannot consider false. Many arrive, multiplying vantage points, exchanging them, until multiple chaos reigns in appearances. The result of their snares is truth in things redundant. The secret of their faces lies outside and time etches the falsehood under their portrait. We shall never find out whether the face betrayed the portrait, the portrait deceived the actor, or whether the face was simultaneously its own prompter and audience. There is only one kind of baseness: realizing one's own deceit.

The poet bids farewell to sleep. The hypocrite keeps picking the names of flowers, but their real image does not exist. The appearance of things could be encompassed by a lyrical monster who has as many eyes as there are points in the space around it. The poet observes the appearance of things from the point at which they have arisen.

Dream landscapes are strange sets with colors waiting to fade, light waiting to be lit, and forms waiting for future gigantic ruins. Life hands out and returns extinguished pawns. Only the child is a viewer, chained to the grass, unable to leave when the game becomes terrible. The secret of magicians lies in the fact that they endure pain, not that they don't feel it.

City fringe dwellers have no microscopes and that's why they are not bothered by bedbugs. If we are drowning, we are irrevocably seduced by mirrors in which we might be able to augment our poverty. The poet is still only walking towards the fools' house; the surrealists had been chased out of it a long time ago. To be enchanted, there is no need to roam Oceania. The poet loves distances. Not distances in space but in time. He loves the earth in its beginning and end. Diluvial seas, only just inventing their language. Wherever a poet goes, he needs nothing more than the world he had brought with him.

Poetry is not the continuation of the image and song first composed by prehistoric man. Mushrooms sprout out in a desire to resemble each other. Poetry comes into being in a desire to shorten one's life.

In times of glory, hyperreality grew a far too thick layer of cheese. Hyperreality cannot revive allusions to modern poets. A tattoo on the deeper layers has come risen to the outer counterweights like a bedsore. The false poet is getting ready to plunder himself. Sleep reproduces the causes of his treacherousness. Cruel consciousness does not play with humility. The lids of the eyes staring from the subconscious are lowered. Mirrors read eyes. The victim is weeping, no longer able to speak by means of gaze. The gardener is growing ribbons for future biers. Many produce critical fleas. It was enough for the poet to watch how those who build on sleep, violating it at the same time, who build on the subconscious, are making their nest, but he is not going to sit on eggs with them. Building on the subconscious means to take pride in losses.

Sleep is a bee gathering honey for a recollection to enjoy its taste. We have no memories, but we are trying to manufacture them. There is only one way to rid oneself of memories. To be abandoned by them.

The poet uses paint or words to dilute what he wants to say. Having no instinct of self-preservation, he lives nevertheless. The engineer is dreaming. Designing a new globe. The poet is no longer surprised by the face of night, of carton boxes and of people. You will not find him in a crowd of gawkers. You will find him in its center, standing over his victim. His victims are unusable forms, trailing colors found on human rubbish tips like spilled out guts.

The misfortune of epigones is comical. It imitates the happiness of poets.

A sensible person arrives at happiness about himself only with difficulties. This borderline is where the poet starts and proceeds in the opposite direction. He enjoys paper, clouds, space and finally emptiness. His joy has no example or model.

The poet does not operate with reality. He is lured by poetry that fills the gaps between real forms, and emptiness emanating from reality. He reacts to the hidden poetry of form interiors, inventing and creating their exterior. Imagination has lost its interest in what is being born and what is dying. It deducts memories and memories of memories, independent of memory and experience. Memory and recollection play a mutual role of executioners.

The poet gives the shape and color to an emotional idea. His perceptions are transfigured at the moment they are born. Recollections pass through consciousness without leaving an imprint or without vanishing. Their form is not real, nor is it artificial. It is natural. The poet cannot be happy in artificial paradises.

Reality and image repulse each other. Between them lies the incantation: the word.
It does not describe the subject. The subject is identified with image. The title gives
direction to excitement. But leaves the viewer abandoned and alone with the image.
Recollection invents.

Translated by Alexandra Büchler

EXCERPTS FROM **POETISM MANIFESTO**   Karel Teige
Originally published as "Manifest poetismu," *ReD* vol. 1, no. 9 (1928)

At the very moment when the last glimmers of the "-isms"—Dadaism, Futurism,
Expressionism, Cubism, Suprematism—were fading, at a time when somber chaos
and dismal stagnation held sway in all studios and studies, amidst tasteless and
excruciating eclecticism, blundering along lost paths and blind alleys, in Prague,
whose gates we wanted to throw open to all the healthy breezes of the world and the
gulf streams of worldwide creative activity, at latitude 50 degrees north and longitude
14 degrees east, in the years 1923 and 1924, i.e. four to five years ago, *Poetism was
proclaimed.* Poetism was proclaimed not in order to supersede some other -ism of
art, literature, painting or music, or to oppose or compete with some other -ism. In
proclaiming Poetism we simply wanted to express and formulate an opinion and fix
a course; we were seeking neither to establish a new -ism for avant-garde studios,
exhibitions and schools, nor to found a movement or school. Poetism was more a
proclamation of "a new era in the history of the human soul," a way out of dismal
aesthetic and philosophical confusion, disorientation and disharmony. Poetism was
conceived as a new aesthetic and philosophical attitude, a creed for the end of the
millennium; the fact that it is has become in addition a school and a poetics, was not
the intention or fault of the authors responsible. Poetism as an art -ism and a school
has gone the way of all -isms and schools: it has found its own artists and epigones;
it has seen a number of superficial fashions; it has been torn to pieces and extolled
by the critics, who one day ring its death knell and the next day hail its re-emergence.
This Poetism as a movement and a school is nothing but a derivative—and in places
a very damaged one—of Poetism as an attitude and aesthetic prognosis. We will not
dwell here on Poetism as a school and an -ism because they are outside our own field
of interest in Poetism as a new aesthetic and philosophy.
[...]
Poetism as an aesthetic prognosis and a philosophy of creation as based on a number
of proven and recognized laws and historical facts. Dissatisfied with and unconvinced
by the existing aesthetic concepts, and the general rules or mythologies of the studios,
we posed afresh the question of art and poetry and are answering it, recapitulating the
results of countless analyses of various phenomena from the recent era of developments in poetry and art.
Our predecessors opened a window on Europe. Discovering modern civilization to be
unequivocally international we decided it was time to abandon provincial and regional
horizons and nationality. We became estranged from the history of Czech literature
and repudiated the heritage of Czech painting. Besides, the legacy of local values
offered us nothing of any worth for the present European moment. (Except, perhaps
for "...the image of all those white towns"...that splendid passage of pre-1848 poetry,

with its free and rhythmic stream of dreamlike images, embodied what we were seeking from poetry).

We integrated ourselves into the rhythm of collective European creation, the rhythm whose metronome—because of the social and cultural situation that arose in the 19th century and laid the basis for today's creation—was Paris. Paris was the focal point of not just French but also international production—its Metropolis and Babylon, the spiritual center of not just the French language and the Latin tradition. It was a successor to Italy and predecessor of Moscow, just as, in history, spiritual hegemony shifts according to changes in first social and then cultural systems. Now that national insularity and parochialism are on the wane, the many national and local literatures are giving way to a global literature (Karl Marx). If we are to work for that international art to materialize, we must seize all the achievements and successes offered by the previous period of development. Modernity, which we defined as an aggregate of present achievements and the present state of the developmental process, requires us to embrace and master the contribution made by the celebrated French creations of the immediate past in the fields of poetry, painting and aesthetics, which is and was the culmination of the spiritual and cultural life of this era of our civilization.

[...]

Contemporary civilization has done most to cultivate sight of all the senses, and photography and film have played a considerable role in attuning the visual sense and making it more flexible. This has steered poetry onto an increasingly optical path. A poem was once sung, now it is read. In the pre-Gutenberg age, rhyme and rhythm, parallelisms and refrains served as technical aids. By the time of Symbolism they were either abandoned (free verse) or had to acquire new (optical or acoustic) emotional functions. With the development of book printing, the spoken language of living speech atrophied, lost its sonic timbre and became a system of graphic ciphers: typographically arranged poems are the outcome of that fact. Marinetti, on the other hand, stresses the total anarchy of words and verbal art which, he maintains, should not be colonized by the optical order: he uses typographic free compositions only to illustrate acoustic values; bold type illustrates fortissimo, narrow type staccato, italic legato and faint type pianissimo. The Futurists are continuing with phonetic poetry, replacing the Debussyesque music of the Symbolists with the noise of the industrial cities. Marinetti actually trusts the proven heresy of onomatopoeia and in the case of Francesco Ganguilla this poetry culminates in poetry set to music, making use of words and a system of notation: Poesia pentagrammata. It would be more consist to make phonograph recordings of such poetic songs rather than using the optical system of book printing and letters.

However "the stock of the auditory poets is falling with the slump in romantic contemplation" (Nezval). Now that Nezval is versifying his Alphabet we stand on the threshold of a new pictorial poetry. Whereas Rimbaud discovered the color values of vowels in their sound value, Nezval transposes the shapes of typographic signs into his poem; he makes poetry from the magic of their form.

By studying the historical development of modern poetry we have come to the following conclusions and perceptions:

That it is necessary above all to demand a poetry that is pure and not allow it to be used for any non-aesthetic purposes; that form must be developed in terms of its function and purpose, i.e. in the direction not of rational comprehensibility, but maximum emotionality, achieved by means of maximum physiological effectiveness. Poetry, which in the Middle Ages made rhyme and verse of scholarly knowledge, only now, in the world of our civilization becomes a sovereign, pure, clean and absolute poesy, that neither has, nor can have, any other purpose than to satisfy people's unbounded thirst for lyricism,

That poetry must be removed from the world of categories and concepts and opened up to the primal psychic sources, whose aesthetic potential is indicated by contemporary psychological and psychoanalytic discoveries;

That it is necessary (particularly in the case of Czech poetic language) to revise the lexical material by means of systematic experimentation, in order to transform words from being vehicles of conceptual content into an independent reality and direct generators of emotion.

That by investigating the correspondence and analogy between the data of individual senses and the qualitative unity of the aesthetic emotion thereby generated, we can open the gates to unlimited possibilities that must be used aesthetically. That in this way the problem of poetry can be posed afresh and its mission may be redefined: poetry for the five senses, poetry for all the senses. Poetism was an attempt to provide an answer to that problem: and that is the essence of Poetism as a new aesthetic.

By continuing with what was foreshadowed by Mallarmé and Apollinaire, we experimented with typographical montage of poems until we eventually came up with a new branch of pictorial poetry, a lyricism of image and reality, and then a new branch of film art: purely lyrical cinematography and dynamic pictorial poetry. We achieved a fusion of poetry freed from literature and the image freed by cubism from representation, and the identification of the poet and the painter. This identification brings the history of painting to an end, i.e. painting in the sense and in terms of the function it fulfilled in the Middle Ages. Painting as a representational art is condemned to extinction.

We proclaimed the extinction of painting in its traditional sense, as we saw that contemporary painting, incapable of continuing powerfully along the trail blazed by Cubism, was caught in a vicious circle of semi-finished products, using uncivilized techniques and old-fashioned materials, and since it failed to understand its own nature, its emotional power was drying up as a consequence.

The history of the human mind, enlightened by psychoanalytical research, has shown us how people's affective needs merged with their material and utilitarian needs, and how the gratification of the one led to the satisfaction of the others; how aesthetic activity first tended to serve a utilitarian function (cave paintings, medieval craftsmanship, folklore) and only later became autonomous. Aesthetic activity and impressionability awaken, in the same way (as Freud has shown) as sexuality, in conjunction with the major vital and physical functions and work.

Painting came into existence as a representational service. The entire history of painting is one of an emancipatory struggle for the freedom and autonomy of non-utilitarian aesthetic values which gradually emerged and gained strength as the craft evolved. In the Middle Ages they were severely repressed by the church. By an edict of the Council of Nicaea, the organization of a picture was a matter for the church as patron; artists were responsible only for the art (i.e. the execution of the work). Fra Angelico painted the Madonna's cloak blue not because he needed that color for a particular area of the picture's composition, but because the Church's rules laid down that the Madonna's cloak had to be blue. Painting conveyed the literary substance of legends and was required to use a priori the prescribed themes, emblems and compositional schemas; it was a Bible for the illiterate. At the end of the Middle Ages in Renaissance mercantile Italy, art's emancipatory strivings proliferated. The first blow against art as a craft and monastic activity (l'art, l'artisanat) was linked with the changing social status of the artist (whereas previously painters were anonymous craftsmen, Charles V used to pick up Titian's brush when it fell from the master's right hand) and the invention of a new painting technique—oil painting, whereby pictures were no longer bound to architecture and were now freer, more graceful and intimate and no longer under the oversight of the church, whose universal power over the human spirit was already undermined. Michelangelo dared to clash openly with Pope Julius III [sic]. That conflict, recorded by Vasari, is historically conclusive: for the first time, a painter demanded a separate order for his works, distinct from the ecclesiastical order. The eye triumphed over prayer. The Dutch still-lives and miniature landscapes of the 17th century are a collection of paintings with indifferent and banal subject-matter; the subject-matter is less important than the composition of color and shapes: a beet is placed where the composition requires the color red, and a white table-cloth or plate where white is needed. The subject is the vehicle of the color scheme. Landscape painting and still-life, genres created in bourgeois Holland, become the vehicles for the further emancipation of painting in the French School of the bourgeois nineteenth century. In the case of the Impressionists the subject and object are even less important. It was a further triumph for sight and the poetry of color. Under the pretext of a subject, the Impressionists painted bright, scintillating and blossoming colored mists, with homogeneous coloring and illumination. The Cubists subsequently pushed the subject and its representation (the original utilitarian function of painting) to extremes and used forms devoid of any meaning in terms of subject; they painted shapes and colors for the emotional response their evoked in the viewer, for their aesthetic and emotional qualities, without any iconic import. Those paintings are artificial optical and physical organisms, which arouse certain sensations in the viewer and arouse their emotions in accordance with the artist's intentions through their physiology, senses and nervous system. The quality of that emotion is the quality of the painting.

Hand in hand with that liberation of painting, whereby the picture has become a vehicle of purely optical, non-literary lyrical values, strides have been made in photography, cinematography, printing and new photochemigraphic methods have been developed that have taken over from painting its documentary, illustrative and imitative function. Moreover, at a time when the ideal of painting as a sovereign and pure art realized by means of a system of specific forms, enormous admiration has been expressed for Negro sculpture—the three-dimensional poetry of tribes who have not been forced by history to subordinate their innate, human and animal poetry and playfulness to the needs of a practical, utilitarian and rationalist hunger over centuries of slave civilization.

In the Cubist era, Picasso declared the epoch of painting finished for good. —Now it was necessary to *formulate the problem of the picture afresh*. We took as the starting point of our analyses and experiments Cubism as a system of lines, colors and forms intended to stir the viewer's emotion through the sense of sight. We discovered within Cubism the historical moment when the aesthetic activity of sight is separated from practical (representational) activity in order to go its own way in future.

Basing ourselves on Cubism we defined the picture as a harmony of color, as a symphony or poem of color. We identified *color* as the fundamental and constitutive element of painting, its mother tongue and lifeblood, its exclusive realizational medium.

So we defined the picture as a perfect system of color on a surface or in space (the statue!) or in space-time (film!) achieved using any technical means. In our search for the laws of color harmony we discovered, by analyzing various schools of painting and works by individual artists that every system has its own laws about complementary colors and virtually its own spectrum, so the contradiction between (psychological) aesthetic laws on color relationships and the laws of color optics remains an unknown quantity in the theory of color in art.

Light—the factor that tells us about colors—has yet to be used directly in painting. It has been expressed by pigment, both material and cloudy. Wherever painting has tried to achieve greater luminosity than is possible with pigment, it has used reflective materials such as metals, gemstones, gilding: the stained glass windows of cathedrals were a first primitive attempt to work with the projection of colored light. Modern technology enables the projection by lamps of actual colored light, the interplay of spotlights, moving shapes, sequential dynamic symphonies of light and color that offer new scope for creation in color: *the projection of moving pictures*, freed from the rigidity of medieval handcraft techniques, born out of light—*the photogenic poem*.

After we departed from Cubism, which we regard as the barrier between old-world painting and modern creation with color, a barrier from which there is no going back to the atavistic representational approach, we eventually managed *to transcend for good the traditional panel picture*: it was superseded by the *dynamically projected light picture* (the interplay of spotlights, film, fireworks) and *static photo- and typo-montage pictures produced serially in book form in thousands of copies; pictorial poetry–the photo- and typo-montage picture in book form identified with the poem and the colored, moving, rhythmical, time-space picture identified with music.*

Having consigned to historians and conservators the job of caring for inherited and moribund branches of art—painting, literature and other arts and crafts—we strove to eliminate those degenerate and extinct areas of art that were appropriate for past societies and civilizations but are not relevant to our mechanical civilization and unacceptable for the modern nerves and psychic make-up of contemporary people, and replace them with that were more appropriate to the present day and present-day people. So we were not seeking a renaissance but *new creative fields*, because new worlds, new disciplines, new reactions, the echoes of the subconscious and the imagination of the superconscious, infra-red and ultra-violet, uncharted territories and *blank spaces on the aesthetic map* attract us and are a spur to the creative experimentation: far removed from the previous artistic and aesthetic conventions, we tried to switch on a new art, a new poetry of color, sound, light, scent and movement—*poetry for all the senses.*

The era of our civilization is a phase in which the various different kinds and branches of art have rid themselves of the roles they played in history, an era in which aesthetic activity is breaking free of the utilitarianism of the crafts of the past and beginning to lead an autonomous existence, and in which these emancipated spheres of artistic activity are becoming closer to each other and combining, so that in future it will be impossible to separate them according to the categories of the former aesthetic systems; at a time when new scientific and technical achievements are giving rise to new aesthetic fields and genres, the idea of the *correspondence and unity of artistic emotion has emerged.*

[...]

It would seem that *our analysis of hearing in color is revealing a profound universal law* applicable to all sorts of other phenomena and forms of human thinking. Psychological experiments have shown that impressions of smell, taste, touch, of skin, of physical pleasure and pain can also be transferred into optical pictures; that color can be attributed to numbers, to the days of the week, to vowels (Rimbaud) and other systems. It has even been discovered that visual oneiric (dream) pictures can be aroused by means of auditory or tactile sensations, which again indicates a certain *correspondence, as well as certain functional supplementarity and sensorial equivalence.* Bergson notes that the sense of touch is above all in dreams an immanent tendency to self-visualization and creation of an optical dream picture. This phenomenon of supplementarity is also common among visual pictures and touch and physical data, and locomotive senses. It is interesting how psychotechnical experiments repeatedly confirm the pre-eminence of sight and the visual type among present-day human characteristics. Acoustic notions are ten times scarcer than visual notions among present-day people. Tactile notions are about as frequent as optical ones. Notional images of taste, smell and movement have not yet been researched in depth.

The aesthetic corollary of these physical and psychotechnical facts is a mutual correlation; the realization that the autonomy of artistic genres may not exceed certain limits and lead to total isolation. On the contrary, these mutual ties between the individual arts, corresponding to sensorial equivalences are increasingly the focus of interest of contemporary aesthetic creation. Impression links sight with the other organs in a new unity, above all with the so-called lower senses, which in consort with sight reveal the deepest mysteries of existence. By its ability to move, sight comprises the functions of two senses: vision and touch; awareness of time and space. It could be that movement is the basis for the inherency of all the sense organs. Even though all the senses have their own energy, can't you sense the wind in Monet's painting, or the scent of the forest or the sea? The activity of sight is just as complex a process of life as thought and vision is a function that involves the entire person. In each sense organ, the others play a part and provide our psyche with its specific data, and thus vision alone can bring the other senses into play and cause all the strings of the modern soul to vibrate. The modern eye has been characterized as an organ in which all the senses reside; "sight that thinks and feels." An equally complex function is fulfilled by the ear, which, as we know, is not an exclusively acoustic organ, but one equipped overall to be a kind of seismic organ for registering vibrations and oscillations.

[...]

This opens up *surprising and amazing prospects*. If this total and universal poetry, this synthesis for all the senses, which was an unattainable absolute and distant utopia for past epochs, is to become a reality, it is necessary above all to define precisely its conditions, to refine and test out its means of expression and investigate its multifarious echoes in the viewer's psyche. In short it must be placed on a scientific footing. We must go on rejecting the imperfect historical materials and techniques of the craft, *create new tools* and invent and create new means of expression, using for that purpose all the tools and achievements of contemporary science and technology. One may indeed assume that the history of art and civilization is not simply a succession of styles and schools but that it represents real progress. One may suppose that a person who has mastered the tools of his trade as well as Rembrandt is capable of producing works with much greater emotional potential than his, quite simply because present-day tools are a thousand times better.

We abandoned historical forms of painting and versification. We abandoned the language of concepts and seized instead the language of reality. We have demonstrated the possibility of poems without words, the possibility of making poems with material which is more reliable, constructive and scientifically verified: making poems of color, shape, light, movement, sound, scent, energy...

We have observed poetry's gradual liberation from literature and hand in hand with that the *trend of poetry towards optical expression until it fuses with painting in the pictorial poem*. We have said that the optical aspect has demonstrated its superiority and greater energy; we noted that among our contemporaries there is an absolute predominance of visual types, probably due to the influence of specific features of present-day civilization, which has brought us the enormous culture of sight. A key role in this has been played by photography and cinematography.

We have created *pictorial poems*: compositions of real colors and shapes within the system of the poem. The animated pictorial poem: photogenic poetry. *Kinography*. We have tried to formulate a proposal for a new art of film—pure cinematography, photogenic poetry, a dynamic picture without precedent. Luminous and glittering poems of undulating light—we saw in them the leading art of our epoch: the magnificent synthetic time-space poem, exciting all the senses and all the sensitive areas of the viewer via sight. We defined film as a dynamic pictorial poem, a living spectacle without plot or literature; black-and-white rhythms and possibly the rhythm of color too; a sort of mechanical ballet of shapes and light that demonstrates its innate affinity with light shows, pure dance, the art of fireworks (and the art of gymnastics and acrobatics). The art of movement, the art of time and space, *the art of the live spectacle*: a new theater.

Hearing—the second of the senses to be considered aesthetic de facto and de jure—demonstrates in the contemporary psyche a lesser potential than the other so-called "inferior" non-aesthetic senses such as touch, smell, etc. However, under the influence of *radiotelephony*, it looks as if it will be rehabilitated. Yet radio at the present time is in the situation film was not long ago, serving solely for reproduction and transmission. But our aim is to claim radiotelephony as a productive medium. In the same manner that poems can be created by film out of light and movement, *radiogenic poetry* can be created as a new art of sound and noise, divorced equally from literature and recitation and from music. We could achieve here more effectively and rationally what Russolo was striving for with his "intoners." Poetism will invent a new radiogenic poetry, similar to photogenic pictorial poetry, whose auditorium will be cosmic space and whose audience will be the world's masses. Auditory, spaceless radiopoetry has wide and viable scope. The radio dramas produced so far are auditory theater in much the same the way that many films are optically transmitted theater. Just like pure kinography and photogenic poetry, radiophonic and radiogenic poems must make use of elementary media (in the former case light and movement, in the latter case sound and noise) and break free of literary and theatrical constraints. Radiogenic poetry as a composition of sound and noise, recorded in reality but woven into a poetic synthesis has nothing in common with music or recitation or literature, nor yet with Verlainesque onomatopoeia. It is also poetry without words and not a verbal art. It bears virtually the same relationship to music as film does to painting. Nezval's first radio scenario "Mobilization" indicates the scope offered by this kind of radiophonic poetry.

By using the analogy of color and sound—as luminous music and orphic painting strove to do—the musical talking movie is coming into being. It was first used to create horribly naturalistic operatic films. Nonetheless this important technical invention can be used for new, undreamed of, totally non-naturalistic compositions. Talking and musical film are based on the idea of using special equipment to convert sound into light and vice versa inasmuch as acoustic, optical and electrokinetic energy essentially differ in terms of frequency; thus acoustic, optical and electrical energy can be converted into each other. This discovery can become the basis of a *new optophonetic art*. Let us divide the process of converting sound into light and light into sound into two separate processes. We will use only the conversion of light into sound. Light rays projected onto a cinema screen induce currents in the equipment and a special telephone converts it into sound. The picture projected onto the screen evokes a sound in the equipment. A square will obviously create a different sound than a triangle, so chords can be created by combining luminous geometrical shapes. And vice versa: what shape and luminosity will be evoked by a specific set of sounds? Converting light into sound or alternatively sound into light—not in the reproductive manner of the musical film but a direct and autonomous optophonetic art (made possible by the new functionalities of the picture [light] and music [tone]) represents an extensive sphere that can give rise to unprecedented aesthetic emotions.

Poetism has advanced proposals for a new poetry, which wants to turn the universe into a poem using all the means made available to it by modern science and industry, a new poetry to capture the entire universe of the human spirit by stirring all the human senses. The holy and healthy thirst of our modern senses and nerves, the hunger of our personae, the lust of our bodies and minds, life's fire burning within us—*élan vital*, libido, or *tropisme vital*—cannot be sated with what was offered by the former art. Our gaze yearns for other spectacles than those offered by the tedious paintings of exhibitions and galleries; our touch wants to be cultivated and charmed by abundant sensations. The previous music does not suit our hearing and possibly only the best cuisine in the world, that of France (which was not by chance the country with the liveliest civilization and culture) could satisfy our taste. We seek a poetry that speaks to all the senses, one that saturates the viewer's sensibility and beguiles and cheers their heart. And we want this poetry to be *based on the sensorial and physiological ABC*, on the infinitesimal vibrations of senses and nerves, those "strings of the soul." Poetism wants to speak to all the senses—albeit on occasions stressing the optical factor for evolutionary reasons—because it seeks to speak to the entire person within this modern culture of the balance of body and spirit.

In place of the old art categories that corresponded to the higher aesthetic senses (sight and hearing) and to people's intellectual and practical needs, which are now better served by other activities and achievements, Poetism creates a poetry for all the senses.

A poetry for SIGHT or "liberated painting": 1. dynamic: kinography, fireworks, light shows and all sorts of live spectacles (= "liberated theater"), 2. static: typo- and photomontage pictures, the new picture as a poem of color.

Poetry for HEARING: the music of loud noises, jazz, radiogenics.

Poetry for SMELL: Poetism plans for a new olfactory poetry, a symphony of smells. Smells exercise a profound influence on our "inferior," instinctive psyche: the smell of blood, dust, perfumes, flowers, the stench of animals, of petrol, of oil, medicines and drugs can exercise a powerful and amazing effect on our emotions. Baudelaire still filtered clusters of smells into a system of poetical language. We want smells to act directly like sounds and colors. The language of smells is probably best known by lovers: gifts of flowers and perfumed love-letters are the first step toward olfactory poetry. Moreover, gardeners were fully schooled in its ABC and its effect on the emotions and it was used in the liturgy of many religions. So let's make poems from smells as directly as me make them from color and sound!

Poetry for TASTE: If, in the case of certain individuals, we do no doubt the direct connection between their sight, sensibility and intrinsic nature, there is every reason to suppose that the great gourmands and gourmets of history—the cordon bleu gastronomes and the Pantagruelesque hedonists—are able to enjoy total communication between taste and soul; that, as Delteil once said, good digestion is as much a source of *joie de vivre* as a good prayer. We are not talking about the poetry of intoxicating drinks and narcotics or alcoholic hallucinations that almost automatically give rise to lyrical tension. The enjoyment of a good *dîner* is no less refined or aesthetic than any other whereas enjoyment is among the supreme human values, measured in terms of life's objective: happiness. We regret that culinary art is no longer taken as seriously as it was in medieval aesthetics and as it deserves. Poetry for taste, culinary art (of which Apollinaire wrote in his "*Poète assassiné*"), apart from its intrinsic gustative values, is intended to affect the entire concert of the senses with its forms and colors and its many and varied aromas.

Poetry for TOUCH. This was discovered by Marinetti, who, in 1921, termed it *tactilism*. There was already a foretaste of it in Rachild's "*La Jongleuse*" and "*Les Hors-nature*." Although the plastic arts also use tactile elements, Marinetti's poems of touch—"tactile pictures"—have nothing in common with painting or sculpture, their aim being to achieve tactile harmony. In our civilization, our touch is trained to a high level of deftness but so far has not been aesthetically cultivated in terms of impressionability. Whereas our visual sensations when looking at materials of different softness or coarseness often arouse in us associative tactile perceptions, merely touching them in the dark fails to arouse intense excitement within us. Tactile poetry, composed of delicate, fine, coarse, warm or cold fabrics, silk, velour, brushes, slightly electrified wires, etc., is capable of cultivating our tactile emotionality and providing us with the utmost sensual and spiritual thrills.

Poetry of *INTERSENSORIAL EQUIVALENCES*: optophonetic, "liberated theater," colored lights and singing fountains.

Poetry of *PHYSICAL AND SPATIAL SENSES*: the sense of orientation, the sense of speed and the time-space sense of movement: *sport* of every possible kind: motoring, aviatics, tourism, gymnastics, acrobatics: our innate thirst for records is slaked by athletics; victory mania flares up at football matches along with the joy of collective teamwork and feeling of strained harmony, precision and co-ordination. The poetry of sport, shining above the educational and orthopedic tendencies of physical exercise develops all the senses and provides a pure sensation of muscular activity, the delight of bare skin in the wind, beautiful physical exaltation and intoxication of the body. *Liberated dance*, sovereign dynamic poetry of the body, independent of music, literature and sculpture, opening the gates of sensuality; the art of physical genius, the most physical and abstract art of all, whose medium is tangible flesh-and-blood physicality, whose movement gives rise to a poem of dance using dynamic and abstract forms. *Poetry of the COMIC SENSE*: Grock, Fratellini, Keaton, Chaplin, etc.

Translated by Gerald Turner

ULTRAVIOLET PAINTINGS, OR, ARTIFICIALISM (NOTES ON THE PAINTINGS OF ŠTYRSKÝ AND TOYEN)   Karel Teige

Originally published as "Ultrafialové obrazy čili artificielismus (Poznámky k obrazům Štyrského & Toyen)" *ReD* vol. 1, no. 9 (1928)

Those approaching Štyrský's and Toyen's new paintings are advised to forget all the tracts on painting written by Leonardo, Vitruvius, German professors or servile reviewers for the Parisian tabloid press. They should realize that the paintings they face here have *nothing to do with the craft called painting by historians, aestheticians and critics*.

We have declared the *demise of painting*. And now we are introducing to you the work of two artists whose occupation might be described as painters. We then have to agree on the following: we have learned that painting, whose works, famous and numerous, are buried in museums, is of no use to us today. We have learned that what Leonardo was interested in and what Picasso was interested in were two things so fundamentally different that from now on, we cannot call both by the same name: painting. And at the same time we have learned that what Leonardo was interested in is today irrevocably a thing of the past.

Medieval artisans and revered old masters were not artists, nor were they poets. The task of medieval painting was to serve: the church, the ruler, education, and morality. Painting depicted; being burdened with iconic, documentary and illustrative functions, it was not allowed to create poetry. The history of painting is an incessant and gradual struggle for emancipation that has been passing through various phases and turns. Only in our century and in our civilization does painting liberate itself from its historical functions and purposes. Photography, film, journalism and advertising relieve painting of its duty to depict and to illustrate. And so it is that the art and craft of painting, born to serve these functions, has lost its *raison d'être* and is dying.

At that time Picasso declared the era of painting definitively over. Painting, which in the past served religion and the state, and depicted the world and the history of mores, is dying to be reborn in a pure, non-applied, specific form.

Liberated painting, the colorful poetry of Artificialism and Poetism in no way resembles the "iconography" of its historical predecessor. It lives in entirely different realms and is created by entirely different means than the works of old masters of and today's lovers of the past.

The art of Toyen and Štyrský is a phenomenon indicative of the contemporary identification of painter and poet. It is poetry of colors, not a colored or drawn illustration of a poem. It sparks off lyrical illuminations without marrying literature. Its lyricism is purely a lyricism of color, which has its source in a collection of luminous color planes and delicate lines.

The poetry of color, optical poetry, is not a mixture of excreta from the painter's palette and inane ink of the writer's pen. It is not a transposition of verse into the speech of lines and colors, nor a pleonastic *Gesamtkunstwerk*. Artificialism does not make the same aesthetic mistake as orphism or color music that translates musical compositions into compositions of color and vice versa. Artificalist painting is a poem in the original Ancient Greek sense of the word poetry: poises, that is, supreme and independent creation. It is an independent, specific poem of color and line, not a reflection of a poem created by others and by different means.

Toyen and Štyrský make poetry by means of color and line in the same way Rimbaud's or Nezval's poetry is made with words. And their poems of blossoming colors fascinate with such emotive power denied to the old craft of painting and to the poetry of literary Parnasists. They are paintings of rare illuminations, infinitesimal vibrations and nuances, a never-ending miraculous kaleidoscope of dancing reflections.

These paintings come into being in an atmosphere of disengagement with nature and with the reality of the world. They do not have a model and constitute their own subject. They are not an artful, sophisticated game to entertain the eye in the same way as post-Cubist abstract compositions, which for all the perfection of their color balance fail to excite the viewer and touch his sensibility. Štyrský and Toyen do not want to charm our eyes; they want to light the fires of highest poetic intuition.

Having renounced the traditional aims of painting, Štyrský and Toyen also renounced its traditional techniques. They have discarded the sauce and paste of academic, gallery-based painting and avoid the vigorous, individualist brush stokes that used to bring false impressionists and their collectors into ecstasy. They covered up the traces that engage the attention of art graphologists and their paintings do not possess individual style. Their paintings therefore represent something entirely different from historical painting, not only as far as technique and medium are concerned, but also in their aim. In the century of polished steel and supreme power of materials it is difficult to understand why Matisse processes his work in the way in which medieval or renaissance painters applied paint. Today, architecture renounces old techniques, methods and materials, stone, timber and bricks, and buildings are constructed with iron, concrete and glass: the body of an automobile is not the work of a master saddler, and in the design of airplanes, timber, the traditional building material, was cultivated to be as strong as steel and duralumin. Štyrský and Toyen have renounced traditional paining methods and they use new means to create works that would charm a person almost obsessively concerned with precision and cultivation of materials. They may not have anything else at their disposal than the traditional material of the oil paint, yet they achieve so many sophisticated effects and manage to make paint, which in the hands of the old masters was heavy and pasty, almost immaterial; thanks to perfect technique they gave each color thousands of nuances and unexpected brilliance. This technique, which perfectly realizes what Impressionists may have dreamt about, is not the aim in itself, but a means to achieve maximum brightness and a charming fête of color. Not even the form of these paintings—contrary to abstract painting—is an aim in itself: it is merely a precondition for the emotion elicited in the viewer. Štyrský's and Toyen's paintings do not tell a story, but by the magic of their lines and colors they awaken in the viewer a dialogue between his consciousness and subconscious. Between the self and memories. And yet these are not images of dreams and hallucinations. Inspired probably by the subconscious, they are realized in the full light of consciousness; they create the poetry of a new reality, new flowers and lights, they direct a film of excitement and high emotion, they create an *ultraviolet superconscious world*; they are works of magic and enchantment, unforgettable jewels, colorful mist of a new dawn of poetry appearing before us.

Toyen's and Štyrský's Artificialism, closely related to Nezval's Poetism, lives in the certainty that *the most artificial existence contains the least illusion and the greatest happiness*. It creates the poetry of colorful games, transfigured, false, and abstract and of future memories: it is not a passive record of the subconscious, nor is it astrology or an explanation of dreams. It is creation, invention, a poem: a work, fact, fruit of poetic superconsciousness. Toyen and Štyrský do not cover themselves with the banner of Artificialism to establish a school or a movement, and they certainly have no intention to leave the word to epigones. Just as they have given each work a name that in itself is an effective lyrical shorthand, to give the viewer's emotion the right direction, to describe their aesthetics and work method, they have chosen a general keynote word that is meant to emphasize their utter independence from the world of nature, as well as the fact that they are not subjected to the forces of the subconscious. At the same time, the name *Artificialism* proclaims that it is distinct from Surrealist painting, which owes too much to Bocklin and Expressionism, and, unable to make use of the legacy of cubism, has descended into literary and formal historicism. Like Poetism, Artificialism is the direct historical successor of cubism, having crossed the barrier that cubism, in its vivisection of the world of phenomena, could not cross. That is why Toyen and Štyrský are contemptuous of today's neo-neo-neo-naturalists and of the classicist "fat muses of the return to nature," and create the poetry of an artificial, irrational world, a golden value of mankind at the end of the millennium, a rainbow of happiness, seeing happiness not as a treacherous gift of fate but as creation.

Toyen's and Štyrský's paintings are the inalienable treasures of the lyrical days and nights of our universe and our calendar.

Translated by Alexandra Büchler

SECTION

4

THE TWILIGHT OF
IDEOLOGIES

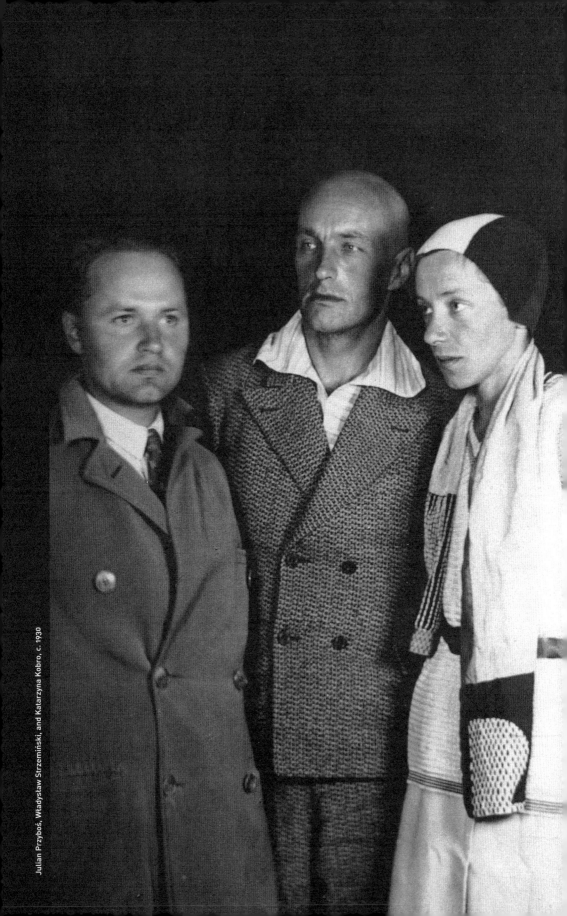

The title of Ernő Kállai's 1925 article, "The Twilight of Ideologies," captures not only the situation of the international avant-garde movements in the mid-1920s, but also the sense of change that was taking place. The utopian expectations of the avant-garde, fueled by the artists' messianic faith in an imminent revolutionary change, peaked around 1922. Already in 1923 the new realism, Neue Sachlichkeit (New Objectivity), was underway in Germany, a manifest reaction to abstract utopianism and optimistic expectations. One of the earliest responses to this change— the acknowledgment of which took another few years for most artists, writers, and intellectuals—came from the painter and Bauhaus master Oskar Schlemmer, who entered in his diary in June 1922: "Turning one's back on utopia. We can and should concentrate only on what is most real, the realization of ideas. Instead of cathedrals, the 'Living-machine.'... Ornamentation necessarily degenerates into unconcrete or aesthetic craftsmanship based on medieval principles; it will be replaced by concrete objects which serve specific purposes."

In 1923 when Kállai wrote his article "Correction: to the Attention of De Stijl" (see Chapter 7) he also, if inadvertently, made a turnabout and, suddenly recognizing the gap between transcendental images and actual reality, opposed pure abstraction. He saw the new art he had championed as stuck in a social vacuum, and made a case for art's living ties to reality at the expense of pure metaphysics. Almost coincidentally, Karel Teige also criticized the pure aestheticism of De Stijl on similar grounds in 1924–25.

Still, the various groups, publications, and art nurtured by ideas and ideologies were alive and well until at least 1924, when pragmatism and the artists' utilitarian efficiency in society became the new objective. Historically, the change was underpinned by the October 1924 implementation of the Dawes Plan (named for American financier and future Vice President Charles Dawes), an international effort that aimed to restore Germany's economic and social stability so it could pay the reparations demanded by the Allies. This relative economic stability gave impetus to modernist design and shifted the focus of many artists from the future to the present. International Constructivism and the grand utopias had been tied to the euphoric moments of the post-World War I years, when such ideas were not tested in reality and practically no architectural production was taking place. Bruno Taut's Stadtkrone plan was the memorable symbol of those years and of the tremendous ambition of the avant-garde. Indeed, in 1924 when Kállai marked the historical changes and outlined the new architectural ideal of simple, healthy, sunny living quarters, he referred back to it: the new building "should not nourish the ambition to become a *Stadtkrone*, an unwieldy idol that towers domineering on the horizon, in the manner of pyramids and cathedrals...let us not conjure additional stone monsters worshipping ideological monumentality over our heads."

Teige expressed an anti-monumental stance in many of his architectural writings in the 1920s, as did the German architecture historian and critic Adolph Behne. His colleague Siegfried Giedion proposed to do away with the word *Architektur* in favor of the less grandiose, lower-case *bauen*, or building. Architecture was indeed the best indicator of the shift from dreams to tangible givens. What had a symbolic meaning in the 1919 Bauhaus Manifesto—the elimination of boundaries between architecture, painting, sculpture, and the crafts—now referred to new metal constructions with "no style, but design." Stanisław Witkiewicz did not welcome the new business mentality in art; he put the bitterly satiric motto "The customer must be satisfied" at the head of his sarcastic lampoon of the rules of a portrait-painting firm (see chapter 11).

With the "twilight of ideologies," art in both Western and Central Europe came to a point similar to Tatlin's Productivism in the Soviet Union. As Kassák wrote in his article "Advertisement," the artist was now expected to become a "social creator" rather than an individualist, becoming engaged in the practical tasks of making objects or pictures such as posters for the masses, rather than for a narrow upper crust.

The newfound pragmatism also brought new hopes. To many artists it appeared that the dreams of the postwar era had come true and technological development had indeed helped to bring about a new sense of community and democratic design. Central Europe also achieved relative stability between the mid-1920s and the years of the Depression. Emphasis in art was now on an early version of mass culture: photography, film, advertisements, and the publicizing of artistic production by various live events in Warsaw, Prague, Bucharest, and Budapest.

Our heading "Twilight of Ideologies" refers only to the demise of the ideological avant-garde movements of the 1910s and 1920s. From the second half of the 1920s, new populist and dictatorial ideologies were on the rise, signaling the ultimate fate of the avant-garde in both Western and Central Europe.

chapter 9

HUNGARIANS IN EXILE

Éva Forgács

The massive wave of emigration of intellectuals following the defeat of the Hungarian Commune in 1919 resulted in irrevocable losses to the culture of the country. The voice of the avant-garde, with the exception of a few vanguard artists such as Ödön Palasovszky or the poet and artist Károly Tamkó-Sirató, disappeared from the Hungarian scene. The avant-garde, with all the scandals and debates it could have generated, did not become integral to the Hungarian cultural tradition, remaining a foreign endeavor largely created by exiles. Many of the Hungarian artists who exhibited in the Der Sturm gallery in Berlin could not exhibit in Budapest during the lifetime of the avant-garde. This is all the more regrettable in the face of the prolific artistic and critical work that Hungarians created abroad.

Ernő Kállai became one of the important art critics in Berlin between 1920 and 1935. László Moholy-Nagy, who had produced just a few drawings prior to his emigration in Germany, became one of the central figures of International Constructivism and one of the pioneers of various new media. Lajos Kassák put the Hungarian avant-garde on the map of European vanguard modernism as a leader in politics, culture, and art. They all responded to the commercialization of the avant-garde around the mid-1920s. Kállai urged the abandonment of utopias and coming to terms with reality. Kassák welcomed commercials and advertisements as a new possibility to reach out for a wide, unsophisticated public—forgetting that in the service of capitalist firms, the avant-garde artist sold himself to his archenemy. Moholy-Nagy, in a 1928 letter to the German painter and architect Erich Buchholz, gave a retrospective account of the spirit of competition and rivalry that characterized the avant-garde artists the early 1920s.

Their lives took different turns. In 1926, once it was possible without risking imprisonment for his participation in the Commune, Kassák returned to Hungary; Kállai escaped Germany and returned to Hungary only after the 1933 Nazi takeover, carefully pondering the choice between Switzerland and his fatherland; and in 1937, Moholy-Nagy emigrated from Germany to the United States via England.

BACK TO THE WORKBENCH   Lajos Kassák

Originally published as "Vissza a kaptafához," *Ma* vol. 9, no. 1 (September 15, 1923)

The artist always draws on himself. Which is to say, each and every productive act of the artist is an additional surplus, something extra added to existing facts and figures. Creation is not making a replica of something *already existing*, but the formation of the picture, the subject itself, out of the unknown, into a unified whole that is a law unto itself. The work of art is the conscious expression of the artist's subconscious surplus. It is a state of equilibrium. It is not a mad rush toward some external goal, but rather a rest stop in the constant rush of power and energy. It is both the living out of life and the possibility of new life.

The creative law of the artist is identical to the law of general manifestation. The artist, the inventor, or the construction engineer all represent the same mathematical and ethical values. They create, each in his own field, according to his gifts, expressing himself through his own unique mix of life. To compare them with each other, to weigh their relative values is therefore an impossible task. Creation is a unique specialty.

Philosophers, politicians, and economists have outlined a new society whose development will be in the hands of specialists. *However, to be a specialist in some field does not mean being deaf and blind in other areas of life.* That would be equal to living an egocentric life divorced from the world at large. Man today lives under the sign of collectivity, or at least would like to. This active, new type of human being is the *collective individuum*. Only simpletons, paid demagogues, or naive romantics refuse to recognize in the present prevalence of dictatorial tendencies man's striving for recognition of his individuality. In place of wanting to imitate something, in place of the irresponsibility of following the herd, the man of today, conscious of his responsibility, has moved into action against everything that stands in the way of his growing awareness of his emotions and self. Political revolution expresses our general discontent, as does any advance made by the engineer, and the artist's will to elemental self-expression without relying on any external themes.

The world is visibly developing in a constructive direction; in the field of creative work, in the wake of the destructive schools beginning with Impressionism, Constructivism has now offered visual art a direct line of advance.

The question is this: what is the most direct path to the total self-realization of Constructive art?

The horrors of the world war and the romantic slogan of the revolutions have sidetracked man from his native, natural ability to act. The first task of the propagandist, and also of the creative forces of science and art, is to lead man, lost and straying, back to himself. But in order to accomplish this, we must have a clear notion of the distinctions between productive and non-productive work. From our point of view, art is a productive, and politics a non-productive, field of work. Art creates and produces whereas the politician merely expropriates. Therefore it would be nonsensical to want to direct any kind of creative work along the lines of any political (that is, external) disciplines.

The fate of the war was decided by specialists in strategy and technology, and the success of the revolutions can only be vouchsafed by the specialists of politics, science, technology, and the arts. By now we have learned that one person attempting to work in all areas can only lead to the most harmful dilettantism. We need specialists to see the revolution through to a successful conclusion. If a creative individual today, in exchange for an opportunity to prophesize, renounces the chance for creative work, he is in fact resigning his revolutionary stance. See what would happen to the Red Army if its specialist engineers abandoned work on perfecting the airplane and decided to go to war against the splendid French air force by delivering dilettantish orations at mass-meetings. And what would happen to the living values of human culture if today's young creative people chose to forget about their opponents on the frontlines of science and art, and decided to cater to the tastes of the culturally underprivileged masses, thereby breaking the back of contemporary art, which could otherwise exert such a powerful fighting force?

Artistic creation, like any primary creative work, can only be defined by its own inner laws, vitality, and constructive unity. There is only one kind of art. There cannot be an art that serves political ends and an art that is utilitarian in purpose—just as there can be no politics with a goal in art, or a utilitarianism with art as its aim. If such a dual-purpose hybrid still crops up in some specialized branch of the struggle for life, it implies a lack of purity in the creative character, and amounts to decadence.

Constructive artists are, given the current possibilities, the most social forces in the field, and have already recognized the untenability of political disciplines. They are right, as far as that goes. But beyond that point they too have strayed from the direct path; to the extent they have liberated themselves from the service of political movements, they have subjugated themselves to another yoke, that of utilitarian tendentiousness, by falling from the trap of political romanticism into the pit of technological romanticism.

For the benefit of the most rabid demagogues we would like to emphasize here that we are not speaking of *l'art pour l'art*—that is not what we want. We want to give ourselves in art, as individual members of human society, as man, who envisions, registers, lives to the utmost the life of today.

The Constructivist movement has arrived at a crossroads at an earlier point in its history than any other art movement. It faces two possibilities: either it will remain on its current course, in which case sooner or later it must drown in a sea of speculative, engineering dilettantism, or else it will find the way toward itself, becoming once more able to give pure expression to its creative nature. Having renounced political alignments they must now renounce the practical mindset. For just as there can be no artistic activity with the preordained purpose of *political agitation*, in the same way no art can be created with the utilitarian purpose of *being lived in*. Both viewpoints mistake the aim for the consequence. Today's art, by virtue of the creative individual's nature tends to be constructive, therefore social, and architectonic, therefore realistically stable.

The manner in which the constructive and architectonic nature of the new art may and indeed must be utilized by society is not *primarily* the concern of the artist as creator. This work is of a political nature and is expropriative. Such expropriative work should not necessarily have to be done by the artist who, as the producer, has already paid his dues to society. It would be utterly inane, for instance, to consider an apolitical person who has invented a method of mining that liberated a portion of humankind from having to descend into underground mines, as any less of a revolutionary, and a less useful human being than a representative in parliament or in a Soviet council. If the improved mines continue to be possessed by capitalists, and the workers themselves continue as miserable beasts of burden, the responsibility for this rests on the shoulders of politicians, the expropriators who are incapable of expropriating extant values in the best interests of humankind.

In the course of the five-year revolutionary period we have had occasion to realize that the serious leaders of the workers' movement must consider as their main task not the making of revolution but the consolidation of the results of revolution, the stabilization of its results and the resumption of production. The era of destruction and putsches is over, replaced by communism, the new constructive ideal taking the leading role in the revolution.

The new slogan is specialize for the fight, in the fight.
In Russian cities special military schools have been established—but at the same time they have not forgotten "that village schools must first of all become specialized in the area of agricultural sciences."
Today we are in the midst of a new preparatory stage of the revolution.
The next successes of the revolution are to be expected not in the realm of destruction but from the new constructive forces.
Politically and ethically the value of the working class lies in the extent to which it can create a new equilibrium for a disjointed, disoriented *humankind*.
The new art will prove its value by creating a new spiritual order for humanity.
The order of our lives has been disrupted; that is why everything hurts us and we hurt all over.
We want order.
We want the order of our own blood and spirit!
We know that everything depends upon us, individual human beings, who make up the masses.
We know that the time of empty speeches and threats daubed in red paint on the walls is over.
And that "we are rabble," not "Thank God"!
We have recovered from the "childhood illnesses" of the revolution.
We want to build!
We need specialists!
Back to the workbench!
Engineers design time machines and open up the caverns of labor and misery!
Scientists, conquer the elements!
Artists, give form to the new human spirit!
Politicians, expropriate for us the possibilities of life!

Translated by John Bátki

ARCHITECTURE   Ernő Kállai
Originally published as "Architektúra," *Ma* (February 20, 1924)

We need an architecture that corresponds to our lifestyle and our intellectual structures. Since the constituents from which the new architecture will have to arise are radically different from those of the time when the old buildings, churches, and castles were erected, the new architecture can not be simply an analogue of the old dressed up in new clothes.
The old architecture occupied the central position in the entire realm of art. And within this architecture there were certain types of buildings that counted as its crowning glory by virtue of their functional and symbolic significance. Such were the cathedral, pagoda, or mosque, serving the highest sacraments of religious ideology. And such were the seats of the highest secular and temporal power, the palaces of pharaohs, sultans, and emperors.
We no longer possess such hierarchic ideological focal points that gather together the various threads of our culture. We do possess the central ideal of a human being fully liberated in both the physical and intellectual senses, living a life of maximal intensity.

But this concept requires the elimination of hierarchies and of exclusive delimitations in the economic, political, and legal, as well as intellectual spheres. The new man is to be no mere solitary figurehead, but is conceived of as a manifold type differentiated into a thousand variants answering to the multitude of practical walks of life. However, he should, even in this multiplicity of forms, retain an openness and availability to connecting into the network of social relations. He must be a conductor of life; he must be a whole man.

It is impossible to elevate this figure of the whole man to such a mythical sphere of psychophysical structuring that a single body and soul should be the bearer and exponent of every single human characteristic and type that we now see swarming around us. It is highly doubtful that the proletarian concept of the new man is capable of accomplishing this abstraction. It would require such a hazy and generalized degree of abstraction that we would not be able to find an equivalent plastic form for it—including its architectural symbol. We lack the kind of spatial concept the structural center of which could serve as a setting for the ideal of the new man as the source and ultimate justification of all arrangement into a spatial order. Since our images of man are vibrant mainly in the multiplicity of concrete types, we cannot transpose them into an arcaded synthesis of architectonic spatial conception that would be a sovereign, quintessential unification of the human multitudes, rather than just a superficial assembling ground. And it is absurd to think of erecting separate, symbolic structures dedicated to the ideas of worker, politician, economist, teacher, physician, engineer, etc.

It is even less likely that we could abstract the various life functions of the new man into architectonic monuments. Work, recreation and entertainment, love or sports—both as concepts and as actual facts of life—cannot serve as the bases for ideological centralization. Our needs and interests are far too complicated, and far too lively in their ramifications for any one of them to swallow up the rest. Neither can their intellectual precipitates be summed up in concepts that in spite of their abstraction are tangible enough to serve as focal points of their own cult. And if there is no cult formed around an ideological abstraction, there can be no architecture in the traditional sense of the word, encompassing all subsidiary forms of art and every detail.

Or let us say that, having liberated it from capitalist exploitation, we attempt to elevate the fact of labor, its essence so vital and full of human dignity, into the most ethereal regions of individual and public interest. Are we justified in expecting to devote a separate housing to this idea, with its own dedicated functionaries and rites? There can be nothing more pathetic or faltering than the sentimentalism oozing from the various "palaces of work" perpetrated by starry-eyed designers, fortunately only on the drafting table. There are plenty of roofs sheltering human labor—forced labor alas—ranging from mines to offices and workshops. But we cannot expect even the most diligent German to erect a monument to and adulate the concept of *Labor*.

Our concrete needs and necessities exert their effects and are dissipated within a terrestrial framework. In time, once architects are liberated from the traditions of ideological representation, they will indeed evolve the pure forms to shelter amours, entertainments, work activities, assemblies, etc. But where do we find the metabolism that could enfold into itself the thousands of concrete energies, tensions, and dynamisms that make up life, life, and yet more life? And were we to find such a central life function, it would still have a long way to go in the processes of intellectual precipitation and transubstantiation to reach the point that marks the beginnings of the transcendentalism that gives rise to architecture. Where is the society that is willing or able to envisage, faithfully accomplish, and consecrate such a journey?

Contemporary architecture also has its own central notion. We judge a building to be successful if it corresponds to our requirements of maximal expediency, materiality, public hygiene, economy, and structural functionality. Today's architecture is governed by an extraordinary number of different purposes. Apartment buildings, factories, malls, theaters, cinemas, spas, terminals, hospitals, warehouses, etc. all serve different aims, and must therefore necessarily assume distinctive structures and forms. The same holds true for materials. On the other hand the requirements of public hygiene demand a certain degree of uniformity. For whatever kind of architecture we are constructing, it cuts off man from the open space and sunlight of the surrounding environment, and hygiene demands that these constrictions be held to a minimum. This requirement, which can be followed through an whole range of solutions starting from the present compromises that take into account contemporary economic, social, and material/technological considerations, all the way to utopian future, will be heeded by communist central planning. In any case current architectural trends include the intention to ensure within an architectonic framework a maximum of open space, fresh air, and sunshine by avoiding vast, heavy masses.

This trend is being realized in the newest plans for urban development, with their emphasis on avoiding crowding, congestion, and traffic jams, and on keeping separate the settings of activities that have special functions. The work district, the public forum for necessary and disciplined activities is one space, distinct from the architectonic environment of rest, the dwelling space. Thus in this respect, too, the end purpose necessarily determines its architectural formulation. The primary nature of organizational tasks does not tolerate in the new city or other type of human settlement the hegemony of a formal uniformity superimposed over the multiplicity of practical purposes, in the way that medieval towns were ruled by the pointed gothic arch and gable, predominant first and foremost in the cathedral. Again, the reason for this is the absence of an ideological center in our lives, the lack of an overweening abstraction arising from concrete details to become a distinct sacrament in contrast to mundane everyday life.

Contemporary life has lost the dualism of the sacrosanct and the profane. We know and live life as a single unity both solemn and lighthearted, free-flowing or constrained. We see architecture likewise as a single entity that vouchsafes an organized space to channel these currents of life; what is more, we see it as a tangible fact that is determined by the components of practical life. A diversity of aims and materials cannot prevent this architecture from being unified in its strict insistence on always documenting its own special mission and content. This requirement includes the notion of structural economy as the de facto rule restraining the autotelic proliferation of forms. The new architecture must be extremely restrained in its massiveness that would diminish light, air, and space, and equally so in the matter of forms aspiring to transcend the primary realities of human life. It must not attempt to be more than an array of inconspicuously employed props or vestments. It should not nourish the ambition to become a "Stadtkrone," an unwieldy idol that towers domineering on the horizon, in the manner of pyramids and cathedrals, forcing to their knees the devout—and downtrodden—working masses. It is sad enough that the monumentality of factory smokestacks, blast furnaces, and tenements rules over our lives. Therefore let us not conjure additional stone monsters worshipping ideological monumentality over our heads. The evolution of life and technology will eventually bring about an architecture that will rise into open spaces beyond the massive straitjackets of stone, steel and concrete.

Translated by John Bátki

Kunst kommt von Können. [Art comes from ability.]

The saying is very old and a commonplace, and has even acquired some ill repute; still, it is high time we pay heed to it and, more important, put it to use.

The age of ferment, of "-isms" is over. The possibilities of creative work have become endless, but at the same time all paths have become obstructed by the barbed wire barriers of ideologies and programs. It takes a man indeed to try and fight one's way from beginning to end, across this horrible cacophony of concepts. Not that all of these theoretical skirmishes, manifestoes and conclusions for the record were not indispensable for the evolution of ideas, or were incomprehensible. Even the wildest flights of pathos, the most doctrinaire stylistic catechisms had their own merit. It was all part of the ferment caused by Impressionism, and the infighting of the various expressive, destructive, and constructive schools.

But all of this turmoil is now finally over. Our awareness of the diverse possibilities has at last been clarified, so that today we are witnessing a time of professional con-solidation and absorption in objective, expert work. This holds true for the entire front: the areas of political, tendentious art and *Proletkult* as well as those of Cubism, Expressionism, Constructivism, Neoclassicism and Neorealism—and also in criticism. The most extreme, most exacting measure of individual vocation and achievement is that which is being employed by each and every school or camp toward its own. The process of selection has begun, and its sole essential guiding principle is this: what is the artist capable of accomplishing in his own field, through his own particular means and message.

What this message consists of, what the artist intends or would like to say not only today but also tomorrow and the day after until, if possible, the end of time at the highest and furthermost extension of utopian perspectives—this we are only too familiar with. We have all participated in the defining of aims and goals, in their expo-sition and propagation. Now at last, the question of "how" becomes all-important. We have discovered that an endless variety of trumpets may be sounded and they all make fine music, if the player knows his business. Therefore let us see the masters. Those who would play the primitive, or work in unconsciously primitive modes, as well as the most self-aware constructivist equipped with the possibilities offered by modern technology must alike be masters in their own m‚tier. This is the only thing that counts. And even if one turns his back on all of art as a bourgeois product and chooses to serve the proletarian tendencies, he will still have to face the requirement of know-how, in the interests of the success of revolutionary agitation acting on the masses. Even among those using the illustrative or caricaturing arsenal of everyday political agitation the most effective ones are those who work at the highest levels of originality and professional accomplishment.

The perfection of stylistic details and workmanship is decisive not only within the artist's particular school. In the competition among the various fully formed, clearly defined stylistic types it is always one quality versus another, in deciding which style survives.

To date, this struggle has by no means been decided by the "triumph" of one or another of the various "-isms." In actuality, each style can only be judged on the basis of its inner needs and not by weighing it against external, incompatible, formalist criteria.

I fully realize that this viewpoint means the surrendering of theories. But only of those theories that purported to apply their own narrow aesthetics and ideologies to the entire gamut of human experience. By espousing, in the name of stylistic and professional perfection, the relativism and free-market democracy of the various schools of art, I am merely acknowledging certain facts that I had previously, along with many others, chose to obstinately ignore.

The artistic monopoly of Constructivism or any other school, or of architecture, film or drama, over all of human existence is an ideological castle in the air, mere utopian fiction. It is confronted by the thousand-faced reality of psychological and objective determinants. It is even questionable whether the new social order that succeeds the decline of the middle class will be able to end this dizzying, chaotic condition. There will still remain the dualism of intellect and emotion, technology and nature, functional efficiency and freedom of impulse. No aesthetically one-sided school will be able to eliminate this dualism; it will perhaps one day be overcome by the evolution of human life itself. In face of the manifoldness of today's psyche the militant, one-sided camps may have possibly catalyzed the process of evolution, this much may be said with certainty. Nonetheless they cannot prevent the multi-layered, conflicted reality of the present from having its own live, suggestively expressive artistic record.

We must once and for all give up seclusion in any of the "-isms" unless we are able to uproot our entire bodily and psychic apparatus, together with its complex of instincts and transpose it into the image of one single ideology, so that it becomes an organic function of that ideology. Therefore only one critical viewpoint can rule over the entire multifaceted spectrum of living art, and that is the viewpoint of quality, embodying the requirements of stylistic and professional perfection.

What good are the ideological perspectives of *Proletkult*, Constructivism, functionalism or Neoclassicism? In place of the great ultimate interconnections that would theoretically project into the skies their monolithic, monumental harmonies, we must decide for each individual work on its own merits whether it is alive and suggestive, today.

We have no illusions regarding the social implications of this struggle. We are aware that the field is littered with the belated, brief efflorescence of retrograde or progressive bourgeois individualism. Only aesthetic narcotics stray consciously among the ambitious aims and great ideological perspectives. But as long as we are inseparably, for better or worse, at one with art, enslaved by a passion or weakness, then any fleeting evidence of life, no matter how infinitesimal, and never mind how abstract or socially conscious, is preferable to any rigid theory bright with promise for a future that may never come.

Translated by John Bátki

EXCERPT FROM **NEW PAINTING IN HUNGARY**   Ernő Kállai
Originally published as *Neue Malerei in Ungarn* (Leipzig: 1925)

INTRODUCTION

"Art is Nature seen through a temperament." If Zola's definition were complete, there would be no more worthy and splendid national school of painting than that of Hungary. For a bounteous Nature has showered us with her richest gifts; as for temperament, we have almost too much of it.

The Hungarian temperament manifests itself in a turbulent dynamism of body and soul, a heady succession of forceful experiences. Such rapidity and intensity of experience necessarily results in emphatic and therefore, in artistic terms, concentrated emotions, which in their turn create a specific kind of structure and set a lively rhythm. But there is another side to the Hungarian temperament. It loves to surrender, with Oriental quietude and inertia, to the hot, brooding power of its senses. Such sensuality all too often reaches a pitch of suffocating excess. It inclines people to a consuming passivity and melancholy, which is liable to shift without warning into an unbridled excess of joy.

Two perils constantly lie in wait for the Hungarian temperament: the blindness of unbridled elation and the abysmal gloom of despondency. Both extremes upset the rhythm of the vital spirits and lead to loss of bearings and inarticulacy. The excessive craving for action dissipates and atomizes experience, or sets it pulsing in sympathy with dynamic associations of emotions and ideas, so that all structured content and stable substance are lost. At the opposite extreme, the overheated temperament and its sensuality rest like a dead weight on every impulse that could ever lead to motion, activity, or vitality. No human predicament is more dismal than those stillborn or broken initiatives that are the defining tragedies of the Hungarian will. Nor, unfortunately, can all of them be blamed on the enervating Romanticism engendered by bourgeois individualism—though such Romanticism has undoubtedly done great harm by causing moral and philosophical disorientation. Nor do our historical and societal misfortunes furnish any adequate explanation—especially since they themselves largely spring from our own national character defects. Destiny, even the destiny of nations, is the result of character. It is fundamental to the Hungarian character that the enduring and practical force of its will seldom harmonizes with the grand perspectives so dear to its enthusiastic temperament—or with the stifling melancholy of its instincts, which so often fatally defeat its better self, its reason, and its soul. Even at full strength, Hungarian will is burdened with inner inhibitions. Even at its most active, Hungarian energy never shakes off the sense of being oppressed and muted, because it is constantly strung between the opposing poles of fatalistic impotence and ecstatic vitality. Almost invariably, the Hungarian national consciousness harbors a deep sense of these elemental impulses—even in its attitudes of statuesque self-containment and stable repose. For this reason, no sooner is the national consciousness thrown off-balance than it is tossed between emotional extremes: it enters upon the famous or notorious rhapsody of tearful self-complacency that is a defining specialty, not only in individual psychology, but also in the Hungarian identity as a whole, and in all the senseless reversals of fate that mark its history.

The psychology of the Hungarian temperament does of course include variations that find an explanation in economic and societal terms. For all its heroic shifts of mood, the temperament of the Hungarian peasant has in its depths incomparably more sureness and firmness, a far more effective instinctual philosophy of cause and function, than that of the bourgeois intelligentsia. It is, above all, in the lower reaches of the provincial gentry—and in those circles where the lifestyle of that deracinated class is still regarded as the ideal of a Hungarian elite consciousness—that the dangers of the Hungarian temperament reveal themselves: the tendencies toward indolence, irresponsibility, and blithe extravagance. It is, however, quite possible to ignore class differences entirely, and to define the Hungarian racial identity as a single, instinctual force, sometimes unruly and domineering, sometimes negligent and slothful, with scant inclination to submit to laws of moderation and discipline. Our frivolity and indolence are all but limitless. All the same, there is one thing that can both awaken the passive, even fatalistic depths of our temperament and curb the playful audacities of our more sprightly moods. And this is not a categorical imperative, or anything of that sort, but our attitude of imperious pride—or, to put it another way, the staying power of our heavyweight instincts, more Asiatic quietude than mental superiority. A proud, masculine bearing and an instinctive, often brutally domineering attitude are the impulses behind the finest and noblest Hungarian deeds. On the other hand, there is in the Hungarian temperament and destiny a kind of calm, Asiatic wisdom that manifests itself in an unshakable sense of purpose, economy, and a priceless sense of humor. Admittedly, this wisdom is not so sober as, say, the Teutonic variety. It does not take life's administrative details quite so seriously. Its interest in modern civilization and its organizational capabilities fall far short of those of the West. In Hungary, much that in the West would be caught up in the hectic business of economic and intellectual production is left to lie fallow. "If you don't come today, you'll come tomorrow," and "Slowly does it," are among the most popular expressions of Hungarian folk-wisdom. No wonder Hungarian life, even in Budapest, still flows with a provincial breadth and deliberation. This leisurely way of life suggests a nation of comparatively simple habits, by contrast with the harried haste of the complicated West.

There is, however, more to this than the contrast between East and West; there is also a state of alienation between agrarian culture, on the one hand, and monopoly capitalist industry and global commerce, on the other. Agriculture and the primacy of natural landscape are essential component factors of the Hungarian character and temperament. The rural Hungarian way of life tends to foster bodily opulence and rich sensuality. People in Hungary like to declare: "We may be poor, but we live well." The agrarian culture upholds and reinforces the ruling trait of Hungarian racial psychology: the concentrated physicality of the Hungarian experience, which emerges intact even where the experience itself points to abstract and intellectual connotations. Undoubtedly the placid life-style of provincial agrarian culture, and its hearty dislike of problematic issues, feed the powerfully instinctual nature of the Hungarian temperament. As a result, there is more scope for the slightly anarchic, often violent, but flamboyantly sensual impulses of the subconscious. This is not so among the masses in the great mercantile and industrial regions of the West, where the vital impulses of the body are far more harshly affected by the rigors of rationalized working and living.

Cushioned by the agrarian fat of the land, the Hungarian tends to be less frequently and less powerfully afflicted by inner conflict than the Westerner. Intellectually inclined toward skepticism, nervously hypersensitive, the Westerner is racked by the thousand crises of psychology and destiny that afflict technological civilization, with its ferment of industrial socialism. Naturally, we, too, pick up echoes of the problems that stir up unrest and threaten disaster in other countries. But the life of the mind, in modern Hungary, has significantly shifted its center of gravity toward diaspora and emigration. Those who have lived or still live at home exhibit nothing like the same extreme and radical dichotomy within bourgeois culture that has found expression in France and Germany. In this respect, the new poets, writers, and artists of Russia—a far more agrarian country still—have gone much farther: this is a consequence of the limitless fanaticism of the Russian soul. The Russians' confession of anti-Christian faith is as ardent and as absolute as their Christian piety and humility once were. We have neither the Russian fanaticism nor the German idealism to break free of our personal limitations and devote ourselves to an idea, a mental demand. Nor, constitutionally, can we muster the same respect as the French for the objective autonomy of the surrounding world. Far down within our national consciousness is an unsleeping instinct that makes us live for our own identities: unassailable, self-contained, imperious, and self-sufficient. For us, the wall between self and not-self remains intact at all times. We lack a center, where—as in some ultimate solution—all the external and internal problems of our being might come to rest. We have no *mystics*, because our imperiousness is far too proud, stiff-necked, and pagan, and we cannot resist the expansionist urges of our temperament. The Hungarian spirit has never submitted so completely as others to Christian or bourgeois constraints. Nothing so well illustrates our pseudo-Christianity as the fact that we, caught between the spheres of the Western and the Eastern Church, have been unable to find our own distinctive form of Christian worship or of church building. Bourgeois life never reached us until long after it had relaxed its initial rigor and made room for a variety of transitions from feudalism and guild organization to liberal democracy. Even so, Hungarian economic and intellectual life during the last century, and in the prewar period, included a number of prominent figures who were as much at home in liberal bourgeois democracy as a bull in a china shop.

The dichotomy between Asiatic origins and European demands subsists to this day. Plainly, this mentality is not conducive to the harmonious clarification and stabilization of a nation's sense of itself.

It is a mark of the proud and well-rounded egocentricity of the Hungarian character that its vital consciousness always distinguishes between the concerns of the ego and those of the world. The external world is a stage backdrop, against which the outlines of the ego stand out with telling clarity. Or else the world is the adversary in a keen trial of strength and endurance; in which case success is announced by ponderous, static monumentality. But any attempt to widen the bounds of this monumentality causes it to dissolve into nebulous imprecision. Our world is not informed with the clear faith of its essential oneness with us. Nor is it a horrific blend of reality and fantasy, ordinariness and miracle, reality and super-reality, manifested in a way that fragments the ego and causes it to merge with objects in many dimensions. To some degree, the gulf that this well-rounded Hungarian egocentricity opens between itself and the world necessarily reveals itself as a fondness for external display. This is not to say that Hungarian egocentricity is incapable of internalizing itself: but this internalization springs more from the confused, intricately entangled instincts of the subconscious than from the radiant purity of psychic enlightenment. Put it this way: as soon as the typically Hungarian experience refines and clarifies itself, it loses depth and coherence and shades over into a plaything of the merely impulsive, joyous temperament, a rootless flowering of our sensuality. On the other hand, the fatalistic Oriental wisdom of the Hungarian soul generally ensures that our experiences of cause and purpose eventually lead us into the realm of ponderous weight and inertia.

FROM ROMANTIC NATIONALISM TO IMPRESSIONISM

At this point in our psychological and philosophical account of the Hungarian soul, it becomes possible to ask what kind of painting might express that temperament and that character.

The history of Hungarian painting is still a very short one. True, some scattered medieval remnants have survived the intervening centuries of almost continuous Turkish and Tartar wars. But it is more than dubious whether these can really be regarded as Hungarian at all, either in origin or in style. Nor have our Renaissance and Baroque paintings anything positive to tell us in this respect. The dawn of the nineteenth century saw a significant increase in the number of Hungarian painters and paintings, but the first fifty years produced little besides a Neoclassicism and a Biedermeier full of Italian or Austrian reminiscences.

Károly Lyka's work on the Hungarian art of the period has much of interest to tell us on the socioeconomic causes of this lack of autonomy. The Viennese court, the court-bound aristocracy, and the Church—insofar as they exerted any artistic patronage— were precluded by their whole mentality from contributing to the emergence of a Hungarian artistic identity. The cultural needs of the local gentry were negligible, and the only public that did exist—the urban bourgeoisie—was almost exclusively German. The social context of our painting was thus so impoverished and so dominated by foreign influences that it could sustain virtually no artists with any aspirations beyond the artisan level. Any Hungarian artist who nevertheless managed to work in his own country was making use of knowledge acquired in foreign academies. The pictures that were painted could be Hungarian only in subject matter, not in style. Even the increasing quantity of paintings on subjects from Hungarian history or folk life depended on a carbon copy of foreign academic formulas. It required the overwhelming national experience of the War of Liberation, and the advent of the Romantic cult of individual feeling, to rid our painting of the sleek, alien skin imposed on it by the Neoclassical canon and by the pedantic, Teutonic, petit-bourgeois love of tidiness and neatness.

The tragic historical compositions of Viktor Madarász embody the revolutionary eloquence of the oppressed Hungarian national consciousness, not only through their subject matter but also through the honest plasticity of their style and the muted expressive force of their gestures and moods. The way in which, in *Zirínyi and Frangepán*, he sets the gentle sadness and devotion of the younger comrade alongside the unbroken, manly defiance of the elder, as they commune with their common destiny in the last hours before the end, is Hungarian lyricism in all its authentic inwardness. This lyrical unity, this inseparable blend of grief and defiance, was the mood of Hungary in the years that followed the suppression of the Revolution. As an adolescent, Madarász had taken part in the bloody struggle against Austrian absolutism, and he shared in the national mood of mingled despair and rage with all the weighty and passionate impulsiveness of his Hungarian temperament. His historical compositions, though they differed widely in subject matter, always sprang from this one basic mood. For Madarász, the motif was not an opportunity for illustration but a means of expression. It was a framework, which the artist filled with rounded form and clothed with the pictorial emblems of defeat (*Frangepán*), of affronted dignity (*Ilona Zirínyi*), or of the rigidity of death (*László Hunyadi on his Bier*). The expressive clarity and suggestive force of his paintings is not solely attributable to Madarász's own personal talent. His paintings gave expression to a national mood that had deep sources in history. Furthermore, that general mood—the lyricism and eloquence of the oppressed and frustrated Hungarian national consciousness—was one that fatefully recurs in Hungarian character and in Hungarian history. Madarász gave visual form to his own, present personal suffering, and thus to the suffering of Hungary in his lifetime. This was the authentic lyricism and eloquence of the ancient laments, transforming historical memories into a true and spontaneous means of present expression...

Impressionism was an extraordinarily mobile, intellectually superior vantage point from which to obtain the most undisturbed enjoyment of the world and life. In place of passionate commitment, truth to objective fact, and devoted fidelity, it chose to play games with objects: delightfully fleet-footed and whimsical, but with very little of substance to offer. The only artists who ever could keep a foothold among all these rarefied and volatile sense-impressions were the French. The analytical acuity and instinctive harmony of the French mind, the ingrained liberal individualism of its bourgeois culture, produced such artists as Manet, Pissarro, Degas, Renoir, Monet, Sisley, and Signac. The Hungarian temperament lacks the ability to subject its instincts to this degree of rational control and intellectual sublimation. Our culture rests on a style of life that is far too plain and provincial to allow us to rise above crude material ties and operate—as the French do—on a superior level of experience and interpretation. The atmosphere of our Impressionist paintings is accordingly denser; their physical framework appears more material, harder, and more rounded. Local tones are not subsumed, as those of the French are, in a shifting veil of complementary colors and reflections. The intensity of color is not so evenly distributed; instead, it builds itself into contrasts of high tension.

We lack the French artists' gray-attuned harmonies of *valeurs*. With us, the liveliest cadences of primary color prevail. Our summary renderings are cruder and more physical in their patch and outline effects. With our Impressionists, mobility resides not so much in subtle, scattered vibrations as in hefted masses. Hungarian Impressionism is both more objective and more expressive than French Impressionism. Often enough, however, this expressiveness takes the form of temperamental impetuosity and a welter of detail: the very same rhapsodic overindulgence and pent-up volcanic force that characterized the studies of Székely and Munkácsy. Modern styles and experiences cannot prevail against the ingrained artistic instincts of the race.

The history of Hungarian Impressionism admittedly affords some exceptions. But— aside from the fact that these serve only to prove the rule—they almost invariably reveal a fading of the Hungarian identity and a reduction in essential content. The classic example here is that of Pál Szinyei Merse.

Translated by David Britt

ADVERTISEMENTS Lajos Kassák
Originally published as "A reklám," in *Tisztaság könyve* (Budapest: 1926)

The prigs of aestheticism, as well as sociologists who move in the scientific and economic spheres of life, all like to speak in negative terms about advertisements. The aesthetes describe them as vulgarly superficial, while the sociologist sees them as destructive and compromising not only with regard to commerce but also with regard to democratic forms of life in general. It is not difficult to refute these two opinions that originate from two different viewpoints but are essentially identical in their foundations.

I.   Beauty as an end in itself is an empty fiction, for beauty is not a primary but a secondary phenomenon. It can only be present as a consequence, only as one of the attributes of some thing. If a certain fact or object is perfect in itself, and fulfills its purpose then it is without a doubt beautiful as well. Thus beauty as a human attribute is the inevitable concomitant of every organic and organized entity. An advertisement, being a human product, also carries within itself the criteria of beauty and ugliness. Thus its anathematization on aesthetic grounds does not constitute a critical stand, but is an irresponsible and anachronistic priggishness.

II. An effective advertisement is aesthetically pleasing, and an effective advertisement is an indispensable requisite from the point of view of society. Advertisements have come into being as a result of commerce, and commerce is a consequence of humankind's constantly increasing living requirements. Naturally, if one were to deliver a judgement of the overall quality of the brunt of advertisements in present-day Europe it would be easy to declare that these advertisements are anti-social and in bad taste. But the same holds true for today's free-market capitalism. Yet this does not mean that we should banish commerce once and for all; it should instead lead to placing it upon foundations that are socially more equitable. There can be no doubt that Russia in our days exerts a far greater amount of cultural and economic propaganda than during the Czarist days. The advertisement has not been eliminated in Russia; it has simply been liberated from the clutches of selfish private interests, so that its hitherto anti-social forces have been converted into propaganda that works in the interests of the community. Thereby it has been reborn not only in an ethical sense but also in its artistic significance.

The Russian advertisement, often in a manner similar to American advertisements, has distanced itself from individualistic graphics by discovering its own character as simplified, economical, and demonstrative.

In this interpretation the successful advertisement has become an active social factor in our lives, and we appreciate its appearance by describing it not as *beautiful* but as *effective*. Even though its essential means of expression are the same as those used by the subjective arts: color, sound, and form—on the whole it is still set apart from even the industrial arts. It is not a lyrical composition, nor does it present a decorative surface. For this reason a well-made poster may, as one of its effects, provide the viewer with an aesthetic experience whereas an artistically successful painting will never stun us at a first glance, to produce a craving for the new and the sensational. The audience viewing an art exhibition enjoys the passive aestheticism of subjective art, whereas if we glance at a wall of advertisements the predominant impression will be made not by the juxtaposed arrangement of posters but by their competition with each other.

The effective advertisement, be it optical (poster, flyer, prospectus, or words projected in electric lights into the night), or acoustical (the scream of a siren, the ringing of a bell), always leaps into the arena like a conqueror, with the speed of an ambush; it is followed by the legions of merchandise offered for sale. It is no mere servile mediator of things extraneous to itself, but asserts itself as a demonstrative complex of energies standing between production and consumption.

The fundamentals of an effective advertisement are sociology and psychology.

Finely nuanced moods and an illustrative loquaciousness are contrary to the essentials of advertising and stand in the way of its instant effect and suggestive force. The effective advertisement is not analytic and is not definitive; it is a synthetic unity of timing, content, and materials. It is this elementary simplicity and purity of the effective advertisement that stops us in our tracks for an instant in the noisy and colorful hubbub of the street; this is what lures us inside a department store that only moments before we had never even heard of; this is what makes us crack open a new book by an unknown author, rouses us from the torpor of daily existence, from the blindness and deafness of wanting nothing—*its primary colors and dynamic articulation of form make us curious and determined.*

The advertisement is one of the most typical expressions of the standards and economic lifeblood of our age. The advertising lights of a metropolis, the illuminated signs resplendent over the rooftops, the eye-catching lettering and strident exclamation marks of window displays and glass advertising pillars on the boulevard say more, and in a more objective manner, to a stranger than all the verbose and reactionarily simple-minded descriptions found in the guide books. A department store prospectus, with its well-designed typography, its clear-cut, easily read lettering, its harmonious balance of light and dark spaces, is a calm and understated object that arouses greater confidence and desire to shop than any individualistic artsiness. An unexpectedly blaring horn will indelibly fix in our memory the car lot or movie theater where we first heard this "senseless" but stunningly simple and hypnotic sound.

The typical advertisement of our age, increasingly characterized by the harmony of its components, a striking simplicity, and technical ease of production, is clearly in the line of progress in the evolution of humankind, not because of any aesthetic objectives, but as a result of its matter-of-fact power.

The advertisement is *applied art* and the advertising artist is a *social creator*.

Translated by John Bátki

dear buchholz,

very many thanks for your frank and honest letter. you, at least, are a comrade who speaks his mind without waiting until my back is turned.

since your opinion matters to me, i would like to tell you about the photogram business, as far as i can, objectively.

in all this, as far as i am concerned, the article in which i am promoted to the status of inventor of the photogram is beside the point. firstly, because i have never written an article making this assertion on my own behalf; secondly, the place where the assertion was made was not an article and is not by me.

623

Hungarians in Exile

in its february issue, *uhu* published a number of photographs and photograms of mine, and for these, without my knowledge or participation in any way, the editors composed headings and captions that did not meet with my approval. the editors—again without my knowledge—even had a photograph taken to show how photograms are made. the whole thing is presented in the manner of an april fool's joke, and i would have been entitled to protest the texts, since the whole thing made fun of a seriously intended piece of work. i did not do this, however, because i realized that, when a magazine pays good fees and consequently acquires the habit of autocratic behavior, it is no use expecting ideal conditions of publication.

so this issue is less important than that of short or long memory, and on this i would like to say something.

to your knowledge, man ray was the first to publish camera-free photographs. as far as the printing of such works is concerned, this is perfectly true. but, as far as the "invention" is concerned, i was there at the same time. When I was in the rhön [mountains], in the summer of 1922, i wrote an article entitled "production–reproduction," which I sent to doesburg in weimar for publication. he published the article in no. 7, 1922.

in that article i described two experiments in which i used two reproductive devices par excellence, the camera and the phonograph, or rather their techniques, for creative and productive purposes. by pursuing a purely theoretical train of thought, production- reproduction, i came up with the idea of camera-free photographs, which i called photograms (light writing). at that time, i had no knowledge of man ray's analogous pieces.

in the fall of 1922, on my return from the rhön, i met with tzara at doesburg's in weimar, and doesburg told him about my article. he mentioned that man ray was working on similar experiments and took an interest in my own experiments. (after the weimar conference he saw these in berlin.)

i was full of enthusiasm at that time and prophesied a splendid future for this type of photography. the presence of "competition" did not bother me at all; on the contrary, it strengthened my conviction that i was on the right lines both with the pieces and with the future plans, since i had made the discovery independently of man ray. the phonograph idea also seemed highly promising to me, and i spent a lot of time trying to turn it into a reality. this thing was in the air, and so it must be right. so i thought.

in those days, however, petty jealousies were rife. i long remained unaware of all this, being too much absorbed in collective work.

later (years later, in fact, and from muche), i found that lissitzky was going around telling everyone that i could never have made photograms if he had not previously shown me man ray's pieces. i liked lissitzky very much, and i honestly helped him in many ways at the beginning of his stay in berlin; i trusted him as a comrade, only to realize in the end that he was a fox.

his stories don't bother me except in so far as they become part of the collective "memory." now it really is time to close the file on the "invention of the photogram."

these days i am not so keen on precedence as to fail to see that claims of precedence always reflect inner insecurities.

the period around 1922 was characterized by embittered arguments and claims as to the ownership of inventions and influences. i no longer want to have any part of this, or to engage in the "falsification of history." i shall take up my work in Berlin in the knowledge that i have many friends and a few enemies there: some earned, some unearned.

i am under no illusions; i know i have my share of faults (i am still young, and there is still time to learn to overcome them); but, for those who dislike me, even my good qualities are no excuse.

thank you again, my dear buchholz, for your frankness. I have responded with a his-torical narrative, based on a premise that was a stupid one from the start. In fact, the photogram is neither man ray's invention nor mine. children have been practicing it for a long time. the fun started only when it came to be exploited.

with best wishes to you and lucia,
yours,
moholy-nagy

Translated by David Britt

chapter 10

BAUHAUS RESONANCES

Éva Forgács

The international student body and stellar faculty of the Bauhaus made the school a particularly important center of exchange in Central Europe—one that also tested the conservative waters of regional governmental support. While bringing together architecture, painting, sculpture, and various fields of design, the Bauhaus also carried on purely experimental activities such as stage work, published a series of books on the most pressing issues of contemporary art, and introduced photography into an official arts curriculum for the first time. In seeking to overcome national interests and traditions for the higher goals of creating rational design, an international idiom, and mode of economic production that would, theoretically, greatly democratize visual culture, it drew close scrutiny from both its regional sponsors and the avant-garde beyond.

If in the early 1920s Theo van Doesburg found it too Expressionist and Karel Teige found it too traditional, the Bauhaus by the end of the decade was nevertheless becoming a legend. It was the only institution of modernism that had heroically realized some the great ideas of the avant-garde. Although publicly funded, the Bauhaus put forward avant-garde ideas and projects on an official curriculum. The technological and economic infrastructure in Germany, along with Gropius's

continual struggle with local authorities, enabled Central European students to work in a way not possible in their home countries. The Bauhaus myth prompted Tadeusz Peiper to accompany Kazimir Malevich on his visit to the Dessau Bauhaus in the spring of 1927. Not everything he had heard was true (for example, Lissitzky had never taught in the Bauhaus), but the sense of awe he felt when sitting in the newly designed armchairs which, he said, "ought to be called sitting apparatuses," explains why he felt that the Bauhaus was "an island of dreams."

Looking back on a decade of the Bauhaus, both Teige and Ernő Kállai (who was then working at the Bauhaus under Hannes Meyer's directorship) put the school's contribution to modern design into perspective. Both were biased toward Meyer's more straightforward approach to architecture and to curriculum. Yet they also pointed out that while the issue of art vs. design, a dilemma since the German Werkbund, was to be left unresolved, it was among the Bauhaus's great merits that it pursued a viable answer. During an era that bid farewell to great ideas, the efforts within the Bauhaus to realize such ideas were seen as monumental.

AT THE BAUHAUS   Tadeusz Peiper
Originally published as "Im Bauhaus," *Zwrotnica* 12 (1927)

Bauhaus, the one in Dessau. So, off to Dessau. Three hours by passenger train from Berlin. We're already there by 5 p.m. Even the feet on the stairs in the hallway of the station make it clear we're in the provinces. But not in the Prussian provinces. Prussian towns differ only in the size of their population, not in their essence. There is almost no trace of Berlin left here. We are in the capital of the duchy of Anhalt. Small one- and two-story houses, almost like those in the Szweska district of Cracow or in the Elektoralna district in Warsaw. Around the city tall red smokestacks shoot up. We are in one of central Germany's coalmining centers.

A café. Frankfurters. Malevich has three cups of tea. Call Kandinsky, not home. Stop in front of every lighted store window. Sighs of longing from Malevich at overcoats, tablecloths, and suitcases. We pretend to purchase a bed. Call Kandinsky, still not home. Back into the street. Damned rain.

No time to lose. Call Gropius, the director of the Bauhaus. We go into a café. I call. He's home! He is very pleased, offers us to let us spend the night at his home, drives up to the café in the director's car. A noble face, veiled in fatigue, hardened by truth.

We are at his place. *Entry hall.* A wall that consists of a thin, sandy cloth curtain behind which stands—as we will see the following day—the dining room, which is directly con-nected to the kitchen, with a sliding window between the two. The walls are painted to match the architectonic divisions of the room precisely. Just as the room is divided into two sections, the ceiling is divided into two rectangular fields of color. One of them is black. Flooded by the milky light from the horizontal ceiling lamps, this black fills the hall with a cool repose. At the edges of an architectonic section the surfaces are equal. Everywhere a taste for the flattest walls possible. No cabinets; everything is in the walls. Even the bookshelf in front of me arouses the ire of the man of the house, who is already thinking of ways to hide this piece of furniture. We sit comfortably in *armchairs that really ought to be called sitting apparatuses.* Their form differs vastly from that of tradi-tional furniture of this sort. They recall medical instruments. That fact suggests that the physiology of the human body was the source of their inspiration. On a skeleton of nickel steel tubes supports and rests have been arranged according to the needs of the seated human body, dispensing with any high-flying invention. We sit comfortably, very comfortably. Frau Gropius enters: pretty, her eyes and mouth simply first-class. We talk about the armchairs. With an easy movement of the hand, Frau Gropius turns my chair into a settee, then sits down on it. Unfortunately, only to demonstrate that the armchair can be moved back and forth effortlessly.

We had arrived on the first day of the Easter holiday. Many of the professors had already left Dessau. Gropius telephoned those still in town to get them together. One by one they arrive. First the Hungarian Moholy-Nagy, painter and photoformer.[1] As he spoke his face

---

1   In the summer of 1923 we sat in a small circle on the balcony of the Esplanade in Cracow. The table was full of empty dishes that the waiter had not yet cleared. One of us built a tower from all the saucers, cups, glasses, and spoons, which everyone found amusing. Bruno Jasieński said at the time that sculpture was superfluous in the face of the beauty of everyday objects. I contradicted him and insisted that the edifice of dishes be photographed, and then proposed that similar compositions of various other similar modern objects for the purpose of photographing them and establishing photo-graphic values. One of the painters became enthusiastic about the idea and began to pursue it method-ically. It became clear to us that we were faced with a new creative realm, and we sought furiously for an expression for it; it did not take long before we baptized the art photoformy, its products photo-forms, and its artists photoformers. After our photoformer had produced his first works, which showed

seemed to be shrunk together by his overexposed teeth. A few moments later the Swiss architect Meyer arrived. The healthy face of a master. Everyone was very interested in Malevich. One of the first professors at the Bauhaus had been Lissitzky, a student of Malevich who had spoken a great deal about his teacher there, translated his articles, and disseminated his ideas. At the mention of the name Malevich at the Bauhaus, hats are removed in profound respect. Even so, the distance between him and the artists gathered here was no less than that between Leningrad and Dessau: Malevich speaks neither French nor German. This only increased the interest in his personality.

After personal information had been exchanged the confrontation over ideas began. Malevich distinguishes between architecture and architectonics; the first has use value, the second only artistic value. Architectonics produces forms that are concerned solely with the artistic combination of spatial forms: the resulting works are not supposed to be inhabited (and therefore architectonics is not concerned with the placement of doors; windows garner attention only because light influences the plasticity of spatial forms). Gropius—who, unlike the sculptor Malevich, is a professional architect—pursues other goals. For him the type of structure is closely dependent on the building's function; the essence of a building determines the technique, and the technique determines the form of the building.

Malevich, by contrast, would be happy if the builders would simply erect structures according to his sculptural models. Strange. Something created for a specific purpose should serve another one! A system of spatial forms based entirely on artistic goals should fulfill the tasks of a utilitarian object! This opposition is perhaps made a little clearer by an anecdote that Malevich told a few days later at lunch. Once for fun he broke a cup into two pieces along its vertical axis. It was a time when his money stretched neither forward nor backward; his wife made a scene. But he liked one half of the cup so much that he kept it. One day he discovered it was no longer in its place. His wife was using it to transfer flour or sugar between containers. This anecdote was intended to demonstrate that something that was not originally created with a utilitarian purpose in mind could turn out to be a utilitarian object. Gropius heard the anecdote and said nothing. One could have objected that *flour can be transferred more easily with a little tin scoop than with half a cup. Let's remember that we are in the realm of things. Here other rules apply than in the world of art.* Because they serve many purposes, as befits the nature of ideas, artworks, however much they may conform to the laws of pure art, doubtless form the reservoir from which the collective life energy is nourished. A poem, if it is a good poem, no matter how "removed from life" it may be, nonetheless serves life. We should not, however, lose sight of the fact that architecture transports us into the world of things. Just as the proper goal of an artwork consists in awakening artistic feelings, so the proper goal of an object lies in its utility. The life of things begins with their use. Like everything created by human hands, a utilitarian object fulfills its purpose when it fulfills it as well as possible. In order to fulfill it as well as possible, it must exhaust all the possibilities that the present age has to offer.

promise of interesting results, despite the unfavorable conditions under which they had been produced, we heard that Man Ray in Paris was doing "something similar." This upset our photoformer so much that he gave the project up. Later we found that Man Ray was concerned primarily with the play of light, and that he gave his compositions nonobjective forms, whereas photoformy was meant to capture the modern objects and the beautiful compositions that could be formed from them. The point was to use the equality of photographs of landscape and photographs of compositions of objects to affect the emotional world of contemporary humanity such that the beauty of nature and the beauty of the products of civilization would be viewed as having equal status. The task that our photoformer abandoned was not continued by anyone else in Poland. In the meanwhile, however, a similar direction has been taken up abroad, along other paths and with better results.

Malevich, however, does not acknowledge the circumstances of our time. A couple of days before we left Dessau we were visiting the German architect Mies van der Rohe. Malevich was making the point that architecture, like the applied arts and art in general, developed exclusively under the influence of aesthetic ideas, independent of historical (social, economic, and other) factors. He told how he had build architectonic models constructed from new architectural elements but according to the Gothic system. Mies remarked that these Gothic buildings weren't suited for anything today. "Who knows!" Malevich replied, and his reply was considered "extraordinarily interesting" by those present. Then he said that the form of furniture would never have changed if not for a transformation in aesthetic perspectives. Mies replied with the assertion that, for example, today's armchair had changed because today's athletic people sit differently than their predecessors. Continuing the topic of the needs of the organism, which someone else had raised, I remarked that the changes in the form of the armchair, and so on, *are dependent even on medical perspectives, even where these relate to breathing and digestion, that is to say—presupposing a universal context for scientific ideas—the form of the armchair will depend on science in general.* I reminded them of the visible influence of bacteriology on interior design.

The conversation, which was meant to serve to get to know one another, bubbled over. There was an excess of controversial questions, and one by one they slipped into silence. It was enough just to touch on them. Gropius called Kandinsky. He was already on his way. One might have expected a curious, if not effusive, greeting between the Russian working in Germany and the Pole working in Russia. But no. Kandinsky made a violent bow, touching the floor quickly with his hand, and its trace disappeared immediately. Even the hope that Kandinsky might at least relieve me of the dull task of translating for a while came to nothing. Of his conversation in Russian with Malevich, Kandinsky translated only the parts that pertained to his own recent failure in Russia.

Twelve o'clock. Sleep! We depart. Herr and Frau Gropius lead us through the apartment. It is smooth and shiny, as if it were made of unbreakable porcelain. The guestroom is on the second floor. Hidden away: two old beds.

The following day a tour of the Bauhaus. The buildings are divided into the trade school, the workshops, and the student apartments. The workshops are an important element of the Bauhaus, and there metalwork, carpentry, architecture, and wall painting are practiced. The overview is impressive. Unusual formal and material effects. Each perspective offers another set of solutions. If more proof is needed of the epochal value of achievements of the new art, here it is. Iron, reinforced concrete, and glass.

The Bauhaus is a school of design. Through instruction in forms, through training in crafts, and through technical instruction it enables the student to build houses, to design interiors and prototypes for industry, and to work in the crafts. *The relationship between the instruction in easel painting and the other scientific goals of the Bauhaus is not entirely clear.* When they show us works that students have created with paper, we understand their significance, even when they do not have any use value whatsoever. The point is to become familiar with the laws of the materials. When the student makes various things from a particular piece of paper and is asked to take care that not even the tiniest edge goes to waste, he comes to know the modern principle of economy of material, while also learning the properties of the material. But the painting instruction?

The question arises whether artistic forms influence technological forms. Should art influence the design of factory products, or should it leave these things to the laws of technical production? Should the artist, even in matters pertaining to very simple forms, be asked to advise on designing forms for products, or should the product be solely the result of technology and its possibilities? *For everyone who acknowledges the realities of time, this question is dependent on the era.* Malevich's standpoint of timelessness leads to solecisms here too; the assertion that it is sufficient to pick up a catalog with illustrations of products from America in order to solve the questions of industrial form design takes into account neither the level of industrialization nor the living conditions current in Poland or Russia. The products from the United States correspond to a great extent to the level of industry there. In countries where industry is far less developed, they could neither be produced and nor utilized in daily life. Such use is also dependent on the era. In countries with a modest level of industrial development, in countries in which the logic of industrial production has not attained some degree of purity, one finds that the products of technology still show influences from the crafts and from the cultural taste of the age of crafts. The art of the present time easily does away with that taste. (It should be noted that the art of the present time is not the same as the art of the present day. The present day is a term borrowed from the calendar; the present time is a term borrowed from physiognomy. Those for whom the present time and the present day are interchangeable speak of the present time as a name; my concern is the present time understood as a description of a person. Need I add that for me the most important rubric in this description of a person is that of "unique features"?) If the art of the present time has the effect of suppressing the artistic influences of the past in the design of factory products in countries with a modest level of industrial development, it can guide machine production to its own essence. With time and with the progress of industry, the laws of amortization and labor productivity become the imperatives of machine and chemistry, which have become intertwined in an irresolvable knot of necessity and will not permit artistic factors to have their say, and certainly that voice would be superfluous at that point anyway. Whether the Bauhaus, in the face of the present development of German industry, is already in arrears, I do not know. To answer that, I would have to know Germany better. For a country like Poland, however, the Bauhaus is still an island of dreams.

Another part of the Bauhaus is the professors' *houses*. They, too, were built by the city and are its property. The lie in a secluded boulevard, far from the school buildings, separated from them by a large section of the city. Their walls are a white glow, surrounded by the green glow of the lawns and trees. Flat roofs—a horizontal line— press them cheerfully down to the ground. The windows find the light where they can. The overhangs catch the shadows. Air and heat bow and scrape on the platforms and terraces. For the first time I see the new architecture not as an illustration but in its inspiring material existence. I look around, pleased, and in all the admiration and all the joy I feel a special satisfaction arise within me that I cannot immediately explain. It swells and swells within me and. . . . Of course, now I know. Personal satisfaction. *The relationship between the rhythm of this architecture and the rhythm of my poetry.* If rhythm has a literary function in my work, then here it has an architectural function. The windows are not placed according to predetermined "feet," nor do they follow "free verse," but rather their arrangement is strictly determined by the logic of the building. The same rhythm in relationship between earth and surface. The "personal rhythm" with which I was concerned in *Neuer Mund* ("Poetry as Architecture") could, *mutatis mutandis*, be applied to this architecture. There, too, this rhythm finds a new confirmation. Aaaah.

After lunch with the Herr and Frau Gropius, a trip to Törten, where Gropius is building workers housing. Two long rows of small houses, each with four small rooms, comprising a dwelling. Modern methods of serial production reduce the costs to such an extent that a work who pays a thousand Reichmarks at the beginning and then the normal rent will be the owner of the little house he occupies after a period of fifteen years. The housing colony in Törten has so many new things for us that we choose not to return for the tea with which Kandinsky awaits us. We return to Dessau half an hour before our train departs. Final farewells in the Bauhaus. Dash over to see Kandinsky in the workshop. We leave. Frau Kandinsky would like to show us the apartment that is "painted using criteria of fine art painting." What to do? The train! The proposal is made a second time. Malevich isn't listening; I am. Fine. "Would I like to see the apartment? With the greatest pleasure." I see it, admire, groan. And then I excuse myself to rush out to the entrance by the shortest possible path and force Malevich into the car. The train!

Translated by Steven Lindberg

TEN YEARS OF THE BAUHAUS   Karel Teige
Originally published as "Deset let Bauhausu," *Stavba* 8 (1929–30)

It is already twenty semesters, or ten academic years, since the Bauhaus school for modern design began its activities. This represents an anniversary of sorts, for this advanced architectural and industrial school of art—a new type of school that underwent a rather dramatic and very instructive development in the ten years of its existence—has experienced many changes, redefining and reforming its own program for work and pedagogy. The Bauhaus has evolved into one of the most important centers of the international modern movement and has quickly become an institution whose work is closely followed in all of Europe and America. Ten years—not a long period but rather an insignificant fragment of history—does not seem to be a sufficient pretext for an anniversary, and yet these ten years of activity represent an entire era in modern architecture and design. Ten years of the Bauhaus that, in essence, is the history of the modern movement in Central Europe.

The Bauhaus was founded in 1919 in Weimar by Walter Gropius. The new school originated as a merger of the Academy of Fine Arts and the School of Applied Arts, both of which were schools where van de Velde had taught years before. It is as if the ghost of van de Velde were still present. In its initial activities the Bauhaus could not free itself from formalism and decorativism and was hindered by a modern form of Jugendstil. As its name indicates, the Bauhaus was supposed to be a new type of architectural school, a school of architecture in the broadest sense, an institute of modern constructional design; nevertheless, in its early years it remained merely a modern version of a school of applied arts. At the time when the Bauhaus was founded, the cultural and ideological situation of Europe was more chaotic than at any other time in our era: a general uncertainty and unrest prevailed, caused by the series of economic and social upheavals that were sweeping through a war-weary Europe.

In the domain of art it was the moment of expressionism's demise, of the emergence of the first proposals of the Suprematists and the Constructivists in the Soviet Union and those of the neoplasticists from the De Stijl group in Holland. The Bauhaus became a kind of crossroads for these tendencies.

In his new school Walter Gropius succeeded in engaging an Outstanding and truly representatjve teaching team. composed of the most important artists of the time. Names such as [Paul] Klee, [Wassily] Kandinsky, [Lyonel] Feininger, Georg Muche, O[skar]

Schlemmer, [Lothar] Schreyer, Johannes Itten, and [László] Moholy-Nagy represented an elite of contemporary German painting. The Bauhaus architectural school was led by Gropius himself, together with his collaborator Adolf Meyer. Adolf Meyer died in the fall of 1929; until recently, he had been active in Frankfurt.

In the beginning, the Bauhaus was viciously attacked by reactionary critics. Yet, the work itself and the names of its teachers helped to gain early and visible success and almost universal recognition. Perhaps by its very ease, this early victory prepared the ground for the later problems of the Bauhaus. Gropius formulated the program of the new school under the slogan the new unity of art and industry; it represented an alliance of all the arts in the service of the highest cultural tasks—for architecture. This represented a new triumvirate of the plastic arts under the protectorate of architecture. The Bauhaus ideology was full of internal obscurities, and these theoretical obscurities in turn caused profound confusion in practice. The unity of art and industry is clearly no more than a somewhat rejuvenated expression of Ruskinism: the union between art and craft. It is a slogan that might have been formulated by van de Velde but one that is an expression of tendencies opposed to modern design, an expression of decorative and applied industry. To have this slogan inscribed above the door of an educational institution that intended to become the center of modern constructive production might have led the institution astray.

In 1923 the Bauhaus produced the first comprehensive exhibition of its work for the international public. Walter Gropius organized an exhibition in Weimar of the first four years of the Bauhaus, which was combined with another exhibition on the new architecture to become one of the first postwar architectural exhibitions organized on an international basis. The exemplary residential house "Am Horn" built in Weimar by G. Muche and Adolf Meyer (see *Bauhausbücher* 3, *Ein Versuchshaus des Bauhauses*) was also part of this exhibition. This was an attempt to reintroduce a Pompeian floor plan into modern housing.

On the occasion of the exhibition a large-scale, exquisitely designed catalog was also published: *Staatliches Bauhaus in Weimar, 1919–1923*, was the first great publication of the modern movement and the first review of Bauhaus activities for the international public. (The Czech periodical *Stavba* published an extensive review of both the publication and the working and pedagogical system of the Bauhaus. Its criticism was subsequently borne out by further developments at the Bauhaus. See *Stavba* 2, no.12.)

By this time the last remnants of expressionism had been dynamically overcome, but Constructivism and neoplasticism, with their preoccupation with form, were becoming competing trends.

In this period of formal decorativism, the Bauhaus produced furniture (à la [Gerrit] Rietveld) as abstract sculpture; rooms were decorated with nonobjective compositions by Mondrian, van Doesburg, or [Kazimir] Malevich; objects of daily use (pots, glasses, carpets, and even toys and chess pieces) were infused with "art;" albeit modern (or rather, modernistic). The prescribed unity of art and industry became in practice nothing but decorativism according to the latest fashion. Malevich's or van Doesburg's square also became a symbol of this latest fashion. At this time the Bauhaus betrayed a very strong influence from members of the de Stijl group. Theo van Doesburg went so far as to found a kind of counterschool in Weimar. The influence of the neoplasticism of de Stijl on the Bauhaus and on Gropius himself was healthy in the sense that it helped to eradicate the surviving expressionist tendencies, but at the same time this imbued its work with the new "orthogonal" formalism. The architectural work of the Bauhaus was then already more advanced than the work of other furniture and design workshops, but it too was subservient to the formula of the square and the cube. However, this architecture was visually powerful and capable of gradually overthrowing the ballast of formalism.

Shortly after the change of government in Saxony the Bauhaus was dissolved by the new right-wing government (in the winter of 1924) for no other reason than political opposition (because it was founded in 1919 under the Socialist government!). The dissolution of the Bauhaus turned into a major scandal. Soon afterward (in the spring of 1925) Gropius succeeded in moving his school to Dessau where he designed and built the outstanding school buildings as well as the less-distinguished housing for its professors. In Dessau the Bauhaus continued its work and clarified its theoretical program. Between 1925 and 1927 the Bauhaus reached the summit of the first stage of its activities: its work was internationally recognized, obtaining wide success and even fame. This success had its downside as well. It gave rise to the so-called *Bauhausstil*, a modernistic fashion that spread through Germany and Central Europe; disseminated by numerous and eager epigones, it became a caricature of the best intentions of the institution and its leaders. The phenomenon of a *Bauhausstil* and the fact that the school became a nursery for epigones indicated problems both in the pedagogical method of the school and in its theoretical and practical program.

This situation required a radical revision. In 1927 the Bauhaus was in turmoil. In 1928 its founder Walter Gropius left the institution, and Moholy-Nagy and Marcel Breuer went with him. Hannes Meyer became the director of the school. Mart Stam, [Anton] Brenner, [Hans] Wittwer, and [Ludwig] Hilberseimer held temporary or permanent positions in the architecture department, and a deep, almost revolutionary change took place in the life and work of the Bauhaus. The Bauhaus was reorganized and became a school worthy of its name: a school of Constructivist design, not just in architecture but in photography, typography, and advertising. The painters' studios operated under the leadership of Kandinsky and Klee as a quasi-separate entity of the Bauhaus. The school quickly divested its work of aesthetic and formalistic speculations and chose rather to build upon a sociologically determined and truly vital oeuvre. Hannes Meyer instituted an in-depth study of the sociology of building, and his students even spoke of "biological architecture." On the occasion of the tenth anniversary of its existence the Bauhaus organized an important major exhibition, not as a retrospective but as a current event. The exhibition demonstrated and described the work of the Bauhaus from the two preceding years. In Dessau it remained open for merely a week but enjoyed numerous visitors. Evening lectures and information sessions took place in the Bauhaus auditorium during the week. From Dessau the exhibition was sent to Essen, and from there it is just about to begin its pilgrimage through many large towns of Central Europe. It would be highly desirable if we could succeed in bringing it to the major cities of Czechoslovakia. This is why it merits a more detailed report.

The core of the exhibition consists of architecture, furnishings, and workshops for photography, typography, and advertising. The exhibitions of painters (students) take second place to the former. In every section of the exhibition the work of both students and professors is shown. The architectural exhibition is naturally led by Hannes Meyer. Among his projects in the exhibition are the little-known design for the Workers' Bank in Berlin (unfortunately not realized, though of considerable interest), and photographs of the Workers' School in Bernau near Berlin, which is currently under completion. It is most interesting to study the work of the pupils of Hannes Meyer. It demonstrates that the director of the Bauhaus is as outstanding a pedagogue as he is an architect, a concordance of abilities that is truly rare. Hannes Meyer teaches without any formulas. He wants, as he says, *"biologisches entfesseltes lebendiges Bauen"* [biological, unleashed, living building]. He teaches the understanding of architecture as a work stemming organically from life and from social conditions; he teaches his students to analyze the environment and the particulars by which each building is determined. The students analyze, for instance, the conditions of workers' housing at the periphery of industrial districts: the direction of wind (smoke, soot), visibility, dust from the road, and noise of transportation. All of this is considered and evaluated before the project itself is undertaken. For example, the students undertook a detailed analysis of the Lüneburg Heath region: geology, climatology, and meteorology; ground cover, fauna, and vegetation in the region; characteristic landscape images. The result was a realization that this piece of land is extraordinarily suitable for the building of resorts, and that schools, sanatoriums, and the like, are ideally situated here. That it is a real *Erholungslandschaft* [landscape for relaxation]. Thus the project of the school in this area included the maximum number of open spaces and the perfect integration of the school's interiors with the natural surroundings. By contrast, a school on the periphery of an industrial district requires a measure of isolation from its surroundings. Another example: in the planning for a garden district the students analyzed the garden as an extension of the living space, as well as the cultivation of vegetables, fruits, and poultry. Such analysis included both the sensuous and the psychological impressions created in the garden. Some studied how the garden makes the experience of the different times of the year more intense; others detailed the social hierarchy of the garden from the flowerpot to the royal park, and so on.

Next to Hannes Meyer, *Ludwig Hilberseimer* is another important architectural faculty member at the Bauhaus. The display of designs by his students is of a very high standard and many of the student projects stand out for the maturity of their conception. An integral part of the *Baulehre* [architectural teachings] is also a course given by the engineer *Alcar Rudelt*, a course that is a novelty at the Bauhaus. It is here that some of the deficiencies in the architectural education of the earlier Bauhaus, in which the technical aspects were the weaker side of the curriculum, have been radically eliminated.

Next to architectural exhibits we find the work of the so-called *Ausbauwerkstatt*, the workshops for interior design into which are integrated the former departments of furniture making, metalwork, wall painting, and so on. The workshop of interior design is now led by [Alfred] Arndt. Among the most remarkable products of the workshop is the excellent "people's dwelling," complete furnishings for a low-cost minimum dwelling, destined for the Museum of Hygiene in Dresden. Among the individual furniture pieces are several remarkable chairs and armchairs designed by [Josef] Albers, a chair by [Peer] Bücking, as well as a kitchen and a workshop chair. The "Bauhaus wallpaper" manufactured by Rasch & Co. in Hanover, inexpensive and—thanks to its durability—much more economical than a painted wall, is also among the products of the workshop. The textile workshops, now led by *Gunta Stölzl-Sharon*, devote much less time to "art" than before. Instead of tapestries and carpets with neoplasticist decoration, the workshop today produces "*geriffelte Silberstoffe*," that is, cellophane fabrics that reflect light and are intended as wall coverings.

The printing and advertising workshops exhibit a number of very interesting publicity brochures, typographical studies, and so on. In addition, photographs of several exhibitions designed by the workshop for the Junkers factory, as well as display windows, are shown here. The workshop includes a photographic studio led by *Walter Peterhans*, whose work is of outstanding quality. In terms of technical perfection, W. Peterhans is without peer among today's photographers. In addition to these technically perfect shots, Peterhans also exhibits here a number of photographs of an almost poetic beauty.

The department of stage design, formerly led by O. Schlemmer, has now become an amateur theater for the students. Among many lively activities, short performances are periodically organized and directed by Albert Mentzel. A series of photographs of the sets, as well as shots of backstage, are included in the exhibition.

Also worthy of note is the *"Vorkurs"* led by J. Albers. This introductory course teaches materials science. Exhibited are a number of interesting material studies, sculpture made of glass, wood and cardboard, montages and compositions, which are often of remarkable artistic value in themselves. The course of analytical drawing taught by *Klee* and *Kandinsky* also belongs among these proseminars. The use of modern pedagogical methods in aesthetic education is truly remarkable. It is a sort of school of elementary and experimental aesthetics. As far as pure artistic design is concerned (which is secondary to the main mission of the Bauhaus), *Klee*, *Kandinsky*, and *Feininger* exhibit larger collections of paintings. This is an elite trio of painters, and the hall in which their works were installed was an exhibition unto itself. It is a genuine rarity in Germany for truly outstanding modern painting to be so powerfully displayed in such a small exhibition.

Recently (in January 1930), Feininger's exhibition came to Prague. Feininger remains faithful to his beliefs and is thus an exception among German artists. He has been in effect the only cubist in Germany and as such stands out sharply amid the former expressionists (now the Neue Sachlichkeit) who, unfortunately, represent German painting. Still young, though over sixty, Kandinsky, the first painter of abstract and nonobjective paintings and a onetime leader of Der blaue Reiter group, shows affinity in his most recent work with the new works of Paul Klee. It is impossible to describe the paintings of Paul Klee in words. We can merely say that, together with the works of [Pablo] Picasso and [Giorgio] de Chirico, they represent the most poetic values of contemporary art. Exhibiting together with the trio of Klee, Kandinsky, and Feininger are also *Joost Schmidt* (with his very original abstract sculptures) and *Albers* (with his compositions on glass).

As a whole, the exhibition gives a very positive picture of today's Bauhaus and its work. It demonstrates that following the departure of Gropius and several other teachers, the Bauhaus not only survived but is very much alive and experiencing healthy development. Its influence abroad has become stronger. The Bauhaus, a school that is unique and unrivaled anywhere, has now grown into an institution that still has every opportunity to become *the model school of architecture and of Constructivist design*—if this has not happened already. Today more than two hundred students from many different countries work here. There is no intention of introducing a regressive quota system; rather, the Bauhaus strives to attract the highest possible number of foreign students. One-third of the student body (including seven from Czechoslovakia) are foreigners. The Bauhaus has become a real Babylon and cosmopolis.

Today's Bauhaus works assiduously on its educational program, refining and modifying it. The school is poised to undertake any needed reforms; it is not a petrified institution with an obsolete curriculum. Even the ambience is livelier and more attractive than in other schools. It is full of optimism and gaiety. It is not just a place for architecture but also for sport, photography, dance, even carnivals.... After its first ten years the Bauhaus is younger, freer, more enterprising and friendlier than ever before.

The Bauhaus Hochschule für Gestaltung [Bauhaus School for Design] is an institution whose work engages the entire international intellectual community of modernists. A traveling exhibition that can display the most recent results of the work of the Bauhaus to many viewers will undoubtedly be received everywhere with interest. Certainly it is one of the most significant exhibitions taking place in Central Europe today. It would be most desirable that it should also come to our country.

Translated by Irena Žantovská Murray

It was ten years ago that Walter Gropius reorganized the Weimar School of Arts and
Crafts and named the new school "Bauhaus." The success of his creation is well known.
What, during the early years at Weimar, used to be the vehemently disputed activity of
a few outsiders has now become a big business boom. Houses and even whole housing
settlements are being built everywhere; all with smooth white walls, horizontal rows of
windows, spacious terraces, and flat roofs. The public accepts them, if not always with
great enthusiasm, at least without opposition, as the products of an already familiar
"Bauhaus style." But in reality the initiative for this kind of architecture originated by
no means at the Bauhaus alone. The Bauhaus is just one part of an international
movement that developed quite a while ago, particularly in Holland. But the Bauhaus
became the first school of this movement. It has been highly effective in disseminating
its ideas and has been extraordinarily successful as a place for experimentation. The
reputation of the institute has quickly spread and reached even the remotest corners
of the country. Today everybody knows about it. Houses with lots of glass and shining
metal: Bauhaus style. The same is true of home hygiene without home atmosphere:
Bauhaus style. Tubular steel armchair frames: Bauhaus style. Lamp with nickel-coated
body and a disk of opaque glass as lampshade: Bauhaus style. Wallpaper patterned
in cubes: Bauhaus style. No painting on the wall: Bauhaus style. Incomprehensible
painting on the wall: Bauhaus style. Printing with sans-serif letters and bold rules:
Bauhaus style. everything written in small letters: bauhaus style. EVERYTHING
EXPRESSED IN BIG CAPITALS: BAUHAUS STYLE.

Bauhaus style: one word for everything. Wertheim sets up a new department for
modern-style furniture and appliances, an arts-and-crafts salon with functionally
trimmed high fashion trash. The special attraction is the name "Bauhaus." A fashion
magazine in Vienna recommends that ladies' underwear no longer be decorated with
little flowers, but with more contemporary Bauhaus-style geometrical designs. Such
embarrassing and amusing misuses in the fashion hustle of our wonderful modern age
cannot be prevented. His Majesty the snob would like something new. Very well. There
are enough architects making the Bauhaus style into a new decorative attraction. The
exhibition of cold splendor is back again. It has just been rejuvenated, has exchanged
the historical robe for a sort of pseudo-technological raciness. But it is just as bad as
before... The new Berlin despises the swollen marble and stucco showiness of the
"Wilhelmian" public buildings and churches, but it revels in the hocus-pocus of mega-
lomaniac motion-picture palaces, department stores, automobile "salons" and gourmets' paradises with their shrieking advertisements. This new architecture, the slender
nakedness of its structure shining far and wide and bathed in an orgy of lights at night,
is by no means, so we are told, ostentatious; it is rather "constructive and functional."
Hence, once more: Bauhaus style. But let us take heart. For small homeowners,
workers, civil servants, and employees the Bauhaus style also has its social application. They are serially packaged into minimum standard housing. Everything is very
functional and economical. Furniture and house- hold articles are within reach and,
according to Westheim: the suicidal gas main is in their mouth...

Let us keep the slogan "Bauhaus style," since it has already become a household word,
even where it is no more than a cover for a corruption of originally more sincere intentions. With all due respect to the difference between these intentions and the commercialization of the Berlin Broadway. It cannot be denied, however, that the work of
the Bauhaus itself is in no way free of esthetic over-cultivation and of dangerous formalism. It is true that discarding all ornamentation and banning each and every curved

plane and line in the design of houses, furniture, and appliances has led to the creation of very interesting, new, and simple forms. But whatever was obvious about these new functional forms has by no means always made as much sense. Rather, the products which were to be expedient and functional, technical and constructive, and economically necessary were for the most part conceived out of a taste-oriented arbitrariness decked out in new clothes, and out of a *bel-esprit* propensity for elementary geometric configurations and for the formal characteristics of technical contrivances. Art and technology, the new unity—this is what it was theoretically called and accordingly practiced—interested in technology, but art-directed. This is a critical "but." Priority was given to the art-directedness. There was the new formalistic willfulness, the desire to create a style at all costs, and technology had to yield to this conviction. This is the way those Bauhaus products originated: houses, furniture, and lamps which wrested attention primarily by their obtrusively impressive form and which, as a logical result of this characteristic, were accepted or rejected by the public and the press as being the products of a new style, namely the Bauhaus style. But they were not accepted or rejected for being the products of a new technical development in the building or furniture industries. Of course the Bauhaus, in numerous programmatical and propagandistic publications, affirmed time and time again that the formal characteristics of its products were no more than the inevitable results of a "strictly relevant" fulfillment of function, rather than an intention to create a style. Yet, a few years of practice were already enough even for the eyes of the younger Bauhaus generation to recognize that these products were outdated handicraft. This may be less florid than customary handicraft. But it is instead inhibited, prejudiced by a doctrinaire mock asceticism, stiff, without charm, and yet pretentious to the point of arrogance. Fellow travelers who are smarter businessmen and are more unscrupulous have not hesitated to make frankly shoddy handicraft out of this somewhat clumsy trouble-child of the new functional design. Where is the dividing line between genuine and false Bauhaus style? The Bauhaus started things rolling with its esthetic ambition; it must now accept the fact that others are going to add all the rest right up to the bitter end. Why is it that a similar fate does not threaten a swivel chair or the "Zeiss" lamp? The reason is that these products are not born of the unity of art and technology but are genuine constructions evolved from industrial technology: they are creations of engineering. It would be revealing to ask one of the "Zeiss" engineers for his opinion on the technical and illumination properties of the Bauhaus lamps.

Gropius established, among others, the following guidelines for the Bauhaus program: "The Bauhaus wants to assist in the development of present-day housing, from the simplest household appliances to the finished dwelling.... The Bauhaus workshops are essentially laboratories in which prototypes of products suitable for mass production and typical of our time are carefully developed and constantly improved.... The prototypes that have been completed in the Bauhaus workshops are reproduced by outside firms with whom the workshops are closely related.... The Bauhaus brings creatively talented people with ample practical experience into the actual course of production, people who have mastered both technical and formal problems, and who are to take over the preparation of models for production in industry and the crafts...

"Particularly with respect to building: the mass prefabrication of houses should be attempted and units should be kept in stock which would be manufactured not on the site but in permanent workshops, to be easily assembled later. These would include ceilings, roofs, and walls. Thus it would be like a children's box of blocks on a larger scale and on the basis of standardization and production of types."

This program is extraordinarily up-to-date and very "social." Modern industry and business have attracted a tremendous number of people to their places of production and distribution. This has caused a social need in the area of housing which can only be overcome by mass production. The industrialization of the building and the home-appliance industry is an urgent socio-economic and socio-political requirement. Industrial production methods, by way of a process of mechanical elimination, inexorably cast off any discrepancies with respect to form which might interfere with the impersonal neutrality and complete fulfillment of the function of the articles. To put Bauhaus production into the service of such standardizing elimination and to train, at the Bauhaus, the leaders of a modern construction and home-building industry is admittedly a highly important and productive idea. But this idea must be followed in reality and not, as has many times been the case in practice at the Bauhaus, deviate into formalism.

It is not enough to force industrial mass production and in so doing, in the design of these products, to allow artistry—despite schematic simplification it is still esthetically willful—to triumph over the engineer. Architecture must strive resolutely to accomplish "social, technological, economic, and psychological organization" (Hannes Meyer). Otherwise architecture will remain—Bauhaus style, a hybrid solution, indecisive about form, neither emotional and free like art, nor straightforward, accurate, and necessary like technology. The result of this ambiguity of the Bauhaus style is the strange and inhibited situation of free art at the Bauhaus, especially that of painting. This inhibition stems from the secret or open hostility between most of the architectural and workshop members. These semi-artists and semi-technicians find arguments to present themselves as superior to the painters with respect to their usefulness and their powers of reasoning. No engineer would ever dare take such a position. It is clear that this hostility is no more than their way of protecting themselves against their own artistic drives which have been repressed by the fact of their association with technology. Bad conscience with respect to the demands of form is thus anesthetized.

Yet, painting is avidly carried on at the Bauhaus, right next door to the imposing reinforced concrete structures and the huge glass planes, in the shadow of these strutting, rationally cold, expedient, and industrially esthetic three-dimensional structures, so to speak. Whoever was to find a chance to peek into the rooms and studios of the Bauhaus people at night would be surprised to see how many painters are standing in front of their easels, painting away at their canvases—some of them secretly, like high-school students who furtively write poems, with a bad conscience perhaps, because instead of sweating over functional modern buildings or folding tables or lamps, they remember just that part of the famous Gropius phrase about "art and technology, a new unity" that deals with art, leaving technology to the technologists. These painters are transcending all rationalized expediency and the principle of esthetic usefulness the Bauhaus preaches, with an indifference as if they were living on some fantastic planet of art where everything is in a state of surrealism. The more the efforts of the Bauhaus workshops and the practice of the building industry focus on the achievement of the kind of straightforwardness that is functionally and structurally directed and mass production and standardization oriented, the more the Bauhaus painting falls into the other extreme. Either it revels in dreams, visions, and blunt confessions of the soul or in paradoxical juggler's tricks between tangible reality and its conversion into metaphysics. It is interesting and curious to note that such art, concerned with psychic introspection and with the skeptical and playful enjoyment of contradictions, was able to develop, particularly in such close contact with the modern, daily practice of the purpose-minded Bauhaus. This development is curious and yet characteristic, for it is to be interpreted as a natural relaxation and compensation. The overemphasis on industrial technology and rational organization, on the other hand, is bound to activate all the powers of the spirit. In this respect the Bauhaus can well be considered a proving ground in the sense of intellectual, cultural activities. The discrepancies between the soul and technology which today exist at the centers of the Euro-American civilization are put to their toughest test at the Bauhaus, where close human contact and close associations in practical work have developed under one roof. Daring balance, cerebral and soul equilibristics: Bauhaus style.

Or is it simply a case of the left hand not knowing, or not wanting to know, what the right hand is doing, and vice versa? Is it a case of not knowing that architecture and art are going separate ways, as husband and wife do in a modern companionate marriage? Antiseptically clean separations are basically very well liked at the Bauhaus. One separates painting from representation. The painting has to be abstract. In Kandinsky's paintings a tree or a face may not even accidentally sneak in. They are immediately contorted past recognition or are expunged altogether and assigned to photography. Everything representational belongs to the realm of photography. Violators of this principle are making punishable reversions into an epoch of art that has been discredited. Still, there are painters at the Bauhaus who dare look at nature. Feininger, Klee, and a good number of younger painters. But they don their visionary protective goggles in order not to shield their spiritual eyes from the crude materialism of reality.

Hence once more: clean separation. Just as between soul and belly. "Eros" has very little influence at the Bauhaus. People are either reserved, straightforward, and cerebral, or they are simply sexual in an unsublimated way. People either pray according to German industrial standards or listen to phonograph records of American jazz hits twanging about sentimental voluptuousness. People are balancing out antitheses: Bauhaus style. There is little human fulfillment, little that is vigorous, genuine, and whole. There is far too much theory, over-exaggeration, and abstraction. What is urgently needed is reform....

Translated by Wolfgang Jabs and Basil Gilbert

chapter 11

POLAND

Piotr Piotrowski

The avant-garde in Poland began to splinter in the mid-1920s. Conflicts within the Blok group led to its break-up. Mieczysław Szczuka (1898–1927) continued his criticism of "pure art." But in response to the development of a mass society, he and Teresa Żarnower (1895–1950) also produced visual propaganda for the Polish left. They both began editing the very ideological *Dźwignia* (Lever). In 1926 their main adversaries—Katarzyna Kobro (1898–1951), Władysław Strzemiński (1893–1952), and Henryk Stażewski (1894–1988)—together with a group of architects that included Szymon Syrkus (1893–1964), founded a new periodical, *Praesens*. It published a series of analyses and program declarations by both the members of their community and by such foreign artists as Kazimir Malevich (who was also invited to Warsaw in 1927, to give a talk and show his pictures), László Moholy-Nagy, Theo van Doesburg, and Hans Richter.

A new conflict quickly surfaced between architects and artists, however. While the former insisted on architecture's need for concrete discussions and practical solutions, the latter stressed the importance of a theoretical discourse concerning the structure of the work of art, its form and function, its connection with its environment, and its historical context. In contrast to Szczuka and Żarnower, the others became progressively less ideological. They continued and developed this line of thinking in the 1930s.

In 1929, Kobro, Stażewski and Strzemiński—this time with a group of avant-garde poets (Jan Brzêkowski, 1903–83, and Julian Przybós, 1901–70)—founded the a.r. group, whose initials referred to the Polish for "real avant-garde" and/or "revolutionary artists." The group's manifesto appeared in a leaflet, later reprinted in *Europa*, while excerpts from it were published in the Parisian *l'Art Contemporain*. Apart from declarations concerning purely artistic problems, it contained the announcement of the foundation of the a.r. library, to publish books on modern art and avant-garde poetry. It was modeled on the earlier Praesens Library, which had published Władysław Strzemiński's *Unism in Painting* (1928), one of the most original and detailed conceptions of painting at its time and one of the most important texts in the history of Polish Constructivism. His next book, *Composition of Space*, written with Katarzyna Kobro, appeared in the a.r. library (1931).

One of the most important initiatives of the a.r. group was the founding, at the end of 1929, of the International Collection of Modern Art, which was formally presented as a gift to the Łódź City Council and deposited, in

1931, at the Municipal Museum of History and Art in Łódź. The Collection transformed the Łódź museum into one of the first museums of modern art. Apart from works by Polish artists, it included works by Jean Arp, Willi Baumeister, Alexander Calder, Sonia Delaunay, Theo van Doesburg, Max Ernst, and Albert Gleizes, among others.

A very different response to the problems of the twilight of the avant-garde and the relationship of modern art to mass society was represented by Stanisław Ignacy Witkiewicz (1885–1939). In the mid-1920s he declared his intention to quit making art, by which he meant painting pictures and writing dramas with a metaphysical dimension—uncovering the "mystery of existence," as he put it. From that point forward, the texts he wrote no longer had (in his opinion) the value of artistic expositions. This was also the case for his paintings from the mid-1920s—almost exclusively portraits—which he regarded as "applied art." That is, he produced them not to satisfy metaphysical needs, but practical "life needs," and he painted them in response to commissions by clients of his one-man, quasi-capitalist enterprise, "The S. I. Witkiewicz Portrait-Painting Firm." He claimed that in a mass society, art (understood as an activity with a metaphysical character) was no longer needed, since metaphysical needs had disappeared. In his view, the utilitarian object, mass-produced for sale—including a portrait commissioned from his "firm"—had taken the place of art.

Translated by Wanda Kemp-Welch

THE CONTEMPORARY STYLE Henryk Stażewski

Originally published as "Styl Współczesnosci," *Praesens* no. 1 (June 1926)

The development of art throughout all epochs basically consisted in a constant rivalry
between the following elements:
the external versus the internal,
the individual versus the universal,
the natural versus the spiritual, etc.
which variably dominated each other or achieved temporary equilibria.

Recent art manifests a very strong and determined desire to reunite those disparate
elements and to bring them to balance. Their unity, broken as it was by naturalistic
art with its materialistic viewpoint, is now being restored by *abstract* art which draws
on inner elements independent of the external reality. This new, abstract art rejects
"descriptiveness." Its sole aim being to present *balanced relations between visual
elements*.

Color and form relations are inherent in nature but obscured by the film of matter.
In ancient, as well as in Renaissance art these relations—and their equilibrium—
were expressed by means of *natural, organic* forms borrowed from the external
reality.

Present-day art expresses these relations in a "purely" visual way. that is by means of
abstract, mechanical forms.

For new art, abstraction is a proper way to express universal elements which shape
the contemporary collective style.

Artists practicing naturalism groped in the maze of their individual techniques and personal experiences of nature. Individualism, with its strictly subjective and unverifiable
interpretation of nature, is unable to generate a *contemporary style*.

A search for an aesthetic based on collectivistic constructivism does not mean a rejection or belittlement of "individuality." But it strives to bring out the most universal
values common to all men, and, by rejecting all non-visual elements, to achieve *well-
balanced relations and proportions*.

Modern approaches to form, which shape the contemporary style, are primarily applied
by architecture.

Painting or sculpture separated from architecture is now quite inconceivable and
unwarranted.

The rapprochement between painting and architecture has been brought about by a new
awareness of the inseparable nature of space, color, and matter. The impact which
color exerts on shapes in the sense of being able to alter their dimensions, creates a
whole new treasury of architectural instruments. Architectural ornamentation is increasingly being replaced by the use of light, colors and different materials.

The contemporary style is also shaped by technology whose products serve as examples of well-constructed forms. Present-day architecture tries to achieve harmony
with technology and industry. Freed of unnecessary ornamentation. it is now able
to create pure structural forms by binding the vertical and the horizontal planes
together.

These are the main foundations on which the great style of modern art is being
built.

Present-day art is closely connected with the economy of thought and perception. As
our life becomes increasingly mechanized, and the intellect progressively masters
impressions, a need arises to systematize forms.

The irrational and abstract forms used by present-day art are but a summary of the
whole ensemble of observed phenomena. Through the medium of abstraction art can

unobstructedly penetrate the depth of pure visuality. Thanks to its direct and disinterested visual awareness art frees itself of all practical and utilitarian considerations associated with objects.

Translation from Three Pioneers of the Polish Avant-Garde

RULES OF THE S. I. WITKIEWICZ PORTRAIT-PAINTING FIRM
Stanisław Ignacy Witkiewicz
Orginally published as *Regulamin firmy portretowej S. I. Witkiewicz* (Warsaw: 1928)

Motto:
The customer must be satisfied.
Misunderstandings are ruled out.

The rules are published so as to spare the firm the necessity of repeating the same thing over and over again.

1. The firm produces portraits of the following types:

1. Type A—Comparatively speaking, the most as it were, "spruced up" type. Suitable rather for women's faces than for men's. "Slick" execution, with a certain loss of character in the interests of beautification, or accentuation of "prettiness."
2. Type B—More emphasis on character but without any trace of caricature. Work making greater use of sharp line than type A, with a certain touch of character traits, which does not preclude "prettiness" in women's portraits. Objective attitude to the model.
3. Type B + s (supplement)—Intensification of character, bordering on the caricatural. The head larger than natural size. The possibility of preserving "prettiness" in women's portraits, and even of intensifying it in the direction of the "demonic."
4. Type C, C + Co, E, C + H, C + Co + E, etc.—These types, executed with the aid of C_2H_5OH and narcotics of a superior grade, are at present ruled out. Subjective characterization of the model, caricatural intensification both formal and psychological are not ruled out. Approaches abstract composition, otherwise known as "Pure Form."
5. Type D—The same results without recourse to any artificial means.
6. Type E—Combinations of D with the preceding types. Spontaneous psychological interpretation at the discretion of the firm. The effect achieved may be the exact equivalent of that produced by types A and B—the manner by which it is attained is different, as is the method of execution, which may take various forms but never exceeds the limit(s). A combination of E + s is likewise available upon request.
   Type E is not always possible to execute.
7. Children's type—(B + E)—Because children can never sit still, the purer type B is in most instances impossible—the execution rather takes the form of a sketch.

In general, the firm does not pay much attention to the rendering of clothing and accessories. The question of the background concerns only the firm—demands in this regard are not considered. Depending on the disposition of the firm and the difficulties of rendering a particular face, the portrait may be executed in one, two, three, and even

up to five sittings. For large portraits showing the upper body or full figure, the number of sittings may even reach twenty.
The number of sittings does not determine the excellence of the product.

#2. The basic novelty offered by the firm as compared to the usual practice is the customer's option of rejecting a portrait if it does not suit him either because of the execution or because of the degree of likeness. *In such cases the customer pays one-third of the price, and the portrait becomes the property of the firm.* The customer does not have the right to demand that the portrait be destroyed. This clause, naturally, applies only to the pure types: A, B, and E, *without supplement (s)*—that is, without any supplement of exaggerated characteristics, or in other words the types that appear in series. This clause was introduced because it is impossible to tell what will satisfy the client. An exact agreement is desirable, based upon a firm and definite decision by the model as to the type requested. An album of samples (but by no means ones "of no value") is available for inspection at the premises of the firm. The customer receives a guarantee in that the firm in its own self-interest does not issue works that could damage its trademark. A situation could occur in which the firm itself would not sign its own product.

#3. Any sort of criticism on the part of the customer is absolutely ruled out. The customer may not like the portrait, but the firm cannot permit even the most discreet comments without giving its special authorization. If the firm had allowed itself the luxury of listening to customers' opinions, it would have gone mad a long time ago. *We place special emphasis on this rule, since the most difficult thing is to restrain the customer from making remarks that are entirely uncalled-for.* The portrait is either accepted or rejected—yes or no, without any explanations whatsoever as to why. Inadmissible criticism likewise includes remarks about whether or not it is a good likeness, observations concerning the background, covering part of the face in the portrait with one's hand so as to imply that this part really isn't the way it should be, comments such as, "I am too pretty," "Do I look that sad?" "That's not me," and all other opinions of that sort, whether favorable or unfavorable. After due consideration, and possibly consultation with third parties, the customer says yes (or no) and that's all there is to it—then he goes (or does not go) up to what is called the "cashier's window," that is, he simply hands over the agreed-upon sum to the firm. Given the incredible difficulty of the profession, the firm's nerves must be spared.

#4. Asking the firm for its opinion of a finished portrait is not permissible, nor is any discussion about a work in progress.

#5. The firm reserves the right to paint without any witnesses, if that is possible.

#6. Portraits of women with bare necks and shoulders cost one-third more. Each arm costs one-third of the total price. For portraits showing the upper body or full figure, special agreements must be drawn up.

#7. The portrait may not be viewed until finished.

#8. The technique used is a combination of charcoal, crayon, pencil, and pastel. All remarks with regard to technical matters are ruled out, as are likewise demands for alterations.

#9. The firm undertakes the painting of portraits outside the firm's premises only in exceptional circumstances (sickness, advanced age, etc.), in which case the firm must be guaranteed a secret receptacle in which the unfinished portrait may be kept under lock and key.

10. Customers are obliged to appear punctually for the sittings, since waiting has a bad effect on the firm's mood and may have an adverse effect on the execution of the product.

11. The firm offers advice on the framing and packing of portraits but does not provide these services. Further discussion about types of frames is ruled out.

#12. The firm allows total freedom as to the model's clothing and *quite definitely does not voice any opinion in this regard*.

#13. The firm urges a careful perusal of the rules. Lacking any powers of enforcement, the firm counts on the tact and good will of its customers to meet the terms. Reading through and concurring with the rules is taken as equivalent to *concluding an agreement*. Discussion about the rules is inadmissible.

14. An agreement on the installment plan or by bank draft is not ruled out. Given the low prices the firm charges, requests for reductions are not advisable. Before the portrait is begun, the customer pays one-third of the price as a down payment.

#15. A customer who obtains portrait commissions for the firm—that is to say, who acts as "an agent of the firm"—upon providing orders for the sum of 100 złotys receives as a premium his own portrait or that of any person he wishes in the type of his choice.

16. Notices sent by the firm to former customers announcing its presence at a given location are not intended to force them to have new portraits painted, but rather to assist friends of these customers in placing orders, since having seen the firm's work they may wish something similar themselves.

Price List
Type A = 350
Type B = 250
Type B + s = 150
Type E = 150–250
Type C = without price
Type D = 100
Children's type = 150–250

Translated by Daniel Gerould

UNISM IN PAINTING   Władysław Strzemiński

Originally published as *Unizm w malarstwie* (Warsaw: 1928)

Our plastic sensibility and our judgments of works of art have been formed under the great influence of the Baroque tradition. It is easy to talk about breaking with tradition. It is easy to defy traditional culture with one's uncouthness, far removed from ever more formidable phenomena, since on the ruins of the destroyed culture there emerges a new one, but only if it is so much more powerful then the existing one that it can effectively replace the old values with the new.

The power of the Baroque does not only rely on the power of its expressive value, or other values related to it such as tradition, past, honor of the ancestors, Romanesque culture and so forth. The Baroque is the honest and intense work of some fifty painters— and such painters that each single one would be sufficient to make the art flourish. The work of Rembrandt, Murillo, Velasquez, Titian, Tintoretto, El Greco, Coreggio, Caravaggio, Poussin, Zurbaran, Ribera, Veronese, Giorgione, Rubens and many other lesser, but nonetheless great painters, contributed to a coherent and unified system of Baroque painting. Breaking away from the Baroque tradition does not only mean the suppression of the tradition itself but the suppression of the extraordinary power of these great and genuine painters.

The power of the Baroque conception and its criteria—sometimes acquiring the power of the seemingly universal and extra-temporal criteria—can be seen from the comparison of the Baroque form with that of Cézanne and with the Cubist form prior to 1918. Baroque emerged when *painting ceased to be part of the wall decoration*. The Renaissance painting was part of architecture and its purpose was to *fill the surface of wall*. The wall, delimited by vaulting above, was symmetrical. Hence the symmetrical composition of the Renaissance picture. The wall had vertical and horizontal directions as well as an arch. The Renaissance picture was to include these directions in variously modified forms in order to repeat the architectural rhythm and in this way unite the picture with architecture. The Renaissance picture was not a self-sufficient entity; it was part of architecture, subordinate to it—linked with architecture through the direct repetition and the modification of its elements. It possessed its full power only in the architectural environment for which it was painted and by which it was conditioned.

The detachment of painting from the wall had to bring about the reassessment of notions of painting. Symmetry does not offer a genuine construction. Symmetrical picture is not constructed, since each axis of symmetry can be infinitely extended. This is why it never results in a complete and coherent whole. It was therefore necessary to propose a new system of construction through *line and color*.

In Baroque [painting] line is seen as a sign of directional tension. Every line is a dynamic sign. Every line is stopped by another. The impact of line against line encloses the painting. The emergent form is the result of the friction of forces, it has its center, formed by the pressure of directional tensions. The central composition is the result of an attempt to base the construction of the picture on its own foundations—to construct the picture not from the elements imposed by architecture but from its own. The construction of the picture through color occurs as if for the second time, independent of the linear construction. Color is placed according to its weight. Weight, balance, pressure—these are dynamic notions. We notice that in the Baroque also color acquires [the function of] a dynamic expression. Color construction is *independent* of linear construction. Linear construction aims at [creating] a network of directional tensions, color construction—an asymmetrical balance of colors.

Line, which the Baroque uses to achieve in the picture a structural connection of shapes so that they form a coherent whole, loses its continuous character which it had previously in Renaissance [painting]. [In the Baroque] a patch of color is no longer closed in itself and unrelated to all other patches—color permeates from one form to the next, breaking contour lines and connecting one shape with another. The Baroque line is broken, it no longer delimits colors but makes up the framework of a pictorial construction, composed of directional tensions. Directional tension is a sign of pressure and this is why its most essential feature is its direction and force, rather than its direct contact. Line can be broken without losing its significance for dynamic expression and for construction: closing off directional tensions is enforced since direction was marked, while, at the same time, there is a greater unity of the painting since not only line but also color connects, permeating from one shape to the next and in this way connecting them in a direct way.

Form [in the Baroque] is conceived by the contrasting juxtaposition of light and dark colors. The stronger the contrast, the more forms stand out. The strength of the color contrast determines the power of the shape's presence. Shape is formed by the color contrast. This contrast sometimes acquires a dynamic force through the strength of the contrast with which two adjoining color patches strike the eye.

The principle of contrast is obligatory not only in relation to color but also to forms: distinct shapes next to less distinct, shapes standing out sharply next to almost indistinct, large shapes next to small ones, shapes of different character, dark shapes on light background, light shapes on dark background, variety of painted surfaces resulting in differences of texture.

Applying the criterion of form when analyzing Cézanne's paintings we notice first of all a significant difference in the treatment of color. Impressionism, reigning then with its principle of multicolors, with its application of the whole range of hues instead of the Baroque color harmony of similar hues (gold, silver harmony and Impressionist) and its theory of complementary colors—was also applied by Cézanne. At a first glance Cézanne's paintings seem entirely different from Baroque paintings. In reality though, the extended range of colors is here only an increase in the number of color contrasts of Baroque painting. Cézanne groups colors according to the principle of contrast (red emphasized by green, etc). The principle of contrast is the main principle of Baroque painting. Cézanne did not break away from it. His deviation from the rule is only apparent. In reality, his color arrangements remain as contrasting as those of Baroque painting. The achievements of Impressionism were absorbed by the Baroque [tradition in painting]. Impressionism could not even develop its own system before it was absorbed by the Baroque [tradition] to enrich and to expand its form.

In every other respect Cézanne remains a follower of Baroque painting. The disappearance of contour line, broken by color (though already in an Impressionist manner, not by tonal values as it was in the Baroque proper), independence of color from line, directional tensions, closing one another off and forming a linear framework, placing colors according to their weight in order to achieve an asymmetrical balance—these are [also] characteristics of Cézanne's painting.

Moreover, applying the same test of an objective form to Cubism, we have to state that Cubism in its early stages—in particular those preceding the important breakthrough of Jeanneret and Ozenfant about 1918—is [essentially] the Baroque, consciously applying the principles that distinguish Baroque painting, though in purified and intensified form.

We notice in Cubism [the use of] directional tensions as the main element of pictorial construction. In the Baroque these tensions have often occurred camouflaged—as external or internal outlines of forms with all their randomness. Cubism, by introducing geometric principles, has enhanced and emphasized these tensions—manifesting the picture's framework and the method of its construction. The aim has remained the same. The means—directional tensions closing one another off—have [also] remained the same.

The [Cubist] range of hues is even richer than Cézanne's. This has been achieved by introducing texture, or rather, through its more conscious and frequent use. Texture is the state of color surface. The way of laying on paint gives such varied color sensations that they cannot be achieved by the juxtaposition of colors alone.

Cubists understood texture in analogy to colors in the Baroque, in a dynamic way. They imbued texture with a dynamic quality seeing it as a trace and sign of movement, or inertness, depending on the arrangement of molecules of color comprising the textural surface. For example—"needle" texture, jagged texture, matte texture, luster texture, dotted texture. Cubists place texture and color in the picture according to the principle of the weight of color or textural mass, independently of linear construction. The independence of color from line in the Baroque found its expression in Cubism, in the independence of *texture and color* from line.

Contrast of shapes, expressed in a more conscious and clear way (contrast of geometric shapes is perceived more readily then contrast of non-geometrical shapes), contrast of colors, and contrast of textures—complete the analogy between Cubist and Baroque elements of the painterly construction. Cubist painting is constructed in such a way that vertical and horizontal directions predominated in the center, placed according to the axes of construction. Curves and diagonals, though sometimes found in the center, predominate near the picture's boundaries. In this way the center of the picture is connected through the rhythm of its directions with vertical and horizontal picture borders and yet, at the same time, separated from them by forms placed near the borders. There occurs a contrast of the pictorial form as a whole with the picture's borders, the contrast which does not allow a complete union of the pictorial form with the picture plane and with its boundaries. The form remains unconnected with the [picture's] frame—it has its own center of gravity, unconnected and contrasting with the picture's borders. The result of the contrast is greater tension of form.

That the phenomenon is not purely coincidental can be seen from the fact that in the oval shaped Cubist pictures straight lines are placed near the borders and curves in the center. It is a common practice [in Cubism] that the center of the picture repeats the rhythm of its borders—and, at the same time, its parts near the borders—through the contrast with the borders' directions. They stand out from the directions of boundaries. It is, therefore, correct to call Cubist construction a *central construction*.

The Baroque tradition has been so attractive that even Cézanne, generally regarded as the initiator of modern art, succumbed to it. He was an Impressionist who continued and expanded the Baroque [tradition]. Cubism, which has been thought of as a movement diametrically opposed to the old art world turns out to be, on [close] analysis of form, the continuation and development of the Baroque—its consistent rectification. The differences in subject matter or content are irrelevant. Non-objective, abstract painting has content like any other. It is form which is decisive, the only value in painting and the only criterion of progress—or retrogression— in art. And the analysis of form proves that Cézanne's Baroque is tantamount to that of Cubism.

A general analysis of a whole variety of Baroque painting leads to conclusion that *baroque [painting] is painting of dramatic tensions*, painting of forces. The drama is the resolution of conflicts. Their force and the power with which concentric and centrifugal tendencies are brought to a unanimous expression, the coercion to unity of expression, the force with which these tendencies are subjugated and forced to cooperate, the coercion imposing the unity of expression—determines the depth and the range of the drama. Baroque [painting] is the drama of painterly conflicts, the resolution of the dualisms of form:

Concentric construction. Form has its center of concentration. Shapes are grouped around this center. Concentric construction tends to be enclosed within a circle or oval and results in a close connection of shapes. At the same time, however, concentric construction, with its arrangement of shapes gravitating towards the center, does not offer any connection with the picture's borders—these are not taken into account since the primary concern is connecting shapes. This is the source of the first conflict: the conflict between painterly form and the space in which it is painted, a flat rectangle of canvas. The treatment of form is such as if it had first been seen in some vision and only then transferred onto canvas. The dualism between painterly form and canvas on which it is painted corresponds to the Baroque conception of the widest possible range of painterly conflicts, dramatic contrasts. The contrast of an elliptical form with the rectangle of canvas intensifies an overall tension of form, adding to the other contrasts. Contrast is the first principle in Baroque painting.

Independence of color from line—the second conflict of Baroque painting. Lines form a framework of construction through the impact against one another and by closing one another. Color and texture are fluid, one passing into the other, placed according to their weight in such a way as to achieve a symmetrical balance. There is contrast of colors not delimited by line (contour). There is contrast of a strong linear framework with a fluid color.

Color and line should cooperate aiming at a shape that is mutually and uniformly defined by both line and color. Their independence, the lack of coordination in defining shape, the diversity in its treatment—all imply a contradiction, conflict, dualism, enriching form and enhancing its dramatic tension.

Impact of lines, the mutual closing of directional tensions [is] the third conflict of Baroque painting. It is the result of the treatment of painting as a sign of dynamic, direct action, and comprehending each shape and each line not just as a line as a sign of force. In reality, line is only a line and nothing more. This is an objective truth. It lies where it is situated and its function is to delimit colors. However, the Baroque imbues line with an illusory movement which in reality it does not possess. This illusory movement tears line away from its proper place forcing it to glide across the picture surface. Hence the conflict between line as a motionless boundary of colors and a moving, gliding, dynamic line as a sign of force. Line begins to move even without altering its position.

Dynamism is not a purely plastic phenomenon. Plastic art moulds space. Only spatial elements belong to the plastic arts. Dynamism signifies movement, and hence it is a space-time phenomenon, the surmounting of space in time. The impact of lines which is the main objective of Baroque construction is a dynamic phenomenon. Lines gliding and striking against one another contain a certain measure of time in which the action occurs. The greater the dynamism the more time contained in the painting. Clear movements, weaker or so weak as almost non-existent, static parts, impacts of different strength, places where line disappears soaked into texture or color—all of this causes such a time content in Baroque picture that we must almost read it, gradually deciphering the impact of shapes to arrive through a gradual synthesis at seeing the whole. However, the picture is, or rather it should be, an object destined to be only looked at. It should not be a dramatic play of struggling forces, but a purely visual phenomenon. The idea alien to painting hinders understanding that the picture is not an illusion of a phenomenon seen elsewhere or simply imagined and then transferred into picture, but that it exists in itself and for itself. The basic premise of the Baroque was that the picture should be a sign of a dramatic pathos. The pathos finds its expression in the dynamism of directional tensions and the dramatic blows struck by lines. This results in the necessity to contain in the picture a great deal of time. The more time the picture contains, the deeper the dynamic drama.

Contrast of shapes grows more pronounced with the development of the Baroque to become the leading principle in Cubist painting. It is not only the contrast of curve next to straight line, the vertical and the horizontal, a small shape next to a larger shape, but also of a clear shape next to an almost indistinct one, of a roughly sketched shape next to one elaborated in detail, and other contrasts deriving from a different treatment of form. The principle of contrast breaking the painting into several unconnectable shapes, detached and opposing one another, results in a general warfare of all shapes, a dramatic conflict of contrasting form. Shape [in the Baroque picture] does not result from the picture's format with which it should be connected. Shape lacks the necessity which would place it in the picture and which would unite it with the picture. Shape exists only to enhance the tension of contrasts between shapes. None of the shapes is derived from a clear necessity of its existence; it is needed indirectly for other shapes but not for itself and for the picture. By looking for contrasts one will not find a connection between shapes that would ensure a uniform painterly organism. The opposing shapes will always remain inimical, forever alien, producing the tension of a condensed, rich and powerful form, full of dramatic contrast of shapes, the form which forces a unity of external connections through coercion but which will never result in a painterly organism whose all parts are connected through inner logic.

Color contrast, irrespective of the type of Baroque painting, occurs always purely as dark-light oppositions (in the Baroque proper), either as a juxtaposition of complementary colors (in Cézanne's Impressionist Baroque: yellow-blue, red-green etc.) or as contrasts in texture in abstract geometrical Baroque [painting]—in Cubism.

Two contrasting colors juxtaposed next to each other break the unity of the picture dividing it into as many parts as there are contrasting patches. The stronger the contrast of colors and their impact—the wider the range of painterly conflicts. The more irrevocably is the picture broken into parts—torn by the impact of colors— the greater the dramatic tension of painterly form. Form, infinitely stressed, saturated but never enough, restrained impetus—this is the intrinsic content of Baroque picture. It is torn by color into parts which cannot be united, though connected in some places as a result of fluidity of color and the disappearance of its outlines.

Contrast of colors not only breaks the picture into unconnectable parts. Contrast of colors produces the greatest tension of form near boundaries of color. The tension of form is not uniformly spread—there are junctions and vofds of form. There are contrasts between parts with dense, condensed form and parts where form is almost nonexistent. The differences in the tension of form divides the picture into parts of different character, mutually alien, united only through the common dramatic pathos.

We must oppose the dualist conception attempting to connect things that cannot be connected and finding its rationale not in achieving its aim but in the power of opposing forces and an excessive effort at their subjugation, this conception of producing forces only to oppose them but never to overcome—with the conception of a uniform and organic painting. *Dualist conception should be replaced by Unist conception.* Not the pathos of dramatic explosions and great forces but the picture as organic as nature itself.

The analysis of all painting in the Baroque tradition should lead to the conclusion that the Baroque has not been capable of creating a genuinely uniform painterly organism. It achieved a maximum of dramatic tensions of contrast which could not be connected. [Baroque painting] confined itself to a potential tendency to connect them. Instead of the actual connection seen directly by the eye, it offered a connection which could only be perceived by the mind.

The appeal of the Baroque has been so strong that we do not notice that our thinking has been under its influence. The main criterion of a good painting "rich form" or "saturated form" is only viable within Baroque values. What is this "rich form"? Where there is a great number of contrasts of form, where there is a great diversity of color, where there is a great deal of dynamic actions, although constrained by other, where there is a great variety and sensitivity in laying on paint, where there are contrasts of textures—there is "rich form." But these are the very notions that define the essence of the Baroque, its ideal, its aim! That is to say a rich form and the picture's perfection are tantamount with its "baroqueness." The more Baroque, the more perfect?

It is time to revise the concept of rich painterly form and other related concepts. [Even] a cursory analysis of these notions should convince that it is the rich form which breaks the uniformity of the picture, its unity; instead of creating an organic unity—mechanically lumps together parts that are unconnectable. Form in painting should no longer be valued for its contrast but for its unity and the means aiming to achieve this unity.

Central composition does not lead to the picture's unity since it results in the contrast of form with the space in which it is placed. In central composition we observe a distinct focus around which form develops—the further away from it, the weaker the tension of form. Form as a whole approximates circle or oval shape, explicitly or in an oblique way. In the first instance curves predominate, in the second—diagonals are placed near the picture's borders. The whole construction of form is designed for the contrast, appearing *post factum*, of form with the picture's borders.

This way of construction contradicts the principle of *equal value of space* in the picture. Every square inch of the picture is of equal value and plays part in the picture's construction in the same degree. Making some parts stand out while neglecting other is unjustified. The picture plane is uniform and so the tension of form should be distributed uniformly. Central construction is the result of a visionary form. Form is seen as something separate from the not bring any other results.

Were it clearly realized that the true uniformity of painting depends not only on the connection of shapes but also on the close unity of these shapes with the space from which they originate, that the true unity of painting is the unity of what had existed before the emergence of the picture with the painted form, then an illusory and subjective form,

a visionary way of experiencing form would give way to an objective and organic construction of the picture. The innate properties of the picture (square boundaries and the flatness the picture plane) should not just be treated as a place to position form, conceived independently. The innate properties (square boundaries and the flatness of the picture plane) are components of a pictorial construction, perhaps even the most important ones since pictorial forms can only emerge in relation to them. They must be dependent and closely connected.

The Baroque picture was constructed through dynamism. Dynamism not only should no longer be a component of a pictorial construction, but should not be used in painting at all.

A dynamic shape is never grown into the picture plane. It does not grow from the place in the picture where it finds itself. Its movement is always directed in some direction, taking the shape beyond the picture's boundaries. A dynamic gliding of the shape on the picture plane detaches it from the place it is positioned and from the picture, throwing it outside the picture. There should be no gliding forms. There should be a complete unity of what is painted with the surface plane on which it is painted. Shapes should form a complete, unbreakable unity with the picture plane.

A genuine pictorial construction cannot be produced through dynamism. The construction relies on shapes growing together and into the pictorial plane so that no shape can break away from the whole forming a separate and distinct part. Since a dynamic shape has a character of a detached part, tries to take off from the whole, is not grown either into the picture plane or to other shapes, then it cannot be used as an element of the pictorial construction. A dynamic construction—impact of all shapes—gives an effect of chaos, momentarily checked in order or rather only maintaining the semblance of order as a result of the destructive effect of the impact of shapes. Shapes do not grow from the picture, they are not grown into it, neither do they form an organism by growing into other shapes. Their position, their inability of leaving their place, is a result of a constraint exerted by other shapes. This constraint is the best proof that [such a] construction is not genuinely organic. Were it organic, constraint would have been unnecessary. Were one of its shapes to be removed, the pressure from that side would decrease, upsetting the balance, and with it the whole elaborate pseudo-construction. Meanwhile, every shape should be grown directly into the picture plane so that it needs no help from any other shapes. Constraint in construction only proves that the construction is not organic.

Movement is a space-time phenomenon. Directional tension is a sign of movement—therefore it contains an element of time. Instead of looking at the picture to see it we are forced to read it. The more directional tensions and their collisions, the more time contained in the picture, the more is the picture removed from a purely plastic art which aims at the simultaneity of spatial-visual phenomena. Our aim is an extra-temporal picture, operating only within the notion of space.

Attempts have been made to remove time in Suprematist and Surrealist paintings. This was achieved by a mutual neutrality of shapes. They are placed in the picture in such a way as not to influence one another. Parallel and independent existence of shapes, the lack of the so-called mutual connection and direct action, mean that we do not feel *duration* of time in these pictures. These paintings cannot, however, be regarded as completely extra-temporal. The system of detached and independent shapes emphasizes parallel, minimally short time spans contained in these shapes, manifested by parallel distances between shapes. Seeing shapes and the distances between them we see not one picture but several, each independent from one another. We need a certain amount of time to connect them into one visual sensation. In this way a seemingly extra-temporal picture becomes spatial and temporal. Every division of the picture means that time is needed to unite it visually. Only a completely uniform painting can be extra-temporal, purely spatial.

In recent times several art movements, in their evolution, have come to the conclusion that plane should be the only constructional element of the picture and that line, in its usual form of a stroke has no place in painting. This should be regarded as a positive sign since line is a far more fluid and dynamic form than plane, not to mention that as an enclosed shape plane grows better into the picture plane while line, having no natural ends, can always be infinitely extended and always shows the tendency to go beyond the picture. The introduction of plane into the picture, several years ahead of all the other modern art movements, was the contribution of Suprematism. Geometrization existed in all painting within the Baroque tradition. In the Baroque proper all shapes were adapted to a form of arch or letter S (the noble roundness of form). Cézanne introduced, and Cubism consistently applied, the simplest and the most distinct forms:

straight line and curve. It was believed that in this way a precise and exact construction can be produced. Geometry cannot construct the picture. Geometry offers clear and precise constructional elements but cannot assign to them their exact place in the picture. As a result, the painter positions shapes according to his intuition. The lack of objective principles forces to look for support in intuition—subjective, inconstant and dependent on individual taste. It is time to put an end to this misconception of geometric construction as a precise, almost engineering construction. Geometric construction is in reality as random and subjective as any other construction. Geometry can make the construction to stand out, show it more clearly, but it cannot construct anything. It does not offer any tangible principles of construction.

Construction of the picture can only be achieved through a uniform numerical expression of the whole picture, i.e. the relationship of the proportions of one shape to those of another is defined by the same number. Naturally, the point of departure is the width and height of the picture. Placing the format of the picture in a sequence of dimensions of pictorial shapes, mutually connected and related through the same numerical ratio offers the most reliable means of connecting the shapes with the picture borders. The same rhythm of the numerical ratio of proportions of all shapes is their most genuine connection. When beginning construction of the picture its basic dimensions— width and height—should be taken as a point of departure for defining the width and height of every shape, as well as its place. In this way the dimensions of the picture become the main components of the construction, decisive for its construction and character, rather then of secondary consideration, outside our consciousness—as it was in Baroque [painting].

One should not assume that by applying arithmetical calculations the idea will follow automatically and painterly activity will become mechanical. Even the best knowledge of the methods of calculation cannot conceive the picture. Calculation should go together with intuition. The picture is the result of both activities, mutually supportive. The advantages of the calculation method are that the picture becomes more objective— doing away with individual methods and graphological quivers transfers the focal point to the picture, its laws, its construction—instead of manifesting whims of individual will, temperament or taste of this or that painter. The law of construction of the picture should stand above an individuality of a painter. The work of art should always take precedence over an incidental and inconstant nature of an artist.

Color contrast, used in Baroque painting to bring out dramatic conflicts, has no place in Unist conception. Instead of division of the picture into mutually opposing parts, a unanimous action of all parts. Just as breaking the unity of an organism causes death, breaking a picture through color kills the painting, makes it dead, forces to search for external measures in order to resuscitate the corpse. This is when directional tensions come to play their role. But the picture is dead, it is decomposing, falling apart. Contrast of colors causes the death of painting. And what use is achieving the tension of form in a corpse?

Colors should not be grouped according to contrast which breaks the picture but to unite and connect the picture. Not according to diversity of color, not according to what divides but to what unites. The range of pure hues does not unify the picture since contrasting brightness of different hues breaks [the unity] of the picture. Contrasts of texture break the picture through a different luminosity contained in textures. Juxtaposition of colors should not be according to different tonal values of the same color since these contain the greatest contrast in brightness. Instead of juxtaposing different tones of the same hue, a variety of hues of the same brightness should be placed together. The same brightness of colors connects the picture, resulting in its uniformity. None of the colors stands out, none falls deeper. What remains is a uniform mass of shapes and the picture plane totally united with the surface of canvas. This treatment of color makes the picture uniform and, as a result, does not require the forcible connection of colors broken up and unconnectable by any other means.

Only then can the independence of color from line be eliminated. It is not line which should mend what color breaks, it is not line which should connect the picture broken up by color—they should both work together aiming at a uniform picture connected in all its parts and derived from its innate components: the square boundaries and the flat picture plane. A uniform painting is not a clash of shapes, it is not a drama, but, like every organism, it is the unanimous action of all parts, the unanimous expression of line and color. Each component of pictorial construction: line, color, texture strive to achieve the same goal, but each in its own way. And since that goal is different—the painting [understood] not as a drama but as an organism, each of these elements has its own means and its own solution.

The flatness of painting is one of the main effects of the unanimous expression of line and color. Color is no longer independent of line. Line is color's boundary. Color no longer permeates through line. It is connected with line, mutually related forms a unity. The removal of this dualism puts an end to the dualism between the flat surface plane of the picture and the three-dimensional form of shapes painted on canvas. The picture aiming at the complete uniformity, should be the result of its innate qualities (flat picture plane and square boundaries). Meanwhile the underlying principle of the Baroque conception was the accumulation of opposing contrasts negating the picture's innate qualities. The picture which contains few contrasts, the picture in agreement with its innate qualities, is, from the point of view of the Baroque [tradition], boring. For Baroque painter a non-organic painting is plenitude, unattainability—an achievement, the result is nothing while the effort used—everything. That is why the partial attempts made within the limits of Baroque [painting] at transition to flat painting have not produced full results. Although there are flat planes in late Cubism, Suprematism or Mondrian's Neoplasticism—the whole [picture] is still not flat. The painters still search for contrasts—painting flat they do not realize what consequences should follow. Hence the color which divides the picture, color contrasts which from a uniformly flat picture make several separate planes. Hence contrasts of shapes which result in their separateness, unconnectability, and instead of a uniform picture—one divided into several shapes. Hence the dynamism leading shapes beyond the picture, unabling [sic] them to grow into the picture plane. Hence central construction so often used by Cubists nowadays. All these errors come from not considering the essence of the picture, [from not realizing] that the flatness of shapes is not enough, that it should [only] be the first step towards the flatness of the whole picture. We must realize the character of the evolution of modern painting which is the transition from the Baroque drama to the mystical conception of the picture as a painterly organism, that Unist painting demands the unanimity of all pictorial elements with its innate qualities. The flatness of pictorial plane belongs to its innate characteristics, therefore the whole painting should form a uniformly flat plane. The picture should be uniform and flat. We must oppose Baroque dramatism with Unism in painting.

Translated by Wanda Kemp-Welch

SCULPTURE AND SOLID Katarzyna Kobro

Originally published as "Rzezba I bryla," *Europa* no. 2 (1929)

There are very few modern sculptors. Are there material reasons? Or is it because sculpture is nowadays too directly involved in architecture, so that each truly modern architect must be a good modern sculptor?

Boccioni in his Futurist sculptures showed us how to liberate sculpture from the burden of solidity. Archipenko opened up the inside of the solid, but he kept the perimeters complete. Vantongerloo feels the need for the harmony of sizes and for modern classicism; he builds up the sculpture out of a few interrelated cubes enclosed in the overall cubic frame.

Van Doesburg, in his few experiments in painting and architecture, promised spatial solutions in the construction of sculpture from flats and solids, but what he promised was neither painting, nor sculpture, nor architecture. It only suggested an idea of what might be achieved. Malevich raises the problem of balance in the distribution of weights and masses in space, in his dynamic-spatial build-ups and in his theoretical discussions. Once he was the prophet of abstract painting; now he announces through architectonic sculptures the new era in architecture arising from modern sculpture.

Sculpture is the shaping of space. If we want to know *the* real tendency in the development of sculpture, we must compare the highest recent achievements. We must not care about what the majority of minor sculptors are doing, but consider only the achievements of those who clear the road. Secondly, we must become radically, beyond recall and once for all, aware that sculpture is neither literature, nor symbolism, nor individual psychology or emotion. Sculpture is exclusively the shaping of form in space. Sculpture appeals to all men and it speaks to all of them alike. Form and space is its idiom. Hence the objectivism of the most economic expression of form. There are no multiple solutions; there is one, the shortest and most appropriate.

Sculpture is a part of the space around it. One must not be detached from the other. Sculpture enters space and space enters sculpture. Spatiality of construction, the link of sculpture with its space, brings out from the sculpture the truth of its existence. Then the shapes in sculpture must not be contingent. Only those shapes should be there which relate it to its space and link up both. The solid is a lie to the essence of sculpture. It closes up the sculpture and separates it from its space: it exists for itself and it regards its inner space like something completely divorced from the outer space. But as a matter of fact space is like everywhere else and always the same. At present, the solid belongs to history and it is just another beautiful tale from the past.

New sculpture, as it becomes united with the surrounding space, should be its most condensed and appealing part. This is achieved, because its shapes, by their mutual interdependence, create a rhythm of sizes and divisions. The unity of rhythm arises out of the unity of its calculated scale.

The harmony of units is the visible revelation of number.

Translation from Three Pioneers of the Polish Avant-Garde

PLASTIC ART AS THE SUMMARY OF CULTURAL LIFE   Henryk Stażewski

Originally published as "Sztuki plastyczne jako streszczenie życia kulturalnego," *Europa*, no. 3 (1929)

The rapid changes that occur in today's life manifest themselves in a new content of artistic consciousness. We live in a period of transforming the form of artistic expression. Today's art can develop by clearing the atmosphere and drawing on the source of—lively and changing—social and scientific ideas. Art, as a result of having lost touch with life, is not very conscious; it falls into routine and convention. The first more crystallized movement, which was out of touch with society, was individualism, expressing the most imperceptible shades of individual psychology. It denied the value of any objective artistic criteria. Individualism is the seed of anarchy since it decisively opposes the necessary discipline. A strong discipline joins the individual centers playing the role of energy uniting separate individualities and does not allow art to become a doctrine—doctrines (as Lemaitre noted) are ossified personal predilections. The so-called strong individualities limited themselves to relatively few cultural and artistic issues. The greater the number of issues the artist occupies himself with, the less individual are his characteristics.

Too rich and colorful a life destroys art since it becomes impossible to master all phenomena. It results in superficial precepts and does not allow for concentration, which is the result of single-track focusing. Internal concentration, a pre-defined artistic consciousness and a simple attitude to life are indispensable to a conception and architectonic plan of the work of art.

The rich and varied impressions find expression in the multitude of forms and dimensions, in individual texture. Today's art, connected with *economy of thought and perception*, cannot bear misunderstandings and demands a good mastery of the subject matter of the work of art—its main quality is *economy of shapes, texture and mathematical relationship of forms*.

Art that is vivid, close to life and original leads to new, exciting connections, it searches for elements not yet worn out and fossilized: it is a negation of inertia. The artist moves away from the conventional colors and shapes which lie useless in the visual field between our eye and reality—he looks for pure form untainted by some marginal considerations or a practical attitude. *We must break off with an instrumental attitude and gain specifically localized disinterestedness of the senses and consciousness.* Such a notion is necessary for the work of art to be real, in order to come into closer contact with reality. Disinterestedness of perception is most pronounced when catching the phenomena in their impersonal form—in non-objective art which brings out the essence of the plastic elements contained in the object, rather than their accidental and variable qualities.

The synthesis of artistic values is achieved by detecting and interpreting the social tension concealed under rational postulates of today's life. *Lyrical experience* is no longer a building material of the work of art. We are bound by the scientific method of development—geometric shapes and their mathematical relationships become the "motif" of art. Under the external shell of the *object* are concealed relations and proportions of shapes and colors that are an expression of the pure and unique elements of plastic art—the live content of art.

Translated by Wanda Kemp-Welch

COMMUNIQUÉ OF THE A.R. GROUP   Władysław Strzemiński, et. al.

Originally published as "Komunikat Grupy 'a.r.'" in *Europa*, no. 9 (1930)

The a.r. group takes up the struggle for modern art in Poland.

The work of *Zwrotnica*, *Blok*, and *Praesens* created the basis for a new art. The achieve-ments of new art were eroded by the chaos of our artistic life and the imitators of modernism who, by adopting superficially some of the means of new art, decreased their revolutionary significance and dulled the senses of the general public to new beauty.

What is praised in Poland nowadays is already some fifty years late.

a.r. declares war on the obsolete, on the falsification of artistic values, on the decrepi-tude of the pseudo-modernists.

a.r. struggles for an art based on laws as constant as the laws of nature.

a.r. announces: organic construction. The logic of form and construction results from the logic of building material. Architecture is the composition of motion in space. Architecture of trajectories that uplift man, and not Corbusier's steam ships which cast anchor by chance on a street at number such and such. Painting the unity of the rectangle, instead of playing with contrived shapes and textures. Spatial sculpture, united with space, and not a four-wall pier. Poetry: the unity of vision, condensed with maximum reference to images and the minimum of words, instead of the lullaby of melodious declamation.

a.r. combines plastic art with poetry. It presents the problems of new art in the broad spectrum, instead of the hitherto existing innovation in one field of art and simultane-ous compromise and ignorance in another, with the result that the idea it gave of the present day was narrow and false.

a.r. constructs art on the principles of conciseness, elimination, concentration. The work of art is the result of the calculation of aesthetic elements.

a.r. propagates plastic art in which every square millimeter and every cubic millimeter is organized.

a.r. creates, it does not imitate, co-operating in the avant-garde movements of Europe, it broadens the field conquered by its ideas. In Poland only a.r. offers both creative work and modernity.

a.r. publishes the Library of Modern Art. So far it has published volume 1, by Julian Przyboś and Władysław Strzemiński. In print: volume 2 of a.r. library: Katarzyna Kobro and Władysław Strzemiński, *Composition Of Space, The Calculations of Time-Space Rhythm*; volume 3 of the a.r. library: Julian Przyboś, *The Creative Elements of Poetry*.

Modern art is not just another style. Modern art is the negation of all that has been before. Modern art is the revolution of all hitherto existing bases of sensation. Modern art changes the relationship of man to all products of his hands.

Translated by Wanda Kemp-Welch

Originally published as *Kompozycja przestrzeni—obliczenia rytmu czasoprzestrzennego* (Łódź: 1931)

Unism in painting tends towards flat visual unity, closed in upon itself and indifferent to its environment. A unistic sculpture aims at accomplishing the unity of the sculpture with the surrounding space, a spatial unity. The general assumption of Unism is the unity of a work of art with the place in which it arises, or with the natural conditions that had already existed before the work of art was made. The terrain on which a painting arises is the flat surface of the canvas and the square of the sides of the picture. It is to this plane, limited, flat and closed, isolated from its environment, that the shapes in the picture must be adjusted. They must be brought to the organic unity that would unite the shapes in the picture with its plane and borders, constituting a flat visual unity, cut off from the environment by the sides of the picture. The visual unity reaches the sides of the picture and it stops there. This kind of organic unity becomes comprehensible for us, when we take into account that the factors that determine it are the flat surface and the clear limits which cannot be infringed. This entails the flatness of the uniform visual phenomenon and its uniformity right up to the borders of the picture.

In sculpture we have no such limits. Nature itself defines the border of a picture as its natural limit, but it offers no natural borders for a piece of sculpture. It has no natural limits at all, and this implies the inevitability of its connection with the whole of infinite space. A unity of what has arisen with what has been prior to the work of art is the main postulate of Unism. This relates to the character of the spatial unity in sculpture. A work of sculpture, arising in space not limited by any frontiers, should compose a unity with the infinity of the space. Any closure of a sculpture, any opposition between it and the space, strips it of its organic character of the uniformity of a spatial phenomenon. by breaking their natural connection and isolating the sculpture.

[...]

The device which gives uniformity to a piece of sculpture without isolating it, is the spatio-temporal calculated rhythm. By rhythm we mean a regular sequence of shapes in space. The rhythm of a unistic sculpture is a complex rhythm of spatial shapes and of colored planes. The regular sequence is attained by reducing the mutual relationships of the consecutive shapes to a common numerical formula. Through reducing the problem to the numerical formula of the relationships of consecutive size we make the rhythm an open one, capable of growth in both directions: towards the greater and towards the smaller shapes. This peculiar rhythm of Unism, the open rhythm, links the shapes, while at the same time linking them to the space.

This rhythm of shapes can grow in any direction; it can add new extensions to existing ones, not contained by the work. These new shapes, being a logical consequence and continuation of the series of already existing shapes must be placed in the space surrounding the sculpture. Thus, an open rhythm arising from the sculpture extends to the space, relating it to the work.

The unity of a sculpture itself and its inherent harmony as a work of art cannot be attained if there is any opposition between it and the space, this would strip it of its only plastic means.

Sculpture is the art of space. However following on from what has been said, sculpture is not a wholly plastic phenomenon, for it assumes the coexistence of space and time within itself. These are the two elements that are united in the concept of motion, which is a synthetic, spatio-temporal concept.

The unlimited number of projected planes can be united only in the spatio-temporal concept of rhythm as an ordered motion, subject to strict and clear laws. No plastic means can establish a connection between an infinite number of projected planes seen from an infinite number of sides, for those means are unable to convey time. Optics are insufficient. Only a rhythm which is a result of spatial changes occurring in time can be the unifying factor.

It is the property of sight that it can see exactly one shape at a single moment. After this shape has been seen, a shift is made to another, and in this way all the shapes which make up a work of art are seen one after another. Depending on the amount of energy inherent in them, these shapes work with more or less strength and they constitute a series of impressions of varying intensity, arranged in a time sequence. This is the rhythm of the simplest type—the spatio-temporal rhythm of a single projected plane. Analyzing this rhythm we must discover its spatio-temporal character. A division of a work of art into parts separating them out from the work, brings about their working against one another which, although it concerns purely spatial phenomena, still occurs in time. This most simple rhythm, the rhythm of a single plane is the point of departure for the building of the rhythm of the whole work of art and of all its sides, for its spatio-temporality is quite peculiar in its character, being the most convenient transition from spatial phenomena to the phenomenon of time. Time is not directly given in it. The whole of what we perceive on a single projected plane is indeed a purely spatial phenomenon, a plastic one. The element of time becomes significant only when the eyes are set in motion. The character of the spatio-temporality of a single projected plane can be defined as potential, as a rhythm having the element of time latent in it. It is only for the different projected planes that the element of time becomes significant in a direct manner, appearing clearly as the pauses dividing a work of art into a series of projected planes separate from each other. It is necessary to understand the potential character of the rhythm of a single projected plane, for only when is has been grasped can we build up a transition from dimensional and spatial phenomena to something as specific as the uniform spatio-temporal rhythm. Time is only potentially inherent within a single plane. In a work of three-dimensional art, it appears in an open manner as a result of the beholding motion around the work of art. The main task is: to build up a transition from individual shapes which are purely spatial and non-temporal, through the potential rhythm, up to the rhythm of the whole work of art or to the overt rhythm which units the whole work into a single spatio-temporal unity.

This entails, as the basic condition: a one-dimensionality of the potential and of the overt rhythm, i.e. the same numerical formula for the rhythm of the projected plane and of the whole work of art. Thus, the rhythm of the whole work is the result of the potential rhythms of the several projected planes which have a common formula with it. Or: the uniformity of the spatio-temporal rhythm through out the whole work of art can be attained, provided that all the potential rhythms of all the projected planes have the same numerical formula.

We can establish the following three periods anterior to the building of a uniform spatio-temporal rhythm connecting the several mutually independent shapes, reducing them to a uniform system and making up an interdependent scale of increases and falls of energy inherent in these shapes, and thus making these shapes into a complete unity of the spatio-temporal phenomenon.

The first period: A uniform potential rhythm within a single projected plane should be established. This is attained by commensurability of all the shapes; which means that the relationships between all of them should be expressed in the same numerical formula. In this way we pass from such or another size of the shapes, from their extensions, from a measurable and purely spatial phenomenon, to a potential rhythm.

The second period: After establishing the same numerical formula for the relationships of all the shapes within the limits of a single projected plane, the same numerical formula must be extended upon all the other projected planes. Each plane is different from the former ones and the disposition of shapes on it is different, but since its rhythm has been built according to the same numerical formula, therefore the consequent result is the resonance of all the potential rhythms.

The third period: We have to pass from the numerical formula common for all the potential rhythms to the sequence of the projected planes. It is only now that we make the transition from the potential rhythms to the higher order rhythm—to the spatio-temporal one which is constituted by the sequence of the consecutive potential rhythms inherent in the several projected planes. This sequence of the projected planes ought to be constructed according with the same numerical formula, according to which each of the projected planes and all of them together have been constructed. If we succeed to embody the same numerical formula into all the parts which constitute the work of art, we shall attain a wholly uniform spatio-temporal rhythm.

The variety of shapes and sizes does not hamper the uniformity of the rhythm, for all the arising contrasts are an effect of the common definition of all the shapes by a common numerical formula n, constituting the essential foundation and the essential description of the spatio-temporal rhythm of the work of art.

The offered way of conduct concerns only the size of the shapes and their arrangement, but it says nothing about the shapes themselves. This is up to the artist who knows himself, what shapes he needs. But the exact magnitude of such shapes, the precise definition of their places, their connections so as to have them make a uniform spatio-temporal rhythm and a construction of a uniform work of art rather than of some fragments—all this can be attained only by an application of a uniform numerical formula comprising the relationships of the shapes.

Consequences:

1. a sculpture is a part of space; its organic quality depends on its incorporation into space,
2. a sculpture is not a formal composition in its own right; it is a composition within space,
3. dynamic qualities of a succession of shapes add up to produce a uniform rhythm within time and space,
4. a harmonious rhythm derives from measure which is based on numbers,
5. architecture helps to organize man's movements in space, hence its character of a spatial composition,
6. architecture is meant not only to design comfortable and functional dwellings,
7. architecture has to combine everything: distribution of everyday utilities, structural inventions and color qualities, as well as to give direction to shapes which will then determine the rhythm of man's life within architecture,
8. a printed page consists of successively arranged (so as to match the content of the text), spatial units (printed planes); that is why its layout should follow numerical measure.

Translation from Three Pioneers of the Polish Avant-Garde

MALEVICH IN POLAND   Tadeusz Peiper
Originally published as "Malewicz w Polsce," *Zwrotnica* no. 11 (1927)

In Russia Kazimir Malevich spent his most creative years; in Russia he found his first disciples. Russia was prepared to be his workshop, and it opened up to him its expanses of influences. Such ties bind an artist so tightly that he cannot free himself even with the greatest effort. For that reason Malevich, a Pole, is only passing through when he comes to Poland.

The name Malevich is not unknown in Poland. The Polish reader encountered it first in *Zwrotnica*, then in *Blok* and *Praesens*, where from the beginning it was associated with an extraordinary intellectual daring, a productive spirit of invention, a precision in grasping artistic problems, and a strong character that, with the utmost tenacity, guided an idea to the highest purity. This intellectual gift was decisive for his conception of art as an activity that remains untouched by utilitarian demands. When a certain group of artists in Russia wanted to allow art to rise in the sourdough of politics, Malevich carefully kept watch over its form.

His work is already impressive solely on the basis of its brilliant results. On his paths toward solutions Malevich was far ahead of the work of European avant-garde artists, and many of the movements that have flooded over young Europe under a variety of names can be traced back to the Suprematism he founded.

Polish artists are overcome with melancholy at the thought that the Pole Malevich is not here working at their side. After all, our artistic life is not exactly rich with artists of his caliber; his collaboration could give new impetus to Polish art and could provide valuable support. We miss Malevich. Our comrades in Warsaw should do everything they can to create at least comparable working conditions to those Russia has offered him. How happy we would be to greet him today with a chorus of joyful cries, but we cannot. The sadness that our countryman comes to us only as a guest stifles our voices! Malevich should not just visit us! Malevich should not just visit us!

Translated by Steven Lindberg

FUNERAL OF SUPREMATISM   Mieczysław Szczuka
Originally published as "Pozgonne suprematyzmu," *Dźwignia*, no. 2–3 (1927)

The retrospective of Kazimir Malevich in the Polish Art Club (end of March and beginning of April), its character and trends remind me vividly of the first steps of modernism in Poland which also made its debut in the Art Club. Personally, I feel very close to the period (1919–24), it was the period of the formation of Polish modernism, its emergence. Later, others (besides its artists) undertook to further the movement giving it different forms.

At that time "Formism" was breaking down. Leon Chwistek was leaving the scene, Tytus Czyżewski was falling into folk primitivism—only the most talented of the Formists, Kamil Witkowski stood by his principles, which he still develops today.

At the time the group of the youngest artists brought to an extreme some of the problems of form in plastic art which had existed in Formism and put forward, independently, slogans so far completely new to Polish art. In 1924 Teresa Żarnower took the initiative to unite the artists in the Blok group. (March 1924—the first exhibition of the group and the first issue of programmatic periodical of the same name.)

It is now 1927. The Blok group has split—there are different aims and tasks ahead of us.

But for our small group from the period before Blok—that did not at that time know Western or Eastern European Suprematism and Constructivism, movements that we were discovering for ourselves independently of outside influences—for us the retrospective exhibition of Malevich echoes and reminds us our own search and strivings from 1919–24.

Malevich's exhibition is a few years too late for our country.

Kazimir Malevich is the founder of Eastern European Suprematism. Malevich was the first to confront the problem of flatness in painting (in consequence of technical possibilities of painterly materials).

Suprematism is the second step (after Cubism) towards creating painting for the sake of painting—painting as a thing in itself—"organically different from its environment." Put forward like that, the issue of painting (agreeing with the slogan "art for art's sake") led to the attempt to change realistic museum painting into abstract museum painting.

Kasimir Malevich expresses this attempt.

"Suprematism finally breaks away from the deformation of nature. Flatness. Abstractionism. Geometrism of forms resulting from geometrism of the canvass stretcher." (*Blok* no.1) In practice Suprematism did not realize all the above postulates.

Most of all it could not achieve (an unattainable objective)—a complete flatness. In Suprematist paintings, even those painted exclusively with one color (e.g. white), parts of the painting differ in texture, i.e. brushwork, since the rough surface of one part of the picture absorbs more light and looks gray, whereas the polished part next to it reflects the light and becomes brighter. The two surfaces differ in the degree of saturation with light and give an illusion of three-dimensionality.

Eastern European Suprematism (Malevich and others) does not contain the picture within its frames—the background, treated as a purely material pictorial means, bearing a complex of geometric forms in close relationship, extends beyond the frame. This mistake is avoided by Western Suprematism, standing on the borderline of Constructivism (Mondrian and others). A certain literary character resulting from juxtaposition of abstract shapes thrown onto unrelated background is another feature of Eastern European Suprematism.

Let us proceed to an evaluation of Malevich's works. Calling to mind the innovative values that he brings into historical perspective, we must state that Malevich is unable to compose the picture. The picture is a thing closed within itself—its boundaries are its frames—within these frames Malevich is unable to compose the surface of the picture: he creates a conflict between the background and an abstract composition thrown onto the background. This reflects on the whole the movement created by Malevich, that is Suprematism. Even in Malevich's pre-Suprematist paintings—the lack of composition skill is clear. The examples could be his two landscapes, a little in Cézanne's style. Both paintings are not contained in the frames, which are something accidental, whereas the boundary that the painting surface should delimit is outright false. Each of these paintings could be added on, it would even do them some good. Malevich's paintings from his early Cubist period are as such—poor. They are a conglomerate of elements loosely connected with each other, and placed within the frames.

Early Cubism built the picture with plane elements—starting from the frame to the center of the surface.

All Malevich understood of this period from the whole process was a superficial linear graphics of Cubism; the essence of Cubism had escaped him, he was satisfied with impressions of Cubist works. (Evidence is the picture he painted under the influence of Picasso's famous Speaker and impressions of the paintings of the Futurist, Severini).

The characteristic feature of Malevich's psychology is an abhorrence of the word "construction," applied to works of art. He is a Romantic who loves painterly means for their own sake. Malevich visualizes his artistic emotions as abstract shapes (somewhat neglected in their form). Not knowing how to create the pictorial whole—he looks around for help. He finds in the literary sensation and muddled metaphysics the material with which to model his pictures— insufficiently connected by their purely formal plastic foundations. His followers made a better Suprematism.

The contribution of Suprematism was to bring certain new plastic possibilities to art and then to end.

Besides paintings Malevich exhibited graphic diagrams—an attempt at a theoretical look at the problem of form in painting—and, on March 25 he gave a talk in which he spoke about himself and his views on art. Malevich strongly opposed a "utilitarian" treatment of art. "Art for art's sake," served by the artist-priest, life barred from demanding anything from art or the artist. Expositions of this kind (convenient for artists because they justified their passivity and laziness for social commitment) have to be quickly passed over. In exchange, I would like to turn Mr. Malevich's attention to, let us say, mistakes that crept into his diagrams.

The first—photomontage—representing elements of Futurist paintings—fails to give any idea of the principles of Futurist pictorial construction. It relies on reproducing a multitude of sensations received from phenomena which surround and penetrate us in space and within (a shorter of longer) time span. From this multitude of phenomena the Futurist attempted to render in painting a simultaneity of phenomena using pictorial means—combining the most contradictory elements (sometimes impossible to express with pictorial means).

Instead, Malevich showed us a couple of photographs laid alongside one another— representing machines, balloons, dance halls etc.

The second mistake—Léger's color scale was wrongly represented etc., etc.

Mystical and theological speculations in which Malevich attempted to contain his conception of art also had a bad effect on his presentation of the problems of artistic technique.

Diagrams included on the pages that follow illustrate our attitude to the kind of art practiced by Mr. Malevich and other artists like him.

Translated by Wanda Kemp-Welch

ART AND REALITY   Mieczysław Szczuka
Originally published as "Sztuka a rzeczywistość," *Dźwignia* no. 4 (1927)

A characteristic feature of evolution that has occurred in the sphere of art in the period of modern capitalism, is the far reaching separation of the activist i.e. the artist from everyday life. This separation is particularly pronounced in the plastic arts. Before we go on to explain the reasons for this separation, it will be necessary to mention the methods and working conditions of artists in past times.

The artist in previous centuries, adapted to an economic system based on small-scale production, remained in a certain harmony with it. The boundaries of artistry were, as is well known, broader than they are today. In some sense, nearly every craftsman producing functional objects, whether a joiner, an ironworker, a carpenter, or a goldsmith was an artist. Having plenty of time, he decorated the objects he was producing with relatively primitive tools, according to certain established canons which were not too far-reaching; neither did they change abruptly—often surviving several generations. Nonetheless, he was left with some initiative within the framework of this canon, allowed by his tools, materials and artistic sensibility.

These relations changed radically as small-scale craft production was replaced by capitalism with its boisterous tempo of development, rapid technological changes, unregulated market—and, above all, mass production in all spheres.[1]

The so-called plastic arts remain directly dependent on architecture which to the greatest extent combines utilitarian content with aesthetic aspect. It is architecture which is most adapted to the living conditions of those for whom it serves as shelter or workplace. Architecture is indicative of the state of their material "standard of life," the range of the demands and requirements of everyday life, culture, and class status.

The harmonious conformity of household utility objects (furniture, kitchen utensils etc.) with the form of the building itself, influences their external qualities (in the aesthetic sense). It is in this way that "style" (i.e. a system of the aesthetic combination of forms) is fashioned. Economically (and thus also culturally) privileged classes create their own architecture—(residential, government buildings, religious, office buildings etc.) where, thanks to the means at their disposal, they can develop the aesthetic aspect to the highest degree, along with comfort and practical function. The emergent style of the privileged class is imposed on the whole of society—regardless of whether other classes had the makings of their own styles (e.g. in our country so called folk art).

The tempo of the development of modern capitalism has not allowed for the accommodation, in the artistic sense, of the forms of the everyday objects produced (apartments, houses, furniture, textiles, plates, spoons etc.) to the new materials, the new technical means and the new living conditions. Every craftsman, since the times of prehistoric man, has attempted to give a beautiful form to the objects he has produced—and the client would choose an object which, apart from its practical aspect, would give him aesthetic pleasure. Also the producer [of mass manufactured goods] has grasped the significance of the aesthetic "bait" on the market. In order to procure this "bait" he employed the easiest, and most importantly, the cheapest method. He reached for models which could be put to use immediately. These models were provided by the past, along with modern "exotic" art, and sometimes our folk art. These sources are then fully exploited, "aesthetic" ornaments are stuck to an often fundamentally different content. The pseudo-classical and the pseudo-gothic are brought back to life, pseudo-Chinese and pseudo-folk styles are imitated, etc. In this way the public's taste is fashioned and the means of production adapted. The interior, beginning with the apartments of the barons of industry, bankers and the like, and ending with the apartment of the petty-bourgeois, is a store, in which a great many (depending on the degree of its owner's affluence) useless knickknacks are chaotically accumulated. Products for

---

1 Even a supposedly "independent" craftsman today is the slave of the perfected tool. It has come to such a point that e.g. making a piece of furniture of a rationally simple shape is more expensive than making this same piece of furniture in the curved shapes of the Secession. Factories producing tools for production adapted to a particular "taste," often make the most rational and modest forms impossible.

the working masses that are supplied are even worse and shoddier because cheaper, and, of course, there are less of them. "Art for the masses" is represented by the reproduction of a pastoral scene or a battle, with patriotic or religious content, intended for workers' dwellings or the premises visited by them.

The development of the plastic arts in the 19th century is undoubtedly influenced by the character of the class which everywhere came to power in this period. The European bourgeoisie has emerged from the so-called "third state," "from the people" as a new, politically and economically privileged, class. On its one side it had the "people," the petty-bourgeoisie and the proletariat, clamoring for its privileges, and on the other, the already formed privileged groups, the feudal lords, whom it was attempting to join—with success, after a short period of ferment and battle. However, it should be noted that as a matter of fact the great-bourgeoisie's battle with the feudalists was never a relentless one.

This social situation, this cowardly sneaking one's way into the ranks of the privileged, results in the great-bourgeoisie having a deeply parvenu attitude to art and life.[2] Typically parvenu is its fixation with all things past, with all kinds of "styles," with outdated fashions, its searching for beauty in that which is old, which has lost all utility value, and its feeling ashamed of those real, utilitarian values which it has brought in. Hence those aesthetic theories which separate beauty and utility—beautiful is only that which has no longer, or never had, any use (the cult of old ruins etc.). The division between that which is "beautiful" and that which is useful had never before reached such horrifying dimensions. On the one hand imitations of outdated styles, on the other hideous brick barracks, built with no regard for hygiene (dwellings, factory premises). The concern is not for the people but for the maximum profit for the owner: in building a factory, a covered enclosure is erected for machines, materials and goods produced— little thought is given to the people who are going to work there. In building dwellings, the elementary rules for creating at the very least bearable living conditions for residents are not taken into account. Tenement houses in which every cubic meter must bring profit, are becoming the main type of urban building. State institutions and office premises, wealthy people's houses, are built in a seemingly luxurious way since it pays off: it attracts the buyer, and ensures the grandeur. Luxury manifests itself especially in external trimmings: cornices, columns, friezes and the like, which cover the facades of buildings with their "stylish" assortment—and do not cost much. Rooms are better and more comfortable. Here and there can be found greenery and some thought is given to provide natural light.[3] All these appearances fall completely by the wayside in buildings in poorer districts, in rooms for servants' and caretakers' rooms, in basements and attics—where conditions are terrible.[4]

2   Sorel remarked on the antechamber/servant traits of French 18th century literature. But even after the French Revolution these symptoms return with characteristic force. The Homer of the bourgeoisie, Balzac, gives evidence in his novels, of an apparently strange, lackey's cult for the aristocracy, which radically diminishes the value of a great number of his works. Interesting symptoms of this can be seen in the philosophy of Comte etc.

3   Capitalism, in its own, well understood, interest shows manifestations of social altruism and concern for the cultural and living demands of the broadest masses. e.g. the new American law concerning the development of cities, in which one can see the first steps on the road to "the urbanization of the city," is explained as a desire to increase the revenue. This is because the apartments on the lower floors of today's skyscrapers, as a result of the complete darkness inside them (resulting from the disproportional narrowness of streets in relation to multi-storey buildings), did not provide revenues high enough to satisfy the capitalists' appetites. So it is not humanitarian considerations, but simply profit which dictates these moves which give the illusion of healthy, modern social tendencies in architecture.

4   Worker's towns—gardens and colonies developed rationally (in England, Austria, Germany, Holland and Belgium) come into existence under the pressure of the demands of the proletariat and ought to be treated as its concrete achievements.

The influence of these determinants: the characteristic traits of capitalism, the psychology of the ruling class, has been increased by the failure of artists to accommodate to higher expectations. The artist, stuck in the old methods of his "creative work," and particularly the artist with initiative, is too slow to keep up with the tempo of developments. He can also be too expensive. As we have noted above as far as architecture is concerned its "aesthetic" aspect remains at the service of speculative considerations. The artist has "pure art" for his consolation. All this cannot be comprised within the framework of "division of labor." The artist is moving increasingly further away from life, practicing "pure art," "art for art's sake."

There were other causes of this "cleansing" of art of earthly elements. The artist of the past worked, almost as a rule, for a known recipient: whether it were a town, an association, the church or a private individual. Later, this type of recipient is replaced. The artist now works for an unknown recipient—he sends his work out to the market, to an exhibition, to an art dealer. This unknown recipient, however, is still not completely anonymous: he must be a person sufficiently well-off to afford a work of art. This is the only point of orientation—besides this there rages the uncontrollable element of the market into which the artist is plunged just as every small-scale manufacturer of luxury goods is.

This market has been fairly receptive: the rapid increase of surplus production, at the expense of the working masses, created whole new categories of recipients, such as connoisseurs; it created the basis for the development of these hitherto unknown relationships. In the past, just as the artist knew the recipient, the recipient also knew the artist. This point of contact has now been broken. Just as the artist is faced with elemental and chaotic market, with a varying degree of self-confidence depending on his popularity, so the "consumer" is faced with the riddle of a completely unknown expression of "artistic creativity."

The artist, irrespective of the tools of his trade: whether poet, painter or sculptor, is now in the position of the high priest, in possession of mysterious powers,[5] to a far greater degree than ever before. His position, in relation to the aesthetically conscious mass of recipients, is somewhat similar to that of the alchemist in the Middle Ages. Part scholar, part charlatan, he separates himself off, with a sweeping and proud gesture, from those matters in which he cannot feel himself a "master" and high priest, matters which he cannot understand, such as the workings of the market. With the same gesture he separates himself from the "crowd."

Here are the roots of Individualism in art (individualism with a capital I, naturally). Various components manifest themselves here. Besides the reasons mentioned above, the desire to fence oneself off from one's competitor—the battle for one's own piece of the market and for one's own adulating recipients, listening and watching with rapt attention, also comes into play.

Let us also recall the phenomenon of the so called bohemia which in the 19th century, it would seem, was a permanent feature of all "broader" manifestations in art. This was a kind of school of life, a necessary preparation in order to become a "real" artist. Bohemia undoubtedly had a de-socializing effect in the preparation of "pure" artists.

City life undoubtedly created the conditions for just this sort of understanding of art, and contributed to the development of certain tendencies. The nostalgia for nature that is characteristic of the city-dweller and is a typical product of the urban environment (lack of healthy conditions, air, sun etc.) finds its expression in landscape painting, in the calm of "still lives," and in genre painting.

5   The medieval craftsman had the same position—"master" of a guild.

The middle classes, suffocating in the city, looked for the source of the force of "rebirth" in the primeval robustness of the "people" or in primitive peoples—hence [the interest in] popular art, the exotic and the primitive.

The rapid pulse of contemporary life, the sudden and profound changes in the formation of social forces on the one hand, and, on the other, the relative ease of propagating the achievements of artistic technique (unavoidably linked with [their] vulgarization)— all this has had effect on the speed and profundity of artistic breakthroughs. In a relatively short period of time a series of breakthroughs has occurred in art: Classicism, Romanticism, Naturalism, Impressionism. In the 20th century, these changes take on a positively merry-go-round pace.

This remains in close relation with technical progress. The need for portraits, landscapes, history and battle painting, illustration of current events etc. are satisfied by photography and film, which are unrivaled in terms of accuracy, speed, and cheapness, as compared to the work of the artist satisfying these needs in the past. The ground is being removed from under the artist's feet, and whole areas of work slip away from him. What remains is formal problems in which he becomes increasingly involved.

First Impressionism—the first movement to emerge in a "purely" bourgeois atmosphere—introduced to art the problem of the analysis of light. Later, comes the period of adulation of the machine. Instead of the expression of individual moods, of dubious value, or the content of the "soul," however poor, in individual artists—often immature, embittered, lacking in even the modest general knowledge—there comes a reaction: the admiration for the wonders of technology (though short-lived).[6]

Work on formal problems makes headway: plastic art liberates itself from the supremacy of naturalism, literary anecdote etc. A period of the collective search for forms ensues, the period of laboratory working methods, endeavoring to build a work of art for its own sake, not expressing anything, existing completely self-sufficiently.[7]

Easel painting has objectively become a luxury, and let us add, a commonplace luxury, imposed on the exhibition market, which has been bringing increasingly poor results. The exhibition, accessible only at certain specified times, has now been surpassed by magazine reproduction.

As we have already noted above, the artist had to, and did, make his existence dependent on the affluent classes, by whom he was variously treated, generally as a cultural luxury, fulfilling a not particularly necessary function, sometimes respected and sometimes outright laughable. Condemned to practice art for its own sake, pure art, the artist nonetheless lived and acted in "society" (meaning the materially and culturally well placed spheres). Hence the artist had, in his work, to give expression to the interests of his clientele. Naturally, this did not preclude the fact that the attitude of individuals to these issues might be different. But we are here concerned with artists as a social group.

6   We shall discuss ideological developments in the plastic arts and the legacy of the influence of bourgeois ideology on contemporary art, in articles devoted to film and advertisement, which best illustrate this ideology.
7   In the flood of formal propositions, problems of material played a decisive role. The artist considering the constructional properties of a material, the variety of surface qualities of a given material, depending on its treatment, the special properties of the material in reaction to light etc. became aware that the character of the object being created should be made dependent on the material being used. The problem of material (not treated fetishistically by the Cubists or the Suprematists) unearthed the problem of the functional qualities of the work of art, a problem which became the turning point for some modern artists.

Naturally, it is no accident that the breakthrough in the attitude of artists to social problems occurred parallel with the ideological and technical crisis in art. The same tendencies are expressed here as in other spheres of contemporary life. Progress in mechanization and technological development have rendered absurd and overturned the existing methods of the working of society and its organization. Technological development has exceeded the strength of the present framework of social organization, hence at every step the absurd contradictions in both ideology and in everyday practice. The modern artist, seemingly in isolation (considering his social position, which we have discussed above), without having clearly grasped these contradictions, has generally followed the path of formal investigation, the path of contributing new values to the achievements of previous generations. Having enough time (lack of practical application) he has been developing formal problems, seeing in them the sense of his labors. The path before him is actually a well beaten track: following the line of the least resistance, satisfying the tastes of people who do not have the time to think over the artistic problems, but have the material means to provide a living for the artist. This is not, naturally, the path for more ambitious, richly endowed, perhaps more conscientious natures. These people rebel, they break out of the established boundaries, and carry the assumptions of the formal experiment right through to the end, thus rendering absurd the fiction of "art for art's sake," "pure art." Disinterested (in the sense of lacking application) work on formal problems (Cubism, Futurism, Suprematism and others), the search for new materials, the awareness of new methods of production, the dependence of the character of the oeuvre on the material used (yes, for this, too, had once been a mystery), all these revealed the monstrous fiction contained in the slogans of "pure art."

The realization of the fact that 19th century art actually had no practical application in life, comes through in slogans—though rather undefined—put forward in the last dozen or so years by artists, such as "art out onto the streets," "art for all." These slogans, proclaimed in the so called new art, were easier to proclaim than to put into action. Consumer society, demoralized by existing practice, saw nothing more in it than an innocent desire for a "new thrill," and at most a reflection of a certain ferment pervading the intelligentsia. What is worse, and what stripped these slogans of their value, was that it was in just this way that a great many artists understood them. The scandals by which the Futurists showed off in the circles of snobbish consumers, testify to this. The nature of the conflict was hidden and was to remain misunderstood for a long time.

The lack of [the artist's] participation in the society contributed to this. The artist, the writer, the intellectual in general (having gone through the experience [with the market] of which we have already spoken), became accustomed to sending "pure art," "pure poetry," "pure thought" and generally only pure cultural goods, out into the uncertain market. But these cultural goods served only a limited number of recipients. This was all right as long as the hitherto existing relations remained unchanged. War and the resulting economic crisis devastated the lower and middle bourgeoisie, which had been the main recipient of the current artistic production (the great bourgeoisie, industrial magnates and landowners, generally bought for their collections the works of old, deceased artists of established reputation). The market became considerably narrower.

A new recipient has come to the fore—the proletariat, which, in time, would make its presence increasingly felt. But this recipient demanded a particular product—he did not want a "pure" product, he demanded utilitarian qualities. Disorientated by the hitherto reigning chaos, he did not define his demands sufficiently clearly, but was, nonetheless, orientated by instinct as to his needs. This instinctive orientation should be stressed. The formation of the modern proletarian consciousness is a unique process in history—its development is hard and complicated by different influences. In the political sphere, the strivings of the working class manifested themselves, as a matter of course, in the way we know, as a result of the urgent necessity of defending itself against the ruling classes. In the sphere of art, as well as in the spheres of many other cultural issues, there was no such urgent necessity. Hence the reigning chaos and absence of a program.

This happened not only because the immediate political struggle—in which almost the whole energy of the working class was absorbed—took precedence and will continue to do so for a long time. It is also necessary to take into account here, that the leading element of the working class grew up and was educated within the framework of bourgeois culture and therefore often considers the products of this culture as supreme phenomena, impossible to surpass. The sharp and deep-reaching criticism of a bourgeois politics and economy disappears, ceasing to be an adequate description of phenomena when applied to the realm of bourgeois culture, art and literature. In a word, revolutionary tendencies in politics are often linked with bourgeois tendencies in culture. Hence tendencies which might be defined as cultural-labeling expansion. This means efforts are made that any typically bourgeois product has a proletarian label applied to it, in the form of a few slogans, some vague call or tendency. Products, particularly of this sort, so long as they are made to order, combine intrinsic bourgeois overtones with shoddy execution. One can in all seriousness find, among proletarian activists, people, in whose minds proletarian is unavoidably linked to shoddiness.

These phenomena could, in a more flowery style, be described as the dirty froth of the oncoming proletarian wave. For this reason, in these matters, it is better to rely upon the instinct of the masses than the existing theories reasoned out in this spirit, which are inadequate because of the incurable bourgeois attitudes of their creators. The proletariat needs art, not as a stucco ornament for special occasions, but an art for everyday. There has to be an end to the division resulting from the bourgeoisie's parvenu shame—the division separating production from life and cultural matters and resulting in the deceptive fetishization of all manifestations of human activity, and horrible lies sticking to everything, beginning with the stock exchange, government institutions and parliamentary democracy, and ending with the most minute, day-to-day matters. This has to disappear as a typical lie of the capitalist world: "art for art's sake." It has to disappear not only in theory, for today hardly anyone would admit to lie, but also in practice.

The artist has begun to think. He has realized the emptiness of his position on social issues. The artist is breaking out of the confines of today's system, he desires and searches for practical goals, a practical application of his work. He does not want to be an empty "ornament" of society, he wishes to participate in the organization of life. The capitalist system will not, and cannot give him all this. Even there where it appears to offer a chance of such work, it turns out to be illusory. Even there where the egoism of individuals, subjecting millions to their will, seems to cede into the background, it always turns out to be a matter of cowardly compromise, the abandoning of some important stance in order to better defend the more remote. Only the new social system will make possible the full use of technological progress, the possibilities now smothered or used wrongly by today's lords of the world. It will facilitate the emergence of new conditions for the human activity which we call art.

Translated by Klara Kemp-Welch

chapter 12

PRAGUE

Karel Srp

The more Karel Teige's concept of Poetism became complex and reached into wider realms of life and art, the more it brought out a stronger counter-reaction. It came not only from critics outside the avant-garde, but from within its own ranks—from the people who had been closest to Teige throughout the 1920s.

Some of the leaders of Devětsil noted the inconsistency between the program and real artistic work. A year and a half after the publication of the "Poetism Manifesto," Štyrský published a harsh, though unspecific polemical reference, "The Generation's Corner," aimed at his own ranks. Teige took up the challenge personally, and initiated one of the most extensive generational discussions of the Czech scene in the 1920s and 1930s. The publication of "The Corner Generation" became an indicator of the coming dissolution of Devětsil. After its demise the tenth and final issue of the third volume of ReD was published (July 1931). Teige's "Poetism Manifesto" (see chapter 8) was the highlight of the 1920s: from 1929 many of the representatives of the avant-garde shifted their orientation toward Surrealism (Štyrský and Toyen, Nezval), and toward different generational groupings, which inspired the origin of many other magazines (for example, *Kvart*, *Rok*, *Levá fronta*, *Zvěrokruh*).

The complex political situation also had a marked effect on clarifying the personal position of various artists: the relationship of avant-garde artists to the Communist Party was reevaluated when many of them spontaneously joined it, although not all avant-garde artists were members (Teige, for example, never joined the Communist Party). The Communist Party went through a distinct crisis in 1929, as pro-Stalinist currents joined it. While this process was taking place on the left side of the political and artistic spectrum, the right wing of the bourgeois First Republic was strengthened, which was expressed through censorship of magazines and books (issues of *ReD* were also subject to confiscation). For these reasons Levá fronta established itself as an interdisciplinary group—partially linked to Devětsil—which was meant to provide a new platform for progressive-minded intellectuals.

Translated by Andrée Collier Záleská

INTRODUCTION TO THE FRONTA ALMANAC   Editors of *Fronta*
Originally published as "Předmluva ke sborníku Fronta," *Fronta* (April 1927)

At a time when political and cultural reaction gains ground; when notions of what is new, good, and modern are opportunistically confused; when our country does not have an uncompromising modern magazine, we are publishing *Fronta* to fill a gap created since the collective manifestations of the young generation two years ago. We are drawing a line where today lies the real front of conquest, development and creation. We do not want to popularize, but rather introduce readers into actual work.

Creative work is full of uncertainty, with ideas for and against making themselves heard. Not wanting to lose any of the vigor of today's creative processes, we did not make a manifesto, but rather placed the ideas of many alongside each other, with all their contradictions. For often the mere finding of a fact is important enough, and polemics sometimes serve to support the view it wants to counter. The key is the readers' opinion—and we publish *Fronta* for people who think.

We live at a historical turning point; where is the ground going to break under our feet? Are we going to remain in the new world or are we going to die with the old? It's necessary to look back—

We are convinced:

In front of us is the only possible society of the future: the socialist society. What will its culture be like?

Today, art does not represent a direct force in life, it is not capable of vital functionality. That is why we must remove all the direct purposes from it, cleanse art of nonfunctional elements and reduce it to the only function it can fulfill. That is one way forward: towards "pure," "abstract," absolute, elementary art. But there is the question: is art still justified? What is its place in life? We have included in *Fronta* all those who had something to say on these questions and wanted to say it, whether they covered the entire problem or just part of it, in our—or their—personal sense, theoretically or by means of creative work.

Where is the place of the "dialectical section" between art and life? Let *Fronta* discuss that. We return to life and its questions. In a new society, we would be unconditional civilizational optimists. Today, we are conditional ones.

Because above all, this is the question of questions, topical and sovereign. And only by answering it, will "culture" move forward.

Translated by Alexandra Büchler

THE GENERATION'S CORNER   Jindřich Štyrský
Originally published as "Koutek generace," *Odeon* no. 1 (1929)

Our generation has matured: it equates the moon with the electric bulb, love with sex and poetry with cash. It measures quality by success and conquers life by seeking favors. Many of its members have aged and grown feeble, and time has turned the once microscopic signs of intellectual poverty into large boils of intellectual destitution. Others have appeased their cowardice, elevating their own wretchedness to be able to pass for lowly layabouts with impunity. And now they enjoy their pieces of silver somewhere in a quiet corner. What is pathetic about their lives is that their real value is far lower than their reputation. Sometimes they still simulate movement the way shadows are reflected on the stagnant surface of a pond. Although they find the world very idyllic, together, they create something much more complex than one would assume, because the more mercenary they become, the more understanding they show for kitsch, or, even better, the more indulgent they become with themselves, the greater quantities of kitsch they produce. They distinguish themselves by their power of perception. A generation dreaming about a bathtub. Today, a true poet's place is nowhere else but on the pillory.

Our generation spoke a lot about adventures and eccentricities, yet one could hardly find a more docile herd than them. They thought that they have encompassed the whole world, but in reality they were unable to gauge their own depth. Their trajectory was from the beginning bound with the disappearance of others' joy, and that was something they enjoyed to the full. Each attempt to widen their horizons resulted in the sacrifice of a lamb. Many are already having their memorials erected by the nation, on which they are portrayed seated, their youth covered with patina.

It is certainly more useful to love illusions because they are possible to penetrate, than it is to believe illusions because we live in them. It seems that we shall be forever contemptuous of others' youth that meanders among departing and arriving groups only to walk quietly back against the general drift of development and progress thus keeping life in balance. Each generation should be driven out by the weapon it deserves. And it seems that our generation does not deserve a butcher's knife or a rapier, just a pinch of strychnine.

The man of today—or his abbreviation or mere suggestion—makes a mistake, because he wants to convince himself by action of the fragility of roses, the image of which he harbors in his subconscious which is in constant movement, imperceptible to the naked eye, and this is why no one can have a reliable idea about roses. Roses shall evoke horror. Even if a single machine were to do the work of thousands of human hands, it would still be crushed by man, simply because his hands will have nothing better to do.

The future of poetry does not lie in the ingenuity with which generations progress. No other generation had so much printed paper, more incense, parasites, clowns, and narcissi, luck and Elberfeld horses than ours, and yet no other generation had fewer poets. Its own ingenuity took revenge on it and every idiot born at a certain time considers himself to be its member.

It is necessary to put an end to the false notion of generations, so that those idiots who are getting ready to comfortably settle in it undisturbed, could, having finished throwing confetti, enjoy the pleasures of the mind, that is, enjoy their own invisibility. And so that those who prostitute themselves could blush for one last time.

Sitting on two chairs is as obscene as secretly wishing to lie in two graves.

Our generation is falling apart. Several poets still live in their own way. The earth is heavy for them and distance is light. Or the other way round.

Translated by Alexandra Büchler

The founding general meeting of the Left Front has agreed on the following program and manifesto:

The Left Front wants to unify and mobilize the cultural left: it wants to become the center of modern creation, creating new cultural conditions and collaborating to rebuild the world so that it achieves a new, rational socio-economic and civilizational equilibrium in a productive community of modern energies organized by a movement that will bring together intellectual workers from all areas of cultural activity who shall maintain contact and co-operate; at the same time, the Left Front wants to break down the narrow, isolating frameworks of professional specialization, in the conviction that only such work has general cultural value and can be seen as modern that has not become rigidly fixed in a narrow specialization, work that can, without losing any of its professional perfection, encompass the entire horizon of modern life, that is aware of its own connections with other cultural and social work, and that therefore has a revolutionary perspective.

Along with a concentration of left-wing intellectual and productive forces Left Front strives to achieve a consistent and direct connection between modern cultural work and its audiences: it wants its readers to become engaged, active collaborators, organizers and propagandists, politically and culturally aware supporters, and together with this modern, left-oriented audience it aims to stand up to the forces of cultural reaction.

Left Front is not an academic association; on the contrary, it wants to organize outstanding events. It does not intend to waste time on paper protests, and whenever it will see intervention as necessary, it will base its intervention on carefully worked-out, concrete counter-proposals. It will support freedom and promotion of scientific and artistic work on behalf of all new scientific, technical, social and aesthetic forms suited to modern man and to the modern spirit. Modern cultural work, today continually silenced and repressed, robbed of any opportunity for real realization, must try, by means of the organized and planned Left Front movement, to break through the blockade of conservatism that surrounds it, especially in our country. Left Front will promote works of modern spirit, introducing its audiences to modern views and directions in all areas, showing the results of collective cultural work to the widest groups, without using the old-fashioned, sentimental "educational" methods—rather it will use modern methods of promotion, clear information and visual demonstration. It will organize lecture series around the whole country, purposefully compiled travelling exhibitions (on the subjects of architecture, housing, painting and sculpture, books, social health, education, etc.), as well as discussion evenings, surveys, etc. Special committees will deal with essential and urgent questions and tasks collectively, and the activities of the Left Front will be international, based on international collaboration.

The Left Front wants to bring together in co-operative activity all those whose work is animated with the modern spirit and expresses the modern will: modern architects, writers, journalists, painters, sculptors, photographers, film-makers, theatre artists, typographers, publishers, lawyers, economists, historians, sociologists, philosophers, natural scientists, medical doctors, hygienists, psychologists, technicians, pedagogues, librarians, organizers, etc.

The basis on which the Left Front is being built is revolutionary: the Left Front is an organized and conscious resistance movement of intellectual productive forces against the ruling, disintegrating culture of liberalism, and takes a stand of resolute non-conformism against its traditions, outdated ideas, academies, esthetics and morals of a disorganized and decaying social system. The Left Front makes a demarcation line between modern creation in the sense of materialist worldview and the old, out-dated aesthetic and idealistic delusions. The Left Front derives its name from its position in the divided cultural world of today and from its social structure. The Left Front is an apolitical association, not connected to any political party, it is an alliance of an international community of intellectuals who want to collaborate effectively on the creation of modern culture and defend modern views and interests against conservatism and reaction.

Among the members of the Left Front we shall, for the time being, name the following: F.X. Šalda, Otakar Chlup, J.L. Fischer, Josef Sokol, Vladislav Vančura, Vítězslav Nezval, Iša Krejčí, Vilém Závada, František Halas, Jaroslav Seifert, Laco Novomeský, Toyen, Štyrský, Václavek, Dr. Ivan Sekanina, Clementis, Dr. Janda, Dr. M. Matoušek, and publishers Fromek and Prokop, and others.

The Left Front calls anyone who agrees with the position and program of its manifesto and who wants to actively take part in its work, to become a member. Applications are accepted by the editorial office of *ReD*.

For the near future, the Left Front is planning the following events: a lecture by F.X. Šalda on Rimbaud, discussion evenings on housing as an architectural and social question, and on the freedom of artistic and scientific expression and censorship, and a travelling exhibition on "minimum dwelling."

Translated by Alexandra Büchler

chapter 13

AMSTERDAM AND STUTTGART

Éva Forgács

Writer, historian, and anarchist Arthur Lehning was editor of the Amsterdam-based *internationale revue i-10*, which he published from 1927 through 1929. In 1926 he visited the Dessau Bauhaus in order to meet one of his future contributors and editor of the film and photography section, László Moholy-Nagy, who would eventually also provide the journal's graphic design. Published in several languages, *i-10* was a leftist, internationalist journal of politics and culture; contributors included the German critic and theorist Walter Benjamin and philosopher Ernst Bloch as well as various artists. Kandinsky, another future contributor whom Lehning met in Dessau, was intensely interested in this journal, which (as Lehning wrote in 1926) seemed to him to embody "what he had wanted ever since the Blaue Reiter: a synthetic journal that encompasses not only art, but the entirety of the intellectual and societal issues."

i-10 was the first international forum to bring the issues of film and photography into focus. In 1927 Moholy-Nagy, a pioneer of new media, launched a debate when he published Ernő Kállai's "Painting and Photography," written in response to Moholy's own "Photography Unparalleled." Kállai's provocative article argued that photography lacked *facture*, or material

texture, which he held as a special value in painting. Fascinated by the infinite possibilities of *Lichtgestaltung*, or designing by light, Moholy-Nagy held photography to be both technically and historically superior to painting. The debate reflected the multiplicity of approaches to the relationship between painting and photography and illumined the range of opinions that cast doubt on the notion of a consensus view within the avant-garde. As Kandinsky underscored, Kállai called attention to the emergence of the moving picture, which he saw as the truly dramatic innovation: "We stand on the watershed between a static culture that has lost all its social influence and a new, kinetic formulation of our own world view."

In addition to the answers that Moholy-Nagy published, we include one that he did not: that of Kasimir Malevich, who, with all his authority, was of a different opinion from Moholy.

Many of the most significant new directions in photography of the latter half of the 1920s in Germany, the Netherlands, Switzerland, the U.S., and the USSR were surveyed in Stuttgart in 1929 in Film und Foto, the first large-scale photography exhibition. Organized for the German Werkbund by Gustaf Stotz with advice from art historian Hans Hildebrandt, architect Bernhard Pankok, graphic designer Jan Tschichold, and Moholy-Nagy, the exhibition explored the relationship of photography to art, advertising, and journalism. It emphasized "new vision" photography over realistically-oriented works with social themes and was widely reviewed in both the trade and popular presses. Many reviewers saw a positive potential in this merger of art with the burgeoning mass media.

To date, all explanations of the means and ends of photography have been on the wrong track. Of all the plentiful topics available for consideration, the one chosen has invariably been that of the relationship between photography and art.

However, the fact of photography is not properly evaluated if it is classified either as a technique of notation of reality, or as an aid to scientific research, or as a means of capturing ephemeral events, or as the basis of reproduction processes, or as an "art." The photographic process is unparalleled by any earlier optical means of expression. It is also unparalleled in its results. In those cases where it relies on its own inherent potential, the infinitely subtle gradations of light and shade that shape the phenomenon of light into an almost immaterial-seeming radiance would in themselves be enough to create a new art of seeing, an art of optical effect.

But there is infinitely more to the photographic process than this.

The prime task of present-day photography is to find a suitable technique based on the inherent laws of the medium. A relatively precise language of photography needs first to be evolved before genuine talent can succeed in elevating it into an "art." the first precondition for this is: no reliance on traditional modes of representation! Photography has no need of that! No painting, past or present, is a match for the unique effects that photography makes possible. Why the "painterly" analogies? Why Rembrandt—or Picasso—imitations?

Without undue utopian enthusiasm, we can safely say that the immediate future will bring a major reevaluation of the objectives of photography. Exploration is already in progress, albeit often along separate lines:

a)   conscious exploitation of chiaroscuro relationships (quantity);

b)   light as active, dark as passive (quality);

c)   use of the textures and structures (facture) of different materials;

d)   reversals: positive-negative;

e)   unknown forms of representation;

f)   introduction of strong contrasts of form, position, direction, and motion.

The areas to be explored may be defined in terms of discrete elements within the photographic process:

1)   unfamiliar views obtained by tilting the camera and by directing it vertically up and down;

2)   experiments with a variety of lens systems: a technique that alters the proportions suggested by prior experience, and on occasion distorts them to the point of "unrecognizability" (concave and convex mirrors, shots of distorting mirrors, etc., were the first steps in this direction). This gives rise to the paradox of the mechanical imagination;

3)   encirclement of the object (a continuation of stereoscope images on a single plate);

4)   new kinds of camera designed to eliminate perspective;

5)   incorporation of the lessons of x-ray photography, as applied to penetration and absence of perspective;

6)   camera-less photographs taken by exposing the sensitive coating;

7)   true sensitivity to color.

One day, only the work that combines all frames of reference, the synthesis of all these elements, will be recognized as true photography.

The evolution of photography receives a powerful impulse from the culture of light that is so much cultivated in so many places today.

683

Amsterdam and Stuttgart

This is the century of light. Photography is the first form of the formal design of light, albeit in a transposed and—perhaps for that very reason—almost abstract form.

Film goes even farther in this direction—just as it can be said in general that photography culminates in film. In film, the exploration of a new optical dimension is carried to a higher power.

Shifting intensities and tempi of light. Variations of movement in space through light. Through light the whole mobile organism darkens and blazes out again. Release of the latent functional charge within our organism, our brain. Tangible light. Light motion. Light near and far. Penetrative and cumulative radiance: the strongest optical experiences available to man.

The groundwork done in still photography is indispensable to the evolution of cinema. A remarkable reciprocity: the master takes lessons from his apprentice. A reciprocal laboratory: photography as a field of experimentation for film, and film as a stimulus to photography.

Translated by David Britt

PAINTING AND PHOTOGRAPHY   Ernő Kállai

Originally published as "Malerei und Photographie," *internationale revue i-10* no. 5 (1927)

I am glad to publish Kállai's highly interesting article. I also find, however, that I do not agree with him in every respect. For this reason, and because the whole question of painting and photography is highly topical at the moment, I would like to open a debate in these pages.
—Moholy-Nagy

The reversion of painting to objective representation is often judged to be an imitation of nature and thus something that can be far more simply and perfectly done by photography. Even that committed theorist of Neue Sachlichkeit [New Objectivity], Franz Roh, warns Post-Expressionism against lapsing into the superficial imitation of objects and thus causing "its significance to shrink, and the whole of painting to be overrun by those magnificent machines" (i.e., photography and film) "that give us such superlative results in terms of imitation." In painting, says Roh, there is no place for the imitation of nature except as raw source material or as a subordinate part of the pictorial design.

Let us suppose for a moment that this is correct. Where are we to draw the line? Where does form cease to be representation and become design? How are we to classify Dürer's meticulous delineation of a lump of turf? Is Holbein's portrait of the merchant Georg Gisze an imitation, or is it rather a work of supreme artistic design? In painting in general, is there a precise stylistic distinction between the outward and the internalized apprehension of nature; or is this distinction independent of period or style and purely dependent on personal commitment—and quality? In a study by Leibl—so faithful to nature in subject and substance, so full of atmosphere—there is more soul and also more design than in a hundred slapdash hangers-on of Expressionism. The same can be said of a whole succession of the best paintings of Neue Sachlichkeit, which present slices of nature in purely perspectival terms, scrupulously avoiding any hint of deliberate composition. For all the sober exactitude with which they imitate the externals of nature, these paintings, too, are indubitably works of design. Their rigorously object-bound representational form is creatively brought to life by a newly awakened love for the intimate and ultimate minutiae of the real.

If the living impulse of painterly design can still, to this day, reside in an attitude of reverent wonder in the face of the humblest manifestations of nature, it follows that we cannot regard imitation and design as irreconcilable opposites. Nor will it do to confine the notion of imitation to the realm of photography, and that of design to painting. Especially since photography has its own way of producing an effect that is—like painting—both representational and formally designed. It needs only to find its master.

To our knowledge, some photographic representations—portraits, landscapes—owe their beauty to such subtle and delicate interventions in the mechanics and chemistry of their making that they demand to be assessed as works of formal design and craftsmanship on an elevated level of artistic culture. This applies, in particular, to the photograms made by such artists as Man Ray, Moholy-Nagy, and Spaemann-Straub, which make the move from submission to the motif to total non-objectivity; they look like ghostly emanations of light.

The difference painting and photography thus has nothing to do with the spurious alternative between "imitation" and "formal design." On both sides, there are representations of nature that have been creatively brought to life—i.e., designed—and other formal designs divorced from any objective reference. Nor is the crucial distinction that between manual and mechanical work. The painter has the option of carrying regularity of form to the borderline of purely mathematical regularity, and making his *facture* approximate to a high polish or to the luster of enamel. There are plenty of works of this kind (Mondrian, Malevich, Moholy-Nagy, Lissitzky, Buchheister et al.), which, despite their creators' mechanistic posturing and theoretical denunciations of painting as an art, are nevertheless painting of outstanding quality. And we have already referred to the wide scope for manual craftsmanship in photography.

These few considerations in themselves suffice to show that the ultimate distinction between painting and photography is not a matter of form. More important than any formal consideration is the material difference: the painter's materials on the one hand, and the photographer's light-sensitive plates, films, and papers on the other. In itself, this difference of substance is enough to distinguish even a perfect painted representation from a photograph of the same motif. This is a more fundamental distinction than that between a bourgeois genre painting on the one hand and a Picasso, or a rigorously intellectual Old Master composition, on the other. It continues to prevail, even where one side or the other attempts to equate painting and photography. Even the boldest efforts in this direction fail to bridge the gap defined by the essential difference between the materials used to create the form: instead, they lose all truth to material, and for that sole reason become stylistically false.

However smooth and polished the facture of a drawing or a painting may be, it nevertheless causes the design to be perceived not just as a union of related forms and colors—with or without spatial illusion—but also, and simultaneously, as a physical substance with a tension and consistency of its own. Old Master paintings elide all traces of the manual craftsmanship that went into their making; nevertheless, their facture is redolent of a material consummation: the sensuous delight of creating substantial objecthood. The same goes for many of the paintings of Neue Sachlichkeit. Not even the oleograph-like smoothness of some of these works can prevent the facture from conveying itself as a fully material, tangible vehicle of the pictorial image.

Photography is not capable of this degree of materiality and objecthood. It creates imitations of reality that can be dazzlingly clear and distinct; but the emotional substrate, defined in real and material terms, is exiguous, indeed almost insubstantial. It extends no farther than the faint breath that mists the photosensitive coating on the plate or film, and the enamel-like gloss or toned texture of the printing paper. At both stages in the process, negative and positive, there is no facture: no optically perceptible tension between the substance of the image and the image itself. Nature's face is reduced to a formula of minimal substance: a light-image. Whether or not the gradations of light in photography, which for the time being are restricted to light and shade, eventually expand to include color, is beside the point. Even a color photograph can never be any-thing but a light-image of nature, neutral in terms of substance. It may match—or even excel—the immediacy of the effect of reality that painting can produce. But to bring that effect to life, to orchestrate it through facture, is beyond its powers.

The involvement of facture in all the effects produced by painting has momentous con-sequences for the specific essence of the art and its laws of pictorial design. The sub-tlest visual values of a composition crucially depend on the tactile values of the facture: that is, on the substance, quantity, plastic structure, and surface texture of the artist's application of material. This is why, in itself, the replacement of these tactile values by the texture of paper and photomechanical printing so detracts from the quality of reproductions, however closely they may approximate to their originals in optical terms.

In the first place, all facture is the residue of psychic impulses. The materials used may vary widely: mosaic or mural painting, thick or fluid paint, drawing on paper or on a printing plate. The facture may be subdued and evened out, as in the various forms of Sachlichkeit, or loose and fragmented, as in subjective and ego-based productions. Such disparities do not affect the underlying essence of all facture: that it is a palpable and organic embodiment, a living focus, of sensibility.

This quality of facture means that even the most elevated spiritual visions in painting are grounded in our substantial sense of reality: incorporated, so to speak, within our existence. Hence the great and exhilarating tension between the—at times—crude tactility of the materials used and the spiritual intention that they embody. In this ten-sion resides the specific creative power, the true beauty of all painting. By contrast, the absence of facture puts even the most exact photographic image of Nature beyond the reach of our substantial sense of reality. However tellingly the photograph may reproduce the appearance of the real, this appearance remains insubstantial and weightless, like a reflection in glass or water. A crucial distinction: painting is able to combine the crudest material means with the most refined spirituality of vision; the means employed by photography possess the utmost physical refinement, and it can nevertheless convey notions of the crudest realism.

The most sparing and pellucid application of color to the support—as in watercolor, for instance—is enough to demarcate and define the material reality of even the most audacious spatial illusions: that is, to localize them in material terms. The optical power of the image, fanning out into illusory depths of space, condenses in the facture into dense, literal foreground presence. Tight and loose factures have, in this respect, precisely the same effect: they liberate the illusion while simultaneously binding it into a web of real, material connections. It is these material connotations that make the paint surface of the image into something more than a window on an illusory world. However fine and smooth the facture, these connotations harden the image surface into a specific and literal dimension of tactile values, thus giving us—even in optical terms—a sense of that surface as a field of tension in its own right, brim-ming with life.

The force of this optical tension can of course vary quite considerably. In the first place, it depends on the tactile values of the facture. The more contrast of relief there is in a particular facture, and the more openly it reveals the creative excitement that went into its making, the more we strongly we perceive its inherent optical vitality within the work as a whole. This optical vitality of the paint surface also depends partly on the degree of illusory depth within the image. In painting, the visual center of gravity may be shifted away from the surface into an imaginary spatial depth. In reality, however, such effects of spatial illusion are anchored within the facture; and this suffices to make us aware—at least at some points—of the surface as the secret support of these illusory depths. At those points, a perceptible pictorial tension arises; the illusion stands out from the material substrate of its making. The more this tension extends across the whole image, the more inherent optical vitality there appears to be in the surface as such. This corresponds to the degree to which the limit of illusory depth in the image advances toward the viewer and thus approximates to the actual two dimensions of the surface. The closer this approximation, the more manifest the presence of the surface, with all its tensions—and the more it is transformed from a subordinate material configuration into the optical plane on which everything within the image exerts its effect. By contrast with illusionistic painting, which set out to conceal the very existence of a surface as far as possible, the aim pursued by all available (and disparate) means in painting today is to consolidate the literal, impermeable, foreground presence of that surface: to fit it as perfectly as possible into the framework of its two dimensions. This restricts, but it does not flatten: it makes for the utmost concentration of meaning and increase of tension. It can be achieved only by gathering all the forces within the painting onto a single plane of from that is not merely optical appearance but tangible substance. Only the materiality and consequent plastic quality of facture can maximize the tension and contrast between the delimited inner field of the painting and its real-world setting. The optical force of resistance that the surface of an image can exert against the creation of illusionistic depth and against flattening extensions ultimately depends on the degree to which that surface is reinforced—concreted, as it were—by its facture. This immediately becomes evident as soon as one begins to draw comparisons between paintings and stylistically similar photographs.

Some photographs seek to confer a two-dimensional structure on their pictorial space. They narrow down the natural vision, working with interlaced diagonals that collide with the edges of the image, or with parallel lines that extend straight across the visual field to echo the vertical or horizontal edges of the image. But, the more strenuous the effort to construct the composition in flat layers and bring it into a structural relationship with the picture plane, the more we realize that all this is in vain, because photography has no facture in to create such stratified relationships. The faint breath of the photosensitive coating and the texture of the paper offer no resistance to the image structure; they give it no purchase. The plane of photographic design is an immaculate, permeable mirror surface, in which all formations and tonal gradations can appear without encountering resistance, only to lose all firm relationship with the picture surface by virtue of that very lack of resistance. Such is the absolute optical neutrality of the constituent photographic materials that even an extreme photographic close-up appears to extend indefinitely into depth behind the surface. Invariably, between the immediate photographic foreground and the surface of the image, there intervenes the impalpable (matte or glossy) apparition of an intervening space full of air. The surface itself affords no place for a photographic gestalt. Optical union with this surface is possible only at the cost of a total blurring and dissolution of form. The photographic image surface has just one application: as an unresisting medium through which to look at spatial emanations of light. By the very nature of its material, there can be no consistency or tension in its optical appearance. This is why all attempts to make that appearance seem to hold its image content in tension are so empty and ineffectual. They are in conflict with the formal potential of the material, and thus stylistically wrong.

After which, it goes without saying that, since a photographic image cannot be structurally connected to the surface of its support, there can be no structural design in a photograph. Of course, photography—cinematography apart—is just as immobile as painting. But that immobility cannot be tautened and expressively emphasized through an interactive system of tensions. In painting structural tensions, like all the other tensions within the image, are validated by the material bonding and hardening conferred by facture. This facture imbues the image—even an entirely naturalistic image—with a material presence that gives special weight and lasting optical balance to its illusory world. By comparison with such naturalistic images in painting, all photographic compositions appear to hang passively in space, with no tension, however rich they may be in structural connections and interconnections of form. A Baroque ceiling painting, or a free-floating construction painted by Lissitzky or Moholy-Nagy, will always exist within the realm of gravitational forces and counterforces; in an earthbound photographic landscape, by contrast, the optical balance reflects not the tensions of an encounter between opposites—not a conflict—but a foregone conclusion. And this is solely because of the lack of facture, the lack of literal, material articulation and weighting of form.

The extent of the possibilities of facture has recently been illustrated in Cubism and kindred phenomena. Picasso, Braque, and Willi Baumeister, among others, take the greatest pains with their facture, making it into a composition of the most diverse tactile values (rough and smooth, sealed and porous, projecting, and receding) and indeed into a structure composed of the most disparate materials (oil, paper, graphite, plaster, etc.) This articulation through facture serves to emphasize the component areas, already defined by color and form, which are layered to form the image as a whole. The Russians Tatlin, Pevsner, Rozanova, and Altman, among others, turn facture almost into an end in itself. They aim to make the image resonate to the full in terms of its literal, material consistency; and to this facturel realism they subordinate all other effects. The resulting works, though uniform and monochrome, are full of vitality. Effects emerge that could never be achieved in photography, with its total absence of facture.

There have been attempts to give photography the livelier look of a facture by the use of grainy paper and ingenious printing methods, and in particular to make it resemble the painting of Rembrandt and of the Impressionists. But such subterfuges only make the void behind the sham even more obvious. A more successful expedient has been to assemble photographic fragments into compositions (Heartfield, Grosz, Hausmann, Moholy-Nagy, Hanna Höch, Citroën, among others). Some powerful effects have been achieved with this technique, especially along Futurist and Dadaist lines. These photographic collages undoubtedly achieve a high degree of surface and structural tension. But, even here, there is a residue of contradiction between the photographic nullity of the fragmentary component surfaces and the overall effect achieved through a literal, material articulation that consists of a surface layer of cut and pasted photographs. Such photomontages are a hybrid between painting and photography.

The attainment of physical objecthood through facture; the visual and tactile values of that facture; the surface tension created by facture; and the expressive value of virtual physical forces: all are beyond the reach of photography. In all of these respects, painting has nothing to fear from photography, irrespective of the degree to which the painting is either composed or confined to the imitation of nature. The only danger here is for photography itself, whenever it attempts to imitate pictorial effects that are exclusive to painting.

The defining limit represented by facture also imposes certain limitations on painting. There are limits beyond which the illusory representation of translucent layers of color, uninterrupted vistas of pictorial depth, and freedom from gravity deprives painting of all the tension created by materiality: the facture remains present, but the demateri-alization of visual values deprives it of its conclusive effect. Constructivists, in their effort to transform painting into the expression of a purely technological, rational, dynamic state of mind and spirit, have sometimes overstepped the material-defined limits of their art. The attempt to eliminate material—and thus surface and structur-al—tensions from painting leads straight into the domain of photography. This kind of free-floating immateriality can be achieved only through light emanations, and specif-ically through the nonobjective light-forms of photography. And those forms manifestly point toward the transition to movement. They divest the visual image of its materiality, and in return for this loss of creative vitality they achieve the miraculous, vital plus of motion: the moving image of light, the film. This is where photography presents the greatest potential threat to painting. Painting or Film: such is the fateful question that confronts the optical creation of form in our time. This alternative defines the historic turning point in our mental existence. We stand on the watershed between a static culture that has lost all its social influence and a new, kinetic formulation of our own world-view: one that already has an unprecedented power to address a mass sensibility.

Translated by David Britt

DEBATE ON ERNŐ KÁLLAI'S ARTICLE "PAINTING AND PHOTOGRAPHY"
Willi Baumeister, et. al.
Originally published as "Diskussionsbeitrag zu Kállai's Artikel 'Malerei und Photographie,'" *internationale revue i-10* no. 6 (1927)

WILLI BAUMEISTER:
Rousseau painted a landscape that includes telegraph poles with white insulators. No painterly eye had previously found any use for such devices. He, however, was free of sentimentality, a realist, and more of a truth-lover than any of his fellow landscapists. His paintings even looked rather like photographs; and yet at the same time they were more abstract.
Quantitatively speaking, his work contained a great deal of naturalism and very little abstraction; qualitatively, however, the abstraction was highly intense. Meanwhile, the painters of the movement known as Synthetism were moving toward abstraction. They eschewed the imitation of Nature and proclaimed the autonomous truth of form, of the artist's means, and of his materials. Photography-as-formal-design and Neo-Naturalism are both attempts to achieve the same combination as Rousseau, with a large quantitative element of Naturalism and a small but intense element of Abstraction. Of the two, it is photography that succeeds in this. So-called Sachlichkeit does not achieve the proportions indicated. The productions of Sachlichkeit remain vague con-figurations. Their literary and sociopolitical value remains acknowledged.

ADOLF BEHNE:
Kállai compares a landscape by Courbet with a landscape photograph picked at ran-dom, and finds—quite correctly—that there is a difference. He defines that difference as follows: the landscape by Courbet has a facture, and the photograph has none. He then generalizes this (in itself disputable) assertion as follows: painting and photography differ essentially and by definition in that one possesses facture and

the other does not. This leads him to the conclusion that Constructivist painting, which lays very little emphasis on facture (not really true, by the way), is in danger of turning into photography—an accusation that has hitherto been leveled only at crass Naturalists.

Kállai has his methodology wrong. The Courbet landscape has not only facture but also a frame; that is to say, it is also—crucially—the organization of a two-dimensional surface. The randomly chosen landscape photograph is not. (Where it exhibits traces of organization, these stem from the same source as Courbet's organization, and thus have nothing to do with photography as such.) If Kállai wants to take a Courbet (manual facture plus organization) as one term of his comparison, his other term ought to be a work that is mechanical facture plus organization. (For photography does have a facture; it is just that this is technical rather than handcrafted, just as a machine-made metal beaker has a facture that bears no traces of the individual craftsman's hand). Kállai himself discusses one approximation to "mechanical facture plus order," namely photomontage; and here he is obliged to admit that it contains "a residue of contradiction." (The presence of such a residue seems entirely understandable, since photography is still working toward an organizational law of its own.)

If Kállai intends to disregard the element of organization in photography, he must do the same in painting in order to draw a viable comparison. In which case, he ought to formulate the antithesis as follows: brushwork facture on one side, light facture on the other. If he did so, he might come to different conclusions.

The most striking feature of Kállai's article is his enthusiasm for individual craftsmanship with the brush. An enthusiasm that impels him to elevate facture to the status of an end in itself. Kállai points to Leibl, whose wondrous craftsmanship is indeed a delight to observe. But what is it that makes a good facture? The less virtuosity there is in it—the less it becomes an end in itself—and the more it serves the needs of the whole, the better. What Leibl thought of his own facture may be seen from the fact that he cut up many of his most technically perfect paintings as soon as he realized that the beauty of the facture had made him lose sight of the whole, the image.

Logically, Kállai's inflated conception of the importance of facture leads to the following conclusions: a photograph of a Mondrian painting belongs together with an amateur photograph of Wannasee bathing beach, since both lack facture; the Mondrian itself belongs together with a photograph overpainted in oils by Arthur Fischer Studio, Berlin, since both possess facture.

MAX BURCHARTZ:

Thanks to the achievements of the exponents of "elementary formal design," the significance and the value of photo-technical representation have become widely known.

Today no defense of those techniques is any longer necessary. the attacks are falling silent. New attempts are made daily—with varying degrees of success—to exploit all the technical possibilities that exist in this area.

As elsewhere, the frequency with which these attempts are made will promote the ability to discern value and skill from slavish ineptitude.

The question whether photo-technical options are superior or inferior to "painting" is a false one, insofar as it implies a principled value judgment. It is impossible to judge the comparative values of a stove and a phonograph.

There are wide areas of formal design in which photography is superior to painting, but there are also some things that only painting can do.

The acquisition of a new and valuable means of formal design is a gain.

The salient achievement of the "elementary formal designers" has been to reassert the value of rational reflection as a requirement in all formal design; the danger, perhaps, is that if we eliminate one highly obvious defect by overemphasizing its opposite, this will lead to a new defect. The largely unconscious urge toward uninhibited expressive movement is suppressed, or even openly denounced. But a full life is impossible without it; it demands to be taken into account even in "elementary formal design."

The advocacy of "facture" is a reflection of the crisis generated by the absence of this aspect of formal design work. as a closer study of photographic technique and facture reveals, it is photographic processes that reveal to us the ultimate and subtlest refinements of facture. Look at microphotographs of, say, handwriting samples: it is here that new areas lie open for elementary formal design.

WILL GROHMANN:

If the means of communication employed in the making of an artwork are irrelevant, and only the outcome counts, it follows that, however different their respective starting and finishing points, there remains a small area of overlap in which art and photography are one and the same. This does not mean, of course, that creative and reproductive art are identical, especially as the area of photography in question—the photogram— is ultimately no more than the end product of a prior process of creative formal design. Its artistic effect depends on composition, differential exposures, and an intuitive use of chance as a substitute for the values of facture. So-called artistic photography rules itself out of the debate, since the most it can do, with the exercise of the utmost ingenuity, is to emulate the subjectively tinged representation achieved by the free use of hand and eye. (Impressionist landscape and portrait photographs.) Clearly, this can on occasion be worth more than certain academic formulations; equally clearly, by descending to this level we are moving away from the fundamental issue and entering the realm of taste and fashion.

For the artistic public at large, the demand for representational imagery is amply satisfied by photographs that emulate works of art; reproductions make up 80 per cent of the art that it lives with, and it has no feeling for facture values. For that public, it is as natural to equate painting with photography as to equate art with Nature; inundated with photographs, it tends more and more to verify art by comparison with optical reproductive technology, thus moving farther and farther away from art itself. It will judge the photogram to be just as arbitrary as abstract art; and so the future prospects of painting and photography will lie in the hands of the minority who can recognize freedom of formal design in whatever disguise, and who can see the representational image for what it is: technology.

WASSILY KANDINSKY:

In issues of "Painting and Photography," much remains unclear—understandably so, given the newness and unfamiliarity of the issues themselves. Only the vastly accelerated tempo of our age could have made issues of this kind—"Painting or Film?" is another—possible and debatable. In the brief space available to me, I would like to approach this extremely complex issue from a single viewpoint: the viewpoint on which Mr. Kállai concentrates.

Mr. Kállai asserts: "We stand on the watershed between a static culture that has lost all its social influence and a new, kinetic formulation of our own world-view." To this it may surely be said that the kinetic force of, for instance, an "easel painting" does not reside in the immobility of that painting, on the wall or elsewhere, but in its "emanation" over a period of time: how it affects a human being, the "experience" of it in time. Today, what really concerns us above all is the theoretical question of how to assess this time element within a painting. The distinction between painting (or, to be more precise, "easel painting") and film, as posited by Mr. Kállai, requires to be understood in strictly relative terms: in essence, the use of "time" in both is the same.

I cannot resist adding another observation. Today, more than ever, the distraught gaze of "Westerners" is often (perhaps too often) turned towards the "East." Not infrequently, they look in that direction in the hope of finding "salvation." In my opinion, we who live in "Western" countries would do well to take to heart one typical characteristic of the "East": the capacity for concentration, which is connected first and foremost with forces in stasis.

Just so long as we pose our questions exclusively in terms of "either/or," we shall not escape from the psychology of yesterday. What gain is there for humankind, in which we all take such an interest nowadays, if it divides itself into two groups, "static" and "kinetic," who refuse to have anything to do with each other?

Please do not come to me with the answer that the stagecoach was superseded by the express train, and that the express train will soon be superseded by the airplane. In every illustrated magazine—and also, not infrequently, on the streets—we see people on foot. These people do not walk everywhere. Sometimes they go by train. It all depends. It depends on the purpose, and the means of locomotion appropriate to that purpose.

I consider one-sidedness of all kinds to be dangerous. And a consistent policy of hopping on one leg will inevitably cripple the other leg.

Nature, however, takes good care of man, and has provided him with two eyes, so that his view can be not only shallow but also deep.

LAJOS KASSÁK:

If we desire to pursue the affinities and disparities between painting and photography beyond the level of technique and outward appearance, we must attend to the true essences of both phenomena. Once we accept that painting is the supreme achievement and distinctive expression of human cultural evolution, and that photography, born of the new age of industrial civilization, is primarily a technical achievement and a strictly material process—and the distinction between painting and photography is plain; it becomes pointless to praise one at the expense of the other. Painting is the art of the cultured individual. From a certain point onward, photography too can be a productive representation, but its claim to exactitude and objectivity means that it can never become an art in the classic sense of that term. This fundamental principle means that no valid conclusion can be drawn from a comparison between the two. The two phenomena have only one thing in common: both derive from, and are an objectivization of, the sense of sight. But the one dies where the life of the other begins. The perfection of the one is defined by the precise and skillful human creative faculty; that of the other by the evolution of technology. The painter paints what he sees, and the photographer fixes what his camera sees. When painting seeks to give an exact image of a thing, it ceases to be art; whereas the perfection of photography consists in providing an exact mirror image of the things photographed. It follows that, as an illustrative art, painting falls far short of the precision obtainable with photography. Looking at a portrait by Holbein or Picasso, we see at once that the painters' individual subjectivity has composed or discomposed the given subject; with a photograph no such variations can exist, unless as a result of a deliberate technical trick. The eye of the painter has subjective visual capacity; the lens of the camera is objective visual capacity. In our age, in which we pursue collectivity and constructive rigor, the camera's objective vision and anti-psychological essence mean that photography is ranked more highly than painting: not only more highly than the naturalistic painting of the past but also more highly than the much-publicized new painting that goes by the name of Neue Sachlichkeit [New Objectvity]. I cannot here enter into a discussion of the basic fallacies of Neue

Sachlichkeit. But the fact is that, by comparison with the recording capacity of the camera, this is painting rejuvenated with monkey glands, which does nothing but make a great deal of trouble for individuals who might well have found a better use for their talents. Even if we look on painting not as something illustrative but as an absolute, we can see that the productive tendency within photography—pure formal creation with light, pursued not with an artistic intention but as objective representation—is in no way inferior.

I repeat: any direct comparison between painting and photography is inadmissible, both in technical and psychological terms.

Painting as art is the expression of culture; photography is a representative of [industrial] civilization. And, by contrast with absolute painting, the light-and-shade compositions of productive photography show, raised to a higher power, the precise purity and aesthetic magnificence of productive creation.

[From a German translation by Eman Fedja Freiberg of a Hungarian original.]

LÁSZLÓ MOHOLY-NAGY:

The nature of the productive process shows itself in the finished object. Its way of showing itself is what we call facture. it would be wrong to apply the name of facture only to the tangible outer surface, just because the manual techniques of the past mostly involved some form of tactile value.

It is precisely because for me facture is not the same as tactile value that the problem as defined in Ernő Kállai's article means nothing to me. i see it as a disguised attempt to rescue manual, representational painting.

Not that there is anything wrong with representation. it is a form of communication that reaches millions. Today optical representation can be achieved with unprecedented accuracy by photography and film. Manual processes cannot compare with these techniques. Not even—indeed least of all—by virtue of their facture values. For, as soon as facture becomes an end in itself, it is ornament.

This is not to say that the contemporary form of abstract—that is, nonrepresentational—painting sets a binding precedent for all times to come. For the time being, it remains much less than that: an intensive quest for the biologically based elements of an optical expression that will mirror us more plainly and more honestly than an oft-regurgitated expressive form.

Likewise photography: this too must be applied—and this is still only an aspiration—in its primal truth. The fanatical zeal with which people in every section of society are taking photographs indicates that in future the illiterate will be the person who lacks expertise in photography. in time to come, photography will be a school subject, as the ABCs and the multiplication tables now are. All the wishes of today's photographic gourmets will be taken for granted, if not carried out automatically.

Furthermore—all prejudices aside—photography justifies its existence as something more than a reproductive technique; it has already led to productive achievements. In its resources of light and shade, it teaches us refinement in our use of means. Through a chemical process, the subtlest gradations of tone appear within a homogeneous layer. The coarse-grained pigment vanishes, and the result is light facture.

This black-and-white effect in the light-sensitive coating—even in the absence of representation (photograms)—has led to a wealth of excellent results. the same will inevitably happen in color. The achievements of the color chemists and the discoveries of the physicists—the use of polarization, interference phenomena, and subtractive mixtures of light—will supplant our medieval painting methods.

This does not mean that the manual activity of painting is to be condemned, wither now or in the future. Having "inspired" earlier ages, it may well serve as a pedagogic instrument for the development of inwardness. But there is no particular merit in recognizing or rediscovering a form of expression that derives from biological factors and is therefore a foregone conclusion. the personal evolution of an individual who gradually and creatively rediscovers forms of optical expression that existed in the past cannot become a compulsory activity for those who have evolved beyond that point, or indeed for people in general.[1]

The "fateful issue," in my opinion, is not "painting or film?" but the grasping of visual formal creativity from every angle that has a contemporary justification: in other words, photography and film, as well as abstract painting and the play of colored light.

The new generation, which has not so much to discard as we have—sentiment and tradition—will turn this issue, thus formulated, to its advantage.

PIET MONDRIAN:

Although I am largely in agreement with Mr. Kállai's interesting remarks on "painting and photography," it seems to me necessary to avoid losing sight of the fact that "the artist" and not "the medium" creates the work of art.

Certainly, the medium is of great importance, and is closely tied up with the plastic expression of a work; but it is the artist who decides on its essence: that the work is purely plastic and not imitative.

Nonetheless, it seems to me that the character of photography is imitative rather than plastic. Photography in the usual sense of the word is the appropriate medium for the reproduction of objective reality, and all art is creation.

But at present it is difficult to define the evolution of photography—such efforts have already been made in the realm of pure plastic creation that there is no limit to what we can expect of photography. It is perfectly possible that the technique of photography will change, as the technique of painting has changed; and the comparisons and observations made by Mr. Ernő Kállai may well help us to reach that change.

GEORG MUCHE:

The human eye is able to perceive 400 trillion variations between 400 and 800 trillion vibrations per second, as a phenomenon of light and color.

The photochemical material used in photography has a far wider range of response. This wider range can be communicated to the eye, but only if it is transposed into the range to which the eye is receptive. in this respect, the "magnificent machine" that is the camera cannot enrich our optical impressions. There is no getting away from the polarity of black and white or from the outer limits represented by red and violet. The superior functionality of the photographic process cannot be passed on to the eye.

But within these limitations the image instantaneously captured by the camera appears to the human observer as a phenomenon that he would never have known without the camera. Photography goes far beyond the manual reproductive techniques of drawing and painting, which are executed through the sense of touch. the presence of a highly efficient reproductive medium—the camera—heightens the effect and mechanizes the method. The division of the photosensitive surface into areas of light and dark is extraordinarily rich in the subtlest nuances. Either in a camera-less photogram or in a photograph, these wonderfully contrived transitions can give rise to effects that make the craft manipulations of painting and drawing appear clumsy.

---

1 The investigations and formulations of Heinrich Jacoby, who has announced his intention of contributing an article to *i-10* on "the common biological foundation of all formal designs," are of the greatest interest in this respect. I consider them to be one of the major intellectual achievements of our time. [Original note]

Painting is a primitive handicraft: true. But it encompasses and masters all of the material color/light phenomena that the eye is capable of perceiving. Additionally, the close association between the senses of sight and touch during the production process makes it possible to feel and spontaneously use the subjective phenomena that take place in the eye. The eye is the organ that generates the impression of light and color. The most sublimated values, which are those most important in the creation of a durably effective formal design—complementary and simultaneous contrasts—are captured by the primitive handicraft. To the camera they are undetectable.

Photography and painting thus differ in artistic value as widely as they do in method, instruments, and materials. Only the effect is similar, and this leads to controversy: "painting?—photography!" "Photography?—painting!"

Now for the essential:

As a reproductive technique, painting is inadequate by comparison with photography. The painted picture derives its justification solely from values that are artistic in nature. As a means to artistic form, painting remains as ideal as ever it was, because the relationship between intention and representation is so eminently "right" in terms of the proportionate interaction of sight and touch. The interposition of the camera and the elimination of the sense of touch remove this salutary tension, thus improving the mechanical effect and detracting from the subjective, creative idea. The blend of chance and intention, of automatic physicochemical processes and creative purpose, is no longer as it should be. The formula for creative achievement is no longer right. Additionally, both photograph and photogram presuppose the existence of an object that has in some way already been designed or shaped. The photograph and the photogram are secondary forms, involving a considerable surprise element. Enthusiasm for photography should not lead to an overestimate of the value of photographic effects. However, one thing makes photography especially valuable: the capability of an objective apprehension of nature. This magnificent achievement on the camera's part is of the utmost importance, particularly for scientific and technological research. in perception via the camera, subjectivity is eliminated. Photography, practiced in a deliberately non-artistic, precise, and illusion-free manner, is the true Neue Sachlichkeit in painting, Neue Sachlichkeit is a petit-bourgeois reaction against the courageous evolution that has taken place in painting from Impressionism to pure, abstract formal creation. In painting there can be no *Sachlichkeit*, no objective interpretation of nature, since this supposed objectivity is always the objectivity of the subjective.

Translated by David Britt

REPLY   Ernő Kállai
Originally published as "Antwort," *internationale revue i-10* (1927)

The statements in response to my article "Painting and Photography" are for the most part valuable contributions, entirely in keeping with the tendency of my own views. I can almost unreservedly subscribe to the views expressed by Willi Baumeister, Burchartz, Grohmann, Kassák, Mondrian, and Georg Muche. The only comment that I would make to Burchartz and Kassák is this: it was never my intention to engage in a comparative evaluation of painting and photography. I am well aware of the full-fledged artistic potential of photography. I say only that this potential differs in kind from that of painting.

My article is an attempt to trace the source of this manifest and essential difference between painting and photography. In so doing, I have deliberately avoided mentioning subjective elements or philosophical and psychological contexts. Not that I intend to deny the essential capacity of these contexts to determine form. It is clear from the outset that the very choice of material—pigment or light—springs from individual creative orientation (Moholy-Nagy!) But to discuss this prime psychological factor would have meant pursuing a broad and complex issue of intellectual history that ranges far beyond the limits of a single article. It was simplest to approach the problem from the other side, and to consider it in terms of works of formal design that were already in existence.

What is the difference between a form in painting, which has passed through the subjective formative process, and a photograph? Here, too, I took a case in which there was a maximum of formal similarity. What is the objective optical difference between a photograph of Nature and a painting of Nature, even where the latter attaches itself as closely as possible to objective appearances?

I concluded that this objective optical difference is, in the first place, a difference of facture, although course it can then be traced in many directions. I confess that in the effort to show the tactile element in painterly facture as a vital quality that photography does not possess, I neglected to enlarge upon the essence of photographic facture, as defined by light. In the process, I let slip a number of formulations that—if taken outside the context of the article as a whole—might have been interpreted as denying that photography possessed any facture at all. This of course would be nonsense. Even the sheer existence of a photograph—the fact that it has somehow been taken, produced, made—means that it possesses a facture. On its surface, it necessarily bears the signs of its making. What counts, however, is the specific nature of those signs: the difference between painterly and photographic facture.

Behne formulates this difference quite correctly: "brushwork facture on one side, light facture on the other." Essentially, this antithesis is what my whole article is about. It underlies my train of thought as a kind of latent blueprint, and the article is really an expansion of this same formula. It is true that I was somewhat one-sided in my development of this train of thought. I presented as positive only the defining qualities of painterly facture, and when it came to photographic facture I contented myself with establishing the qualities that it lacks. Even so, there remain plenty of passages in which stress is laid on the light-defined nature of photographic facture. At all events, one thing is clear: that painterly facture, being brushwork facture, is a tactile facture. I consider that this fact has decisive consequences for the visual definition of painting, its entirely specific ocular vitality. None of which applies where the ground of the image is essentially different: that is, in the photographic facture of light. It is not the material but the artist that "makes" the work: Mondrian's statement is entirely right and requires no further comment. But materials do have their living identities, and the artist's creative work consists in creating form from and not against the identity in question.

As for Behne's statement that facture is not an end in itself but simply a means of giving material substance to a vision: this is a truism, and it would not be easy to find anything to the contrary in my article. Equally, however, facture is not some neutral factor that takes the same form irrespective of the painting materials and the style employed. True enough, Leibl had his reasons for cutting up one or the other of his paintings even though—as always with him—it had a beautiful facture: i.e. it was beautifully crafted. But in such cases he had failed to achieve a coherent whole not because of the beauty of the facture but simply because his pictorial conception had been insufficiently clear and well considered.

"Facture plus organization equals image." Behne's formula is right, with the proviso that facture is not some chaotic raw material but is in itself organized material. How else could it prompt an organized notion of color and form? Facture organization plus color and form organization: this expansion of the equation, at least, is necessary in order to make Behne's formula hold good.

Behne points to a conclusion that, in his view, I ought to have drawn from my own supposedly inflated valuation of facture and manual craft. According to Behne, it would be logical to conclude from my remarks that a painting by Mondrian belongs to the same category as a kitsch photograph overpainted in oils, since both possess facture. Behne supposes that this is a reductio ad absurdum of an erroneous statement in my article. On close inspection the apparently paradoxical pairing of Mondrian with a kitsch overpainting turns out to be a statement of the obvious: misapplied, perhaps, but in itself entirely truthful. Why should Mondrian and the kitsch overpainting not belong together? The connection would be nonsensical only in the absence of any discrimination between quality and trash. Behne supposes me to assert that Mondrian and the kitsch painter belong together because both possess facture, which is supposedly my principal criterion. Criterion or no criterion, this is beside the point. All images with a brushwork facture do indeed belong to painting, regardless of their merit or lack of it. The same goes for stylistic variations. What the most disparate stylistic epochs have in common—so that even artists as infinitely dissimilar Duccio and Kandinsky can both be described as painters—may be left on one side for the moment; but, here as in the former case, brushwork facture is basic to both. According to Behne, my excessive concentration on facture points to the conclusion that a photographic reproduction of a Mondrian and an amateur snapshot from Wannsee beach belong together, since both are lacking in facture. This thrust, too, misses its mark. Of course all photographs belong together, whatever they may show. All photographs are light images. All photographs have the common quality of light facture. That a photographic reproduction of a Mondrian differs in subject matter from a direct photograph of real life: this knotty proposition is, I fancy, outside the scope of our problem.

The inherent light facture of a reproduction must be distinguished from the painterly facture that has been illusionistically imitated by photographic means. If this illusion of the materiality of the object reproduced were to be accepted as facture, then photographic facture would of course be superior to all the tactile values of painting. But we are concerned not with the objective and literal ability of photographic light facture to mirror reality but with the distinction between the formal design possibilities of such facture and those of painterly facture.

The tactile values of painterly facture endow it with the capacity of exerting a material, expressive power of its own, which serves to multiply, as it were, all other pictorial factors, whether representational or nonobjective. These tactile values are the unifying physical factor that maximizes the surface tension of the painting. Above all, the tangible, literal deposit of material represents the process of creative realization in the form that is basic to painting. The light facture of photography cannot contribute to formal design in this sense. Its possibilities are of a different kind. It would be wrong to allow an emotional love of the manual craft of painting to lead us to ignore the artistic possibilities of photography. Any such "enthusiasm" is foreign to my nature.

Equally inappropriate, however, is the doctrinaire technomania that rejects hand craftsmanship, lock, stock, and barrel. Craftsmanship is a means: an aid to the creative confrontation between man and Nature, man and spirit. Photography cannot replace, let alone "progressively improve on," the specific creative possibilities of the manual craft of painting. At the same time, however, photography is well suited to become the medium that gives formal expression to a new emotional experience of the world, especially in the form of motion pictures. This was what I meant by my remarks on film at the end of my article. The spiritual and artistic potential of painting is not in question. Kandinsky's remarks on this subject suggest to me that he has misunderstood my article. I spoke of painting's lack of social influence and the enormous popularity of film. This significant and far-reaching difference in effect between the two art forms is of course obvious to any impartial observer. At the same time, the whole art of film is still in its infancy, and it is also virtually defenseless against the vilest commercial speculations.

By comparison with the categorical difference that separates light facture, with its various formal design possibilities—those of film above all—from painting, the contest between representational and abstract painting, so keenly fought by partisans on both sides, dwindles into insignificance. As long as painting remains formal design by means of brushwork facture or tactile facture, even its most extreme contrasts are no more than divergences, not differences of kind. From easel painting to mosaic and mural fresco, from the academic traditionalists to the exponents of Absolute Painting and Constructivism, all painters should form a common front. That which is truly, fundamentally new stands on the other side and bears the names of photography and film.

Translated by David Britt

LETTER TO LÁSZLÓ MOHOLY-NAGY   Kazimir Malevich
April 12, 1927

Dear Moholy-Nagy,

I have received your invitation to take part in a discussion about the article in *i10* and having learnt its contents, I see that it deals primarily with defending painting, but not with the juxtaposition of photography with the latter.

There is an interesting passage in this article concerning me, in which I am in some way found guilty of holding heretical views on painting, and consequently on Art, and on the transfer to the mechanical type of production of plastic phenomena. I hereby make haste to deny the misunderstandings that have crept in. I have never supported and approved the dead mechanical glazed photographic objective and have never written in my theory against painting, on the contrary, I have always upheld the painterly beginning as one of the elements of Art, as a complete plastic sensation of the painterly world, of course I insist on non-objective painting as such.

If the author feels that in my present works painting can be perceived, in other words an element of Art, this is proof that the sensations conveyed by Suprematist elements cannot be conveyed in any other way but through the prism of Art, which he understands as painting; but here I must mention that there is no painting in Suprematist elements, for under the name of painting I understand something else, i.e. the painting of Cézanne and the first stage of Cubism. The element of Suprematist planes is different, but we are not talking now about painting, but only about a method of Art, a spiritually organic means of conveying various sensations. And if it will be possible to convey the same sensations by the photographic method, then photography will become a similar technical medium such as the brush, the pencil, nothing more.

The question raised by the author of the article on photography and art would be meaningless at any other time, but it is obvious that the author has noticed at present a movement as though against painting, against Art. It is true that there cannot be smoke without fire; materialization, mechanization, "lithographization," "photographization," simplification—are being put forward mainly by the Constructivists, and this is truly

dangerous, inasmuch as the machine cannot express spiritual sensations, cannot be considered a good medium, when both brush and pencil are superlative to it in a technical
sense, for through them various sensations can flow in all their force.

For the upholders of photo-mechanization the printed square Suprematist plane (cf.
the journal *Merz*) is enough, but for me this is a dead element and whatever montages
may exist of photographed elements—as such they will be dead for Art; the contents
of Art embrace various non-objective sensations and through them I keep in complete
contact with the world.

With reference to texture: from my point of view it is irrelevant if observed in isolation,
for it is not an aim in itself, but can be viewed only in the light of "the spiritual excitation of the soul" as says the author of the article, I would add to this, that any excitation
of the soul is produced by some sensations and is the direct result of that and takes
on an appropriate texture.

Further on the author writes that "thanks to the specific texture painterly visions
of *lofty spirituality* fall immediately into the realm of the material concept of reality."
I should certainly argue this position, such a realm of material reality does not
exist for me, only sensations outside the reality of their own conceptual world exist
for me.

In this way, says the author, is created the intensity of inspiration; or, it is created
because there exists a discrepancy between the painterly means and ideological aims
with regard to their essential meaning and the means of their realization.

With the New Art this point of view has become obsolete, for New Art is non-ideological,
non-objective; today Art exists only as such, but intensity is not excluded, the intensity
that depends on various sensations.

Regarding the fact that the author thinks that "the more the surface of a picture abounds
in types of texture, the more obvious is the inspired formative course of the painterly
process," I doubt this very much, for the latter depends not on the number of different
textures, but only on the most economical juxtaposition of contrasting moments in the
latter.

Thus photography and cinema from my point of view are only technical new media,
which painters must utilize, as in the past they used and even now they use bristle
brushes, and graphite, and paint. They must become similar sensation-conductors
as the pencil, charcoal and the brush.

If you are interested in my letter and find an answer to your questions you may publish
the whole letter or some ideas I have noted down.

Translation from Krisztina Passuth, Moholy-Nagy

VANGUARD SKIRMISH IN STUTTGART   Andor Kraszna-Krausz
"Vorpostengefecht in Stuttgart," *Filmtechnik* vol. 5 (July 20, 1929)

The exhibition *Film and Photo* was held in Stuttgart from May 18 through July 2, 1929.
The official representatives of the motion picture industry took very little notice of it.
No doubt this was largely because they doubted from personal experience the practi-
cability of holding an exhibition of film. The fact that this exhibition was, furthermore,
organized in the so-called provinces, and by people who could be described as outsiders, was calculated to reinforce their skepticism....

Here lies the core of the avant-garde problem. (Marginal note: vanguards without armies.) This was plainly evident on this occasion. With the avant-garde, the lack of firm discipline brings lack of organization and disorganization. Casual ideas, which in the context of regular creative work might have contributed nuances, expand into fundamental issues of principle. Turns of phrase act as if they were themes in their own right. Forms are stretched out so far that they become transparently thin, and the void behind them shows through.

In itself this would do no harm. Studies are useful things, if used as a preparation for great works. But this has to be done tirelessly and systematically.... The tragedy of the avant-garde springs from its lack of system. Instead of skirmishing in advance of the main army, this vanguard is firing off its ammunition in guerrilla wars.

Translated by David Britt

PHOTOGRAPHY—THE PICTORIAL ART OF THE PRESENT DAY
Ludwig Neundörfer
Originally published as "Photographie—Die Bildkunst der Gegenwart" in *Kölnische Volkszeitung* (June 23, 1929)

The first representative showing of this kind of photography to come before the German public is the Stuttgart exhibition *Film and Photo* (May 18–July 7, 1929). The exhibition is organized by the German Werkbund, and this in itself places it a notch above the normal run of photographic exhibitions. The jury accepted only those photographs in which the camera is used as a new medium of formal design.... At the same time, it was intended to demonstrate the new fields of operation in which photography now works. This took place in a single room, for which Moholy-Nagy was responsible....

At the end, Moholy-Nagy draws attention to "the profound social responsibility of the photographer, who with the given, elemental materials of photography, carries out a task that could never be performed by other means: the task of providing an undistorted documentary record of contemporary reality. The criterion of value in photography must not reside in a photographic aesthetic but on the human and social intensity of the content that is optically expressed; this is the sole criterion of any productive work." Unfortunately, in the other rooms, the most interesting areas—reportage, scientific photography, and motion photography—are not included....

The majority of the images on show are objective representations of persons and objects. (Landscape is almost entirely absent.) They clearly show the specific formal design possibilities of the new photography....

The question remains: which way will photography now go? If it turns toward "Art," it will become one of the visual fine arts that are taught at art institutes and academies, and it will share the fate of the other arts.... If photography remains aware of its own true task, that of operating through reportage, advertising, and objective images—if photographers remain professionals, but with a strong formal design impulse—then perhaps photography may one day lead us back to a pictorial art that will be for the people as a whole.

Translated by David Britt

OPENING OF THE WERKBUND EXHIBITION FILM AND PHOTO
(Anonymous)
Originally published as "Eröffnung der Wekbundausstellung 'Film und Foto'"
in *Schwäbische Tagwacht* (May 18, 1929)

What sets *Film and Photo* apart from the ordinary and now fashionable run of photographic exhibitions is that it is the first to offer a systematic review of major achievements in these still comparatively new fields of visual activity. The exhibit blurs the
distinctions between what is customarily called "Art" and "Technology" and contributes
to the debate a new and—one may say without exaggeration—a still evolving definition
of art. Here before us are the beginnings of a new image of the world, based on a
new mode of seeing: an image of the world which is fundamentally distinct from the
painterly and impressionistic image, and which seeks to employ reproductive technology to capture the ambient world of matter and the coloring of nature.

Translated by David Britt

"FORM," PHOTO AND FILM   W. Riezler
Originally published as "'Form,' Foto und Film," *Die Form* (1929)

It was quite right to show some samples of the "feature film," since for the time being
this is the mainstay of public showings. And here something of a historical retrospect
is already possible: *The Cabinet of Dr. Caligari* already looks like a document from a past
age, which might be referred to as "classic," did it not retain so many primitive characteristics…. From this to the great Russian film *Ten Days that Shook the World* marks
another vast step. Here, the element of theatricality is almost entirely eliminated;
invented or composed action is replaced by history, presented with a claim to truth
and "reality," and affecting every receptive viewer accordingly, despite the admixture
of a tendentious "message."….
What was almost more important, and certainly newer, was the showing of what are
called "avant-garde films": the work of those who hope to develop film into an entirely
autonomous art form. This was fascinating and thought provoking in the extreme—
although one feels that the course of future evolution is far from clear. On the contrary,
paths lead off in all directions, and it is certain that some of them will lead nowhere….
It was a strange sensation to observe such disparate experiments in such rapid succession. One thing was surprising: even in this new "art," which seems to be so much
the product of modern "civilization," distinctions of nationality remained unexpectedly
clear.

Translated by David Britt

The second half of the 1920s posed important problems of national organization and internal development for Romania. In particular, this was a period of heightened nationalist turmoil, during which modernity and tradition emerged as two increasingly polarized alternatives. In what has been called "the Great Debate," Romanian intellectuals envisioned the nation's future either by posing the urbanized and industrialized West as a model or by rejecting the West, emphasizing instead Romania's agrarian character, its local values, and its Eastern spirit.

On an artistic level, this conflict translated into attempts to define the specificity of a Romanian avant-garde. The following texts, while never openly addressing the debate over national character, all indirectly address the problem of an indigenous modernism. Nenițescu and Vinea's texts, for instance, belong to the project of reconciliation between modernism and the expression of an innate Romanian artistic sensibility. Emblematic of the effort in those years to provide the avant-garde with a local history is the text from critic Ionel Jianu (later to be instrumental in claiming Brâncuși as a national figure), who wrote an idealized narration of the origins of the Romanian avant-garde.

From 1925 on, the Romanian artistic scene also began to split along generation lines. Increasingly, founding figures such as Vinea, Voronca and Janco distanced themselves from avant-garde activity. Vinea and Voronca sought to establish themselves as important national writers; Janco, who had studied architecture at the Eidgenössische Technische Hochschule while part of the Zurich Dada, was a prominent modernist architect from 1927 on. Janco's revived interest in Cubism in 1928, at a time when the art scene in Bucharest was more and more weary of Western importations, has to be read as a manifesto for an architecture that would integrate the lessons of modernist painting.

By 1930, at the time of Marinetti's visit to Romania, the younger avant-garde generation (comprised of such figures as Geo Bogza, Gherasim Luca, Paul Păun and the painter Jules Perahim) had largely rejected the older generation as representatives of an "official," compromised, and obsolete art. Bogza's writings and Perahim's artwork appeared in *Unu* (along with work from such contributors as Stephan Roll and B. Herold), a new avant-garde journal first published in 1928. Edited by poet and doctor Saşa Pană, it emerged at a time when the Constructivist journals were betraying signs of exhaustion. But while *Unu* included contributions from both these newer avant-garde artists, it still included some of the established avant-garde figures, such as M.H. Maxy, Victor Brauner, and Ilarie Voronca.

Although information concerning Surrealism had not been entirely absent from previous avant-garde journals, the movement had not, up to that point, figured prominently in Romanian literary or artistic practice. In the pages of *Unu*, however, a shift from the prevailing Constructivist program to Surrealism became evident. Elsewhere, justifying the new Surrealist orientation of Brauner's painting, Voronca argued that painters were threatened by two traps: one, the imitation of nature; the other, abstraction, a limitation imposed by architecture. Thus, while the revolutionary mission remained intact, the turn to Surrealism meant that artists had to investigate the unseen world of the imagination and dreams.

Originally published as "Răsfrângerea cubismului," *Cuvântul* vol. 4, no. 979
(January 8, 1928)

"Cubism" is a moniker thrown about by the press regarding a canvass exhibited by
Braque in Paris two thousand decades ago. This moniker turned into the struggle's
banner.

That is why the new art has only a symbolic relationship with this title: the cube.

Cubism represents the new human being's attempt to bring back clarity to the chaos
of thought and feeling.

Chased out of life itself, replaced in its social functions by the printing press
and photography, the plastic arts retain their function as plastic poetry, that is,
lyricism.

This is what it gained after a difficult discord with itself and with its enemy: the
academic ghost.

Public opinion, which does not follow the facts, is deadlocked and today is still perplexed
over the stages of evolution, which in every work of plastic art is nothing but an instant
in the motion towards the new ideal.

Cubism, for this moment of purification, had to pass from the simplification of form
to the recovery of its elements: line and color. Redeeming of craft through seeking
the specific of the plastic emotion and clearing away of dross left behind from its old
functions.

At first destructive, even chaotic, revolutionary (see Dada and Futurism), the
positive effort begins with the gigantic work of art of the greatest painter of our
time, *Picasso*.

But craft redeemed through the gains of the young artists was insufficient; a
new yearning manifests itself in the realm of the spirit, a yearning befitting the preoccupations of the new man. Art cannot imitate or copy anymore; it must create,
because in truth, what directs the plastic laws are spiritual laws, which are always
different than the material laws, and art cannot circumscribe itself to giving
the illusion of the "real." Art creates a new reality. These grand ideas are not the
property of one man but emerge out of the evolution towards which art aspires
since Cézanne, since Rimbaud and Mallarmé, and reaching fruition in today's
Surrealism.

It is the French spirit alone that is responsible for this novel and powerful orientation
in the arts. These explorations and fumblings in the dark inherent to these new changes
have appeared to many to be nothing but childish adventures.

All those who heaved a sigh of relief when Cubism was absent from the autumn Salon,
found themselves unexpectedly dragged along in the midst of an entire current of
modern life.

Wasn't perhaps the exhibit of decorative arts a victory for the modern pulse? The whole
of decorative arts, this time official, was in concert with the explorations of the plastic
masters, which some of them even collaborated with: Cubism.

It was impossible that the reflection of cubist concepts in other arts, which claim an
independence of inspiration and recovery of ideal craft, would not occur.

Architecture itself was "contaminated" by the decorative arts. It can certainly be
claimed that the groundwork for this event was prepared by a multitude of factors;
still, without the cubist experiment it would not have been brought to birth. Certainly
the architects Perret and the builder of the abattoirs from Lyon were the inspired
forgers of revolutions, but the one who formulated in genial fashion the time's sentiment, its needs, was Le Corbusier—Saugnier: "The home is a machine for living."

The shout of hatred rising against aestheticism was the unification signal that caused architectonic Europe to gather around it.

Today, because of the little resistance encountered by it in France, we have many modern accomplishments in Holland, Belgium and Russia. The guiding force emerges from the world of art. The reflection of Cubism in music occurred as a consequence the School of Seven and then the school from Auteuil [near Paris]. Erik Satie was most certainly the backbone and guiding spirit of the new music: the reduction of melody to elements, the restoration of rhythm to jazz-like cadence, the wealth of invention in coloratura leading to the invention of new instruments.

As far as Cubist theatre, its greatest development occurred in Russia as a flowering of Meierhold's theatre and in that school where the actor's role takes precedence over the text, décor, and the three unities.

The same emphasis of detail, the same evasion of "reality" giving rise to artistic reality.

We will not address bibilophily, poster design, printed fabric, fashion, advertising and others, where, from a superficial point of view, Cubism modified their aspect, totally or in part.

And no one can truly discern the quintessential transformation of life itself and the human spirit.

With the invention of mechanization the entire aspect of things changed; along with this our optics, causing an Americanization of the spirit to the detriment of idealism. The modern ubiquity and the sensation of time's nonexistence brought about by the inventions of Edison, will these not contribute essentially to the modification our consciousness? An emphatic yes. It seems to us that out of today's inebriation of the arts germinates an all-encompassing foundation of a spiritual domain upon which will rise a new culture. We close in complete agreement with Mr. Cisek, with the belief that our new style is in the process of formation, engendering at least that identification with life itself without which art will not exist.

Translated by Julian Semilian

FRAGMENTS FROM **A CONTRIBUTION TO OUR HISTORY OF MODERNISM: WHAT A YOUNG PAINTER TELLS US**   Ionel Jianu

Originally published as "O contribuție la istoria modernismului la noi: Ce ne spune un pictor tânăr," *Rampa* no. 3057 (March 31, 1928)

[...]

A band of children that follow a chimera with all the naivete and all the enthusiasm of their tender years.

[...]

Our modernism appeared enriched by all the advantages of a fashion.

An intelligent librarian sold on account Herwarth Walden's magazine *Sturm*.

The books with impossible reproductions of the plastic arrangements of Picasso, Juan Gris, Dunoyer de Segonzac, Oscar Kokoschka and so many others scandalized and charmed our Bucharest dwellers.

And then the magazine *75HP* was launched which sounded the signal for the manifestation of our modernity.

That's where the painter Victor Brauner was presented for the first time.

[. . .]

Then I made the acquaintance of Ilarie Voronca. An enthusiast. You know, a fighter among those who step down into the arena, who combat, who throw themselves body and soul into the vortex from which emerges the triumph of their ideas.

You remark, perhaps, isn't it curious?

Everywhere, modernism was launched by groups of friends who understood life as a path to be traveled together.

There is a new contemporary Bohemianism. That which idealizes friendship, practices it, and works under its urges and warmth.

In France the Fauves were a group of friends who suffered together the disadvantages of a poverty-stricken but enthusiastic existence, and who, together, took off to conquer the world.

In Germany, in Italy, in Russia, everywhere, modernism emerged from such artistic and literary circles.

The other art movements had no need of such collective initiative.

Impressionism, for instance, was a personal attitude, which didn't unite at all the disparate artists who practiced it.

And so on and so forth.

We emerged as a group.

In the literary arena, Gheorge Dinu, Stephan Roll, Mihai Cosma, Ilarie Voronca and I.

We began by originating *75HP*, a magazine/manifesto, which was meant to stir up indignation in the old system. We didn't want to start out by making up subtle but fastidious aesthetic theories. We created scandal around us, which is the only modern means of launching yourself.

It was certainly a young and enthusiastic emergence.

It was from *75HP* that laid the foundation, occidental modernist, for *Contimporanul* and the other magazines, *Punct* and *Integral*.

At *Contimporanul* Marcel Iancu ruled, together with Vinea. At the start, inspired by Arghezism, they were not precisely modernist. But when they felt they were supported, they hazarded to follow the modernist path in full.

Thus, we had Vinea's second period, which will certainly result in his seizing an important place in the history of our literature.

And then we took of for Paris. There we worked with Robert Delaunay, with Marc Chagal, and we formed a Romanian literary circle, together with Ilarie Voronca, Fundoianu and Cosma.

Our group was joined at times by other modernist militants: Man Ray, Kassák— with whom we planned to organize a Hungarian-Romanian magazine—and others.

Translated by Julian Semilian

MANIFESTO Saşa Pană
Originally published as "Manifest," *Unu* no. 1 (April 1928)

"readers, disinfect your brains!"
kettledrum cry
airplane
wireless telegraphy—radio
television
76 h.p.
marinetti
breton
vinea
tzara
ribemont-dessaignes
arghezi
brancusi
theo van doesburg
hurraaay hurraaay hurrraaaaaaay
the library trash is burning
a. et p. Chr. n.
123456789000,000,000,000,000 kg
or rats get fat
scribes
dodges
sterility
amanita muscaria
eftimihalachisms
brontosaurs
booooooooooooo
verb combine
abcdefghijklmnopqrstuvwxyz
= art rhythm speed unexpected granite
gutenberg, you're coming back to life

Translated by Monica Voiculescu

M. H. MAXY Ilarie Voronca
Originally published as "M. H. Maxy," *A doua lumină: proze* (Bucharest: 1930)

The delight of experiencing my ebullience not chained by any consideration of a professional gravity: I will not be forced to render nasally sonorous commonplaces about line or color, I will not have to point out the catalogue placing of the canvass which, like the albatross, the heart aspires towards.
For me the silhouette and vigor of Mr. Maxy cannot be separated from the emotion I experienced that day when, in a gallery without a signboard on the door to indicate anything about the revelation to follow inside, I was to discover an interpretation of the

world and of intelligence entirely unexpected, entirely invigorating. The Constructivist vision acquires through Mr. Maxy, for the first time, its voice in Bucharest. Marcel Iancu, entitled to the role of the first to breathe new life into, over here (and among those of other countries), into the possibilities of creation and invention in painting, will join H. M. Maxy in associating bodies and abstract planes with the colors clinking against each other like clear crystals, traversing across hallucinatory fields, where the air like an ungraspable bubble tumbles over scaffoldings and handwriting dilating towards an architecture of shadows.

Painting, which sensed its own perdition, was seeking a fire escape, a pretext to evade. Constructivism, a logical consequence of Cubism, pushed between the narrow space of its branches a voluminous space. A rest and an attempt only. Attempts need not be unfruitful, but persisting, will reduce the exaltation of lines to a drafting engineer's plane. As for the placing of architecture (in painting) on the poem's staves, one single name, one single sublime revelation: Giorgio de Chirico. But Chirico introduced an agitation, a tragic unease, a nightmare categorical as sentence of supreme condemnation. Next to the colonnades of an oneiric Parthenon, horses, galloping with mane unfurled. Next to the philosopher's mask, an artichoke.

To pause, thus, in recollection of the hours spent in meditation before the abstract canvasses of M. H. Maxy. The surprise at the conjunction of forms doesn't diminish at all our comprehending of the science and amorous play the lines separated or embraced each other with, like some artesian fountains over a twilight forest. And even above all this, a sketching in an air which fatigued us, mechanized us, a will and attitude of renewal. Constructivism would opened up the path towards that immense freedom of the spirit, would, after the symphony of volumes painted in crude colors, lead us towards that detailed knowledge of the reactions of objects to one another, towards those charging attacks of personages and landscapes of our illusive imagination and suffering. With a fully mastered craft, with his floating above things, with smile of intelligence, M. H. Maxy has succeeded, in accents fully personal and freshly tender, a fresco of aboriginal countenances, from the singers with the star, to the bear trainers of frost.

I couldn't, in these lines which my friendship would fling over the shoulders of M. H. Maxy like a fistful of confetti, underline the significance of his name in the development of the plastic arts over here: M. H. Maxy wears in his buttonhole a mirror where you can foresee the flight of metal and the clouds of flight. A sky awakens each time he touches it with his brush. But M. H. Maxy is also a friend who received and adoringly tasted on his lips the bitter sugar of poetry, who tirelessly navigated quartier-maître on the *Integral*, into the foam of his dissolution. In his recent painting, M. H. Maxy unfurls in cascades silks and woolens of murmurs, lithe bodies cleave the waters like oysters from which the pearl of an aurora will tumble, dear reader, on your plate.

M. H. Maxy paints with his eyes open like a hunter who knows that from the charge of colors on his palette a raspberry quail will burst out, will transmute into a shout or a dandelion. He is not terrified of the obstacles that unanimous existence places before him, and crosses further into inspiration and creation like a seed which, quaint and concealed, metamorphoses into branch and leaf.

Translated by Julian Semilian and Sanda Agalidi

VICTOR BRAUNER Ilarie Voronca

Originally published as "Victor Brauner," *A doua lumină: proze* (Bucharest: 1930)

Victor Brauner rummages with his brush through all the thoughts' feathers, agitates in his palms all the little bells of ecstasy. His eye like a hound without collar or chain tramps the sky's fields, returns with the dream's quail in his teeth. For thirst, for the heart, Victor Brauner is tonic balsam, is reassurance. Where the hour's restlessness burns and cleaves, Victor Brauner's finger makes out through the ash a forest path over which the seasons have ripened bracken and bison. A world of Other, without the hamper of materialism, without the crutch of the code of manners or rules. The pencil may then be a stiletto or a nightingale, a mirror over the water above which swans flew, or clouds; in the fish pond clenched like a pearl in mountain's oyster you can divine trout with tiny wings like crimson pods; over there the stags lift up their moist muzzles, sniff the approach of the hunter; the wind like a hand caresses the creatures' brows, straightens the forest's curls.

Who gave Victor Brauner the magic herb?

All the creatures come to him, lick his palms, glue themselves like leaves upon the eyelid's album. His step awakens the weeds' piccolos, blows up like a peacock, calls out; the imagination's gates gape apart. Victor Brauner domesticates the wild creatures of unease, captures with a lasso of images all the wild horses of the blood. Victor Brauner: a hymn to the death and rebirth of painting! The poet in him has understood early on that the path of the gatherer of colors and signs is crowded between two chasms without forgiveness: on one side: reproduction of nature—plasticity—which photography itself succeeds in shedding—the photography of the last decades. Man Ray gropes an alphabet beyond the thickets of visual illusion; on the other: the architecture that brought to painting the hermaphroditics of Constructivism. Victor Brauner's pause at the juncture confined by volume or abstraction (even abstraction is a confinement) can only end in a suffocation, can never satiate our hunger for truth and significances. Like a poem, a drawing or a painting must enrich the sensibility and the eye with new revelatory possibilities.

REVELATION. With a fishhook of light Victor Brauner brings to the surface, from the darkness within or without him, the fish of forms which will shatter the habitual or quotidian's crusty shell, to place on the tables with manuals and magazines the writhing of a worm of azure. So many dreams, so many sunk galleons within us.

But look at me now preceded by the prophets of Victor Brauner's dream, trailed by the deluge of plants and creatures, culled from the slumber's swamps; by the caravans with embroideries and carpets of morning stars collected from imagination's steppes. Victor Brauner forges through the marrow of things, awakens with a touch fresh harmonies, fresh infusions of vitality. Look, here's the copper forest, there the emerald forest, beyond the forest of silence. One gesture and the ocean's cello sings. Inside the veins flows a confetti shop where all the twilight's serpentines crepitate. But, silence! Wind up the bow of your nerves, soon the word's arrow will shriek: Victor Brauner approaches, caresses, catches in his arms, the majestic bird of the unforeseen.

Translated by Julian Semilian and Sanda Agalidi

MARINETTI Ion Vinea and Marcel Janco
Originally published as "Marinetti," *Rampa* no. 3688 (May 11, 1930)

Marinetti, the herald of modernism, is among us.

But his thought has long preceded him.

In Italy, more than anywhere else, art suffered the burden of *tradition*. The country of old booksellers and antiquity, the country of multitudes of curiosities for billionaires and Americans, wheezes under the ballast of past genius. The past's specter paralyzed the arts.

Nearly a quarter century ago, Marinetti sounds the alarm signal, and together with Russolo, Carra, Severini, Prampolini, Balla, Soficci, Pisis and others, hurls the most audacious desiderata of the arts of the future: Futurism.

The death of official art

Setting fire to museums

The poetry of liberated words

The music of mechanization

The simultaneous theatre

Velocity: art's expression

Architecture in motion

The abolition of the nude in art...

These slogans produced in the torpor and confusion of two decades ago, the effect of an infernal machine. The Futurist earthquake transfigured the world's artistic soil, fertilized the landscape, manifesting everywhere new and undiscovered aspects, in music, in painting, in the theatre, in architecture, in literature, in choreography. Cubism, Dadaism, Constructivism, the Russian Suprematism, are the repercussions of this spiritual seismic phenomenon: Futurism.

From then on, the liberated lyrical consciousness of humanity reshaped itself according to new data. Still, Marinetti's violence and frenzy continue to sustain the revolutionary state, the spirit of exploration, the unflagging nerve, in the struggle with the official tendency to return to "passé-ism": that is, a return to cemeteries, through imitation, duplication, hypocrisy. Our past is admirable, Mussolini said once, but it must not thwart the paths of the future.

Marinetti is the live symbol of eternal youth, antagonist of senile stuttering, contemptuous of tradition's crutches and dentures, architect of the unknown.

Translated by Julian Semilian

F. T. MARINETTI Ilarie Voronca
Originally published as "F. T. Marinetti," *Rampa* no. 3688 (May 11, 1930)

A name like a slingshot shattering all of mediocrity's windows, flinging anxiety and distress amidst the sedentary paralytics with race horse pretensions, unfurling over centuries and horizons a multicolored tinsel sash of shouts and vanquishments. From its incipience and all the way into its entrails, the twentieth century will always bear the firebrand of this name, of this surgeon who operated with astral violence upon its sensibility and all its forms of art, upon the appendicitis of the *claire de lune* ankylosis of a vocabulary and an obsolete sentimentalism. "We will sing," spoke Marinetti in the "Futurist Manifesto," published by Le Figaro on February 20, 1909, "we will sing the great multitudes roiled by labor, by pleasure, by revolt, the polyphonic and multicolored vortices of revolutions in modern capitals; the nocturnal quiver of arsenals and construction sites under the homicidal electrical stars; the voracious train stations, devourers of fumigating reptiles; power plants suspended in the clouds through the columns of smoke." And likewise bridges, steamers, locomotives neighing like gargantuan steeds of steel, airplanes, multitudes applauding like fanatics.

F. T. Marinetti, the first to fling the mitt of affront before the museums and the art collections and the narcoleptic literature that mundanely begged for the admiration of the visitor, barren and mechanized. From him began the great transformations of the contemporary spirit, the thought of the war with universal reflexes, which would purify our vision of the residue of a past with castles and parks in ruins. "Guerra unica igiene il mundo." ["War is the world's only hygiene."] All his work, all his manifestoes are impregnated simultaneously by the breath of great inspiration, prophecy, and veritable and spatial poetry. Along with the fulgurating associations of ideas and novel aspects, an incendiary eruption of unforeseen art asserts itself, an image, an infinity of images, fluttering between planets and terrestrial inventions a gigantic carpet of poems.

The first poet (how long we waited for this!) who lifted his brow proudly against the great enigmas of the skies and thought! The first poet to choke with a fistful of sand and confetti, with a sarabande of hues and poems, the mouth open in the stereotypics of a tradition depleted of the potency of a novel and revitalizing vision. The first to attempt to grasp the proximity of the ambrosial source of creation, of unforeseen and dauntless invention.

The first to extricate poetry and art from the inoffensive and putrid sarcophagus where they were preserved along with embroideries of old maids and grandmother's needle-work crotchet. Poetry and art, unleashed like the peacock's tails over years and conti-nents, penetrating all forms of thought and life, realizing a novel mentality, novel religion.

How can you pass over all these when you speak of F. T. Marinetti? How can you forget that Marinetti was the one to throw open all doors to the arts, synthesized and universalized through futurism, that he is the one to offer the most unforeseen wealth of possibilities? Perhaps only D'Annunzio—but only in a far smaller measure than Marinetti—accomplished this miracle of erasing all borders and banding peoples in a vigorous cult of poetry and art, of adventure and youth. Because indeed, this must be thought of as a miracle of our century, the eruption of poetry and art out into the streets, the carpeting of fields and cities with immense symphonies of hues, of musics, of words, leading towards the architecture and all life's aspects of today. Marinetti conjectured this form of life, he prepared its development, he sang it in a time when most couldn't see it or refused to. Marinetti, in 1909, already gave the signal for the great ball.

In every country generation of young people would hearken his shout, would, in the high-wire dance of liberated words, to head towards a cogitation disburdened of impedi-ments, hoisted towards the robust and muscular sky of a new world.

"The essential elements of our poetry will be courage, audacity and revolt." No one may contest that all the post-war achievements in the arts in Germany, France, and all the other countries bloomed, in their essence, out of F. T. Marinetti's principles and vitality. Music, the plastic arts, the written or spoken arts, theatre, architecture, were lifted to a potency and unity of sound which bewildered the spectator, perplexed him in order to vanquish him, to fortify him with ample and novel vision. F. T. Marinetti attempted likewise an enlargement of the senses of artistic perception. His imagination craved to augment sight and hearing—the only senses that, through their development, led to artistic achievements—with Tactilism. He fashioned Tactilist poems and paintings, along with the comrades of his group—all individuals of renown and considerable achievement—imagined polyformal music, the russolophone, the Futurist painting, shock theatre.

Nothing is more consequential and logical than the birth of this new tradition, this new Renaissance, this new *Cinquecentissimo*—namely Futurism—to occur in the country of serene traditions, the country of renaissance and fecund arts, in Italy with its dream gondolas and its painting resembling the sky and the flight of maritime birds.

From the activities unleashed in the past twenty-five years—the manifestoes in French and Italian and the vitality briefly mentioned above—one can sketch Marinetti's silhouette in fulgurant and all-encompassing manner. No one can escape his intelligence and sensibility.

He conjectured the triumphant arrival of the music hall, and his actual successes in the great capitals of the world, during a time when the music hall shielded itself and evolved under the cupolas of traveling circuses. He sang the impressive adventure of trajectories inscribed in the skies by airplanes that ferried our yearning and vitality. Like a modern alchemist, but like an alchemist with tresses of sprightly and youthful storms, an alchemist like a young Faustus, he sang and anticipated—through poems— all the audacious discoveries of the man of science. F. T. Marinetti explodes, is grander than, more powerful than his own self, cannot be reduced, cannot be constrained inside his own self.

F. T. Marinetti represents an entire era, an entire inner universe. He is the complete human being.

He is ready for any expedition, any experience, no matter how reckless.

For the force which unleashes out of himself, for the novelty which he has engendered and still engenders out of himself, for his power as a poet, as an orator, as a lecturer, as a firebrand, propagandist, ever unequalled athletic Futurist, on the occasion of his visit among us, let us receive and greet him with the greatest enthusiasm.

Translated by Julian Semilian

OUR OWN FUTURISM   Marcel Janco
Originally published as "Futurismul nostru," *Facla* no. 358 (May 19, 1930)

After Ruskin, the lethargy of art would have overwhelmed the entire world if it hadn't been for Marinetti to end this agony.

To all sorts of *regrets, laments, despondency, and despair* he opposed the *optimism and presentness of living*, thus creating Futurist art with lively elements. Then the revolutionary squadron started the noble and generous battle that freed modern man's feelings and verb.

Futurism has set a great store on the courage and the undeniable right of the young age.

Futurism has chased art away from libraries and museums. Futurism has urged art into action, a true incentive for life.

Futurism shows the value of creation and the amount of novelty, sensation, and expression contained by the new art.

Futurism promotes art as a guide for life while the artist assumes his responsibility for human happiness.

Our Futurism has its own features: We haven't published any sort of manifestoes, since they are never read.

We haven't had any street riots because everybody is a modernist over here.

We haven't brought poetry down in the street because our rhythm of life is slower.

Our opposition has never gone beyond irony and subversion.

We have neither indulged ourselves in exuberant acts of those unrestrained temperaments, nor have we spoken overtly for fear we might lose our poise.

We have leashed our revolt because we were instructed at a skeptical school.

We haven't overtly spoken our love for [the verbal], for form, because it is a "shame" to confess your feeling.

We haven't tasted the joy of our victory, because we are systematically surrounded by that type of "mute" admiration.

We never worship our leaders because our foes "worship" them too.

We have no profession of faith because we flee the "ridicule." We are "ashamed" to trust something: a pure intellectual disposition. However, Futurism was our school. Its symbol has energized everyone, just like any other avant-garde. We have fed on its ideas and strengthened our enthusiasm.

Ours is a creative, optimistic, iconoclastic Futurism.

Translated by Magda Teodorescu

THE REHABILITATION OF THE DREAM   Geo Bogza
Originally published in *Unu* (1931)

And I'm considering an anthology of the dream, told the simple way, without any skills, because a dream is beautiful owing to its very substance that shouldn't be deteriorated by any one style or fantasy.

The dreams of ancient kings passing through legend, from one generation to another. The dreams of Robin Hoods and people on death row. The tortured dreams of ascetics. The wonderful dreams of prisoners getting ready to escape. The red dreams of anarchists. The dreams of card players: hope and illusion. The glutinous dreams of prostitutes. The dreams of sailors and of black people. Dreams in tropical lands and at the North Pole. The lascivious dreams of teenagers. Halo dreams and dreams descended to hell.

And I love dreams because they are subversive. Because they drill into the flesh and re-establish the imminences of a blind justice. You, humble servant that the lady of the manor has slapped in her vanity, know this, during the night her body twisted and gasped seeing you bending over her, rough like a tree trunk, abolishing her dress, slowly, sadistically, in a ritual of the last judgment. You were asleep somewhere, not knowing anything, but the dream made sure you exacted your revenge. Next morning, the lady must have been angry to see the dark circles around her eyes and the rumpled sheets—the sheets you rumpled—and she must have bitten her lips consuming the snake venom enclosed in her very biological formula.

And then there are the revenge tricks against those who use the polite plural when they talk about themselves, to boost their own ego. I confess I'm happy when I see a rigid, stern cabinet minister or university professor any I think maybe tonight he'll dream of masturbating like a boy. Or a majestic metropolitan bishop, finding himself gasping in sweat in the room of some cheap neighborhood prostitute.

Translated by Monica Voilculescu

715

Bucharest

chapter 15

GERMANY

Éva Forgács

The tenth anniversary of the November Group in 1929 prompted the art critic Ernő Kállai to discover that "it is a sobering experience to look back," to take stock of the legacy of the past decade "now that all the messianic dreams have faded." Amidst the pragmatism and functionalism of the late 1920s the question asked in Kállai's own short-lived periodical *Der Kunstnarr* (The Art Fool) was one that could apply to the whole German cultural scene: "What has become of the social, ethical, and religious activism of the early years of the November Group?"

The messianic dreams had turned into streamlined design and industrial production, while in painting, they were replaced by the Surrealists' attempts to fathom the unconscious. Clarity and transparent order in art were still found in geometric abstraction, but darker visions of anxiety and anticipation now emerged in Surrealism as well as in New Objectivity.

The question of whether art should be redefined in the face of popular culture also loomed. The beginnings of mass production and mass consumption absorbed authentic "primitive" folk, peasant, and tribal art and flooded the market with cheap versions of what had once been high art.

German society and culture were polarized throughout the second half of the 1920s. The right and left hardened their political positions and used art as a means to voice them. The communists of the Malik Verlag (Malik Publishing House), John Heartfield, Wieland Herzfelde, George Grosz, and a great many other artists, adopted *Tendenzkunst* (or politically committed leftist art), while Nazi populism and propaganda "art" were also on the rise. Proletkult agitation competed with the expression of populist-nationalist attitudes to address the mass audience.

Theo van Doesburg's death in 1931 was the symbolic closure of the period of agitation for the avant-gardes in Germany. The cessation of his vigorous and ubiquitous publishing, painting, writing, and organizing activity, as well as the absence of his controversial and charismatic persona, marked the end of an era. By the time Kállai reflected on the politics of culture of the Third Reich, he had to use a pseudonym ("Danubius"), but his manuscript remained unpublished nonetheless.

TEN YEARS OF THE NOVEMBER GROUP   Ernő Kállai
Originally published as "Zehn jahre Novembergruppe," *Der Kunstnarr* (April 1929)

What has become of the social, ethical, and religious activism of the early years of the November Group? "The work of the November Group had the purpose of rescuing art from irrelevance, finding a place for it in contemporary life. For this very reason, it involved itself in working out the possibilities of major collective undertakings. As yet, the time does not seem to be ripe for this, either economically or artistically, and so there is nothing for it but to create art for the sake of acquiring a deeper understanding, until the necessity for it within human society is grasped." (W[ill] Grohmann.) This brings us back to the "cruel isolation of the outsider who is dismissed as unworldly." The journey to the State and the Nation, on which the November Group set out with such overwhelming enthusiasm, was a quixotic exploit. Not only in theoretical mani-festoes but also in practice, in the style of those stormy years. Almost without excep-tion, the Group's artistic productions now seem grotesque: a failure of effect that must be ascribed not to noble delusions but to a lack of quality. There is much in modern art that springs from the same spirit as the impotent gesturing of the average November Group member—and nevertheless remains great art, even now that all the messianic dreams have faded. The November Group itself has some things to show that have succeeded in outlasting the Romantic mists of Activism. On the whole, however, it is a sobering experience to look back at the heroic period of the November Group. The works of more recent years are mostly more effective. They evidently reflect more lucidity and self-control on the artists' part. We less frequently encounter that fatal mismatch between desire and capacity that so often causes revolutionary efforts to distort and go into spasm.

The most consistent progress is to be found among the architects of the Group. With few exceptions, they have been spared the fantastic vagaries of their painter and sculp-tor comrades, and have found access to the great collective tasks that confront society. Today, they are engaged in building functional organizations of space and helping to relieve the housing crisis; they are entirely useful citizens and taxpayers. But, even though the November painters and sculptors cannot claim this degree of social useful-ness, they too have a justification for their existence, which can be accepted all the more unreservedly since Will Grohmann endorses it in his intelligent Foreword to the jubilee publication. Art is created not only "for the sake of deeper insight" but also out of intense passion and as a psychic sport: a superior form of private activity, if you like. It is wrong to underestimate the positive human significance of private activities. Paul Klee once jokingly referred to his painting as "small-animal breeding." Painting, rab-bit breeding, flower gardening, cactus cultivation, and all other hobbies, great and small, are—if nothing else—reserves of private territory from which one can defy the *great powers of government, national economy, politics,* and other *collective forms of human degradation* and allow free play to primal instincts. There are some essential affinities between a Bach fugue and a game of chess.

Translated by David Britt

ART AND THE GENERAL PUBLIC   Ernő Kállai

Originally published as "Kunst und großes Publikum," *Der Kunstnarr* (April 1929)

You seldom comprehended me, 'tis true,
And I as seldom comprehended you;
We reached an understanding when we found
That Kitsch it was that gave us common ground.

(Freely after Heine)

One of the many arguments used today to demonstrate the general uselessness and
asocial nature of personality in art, literature, and philosophy is this: that such values
have nothing to say to the masses. And indeed the most profound and responsible creative talents must suffer most from such isolation. But the incomprehension and ignorance of the crowd proves nothing—in any argument. Above all, one thing is undeniable:
that even the crowd has its artistic needs. Otherwise why are the movies, the music
cafés, and the radio doing so well? Why do the weeklies and magazines publish in editions of millions of copies? And, in the last resort, what is this mass trade there for, but
to purvey art, literature, and practical philosophy with a hint of the ideal? In suitably
popular forms, of course: that is, as a watered-down version of what were originally
"exclusive" and "socially unacceptable" works of genius. Pseudo-art and pseudo-
philosophy are the more or less grubby small change that endlessly circulates from
hand to hand, while the gold reserves of the great spiritual enterprise lie locked up
in exalted creative masterworks, inaccessible except to the few.

This state of affairs can to some extent be explained in terms of the wedge driven by
the technological and economic revolution between the bare necessities of survival
and the leisure required for mental pursuits. Much of the mindless claptrap that the
masses of the so-called middle-class public and of the proletariat unresistingly accept
is the fault of our wonderful [industrial] civilization, which has turned man into an
abject, harassed slave of work, a defrauded fraudster, an oppressed oppressor of his
neighbor. There is no predicting how far this situation can be radically remedied by a
revolution that brings purely economic and social benefits to the proletariat; perhaps
the remedy is more likely to come from technological improvements still to come,
and from the longed-for "comfortable surplus" for everyone. Nevertheless, even the
total fulfillment of the most extravagant technological fantasies cannot eliminate
one obstacle that will continue to stand between the public at large and the supreme
achievements of the human mind. This is the necessity of winning access to a mental
world through empathy, creative work, devotion, and rigorous concentration. It may
well be that in earlier cultures the capacity or the passion that affords such depth of
vicarious mental experience was common property and, as it were, a gift of nature.
Perhaps we are moving toward a new age in which even supreme creative achievements will be self-evidently accessible to all. Perhaps the divide between mind and
reality will disappear again, and—after paradise—man will experience a second
transformation of his earthly life: a technological one. For the time being, these are
utopian prospects. The present day knows no paths to the Center other than those of
specialized aptitude, talent, and commitment. This observation does not spring from
any sectarian obsession; nor does it stand for high-flown hero-worship or pedigree
dandyism. It is objectively based, no more and no less. It acknowledges the obstacles
that prevent creativity from gaining undistorted access to a wider collective consciousness, and treats the isolation of creativity behind such high walls as anything but a
privileged position. Rather as an unwanted burden that is both morally *and* materially
hard to bear.

Times have changed. Where is the much-maligned arrogance of the artist now? Even talented individuals are now losing courage and turning petty and ugly. Only recently, a *Berliner Tageblatt* survey of leading writers and poets revealed a surprising number of inferiority complexes. Rightly, Béla Balázs in *Die Weltbühne* lectured them for their pusillanimity and denounced such slogans as Objectivity [*Sachlichkeit*] and Functionalism as capitalist crimes against humanity and against the human spirit. As with writers, so with artists. There is no arrogance in artists nowadays; at best, there is a dour, defiant defensiveness. Understandably so, for the philistinism of the good old days, which dismissed any artist who went his own way as a fool and a wastrel, now has a host of new allies in the shape of clever-clever technomaniacs, snobbish America-worshipers, and utilitarian fanatics. Not to speak of the apostles of *Proletkult* and the oafs of ideological art. These are the circles in which arrogance is to be found, and among them there are quite a few Modernist architects[1] and architectural aesthetes.

At best, the art-hating, horribly patronizing attitudes of such people rest on a social superstition: the argument quoted at the beginning of this article. This is that the masses have no time for the highly personal, "eccentric" creations of art and philosophy. These hostile intellectual critics fail to acknowledge the sources from which the—undeniable—artistic needs of the masses are ultimately supplied. If it were not for the thinkers and artists of genius, whose creations represent the utmost concentration of their vital energies and the revelation of ultimate realities, then one fine day the whole popular trade in spiritual surrogates would dry up. The countless makers of art and literature, and the more or less shallow popular philosophers, would have no sources from which to derive the specialties that now reach them in mangled form at the end of a long, intermediate supply chain. The closure of the great powerhouses of the mind would lead, at lengthening intervals, to the extinction of all the lights that draw power from them. The mass production and mass consumption of contemporary culture surrogates would be in the same plight as contemporary European folk art. This, too, was never anything but an adaptation of the art of the upper classes; it can no longer receive any stimulus from those sources, now that machine technology and capitalist production have made all art bourgeois and proletarian. This process has already worked its way through the system and is supplanting peasant art, in countries like Hungary and Russia, with utterly cretinous offshoots of "urban fashion."

In the beginning, Impressionist painting was of course an exclusive and individualistic phenomenon, even for the academicians. Now, kitsch derivatives of that same Impressionism can be seen in hundreds of thousands of dirt-cheap color prints in every petty-bourgeois parlor and barbershop. Even the mass production of art is "progressive" in its own way. Especially in Germany, where machines extrude thousands of kilometers of wallpaper like monstrous tapeworms, with ornamental appliqués in the "Expressionist" or "Neoplasticist" style. A few days ago, a wallpaper manufacturer suggested to the Bauhaus that its students should make designs for new wallpaper patterns. To the credit of the *Bauhäusler*, be it said that they showed no great inclination for this kind of arty-crafty formal stereotyping. Of course, the linoleum manufacturers have their own up-to-the-minute stylistic ambitions, and now they give their products not only the semblance of Persian carpets but also a décor of brightly colored squares. The triumphal progress of Bauhaus geometry, with its Dutch and Suprematist antecedents, has now reached as far as the nightwear of the "modern lady of taste" —

---

1 Dear Mr. Mart Stam, It is said that you are at work on a project for the Standard City of the Future. In this city, everything that pertains to the mind, without exception, will have been organized on a functional basis. For those few hopeless dolts who are unable to let things be, there will be public comfort stations in which they can perform their menial mental functions at low cost: First Class (with abstract painting and atonal music), 20 pfennigs; Second Class (with Magic Realism and demoniac idyll or idyllic demonism), 10 pfennigs. Press pigs, free of charge.

presented for our inspection by a Viennese women's magazine. The painters Malevich and Mondrian, a whole international school of architects, and the Viennese lingerie industry, can all join hands in the sign of the Square. If that isn't popular...

A word on the popularity of motion pictures. If we ignore for a moment the overwhelming preponderance of kitsch products, there are still many films that appeal equally to the most jaded intellectual and the most naïve movie-going audience. Even in such cases of universal popularity, however, reactions differ widely. An example: for the ordinary man in the audience, Chaplin is only an amusing joker. For the person of greater insight, he is infinitely more than that. An eternal icon of humanity, a hero with a tragicomic destiny, as profound, even in his wildest grotesques, as any quixotic creation of the human imagination.

The experience of true art is a matter of mental passion: it is both ecstasy and supreme insight. It cannot lie around on every street corner, to be picked up by any rubberneck who happens to come along (no class distinction intended).

Every nation has the government—and the art—that it deserves.

Translated by David Britt

VISION AND THE LAW OF FORM   Ernő Kállai
Originally published as "Vision und Formgesetz," from Ferdinand Möller Gallery catalogue (1930)

The turn away from Impressionism was also a turn away from the visual appearance of things and toward their essence, from perspective to vision, from representation to construction. Art was no longer content to produce a perspective from cross sections of nature. Art came to realize that it bore the experience of totality in its own blood and spirit. As the raging force of primal urges and as the harmony of objective law. As Expressionism it rooted up all the passions of color and as Constructivism it revealed the most delicate relationships of number and scale among surface, space, and form. If we trace it back to its first definitive beginning in the work of Cézanne and van Gogh, its first portents in the lightning flashes of Redon and Ensor, then this much-debated art has passed through fifty years of evolution and through other unforeseeable possibilities. Even so, from every rooftop one hears the critical cackling of crows: the isms are dead, back to nature, back to reality. Granted, visionary depth and strict laws of construction are ideals that in the stilted intellectual alienation of our social forces—no matter whether they are petty bourgeois, chic, or Marxist—demand from every painter and sculptor an unusual degree of intellectual distance and the courage to be isolated. These are virtues that are less frequent today than ever before. Their representatives in the arts are incomparably rarer than the academics and genre painters of modern stripe. Nothing is easier than to overlook or make light of the relatively few examples of abstract design among the generous offering of easily absorbed realisms.

This makes it all the more urgent to demonstrate that there are also outsiders at work who fulfill the visionary and constructional aspects of art with new creative impulses and convincingly disprove the banal chatter about the end of Expressionism and "isms of that sort." The exhibition at Ferdinand Möller's gallery shows only a limited selection of very recent works. Fundamental creations are missing—like the works of Hans

Arp, Meyer-Amden and Ozenfant, Mondrian, Lissitzky, and Gabo, to name but a few. The impression is nevertheless lively. Rich in stimulating forms that reveal the decisive impulse in the essence and consciousness of our time. Their technical vivacity. Their utopian faith in the bold intellectual perfection of life. At the same time, though, their expanded and penetrating insight into physical and spiritual qualities. Its hotly overflowing feeling of being deeply connected to every creature in a community of beings. Human beings are spiritual powers, perceivers, and constructors of high rank. And still they function in the same circulation of the natural forces of blood, sex, and hunger, of reproduction and death that animals and plants do. We have recognized— as artists, writers, and metaphysicians have long since suspected—that our most literal daily actions are permeated and fatefully codetermined by the irrationalities of the subconscious. What spaces and dimensions, hitherto imagined at most only by visionaries, are ready to enter into scientific and practical consciousness? What kind of new questions, new abysses of existence, lurk behind them as unseen directors of our reality, which we consciously try to master in ever bolder systems of order, which we tirelessly seek to civilize? We carry all the urgent currents and nocturnal inventions of the formless in us, and all the luminosity of organizing thought. Heaven and hell— with their transfiguring and obscuring spirits, with their saints and demons—have more effect on us now than in any period since the Middle Ages. The difference is simply that we localize and label these forces differently. We do not believe in gods and devils, but we are aware of enormous dialectical tensions within existence—social tensions are merely one resultant of them. We know the creative aspect of contradiction, the fundamental condition of the dissonant pairing of instinct and spirit, of chaos and construction in the structure of our world. This image of the world, which explodes the confines of the bourgeois settlement of 50 percent materialism–idealism, was buried for centuries until Nietzsche brought it to its violent new dawn, and now it will celebrate unimaginable triumphs of culture. The decisive creative achievements that have been accomplished in the visionary and constructivist art of the past fifty years are already its triumph. A magnificent advance in several ranks and stages: Les Fauves, Die Brücke, the futurist manifesto, Der Blaue Reiter, Der Sturm, L'Esprit nouveau, De Stijl in Holland, Obmochu, the Realist manifesto in Moscow, and last but not least the Bauhaus...a tremendous series of artistic creations and stimuli.

The exhibition at the Möller gallery is dedicated mainly to more recent examples of this development. The simultaneous presence of several representative works by masters like Kirchner, Nolde, Schmidt-Rottluff, Heckel, Otto Müller, Feininger, Kandinsky, and Klee is intended to attest to how much the work of younger artists is indebted to these pioneers. This debt does not take the form of personal dependencies; rather, a trenchant breakthrough into world of realistic and impressionistic pictorial forms was necessary in order to make the field fertile for a freely blossoming intellectual landscape of art. Kandinsky and Klee are not merely pioneers, they are already productive figures in this landscape. Their closeness makes particularly clear the new turn that the visionary element has taken in the work of younger painters like Kuhr and Winter. It is not a romantic rapture over distant worlds—no ghosts any longer—but is instead dominated by an awareness of the real presence of irrational elements pushing and germinating inside us, in our flesh and blood. Held together, condensed. In Klee's work the element of the miraculous is still motivated by sorcerer's masks and physiognomies, far removed from the earth. Even the landscape, the figure of the real motif, becomes fairytale-like, dreamlike. In the work of Kuhr and Winter even the most concealed flicker of the soulful has its own fleshy, as it were, sensual closeness and physical lust. A new naturalism is afoot, certainly not one of bourgeois realist perspective but of universal perception. A stripping away of studied superiority, as if the complicated circumstances of our lives, conflicts, achievements, our artfully constructed bridges from birth to death were in essence something else, something "better" or "more perfect" than the living space and life practice that characterize the fates of animals and plants. In the work of Fritz Winter in particular one sees forms that are reminiscent of microorganisms and that contain a sensibility that establishes space and image, occasionally achieving the monumental (his *Bird's Head!*) Behind all the external limits and value judgments of our reality a great unified stream of more profound life runs rampant— no less effective, no less real. Otto Coester explodes the shells or makes them transparent; the spaces of his etchings and drawings are populated with turbulent reality, enlivened by shapes and fates that we have carried with us in our blood, in our forms, since the beginning of time. No more sunken stars, no more sunken bells. The great enigma of existence is truly revealed only in the visible.

Even when it appears in forms of ultimate simplicity and constructional stability. The exhibition presents a considerable number of works that know how to affect the deepest sources of the lyrical and the musical in us, even though they are dominated by a clear, logical tension of the pictorial idea. Take the woodcuts of Mataré. They superimpose a few planar contrasts and animal contours in infinite distance as a deeply concealed animal peace: broad and deep. What naturalist ever placed us so lovingly at the heart of nature as Mataré has, with his simple forms of the most austere restraint? Or look at the paintings of Schlemmer, Nebel, Muche, Neugeboren, Hoerle, Seiwert, and Bortoluzzi. In varying degrees of depth and delicacy or strength, all of them share an absolutely transparent, often architecturally conceived order of colors and forms. Surfaces are laid bare equally, which allows all the relationships of spatial depth to resolve into a two-dimensional plane, and this plane remains flat because it is compressed and self-contained in the total rhythmic correspondence of all its parts to one another. Rhythm: it runs through the circulation of colors and forms in these paintings like an invigorating pulse, like an intensity that both stimulates and regulates.

Rhythm: the common denominator of such extreme contrasts in the exhibition like Coester, Kuhr, Scholz, Tinzmann, and Winter, on the one hand, and Baumeister, Vordemberge-Gildewart, Nerlinger, and Engelien, on the other. Here a visionary passion that flows like nature; there a coolness that is enthusiastic about reason. Precision in the spirit of the engineer, a joy in movement that is stimulated by sports and technology, hard, energetic tension. Is it still proper to speak of abstractions where the relationships to the most immediate reality of our time are so clear? Nerlinger's industrial painting, with its oppressive superiority of object over human being, reveals social issues more mercilessly and more fundamentally than all the so-called Proletkult paintings of the new art of the poor. The fact that paintings by Nerlinger or Vordemberge-Gildewart could be made into posters without further ado is not the ultimate advantage of their appropriateness, mirroring and intensification, even a utopian and optimistic transfiguration of our technological and intellectual civilization. Vordemberge-Gildewart in particular brings extreme reduction and condensation to formulas that could be considered the aesthetic analogy to the whole obsession with planning and construction of our age.

A wise old saying notes that extreme contrasts converge in their essentials. An Expressionist like Fritz Winter is contrasted with a Constructivist like Vordemberge-Gildewart. It becomes clear that both the most profound animal contemplation and highest intellectual exuberance of art, both vision and architectural form, must be enlivened by the same heartbeat if they wish to grow to become the purest expression of themselves: of rhythm. The circle is closed.

Translated by Steven Lindberg

Walter Dexel

Originally published as "Theo van Doesburg," *Das neue Frankfurt* no. 6 (1931)

On March 7, Theo van Doesburg died at Davos. He was a highly significant and almost a tragic figure, since the opportunity to realize his potential to the full was largely denied him—a fact that is hard to understand if one looks at some of those who are permitted to work.

He was a painter, an architect, a typographer, and from 1917 the founding editor of the magazine *De Stijl*, the first ever to campaign consistently for new formal design. (The cover of *De Stijl* remains an exemplary piece of modern typography—think of the visual changes that have overtaken our periodicals in the past decade, and you have one small illustration of Van Doesburg's startling anticipation of present-day design principles.) He fought in the foremost ranks of the Dutch shock troops alongside Mondrian, Oud, Rietveld, Wils, Huszár, Van t'Hoff and others. What they stand for is well known. Now that he is dead, let us reflect for a moment on what we in Germany owe to Doesburg. Historical justice and the memory of an important man demand that we remember.

In 1921 Theo van Doesburg came to Weimar, with his vital energy and his clear critical mind—Weimar, where the Bauhaus had been in existence since 1919, and where a considerable number of modern artists were living, attracted by the wind of progress that used to blow—in those far-off days—through Thuringia. The credit for inviting Doesburg to Weimar goes to Adolf Meyer; straightforward, phlegmatic, and consistent, Meyer never diverged from the straight line that led from the buildings designed in cooperation with Gropius in Cologne and Alfeld to the works of his later, mature period in Frankfurt. The teaching appointment as such was not a success, since it proved impossible to bridge the gap between Doesburg's views and those of the then dominant Bauhaus personalities.

But Doesburg did not lose heart. True prophet that he was, he passed on what he had to say to anyone who wanted to learn. We had lived through the war in ignorance of the living forces at work in other countries; he was engaged in a constant exchange of views with members of the avant-garde everywhere, and he brought the whole world with him into our seclusion. All that Holland, France, Italy, America, and Russia possessed, by way of major progressive work and new ideas, was there in the countless illustrations and publications in all languages that lay piled up in Doesburg's Weimar studio.

In countless private conversations, but also in systematically constructed courses, he clarified the fundamental concepts of new design in every area of work. These courses were regularly attended by numerous Bauhaus students, among others; and the fundamental reorientation that took place at the Bauhaus in 1922–23 would have been unthinkable without Doesburg's influence. His personality was essentially that of a teacher. As a teacher, he was a spellbinder, who swept his hearers along with him. Energized by his subject like no other teacher, he was always at pains to establish universally comprehensible basic principles, and to give his hearers not subjective impressions but a method. He provided, at least for Germany, the first valid formulation of the ABC of the new impulse in design. Consciously and deliberately, Doesburg was an artist/theoretician. As an artist, he was one of a select few; but as a theoretician he is, in his own field, as unique as Adolf Loos. He had no interest in exploiting artistic individuality as a means of gaining attention; he strove with all the means at his command to enact a universally valid stylistic impulse with the utmost clarity and purity. By imposing an at times disabling burden of—perfectly sound—theory on his own work, Doesburg the thinker eased the way for others to gain, through more accessible words and works, the popularity that was always denied him. But if the criterion of priority has anything like the status in artistic matters that it has in science, Doesburg's contribution to the evolution of the new formal design has yet to receive its due.

His lectures of 1921–22 anticipated most of the ideas purveyed in subsequent years by leading artistic personalities: ideas that are now current coin. He identified the characteristic signs of today's world-view as against yesterday's—

openness, not closure
clarity, not vagueness
religious energy, not faith and religious authority
truth, not beauty
simplicity, not complexity
proportion, not form
synthesis, not analysis
logical construction, not lyrical conjunction
mechanics, not handicraft
formal design, not imitation and decorative ornamentation
collectivism, not individualism

—as applied to painting, sculpture, architecture, literature, film, music, and life in general. He sought to resolve the problem of architecture on a scientific basis of social and biological fact. By 1921 he proclaimed housing as a vital function that affects our mental as well as physical activity. At that early date, he clearly understood that any attempt at renewal that concentrated exclusively on one factor was impoverished and doomed to perish. He prophesied the early demise of utilitarianism unless it once more acknowledged our psychological needs. Sadly, this hope has yet to be fulfilled—as can be seen from many modern housing projects, which, sailing under the colors of function and fitness for purpose, often do no more than revive yesterday's back elevations and put them along the street frontage. Doesburg unmasked the decorative and dilettante uses of Modernist methods, at a time when there was a general inability to tell the difference. He was one of the first to recognize that craftsmanship has become steeped in individualism, and that collectivist formal design needs the machine in order to fulfill the new aesthetic needs that arise from the remodeling of society.

The ideas of Doesburg's final half-decade have yet to be fully realized. Partly put into practice at the Aubette in Strasbourg and at his own house in Meudon, they offer endless material for the theoretician above all. For Doesburg, color was a design material, an architectural element. Ever more clearly, he saw that, although nakedly structural— or, as he called it, "anatomical"—architecture had banished the decorative principle of the past, its exclusive utilitarianism had led it to neglect optical, tactile and psychological needs. Doesburg calls for architecture and painting to operate synoptically, so that architectural and painterly elements relate to each other: a process that involves the materials of glass, concrete, steel, etc., together with horizontals and verticals, light and shade, color and gray/black/white. He knew that the fundamentals of a new theory of formal design must necessarily rest on the scientific and artistic exploitation of these antitheses.

Translated by David Britt

POLITICS OF ART IN THE THIRD REICH Ernő Kállai (under the pen name Danubius)

Unpublished manuscript, "Kunstpolitik im Dritten Reich" (1934)

Whatever area one chooses in which to observe the effect of National Socialism, it is difficult to make sense of its contradictory image. It is baffling the extent to which it wishes to locate and follow the golden mean between free competition and a state-planned economy. It is a mystery what it will do to achieve the subdivision of classes given its proclaimed distance from both the "individual of liberalism" and the "masses of Marxism." Its devout cult of the *Führer* aims at a political aristocracy of a new breed, but its bond to the *Volk* knows to adhere to the Roman principle of *"panem et circenses"* [bread and circuses], but with all the advertising and organizational practices of modern mass psychology. Its cultural policies have driven the Protestant Church into a chaotic process of disintegration. Monist associations, which are suspected of harboring "Marxist freethinkers," are forbidden, but the pantheism to which those groups essentially paid homage enjoys a freedom of conscience attested by the authorities, so long as it belongs to the association of the German faith movement. Although a "chamber of horrors" of modern German art with the finest works of the "cultural Bolshevism" of expressionism is just opening in Breslau, the Dresden chamber of horrors with the same demagogic tendencies is closed by the police. The result of superior, if admittedly rather belated knowledge? The result of disappointment over the avid interest with which the large crowds that were rushed in to denounce this form of art—so condemned and despised, so evil and dangerous—instead studied it and thus neglected to exhibit the indignation that was expected of them?

Let us stick to the topic of policies on the arts. The National Socialist state lays claim to totality. It wants to possess the soul of the entire people as well as this soul in its visible form: art. State and art should work toward the same demonstration of the essence of the people. Who would not want to support enthusiastically the powerful perspectives of such a synthesis? Admittedly, because the National Socialist state, with a clear-eyed view of economic considerations, must take cover against private capitalism, it can only partially fill the ideal of totality it seeks. Broad swaths of this totality remain, for the moment, unoccupied by the state, because they must serve as the space for the free play of the private economic forces of capitalism. It is thus a totality with bourgeois provisos. The rationale of economic goals may respect these provisos. The coming into line [*Gleichschaltung*] that National Socialism expects of art cannot possibly mean that the imaginative free play of design will also accommodate itself to the limited perspectives and range of operations inherent in these bourgeois provisos. Such a limitation on art would with time lead to a homespun realism. National Socialism, however, is constantly calling for mythical visions, in order to provide a visual emblem for the irrational abysses of its connection to nature and the *Volk*. It is in keeping with its antimaterialist and antirationalist ideals that National Socialism must seek symbols that extend down to the maternal depths of creation and up to the stars of eternity. Therefore, it must have an art that wants to tie itself to the state and yet remain free for the limitless perspectives that represent the only place its ideals of totality can be fulfilled. This is because an art that wants to be national and socialist, that wants to create the "Myth of the Twentieth Century,"[1] can, of course, only begin where the bourgeois ends. The artistic principle of the bourgeois is dominated by the drive to establish the distinctiveness of personality, never in the symbols of

---

1 *The Myth of the Twentieth Century* was the title of a 1930 book by Nazi ideologue Alfred Rosenberg. [Ed.]

totality but in depictions of "a corner of creation seen through a temperament" (Zola). For the German version, the word *temperament* should probably be replaced by *disposition* [*Gemüt*].

For some twenty-five years now there has been a form of German art whose imagery has increasingly overcome the corner of creation limned by the bourgeois and personal and instead sought visions of the profound beyond and symbols of far-reaching meaning. I mean the Expressionism of Nolde, Kirchner, Franz Marc, Feininger and Paul Klee, Barlach and Lehmbruck. It also includes the work of a whole series of young artists who have developed this Expressionism with utmost compression and discipline, without losing sight of its vital force and depth. One might think that National Socialism in particular, with its blustering professions of the irrational force of blood and soil, would have to appreciate this Faustian art of primal images and history. Indeed, there are National Socialists for whom Expressionism is the profoundest revelation of their *völkisch* nature. They are, however, a minority in opposition, with little influence. Under the protection of Hitler and Frick, the National Socialist *Kampfbund für deutsche Kultur* [Combat league for German culture] leads a struggle against Expressionism with a hatred and venom that it displays nowhere else, and it slanders Expressionism as a destructive work of cultural Bolshevism, a spirit foreign to the nation. Even if the Kampfbund is not considered an official institution of the party, this is nevertheless the reactionary tendency that dominates the government's policies on the arts.

The Kampfbund caused the downfall of Dr. Alois Schardt, because as interim director of the *Nationalgalerie* he professed in word and deed a glowing enthusiasm for expressionism. Schardt had to go shortly before a large programmatic exhibition he had organized was to open at the *Kronprinzenpalais*. Admittedly, his successor, Dr. Hanfstaengl, who was approved by the Kampfbund and the cultural reactionaries around Hitler and Frick, let stand much of what Dr. Schardt had wanted to show. After all, it was not possible, if only with an eye to the impression it might createabroad, to proceed in Berlin in 1933 in precisely as Herr Frick, following the bad advice of Schultze-Naumburg, had done at the museum in Weimar in 1929, when he banished the entire expressionist collection to the museum's basement. Dr. Schardt's exhibition plan was, however, in important respects weakened or entirely cut and altered. And, as if in a mocking grimace at his predecessor's "cultural Bolshevist" ideals, the new director of the Kronprinzenpalais opened with a special exhibition of Karl Leipold. That is to say, with the work of a painter from Munich who is at best an academic cross between plein air painting and second-hand romanticism and belongs precisely to that "new incarnation of bourgeois philistinism" in the arts against which the National Socialist advocates of Expressionism—first and foremost the National Socialist student association—have repeatedly protested with indignation.

The programmatic debates on the arts in the Third Reich that raised such a clamor among the German public last summer are now carried out with less noise but no less tenacity and bitterness. The conflict within that National Socialist camp itself that has died down least of all could, on superficial observation, be seen as a struggle between the competing adherents of two movements, like Romanticism opposed to Classicism. However, they are not movements. They represent two different interpretations of National Socialism in general. Both sides profess themselves supporters of the Third Reich. But each of them understands that claim in a different way. A bourgeois and conservative interpretation is opposed to a socialist and revolutionary interpretation, even if it is one of a highly nebulous and Romantic sort. We are faced with adherents of German socialism, which seeks not an "economic structure" but a "spiritual attitude."

The results are strangely disappointing when one attempts to trace this spiritual attitude in the works of those young German artists who are in many cases members of the NSDAP [National Socialist German Workers' Party] or at least openly and aggressively express the attitudes that the party backs. One is usually confronted with a typical juste milieu art, a tempered, faded Post-Expressionism that is distinguished from the new sentimental and pedantic Biedermeier art of a Schrimpf, Kanoldt, or Lenk only by trifling nuances in style and mood. In both cases we find excerpts of native landscape, observed with tempera-ment and disposition, now more static and linear, now more dynamic and painterly. Admittedly, some of them are quite pretty, very congenial. Still, it is difficult to comprehend the big words that gather like momentous cloud formations around these harmless, peaceful, and bourgeois spheres of art. "Myth of the native soil"..."miracles and mysteries of the cosmos"..."*völkisch* eros in blood and soil," and so on, and so on—*tant de bruit pour une omelette!* [a lot of noise over an omelette]. As elsewhere in the Third Reich, here too the proclivity for self-corroboration by means of grand, ornate phraseology is an alarming indicator of instincts that are at bottom unclear, uncertain, and fusty.

Be that as it may, this new Biedermeier, this triflingly guarded perspectival restoration of the object in painting, should clearly be seen as the officially preferred sector for German art. Its painters, belated recollections of the art of a hundred years ago, have been frequently granted professorial honors in recent appointments to the academies. By contrast, the forces that have been creating out of the depths of our age— painters like Klee and Campendonk, Hofer and Dix, Schlemmer and Baumeister, Muche, Molzahn, and Mohl; sculptors like Marcks and Mataré—have been dismissed from their positions on short notice. Without any artistic, pedagogical, or political justification, these artists, all of whom are at the peak of their (significant) creativity, were all cut down with summarily through the despised Weimar "system." A chapter unto itself, about which much more could be said.

All in all the National Socialist policies on the arts have always represented and continue to represent a ruthless poisoning of the well. Even where the policies at the national or state level may perhaps be better intentioned, the situation is ultimately made completely intolerable by the arrogance of the many petty local leaders and their self-important advisers who take things into their own hands like grotesque potentates and issue orders, decrees, and prohibitions. They eagerly and enthusiastically seek to pull the wool over German eyes and minds—eyes that can in any case hardly be called clear-sighted where the arts are concerned. It is impossible to describe the confusion that results from these policies on the arts based on resentment, slogans, and overturned principles. It will not be so easy to cope with this chaos.

Translated by Steven Lindberg

CREDITS

Most illustrations and previously published translations are included here courtesy of the copyright holders. Every effort was made to locate copyright holders by the time of publication. The publishers apologize in advance for any unintended errors or omissions, and would appreciate notification of additional credits for acknowledgment in future editions.

ILLUSTRATIONS:

16: McCormick Library of Special Collections, Northwestern University Library

24, 25: Los Angeles County Museum of Art, The Robert Gore Rifkind Center for German Expressionist Studies, purchased with funds provided by Anna Bing Arnold, Museum Associates Acquisition Fund and deaccession funds; 24, photo © 2002 Museum Associates / LACMA; 25 © 2002 Artists Rights Society (ARS), New York / HUNGART, Budapest, photo © 2002 Museum Associates / LACMA

27, 31: Library, Getty Research Institute, Los Angeles; © 2002 Artists Rights Society (ARS), New York / VG Bild-Kunst, Bonn

28: M. Szarvasy Collection, New York; courtesy The Estate of Lajos Kassák, photo by University Gallery, University of Delaware

30: National Museum, Belgrade

33: Neues Museum—Staatliches Museum für Kunst und Design, Nürnberg; courtesy The Estate of Lajos Kassák, photo by Kurt Paulus

34, top: The Mitchell Wolfson Jr. Collection, The Wolfsonian Florida International University, Miami Beach, Florida; courtesy The Estate of Lajos Kassák

34, bottom; 35, top: Courtesy The Estate of Lajos Kassák

36, top: Ceskoslovenská akademie ved, © Estate of Karel Teige, photo by František Krejcí

36, bottom: Zdenek Primus Collection, Prague, © Estate of Karel Teige

38: Polska Akademia Nauk, Instytut Sztuki, photo # 17.588 PL

39, top, 605, 641: Muzeum Sztuki w Łódźi, photo by Piotr Tomczyk

39, bottom: National Museum, Belgrade

45: Ceskoslovenská akademie ved, photo by Tatána Billerová

140: Biblioteka Narodowa (National Library of Poland)

141: Muzeum Narodowe w Krakowie (The National Museum in Cracow, Poland), photo by Marek Studnicki

199: Biblioteki Jagiellonskiej (Jagiellonian University Library, Cracow)

303, 304: Netherlands Architecture Institute, Rotterdam/collection Van Eesteren-Fluck en Van Lohuizen-Foundation, The Hague, photo by Retina

305, 625: Collection of Vladimir Panǎ

306: Hungarian Academy of Sciences—Archives of the Research Institute for Art History, photo © György Makky

PREVIOUSLY PUBLISHED TRANSLATIONS:

50, 52, 300, 457: from Rose-Carol Washton Long, ed., *German Expressionism: Documents from the End of the Wilhelmine Empire to the Rise of National Socialism* (New York: G.K. Hall, 1993), with translations from the German edited by Nancy Roth. Copyright © 1993 by G.K. Hall & Company.

125, 427: translated by George Cushing, from *The Hungarian Avant Garde: the Eight and the Activists*, exh. cat. (London: Arts Council of Great Britain, Hayward Gallery, 1980). © 1980 Arts Council, John Willett, Júlia Szabó, Krisztina Passuth, János Brendel, Tamás Aknai.

204: translated by Wolfgang Jabs and Basil Gilbert; 204, 207, 408: translated by Don Reneau; from Anton Kaes, Martin Jay, and Edward Dimendberg, eds., *The Weimar Sourcebook* (Berkeley: University of California Press, 1994). Copyright © 1994 by the Regents of the University of California.

313, 318: translated by Ralph Manheim, from Robert Motherwell, ed., *Dada Painters and Poets* (Boston: G.K. Hall, 1951, 1981). Copyright © 1951 by Wittenborn, Schultz, Inc.

359: translated by Stephen Rudy, from Roman Jakobson, *Language in Literature*, eds. Krystyna Pomorska and Stephen Rudy (Cambridge and London: The Belknap Press of Harvard University Press, 1987). Copyright © 1987 The Jakobson Trust

389, 470: translated by Nicholas Bullock; 496: translated by John Bowlt; from Stephen Bann, ed., *The Tradition of Constructivism* (New York: The Viking Press, 1974). Copyright © 1974 by Stephen Bann.

424, 443, 454, 471: from Krisztina Passuth, *Moholy-Nagy* (New York: Thames and Hudson, 1985), with translations from the Hungarian by Éva Grusz, Judy Szöllősy, and László Baránsky Jób, and from the German by Mátyás Esterházy. Copyright © 1985 Thames and Hudson, Ltd.

497: from *Vision and Unity: Strzeminski, 1893–1952, and 9 Contemporary Polish Artists*, exh. cat. (Muzeum Stucki w Łódźi and Van Reekum Musuem Apeldoorn, 1989).

533, 566, 567, 705, 713: translated by Magda Teodorescu, from *Marcel Janco 1895–1995*, exh. cat. (Bucharest: The Union of Architects of Romania and the National Museum of Art of Romania, 1996).

535, 537, 538, 554, 708, 714: translated by Monica Voilescu, from *Plural 3* (Bucharest: The Romanian Cultural Foundation, 1999).

579: translated by Alexandra Büchler, from Eric Dluhosch and Rostislav Švácha, *Karel Teige: L'Enfant Terrible of the Czech Modernist Avant-Garde* (Cambridge and London: The MIT Press, 1999). Copyright © 1999 The Massachusetts Institute of Technology

632: translated by Irena Žantovská Murray, from Karel Teige, *Modern Architecture in Czechoslovakia and Other Writings* (Los Angeles: The Getty Research Institute, 2000). Copyright © 2000 by The Getty Research Institute.

637: translated by Wolfgang Jabs and Basil Gilbert, from Hans M. Wingler, *The Bauhaus: Weimar, Dessau, Berlin, Chicago* (Cambridge and London: The MIT Press, 1969). English edition Copyright © 1969 by The Massachusetts Institute of Technology

646: from Daniel Gerould, ed. and trans., *The Witkiewicz Reader* (Evanston: Northwestern University Press, 1992). Copyright © 1992 by Northwestern University Press.

649: translated by Wanda Kemp-Welch, from Władysław Strzeminski, *Unism in Painting*, reprint (Muzeum Stucki w Łódźi, 1994).

658, 659, 661: from *Three Pioneers of the Polish Avant-Garde*, exh. cat. (Odense: Fyns Kunstmuseum, 1985), with translations from the Polish by Piotr Graff, Ewa Krasinska, and John Szelmkier.

Felix Aderca (1891–1962) Romanian writer and critic

Jankiel Adler (1895–1949) Polish painter

Dragan Aleksić (1901–1958) Yugoslav writer

Hans [Jean] Arp (1886–1966) German-French sculptor, printer, painter, and poet

Béla Balázs [born Herbert Bauer] (1884–1949) Hungarian writer, librettist, critic, and filmmaker

Sándor Barta (1897–1938) Hungarian poet

Willi Baumeister (1889–1955) German painter and writer

Adolf Behne (1885–1848) German art and architecture critic

Henryk Berlewi (1894–1967) Polish painter, designer, and writer

Lucian Blaga (1895–1961) Romanian poet and philosopher

Geo Bogza (1908–1993) Romanian poet and journalist

György Bölöni (1882–1959) Hungarian writer, critic, and editor

Sándor Bortnyik (1893–1976) Hungarian painter, printmaker and poster designer

Constantin Brâncuşi (1876–1957) Romanian-French sculptor, draftsman, painter, and photographer

Nikolaus Braun (1900–1950) German painter and sculptor

Victor Brauner (1903–1966) Romanian painter and sculptor

Max Burchartz (1887–1961) German photographer, painter, and printmaker

Scarlat Callimachi (1896–1975) Romanian writer and editor

Josef Čapek (1887–1945) Czech painter, printmaker, and writer

Avgust Černigoj (1898–1985) Slovenian painter and designer

Leon Chwistek (1884–1944) Polish painter, theorist, philosopher, and logician

Oscar Walter Cisek (1897–1966) German-Romanian writer and poet

N. D. [Nicolae] Cocea (1880–1949) Romanian writer and journalist

Theodor Cornel (1873–1911) Romanian writer and critic

Mihail Cosma [later Claude Sernet] (1902–1968) Romanian-French writer and poet

Tytus Czyżewski (1880–1945) Polish painter, critic, and poet

Honoré Daumier (1808–1879) French graphic artist, painter, and sculptor

Ferdinand [also Ferdo] Delak (1905–1968), Slovenian actor, director, and writer

Walter Dexel (1890–1973) German painter, graphic artist, and teacher

Theo van Doesburg [born Christian Emil Marie Küpper] (1883–1931) Dutch painter, architect, designer, and writer

Viking Eggeling (1880–1925) Swedish draftsman, filmmaker, painter, and writer

Ilya Ehrenburg (1891–1967) Russian writer and journalist

Emil Filla (1882–1953) Czech painter, printmaker, sculptor, and writer

Lajos Fülep (1885–1970) Hungarian writer, critic, and philosopher

Sándor Galimberti (1883–1915) Hungarian painter

Valéria (Dénes) Galimberti (1877–1915) Hungarian painter

Endre Gáspár (1897–1943) Hungarian writer

Ivan Goll [born Isaac Lang] (1891–1950) French writer and poet

Jefim Golyscheff (1897–1970) Ukrainian writer, artist, and composer

Will Grohman (1887–1968) German critic and art historian

Walter Gropius (1883–1969) German-American architect, designer, and teacher

Otto Gutfreund (1889–1927) Czech sculptor and draftsman

František Halas (1901–1949) Czech writer and poet

Raoul Hausmann (1886–1971) Austrian painter, printmaker, photographer, designer, and theorist

Iván Hevesy (1893–1966) Hungarian critic, art historian, and writer

Vlastislav Hofman (1884–1964) Czech designer and theorist

Richard Huelsenbeck (1892–1974) German writer, painter, and doctor

Jerzy Hulewicz (1886–1941) Polish writer, graphic artist, and publisher

Roman Jakobson (1896–1982) Russian-American linguist and theorist

Pavel Janák (1882–1956) Czech architect, designer, theorist, and teacher

Marcel Janco (1895–1984) Romanian painter, printmaker, architect, and writer

Bruno Jasieński [born Wiktor Zysman] (1901–39) Polish writer and poet

Ionel Jianu (1905–1993) Romanian critic and art historian

Miloš Jiránek (1875–1911) Czech painter, graphic artist, critic, and writer

Juliusz Kaden-Bandrowski (1885–1944) Polish writer

Ernő Kállai (1890–1954) Hungarian writer, critic, and theorist

Wassily Kandinsky (1866–1944) Russian painter, printmaker, designer, and theorist

Lajos Kassák (1887–1967) Hungarian writer, theorist, publisher, painter, printmaker, and designer

Alfréd Kemény (1896–1945) Hungarian critic and theorist

Károly Kernstok (1873–1940) Hungarian painter and decorative artist

Katarzyna Kobro (1898–1951) Latvian-Polish sculptor

Marij Kogoj (1892–1956) Slovenian composer

Vincenc Kramář (1877–1960) Czech critic, writer, and collector

Andor Kraszna-Krausz
(1904–1989) Hungarian-
British photographer

Stanisław Kubicki
(1889–1942) Polish graphic
artist and poet

Bohumil Kubišta
(1884–1918) Czech
painter, printmaker,
and draftsman

Georg Kulka (1897–?)
German writer

**El [Lazar Markovich]
Lissitzky** (1890–1941)
Russian architect, painter,
printmaker, photogra-
pher, designer, typogra-
pher, and theorist

György Lukács
(1885–1971) Hungarian
writer, critic, and
theorist

János Mácza (1893–1974)
Hungarian-Russian
writer and critic

Jacek Malczewski
(1854–1929) Polish painter
and teacher

Kasimir Malevich
(1878–1935) Russian
painter, printmaker, dec-
orative artist, and writer

Josef Mánes (1820–1871)
Czech painter, illustrator,
designer, and draftsman

**F. T. [Filippo Tommaso]
Marinetti** (1876–1944)
Italian writer and theo-
rist

Jan Matejko (1830–1893)
Polish painter

János Máttis-Teutsch
(1884–1960) Hungarian
painter, printmaker,
sculptor, and writer

**M. H. [Max Hermann]
Maxy** (1895–1971)
Romanian painter and
theater designer

Corneliu Michăilescu
(1887–1965) Romanian
painter and sculptor

Ljubomir Micić
(1895–1971) Yugoslav
writer, publisher, and
artist

Ion Minulescu
(1881–1944) Romanian
poet and writer

László Moholy-Nagy
(1895–1946) Hungarian-
American designer, sculp-
tor, painter, filmmaker,
theorist, and educator

Farkas Molnár
(1897–1945) Hungarian
architect and lithographer

Piet Mondrian
(1872–1944) Dutch
painter, theorist, and
draftsman

Georg Muche (1895–1987)
German painter and
teacher

Václav Nebeský
(1889–1949) Czech writer
and theorist

Stanislav K. Neumann
(1875–1947) Czech poet
and writer

Ludwig Neundörfer
(1901–?) German
sociologist

Ödön Palasovszky
(1899–1980) Hungarian
actor, poet, and
playwright

**Saşa Pană [born
Alexander Binder]**
(1902–1981) Romanian
poet and writer

Tadeusz Peiper
(1895–1969) Polish
poet, critic, theorist,
and publisher

László Péri (1889–1967)
Hungarian-British
sculptor, painter, and
printmaker

Militsa Petraşcu
(1892–1976) Romanian
sculptor, graphic artist,
and illustrator

Franz Pfemfert
(1879–1954) German
editor and writer

Mirko Polić (1890–1951)
Slovenian composer and
conductor

**Branko Ve [also Virgil]
Poljanski [born Branko
Micić]** (1898–1947)
Yugoslav writer, poet,
graphic artist

Zbigniew Pronaszko
(1888–1961) Polish
painter, sculptor, and
theater designer

**Ivan Puni [also Jean
Pougny]** (1892–1956)
Russian painter, illustra-
tor, and designer

Tivadar Raith (1893–1958) Hungarian poet and writer

Risto Ratković (1903–1954) Yugoslav poet

Hans Richter (1888–1976) German-American painter, filmmaker, writer, and theorist

Walter Riezler (1878–1965) German art historian and musicologist

Ludwig Rubiner (1882–1920) German poet, writer, and critic

Oskar Schlemmer (1888–1943) German painter, sculptor, choreographer, and theater designer

Kurt Schwitters (1887–1948) German painter, designer, sculptor, and writer

Henryk Stażewski (1894–1988) Polish painter, designer, and theorist

Václav Vilém Štech (1885–1974) Czech art historian

Władysław Strzemiński (1893–1952) Polish painter, theorist, and typographer

Jindřich Štyrský (1899–1942) Czech painter, graphic artist, photographer, publisher, and theorist

Dezső Szabó (1879–1945) Hungarian writer and critic

Mieczysław Szczuka (1898–1927) Polish painter, designer, typographer, and writer

Árpád Szélpál (1897–1987) Hungarian photographer and writer

Vladimir Tatlin (1885–1953) Ukrainian painter, designer, and sculptor

Karel Teige (1900–1951) Czech critic, theorist, graphic designer, and typographer

Lajos Tihanyi (1885–1938) Hungarian painter, lithographer, and draftsman

Boško Tokin (1894–1953) Yugoslav poet, writer, and film critic

Toyen [born Maria Čerminová] (1902–1980) Czech painter, illustrator, and theorist

Tristan Tzara [born Samuel Rosenstock] (1896–1963) Romanian-French writer and poet

Béla Uitz (1887–1972) Hungarian painter, draftsman, and writer

Bedřich Václavek (1897–1943) Czech literary critic, historian and theorist

Tudor Vianu (1897–1964) Romanian poet, writer, and critic

Ion Vinea (1895–1964) Romanian writer and poet

Carl Vinnen (1863–1922) German painter

Ilarie Voronca [born Eduard Marcus] (1903–1946) Romanian poet and writer

Herwarth Walden [born Georg Lewin] (1879–1941) German writer, editor, and critic

Paul Westheim (1886–1963), German-Mexican critic, writer, and publisher

Stanisław Witkiewicz (1851–1915) Polish architect, painter, and critic

Stanisław Ignacy Witkiewicz ["Witkacy"] (1885–1939) Polish writer, painter, photographer, and theorist

Wilhelm Worringer (1881–1965) German art historian

Stanisław Wyspiański (1869–1907) Polish painter, poet, and dramatist